THE STATE OF
NONPROFIT AMERICA

THE STATE OF NONPROFIT AMERICA

SECOND EDITION

LESTER M. SALAMON

Editor

BROOKINGS INSTITUTION PRESS

Washington, D.C.

Published in collaboration with the Aspen Institute

ABOUT BROOKINGS

The Brookings Institution is a private nonprofit organization devoted to research, education, and publication on important issues of domestic and foreign policy. Its principal purpose is to bring the highest quality independent research and analysis to bear on current and emerging policy problems. Interpretations or conclusions in Brookings publications should be understood to be solely those of the authors.

ABOUT ASPEN

Founded in 1950, the Aspen Institute is a global forum for leveraging the power of leaders to improve the human condition. Through its seminar and policy programs, the Institute fosters enlightened, morally responsible leadership and convenes leaders and policymakers to address the foremost challenges of the new century.

Library of Congress Cataloging-in-Publication data

The state of nonprofit America / Lester M. Salamon, editor.—2nd ed.
   p. cm.
Includes index.
Summary: "Examines the private nonprofit sector and the tax-exempt institutions that make up this sector providing important services and benefits to all Americans, with histories behind different institutions and the forces and developments that have buffeted them and what they have done to retain their resilience"—Provided by publisher.
  ISBN 978-0-8157-0330-3 (pbk. : alk. paper)
  1. Nonprofit organizations—United States. I. Salamon, Lester M.
HD62.6.S734 2012
338.7'4—dc23   2012011884

9 8 7 6 5 4 3 2 1

Printed on acid-free paper

Typeset in Adobe Garamond

Composition by Cynthia Stock
Silver Spring, Maryland

Printed by R. R. Donnelley and Sons
Harrisonburg, Virginia

This book is dedicated to the memory of
Peter Goldberg
visionary nonprofit leader, effective manager, and trusted friend,
whose life-work perfectly embodied the values
that make nonprofit America so special.

Contents

Preface   ix

Part I: Overview

1   The Resilient Sector: The Future of Nonprofit America   3
    Lester M. Salamon

Part II: Major Fields

2   Health Care   89
    Bradford H. Gray and Mark Schlesinger

3   Education and Training   137
    Donald M. Stewart, Pearl Rock Kane, and Lisa Scruggs

4   Social Services   192
    Steven Rathgeb Smith

5   Arts and Culture   229
    Stefan Toepler and Margaret J. Wyszomirski

6   Housing and Community Development   266
    Avis C. Vidal

7   Environmental Organizations   294
    Carmen Sirianni and Stephanie Sofer

8 International Assistance   329
   Abby Stoddard

9 Religious Congregations   362
   Mark Chaves

10 Civic Participation and Advocacy   394
   Elizabeth T. Boris with Matthew Maronick

11 Infrastructure Organizations   423
   Alan J. Abramson and Rachel McCarthy

12 Foundations and Corporate Philanthropy   459
   Leslie Lenkowsky

13 Individual Giving and Volunteering   495
   Eleanor Brown and David Martin

Part III: Major Challenges

14 Commercialization, Social Ventures,
   and For-Profit Competition   521
   Dennis R. Young, Lester M. Salamon, and Mary Clark Grinsfelder

15 Devolution, Marketization, and the Changing Shape
   of Government-Nonprofit Relations   549
   Kirsten A. Grønbjerg and Lester M. Salamon

16 Accountability in the Nonprofit Sector   587
   Kevin P. Kearns

17 Demographic and Technological Imperatives   616
   Atul Dighe

18 Nonprofit Workforce Dynamics   639
   Marla Cornelius and Patrick Corvington

19 For Whom and for What? Investigating the Role
   of Nonprofits as Providers to the Neediest   657
   Pascale Joassart-Marcelli

Contributors   683

Index   685

Preface

The literature on America's nonprofit sector has burgeoned in recent years. Long an obscure academic backwater inhabited by a small band of dedicated mavericks, the field of nonprofit studies has swelled into a mighty stream fed by growing doubts about the capabilities of government, political and ideological resistance to expanded public spending, and concerns about America's civic health.

While this increased attention has substantially expanded the base of information available about America's nonprofit organizations, it has not yet generated the clear understanding that is needed of the sector's changing position and role. For one thing, nonprofit organizations continue to be caught up in the long-standing political conflict over the relative roles of the state and the market in responding to public problems, creating a heavy ideological overlay that distorts our view and systematically blocks out uncomfortable facts. Beyond this, the sheer outpouring of information creates its own confusion. Once starved for information, nonprofit practitioners are now deluged by it. Fitting the bits and pieces together into an integrated understanding thus becomes a full-time occupation, something that few harried practitioners or volunteer board members have the luxury to pursue.

The project of which this volume is the second installment was conceived as a response to this dilemma. It seeks to provide a comprehensive, but readable, assessment of the state of America's nonprofit sector at what turns out to be a pivotal moment in its development. More than a compilation of facts and figures, the book seeks to interpret what is going on and make it understandable to the broad cross-section of informed opinion on which the future of this sector ultimately rests.

To be sure, this is no mean undertaking, which may explain why it has never been undertaken before. Nonprofit organizations are almost infinitely varied. They come in different sizes, operate in widely different fields, perform different functions, and support themselves in varied ways. What is more, all of these features are in flux. Like the elephant in the ancient tale, this beast thus appears different depending not only on who touches it and where, but also when.

To assist me in this mission impossible, I was fortunate enough to forge a partnership with the Aspen Institute's Nonprofit Sector and Philanthropy Program and to recruit an extraordinary group of colleagues who have worked with me over the past two-and-a-half years to produce an updated portrait of America's nonprofit sector and its component parts that is factually grounded and sensitive to the sector's diversity while still reaching for the broad interpretive judgments that are needed to make sense of the swirling cross-currents of daily events.

When this project began, the American stock market was at historic highs, the central political question was what to do with a burgeoning federal surplus, dot-com entrepreneurs were transforming philanthropy with the windfall profits of their ingenuity, and America was bursting with a confidence born of apparent omnipotence. This second edition of our pioneering book appears, however, in the wake not only of September 11, the resulting wars in Iraq and Afghanistan, and the loss of American innocence, but also of the precipitous bursting first of the dot.com bubble and then of the housing bubble, followed by the disastrous financial crash of 2008–09 and the lingering economic decline it has brought with it. Inevitably, these developments hold immense implications for the nation's nonprofit institutions, but implications that are still too rarely considered in the fractious policy debates that these developments have triggered.

While we have attempted to accommodate many of these developments, inevitably it has not been possible to make this account as current as yesterday's newspaper. Far from diminishing the value of this book, however, these shifts make it clear why the kind of interpretive perspective we have sought to produce is so useful. Readers can judge for themselves whether the trends and developments we have highlighted are the ones that will prevail in the years immediately ahead, but we are convinced that the central themes we have identified will meet the test of time and prove every bit as germane today as they were when the project was originally conceived. Those themes emphasize the enormous resilience that the American nonprofit sector has displayed over the past several decades, the significant process of re-engineering that the sector has undergone as a consequence, the vast opportunities that this process has opened, but also the enormous risks that the sector now faces as it struggles to adjust to potentially radical shifts in government funding and support. Not only are these trends important for the future of the nonprofit sector, they also hold enormous implications for the society of which these institutions are an increasingly pivotal part.

In addition to the colleagues who contributed chapters to this volume and who put up with the extensive consultations required to fashion it into an integrated book, I want to express my appreciation as well to Eric Boehm of the Aspen Institute's Philanthropy and Social Innovation Program, who handled a variety of administrative tasks associated with this project; to Janet Walker of the Brookings Institution Press, who patiently oversaw the editing of the manuscript and production of the finished product; and to the Carnegie Corporation of New York, the Nathan Cummings Foundation, The John D. and Catherine T. MacArthur Foundation, the Charles Stewart Mott Foundation, the David and Lucille Packard Foundation, and the Rockefeller Brothers Fund for the financial support that made both the initial volume of this project and this second edition possible. I also want to express my gratitude to the numerous students of the nonprofit sector whose reliance on this book have more than fulfilled our expectations about its usefulness. Needless to say, however, the opinions and interpretations offered here are those of the authors and editor only, and may not represent the views of any of the organizations with which we may be affiliated or that have supported or published the work.

Finally, this book is dedicated to the memory of Peter Goldberg, a colleague and friend whose passion for the nonprofit sector knew no bounds, and whose creativity and energy in support of it were an inspiration to us all. Peter was always one step ahead of the rest of us in conceiving imaginative ways to address the nonprofit sector's challenges. In this he embodied the spirit and resilience that underlies the nonprofit sector and that makes it so crucial a part of American life to understand and preserve.

LESTER M. SALAMON

Annapolis, Maryland
April 15, 2012

PART I

Overview

1

The Resilient Sector: The Future of Nonprofit America

LESTER M. SALAMON

A struggle is under way at the present time for the "soul" of America's non-profit sector, that vast collection of private, tax-exempt hospitals, higher-education institutions, day care centers, nursing homes, symphonies, social service agencies, environmental organizations, civil rights organizations, and dozens of others that make up this important, but poorly understood, component of American life.

This is not a wholly new struggle, to be sure. From earliest times nonprofits have been what sociologists refer to as "dual identity," or even "conflicting multiple identity," organizations.[1] They are not-for-profit organizations required to operate in a profit-oriented market economy. They draw heavily on voluntary contributions of time and money yet are expected to meet professional standards of performance and efficiency. They are part of the private sector yet serve important public purposes.

In recent years, however, these identities have grown increasingly varied and increasingly difficult to bridge, both in the public's mind and in the day-to-day operations of individual organizations. In a sense, America's nonprofit organizations seem caught in a force field, buffeted by a variety of impulses, four of which seem especially significant. For the sake of simplicity I label these voluntarism, professionalism, civic activism, and commercialism, as shown in figure 1-1, though in practice each is a more complex bundle of pressures.

Figure 1-1. *Four Impulses Shaping the Future of Nonprofit America*

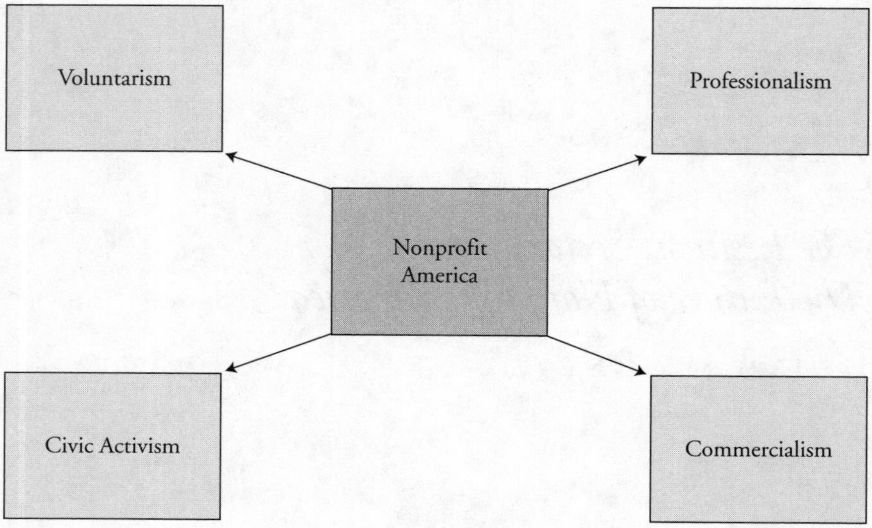

What makes these four impulses especially important is that their relative influence can profoundly affect the role that nonprofit organizations play and the way in which they operate. Understanding this force field and the factors shaping its dynamics thus becomes central to understanding the future both of particular organizations and of the nonprofit sector as a whole.

Sadly, far too little attention has been paid to the significant tensions among these impulses. The nonprofit sector has long been the hidden subcontinent on the social landscape of American life, regularly revered but rarely seriously scrutinized or understood. In part, this lack of scrutiny is due to the ideological prism through which these organizations are too often viewed. Indeed, a lively ideological contest has long raged over the extent to which we can rely on non-profit institutions to handle critical public needs, with conservatives focusing laserlike on the sector's strengths in order to fend off calls for greater reliance on government, and liberals often restricting their attention to its limitations to justify calls for expanded governmental protections.

Through it all, though largely unheralded—and perhaps unrecognized by either side—a classically American compromise has taken shape. This compromise was forged early in the nation's history, but it was broadened and solidified in the 1960s. Under it, nonprofit organizations in an ever-widening range of fields were made the beneficiaries of government support to provide a growing array of services—from health care to scientific research—that Americans wanted but were reluctant to have government provide directly.[2] More, perhaps, than any other single factor, this government-nonprofit partnership is responsible for the growth of the nonprofit sector as we know it today.

Since about 1980, however, that compromise has come under considerable assault. Conservative critics, concerned about what they see as an unholy alliance between the once-independent nonprofit sector and the state, have called for a return to the sector's supposed purely voluntary roots.[3] Liberal critics have bewailed the sector's departure from a more socially activist past and its surrender to professionalism.[4] At the same time, the country's nonprofit managers, facing an extraordinary range of other challenges as well—significant demographic shifts, fundamental changes in public policy and public attitudes, new accountability demands, massive technological developments, and changes in lifestyle, to cite just a few—have been left to their own devices and have turned increasingly to the market to survive. Through it all, nonprofit America has responded with considerable creativity to its many challenges, but the responses have pulled it in directions that are, at best, not well understood and, at worst, corrosive of the sector's special character and role.

Despite the significance of these developments, little headway has been made in tracking them systematically, in assessing the impact they are having both generally and for particular types of organizations, and in effectively getting the results into the hands of nonprofit managers, policymakers, the press, and the public at large. This book seeks to fill this gap: to offer an overview of the state of America's nonprofit sector, to examine the forces that are shaping its future, and to identify the changes that might be needed to promote its long-term health. The result is a comprehensive analysis of a set of institutions that we have long taken for granted but that the Frenchman Alexis de Tocqueville recognized over 175 years ago to be "more deserving of our attention" than any other part of the American experiment.[5]

The purpose of this chapter is to set the stage for the detailed examination of key components of the nonprofit sector that follows. To do so, the chapter first introduces this set of institutions and explains the stake the nation has in its operations. I then look in a bit more detail at the four impulses identified earlier that are shaping this sector at the present time and the implications they have for a number of the key facets of nonprofit operations. Against this backdrop, the chapter then examines the challenges and opportunities that constitute the drivers behind these impulses, the responses nonprofits have generally made to them, and the risks that have arisen as a consequence. A final section then offers some suggestions for steps that would help ensure that a vibrant nonprofit sector, performing the functions for which the country has long relied upon it, survives into the future.

Perhaps the central theme that emerges from this account is one of *resilience*. The overwhelming impression that emerges from this book's chapters is that of a set of institutions and traditions facing not only enormous challenges but also important opportunities, and finding ways to respond to both with considerable creativity and resolve. Indeed, nonprofit America appears to be well along in a fundamental process of reengineering that calls to mind the similar transformation that large segments of America's business sector have been undergoing since the late 1980s.[6] Faced with an increasingly competitive environment, nonprofit organizations have been called on to make fundamental changes in the way they operate. And that is just what they have been doing.

The problem, however, is that, although the sector's organizations have been responding resiliently, those responses are taking a toll on their ability to perform some of their most important functions. In a sense, nonprofits have been forced to choose between two competing imperatives: a *survival imperative* and a *distinctiveness imperative,* between the things they need to do to survive in an increasingly demanding market environment and the things they need to do to retain their distinctiveness and basic character.[7] How the country's nonprofit organizations balance these demands, and how much understanding and help they receive from the broader society in doing so, will shape the condition in which the country's nonprofit institutions survive into the future.

But first we need to clarify what the nonprofit sector is and what makes it so deserving of our attention.

What Is the Nonprofit Sector and Why Do We Need It?

The nonprofit sector is one of the most important components of American life, but it is also one of the least understood. Few people are even aware of this sector's existence, though most have some contact with it at some point in their lives. Included within this sector are most of the nation's premier hospitals and universities; almost all of its orchestras and opera companies; a significant share of its theater companies; all of its religious congregations; the bulk of its environmental advocacy and civil rights organizations; huge numbers of its family service, children's service, neighborhood development, antipoverty, and community health agencies; not to mention its professional associations, labor unions, and social clubs. Also included are the numerous support organizations, such as foundations and community chests, which help to generate financial assistance for these organizations and to encourage the traditions of giving, volunteering, and service that undergird them.

More formally, the nonprofit sector consists of a broad range of private organizations that are generally exempted from federal, as well as state and local, taxation on the grounds that they serve some public purpose.[8] The term *nonprofit,* which is commonly used to depict these organizations and which will be used here, is actually a misnomer: these organizations are permitted to earn profits—that is, end up with an excess of income over expenditures in a given year; what is prohibited is the distribution of any such profit to organizational directors or managers. Technically, then, we might more accurately refer to these organizations as *non-profit-distributing* organizations.

Within this complex array of organizations are two broad types: first, *member-serving organizations,* such as labor unions, business associations, social clubs, and fraternal societies; and second, *public-serving organizations,* such as hospitals, universities, social service agencies, and cultural venues. For the purpose of this volume, we focus exclusively on the second type, the public-serving organizations, which make up by far the largest, and most visible, component of the tax-exempt-organization sector. Also known as charitable organizations, most of these organizations earn their exemption from federal income taxation under section 501(c)(3) of the Internal Revenue Code, which is reserved for organizations that operate "exclusively for religious, charitable, scientific, or educational purposes." Alone among tax-exempt organizations, the 501(c)(3) organizations are eligible to receive tax-deductible donations from individuals and businesses, that is, gifts that the individuals and businesses can deduct from their income when computing their income taxes. This reflects the fact that the recipient organizations are expected to serve broad public purposes, not just the interests and needs of the organizations' members. The public-serving component of the nonprofit sector also includes another set of organizations, however, which are eligible for tax exemption under section 501(c)(4) of the Internal Revenue Code, which is reserved for so-called social welfare organizations. The major difference between 501(c)(4) and 501(c)(3) organizations is that the former are permitted to engage in lobbying without limit, whereas the latter have limits on the extent of their lobbying activity. Because of this, however, contributions made to 501(c)(4) organizations are not tax deductible.[9]

Size of the Sector

No one knows for sure how many tax-exempt nonprofit organizations exist in the United States, since large portions of the sector are essentially unincorporated and the data available on even the formal organizations are notoriously imperfect.[10] A conservative estimate would put the number of formally constituted tax-exempt organizations, as of the late 2000s, at nearly 2 million, of which 1.6 million are in the public-serving component of the sector.[11]

Within this public-serving portion of the entire tax-exempt universe, moreover, are four subgroups of organizations:

—About 1 million service and expressive organizations, ranging from hospitals to advocacy organizations and cultural institutions;

—A little over 100,000 501(c)(4) social welfare and lobbying organizations;

Figure 1-2. *Employment, Nonprofit Sector and Selected Industries, 2006*

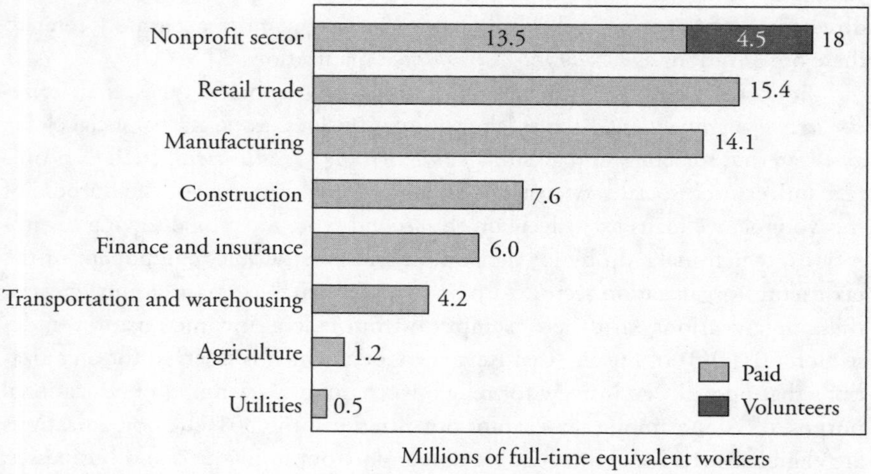

Millions of full-time equivalent workers

Source: Lester M. Salamon, *America's Nonprofit Sector: A Primer,* 3rd ed. (New York: Foundation Center, 2012).

—Approximately 114,000 foundations, federated funders, and other "support organizations"; and

—Over 400,000 religious congregations.

As of 2007 these public-serving nonprofit organizations employed close to 13.5 million paid workers. This represents 10 percent of the entire U.S. labor force and makes the nonprofit paid workforce the third largest of any U.S. industry, behind only retail trade and manufacturing, but ahead of such industries as construction, finance and insurance, and transportation (figure 1-2). With volunteers included, and their volunteer time translated into the equivalent number of full-time workers, the workforce of nonprofit, public benefit organizations swells by another 4.5 million full-time-equivalent workers, making it the largest workforce of any U.S. industry—larger than construction, larger than finance and insurance, even larger than retail trade and all the branches of manufacturing combined, as figure 1-2 also shows.

Employment provides just one measure of the scale of America's public-serving nonprofit organizations. Also impressive are the financial resources that these organizations command. As of 2007 the revenue of public benefit, nonprofit organizations stood at slightly over $1.7 trillion. Most (76 percent) of this revenue, a sizable $1.3 trillion, accrued to the service and expressive organizations, which form the economic core of the sector. The balance went to the

Figure 1-3. *Share of Organizations and Share of Revenue, Nonprofit Service and Expressive Organizations, by Field, 2007*

Percent

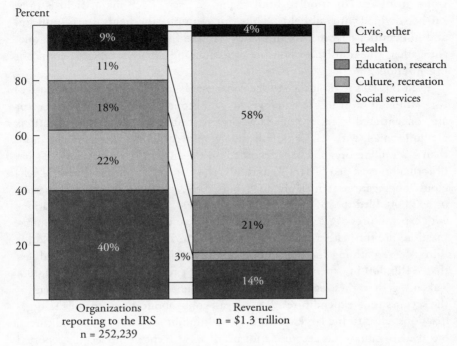

Source: Lester M. Salamon, *America's Nonprofit Sector: A Primer,* 3rd ed. (New York: Foundation Center, 2012).

funding intermediaries ($211 billion), religious congregations ($119 billion), and 501(c)(4) social welfare agencies ($85 billion).

Among the service and expressive organizations, most of the revenue flows to health-related organizations. With 11 percent of the organizations, this field captured 58 percent of all nonprofit service and expressive organization revenue in 2007, as shown in figure 1-3.[12] Education and research organizations make up the second-largest component in terms of revenue, with 21 percent of the total. By contrast, social service providers, although the most numerous of the service and expressive organizations, making up 40 percent of the reporting organizations, accounted for a considerably smaller 14 percent of the revenue (though this was still a substantial $182 billion).

These large categories disguise the huge array of separate services and activities in which nonprofit organizations are involved, however. A classification system developed by the National Center for Charitable Statistics, for example, identifies twenty-six major fields of nonprofit activity, and sixteen functions, from accreditation to fundraising, in each. Each major field is then further divided into subfields. Thus, for example, the field of arts, culture, and humanities has fifty-six subfields, and the field of education, forty-one. Altogether, this translates into close to a thousand different types of nonprofit organizations.[13]

Even this fails to do justice to the considerable diversity of the nonprofit sector. Although most of the employment and economic resources of this sector are concentrated in the sector's large organizations, most of the organizations are quite small, with few or no full-time employees. For example, of the more than 1.2 million organizations recorded on the Internal Revenue Service's list of formally registered 501(c)(3) and 501(c)(4) organizations (exclusive of religious congregations, which are not required to register), only about a quarter, or 332,000, filed the information form (form 990) required of all organizations with expenditures of $25,000 or more. The remaining three-fourths of the organizations are thus either inactive or below the $25,000 spending threshold for filing.[14] Even among the filers, close to 45 percent, nearly half, reported less than $100,000 in expenditures, and 75 percent reported less than $500,000. Taken together, these small organizations accounted for a mere 2.6 percent of the sector's total expenditures. By contrast, only about 4 percent of the organizations fell into the largest category ($10 million or more in expenditures), but these organizations accounted for nearly 83 percent of the sector's reported expenditures.[15] The overwhelming majority of the sector's organizations therefore account for only a tiny fraction of the sector's activity.

Revenue Sources

While most of its organizations are small, America's nonprofit sector is still a major economic presence, with over $1.3 trillion in revenues just in its core service and expressive organizations. Where does this revenue come from? According to popular mythology, the sector is mostly supported by private philanthropy. In reality, however, the revenue structure of the nonprofit sector differs strikingly from this popular conception. In particular, the major sources of revenue of nonprofit service and expressive organizations are fees and charges paid by their clients or customers (figure 1-4). This source alone accounted for 52 percent of nonprofit service and expressive organization revenue as of 2007. Nor was philanthropy the second major source of revenue. Rather, that position was filled by government, which accounted for another 38 percent of overall service and expressive organization revenue.[16] Philanthropy from all sources—individuals, foundations, and corporations—came in third among nonprofit revenue sources, accounting for only 10 percent of the total.

Figure 1-4. *Revenue Sources, Nonprofit Service and Expressive Organizations, 2007*

Total revenue: $1.323 trillion

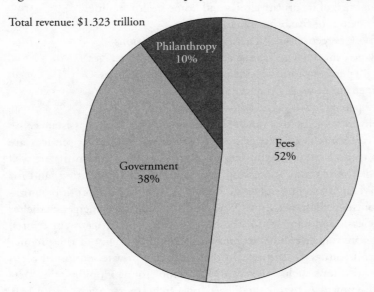

Source: Lester M. Salamon, *America's Nonprofit Sector: A Primer,* 3rd ed. (New York: Foundation Center, 2012), chap. 3, n. 18.

To be sure, philanthropy plays a more substantial role in some parts of the sector than in others. In particular, it is far more important in the expressive fields (arts and recreation) and civic affairs, where it accounts for 37 and 54 percent of the revenue, respectively. Even in the field of social services, long considered a major destination of charitable support, philanthropy's lead revenue role has been eclipsed by fees and government support.

Functions

Quite apart from their economic importance, nonprofit organizations perform major functions in national and community life, functions that define the stakes that the nation has in these institutions. Five such functions in particular deserve mention.[17]

THE SERVICE FUNCTION. In the first place, nonprofit organizations are service providers: they deliver much of the hospital care, higher education, social services, cultural entertainment, employment and training, low-income housing, community development, and emergency aid available in this country. More concretely, these organizations constitute:

—Half of the nation's hospitals
—Nearly a third of its private clinics and home health facilities
—Nearly one out of five of its nursing homes
—Close to 40 percent of its higher education institutions
—Seventy percent of its individual and family service agencies
—Nearly 80 percent of its vocational rehabilitation facilities
—Thirty percent of its day care centers
—Over 90 percent of its orchestras and operas
—The delivery vehicles for a major share of its foreign disaster assistance.

While disagreements exist over how "distinctive" nonprofit services are compared to those provided by businesses or governments, nonprofits are well known for identifying and addressing unmet needs, for innovating, and for delivering services of exceptionally high quality. It was thus nonprofit organizations that pioneered assistance to AIDS victims, hospice care, emergency shelter for the homeless, food pantries for the hungry, drug abuse treatment efforts, and dozens more too numerous to mention. Similarly, many of the premier educational and cultural institutions in the nation are private, nonprofit organizations—institutions such as Harvard, Princeton, Johns Hopkins, the Metropolitan Museum of Art, and the Cleveland Orchestra, to name just a few. To be sure, public and for-profit organizations also provide crucial services, but the country's thousands of private, nonprofit groups add an extra dimension in meeting public needs, often responding to needs that neither the market nor the government is adequately addressing.

THE ADVOCACY FUNCTION. In addition to delivering services, nonprofit organizations also contribute to national life by identifying unaddressed problems and bringing them to public attention, by protecting basic human rights, and by giving voice to a wide assortment of social, political, environmental, ethnic, and community interests and concerns. Most of the social movements that have animated American life over the past century or more operated in and through the nonprofit sector. Included here are the antislavery, women's suffrage, populist, progressive, civil rights, environmental, antiwar, women's, gay rights, and conservative movements. The nonprofit sector thus operates as a critical social safety valve, permitting aggrieved groups to bring their concerns to broader public attention and to rally support to improve their circumstances. This advocacy function may, in fact, be as important to the nation's social health as the service functions the sector also performs.

THE EXPRESSIVE FUNCTION. Political and policy concerns are not the only ones to which the nonprofit sector gives expression. Rather, an enormous variety of other concerns—artistic, religious, cultural, ethnic, social, recreational—also find expression through this sector. Opera companies, symphonies, soccer clubs, churches, synagogues, fraternal societies, book clubs, and Girl Scouts are just some of the manifestations of this expressive function. Through them nonprofit organizations enrich human existence and contribute to the social and cultural vitality of American life.

THE COMMUNITY-BUILDING FUNCTION. Nonprofit organizations are also important in building what scholars call "social capital," those bonds of trust and reciprocity that seem to be prerequisites for a democratic polity and a market economy to function effectively.[18] Alexis de Tocqueville understood this point well nearly two hundred years ago when he noted in *Democracy in America* that: "Feelings and opinions are recruited, the heart is enlarged, and the human mind is developed, only by the reciprocal influence of men upon one another. . . . These influences are almost null in democratic countries; they must therefore be artificially created and this can only be accomplished by associations."[19] By establishing connections among individuals, involvement in associations teaches norms of cooperation that carry over into political and economic life.

THE VALUE GUARDIAN FUNCTION.[20] Finally, nonprofit organizations embody, and therefore help to nurture and sustain, a crucial national value emphasizing individual initiative in the public good. They thus give institutional expression to two seemingly contradictory principles, both important parts of American national character: the principle of individualism, the notion that people should have the freedom to take the initiative on matters that concern them; and the principle of solidarity, the notion that people have responsibilities not only to themselves, but also to their fellow human beings and to the communities of which they are part. By fusing these two principles, nonprofit organizations reinforce both, establishing an arena of action through which individuals can take the initiative not simply to promote their own well-being but also to advance the well-being of others. This is not simply an abstract function, moreover. It takes tangible form in the billions of dollars in private charitable gifts that nonprofit organizations help to generate from the American public annually and in the 15.8 billion hours of volunteer time they stimulate.

The Four Impulses

While these key functions and roles continue to characterize the nonprofit sector, powerful forces are at work challenging and reshaping a number of them. Indeed, as noted earlier, the nonprofit sector appears caught in a difficult force field controlled by four partially conflicting impulses– voluntarism, professionalism, civic activism, and commercialism—that are pulling it in somewhat different directions. These impulses have implications, moreover, for a broad swath of nonprofit features, from the *roles* that nonprofits play and the *strategies* they use to their *style* of operation, their principal *reference groups,* their *organizational structure,* their *management style,* and their *resource base.* The power of these impulses is hardly identical in all fields, or in all organizations even within fields, but there is enough commonality to the impulses to warrant a general characterization of their major features as a prelude to examining the drivers that are supporting or retarding each.

Voluntarism

Perhaps the most fundamental of these impulses, and the one that has fixed itself most securely onto popular conceptions of the nonprofit sector, is the voluntaristic impulse. This impulse carries much of the distinctive value claim of the nonprofit sector—its function as the vehicle through which individuals give expression to a wide assortment of social, cultural, religious, and other values and exercise individual initiative for the common good. But in recent years the voluntaristic impulse has come to be associated with a more stridently ideological conception of this sector. Indeed, as historian Waldemar Nielsen has shown, a "simplistic folklore" has attached itself to the American belief system with regard to this impulse. According to this folklore, the sectors of American society, including particularly the nonprofit sector, "are neatly separated and exist in a static, ideologically partitioned relationship to each other, always have been, and ideally always should be." [21] This has given rise, particularly in conservative circles, to an ideal image of a nonprofit sector that eschews involvement with government, is mostly staffed by selfless volunteers, many of them religiously inspired, and wholly, or nearly wholly, supported by charitable giving.[22]

Whether in its more ideological or its more balanced forms, this voluntaristic impulse continues to exert a strong gravitational pull on public perceptions of the nonprofit sector, if less so on the actual operations of the sector's organizations. More specifically, as summarized in table 1-1, the voluntaristic impulse has come to be associated with a nonprofit sector whose *primary role* is to express and inculcate values. While a wide assortment of values can find resonance with this impulse, in recent years an especially strong current has arisen from the religious right and has found expression in the faith-based charity movement. Adherents to this perspective tend to attribute a wide range of human problems to the absence or underdevelopment of appropriate normative values. The *strategies* of intervention associated with this impulse therefore often emphasize values counseling and self-help, coupled with temporary material assistance until the needed value messages are internalized and absorbed.

Table 1-1. *Implications of Four Impulses for Nonprofit Operations*

Feature	Voluntarism	Professionalism	Civic activism	Commercialism
Role/ objectives	Overcome value deficits Transform individuals Relieve suffering	Overcome physical, educational, or psychological deficits Offer treatment	Change structures of power Change basic policies	Use market means for social ends Efficiently address social needs
Strategy	Inculcate values Counseling, personal renewal Self-help Temporary material assistance	Medical model Deliver services Establish services as rights	Asset model Advocacy strategy Organize citizens/build leadership Access media/ elites	Promote social entrepreneurs Locate market niches Pursue self-sustaining income Measure results
Style	Pastoral Normative Paternalistic Particularitistic Holistic	Programmatic Technocratic Therapeutic Universalistic Secular	Participatory Confrontational Critical	Entrepreneurial Efficiency oriented Profit focused Measurement driven
Principal reference group	Donors/volunteers Members	Staff Profession Clients	Citizens Community assets	Corporate donors Customers Entrepreneurs
Organizational structure	Fluid Ad hoc	Hierarchic Segmented	Modular Federated Alliances	Product focused Networked Flexible
Management style	Informal Volunteer dominant Spiritual	Bureaucratic Formal Rule bound	Consensual Collaborative Participatory	Responsive Bottom-line focused Disciplined
Resource base	Voluntarism Individual philanthropy	Government Fees Institutional philanthropy	Philanthropy Voluntarism Government	Venture philanthropy Sales Vouchers

The *style* of intervention emphasized in the voluntaristic impulse therefore tends to be pastoral, normative, nonprofessional, holistic, and at times paternalistic. The stakeholders or *reference groups* most closely associated with this impulse are often individual donors and volunteers, who serve as role models for the disadvantaged and whose religious faith and values of hard work and personal responsibility are to be transmitted to those lacking them. The *organizational* structures associated with the voluntaristic impulse tend to be fluid and ad hoc, and the management style flexible and informal, as befits a volunteer-based staffing pattern. Finally, the resource needs of organizations imbued with the voluntaristic impulse are different in both scale and kind from those of other types of organizations, relying much more heavily on volunteers and charitable contributions rather than fees or government support.[23]

Professionalism

While the folklore of voluntarism remains dominant in much of the belief system surrounding the American nonprofit sector, a second impulse has profoundly shaped the reality of nonprofit operations. This is the impulse of *professionalism.* By professionalism, I mean the emphasis on specialized, subject-matter knowledge gained through formal training and delivered by paid experts.[24]

Professionalism has had a profound effect on the nonprofit sector, strengthening its capacities in important respects but at least partially displacing the sector's voluntaristic character.[25] While many of these effects have been attributed to the sector's involvement with government, in truth professionalism has probably had as much impact on government as government has had on professionalism since a push by professionals to establish government licensing or program-staffing requirements is one of the crucial steps in establishing a profession.[26] At the least, the rise of professionalism within the nonprofit sector clearly predated the expansion of government involvement in the fields in which nonprofits are active. The transformation of private hospitals from small community institutions addressing the primary-care needs of communities into large bureaucratic institutions dominated by professionally trained doctors took place between 1885 and 1915, decades before Medicare and Medicaid had even been contemplated.[27] So, too, the professionalization of social work and the rise of "case work" rather than community organizing and social reform as the primary social-work mode of intervention was well along by the turn of the twentieth century and firmly in place by 1920.[28] What is more, the engine for this change was private philanthropy (in the form of local community chests) rather than government, as the scientific charity movement sought to replace what was widely perceived to be the inadequacies of well-meaning volunteers with the "trained intelligence" of professionals.[29]

While government did not introduce the professional impulse into the nonprofit sector, it has certainly helped to nurture and sustain it, both by providing professions with a mechanism through which to enforce professional standards in government-funded programs and by providing the funds needed to hire professional staff. In the process, it has helped push nonprofit organizations in directions quite different from those imparted by the voluntaristic impulse. While it shares with voluntarism a deficit model emphasizing individual shortcomings as the cause of human problems, professionalism emphasizes not normative shortcomings but social, educational, physical, and psychological ones. The *role* of the nonprofit sector in this view is thus to offer professional services to disadvantaged clients (see table 1-1). "Not alms but a friend," the long-standing slogan of the voluntaristic Boston Associated Charities, thus came to be replaced in professional social-worker circles by the mantra, "Neither alms nor a friend, but a professional service."[30]

Professionalism's *strategy* thus relies on a medical model, treating beneficiaries essentially as "patients" needing some form of "treatment," whether physical, or educational, or psychological. Unlike the pastoral and holistic *operating style* characteristic of the voluntaristic impulse, the professional style is thus therapeutic, technocratic, segmented, and secular. The principal *reference group* for the professional impulse is not donors or beneficiaries but professional staff and the profession itself. Consistent with these features, professionalism creates organizational structures that are hierarchic and segmented; uses a management *style* that tends toward the bureaucratic, formal, and rule-bound; and requires the more ample and reliable *resources* of government and fees for support.

Civic Activism

Far different from both the voluntaristic and professional impulses is a third impulse coursing through the nonprofit sector: the impulse of *civic activism*. According to this perspective, the real source of the social ills besetting significant segments of the American public does not lie in the values, or in the psychological or skill deficits, of disadvantaged individuals. Rather, it lies in the structures of social, economic, and political power that such individuals confront in the broader society and in the unequal access to opportunities that result. The solution to these social ills therefore does not depend on moral preachment by well-meaning volunteers or treatments administered by trained professionals but on the mobilization of social and political pressure to alter the structures of power and correct the imbalances of opportunity.[31]

The settlement house movement of the late nineteenth and early twentieth centuries clearly embodied this approach. Although providing immediate services to residents of the neighborhoods in which they were located, the real focus of the settlements, according to their historian, was to "bring about social reform, thus alleviating the underlying causes of social problems."[32] Seventy-five years later, this perspective remained uppermost in the mind of the first president of Independent Sector, the national umbrella group for American nonprofit organizations, who referred to "efforts to influence public policy" as "the role society most depends on [the voluntary sector] to perform."[33]

Instead of expressing values and transforming individuals, the social activism impulse thus sees the fundamental *role* of the nonprofit sector to be eliminating the need for services by changing the balance of power in society and opening channels of opportunity to a broader swath of the population (see table 1-1). Unlike the deficit strategies embodied in both the voluntaristic and professional impulses, the civic activism impulse embodies an "asset model," using a *strategy* that sees in the disadvantaged population an enormous resource that can be mobilized and organized to bring about significant societal change. The basic *operating style* favored in this impulse is thus at once participatory, empowering, and confrontational, bringing pressures on the powers that be to establish worker rights and offer access to education and other services that those on the bottom of the economic pyramid are unable to secure through market means. The principal *reference groups* for advocates of this perspective are ordinary citizens and those in greatest need plus, where available, the media to amplify the voice of otherwise voiceless constituencies. To achieve its empowerment objectives, the civic activism impulse fosters a modular *organizational structure*, with multiple linked nodes of action and mobilization. Its *management style* is consensual, participatory, and, where possible, collaborative, building alliances wherever willing partners can be located. And its *resource base* tends to be engaged individuals and, paradoxically in recent decades, government support.

Commercialism/Managerialism

Finally, in the past several decades, a fourth impulse has burst upon the non-profit scene, *commercialism*—and its next-of-kin, *managerialism*.[34] This impulse, too, has its distinctive features and its distinctive implications for the operation of nonprofit organizations, some of which are consistent with the other impulses, but others of which are clearly in tension. The *role* that the commercial impulse presses on the nonprofit sector is a service role, but one that emphasizes managerial efficiency, innovation, and cost containment—dimensions that run counter to professionalism's emphasis, first and foremost, on effectiveness. The *strategy* embodied in the commercial impulse is the injection of a different type of professionalism into the operation of nonprofit organizations, not the subject-matter professionalism of doctors, social workers, and educators, but the business-oriented skills of the managerial professional. This includes the use of strategic planning, quantitative measurement of outcomes, identification of market niches, and heightened attention to operational efficiency (see table 1-1).

The *style* emphasized by the commercial/managerial impulse is entrepreneurial and businesslike, efficiency oriented and measurement driven. The *principal reference groups* for those espousing the commercial impulse are business leaders, entrepreneurs, and actual or potential beneficiaries of an agency's services, who are reconceptualized as "customers." The commercial/managerial impulse calls for *organizational structures* that are focused on individual "products" or "lines of business," with metrics that track each line of business separately and network structures that encourage coordination but allow considerable autonomy for "product managers." The *management style* consistent with this impulse emphasizes clear lines of authority and disciplined performance, which is achieved through regular measurement against preset targets and the flexibility to advance and dismiss staff on the basis of performance rather than professional credentials. In terms of *revenue,* the commercial impulse drives its adherents to search out sustainable revenue streams that can attract private investment capital for start-up and expansion. This means fee income and government entitlement program support, particularly such support delivered through vouchers and other market-based, consumer-side subsidies.

Navigating the Force Field

To be sure, these brief descriptions cannot do justice to the nuances and complexities of these various impulses. They are presented here as heuristic devices to suggest some of the major pressures to which nonprofit organizations are being subjected. What is more, while the impulses are in some tension with each other, there are also clearly points of mutual reinforcement. For example professionalization and the growth of nonprofit paid staff have not displaced the nonprofit involvement in advocacy, though they may have changed its character in certain ways. Similarly, the emergence of social entrepreneurs and social ventures, while a manifestation of the commercial impulse, also reinforces the voluntaristic impulse emphasizing private initiative in the common good. The challenge, therefore, is not to find the single best impulse to follow but rather the combination that produces the most meaningful and appropriate balance needed to allow organizations to survive and grow while still holding true to their distinctive attributes.

These impulses are not, moreover, disembodied concepts floating in space. Rather, they take concrete form in the actions of the sector's stakeholders— those who provide the resources, set the regulations and incentives, serve on the boards, operate the organizations, frame public perceptions, and lend their support in countless other ways. Lacking the firm anchor of a single clear, dominant, raison d'être—such as maximizing profit in the case of business and securing popular political support in the case of government—nonprofits are especially vulnerable to being pulled this way and that by whichever pressure is dominant at the moment.

And this is just what appears to be happening at the present time. Responding brilliantly and resiliently to a variety of dominant challenges and pressures, significant components of the nonprofit sector have moved far from the sweet spot that has historically earned the sector public trust, and too little attention has been given to bringing public understanding in line with operating realities or to finding a more appropriate balance among the impulses that are pressuring the sector and its leaders. In a sense, to survive in a demanding environment, nonprofit organizations are being forced to surrender what may be too many of the things that make them distinctive and worthy of the special advantages they enjoy. Of special note in recent years has been the growing impact of the commercial/managerial impulse, eclipsing the professional emphasis on effectiveness and the voluntaristic emphasis on expressiveness, and potentially undermining as well much of the sector's historic attention to civic activism.

Nonprofit leaders are not without choices in this process, of course. But their choices are highly constrained by the balance of challenges and opportunities they face. Any account of the "future of nonprofit America" in the face of these impulses must therefore be a story in three parts, focusing first on these challenges and opportunities and the extent to which they support or retard these impulses, then examining how the sector's leaders have responded, and finally assessing the consequences of these responses both for individual organizations and subsectors and for nonprofit America as a whole. Only then will it be possible to suggest what alternative options might be worth considering to achieve a more appropriate balance than seems to be emerging among the impulses at play. It is to these tasks that we therefore now turn.

Six Challenges

Writing in 1981, at the end of a decade that witnessed a renaissance of interest in America's nonprofit organizations, Stuart Langton found reason to declare the dawn of a "new voluntarism" in America and to see in the nation's voluntary organizations "a sector of hope in an age of diminishing expectations" and "a corrective force in American society."[35] Exactly three decades later, Langton's "sector of hope" has become, if not quite a sector of despair, at least one of serious concerns. Despite the important contributions they make, nonprofit organizations find themselves at present in a time of testing. Once-sacrosanct tax deductions for charitable contributions have been offered up as part of deficit reduction deals; entitlement programs that fueled nonprofit growth for decades are on the chopping block; and new competitors, some of them taking new institutional forms, are challenging not only the nonprofit sector's market share in fields that nonprofits once dominated, but also its claim to distinctiveness as the sector that uniquely mobilizes private initiative for the common good.

To be sure, nonprofits are not alone in facing significant challenges at the present time. But the challenges facing nonprofit organizations are especially daunting since they go to the heart of the sector's operations and raise questions about its very existence. Against the backdrop painted above, it is therefore necessary to look more closely at these challenges before turning, in a subsequent section, to the opportunities the sector also faces. Fundamentally, six such

Figure 1-5. *Government Social Welfare Expenditures, 1965–2000*

Percent

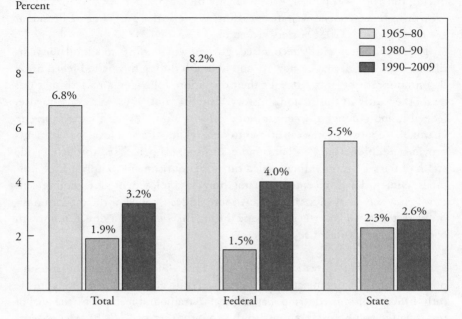

Source: U.S. Bureau of Economic Analysis, *National Income and Product Accounts,* table 3.16.

challenges seem especially significant. From all indications, moreover, these challenges seem likely to persist, and in some cases to intensify, in the years ahead.

The Fiscal Challenge

In the first place, America's nonprofit organizations confront a significant fiscal squeeze. This fiscal squeeze has waxed and waned over the sector's recent history stretching from 1965 to the present, but the current period appears to mark a new level of severity. To see this, the discussion here examines the period of government-fueled fiscal growth from 1965 to 1980, the period of retrenchment that followed in the 1980s, the partial recovery that ensued from 1990 to 2009, and the further retrenchment that seems in store for the second decade of the twenty-first century.

THE GREAT SOCIETY AND BEYOND, 1965–80. Fiscal distress has been a way of life for the nonprofit sector throughout its history, but this eased significantly during World War II and even more so during the 1960s, when the federal government expanded its funding, first, of scientific research, and then of a wide range of health and social services. Thus, as shown in figure 1-5, government social welfare spending grew at a robust average annual rate of 6.8 percent during the 1965–80 period, driven largely by the 8.2 percent average annual growth in federal social welfare spending as the social programs of President Lyndon Johnson's Great Society kicked in.

Though it is not widely recognized, governmental efforts to stimulate scientific advance and overcome poverty and ill health during this period relied heavily on nonprofit organizations for their operation, following a pattern that was established early in this nation's history.[36] By the late 1970s, as a consequence, federal support alone to American nonprofit organizations outdistanced private charitable support by a factor of two to one, while state and local governments provided additional aid.[37] What is more, this support percolated through a wide swath of the sector, providing needed financial nourishment to universities, hospitals, clinics, day care centers, nursing homes, employment and training centers, family service agencies, and many more. Indeed, much of the modern nonprofit sector as we know it took shape during this period as a direct outgrowth of expanded government support.

FEDERAL RETRENCHMENT, 1980–90. This widespread government support to nonprofit organizations suffered a significant shock, however, in the early 1980s. Committed to a policy of fiscal restraint and inspired by the goal of restoring the voluntaristic impulse to the nonprofit sector ("We have let government take away too many of the things that were once ours to do voluntarily," is how Ronald Reagan put it in one of his first speeches as president), the Reagan administration launched a serious assault on federal spending in precisely the areas where federal support to nonprofit organizations was most extensive— social and human services, education and training, community development, and nonhospital health care.

Although the budget cuts that occurred were not as severe as proposed, federal support to nonprofit organizations, outside of Medicare and Medicaid, declined by approximately 25 percent in real dollar terms in the early 1980s and did not return to its 1980 level until the latter 1990s.[38] Some state governments boosted their own spending in many of these fields but not nearly enough to offset the federal cuts. Indeed, as figure 1-5 shows, total government social welfare spending grew at an anemic average annual rate of 1.9 percent during the 1980–90 decade, well below the growth of the population, and even this was largely due to the growth of the major entitlement programs of Social Security and Medicare, which the Reagan administration chose not to touch. Outside of pensions, public education, and health, however, overall government social welfare spending declined by more than $30 billion between 1981 and 1989. Nonprofit organizations in the fields of community development, employment and training, social services, and community health were particularly hard hit by these reductions.

PARTIAL RESUMPTION OF GOVERNMENT SOCIAL WELFARE SPENDING GROWTH, 1990–2007. Government social welfare spending resumed its growth in the 1990s and into the new century but at a much slower average rate than during the 1965–80 period. A number of factors seem to have been responsible for this growth:

—*Expansion of entitlement program coverage.* Responding to various constituencies whose needs remained inadequately addressed by the social programs of the Great Society, especially in the wake of the Reagan retrenchment of the 1980s and the Contract with America cuts introduced in the mid-1990s, Congress expanded eligibility under the basic government entitlement programs for health and income assistance. For example, coverage under the federal Supplemental Security Income program, which was originally created to provide income support to the elderly poor, was expanded to cover people with disabilities, including children and youth, increasing the number of recipients by 50 percent, from 4.1 million in 1980 to 6.6 million by 1999.[39] And similar extensions of coverage occurred in Medicaid and other entitlement programs.[40]

—*New federal initiatives.* In addition to expanding coverage under existing programs, federal policymakers also created programs to address long-standing or newly emerging social ills. For example, four federal child care programs were added in 1988 and 1990 alone, and special programs were added as well for homeless people, AIDS sufferers, children and youth, people with disabilities, voluntarism promotion, drug and alcohol treatment, and home health care.[41]

—*Medicalization of aid.* In the face of cuts to discretionary grant programs, many states found ways to shift activities previous funded from state resources or federal discretionary programs subjected to Reagan-era budget cuts, and reconfigure them to make them eligible for funding under the more lucrative Medicaid or SSI entitlement programs.[42]

—*The welfare reform windfall.* Passage in 1996 of the Personal Responsibility and Work Opportunity Reconciliation Act (welfare reform) produced its own windfall of resources in program areas of interest to nonprofits. This was so because the act replaced the existing program of entitlement grants for welfare recipients channeled through states with fixed, six-year federal grants to states for use in both direct payments to welfare recipients and, if funds were available, programs supporting work readiness, child care, and human services to help welfare recipients transition into work. When welfare rolls began to fall sharply in the late 1990s thanks to the economic boom then in progress, the funds needed for direct payments to beneficiaries declined, and states found themselves with a fiscal windfall that they were able to invest in expanded service programs designed to prepare even more welfare recipients for work. As a result, the social welfare system was temporarily awash with funds.[43]

RETURN OF RETRENCHMENT, 2009 ONWARD. Although government support of the nonprofit sector resumed its growth in the 1990s and into the new millennium, albeit at a slower pace, the experience of the 1980s and early 1990s left behind a lingering residue of anxiety that has still not subsided. This anxiety was reignited, moreover, by the conservative revolt that produced the Contract with America experience of the mid-1990s, with its calls for further sharp reductions in government social welfare spending, and by the additional significant cuts in discretionary programs of interest to nonprofits proposed by the Bush administration beginning in 2002.[44]

More recently, the banking crisis and resulting recession that began in 2008 added new causes for concern. Although the economic recovery program passed by Congress in early 2009 helped to buffer many human service nonprofits from the early effects of this recession, a shift in the country's political climate following the 2010 election all but slammed the door on additional antirecessionary assistance. More seriously, concern about the substantial federal deficit bequeathed by the Bush-era tax cuts, the costly wars in Iraq and Afghanistan, and the efforts to combat the recession has made it increasingly clear that government's past role as a major source of nonprofit revenue growth is likely to be scaled back extensively. With powerful political forces insisting that deficit reduction proceed entirely, or at least chiefly, through spending cuts as opposed to revenue increases, the stage was set for another extended period of retrenchment focusing on precisely the public programs of most concern to nonprofit organizations. This time, however, it seems likely that retrenchment will also carve into the once-sacrosanct entitlement programs of Medicare and Medicaid, two of the major sources of federal support not just to nonprofit hospitals but also to assisted living facilities and providers of day care, home health, supportive services for the developmentally disabled, and many more.[45] Given the fiscal pressures facing state and local governments as well, the prospects for continued growth in nonprofit revenue from government sources at anything like even recent rates thus appear dim.

FROM PRODUCER SUBSIDIES TO CONSUMER SUBSIDIES. Not just the amount, but also the form, of public sector support to the nonprofit sector changed during this period, moreover. Where in the 1960s and 1970s government offered grants and contracts to nonprofit organizations and gave nonprofits the inside track, the ascendance of conservative political elements in the 1980s and beyond brought with it a conscious effort through executive office

Table 1-2. *Federal Tax Expenditure and Loan Programs in Fields of Nonprofit Activity, 1990 and 2010*

Type of program	Amount (billions of constant 2010 dollars)		Percent change, 1990–2010
	1990	2010	
Tax expenditures	201.2	292.5	45.4
Direct loans	0.2	149.4	84,846.2
Loan guarantees	47.3	42.3	−10.6
Total	248.7	484.1	94.7

Source: U.S. Office of Management and Budget, *Budget of the U.S. Government, FY 2012,* supplemental tables; *Budget of the U.S. Government, FY1992,* special analyses.

circulars and other vehicles to encourage government program managers to promote *for-profit* involvement in government contract work instead, including that for human services.[46] At the same time, given the prevailing climate of tax cuts and hostility to expanded government spending throughout the 1980s and into the 1990s, policymakers increasingly responded to social welfare and related needs by relying more heavily on unconventional tools of government action, such as loan guarantees, tax expenditures, and vouchers, which do not appear as visibly on the budget and which channel aid to the consumers of services instead of the producers, thus requiring nonprofits to compete for clients in the market, where for-profits have traditionally had the edge.[47]

The use of such tools is by no means entirely new, of course. The deduction for medical expenses and the exclusion of scholarship income, for example, have long been established features of the tax code. But the use of such tools in fields where nonprofits are active expanded considerably over the past decade or more with the addition or extension of programs such as the child care tax credit, the credit for student loan interest payments, the low-income housing tax credit, and the new market tax credit. Just three of these tools—tax expenditures, loan guarantees, and direct loans—amounted to $484.1 billion in federal assistance in fields where nonprofits are active as of 2010 (see chapter 15, this volume). This is double their scale two decades earlier, as shown in table 1-2, and roughly equivalent to the more than $500 billion in total direct government support flowing to nonprofits. In many fields, such as day care, the indirect subsidies available through the tax system easily exceed those supported by the outright spending programs.[48]And these figures do not even include the massive sums spent through the two sizable federal voucher programs, Medicare and Medicaid. Already by 1980 as a consequence, the majority (53 percent) of federal assistance to nonprofit organizations took the form of such consumer-side subsidies, much of it through the Medicare and Medicaid programs. By 1986 this stood at 70 percent, and it continued to rise into the 1990s and beyond.

In part, this shift toward consumer-side subsidies resulted from the concentration of budget cuts almost exclusively on the so-called discretionary spending programs, which tend to be producer-side grant and contract programs, while Medicare and Medicaid—both of them demand-side subsidies—continued to grow.[49] In part also, however, the shift toward consumer-side subsidies reflects the ascendance of conservative political forces that favor forms of assistance that maximize consumer choice. The price of securing conservative support for new or expanded programs of relevance to nonprofit organizations in the latter 1980s and 1990s, therefore, was to structure them as vouchers or tax expenditures. The new Child Care and Development Block Grant enacted in 1990, and then reauthorized and expanded as part of the welfare reform legislation in 1996, thus specifically gave states the option to use the $5 billion in federal funds provided for day care to finance voucher payments to eligible families rather than grants or contracts to day care providers, and most states have pursued this option. As of 1998, therefore, well over 80 percent of the children receiving day care assistance under this program were receiving it through such voucher certificates, and another $3.5 billion in federal day care subsidies is delivered through a special child care tax credit.[50] Compared to this $7 billion in consumer-side subsidies for day care, the total that the federal government makes available through its producer-side social services block grant for the full range of social services, including day care, stood at only $2.8 billion.

Nonprofit day care providers, like their counterparts in other fields, have thus been thrown increasingly into the private market to secure even public funding for their activities. As a result, they have been obliged to master complex billing and reimbursement systems and to learn how to "market" their services to potential "customers." Worse yet, the reimbursement rates in many of these programs have often failed to keep pace with rising costs, putting a further squeeze on nonprofit budgets and making it harder to sustain mission-critical functions such as advocacy and charity care, as reflected in chapters 2 and 4 on health and social services in this volume.

Not only did government support to nonprofit organizations change its form during this period but so did important elements of private support. The most notable development here was the emergence of "managed care" in the health field, displacing the traditional pattern of fee-for-service medicine. Medicare provided an important impetus for this development by replacing its cost-based reimbursement system for hospitals in the early 1980s with a system of fixed payments for particular procedures. Corporations, too, responded to the rapid escalation of health care benefits for their workers by moving aggressively during the 1980s to replace standard fee-for-service insurance plans with managed care plans that featured up-front capitation payments to managed care providers. These providers then inserted themselves between patients and health care providers, negotiating rates with the latter and deciding which procedures were truly necessary. By 1997 close to 75 percent of the employees in medium and large establishments, and 62 percent of the employees in small establishments, were covered by some type of managed care plan.[51] More recently, managed care has expanded into the social services field, subjecting nonprofit drug treatment, rehabilitation service, and mental health treatment facilities to the same competitive pressures and reimbursement limits as hospitals have been confronting.

Taken together, these shifts added significant force to the commercialism impulse pressing on the nonprofit sector. The new forms of public action put a premium on skills and capacities far different from those advantaged by the other impulses outlined above. To survive in this new government marketplace, nonprofits had to adapt to the new commercial realities, find new market niches, or surrender market share. As we will see, most did some of each.[52]

CHANGES IN PHILANTHROPIC SUPPORT. Adding to the fiscal pressure nonprofits face has been the inability of private philanthropy to offset cutbacks in government support and finance expanded nonprofit responses to community needs. To be sure, private giving has grown considerably over the recent past. Between 1977 and 1997, for example, total private giving grew by some 90 percent after adjusting for inflation, roughly equivalent to the growth of gross domestic product. However, this lumps the amounts provided for the actual operations of charities in a given year with large endowment gifts to foundations, universities, and other institutions—gifts typically not available for use in a given year—as well as with gifts to religious congregations, most of which goes to the upkeep of the congregations and clergy.[53] When we focus on the private gifts available to support nonprofit human service, arts, education, health, and advocacy organizations over this twenty-year period the growth rate was closer to 62 percent, still impressive, but well below the 96 percent growth in overall nonprofit revenue.[54] Indeed, as a share of personal income, private giving declined steadily in the United States between the 1970s and the early 1980s, from an average of 1.86 percent in the 1970s, to 1.78 percent in the 1980s, and to 1.72 percent in the early 1990s. As a share of total sector income, private giving thus actually lost ground between 1977 and 1997, falling from 18 percent of the total in 1977 to 10 percent in 1997 excluding religion, and from 26 percent to 17.5 percent with religion included.[55]

Giving grew somewhat more robustly in the more recent 1997–2007 period, but the amounts reaching nonprofit service, expressive, and religious organizations still lagged behind the overall growth of these organizations. Thus,

Table 1-3. *Charitable Giving to Nonprofit Operating Organizations,*
1997 and 2007
Percent

Type of recipient organization	Percent increase, 1997–2007 (in constant dollars)		Giving as percent of total revenue	
	Private giving	*Total revenue*	*1997*	*2007*
Service and expressive	64	53	9.5	10.2
Religious congregations	21	25	88.0	85.0
All	42	50	17.5	16.6

Source: Murray S. Weitzman and others, *The New Nonprofit Almanac and Desk Reference, 2002* (San Francisco: Jossey-Bass, 2002), pp. 96–97; Lester M. Salamon, *America's Nonprofit Sector: A Primer,* 3rd ed. (New York: Foundation Center, 2012), chap. 3, n. 18.

as shown in table 1-3, with religious congregations included, giving to these operating nonprofit organizations increased 42 percent between 1997 and 2007 after adjusting for inflation, while overall revenue for these organizations increased by 50 percent. Giving's share of the total, with religion included, thus shrank further, to 16.5 percent. Outside of religion, giving to nonprofit service and expressive organizations registered a more sizable 64 percent growth during this decade, compared to a growth of 53 percent in the overall revenue of these organizations. However, because it started from such a small base, giving barely held its own as a share of total revenue for these organizations, increasing from 9.5 percent of the total in 1997 to 10.2 percent in 2007. And with the onset of the 2008 recession and the shrinking of assets caused by the housing bust and the banking crisis, the growth rate of private giving has slowed again. Indeed, overall private giving actually declined in absolute terms in 2008.[56]

The Competition Challenge

In addition to a fiscal challenge, nonprofit America has also faced a serious competitive challenge as a result of a significant growth of for-profit involvement in many traditional fields of nonprofit activity, from health care and welfare assistance to higher education and employment training. This, too, is not a wholly new development. Thus the nonprofit share of day care jobs dropped from 52 percent to 38 percent between 1982 and 1997, a decline of some 27 percent. And as shown in table 1-4, similarly sharp declines in the relative nonprofit share occurred among rehabilitation hospitals (down 50 percent), home health agencies (down 48 percent), health maintenance organizations (down 60 percent), kidney dialysis centers (down 45 percent), hospices (down 15 percent), and mental health clinics (down 11 percent). In many of these fields the absolute number of nonprofit facilities continued to grow, but the for-profit growth

Table 1-4. *Nonprofits' Share of Private Employment and Facilities,*
Selected Fields, 1997 and 1982
Percent

	Nonprofit share		Percent change in relative non-profit share
Measure	1982	1997	
Employment			
Child day care	52	38	−27
Job training	93	89	−4
Individual and family services	94	91	−3
Home health	60	28	−53
Kidney dialysis centers	22	15	−32
Facilities/enrollment			
Dialysis centers	58[a]	32	−45
Rehabilitation hospitals	70[a]	36	−50
Home health agencies	64[a]	33	−48
Health maintenance organizations	65[a]	26	−60
Residential treatment facilities for children	87[b]	68	−22
Psychiatric hospitals	19[a]	16	−16
Hospices	89[c]	76	−15
Mental health clinics	64[b]	57	−11
Higher education enrollments	96	89	− 7
Nursing homes	20[b]	28	40
Acute care hospitals	58[a]	59	2

Source: *U.S. Economic Census,* 1999, fig. 2.1; *Digest of Education Statistics, 2000,* pp. 209, 202–03.
a. Initial year for data is 1985, not 1982.
b. Initial year for data is 1986, not 1982.
c. Initial year for data is 1992.

outpaced it. And in at least one crucial field—acute care hospitals—while the nonprofit share increased slightly, a significant reduction occurred in the *absolute number* of nonprofit (as well as public) facilities, so that the for-profit share of the total increased even more.[57]

But the scope of competition appears to have broadened considerably in more recent years, and in an increasing range of fields nonprofits have been losing market share. Thus, as table 1-5 reveals, between 1997 and 2007 the nonprofit share of employment declined relative to that of for-profit providers in the fields of individual and family services (down 23 percent), community care facilities for the elderly (down 20 percent), home health care (down 19 percent), specialty hospital care (down 13 percent), outpatient care centers (down 8 percent), nursing care facilities (down 3 percent), and day care (down 2 percent).[58]

Table 1-5. *Change in Nonprofits' Share of Employment, Selected Fields,*
1997–2007
Percent

Field	Change in nonprofit share
Individual and family services	−23
Community care facilities for the elderly	−20
Home health care facilities	−19
Specialty hospitals (other than psychiatric)	−13
Outpatient care facilities	−8
Nursing care facilities	−3
Other residential care facilities	−3
Child day care	−2

Source: U.S. Census Bureau, *Economic Census, 1997; Economic Census, 2007.*

The range of for-profit firms competing with nonprofits has broadened, moreover. For example, the recent welfare reform legislation, which seeks to move large numbers of welfare recipients from welfare dependence to employment, attracted defense contractors like Lockheed Martin into the social welfare field. What these firms offer is less knowledge of human services than information-processing technology and contract management skills gained from serving as master contractors on huge military system projects, precisely the skills now needed to manage the subcontracting systems required to prepare welfare recipients for work.[59] Similarly, for-profits have made substantial inroads in the field of higher education. Between 1980 and 2005, while enrollment in public and nonprofit higher education institutions each grew by roughly 37 percent, enrollment in for-profit institutions expanded by 800 percent—from just over 110,000 to more than 1 million students.[60] Even the field of charitable fund-raising has recently experienced a further significant for-profit incursion in the form of financial service firms such as Fidelity and Schwab, which have created their own charitable gift funds. By 2000 the Fidelity Charitable Gift Fund had attracted more assets than the nation's largest community foundation and distributed three times as much in grants.[61] Taken together, the assets held in the donor-advised funds managed by the 38 corporate-originated charitable funds as of 2007 exceeded the donor-advised-fund holdings of all 600 of the nation's community foundations.[62]

The reasons for this striking for-profit success are by no means clear and vary from field to field. The shift in forms of public funding mentioned earlier has very likely played a significant role: by shifting from producer-side subsidies to consumer-side subsidies, government channeled more of its assistance through the marketplace, where for-profit firms have a natural advantage. The rise of HMOs and other "third-party payment" methods has had a similar effect, chapter 2 below shows, since such organizations put a special premium on price rather than quality or community roots in choosing providers, thus minimizing the comparative advantages of nonprofits.

Perhaps most decisive in explaining why nonprofits have lost market share to for-profits in so many of these markets is the uneven playing field nonprofits confront in accessing the investment capital required to establish new facilities and new operations in response to technological changes or rapid surges in demand, such as often occur when new government programs are created. A recent survey by the Johns Hopkins Listening Post Project found, for example, that the overwhelming majority of nonprofit organizations in the core human service, arts, and community development fields need investment capital to acquire facilities, equipment, and strategic planning.[63] Because they are prohibited from distributing profits to their "owners" (and indeed are not allowed to have "owners" in the market sense of the word), nonprofits lack access to the essentially "free" capital that for-profit businesses can generate merely by issuing and selling stock. Most of these surveyed organizations therefore encountered difficulties accessing the investment capital they needed, and those that did manage to access it were restricted to borrowing from commercial banks, typically the most expensive sources.

When surges in demand occur, such as accompanied the decision by the Medicare program to make home health care a reimbursable expense in 1980 as a way to reduce the spiraling cost of hospital care, it was thus for-profit providers who were in the best position to respond by floating IPOs (initial public offerings) and generating the capital to build thousands of new facilities. And this pattern has been repeated in numerous other spheres. While efforts have recently been launched to attract private investment capital into "social enterprises" and other social-purpose organizations, and to entice foundations to function like "philanthropic banks" by leveraging their assets to incentivize such flows of private investment capital into nonprofit and for-profit social ventures, such efforts remain on the "frontiers" of philanthropic and private-investment practice and have yet to be fully mainstreamed.[64]

The Effectiveness Challenge

One consequence of the increased competition nonprofits are facing has been to intensify the pressure on them to perform—and to demonstrate that performance. The result is a third challenge: the effectiveness challenge. As the management expert William Ryan writes, "Nonprofits are now forced to reexamine their reasons for existing in light of a market that rewards discipline and performance and emphasizes organizational capacity rather than for-profit or nonprofit status and mission. Nonprofits have no choice but to reckon with these forces."[65] This runs counter to long-standing theories in the nonprofit field that emphasize this sector's distinctive advantage precisely in fields where normal market mechanisms do not operate because the consumers of services are not the same as the people paying for them, and where trust is consequently needed instead. Because they are not organized to pursue profits, it is argued, nonprofits are more worthy of such trust and therefore more reliable providers in such difficult-to-measure fields.[66]

In the current climate, however, such theories have few remaining adherents, at least among those who control the sector's purse strings. Government managers, themselves under pressure to demonstrate results as a consequence of the recent Government Performance and Results Act, are increasingly pressing their nonprofit contractors to deliver measurable results, too. Not to be outdone, prominent philanthropic institutions have jumped onto the performance bandwagon. United Way of America, for example, thus launched a bold performance measurement system in the mid-1990s complete with website, performance measurement manual, and video in order to induce member agencies to require performance measurement as a condition of local funding. Numerous foundations have moved in a similar direction, increasing the emphasis on evaluation both of their grantees and of their own programming.[67] Indeed, a new foundation affinity group, Grantmakers for Effective Organizations (GEO), was recently formed, and a new "venture philanthropy" model has been attracting adherents.[68] The key to this model is an investment approach to grant making that calls on philanthropic institutions to invest in organizations rather than individual programs, to take a more active hand in organizational governance and operations, and to insist on measurable results. This same emphasis on "metrics" as the new elixir of nonprofit performance has taken root in the social enterprise movement that has lately swept the nonprofit field, with support from a new class of dot.com entrepreneurs turned philanthropists.[69]

The resulting "accountability environment" in which nonprofits are having to operate will doubtless produce many positive results. But it also increases the pressures on hard-pressed nonprofit managers for demonstrations of progress that neither they, nor anyone else, may be able to supply, at least not without far greater resources than are currently available for the task. What is more, as chapter 16 of this volume suggests, accountability expectations often fail to acknowledge the multiple meanings that accountability can have and the multiple stakeholders whose accountability demands nonprofits must accommodate. The risk is great, therefore, that the measures most readily at hand, or those most responsive to the market test, will substitute for those most germane to the problems being addressed. That, at any rate, is the lesson of public sector experience with performance measurement, and the increased focus on price rather than quality or community benefit in third-party contracting with nonprofit health providers certainly supports this observation.[70]

The Technology Challenge

Pressures from for-profit competitors have also accelerated the demands on nonprofits to incorporate new technology into their operations. Indeed, technology has become one of the wild cards of nonprofit evolution.

But enticing as the opportunities opened by technological change may be to the nation's nonprofit institutions, they pose at least equally enormous challenges. Most obvious, perhaps, are the financial challenges. As one recent study has noted: "Information technologies are resource intensive. They entail significant purchase costs, require significant training and upkeep, and yet become obsolete quickly."[71] Because of the structural disadvantages nonprofits face in raising capital due to their inability to enter the equity markets, however, the massive intrusion of new technological requirements into their work puts them at a distinct disadvantage vis-à-vis their for-profit competitors. We have already seen the consequences of this in the health insurance industry, where the lack of capital following the discontinuation of government funding led to loss of market share to for-profit firms, which were better able to capitalize the huge investments in information-processing equipment required to manage the large risk pools that make managed care viable. Similar pressures are now at work in the social services industry, where managed care is also taking root.

Not only does technology threaten to alter further the balance between nonprofits and for-profits, but also it threatens to alter the structure of the nonprofit sector itself, advantaging larger organizations over smaller ones. This is due in part to the heavy fixed costs of the new technology. Already, concerns about a "digital divide" are surfacing within the sector, as survey after survey reveals the unequal distribution of both hardware and the capacity to adapt the hardware to organizational missions.[72] Though it initially stimulates competition by giving even small start-ups access to huge markets, information technology also creates "network effects" that accentuate the advantages of dominant players.[73] Concern has thus surfaced that e-philanthropy will allow large, well-known national nonprofits to raid the donor bases of local United Ways and operating charities and that information technology more generally advantages large, nationally prominent agencies in the competition for business partners, government funding, and charitable support. Although recent data suggest that more nonprofits are managing to catch up to the early adopters with respect to core IT tools, such as computers and Internet access, many fewer nonprofits are using newer technologies, such as hand-held devices and web applications. What is more, technology is being applied more extensively to basic administrative and accounting functions than to more complex programmatic ones.[74]

But the challenges posed by technology go far beyond financial or competi-tive considerations. Also at stake are fundamental philosophical issues that go to the heart of the nonprofit sector's mission and modes of operation. Indeed, technology has been one of the doors through which the commercial impulse has entered the nonprofit sector in a major way. As shown in chapter 5 such issues have surfaced especially vividly in the arts, where the new technology raises fundamental questions of aesthetics, creative control, and intellectual property rights. Similar dilemmas confront educational institutions that are tempted by the new technologies to brand their products and package them for mass consumption but at the risk of alienating their professorate, losing the immediacy of direct student-faculty contact, and giving precedence to the pack-aging of knowledge rather than to its discovery. How these commercial/tech-nological dilemmas are resolved could well determine how the nonprofit sector evolves in the years ahead.

The Legitimacy Challenge

The moral and philosophical challenges that American nonprofit organizations are confronting at the present time go well beyond those posed by new technol-ogy, however. Rather, a serious fault line seems to have opened in the founda-tion of public trust on which the entire nonprofit edifice rests. This may be due in part to the unrealistic expectations that the public has of these institutions, expectations that the charitable sector ironically counts on and encourages. Also at work, however, have been four other lines of argument.

SPECIAL INTEREST ARGUMENT. The first is the strident indictment that con-servative politicians and commentators have lodged against many nonprofit organizations over the past decades on grounds that nonprofit charitable orga-nizations have become just another special interest, regularly conspiring with government bureaucrats to escalate public spending, and doing so not so much out of real conviction about the needs being served than a desire to feather their own nests. The Heritage Foundation president Edward Fuelner put this case especially sharply in 1996, criticizing charities for urging Congress to expand social welfare spending while themselves "feeding at the public trough."[75] Entire organizations have been formed, in fact, to remove the halo from the nonprofit sector in this way, charging that a "new kind of nonprofit organization" has emerged in recent years "dedicated not to voluntary action, but to an expanded government role in our lives."[76]

Worse than that, the very motives of nonprofit agencies have been called into question. Involvement in government programs "changes charities' incentives," charges one critique, "giving them reasons to keep caseloads up instead of get-ting them down by successfully turning around people's lives."[77] Nonprofits thus stand accused not only of being ineffective but also of preferring not to solve the problems they are purportedly addressing. In part to remedy this, advocates of this view rallied behind the so-called Istook amendment, which sought to limit the advocacy activity of nonprofit organizations by prohibiting any nonprofit organization receiving government support from using any more than 5 percent of its *total* revenues, not just its public revenues, for advocacy or lobbying activities.

THE PROGRAMMATIC CRITIQUE. Feeding into this critique, moreover, has been a second line of argument that has caught nonprofit organizations, particularly in the human service field, in the more general assault on public social programs that has animated national political debate for more than three decades now. In the minds of many, the persistence of poverty, urban crime, teenage pregnancy, and numerous other problems have been taken as evidence that publicly funded social programs do not work, despite considerable evidence to the contrary.[78] The resulting open season on government social programs has caught significant components of the nonprofit sector in the crossfire, particularly since the sector has been involved in administering many of the discredited efforts. Underlying this argument is a profound rethinking of the causes of poverty and of the interventions likely to reduce it. The central change here involves a loss of faith in the traditional premise of professional social work, with its emphasis on casework and individualized services as the cure for poverty and disadvantage. During the 1960s, this precept was translated into public policy through the 1962 amendments to the Social Security Act and, later, through portions of the Economic Opportunity Act of 1964, both of which made federal resources available to purchase social services for poor people in the hope that this would allow them to escape the "culture of poverty" in which they were enmeshed. In the process, the professionalism impulse was firmly implanted in the nation's nonprofit sector.

This "services strategy," and the professionalism impulse it encouraged, has subsequently been challenged by critics on both the right and the left. Those on the right argue that the growth of supportive services and income assistance for the poor ultimately create disincentives to work and undermine fundamental values of self-reliance.[79] Those on the left, by contrast, point to the structural shifts in the economy, which have eliminated much of the market for blue-collar labor, as the real causes of poverty, unemployment, and the social maladies that flow from them. Both sides seem to agree, however, that the traditional skills of the nonprofit human service sector have become increasingly irrelevant to the problems facing the poor. More important than social services in the new paradigm is job readiness and, ultimately, a job.

Under these circumstances, the employer rather than the social worker becomes the pivot of social policy. While private nonprofit organizations may still play a role in the alleviation of poverty, the real action has shifted to the business community, the educational system, and in the conservative view, the faith community. This is clearly reflected in the welfare reform law of 1996, which ended the entitlement to income assistance and emphasized employment as a condition of assistance.

These views also echo loudly in the Bush administration's 2001 proposal to privilege "faith-based charities" in the distribution of federal assistance. A principal appeal of this idea is the prospect of replacing formal, professionalized, nonprofit organizations with informal church groups, staffed by well-meaning volunteers, who can help individuals gain the life skills and moral backbone thought to be needed to succeed in the workplace. This reinforces a quaint, nineteenth-century image of how charitable organizations are supposed to operate, an image that competitive pressures, accountability demands, and technological change have made increasingly untenable. This jobs focus also lies behind the recent enthusiasm for "social enterprises," which, unlike standard human service agencies, use the market to pursue social objectives.[80] All of this has pushed the traditional nonprofit sector toward the periphery of social problem solving, at least in much of the prevailing political rhetoric, undermining the professional impulse and strengthening the civic activism, voluntaristic, and commercial impulses at work in the sector.

THE OVERPROFESSIONALIZATION ARGUMENT. Similar challenges to the legitimacy of nonprofit organizations and to the professional impulse that gained ascendance in much of the nonprofit sector over the previous half-century arise from critics who take nonprofits to task for becoming overly professional and thus losing touch with those they serve. This line of argument has a long lineage in American social science, as evidenced by the brilliant analysis by the historian Roy Lubove of the professionalization of social work, which led social workers away from social diagnosis, community organizing, and social reform toward a client-focused, medical model of social work practice.[81]

More recently, critics on the left have implicated nonprofit organizations more generally for contributing to the overprofessionalization of social concerns, redefining basic human needs as "problems" that only professionals can resolve, and thereby alienating people from the helping relationships they could establish with their neighbors and kin.[82] By embracing professionalism, these critics charge, nonprofit organizations destroy community rather than building it. Critics on the right, moreover, have been equally derisive of the professionalized human service apparatus, charging it with inflating the cost of dealing with social problems by "crowding" out lower-cost, alternative, mechanisms that are at least as effective.[83] This, in turn, has added further fuel to the voluntarism engine.

THE ACCOUNTABILITY ARGUMENT. Complicating matters further is the fact that nonprofit organizations generally lack meaningful bases for demonstrating the value of what they do. "Unlike publicly traded companies," the management expert Regina Herzlinger notes, "the performance of nonprofits and governments is shrouded behind a veil of secrecy that is lifted only when blatant disasters occur."[84] This is problematic, she argues, because nonprofit organizations generally lack the three basic accountability mechanisms of business: the self-interest of owners, competition, and the ultimate bottom-line measure of profitability. This view has prompted calls even from advocates of the sector for more formal mechanisms for holding nonprofit organizations accountable and suggestions from political leaders that the nonprofit sector is in serious need of additional regulation.[85]

CONSEQUENCES. These criticisms, coupled with a spate of high-profile scandals in the early 1990s, seem to have shaken public confidence in charitable institutions. Surveys taken in 1994 and 1996 found only 33 percent and 37 percent of respondents, respectively, expressing "a great deal" or "quite a lot" of confidence in nonprofit human service agencies, well behind the proportions expressing similar levels of confidence in the military and small business.[86] This improved considerably in the latter 1990s, perhaps as a consequence of the perceived success of welfare reform. Yet even at this latter date, while a substantial majority of respondents agreed that "charitable organizations play a major role in making our communities better places to live," only 20 percent "strongly agreed" with this statement. And only 10 percent agreed "strongly" that most charities are "honest and ethical in their use of donated funds," a figure that remained at this low level seven years later, in 2006.[87] All of this suggests that America's nonprofit institutions are delicately balanced on a knife edge of public support, with most people willing to grant them the benefit of the doubt, but with a strong undercurrent of uncertainty and concern. As a consequence, a relative handful of highly visible scandals—such as the United Way scandal of the early 1990s, the New Era Philanthropy scandal of the mid-1990s, or the Red Cross difficulties in the wake of September 11—can have an impact that goes well beyond their actual significance.

Taking advantage of the resulting questioning, local governments are increasingly emboldened to challenge the tax exemptions of nonprofit organizations. Such challenges have surfaced in Pennsylvania, New York, New Hampshire, Oregon, Maine, Wisconsin, Colorado, Massachusetts, and Illinois.[88] A recent survey showed, in fact, that among one sample of mostly mid-sized and large nonprofits operating in the fields of social services, community development, and arts and culture, a striking 63 percent reported paying some kind of tax, payment in lieu of taxes, or other fee to state or local government.[89] And challenges to the favorable tax treatment of nonprofits is not restricted to state and local governments. As noted earlier, the Obama administration, hardly a foe of the nonprofit sector, proposed a cap on the tax deduction available for charitable contributions in its 2011 budget proposal and repeated this idea in the deficit reduction proposals it advanced during the debt crisis debate of 2011.

One additional reflection of the legitimacy cloud under which nonprofits have been obliged to operate concerns their political advocacy activities, another crucial function of the nonprofit sector, as outlined above. To be sure, restrictions on nonprofit campaign activities and lobbying have long been a part of the basic federal tax exemption law. But as noted in chapter 15, *lobbying* is defined rather narrowly in the tax law, and even then nonprofits are allowed to engage in it as long as it does not constitute a "significant" part of their activities. Beginning in the late 1960s, and then gathering pace in the 1980s and over the next twenty-five years, however, nonprofits have been subjected to an increasing set of restrictions on their advocacy and lobbying activities. These restrictions are all the more troubling for nonprofits in view of the 2010 Supreme Court ruling in *Citizens United* v. *Federal Election Commission,* which removed all restrictions on corporate financing of election campaigns.[90]

An opening salvo in this line of restrictions came with the passage of the landmark 1969 Tax Reform Act, which penalized foundations for their involvement in the civil rights struggle of the 1960s by prohibiting foundations from financing nonprofit efforts to influence legislation, thus eliminating one of the more important sources of funding for nonprofit lobbying activities.[91] This was followed by an Office of Management and Budget Circular (A-122) promulgated by the Reagan administration in 1984, which essentially prohibits nonprofits from using federal grant dollars to support "political advocacy," a concept that embraces far more than the narrower concept of "lobbying."[92] The Lobbying Disclosure Act of 1995 then extended restrictions on lobbying to 501(c)(4) organizations, which are specifically permitted to lobby even if they receive federal grants, loans, or awards. A spate of campaign finance and lobby disclosure restrictions in 2002, 2004, and 2007 also caught nonprofit organizations in their crossfire.[93] And nonprofits have also confronted additional challenges, so far unsuccessful, to bar organizations receiving federal funds not only from attempting to influence legislation but also from engaging in litigation or participating in administrative agency proceedings, activities long considered fundamental forms of expression in a free society.

The Human Resource Challenge

Inevitably, fiscal stress and signs of public ambivalence toward the nonprofit sector have taken their toll on the sector's human resources. Experts in the child welfare field, for example, identify "staff turnover" as "perhaps the most important problem" facing the field, and cite "stress . . . overwhelming account-ability requirements, and concern over liability" as the principal causes.[94] As chapter 8 shows, similar problems afflict the international relief field due to the explosion of complex humanitarian crises that intermix enormous relief challenges with complicated political and military conflicts.

Especially difficult has been the recruitment and retention of frontline service workers, for whom salary, benefit, and safety issues are particularly important, but retention of managerial personnel has also grown increasingly problematic. One study of graduates of public policy programs reports, for example, that the proportion of these public-spirited young people who took their first jobs in nonprofit organizations doubled between the early 1970s and the early 1990s.[95] However, the nonprofit sector's retention rate for these personnel has declined over time, with more turning to the for-profit sector as an alternative. Of special concern is the turnover of talent at the executive director level. Executive directors, who came into the field to pursue the social missions of their agencies, find themselves expected to function instead as aggressive entrepreneurs, leading outward-oriented enterprises able to attract paying customers while retaining the allegiance of socially committed donors and boards, all of this in a context of growing public scrutiny and mistrust. According to one study, a surprising two-thirds of the executive directors in a national sample of nonprofit agencies were in their first executive director position, and over half of these had held the job for four years or less.[96] While most reported enjoying their jobs, a third indicated an intention to leave it within two years; and even among those likely to take another job in the nonprofit sector, only half indicated that their next job was likely to be as an executive director. As Stefan Toepler and Margaret Wyszomirski report in chapter 5, leadership recruitment has become a particular challenge in the arts field, where the vacancy rate for art museum directors hit a fifteen-year high in 1999.

Opportunities

But challenges are not all that nonprofit America has confronted in the recent past. It has also had the benefit of a number of opportunities, many of which also seem likely to persist. Four of these in particular deserve special attention.

Increased Demand

In the first place, nonprofit organizations are being affected by a number of demographic trends that are boosting the demand for the kinds of services these organizations provide. Among the more salient of these trends are the following:

—Aging of the population. The country's population of seniors seventy-five years and older doubled between 1980 and 2008, on top of a doubling of the sixty-five and older population between 1960 and 2000. This trend seems likely to continue, moreover, with the prospect that the over-seventy-five population will grow by 77 percent between 2010 and 2030, while the overall population of the country will grow by only 20 percent.[97] This will boost the need for nursing home care, assisted living, and other elderly services, fields in which nonprofits have a considerable presence. At the same time, as noted in chapter 17, the lengthened life span of the average American is changing the normal education-work-retirement trajectory to something closer to an education-work-contribute trajectory, as baby boomers show up at the doors of nonprofit organizations as volunteers eager to put their skills at the service of others in so-called encore careers.

—*Expansion of the labor force participation rate of women.* The labor force participation rate for women jumped from less than 20 percent in 1960 to over 60 percent in 1998 and has been holding at that level ever since. Even more dramatically, the labor force participation rate for married women with children under the age of six rose from 18.6 percent in 1960 to 62.0 percent in 2009, and for single women with children under six it reached nearly 68 percent.[98] While it is far from clear what impact the job losses that accompanied the recession that began in 2008 will have on this pattern, it seems likely that the increased demand for child care and other household-related services, another significant arena of nonprofit activity, will persist.

—*Shifts in family structure.* Significant changes that have occurred in the American family structure also have important implications for nonprofit agencies. In 1960 there was one divorce for every four marriages. By 1980 this figure had jumped to one divorce for every two marriages, and it has remained there into the new millennium. During this same period, the number of children involved in divorces increased from 463,000 in 1960 to more than 1 million throughout the 1980s and 1990s. Since divorce typically involves a certain amount of emotional trauma and often brings with it significant loss of economic status, this shift also translates into increased need for human services of the sort that many nonprofit agencies offer. Also contributing to this increased demand is the tremendous surge in out-of-wedlock births. Between 1960 and 1980 the proportion of all births that were to unwed mothers increased from 5 percent to 18 percent, and by 1994 it had reached 33 percent. This represents an eightfold increase in the number of out-of-wedlock births, from 224,000 in 1960 to 1.3 million in 1995, and to 1.7 million in 2007. Although this phenomenon is sometimes perceived to be concentrated in minority populations, in fact the vast majority of these births (68 percent) are to white mothers.[99]

—*Substance abuse.* Changes have also occurred in the prevalence of substance abuse in American society. One reflection of this is the striking increase in the number of people receiving substance abuse treatment over the past several decades. As recently as 1977 the number of people using such services stood at approximately 235,000. By 1995 it was over 1 million, and by 2009 it was close to 1.2 million.[100]

—*Surge of immigration.* A significant expansion has also occurred in the number of people obtaining legal permanent resident status in the United States. This number rose from 3.3 million in the 1960s to 9.5 million in just the first nine years of the new millennium, and this does not include the continued surge of illegal immigration.[101] These developments, too, have created increased demands for a variety of acculturation and resettlement services, not to mention related human and health services, that nonprofits have long provided.

—*Cultural subgroups.* Equally important is the emergence of at least one demographic subgroup that may hold some promise of helping the nonprofit sector meet some of this expanded demand. The subgroup in question is what demographers have termed "cultural creatives," an estimated 50 million people distinguished from others in the population by their preference for holistic thinking, their cosmopolitanism, their social activism, and their insistence on finding a better balance between work and personal values than the two other prominent population groups in American society, the "moderns" and the "traditionalists," seem to have found.[102] Though they have yet to develop a full self-consciousness, cultural creatives are powerfully attracted to the mission orientation of the nonprofit sector and could well help resolve some of the sector's human resource challenges.

Taken together, these and other sociodemographic changes have expanded the demand for many of the services that nonprofit organizations have traditionally provided, such as child day care, home health and nursing home care for the elderly, family counseling, foster care, relocation assistance, and substance abuse treatment and prevention. The demand for these services has spread well beyond the poor, moreover, and now encompasses middle-class households with resources to pay for them, a phenomenon that one analyst calls "the transformation of social services."[103] The foster care system alone, for example, has ballooned, as the number of children in foster care doubled between the early 1980s and the early 1990s, though the growth subsided somewhat in the new millennium. At the same time, the welfare reform legislation enacted in 1996, with its stress on job readiness, has created additional demand for the services that nonprofits typically offer.

While the demographic developments have increased the demand for nonprofit services, they may also be contributing to the supply of personnel willing to help meet this demand, as the growing elderly population cycles out of full-time work and into greater volunteer involvement and as cultural creatives find in the nonprofit sector a combination of work and meaning that fulfills their own sense of worth.

Greater Visibility and Policy Salience

Another factor working to the advantage of nonprofit organizations has been a spate of political and policy developments that has substantially increased the visibility of these organizations. This has included the neo-liberal ideology popularized in the 1980s by Margaret Thatcher in the United Kingdom and Ronald Reagan in the United States with their antigovernment rhetoric and their emphasis on philanthropy and the private sector, including the private nonprofit sector, as better vehicles than government for addressing human needs; the revival of these notions with the rise of the Tea Party movement in the United States in 2008 and beyond despite the evidence of for-profit excesses that produced the 2008 economic crisis; the significant credibility that the concept of "civil society," of citizen self-organization, gained during the uprisings that brought down communism in Central Europe in the latter 1980s and again in the citizen movements challenging authoritarian regimes in the "Arab spring" of 2011; the recent emphasis on the importance of "social capital" in promoting democracy and economic growth and the linkage of social capital to the presence of associations; the growing enthusiasm over the emergence of "social entrepreneurs" and the "social ventures" they are creating; and the Obama administration's support for "social innovation" and the "social entrepreneurs" that promote it.

Responding to the buzz surrounding civil society and the nonprofit sector, the academic community has taken a newfound interest in these organizations. Research centers focusing on nonprofit organizations and philanthropy have been established at such institutions as Yale University, Johns Hopkins University, Indiana University, Harvard University, and the Urban Institute beginning as early as 1975 and extending into the 1990s. In addition, nonprofit studies has slowly penetrated the academic curriculum. As of 2009, 168 U.S. colleges or universities had graduate degree programs with a concentration in the operation of nonprofit organizations, up from only 17 as recently as 1990.[104] Despite the evidence of declining confidence in nonprofit organizations, moreover, other evidence points to continued popular support. Public opinion polls thus reveal continued widespread involvement in charitable giving and volunteering, key supports for the country's nonprofit organizations.[105] What is more, as chapter 11 shows, a robust set of infrastructure organizations has grown up to support various types of nonprofit organizations and the nonprofit field as a whole.

New Technology

A third factor at least potentially of assistance to the nonprofit sector is the extraordinary array of technological advances that has become available thanks to the communications and biotechnology revolutions of the past several decades. To be sure, as noted earlier, technology is a two-edged sword for the nonprofit sector. On the one hand, it poses challenges to nonprofits because of its associated capital requirements. But as labor-intensive organizations, nonprofits stand to benefit greatly from the technology revolution if they can find the resources of capital and knowledge to do so. "Distributed learning" that provides new options for small liberal arts colleges, the promotion of newly developed green technologies by nonprofit environmental organizations, "social networking civic activism" to transform nonprofit advocacy, and developments in biosciences that could revolutionize medical treatment in nonprofit hospitals and clinics are just some of the opportunities that new technologies offer to nonprofits, as chapter 17 notes.

The New Philanthropy

Also working to the benefit of the nonprofit sector is a series of developments affecting private philanthropy. These include

—A widely anticipated *intergenerational transfer of wealth* between the baby boom generation and its offspring over the next twenty to thirty years, though the sharp drop in home prices beginning in 2008 and the rising cost of health care for the baby boom generation seem likely to take a large bite out of this rather optimistic scenario.[106]

—The greater corporate willingness to engage in partnerships and collaborations with nonprofit organizations, which has resulted from globalization and the resulting importance of corporate "reputational capital."[107]

—The dot.com phenomenon, which led to the accumulation of enormous fortunes in the hands of a small group of high-tech entrepreneurs, some of whom have turned their newfound wealth into charitable activities.[108]

—The parallel emergence of a robust group of "social entrepreneurs" who are finding new ways to use business means to serve social ends and an inventive group of philanthropists and social investors who are developing new tools through which to leverage philanthropic capital and thereby channel private investment capital into the resulting social ventures.[109] Together, these developments are injecting a substantial amount of new blood and new energy into the philanthropic field, creating new opportunities for meeting the nonprofit sector's fiscal needs.

The Nonprofit Response: A Story of Resilience

How has nonprofit America responded to the extraordinary combination of challenges and opportunities it has faced over the past several decades? Has the sector been able to cope with the challenges and take advantage of the opportunities? And with what consequences for its current health and character and for its likely evolution? More significantly, have the responses advantaged any of the four impulses identified earlier, and if so, what implications does this have for the role that nonprofits are likely to play in national life?

The answers to these questions are especially important in light of the conventional wisdom about the responsiveness of nonprofit organizations. "Profit-making organizations are more flexible with respect to the deployment and redeployment of resources," management experts Rosabeth Kanter and David Summers wrote in 1987. "But the centrality of mission for nonprofit organizations places limitations on their flexibility of action."[110] Nonprofits are not to be trusted, Regina Herzlinger similarly explained to readers of the *Harvard Business Review* in 1996, because they lack the three basic accountability measures that ensure effective and efficient business operations: the self-interest of owners, competition, and the ultimate bottom-line measure of profitability.[111]

Contrary to these conventional beliefs, however, nonprofit America has responded with striking resilience to the complex challenges and opportunities it has recently confronted and continues to confront. Though largely unheralded, nonprofit America has undergone a quiet revolution during this period, a massive process of reinvention and reengineering that is still under way. To be sure, the resulting changes are hardly universal. What is more, there are serious questions about whether the resulting changes are in a wholly desirable direction or whether they have exposed the sector to unacceptable risks. While important shadings are needed to do justice to the considerable diversity that exists, there is no denying the dominant picture of resilience, adaptation, and change. More specifically, four broad threads of change are apparent.

Overall Sector Growth

In the first place, despite the cutbacks of the early 1980s, nonprofit organizations have registered substantial growth over the past thirty years, through 2007, the latest year for which data are available as of this writing.[112] This growth was already evident in the early part of this period. Thus as figure 1-6 shows, between 1977 and 1996 nonprofit revenues swelled by 96 percent after adjusting for inflation, for an average annual growth rate of 3.6 percent. By comparison, during this same period the GDP grew by a significantly smaller 75 percent, or about 3.0 percent a year. Put somewhat differently, nonprofit revenues increased at a rate that was 20 percent faster than the overall U.S. GDP.

What is more, this growth was not restricted only to nonprofit health organizations. Rather, while nonprofit health organizations boosted their revenue by 109 percent between 1977 and 1996, nonprofit arts organizations grew by 114 percent and nonprofit social service organizations by 117 percent.[113]

Figure 1-6. *Average Annual Growth in Nonprofit Revenues and U.S. GDP, 1977–96 and 1997–2007*

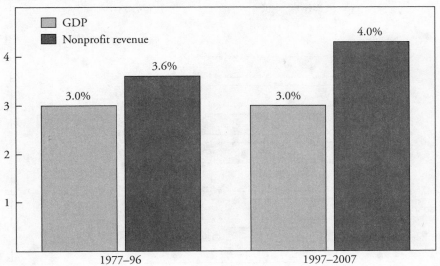

Source: See note 112 on page 82.

But the growth in nonprofit revenue has accelerated even further in more recent years. Thus as shown in figure 1-6, during the ten years between 1997 and 2007 nonprofit revenues grew by another 53 percent after adjusting for inflation for an average growth rate of 4.3 percent a year, well above the 3.6 percent in the earlier 1977–96 period. During this recent period as well, moreover, the growth of the nonprofit sector continued to outpace the growth of the U.S. economy as a whole. Thus, compared to the 53 percent increase in nonprofit revenues between 1997 and 2007, the U.S. GDP grew by a smaller 32 percent, or about 3 percent a year.

As figure 1-7 shows, moreover, this recent growth too was not restricted to any one component of the nonprofit sector. Although the category of "other" organizations—civic, international, and other—appears to have surged ahead of other fields, this is likely a reflection of the small base against which these percentages are computed. More generally, the growth pattern of most fields of nonprofit activity hovered around 50 percent during this 1997–2007 period, and the one laggard—culture and recreation—still had a growth rate (41 percent) that beat that of the U.S. GDP.

Figure 1-7. *Changes in Nonprofit Revenues, by Field, 1997–2007 (constant 2007 dollars)*

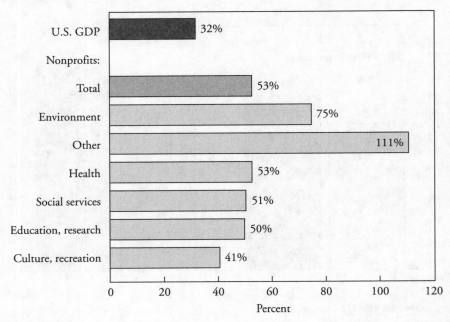

Source: See note 112 on page 82.

While the *rate* of growth in the nonprofit sector was quite uniform across components, the share of the growth captured by the various segments differed markedly, reflecting the divergent scale of these segments. Thus health care nonprofits generated 57 percent of the growth of the nonprofit sector between 1997 and 2007, roughly equivalent to the share of the total with which they started the period. Education organizations accounted for 21 percent of the growth, and social service providers, 14 percent. The remaining organizations—culture and recreation, environment, and international—accounted for the remaining 8 percent.

Evidence of the vibrancy of the nonprofit sector extends well beyond financial indicators, however, which are heavily influenced by the performance of the largest organizations. Equally revealing is the record of organizational formation. Between 1977 and 1997 the number of 501(c)(3) and 501(c)(4) organizations registered with the Internal Revenue Service increased by 115 percent, or about 23,000 organizations a year.[114] By comparison, the number of business organizations increased by only 76 percent during this same period. The rate of nonprofit organization formation seems to have accelerated in more recent years, moreover, jumping to an average of 45,000 a year between 1997 and 2009, and this despite increased pressures for organizational mergers and the onset of the 2007–09 recession. Evidently, Americans are still finding in the nonprofit sector a convenient outlet for a wide assortment of social, economic, political, and cultural concerns.[115]

Commercialization

What accounts for this record of robust growth? While many factors have played a part, the dominant one appears to be the vigor with which nonprofit America has embraced the spirit and the techniques of the market. The impact of the commercial and managerial impulse on the nonprofit sector has increased enormously over the past two decades and manifests itself in a number of ways.

GROWTH OF COMMERCIAL INCOME. Perhaps the clearest indication of the penetration of the commercial impulse into nonprofit operations has been the substantial rise in nonprofit commercial income, that is, income from service fees, investment earnings, and sales of products.[116] This reflects the success with which nonprofit organizations took advantage of the demographic trends noted above by marketing their services to a clientele both increasingly in need of non-profit services and able to pay for them. In fact, nonprofit income from these commercial sources surged 64 percent in real dollar terms between 1997 and 2007, accounting in the process for nearly 60 percent of the sector's revenue growth during this period—twice as much as their nearest competitor, as shown in figure 1-8. In the process, commercial income strengthened its position as the dominant source of nonprofit service and expressive organization revenue, with 52 percent of the total as of 2007.

Fees and other commercial sources of nonprofit income not only grew in overall scale but also spread to ever-broader components of the sector. Already dominant in health, higher education, and the arts by 1997, commercial income spread its reach to other areas of nonprofit activity as well. Thus for example, as figure 1-9 shows, commercial income also accounted for 40 percent of the revenue growth of nonprofit social service organizations during the 1997–2007 period. Even religious organizations boosted their commercial income during this period, largely, as chapter 9 below shows, through the sale or rental of church property.

In only one field—culture and recreation—did the commercial tide weaken in the most recent period for which data are available. While fees and charges remained the largest source of revenue growth for culture and recreation organizations as they did for the nonprofit sector as a whole between 1997 and 2007, that dominance actually slipped somewhat. Thus, while fees and charges accounted for 57 percent of the income of these organizations as of 1997, they

Figure 1-8. *Sources of Nonprofit Growth, 1997–2007*

Total growth: $457 billion

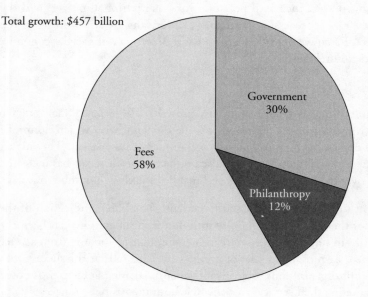

Source: See note 112 on page 82.

accounted for a much smaller 45 percent of the revenue growth between 1997 and 2007, as culture and recreation organizations, feeling some pushback from patrons, made a concerted effort to boost their philanthropic support instead. Whether arts organizations can continue to rely on growth in philanthropy in the wake of the stock market turmoil and economic distress that followed the banking crisis of 2008, however, remains an open question going forward.

To secure such commercial income, nonprofits have naturally had to go where the "customers" are, which has meant a migration of nonprofit jobs to the suburbs and the Sun Belt. This is evident in the growing suburbanization of philanthropy during the 1980s and in the geographic spread of nonprofit employment.[117] Seventy percent of the substantial growth of nonprofit employment in the state of Maryland between 1989 and 1999, for example, took place in the Baltimore and Washington suburbs, whereas the city of Baltimore, which started the period with nearly half of the state's nonprofit employment, accounted for only 17 percent of the growth. This pattern has continued into more recent years as well. Thus the Baltimore and Washington suburbs, with 53 percent of the state's nonprofit employment as of 2008, accounted for 58 percent of the state's nonprofit employment growth between 2008 and 2010,

Figure 1-9. *Sources of Nonprofit Revenue Growth, by Field, 1997–2007*

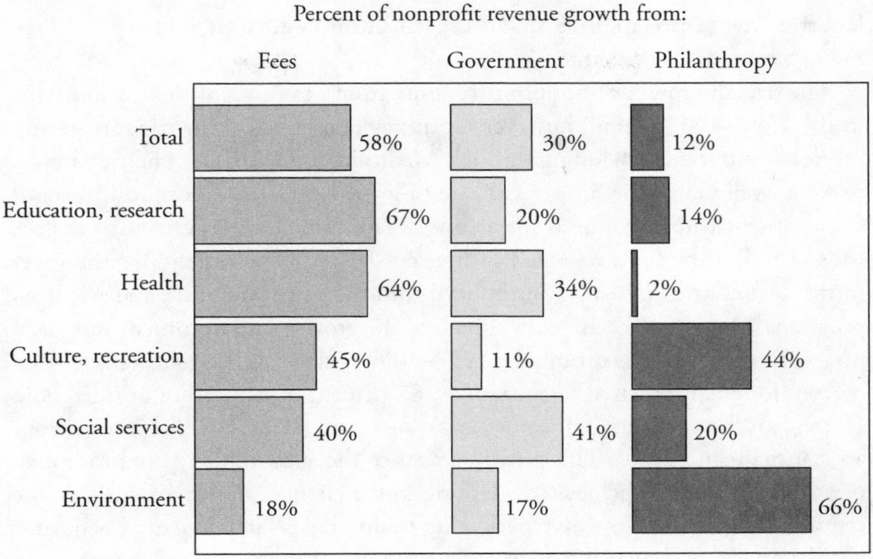

Percent of nonprofit revenue growth from:

	Fees	Government	Philanthropy
Total	58%	30%	12%
Education, research	67%	20%	14%
Health	64%	34%	2%
Culture, recreation	45%	11%	44%
Social services	40%	41%	20%
Environment	18%	17%	66%

Source: Regina Herzlinger, "Can Public Trust in Nonprofits and Governments Be Restored?" *Harvard Business Review* 74, March/April (1996).

while the city of Baltimore, with 37 percent of the nonprofit jobs, accounted for a much smaller 29 percent of the nonprofit job growth.[118]

ADAPTATION TO THE NEW TERRAIN OF PUBLIC FUNDING. Another reflection of the commercialization of the nonprofit sector is the success with which nonprofits have adapted to the new terrain of public funding, which has grown more commercial as a consequence of the shift to consumer-side subsidies discussed earlier. Despite this shift, nonprofits managed to boost their government support 195 percent in real dollar terms between 1977 and 1997. Government accounted for 42 percent of the nonprofit service and expressive organizations' substantial growth during this period as a consequence.

Behind these numbers lie some creative nonprofit responses to the enormous shifts in the forms of public sector support. Social service agencies had to be particularly nimble in adjusting to the new realities, as states shifted their social service spending from stagnant or declining discretionary grant programs to the rapidly growing Medicaid and SSI programs, both of which deliver their benefits to clients and therefore require agencies to master new marketing, billing, and reimbursement-management skills. Similarly impressive is the success of nonprofit housing and community development organizations in taking advantage of the new Low Income Housing Tax Credit program designed to stimulate the flow of private investment capital into low-income housing, as documented more fully in chapter 6.

The overall growth of nonprofit revenue from government slowed somewhat in the 1997–2007 period, however, during which government support to nonprofit organizations, including through Medicaid and Medicare, increased by 38 percent, well below the 53 percent rate of growth of overall nonprofit revenue. Government thus accounted for a considerably smaller 30 percent of the sector's overall growth, as reflected in figure 1-8. This was largely due, however, to the cost control measures introduced into the huge Medicare and Medicaid programs. Outside of health care providers, the growth in government support to nonprofit organizations during the 1997–2007 period has been substantial—149 percent for environmental organizations, 82 percent for education organizations, 69 percent for social assistance organizations, and 61 percent for international assistance organizations. This growth attests to the success many nonprofit organizations continue to achieve in adapting to the changes in the structure of government funding streams by repackaging traditional social services as behavioral health services and securing government support through the expanding health programs. At the same time, because the government share of total income is somewhat small for some of these fields (for example, arts and culture), the government contribution to overall revenue growth in a number of these fields remained limited despite the growth that occurred, as figure 1-9 shows.

The significant expansion of government support, particularly in health and social services, has had its downside, of course. Particularly problematic is the tendency for Medicaid (and to some extent Medicare) reimbursement rates to fall behind the actual costs of delivering the services they are intended to support.[119] For-profit vendors can respond to these cuts by pulling out of the affected lines of business, but nonprofits often find this difficult. As a consequence, nonprofit organizations often end up subsidizing, with scarce private charitable resources, services they have undertaken to help fulfill federal program priorities.

Even so, the success with which nonprofit organizations have adapted to the new government funding realities is another indication of the penetration of the commercial impulse into the nonprofit sector, since so much of government aid now takes the form of consumer-side subsidies. When this voucher-type government support is added to the fee income that nonprofits received in 2007 (as it is in the data on program service revenue that nonprofit organizations report to the Internal Revenue Service), it turns out that 81 percent of the reported income of nonprofit 501(c)(3) organizations, exclusive of churches, shows up as commercial or quasi-commercial revenue. Even among nonprofits in the social service field, the combination of consumer-side government subsidies plus fee income accounted for three-fifths (61 percent) of total revenue in 2007.

EXPANDED VENTURE ACTIVITY. A third manifestation of the penetration of commercial impulses into the nonprofit sector is the sector's increased involvement in commercial ventures. Such ventures differ from the collection of fees for standard nonprofit services in that they entail the creation and sale of products and services primarily for a commercial market. Examples include museum gift shops and on-line stores, church rentals of social halls, licensing agreements between research universities and commercial firms, and in recent years, the growth of so-called social-ventures—that is, organizations that pursue their social or environmental missions through businesses that generate revenues from the sale of goods or services.

Existing law has long allowed nonprofit organizations to engage in commercial activities as long as these activities do not become the primary purpose of the organization. Since 1951 the income from such ventures has been subject to corporate income taxation unless it is "related" to the charitable purpose of the organization.

Solid data on the scope of this activity are difficult to locate, however, since much of it is considered "related" income and buried in the statistics on fees, but the clear impression from what data exist suggests a substantial expansion over the past two decades. One sign of this is the growth in so-called unrelated business income reported to the Internal Revenue Service. Although the IRS is notoriously liberal in its definition of what constitutes "related," as opposed to "unrelated," business income, the number of charities reporting such income increased by 35 percent between 1990 and 1997, and the amount of income they reported more than doubled.[120] In 1997 gross unrelated business income reported by all types of nonprofit organizations reached $7.8 billion, an increase of 7 percent over the previous year—and following even larger percentage increases over the previous two years. Much of this income flows to member-serving nonprofits, but 501(c)(3) and 501(c)(4) organizations accounted for 57 percent of it. The unrelated business activity of nonprofits grew even further in recent years. Thus the number of 501(c)(3) and 501(c)(4) organizations reporting such unrelated business income increased by another 32 percent between 1997 and 2007, and the value of their earnings increased by nearly 25 percent after adjusting for inflation.[121] Still, only about 5 percent of all charitable nonprofits reported any unrelated business income in 2007, and for most of those that did, the deductions taken against this income came very close to balancing out the income earned, suggesting either that such enterprises are not very "profitable" or that nonprofits have learned how to allocate expenses so as to minimize tax obligations.

Far more widespread than "unrelated" business activity in the nonprofit sphere is the "related" business activity that many nonprofits are undertaking. Cultural institutions seem to be especially inventive in adapting venture activities to their operations, perhaps because they have the clearest "products" to sell. The Guggenheim Museum has even gone global, with franchises in Italy, Germany, and Spain, while elaborate touring exhibitions and shows have become standard facets of museum, orchestra, and dance company operations. Cultural institutions also actively exploit the new digitization technologies, often in collaboration with commercial firms. In the process, as chapter 5 notes, arts organizations are being transformed from inward-oriented institutions focused primarily on their collections to outward-oriented enterprises competing for customers in an increasingly commercial market, though the enthusiasm for venture-type activities in the arts world has cooled somewhat in recent years.

Other types of nonprofit organizations are also increasingly involved in commercial-type ventures. Thus hospitals are investing in parking garages, universities establishing joint ventures with private biotechnology companies, and social service agencies operating managed care and crisis intervention businesses financed by corporate customers.[122] The business activities of nonprofit hospitals have grown especially complex, with elaborate purchasing and marketing consortia linking hospitals, medical practitioners, insurance groups, and equipment suppliers.[123]

Perhaps the most interesting facet of this venture activity in the nonprofit arena, however, is the recent tendency of some nonprofit organizations to utilize business ventures not simply to generate income but to carry out their basic charitable missions.[124] This reflects the broader transformation in prevailing conceptions of how to address poverty, from one focused on providing services to one focused on providing jobs. Thus, as chapter 14 shows, rather than merely training disadvantaged individuals and sending them out into the private labor market, a new class of "social purpose enterprises," or "social ventures" has emerged to employ former drug addicts, inmates, or other disadvantaged persons in actual businesses as a way to build skills, develop self-confidence, and teach work habits. Other such ventures are manufacturing and distributing products or services that ease environmental pollution, overcome disabilities, or serve other social or environmental purposes. Examples here include the Greyston Bakery in Yonkers, New York, which trains and hires unemployable workers in its gourmet bakery business; Pioneer Human Services, a nonprofit in Seattle, Washington, that operates an aircraft parts manufacturing facility, food buying and warehousing services, and restaurants that employ disadvantaged workers and prepare them for the labor market; and Bikeable Communities in Long Beach, California, which promotes bicycle use by offering valet and related services to cyclists.[125] The result is a thoroughgoing marriage of market means to charitable purpose and the emergence of a new hybrid form of non-profit business.

The emergence and expansion of social enterprises has also brought with it a significant degree of institutional innovation in the nonprofit arena. Because social enterprise managers have found their expansion constrained by the lack of access that nonprofit organizations have to the equity markets, and because for-profit companies are bound by law to maximize profits instead of pursuing social purposes, social entrepreneurs have begun experimenting with a variety of "flexible purpose" corporate forms. Thus, for example, eight states have adopted statutes permitting the formation of so-called L3C, or low-profit, limited liability companies, and other innovative hybrid forms are being actively explored.[126]

Taken together, these developments have created a certain "buzz" in the nonprofit and social-purpose arena, as "social entrepreneurs" and the social enterprises they create have become the change agents of the new millennium, displacing traditional nonprofit managers as role models for socially and environmentally oriented activists. The award of the Nobel Peace Prize to the social entrepreneur Muhammad Yunus in 2006, the appearance of books on social enterprise with titles such as *How to Change the World* and *The Power of Social Innovation,* and the creation of a Social Innovation Fund in the early days of the Obama administration provide evidence of the energy and enthusiasm this movement has unleashed.[127]

MANAGERIAL PROFESSIONALIZATION. A fourth manifestation of the commercial impulse in the nonprofit sector is the growing professionalization of nonprofit operations. *Professionalization* may be too blanket a term to depict the recent shifts in the staffing and operation of nonprofit organizations, however, for it has at least three different meanings. The first is the basic expansion of paid staff, not necessarily replacing volunteers but certainly displacing them as the backbone of nonprofit operations. Though volunteers continue to play important roles in the nonprofit sector, the myth that portrays these organizations as principally operated by volunteers now no longer comes close to portraying reality, at least for the bulk of nonprofit activity if not for the bulk of the organizations. In point of fact, nonprofit organizations had become major employers by the late 1970s, and their attraction of paid staff has continued into the new century. Indeed, between the late 1970s and the mid-1990s, the paid staff of nonprofit organizations grew at an annual rate more than 70 percent higher than that of all nonagricultural employment.[128] This disparity in employment growth has not only continued but accelerated in the new millennium, as the U.S. economy continues its structural shift from manufacturing to services. Thus nonprofit employment grew two and one-half times faster than overall nonfarm employment between 1998 and 2005, and it appears to have sustained this growth through much of the economic recession of 2008 and beyond.[129] Indeed, if the nonprofit sector were itself one of the eighteen "industries" into which statisticians divide economies, as of 2007 it would be the third largest such industry in the U.S. economy in terms of employment, behind only retail trade and manufacturing.

The second meaning of *professionalization* involves the penetration of subject-matter professionals into leadership positions in organizations. This, too, is an old story. As noted earlier, the professionalization of the health, education, and even social service spheres in this sense occurred fairly early in the twentieth century. This type of professionalization was a later arrival in the arts field, as noted in chapter 5, though it has had its characteristic results of creating an inward-looking performance culture, which stands accused of pushing contemporary composers to the sideline, constraining musical innovation, and losing touch with younger and more diverse audiences.[130] More generally, as one scholar notes, "Although some nonprofit industries, such as education and health care, had been professionally managed for decades, by the end of the Reagan era, professionalization had penetrated every area in which nonprofits operated, including religion."[131]

As noted earlier, however, the professionalism impulse has encountered significant resistance in recent years and subject matter professionals have been put on the defensive. At the same time, a third, more commercial-oriented type of professionalism—managerial professionalism—has arisen to challenge subject-matter professionals.[132] Rather than substantive training in health or education or case work, managerial professionals are trained in the techniques of rational management, such as strategic planning, management by objectives, segmentation of operations along individual lines of business, and the use of metrics. Indeed, substantive professionals are now increasingly being managed by managerial professionals, who hold them accountable for performance goals and productivity gains.

All of this suggests a broader and deeper penetration of the market culture into the fabric of nonprofit operations. Nonprofit organizations are increasingly "marketing" their "products," viewing their clients as "customers," "segmenting their markets," differentiating their output, identifying their "market niches," formulating "business plans," and generally incorporating the language, and the style, of business management into the operation of their agencies. As one student of the field has remarked, nonprofit executives are now "among the most entrepreneurial managers to be found anywhere, including the private for-profit sector."[133]

How fully the culture of the market has been integrated into the operations, as opposed to the rhetoric, of the nonprofit sector is difficult to determine. However, a survey of a core set of nonprofit human service, arts, and community development organizations by the Johns Hopkins Listening Post Project finds widespread adoption of at least one aspect of the market mantra: the need for improved performance metrics, with 85 percent of surveyed agencies reporting measuring the performance of at least a portion of their programs and 70 percent reporting use of "outcome," and not just "output," measures.[134] Certainly the appetite for market-oriented materials has been robust enough to convince commercial publishers like John Wiley and Sons to invest heavily in the field, producing a booming market in "how-to" books offering nonprofit managers training in "strategic planning," "financial planning," "mission-based management," "social entrepreneurship," "street-smart financial basics," "strategic communications," "high-performance philanthropy," and "high-performance organization," to cite just a handful of recent titles.[135]

The Drucker Foundation's Self-Assessment Tool, with its market-oriented stress on the five questions considered most critical to nonprofit-organization performance (What is our mission? Who is our customer? What does the customer value? What are our results? What is our plan?), was reportedly purchased by more than 10,000 agencies in the first five years following its publication in 1993, suggesting the appetite for business-style management advice within the sector.[136] The cross-organizational spread of these market-oriented management tools is such that researchers in San Francisco stumbled upon a religious organization whose training materials feature a PowerPoint urging Christian leaders to "Build Market Share for God."[137]

Beyond this, there is growing evidence that the market culture is affecting organizational practices, organizational structures, and interorganizational behavior. This process began, ironically enough, in the most voluntaristic component of the nonprofit field—the charitable fundraising sphere. A veritable revolution has occurred in this arena of nonprofit action, as reflected in the emergence and growth of specialized fundraising organizations, such as the National Society of Fund-Raising Executives (1960), now the Association of Fund-Raising Professionals (AFP); the Council for the Advancement and Support of Education (1974); the Association for Healthcare Philanthropy (1967); and the National Committee for Planned Giving (1988). As recently as 1979, the AFP, the largest of these organizations, boasted only 1,899 members. By 2011 it could claim over 30,000 members in 225 chapters around the globe.[138] Equally impressive has been the transformation in the technology of charitable giving through the development of such devices as workplace solicitation, telethons, direct mail campaigns, telephone solicitation, a host of complex planned-giving vehicles such as charitable remainder trusts, and more recently e-philanthropy. Entire organizations have surfaced to manage this process of extracting funds, and, as we have seen, for-profit businesses, such as Fidelity Investments, have also gotten into the act with their own charitable funds, offering their investors an opportunity to manage their charitable resources through a nonprofit with ties to the firm that handles their regular investments.[139]

How much of the surge in philanthropic support between 1997 and 2007 can be attributed to these developments is difficult to say, but it is notable that private philanthropic support to nonprofit service and expressive organizations kept pace, at least in percentage terms, with the growth of fee income to the sector, though it started from a much smaller base. Also notable is the emergence in philanthropic space of a host of new actors, who are focused on channeling private investment capital from banks, insurance companies, pension funds, and high-net-worth individuals into social purpose activities. Included here are entities known by such nontraditional charitable terms as *capital aggregators, social-purpose secondary markets, social stock exchanges, enterprise brokers,* and *multiwindow philanthropic banks,* all of them using financial instruments that go well beyond the normal mechanism of the charitable grant.[140] How successfully these developments will withstand the effects of the recent economic turmoil remains to be seen, but they have clearly established a beachhead that augurs well for their future.

These developments in the field of fundraising hardly begin to exhaust the changes in organizational behavior and structure ushered into the nonprofit field by the powerful commercial and managerial impulse. Hospitals, for example, are increasingly advertising their capabilities, universities investing in off-campus programs, museums and symphonies establishing venues in shopping centers, and even small community development organizations engaging in complex real estate syndications. Significant changes are also occurring in the basic structure and governance of nonprofit organizations. Boards are being made smaller and more selective, substituting a corporate model for a community-based one. Similarly, greater efforts are being made to recruit business leaders to serve on boards, further solidifying the dominant corporate culture. In addition, the internal structure of organizations is growing more complex. To some extent this is driven by prevailing legal restrictions. Thus, as reported in chapter 10, many nonprofit advocacy organizations have created 501(c)(4) subsidiaries to bypass restrictions on their lobbying activity as 501(c)(3) charities. Similarly, nonprofit residential care facilities are segmenting their various activities into separate corporate entities to build legal walls around core operations in case of liability challenges. And universities, freed by the Bayh-Dole Act and subsequent legislation to commercialize patent discoveries developed with federal research funds, are turning to complex consortium arrangements to market the products of university-based scientific research.[141]

Behind the comforting image of relatively homey charities, nonprofit organizations are thus being transformed into complex holding companies, with multiple nonprofit and for-profit subsidiaries and offshoots, significantly complicating the task of operational and financial management and control. Not surprisingly, to cope with this increased complexity, nonprofit management has had to become increasingly professional. These developments have thus helped to fuel the growth of the new nonprofit management training programs mentioned earlier, 168 of which were in existence in colleges and universities across the country as of 2009.[142] Other evidence of the growing managerial professionalization of the nonprofit field includes the construction of a set of sectorwide infrastructure institutions, such as Independent Sector, the Council on Foundations, the Association of Small Foundations, the Forum of Regional Associations of Grantmakers, and state nonprofit organizations; as well as the emergence of a nonprofit press: *Chronicle of Philanthropy, Nonprofit Times, Nonprofit Quarterly,* and *Stanford Social Innovation Review* (see chapter 11 for additional detail).

What was once a scatteration of largely overlooked institutions has thus become a booming cottage industry, attracting organizations, personnel, publications, services, conferences, websites, head-hunting firms, consultants, rituals, and fads—all premised on the proposition that nonprofit organizations are distinctive institutions with enough commonalities, despite their many differences, to be studied, represented, serviced, trained, and, most important, managed using a similar set of concepts and tools, but a set inspired in important part by those in use in the business sector.

NEW BUSINESS PARTNERSHIPS. As the culture of the market has spread into the fabric of nonprofit operations, old suspicions between the nonprofit and business sectors have significantly softened, opening the way for nonprofit acceptance of the business community not simply as a source of charitable support but as a legitimate partner for a wide range of nonprofit endeavors. This perspective has been championed by charismatic sector leaders such as Billy Shore, who urge nonprofits to stop thinking about how to get donations and start thinking about how to "market" the considerable "assets" they control, including particularly the asset represented by their reputations.[143] This has meshed nicely with the growing readiness of businesses to forge strategic alliances with nonprofits in order to generate "reputational capital," demonstrating that the penetration of the business culture into the nonprofit sector has been accompanied by a significant penetration of the nonprofit culture into business operations, as businesses have begun developing "mission statements" and aligning products with good causes. The upshot has been a notable upsurge in strategic partnerships between nonprofit organizations and businesses.

One early manifestation of this was American Express's invention of "cause-related marketing" in the early 1980s. Under this technique, a nonprofit lends its name to a commercial product in return for a share of the proceeds from the sale of that product. Research demonstrates that such arrangements bring substantial returns to the companies involved, boosting sales, enhancing company reputations, and buoying employee morale. Coca-Cola, for example, experienced a 490 percent spurt in the sales of its products at 450 Wal-Mart stores in 1997 when it launched a campaign promising to donate 15 cents to Mothers Against Drunk Driving for every soft drink case it sold. More generally, a 1999 Cone/Roper survey found that two-thirds of Americans have greater trust in companies aligned with a social issue and that more than half of all workers wish their employers would do more to support social causes. This evidence has convinced a growing number of corporations to associate themselves and their products with social causes and the groups actively working on them. The apparel retailer Eddie Bauer has thus entered cause-related marketing arrangements with American Forests, Evian with Bill Shore's Share Our Strength, Liz Claiborne with the Family Violence Prevention Fund, Mattel with Girls Incorporated, Timberland with City Year, Yoplait with Susan G. Komen for the Cure, and many more. Indeed, an entire cottage industry has sprung up around cause-related marketing, including the web-based Cause Marketing Forum, the website onPhilanthropy for "professionals working on the social commons," and regular tracking of cause-related marketing proceeds by marketing research firm IEG, LLC. By 2010 cause sponsorship was delivering an estimated $1.62 billion in proceeds to nonprofit organizations, up from $120 million in 2002.[144]

Increasingly, moreover, cause-related marketing relationships have evolved into broader partnerships that mobilize corporate personnel, finances, and know-how in support of nonprofit activities. The most successful of these efforts deliver benefits to both the corporation and the nonprofit. Thus for example, when the Swiss pharmaceutical manufacturer Novartis contributed $25 million to the University of California at Berkeley for basic biological research, it secured in the bargain the right to negotiate licenses on a third of the discoveries of the school's Department of Plant and Microbial Biology, whether it paid for these discoveries or not.[145] The management expert Rosabeth Kanter even argues that businesses are coming to see nonprofits not simply as sources of good corporate images but also as the "beta site for business innovation," a locus for developing new approaches to long-standing business problems, such as how to recruit inner-city customers to the banking system and how to locate and train entry-level personnel for central-city hotels.[146] In these and countless other ways nonprofit organizations and businesses have begun reaching out to each other across historic divides of suspicion to forge interesting collaborations of value to both, leading the Aspen Institute's Nonprofit Sector Strategy Group to "applaud the new strategic approach that businesses are bringing to societal problem-solving and the expansion of business partnerships with nonprofit groups to which it has given rise."[147]

In short, a massive and multifaceted commercial surge has enveloped the country's nonprofit sector, affecting its internal operation, its revenue base, its organizational structure, and its entire modus operandi.

Meeting the For-Profit Competition

One interesting consequence of the nonprofit absorption of the market culture is an enhanced capacity of nonprofits to hold their own in the face of the rising tide of for-profit competition. To be sure, the credit for this does not belong to nonprofits alone. Rather, the for-profit sector has proved to be far less formidable a competitor in many of the spheres in which both operate than initially seemed to be the case. As Gray and Schlesinger point out in chapter 2, a "life-cycle" perspective is needed to understand the competitive relationship between nonprofit and for-profit organizations in the health field, and a similar observation very likely applies to other fields as well. For-profit firms have distinct advantages during growth spurts in the life cycles of particular fields, when new services are in demand as a result either of changes in government policy or of shifting consumer needs. This is so because these firms can more readily access the capital markets to build new facilities, acquire new technology, and attract sophisticated management. In addition, they are better equipped to market their services and achieve the scale required to negotiate favorable terms with suppliers (for example, pharmaceutical companies).

However, once they become heavily leveraged, the continued success of these enterprises comes to depend on the expectation of continuing escalation of their stock prices. When this expectation is shaken, as it often is thanks to shifts in government policies—such as reimbursement policies for Medicare and Medicaid—the results can be catastrophic and precipitous. In such circumstances, for-profit firms can go bankrupt or exit particular fields—for example, by refusing to serve Medicaid recipients. In some cases they have also shown a distressing tendency to engage in fraudulent practices. In the 1990s, for example, some for-profit nursing homes, squeezed by new state policies designed to reduce Medicaid costs, turned to misleading billing practices to sustain their revenues and ultimately got caught. A similar scenario played out in the hospital field twice in the past several decades—first in the latter 1980s and again in the mid-1990s. In both cases overly optimistic for-profit entrepreneurs found it impossible to sustain the growth paths that their stock valuations required and ended up being discredited when government agencies and private insurers found that they had fraudulently inflated their costs and overbilled for services.[148] This boom and bust cycle seems to operate as well in the social service field, particularly where government support is a crucial part of the demand structure of agencies. For-profit involvement grows in response to increased public funding but then suffers a shakeout when government reimbursement contracts.

All of this demonstrates why nonprofit involvement is so crucial, especially in fields where vulnerable populations are involved and the reliable maintenance of a basic level of quality care is essential. At the same time, such involvement is far from guaranteed, even where nonprofits pioneer the service. Given the intensity of competition at the present time and the expanded access of for-profits to government support, nonprofits can hold their own only where they have well-established institutions, where they can secure capital, where they manage to identify a meaningful market niche and a distinctive product, where they respond effectively to the competitive threat, and where individual consumers or those who are paying on their behalf value the special qualities that the nonprofits bring to the field.[149] The fact that nonprofits have continued to expand substantially in the face of competition suggests that many nonprofits have been up to this challenge. What is more, the not-for-profit form is staging a renaissance in some unexpected places. One of these is the emergence of non-profit, multispecialty, physician groups, reflecting the reluctance of many young doctors, already burdened by heavy medical school debt, to take on the additional debt involved in opening their own practices or to handle the increasingly complex business dimensions of medical practice. One estimate is that a quarter of all practicing physicians now belong to such groups.[150] At the same time, recent reports indicating problems for nonprofit hospitals in generating capital to respond to a spurt in admissions make it clear that competitive challenges remain even for quite large and sophisticated nonprofit providers.[151]

Sustaining an Advocacy Role

In addition to growing robustly, finding ways to market their services to paying customers, adjusting to a new terrain of government funding, and reengineering key features of their operations in response to the dominant market culture, American nonprofits have also demonstrated their resilience by maintaining a considerable presence in the realm of advocacy and citizen engagement. In this their performance stands in stark contrast to concerns about the decline of social capital and the disappearance of nationally integrated civic associations voiced by scholars such as Robert Putnam and Theda Skocpol.[152] One explanation for this lies in the impact of the communications revolution of the past two decades. As chapters 10 and 17 make clear, Internet activism has fundamentally reshaped civic participation and advocacy, providing through social media, blogs, chat rooms, and other vehicles new ways for citizens to connect, share ideas, mobilize, and inform; and for organizations to reach out to members and to form and manage advocacy coalitions.

Also at work, however, is the professionalization of nonprofit advocacy activity. This was particularly in evidence during the period from the early 1960s through the early 1990s, perhaps the high point of nonprofit, public interest advocacy involvement. During this period a variety of public interest advocacy groups effectively advanced agendas seeking improvements in civil rights, consumer protection, environmental protection, health care, and relief from hunger and poverty. As reflected in Jeffrey Berry's careful analysis of the role of such groups in shaping the congressional agenda during this period, with only 7 percent of the Washington interest group universe throughout this period, these groups accounted for 24–32 percent of congressional testimony, generated 29–40 percent of the press coverage of pending legislation, and were nearly 80 percent as effective in passing legislation they favored as the business lobbies against which they were often arrayed.[153]

But nonprofit involvement in citizen engagement has persisted well beyond this period. Mainline civic and civil rights membership organizations such as the League of Women Voters, the Jaycees, Kiwanis, the National Association for the Advancement of Colored People, the National Council of La Raza, and the Urban League have now been joined by new organizations committed to strengthening democracy by promoting voting, civic participation, and community problem solving.

Citizen activism is particularly evident in the environmental area, as detailed in chapter 7. Close to 680 watershed associations operate in the Chesapeake Bay watershed alone, for example, sampling water and checking for illegal discharges; and similar associations operate in other watersheds across the country, all of them linked together in the River Network. Land trusts, multi-stakeholder climate change and ecosystem partnerships, and environmental education coalitions fill out the rich organizational and associational tapestry of the contemporary environmental movement.[154] Beyond these citizen engagement activities, more traditional nonprofit advocacy organizations continue to grow. For example, the Sierra Club, a leading nonprofit environmental organization, boasted 1.3 million members in 2008–09, up from 246,000 in 1980, and other organizations are not far behind.[155]

In the process, nonprofit advocacy organizations have grown increasingly complex and professional. The Sierra Club, for example, is a 501(c)(4) organization that operates six other organizations: a legal defense fund, a foundation, a political action committee, a student coalition, a book club, and a property management company. In addition, it operates twenty-two regional offices and chapters in every state. Nor is this type of development restricted to the environmental arena. NOW, the National Organization for Women—like the Sierra Club a 501(c)(4) organization—also has a separate 501(c)(3) foundation, a number of PACs, a network of local chapters, and an active online presence through Facebook and Twitter.

More generally, research demonstrates that sizable proportions of nonprofit service-providing organizations engage in some type of advocacy activity. Thus a 2000 survey of a cross-section of nonprofit organizations found three-fourths reporting some engagement in public policy activity. This general finding was confirmed in a more recent survey by the Johns Hopkins Listening Post Project, which found that nearly three-quarters (73 percent) of a core set of human service, arts, and community development organization executives reported involvement in some type of policy advocacy or lobbying during the year leading up to the survey, with three out of five of these indicating some advocacy involvement almost every month.[156] This involvement is all the more impressive in light of the legal limitations on nonprofit political action—limitations that bar nonprofit organizations from engaging in electoral activity, from contributing to political campaigns, from devoting more than a limited share of their resources to lobbying, and from engaging in "political activity" if they receive government funds.[157]

Not only have nonprofit citizen groups proved effective in national political advocacy, but also they have extended their reach upward to the international level and downward to states and localities. The same new communications technologies that facilitated the rise of global corporations have permitted the emergence of transnational advocacy networks linking nonprofit citizen groups across national borders. This "third force" is rapidly transforming international politics and economics, challenging government policies on everything from land mines to dam construction and holding corporations to account in their home markets for environmental damage or labor practices they may be pursuing in far-off lands.[158] Indeed, the recent eagerness multinational corporations have shown for cause-related marketing arrangements and broader strategic partnerships with nonprofit organizations has been driven in important part by the threat these networks pose to these corporations' "license to operate" and to their reputations among both consumers and their own staff. Similarly, nonprofits have forged advocacy coalitions at the state level to make sure that devolution does not emasculate policy gains achieved nationally. The expansion of state social welfare and arts spending cited earlier can probably be attributed in important part to this nonprofit policy advocacy at the state level.

Impressive as the scope and scale of nonprofit involvement in civic engagement and advocacy may be, however, so too are its limitations. For one thing, lobbying and advocacy, while widespread and varied, tend to involve relatively limited commitments of time and resources for most organizations most of the time. Only about half of the organizations in the Listening Post survey, for example, report doing even the least-demanding forms of lobbying or advocacy during the year preceding the survey, and the proportions that are involved three or more times in the course of a year exceeded one-third of the organizations for only the least-demanding of all forms (signing correspondence to a government official).[159]

One reason for this fairly limited involvement appears to be the limited resources and resulting limited staff time available to support advocacy in most organizations. The vast majority (85 percent) of Listening Post Project respondents reported devoting less than 2 percent of their budgets to either lobbying or advocacy, and in most organizations the advocacy function is left largely to the executive director, with little effort to rally clients or patrons let alone engage other staff. Simple lack of resources was thus the most common barrier to greater policy engagement cited by respondents in both surveys cited above, outdistancing concerns about restrictive regulations by far, at least in the Listening Post survey.

Data on nonprofit expenditures on lobbying recorded on nonprofit form 990 filings confirm these findings. As noted in chapter 10, only 6,502 nonprofit 501(c)(3) organizations reported any lobbying expenditures in 2005, twice the number ten years earlier but still a mere 2 percent of all reporting organizations, and this despite the fact that all 501(c)(3) organizations are allowed to do some lobbying. What is more, the amount these organizations reported spending on lobbying remained below 0.1 percent of their total expenditures. This pattern has certainly been true in the environmental arena. As Siriani and Sofer report in chapter 7, 40 percent of watershed groups sampled by the River Network had no budget, and three-fourths had no fundraising strategy. As a consequence, these groups lack the capability to engage substantial numbers of citizens for restoration efforts or to tackle the complex challenges of climate change, and similar problems confront land trusts and groups addressing toxics and environmental justice issues.

Incredibly, and perhaps paradoxically, the major source that organizations have been able to count on to finance their advocacy and citizen engagement activity has been government, and study after study confirms a positive relationship between receipt of public funding and policy engagement. On the other hand, foundation funding seems to constrain advocacy activity, perhaps as a result of the restrictions on foundation support of lobbying written into the 1969 Tax Reform Act.[160]

In short, while the advocacy fire still burns within the nonprofit sector, it simmers at a relatively low temperature. What is more, it is increasingly selective in its focus. The public interest groups that made such a powerful political impact during the 1970s and 1980s differ markedly in their focus from the traditional working-class-oriented liberal and labor groups of the 1930s to 1950s. The political scientist Jeffrey Berry characterizes this as a shift from "materialism" to "postmaterialism," from the pocketbook concerns of middle- and working-class voters to the social concerns of more affluent ones.[161] The political awakening of the Christian Right has had a similar result, as Jacob Hacker and Paul Pierson observe in their powerful book, *Winner-Take-All Politics.* "Like the public interest groups on the left," Hacker and Pierson note, "the Christian Right has engaged voters on nonmaterial grounds. Moral values issues like abortion and gay marriage are the focus. And this concentration on moral issues has had a paradoxical consequence: It has aligned a large bloc of evangelical voters whose incomes are generally modest with a political party attuned to the economic demands of the wealthy."[162] Coupled with the emasculation of private sector unions, the result has been to open a significant vacuum with regard to advocacy and lobby support for issues relating to the poor and to the economic security of working-class people.

At the same time, business interests responded to the liberal environmental, consumer, and workplace safety victories of the 1960s and 1970s with a concerted organizational counterattack shepherded by a reinvigorated U.S. Chamber of Commerce and newly formed Business Roundtable. By 1982, 2,500 firms had registered lobbyists in Washington, up from 175 in 1971. The number of corporate PACs quadrupled between 1976 and 1980, and money poured into them. Despite efforts to impose legal limits on corporate and union campaign contributions, between the late 1970s and the late 1980s, corporate PAC contributions in congressional elections swelled by 500 percent, easily outdistancing labor contributions, even to Democratic candidates.[163] And this was before the landmark Supreme Court decision in *Citizens United* v. *Federal Election Commission* (2010), which freed corporations from any restrictions on their support of political candidates. And if labor has been outgunned as a consequence, so have public interest advocacy and plain-vanilla nonprofit service organizations, held back not only by legal and administrative limits on their involvement in policy activity, but also by limited resources of time and money. Under the circumstances, the prospects for a level playing field for nonprofits in the political arena seem increasingly remote, even given the advantages afforded by the new communications technologies and Internet-promoted demonstrations of the sort embodied in the Occupy Wall Street movement of 2011.

Summary and Implications

Nonprofit America has thus responded with extraordinary creativity and resilience to the challenges and opportunities it has confronted over the past thirty or so years. The sector has grown enormously as a consequence—in revenues, in number of organizations, and in the range of purposes it serves. In addition, the competencies and management of the sector's organizations have improved, though these are more difficult to gauge. To be sure, not all components of the sector have experienced these changes to the same degree or even in the same direction. Yet what is striking is how widespread the adaptations seem to have been.

In large part, what allowed nonprofit organizations not only to survive but to thrive during this period was that they moved, often decisively, toward the market. In the terms introduced earlier, the commercial impulse clearly gained the upper hand in nonprofit operations across a broad front. This did not mean, of course, that the other impulses pressing on the sector ceased to operate. To the contrary, nonprofits continued to promote advocacy and citizen engagement, though with somewhat subdued firepower; the voluntary impulse remained alive and well in the sector's public persona and in its attraction of charitable resources, volunteer effort, and new public programs supporting community service and faith-based organizations, even as the sector's center of gravity moved in a different direction; and professionalism continued to influence the sector's organizations, though more in their management than in the substance of their programs, thus moving nonprofit organizations ever closer to their for-profit cousins rather than their public-sector next of kin.

In short, while these other impulses continued to be felt, the commercial one seemed to gain the ascendance. Nonprofit organizations thus took advantage of the growing demand for their services, expanded their fee income, launched commercial ventures, forged partnerships with businesses, adopted business management techniques, mastered new consumer-side forms of government funding, reshaped their organizational structures, incorporated sophisticated marketing and money management techniques into even their charitable fundraising, and generally found new ways to tap the dynamism and resources of the market to promote their organizational objectives. This move toward the market has by no means been universal. Nor is it entirely new. What is more, it did not exhaust the range of responses the sector made to the challenges it faced. Yet it has clearly been the dominant theme of the past several decades, and its scope and impact have been profound, affecting all parts of the sector to some extent. As a result, the nonprofit sector that is entering the second decade of the twenty-first century is not your father's nonprofit sector. Rather, it has been substantially reengineered, and this process is still very much under way, though it has yet to be fully appreciated by the sector itself or by the nation at large.

On balance, these changes seem to have worked to the advantage of the nonprofit sector, strengthening its fiscal base, upgrading its operations, enlisting new partners and new resources in its activities, and generally improving its image for organizational effectiveness. But they have also brought significant risks, and the risks may well overwhelm the gains. Before drawing up the final balance sheet on the state of nonprofit America or its likely future evolution, therefore, it is necessary to weigh the gains against these risks. More specifically, the nonprofit sector's response to the challenges of the past thirty years, creative as it has been, has exposed the sector to at least five new problems: a growing identity crisis, increased managerial demands, mission creep, disadvantaging small agencies, and a loss of public trust.

Growing Identity Crisis

In the first place, the nonprofit sector is increasingly confronting an identity crisis as a result of a growing tension between the market character of the services it is providing and the continued nonprofit character of the institutions providing them. As Gray and Schlesinger show in chapter 2, this tension has become especially stark in the health field, where third-party payers, such as Medicare and private HMOs, refuse to consider values other than actual service cost in setting reimbursement rates and where bond-rating agencies discount community service in determining what nonprofit hospitals have to pay for the capital they need to expand. Left to their own devices, nonprofit institutions have had little choice but to adjust to these pressures, but this adjustment comes at some cost to the features that make the institutions distinctive.

Under these circumstances, it is no wonder that scholars have been finding it difficult to detect real differences between the performance of for-profit and nonprofit hospitals and why many nonprofit HMOs and hospitals have surrendered the nonprofit form or sold out to for-profit firms.[164] Private universities are similarly experiencing strains between their mission to propagate knowledge and the expansion of their reliance on corporate sponsorship, which has brought with it demands for exclusive patent rights to the fruits of university research.[165] Marketing pressures are also intruding upon nonprofit arts and cultural institutions, limiting their ability to focus on artistic quality and transforming them into social enterprises focusing on market demands (see chapter 5, this volume). So intense has the resulting identity crisis become, in fact, that some scholars are beginning to question the long-standing belief that nonprofits are reluctant participants in the market, providing only those "private goods" needed to support their "collective goods" activities, and are coming to see many nonprofits functioning instead as out-and-out commercial operations dominated by "pecuniary rather than altruistic objectives."[166]

Increased Demands on Nonprofit Managers

These tensions have naturally complicated the job of the nonprofit executive, requiring these officials to master not only the substantive dimensions of their fields but also the broader private markets within which they operate, the numerous public policies that affect them, and the massive new developments in technology and management with which they must contend. Nonprofit executives must do all this, moreover, while balancing a complex array of stakeholders that includes not only clients, staff, board members, and private donors but also regulators, government program officials, for-profit competitors, and business partners; and while also demonstrating performance and competing with other nonprofits and with for-profit firms for fees, board members, customers, contracts, grants, donations, gifts, bequests, visibility, prestige, political influence, and volunteers.[167] No wonder that burnout has become such a serious problem in the field despite the excitement and fulfillment the role entails.

The Threat of Mission Creep

Inevitably, these pressures pose threats to the continued pursuit of nonprofit missions. Nonprofit organizations forced to rely on fees and charges naturally begin to skew their service offerings to clientele that are able to pay. What start out as sliding-fee scales designed to cross-subsidize services for the needy become core revenue sources essential for agency survival. Organizations needing to raise capital to expand are naturally tempted to locate new facilities in places with a client base able to finance the borrowing costs. When charity care, advocacy, and research are not covered in government or private reimbursement rates, institutions have little choice but to curtail these activities. Similarly, when new "impact investors" interested in measurable results for specific beneficiaries hold the upper hand in agency survival, hard-to-measure activities like advocacy and community organization may cease to seem important.

How far these pressures have proceeded is difficult to say. As Joassart-Marcelli shows in chapter 19, support for the poor has never been the exclusive, or the primary, focus of nonprofit action. Nor need it be. What is more, many of the developments identified above have usefully mobilized market resources to support genuinely charitable purposes. Yet the nonprofit sector's movement toward the market is creating significant pressures to move away from those in greatest need, to focus on amenities that appeal to those who can pay, and to apply the market test to all facets of their operations.[168] The influence of the market impulse may thus be working at cross-purposes with the impulses to promote social justice and serve the poor—the impulses that government support, with all its limitations, opened up for significantly broader segments of the nonprofit sector in the post–World War II period.

Disadvantaging Small Agencies

A fourth risk resulting from the nonprofit sector's recent move to the market has been to put smaller agencies at an increasing disadvantage. Successful adaptation to the prevailing market pressures requires access to advanced technology, professional marketing, corporate partners, sophisticated fundraising, and complex government reimbursement systems, all of which are problematic for smaller agencies. Market pressures therefore create not simply a digital divide but a much broader "sustainability chasm," one that smaller organizations find difficult to bridge. Although some small agencies can cope with these pressures through collaborations and partnerships, these devices themselves often require sophisticated management; further, they absorb precious managerial energies.[169] As the barriers to entry, and particularly to sustainability, rise, the nonprofit sector is thus at risk of losing one of its most precious qualities—its ease of entry and its availability as a testing ground for new ideas.

Loss of Public Trust

All of this, finally, poses a further threat to the public trust on which the nonprofit sector ultimately depends. Thanks to the pressures they are under and the agility they have shown in response to them, American nonprofit organizations have moved well beyond the quaint Norman Rockwell stereotype of selfless volunteers ministering to the needy and supported largely by charitable gifts. Yet general public and media images remain wedded to this older stereotype and far too little attention has been given to bringing popular perceptions into better alignment with the realities that now exist, and to justifying these realities to a skeptical citizenry and press. As a consequence, nonprofits find themselves vulnerable when highly visible events, let alone instances of mismanagement or scandal, reveal them to be far more complex and commercially engaged institutions than the public suspects. The more successfully nonprofit organizations respond to the dominant market pressures, therefore, the greater risk they face of sacrificing the public trust on which they ultimately depend. This may help explain the widespread appeal of the Bush administration's "faith-based charities" initiative. What made this concept so appealing is its comforting affirmation of the older image of the nonprofit sector, the image of voluntary church groups staffed by the faithful solving the nation's problems of poverty and blight, even though this image grossly exaggerates both the capacity and the inclination of most congregations to engage in meaningful social problem solving, as chapter 9 powerfully reveals.

The Road Ahead

What this discussion suggests is that a different balance may need to be struck between the nonprofit sector's "distinctiveness imperative" (the things that make nonprofits special) and the sector's "survival imperative" (the things nonprofits need to do in order to survive). To be sure, these two imperatives are not wholly in conflict. Nevertheless, the tensions between them are real, and there is reason to worry that the survival imperative may be gaining the upper hand. In the terms introduced before, the commercial and professional impulses may be squelching the voluntaristic and civic activist ones, posing a challenge to the sector's future.

How these competing impulses will play out will likely depend to a considerable extent on forces outside the sector's control—the shifting realities of political life, the resulting patterns of government policy, and broader economic trends. Nevertheless, sector leaders also have important choices. Broadly speaking, at least three scenarios seem possible.

Celebration and Drift: The Status Quo Scenario

In the first place, the nonprofit sector can continue its historic posture of self-celebration and drift, emphasizing the virtues of charitable giving and volunteering, while drifting toward ever greater reliance on commercial, or quasi-commercial, sources of support. Given the obvious strength of nonprofit organizations in a number of spheres, the reliance placed upon them by governments in crucial policy arenas, and the growing capability of nonprofit managers to balance the competing pressures they are facing, it seems likely that this scenario could sustain the sector for some time to come.

However, it is equally likely that a policy of drift will cause nonprofits to lose more of their market share, surrender more of their mission-critical functions such as advocacy and community organizing, and see the raison d'être for many of their special advantages, such as tax exemption, slip further away.

Social Enterprise Scenario

A second scenario, especially attractive to younger activists and the socially conscious entrepreneurs from the dot.com industry, is to give up on the traditional nonprofit sector as it now exists and work toward the creation of a self-consciously new "social enterprise," or "fourth sector," one that explicitly merges social purpose with business methods and taps into the much larger resources available through socially focused private investment capital.

Hundreds of such social enterprises have surfaced in recent years both in the United States and around the world. Supporting this new wave of social-purpose businesses are capacity builders like New Profit and Community Wealth Ventures, enterprise brokers, as well as a growing number of investment funds and investment vehicles.[170] Already, one portion of this "fourth sector," composed of microenterprises and the "microfinance institutions" that support them, is estimated to have generated between $75 billion and $150 billion in investments, with prospects of growing into a much broader "microfinancial services" industry on a global scale.[171] Another branch is incubating a host of so-called bottom-of-the-pyramid businesses. These are businesses that design products and distribution channels that fit the economic resources of the millions of people at the bottom of the economic pyramid.[172] In the minds of many, these types of entities hold far more promise for solving the world's social and environmental problems than do traditional nonprofit organizations.

The Renewal Scenario

A third possible path of nonprofit evolution might be characterized as the "renewal option," and it is the option that this author favors. The key to this approach is to see the challenges facing the nonprofit sector not as an excuse for retreat into some pretended golden age of nonprofit independence, or as a time for continued drift toward greater commercialization, but rather as an opportunity for renewal, for rethinking the nonprofit sector's role and operations in light of contemporary realities, and for achieving a new consensus regarding the functions of these organizations, the relationships they have with citizens, with government, and with business, and the way they will operate in the years ahead.

CLARIFYING THE NONPROFIT VALUE PROPOSITION. At the center of the renewal scenario must be a clarification of the sector's "value proposition," the distinctive qualities and attributes nonprofit organizations bring to American society.[173] The voluntaristic impulse, after all, is not just about charitable giving and volunteer effort. This impulse is the carrier for the broader set of values that define the nonprofit sector's distinctive contributions—values of equity, openness, empowerment, participation, responsiveness, and commitment to the enrichment of human life. Thanks in part to the ascendance of the commercial impulse and its accompanying emphasis on metrics, however, many of these other values have been downplayed, and the value of the nonprofit sector reduced to the sector's service functions. While these functions are important, they hardly exhaust the value that Americans derive from nonprofit institutions. Clarifying these contributions and articulating them forcefully both for the sector as a whole and in particular organizations will be pivotal to the sector's ability to retain its special place in American life.

IMPROVING THE GOVERNMENT-NONPROFIT PARTNERSHIP. Equally important to the renewal scenario is the acknowledgment, indeed celebration, of the nonprofit sector's role as a partner in public service along with government.[174] The sector's role as the delivery system for publicly funded services, which expand opportunities and improve the quality of life for millions of citizens, needs to be made clear. As noted, government has emerged as the second most important source of nonprofit revenue, outdistancing philanthropy by a factor of nearly four to one. Yet the nonprofit sector's relationship with government remains suspect in the minds of many and poorly understood among most of the rest. At the same time, this relationship, for all its strengths, remains in need of restructuring and reconstruction. As a declaration by leaders representing over 100,000 nonprofit organizations noted recently, "The relationships between government and the nonprofit sector have evolved in ad hoc fashion, with too little attention to their operational inefficiencies or to their tendency to put valued characteristics of the citizen sector at risk."[175]

Other countries have dealt with these problems by forging compacts between government and nonprofit organizations in order to make their collaborations operate better for both sides. While such overarching policy prescriptions are difficult to establish in America's fragmented political system, more explicit recognition is needed that this partnership offers enormous advantages to government, to nonprofits, and to the citizens they both serve, but that significant improvements are needed to allow it to achieve its promise. Such a recognition would begin by acknowledging government's stake in the nonprofit delivery system for its programs and the resulting need for governmental investment in the capacity of its nonprofit partners.

Equally important is explicit acknowledgment in government grants, contracts, and reimbursement systems of the need to protect the mission-critical functions of nonprofits, such as advocacy and community organizing. Whether nonprofit hospitals can continue to support their teaching and research functions, for example, is significantly affected by whether Medicare considers this function vital enough to cover in the reimbursement rates for nonprofit hospitals. But rather than protecting and encouraging these important nonprofit functions, government policy in recent years has moved in the direction of constraining them, especially in the advocacy area. In the prevailing deregulation climate, some significant deregulation of nonprofit advocacy also therefore seems in order.

Beyond this, government needs to commit to full coverage of the costs of the services it depends on nonprofits to deliver, and timely payment on grants and contracts.

STRENGTHENING NONPROFIT FINANCE. Any serious renewal scenario must also address the perennial problems of nonprofit finance, and particularly the problem of nonprofit access to investment capital. As we have seen, nonprofits confront an uneven playing field in this area due to their lack of access to the equity markets. As a consequence, they have frequently lost market share even in fields in which they pioneer. Significant developments on the "frontiers of philanthropy" hold promise for improving nonprofit access to investment capital, but these could benefit greatly from government encouragement.

The experience of nonprofit hospitals, higher education institutions, and low-income housing organizations is instructive in this regard. The experience of the first two demonstrates that nonprofit organizations can often hold their own in the face of stiff for-profit competition when they can gain access to needed capital at competitive rates. In both of these cases, special tax incentives have been available to subsidize bonds issued to finance nonprofit facilities.

The example of the nonprofit housing organizations described in chapter 6 of this volume demonstrates that the same approach can be successfully used for organizations serving disadvantaged groups. Here, passage of the Low-Income Housing Tax Credit program, coupled with the emergence of nonprofit intermediary institutions that package the resulting tax breaks for sale to investors, has opened a significant flow of private investment capital into low-income housing.[176] Broadening this tax credit to cover investments in other nonprofit facilities or equipment serving disadvantaged persons would go a long way toward keeping nonprofits competitive in a wider range of fields.

Also needed—given the likely near-term constraints on government funding—is some way to stimulate greater charitable giving. The recent expansion of web-based giving seems likely to help in this, though experience suggests that such giving is episodic and crisis related. Another approach might be to move toward a system of tax credits instead of tax deductions. Unlike deductions, which deliver more tax benefits per dollar contributed to persons in high tax brackets than in low ones, tax credits provide the same tax benefits to all contributors regardless of their income.[177] In addition, tax credits can be made available to all contributors regardless of whether they itemize their tax deductions. Since 75 percent of taxpayers currently take the so-called standard deduction and therefore do not itemize, a shift to a tax credit system would further democratize giving.

The major obstacle to this approach is that it could provide a windfall benefit to people who would be making contributions anyway, but this could be remedied by setting a floor under the amount of gifts that would qualify for credits. American charitable giving has been stuck at 2 percent of personal income, or less, for some time. It is worth considering approaches that might boost this level in the future, and a system of tax credits instead of deductions might well be one of those worth trying.

IMPROVING PUBLIC UNDERSTANDING. Finally, any renewal scenario will require a major investment in public education. What is needed here, however, is not another celebration of private giving and volunteering, important though these are. Rather, the public must be introduced to the broader realities of current nonprofit operations, to the impressive resilience that the sector exhibits, and to the special qualities that make nonprofit organizations worth protecting. Also required is a better public defense of the sector's long-standing partnership with government and a clarification of the crucial role nonprofits play as key links working collaboratively with government and the business sector to solve public problems. This may be a complex message to convey, but it is the one that best reflects the current realities, and perhaps the best hope for the nonprofit sector's future.

Conclusion

It has been said that the quality of a nation can be seen in the way it treats its least advantaged citizens. But it can also be seen in the way it treats its most valued institutions. Americans have long paid lip service to the importance they attach to their voluntary institutions, while largely ignoring the challenges these institutions face. During the past two decades, these challenges have been extraordinary. But so too has been the nonprofit sector's response. As a result, the state of nonprofit America is surprisingly robust as we enter the second generation of the new millennium, with more organizations doing more things more effectively than ever before.

At the same time, the movement to the market that has made this possible has also exposed the sector to enormous risks. What is more, the risks go to the heart of what makes the nonprofit sector distinctive and worthy of public support—its basic identity, its mission, and its ability to retain the public's trust.

Up to now, nonprofit managers have had to fend for themselves in deciding what risks it was acceptable to take in order to permit their organizations to survive. Given the stake that American society has in the preservation of these institutions and in the protection of their ability to perform their distinctive roles, it seems clear that this must now change. Americans need to rethink whether the balance that has been struck among the four impulses driving the nonprofit sector, and between the survival and distinctiveness imperatives that lie behind them, is the right one for the future—and if not, what steps might now be needed to shift this balance for the years ahead.

The argument here is that some such adjustments are needed, that America's nonprofit institutions require broader support in preserving the features that make them special. Whether others agree with this conclusion remains to be seen. What seems clear, however, is that better public understanding of the state of nonprofit America is needed if such judgments are to be possible. It is our hope that the analyses in this book will contribute to such understanding. That, at any rate, is our goal.

Notes

1. D. A. Whetten and P. C. Godfrey, *Identity in Organization* (London: Sage, 1998); M. A. Glynn, "When Cymbals Become Symbols: Conflict over Organizational Identity within a Symphony Orchestra," *Organizational Science* 11, no. 3 (2000): 285.

2. For a discussion of this partnership, see Lester M. Salamon, "Partners in Public Service," in *The Nonprofit Sector: A Research Handbook,* edited by Walter W. Powell (Yale University Press, 1987), pp. 99–117; and Lester M. Salamon, *Partners in Public Service: Government-Nonprofit Relations in the Modern Welfare State* (Johns Hopkins University Press, 1995).

3. Michael S. Joyce and William A. Schambra, "A New Civic Life," in *To Empower People: From State to Civil Society,* edited by Michael Novak, 2nd ed. (Washington: AEI

Press, 1996), pp. 11–29; Robert Nisbet, *Community and Power,* 2nd ed. (Oxford University Press, 1962).

4. Carmen Sirianni and Lewis Friedland, *Civic Innovation in America: Community Empowerment, Public Policy, and the Movement for Civic Renewal* (University of California Press, 2001); Harry Boyte, *Commonwealth: A Return to Citizen Politics* (Galway: MW Books, 1989); John McKnight, *The Careless Society: Community and Its Counterfeit* (New York: Basic Books, 1995).

5. Alexis de Tocqueville, *Democracy in America,* vol. 2, trans. Henry Reeve, rev. Francis Bowen (1835; reprint, New York: Vintage Books, 1945), p. 118.

6. On the reengineering movement in the corporate sector, see Michael Hammer and James Champy, *Reengineering the Corporation: A Manifesto for Business Revolution* (London: Nicholas Brealey, 1994); David K. Carr and Henry J. Johnson, *Best Practices in Reengineering: What Works and What Doesn't in the Reengineering Process* (New York: McGraw-Hill, 1995).

7. This concept is developed in chapter 2 of this volume by Bradford Gray and Mark Schlesinger.

8. Federal tax law identifies at least twenty-six classes of such organizations, ranging from political parties to cemetery companies. Nonprofits are required to pay taxes on any so-called "unrelated business" profits they may earn. For a fuller discussion of the legal definition of a tax-exempt or nonprofit organization, see Bruce R. Hopkins, *The Law of Tax-Exempt Organizations,* 9th ed. (New York: Wiley, 2007), pp. 3–23. See also Lester M. Salamon, *America's Nonprofit Sector: A Primer,* 3rd ed. (New York: Foundation Center, 2012).

9. This difference between 501(c)(3) and 501(c)(4) organizations with respect to lobbying activity is notoriously unclear. The difference hinges on the definition of lobbying as opposed to advocacy, and that definition is rather complex. Advocacy refers to any effort to inform policymakers or the public about public problems and possible government or private actions that might be needed to resolve them. Lobbying is a more narrow concept and refers to specific attempts to influence the passage or defeat of particular laws, either directly, through influencing legislators, or indirectly, by mobilizing broader public efforts to influence legislators. Both 501(c)(3) and 501(c)(4) organizations are free to engage in advocacy activities without limit, but 501(c)(3)s are only allowed to participate in lobbying activities to an "insubstantial" extent. What an insubstantial extent actually consists of has never been fully explicated in legislation or court interpretations, though recent legislation has given 501(c)(3) organizations the option of accepting a legislative schedule of permissible resources that can be devoted to such activity. For further details, see Hopkins, *Law of Tax-Exempt Organizations,* pp. 400–04.

10. This section draws heavily on data reported in Salamon, *America's Nonprofit Sector.* Unless otherwise noted, all data in this chapter derive from this work and the sources on which it relies.

11. Although churches are actually member-serving organizations, we include them in the public-serving portion of the sector because religious purposes are among those qualifying an organization as eligible for tax-deductible gifts under section 501(c)(3) of the Internal Revenue Code.

12. The data here apply only to organizations that filed form 990, which is required by all nonprofit organizations with revenue in excess of $25,000.

13. Kennard T. Wing, Thomas H. Pollack, and Amy Blackwood, *The Nonprofit Almanac, 2008* (Washington: Urban Institute, 2008), pp. 228–35.

14. Based on Internal Revenue Service, "SOI [Statistics of Income] Tax Stats—Charities & Other Tax-Exempt Organizations Statistics" (www.irs.gov/taxstats/charitablestats/article/0,,id=97176,00.html#2).

15. Wing, Pollack, and Blackwood, *Nonprofit Almanac, 2008*, p. 142.

16. The data reported here draw primarily on microdata files prepared by the Internal Revenue Service from form 990 filings required of all nonprofit organizations with $25,000 or more of annual income. Foundations and other funding intermediaries, as well as religious congregations, are removed from the data to avoid double counting of contributions and to zero in on the service and expressive organizations of principal concern to us. The microdata files were accessed at Internal Revenue Service, "SOI Tax Stats." Because form 990 lumps together as "program service revenue" government contract payments, government voucher payments such as Medicare and Medicaid, and direct purchases paid for by consumers, the data obscure the true extent of government support flowing to nonprofit organizations. Since these government "purchases" are huge, it was necessary to disentangle this "program service revenue" category and provide a clearer picture of the totality of direct government support to nonprofit service and expressive organizations. For further detail on how this was done, see Salamon, *America's Nonprofit Sector*, chapter 3, n. 18.

17. The discussion here draws heavily on ibid.

18. See for example James S. Coleman, *Foundations of Social Theory* (Harvard University Press, 1990), pp. 300–21; Robert Putnam, *Making Democracy Work: Civic Traditions in Modern Italy* (Princeton University Press, 1993), pp. 83–116, 163–85.

19. De Tocqueville, *Democracy in America*, p. 117.

20. The term *value guardian* was first used by Ralph Kramer, *Voluntary Agencies in the Welfare State* (University of California Press, 1981), pp. 193–211, to describe one of the crucial roles of nonprofit organizations. Kramer refers mostly to volunteering, but it has a broader meaning as well.

21. Waldemar Nielsen, *The Endangered Sector* (Columbia University Press, 1979), pp. 24–25.

22. See for example Nisbet, *Community and Power;* Peter D. Berger and Richard Neuhaus, *To Empower People: The Role of Mediating Structures in Public Policy* (Washington: AEI Press, 1977); Joyce and Schambra, "New Civic Life"; Leslie Lenkowsky, "Philanthropy and the Welfare State," in *To Empower People: From State to Civil Society*, edited by Novak, pp. 90–91.

23. This portrait of the characteristics of the voluntaristic impulse draws on a variety of sources, including Stuart Langton, "The New Voluntarism," *Nonprofit and Voluntary Sector Quarterly* 10 (January 1981): 7–20; Barry D. Karl, "Volunteers and Professionals: Many Histories, Many Meanings," in *Private Action and the Public Good*, edited by Walter W. Powell and Elizabeth Clemens (Yale University Press, 1998), pp. 248–57; Peter Frumkin, *On Being Nonprofit: A Conceptual and Policy Primer* (Harvard University Press, 2002); Joyce and Schambra, "New Civic Life"; Karin Kreutzer and Urs Jäger, "Volunteering versus Managerialism: Conflict over Organizational Identity in Voluntary Associations," *Nonprofit and Voluntary Sector Quarterly* 40, no. 4 (2011): 634–61; Robert L. Woodson Sr., "Success Stories," in *To Empower People*, edited by Novak, pp. 105–15.

24. The usage of the term *professional* here thus corresponds to what Hwang and Powell refer to as "traditional ideal-type professionals" or "subject-matter professionals," as opposed to those whose expertise is in general management. See Hokyu Hwang and Walter W. Powell, "The Rationalization of Charity: The Influences of Professionalism in the Nonprofit Sector," *Administrative Science Quarterly* 54, no. 2 (2009): 268–75. I refer to this latter as *managerial professionalism* as opposed to *professionalism*. On the definition of *subject-matter professionalism*, see Karl, "Volunteers and Professionals," p. 246; Harold Wilensky, "The Professionalization of Everyone?" *American Journal of Sociology* 70, no. 2 (1964): 137–58; Hwang and Powell, "Rationalization of Charity." For a definition of managerialism, see Kreutzer and Jäger, "Volunteering versus Managerialism."

25. See for example J. A. Trolander, *Professionalism and Social Change* (Columbia University Press, 1987), pp. 39, 238–39; Roy Lubove, *The Professional Altruist: The Emergence of Social Work as a Career, 1880–1930* (Harvard University Press, 1965), pp. 49–53; David Rosner, *A Once Charitable Enterprise: Hospitals and Health Care in Brooklyn and New York, 1885–1915* (Cambridge University Press, 1982), pp. 6–12.

26. According to Harold Wilensky, there are at least five steps crucial to the establishment of a profession: full-time work, a curriculum and training schools, a professional association, official licensing or certification requirements, and a formal code of ethics. Wilensky, "Professionalization of Everyone," 142–46.

27. Rosner, *Once Charitable Enterprise,* p. 6.

28. Lubove, *Professional Altruist,* p. 48.

29. Trolander, *Professionalism and Social Change,* p. 40; Karl, "Volunteers and Professionals," p. 256.

30. Lubove, *Professional Altruist,* p. 23.

31. The portrayal of the civic activism impulse here draws on Vernon Jordan, "Voluntarism in America," *Vital Speeches* 43, no. 16 (1977): 493; Langton, "New Voluntarism," 10–11; Theda Skocpol, *Diminished Democracy: From Membership to Management in American Civic Life* (Oklahoma University Press, 1987); Frumkin, *On Being Nonprofit,* pp. 29–31, 53–61; Sirianni and Friedland, *Civic Innovation in America;* Boyte, *Commonwealth.*

32. Trolander, *Professionalism and Social Change,* p. 1.

33. Brian O'Connell, "From Service to Advocacy to Empowerment," *Social Casework* 59 (April 1978): 198.

34. The description of the characteristics of this impulse here draws on the following sources, among others: Hwang and Powell, "Rationalization of Charity"; Kreutzer and Jäger, "Volunteering versus Managerialism"; Frumkin, *On Being Nonprofit,* pp. 129–62; Lester M. Salamon, "The Marketization of Welfare: Changing Nonprofit and For-Profit Roles in the American Welfare State," *Social Service Review* 67, no. 1 (1993): 17–39; Angela Eikenberry and Jodie Drapal Kluver, "The Marketization of the Nonprofit Sector: Civil Society at Risk?" *Public Administration Review* 64, no. 2 (2004): 132–40; Howard P. Tuckman, "Competition, Commercialization, and the Evolution of Nonprofit Organizational Structures," in *To Profit or Not to Profit: The Commercial Transformation of the Nonprofit Sector,* edited by Burton A. Weisbrod (Cambridge University Press, 1998), pp. 25–46; Burton A. Weisbrod, "Modeling the Nonprofit Organization as a Multiproduct Firm: A Framework for Choice," in *To Profit or Not to Profit,* edited by Weisbrod, pp. 47–64; Kevin P. Kearns, *Private Sector Strategies for Social Sector Success: The Guide to Strategy and Planning for Public and Nonprofit Organizations* (San Francisco: Jossey-Bass, 2000).

35. Langton, "New Voluntarism," p. 9.

36. For a more complete analysis of this system of government-nonprofit relations and the broader pattern of third-party government of which it is a part, see Salamon, "Partners in Public Service"; and Salamon, *Partners in Public Service.* For a discussion of the federal government's support of nonprofit research universities, see Don K. Price, *The Scientific Estate* (Harvard University Press, 1965). For the early roots of government support to nonprofit organizations in the United States, see John S. Whitehead, *The Separation of College and State: Columbia, Dartmouth, Harvard, and Yale* (Yale University Press, 1973), pp. 3–16; Amos Warner, *American Charities: A Study in Philanthropy and Economics* (New York: Thomas Y. Crowell, 1894), pp. 400–05.

37. Lester M. Salamon and Alan J. Abramson, *The Federal Budget and the Nonprofit Sector* (Washington: Urban Institute, 1982).

38. Lester M. Salamon and Alan J. Abramson, "The Federal Budget and the Nonprofit Sector: Implications of the Contract with America," in *Capacity for Change? The Nonprofit World in the Age of Devolution,* edited by Dwight F. Burlingame and others (Center on Philanthropy, Indiana University, 1996), pp. 8–9; Alan J. Abramson, Lester M. Salamon, and C. Eugene Steuerle, "The Nonprofit Sector and the Federal Budget: Recent History and Future Directions," in *Nonprofits and Government: Collaboration and Conflict,* edited by Elizabeth T. Boris and C. Eugene Steuerle (Washington: Urban Institute, 1999), pp. 110–12.

39. U.S. House of Representatives, Committee on Ways and Means, *2000 Green Book: Background Material and Data on Programs within the Jurisdiction of the Committee on Ways and Means,* 106 Cong. 2 sess., p. 214. As a consequence, the number of children covered by SSI increased from 71,000 in 1974 to over 1 million in 1996, boosting expenditures in real terms from $16.4 billion in 1980 to $30.2 billion in 1999.

40. Medicaid coverage was extended to fifty distinct subgroups during the late 1980s and early 1990s, including the homeless, newly legalized aliens, AIDS sufferers, recipients of adoption assistance and foster care, and broader categories of the disabled and the elderly. Between 1980 and 1998, as a consequence, Medicaid coverage jumped from 21.6 million people to 40.6 million. At the same time, the services these programs cover also expanded dramatically. Thus skilled nursing care, home health care, hospice care, and kidney dialysis services became eligible for Medicare coverage. Intermediate care for the mentally retarded, home health care, family planning, clinic care, child welfare services, and rehabilitation services were added to Medicaid. These changes, coupled with state options to add additional services (such as physical therapy, medical social worker counseling, case management, and transportation), transformed Medicaid from a relatively narrow health and nursing home program into a social service entitlement program. Reflecting these changes, spending on the major federal entitlement programs jumped nearly 200 percent in real terms between 1980 and 1999, more than twice the 81 percent growth in GDP. House Committee on Ways and Means, *Green Book 2000,* pp. 924, 927.

41. Ibid., pp. 597, 953–54.

42. Mental health, mental retardation, maternal and child health rehabilitation, and AIDS services were special targets for this strategy, particularly as Medicaid expanded eligibility for pregnant women and children, and SSI (and hence Medicaid) expanded coverage for AIDS patients and the disabled. Teresa Coughlin, Leighton Ku, and John Holahan, *Medicaid since 1980* (Washington: Urban Institute, 1994), p. 87. For further detail, see chapter 4, this volume.

43. The number of people on welfare fell by half between 1994 and 1999, from 14.2 million to 7.2 million. In addition, the portion of those remaining on the rolls requiring full cash grants also declined, because more of them were working. Since states were guaranteed federal grants under the new Temporary Assistance for Needy Families (TANF) program at their peak levels of the early 1990s, and were also obligated to maintain their own spending on needy families at 75 percent of their previous levels, funding for services increased. By 1999, for example, spending on direct cash assistance under the welfare program had fallen to 60 percent of the total funds available, leaving 40 percent for child care, work readiness, drug abuse treatment, and related purposes. House Committee on Ways and Means, *Green Book 2000,* pp. 376, 411.

44. Elizabeth Schwinn, "Bush's Budget Plan," *Chronicle of Philanthropy,* February 27, 2007 (http://philanthropy.com/article/Charities-Face-Challenges-From/126375/); Brennen Jensen and Suzanne Perry, "A Budget Squeeze Hits Charities: Bush's 2009 Plan Calls for Cuts in Social Services and the Arts," *Chronicle of Philanthropy,* February 21, 2008 (http://philanthropy.com/article/A-Budget-Squeeze-Hits/61350/).

45. Federal Budget (2011 and 2012)—Obama and Ryan Budget Plans," *New York Times,* May 5, 2011; Robert Pear, "Obama Proposes $320 Billion in Medicare and Medicaid Cuts over 10 Years," *New York Times,* September 20, 2011, p. A15; Jackie Calmes, "Obama Confirms New Hard Stand with Debt Relief," *New York Times,* September 20, 2011, p. A1.

46. Office of Management and Budget, "Enhancing Governmental Productivity through Competition: A New Way of Doing Business within the Government to Provide Quality Government at Least Cost," cited in Donald Kettl, *Shared Power: Public Governance and Private Markets* (Brookings, 1993), p. 46.

47. Vouchers essentially provide targeted assistance to eligible recipients in the form of a certificate or a reimbursement card that can be presented to the provider of choice. The provider then receives payment for the certificate or reimbursement from the government. Tax expenditures use a similar method except that no actual certificate is used. Rather, eligible taxpayers are allowed to deduct a given proportion of the cost of a particular service (such as day care) either from their income before computing their tax obligations (tax deduction) or directly from the taxes they owe (tax credit). For a general discussion of these alternative tools of public action, see Lester M. Salamon, "The New Governance and the Tools of Public Action: An Introduction," in *The Tools of Government: A Guide to the New Governance,* edited by Lester M. Salamon (Oxford University Press, 2002), pp. 1–47. For specific discussions of such tools as loan guarantees, tax expenditures, and vouchers, see chapters 6, 7, and 8, respectively, this volume.

48. In day care, for example, the $3.5 billion in subsidies made available to middle-income and lower-middle-income families through the child and dependent care tax credit in 2010 exceeds the roughly $3.5 billion in subsidies provided to poor families through the Child Care and Development Block Grant. Even this understates the change, since, as noted below, most states have taken advantage of the option provided in the block grant law to deliver block grant assistance in the form of vouchers. Data on tax expenditures for child care are from U.S. Bureau of the Census, *Statistical Abstract of the United States, 2011,* p. 322; information on the Child Care and Development Block Grant is from www.gpoaccess.gov/usbudget/fy10/pdf/appendix/hhs.pdf, p. 488.

49. Salamon, *Partners in Public Service,* p. 208. Both Medicare and Medicaid are essentially voucher programs since consumers are entitled to choose their provider and the government then reimburses the provider. Spending on Medicaid, for example, swelled more than fourfold in real dollar terms between 1975 and 1998, while discretionary spending stagnated or declined. Computed from data in House Committee on Ways and Means, *2000 Green Book,* pp. 912, 923.

50. House Committee on Ways and Means, *2000 Green Book,* pp. 599, 617, 912, 923.

51. Of these, 40 percent of employees of large establishments and 35 percent of employees of small establishments were covered by preferred provider plans; the balance were covered by true HMOs. U.S. Bureau of the Census, *Statistical Abstract of the United States, 2000,* table 180.

52. For further detail on how these pressures have affected nonprofit organizations, see particularly chapters 2, 3, 4, and 5 on health, education, social welfare, and the arts, respectively, this volume. For an interesting analysis of the pressures on nonprofits to find new market niches, see Peter Frumkin and Alice Andre-Clark, "When Missions, Markets, and Politics Collide: Values and Strategy in the Nonprofit Human Services," *Nonprofit and Voluntary Sector Quarterly* 29, no. 1 (2000): S141–S163.

53. See chapter 8, this volume.

54. Author's estimates based on data in Murray S. Weitzman and others, *The New Nonprofit Almanac and Desk Reference, 2002* (San Francisco: Jossey-Bass, 2002), pp. 96–97.

55. Computed from data in ibid., pp. 96–97. For further discussion of trends in private giving, see chapter 13, this volume. Data on giving to religious congregations here are based on *Giving USA, 2009* (Indianapolis: Giving USA Foundation, 2009), p. 214.

56. Sources of data on the growth of private giving and overall revenue of nonprofit service and expressive organizations are from Salamon, *America's Nonprofit Sector,* chapter 3, n. 18. Data on religious giving and on total giving in 2008 are from *Giving USA, 2009,* pp. 1, 214. Estimates of the share of religious congregation revenue from giving are based on chapter 9, this volume.

57. Based on data in U.S. Census Bureau, *Economic Census, 1999;* see also chapter 2, figure 2-1, this volume; U.S. Department of Education, *Digest of Education Statistics, 2000,* pp. 209, 202–03.

58. U.S. Census Bureau, *Economic Census, 1997; Economic Census, 2007.*

59. Frumkin and Andre-Clark, "When Missions, Markets, and Politics Collide."

60. U.S. Department of Education, *Digest of Education Statistics, 1981; Digest of Education Statistics, 2007.*

61. The Fidelity Gift Fund recorded assets of $2.2 billion as of early 2000 and made grants of $374 million in the 1998–99 fiscal year. By comparison, the New York Community Trust reported assets of $2.0 billion as of the end of 1999 and grants during 1999 of $130.7 million. *Giving USA, 2001,* p. 53; Foundation Center, *Foundation Yearbook, 2001* (New York), pp. 67–68.

62. Andrew W. Hastings, ed., "Donor Advised Fund Market" (Jenkintown, Pa.: National Philanthropic Trust, 2008) (www.nptrust.org/images/Generic/DAF_White_Paper_12.03.08).

63. Lester M. Salamon and Stephanie L. Geller, "Investment Capital: The New Challenge for American Nonprofits," Communiqué 5, Listening Post Project (Center for Civil Society Studies, Johns Hopkins University, 2006).

64. For a discussion of these efforts, see Lester M. Salamon, ed., *New Frontiers of Philanthropy: A Guide to the New Tools and Actors That Are Reshaping Global Philanthropy and Social Investing* (San Francisco: Jossey-Bass, 2012).

65. William P. Ryan, "The New Landscape for Nonprofits," *Harvard Business Review* 77 (January/February 1999): 128.

66. Henry Hansmann, "The Role of Nonprofit Enterprise," *Yale Law Journal* 89, no. 5 (1980): 835–901.

67. See for example Paul Brest and Hal Harvey, *Money Well Spent: A Strategic Plan for Smart Philanthropy* (New York: Bloomberg Press, 2008); Michael Porter and Mark R. Kramer, "Philanthropy's New Agenda: Creating Value," *Harvard Business Review* 77 (November/December 1999): 121–30; Gar Walker and Jean Grossman, "Philanthropy and Outcomes," in *Philanthropy and the Nonprofit Sector in a Changing America,* edited by Charles Clotfelter and Thomas Ehrlich (Indiana University Press, 1999), pp. 449–60.

68. Christine W. Letts, William Ryan, and Allen Grossman, "Virtuous Capital: What Foundations Can Learn from Venture Capitalists," *Harvard Business Review* 75 (March/April 1997): 2–7.

69. See for example Matthew Bishop and Michael Green, *Philanthrocapitalism: How the Rich Can Save the World* (New York: Bloomsbury Press, 2008).

70. H. George Frederickson, "First, There's Theory Then, There's Practice," *Foundation News and Commentary* (March/April 2001), p. 38. See also Doug Easterling, "Using Outcome Evaluation to Guide Grant Making: Theory, Reality, and Possibilities," *Nonprofit and Voluntary Sector Quarterly* 29, no. 3 (2000): 482–86; Walker and Grossman, "Philanthropy and Outcomes."

71. Andrew Blau, "More than Bit Players: How Information Technology Will Change the Ways Nonprofits and Foundations Work and Thrive in the Information Age" (New York: Surdna Foundation, 2001), p. 10.

72. Stephen Greene, "Astride the Digital Divide: Many Charities Struggle to Make Effective Use of New Technology," *Chronicle of Philanthropy,* January 11, 2001 (http://philanthropy.com/article/Astride-the-Digital-Divide/54079/).

73. Blau, "More than Bit Players," p. 9.

74. Stephanie Geller, Alan J. Abramson, and Erwin de Leon, "The Nonprofit Technology Gap: Myth or Reality," Communiqué 20, Listening Post Project (Center for Civil Society Studies, Johns Hopkins University, 2010).

75. Edwin Feulner, "Truth in Testimony," *Heritage Foundation Testimony,* August 22, 1996 (www.heritage.org/research/commentary/1996/08/truth-in-testimony).

76. Capital Research Center, "Our Mission" (http://capitalresearch.org/).

77. Kimberly Dennis, "Charities on the Dole," *Policy Review: Journal of American Citizenship* 76, no. 5 (1996): 5.

78. See for example Lisbeth Schorr, *Within Our Reach: Breaking the Cycle of Disadvantage* (New York: Anchor Books, 1988).

79. See for example Charles Murray, *Losing Ground: American Social Policy, 1950–1980* (New York: Basic Books, 1984).

80. For a discussion of the social enterprise phenomenon, see chapter 14, this volume; David Bornstein, *How to Change the World: Social Entrepreneurs and the Power of New Ideas* (Oxford University Press, 2004). For examples of social ventures, see www.community-wealth.org/strategies/panel/social/models.html. For a discussion of the broader array of financial instruments and institutions supporting this development, see Salamon, *New Frontiers of Philanthropy*. For a conceptualization of this development as a fourth sector, see Heerad Sabeti and the Fourth Sector Network Concept Working Group, "The Emerging Fourth Sector," executive summary (Washington: Aspen Institute, 2009). For an analysis of proposed new legal forms for the emerging social enterprise sector, see Marc Lane, *Social Enterprise: Empowering Mission-Driven Entrepreneurs* (Chicago: American Bar Association, 2011).

81. Lubove, *Professional Altruist*.

82. McKnight, *Careless Society,* p. 10.

83. Stuart Butler, *Privatizing Federal Spending* (New York: Universe Books, 1985); Martin Anderson, *Imposters in the Temple: American Intellectuals Are Destroying Our Universities and Cheating Our Students* (Englewood Cliffs, N.J.: Simon and Schuster, 1992).

84. Regina Herzlinger, "Can Public Trust in Nonprofits and Governments Be Restored?" *Harvard Business Review* 74 (March/April 1996): 96.

85. Joel Fleischman, "To Merit and Preserve the Public's Trust in Not-For-Profit Organizations: The Urgent Need for New Strategies for Regulatory Reform," in *Future of Philanthropy in a Changing America,* edited by Clotfelter and Ehrlich, pp. 172–97. For a recent congressional challenge to the accountability features of nonprofits, see U.S. Senate Finance Committee, "Staff Document on Regulation on Tax-Exempt Organizations," June 22, 2004.

86. Independent Sector, *Giving and Volunteering, 1999* (Washington: 1999), pp. 3, 5.

87. "While a third of adults think the nonprofit sector in the United States is headed in the wrong direction, a vast majority of households have donated to charities in the past year," Harris Poll 33, April 27, 2006 (www.harrisinteractive.com/harris_poll/printerfriend/index.asp?PID=657). See also Paul C. Light, "How Americans View Charities: A Report on Charitable Confidence, 2008," Issues in Governance Studies 13 (Brookings, 2008). For an

alternative view emphasizing Americans' continued willingness to make charitable contributions, see Michael C. O'Neill, "Public Confidence in Charitable Nonprofits," *Nonprofit and Voluntary Sector Quarterly* 38, no. 2 (2009): 237–69.

88. Michael Cooper, "Squeezed Cities Ask Nonprofits for More Money," *New York Times,* May 12, 2011, p. A1.

89. Lester M. Salamon, Stephanie L. Geller, and S. Wojciech Sokolowski, "Taxing the Tax-Exempt Sector: A Growing Danger for Nonprofit Organizations," Communiqué 21, Listening Post Project (Center for Civil Society Studies, Johns Hopkins University, 2011).

90. Adam Liptak, "Justices, 5-4, Reject Corporate Spending Limit," *New York Times,* January 21, 2010, p. A1.

91. Hopkins, *Law of Tax-Exempt Organizations,* p. 381.

92. Gail Harmon, Diane Curran, and Anne Spielberg, "Regulation of Advocacy Activities for Nonprofits That Receive Federal Grants" (Washington: Alliance for Justice, n.d.).

93. See for example Peggy Gavin and Deanna Gelak, "Lobbying Disclosure Databases: A User's Guide," *Online* 32, no. 5 (2008): 34–38; Campaign Finance Institute, "Fast Start for Soft Money Groups in 2008 Election: 527s Adapt to New Rules, 501(c)(4)s on the Upswing" (Washington: Campaign Finance Institute, 2008).

94. Phillip Howe and Corinne McDonald, "Traumatic Stress, Turnover, and Peer Support in Child Welfare" (Washington: Child Welfare League of America) (www.cwla.org/programs/trieschman/2001fbwPhilHowe.htm).

95. Paul Light, *Making Nonprofits Work: A Report on the Tides of Nonprofit Management Reform* (Brookings, 2000), p. 10. Among public policy program graduates in the classes of 1973 and 1974 and 1978 and 1979 an average of 14 percent took their first jobs in the nonprofit sector and 14 percent remained employed in the nonprofit sector in the mid-1990s. By contrast, an average of 16 percent of these graduates took their first job in the private business sector, and 33 percent were employed in the business sector as of the mid-1990s.

96. Jeanne Peters and Timothy Wolfred, *Daring to Lead: Nonprofit Executive Directors and Their Work Experience* (San Francisco: CompassPoint, 2001), pp. 13–14, 20–21.

97. U.S. Census Bureau, *Statistical Abstract of the United States, 2011,* table 8.

98. *Statistical Abstract of the United States, 2000,* pp. 408–09; *Statistical Abstract of the United States, 2011,* table 598.

99. *Statistical Abstract of the United States, 2000,* p. 71; *Statistical Abstract of the United States, 2011,* tables 129, 85.

100. *Statistical Abstract of the United States, 1983,* table 197; *Statistical Abstract of the United States, 2011,* table 202.

101. *Statistical Abstract of the United States, 2011,* table 43.

102. Paul Ray and Sherry Ruth Anderson, *Cultural Creatives: How 50 Million People Are Changing the World* (San Francisco: Harmony Press, 2000).

103. Neil Gilbert, "The Transformation of Social Services," *Social Services Review* 51, no. 4 (1977): 624–41.

104. Roseanne Mirabella, "Nonprofit Management Education: Current Offerings in University-Based Programs" (http://academic.shu.edu/npo/). See also Roseanne Mirabella, "University-Based Educational Programs in Nonprofit Management and Philanthropic Studies: A 10-Year Review and Projections of Future Trends," *Nonprofit and Voluntary Sector Quarterly* 36, no. 4 (2007): S11–S27.

105. For a discussion of the competing evidence on public confidence in nonprofit organizations, see Michael O'Neill, "Public Confidence in Charitable Nonprofits," *Nonprofit and*

Voluntary Sector Quarterly 38 (2009): 237–69. For a statement of the importance of social capital and the nonprofit sector's contribution to it, see Robert Putnam, *Making Democracy Work: Civic Traditions in Modern Italy* (Princeton University Press, 1993).

106. John J. Havens and Paul G. Schervish, "Millionaires and the Millennium: New Estimates of the Forthcoming Wealth Transfer and the Prospects for a Golden Age of Philanthropy" (Social Welfare Research Institute, Boston College, 1999).

107. Craig Smith, "The New Corporate Philanthropy," *Harvard Business Review* 72 (May/June (1994): 105–16; Jane Nelson, *Business as Partners in Development: Creating Wealth for Countries, Companies, and Communities* (London: Prince of Wales Business Leaders Forum, 1996); Lester M. Salamon, *Rethinking Corporate Social Engagement: Lessons from Latin America* (Sterling, Va.: Kumarian Press, 2010).

108. Bishop and Green, *Philanthrocapitalism: How the Rich Can Save the World*.

109. Salamon, ed., *New Frontiers of Philanthropy;* Antony Bugg-Levine and Jed Emerson, *Impact Investing: Transforming How We Make Money while Making a Difference* (San Francisco: Jossey-Bass, 2011).

110. Rosabeth Moss Kanter and David V. Summers, "Doing Well While Doing Good: Dilemmas of Performance Management in Nonprofit Organizations and the Need for a Multiple-Constituency Approach," in Powell, *Nonprofit Sector,* p. 154.

111. Regina Herzlinger, "Can Public Trust in Nonprofits and Governments Be Restored?" *Harvard Business Review* 74 (March/April 1996): 98.

112. Estimates of nonprofit revenue in this section are drawn from two broad sets of sources. For the period 1977–96, author's estimates are based on data in Virginia Hodgkinson and others, *Nonprofit Almanac, 1996–1997* (Washington: Independent Sector, 1997), pp. 190–91; on unpublished data supplied by Independent Sector; and on U.S. Bureau of the Census, *Service Annual Survey, 1996.* For these estimates, social and fraternal organizations are deleted from civic, social, and fraternal, and social services are grouped with civic. Inflation adjustment is based on the implicit price deflator for the services component of personal consumption expenditures as reported in the *Economic Report of the President* (February 1998), p. 290. For the period 1997–2007, estimates were developed from special tabulations available from the Internal Revenue Service, *Statistics of Income,* supplemented by data from the U.S. Census Bureau, *Census Annual Survey, 2006,* on government voucher payments (Medicare and Medicaid) to nonprofit organizations. Reported nonprofit program service revenue (that is, market sales) is adjusted for both health and social service organizations to take account of government voucher payments recorded as market sales or fees in IRS data. Even so, the fee portion of nonprofit revenue may still be overstated somewhat due to the fact that government contract and voucher payments are treated as program service revenue on form 990 (filed by nonprofits and used by the Internal Revenue Service in its data). For further detail, see Salamon, *America's Nonprofit Sector,* 3rd edition, chapter 3, n. 18.

113. Based on Lester M. Salamon, *America's Nonprofit Sector,* 2nd ed. (New York: Foundation Center, 2009), p. 68.

114. U.S. Internal Revenue Service, *Data Book,* various years. Recent editions accessed at ⟨www.irs.gov/taxstats/article/0,,id=102174,00.html⟩. Nonprofit organizations are not required to incorporate or register with the Internal Revenue Service unless they have annual gross receipts of $5,000 or more and wish to avail themselves of the charitable tax exemption. Religious congregations are not required to register even if they exceed these limits, though many do. It is therefore likely that more organizations exist than are captured in IRS records. It is also possible, however, that some of the new registrants are organizations that have long

existed but have chosen to register only in recent years. Because the legal and financial advantages of registration are substantial, however, it seems likely that the data reported here represent real growth in the number of organizations despite these caveats.

115. This same picture of organizational vitality emerges as well from detailed scrutiny of the form 990 that registered nonprofit organizations are obliged to file with the Internal Revenue Service. Because these forms are only required of organizations with $25,000 or more in revenue, it might be assumed that older and larger organizations would dominate the reporting agencies. Yet a recent analysis of these reporting organizations reveals that about half of those in existence as of 2005 had been founded since 1992, though among organizations with at least $5 million in expenditures, this was true of fewer than one-quarter of the organizations. Wang, Pollack, and Blackwood, *Nonprofit Almanac, 2008,* p. 143.

116. This phenomenon was already apparent in the early 1990s. See for example Salamon, "Marketization of Welfare."

117. Julian Wolpert, *Patterns of Generosity in America: Who's Holding the Safety Net?* (New York: Twentieth Century Fund, 1993), pp. 7, 27, 39–40; Sarah Dewees and Lester M. Salamon, "Maryland Nonprofit Employment, 1999," Nonprofit Employment Bulletin 3 (Center for Civil Society Studies, Johns Hopkins University, 2001).

118. Lester M. Salamon and Wojciech Sokolowski, "Maryland Nonprofit Employment: 2010" (Center for Civil Society Studies, Johns Hopkins University, 2011).

119. See for example Raymond Hernandez, "A Broad Alliance Tries to Head off Cuts in Medicare," *New York Times,* May 13, 2001, p. Al.

120. Harvey Lipman and Elizabeth Schwinn, "The Business of Charity: Nonprofit Groups Reap Billions in Tax-Free Income Annually," *Chronicle of Philanthropy,* October 18, 2001, p. 25 (http://philanthropy.com/article/The-Business-of-Charity/52259/).

121. Margaret Riley, "Unrelated Business Income of Nonprofit Organizations, 1997," IRS, Statistics of Income Bulletin (2008), p. 125; Jael Jackson, "Unrelated Business Income Tax Returns, 2007," IRS, Statistics of Income Bulletin (2011), p. 154.

122. On the latter, see the website of FEI Behavioral Health, a subsidiary of Families International, a holding company for an association of nonprofit family and children service organizations (www.feinet.com).

123. See for example Mary Williams Wals, "Hospital Group's Link to Company Is Criticized," *New York Times,* April 27, 2002, p. B1; Walt Bogdanich, "Two Hospital Fundraising Groups Face Questions over Conflicts," *New York Times,* March 24, 2002, p. A1.

124. This conception of social enterprises follows the definition used by the Social Enterprise Alliance: a social enterprise as an organization that achieves its primary social or environmental purpose through a business. Other definitions of social enterprises are not this demanding. For a discussion of the alternative definitions of social enterprises, see Lane, *Social Enterprise.*

125. Roberts Enterprise Development Fund, *Social Purpose Enterprises and Venture Philanthropy in the New Millennium* (San Francisco: 1999). For other examples of social enterprises, see Lane, *Social Enterprise,* pp. 1–2; and www.community-wealth.org/strategies/panel/social/models.html.

126. Lane, *Social Enterprise,* pp. 9–13; Stephanie Strom, "A Quest for Hybrid Companies That Profit, but Can Tap Charity," *New York Times,* October 13, 2011, p. B1.

127. David Bornstein, *How to Change the World: Social Entrepreneurs and the Power of New Ideas* (Oxford University Press, 2004); Stephen Goldsmith, *The Power of Social Innovation: How Civic Entrepreneurs Ignite Community Networks for Good* (San Francisco: Jossey-Bass, 2010).

128. The paid employment of public-benefit nonprofit organizations grew at an annual average rate of 3.3 percent between 1977 and 1994, compared to 1.9 percent for all nonagricultural employment. Bureau of Labor Statistics data as reported in Hodgkinson and others, *Nonprofit Almanac, 1996–1997,* p. 129.

129. Nonprofit employment grew by an estimated 16.4 percent between 1995 and 2008 while total nonfarm employment grew by only 6.2 percent. Wing, Pollack, and Blackwood, *Nonprofit Almanac, 2008,* table 1.8. Evidence on twenty-one states across the country indicates that nonprofit employment actually grew by an average of 2.5 percent a year between the second quarter of 2007 and the second quarter of 2009, the worst part of the recent recession. By contrast, for-profit employment in these states fell during this same period by an average of 3.3 percent a year. And this pattern held for every single state examined. See news release, Center for Civil Society Studies, Johns Hopkins University, 2010 (http://ccss.jhu.edu/publications-findings?did=271).

130. Joseph Horowitz, *Classical Music in America: A History of Its Rise and Fall* (New York: W. W. Norton, 2005), p. 534

131. Peter Dobkin Hall, "Historical Perspectives on Nonprofit Organizations," in *The Jossey-Bass Handbook of Nonprofit Leadership and Management,* edited by Robert D. Herman (San Francisco: Jossey-Bass, 1994), p. 28.

132. Hwang and Powell, "Rationalization of Charity," pp. 286–92.

133. Kevin P. Kearns, *Private Sector Strategies for Social Sector Success: The Guide to Strategy and Planning for Public and Nonprofit Organizations* (San Francisco: Jossey-Bass, 2000), p. 25.

134. Lester M. Salamon, Stephanie L. Geller, and Kasey L. Mengel, "Nonprofits, Innovation, and Performance Measurement: Separating Fact from Fiction," Communiqué 17, Listening Post Project (Center for Civil Society Studies, Johns Hopkins University, 2010).

135. Based on recent offerings from John Wiley and Sons' website (www.wiley.co.uk/products/subject/business/nonprofit/management.html).

136. Frances Hesselbein, "Foreword," in Peter Drucker, *The Drucker Foundation Self-Assessment Tool,* rev. ed, (San Francisco: Jossey-Bass, 1999), p. vi.

137. Hwang and Powell, "Rationalization of Charity," p. 288.

138. See www.afpnet.org/about/?navItemNumber=500.

139. For an analysis of these corporate-initiated charitable funds, see Rick Cohen, "Corporate-Originated Charitable Funds," chapter 5 in Salamon, *New Frontiers of Philanthropy.*

140. For an analysis of these new actors and new tools, see Salamon, *New Frontiers of Philanthropy.*

141. See for example Walter W. Powell and Jason Owen-Smith, "Universities as Creators and Retailers of Intellectual Property," in Weisbrod, *To Profit or Not to Profit,* pp. 169–93.

142. Mirabella, "Nonprofit Management Education"; Mirabella, "University-Based Educational Programs in Nonprofit Management and Philanthropic Studies."

143. Tracy Thompson, "Profit with Honor," *Washington Post Magazine,* December 19, 1999, pp. 7–22.

144. Susan Gray and Holly Hall, "Cashing in on Charity's Good Name," *Chronicle of Philanthropy,* July 20, 1998, p. 26 (http://philanthropy.com/article/Cashing-In-on-Charitys-Good/53390/); *Cause Related Marketing* (San Francisco: Business for Social Responsibility Education Fund, 1999); *IEG Sponsorship Report,* April 16, 2012 (www.sponsorship.com/IEGSR/2009/07/27/Sponsorship-Spending-On-Causes-To-Total-$1-55-Bill.aspx); Cause Marketing Forum (www.causemarketingforum.com/site/c.bkLUKcOTLkK4E/b.6452355/apps/s/content.asp?ct=8965443).

145. Eyal Press and Jennifer Washburn, "The Kept University," *Atlantic Monthly*, March 2000, pp. 39–40.

146. Rosabeth Moss Kanter, "From Spare Change to Real Change: The Social Sector as Beta Site for Business Innovation," *Harvard Business Review* 77 (May/June 1999).

147. Nonprofit Sector Strategy Group, "The Nonprofit Sector and Business: New Visions, New Opportunities, New Challenges" (Washington: Aspen Institute, 2001), p. 1.

148. See for example Kurt Eichenwald, "Columbia/HCA Fraud Case May Be Widened, U.S. Says," *New York Times,* February 28, 1998; and chapter 2, this volume.

149. For an interesting example of a nonprofit strategy for meeting the for-profit competition in the field of welfare services, see Frumkin and Andre Clark, "When Missions, Markets, and Politics Collide."

150. Arnold Relman, "How Doctors Could Rescue Health Care," *New York Review of Books,* October 27, 2011, p. 16.

151. Since the beginning of 2000, Moody's Investors Service has downgraded the bonds of 121 nonprofit hospitals, affecting $24 billion in bonds. See Reed Abelson, "Demand, but No Capital, at Nonprofit Hospitals," *New York Times,* June 12, 2002, p. B1.

152. Robert D. Putnam, *Bowling Alone: The Collapse and Revival of American Community* (New York: Simon and Schuster, 2000); Theda Skocpol, *Diminished Democracy: From Membership to Management in American Civic Life* (Oklahoma University Press, 1987).

153. Jeffrey Berry, *The New Liberalism: The Rising Power of Citizen Groups* (Brookings, 1999).

154. For further detail on these and other citizen engagement activities, see Sirianni and Friedland, *Civic Innovation in America.*

155. The National Audubon Society thus claims 600,000 members, the Natural Resources Defense Council, 564,000, and the Wilderness Society, 400,000.

156. Gary D. Bass and others, *Seen but Not Heard: Strengthening Nonprofit Advocacy* (Washington: Aspen Institute, 2007); Lester M. Salamon and Stephanie Lessans Geller, "Nonprofit America: A Force for Democracy?" Communiqué 9, Listening Post Project (Center for Civil Society Studies, Johns Hopkins University, 2008).

157. As detailed more fully in chapter 10, lobbying differs from advocacy in that it is directed at specific pieces of legislation. No limitations impede nonprofit involvement in advocacy activity. Only lobbying is restricted.

158. See for example Margaret E. Keck and Kathryn Sikkink, *Activists beyond Borders: Advocacy Networks in International Politics* (Cornell University Press, 1999); Anne M. Florini, ed., *The Third Force: The Rise of Transnational Civil Society* (Washington: Japan Center for International Exchange and the Carnegie Endowment for International Peace, 2000).

159. This finding is wholly consistent with the prior Strengthening Nonprofit Advocacy Project (SNAP) findings. See Bass and others, *Seen but Not Heard.*

160. Salamon and Geller, "Nonprofit America: A Force for Democracy?"

161. Berry, *The New Liberalism*, p. 57.

162. Jacob S. Hacker and Paul Pierson, *Winner-Take-All Politics: How Washington Made the Rich Richer—And Turned Its Back on the Middle Class* (New York: Simon and Schuster, 2010), p. 147.

163. Ibid., pp. 118, 121.

164. A classic statement of this tension, focusing on a much earlier period, can be found in David Rosner, *A Once Charitable Enterprise: Hospitals and Health Care in Brooklyn and New York, 1885–1915* (Princeton University Press, 1982). For more recent analyses, see

Regina Herzlinger and William S. Krasker, "Who Profits from Nonprofits?" *Harvard Business Review* 65 (January/February 1987): 93–106; David S. Salkever and Richard G. Frank, "Health Services," in *Who Benefits from the Nonprofit Sector,* edited by Charles T. Clotfelter (University of Chicago Press, 1992), pp. 24–54.

165. Press and Washburn, "Kept University." See also chapter 3, this volume.

166. Estelle James, "Commercialism among Nonprofits: Objectives, Opportunities, and Constraints," in Weisbrod, *To Profit or Not to Profit,* p. 273. For the alternative theory, see Weisbrod, "Modeling the Nonprofit Organization as a Multiproduct Firm."

167. Evelyn Brody, "Agents without Principals: The Economic Convergence of the Nonprofit and For-Profit Organizational Forms," *New York Law School Law Review* 40, no. 3 (1996): 457–536. See also chapter 16, this volume.

168. James, "Commercialism among Nonprofits," p. 279.

169. Amelia Kohm, David La Piana, and Heather Gowdy, *Strategic Restructuring: Findings from a Study of Integrations and Alliances among Nonprofit Social Service and Cultural Organizations in the United States* (Chicago: Chapin Hall Center for Children, 2000).

170. For other examples of social ventures, see www.community-wealth.org/strategies/panel/social/models.html. For a discussion of the broader array of financial instruments and institutions supporting this development, see Salamon, *New Frontiers of Philanthropy.* For a conceptualization of this development as a fourth sector, see Sabeti and the Fourth Sector Network Concept Working Group, "Emerging Fourth Sector."

171. Sam Daley-Harris, *State of the Microcredit Summit Campaign Report* (Washington: Microcredit Summit Campaign, 2009), p. 3.

172. See C. K. Prahalad, *The Fortune at the Bottom of the Pyramid: Eradicating Poverty through Profits* (Philadelphia: Wharton School Publishing, 2004).

173. As John Gardner put it in his influential book on self-renewal, "Anyone concerned about the continuous renewal of society must be concerned for the renewal of that society's values and beliefs." John Gardner, *Self-Renewal: The Individual and the Innovative Society,* rev. ed. (New York: W. W. Norton, 1981), p. 115.

174. This term is drawn from the title of Salamon, *Partners in Public Service.*

175. "Forward Together: Empowering America's Citizen Sector for the Change We Need," p. 2 (http://ccss.jhu.edu/publications-findings?did=322).

176. See also David J. Erickson, *The Housing Policy Revolution: Networks and Neighborhoods* (Washington: Urban Institute, 2009).

177. Under the existing tax deduction system, taxpayers are allowed to subtract their charitable contributions from their taxable income if they itemize their deductions. Since higher income taxpayers face higher tax rates, however, the resulting deductions are worth more to them than to lower income taxpayers and those who do not itemize their deductions. Tax credits, however, are deducted from the actual taxes a taxpayer owes. Credits can be set equal to the contribution or at some fraction of the contribution (for example, 40 percent of the contribution can be deducted from the tax bill).

PART **II**

Major Fields

2

Health Care

BRADFORD H. GRAY AND MARK SCHLESINGER

The American health care system is characterized by paradox. At its best it offers technological care at a level that is unmatched in the world, yet the United States ranks far down the list of countries in basic measures of population health such as infant mortality and life expectancy. Hundreds of state laws require health insurers to provide coverage for particular types of services (for example, fertility treatment) or types of providers (for example, chiropractors), yet some 46.3 million Americans had no health insurance in 2008 and tens of millions will remain uninsured even after the implementation of "comprehensive" federal health care reform. Although health care is widely recognized as a *social* good that places a substantial claim on public resources, public policy in recent decades has sought to make health care a market good based on *individual* choices. Although American health care is extraordinarily costly, it is still thought of as a charitable field, since the organizations that absorb the largest share of the expenditures, hospitals, are predominantly nonprofit, taxexempt organizations.

Health care must occupy a central place in any account of the American nonprofit sector. Although health care organizations make up only 14 percent of all nonprofit organizations, they account for almost 60 percent of all nonprofit revenues, and their share has been increasing.[1] For many Americans, hospitals may be the most readily recognized nonprofit entities, because of the vital services they provide, their visible physical presence, and their history as objects of civic commitment. But nonprofits also provide most other health-related services not provided in hospitals.

There has been great disquiet in the nonprofit health care sector in recent years. Financial pressures have forced some well-established nonprofit hospitals to choose among merging with a competitor, selling to a for-profit company, or closing. Entire categories of health care organizations (home health agencies, managed-care plans, rehabilitation hospitals) have gone from predominantly nonprofit to mostly for-profit. Major hospitals long viewed as pillars in their communities have faced new demands from federal, state, and local officials to document that they are sufficiently charitable to deserve their tax exemptions. Academics have published learned articles questioning the rationale for tax exemptions for nonprofit organizations whose revenues come mostly from the sale of services (so-called commercial nonprofits), as is the case with most health care organizations.[2] The fact that they often compete with tax-paying, for-profit firms has generated additional questions.

Thus, despite the size, vitality, and historical importance of the nonprofit sector in health care, it faces serious financial, competitive, regulatory, and intellectual challenges. These challenges are neither superficial nor transitory. They are inevitable byproducts of public policies that expect nonprofit health care organizations to engage in substantial charitable activities while operating in competitive markets successfully enough to be deemed debt-worthy by providers of private capital. These ambiguous expectations seem unavoidable, given the diversity of the health care sector with its many kinds of organizations—hospitals, nursing homes, health maintenance organizations (HMOs), drug treatment centers, and so forth. Each of these subfields—or *domains*—each has its own history, meets particular kinds of needs, and faces distinctive regulatory and payment regimes.

The experiences of nonprofit enterprises in the different health care domains have been quite varied in recent decades. The relative presence of nonprofits compared to for-profits has declined sharply over the past twenty-five years in several domains but remained stable or increased in others. In this chapter we suggest that these patterns can be understood by viewing services from a life-cycle perspective that takes account of the highly policy-sensitive context in which American health care organizations operate. As particular services move through different stages from innovation to institutionalization, the relative potential for nonprofit and for-profit involvement changes, as does the nature of their comparative performance.

In addition to developments that have shaped particular service domains, a broader set of institutional changes has swept through American health care over the past three decades. Some of these threaten the viability of the nonprofit sector. Others create new, potentially valuable niches for nonprofit enterprise, albeit with characteristics that are different from those that the government historically has recognized as justifications for tax exemptions.

As with the comparisons across domains, these comparisons over time reveal how profoundly the consequences of nonprofit ownership are mediated by the contexts within which these organizations operate. Nonprofits' performance is affected by differences in community needs, available resources, and contextual constraints, including some that affect both nonprofit and for-profit enterprises alike and that therefore affect the extent to which their behaviors are distinctive. This chapter seeks to identify systematically the contextual factors that influence today's health care organizations, analyze how nonprofit health care providers have responded to them, and consider future options.

The discussion falls into four parts. In the first section we examine the role of nonprofits in health care and the context within which they operate. The goal is to establish why concerns about the future of the nonprofit form have arisen in this field. Against this backdrop, in the second section we take up some of the central challenges that confront nonprofit organizations in health care. These challenges revolve around the fundamental tension between the market character of health services and the nonprofit character of many of the institutions that provide them. In the third section we examine how nonprofits have been responding to these challenges. These responses have taken two rather different forms: first, a slow but steady incorporation of essentially commercial practices and, second, a rearguard effort to preserve the distinctiveness of the nonprofit form. In the final section we consider alternative approaches that nonprofit organizations in health care might use to protect or enhance their distinctive contributions.

Prevailing Realities about the Role of Nonprofits in Health Care

Notwithstanding the many domains that heath care comprises, several broad generalizations can be made about the field. This section describes six realities. Though each can be found in other arenas of nonprofit activity, in combination these six factors make health care a particularly challenging setting for making sense of the role of nonprofits.

Reality 1: A Major but Varied Role for Nonprofits

Nonprofit organizations occupy a major place in the health field. Table 2-1 shows the ownership composition of twelve major service domains in three recent periods—the mid-1980s, the late 1990s, and, where comparable data are available, in the late 2000s. Nonprofit organizations are the predominant providers in several domains. These include clinics that provide mental health services, acute-care hospitals, residential treatment facilities for emotionally

Table 2-1. *Ownership Trends, by Health Care Domain*

Domain	Year	Mid 1980s Number	Percent	Year	Late 1990s Number	Percent	Year	Late 2000s Number	Percent
Domains of for-profit expansion									
Dialysis centers	1985			1997			2008		
For profit		616	42		2,322	68		3,945	78
Nonprofit		847	58		1,101	32		1,001	20
Government		n.a.	n.a.		n.a.	n.a.		96	2
Subtotal		1,463	100[a]		3,423	100[a]		5,042	100*
Rehabilitation hospitals	1985			1998			2008		
For profit		11	15		119	58		134	61
Nonprofit		51	70		71	35		76	31
Government		11	15		14	7		8	4
Subtotal		73	100[b]		204	100[c]		218	99*
Home health agencies	1985			1997			2008		
For profit		2,055	36		6,290	67		6,323	68
Nonprofit		3,653	64		3,123	33		2,046	22
Government								866	9
Subtotal		5,708	100[d]		9,413	100[d]		9,235	99*
Health maintenance organizations	1985			1997			2008		
For profit		137	35		481	74		n.a.	n.a.
Nonprofit		256	65		167	26		n.a.	n.a.
Subtotal		393	100[e]		648	100[f]			
Outpatient mental health clinics	1986			1997			2008**		
For profit		45	6		322	18		185	30
Nonprofit		502	64		1,007	57		367	59
Government		242	31		426	24		75	12
Subtotal		789	100[g]		1,755	100[g]		627	101
Hospice programs	1992			1999			2006		
For profit		151	13		593	28		1,613	53
Nonprofit		957	82		1,365	65		1,217	40
Government		63	5		146	7		191	6
Subtotal		1,171	100[h]		2,104	100[h]		3,021	99
Domains of nonprofit resurgence or for-profit decline									
Nursing homes	1986			1997			2006		
For profit		14,300	75		11,250	65		10,159	68
Nonprofit		3,800	20		4,792	28		4,118	27
Government		1,000	5		1,134	7		751	5
Subtotal		19,100	100[i]		17,176	100[i]		15,028	100
Psychiatric hospitals[j]	1985			1998			2006		
For profit		233	67		275	73		147	33
Nonprofit		117	33		102	27		97	22
Government		n.a.	n.a.		n.a.	n.a.		207	46
Subtotal		350	100[b]		377	100[c]		451	100

Domain	Mid 1980s			Late 1990s			Late 2000s		
	Year	Number	Percent	Year	Number	Percent	Year	Number	Percent
Domains of nonprofit stability									
Community health centers	n.a.			1997			2007		
For profit		n.a.	n.a.		0	0		0	0
Nonprofit		n.a.	n.a.		641	100		1,076	100
Government		n.a.	n.a.		0	0		0	0
Subtotal			100		641	100[k]		1,076	100
Residential treatment facilities for emotionally disturbed children	1986			1997			n.a.		
For profit		31	7		69	8		n.a.	n.a.
Nonprofit		378	87		590	68		n.a.	n.a.
Government		27	6		211	24		n.a.	n.a.
Subtotal		436	100[l]		870	100[m]			
Acute care hospitals	1985			1997			2006***		
For profit		805	14		797	16		1,890	18
Nonprofit		3,349	58		3,000	59		2,919	59
Government		1,578	28		1,260	25		1,119	23
Subtotal		5,732	100[b]		5,057	100[n]		4,928	100

n.a. Not available.

a. U.S. Department of Health and Human Services, Centers for Medicare and Medicaid Services, Office of Clinical Standards and Quality, data from the Program Management and Medical Information System, 1985–97, Baltimore.

b. American Hospital Association, Hospital Statistics 1986 Edition, tables 2A and 2B (Chicago, 1986).

c. American Hospital Association Resource Center, American Hospital Association Annual Survey (Chicago, 1998).

d. Health Care Financing Administration, 1998 Profile of Medicare Chart Book (www.hcfa.gov/stats/stats.htm/98datacmp.pdf).

e. InterStudy Publications, InterStudy 1985 Guide to National Firm HMOs (St. Paul, Minn.).

f. InterStudy Publications, InterStudy Competitive Edge 8.1 (Excelsior, Minn.).

g. U.S. Department of Health and Human Services, Substance Abuse and Mental Health Services Administration, data as reported to the Center of Mental Health Services, Rockville, Md.

h. General Accounting Office, Medicare: More Beneficiaries Use Hospice but for Fewer Days of Care. GAO/HEHS-00-182 (Washington: GAO, September 2000).

i. National Center for Health Statistics, National Nursing Home Survey (Hyattsville, Md., 1997).

j. Not revealed in the table is an increase (from 24 to 27 percent) in nonprofits' market share that occurred between 1991 and 1998. During that period, the number of for-profit psychiatric hospitals declined from 405 to 275.

k. U.S. Department of Health and Human Services, Health Resources and Services Administration, Bureau of Primary Health Care (www.bphc.hrsa.dhhs.gov/databases/fqhc/default.htm).

l. U.S. Department of Health and Human Services, Substance Abuse and Mental Health Services Administration, data as reported to the Center for Mental Health Services, Rockville, Md.

m. U.S. Department of Health and Human Services, Substance Abuse and Mental Health Services Administration, Center for Mental Health Services, Survey and Analysis Branch, Inventory of Mental Health Organizations, unpublished data, 1988, Rockville, Md.

n. American Hospital Association, Hospital Statistics 1999 Edition (Chicago, 1999).

* Providers of Service File, Center for Medicare and Medicaid Services, 2008.

**2007 data are for community Mutual Health Centers.

*** American Hospital Association, Hospital Statistics 2006 Edition (Chicago 2006).

disturbed children, and community health centers. Some domains are predominantly for profit, with nonprofit organizations accounting for only one-quarter to one-third of the providers. Included here are HMOs, home health agencies, dialysis centers, and rehabilitation hospitals.

Table 2-1 also demonstrates that the stability of the nonprofit share has varied markedly among health care domains in recent years. With the exception of nursing homes, all these health care services were historically provided predominantly in nonprofit settings. Yet the mix of ownership in health care cannot be accurately characterized as following a grand historical arc of increasing commercialization. For-profit firms have become predominant in some but not all traditionally nonprofit domains. We explore more fully the meaning of these complicated trends later in this chapter.

Reality 2: Importance of Trustworthiness and Professional Values

Trustworthiness is particularly salient in health care because obtaining timely, skillful, and appropriate services may be a matter of life and death for patients who are often poorly situated to judge the appropriateness or quality of services. Patients are vulnerable to unscrupulous or incompetent service providers, who may misdiagnose symptoms, provide unnecessary services, or skimp on quality of care.[3] Purchasers such as insurance companies, Medicare, and Medicaid are third parties in most transactions between providers and patients and are vulnerable to fraud and abuse because they are not present when services are provided.[4]

Because nonprofit organizations are prohibited from distributing profits to those who control the organization, they have been posited to be less likely than for-profits to exploit informational advantages for economic gain.[5] Some commentators question the relevance of organizational trustworthiness in the field of health care since service recipients (patients) have knowledgeable agents: physicians whose professional values include a sense of responsibility for patients and who can deter organizational actions that do not serve patients' interests.[6] For several reasons, however, professionalism is an inadequate protector of vulnerable patients. Many patients have no identified physician. Physician autonomy has declined in the face of managerial imperatives, and some physicians have economic and organizational entanglements that create conflicts of interest.[7] Moreover, many organizational decisions that affect patient care—such as the ratio of nurses to patients on a hospital floor—are beyond the physician's control. Finally, some health care organizations (such as clinical labs, dialysis centers, and custodial long-term care) provide quite routinized services and may not have to accommodate themselves to physicians' values.

For all of these reasons, organizational as well as professional values may be important when medical services are provided. Nonprofit ownership promotes objectives that seem more compatible with professional norms than does for-profit ownership.[8] There is some evidence that nonprofit health care providers are more trusted by patients and are, at least under certain conditions, more trustworthy in their behavior than are for-profits, but evidence about this is mixed.[9] Apart from an inherent motivation to behave in a trustworthy manner, nonprofits may also allow their affiliated health professionals greater freedom to protect the well-being of vulnerable patients. Some studies find that nonprofit health care providers allow for greater professional *autonomy* (for example, the freedom to practice without organizational constraints);[10] others suggest that there are few ownership-related differences in professional *authority* (influence over organizational policies).[11]

Additional trustworthiness concerns arise because of third-party payment, a necessity in health care because expensive services are impossible for most individuals to budget and pay for on their own. But third-party payers are poorly situated to assess the necessity and quality of billed-for services, so they are vulnerable to fraud.[12] With health care costs threatening budgets among both public and private purchasers, fraud has become a serious problem.[13] Although some fraudulent activities have occurred among nonprofit providers, fraud as a large-scale organizational strategy for generating profits appears to be most common among for-profit organizations.[14] Indeed, in recent years leading investor-owned hospitals, psychiatric hospitals, nursing homes, and dialysis companies have all paid penalties in the hundreds of millions of dollars to settle Medicare fraud charges.[15] Moreover, there is considerable evidence that nonprofit health care providers are less aggressive in seeking to maximize revenues generated from third-party payers than are their for-profit counterparts.[16]

In short, the distinctive need for trustworthiness in the health arena may enhance the societal value of the nonprofit form for these services. Although policymakers concerned with health recognize the importance of trustworthiness, the question of comparative trustworthiness has received little attention from researchers, and trustworthiness itself has never been offered as a reason for granting nonprofit organizations tax-exempt status (in part because the policymakers and regulators with jurisdiction over tax policy are typically different from those with responsibilities for health care).

Reality 3: An Extremely Dynamic Arena

The health care field is characterized by specialized knowledge, high client expectations, extensive technological development, and rapid changes in services, treatment capacities, organizational infrastructure, regulatory provisions, and, as the 2010 health reform demonstrated, even occasional major changes in the rules of the game. The push for innovation involves new technologies, changing concepts of appropriate care, and new or expanded funding programs that open or expand markets for particular services (for example, in recent decades, hemodialysis and hospice care). Cost containment pressures are another source of change, leading to new payment methods and organizational arrangements (for example, managed-care plans). Thus, survival of nonprofit organizations in health care depends upon their ability to adapt. The need to adapt to changing technologies and expectations also means that hospitals and some other health care organizations are very capital-intensive and require regular infusions of capital.

Reality 4: A Capital-Intensive Market Good

Private contributions account for a small share of the revenues of the nonprofit sector as a whole (about 12 percent in 2005), and this percentage is particularly small for organizations that provide health services (less than 4 percent).[17] Contributions to organizations that provide health services tend to be for capital projects rather than for operating costs. To meet their operating expenses, nonprofits in health care rely heavily on—and compete for—revenues generated from the sale of services.[18] Survival requires commercial success in crowded markets that often include for-profit competitors. Hospitals traditionally competed on the basis of reputation, location, and the historical loyalties of doctors and patients, but in recent decades third-party purchasers have sought to encourage price competition by negotiating discounts from hospitals and by limiting the number with which they contract for services. This selective contracting strategy of purchasers led to a wave of mergers among hospitals and other service providers. Most hospitals today are part of larger organizations that own multiple facilities.

The capital needs of health care organizations contribute further to this competitive reality. Even though most donations to nonprofit health care providers are for capital funding, most of the capital needs of contemporary health care nonprofits are met from retained earnings and borrowed money. The availability and cost of debt financing are heavily influenced by an organization's creditworthiness, evaluated in cold economic terms. Bond-rating firms on Wall Street do not take favorable notice of an institution's charity care or service to the community.[19] Their concern is sound financial performance, measured in terms of keeping costs lower than the revenues generated through the sale of services. Nonprofits' dependence on private capital while selling services in the marketplace means that, notwithstanding their nonprofit status, they must adapt to economic imperatives and constraints that are similar to those faced by their for-profit competitors.

Reality 5: Charitable Roots Matter

Understanding the modern meaning of health care's charitable roots is important for particular organizations and for the field itself. Today's nonprofit health care sector developed out of eighteenth- and nineteenth-century charitable initiatives to serve the poor and infirm, and nonprofits are tax-exempt under federal law as charitable organizations.[20] The need for charity care has never disappeared. Hospital insurance programs began in the 1930s but were tied to employment and thus did not cover many people with significant health care needs and limited ability to pay, such as the elderly, the disabled, and poor women with dependent children. When these groupings gained coverage after passage of Medicare and Medicaid in 1965, the health care sector began to attract interest from serious investors, but the system of health insurance remained incomplete. By the time that major health reform legislation was enacted in 2010, some 46 million people (15 percent of the population) were uninsured and 25 million more had seriously inadequate health insurance.[21] The coverage expansions of the health reform legislation will not be fully implemented until 2014, but even then it is projected that 6 percent of the American population will remain uninsured.

Notwithstanding the commercial, competitive nature of today's health care, expectations of charitability still apply to nonprofit health care organizations, and these expectations were expanded under the 2010 health reform legislation, as we will see more fully in the next section. The coherence and strength of charitable expectations vary by type, age, and location of institutions, and some institutions clearly feel them more strongly than others.

Reality 6: A Policy-Sensitive Field

American health care is powerfully shaped by government policy. Dozens of local, state, and federal agencies have regulatory oversight of quality standards and business practices of health care organizations. The federal and state governments also have great influence through their requirements as purchasers of care; the Medicare and Medicaid programs pay for 28 percent of all medical care, 40 percent of all hospital care, 60 to 70 percent of long-term care, and virtually all costs for certain services (dialysis and hospice care). The coverage expansions and other provisions of the Patient Protection and Affordable Care Act of 2010 will further expand the governmental role—half of the newly insured population will be covered by Medicaid, the other half through private policies offered through government-regulated insurance "exchanges." Public policy also affects countless other matters, such as the terms on which relationships between providers and private insurers are negotiated. Both new funding programs and regulatory changes can stimulate important changes in organizational behavior or even cause shifts in the mix of ownership in a particular domain. In recent decades, public policy attention has increased regarding ownership-related issues, particularly the justification of nonprofits' tax-exempt status and the sale of nonprofits to for-profit purchasers.

Recent Challenges

These realities shape and intensify the challenges that face today's nonprofit health care organizations. Sources of five of the most important challenges are the following:

—Institutional change and growing constraints on the services that nonprofit health care organizations provide

—The changing nature of for-profit competition

—New expectations regarding accountability

—Limitations in public understanding of nonprofits

—Changing ideas about health and health care

In this section we examine each of these challenges in turn.

Fiscal Pressures and Institutional Constraints

Health care is shaped in many ways by payment systems. When the Medicare and Medicaid programs were established, in addition to existing employment-based insurance, more than 85 percent of Americans had third-party coverage for some or all of their medical care. Medical costs grew from 5 percent of gross national product in 1960 to 16 percent by the mid-2000s. Cost containment became a major policy concern.

The system of third-party payment also means that a small number of payers (Medicare, Medicaid, private health plans) generally account for the bulk of health organizations' revenues. Changes in purchasers' policies and practices can quickly change providers' circumstances. Some such changes have been significant.

Prior to the 1980s, Medicare, Medicaid, and the health insurance industry had few levers of control over what they paid for, how much they paid, or both. Medicare reimbursed hospitals for allowable costs, unintentionally creating incentives to generate more costs. Medicaid paid via an often low fee schedule but had little means of controlling the provision of unnecessary care. Insurance companies paid providers on the basis of their bills, so there was no constraint on cost there. This situation reflected the once predominantly nonprofit nature of the field, but it attracted for-profit competitors in the years after Medicare and Medicaid were enacted. As a Wall Street analyst reportedly said of the investor-owned hospital companies in the 1970s, it would have been difficult *not* to make money in this industry.

This profitable situation for providers proved untenable for those paying the bills, leading to new payment methods, new forms of oversight and accountability, and consolidation among payers. For example, in 1983 Medicare stopped reimbursing hospitals for the costs incurred in caring for patients and began paying fees on the basis of average costs for the "diagnosis related group" into which each patient's malady fit. Being paid a set amount for a patient's hospital stay reversed the incentive to generate more costs and enabled Medicare to make annual decisions regarding the rates it would pay for hospitalized patients.

Also in the 1980s, new managed care organizations began to carry out various forms of utilization review, including prior authorizations of elective hospitalizations and specialty referrals, and reviews of the appropriateness of services and patterns of care.[22] Payment denials for services deemed to be medically unnecessary became common, provoking outrage among providers and patients and a policy "backlash" against some cost containment techniques.[23] Payers' search for new cost containment strategies then led them to the use of contracts with selected providers with whom they negotiated price discounts, thereby generating price competition among providers. The resulting economic battles between purchasers and providers led to consolidation on both sides.

Health plans covering insured populations consolidated into a handful of national companies (such as Aetna and Wellpoint) that operated health plans in multiple states.[24] As a result, providers lost much of their power to pass along cost increases, and the effective decisions about the purchase of some services became concentrated into fewer hands, resulting in revenue losses for some providers. Obtaining payment for services provided became more difficult, with claims for payment being challenged on many grounds. Providers' complaints led several states to impose penalties on payers for untimely payment of "clean" claims.

The changing payment environment led to concerns about the ability of nonprofit providers to finance charitable or community-benefit activities that had long been supported in part from patient-care dollars. Studies showed, for example, that relatively few managed-care plans were willing to pay for activities related to research or medical education and that in locations with heavy managed-care penetration, the amount of uncompensated medical care declined and the dumping (economically motivated discharges) of unprofitable patients increased.[25] The economic pressures brought about by consolidation among payers provided additional stimulus to a long-standing trend of merger and consolidation among provider organizations, including nonprofits. The number of providers of some services (such as hospital care) declined (this can be seen in table 2-1); the percentage of providers that were part of multi-institutional organizations grew. Today, about two-thirds of nonprofit hospitals are in organizations that own multiple hospitals.

Consolidation among providers strengthened their position in contract negotiations with purchasers, but it also led to an unprecedented level of antitrust scrutiny of nonprofit organizations.[26] It also led to concerns that nonprofits might be losing touch with the needs of the communities that they serve, a topic to which we will return.

But a new and potentially important role—the role of quality leader–was created for nonprofit organizations by the changes stimulated by managed care. Because large health plans can have a profound impact on the delivery of medical services, concerns grew about the exercise of such power by organizations motivated primarily by the profit motive. Industry surveys showed (and continue to show) that nonprofit plans rated highest on measures of quality, and research on plan performance shows that nonprofit plans such as Kaiser Permanente tend to outperform for-profit plans.[27]

Although policymakers' views of the nonprofit health care sector remain mixed (some accusing nonprofits of failing to uphold their historically distinctive role), several of the provisions of the Patient Protection and Affordable Care Act of 2010 seemingly acknowledge that nonprofit ownership yields distinctive benefits in the provision of health insurance. After much debate in Congress, a government-run insurance plan (the so-called "public option") was not incorporated into the legislation. Its proponents, however, concluded that nonprofit ownership offered some of the same virtues. As a result, the final legislation incorporated requirements that the federal government ensure that at least one nonprofit insurance plan be offered in each of the state-run insurance exchanges. And it established a $6 billion loan fund to support the creation of new nonprofit health insurance plans to be operated as consumer cooperatives.

Expanded For-Profit Competition

A second major challenge facing nonprofit health care organizations stems from for-profit competition. The nature of competition from for-profits changed in several ways over the past thirty years. For-profit firms became much more prominent. A different form of for-profit organization came to the fore, with investor-owned corporations replacing local proprietors as the typical owners. And for-profits became competitive in the public policy arena as well as in the marketplace.

As can be seen in table 2-1, substantial for-profit growth has occurred since the mid-1980s in several health domains, with for-profit firms displacing non-profits as the predominant form among dialysis centers, rehabilitation hospitals, home health agencies, HMOs, private psychiatric hospitals, and, most recently, hospice programs.

This change has presented several challenges for the nonprofit sector.[28] Many nonprofits faced a competitive challenge from organizations that were frequently much more active and sophisticated in marketing. In some fields, for-profits also presented a takeover challenge, with for-profit organizations aggressively seeking to gain market share by purchasing nonprofit competitors. Finally, the growth of for-profits has sometimes presented a *legitimacy* challenge to nonprofits, as some research has shown that the measurable charitable activities of nonprofits differed little from those of their tax-paying for-profit counterparts.[29]

THE SHIFT TO INVESTOR OWNERSHIP. Until recent decades, for-profit health care organizations were generally local owner-operated facilities, such as doctor-owned hospitals and mom-and-pop nursing homes. The creation of Medicare and Medicaid in 1965 led to incentives that led to the establishment and growth of health care companies that built some hospitals and acquired most proprietary ones. The stockholders in these firms had little or no contact with the facilities owned by their company.[30] Publicly traded investor-owned companies that own multiple facilities are now typical in the for-profit component of the health care field, including hospitals, nursing homes, home health agencies, HMOs, dialysis centers, and hospices.

The shift from proprietary to investor ownership had important consequences for nonprofits. These new investor-owned organizations were generally much better capitalized than the proprietary organizations had been, and they could compete much more aggressively. It was common for a marginal proprietary facility to be bought by an investor-owned company that then renovated or replaced it. Moreover, companies that own multiple facilities are able to bring in more sophisticated management and gain advantages of scale and scope. In some domains, size could be important in gaining access to certain markets, such as national employers that purchase managed-care services, and in negotiating favorable terms with suppliers of goods and services.

Investor ownership also changed the dynamics of for-profit involvement. The stock price of publicly traded companies is a function of both the company's earnings and investors' expectations of future earnings. Since a company's access to capital and the wealth of its executives are a function of stock price, investor-owned corporations have strong incentives to grow. The most rapid path is via acquisitions, and many of the publicly traded health care companies have gone through periods of omnivorous growth, fed by high stock prices, which in turn were fed by the expectations and fact of further growth. In some domains, nonprofits faced strong pressures and enticements to sell when companies were in such a growth period, and some conversions to for-profit status resulted.

Experience in health care has also shown, however, that when a company's growth is curtailed by stagnant demand, scandal, or regulatory barriers, stock values can decline precipitously.[31] Virtually all investor-owned health care companies have experienced this boom-bust cycle, which led to the resale, closure, or conversion back to nonprofit status of many for-profit facilities, particularly hospitals. A similar market exit occurred in the massive withdrawal in the early 2000s of for-profit HMOs from participation in Medicare, as had happened with Medicaid in the late 1990s. When continuity of medical care is important for patients, the closure of facilities during the bust periods can seriously disrupt treatment and threaten patient well-being.

COMPETITION IN THE PUBLIC POLICY ARENA. The shift to investor owner-ship also enhanced the political influence of the for-profit sector. Large corpora-tions use their financial resources to influence regulatory actions, policy deci-sions, and even electoral outcomes at the local, state, and national levels.[32] The interests of for-profit and nonprofit organizations sometimes diverge. In our own research, we have learned of lobbying activities encouraging state and local attacks on nonprofit hospitals' tax exemptions and against new state laws to reg-ulate the sale of nonprofit hospitals to for-profit purchasers. At the federal level, the trade association of for-profit hospitals has sought rule changes in Medicare to allow payments, from a fixed pot of money from which all hospitals are paid, to reimburse for-profit hospitals for their local property tax payments. Multiple-state corporations often can circumvent state regulation, either by shifting cer-tain activities to less regulated states or by threatening to avoid a state entirely if regulations are enforced against them.

New Expectations for Accountability

The past two decades have seen a surge in demands that nonprofit organizations document practices that justify their tax preferences. Such demands are neither new nor limited to health care organizations, but they have been especially strong and insistent in health care. Some two dozen states initiated reporting require-ments regarding charitable expenditures of nonprofit hospitals, and the Inter-nal Revenue Service's revision of its Form 990 for Tax-Exempt Organizations, which was released in 2008, included a special section (Schedule H) for hospitals to report their expenditures on community benefit (that is, charitable) activities). At about the same time, the minority (Republican) staff of the Senate Finance Committee proposed that nonprofit hospitals be required to devote a minimum of 5 percent of their expenditures to charity care, narrowly defined. At the local and state levels, there have been scattered attacks (occasionally successful) on individual hospitals' tax exemptions, complemented by a handful of states that set expenditure requirements regarding hospitals' charitable activities.[33]

Several factors led to the new demands and criticisms. One important stimu-lus was a series of press accounts about the billing and debt-collection practices of hospitals, beginning with a 2003 *Wall Street Journal* article about Yale–New Haven Hospital. It became apparent that various nonprofit and for-profit hos-pitals were charging uninsured patients more than insured patients (a conse-quence of insurers' success in negotiating discounts from list prices) and using aggressive methods to try to collect bill payment from patients, including some who lacked means to pay. Although these practices may not have been typical, the published accounts led several states to pass laws to limit hospitals' charges and collection practices regarding uninsured patients.[34] At the national level, the issue stimulated several congressional hearings, studies by the Government Accountability Office, the Senate Finance Committee, and the Internal Revenue Service, and provisions in the Affordable Care Act.

Several issues were thrown into high relief by these various activities. First, some nonprofit hospitals had engaged in practices that seemed inconsistent with their charitable status, although hospitals' policies and practices were quite variable. Second, it became apparent that there was disagreement and a lack of clarity among policymakers and critics of nonprofit hospitals about what expectations should be tied to nonprofits' tax exemptions. Third, meaningful charitable accountability was complicated by a lack of agreement and standardization regarding what should be counted as a charitable (or community benefit) expense. As Senator Chuck Grassley of Iowa put it, trying to compare the charitable activities of different hospitals was less like comparing apples to oranges than like comparing apples to farm tractors.[35]

The Internal Revenue Service's release of its reporting requirement (Schedule H of Form 990) regarding community-benefit expenditures for organizations that operate nonprofit hospitals brought some clarity to this issue by including a standardized set of categories and reporting rules based on reporting guidelines that had been developed by the Catholic Health Association and the Voluntary Hospitals of America. The categories include charity care and unreimbursed expenses for means-tested government programs such as Medicaid, community health improvement activities, subsidized health services, health professions education, research, and charitable contributions to community organizations. Schedule H also contains other provisions to improve the accountability of nonprofit hospitals such as requesting information about their policies regarding eligibility for charity care and about debt collection practices.

Although Schedule H represented a significant step in charitable accountability, it has three significant limitations. First, expenses for community building (investing in community infrastructure) are not counted as community benefit expenses.[36] Second, dollars expended are a poor measure of some community benefit activities, such as those intended to reduce the burden of illness or the unnecessary use of emergency departments. Finally, Schedule H applies to the entire organization that files a Form 990, and some such organizations operate multiple hospitals and many other kinds of entities (foundations, nursing homes, outpatient clinics, and so forth). These differences in the reporting entities greatly reduce the usefulness of Schedule H as a tool with which to make cross-organizational comparisons and thus for localities to hold accountable the facilities that are serving their health needs.

Notwithstanding the importance of accountability reforms of the 2000s, it should be recognized that the demand for greater accountability in nonprofit health care organizations, particularly hospitals, has roots that go much deeper than the controversies of the 2000s or the demands for better reporting requirements. For a quarter century, some legal scholars have challenged the fundamental rationale for tax exemptions, with hospitals often cited as a case in point.[37] A body of empirical research developed since the 1980s has showed only modest and inconsistent differences between for-profit and nonprofit hospitals regarding the amount of uncompensated care that they provide.[38] This all occurred in the context of a growing American sense of distrust in all social institutions, and a public that expected to see evidence to back up institutional claims about social benefits.[39]

Within the health care field, the demand for accountability has been embodied in the growing use of report cards for grading the performance of various organizations, particularly HMOs and nursing homes. The expansion of for-profit involvement in the health field has helped to stimulate this demand, raising awareness of providers' mixed motives and also creating an organized political interest with a stake in raising doubts about nonprofits' tax exemptions or other forms of preferential treatment that create "unfair" competition.[40] Beneficiaries of nonprofits' charitable and community service activities (indigent patients, those with the most complex and costly cases, those in need of unprofitable services, those who benefit from experimental techniques) rarely have an equivalent capacity to organize and voice their concerns in a politically effective manner. Thus, ironically, arguments about the need to eliminate tax exemptions so as to create a level playing field in the provision of health services have often been made in the absence of a level playing field in political representation.

Before the issuance of the Internal Revenue Service's Schedule H in 2008, most changes in nonprofit accountability in health care had occurred at the state level.[41] The state requirements mentioned earlier use one of two approaches, primarily applying them to hospitals rather than health care organizations more generally.[42] One requires nonprofits to assess community needs and develop plans for addressing them. The other requires reporting on the amount of charity care that is provided, with a handful of states setting some variation of a threshold.

New reporting and threshold requirements for nonprofit hospitals were on the table during the larger national health reform debate in 2009. A proposal from the Republican staff of the Senate Finance Committee to create a uniform threshold requirement for charity care went nowhere, probably because of practical complexities (the variability in need in different states and communities) and because insurance reform can be expected to reduce, though not eliminate, the need for charity care. In addition, Schedule H partially filled the need for better accountability.

The Patient Protection and Affordable Care Act of 2010 included provisions that require tax-exempt hospitals to conduct community health needs assessments every three years and to develop an implementation strategy to meet those needs. It also requires hospitals to have written financial assistance policies regarding eligibility for free or discounted care and setting limits on charges and collection practices for patients who are eligible for financial assistance. As with Schedule H, these requirements clarify what is expected of nonprofit hospitals, but do not break with long-standing policies regarding expectations of nonprofit health care organizations. There are no threshold requirements for any particular kind of charitable activity, and charitability continues to be defined in terms of community benefit rather than charity care, as we will discuss further.

The central purpose of the Patient Protection and Affordable Care Act of 2010 was to decrease quite substantially the percentage of Americans who lack health insurance protection; projections saw reductions in the percentage from more than 15 percent to about 6 percent. This raises questions about the future of organizations such as community health centers that have been funded to serve low-income populations, particularly the uninsured. Questions have also been raised as to whether a reduced demand for charity care will obviate the rationale for tax exemptions for nonprofit hospitals.

On the other hand, the legislation also reduces direct government subsidies to hospitals that serve largely low-income populations (the "disproportionate share" hospitals), so that continued treatment for the tens of millions of Americans expected to remain uninsured after the reforms are fully implemented may actually depend increasingly on the charitable motivations of health care providers. Although the full effects of reform on charity care are yet to be determined, such questions point to the need for greater clarity about what it means for an organization to be tax-exempt as a charity.

The Changing Definitions of Charity

Considerable confusion and disagreement about what should constitute charitability and community service for nonprofits in the health care arena has been in evidence in debates over the accountability of nonprofit health providers. As noted, nonprofits in health care have a history of providing free or reduced-price care to people who lack the means to pay. Moreover, many of today's nonprofit hospitals benefited from construction funds provided in the post–World War II period under the federal Hill-Burton Act, which subsidized construction of nonprofit hospitals. These funds carried obligations (often poorly enforced) that hospitals provide a certain level of free care.

Nonprofit health care organizations have always been tax-exempt as charitable organizations, but the operational meaning of "charitable" in the health care field has undergone important changes among tax authorities over the years. First, after the number of Americans without health insurance was dramatically reduced by the enactment of Medicare and Medicaid in 1965, the Internal Revenue Service (IRS), in 1969, changed the criteria for tax exemption for hospitals (and, by extension, for other health care organizations) from a definition focused on serving the poor (a so-called relief-of-poverty definition of charity) to a definition that emphasized serving the community at large (the community-benefit standard). The community-benefit definition did not make any reference to service to patients who were unable to afford medical services, and there has been considerable disagreement about what should count as "community benefit." This broader definition of community benefit was explicitly adopted by the tax authorities or legislatures in a number of states—most notably California, Minnesota, Massachusetts, New York, and Maryland—and by the IRS.

With community benefit defined broadly enough to include a variety of health promotion and disease prevention activities unrelated to providing free care to the needy, judgments about whether health institutions deserve their tax-exempt status became increasingly contentious. Many legitimate demands compete for the operating revenues that organizations generate. In addition to the care of indigent patients, the expenses of an academic medical center, for example, might include various other activities that provide social benefit, including research or educational activities, the development of new services that are not yet covered by insurance, or various kinds of health promotion and disease prevention activities in the community.

Not all of these activities might count under the community-benefit criteria established by state legislatures or attorneys general, and only some might benefit the community within which the hospital is located, as opposed to the broader health care system or country as a whole, as do research or health professional education. No established criteria in law or the academic literature make it clear which, if any, of these activities are most compatible with a nonprofit mission, although many different ideas have been published.[43] Leadership in defining what counts as community-benefit activity has been taken in the past two decades by the Catholic Health Association (CHA) and the Voluntary Hospitals of America (VHA), which have published guidance for their members regarding the conduct and reporting of community-benefit activities. Some states and the Internal Revenue Service build upon CHA's and VHA's efforts in developing their own reporting requirements. Areas of disagreement remain, particularly with regard to counting bad debt—some but not all of which results from service to low-income uninsured patients—and gaps between costs and payment rates for the Medicaid program. Clarification is provided by the categories and instructions in the IRS's Schedule H, which contain practical guidance to what hospitals should count and report as a community-benefit activity. The reporting in Schedule H may stimulate new debates about what should be counted and how much is enough.

Beyond this, there is a tension between approaches to accountability that rely on countable forms of community benefit and those that rely on newly emerging concepts of community benefit.[44] Calculating expenditures for charity care is easy compared to measuring the benefits that result from greater trustworthiness, preserving professional ethics in patient care, or addressing the social determinants of health. Yet these forms of community benefit may be just as important as charity care. Similarly, although Schedule H represents a major advance in the accountability of nonprofit hospitals, it is based on the reporting of expenditures, which may be a poor measure of the benefits of certain activities, such as programs to reduce teenage pregnancy, obesity, or substance abuse or to prevent hospitalizations for uncontrolled diabetes or childhood asthma.

Limited Public Understanding

Nonprofit organizations are easily misunderstood, and this is perhaps particularly the case in health care. Even though profit is not their raison d'être, in fact they generate most of their revenues from the sale of services. Even though they don't have owners, investors (in this case, lenders) provide much of their needed capital. Even though "charitable," they are not required to provide charity care to people who do not have the means to pay. Health care organizations share various of these characteristics with some other kinds of nonprofits (particularly, private educational institutions), but the prominence of the problem of America's uninsured population gives a special flavor to expectations and assumptions about what it means to be tax-exempt as a charity.

Survey data from recent years illustrates why public understanding presents a challenge for nonprofit health care organizations. In simple terms, the very nature of a nonprofit organization is not understood by a large share of the public, and the imagery associated with the idea of a nonprofit organization is decidedly mixed. About a third of the American public has no coherent conception of what a nonprofit organization is, and explanations tend to lead to less favorable views about performance.[45]

Most of the public believes that ownership form affects the behavior of hospitals and HMOs.[46] However, although most of the public views nonprofit hospitals and HMOs as better than for-profits in terms of trustworthiness and humaneness, nonprofit ownership is seen by the public as offering lower quality of care than for-profit ownership, even though a large body of research shows nonprofits' quality to be better than or similar to for-profits'.[47] It appears that the nonprofit form's association with charity has some negative connotations for many people.

Changing Interpretations of Health and Health Care

Finally, nonprofit health care providers have been affected by a broader set of changes in American medicine over the past two decades that have altered the nature of health services and the norms of performance against which those services are judged.

THE GROWTH OF CONSUMER CHOICE IN MEDICAL CARE. Public policy in recent decades has encouraged individuals to choose among health insurance plans that have differing networks of providers. For example, the federal HMO Act of 1973 encouraged employers to offer employees choices among plans. Public programs such as Medicare and Medicaid began to incorporate similar choices in the mid-1980s, and the role of consumer choice was expanded considerably in the 1990s.[48] Over the past ten years, "report cards" designed to promote consumer choice have proliferated to cover hospitals, doctors' practices, nursing homes, home health agencies and renal dialysis centers.[49]

Consumer choice has been lauded as empowering individuals by increasing their control over the types of medical care they consider most important. But consumer empowerment also creates the potential for misinformed choices and problematic consequences if individuals act on insufficient or inaccurate information about the options they face. To the extent that nonprofit organizations are more trustworthy in representations about their services and performance, a larger nonprofit presence may enhance the odds that consumers can make effective decisions.

The continuing increase in public information about performance of health care organizations may reduce the likelihood that for-profits will skimp on dimensions of quality that are difficult for individual consumers to assess, but that can be measured in quantifiable measures on report cards. This would reduce future quality-related differences between for-profits and nonprofits in these aspects of care. Conversely, however, dimensions of quality that are less effectively quantified (and thus less appropriate candidates for inclusion on report cards) may get even shorter shrift by for-profits, increasing the magnitude of these ownership-related differences.

THE DEPROFESSIONALIZATION OF MEDICAL SERVICES. As was noted earlier, the professional training of health providers, particularly physicians, has always emphasized the vulnerability of patients and hence the need to instill in doctors not only technical competence but also a fiduciary ethic, a concern for protecting the well-being of patients.[50] To the extent that these professional norms held, the influence of professionals within health care organizations could mitigate some of the dangers that the profit motive could pose to patients.[51]

Some four decades ago cracks began to appear in the foundation on which claims to the authority of medical professionals had been erected. "Medicine, like many other American institutions, suffered a stunning loss of confidence in the 1970s."[52] By the mid-1980s, both sociologists and doctors themselves were writing about the "deprofessionalization" of medicine, as practitioners lost autonomy under the oversight of managed-care plans, and public confidence in the motives of the profession continued to erode.[53] By the mid-1990s, a sociologist studying the professions in a number of different countries wrote, "No profession in our sample has flown quite as high in guild power and control as American medicine, and few have fallen as fast."[54]

The challenge to professionalism in American medicine holds two potential implications for the role of nonprofit enterprise in this field. First, if professionals become less willing or able to act as effective agents for their patients (or are so perceived by those patients), the trustworthiness of health care organizations becomes increasingly important for protecting patients from exploitation. Second, as professional autonomy and authority are circumscribed by managed-care arrangements, the motives driving managed-care plans become increasingly important. If, as some limited evidence suggests, nonprofit plans are more likely to preserve professional prerogatives, ownership may play an important, albeit indirect, role in safeguarding patient welfare.[55]

NEW UNDERSTANDINGS OF THE DETERMINANTS OF POPULATION HEALTH. Since the beginning of the twentieth century, public health advocates have recognized the importance of nonclinical factors, including economic, social, and environmental conditions, in shaping the health of populations.[56] But these perspectives have been incorporated only episodically into health policy, which remained focused on the delivery of medical care and the ways in which individual behaviors affect the prospects for health, while downplaying the role of community infrastructure, corporate practices, or other social factors.[57]

Policymakers are becoming more aware of evidence linking health to societal characteristics and are becoming increasingly frustrated by the modest returns from high levels of spending on medical care.[58] For example, compelling evidence has accumulated to show that community characteristics exert a powerful independent influence on the health of residents.[59] The important role of community resources has been reinforced by the growing prevalence of chronic medical conditions.[60] The success of interventions for people with chronic conditions often depends on the availability of social and other health-related services in the community as well as on the willingness of family caregivers to help meet relatives' needs.[61]

Recognizing these social determinants suggests avenues for redirecting the resources that nonprofit health care organizations devote to community-benefit activities. For example, the most effective approach to improving the health of residents in low-income communities may not involve the provision of charitable medical services to the infirm. Instead, it may require the allocation of resources to programs designed to improve the nutritional content of the meals in neighborhood restaurants and schools, reducing the prevalence of local traffic accidents, or installing smoke detectors in residences whose inhabitants cannot otherwise afford them.[62]

Nonprofits' Responses to These Challenges

How have these challenges affected the role of nonprofits in the health field? Broadly speaking, three sets of responses are evident. First, the role of nonprofits in various domains of the health field has shifted in response to the entry of well-financed for-profit organizations, although this has varied greatly by domain. Second, changes have taken place in the structure and practices of nonprofit providers, mostly in the direction of convergence with for-profit providers. And third, efforts have been made to maintain a distinctive role for nonprofits.

Shifts in the Nonprofit Role

Since the 1980s, several health care domains have undergone a rapid transformation from predominantly nonprofit to predominantly for-profit ownership (see table 2-1). This pattern is unusual within the nonprofit sector, and it is important to understand what has been driving this shift and what it might portend for the future of nonprofit involvement in this field and potentially in others.

Having studied the health field for roughly thirty years, we think that such understanding cannot be derived from any existing general theory about the role of nonprofit organizations or about the types of social needs that nonprofit organizations meet, whether these theories focus on the "public goods" character of the services, the asymmetries of information between client and service provider, or the inability of organizations to distribute their surplus.[63]

Nor does the record support the view that the entry or growth of a for-profit element in a nonprofit field necessarily initiates a cascade of events leading to the disappearance of nonprofits. On the contrary, table 2-1 shows that in some domains—nursing home care and general hospitals—nonprofits have at least been holding their own, even while for-profits have replaced, or at least outdistanced, nonprofits in several domains. Among psychiatric hospitals, the nonprofit share of those that are not governmental has increased in the past decade because of shrinkage in the number of for-profits. Even in some fields in which the nonprofit share has declined, the absolute number of nonprofit organizations has increased.

All of this points to the need to complement theoretical explanations for the presence of nonprofit or for-profit organizations in a field with a more careful understanding of the varying contexts within which services are provided, reasons for the rapid for-profit increase in some domains, and reasons for the persistence or resurgence of nonprofits in others.

We suggest that ownership patterns are influenced by a combination of three contextual factors: the historical era in which a service first emerges, prevailing market conditions, and government policies that intentionally or unintentionally advantage certain types of providers.

WHEN FOR-PROFITS EXPAND. The interplay of these factors can be seen vividly in the experience of four domains in which for-profits came to outdistance nonprofits between the mid-1980s and the late 1990s: dialysis centers, rehabilitation hospitals, home health agencies, and HMOs. These domains lend credence to a view advanced by scholars two decades ago that for-profit growth results in part from nonprofit organizations' inability or failure (as a result of either limited access to capital or weak entrepreneurial incentives) to respond quickly when demand for a service substantially increases.[64] As can be seen in table 2-1, the domains in which the for-profit share grew dramatically experienced rapid increases in the total number of organizations. These increases resulted from public policy changes that substantially increased the number of paying (or insured) patients seeking services.

Several of these domains were also affected by federal policies that either inhibited the growth of nonprofit organizations or stimulated the expansion of their for-profit competitors. These policies reflected insensitivity, ambivalence, or perhaps even skepticism, among policymakers about the merits of nonprofit enterprise in medical care.[65]

Dialysis centers illustrate the pattern of for-profit expansion following a policy reform that stimulated demand for services. As of 1970, less than 5 percent of all dialysis—which was then a very new technology—was provided under for-profit auspices.[66] Passage of the federal end-stage renal disease program in 1972 gave patients suffering from chronic kidney failure coverage under Medicare. The number of patients whose care was paid for by this program immediately surged and continued to increase at a relatively steady 7 to 9 percent a year.[67] The number of providers of dialysis services grew, as did the market share of for-profit agencies, going from 20 percent by 1977 to 68 percent by 1997 to 78 percent in 2007. The number of nonprofit providers also increased, but at a much slower pace.

The more recent trajectory of *hospice programs* is similar to that of dialysis centers: both involve a service for which a new federal payment program began. The hospice benefit was added to the Medicare program in 1982. However, as we discuss later, there were already a substantial number of nonprofit hospices in place when the new benefit was created.

The rapid increase in demand for *rehabilitation hospitals* was partially a product of technology and partially a result of policy change. Technological improvements in physical medicine had led over many years to much more concerted efforts to rehabilitate patients with severe head and spinal cord injuries. Once Medicare shifted to paying hospitals on a per-case basis in 1983, patients requiring rehabilitation services began to be transferred out of acute-care beds and into rehabilitation units (often in the same hospital) or into rehabilitation hospitals. This led to almost a tripling in the number of rehabilitation hospitals over the next fifteen years and a corresponding increase in the market share of for-profit facilities.

Demand for *home health care* was also stimulated by the Medicare payment change that created powerful incentives for the rapid discharge of hospitalized patients. New technologies had made it possible to provide drug infusion and other services in the home that had previously been provided only in the hospital. Further stimulating demand was a 1989 court case that required the federal government to apply less restrictive standards for qualifying Medicare beneficiaries for home care.

The ownership mix among home health care providers was also affected by policies targeted to ownership form. Prior to 1981, Medicare required for-profit home-care agencies to have state licenses to participate in the program. This quality-of-care protection was not required of nonprofit agencies. Many states did not actually have licensure procedures for home-care agencies, so this regulation effectively inhibited the expansion of for-profit home care. It was repealed early in the Reagan administration, opening the market to entry by for-profit agencies at the same time that changes in the rules for hospital payment were stimulating demand.

In the case of *health maintenance organizations,* the expansion of the for-profit role in the 1980s was a product of employers' desire for cost containment assistance as well as several policy decisions.[68] Early in the Reagan administration, a federal program was ended that had provided start-up capital for nonprofit HMOs, making it difficult for the nonprofit sector to respond to growing demand. Coupled with this were IRS reservations about whether nonprofit HMOs deserved tax exemptions; in the IRS view, HMOs provided *private* benefits (either to the enrolled population or to physicians) rather than benefits to the community at large. These concerns were particularly pronounced for certain forms of HMOs that existed largely as contractual affiliations among a set of clinicians; those were effectively ruled out of bounds for nonprofits. But since these were the very plans that could be expanded most quickly (due to their minimal capital requirements), this put a damper on the expansion of nonprofit HMOs. Whereas the developers of new plans in the 1970s had reasons to choose the nonprofit form (to secure funding under the HMO Act), in the 1980s the federal government became an obstacle to the creation of new nonprofit plans due to uncertainty about whether they could obtain a tax exemption.

Finally, lax oversight at the state level facilitated the conversion of plans from nonprofit to for-profit. Approximately one-third of nonprofit HMOs converted to for-profits in the 1980s, either by selling their assets to a for-profit purchaser or by reorganizing the corporation.[69] For-profit conversions of HMOs were motivated both by their need for capital to facilitate growth and by insiders' ability to acquire the assets at bargain prices. Few states had experience with for-profit conversions, and most had little or no regulatory staff to review such transactions, which apparently often occurred for much less than fair market value.[70]

DOMAINS OF NONPROFIT PERSISTENCE OR RESURGENCE. The powerful forces that have encouraged the growth of for-profit involvement in health care are not inexorable. The cases of general hospitals, hospice programs, nursing homes, and psychiatric hospitals provide examples of periods of nonprofit persistence, nonprofit resurgence, and for-profit decline. The patterns exhibited here are instructive.

General hospitals constitute a domain in which nonprofit providers have resisted the pressures of for-profit incursion. Despite fears in the past three decades that these facilities would be swallowed by investor-owned companies, about 60 percent of community hospitals have been under nonprofit auspices for forty years, even as the number of hospitals in the country has shrunk substantially.[71]

Hospitals have had a mix of ownership since the first surveys were conducted early in the twentieth century, when about half of all hospitals were for-profit—mostly small hospitals owned by individual doctors and operated as adjuncts to their offices.[72] As the technology of health care developed over the course of the century and as quality and life safety rules became more demanding, operation of these small-scale hospitals became increasingly difficult. In each successive survey, the for-profit sector was smaller—36 percent in 1928, 25 percent in 1941, 18 percent in 1950, and 12 to 14 percent when Medicare was passed in 1965.[73] Toward the end, this decline was fostered by the Hill-Burton program (by subsidizing construction of nonprofit hospitals).

Equity capital was attracted to hospitals by the investment opportunity resulting from the passage of Medicare and Medicaid, which covered the elderly, the disabled, and many of the poor. Medicare also facilitated access to capital for hospitals and nursing homes by including capital costs (interest, depreciation, and, for for-profits, return on equity) in the cost-based reimbursement system of paying for services. Investor-owned hospital companies began to be formed in the middle to late 1960s.[74]

In spite of the great increase in the number of people with insurance coverage, the ability of these companies to grow was limited by a combination of factors. First, no shortage of hospital beds developed after the Medicare and Medicaid programs came on line.[75] After almost twenty years of Hill-Burton support for hospital construction, the country had an ample stock of hospitals and beds that was easily able to absorb the 5 to 10 percent increase in utilization that occurred. Second, the new programs also enhanced the financial health of nonprofit hospitals and facilitated their access to debt as a source of capital. Their boards of trustees had little reason to consider the sale of their hospitals. Third, by the time that the initial set of investor-owned companies began to develop some real size and heft in the mid-1970s, the federal government and the states had put in place a health planning program under which a certificate of need had to be obtained before a new hospital could be constructed.

Thus, although the Medicare and Medicaid programs created a stimulus for demand, even well-capitalized companies faced limited paths for growth in the hospital domain. Nevertheless, several new investor-owned hospital companies did grow by signing contracts to manage nonprofit and public hospitals, acquiring most remaining proprietary hospitals owned by physicians, building specialized institutions such as psychiatric facilities, and building new community hospitals in parts of the country that were experiencing rapid population growth and had a relatively underdeveloped nonprofit infrastructure. The share of hospital beds that were for-profit has increased gradually over the years, but as a result of a decrease in the public hospital share.

The persistence of the nonprofit share has not always been steady. Changes in economic circumstances have twice produced alarm bordering on panic among nonprofit hospitals, prompting some mergers among nonprofits or sales to for-profit purchasers. The first wave occurred in the early 1980s, when Medicare replaced a hospital payment system based on reimbursing for incurred costs with a system that set rates in advance for hospitalizations. Deeply worried about their institutions' ability to cope with the new payment method, which contained no assurances that a hospital's costs of caring for Medicare patients would be covered, the trustees of some nonprofit hospitals decided to sell to one of the rapidly growing investor-owned hospital companies, which had high stock prices and abundant capital. With dire predictions that hospital care would go entirely for-profit, the Institute of Medicine (IOM) at the National Academy of Sciences appointed an expert panel in 1984 to assess the likely consequences.[76] When the IOM report was published in 1986, however, it found that the risk of a for-profit takeover was seriously overstated. By then, the hospital companies had experienced serious setbacks.[77] Having mastered the tricks of maximizing revenues under the cost-based reimbursement system, for-profit companies struggled under the new payment system. The companies' high stock prices came back to earth; some of their hospitals closed, while some reverted to nonprofit control.

A second wave of panic selling by nonprofit hospitals occurred in the mid-1990s, again in the face of a serious threat to the hospitals' economic well-being. This time it was the growth and increasing aggressiveness of managed care. And, again, some investor-owned companies (most notably, Columbia/HCA and Tenet) had grown rapidly by acquiring the remnants of the struggling companies from the 1980s, and had high stock prices and abundant capital. These companies became active purchasers of nonprofit hospitals, and Richard Scott, chief executive officer of Columbia/HCA, launched outspoken attacks on the legitimacy of tax exemptions for nonprofit hospitals. Then, in early 1997, Columbia/HCA became enmeshed in a series of major investigations by government agencies and insurance companies into allegations of fraud involving overbilling and charging for unnecessary services.[78] The company's stock price tumbled, Scott was fired, and the company became a net seller of hospitals, some of which again became nonprofit. The company made a $745 million payment to settle the federal fraud case in 2000, and it also followed the strategy used by previously discredited companies of changing its name. Tenet encountered a similar fate, settling three fraud cases a few years later for $900 million.

These two waves of highly publicized acquisitions of nonprofit hospitals by for-profit companies attracted considerable controversy, and by the late 1990s some twenty-five states had adopted legal reforms to increase public scrutiny of and mitigate conflicts of interest in the sale of nonprofit hospitals. Yet despite much concern about the activities of investor-owned hospital companies, the overall composition of the hospital domain changed very little.[79] Some for-profit acquisitions eventually turned into closures, and some conversions have occurred in the opposite direction.[80]

Regarding *hospice* services, legislation created a growth opportunity in the early 1980s that appears similar to examples where rapid for-profit expansion ensued, particularly renal dialysis services. As with dialysis, the legal change provided Medicare payment (beginning in 1983) for a service in a new field that was almost entirely nonprofit (only 2 percent of hospice programs operated under for-profit auspices in the early 1980s).[81] Yet this new source of payment led to a much more limited initial for-profit increase among hospice providers than had occurred for dialysis services.

Two factors appear to account for the difference. First, in contrast to the dialysis case, more than a thousand nonprofit hospice programs were already in operation by the time Medicare coverage was enacted. The hospice concept had come to this country from England in the late 1970s and struck a responsive chord. Through grassroots charitable and voluntary activity, nonprofit hospice programs were created all over the country before third-party coverage was available. Some were independent organizations; some were creations of other organizations, such as nonprofit hospitals.

Second, because of concerns about cost and quality and the desire of leaders of the hospice movement to assure the differentiation of hospice services from those of hospitals, the law set stringent requirements for hospice programs to be eligible for Medicare funding.[82] This created a barrier to entry. Moreover, some of the requirements themselves—the provision of ministerial, bereavement, and volunteer services that were not directly reimbursable—signaled that entrepreneurs were not welcome. These two factors combined to enable the nonprofit sector to absorb most of the expanding demand, leaving a smaller market opportunity for new for-profit competitors. Thus, even nine years later, in 1992, the total number of Medicare-certified hospice providers was 1,208, of which only 13 percent were for-profit.

The use of hospice services subsequently grew much more rapidly, with the number of persons using Medicare hospice benefits alone doubling, from 143,000 to 295,000, between 1992 and 1996 and continuing to grow thereafter. No single cause can be identified, but there are several indications that a consensus had developed—among the health professions, the public, and policymakers—that our growing technological ability to prolong life was creating needless suffering at very high cost. For example, the Patient Self-Determination Act was enacted in 1991, requiring health care organizations to educate patients and staff about end-of-life treatment and to document patients' wishes. A palliative-care physicians' group was established in the early 1990s. In any event, the increasing demand for hospice services was accompanied by growing numbers of hospice programs, with the for-profit sector increasing most rapidly.[83] The much larger nonprofit sector also grew, but at a slower rate since the 1990s.

The hospital and hospice examples show that new funding in a domain does not necessarily change its nonprofit character. The nursing home and psychiatric hospital examples show that the growth of the for-profit sector within a domain is not immutable.

Between 1986 and 1997, the market share of for-profit *nursing homes* fell from 75 to 65 percent, while the share and absolute number of nonprofit facilities was increasing. This pattern contrasts sharply with earlier periods in which the for-profit share increased dramatically. The first increase predated World War II, a largely unforeseen consequence of the Social Security Act of 1935, which established a new cash assistance program to enable the elderly poor to purchase needed institutional care.[84] The act stipulated that such funds could not be paid to any "inmate of a public institution," thereby opening a marketing opportunity for proprietors. By the time of the earliest survey of ownership of nursing homes (in this case, skilled nursing facilities) in 1954, the pattern was set: 71 percent were for-profit (many of them essentially boarding houses), 14 percent were nonprofit, and the rest were public.[85]

The for-profit market share subsequently declined during the 1950s, as nonprofit nursing homes gained access to federal construction subsidies.[86] But demand for services (and thus the market share of for-profit nursing homes) received a second boost when Medicare and Medicaid were created. The Medicaid program, which became the largest purchaser of nursing home care, stimulated a major increase in nursing home capacity. The total number of beds roughly doubled between 1963 and 1971, and the for-profit share of nursing home beds grew from 60 to 72 percent.[87] Ownership by investor-owned companies became typical.

By the 1990s, however, the growth dynamic in the nursing home industry was reversed, as state and federal governments began to pay for more home health services and states enacted various policies designed to reduce institutionalization of the elderly and disabled. With demand stagnant, investors began to look elsewhere and the number of for-profit facilities began to decline, reflecting the dynamics associated with stock valuation in investor-owned corporations, a process we described earlier. The pressure to sustain growth also led some for-profit entrepreneurs to engage in fraud. This pattern, which also arose among psychiatric hospitals, involved everything from inappropriate billing to repurchasing arrangements through which homes were sold multiple times to overstating the capital costs on which their reimbursement was partially based.[88]

For *psychiatric hospitals,* as for general hospitals, there has long been a small proprietary sector. It began to grow in the 1960s as the deinstitutionalization movement was emptying many beds in state and county psychiatric hospitals and states began requiring private insurance plans to include coverage for mental health care. There had long been epidemiological evidence of unmet need for psychiatric services, especially among the poor, the elderly, and children. Thus a combination of factors in the late 1960s and 1970s stimulated demand for psychiatric services.[89] Public hospitals continued to house the chronically mentally ill who were public charges but private psychiatric hospitals served a growing market of insured "short stay" patients.

Investor-owned companies that owned multiple facilities appeared in the late 1960s. The number of for-profit psychiatric hospitals grew 80 percent, from 81 to 146, between 1969 and 1979, while the number of nonprofits increased 8 percent, from 87 to 94.[90] The pace of for-profit growth quickened in the 1980s. One reason was that Medicare exempted psychiatric hospitals from the prospective payment system that was introducing new cost constraints. Also, managed care did not have effective tools for identifying inappropriate psychiatric admissions that would be ineligible for payment. Investor money moved into psychiatric hospitals, and at least two major hospital companies, National Medical Enterprises and Hospital Corporation of America, shifted their corporate focus in that direction. The number of for-profit psychiatric hospitals increased to 233 by 1995 and peaked at 405 in 1991. By comparison, 130 nonprofit hospitals were in operation that year.

The rapid increase signified by those numbers—from 146 to 405 hospitals in twelve years—is characteristic of the for-profit sector when new demand appears. But what followed is another side of the for-profit sector in health care. By 1998, there were only 275 for-profit psychiatric hospitals, and by 2007 the number had declined to fewer than 150. Treatment capacity under nonprofit auspices declined as well, but far less dramatically than on the for-profit side.

Two factors prompted the decline. One affected all psychiatric hospitals: the increased effectiveness of the cost containment methods of managed-care and health benefit design. The other affected the major for-profit companies: widespread fraud investigations followed by successful prosecutions and settlements. The charges included unnecessary admissions, hospital stays involving high charges and little treatment of patients while their insurance benefits were exhausted, and kickbacks to referring physicians. With all of the leading companies—National Medical Enterprises, Community Psychiatric Centers, Charter Medical, and Hospital Corporation of America—engaged in some or all of these practices, investor money fled this field. Nonprofit market share then grew.

A Life-Cycle Perspective on the Roles of Nonprofit and For-Profit Medical Care

We have described several forces that have encouraged the expansion of for-profit involvement in the health care market. The most important appears to have been public policies that expanded demand for services, demand that was not met by existing nonprofit providers. For-profit expansion has been most dramatic when demand has expanded rapidly in undeveloped domains. In many instances, the public policies that changed the ownership composition of health care domains did so only inadvertently, as with Medicare's original capital payment rules that facilitated the creation and growth of the investor-owned sector among hospitals. But there are also examples in which public policies directly targeted to ownership contributed to the for-profit shift, as in the home health and HMO domains, where preferential policies that had favored nonprofit agencies were stripped away or policies that favored their for-profit competitors were implemented. The lack of recognition of a distinctive role of nonprofit enterprise in health care has contributed to a policy environment in which nonprofits have a diminishing overall share in the delivery of services.

But the for-profit expansion is far from inevitable or universal. The stability of the nonprofit sector among community hospitals, even after passage of the demand-stimulating Medicare and Medicaid programs, is a prime example. It is noteworthy that public policies to facilitate nonprofit hospitals' access to capital meant that an ample supply of hospital beds was in place when the Medicare and Medicaid legislation was passed, and that the Medicare law included provisions to pay hospitals for their capital costs. There was no void to be filled by for-profit companies with their access to equity capital. The growth of for-profit health care in any given domain also appears to have limits. The very sensitivity to profitability that attracts investor capital quickly to arenas of increased demand also makes investor-owned facilities particularly likely to leave markets that are no longer profitable. Because third-party payment concentrates purchasing power in health care, and because two of the largest purchasers are government programs, the profitability of health care providers is monitored and responded to. Moreover, the aggressive pursuit of profit provides incentives within companies that may induce illegal or unethical behavior, which in a whole series of well-publicized cases has induced offending corporations to downsize, drop lines of business, or merge into other companies and disappear.

A life cycle thus seems to exist in the health field. In the initial stage of service development, fledgling organizations try new approaches, responding to emerging needs or making use of newly available technologies. This initial experimentation stage has occurred almost exclusively in the nonprofit sector, with support from philanthropy, government grants, or existing nonprofits. The earliest hospitals, the original forms of health insurance, the first HMOs, the first renal dialysis facilities, the earliest drug treatment centers, and the pioneering forms of hospice were all operated under nonprofit auspices.[91] None of the early examples was motivated by perceptions of potential financial returns. The nonprofit form provided the mechanism that facilitated pioneering experiments that antedated formal government funding programs.

The availability of government funding for services opens a new stage in the life cycle. A stable source of revenues is essential to the survival and growth of a nascent field, but when a government program begins to pay for a service, investor capital is immediately attracted and the composition of the field changes toward investor ownership. However, the conditions that favor the expansion of the for-profit sector do not eliminate the role for nonprofit organizations, even for commercialized services. The for-profit expansion is checked in part by payers' ability to react when providers become too profitable. Moreover, there will always be some patients (for example, the most complex and costly cases), some communities (typically the most geographically isolated or economically deprived), or some circumstances under which treatment proves unprofitable.[92] And as noted, the for-profit role is further circumscribed by companies' tendency to succumb to incentives for fraudulent behavior, resulting in a loss of legitimacy and capital for investor-owned enterprises in the domain. Trustworthiness may come to be seen as an important factor in preserving a nonprofit role in health care after all.

Toward Convergence: Shifts in Organizational Practices and Structure

Even where nonprofits have maintained their role in health care, they have often responded to the challenges confronting them by becoming institutionally more like commercial enterprises. These changes have involved organizational practices, organizational structure, and interorganizational linkages.

Changes in Organizational Practices

Today's nonprofit health care providers engage in advertising, marketing, and other business practices that have long typified for-profit companies. One symbolically powerful example involves the efforts of some hospitals to attract affluent patients by establishing plush concierge floors with private chefs and antique furniture. Many nonprofit health care organizations have invested some surplus revenues in commercial enterprises chosen for their profit-generating potential. Some of these investments bear some relationship to the core mission (as with a hospital's parking garage), but not all do so. Such practices do not necessarily undermine the organization's focus on community benefits; indeed, the revenues from profitable services may be used to subsidize community-benefit activities. But they can induce a subtle shift in the perceptions of consumers and third-party purchasers, who may come to consider nonprofit health care agencies as indistinguishable from their for-profit counterparts.

Changes in Organizational Structure

A second area of convergence involves changes in organizations themselves. An example is the composition of the governing boards of nonprofit health care organizations. Historically, nonprofits had large boards, selected to facilitate fundraising in the community. Many still do, but nonprofit boards have been coming to resemble those in the for-profit world—smaller and selected to emphasize strategic planning and technical expertise in areas such as finance and marketing.[93] This change is attributed to the demands of the competitive environment. The consequences for the charitable side of nonprofit enterprise are poorly understood.

Many nonprofit health care organizations have also created for-profit subsidiaries to develop new service areas. Joint ventures with proprietary physician groups or other specialized for-profit companies are common. Some of these joint ventures involve services that were once provided within hospitals and are now provided on an outpatient basis in specialized facilities or in patients' homes. These joint ventures seek to capture revenues that would otherwise be lost. Some joint ventures link hospitals with other kinds of providers, particularly physicians, who are seeking to achieve either economies or bargaining power in the face of managed care. Many of these entities have failed, and the growing conventional wisdom seems to be that hospitals do best by maintaining their core focus.

Interorganizational Linkages

A third type of convergence involves interorganizational linkages. Responding to the entry of investor-owned companies, many nonprofits have sought to gain comparable economies of scale by banding together in one of several ways. One way has been by creating cooperative purchasing arrangements such as VHA, Inc. (formerly Voluntary Hospitals of America), a for-profit organization owned by a consortium of major nonprofit hospitals. Many nonprofit facilities have also formed multi-institutional systems that operate at a state or regional level. According to the American Hospital Association, some two-thirds of nonprofit hospitals now belong to such systems.[94] Most are small (two-thirds of nonprofit systems have fewer than five hospitals), but sixteen nonprofit systems operate twenty-five or more hospitals. Multifacility systems are also found among many other types of nonprofits, including HMOs and nursing homes.

The creation of joint ventures and multiple-facility systems requires changes in governance structures. Commonly, a system-level board is created, which may include representatives from the component institutions, whose own boards typically have only limited powers. In these arrangements, important decisions (say, regarding capital investments) may be moved to the system, creating a challenge for meeting community needs.[95]

Another form of convergence involves trade associations that once gave moral shape to particular domains and were exclusively nonprofit or dominated by nonprofits. Now, many have major for-profit constituents and avoid taking positions that might alienate members on the other side of the for-profit/nonprofit divide. Leadership on many social issues has passed to smaller associations made up of segments from within the nonprofit side of the domains, such as the Catholic Health Association or the Alliance of Community Health Plans.

Efforts to Maintain a Distinctive Nonprofit Role

Notwithstanding the many responses to the challenges facing nonprofit health providers that have moved nonprofits toward convergence with their for-profit competitors, efforts to maintain or enhance the distinctiveness of nonprofit providers are also evident. These have taken two principal forms. Most visible have been projects from within the industry to encourage nonprofits to provide and document the provision of more public goods and to engage in more community-benefit activities. In response to growing disquiet among scholars, policymakers, and even their own members about the drift toward commercialization and the justification for nonprofit hospitals' tax exemptions, the American Hospital Association (AHA), the Catholic Hospital Association (CHA), and the Voluntary Hospitals of America (VHA) all undertook initiatives in the late 1980s to define an appropriate and measurable scope for community-benefit activities.[96] All emphasized community participation in determining a hospital's mix of community-benefit activities, in accordance with the commonly held view that health needs vary substantially across communities. Beyond this commonality, however, there were differences among the three organizations in how they framed of community benefit.[97] Furthermore, all diverged in some ways with the community-benefit ideas being developed by state officials.

From the perspectives of critics both inside and outside government, these early efforts had serious shortcomings: they did not lend themselves to rigorous quantification and they were voluntary. The VHA and CHA continued to work on refining approaches, issuing joint guidelines for their members. CHA eventually insisted that their members adopt the association's approach for the planning and reporting of community-benefit activities. Their approach became very important in the 2000s, when even the strongest congressional critic of the nonprofits, Senator Chuck Grassley, praised the CHA, and the Internal Revenue Service modeled its Schedule H reporting requirement for hospitals on the CHA approach.

Paths toward the Future

In 2002 we observed:

> A significant and potentially dangerous drift is evident in the health field toward diminished nonprofit distinctiveness and convergence toward the for-profit form. Whatever benefits may arise from this trend—for example, regarding ability to compete and to gain access to capital—our analysis suggests that much that is important would be lost if nonprofit institutions were to disappear from the health care field or surrender their distinctive features too completely. Among other things, the potential losses would include a commitment to the more intangible aspects of quality, an important degree of institutional stability, a significant element of trustworthiness, and support for community benefit, broadly conceived.[98]

The concern we expressed in 2002 was validated to some extent by the scrutiny that we described earlier from various congressional committees and federal agencies in the years since 2002. It remains to be seen whether the new era of accountability signified by the IRS's Schedule H for community-benefit reporting by hospitals will slow or reverse the trend that concerned us in 2002.

The community-benefit standards that have been developed and that are reflected in Schedule H are most applicable for hospitals and have shortcomings when applied to other service domains.[99] Individual organizations acting on their own seem more enamored of approaches that move them in the direction of convergence than ones that establish their distinctive characteristics. An approach is needed that takes into account the sort of tensions and complexities that characterize the contemporary role of nonprofit enterprise in American health care. Practically speaking, this will involve addressing simultaneously two imperatives: to survive and to maintain distinctiveness. Let us examine each of these imperatives and explore the steps needed to respond to them.

The Survival Imperative

Nonprofit organizations confront two central challenges to economic sustainability: establishing the value of nonprofit services and responding to expansions in demand.

ESTABLISHING THE VALUE OF NONPROFIT SERVICES. Most nonprofits in health care will not survive if large purchasers do not want to contract with them. Nonprofits need to establish that the services they offer are a reasonable value. For some services, such as hospitals and managed-care plans, past research suggests that nonprofit services are on average no more costly than those provided by for-profit competitors.[100] In these cases, if nonprofit providers can establish that their services are better in quality or more reliable, they would have a competitive advantage. For other services, such as nursing home care, nonprofit services are consistently more expensive than services under for-profit auspices.[101] In these cases, establishing that additional benefits are associated with nonprofit control is vital to maintaining the long-term viability of the nonprofit sector.

Nonprofit providers can make this case most obviously in terms of the quality and reliability of the services they provide—for example, their trustworthiness. These matters are increasingly subject to measurement and public reporting, though it remains unclear how to capture some of the most consequential forms of trustworthiness, which by their very nature are related to practices that are difficult for outsiders to observe, let alone objectively measure. For example, it is hard to measure the level to which promises are kept regarding the relational aspects of care provided to individual patients. Nonprofits also need to make the case that broader community benefits are associated with their enterprise. Hospitals' reporting on the IRS's Schedule H should be helpful in this regard.

But nonprofits need to do more than merely tell their story. They must also convince purchasers that it is the purchasers' responsibility and in *their* interest to care about community benefits. Certainly some employers and some state Medicaid agencies that contract selectively have accepted these responsibilities.[102] Even if there is an effective campaign to broaden this commitment, nonprofit providers will have to document their comparative advantages more effectively on both community-benefit and quality grounds. The evidence summarized in our recent review of the comparative research literature is somewhat supportive concerning these matters, but nonprofits' advantages are far from consistently demonstrated.[103] The story told on the new Schedule H may make either a positive or negative difference.

RESPONDING TO EXPANSIONS IN DEMAND. A second challenge to economic sustainability involves nonprofits' responses to large increases in demand for services. The nonprofit sector's past slow response to increasing demand resulting from changes in public policy raises doubts about the reliability of the nonprofit sector as a source of vital services.

On the other hand, as we have shown, the greater responsiveness of investor-owned corporations carries some liabilities. One involves the boom-bust cycle associated with stock valuation, with waves of hyperexpansion followed by a collapse in capacity. The resulting turbulence in the delivery system can disrupt continuity of services for patients and communities. As the prevalence of chronic illness increases with the aging of the American population, the costs in terms of disrupted caregiving relationships may become more problematic. An additional liability involves the risks of fraudulent behavior associated with the relentless pressures for growth and profits in investor-owned health care. Although these drawbacks of for-profit health care have not been sufficient to convince policymakers of the need for a prohibition on investor ownership, they could be used to justify government programs to enhance access to capital for nonprofit health care organizations, particularly in emerging domains. In domains where such subsidies once existed, nonprofit organizations had the capacity to meet sizable increases in demand. Such public policies can lessen the pressures that produce hyperexpansion in the for-profit sector, stabilizing both sectors simultaneously.

The Distinctiveness Imperative

Nonprofits in health care must do more than survive. They must also maintain their distinctiveness while surviving. The growing demand for more accountability, as represented in community-benefit reporting requirements in many states and the IRS's Schedule H, may prove quite beneficial in this regard by making nonprofit leaders more aware of the need to carry out and document community-benefit activities. Still, a tension may emerge between policies that encourage quantifiable forms of community benefit—particularly if such policies come to be accompanied by threshold requirements for charity care or other community-benefit activities—and the considerable heterogeneity of the institutions that compose this sector.

This potential tension can perhaps be resolved if policymakers take account of two fundamental attributes of the contemporary health scene identified earlier: the presence of multiple concepts of community benefit in the health field and the different stages of development that health organizations go through. It is possible that the standards of community benefit that are appropriate for different institutions vary depending on their stage of development. The task of ensuring institutional distinctiveness may therefore differ at different stages of the process.

ALTERNATIVE CONCEPTIONS OF COMMUNITY BENEFIT. Because policy discussions about nonprofits' community-benefit activities have commonly arisen in debates about tax exemption, a strong push developed for quantified measures of community-benefit activities. The IRS's Schedule H provides for the reporting of a variety of community-benefit activities involving charity care, community health improvement, education and research, and charitable contributions. Although such forms of community benefit have been represented in various tax court decisions, state requirements, and IRS rules, they represent only a subset of the ways that health care organizations can benefit the communities they serve.

We have previously urged that attention focus on three alternative paradigms of community benefit in health care that go beyond conventional legal definitions.[104] These paradigms are only partially reflected in the reporting requirements of Schedule H, which focus on hospitals rather than the full range of health care organizations.

The first paradigm we term the *community health* orientation, which has been largely advanced by clinicians and embodied to varying degrees in past policies associated with neighborhood health centers, community mental health centers, and community-oriented primary care.[105] At its core, the community health approach emphasizes responsibilities of health care professionals and organizations to inform the community about their practices and performance, share their resources and expertise to meet local needs, and assume a fair share of the costs of unprofitable patients and services. Schedule H partially captures activities that grow out of this orientation in its charity-care, subsidized health services, and community health improvement categories.

A second approach, the *healthy community* paradigm, draws on conceptual frameworks of sociology and social epidemiology.[106] Emphasizing social and environmental factors that affect population health, this approach calls for health care organizations not simply to be responsive to community needs but also to help build each community's own capacity to respond to those needs.[107] It also encourages health care organizations to act as catalysts to enhance the capacity of community groups and agencies to determine appropriate priorities for health care spending and policies. The community-benefit categories in Schedule H do not shed light on how priorities will be set; furthermore, although it requests information about hospitals' expenditures for community development, it does not include this in the calculation of community-benefit expenditures.

A third approach, which emphasizes the community benefit that flows from responding to *market failures,* derives from economic models of markets applied to the delivery of medical services and highlights circumstances under which the costs and benefits that face a health care organization differ from the impact that their decisions have on society as a whole.[108] It also directs attention to the role of public goods, such as training certain medical professionals or supporting clinical research, that generate substantial collective benefits beyond local geographic boundaries. At best, Schedule H only partially captures community benefits provided by health care organizations as a result of market failures.

STAGES IN A DOMAIN'S LIFE CYCLE. The need for different kinds of community-benefit activities may vary with the stage of development of the domain in question. For example, in the first stage, when services are largely experimental in nature, the knowledge building that occurs almost exclusively in the nonprofit sector is itself an important public good. Organizations that generate research findings and innovation should be recognized as important sources of community benefit—benefit that is not limited to one locality.

In the second stage of the life cycle, private demand for the service expands, while third-party coverage remains incomplete. At this stage, patients with limited financial means often lack financial access to treatment. Charity care, in its traditional sense, could be the primary priority for nonprofits at this stage.

In the third stage of the life cycle, insurance coverage becomes more complete and charity care of indigent patients may become a less relevant standard for assessing community benefit in some locales. When fully implemented, the health reform legislation of 2010 will greatly reduce the need for charity care for hospital services, but the need for charity care is already very limited for some types of services, such as nursing home care and end stage renal disease services—now covered by Medicare and Medicaid. But even with regard to charity care, needs vary from state to state and community to community. In many communities the portion of the population that is both uninsured and unhealthy is quite small, and many communities have publicly funded institutions whose explicit mission is to serve the poor and uninsured.

For populations that are fully and adequately insured for coverage, other forms of community benefit are more relevant, such as those suggested by the community health orientation. The propensity of nonprofit organizations to behave in a more trustworthy fashion or to protect professional values may prove important safeguards for patient welfare, particularly when third-party purchasers are unwilling or unable to effectively monitor the well-being of the population whose treatment they are financing. Such trustworthiness is difficult to document by conventional methods. But it is possible to develop new measures for report cards on organizational performance, measures that focus on outcomes rather than expenditures.

The final stage of the domain life cycle, when demand for services in the domain stagnates or even declines, creates a difficult challenge for nonprofit organizations. Boards of trustees typically see their responsibilities in terms of building or at least sustaining their institution, so it is out of character for them to consider whether their community would be better off with less capacity.

At this stage, community benefit can perhaps be best assured by incorporating our emerging understanding of the social determinants of health. As long as trustees see their organization's mission as locked into a particular set of clinical services, they have little flexibility to respond to declining demand. However, if they instead see its mission as meeting the health needs for which those services are relevant, other opportunities emerge. For example, it may benefit the community if some hospital resources are shifted to dealing with nutritional issues, health education programs, or primary care that might reduce the need for hospital use. At this stage, the challenge for accountability becomes less one of measuring the organizations' expenditures for such activities and more one of assessing how those activities actually affect health outcomes—and whether more creative alternatives exist through shifting resources to new purposes while retaining the commitment to promote a healthier community.

This life cycle perspective can assist policymakers to consider the sorts of community-benefit activities that are appropriate for particular service domains. In reality, of course, this assessment will be more complicated than suggested here. But this is not inconsistent with notions of accountability. It simply calls for nonprofit organizations to be clear about the needs that they are meeting through their community-benefit activities and to accept responsibility for documenting them. And it requires that community benefits be viewed more broadly than has been true in the past. How this will comport with the constraints of the marketplace and the new demands for public accountability are great challenges for the future.

Conclusions

As organizations that are simultaneously commercial and charitable entities, nonprofit health care organizations must play to two audiences. The first audience looks at them as fee-collecting, service-providing organizations. The second audience sees them as tax-exempt charitable organizations. The future of nonprofit health care depends on satisfactory reconciliation of these two roles. The ever-evolving nature of that balance reflects the interwoven influence of the four cross-sectoral trends that Lester M. Salamon identifies in his introductory chapter: commercialization and professionalization are blended to define a distinctive nonprofit "niche" in terms of the quality and innovativeness of service provision; voluntarism and civic activism are blended to shape the distinctive ways in which nonprofit health care providers connect to the communities in which they are located.

On the commercial side, nonprofits in health care are judged by the people they serve, by third-party purchasers, and by the providers of capital. They must operate successfully in business terms, often in competition with for-profit organizations. Notably, even as particular health services have undergone a growth-driven shift toward for-profit control, it is rare to see a decline in the absolute numbers of nonprofit providers, which gives evidence of their capacity to maintain a distinctive position even in increasingly competitive markets.

Will nonprofits continue to maintain positions in the various competitive domains within health care? We believe that this will depend on their ability to be part of the solution to the many difficult problems that confront the numerous stakeholders in the system. From the patient's standpoint, will nonprofits be more trustworthy regarding quality, and will they not exploit patient vulnerabilities? From the physician's standpoint, will nonprofits operate in ways that are compatible with professional values regarding quality and service? From the payer's standpoint, will nonprofits provide greater value and fewer propensities for fraud and abuse? There are theoretical reasons to expect superior performance by nonprofits on these dimensions, and there is some supportive empirical evidence. But market trends will not turn on the work of scholars. Key questions for the future will be whether (a) nonprofits behave differently than for-profits, (b) whether purchasers detect these differences, and (c) whether purchasers care about the differences enough to be influenced in their purchasing decisions. Although the research base for the first of these three points is well established, too little is known about the latter two considerations for us to be confident about the outcomes of these developments.

As regards charitable expectations, health care nonprofits must meet the expectations of the public, actual and potential donors and volunteers, policymakers, and regulators. They face growing pressure to demonstrate that they deserve the tax benefits that they receive from government. Because these tax benefits can be stated in numerical terms, there has been a tendency to demand evidence of community benefit in similar terms, as is done with the IRS's Schedule H for hospitals. Yet many important health-promoting activities that organizations can engage in are not quantifiable in terms of their effects, only in terms of expenditures. Nonprofits in health care will therefore face the dual challenge of (a) educating policymakers about the types of activities that are appropriately viewed as meeting organizations' community-benefit obligations and (b) demonstrating that they are indeed engaged in such activities. What gets reported on Schedule H will undoubtedly affect this, though it remains to be seen how.

A final challenge facing the nonprofit sector in health care comes from an ironic confluence of trends regarding expectations and regulations. The health care system once operated substantially on trust. Physicians and hospitals were expected to take care of people who otherwise could not afford medical care, and providers were trusted to provide the services for which they were billing insurance plans. These expectations and this trust were not always well founded, but they had a degree of plausibility because of their consistency with prevailing beliefs about the meaning of professionalism and the nonprofit nature of medical institutions.

The growing prevalence of for-profit organizations and the decline of confidence in assumptions about professionalism have been accompanied by a stream of regulatory actions aimed at blocking negative excesses in the pursuit of profits, excesses that are not necessarily limited to for-profits. Thus legislation was passed in 1986 requiring hospitals to provide emergency services without regard to ability to pay, waves of cost containment and antifraud legislation have been implemented, and several types of managed-care reforms have been passed. Stopgap legislation over the years filled some of the worst holes in insurance coverage left after the passage of Medicare and Medicaid, most notably expanded coverage in the late 1980s and mid-1990s to cover additional poor children and pregnant women. Most important, the Patient Protection and Affordable Care Act of 2010 is projected to bring insurance coverage to 94 percent of the American population when it is fully implemented in 2014.

Taken together, these legislative and regulatory changes are addressing dimensions of performance that were once managed largely through reliance on the nonprofit form. Thus nonprofits are being challenged to justify their distinctiveness at a time when public policy is forcing their for-profit competitors to act in accord with the same high ideals that nonprofits were expected to exhibit automatically. Ironically, therefore, these formal requirements may ultimately undermine the very distinctiveness of the institutions that once best embodied them.

Yet after each wave of health care reform the opposite side of the coin is also evident. Given the complex, heterogeneous, and constantly shifting nature of medical care, efforts by policymakers to formalize and regulate good practices will always lag behind—often substantially behind—our understanding of the factors that lead to the most effective and equitable medical care, as well as those that most robustly and comprehensively promote the health of individuals, communities, and the population as a whole. The capacity for nonprofit health care to situate itself on this dynamic margin, to embody a conception of the public good that has been so difficult to codify in public policy, remains the greatest hope for the future resilience of nonprofit health care in the United States.

Notes

1. Elizabeth T. Boris and C. Eugene Steuerle, "Scope and Dimensions of the Nonprofit Sector," pp 66–87, in *The Nonprofit Sector: A Research Handbook,* 2nd ed., edited by Walter W. Powell and Richard Steinberg (Yale University Press, 2006), p. 74.

2. Henry B. Hansmann, "The Role of Nonprofit Enterprise," *Yale Law Journal* 89 (1980): 835–901; Frank A. Sloan and others, "Hospital Ownership and Cost and Quality of Care: Is There a Dime's Worth of Difference?" *Journal of Health Economics* 20 (2001): 1–21; M. G. Bloche, "Should Government Intervene to Protect Nonprofits?" *Health Affairs* 17 (1998): 7–25.

3. Mark A. Hall and others, "Trust in Physicians and Medical Institutions: What Is It, Can It Be Measured, and Does It Matter?" *The Milbank Quarterly* 79, no. 4 (2001): 613–39; David Mechanic, "The Functions and Limitations of Trust in the Provision of Medical Care," *Journal of Health Politics, Policy and Law* 23, no. 4 (1998): 660–86.

4. Jack Meyer, *Fighting Medicare Fraud: More Bang for the Federal Buck* (Washington: Economic and Social Research Institute, 2006).

5. Hansmann, "Role of Nonprofit Enterprise"; Richard Steinberg and Bradford H. Gray, "'The Role of Nonprofit Enterprise' in 1992: Hansmann Revisited," *Nonprofit and Voluntary Sector Quarterly* 22 (1993): 297–316.

6. John Kultgen, *Ethics and Professionalism* (University of Pennsylvania Press, 1988); Hansmann, "Role of Nonprofit Enterprise."

7. Bradford H. Gray, *The Profit Motive and Patient Care* (Harvard University Press, 1991): 111–51; Marc Rodwin, *Medicine, Money, and Morals: Physicians' Conflicts of Interest* (Oxford University Press, 1993): 204–41.

8. Giandomenico Majone, "Professionalism and Nonprofit Organizations," *Journal of Health Politics, Policy, and Law* 8 (1984): 639–59.

9. Andreas Ortman and Mark Schlesinger, "Trust, Repute, and the Role of Nonprofit Enterprise," *Voluntas* 8 (1997): 97–118.

10. Mark Schlesinger, Bradford H. Gray, and Elizabeth Bradley, "Charity and Community: The Role of Nonprofit Ownership in a Managed Health Care System," *Journal of Health Politics, Policy, and Law* 21 (1996): 697–752.

11. Institute of Medicine, "The Changing Nature of Physician Influence in Medical Institutions," in *For-Profit Enterprise in Health Care: A Report of the Institute of Medicine,* edited by Bradford H. Gray (Washington: National Academy Press, 1986): 171–81

12. Bradford H. Gray, "Trust and Trustworthy Care in the Managed Care Era," *Health Affairs* 16 (1997): 34–49.

13. Theda Skocpol, *Boomerang: Health Care Reform and the Turn against Government* (New York: W. W. Norton, 1997); Malcolm Sparrow, *License to Steal* (Boulder: Westview, 2000).

14. Gray, *Profit Motive and Patient Care,* pp. 111–51.

15. Mark Schlesinger and Bradford H. Gray. "Nonprofit Organizations and Health Care: The Paradox of Persistent Attention," in Powell and Steinberg, *Nonprofit Sector: A Research Handbook,* pp. 378–414.

16. Constance M. Baker and others, "Hospital Ownership, Performance, and Outcomes," *Journal of Nursing Administration* 30 (2000): 227–40; Mark Schlesinger and Bradford H. Gray. "How Nonprofits Matter in American Medicine, and What to Do about It?" 25, no. 4 (2006): 287–303.

17. Kennard T. Wing, Thomas H. Pollak, and Amy Blackwood, *The Nonprofit Almanac 2008* (Washington: Urban Institute, 2008), pp. 145, 181.

18. Rosemary Stevens, *In Sickness and in Wealth: The American Hospital in the Twentieth Century* (New York: Basic Books, 1988); Paul Starr, *The Social Transformation of American Medicine* (New York: Basic Books, 1982).

19. Gray, *Profit Motive and Patient Care,* pp. 20–22.

20. Charles E. Rosenberg, *The Care of Strangers: The Rise of America's Hospital System* (New York: Basic Books, 1987).

21. Sara R. Collins and others, *Losing Ground: How the Loss of Adequate Health Insurance Is Burdening Working Families* (New York: Commonwealth Fund, 2008).

22. Schlesinger, Gray, and Bradley, "Charity and Community."

23. David Mechanic, "The Managed Care Backlash: Perceptions and Rhetoric in Health Care Policy and the Potential for Health Care Reform." *Milbank Quarterly* 79 (2001): 35–54; Alice A. Noble and Troyen A. Brennan, "The Stages of Managed Care Regulation: Developing Better Rules." *Journal of Health Politics, Policy and Law* 24 (1999): 1275–1305

24. James S. Robinson, "The Future of Managed Care Organization," *Health Affairs* 18, no. 2 (1999): 7–24.

25. Robert E. Mechanic and Allen Dobson, "The Impact of Managed Care on Clinical Research: A Preliminary Investigation," *Health Affairs* 15 (1996): 72–89; Peter Cunningham and others, "Managed Care and Physicians: Provision of Charity Care," *Journal of the American Medical Association* 281 (1999): 1087–92; Mark Schlesinger and others, "The Determinants of Dumping: A National Study of Economically Motivated Transfers Involving Mental Health Care," *Health Services Research* 32 (1997): 561–90.

26. See *Journal of Health, Politics, and Law* 31, no. 3 (June 2006) (special issue on the Federal Trade Commission Report).

27. Robin R. Gillies and others, "The Impact of Health Plan Delivery System Organization on Clinical Quality and Patient Satisfaction," *Health Services Research* 41(2006): 1181–99; Ha T. Tu and James D. Reschovsky, "Assessments of Medical Care by Enrollees in For-Profit and Nonprofit Health Maintenance Organizations," *New England Journal of Medicine* 346 (2002): 1288–93; Bruce E. Landon and others, "Health Plan Characteristics and Consumers—Assessments of Quality," *Health Affairs* 20 (2001): 274–86; David U. Himmelstein and others, "Quality of Care in Investor-Owned and Not-for-Profit HMOs," *Journal of the American Medical Association* 282 (1999): 159–63.

28. Bradford H. Gray, "Tax Exemptions as Health Policy," *Frontiers of Health Services Management* 12 (1996): 37–42.

29. Frank A. Sloan and others, "Hospital Ownership and Cost and Quality of Care: Is There a Dime's Worth of Difference?" *Journal of Health Economics* 20 (2001): 1–21.

30. Gray, *Profit Motive and Patient Care,* p. 32.

31. Ibid., p. 24.

32. Ibid., pp. 152–65.

33. Fred J. Hellinger, "Tax-Exempt Hospitals and Community Benefits: A Review of State Reporting Requirements." *Journal of Health Politics, Policy and Law* 34 (2009): 37–61.

34. Glenn A. Melnick and Katya Fonkych, "Hospital Pricing and the Uninsured: Do the Uninsured Pay Higher Prices?" *Health Affairs* 27 (2008): w116–w122.

35. Senator Charles Grassley, Opening Statement at Senate Finance Committee hearing, "Taking the Pulse of Charitable Care and Community Benefits at Nonprofit Hospitals, September 13, 2006."

36. Mark Schlesinger and others, "A Broader Vision for Managed care, Part 2: A Typology of Community Benefits," *Health Affairs* 17 (1998): 210–21.

37. John D. Colombo and Mark A. Hall, *The Charitable Tax Exemption* (Boulder: Westview, 1995); Hansmann, "Role of Nonprofit Enterprise"; Robert C. Clark, "Does the Nonprofit Form Fit the Hospital Industry?" *Harvard Law Review* 93 (1980): 1416–89.

38. Gray, *Profit Motive and Patient Care.*

39. Robert D. Putnam, *Bowling Alone: The Collapse and Revival of American Community* (New York: Simon and Schuster, 2000); Orlando Patterson, "Liberty against the Democratic State: On the Historical and Contemporary Sources of American Distrust," in *Democracy and Trust,* edited by M. E. Warren (Cambridge University Press, 1999): 151–207.

40. Burton A. Weisbrod, ed., *To Profit or Not to Profit: The Commercial Transformation of the Nonprofit Sector* (Cambridge University Press, 1998); Small Business Administration, *Unfair Competition by Nonprofit Organizations with Small Business: An Issue for the 1980s* (Washington: Small Business Administration, 1983).

41. Three pieces of federal legislation that would have toughened the standards for tax exemptions for hospitals were proposed in 1990, but none passed. Less demanding standards were incorporated in President Clinton's ill-fated health reform proposals in 1994.

42. Fred J. Hellinger, "Tax-Exempt Hospitals and Community Benefits: A Review of State Reporting Requirements," *Journal of Health Politics, Policy and Law* 34 (2009): 37–61; for an examination of how such requirements actually work, see Bradford H. Gray and Mark Schlesinger, "The Accountability of Nonprofit Hospitals: Lessons from Maryland's Community Benefit Reporting Requirements," *Inquiry* 146 (2009): 122–39.

43. Schlesinger and others, "Broader Vision for Managed Care, Part 2."

44. For a systematic analysis of four different frameworks within which the meaning of community benefit might be defined, see ibid.

45. Mark Schlesinger, Shannon Mitchell, and Bradford H. Gray, "Restoring Public Legitimacy to the Nonprofit Sector: A Survey Experiment Using Descriptions of Nonprofit Ownership, " *Nonprofit and Voluntary Sector Quarterly* 33 (2004): 673–710.

46. Ibid.

47. Mark Schlesinger, Shannon Mitchell, and Bradford H. Gray, "Public Expectations of Nonprofit and For-Profit Ownership in American Medicine: Clarifications and Implications," *Health Affairs* 23 (2004): 181–91; see also Schlesinger and Gray, "How Nonprofits Matter in American Medicine."

48. Amy Bernstein and Anne Gauthier, "Choices in Health Care: What Are They and What Are They Worth?" *Medical Care Research and Review* 56, supplement 1 (1999): 5–23.

49. C. Darby, C. Crofton, and C. M. Clancy, "Consumer Assessment of Health Providers and Systems (CAHPS®): Evolving to Meet Stakeholder Needs," *American Journal of Medical Quality* 21 (2006): 144–47.

50. Kultgen, *Ethics and Professionalism.*

51. Hansmann, "Role of Nonprofit Enterprise."

52. Starr, *Social Transformation of American Medicine,* p. 379.

53. Dahlia K. Remler and others, "What Do Managed Care Plans Do to Affect Care? Results from a Survey of Physicians," *Inquiry* 34 (1997): 196–204; Mark Schlesinger, Bradford H. Gray, and Kristin Perreira, "Medical Professionalism under Managed Care: The Pros and Cons of Utilization Review," *Health Affairs* 16 (1997): 106–24; Robert J. Blendon, T. S. Hyams, and J. M. Benson, "Bridging the Gap between Expert and Public Views on Health Care Reform," *Journal of the American Medical Association* 269 (1993): 2573–78.

54. Elliot A. Krause, *Death of the Guilds: Professions, States, and the Advance of Capitalism: 1930 to the Present* (Yale University Press, 1996), p. 36.

55. Nancy Wolff and Mark Schlesinger, "Risk, Motives, and Styles of Utilization Review," *Social Science and Medicine* 47 (1998): 911–26; Schlesinger, Gray, and Bradley, "Charity and Community."

56. Thomas McKeown, *The Role of Medicine: Dream Mirage or Nemesis?* (Princeton University, 1979); Richard Meckel, *Save the Babies* (Johns Hopkins University Press, 1991); Benjamin Amick and others, "An Introduction," in *Society and Health,* edited by Benjamin Amick and others (Oxford University Press, 1995).

57. Deborah Lupton, *The Imperative of Health: Public Health and the Regulated Body* (London: Sage, 1995); Deborah Stone, "The Resistible Rise of Preventive Medicine," in *Health Policy in Transition,* edited by Lawrence Brown (Duke University Press, 1987): 103–28.

58. Sally MacIntyre, "The Black Report and Beyond: What Are the Issues?" *Social Science and Medicine* 44 (1997): 723–45.

59. Debebar Banerji, "Serious Crisis in the Practice of International Health by the World Health Organization: The Commission on Social Determinants of Health," *International Journal of Health Services* 36, no. 4 (2006): 637–50; S. E. D. Shortt, "Making Sense of Social Capital, Health and Policy" *Health Policy* 70, no. 1 (2004): 11–22; Ichiro Kawachi and others, "Social Capital, Income Inequality, and Mortality," *American Journal of Public Health* 87 (1997): 1491–98.

60. Catherine Hoffman, Dorothy Rice, and Hai-Yen Sung, "Persons with Chronic Conditions: Their Prevalence and Costs," *Journal of the American Medical Association* 276 (1996): 1473–79.

61. Susan M. Allen and Vincent Mor, "Unmet Need in the Community: The Springfield Study," in *To Improve Health and Health Care, 1998–1999,* edited by Stephen L. Isaacs and James R. Knickman (San Francisco: Jossey-Bass, 1997), pp. 132–60; Dorothy Rice and others, "The Economic Burden of Alzheimer's Disease Care," *Health Affairs* 12 (1993): 164–76.

62. John McKnight, *The Careless Society: Community and Its Counterfeits* (New York: Basic Books, 1995).

63. Helmut K. Anheier and Avner Ben-Ner, eds., "Economic Theories of Non-Profit Organizations: A *Voluntas* Symposium," *Voluntas* 8 (1997): 93–96.

64. Theodore R. Marmor, Mark Schlesinger, and Richard W. Smithey, "Nonprofit Organizations and Health Care," in Powell and Steinberg, *Nonprofit Sector: A Research Handbook:* 221–39.

65. M. Greg Bloche, "Should Government Intervene to Protect Nonprofits?" *Health Affairs* 17 (1998): 7–25; Schlesinger, Gray, and Bradley, "Charity and Community."

66. Mark Schlesinger, "Public, For-Profit, and Private Nonprofit Enterprises: A Study of Mixed Industries," Ph.D. dissertation, University of Wisconsin–Madison, 1984.

67. Richard A. Rettig and Norman G. Levinsky, eds., *Kidney Failure and the Federal Government* (Washington: National Academy Press, 1991), p. 111.

68. Bradford H. Gray, "The Rise and Decline of the HMO: A Chapter in U.S. Health Policy History," in *History and Health Policy in the United States,* edited by Rosemary A. Stevens, Charles E. Rosenberg, and Lawton R. Burns (Rutgers University Press, 2006).

69. Ari Ginsberg and Ann Buchholtz, "Converting to For-Profit Status: Corporate Responsiveness to Radical Change," *Academy of Management Journal* 33 (1990): 445–77.

70. Anne L. Bailey, "Charities Win, Lose in Health Shuffle," *Chronicle of Philanthropy,* June 14, 1994, p. 1.

71. Robert Kuttner, "Columbia/HCA and the Resurgence of the For-Profit Hospital Business," *New England Journal of Medicine* 335 (1996): 362–67, 446–51.

72. Bruce Steinwald and Duncan Neuhauser, "The Role of the Proprietary Hospital," *Law and Contemporary Problems* 35 (1970): 817–38; Stevens, *In Sickness and in Wealth.*

73. Steinwald and Neuhauser, "Role of the Proprietary Hospital," p. 819. Different sources report slightly different percentages.

74. Gray, *Profit Motive and Patient Care,* pp. 32–37.

75. Herman Somers and Anne Somers, *Medicare and the Hospitals: Issues and Prospects* (Brookings, 1967).

76. Gray, *For-Profit Enterprise in Health Care.*

77. Ibid., pp. 37–48.

78. Lucette Lagnado, Anita Sharpe, and Greg Jaffe, "States Review Columbia/HCA Billing Practices," *Wall Street Journal,* July 22, 1997; Lucette Lagnado, "Insurance Companies Start an Independent Probe into Billing Practices," *Wall Street Journal,* July 31, 1997.

79. Cutler and Horwitz count 330 conversions of nonprofit hospitals between 1970 and 1995. David M. Cutler and Jill R. Horwitz, "Converting Hospitals from Not-for-Profit to For-Profit Status: Why and What Effects?" in *The Changing Hospital Industry: Comparing Not-for-Profit and For-Profit Institutions,* edited by David M. Cutler (University of Chicago Press, 2000).

80. Jack Needleman, Deborah J. Chollet, and JoAnn Lamphere, "Hospital Conversion Trends," *Health Affairs* 16 (1997): 187–95.

81. Vincent Mor, *Hospice Care Systems: Structure, Process, Costs, and Outcome* (New York: Springer, 1987).

82. Ibid.

83. U.S. General Accounting Office, *Medicare: More Beneficiaries Use Hospice but for Fewer Days of Care* (Washington: U.S. General Accounting Office, 2000).

84. Cathy Hawes and Charles D. Phillips, "The Changing Structure of the Nursing Home Industry and the Impact of Ownership on Quality, Cost, and Access," in Gray, *For-Profit Enterprise in Health Care,* pp. 492–541.

85. Schlesinger, "Public, For-Profit, and Private Nonprofit Enterprises."

86. Bruce Vladeck, *Unloving Care: The Nursing Home Tragedy* (New York: Basic Books, 1980).

87. Schlesinger, "Public, For-Profit, and Private Nonprofit Enterprises."

88. Mark Schlesinger and Bradford H. Gray, "Institutional Change and Its Consequences for the Delivery of Mental Health Services," in *A Handbook for the Study of Mental Health:*

Social Contexts, Theories, and Systems, edited by Allan V. Horwitz and Teresa L. Scheid (Cambridge University Press, 1999), pp. 427–48; Vladeck, *Unloving Care.*

89. Robert A. Dorwart and Mark Schlesinger, "Privatization of Psychiatric Services," *American Journal of Psychiatry* 145 (1988): 543–53.

90. Alan I. Levenson, "The Growth of Investor-Owned Psychiatric Hospitals," *American Journal of Psychiatry* 139 (1982): 902–07.

91. Many early hospitals that are considered nonprofit organizations today were established before today's distinction between public and private nonprofit organizations existed.

92. Nancy Wolff and Mark Schlesinger, "Access, Hospital Ownership, and Competition between For-Profit and Nonprofit Institutions," *Nonprofit and Voluntary Sector Quarterly* 27, no. 2 (1998): 203–36.

93. Jeffrey Alexander, "Hospital Trusteeship in an Era of Institutional Transition: What Can We Learn from Governance Research?" in *The Ethics of Hospital Trustees,* edited by Bruce Jennings and others (Washington: Georgetown University Press, 2004).

94. American Hospital Association, *Hospital Statistics* (Chicago: American Hospital Association, 2008).

95. Jeffrey A. Alexander, Bryan J. Weiner, and Melissa Succi, "Community Accountability among Hospitals Affiliated with Health Care Systems," *Milbank Quarterly* 78 (2000): 157–84.

96. Bradford H. Gray, "The Future of the Nonprofit Form for Hospitals," *Frontiers of Health Services Management* 8 (Summer 1992): 3–32.

97. Robert Sigmond and J. David Seay, "In Health Care Reform, Who Cares for the Community?" *Journal of Health Administration Education* 12 (1994): 259–68; Daniel R. Longo, "The Measurement of Community Benefit: Issues, Options, and Questions for Further Research," *Journal of Health Administration Education* 12 (1994): 291–318.

98. Bradford H. Gray and Mark Schlesinger, "Health," in *The State of Nonprofit America,* edited by Lester M. Salamon (Brookings, 2002), p. 95.

99. Schlesinger and others, "Broader Vision for Managed Care, Part 2."

100. Schlesinger and Gray, "How Nonprofits Matter in American Medicine."

101. Schlesinger, "Public, For-Profit, and Private Nonprofit Enterprises."

102. Raymond J. Baxter and Robert E. Mechanic, "The Status of Local Health Care Safety Nets," *Health Affairs* 16 (1997): 7–23.

103. Schlesinger and Gray, "How Nonprofits Matter in American Medicine."

104. Schlesinger and others, "Broader Vision for Managed Care, Part 2."

105. Jonathan Showstack and others, "Health of the Public: The Private Sector Challenge," *Journal of the American Medical Association* 276 (1996): 1071–74; David R. Lairson and others, "Managed Care and Community-Oriented Care: Conflict or Complement," *Journal of Health Care for the Poor and Underserved* 8 (1997): 36–55; Eileen Connor and Fitzhugh Mullan, eds., *Community-Oriented Primary Care: New Directions for Health Services Delivery* (Washington: National Academy Press, 1983); Alice Sardell, *The U.S. Experiment in Social Medicine* (University of Pittsburgh Press, 1988).

106. This is enunciated most clearly in David G. Whiteis, "Unhealthy Cities: Corporate Medicine, Community Economic Underdevelopment, and Public Health," *International Journal of Health Services* 27 (1997): 227–42. Some aspects also are captured in Kevin Barnett, *The Future of Community Benefit Programming: An Expanded Model for Planning and Assessing the Participation of Health Care Organizations in Community Health Improvement Activities* (Berkeley: Public Health Institute, 1997).

107. McKnight, *Careless Society.*

108. This has been applied explicitly to notions of community benefit by Mark V. Pauly, "Health Systems Ownership: Can Regulation Preserve Community Benefits?" *Frontiers of Health Services Management* 12 (1996): 3–34; Carolyn Madden and Aaron Katz, *Community Benefits and Not-for-Profit Health Care: Policy Issues and Perspectives,* a report prepared for the Catholic Health Association (University of Washington, School of Public Health and Community Medicine, 1995); Schlesinger, Gray, and Bradley, "Charity and Community"; and Susan Sanders, "The Common Sense of the Nonprofit Hospital Tax Exemption: A Policy Analysis," *Journal of Policy Analysis and Management* 14 (1995): 446–66.

3

Education and Training

DONALD M. STEWART, PEARL ROCK KANE, AND LISA SCRUGGS

F urnishing the knowledge, skills, and dispositions that enable citizens to make meaningful contributions to the workforce and society, educational organizations are among the foremost social institutions in the United States. In comparison with other industrialized countries, one of the most distinctive characteristics of America's constellation of schools, colleges, universities, and related organizations is its longtime inclusion of diverse institutional types—private nonprofit, public, and for-profit institutions.

Though not as numerous or large as their public education counterparts, the country's private, nonprofit education and training organizations still reach over 10 million students annually at the primary, secondary, and postsecondary levels and are among the most highly respected institutions in the country. Despite being relatively small and especially susceptible to economic and other challenges, the private nonprofit arm of education in the United States has proven time and again to be responsive and resilient. These qualities, so important in the past, remain equally important in the present, since the survival of the private, nonprofit component of America's educational establishment is hardly a foregone conclusion.

The authors wish to express their appreciation to Jason Johnson for help in updating the higher education portion of this chapter and to Lester Salamon for important editorial assistance throughout.

Like other institutions, America's private nonprofit education institutions have been shaken in recent years by an array of significant challenges, including the formidable economic crisis of the late 2000s and the increasing demands from students as well as institutions, public and private, for greater quality and accountability. They are also experiencing enrollment competition from public and for-profit institutions. As a consequence, the question is not simply one of survival, but also one of maintaining historic commitments to the traditions and values of liberal arts education. Indeed, one can imagine a scenario in which the private nonprofit educational organizations we know today continue to thrive, but without the venerable commitment to academic quality and intellectual inquiry that have characterized many of them for centuries.

The purpose of this chapter is to address the following questions: What is the state of private nonprofit education and training in America today? What are its major challenges? How is it responding, and how should it respond, to these challenges in order to ensure its future? These questions are taken up in the context of three sections, namely, higher education, primary and secondary education, and workforce development.

Higher Education

Higher learning in America has long been distinguished by a robust configuration of public and private colleges and universities as well as training institutions, which together constitute the nation's higher education sector. According to the National Center for Education Statistics, in 2009–10 there were 1,672 public degree-granting institutions and 1,624 private nonprofit degree-granting institutions operating in the United States.[1] In the fall of 2009, the public institutions enrolled approximately 14.8 million students while the private nonprofit ones enrolled approximately 3.8 million students.[2] Completing this higher education enrollment picture in 2009–10 were the approximately 1.8 million students enrolled in the 1,199 private, for-profit colleges and universities throughout the country. These for-profit institutions, whose students are eligible to receive federal loans and grants, have changed the nomenclature of American higher education to include postsecondary education as their descriptive term.

Accounting for 35 percent of all degree-granting institutions and enrolling nearly 20 percent of all degree-seeking students, the private nonprofit component of higher education in America is especially prominent, and not only for its numbers. This component contains many of the country's—indeed, the world's—most respected institutions of higher learning (Harvard, Princeton, Johns Hopkins, University of Chicago, Swarthmore, Yale). Further, this sector adds a measure of diversity to the American system of higher education, containing as it does a wide assortment of institutional types—small liberal arts colleges, major research universities, two-year colleges, religiously affiliated institutions, minority-serving institutions, and women's colleges and universities. It offers a far wider array of educational choices than would otherwise be available and preserves educational values that might otherwise disappear if political or market imperatives were the only ones operating on the postsecondary educational scene.

But despite their special contributions, nonprofit higher education institutions face some formidable challenges. Fiscal concerns are paramount, of course, as rising costs coupled with resistance to ever-increasing tuition fees and recession-induced restraints on both government and private assistance combine to produce a perfect storm of financial pressures. Along with emergent money concerns have come a host of other difficulties, some recession related, some enduring, and some endemic to the private nonprofit sector. Accompanying these challenges, however, are some significant opportunities, and America's private colleges and universities have proven time and again their ability to take advantage of such opportunities, providing powerful support to one of the central themes of this volume: the resilience of nonprofit America more generally.

Background and Contemporary Landscape

To understand the challenges and opportunities nonprofit higher education faces at the present time, however, it is necessary to provide a bit of the background that has shaped the current contours and operations of this diverse component of American higher education.

EARLY ORIGINS. Among the first institutions of higher learning in America were what students of higher education commonly refer to as the "colonial nine": Harvard (1636), William and Mary (1693), Yale (1701), Penn (1740), Princeton (1746), Columbia (1754), Brown (1765), Rutgers (1766), and Dartmouth (1769).[3] While the various models of higher learning predominant throughout Europe in the seventeenth and eighteenth centuries heavily influenced the purposes and structures of the colonial colleges, none of the colonial colleges could be considered to have been replicas by default or by intent. Rather, just as the colonists invented mechanisms to embody their ideals of self-government, "they had to reinvent . . . educational forms as they went along."[4] For example, students were given much less authority in the governance of the colonial colleges in comparison to their European counterparts, and the influence of religious denominations, though present, lacked the tightly coupled nature of many church-college relationships in the old world. Whatever their particulars and idiosyncrasies, the colonial colleges, "all developed around notions of acculturating the young, passing on the wisdom of the classics, and preparing people not only for service as clergymen, but as public servants as well."[5]

Contrary to many current beliefs, these early institutions were not purely private. Rather, they blended public and private action and support. America's first nonprofit organization, Harvard College, reflected this blending clearly. Soon after Harvard's founding in 1636, the colonial government of Massachusetts enacted a special tax, "the college corn," to support this institution. The commonwealth government also paid part of the salary of Harvard's president until 1781 and elected the college's board of overseers until after the Civil War. The state of Connecticut had an equally intimate relationship with Yale, and the state's governor, lieutenant governor, and six state senators sat on the Yale Corporation board from the founding of the school until the late 1800s. While at the outset they were governed largely by the clergy, the colleges received some form of assistance from the local colonial government and, later, state authorities, a situation that prompted historian Frederick Rudolph to comment wryly that "one great barrier to determining who paid the bill of the American college is the myth of the privately endowed independent college, a myth that was not encouraged until the colleges discovered that they could no longer feed at the public trough and had in one sense, indeed, become private."[6]

Not until the Supreme Court decision of 1819, in *Trustees of Dartmouth College* v. *Woodward,* did a sharp line begin to be drawn between public and private institutions. In this case, the Court ruled that actions undertaken by the state of New Hampshire to alter Dartmouth's original charter (with England) were unconstitutional because the original charter was an agreement between two private parties (the Dartmouth trustees and the king of England), and therefore any alteration of it would be in violation of the "contract clause." The implication was that a state could not impinge upon the charter of a private institution of higher education unless the state itself had formed the charter, even if the state had a record of providing resources to the institution (as was the situation with Dartmouth). While historians disagree over whether the Dartmouth case drew a clear or a faint line in the sand between public and private institutions (to wit, many "private" institutions of higher education, including Dartmouth, continued receiving direct support from their respective states), it is clear that the decision preceded a major increase in the number of colleges founded throughout the remainder of the nineteenth century (from 11 in 1790 to 240 in 1869 alone) as well as significant declines in state subsidies and involvement overall.[7]

GROWTH OF GOVERNMENT INVOLVEMENT. After the Civil War, state governments discovered more appealing outlets for their public largess than the "old-time" colleges, with their religious orientation and adherence to a classical course of study. With the passage of the first Morrill Act in 1862 and the second in 1890, state legislatures turned to state-created land-grant universities and federally endowed agricultural and mechanical colleges to develop practical and applied studies as well as to provide trained manpower for the agricultural, scientific, and industrial revolution beginning to take place at the dawn of the twentieth century.

In this process, public higher education began its growth and expansion in earnest. State colleges, or "normal schools," were opened to train public school-teachers. Of special note in the 1890 Morrill Act was the provision that, in accordance with the 1896 Supreme Court decision of *Plessy* v. *Ferguson,* black Americans subsequently would attend "separate, but equal institutions of higher education," thus opening the way for the creation of public black colleges and universities, complementing the numerous private, nonprofit black colleges started in the aftermath of Reconstruction, such as Spelman College in 1881.[8] Thus opened what came to be called the Jim Crow era in American education, a period of inferior education for black Americans, which did not legally come to an end until the Supreme Court's decision in the 1954 *Brown* v. *Board of Education* case, which sought to integrate schools racially.

Nationally, private colleges, with their large number of institutions spread across the country, held their own competitively for the first half of the twentieth century against the increasing number of state-supported public institutions that were created thanks to the Morrill legislation. From the end of World War II until the early 1950s, enrollment was evenly divided between the two sectors. From 1950 through 1967, however, both public and private institutions experienced exponential growth in enrollment, but the public sector grew far more rapidly than the private one. In 1968 private enrollment leveled off at slightly more than 2 million students, while public enrollment reached 5 million and continued to grow, reaching 9 million by 1977 and 11 million by 1997.[9]

A major engine for this growth was the expansion of state and federal support. Following World War II the Servicemen's Readjustment Act of 1944 (Public Law 78-346 and amendments), also called the GI Bill, injected massive new resources into the higher education sector.[10] Returning GIs flooded university and college campuses with their "vouchers," which could be used at both private and public institutions. Initially, the federal government was willing to pay additional dollars to meet the higher tuition at private schools. However, competition for students between tuition-dependent, private nonprofit institutions and state-subsidized public institutions, coupled with complaints from state congressional delegations as well as governors, culminated in the early equalization of payments to public and private institutions. Since tuition at the public institutions was lower, an increasing number of GIs went to public institutions, a trend that only accelerated following the Korean War. Over time, private institutions found it difficult to attract and hold large numbers of veterans because of the cost-price differential with public institutions, and this pattern continues today.[11]

The structure of American higher education underwent further expansion following the report in 1947 of President Truman's Commission on Higher Education, which recommended that education through the fourteenth grade be made available to all students in the same way that high school by then was available.[12] Here was the opening wedge for the community college movement, which picked up momentum through the 1950s, 1960s, and early 1970s in states and cities all across the country. Public higher education's greatest growth has largely taken place in the community college subsector, which now accounts for 35 percent, or 7 million, of all postsecondary students in the United States.[13]

Additional public support was provided to public and private institutions through the National Defense Education Act (Public Law 85-864 as amended), which was enacted in response to the launch of the Soviet Union's Sputnik in 1957.[14] It provided scholarships and training grants as well as federally subsidized loans for academically able students who demonstrated financial need. Subsequently, the Higher Education Act of 1965 (Public Law 89-329), part of the Great Society surge, provided education opportunity grants of up to $1,500 in federal funds to students with "exceptional need." The funds were allocated to the receiving institution, not to individual students, as was the case with GI Bill payments. In neither case, however, did the aid offset the financial advantages that public institutions enjoyed thanks to their state-subsidized tuition, capital, and operating costs.[15]

With the passage of the 1972 amendments to the Higher Education Act of 1965 (Public Law 92-318), Congress shifted the focus of federal higher education away from institutions to students, creating the basic education opportunity grants program, which funneled financial aid directly to poor students. Although these grants were means tested, the program was large enough to pay tuition at both public institutions and a number of private institutions in 1972–73, but a decade later, rising costs and prices meant that the grants barely covered tuition at public community colleges (the grants are now called Pell grants in honor of Senator Claiborne Pell, Democrat of Rhode Island). Federal grant aid to students continued to decline during the 1980s and 1990s and reached its lowest level in 1995–96, by which time federal aid had shifted significantly from grants to loans.[16]

Yet student reliance upon federal monies to attend college has become increasingly significant since the mid-1990s. According to the College Board, the federal government provided 51 percent of all undergraduate grant aid in 2010–11 through a combination of tax credits and deductions as well as Pell grants and special benefits for veterans.[17]

On the loan side, in the 1999–2000 academic year, over $42 billion was borrowed by students through the U.S. government's various student loan guarantee programs.[18] For the 2009–10 academic year, that figure was $95 billion (one assumes unadjusted for inflation). Parents of students enrolling at private nonprofit institutions of higher education have become particularly reliant upon federal loan sources: Private nonprofit colleges and universities accounted for 54 percent of the total amount distributed through the Parent Loan for Undergraduate Student (PLUS) loan program.[19] In addition, with roughly 20 percent of the enrolled students, private nonprofit colleges and universities' students nevertheless received 30 percent of both the subsidized and unsubsidized Stafford loans. What this also means, of course, is that students attending private, nonprofit colleges and universities are leaving school with much higher indebtedness.

Given that federal grants, loan guarantees, and other financial supports to students (such as federal work-study programs and education tax benefits) increased 136 percent between 1999 and 2010, it is not surprising that the most recent (2008) reauthorization of the Higher Education Act produced a number of new accountability methods and measures.[20] While public and private higher education alike continue to enjoy greater freedoms from direct governmental control when compared to primary and secondary education, the pendulum is swinging toward greater governmental involvement.

STRUCTURE OF PRIVATE NONPROFIT HIGHER EDUCATION. This pattern of public and private support has produced a diverse array of private nonprofit higher education institutions. Each of the 1,624 private, nonprofit institutions has its unique qualities, yet the group can be categorized in a number of useful ways in order to capture some essential commonalities.

Most private nonprofit institutions of higher education are four-year institutions, according to the National Center for Education Statistics, meaning that they offer baccalaureate or higher degrees. In 2009–10, however, eighty-five private nonprofit two-year colleges offered subbaccalaureate degrees, namely, associate's degrees and related credentials.[21] These last range from being highly vocational in orientation (like the Alegent Health School of Radiologic Technology in Omaha and the Commonwealth Institute of Funeral Service in Houston) to being grounded in traditional liberal arts courses of study (the Ancilla College in Donaldson, Indiana, and Marymount College in Rancho Palos Verdes, California). While their student bodies are relatively small in comparison to the millions of students engaged in postsecondary education across the country, such two-year institutions enrolled nearly 35,000 students in the fall of 2009.[22]

There is substantial variation among private nonprofit colleges and universities offering baccalaureate degrees and beyond. The majority are small, nonselective, underendowed undergraduate institutions descended from the independent colleges that emerged in the nineteenth century. These institutions today rely overwhelmingly on tuition revenues for their survival and often appeal to prospective students on the basis of special religious, regional, gender, or racial values. Within the private nonprofit sector of American higher education, students may thus find institutions through which they may connect with others who share similar identities. While the sectarian roots of the colonial nine are largely historical icons, the tradition of the strongly sectarian campus has persisted into the present day. For example, the Carnegie Foundation for the Advancement of Teaching, through its venerable Carnegie classification system, lists 302 theological seminaries, Bible colleges, and other faith-related organizations that are private nonprofit institutions. All but one of the nation's 48 women's colleges are private nonprofit institutions.[23] In 2004 private nonprofit institutions of higher education made up approximately 48 percent of historically black colleges and universities, 20 percent of predominantly black-serving institutions, 16 percent of Hispanic-serving institutions, 34 percent of Asian-serving institutions, and 28 percent of American Indian–serving institutions.[24]

These generally small higher education institutions have a traditional commitment to teaching the liberal arts, but many have introduced preprofessional and vocational classes needed to attract a larger, more job-oriented student applicant pool. They have been classified by the Carnegie Foundation since 2005 as baccalaureate, rather than liberal arts, colleges, and their degree programs in the liberal arts account for fewer than half of their bachelor degrees awarded. The rest are in such fields as business, nursing, communications, and social work. While these institutions are not strong in any single or combination of revenue sources, they continue to benefit from a deep commitment in American culture and society to individualism and choice. Not all students and their families want to attend public institutions, even if they are cheaper, particularly when a private liberal arts college leads to a job.

At the other end of the pecking order of nonprofit higher education institutions are the large research universities. In fact, one of the most notable developments in private, nonprofit higher education since the turn of the twentieth century is the creation of the research university offering undergraduate, graduate, and graduate professional degrees. Johns Hopkins University (begun in 1876 and modeled after the great graduate research universities of nineteenth-century Germany) was the first—quickly followed by Harvard, Yale, Princeton, Columbia, Brown, Cornell, and Penn.[25] These were joined by the University of Chicago in the late nineteenth century, supported by John D. Rockefeller Sr., and the Massachusetts Institute of Technology. Stanford University, funded by railroad magnate Leland Stanford, was founded during the same period. To be sure, a number of public land-grant universities created by the two Morrill Acts (the Universities of Michigan, Wisconsin, Illinois, Minnesota, and California) quickly followed suit and gained a status comparable to that of private universities, but the premier research universities in the private sector were already at the forefront of scientific discovery, and they remain there today. Indeed, of the 262 institutions identified by *U.S. News & World Report* as being among "America's 262 Best National Universities," 37 percent are private, nonprofit institutions, and this includes the top twenty institutions in this listing.[26]

Major Challenges

Although a richly diverse network of private nonprofit higher education institutions has clearly survived, this set of institutions faces considerable challenges at the present time. Some of these challenges have been in place for some time, though they have been exacerbated by recent economic circumstances. Others are relatively new. Seven such challenges are especially deserving of attention here.

AFFORDABILITY. Perhaps the most basic challenge facing private higher education has been keeping tuition prices affordable for students and their families while coping with ever-increasing operating costs. According to the National Center for Education Statistics (NCES), between the 1998–99 and 2008–09 academic years, total expenditures of private nonprofit colleges and universities nearly doubled after adjusting for inflation, growing from $75 billion to $141 billion.[27] In terms of constant dollars per student, these institutions' total expenditures increased by 14 percent, from roughly $39,000 to $45,000 per student, reflecting an increase in virtually every category tracked by the NCES (instruction, research, academic support, student services) with the exception of the categories public service and net grant aid to students. While public service expenditures per student dropped a relatively modest 6 percent, the grant aid awarded per student on average dropped from $640 to $246, a 61 percent decrease. The corollary is not surprising: Between 2000–01 and 2009–10, prices for tuition, room, and board at private nonprofit institutions rose nearly 22 percent (in constant 2008–09 dollars), from $26,197 to $31,876.[28]

What accounts for increased costs and related increases in prices for students at private, nonprofit colleges and universities? The culprits are numerous: the labor-intensive nature of teaching and research; the competition among elite institutions for faculty, students, and research funding; and library and technology costs.[29] With a faculty culture that expects excellence and also full participation in all decisions, and with a self-perpetuating board of directors (often made up of alumni) not able to exercise corporatelike, top-down decisionmaking, cost containment is difficult to achieve. Quality—as demonstrated by new programs, prestigious professors, and the most competitive students—is expensive.[30]

In recognition of the bureaucratic and cultural inertia affecting higher education organizations, trade associations representing private nonprofit colleges and universities, like the National Association of Independent Colleges and Universities (NAICU), have designed special initiatives to assist institutions in their efforts to address the issues of rising costs and prices and to highlight exemplary work being done by particular institutions. For example, NAICU has called attention to institutions like Catawba University (Salisbury, N.C.) and the Sage Colleges (Albany, N.Y.), which have frozen their tuition rates; and others like Sewanee, the University of the South, which have actually cut tuition rates.[31] Along similar lines, NAICU has highlighted several institutions' efforts to control costs.[32] Clark University (Worcester, Mass.), Denison University (Granville, Ohio), and Georgetown College (Georgetown, Ky.) are but three of many institutions that have instituted a whole menu of cost-cutting techniques—outsourcing, streamlining administration, and adopting alternative budgeting models.

Such exemplary actions notwithstanding, it is clear that managing the affairs of private nonprofit colleges and universities in cost-effective ways and offering reasonable prices to students will continue to be a significant challenge to the leaders of these institutions. In this environment, private nonprofit higher education risks being less attractive than public higher education to the middle class and even to the more affluent. "Middle-class melt" is a phrase often used by private institutions as they see students and families "who can pay" choose lower-priced public institutions.[33]

SUSTAINING LIBERAL ARTS COLLEGES. A second challenge confronting nonprofit higher education involves how to maintain liberal arts colleges, and the core liberal arts curriculum, in the face of recent assaults on liberal education from those encouraging a professional or vocational approach to higher education. The central concern here is the fear that traditional liberal education norms and values—emphasizing learning for the sake of learning, rather than learning to earn, and stressing breadth, rather than specialized subject matter—are being eclipsed by a form of teaching and learning more tightly coupled with the marketplace.[34] W. Norton Grubb and Marvin Lazerson evocatively term this trend "the triumph of the education gospel." "In American higher education," they write, "the Education Gospel has led to a dramatic expansion of access and to a greater emphasis on vocational purposes. As higher education became a mass institution in the last half of the twentieth century," its promised "private benefits in giving individuals access to income and professional status" took precedence over its broader function of creating a broadly educated citizenry. As a result, higher education "is now the clearest embodiment of the American dream of getting ahead, especially getting ahead through one's own labor."[35]

As individuals have sought to get ahead, the higher education market has fundamentally changed, according to Grubb and Lazerson, compelling institutions to adapt their educational programs to the vocational, occupational, and professional aims of prospective students. This has naturally put the liberal arts subsector of private nonprofit higher education at a particular disadvantage. Indeed, this subsector may well be shrinking. Although "liberal arts college" as a formal category has been dropped by the Carnegie Classification of Institutions of Higher Education for some time now, it persists in discourse about colleges and universities in America, a discourse that is more and more concerned with the possible demise of this traditional institutional form.[36] David Breneman finds that only 212 of the 540 institutions classified as liberal arts colleges in 1970 deserved that designation in 1994.[37] In a 2008 essay in "Inside Higher Education," Victor E. Ferrall Jr., president emeritus of Beloit College, asks the question "Can Liberal Arts Colleges Be Saved?"[38] Given that the term *liberal arts college* has long been used to mean the private nonprofit sector of higher education, a change in this designation surely would be a blow.

Lest anyone become concerned that liberal education has been or soon will be wholly eradicated, however, David Labaree shows that, while the aims of higher education have indeed come to be dominated by professional rather than liberal philosophies, the content of education (its professional curricula) has become increasingly liberal. In fact, as he notes, "professional education may be the biggest recurring loser in the history of American higher education. Responding to the rhythms of the educational status order, the professional keeps surging forward as the central thrust of new colleges and then retreating, as new institutions revert to the liberal norm."[39] This is not wholly accidental, of course. Major efforts have been launched by national organizations like the Association of American Colleges and Universities and its Liberal Education and America's Promise initiative to keep liberal arts education alive in the face of the vocational pressures.[40] The liberal arts may thus have made only a tactical retreat, surrendering some ground to the forces of vocationalism but remaining in command of the high ground of curricular content. Revealingly, fewer than 30 of the 540 liberal arts institutions that Breneman identified in 1970 had ceased operation as of 2009, and most of the remaining ones had maintained, or boosted, their enrollment while retaining a significant—if somewhat less dominant—liberal arts presence in their curricula.[41]

SUSTAINING RESEARCH UNIVERSITIES. Where private nonprofit higher education continues to establish its own distinctive competence is with the research university model, which it planted in American soil before the turn of the twentieth century. Each year the *Chronicle of Higher Education Almanac* lists those higher education institutions receiving the most federal research-and-development funds. In 2011 private, nonprofit Johns Hopkins University topped the list, as it has in years past, with twice as much support as that received by the runner-up, the University of Michigan.[42] Rounding out the remaining 23 of the top 25 were 10 additional private nonprofit institutions, which is considerable given that only 35 of the 108 institutions designated in the current Carnegie classifications as research universities ("very high research activity") are private nonprofit institutions.[43]

Yet while many of these universities remain viable, a third set of challenges exists. Foremost among the challenges has been the steady decline of federally funded scientific research. According to the American Association for the Advancement of Science,

> after tremendous growth during the National Institutes of Health (NIH) doubling campaign between 1998 and 2003, federal support of R&D at colleges and universities flattened out in FY 2005 and then failed to keep pace with inflation in 2006 and 2007, resulting in real declines for federal support of university R&D for two years in a row in 2006 and 2007. . . . Total university R&D grew to $49.4 billion in FY 2007, a slight increase after adjusting for inflation because of continuing growth in non-federal support.[44]

Further complicating matters for nonprofit private research universities are the special challenges faced by academic health centers, which many nonprofit research universities house. The major challenges faced by these institutions are cost containment and cost reimbursement under the Medicaid program (Public Law 89-97). Caught by surprise in the early 1990s by increased economic competition from managed care companies working on behalf of cost-conscious employers and private insurance companies, these academic health centers find themselves in a cost-price squeeze that they cannot control. Often serving large, uninsured, and poor communities, these centers also depend on state-provided Medicaid reimbursement in order to provide primary care and graduate medical education. In addition, continued reductions in Medicare reimbursement and in fees from privately insured patients have made it virtually impossible to cross-subsidize Medicaid patients, for whom states rarely cover full costs, thereby adding one more cost burden to the academic health centers of private research universities. This cost pressure in research universities with academic health centers not only applies to patient care, it comes on top of the cost pressures in teaching and research.[45] Given the growing concerns about the federal debt that ballooned as a result of the Bush-era budget cuts, the wars in Iraq and Afghanistan, and the efforts to contain the 2008–09 recession, these fiscal pressures are likely to intensify as federal and state governments look to reductions in Medicare and Medicaid as important sources of savings.

One potential source of relief, as reflected in the data quoted above, is non-federal research support, much of it corporate. While this has offset at least some of the reductions in federal research support, it is not without its own challenges. Indeed the commercialization of research gives a new twist to the long-standing tension between what Donald E. Stokes calls "general understanding"—knowledge for the sake of knowledge—and "applied use"—the solution of practical problems through the application of technological innovation.[46]

Under the framework put in place by President Roosevelt's wartime director of the Office of Scientific Research and Development, Vannevar Bush, a professor at MIT, in his pivotal 1944 report, *Science: The Endless Frontier,* federal policy consciously sidestepped this distinction and committed itself to the funding of basic research in the confident expectation that practical consequences would eventually flow from it.[47]

Under this structure, the autonomy of faculty and the rigor of proposal review for those seeking grants from the National Science Foundation and National Institutes of Health were to be safeguarded through the peer review process. In theory, peer review and collegiality safeguarded the creation and open dissemination of knowledge that commercial competition often negates. The issue is whether—as nonprofit institutions that still require tax-exempt contributions to support their mission of research, teaching, and service—universities should engage in the pursuit of profits through the marketing of exclusively patented discoveries made by their faculty members, who are supposed to be engaged in the pursuit of knowledge for knowledge's sake. This conflict in values is particularly evident in the life sciences, in which important new connections have been made to the commercial fields of pharmaceuticals and biotechnology.[48]

The Patent and Trademark Amendments of 1980, better known as the Bayh-Dole Act (Public Law 96-517), which grants patent ownership rights to universities and their faculty principal investigators for research results supported with federal R&D funds, has intensified this reorientation by giving universities a strong incentive to treat "knowledge as property," according to Walter Powell and Jason Owen-Smith.[49] New for-profit subsidiaries and partnerships get formed, as does a new culture within the university, advantaging the pursuit of profits over the traditional intellectual values, such as discovery and peer recognition in refereed journals leading to promotion and tenure based on merit.[50] It remains to be seen what the impact of the nation's 2007–09 economic recession and decline of endowment income will have on the traditional academic incentive systems of private universities.

FOR-PROFIT COMPETITION. A fourth challenge facing America's private nonprofit higher education sector is competition for students brought on by the rise of private for-profit colleges and universities. As previously noted, in

2009–10 there were 1.8 million students enrolled in 1,199 private for-profit colleges and universities throughout the country, compared with 3.8 million students enrolled in the 1,624 private nonprofit degree-granting institutions.[51] But the tide has been running with the for-profit institutions, at least until very recently. Thus compared to the nearly 1,200 for-profit institutions enrolling 1.8 million students in existence as of 2010, there were only 343 such institutions enrolling 450,000 students a mere twenty years before. While the for-profit higher education sector has been growing robustly, however, the private nonprofit one has experienced a slight decline in number of institutions, if not in number of students.

More recently, a spate of controversies over the admissions policies and loan default rates at these for-profit institutions, coupled with the economic recession, has led to a 14 percent decline in enrollment at several of the largest for-profit education companies (Kaplan, Apollo, Corinthian, Strayer) as of the middle of 2011. But it is too early to jump to any conclusion that this signals an outright reversal of growth in the for-profit component of the field.[52] Nor does the growth in enrollment in private for-profit institutions necessarily mean that the nonprofit and for-profit sectors of private higher education are competing with one another. Enrollment in both sets of institutions has grown over the recent past. Though the growth at for-profit institutions has been far more robust, there is reason to believe that these different components of the higher education field are drawing from far different pools of students—the nonprofits from traditional college attendees and the for-profits from older returnees or persons who went straight into the workforce without getting either a baccalaureate or advanced degree.[53]

Still, a threat of competition, if not actual competition, looms large. Associations like NAICU have been quick to criticize the for-profit sector, as have many higher education leaders from the private and public sectors. Moreover, given that the average tuition and required fees for undergraduates enrolled at public, private nonprofit, and private for-profit colleges and universities were recently $4,751, $25,413, and $15,166, respectively, it is reasonable to believe that for-profit institutions may well get more and more consideration from would-be nonprofit college-goers in the coming years.[54]

SHIFTING PRIORITIES OF PRIVATE PHILANTHROPY. A fifth challenge facing private nonprofit higher education is the apparent shift in priorities on the part of private charitable institutions, especially foundations. Private, nonprofit higher education has traditionally been valued and well supported by philanthropy. The era of big philanthropy in the early twentieth century commenced with the Rockefeller Foundation's support of schools of medicine and public health. Andrew Carnegie followed by establishing free public libraries. And philanthropic support continued into the twenty-first century, increasing annually despite fluctuations in the stock market. At the same time, a number of the largest foundations, such as Gates, Pew, and Atlantic Philanthropies, began turning their attention away from higher education and toward the K–12 education sector.

The late-2000s recession has further significantly changed the landscape of philanthropic support of higher education. According to the Council for Aid to Education's Voluntary Support of Education survey, philanthropic support to higher education dropped nearly 12 percent between 2008 and 2009, and the 2008 level was already depressed. Although giving to higher education rose somewhat in 2010, in inflation-adjusted terms it remained 8 percent lower in 2010 than it had been in 2006.[55]

Still, private nonprofit colleges and universities continue to be well represented among the nation's top fundraising institutions. According to the survey, twelve of the top twenty fundraising educational institutions in 2010 were private nonprofit universities. And private nonprofit four-year institutions fared best among other institutional types, reporting "the largest increase in giving in 2010 (2.9 percent) after experiencing one of the largest declines (18.3 percent) the year before."[56] Still prominent among the sources of this giving were foundations, accounting for 30 percent of the total, followed by alumni (~25 percent), other individuals (~18 percent), corporations (~17 percent), and other sources (10 percent).

What the shifts in levels of both individual and foundation giving will mean for higher education into the future remains to be seen. What is clear, however, is that the most vulnerable institutions, given the shifting priorities of foundations and the need for both an endowment and a strong alumni giving base, are the small, often nonselective, underendowed private liberal arts colleges. Shortfalls in enrollment at small regional colleges like Beloit in Wisconsin (with a modest endowment of $50 million) mean financial disaster when tuition and fees are the only real source of income. Institutions like Beloit make up the vast majority of the 1,600 private liberal arts colleges in the United States. Many of these institutions may be forced to close their doors. The trustees of Notre Dame College in New Hampshire, Marycrest International University in Iowa, and Antioch College in Ohio have already decided to follow this path rather than face mounting faculty and staff layoffs along with growing debt. Even for the larger institutions, however, it seems likely that their long-standing near lock on private philanthropic support of education is no longer a certainty, and they will have to share this support increasingly with the public and private elementary and secondary education field.

GOVERNMENTAL ACCOUNTABILITY. The sixth challenge facing private, non-profit higher education arises from the growing strength of demands for the imposition of external performance standards on higher education institutions. As noted, the federal government's financing of student participation in higher education has increased substantially over the past decade. In turn, the federal government's interest in higher education operations and outcomes has also grown apace, most notably as reflected in the 2008 Higher Education Opportunity Act (Public Law 110-315) as well as other actions initiated by the U.S. Department of Education.

While the regulations implementing the 2008 act are still being worked out, it is clear that colleges and universities are having to become more transparent in their academic business practices. For example, colleges and universities must disclose their transfer credit policies (such as the criteria upon which decisions are made to award credit from other institutions); lists of institutions with which they have articulation agreements; bibliographic and pricing information for all textbooks required or recommended by their faculty; and various other pieces of information, such as demographic characteristics of their student populations, employment and education status of graduates, student retention rates, and disaggregated graduation data; and a net cost calculator that allows students to compute the cost of the education they seek.[57] Institutions that report the highest price increases are required to submit an explication and justification. In addition, institutions are required to report several new points of information to the National Center for Education Statistics so that the information may be made available to the public (especially for students searching for colleges or universities that meet their preferences) via the Integrated Postsecondary Education Data System (IPEDS) and the College Navigator website, which is built from it.

As the Department of Education began to implement the 2008 act, it also generated a number of program integrity regulations. Ostensibly motivated by the practice of some for-profit institutions identified as producing graduates with little by way of job prospects yet much by way of loan debt, thanks to high-pressure recruitment, one set of rules, issued in June 2011, establishes reporting requirements for "gainful employment" programs (that is, those that do not lead to a degree but that offer students a course of study that leads to "gainful employment" in a recognized occupation). Because some for-profit institutions offering such programs have been accused of misleading students and leaving them deeply in debt but with no job prospects, the new regulations require institutions' gainful employment programs to meet or exceed certain postgraduation performance thresholds. Institutions that fail to meet the thresholds for three of four consecutive years will lose eligibility as sites at which students can use Title IV higher education loans, a crucial source of revenue for these for-profit schools.[58]

Taken together, these new regulatory provisions constitute a significant shift in the relationship between the federal government and the higher education community. Colleges and universities are being called on to provide the government (and by extension, the public) with more and more information in standardized forms.

To be sure, the higher education community has dodged even worse bullets, such as sweeping controls on admission standards, tuition prices, accreditation, and credit articulation.[59] What is more, several of the requirements promise to provide useful information for students and to discourage deceptive advertising and recruitment practices that have victimized a number of students. But the increased accountability and reporting standards being required of private, nonprofit colleges and universities are likely to have some downsides as well. First, of course, collecting and reporting information is not without its costs. For smaller colleges, where the staff available to compile and communicate such information is limited, other facets of educational administration may suffer. Second, standardized approaches to communicating information can be risky. For example, while requiring a "net price calculator" seems like good policy, it may well undermine the successful and ethical practices that many private nonprofit colleges and universities have developed to help prospective students understand the added benefits they receive in return for the higher prices they pay for their education at such institutions. Third, and most significantly, the education act and related Department of Education regulations (not to mention state-level accountability initiatives) largely treat all sectors of higher education identically when in fact the problems may really be concentrated in one or two subsectors. Private nonprofit schools are particularly concerned that they are being subjected to restrictions designed to resolve problems in the for-profit segment of the higher education field.

INSTITUTIONAL ISOMORPHISM. One additional challenge that is emerging for the private nonprofit sector of higher education is a growing institutional isomorphism, or blurring of the distinctions among the different segments of the higher education or postsecondary universe.

One piece of evidence of this phenomenon can be found in shifts in tuition at public universities. Between the 2000–01 and 2009–10 academic years, the average cost for tuition, room, and board at public colleges and universities rose by 36 percent, from $9,300 to $12,681, after adjusting for inflation. While the average cost of tuition, room, and board for private nonprofit institutions, at $31,876, was well above this latter figure, the rate of increase among public institutions outpaced that of private nonprofit institutions 36 percent to 22 percent. In some states, moreover, the difference between the public and private nonprofit institutions' costs is even narrower. For example, estimated college costs (tuition, room, board, books, and fees) for an entering freshman in 2011–12 at Penn State University were over $27,000.[60] Although Penn State is an extreme example, it is widely regarded as a case study in declining public financing of public higher education and the growing reliance on tuition income. As such, it may prove to be an unwitting exemplar for the public higher education sector, should trends toward privatization continue, as many suspect they will.[61]

While this narrowing of the price differential between nonprofit and public institutions could be perceived as a windfall for the private nonprofit higher education sector, all the outcomes may not be positive. If public institutions, by virtue of becoming less and less financially dependent on state dollars, loosen their grip on being generic, comprehensive institutions and instead further develop their own market niches, they may in effect become "more private" in terms of how they organize themselves and project their identities in the marketplace. For instance, some public institutions may find a market advantage in rehabilitating a liberal arts college identity, thus capitalizing on, and expediting, the dissolution of the private nonprofit sector's hold on that market corner. Although it may seem improbable, it does not take too much creativity to imagine a time when Evergreen State College or UC Santa Cruz, two public institutions known for their resistance to status quo models of public higher education, could rival Reed College, Willamette University, or Pomona College for the hearts and minds of liberal arts college aspirants.

As public institutions become increasingly privatized, it also stands to reason that competition between the public and private nonprofit institutions for investments and gifts may intensify. Already many public institutions have created foundations to receive charitable gifts on which donors can claim tax deductions and foundations can claim payout credits. Just as some public institutions may embrace liberal arts college ideals, some others may fortify and specialize their research missions in ways that rival private nonprofit competitors. Further, assuming it has long been common practice in private nonprofit college and university fundraising to remind prospective donors that they are at a disadvantage relative to their public institution counterparts, it is fair to presume that prospective donors will hear the reverse of that message from public institutions, as state schools see their public funding decrease with each state legislative session.

Similar challenges confront private nonprofit higher education institutions as a result of the rapid growth of for-profit higher education. As the for-profit sector strives for legitimacy, it is not hard to imagine for-profit institutions emulating their nonprofit counterparts so closely that no discernible differences remain between the two. And if so, what difference will nonprofit status really mean in the eyes of the government? Indeed, some semblance of this development is already evident in the recent actions taken by some for-profit higher education leaders, who have banded together to create "codes of conduct" for their institutions, reminiscent of honor codes that have endured at nonprofit colleges and universities for generations.[62]

Finally, increased governmental accountability requirements impose a significant degree of uniformity on all higher education institutions, thus potentially challenging both the prized diversity of the private nonprofit institutions and the features that distinguish these institutions as a group from their for-profit and public counterparts. Continuous publication and circulation of tuition prices and other institutional information may create powerful pressures toward homogenization, as institutions find it more and more difficult to be seen as outliers and as the identity of the institutions as private nonprofits moves further into the background.

Toward the Future

Private nonprofit higher education institutions thus face some fundamental developments that challenge their long-standing distinctive position in the American higher education world. Long the carriers of a proud tradition of liberal arts education, they are increasingly finding that tradition challenged by a powerful push toward more vocational fields of study. Historically distinguished for their diversity and creativity, they are increasingly being forced into a common mold dictated by accountability demands shaped by shortcomings in the burgeoning private, for-profit component of the field. Faced with declining governmental support, they are confronted with challenges from public institutions for charitable resources that are being siphoned away as well by newfound philanthropic interest in K–12 education.

But private nonprofit institutions initiated America's experiment with higher learning, engaged an agenda of expansion rather than retreat as states established public forms of higher learning, and continue to persevere and grow, however modestly, in the face of this withering array of challenges. The research universities and highly selective colleges (that is, the elite institutions) lead the way. The institutions at all tiers continue to survive and offer access, choice, diversity, innovation, and postsecondary education experiences of overall quality. Quality teaching and learning remain at the heart of the enterprise, at the undergraduate, graduate, and professional levels, with research an important stimulus for all three. In addition, these institutions are affordable to many middle-income families when appropriate grant aid, loans, tax credits, tax deductions, or discounting arrangements are made available. To be sure, many middle-income families are opting for public rather than private institutions as a consequence of changing values, improved public higher education (such as honors colleges), and limited discretionary income.[63] While stopping this loss is a challenge, the private colleges are not in fact the endangered breed that the former University of Pennsylvania president Martin Meyerson feared, a half century ago, they might become. They are instead a special breed of institution, one that is eminently well worth preserving.[64] And there is reason to hope that the resilience and creativity that have allowed these institutions to survive previous twists and turns will enable them to continue their distinguished record of contributions in the future. The key lies in the maintenance and enhancement of their liberal arts base.

K–12 Education

Higher education is only one component of the private nonprofit sector's involvement in the education sphere. Also important is the nonprofit involvement in elementary and secondary education.

A Brief History

The first elementary and secondary schools in America were private and nonprofit, often relying on a combination of funding from tuition and taxes for their existence. Long before Horace Mann championed free public education for the towns of Massachusetts, a variety of private schools existed to serve a diversity of family orientations and preferences. Some schools were rooted in Puritan traditions, while others were operated by churches, chartered corporations, or enterprising individuals. These schools competed for the students whose families could afford the cost of tuition.

A small number of private schools, supported by philanthropy, educated students who were excluded from other school options, such as students of color.[65] In fact, the Protestant ethos of mass education in America felt culturally alienating to some groups, who, believing their survival was at stake, did what "beleaguered or dissenting" minorities have done throughout history; they built their own schools, resisting state intervention.[66] To this day, families of a particular faith or value orientation exit public schools when their educational preferences are contrary to what is being taught.[67] Their right to do so has been firmly enshrined at least since the landmark 1925 Supreme Court decision in *Pierce* v. *Society of Sisters,* in which Justice McReynolds, writing for the Court, established the principle, "The liberty of parents and guardians to direct the upbringing and education of children under their control is vital to the health of America, as long as the State maintains the power to regulate all schools."[68] Often called the Magna Carta of private schools, this decision established the private school's right to exist and a parent's right to choose a private school.[69]

Today, and with very few exceptions, private schools, both religious and nonsectarian, exist as 501(c)(3) nonprofit organizations. The benefits of exemption from property, sales, and income tax, as well as the ability, granted by the

IRS code of 1917, to accept tax-deductible contributions, outweigh the limitations on the distribution of profits that such organizations confront.

This section provides an overview of the private component of the nation's elementary and secondary education universe and then explores some of the challenges to private elementary and secondary education in America, focusing particularly on two prominent types of private schools: Catholic and independent.

The Diversity of Private Schools

In 1899, the first year that the federal government collected statistics on private schools, approximately 11 percent of all elementary and secondary school students attended private schools. Despite minor fluctuations, private school enrollment hovered at roughly 10 percent during most of the twentieth century, and by 2007 some 11 percent of all American students (5,072,451) attended 33,740 private (nonpublic) elementary and secondary schools.[70] Despite the appearance of stability, these numbers actually reflect the success with which the private component of the elementary and secondary education field has kept pace with overall growth in this field. Between 1980 and 2007, in fact, the number of private elementary and secondary school students jumped by 20 percent in the United States, and the number of private schools increased by 4 percent.[71]

CATHOLIC SCHOOLS. Broadly speaking, the private school universe can be divided into two major types, religious and nonsectarian. Fully 81 percent of private school students attend religious schools, 43 percent of which are Catholic.[72] Catholic schools therefore serve the largest population of private school students.

These schools have their origins in the nineteenth century, when waves of Catholic immigrants, many uneducated and impoverished, precipitated militant anti-Catholic bias in heavily Protestant America and its Protestant-oriented public schools.[73] Catholic leaders responded by developing their own school system, by mandating "a Catholic school for every parish," and by dedicating themselves to placing "every Catholic child in a Catholic school."[74] Reaching peak enrollment in the mid-1960s, Catholic schools served half of all elementary-age Catholic children and one-third of secondary-school-aged Catholics.

As the number of teachers available from religious orders decreased and the upward mobility of Catholics made religious schools less appealing to them, Catholic school enrollment declined. Then in the mid-1960s, the Second Vatican Council proclaimed an enlarged mission for Catholic schools, identifying the schools as instruments of social justice focused on building communities and fostering emotional, as well as academic, development. As a result, the schools have been welcoming an increasing number of racial minorities and non-Catholic students.[75]

Catholic school leaders say, "We don't educate the poor because they are Catholic, we educate them because *we* are Catholic."[76] While some scholars believe that "the Catholic school advantage" for inner-city poor and minority children is "a sense of spiritual mission" that informs Catholic school culture, others believe that it is the core academic curriculum that all students are expected to master. Still others believe that the personal and academic discipline that Catholic schools instill provides the foundation for the civic activism that religious leaders hope to create in their communities and in the larger world. Edmund Rice High School, a Catholic boys' school in Harlem, is an example of how the Second Vatican Council's mission has been realized. At Rice, which serves the highest proportion of black students of any Catholic high school in the city, a plaque above the door reads, "The 'Street' ENDS Here!" The commandment, though far from biblical, is sacred at Rice High School. Rice men are exhorted to succeed and, through their success, to drive "another nail in the coffin of racism." All seniors are required to apply to college, and over 90 percent attend.

Catholic schools today are characterized by a focused academic curriculum, small size, decentralized governance, and the concept of school as community, with a strong ethos of spirituality. Requiring the same core curriculum, including advanced academic coursework, for all students results in higher academic achievement in Catholic schools than in public schools.[77]

INDEPENDENT SCHOOLS. Independent schools are a small group of private, nonsectarian schools that educate 8 percent of all students who attend private schools.[78] In spite of their small numbers, these schools have exerted significant influence, for they rank among the most prestigious institutions in the country. Beginning in the seventeenth century, a variety of quasi-private schools existed in the United States. Though most depended on public funds for survival, these schools were private in terms of governance and ownership. Some were maintained by churches as adjuncts of religious programs. Others were private ventures run by individuals or groups of teachers. Still others, known as academies, were founded by self-perpetuating boards of trustees to offer instruction that went beyond rudimentary literacy and computation. Most of these schools were also public in the sense that they were open to children with the desire and means to attend.[79]

With the evolution of common schools—free schools providing basic education for all—many of these private schools lost constituents and public support. Yet families remained who were willing to pay for education reflecting their own values. These private schools evolved into independent boarding and day schools. Independent boarding schools, which grew out of the academy movement, were patterned after the European upper-class model. Emphasizing physical, intellectual, and moral education, independent boarding schools included both classical and modern curricula. Independent day schools developed from proprietary schools (schools operated for profit), town and church schools, and country day schools, which were designed to provide an education comparable to the boarding schools.[80]

Today's independent boarding and day schools reflect this range of origins. Some are traditional, some progressive, some single sex, some coeducational, some highly selective, some designed to offer struggling students a second chance, some with impressive endowments, some reliant on tuition, and some fully dependent on philanthropy to educate disadvantaged children. The defining characteristic of an independent school is its "self-selecting and thus self-perpetuating board of trustees [which] bears ultimate responsibility for [its] philosophy, resources, and programs."[81] Mission-driven, independent schools are mostly small and self-supporting, avoiding public monies to protect against government interference. They determine their own curricula, devise their methods for selecting faculty and students, and strive for personalized environments.

The schools in the National Association of Independent Schools, an affiliation of 1,228 independent schools, serve approximately 586,000 students.[82] These schools, which are among the most costly private schools, are known as "prep" schools, for their purpose is to prepare students for college. Requiring a rigorous curriculum, independent prep schools enjoy influence disproportionate to their numbers due to the quality of their programs, the success their graduates have matriculating at competitive colleges, and the substantial social, economic, and political capital of their alumni.

Historically, independent schools have served as incubators of both pedagogy and curriculum for several educational innovations in the last century. At Phillips Academy Andover, more commonly known as Andover, the first advanced placement exams were administered by the College Board in 1954.[83] Earlier in the century, shortly after World War II, Andover's foreign language department borrowed the intensive immersion model of the U.S. military and began instructing students entirely in the language being taught. Andover has modeled interdisciplinary studies in courses that combine history and literature, for example, and the array of sports offerings that have engaged students influenced schools to consider the value of extracurricular experiences.[84]

CONSERVATIVE CHRISTIAN SCHOOLS. Among the fastest growing components of the private school field in recent years have been conservative Christian schools: 16 percent of all private school students (823,696) attended such conservative Christian schools in the academic year 2005–06.[85] The formation and growth of these schools is fueled by the perception that public schools are increasingly secular and give insufficient attention to Christian values.[86] Christian day schools in 2007 made up a sizable segment of the private school landscape, as enrollment in other religious schools declined.[87] Generally, Christian schools vary in many respects. Most Christian schools are attached to a local church, and facilities range from poorly equipped church basements to modern campuses. The majority are elementary schools. Programs of study vary, as does enrollment: average enrollment has been betweem 150 and 200 students, but it has ranged from less than 10 students to more than 2,000.[88] The long-term prospect of Christian day schools will depend on "maintaining the dissenting spirit and alternative vision of education" that prompted their creation, as well as on sustaining them financially.[89]

CHARTER SCHOOLS. Forty-two states and the District of Columbia have passed laws allowing individuals or groups to set up autonomous public schools under state charters.[90] Charter schools, numbering 5,714 in America in 2011, must follow state guidelines and select students based on a lottery, as they are not permitted to select their students on any other basis.[91] Yet they choose their instructional approaches freely, and they make financial and hiring decisions without bureaucratic intervention. Usually run as nonprofit organizations, charter schools resemble private schools in that they are typically small, have specific curriculum goals, and attract like-minded families, creating value communities characteristic of private schools. In urban areas, charter schools often resemble Catholic schools in that they require uniforms, stress disciplined behavior, and teach a focused curriculum.

Challenges to Private Schools

Catholic and independent schools provide useful lenses for examining the status of American private schooling. As different as these schools may be in terms of clientele and economics, Catholic and independent schools share similar threats to their stability. Four issues in particular deserve particular attention here: diversity, teacher shortages, competition, and their own affordability.

DIVERSITY. Both Catholic and independent schools recognize the philosophical and pragmatic reasons for enrolling a diverse population. Not only are these schools responding to a moral imperative to promote social justice by educating all Americans, but they are reacting to economic and demographic realities. Nearly 13 million American children live in poverty; 39 percent of them live in low-income families.[92] Children of color make up 44 percent of children under the age of seventeen in the United States; by 2020 it is projected that almost half of American children will be children of color.[93]

Efforts to educate a more diverse student body have played out differently in Catholic and independent schools. The Catholic schools, already established in inner cities to educate European immigrants, continue to focus on educating the poor, both Catholic and non-Catholic. Because of the high cost of running their schools and the reliance on tuition, independent schools have made more modest progress in recruiting economically and racially diverse students, often choosing those with high potential from neighborhoods outside of the schools' immediate locations.

The changing Catholic school demographics have created both financial pressures on Catholic education and challenges to its definition. Students of color compose 29 percent of Catholic school enrollment, and 14 percent of students are non-Catholic.[94] Since approximately 39 percent of urban Catholic schools are situated in inner cities (880 of the 2,277 schools), these figures belie the reality that many schools' student bodies are composed of 90 to 100 percent of students of color and are frequently predominantly non-Catholic. At Edmund Rice High School in Harlem, for example, where all students are African American or Latino, 75 percent are non-Catholic; 80 percent receive financial aid. Suburban Catholic schools, which typically serve largely white populations, report an increase in enrollment, attributable, in part, to the schools becoming "a little less Catholic," thereby attracting more non-Catholic children.[95]

Ever since national interest in social justice emerged in the 1960s, independent schools have sought more religious, racial, and economic diversity. At independent schools today, religious prejudice appears to be a thing of the past, and the enrollment of students of color, from the full economic spectrum, has increased to about 22 percent. About 18 percent of all students at independent schools receive need-based financial aid, and 38 percent of those receiving aid are students of color.[96]

Independent schools, which pride themselves on preparing students for leadership, must consider that their graduates will live and work in a diverse society. Yet the extent and nature of diversity in any school depends on the availability of resources as well as on the disposition of trustees and parents. At Phillips Academy Andover, a school with a large endowment, where there is a serious commitment to economic, racial, and ethnic diversity, 35 percent of students are students of color, and 41 percent of all students receive financial aid. Schools with more limited resources must reconcile their desire for a student population that reflects the broader society with their ability to provide for it, and the uncertain economy that followed the banking crisis of 2008 has only exacerbated the problem.

FACULTY RECRUITMENT. Private schools rely heavily on capable faculty to provide a challenging academic program and promote school values. Characteristically, private schools, even the most well-endowed schools, offer lower salaries than public schools. Private schoolteachers forgo higher income for the opportunity to work with small classes and motivated students, in safe environments, and in settings that reflect their religious or moral values.

A looming teacher shortage may soon make it difficult for private schools to hire able faculty. The National Center for Education Statistics predicts that, nationwide, 1.7 million to 2.7 million teachers will be needed by the end of the decade because of teacher attrition, retirement, and increased student enrollment.[97] State and local governments are attracting teachers, particularly to urban areas, by offering incentives like fellows' programs, sign-on bonuses, tuition forgiveness plans, and alternative certification arrangements that allow teachers to earn credentials while teaching. Additionally, high-profile service programs such as Teach for America attract capable liberal arts graduates to high-need, inner-city areas. As entry into public school teaching becomes easier and more appealing, Catholic and independent schools may find it more difficult to recruit able teachers.

The diminishing number of clerics working in Catholic schools has exacerbated the need for hiring lay teachers. Lay faculty, which has increased from 52 percent in 1970 to nearly 97 percent in 2011, creates a demand for increased wages and benefits.[98] Since most Catholic schoolteachers hold state certification, hiring incentives in public schools may lure away these teachers.

Independent schools have traditionally drawn from a large pool of teachers with liberal arts degrees who do not necessarily hold teaching certificates. Whereas independent schools have attracted those unwilling to undergo teacher education programs, curtailed requirements for public schoolteachers may lure teachers from independent schools to higher paying public schools.[99] This eased access to public school teaching jobs, however, may be counterbalanced by the curricular focus on standardized tests, which many teachers find objectionable. Compensation at independent schools, which sometimes includes housing subsidies and tuition waivers or tuition remission for faculty children, may have to be more competitive with public schools, especially in hard-to-staff fields such as physics, chemistry, math, computer science, and Spanish.[100]

SCHOOL CHOICE AND COMPETITION. Public school reform efforts that emphasize choice and competition are affecting private schools, which have always been influenced by market forces. Designed initially to offer low-income families escape from low-performing public schools and to spark improvement through market competition, charter schools and, to a lesser degree, vouchers are currently the most significant school choice alternatives. In urban areas, the growth of small schools—public schools that are theme based—provide another school choice option for families seeking more personalized environments for their children.[101] While independent schools remain largely unaffected, urban Catholic schools appear to be more vulnerable.

Besides charter schools, vouchers are another instrument of school choice. These are given to families to allow them to choose schools. Privately funded vouchers have served more than 13,000 low-income families in thirty-three states.[102] Publicly funded vouchers, a hotly debated choice option, allow parents to use taxpayer money for private school tuition. Voucher programs in Milwaukee, Cleveland, and Florida, which have allowed use of public monies for secular or religious schools, have been embroiled in litigation concerning their constitutionality. While the U.S. Supreme Court in 2002 upheld the right of Cleveland families to use vouchers for religious or secular schools, the Florida Supreme Court struck down a voucher program for students attending failing public schools, saying the state constitution bars Florida from using taxpayer money to finance a private alternative to the public system.[103] Any vouchers attempted in the future that include private schools will thus almost assuredly involve legal issues and will have to be resolved at the state level.

Catholic schools make up the largest group of schools participating in voucher programs.[104] Such vouchers have made Catholic schools, which are a strong presence in urban areas, an affordable choice for inner-city parents. However, neither the long-term commitment of private contributors nor public funds for vouchers can be counted on, leaving the long-term future of Catholic schools uncertain.

Charter schools also pose a competitive challenge to Catholic schools. The cost-free alternative of charter schools may be particularly attractive to families who choose a Catholic school for nonreligious reasons.[105] Most charter schools are located in inner cities where there is a predominance of Catholic schools and a high percentage of non-Catholics attending. In New York State, for example, emerging research indicates that transfers to charter schools account for 37 percent of the decline in Catholic school enrollment. About 180 charter schools in the state have drawn roughly 32,000 students away from the Catholic school system.[106]

Charter schools and vouchers are likely to have less impact on independent schools. The amount of a voucher is not significant when compared to the high tuition of most independent schools, and vouchers often come with stipulations that prohibit selective admissions policies. In Washington, D.C., for example, private schools that accept students participating in the voucher program may not choose students or require additional funds. Similarly, given the preponderance of charter schools that serve the poor, and their location in the inner city, enrollment of affluent families at independent schools is unlikely to be significantly affected by charters. Yet charter schools in middle-class communities may draw families struggling with high tuition costs or families of color who are seeking a more balanced racial environment. Charter schools may also attract away from independent schools faculty committed to educational equity who want to work in a small, safe, nonbureaucratic environment.

AFFORDABILITY. Catholic and independent schools also face rising costs associated with the demands of educating students for the twenty-first century. For example, the demand for updated technology, along with a need for technology maintenance and personnel training, puts significant pressure on schools' resources. Though a few private schools can rely on large endowments to meet operating costs, most schools are heavily dependent on student tuition.

Competing with free public schools, as well as with other private schools, Catholic and independent schools need to be adept at determining what the market will bear for the services they offer. Furthermore, since tuition does not fully cover operating costs at most of these schools, ever-greater fundraising efforts are needed to cope with rising costs. In the period 2007 to 2008 it cost on average $6,906 to educate each student in a Catholic secondary school, $1,837 less than the average tuition.[107] At schools serving the poor, such as Rice High School, the gap is greater. Rice's tuition was $5,550 plus a student fee of $500, but the actual cost was $11,291, creating a shortfall of approximately $5,000 per student—which must be met through external sources of support, including federal supplements for services for low-income families, fundraising, and contributions from affiliated religious orders. Parish and diocesan schools also receive community contributions, but all schools that must supplement tuition are obliged to limit their enrollment by the amount of funds they are able to raise.

On average, in the school year 2006–07, it cost independent secondary schools $17,960 to educate each student, $2,066 more than the average tuition charged.[108] Independent schools seldom accept government funds for fear of intervention but rely instead on contributions, mostly from parents of current students, alumni (who provide the largest share of annual giving dollars), and trustees (94 percent of whom contribute to their schools).[109] Perhaps because fundraising is so time consuming and labor intensive, most schools employ fundraising professionals.

In setting tuition charges, boards of trustees struggle to maintain an appropriate balance between covering the expenses associated with small class sizes and the upkeep of expensive facilities and not pricing themselves out of the market for middle-class and upper-middle-class families. Since many families are unaware of what independent schools offer, identifying new populations and educating them as to the benefits of a private school is a constant challenge for admissions officers. Success in attracting families and raising funds to balance the budget is directly linked to the state of the economy, moreover, so the economic difficulties that followed the banking crisis of 2008 have further complicated the funding picture for these schools.

Private School Lessons for Public School Reform

The private sector, which has greater latitude in shaping practices than the public sector, may provide a source of research and development for public schools.

Policies that tap into the best models of private education can inform public educational practice and thereby hold the promise of benefiting the greater good.

As public education has come under fire for failing to educate a large portion of America's children, particularly in inner cities, policymakers, politicians, and business leaders have begun to look to private schools as a source of lessons about education that works. Private school educators who choose to work in charter schools bring with them knowledge and experience of effective practices and the culture of high expectations for students and faculty. In the past, claiming that the ability to select students is a key element of private school success, public school officials have dismissed the outcomes of private schooling, ignoring the reality that most Catholic schools are not selective and that independent schools are only modestly so.

There are five important lessons from the experience of Catholic and independent schools that may be instructive for public schools:

—Allowing families to choose schools not only offers psychological advantages but also creates a cohesive community of families attracted to the school's mission.[110]

—Expecting all students to master the curriculum produces results because, given an opportunity and high expectations, most students are likely to learn.[111]

—A nurturing environment with personal attention has a positive influence on learning.[112]

—Allowing academic and organizational decisions to be made expediently at the school level rather than dictating them from a centralized bureaucracy is effective in increasing student achievement.[113]

—Having a strong mission, whether based on religious ideology or moral conviction, is necessary for directing and aligning institutional action.[114]

Even as public schools move toward providing a variety of choices, private schools will continue to exercise their historic role in the educational fabric of America. There will always be families that want their children educated with a particular religious or moral persuasion, families that desire more personalization and academic rigor than is found in most public schools, and families that can afford the cost of tuition. And private schools are likely to display resilience in confronting the twenty-first century's challenges of increased diversity, recruitment of capable teachers, school choice, and affordability.

Private schools serve the interests of families, but they also serve the public good because a better-educated populace is in the best interests of a democracy. The economist Milton Friedman points to the "neighborhood effect" of schooling, in which the benefits of education are applicable not only to the individual but also to the community as a whole.[115] In *Pierce* v. *The Society of Sisters,* the U.S. Supreme Court held that the child is not the creature of the state.[116] Choosing from a diversity of schools the ones that fit with their values is one of the most important declarations of independence Americans can make. The United States was founded with the intention of protecting the exercise of choice, and the right to choose a school—be it public or private—is a direct expression of the fundamental democratic freedoms of this country.

POSTSCRIPT. Edmund Rice High School closed for financial reasons, effective September 2011.

Workforce Development and Training

Nonprofit organizations play a role in the education field not only by providing education at colleges, universities, and elementary and secondary schools, but also through less formal institutions formed to help individuals overcome the barriers to work and the disadvantages that exist for those who have been left behind by the educational system. Job training legislation can be traced back to the 1960s, when training programs were established for workers dislocated by changes in federal trade, environmental, space, and defense policies. Growing concerns about sex equity, the needs of the disadvantaged, and the high cost of providing welfare benefits stimulated the expansion of these programs to provide job placement and training for persons other than dislocated workers. In 2004 one researcher estimated that between 15 million and 50 million people in the United States needed workforce services.[117] Following the Great Recession of 2008 and 2009, those numbers grew substantially, as over 8 million Americans lost their jobs.[118] The field of workforce development and training has evolved into a substantial area of public policy, involving all levels of government, thousands of educational institutions, agencies, and nonprofit organizations, and to an increasing degree, businesses and business organizations.[119]

The federal government has often taken the lead in this area, providing funding and spurring the creation of support agencies and service providers.[120] Since Congress enacted the first piece of workforce development and training legislation, hundreds of federal programs have been created. However, both federal and state governments sponsor programs designed to provide job training and other workforce development services to those whose previous education has left them unprepared for work. Some of these state and federal programs are voluntary, while others condition receipt of government benefits on participation. However, each of them has led to the increased involvement of nonprofits in workforce development and training.

The nonprofits that provide workforce development and training come in a variety of forms. They use a variety of methods to create employment opportunities for workers who face barriers to entering or reentering the labor force or who seek better jobs. Many are community-based organizations. Others are workforce development agencies formed in direct response to government funding, and in recent years a number of collaborative organizations, joint venture entities, and even labor unions have entered the arena.[121] Many nonprofits that provide workforce development services are, however, vulnerable to changes in government expenditures and policies. As government funding has failed to keep pace with demand, these organizations must constantly adapt in order to respond to changing government policies, programs, and spending at all levels—federal, state, and local.[122] In addition, the widespread joblessness that resulted from the Great Recession of 2008 and 2009 has intensified reliance on nonprofit organizations to provide effective workforce development and training programs.[123]

A New Environment for Workforce Development and Training

By and large, the world of workforce development and training has been characterized by an entrenched division of labor, whereby programs are divided into two subsystems. One is the subsystem of public, nonprofit, and for-profit educational institutions; and the other is the subsystem of training institutions, usually nonprofit and community-based organizations but also for-profit firms. In the past, competition for resources was extremely limited. In a 1996 study, W. Norton Grubb and Lorraine M. McDonnell concluded that competition among service providers from the different subsystems was uncommon.[124] More recent studies suggest, however, that this is no longer true.[125] Substantial changes in federal workforce development and training policies and in the private sector have stimulated a movement away from a nonprofit monopoly. Nonprofits now compete with one another and with for-profit firms for government funding, employer contracts, and clients.

Government agencies now have more options than ever for service providers. Although, historically, community colleges and for-profit institutions served a different purpose and a different clientele than traditional nonprofits, this too is changing. Current federal policy and programs give community colleges a prominent role in workforce development. As a result, community colleges have become a principal source of competition for community-based service providers.[126] Community colleges usually have more resources than nonprofit organizations and also can design quality programs for career advancement and have better links to community employers.[127] Moreover, one influential scholar posits that increasingly, nonprofits compete directly with for-profit firms in a variety of ways.[128]

Many employers have now joined the government effort, becoming the primary contractors of workforce development and training services.[129] Employers now seek out community colleges, for-profit schools, community-based organizations, and other nonprofits to assist potential employees in everything from transportation and child care provision to basic job and social interaction skills. Those firms without the skill, experience, or resources to provide the services needed to improve retention and advancement of nontraditional workers are the most likely to rely on nonprofit organizations for assistance.[130] Labor unions have also increasingly entered the picture, serving as direct links to skilled workers for employers and industry. They now offer workforce development opportunities to low-income workers and can provide training and career ladders to both members and potential members.[131]

More recently, workforce development providers have joined forces to establish what are commonly known as workforce intermediaries. These organizations tend to be homegrown, local partnerships that work together with employers and workers to utilize private and public funding streams and other partners to implement workforce development strategies.[132] They are outgrowths of community organizations, community colleges, labor unions, and employer associations. These intermediaries that can form long-term relationships with employers are now seen as critical elements of a successful workforce development strategy.[133] Advocates of workforce intermediaries argue that they reflect the failure of government-led initiatives and serve five unique and critical functions:

—They take a dual customer approach, addressing needs of employers and low-income and less-skilled workers and job seekers.

—They go beyond job matching to host interventions (work with both supply and demand sides to improve each).

—They act as integrators of funding streams, public and private sector services and programs, and information sources.

—They generate ideas and innovations.

—They provide a bundle of services rather than serve only a single purpose.[134]

Whether they work as part of a formal or informal network, in collaboration with others or independently, nonprofit organizations continue to play a central role in the delivery of workforce development and training services.

Impact of Federal Policy on Workforce Development and Training

Changes in public policy can have a significant impact on a nonprofit's priorities and ability to pursue its mission. In 1998, with the adoption of the Workforce Investment Act (WIA) of 1998, Congress introduced a focus on increased accountability and choice within public workforce development and training policy. The WIA replaced many aspects of its predecessor, the Job Training Partnership Act of 1982, and included provisions that stress the importance of local governance, accountability, and customer choice.[135]

The WIA was created primarily to address chronic individual use of welfare funding in place of working. Before the implementation of the WIA, workforce development policy was not addressed comprehensively at either the federal or local levels. Job training programs often operated with a single purpose: training primarily underemployed or unemployed workers for projected high-demand occupations in the local or national labor market. There were few supportive services for workers in these programs after they obtained their first job and almost no policies to support employers after they hired the workers. Through tougher accountability measures, choice, and efforts to force nonprofits and other groups to collaborate, the WIA sought to create incentives for workforce training providers to offer comprehensive social and supportive services.

Although the WIA was set to expire in 2003, to date, each year, Congress has continued to fund WIA programs without officially reauthorizing the legislation, albeit at lower levels of funding.[136] In 2009, after years of budget cuts in WIA funding, the Obama administration secured substantial new funding for federal workforce development programs through the American Recovery and Reinvestment Act of 2009 (ARRA)[137] In the early months of 2012, Congress appears ready to consider reauthorization of WIA after years of inaction. Most calls for reform highlight the need for increased funding and the need to lessen the administrative burden associated with receiving WIA funding, but until new legislation is enacted, federal workforce development and training policy continues to focus on accountability, choice, and collaboration. Each of these policy components has an impact on the nonprofits that provide workforce development and training.

ACCOUNTABILITY. The concept of accountability in workforce development and training is not new. As with all programs born out of legislation, the government has always conditioned funding upon some demonstrable evidence that the program's goals are being realized. However, as legislative budgets tighten and questions about the effectiveness of workforce development and training programs persist, scholars and policymakers are under pressure to hold nonprofits more accountable and to enforce strict performance standards. The WIA contains a number of provisions designed specifically to enhance the level of accountability for service providers. At the heart of the law is a system of performance-based contracting, whereby an organization's funding is tied directly to the performance of the clients it serves.

At the time of the WIA's enactment, there was some evidence that the move toward higher accountability measures was warranted. One study finds, for example, that while neither for-profit nor nonprofit providers were consistently successful in increasing clients' earnings and employment rates, the inclusion of performance incentives in a providers' contract with the government improved effectiveness.[138] Early evaluations of the WIA's accountability measures indicated that the act had not significantly changed the way traditional workforce development and training providers operate. The focus remained on program inputs, like classroom time, rather than on outcomes. In addition, workforce goals, rather than strategies, were modified when an organization encountered difficulty meeting the performance standards; and the high stakes involved tend to discourage organizations from setting ambitious goals related to job retention and advancement.[139]

However, other data suggest that WIA's introduction of a performance-based system has had a profound effect, particularly on community organizations and small nonprofits.[140] Moreover, a number of more recent studies evaluating the effectiveness of programs funded through WIA indicate that the evidence on cost-effectiveness of job training for disadvantaged workers is positive.[141] As policymakers intended, the move toward more performance-based contracting caused some funding instability for those nonprofits that traditionally received funding commitments on the basis of reputation or politics alone.[142] Yet opponents of performance-based funding point to the unintended effects and argue that tying payments and bonuses to contractors' performance on short-term outcome measures may force nonprofits to abandon their workforce development efforts or move away from their charitable mission and toward shorter term financial goals or may otherwise have an impact on program administrators' decisions to terminate a client's participation.[143]

The WIA also includes performance standards that require the evaluation of program outcomes over a longer postprogram period. Still, an enduring concern with high-stakes accountability measures and universal access (rather than programs targeted to special populations) is that the pressure to secure or protect funding forces providers to serve only those individuals with the fewest barriers to employment and long-term placement and punishes those whose mission is to serve individuals with multiple barriers to employment.[144] A potential means to address this concern would be to institute differentiated performance standards that account for the additional challenges a provider may have in serving certain client populations. Or the law could provide for an evaluation process that measures, recognizes, and rewards incremental improvement or gains, in addition to performance on overall placement and retention targets.

Another unwanted byproduct of increased accountability is higher administration costs. The act's accountability system requires nonprofits to institute information technology systems that track and verify the progress of all clients. All too often, this requires costly technology and management systems, which may be too expensive for smaller, community-based nonprofits.[145] Additionally, most nonprofits need upfront capital to undertake a government contract. Ultimately, this means that these organizations are more vulnerable if the government entity is slow to pay and if they cannot survive until after an evaluation for payment.[146]

Another consequence of the accountability measures is that all of the reporting mechanisms may keep certain nonprofits from participating. Often local government officials are the ones who evaluate whether a nonprofit has met the performance standards, and a politically active organization may fear that, in the wrong hands, the information may "narrow the range of inclusion."[147] One study reveals that, for many nonprofits, the decision to participate in the WIA often rests upon the group's determination that it is likely to be able to comply with the new performance standards.[148] Other nonprofits opt out of the WIA altogether by deciding to forgo federal funding or by becoming a subcontractor to a group that receives WIA funding. Some posit that WIA's focus on accountability has consequently led to a smaller number of organizations becoming workplace development service providers, as these organizations opt to become niche service providers, working only with those workers who are hardest to serve or as subcontractors to larger, more established, nonprofits.[149] This leaves only these established organizations, those that are not reliant solely on government funding for survival.[150] This outcome evidences the need for additional incentives for workplace development and training providers who will serve such populations as ex-offenders, working mothers, and immigrants.[151]

CHOICE. The WIA introduced the concept of choice into workforce development and training programs through individual training accounts (ITAs), which permit clients to select the services they need. This client choice affects the choices that nonprofits make about which services they offer. The decision as to whether to use a comprehensive services approach, like Project Match, or to concentrate on offering clients a single service is likely to be influenced by the demand generated by clients' use of their accounts.

The arguments for and against more choice are complicated and varied. Initially, the new ITA system raised significant concerns among some nonprofits. According to the Chicago Jobs Council executive director, Robert Wordlaw, because these accounts enable individuals to contract directly with service providers, the traditional nonprofit is significantly weakened.[152] There is some evidence to substantiate the concern that the increased competition among nonprofits for clients has forced small, relatively low-capacity, community-based organizations to leave the workforce development business.[153] Yet proponents of the ITA system suggest that forcing nonprofits to diversify their funding base may have yielded positive effects.[154] Choice, via the ITA system, is designed to encourage service providers to streamline and improve their services. If an organization is successful, clients will come and bring the funding with them. Critics of this view point out, however, that if success is measured by such indicators (which do not account for the severity of barriers facing many clients), those organizations dedicated to working with the long-term unemployed and other hard-to-place populations will find it very difficult to survive.

It is also contended that the account system breeds inefficiency. Nonprofits that can afford to expend resources trying to attract clients might engage in reverse referrals to attract customers, investing resources on the front end (in initial recruiting and training) before they send clients to a center to be certified.[155] They then hope, but have no guarantee, that the client will return for more intensive services. The process is costly and prevents nonprofits from allocating their resources in a more targeted fashion.

Regardless of continuing policy discussions on the merits of the individual training accounts, the WIA made them central to the nation's system of workforce development and training. For the market forces to work as intended, clients must have better information about the quality of services available.[156] Additionally, as workforce development providers favor collaborating with partners or as part of an intermediary, it will be important to ensure that these partnerships are able to access WIA funds through the ITA system as well.[157] Under current federal policies, nonprofits must be proactive in developing relationships with other organizations and agencies to ensure that other service providers know about and can recommend their services to clients. In addition, where available, organizations should seek certification or accreditation to make certain that they will have access to clients with training accounts and can improve their capacity to meet higher performance standards.

CALLS FOR COLLABORATION. The pressure to compete in the face of performance-based contracting and greater choice for clients has brought about new strategies of adaptation by nonprofits. Many nonprofits, after being forced out of business as independent providers of workforce development, have begun to collaborate with one another and other entities to enhance their services. Two examples of coordination that have become prevalent are One-Stop career centers and formal community alliances. Recent research indicates that the nonprofit organizations that thrive in this new regulatory environment are those that have formed strong, formal partnerships with other entities, especially employers.[158]

The One-Stop centers were designed in part to assist service providers to become more efficient and to increase their capacity to serve a client's various needs. Yet some providers find that, by giving greater control to the client to determine which services he or she will receive, the centers make their job more difficult.[159] In more traditional programs, a caseworker designs an individualized plan for each client, and they work together to realize the goals set forth in the plan and to alter the plan when necessary. Therefore, those groups serving the hardest-to-employ may view the one-stop system's focus on universality as detrimental to the principal goal of many workforce development and training programs, that of moving people out of poverty and into self-sufficiency.

One-Stop centers have become one of the most influential and enduring components of the WIA. Some contend that reliance on these centers as the primary service delivery mechanism has generated several unintended and negative results. The principal criticism is that the centers may lack the capacity to serve all those who need workplace development and training services, both employers and job seekers. Another criticism is that most participants do not use the centers for employee recruiting, training, or retention services.[160] Where a One-Stop center is operated solely by one organization, the provision of all services by a single nonprofit increases the risk that the organization will serve fewer job seekers and become disconnected from other labor market players and informal networks that bring employers and job seekers together.[161] Thus, the establishment of One-Stop centers has not alleviated the need for more effective collaboration among workforce development providers.

Some nonprofits that act as One-Stop career centers do reach out to other organizations and rely on subcontractors to make these connections and provide the actual services. However, subcontracting can leave these organizations vulnerable.[162] When acting as a subcontractor, a nonprofit organization becomes dependent on timely payments by the primary vendor. Slow payment can force the organization to shut its doors or discontinue workplace development services, as there is often no recourse against a government agency for slow or missed payments, and the nonprofit's only option is costly litigation.[163]

A New Era in Workforce Development and Training

Just like their counterparts in higher education and elementary and secondary education, community-based and nonprofit organizations necessarily found ways to adapt to the changing times in order to continue fulfilling their role as the principal providers of workforce development and training. The WIA was first passed during the booming economy of the mid- and late 1990s. During this era, federal funding for social services was high, jobs were growing, and consumer confidence and corporate spending were high.[164] Although the WIA encouraged greater accountability and introduced more stringent performance management mechanisms, those measures were not accompanied by increased funding. In fact, after the passage of the act, there actually was a reduction in training dollars available. The economic downturn of 2001, coupled with federal policies for much of the decade favoring devolution and partnerships among service providers, led to a much different landscape for those engaged in workforce development.[165] The Great Recession of 2008 and 2009 has led to even greater and more dramatic changes to the landscape. Although funding for workforce development policies at the federal level has been increased through the American Recovery and Reinvestment Act of 2009, so too has the number of displaced workers and the challenge of providing appropriate training for those workers.[166]

DEMOGRAPHIC SHIFTS IN THE AMERICAN WORKFORCE. Some critics suggest that the WIA fails to address the growing number of mismatches that now exist due in part to changes in the demographic landscape.[167] Even before the job losses brought on by the Great Recession, changes in the economy and the labor market—including increased diversity, a younger workforce, greater reliance on technology, increased relocation of jobs to suburban areas, and shifting governance priorities—directly influenced how all the participants in workforce development and training operate.[168]

While explorations of a mismatch between workforce demands and the skills of workers were common before the WIA, in later years, the literature reflects an even greater mismatch between the needs of most employers and workers' skills, geographic location, and training.[169] A number of academics point to the fact that the workforce is younger and more and more diverse and urban.[170] Meanwhile, rapidly changing technology requires a more skilled workforce, and urban offices have been moving out of cities and into the suburbs.[171] The need for effective and comprehensive support programs that can fill these gaps has therefore emerged.[172] Many employers "lack experience in dealing with a demographically diverse workforce. And the workforce development programs that currently assist these employers often lack a key 'cultural competence' component, making them unable to tackle these challenges effectively."[173]

These mismatches and attendant gaps between labor supply and employer demand have expanded and become more complex due to the Great Recession of 2008 and 2009. Lower-skilled workers are now joined by an array of skilled workers who were laid off during the Great Recession. Many workers now find that they need a higher skill set, sector- and firm-specific skills and connections to employers in order to secure a well-paying job.[174] Individuals in both groups seek workforce development training that will enable them to secure and retain a high-quality job in a high-growth field.[175] Additionally, education levels are not keeping up with demand for skilled labor; there are fewer "good jobs" available in manufacturing and more that are found in the professional, financial, health care, and construction fields, where postsecondary training is essential.[176]

Traditional employment practices fostered by the WIA and other government workforce development initiatives arguably leave employers with limited resources for engaging and retaining the new workforce and its workers. This need has stimulated the development of strategies and practices aimed at bridging the gap between employers and workers. They include interventions and programming that address cultural competence, antidiscrimination laws, and supportive workplace policies. Job programs, diversity consultants, and universities are among the organizations that are providing specific training to employers on issues of cultural competence. More recently, the focus has shifted to targeting employers and industries and engaging them in partnerships or sector projects.[177] For some community-based organizations with strong ties within a particular community or with a long history of working with a certain population, the mismatch problem presents a unique opportunity to contract with employers and provide the necessary training or to act as intermediaries between employer and employee.

CHANGING FACE OF COMPETITION: FOR-PROFIT FIRMS. The advent of individual training accounts and the entry of new providers into the workforce development arena increased choice and competition among nonprofit organizations.[178] Traditional nonprofits compete with one another and against community colleges; large, well-established nonprofits; and even labor unions. Interestingly, nonprofit organizations have also seen a rise in competition from for-profit companies.[179]

Temporary employment firms and trade schools have entered the marketplace in increasing numbers. While unions may be positioned to compete with for-profit firms that provide workplace development services to employers, many other nonprofit organizations find it a challenge.[180] And while they do happen, mutually beneficial partnerships between traditional nonprofits and for-profit firms tend to be more the exception than the rule.[181] Those nonprofits that do survive competition with for-profit firms improved their organizational systems, staff, programming, and service delivery and tend to compete on price.[182] Yet they continue to struggle with government agency demands that compromise their organizations' values and challenge their long-standing missions.[183]

The increased competition particularly affects those nonprofits that are not fiscally sound or that do not have a broad base of funding to improve and to innovate.[184] Those that have been unable or unwilling to accept the challenges that a performance-based system brings have been seriously weakened by the WIA's emphasis on choice and performance-based policy and are less likely to survive. Simply put, the policy shift to a work-first, choice- and performance-based system has changed the way most nonprofits that provide workforce development services do business.

The Future of Workforce Development and Training

Most scholars acknowledge that the implementation of the WIA has had a profound effect on the environment in which most workforce development and training providers operate. However, questions about the overall effectiveness of this nation's workforce development and training system persist. Some scholars point to concerns that service providers fail to connect training and education to the specific job skills that employers need. Yet others focus on the need to find ways to fulfill the unmet needs of the hardest-to-serve job seekers. There is a consensus developing, however, that even with the investment of ARRA stimulus dollars in 2009, a more significant investment from public and private sources will be needed to develop workforce development strategies sufficient to address concerns about the needs of employers and hard-to-serve job seekers and at the same time, reintegrate the millions of workers who lost their jobs during the Great Recession of 2008 and 2009.

EMPLOYER AND INDUSTRY DEMAND-DRIVEN WORKFORCE DEVELOP-MENT SYSTEMS. For years, policymakers have responded to critics who argue that employers have not been sufficiently engaged in workforce development programs by promoting increased coordination among service providers. WIA called for the creation of Workforce Investment Boards, or WIBs. These boards, which include representatives from local industries, distribute and monitor WIA contracts. They oversee each local training system and attempt to bring local employers together with the policymakers charged with implementing workforce development and training laws and the nonprofits and other service providers that work directly with the individuals in need of assistance. Yet even with the establishment of WIBs, questions linger about the extent to which the boards actually bring employers into the process in a way that is meaningful.[185]

Experts continue to urge providers and policymakers to institute more employer-centered programs and to engage employers in issues beyond job placement, such as retention, advancement, financing for workforce development programming and training, and how to shape the civic workforce agenda more broadly.[186] Employer-centered programs refer to training programs that are both employer initiated and customized to meet employer needs and that emphasize working directly with employers and unions, where available, and treating employers and firms as clients.[187] In the late 1990s, Edwin Meléndez and others predicted that a key to successful workforce development and training would be the involvement of employers in the workforce development process.[188]

Over a decade later, the calls for more sustained engagement of employers and the creation of workforce development strategies that address employer needs continue.[189] As one funder put it, "Workforce development programs must be demand driven and willing to learn about changes in demand, not just client needs. Employers need to trust that the [nonprofit organization] will provide their workforce and human resource needs. This includes delivering on their needs and providing the appropriate screening for the workforce."[190]A strong employer-based program is one that begins with a careful analysis of an employee's (or potential employee's) performance on the job and directly supports the employer's institutional culture and strategic goals.[191] In addition to becoming more responsive to employer demands, employer-centered programming also means permitting oneself to be evaluated according to business metrics of performance and profitability.[192]

One organization that serves as a model for many groups seeking to develop an employer-centered program is Goodwill Industries.[193] Goodwill has proven to industry that it has the capacity to train individuals. Goodwill itself runs a thrift shop that recycles, repairs, and cleans donated items that are then sold in its retail shops. Goodwill uses these businesses to train some of the hardest-to-serve workers. Traditionally, Goodwill works hard to establish a presence within the community, takes a comprehensive approach to service provision, and forges partnerships with employers to better understand their needs. The CEO has said, "We run businesses and embrace business-oriented management techniques. We are reliable, and our results are predictable. We have the lowest overhead in the country and can fund our operations up front through high capitalization."[194]

Other examples of extensive employer engagement can be found in sector projects being implemented around the country.[195] A sector project strategy necessarily involves employers by targeting a specific industry or cluster of occupations, pulling together a set of organizations that work specifically to support workers' efforts to improve their range of employment related skills and to meet the needs of employers within the identified industry or cluster of occupations.[196] Nonprofit organizations often play a pivotal role within a sector project. Yet in a departure from previous workforce development strategies, organizations engaged in a sector project focus on comprehensively meeting the needs of dual customers—both employers and job seekers. This has required nonprofit organizations to engage employers in new ways, such as inviting employers to participate in program design and operation and to become instructors to ensure that training meets employer needs.[197] The challenge of serving employer needs, while simultaneously fulfilling a mission to provide services to lower-skilled workers or hard-to-serve individuals, can create problems for even the most effective nonprofit organization.[198]

WORKFORCE DEVELOPMENT AND TRAINING FOR THE HARDEST TO SERVE. Notwithstanding a more focused effort by nonprofits to institute more employer-centered programs, to be successful, nonprofit organizations must maintain a dual focus and continue to cater to the needs of individual clients. However, doing so remains a significant challenge. A by-product of WIA's performance-based contracting requirements is that federally funded service providers end up working mainly with job seekers who are easier to train and place.

For-profit organizations, unions, and community colleges frequently serve workers who have attained some skill and have fewer barriers to employment. Therefore, many nonprofit organizations must find ways to provide programs and services for the hardest to serve—people from low-income homes, high school dropouts, ex-offenders, the homeless, and workers for whom English is a second language. In other words, while web-based job-matching firms, temporary worker firms, and employer-run training programs focus their efforts on the easier-to-help more skilled workers, community based organizations and other nonprofits have become the providers of workplace development services to the most disadvantaged job seekers.[199] After the Great Recession, the ranks of the hard-to-serve have expanded to include newly unemployed workers recently displaced from jobs that were modernized or eliminated altogether and who must be retrained in order to qualify for a job with similar pay.[200]

Some federal policies, like those enacted as part of the YouthBuild Transfer Act and the Jobs for Veterans Act, seek to address the need for additional resources and programs for the hardest-to-serve. Both the YouthBuild Transfer Act and the Jobs for Veterans Act provide supplemental services and a comprehensive approach to job training for specific populations. In 2007, Congress passed the Second Chance Act to improve reentry planning and implementation for ex-offenders. This legislation authorizes grants for employment assistance, substance abuse treatment, housing assistance, family programming, mentoring, victim support, and other services that help reduce recidivism. However, even with the investments in these programs, and more recent investments like funding from the ARRA stimulus of 2009, the demand substantially outpaces the supply of funding that would be required to reach these job seekers. In addition, workforce interventions alone may not be sufficient to support low-income, low-skilled, or other workers with special needs.[201] Additional economic and social supports must be provided to enable the hardest-to-serve to get the training they need and to find and keep good jobs.[202]

Workforce development policy expert Robert Giloth contends that an even greater investment of resources will be necessary to build upon recent successes in workforce development and to meet the new challenges posed by the Great Recession. "Investment in the capacity of community organizations to become effective workforce partners is important because outreach and recruitment, assessment, support, and follow-up are desperately needed, not only to achieve job placement but also for retention and advancement."[203] These investments need not come solely from the government. One organization, the Cara Program in Chicago, has leveraged the emerging trend of social enterprise and implemented an aggressive fundraising strategy to build a diverse base of funding. Using a combination of results-driven decisionmaking, an innovative approach to client service, creative fundraising strategies, and sustained partnerships with industry and local businesses, the Cara Program found a way to keep its reliance on government dollars to less than 20 percent of its overall revenue stream. Its former vice president of program services, Brandon Crow, explains the program's commitment to a diversified funding base: "We simply [avoid] most of the government funds so we have the freedom to adapt to the populations that we are working with and serving pretty well."[204] Freedom from an overreliance on government funding has worked well for the Cara Program. Since 1991 the program has placed over 2,500 individuals in full-time quality jobs, and in 2011, 77 percent of those placed in full-time jobs remained in their job after one year.[205]

To meet the needs of populations that are harder to serve, more nonprofits will undoubtedly have to alter their strategies and innovate. This innovation will likely take the form of diversified funding, creative initiatives and partnerships, streamlining, expanding or changing missions, revamping corporate structures, and even merging with other organizations.

Summary

It is clear that the organizations that operate workforce development and training programs will, for years to come, be forced to do their work in the face of increased accountability, tight government budgets, greater competition, enhanced choice for individual clients, and a more substantial role for employers in shaping workforce development and training programs. To sustain the important role that these organizations play in the provision of workforce development and training, they will have to find a way to balance the need to provide individual client service with the need to meet employer and industry demand.

They must learn what employers require and then prepare individuals to fill those needs, while still connecting these individuals to the comprehensive services they must have to succeed in today's workplace. To do so will require the development of partnerships with employers and others as well as a willingness to move in new directions, to break with tradition, to form new structures, and to find new sources of funding and support. Employers and their firms must continue working to bridge the gap between the jobs available and the needs and skills of a younger, more diverse workforce. Both employers and workers have to be ready to embrace change and build strong internal support for existing workforce development practices.[206]

Notes

1. National Center for Education Statistics, *Digest of Educational Statistics: 2010* (Washington, D.C.: Department of Education, Institute of Education Sciences, 2010), table 275 (http://nces.ed.gov/programs/digest/d10/tables/dt10_275.asp).

2. National Center for Education Statistics, *Digest of Educational Statistics: 2010,* table 202.

3. There were other institutions of higher education founded in this time period (St. John's College in 1696, University of Delaware in 1743), but they are not typically included in lists of firsts because they operated without formal charters for a significant period of time.

4. Arthur M. Cohen and Carrie B. Kisker, *The Shaping of American Higher Education: Emergence and Growth of the Contemporary System* (San Francisco: Jossey-Bass, 2010), p. 21.

5. Cohen and Kisker, *The Shaping of American Higher Education.*

6. Frederick Rudolph, *The American College and University: A History* (University of Georgia Press, 1990), p. 185.

7. Cohen and Kisker, *The Shaping of American Higher Education,* p. 58; Christopher J. Lucas, *American Higher Education: A History* (New York: Palgrave Macmillan, 2006), pp. 114–16.

8. *Plessy* v. *Ferguson,* 163 U.S. 537 (1896).

9. National Center for Education Statistics, *Fall Enrollment Surveys, 1998,* table 157.

10. Michael J. Bennett, *When Dreams Come True: The GI Bill and the Making of Modern America* (Washington: Brassey's, 1996), pp. 237–76.

11. Bennett, *When Dreams Come True.*

12. President's Commission on Higher Education, *Higher Education for Democracy* (1947).

13. National Center for Education Statistics, *The Condition of Education 2010,* NCES 2010-028 , p. 37.

14. On October 4, 1957, the Soviet Union launched Sputnik I, the world's first earth-orbiting, artificial satellite, marking the beginning of the space age.

15. Donald M. Stewart, *The Politics of Higher Education and Public Policy: A Study of the American Council on Education* (Cambridge, Mass.: Harvard Kennedy School of Government, 1975), p. 243.

16. College Board, *Trends in Student Aid, 2000* (New York, 2000), pp. 2–3.

17. College Board, *Trends in Student Aid, 2011* (New York, 2011).

18. College Board, *Trends in Student Aid, 2010* (New York, 2010), p. 13. Measure is in constant 2009 dollars, and the figure is inclusive of loans distributed through several loan programs, among them the subsidized Stafford, the unsubsidized Stafford, the Parent PLUS, the Grad PLUS, and Perkins. Nonfederal loans accounted for an additional $5 billion in 1999–2000 and $8 billion in 2009–10.

19. College Board, *Trends in Student Aid, 2010,* p. 16.

20. College Board, *Trends in Student Aid, 2010,* p. 10.

21. National Center for Education Statistics, *Digest of Educational Statistics: 2010,* table 275.

22. National Center for Education Statistics, *Digest of Educational Statistics: 2010,* table 202.

23. National Center for Education Statistics, *Digest of Educational Statistics: 2010,* table 247 (http://nces.ed.gov/programs/digest/d10/tables/dt10_247.asp).

24. National Center for Education Statistics, "Characteristics of Minority-Serving Institutions and Minority Undergraduates Enrolled in These Institutions" (Washington, D.C.: Department of Education, Institute of Education Sciences), p. 20.

25. Rudolph, *The American College and University,* pp. 99–330.

26. U.S. News, *America's Best Colleges, 2010,* pp. 88–93.

27. National Center for Education Statistics, *Digest of Educational Statistics* (2010), table 375 (http://nces.ed.gov/programs/digest/d10/tables/dt10_375.asp)

28. National Center for Education Statistics, "Fast Facts: What Are the Trends in the Cost of College Education?" (http://nces.ed.gov/fastfacts/display.asp?id=76). See College Board,

Advocacy and Policy Center, "Trends in College Pricing, 2011," which further details the pricing patterns and cost pressures of private, nonprofit colleges and universities.

29. Charles T. Clotfelter, *Buying the Best: Cost Escalation in the Arts and Sciences* (Princeton University Press, 1996), p. 12; Derek Bok, note to author, August 12, 2002.

30. Clotfelter, *Buying the Best,* pp. 28, 32.

31. See www.naicu.edu/special_initiatives/affordability/about/enhancing-affordability.

32. See www.naicu.edu/special_initiatives/affordability/news_room/controlling-costs.

33. Michael S. McPherson and Morton O. Schapiro, "End of the Student Aid Era? Higher Education Finance in the United States," in *A Faithful Mirror: Reflections on the College Board and Education in America,* edited by Michael C. Johanek (New York: College Board, 2001), p. 234.

34. Victor E. Ferrall, "Can Liberal Arts Colleges Be Saved," *Inside Higher Education* (February 11, 2008) (www.insidehighered.com/views/2008/02/11).

35. W. Norton Grubb and Marvin Lazerson, "Vocationalism in Higher Education: The Triumph of the Education Gospel," *Journal of Higher Education* 76, no. 1 (2005): 2.

36. See http://classifications.carnegiefoundation.org. The Carnegie Classification of Institutions of Higher Education, commonly referred to as the Carnegie classification system, or simply the Carnegie classifications, "has been the leading framework for recognizing and describing institutional diversity in U.S. higher education for the past four decades. Starting in 1970, the Carnegie Commission on Higher Education developed a classification of colleges and universities to support its program of research and policy analysis. Derived from empirical data on colleges and universities, the Carnegie classifications were originally published in 1973 and subsequently updated in 1976, 1987, 1994, 2000, 2005, and 2010 to reflect changes among colleges and universities. This framework has been widely used in the study of higher education, both to represent and control for institutional differences and to design research studies to ensure adequate representation of sampled institutions, students, or faculty."

37. David W. Breneman, *Liberal Arts Colleges: Thriving, Surviving, or Endangered?* (Brookings Institution Press, 1994), p. 13.

38. See www.insidehighered.com/views/2008/02/11/ferrall.

39. David F. Labaree, "Mutual Subversion: A Short History of the Liberal and the Professional in American Higher Education," *History of Education Quarterly* 46, no 1 (2006): 13.

40. See www.aacu.org. The Association of American Colleges and Universities is a Washington, D.C.–based membership association. It calls itself a "Voice and a Force for Liberal Education in the 21st Century" and has been increasingly active through initiatives like Liberal Education and America's Promise.

41. Data on closings through 1998 are from information provided to Don Stewart by Frank J. Baly, vice president for research and policy analysis, National Association of Independent Colleges and Universities, 1998. Data on closings since 1998 are based on Stewart's conversations with private college presidents in 2009.

42. "A Key Research Yardstick: The Top 100 Institutions in Federal Dollars for Science, 2009," *Chronicle of Higher Education, Almanac of Higher Education 2011* (http://chronicle.com/article/A-Key-Research-Yardstick-The/128218).

43. See http://classifications.carnegiefoundation.org/lookup_listings/standard.php.

44. American Association for the Advancement of Science, "Guide to R&D Funding Data, R&D at Colleges and Universities" (Washington, D.C., August 2008) (www.aaas.org/spp/rd/guiuniv.htm).

45. David Blumenthal, "Unhealthy Hospitals: Addressing the Trauma in Academic Medicine," *Harvard Magazine* 103, no. 4 (2001), p. 30.

46. Donald E. Stokes, *Pasteur's Quadrant: Basic Science and Technological Innovation* (Brookings Institution Press, 1997), p. 9.

47. Association of American Colleges and Universities, "The Quality Imperative: Match Ambitious Goals for College Attainment with an Ambitious Vision for Learning," news release, January 20, 2010.

48. Association of American Colleges and Universities, "The Quality Imperative."

49. Walter W. Powell and Jason Owen-Smith, "Universities as Creators and Retailers of Intellectual Property: Life-Science Research and Commercial Development," in *To Profit or Not to Profit: The Commercial Transformation of the Nonprofit Sector* (Cambridge University Press, 2000), pp. 175–82.

50. Powell and Owen-Smith, "Universities as Creators and Retailers of Intellectual Property," pp. 172–79.

51. National Center for Education Statistics, *Digest of Educational Statistics: 2010,* tables 275 and 202.

52. Rachel Wiseman, "Enrollments Plunge at Many For-Profit Colleges," *Chronicle of Higher Education,* August 16, 2011.

53. For-profit institutions boosted their enrollments by 326 percent between the fall of 2000 and the fall of 2008, while nonprofit institutions boosted their enrollment by only 20 percent. National Center for Education Statistics, *Digest of Educational Statistics: 2010,* table 205 (http://nces.ed.gov/programs/digest/d10/tables/dt10_205.asp).

54. National Center for Education Statistics, *Digest of Educational Statistics: 2010,* table 345 (http://nces.ed.gov/programs/digest/d10/tables/dt10_345.asp).

55. Council for Aid to Education, "Colleges and Universities Raise $28 Billion in 2010— Same Total as in 2006," news release on February 2, 2011, New York, from the Voluntary Support of Education Survey (www.cae.org/content/pdf/VSE_2010_Press_Release.pdf).

56. Council for Aid to Education, "Colleges and Universities Raise $28 Billion in 2010."

57. Higher Education Act, Title I, secs. 132 (i), 133; Title IV, pt. G, sec. 485 (a and h); and Title IV, pt. H, sec. 496(c)(9).

58. "Obama Administration Announces New Steps to Protect Students from Ineffective Career College Programs" (www.ed.gov/news/press-releases/gainful-employment-regulations).

59. "What Didn't Happen but Just Might in the Future" (www.naicu.edu/special_initiatives/hea101/what_didn't_happen).

60. Derived using Penn State's College Cost Calculator (http://collegecostestimate.ais.psu.edu/cgi-bin/CollegeCostEstimate.exe/launch/CollegeCC/fullcalc).

61. For but one example, see Katharine C. Lyall and Kathleen R. Sell, *The True Genius of America at Risk: Are We Losing Our Public Universities to De Facto Privatization?* (Lanham, Md.: Rowman and Littlefield, 2005).

62. See http://chronicle.com/article/News-Analysis-Codes-of/129126.

63. Caralee Adams, "Students and Higher Education Prepare for Direct Lending," *Education Week,* June 9, 2010, p. 6.

64. Martin Meyerson, "An Endangered Breed: The Private University," unpublished speech presented to the Education Writers Association of Philadelphia, February 9, 1972.

65. Andrew J. Coulson, *Market Education: The Unknown History* (New Brunswick, N.J.: Transaction Publishers, 1999), pp. 73–81.

66. Otto F. Kraushaar, *American Nonpublic Schools: Patterns of Diversity* (Johns Hopkins University Press, 1972), pp. 6–7.

67. James C. Carper and Thomas C. Hunt, *The Dissenting Tradition in American Education* (New York: Peter Kang, 2007), p. 192.

68. E. Edmund Reutter Jr. and Robert R. Hamilton, *The Law of Public Education* (New York: Foundation Press, 1976), p. 14.

69. Kraushaar, *American Nonpublic Schools,* pp. 13–14.

70. Stephen P. Broughman, Nancy L. Swaim, and Patrick W. Keaton, *Characteristics of Private Schools in the United States: Results from the 2007–08 Private School Universe Survey,* NCES 2009-313 (Washington, D.C.: Department of Education, National Center for Education Statistics, March 2009), table 1. (http://nces.ed.gov/pubsearch/pubsinfo.asp?pubid=2009313).

71. Broughman and others, *Characteristics of Private Schools in the United States,* table 2.

72. Broughman and others, *Characteristics of Private Schools in the United States,* table 1.

73. Lloyd P. Jorgenson, *The State and Non-Public School: 1825–1925* (University of Missouri Press, 1987), pp. 146–54.

74. Neil McCluskey, *Catholic Education Faces Its Future* (Garden City, N.Y.: Doubleday, 1969), pp. 78, 263.

75. Anthony S. Bryk, Valerie E. Lee, and Peter B. Holland, *Catholic Schools and the Common Good* (Harvard University Press, 1993), pp. 51–54.

76. Sol Stern, "Save the Catholic Schools!" *City Journal* (Spring 2007): 74–83. This work is referenced throughout this paragraph.

77. William Carbonaro and Elizabeth Covay, "Sector Differences in Student Experiences and Achievement: An Update," *Sociology of Education* 83 (2010):160–82 (www.allacademic.com//meta/p_mla_apa_research_citation/1/8/3/0/1/pages183012/p183012-1.php).

78. Council for American Private Education, "Private Education: A Changing Landscape" *CAPE Outlook* 48 (Germantown, Md., October 2009) (www.capenet.org/facts.html).

79. Theodore R. Sizer, ed., *The Age of the Academies* (New York: Bureau of Publications, Teachers College, Columbia University, 1964), pp. 1–48; Lawrence A. Cremin, ed., *The Republic and the School: Horace Mann on the Education of Free Men* (Teachers College Press, 1957), pp. 23–25.

80. Kraushaar, *American Nonpublic Schools,* pp. 56–68.

81. Pearl Rock Kane, ed., *Independent Schools, Independent Thinkers* (San Francisco: Jossey-Bass, 1992), p. 7.

82. National Association of Independent Schools, "Independent School Facts at a Glance for: All NAIS Members Schools, 2007–2008" (Washington, D.C., 2008). (www.nais.org/resources/statistical.cfm?ItemNumber=146713).

83. Jeff Archer, "A League of Its Own," *Education Week* (October 20, 1999), pp. 34–41.

84. Archer, "A League of Its Own."

85. Stephen P. Broughman, Nancy L. Swaim, and Patrick W. Keaton, *Characteristics of Private Schools in the United States: Results from the 2005–2006 Private School Universe Survey,* NCES 2008-315 (Washington, D.C.: Department of Education, National Center for Education Statistics, 2008).

86. Mary Ann Zehr, "Evangelical Christian Schools See Growth," *Education Week,* December 8, 2004.

87. Carper and Hunt, *The Dissenting Tradition in American Education,* p. 212. Christian day schools, as defined by Carper and Hunt, include Lutherans, Friends, Methodists, Moravians, Baptists, German and Dutch Reformed, Presbyterians, and Anglicans.

88. Carper and Hunt, *The Dissenting Tradition in American Education,* p. 205.

89. Carper and Hunt, *The Dissenting Tradition in American Education,* p. 211.

90. Center for Education Reform, "Charter School Law" (Washington, D.C.). The nine states that do not have charter school laws are Alabama, Kentucky, Montana, Nebraska,

North Dakota, South Dakota, Vermont, Washington, and West Virginia. Maine passed its first charter school law in the summer of 2011 (www.edreform.com/index.cfm?fuseAction=document&documentID=1964).

91. Center for Education Reform, "The State of Charter Schools: What We Know—and What We Do Not—About Performance and Accountability" (Washington, D.C., December 2011), Appendix C, Charter School Growth over Time, 2000–2011 (http://www.edreform.com/2012/01/26/charter-school-closure-report/).

92. National Center for Children in Poverty, "Basic Facts about Low-Income Children: Birth to Age 18" (New York: Columbia University, 2007) (www.nccp.org/publications/pub_762.html).

93. Federal Interagency Forum on Child and Family Statistics (Forum), "America's Children: Key National Indicators of Well-Being, 2008" (Washington, D.C.) (www.childstats.gov/AMERICASCHILDREN/demo.asp).

94. National Catholic Educational Association, *United States Catholic Elementary and Secondary Schools: 2007–2008, The Annual Statistical Report on Schools, Enrollment, and Staffing* (Arlington, Va.) (www.ncea.org/news/AnnualDataReport.asp#full).

95. Nancy Trejos, "Suburban Boom Helps Revive Catholic Schools," *Washington Post*, August 13, 2000, p. M1.

96. National Association of Independent Schools, "Independent School Facts at a Glance for All NAIS Members Schools, 2007–2008."

97. William J. Hussar, *Predicting the Need for Newly Hired Teachers in the United States to 2008–09* (Washington, D.C.: Department of Education, National Center for Education Statistics, 1999).

98. Dale McDonald and Margaret M. Schultz, "Executive Summary," in *United States Catholic Elementary and Secondary Schools, 2011–2012* (Arlington, Va.: National Catholic Educational Association), p. 3.

99. Pearl Rock Kane, *Public and Independent Schools: A Comparative Study* (New York: Esther A. and Joseph Klingenstein Center for Independent School Education, 1986), p. 28.

100. Higher pay for hard-to-staff areas is already occurring, according to Jonathan K. Ball of Carney Sandoe and Associates in Boston, e-mail to author, August 17, 2008.

101. Howard S. Bloom, Saskia Levy Thompson, and Rebecca Unterman, *Transforming the High School Experience: How New York City's New Small Schools Are Boosting Student Achievement and Graduation Rates* (New York: MDRC, June 2010) (www.mdrc.org/publications/560/overview.html).

102. Children's Educational Opportunity Foundation of America, "Just Doing It 4: 1998 Annual Survey of the Private Voucher Movement in America" (Bentonville, Ariz., and Washington, D.C.: National Scholarship Center, 1998), pp. 1–3.

103. Sam Dillon, "Florida Court Strikes Down School Voucher Program," *New York Times*, January 5, 2006.

104. Children's Educational Opportunity Foundation of America, "Just Doing It 4," pp. 28–30.

105. Scott J. Cech, "Catholic Closures Linked to Growth of City Charters: Planned White House 'Summit' Raises Enrollment-Trend Issues," *Education Week* (February 13, 2008), p 1.

106. Corinne Lestch, "Charter vs. Catholic Schools: New Research Says Charters Are Siphoning Students from Parish Schools," *New York Daily News*, February 22, 2012 (www.nydailynews.com/new-york/bronx/charter-catholic-schools-research-charters-siphoning-students-parish-schools-article-1.1026463#ixzz1p98JxC2I). The article is based on preliminary research presented by Abraham M. Lackman, "The Collapse of Catholic School

Enrollment: Dissecting the Causes," an unpublished study presented at St.Francis College, Brooklyn, N.Y., March 7, 2012. Lackman is scholar in residence at the Albany Law School.

107. National Catholic Educational Association, *United States Catholic Elementary and Secondary Schools 2007–2008.*

108. The figures in this paragraph are taken from National Association of Independent Schools, "NAIS Independent School Facts at a Glance 2006–2007" (Washington, D.C., 2007) (www.nais.org/resources/statistical.cfm?ItemNumber=146713).

109. National Association of Independent Schools, "NAIS Independent School Facts at a Glance 2006–2007," table 32a.

110. James S. Coleman and Thomas Hoffer, *Public and Private High Schools: The Impact of Communities* (New York: Basic Books, 1987), pp. 6–10.

111. David Perkins, *Smart Schools: Better Thinking and Learning for Every Child* (New York: Free Press, 1992), pp. 43–72.

112. Arthur G. Powell, *Lessons from Privilege: The American Prep School Tradition* (Harvard University Press, 1996), pp. 239–47; Bryk and others, *Catholic Schools and the Common Good,* pp. 274–94.

113. John E. Chubb and Terry M. Moe, *Politics, Markets, and America's Schools* (Brookings Press, 1990), pp. 190–91.

114. Jim Collins, *Good to Great and the Social Sectors: A Monograph to Accompany Good to Great* (New York: Harper-Collins, 2005), pp. 17–23.

115. Milton Friedman, *Capitalism and Freedom* (1962, repr., University of Chicago Press, 2002), pp. 85–98.

116. E. Edmund Reutter Jr. and Robert R. Hamilton, *The Law of Public Education* (New York: Foundation Press, 1976), p. 14.

117. Robert P. Giloth, *Workforce Intermediaries for the Twenty-First Century* (Temple University Press, 2004), p. 372.

118. Harry J. Holzer, "Raising Job Quality and Skills for American Workers: Creating More-Effective Education and Workforce Development Systems in the States," The Hamilton Project, Policy Brief 2011–10 (Brookings Institution, November 2011), p. 5.

119. Ronald. L. Jacobs and Joshua D. Hawley, "The Emergence of 'Workforce Development': Definition, Conceptual Boundaries, and Implications," in *International Handbook of Education for the Changing World of Work,* vol. 1, edited by R. Maclean and D. Wilson (Springer, 2009), pp. 2537–552; W. Norton Grubb and Lorraine M. McDonnell, "Combating Program Fragmentation: Local Systems of Vocational Education and Job Training," *Journal of Policy Analysis and Management* 15 (1996): 252–70; Kellie Isbell and others, "Involving Employers in Training: Best Practices," Research and Evaluation Report Series 97-I (Washington, D.C.: Education Resources Information Center, 1997); Kellie Isbell and others, "Involving Employers in Training: Case Studies," Research and Evaluation Report Series 97-J (Washington, D.C.: Education Resources Information Center, 1997).

120. Anthony P. Carnevale, "Beyond Consensus: Much Ado about Job Training," *Brookings Review* 17, no. 4 (Fall 1999): 40–43.

121. Joshua D. Hawley, Lynn McCormick, and Edwin Meléndez, "The Core Model: What Factors Influence Associational Involvement in Workforce Development?" (Boston: Jobs for the Future, 2005); Joshua D. Hawley and Judith C. Taylor, "Business Associations and Workforce Development: Implications for Human Resource Development" (Boston: Jobs for the Future, 2003).

122. Of course those organizations that find ways to diversify their funding streams have shown greater resiliency during times of contracting government spending and adapt

to changing policy demands and economic fluctuations much more readily. See M. Bryna Sanger, "Competing for Contracts: Nonprofit Survival in an Age of Privatization," in *Communities and Workforce Development,* edited by Edwin Meléndez (Kalamazoo, Mich.: Upjohn Institute for Employment Research, 2004), p. 43.

123. Holzer, "Raising Job Quality and Skills for American Workers," p. 5.

124. Grubb and McDonnell, "Combating Program Fragmentation."

125. Scott Cheney, "Keeping Competitive: Hiring, Training, and Retaining Qualified Workers" (Washington, D.C.: U.S. Chamber of Commerce, Center for Workforce Preparation, 2001) (www.workforceatm.org/sections/pdf/2001/KeepingCompetitive. pdf); Judy McGregor, David Tweed, and Richard Pech, "Human Capital in the New Economy: Devil's Bargain?" *Journal of Intellectual Capital* 5 (2004): 153; Carl E. Van Horn and Aaron R. Fichtner, "An Evaluation of State-Subsidized, Firm-Based Training: The Workforce Development Partnership Program," *International Journal of Manpower* 24 (2003): 97.

126. Under the Obama administration, there have been significant investments in community colleges, including $500 million through the Trade Adjustment Assistance Community College and Career Training Initiative. Trade Adjustment Assistance Community College and Career Training, Division B, Title I, Subtitle I of the American Recovery and Reinvestment Act of 2009, P.L.111-5, codified at 19 U.S.C. §§ 2372–2372a. In his 2012 State of the Union address, the president announced plans for another $8 billion investment for the Community College to Career Fund. That program would create new partnerships between community colleges and businesses to train 2 million workers for jobs in high-growth and high-demand industries. See transcript of the Remarks by the President, 2012 State of the Union Address (www.whitehouse.gov/the-press-office/2012/01/24/remarks-president-state-union-address). Edwin Meléndez, "Matching the Disadvantaged to Job Opportunities: Structural Explanations for the Past Successes of the Center for Employment Training," *Economic Development Quarterly* 12, no. 1 (1998): 3–11; Edwin Meléndez, Luis K. Falcon, Carlos Suarez-Boulangger, Lynn McCormick, and Alexandra de Montrichard, "Community Colleges, Welfare Reform, and Workforce Development," in *Communities and Workforce Development,* p. 298.

127. Meléndez and others, "Community Colleges, Welfare Reform, and Workforce Development," pp. 299–300.

128. B. A. Weisbrod, "The Future of the Nonprofit Sector: Its Entwining with Private Enterprise and Government," *Journal of Policy Analysis and Management* 16 (1997): 541–55; Judith L. Bosscher, "Commercialization in Nonprofits: Tainted Value?" *SPNA Review* 5, issue 1 (2009).

129. Stacey A. Sutton, "Corporate-Community Workforce Development Collaborations," in *Communities and Workforce Development,* p. 446.

130. Sutton, "Corporate-Community Workforce Development Collaborations," p. 440.

131. Beverly Takahashi and Edwin Meléndez, "Union-Sponsored Workforce Development Initiatives," in *Communities and Workforce Development,* p. 140–41.

132. Giloth, *Workforce Intermediaries for the Twenty-First Century,* p. 7.

133. Holzer, "Raising Job Quality and Skills for American Workers," p. 12.

134. Giloth, *Workforce Intermediaries for the Twenty-First Century,* p. 7.

135. Some argue that Congress's adoption of welfare reform legislation also had a major impact on the not-for-profit sector, which provides workforce development and training services. The shift to a work-first approach to welfare has forced many service providers to transform from a supply side, training-and-education-first philosophy to one that incorporates the needs of job seekers and employers and focuses on finding entry-level jobs for clients, even before they have received education or training.

136. Until the infusion of stimulus funds from the ARRA in 2009, the level of funding for WIA had steadily declined each year. Goodwill Industries reports that the level of combined funding that the Bush administration proposed for WIA for fiscal year 2009 was 15 percent less than the funding level for the previous fiscal year (Goodwill Industries, "Public Policy Fact Sheet," June 2008). The decrease in funding had a significant impact on those nonprofits that do not have diversified sources of funding. A substantial number of them likely fall into this category: by 1982 almost half of the employment and training services financed by the federal government were delivered by nonprofits. Between 1992 and 1998 public support for employment and training nonprofits grew by 44 percent. A 1997 study of nonprofit social service organizations indicates that those nonprofits received over 52 percent of their revenue from government sources. See Linda M. Lampkin and Thomas H. Pollak, *The New Nonprofit Almanac and Desk Reference: The Essential Facts and Figures for Managers, Researchers and Volunteers* (Washington, D.C.: Urban Institute Press, 2002), table 5.8, pp.100–101. "This figure probably underestimates the percentage among employment and training providers, where nonprofits still provide the bulk of services to state and local governments and for whom government funding historically made up the single largest source of funding." See Sanger, "Competing for Contracts," p. 43.

137. Robert P. Giloth, "Lessons for a New Context: Workforce Development in an Era of Economic Challenge" (Baltimore, Md.: Annie E. Casey Foundation, March 26, 2009), p. 12.

138. Sanger, "Competing for Contracts," pp. 38–39.

139. Giloth, *Workforce Intermediaries for the Twenty-First Century,* p. 12.

140. Edwin Meléndez, "Communities and Workforce Development in the Era of Devolution," in *Communities and Workforce Development,* p. 14.

141. Holzer, "Raising Job Quality and Skills for American Workers," p. 9; Carolyn J. Heinrich, Peter R. Mueser, Kenneth R. Troske, Kyung-Seong Jeon, Daver C. Kahvecioglu, "New Estimates of Public Employment and Training Program Net Impacts: A Nonexperimental Evaluation of the Workforce Investment Act Program," Discussion Paper 4569 (Bonn, Germany: Institute for the Study of Labor,November 2009); Carolyn J. Heinrich and Christopher King, "How Effective Are Workforce Development Programs?" paper presented at the 40th Anniversary Conference of the Ray Marshall Center, University of Texas at Austin, October 19, 2010; Harry Holzer, "Workforce Development Programs as an Antipoverty Strategy: What Do We Know? What Should We Do?" in *Changing Poverty, Changing Policies,* edited by Maria Cancian and Sheldon Danziger (New York: Russell Sage Foundation, 2009).

142. See Carolyn J. Heinrich, "Organizational Form and Performance: An Empirical Investigation of Nonprofit and For-Profit Job-Training Service Providers," *Journal of Policy Analysis and Management* 19, no. 2 (2000): 233–61.

143. Sanger, "Competing for Contracts," p. 60.

144. Sanger, "Competing for Contracts," p. 45; Chicago Jobs Council, "Recommendations for Chicago's Local Plan Title I of the Workforce Investment Act of 1998" (2000); David M. Kennedy, "The Ladder and the Scale: Commitment and Accountability at Project Match" (Cambridge, Mass.: Harvard University, 1992).

145. Meléndez, "Communities and Workforce Development in the Era of Devolution," p. 14. Those providers that lack the resources to purchase and implement sufficient technology and management systems may be unable to demonstrate the effectiveness of their programs to funders, even if the programs are effective. In a July 2008 interview with Matthew McGuire, former chair of the board of directors for Public Private Ventures, now assistant to the secretary and director of the office of business liaison at the U.S. Department of Commerce, he spoke about his experience at Public Private Ventures: "Something that's one- to

three-years-old could be working fantastically, but they don't have all the things in place to show that it's working well. It may not be responding in terms of numbers immediately because people are overwhelmed. It may not be tracking [the] data, [its] IT systems may be a wreck. . . . Where if you get a more mature organization, they can be running the exact same program, but they'll have all those other things in place that will make them look to the evaluator as though they are much more successful."

146. Sanger, "Competing for Contracts," pp. 61–62.

147. Ramón Borges-Méndez and Edwin Meléndez, "CBOs and the One-Stop Career Center System," in *Communities and Workforce Development,* p. 106.

148. Borges-Méndez and Meléndez, "CBOs and the One-Stop Career Center System," p. 109.

149. Meléndez, "Communities and Workforce Development in the Era of Devolution," pp. 15–16.

150. Sanger, "Competing for Contracts," pp. 63–64; Carol Clyner, Brandon Roberts, and Julie Strawn, "State Policies and Programs Promoting Low-Wage Workers' Steady Employment and Advancement," in *Low-Wage Workers in the New Economy,* edited by Richard Kazis and Marc S. Miller (Washington, D.C.: Urban Institute, 2001), pp. 169–79.

151. The Second Chance Act attempts to do so by expanding the ways in which state and local governments can fund programs that provide job training and related services to people who are released from prison.

152. Robert Wordlaw, Chicago Jobs Council, telephone interview with author, December 2000. The Chicago Jobs Council is a community coalition dedicated to helping community-based organizations prepare low-income Chicago residents to enter and to advance in the workforce.

153. Sanger, "Competing for Contracts," p. 60.

154. Since the implementation of WIA, there has been an increase in the number of workforce intermediaries. Although some participating nonprofit organizations may find it difficult to access WIA funds because they come from ITA vouchers and are driven by consumer choice, successful nonprofits engaged in long-term or sector workforce development projects are finding and drawing upon multiple funding sources. See Sarah Griffen, "Sustaining the Promise: Realizing the Potential of Workforce Intermediaries and Sector Projects" (Boston: National Fund for Workforce Solutions, December 2008), pp. 8, 17.

155. Sanger, "Competing for Contracts," p. 60.

156. Heinrich, "Organizational Form and Performance: An Empirical Investigation of Nonprofit and For-Profit Job-Training Service Providers."

157. Griffen, "Sustaining the Promise," p. 32.

158. Hawley, McCormick, and Meléndez, "The Core Model: What Factors Influence Associational Involvement in Workforce Development?" p. 747; Griffen, "Sustaining the Promise," pp. 26–27.

159. Borges-Méndez and Meléndez, "CBOs and the One-Stop Career Center System," pp. 102–103.

160. Giloth, *Workforce Intermediaries for the Twenty-First Century,* p. 15; Ronald D'Amico, Kate Dunham, Annelies Goger, Charles Lea, Nicole Rigg, Sheryl Ude, Andrew Wiegand, "Findings from a Study of One-Stop Self-Services: A Case Study Approach," Final Report (Oakland, Calif.: Social Policy Research Associates, December 2009), p. III16–III18.

161. Louis S. Jacobson, "Strengthening One-Stop Career Centers: Helping More Unemployed Workers Find Jobs and Build Skills," Discussion Paper, Hamilton Project (Washington, D.C.: Brookings Institution, April 2009), p. 8, n. 3.

162. Jacobson, "Strengthening One-Stop Career Centers," pp. 19, 107–10. "Small CBOs, mainly recently founded ones, seem to be more likely to become subordinate subcontractors to the extent that they have less resources and organizational capital to invest in program restructuring without significant shifts in their overall mission objectives." See Borges-Méndez and Meléndez, "CBOs and the One-Stop Career Center System," p. 107.

163. Sanger, "Competing for Contracts," p. 62.

164. Robert P. Giloth, "Learning from the Field: Economic Growth and Workforce Development in the 1990s," *Economic Development Quarterly* 14 (4) (2000): 354.

165. Meléndez, "Communities and Workforce Development in the Era of Devolution," p. 14.

166. Giloth, "Lessons for a New Context," p. 12–13.

167. Giloth, "Lessons for a New Context," p. 4.

168. Holzer, "Raising Job Quality and Skills for American Workers," p. 6–7; Griffen, "Sustaining the Promise," p. 2.

169. Annie E. Casey Foundation, "Strengthening Workforce Policies: Applying the Lessons of the Jobs Initiatives to Five Key Challenges" (Baltimore, Md., 2007), p. 1–2. The greater attention to the mismatch can be attributed, at least in part, to the inclusion of concerns for employers' needs or the demand side when one is framing workforce development and training programs and policies. See Sutton, "Corporate-Community Workforce Development Collaborations," p. 443; see also Giloth, *Workforce Intermediaries for the Twenty-First Century,* p. 11: "Many low-skilled jobseekers do not have the basic skills, job readiness skills, or informal network connections required to navigate today's labor market. . . . Indeed, many inner-city residents do not have the necessary skills, role models for advancing in the labor market, nor faith in training institutions and in the payoff of investing in their own human capital. The pressures of supporting a family, the current policy environment of reducing social welfare supports, and the inflexibility of many training institutions reinforce the unwillingness of many working poor families to seek higher paying skilled employment."

170. See Judy McGregor, David Tweed, Richard Pech, "Human Capital in the New Economy: Devil's Bargain?" *Journal of Intellectual Capital* 5 (1) (2004): 153; Phillip Moss and Chris Tilly, *Stories Employers Tell: Race, Skill and Hiring in America* (New York: Russell Sage Foundation, 2001); Barbara F. Reskin, "Occupational Segregation by Race and Ethnicity among Women Workers," in *Latinas and African American Women at Work: Gender and Economic Inequality,* edited by I. Browne (New York: Russell Sage Foundation, 1999), pp.183–204; Michael A. Stoll, Stephen Raphael, and Harry J. Holzer, "Black Job Applicants and the Hiring Officer's Race," *Industrial and Labor Relations Review* 57 (2) (2004): 267–87. According to Stacey A. Sutton, "Racial and ethnic minorities pursuing entry-level jobs frequently have the misfortune of being connected to the wrong types of networks" and lack the resources and connections to obtain information about living wage jobs; see Sutton, "Corporate-Community Workforce Development Collaborations," p. 444. See also Kazis and Miller, *Low-Wage Workers in the New Economy;* Harry J. Holzer, "Employer Skills Demand and Labor Market Outcomes for Blacks and Women," *Industrial and Labor Relations Review* 52 (1) (1998): 82–98.

171. Frank Levy and Richard J. Murnane, *The New Division of Labor: How Computers Are Creating the Next Job Market* (Princeton University Press, 2004), pp. 1–9.

172. Evidence suggests that important progress has been made under the law, however. See Giloth, *Workforce Intermediaries for the Twenty-First Century,* p. 17.

173. Annie E. Casey Foundation, "Strengthening Workforce Policies," p.1. Again, Giloth sums up the situation aptly: "On the firm side, many established companies have closed their

human resource departments, outsourced entry-level jobs to contingent workers, flattened job ladders in the search of lowering costs and higher productivity, and deskilled jobs at the same time they adopt new technologies. Cutbacks and aging workforces have left them unprepared to incorporate new workers, many of whom come from more diverse backgrounds than their current workforce. Smaller firms . . . share similar problems, but with fewer resources and frequently without a history of hiring entry-level workers. . . . Both firms and jobseekers are further inhibited by their sheer spatial separation—firms in the suburbs and jobseekers in inner city neighborhoods. Low levels of car ownership, driver's license revocations and penalties, inflexible and time intensive public transportation, and the necessities of childcare and family support make the matching of good jobs and low-skilled jobseekers even more difficult, even for the many job openings in central cities." See Giloth, *Workforce Intermediaries for the Twenty-First Century,* p. 11.

174. Fred Dedrick, "The National Fund for Workforce Solutions: The Impact and Challenges of Its Workforce Partnership Model," *Cascade, A Community Development Publication* 79 (Winter 2012): 10–11.

175. Giloth, "Lessons for a New Context," p. 9.

176. Holzer, "Raising Job Quality and Skills for American Workers," p. 6–7.

177. Giloth, "Lessons for a New Context," p.13; Griffen, "Sustaining the Promise," p. 3.

178. Scott Cheney, "Keeping Competitive"; Paul Osterman and others, "Reframing the Debate," in *Working in America, A Blueprint for the New Labor Market,* edited by Paul Osterman, Thomas Kochan, Richard M. Locke, Michael J. Piore (MIT Press, 2002), pp. 1–26; Carl Van Horn and Aaron Fichtner, "An Evaluation of State-Subsidized, Firm-Based Training: The Workforce Development Partnership Program," *International Journal of Manpower* 24 (1) (2003): 97.

179. Meléndez, "Communities and Workforce Development in the Era of Devolution," p. 17.

180. "One advantage to having unions provide training is their access to on-the-ground skills and experience among their members. Union members 'get' the working environment because they are workers as well as training providers. Moreover, they understand how the skills they are teaching are used in the workplace." See Stacey Wagner, "Unions as Partners: Expanding the Role of Organized Labor in Workforce Development" (Boston: National Fund for Workforce Solutions, November 2010), p. 3.

181. Sanger, "Competing for Contracts," p. 39.

182. Meléndez, "Communities and Workforce Development in the Era of Devolution," p. 17.

183. Sanger, "Competing for Contracts," pp. 39–42.

184. Meléndez, "Communities and Workforce Development in the Era of Devolution," p. 17.

185. Working for America Institute, "Fulfilling the Promise of the Workforce Investment Act: A Survey of Labor Representatives on Workforce Investment Boards" (Washington, D.C., November 2009), p. 8; Holzer, "Raising Job Quality and Skills for American Workers," p. 7.

186. Giloth, "Lessons for a New Context," p.13; Griffen, "Sustaining the Promise," p. 3.

187. Robert R. Reich, *Involving Employers in Training: A Literature Review* (Washington, D.C.: U.S. Department of Labor, Employment and Training Administration, 1996); Anthony P. Carnevale, "The Learning Enterprise," *Training and Development Journal* (February 1989): 26–33.

188. Edwin Meléndez and Bennett Harrison, "Matching the Disadvantaged to Job Opportunities: Structural Explanations for the Past Successes of the Center for Employment

Training," *Economic Development Quarterly* 12 (1) (1998): 3–11; Paul Osterman, "Employer-Centered Training for International Competitiveness," *Journal of Policy Analysis and Management* 12 (1998): 456–77.

189. Giloth, "Lessons for a New Context," p. 13; Griffen, "Sustaining the Promise," p. 3; Heinrich and others, "New Estimates of Public Employment and Training Program Net Impacts"; Heinrich and King, "How Effective Are Workforce Development Programs?"; Holzer, "Workforce Development Programs as an Antipoverty Strategy."

190. Rosanna Marquez, Eleanor Foundation, interview with author May 2008.

191. Carnevale, "The Learning Enterprise."

192. Maria Kim and Brandon Crow, Cara Program, Chicago, Illinois, interview with author May 2008.

193. Goodwill Industries International, "1999 Annual Report for Goodwill Industries of Southeastern Wisconsin and Metropolitan Chicago, Inc." (Rockville, Md., 1999).

194. Sanger, "Competing for Contracts," p. 51.

195. Griffen, "Sustaining the Promise," p. 3.

196. Maureen Conway, Amy Blair, Steven L. Dawson, and Linda Dworak-Munoz, *Sector Strategies for Low-Income People: Lessons from the Field* (Washington, D.C.: Aspen Institute, 2007), p.11.

197. Giloth, "Lessons for a New Context," pp. 9–10.

198. Griffen, "Sustaining the Promise," pp. 26–27; Fred Dedrick, "The National Fund for Workforce Solutions: The Impact and Challenges of Its Workforce Partnership Model," *Cascade* 79 (Winter 2012): 10–11.

199. Meléndez, "Communities and Workforce Development in the Era of Devolution," pp. 15–16.

200. Holzer, "Raising Job Quality and Skills for American Workers," pp. 7–8.

201. Giloth, "Lessons for a New Context," p. 12.

202. Giloth, "Lessons for a New Context," p. 12.

203. Giloth, "Lessons for a New Context," p. 13.

204. Maria Kim and Brandon Crow, Cara Program, Chicago, Illinois, interview with author, May 2008.

205. Cara Program, "Performance Update as of December 31, 2011" (Chicago, December 2011).

206. Sutton, "Corporate-Community Workforce Development Collaborations," pp. 439–71.

4

Social Services

STEVEN RATHGEB SMITH

Nonprofit social service agencies are a central and vitally important part of
America's social policy agenda and service delivery system. The number
of nonprofit social service agencies has risen rapidly since the late 1990s, reflecting many key trends in social policy. Welfare reform in 1996 sharply reduced
the importance of cash assistance for the poor and concomitantly greatly
boosted the importance of effective community-based social services to help
poor and disadvantaged citizens.[1] The Bush administration aggressively pushed
government funding of faith- and community-based agencies that provide
social services as a strategy to resolve urgent social problems, and the Obama
administration continues to seek partnerships with local community- and faith-
based organizations through a variety of important federal initiatives, including the newly created Office of Social Innovation, which has funded many
high-profile social service agencies around the country. In addition, programs

The author is indebted to the Nancy Bell Evans Center on Nonprofits and Philanthropy at the
University of Washington's Evans School of Public Affairs, the Georgetown Public Policy Institute,
and the Aspen Institute for funding in support of the research for this chapter. Excellent research
assistance was provided by Luisa Boyarski, Timothy Cormier, Lauren Marra, Kate Simons, and
Nina Tantrapol. The author is also grateful to Scott Allard, Putnam Barber, Elizabeth Boris, Harold
W. Demone, Jr., Julita Eleveld, Jack Krauskopf, Kathy Kretman, Lester M. Salamon, Cory Sbar-
baro, and Melissa Walker for their feedback on earlier versions of this chapter.

providing community service such as those of AmeriCorps, Teach for America, YouthBuild, and City Year have received broad support from across the political spectrum. The concerted push by policymakers and advocates to develop community care for the mentally ill, developmentally disabled, and aged over a period of many years has led to the establishment of thousands of new nonprofit community agencies and programs supported extensively with government funds. United Way chapters around the country rely almost exclusively on nonprofit social welfare agencies to solve urgent social problems. And private grant-giving foundations—which grew substantially until the financial crisis hit—depend heavily upon local nonprofit social service agencies for their social-purpose grant making.

The vital role of nonprofit social service organizations within American social policy fits with the discourse on privatization, devolution, and the long-standing view of the United States as a liberal welfare state regime reliant upon private philanthropy and voluntarism to deal with social problems.[2] However, this viewpoint tends to mask the extensive direct and indirect government support of nonprofit social service agencies and the broad expansion of social services in recent decades. Indeed, major federal funding programs such as Medicaid are an increasingly important funder of many valued social service programs.

Unfortunately, this public funding support is now beset by uncertainty. Faced with severe budget problems caused by the recession, state and local governments are slashing spending to countless agencies. Major federal programs face uncertain futures because of concerns about taxes and the federal budget deficit. Adding further to the fiscal pressure on nonprofits, the assets of foundations have declined, leading them to cut their grant levels. Individual donors, too, are facing declines in their asset values at a time of growing layoffs and economic uncertainty. A by-product of this dramatic shift in the revenue of nonprofit social service organizations is heightened competition for public and private funding resulting from the sharp rise in the number of nonprofit agencies.

Against the backdrop of these important organizational and economic trends, this chapter examines in detail the characteristics of nonprofit social service agencies and situates these agencies within broader changes in American social policy. The basic argument aligns with the work of researchers who suggest that the characteristics of the nonprofit social services are substantially dependent upon public policy and, more broadly, the welfare state.[3] In particular, in this chapter, I devote special attention to the different roles and pressures faced by nonprofit social service agencies in light of the four impulses affecting the future of nonprofit agencies: voluntarism, professionalism, civic activism, and commercialism. The next section offers a detailed mapping of the universe of nonprofit social services followed by an overview of the development of nonprofit social service organizations, primarily since the 1960s. I subsequently examine important challenges and opportunities facing nonprofit social service agencies. I conclude with suggestions for social policy and nonprofit organizations, taking into account the increased centrality of nonprofit service agencies at a time of economic crisis, increased competition, and government cutbacks.

Mapping Nonprofit Social Services

The field of nonprofit social services is diverse with many sub-sectors. Indeed, the makeup of this field remains a matter of dispute. The term "social services" came into widespread usage in the post–World War II period, especially in the United Kingdom, where the term "personal social services" was used to refer to the governmentally supported provision of a "wide range of services designed to promote the health and well-being of the community."[4] In the United States, "social services" generally refers to the social care provided to deprived, neglected, or handicapped children and youths, the needy elderly, the mentally ill and developmentally disabled, and disadvantaged adults. These services include daycare, counseling, job training, child protection, foster care, residential treatment, homemakers, rehabilitation, and sheltered workshop assistance.[5] Nonetheless, the boundaries of social services are increasingly fluid, especially given the pressure for social services to be more fully integrated into other public and nonprofit programs such as health, housing, and corrections. At its core, however, the social services universe encompasses a diverse array of programs designed to enhance the life of families and individuals, including community care for the aged and individuals with developmental disabilities and mental illness, and programs to address domestic violence, AIDS, poverty, homelessness, drug and alcohol addiction, and re-entry into society from prison.

Types of Organizations

Nonprofit organizations are on the front lines of the social services field. However, these organizations vary greatly in scale, character, and degree of formality. Indeed, it is possible to distinguish three broad categories of nonprofit social service agencies.

Informal Organizations

A significant number of nonprofit social service agencies are informal community-based groups and associations. Typically these groups lack legal status and depend upon small cash and in-kind donations to support their activities. Some also collect fees for service that vary greatly depending upon the circumstances.

Classic examples of such informal associations are self-help groups such as Alcoholics Anonymous and support groups for survivors of diseases such as cancer. These informal groups usually accept no external grant funds and depend completely on volunteers, although they may receive periodic support from more formal institutions and may collaborate with established public and nonprofit institutions.[6] Other social service associations that can exist as informal organizations are soup kitchens and shelters (especially programs that are affiliated with churches), daycare programs, recreational programs, and emergency assistance. Many churches also have programs that do not exist as formal organizational entities apart from the church. For instance, an interfaith soup kitchen may operate in different locations during the week and depend completely on volunteers from the member churches' congregations.

Formal Agencies

Beyond these informal entities are a wide variety of agencies with formal legal status as 501(c)(3) public charities. At one end of the formal continuum are large, multiservice agencies with diversified funding that can include sizable private donations and endowment funds as well as substantial government funds. Agencies in this category include many long-standing child and family service agencies, Catholic Charities, Lutheran Social Services, Jewish Family Services, Volunteers of America, the Boys and Girls Club, Goodwill Industries, the American Red Cross, and the Salvation Army. These agencies usually have large boards with up to forty or fifty directors. They are often members of larger national associations such as the Child Welfare League of America, the Alliance for Children and Families, or the YWCA. These organizations vary in their public and private revenue mix, but many of these organizations grew substantially between 1990 and 2008 as a result of increased government funding of their core services such as foster care, community care, and welfare-to-work programs. Other organizations, such as the Salvation Army and the YWCA, differ greatly in their service offerings, depending upon the policies and history of the local chapter. Some Salvation Army and YWCA chapters, for instance, receive substantial government support, whereas other chapters refuse to accept any government funds and thus tend to have a narrower range of services.

The "formal organization" category includes a number of recent additions to the nonprofit social services field that started as informal agencies and then became more formalized organizations with nonprofit legal status after the agency was awarded a sizable public or private grant. Large and small agencies of this type include AIDS service agencies, domestic violence shelters, rape crisis centers, immigrant assistance agencies, drug and alcohol treatment programs, community care for the developmentally disabled, mentally ill, and the aged, early childhood programs, and services for delinquent youths. Many of these agencies rely heavily on government funds; others depend upon modest private grants and donations. Overall these agencies tend to be undercapitalized, with modest budgets and relatively small boards of eight to fifteen directors. They face formidable challenges in attracting and recruiting talented staff and effective board members. Furthermore, they may be highly dependent on a single government agency, foundation, or donor for their funding, which can create serious imbalances in power and recurrent management problems. In the current fiscal environment, it can also lead to severe program instability. Indeed, many social service agencies experience substantial volatility in their revenues from year to year.[7]

Scope of the Nonprofit Social Services Sector

Because informal organizations do not have legal status, it is virtually impossible to accurately estimate how many of these informal groups exist. Available research does indicate, though, that in many service categories where voluntarism and self-help are important, such as daycare, emergency assistance, and recreation for youths, informal groups and associations are very important, even though they may individually provide a relatively modest level of services.

An important step in the formalization process is legal incorporation and registration with the Internal Revenue Service as a 501(c)(3) organization, eligible for tax-deductible contributions. Reflecting the growth of social services, the National Center for Charitable Statistics (NCCS) at the Urban Institute reports that the number of registered nonprofit human service agencies incorporated as 501(c)(3) organizations grew sharply from 1995 to 2010, more than doubling, to 271,163 The number of reporting agencies, those with revenues above $25,000, rose even faster, from 62,530 to 163, 961, or almost 262 percent.[8] The nonreporting agencies do not provide extensive services and many are completely volunteer organizations such as soup kitchens or a new start-up crime prevention agency in a distressed community. These small organizations can nevertheless play an important, albeit targeted, role in many communities and contribute to the enhanced competition for public and private funding among social service agencies. Further, the widespread interest in capacity building is often directed at the smaller agencies (both reporting and nonreporting), which face resource and staff challenges in responding to the increasing pressures for professionalization and accountability. One drawback of this NCCS dataset is that it also includes programs and services that are not conventionally considered human services, such as camps, sports clubs, and public safety programs. Even so, the data usefully underscore the increase in the number of nonprofit human services agencies in recent years.

Table 4-1, showing the growth of employment in the nonprofit sector, provides an even more vivid picture of the growth of nonprofit and for-profit social services over a longer period of time. These data are from the U.S. Census Bureau, which conducts a comprehensive national survey of economic activity every five years. As indicated in the subtotal for social services, employment in social services agencies rose at an average annual rate of 5 percent over the twenty-five-year period between 1977 and 2002, for a total increase of 203 percent. Behind this dramatic growth lay several factors: the influx of government funding into social services as a result of welfare reform, the expansion of community care, the broad interest in community service, and the growth of private philanthropy. It is significant that between 2002 and 2007 the growth rate of social services appears to have slowed markedly, dropping from an average annual rate of 5 percent over the previous twenty-five years to only 1 percent during the five years from 2002 to 2007. Equally important, the growth rate of employment in for-profit social services outdistanced the growth rate in nonprofit social services in both the earlier period and the more recent one, a topic to which we will return later in the chapter.

The growth trajectory for employees of nonprofit providers of related services, which include home health, family planning, and outpatient mental health and substance abuse, is also noteworthy. As will be discussed in the following pages, the line between traditional social services such as counseling and community care, and health care has become much blurrier in recent years because of the expansion of public funding for services such as mental-health care, outpatient counseling, home health services, and home care. What is apparent from the data provided in table 4-1, however, is that nonprofit employment growth in these fields has been relatively tepid in recent years while for-profit employment has been rising sharply.[9]

These figures underline the important shift that has been under way in the social services field over the past several decades, a shift that has affected both the substance of the services and the type of providers. Until the 1960s, the overwhelming percentage of social service agencies was nonprofit, as exemplified by well-known nonprofits such as the American Red Cross, the Salvation Army, and Goodwill Industries. Beginning in the 1960s, for-profit social service agencies entered many services previously dominated by nonprofits, including child care, home care, home health, mental health, and drug and alcohol treatment. This occurred simultaneously with the rapid growth of programs such as home health and residential care during the 1977–2002 period, reflecting a shift within the universe of social services from traditional social services to social services that overlap, at least to an extent, with health services, partly spurred by financing from Medicaid and Medicare. Indeed, traditional social service programs such as residential foster care or counseling have been eclipsed by the sharp escalation in

Table 4-1. *Employment Trends in Social Services, 1977–2007*

	1977		2002		2007		Compound annual rate of change (percent)	
Type of service	Number	Percent of total number	Number	Percent of total number	Number	Percent of total number	1977– 2002	2002– 07
Social services								
Child daycare[a]	189,918	100.0	751,733	100.0	851,624	100.0	6	3
Nonprofit	102,408	53.9	314,436	41.8	319,144	37.5	5	0
For-profit	87,510	46.1	437,297	58.2	532,480	62.5	7	4
Individual and family services[b]	182,947	100.0	907,796	100.0	1,147,521	100.0	7	5
Nonprofit	167,384	91.5	768,586	84.7	797,269	69.5	6	1
For-profit	15,563	8.5	139,210	15.3	350,252	30.5	9	20
Job training and vocational education[c]	151,525	100.0	317,045	100.0	304,836	100.0	3	−1
Nonprofit	138,368	91.3	283,655	89.5	272,850	89.5	3	−1
For-profit	13,157	8.7	33,390	10.5	31,986	10.5	4	−1
Residential care[b]	184,770	100.0	911,996	100.0	1,026,529	100.0	7	2
Nonprofit	135,144	73.1	537,570	58.9	599,853	58.4	6	2
For-profit	49,626	26.9	374,426	41.1	426,676	41.6	8	3
Emergency relief and miscellaneous services[b]	144,762	100.0	145,929	100.0	164,633	100.0	0	2
Nonprofit	133,169	92.0	144,497	99.0	158,382	96.2	0	2
For-profit	11,593	8.0	1,432	1.0	6,251	3.8	−8	34
Subtotal, social services	853,922	100.0	3,034,499	100.0	3,495,143	100.0	5	3
Nonprofit	676,473	79.2	2,048,744	67.5	2,147,498	61.4	5	1
For-profit	177,449	20.8	985,755	32.5	1,347,645	38.6	7	6
Related services								
Home health[c]	n.a.	n.a.	777,128	100.0	972,791	100.0		5
Nonprofit	n.a.	n.a.	224,021	28.8	223,583	23.0		0
For-profit	n.a.	n.a.	553,107	71.2	749,208	77.0		6
Family planning[b]	n.a.	n.a.	18,439	100.0	22,228	100.0		4
Nonprofit	n.a.	n.a.	14,675	79.6	16,708	75.2		3
For-profit	n.a.	n.a.	3,764	20.4	5,520	24.8		8
Outpatient mental health and substance abuse[b]	n.a.	n.a.	165,089	100.0	194,204	100.0		3
Nonprofit	n.a.	n.a.	138,312	83.8	153,773	79.2		2
For-profit	n.a.	n.a.	26,777	16.2	40,431	20.8		9
Subtotal, related services	n.a.	n.a.	960,656	100.0	1,189,223	100.0		4
Nonprofit	n.a.	n.a.	377,008	39.2	394,064	33.1		1
For-profit	n.a.	n.a.	583,648	60.8	795,159	66.9		6
Total services	n.a.	n.a.	3,995,155	100.0	4,684,366	100.0		3
Nonprofit	n.a.	n.a.	2,425,752	60.7	2,541,562	54.3		1
For-profit	n.a.	n.a.	1,569,403	39.3	2,142,804	45.7		6

Sources: U.S. Census Bureau, Economic Census, selected years.

Qualifiers: Data from 2002 and 2007 use the new NAICS (North American Industry Classification System) codes, which replaced the earlier SIC (Standard Industrial Classification) codes for specific service categories.

a. 2002 and 2007 NAICS data almost comparable to SIC data (within 3 percentage points of sales or receipts from SIC).

b. 2002 and 2007 NAICS data are not comparable (cannot be estimated within three percentage points of SIC data).

c. 2002 and 2007 NAICS data are comparable to or derivable from SIC data.

health-related programs. Moreover, many traditional social service agencies, such as Catholic Charities, Lutheran Social Services, and the Jewish Family Services, now offer these health-related social services including home health. But, as suggested by table 4-1, for-profit organizations have increased their overall role in service provision in the 2002–07 period, while the nonprofit role has diminished slightly. For example, in many communities, the field of home health has become dominated by large for-profit providers. The reasons for this changing mix are complex, but relate in part to the growth of government funding through programs such as Medicaid, the expansion of for-profit regional and national chains that have access to capital, and the relatively small size of many newer nonprofits, placing them at a competitive disadvantage vis-à-vis for-profits.

Importantly, though, the nonprofit–for-profit mix can vary widely depending upon the state and locality. For instance, California had a total of 2,829 residential-care agencies in 2007, of which 1,869 were for-profit. In the same year, Connecticut had a total of 532 residential care agencies, of which only 16 were for-profit.[10] (Some for-profit services such as home health are quite prevalent throughout the country.) This great variation in the mix between nonprofits and for-profits generally reflects differences in market conditions in various states ascribable to the historical position of nonprofits and state funding and regulatory policy.

The expansion of nonprofit and for-profit services is also indirectly reflected in the incremental growth of public employment in public welfare. For example, state and local governments employed 491,577 people in the broad category of public welfare in 2007, an increase of 42,970 since 1997 (or just over 10 percent over ten years),[11] despite the growth in public funding of social welfare services broadly defined (at least until 2008). Thus, the expansion of nonprofit (and for-profit) social services does not primarily represent the privatization of previously public social services. Instead, this growth has been mostly in new programs and services. The exception, perhaps, is in mental health and services for the mentally retarded, where the relative decline in public sector employment resulted from a shift from public institutional settings to nonprofit (and for-profit) community care.

Finally, the growth of for-profit services also indirectly reflects the declining importance of private philanthropy as a revenue source for the larger and more formal social service agencies, although some agencies, such as food banks and emergency assistance programs, receive substantial private support. As will be discussed in the following pages, the growth areas in social services do not depend extensively on private philanthropy: child daycare, for example, relies upon client fees and direct and indirect government funding (including vouchers and tax credits), whereas home health and related programs rely heavily upon Medicaid and Medicare and, to a much lesser extent, private fees.

Nonprofit Organizations and Social Services Policy

In the nineteenth century, American social welfare services were actually quite similar to those of many European countries, featuring extensive reliance on voluntary agencies, especially faith-related agencies such as Catholic Charities and the Salvation Army and a dependence on a mix of public funding and private fees.[12] But in the late nineteenth century and first half of the twentieth century, most European countries developed an extensive public safety net. Germany and the Netherlands created tight partnerships between government and voluntary agencies and Denmark and Sweden essentially created a public social service system with nonprofit agencies playing a relatively small niche role.[13] By contrast, the United States at mid-century remained committed to a relatively small, by European standards, government-supported safety net. Thus, in the 1950s the federal government provided extremely limited funding for social services, leaving state and local governments very constrained in terms of their ability to fund social services. The exceptions were very small grant-in-aid programs for child welfare and vocational rehabilitation.[14] State and local governments, to varying extents, funded welfare-related services for the very poor and a network of institutional facilities for the mentally ill, disabled, and elderly poor.[15] With extremely limited federal funding, most state and local governments relied upon their own revenues to fund these programs. Nonprofit social service agencies relied primarily on private donations (especially through the Community Chest, the forerunner of the United Way) and modest fees paid by clients (recipients of the service). Public funding of these nonprofit agencies tended to be restricted to a few specific categories such as child welfare. In any given community, the universe of social service agencies was also dominated by long-standing agencies such as the Salvation Army, Goodwill Industries, the American Red Cross, the Volunteers of America, the Boys and Girls Club, Catholic Charities, and Lutheran Social Services.

This limited public support for social welfare services led many commentators at the time to regard the American welfare state as a "laggard" in comparison to European countries.[16] But this government-nonprofit relationship in social services changed dramatically in the 1960s. During this period, state and local governments were roundly criticized for inequitable and racist policies that denied equal opportunity to countless citizens who needed supportive services.[17] To address these problems, which were perceived as deriving from excessive decentralization to state and local government in the funding and delivery of public services, the Kennedy and Johnson administrations initiated a wide range of social initiatives at the federal level with profound effects on social service delivery. The new federal initiatives had four overlapping purposes: expand opportunity, stimulate citizen action, provide new services, and expand cash-transfer payments.[18] As a result, federal funding for a diverse array of social services delivered at the local level expanded rapidly in the late 1960s and 1970s, from $416 million in 1960 to $8.5 billion in 1980 (in nominal, or noninflation adjusted, dollars).[19]

Although some federal programs provided direct grants to local nonprofit and public organizations, most of the new federal funding took the form of intergovernmental grants to state and local governments. Thus, the federal government would provide a grant to the states for child welfare services (on a formula basis) that was then used by the state and local governments to fund direct services through government agencies or contracted services with local nonprofits. A few federal programs also had matching provisions between the state and federal government. For example, the Public Welfare Amendments of 1962 provided federal funding for 75 percent of the costs of state and local programs providing services to prevent people's dependency on welfare, 25 percent of the costs to be matched by the states. The vague guidelines on eligible services allowed many states to use this federal program to refinance or expand state and local programs as well as eligible nonprofit programs.[20] The amendments of 1962 were open-ended, so that any claim for reimbursement by the states for an eligible client required the federal government to provide the matching funds. This open-ended character and the expansive eligibility standards were key reasons for the dramatic increase in federal social services spending that resulted from these 1962 amendments.

The sharp overall increase in federal social service spending led to the rapid establishment and growth in nonprofit social service organizations, including community mental health centers, community action agencies, new child welfare agencies, drug and alcohol treatment centers, domestic violence programs, legal services for the poor, home care, emergency shelters for youth, and workforce development programs. Most of the funding for these agencies and programs was federal, although the additional spending also spurred more spending by state and local government.[21]

As a result, the federal percentage of total public social service spending grew substantially, leading to a marked shift away from the voluntaristic roots of the nonprofit sector characteristic of the pre-1960s period. One indicator was the beginning of a long-term decline in the reliance of private nonprofit social service agencies on funds from private donative entities such as the United Way. In the 1960s, many agencies receiving United Way grants often relied upon these grants for well over 50 percent of their much more limited total revenue. With the growth of federal funding, the share of agency revenue from the United Way has steadily declined. These same agencies might receive less than 5 percent of their funding from the United Way today. United Way funding has also declined in real terms since the late 1960s, and now most social service agencies in a given community do not receive any United Way funding, a fundamental change from the pre-1960s era.

The rise in federal social service spending occurred through capped categorical grants such as the Community Mental Health Centers Act of 1963 and open-ended programs such as the 1962 Amendments to the Social Security Act.[22] Alarmed at the dramatic rise in spending, Congress capped the latter program at $2.5 billion in federal spending in 1972. Three years later, Congress folded this program into Title XX of the Social Security Act as a capped block grant to the states, which gave the states even greater flexibility in the expenditure of federal funds for social services. The changes enacted by Congress slowed the growth of federal spending on social services, and after 1978, total federal funding started to decline, albeit slowly.[23] In essence, the creation of Title XX was an attempt by Congress to get control of spending for social services.[24]

Implicitly, constraints on spending would also slow the "drift toward universalism," a tendency that started in the early 1960s to broaden eligibility for different social services in a way that began to move the United States toward the European pattern of universal eligibility for various social services.[25] For example, eligibility for services was opened for more individuals of middle-class means, especially if they had a special condition such as mental illness. This shift also encouraged greater professionalism within nonprofit organizations, since federal funding was accompanied by new regulations and expectations regarding the quality of service delivery.

Title XX, then, represented an effort begun in the 1960s to move away from reliance on voluntarism in response to social problems toward more professionalized service delivery, although the reliance on nonprofit agencies remained. At this time, social service agencies did not face substantial competition because of the relatively limited number of agencies in most jurisdictions and the long-standing relationships many social service agencies enjoyed with state and local officials. Consequently, little incentive existed for nonprofits to be engaged in commercial activity and to generate substantial earned income.

The election of Ronald Reagan brought important changes to this evolving pattern of federal funding of social services, however. Under the Omnibus Budget Reconciliation Act (OBRA) of 1981, funding for social services was cut and many categorical federal grants were consolidated into the Social Services Block Grant (SSBG). Overall, the Reagan administration hoped that block grants and other policy changes could reverse the rise of federal spending and expansion of eligibility for social services. These policy changes meant that many local social service agencies almost immediately lost substantial funding.

These Reagan administration changes were the culmination of an effort by conservatives and many members of Congress to reconfigure social services to fit the pre-1960s emphasis on voluntarism, dependence on state and local funding, and private charity. The political problem with this new approach was that the new federal role had created an entirely new configuration of interests in social services policy. First, thousands of new nonprofit human services agencies had been established since the early 1960s; these agencies were now vocal advocates of continued public funding. Second, a new constituency existed for expanded services as the growth of federal spending was encouraged by advocates for the poor, disabled, and disadvantaged, many of them family members seeking more services for their relatives and children. Third, federal spending had created another important constituency for federal social service spending: state and local government officials, especially the administrators of line agencies such as state departments of social services. Federal spending directly supported many positions in these agencies as well as many private nonprofit agencies on which these agencies depended for vital public services. Thus, the expansion of subcontracting during the 1960s and 1970s had created relationships, often tight, between state and local agencies and nonprofit service providers in support of more funding. Fourth, the courts had slowly started to get behind expanded social services in the community, especially through landmark court decisions in the 1970s that mandated deinstitutionalization of the developmentally disabled and mentally ill from large state institutions to community-based settings.[26]

This new configuration of political interests, as well as the rising demand for services such as community care for the disabled, encouraged nonprofit agencies and state and local government officials to seek alternative sources of funds to offset declining revenue from federal programs such as SSBG.[27] One such source was Medicaid, the program created in 1965 as the health program for the poor. Until the 1980s, Medicaid was a very limited source of funding for traditional social services.

But starting in the 1980s, this changed sharply.[28] This is vividly evident in services for the developmentally disabled and mentally ill. In 1980, most government funding for services for the developmentally disabled were state dollars, primarily for institution-based programs. Now most public spending for such programs goes for community-based programs such as home care, apartment-style residential living, and employment training, much of it funded primarily by Medicaid, especially through the Home and Community Based Waiver program (which allowed states to fund community programs for individuals who did not meet the very stringent existing Medicaid eligibility rules). In just the period 1999 through 2006, the number of recipients in this waiver program rose from 1.9 million to 2.9 million.[29] In essence, Medicaid has supported the shift from a public institutional system for the developmentally disabled operated by state government with state employees to a community-based system provided by nonprofit and for-profit service agencies.[30] To an increasing degree, Medicaid also funds child welfare, home care, hospice care, counseling, residential foster care, drug and alcohol treatment, and services for the mentally ill (although the extent of coverage varies from state to state).[31]

In addition, other new sources of federal financing enacted as part of the landmark welfare reform legislation of 1996 spurred the expansion of job training, child care, and other social services. This legislation replaced the older Aid to Families with Dependent Children (AFDC) program with the Temporary Assistance for Needy Families (TANF) program. As part of these legislative initiatives, the federal government also gave greater administrative discretion to state and local governments to spend the new money, including much greater flexibility by local administrators to shift money from cash assistance to services. With these new requirements and funding streams, the welfare rolls and the expenditure of funds on welfare-related programs changed dramatically: the number of families and teen parents on welfare dropped and the share of AFDC and TANF dollars spent on direct cash assistance declined rapidly, from 73 percent to 44 percent between 1996 and 2001, while the share spent on social services rose.[32] Thus, in 1993, for every dollar spent by state and local governments on cash assistance (primarily through AFDC), $1.24 was spent on social services and $3.63 on medical assistance. By 2002, for every dollar of cash assistance, $3.52 was spent on social services and $9.96 on medical assistance.[33] Overall, a large percentage of this additional service funding went to support services provided by nonprofit organizations, including daycare, welfare-to-work, job training, and counseling.[34]

In addition to Medicaid and TANF-related funding, other federal programs for at-risk youths, community services, drug and alcohol treatment, prisoner reentry, and community care also experienced substantial growth. The overall effect of the rise in federal funding for social services was fiscal centralization, even as the federal government was devolving responsibility for service decisions to the states—which were often given substantial discretion on specific spending decisions for the federal grant money, often channeled through state and local governments.[35]

To an extent, the shift toward fiscal centralization is welcomed by nonprofit agencies and state and local governments because it overcomes some of the constraints of state and local funding. For instance, the federal government contributed 62.8 percent of total state and local government spending on social welfare (including social services, cash assistance, and medical assistance) as of 2007.[36] Medicaid is a critical part of this prominent role for the federal government.[37] From just 2002 to 2008, federal Medicaid expenditures rose from $146 billion to $201 billion, while state expenditures increased from $101 billion to $146 billion.[38] Through Medicaid, state and local government can shift costs for services such as child welfare previously borne primarily by them (or other public and private funding programs) to the federal government, which pays at least 50 percent of the program costs, and substantially more in poorer states such as Alabama. To be sure, the rise in Medicaid expenditures is partially fueled by higher costs for acute care in hospital settings, yet spending on home health and personal care services such as home care for the disabled continued to rise even as spending on institutional services declined.[39] This escalation in Medicaid spending continued during the recent recession, thanks in important part to the Economic Recovery Program, which included a significant federal supplement designed to offset state cutbacks and preserve critical services and jobs.[40]

Arguably, the growth of fiscal centralization through Medicaid and other federal programs in service categories such as mental health and child welfare has been facilitated and enabled by nonprofit organizations, especially community agencies. The latter are perceived as legitimate, neutral organizations with community roots. This community connection is perceived as especially valuable in providing support for Medicaid expansion, especially through the Medicaid waiver programs for community care and alternatives to institutional care.

The growth of nonprofit social service agencies since the 1990s also directly connects with the recent widespread interest in voluntarism, citizen engagement, and community services. National programs such as AmeriCorps depend heavily upon local nonprofits for the placement of young people undertaking their community service. Nationally prominent nonprofits such as Teach for America, City Year, the Harlem Children's Zone, and YouthBuild rely on partnerships with government for funding and referrals. Indeed, the Edward Kennedy Serve America Act of 2009 could eventually fund up to 250,000 additional volunteers through AmeriCorps and other federal service programs. More broadly, many nonprofits such as Habitat for Humanity, local food banks, and emergency shelters rely extensively upon volunteers to help provide various types of direct and supportive services.

Nonprofit social service agencies have also been on the forefront of the broad movement to promote social innovation and social entrepreneurship.[41] Since 1997, public and private funders have been increasingly interested in the potential of nonprofit organizations to develop solutions to social problems that are more effective and efficient than government programs. Reflecting this sentiment, the Obama administration created the Office of Social Innovation in early 2009, with the goal of supporting innovative social programs. Many leading nonprofit social service organizations such as the Harlem Children's Zone and YouthBuild have received widespread government support and attention as prominent examples of nonprofits that create effective programs through the use of innovative programmatic and revenue diversification strategies, including partnerships with government and the for-profit sector.

In sum, nonprofit social service agencies have been in the midst of a profound transformation in the last fifty years. Prior to the 1960s, these agencies were small and largely reliant on private contributions (especially the United Way) supplemented with client fees; their services were relatively narrow and restricted. Many agencies depended on volunteers and were short on professionalism and accountability. The growth of government funding, the restructuring of the American state, key changes in social policy such as welfare reform, and the growing interest in community service and social innovation have fueled a sharp rise in the number of nonprofit social service agencies and an increase in their importance in the development and implementation of American social policy. In a sharp departure from the pre-1960s era, many social service agencies are now primarily reliant on government funds, especially in service areas such as community care, foster care, and drug and alcohol treatment. Still, many social services such as emergency assistance, recreation, youth mentoring, and child care continue to rely on a mix of public funds, private fees from individuals, and charitable contributions.[42] Given this restructuring of social policy, an individual citizen in need is much more likely to encounter a staff person or volunteer from a nonprofit social service agency than a public sector worker. In this sense, nonprofit social service agencies are critical to social citizenship—meaning that an individual citizen's life chances hinge on his or her access to quality social services such as job training, affordable housing, and mental health care.

Challenge and Opportunity

The centrality of nonprofit social service agencies in social policy also means that the citizenry now depends more extensively on the capacity and leadership of nonprofit social service agencies than ever before to provide adequate quality services to individuals in need. Yet at precisely the moment that America needs nonprofits as never before to meet urgent problems such as unemployment, worker retraining, and helping at-risk youth, these same agencies are wrestling with a wide range of enormous challenges that have been exacerbated by the recent economic crisis.

Regulation and Accountability

Even before the current financial crisis, important shifts were occurring in the relationship between government and nonprofit social service agencies. First, government contracts have become more performance-based. In the initial buildup of government contracting with nonprofit agencies in the 1960s and 1970s, government administrators tended to emphasize "process" accountability, which focused on the outputs and activities of the contract agencies. The advent of the government reform movement of the 1990s encouraged government administrators to restructure their contracts with social service agencies to be more performance- or outcome-based.[43] To varying degrees, many key social service contracts, including welfare-to-work, mental health, workforce development, and child welfare, are now performance-based contracts wherein agencies are reimbursed for services only if they meet specific performance targets.[44] Many private funders such as local United Way chapters and national foundations such as the Edna McConnell Clark Foundation are also tying their grants to an expectation of meeting certain agreed-upon performance targets.

This heightened interest in performance has a number of implications for the governance of nonprofit social service organizations, including for the role of voluntarism within these agencies. First, the shift to outcome evaluation often involves a revolution in management thinking. Agencies need new investments in information systems in order to track outcomes and compile relevant programmatic and financial data. A key ripple effect is the "professionalization" of the administrative and programmatic infrastructure of nonprofits, especially for smaller community organizations that may have roots in local voluntarism. Greater investment in administration and programs can be a severe challenge for these community organizations, given their relative undercapitalization. Also, the resources necessary to comply with performance contracts can raise questions about mission and programmatic focus, since the performance contracts may contain expectations that are at variance with the previous client and program emphases, although some agencies may be able to shape these contract requirements to fit their previous client and program goals. For example, a community agency for youths may have to shrink its counseling program and target youths who match specific contract expectations in order to meet the performance contract requirements.

Despite the push for professionalization and performance management, many nonprofit social service agencies continue to rely on volunteers, who tend to be involved in support activities such as board service and fundraising, or less intensive direct service roles such as staffing soup kitchens, crisis hot-lines, and youth tutoring programs.

The shift to professionalization and performance-based contracting can be especially consequential for social service agencies because such agencies often emerge out of a desire of a like-minded "community" of people to deal with a problem or social need such as homelessness. These individuals create a service agency that regards its mission as logically responsive to their community of interest.[45] Government, by contrast, tends to approach services and clients from the norm of equity, consistent with the need of government officials to treat groups and individuals fairly. Equity can be interpreted in a variety of ways, but in social and health services, it usually means defining need in order to allocate resources by criteria deemed to be fair. Thus, an agency founded to serve a particular neighborhood or community may be required to expand its geographic reach significantly because government needs to allocate resources across a broader region.

This emphasis on responsiveness may lead the staff of nonprofit agencies to disagree with government, especially on policy matters relating to services, clients, and staff. This clash can be especially pronounced under a performance contracting regime, which can leave nonprofit social service agencies little discretion on the performance targets to be met and may require an agency to shift its focus toward programmatic goals and client groups at variance with its original community of interest.[46] For instance, welfare-to-work programs might prefer to work intensively with clients from a specific neighborhood or ethnic group; however, many performance contracts for welfare-to-work programs require agencies to meet short-term placement goals in order to be reimbursed for services, greatly reducing the ability of agencies to work with clients on a longer-term, more holistic basis.

Performance contracting with nonprofit social service agencies and, more generally, the focus on program outcomes and evaluations is likely to continue to gain prominence in the coming years. Fiscal pressures on state and local government will encourage government administrators to deploy their scarce dollars on their highest priorities and maximize the likelihood of achieving the desired outcomes. Advances in technology have also allowed government and nonprofit agencies to more easily track expenditures, client services, and outcomes. Private donors and funders are also supportive of various performance management strategies. For example, the Nurse Home Visiting program and the Harlem Children's Zone are widely recognized for their positive results and willingness to report their outcomes.[47] Each agency has received concerted support from leading foundations and the Obama administration, including funding for expansion and replication.

Given the emphasis on performance by funders, a central challenge facing nonprofit social service agencies is to develop the capacity to be able to respond effectively to performance expectations, especially since neither public nor private funders typically provide adequate funding for evaluation in their grants and contracts. Consequently, nonprofits face big challenges in obtaining adequate resources to fund their evaluation- and performance-related activities. Whereas larger agencies tend to have more diversified income streams and the capability to use private philanthropic support to fund evaluation, many smaller and newer agencies are at a special disadvantage because of their relative undercapitalization. Technical assistance by government and private funders for these private agencies is thus imperative if smaller agencies are to compete effectively for government contracts and private philanthropic grants. Almost inevitably, though, technical assistance tends to promote greater professionalization within nonprofit social service agencies, since the advice and support typically involves

helping position nonprofits to meet the higher professional expectations attendant on performance management regimes.[48]

The widespread interest in performance is also evident in growing support
for improved self-regulation, including new forms of accreditation. Toward
this end, the Maryland Association of Nonprofit Organizations has developed
"Standards of Excellence" to promote high standards of ethical behavior and
good governance in nonprofits. Nonprofit agencies in specific service fields such
as addiction services are also using accreditation to help support their efforts to
enhance their impact and effectiveness. In some jurisdictions, policymakers are
also encouraging or requiring nonprofit social service agencies to adhere to "evidence-based practices," that is, practices that have been proved effective through
research and field testing.[49] The state of Oregon, for example, mandated that by
fiscal year 2011–12, 75 percent of the funds spent by five state agencies, including the Oregon Department of Human Services, must be spent on services
using "evidence-based practice."[50] Professionals such as social workers increasingly embrace evidence-based practice as a norm guiding service delivery. As
nonprofits embrace evidence-based practice—even if only to obtain a government contract or foundation grant—they are likely to further professionalize the
agency through additional staff qualifications and training. Even agencies with
volunteers in direct service roles are likely to invest in more professionalized
management of their volunteers. In a sense, evidence-based practice represents
an attempt to overcome the vagaries of program implementation by public nonprofit and for-profit service agencies. In the nonprofit sector, program effectiveness can be undermined by the voluntarism of many agencies, the discretion of
direct service workers, and the commitment of staff and volunteers to a particular mission and program model. The evidence-based practice movement, like
other performance management strategies such as performance contracting, is
an effort to standardize service and reduce the discretion of service agency workers. Some jurisdictions, such as Oregon, are requiring evidence-based practice
as a condition of financial support, but meanwhile many nonprofit agencies are
voluntarily adopting these practices in response to evolving professional norms
and expectations.

Competition for Clients and the Market for Social Services

Nonprofit social service agencies face not only rising expectations on accountability and evaluation but also an increasingly complicated, turbulent, and competitive organizational environment. The economic crisis has clearly created
tremendous uncertainty for nonprofit social service agencies. The federal government provided hundreds of millions of dollars of funding support through
the American Recovery and Reinvestment Act (ARRA), but this funding was
temporary. State governments have, to varying degrees, cut funding, even in

some cases on existing contracts. The increase in joblessness and foreclosures has produced rising demand for the services of many nonprofits, especially services focused on emergency assistance and shelter. And the demand for many other services provided by nonprofits, such as child care and community care for the aged and disabled, continues to grow.

Even before the economic crisis, however, nonprofit social service agencies were facing important shifts in their funding and their relationship with other nonprofit and for-profit organizations. During the take-off period for government contracting, in the 1960s and early 1970s, most nonprofit social service agencies did not really compete with other agencies for contracts. "Block" contracts with the agency for a certain level of service were the norm. Most contracts were cost-reimbursement contracts that essentially paid agencies for their costs on the basis of the contract terms and budget. Reimbursement was not linked to outcomes, and most agencies recovered their costs (at least as specified in the contract). Little incentive existed for agencies to compete with other agencies since contracts were unlikely to be moved from one agency to another unless egregious problems existed.

Since then, government itself has shifted away from the traditional contracts that were the hallmark of the initial period of widespread government contracting. Increasingly, many new "tools" of government support have come into widespread use, many of them tied to the client of the agency rather than to the producer of services.[51] The most vivid example is Medicaid, which functions like a "quasi-voucher" because eligibility is tied to the client. Thus, agencies are reimbursed for providing qualifying services to eligible clients, and their reimbursement rate is set at a predetermined amount for a specific service. For some routine services, such as home care, each new Medicaid-eligible client means more revenue for the agency at only marginally more cost, so it may be possible to generate surpluses only at high levels of service volume. This financing arrangement thus encourages competition for clients, and is dramatically different from the traditional cost-reimbursement contract, in which agencies actually experienced disincentives for service expansion because they might have difficulty recovering the full cost of additional service units in excess of the original contract terms. Other government funding programs, such as child care and housing vouchers, also encourage this competition for clients.

The growing use of tax-exempt bond money to help with the capital needs of nonprofit social service agencies has also introduced a more competitive element for resources. States are typically responsible for administering this bond money and competition for the funds is often very keen. The economic crisis has dampened demand for these funds but this bond money is likely to continue to be important, given the need for capital among nonprofit agencies. Another spur for more competitive behavior among nonprofit agencies is performance contracting, which creates the threat that nonprofits could lose their contracts for poor performance (although in practice losing contracts is still relatively rare). The net effect is to increase the funding uncertainty facing nonprofits. Nonprofits also face competition from for-profit firms, although this competition tends to vary tremendously by the service field and location. Many traditional social services, such as foster care, youth services, and emergency assistance, remain dominated by nonprofits. However, as shown in table 4-1, for-profit firms now compete with nonprofit agencies in many key service fields such as child care, home care, and community programs for the mentally ill and developmentally disabled. For-profits possess some advantages vis-à-vis nonprofits in the competition for government and private client funds. First, for-profit chains have access to capital and are of a sufficient size to promote substantial economies of scale, allowing them to operate at least some programs more efficiently. Second, many nonprofits are mission-based and small and are unwilling to serve certain types of clients or certain regions, thus reducing the opportunities for them to cross-subsidize their operations through growth or a diversified client mix. Many community-based nonprofits may also be very ambivalent about expansion or may lack the capacity for expansion. For-profits typically do not have such mission constraints and are thus more willing to serve a diverse mix of clients, including controversial ones.

Variation in the mix of nonprofits and for-profits in particular social service fields can be due to several factors. Some states discourage or restrict the entry of for-profits into certain fields. In some states, the nonprofit provider community is so large and entrenched that for-profits are discouraged from even trying to enter specific service markets. The for-profits also tend to avoid financially risky services, such as serving the homeless mentally ill. Further, reimbursement rates for some services may be so low that for-profits may find it difficult to make a profit, so nonprofits that can cross-subsidize their services with private donations or earned income may have a competitive advantage. This issue of low reimbursement rates is one explanation for the relative lack of for-profit services in various welfare-to-work programs that emerged in the wake of the welfare reform bill of 1996. The payment levels and the incentives to place clients in permanent employment make it very difficult for for-profit firms to generate a profit. Furthermore, many of the remaining clients on welfare have complicated needs that require intensive services. For-profit firms tend to dominate in more routine services such as daycare and home care, where it is also possible to generate significant volume and the barriers to entry are not as high as in other social services such as child protective services or low-income housing.

Greater competition in social services is also encouraged by the growing support for more client choice in the selection of service providers, especially in service categories such as mental health, developmental disabilities, and chronic illness. This movement is evident in the sharp drop in institutional care in favor of more flexible community service options requiring a variety of personal social services such as home care and counseling. For instance, nationwide, the number of developmentally disabled individuals living in settings of one to three residents has risen, from 18,304 in 1996 to 195,450 in 2006. At the same time, the number of individuals living in settings of sixteen or more people dropped from 95,345 in 1996 to 64,864 in 2006.[52] In publicly funded mental health care, community care made up 33 percent of all expenditures in 1981 but rose to 70 percent in 2005.[53] In terms of setting, the fastest-growing component of Medicaid mental health expenditures from 1991 to 2001 was multiservice mental health organizations in the community.[54] Reflecting this interest in smaller, community settings and independent living, the Bush administration in 2003 established the New Freedom Initiative, which provides funding support for more independent living options for the disabled and elderly, including individual funding accounts for them to purchase services such as home care from local community agencies.[55]

The use of managed-care arrangements by government in selected social services has created further competition and uncertainty among the affected social service agencies. The basic principle underlying managed care is that government and private insurers can save money by paying a nonprofit or for-profit managed-care firm on a per person basis to care for a specified number of individuals, rather than reimbursing providers through traditional fee-for-service arrangements. Thus, the firm has an incentive to control costs because cost overruns will not be covered and the firm can keep any surplus. Initially, managed care was employed in the health care sector, starting in the 1970s. Then, during the 1990s, many state governments embraced managed care for their Medicaid programs.[56] In addition, some states and localities created managed-care programs for mental health that were "carved out" of the regular Medicaid program.[57] In this arrangement, state or local governments might contract with a managed-care firm that would then subcontract with local nonprofit and for-profit service agencies to provide services to eligible individuals. Some states have also created managed-care arrangements in child welfare.[58] As Medicaid has expanded beyond traditional health services to include social services such as community care, counseling, and home care, many nonprofit social service agencies are providing services to eligible clients through regular Medicaid managed care.

In practice, managed care tends to create a more uncertain and competitive environment for nonprofit social service agencies. Previously, agencies had a direct relationship with state or local contract administrators—a relationship that usually involved long-term contracts that agencies could depend on being renewed. The managed-care firm, by contrast, is essentially an intermediary entity between the service agency and government. The capitation payment system of managed care means that these firms have an incentive to reduce costs, even if the service demand exists. Overall, nonprofit agencies experience greater uncertainty on their revenues than they did under the old direct contract system.

Revenue Diversification and Organizational Restructuring

Greater competition, the diversification of government support, managed care, and the economic crisis require nonprofit social service agencies to alter their governance to effectively manage financial risk. Toward this end, nonprofit social service agencies are adopting a more corporate management style that emphasizes growth opportunities, revenue diversification, and reduction of programs that may place the organization at financial risk. Revenue growth opportunities can include levying new client fees, selling ancillary services such as technical assistance, obtaining government contracts for services that the agency previously did not provide, and expanding beyond the existing geographic service boundaries of the agency.

Earned income has received widespread attention as a source of new revenue for nonprofits.[59] For example, some nonprofits have established retail businesses in which clients are also employed or receive training. Good examples include Farestart in Seattle, which operates a restaurant employing disadvantaged workers; Goodwill Industries and the Salvation Army, which operate thrift shops throughout the country; and Delancey Street, a drug rehabilitation agency based in San Francisco, whose revenues are entirely from the sale of client-run services, including a moving business and a restaurant. Many newer nonprofits with this related business income such as Farestart have received well-deserved praise for their innovative programs and positive outcomes.

The interest in earned income is reflected in the growth of nonprofit social service organizations with various hybrid structures that mix nonprofit and for-profit elements.[60] For example, the Greyston Bakery in Yonkers, New York, is a for-profit bakery employing disadvantaged workers that has an affiliated foundation that operates various social service programs for the local community. Share Our Strength, a national nonprofit focused on reducing hunger, has a for-profit arm, Community Wealth Ventures, to help other nonprofits develop more "market-oriented approaches to social change."[61] The Manchester's Craftsmen Guild, a large multiservice organization in Pittsburgh, operates a for-profit jazz music label to help support its employment and training programs. Many other social service nonprofits have created for-profit subsidiaries to provide earned income.

The push for earned income through market-oriented activity by nonprofit social service organizations is due to several factors. Certainly the relative scarcity of public and private charitable contributions has spurred nonprofits to seek alternative sources of revenue, and the extensive interest and support for a greater market orientation by nonprofits certainly has also played a key role. For instance, Leslie R. Crutchfield and Heather McLeod Grant argue in their widely read book, *Forces for Good,* that nonprofits with a market orientation are more likely to be effective and efficient.[62] Many scholars, policymakers, and donors are also keenly interested in social enterprises that mix nonprofit and for-profit activities in support of innovative programming.[63] Greater competition from for-profits has also encouraged nonprofits to adopt a stronger market orientation.

Despite the ongoing attention to earned-income possibilities and social enterprises, many social service nonprofits (if not most) are not well positioned to generate substantial earned income from nongovernment sources. As noted, many community agencies are quite small and thus do not have the capital to launch a new market venture. The creation of a for-profit subsidiary requires extensive legal and accounting consultation and an investment in greater staff capacity, and these initiatives simply cannot be attempted by grass-roots agencies that have a higher dependence on volunteers and small paid staffs. Also, the clientele of many nonprofit social service agencies are poor and disadvantaged and consequently are unable to pay substantial service fees. Many community nonprofits may also view new earned-income activities as contrary to their mission, since it might suggest a move away from free or subsidized services for local citizens. Smaller-scale earned-income ventures such as fees paid for parent trainings or the sale of technical assistance videos are less controversial, but typically generate very modest amounts of money.

Data on nonprofit revenues reported on Form 990, which nonprofits are required to submit to the Internal Revenue Service, suggest substantial fee income in the revenue base of nonprofit social service providers. However, these data are quite inaccurate and misleading. Much of this income actually comes from government programs such as Medicaid, which is recorded on these forms as "program service revenue" along with true private market purchases. Voucher payments and fees paid to residential programs from government income maintenance payments such as Supplemental Security Income (SSI) are also reported as program service revenue. For example, one large innovative multiservice agency in Seattle, Pioneer Human Services, which provides correctional, housing, and behavioral health services, had $2.3 million in revenue from the sales of goods and services and over $35 million in funding from government as part of its program fee revenue in 2008. (This agency is also regarded as on the cutting edge of social enterprise activity in social services.)

In short, the pressure for revenue diversification, greater market orientation, more intense competition, and greater scale and complexity are all having important effects on social service nonprofits. Many nonprofits, especially long-standing agencies such as Catholic Charities, have evolved into complex multiservice organizations. For example, Catholic Community Services of Western

Washington and its affiliated organization, Catholic Housing Services, had combined revenues of over $121 million in 2009.[64] Newer agencies with roots in the social entrepreneurship and community service movement such as City Year, YouthBuild, and Pioneer Human Services have grown large through close partnerships with government, supplemented with grants from foundations and individuals. Community Voice Mail, an agency to help the homeless obtain employment, was established in 1991 and now has sites in forty-seven cities, many of them incorporated as separate 501(c)(3) organizations.

This shift toward greater size and complexity reflects the changed funding and political environment of nonprofit social service agencies. Low government payment rates in programs such as Medicaid encourage nonprofits to grow because it helps them achieve greater efficiencies and cross-subsidize their administrative costs. Many foundations are increasingly interested in leveraging their funding and enhancing their impact, so they have often been pushing nonprofits with proven results to "go to scale."[65] Two notable examples are the Harlem Children's Zone (www.hcz.org) and YouthBuild (www.youthbuild.org), which have received major support for expansion from foundations and government.[66]

Larger size is also a ripple effect of increased competition from for-profits and other nonprofits. As noted, for-profit agencies in home care, community care for the developmentally disabled and mentally ill, and child care have proliferated, to varying extents, throughout the country. Although some for-profit agencies are relatively small and localized operations—such as a group home for the disabled—many national and regional chains have expanded their scope significantly. These chains have access to capital that may give them a competitive advantage vis-à-vis smaller nonprofit agencies that face serious constraints on their ability to raise capital, particularly in the current tight credit markets. Thus, bigness confers some advantages on nonprofits in terms of capital and the ability to match for-profits on the cost of service. Also, larger nonprofits may have the ability to react more quickly to new funding or service opportunities than smaller ones. The economic crisis has undermined the ability of many smaller nonprofits to continue as viable enterprises, so larger organizations often grow through the acquisition of smaller ones.

Greater scale and greater market orientation raise the specter of the commercialization of nonprofit social service agencies, which is typically regarded as a management focus on the market for organizational services rather than on the charitable mission of the agency. In this context, commercialization is evident in the greater dependence on user fees and earned income and less reliance upon volunteers, private contributions, and government grants.[67] In the context of social services, commercialization is also associated with straying from the original mission of the organization such as serving the poor and moving into services for paying customers with higher incomes. Yet there is reason to ask whether this interpretation really reflects the dynamic under way. To be sure, many nonprofit social service agencies have changed their mission in recent years or moved into new program areas. An agency originally founded as a mental health agency may decide to provide correctional services with different government contracts. Or a drug treatment agency, faced with cutbacks in its core funding, might elect to contract with the county government to provide education and training for DUI offenders. If these new program opportunities do not exist for particular agencies, the most likely programmatic response to cutbacks in government funding or declines in charitable donations or foundation grants is to reduce services and staff and remain mission-based but serving fewer clients with a smaller staff. Agency movement into new fields can therefore be seen as effective adaptations to new funding realities rather than surrender of core missions.

Yet another response to the current competitive environment is new investments in capacity. Toward this end, nonprofits are taking increasing advantage of capacity building and technical assistance provided by public and private funders. For example, the Compassion Capital Fund, created by the Bush administration, was specifically designed to improve the capacity of faith-based and community organizations to obtain government contracts and grants. The Obama administration has inaugurated a successor program, called the Strengthening Communities Fund, with the goal of improving the capacity of community-based social welfare agencies to provide effective and sustainable services.[68] Countless private funders, consulting firms, and intermediary associations also provide capacity-building services.

Capacity building can include a wide variety of initiatives: new IT systems; more professionalized administrative and program staff; added development and marketing staff; new procedures and practices governing agency operations; improved ability to track clients and outcomes; and board and organizational restructuring. Many agencies are even creating affiliated 501(c)(3) public charities with the sole purpose of raising private contributions. (Often these affiliated organizations are called foundations.) Many social service agencies have also created advisory committees and support groups to help the agency raise funds and develop deeper community support. In the current environment, this effort can be especially important for smaller community organizations since many of them are relatively new and at least initially may lack broad-based community support. For these organizations, though, enhancing capacity may require professionalization and changes in the structure of the organization that can displace the initial organizing volunteers and staff. Thus, successful capacity building requires skilled management to effectively guide the organization through this delicate stage of organizational development.

The challenge of capacity building can also be met through greater collaboration among organizations. Given the growth of nonprofit social services delivery, many organizations in the same field—such as housing, workforce development, or child welfare—may have overlapping administrative and program areas. Moreover, many nonprofits are relatively small and isolated from other social service organizations, owing in part to program-based funding which promotes a "silo" mentality in the provision of services and creates challenges for integrating and coordinating services.[69]

In an era of very scarce resources, cooperation and greater coordination among nonprofits might permit a higher level of administrative capacity and more effective program services. This cooperation can be conceptualized along a continuum from lesser to greater integration: less intensive strategies might be sharing a staff person with another nonprofit or cooperating in support of an advocacy campaign; more intense cooperation might be sharing all back-office functions among several organizations and sharing client data to develop a more integrated set of services. (Some agencies are also required to collaborate as a condition of getting their grants from a public or private funder.) Ultimately, some organizations may decide that they, and their clients, are better served through a complete merger, although this strategy is usually difficult and frequently contentious. Regardless of the strategy, though, social service nonprofits will need to embrace appropriate collaboration in the coming years to cope with the increasingly austere funding environment and the expectations of public and private funders.

Voluntarism, Community Service, and Civic Engagement

Social service nonprofits have to an extent always relied on volunteers, since most board members are volunteers. Countless informal and newer social service nonprofits such as soup kitchens and self-help groups are entirely staffed by volunteers. Furthermore, wages and benefits are often lower than the wages in the public sector, so even the staff are effectively donating services in kind. Societal attention to voluntarism, especially through social service organizations, is arguably at an all-time high.[70] The Corporation for National and Community Service (CNCS) continues to have a big impact. CNCS was created in 1993 as one of the signature pieces of legislation of the Clinton administration. During its early years it was an embattled agency, although its AmeriCorps program provided stipends for thousands of young people to work primarily in social service programs throughout the country. CNCS fueled the rise of many nationally prominent social service programs, such as City Year, YouthBuild, the Harlem Children's Zone, and STRIVE. Several other national associations and groups, including the Points of Light Foundation and Hands On America (now one organization), have championed community service and voluntarism through nonprofit organizations. The combined efforts of these national organizations and leading nonprofit social service organizations culminated in the passage of the Edward T. Kennedy Serve America Act of 2009, which has the potential to fund up to 250,000 AmeriCorps volunteers.

Second, the broad interest in community service dovetails with the extensive interest in social innovation and social entrepreneurship. High-profile nonprofit social service organizations such as Parents As Teachers, Share Our Strength, Jumpstart, and Harlem Children's Zone have received well-deserved credit for their innovative programming. These groups also have many volunteers in a wide variety of roles and they have tried to use volunteers in novel ways that depart from traditional professional roles and responsibilities.

Third, encouraged by organizations such as the Campus Compact and the CNCS, secondary schools and universities have embraced community service as an expectation and an obligation of their students, often with specific requirements within the overall curriculum. The ongoing support for community service has certainly broadened the engagement of young people in nonprofit social service agencies and provided support for many local projects and initiatives.

Fourth, social service nonprofits have invested in more capacity to raise private donations. As part of this effort, the reliance on various types of special-event fundraising such as benefit auctions, breakfasts and dinners, and walk-a-thons has increased substantially. These efforts are often the most significant fundraising event for an agency, requiring the volunteer efforts of many individuals, especially in larger organizations. So in essence, the pressure on agencies for revenue diversification through private fundraising has enlisted more individuals in a volunteer support role.

Fifth, voluntarism through social service agencies received a big boost from the Bush administration's widely publicized Faith-Based and Community Initiative, through which the administration devoted millions of dollars to faith-based organizations so they could provide public services, particularly social services. One of the key targets of Bush administration funding was smaller social service organizations that often relied significantly on volunteers and in-kind and cash donations, and had smaller professional staffs. The overall goal was to offer faith-based organizations an opportunity to provide more effective services than traditional, more professionalized agencies. The Bush administration created the Compassion Capital Fund (CCF) with the express purpose of enhancing the capacity of smaller organizations to compete for public and private funding. The actual impact of CCF remains unclear, since most of the technical assistance was short-term trainings rather than longer-term capacity building.[71] The Obama administration continues to support greater engagement with faith-based organizations, although this effort has a much lower profile than it had during the Bush years.

Civic engagement is of course broader than voluntarism and participating in a direct service role in a social service agency, although the community service movement has arguably redefined civic engagement as volunteering in a direct service capacity rather than civic participation through advocacy and community organizing. This result is surprising, given that many social service agencies essentially started as advocacy organizations with community members organized to advocate for an urgent community need such as more services for at-risk youth, or to address a serious social problem such as drug abuse or the lack of affordable housing. So at least initially, the agency was primarily engaged in changing local policies rather than providing a service. As advocacy organizations, these agencies were often engaged in mobilizing the community and generating community support for their priorities. Eventually, many of these advocacy groups evolved into direct service organizations with much less focus on community mobilization and advocacy.

The current economic crisis and the increased competition for public and private funding, however, encourages nonprofit social service organizations to develop broad-based community support in order to better position themselves to land government contracts and private foundation grants and win policies favorable to agency goals and services. Unfortunately, many newer nonprofit service organizations are not well positioned to mobilize community support. Many of these agencies were founded by social entrepreneurs with innovative ideas on changing policies or providing services to the citizenry. At their inception, these agencies usually had small boards and lacked broad-based community support. An infusion of government or private funds allowed growth, but the board did not typically expand and the agency was often oriented toward its funders, especially the government, rather than toward the community.

In the current fiscal and political climate, nonprofit social service agencies need to engage their communities more deeply on their own behalf. This engagement needs to have several components. The first is political: agencies need to enlist their boards, staff, volunteers, and community members to support the organization in the political arena. Many nonprofit organizations, including social service agencies, are relatively inactive politically; many worry that advocacy will create legal and political problems in light of the restrictions on advocacy in federal law. Service providers may worry that advocacy will have a deleterious effect on their relationship with government, including future funding and regulatory decisions. Perhaps even more important, newer and smaller community organizations often lack the resources and expertise to be effective political advocates. Also, some social service agencies, such as emergency shelters or food banks, may not necessarily view political activity and civic engagement as activities that align with their mission and program goals.[72]

Despite these obstacles and limitations, many social service organizations are striving to be more effective advocates and to develop broader community support. One strategy is through active participation in coalitions and associations, especially at the state level, in service fields such as home care, child welfare and mental health, where state regulations and policy are especially important. These statewide or regional associations typically are membership organizations with limited budgets that strive to build long-term relationships with legislators and government contract administrators in support of the funding and regulatory priorities of their members. These associations usually do not engage in more generalized advocacy on social policy issues such as higher welfare payments or more Section 8 vouchers for poor people but instead focus their policy agendas on organization-related issues such as more contract funding or client eligibility criteria.[73]

Many of the larger nonprofit social service agencies also have ongoing contact and relationships with state and local legislators and administrators. This contact can include direct lobbying and advocacy pertaining to agency programs and funding needs as well as more broad-based public education in support of better funding for social service programs. The staff and board may also be mobilized to protest funding cutbacks or argue for rate and funding increases. Also, many human service agencies participate in an advocacy day at the state capitol to push for their legislative priorities and agenda. Increasingly, these larger agencies employ former government officials in key leadership positions in order to help promote their programmatic and policy goals.

Civic engagement by nonprofit social service organizations also occurs through the board of directors, although evidence from the Johns Hopkins Listening Post Project suggests that most board members are not engaged in advocacy on behalf of the organization.[74] However, the economic crisis and increased competition is pushing social service agencies to revisit their prevailing governance structures in the interest of financial and programmatic sustainability and improved civic engagement. Several strategies are evident, although great variation exists on the application at the agency level. Many newer social service organizations have small boards, placing them at a disadvantage regarding civic engagement. In response, many community organizations providing social services are striving to attract larger, more diverse boards that include more community members, client representatives where appropriate, and civic leaders. Research shows that nonprofits are more likely to be effective in their advocacy when they have a committee or staff person responsible for advocacy and government relations. Hence some larger social service organizations have established public policy committees comprising board members and staff.[75]

The Future of Nonprofit Social Services

The nonprofit social services field is in the midst of an important transition period. The number of agencies more than doubled between 1996 and 2011 and the reliance of government and the citizenry upon social services increased as cash assistance for the poor declined sharply. There is broad support for community service, voluntarism, and social innovation through community-based service agencies such as City Year and YouthBuild. Yet many challenges exist: public and private funding has been cut to many agencies, although the extent of cutbacks varies widely across the country and service fields. Indeed, public funding for some social services, such as welfare-to-work and workforce development, has been declining for some time.

Furthermore, the economic crisis has exposed the vulnerabilities of nonprofit social service agencies in a devolved service system. Federal financing is higher, especially given the prominent role of Medicaid as a funder of a wide range of social services. But decisions on eligibility and funding, especially given the prominence of Medicaid, are at the state level, leaving social service agencies extremely vulnerable to the economy and state finances in particular. The core problem is not a reliance on nonprofit agencies for service delivery. For instance, many European countries—the Netherlands and Germany are two—have relied on nonprofit social service organizations supported by government for decades. Evidence also suggests that government funding is associated with higher levels of effectiveness by nonprofit social service agencies.[76] The challenge facing nonprofit social services in the United States is a federalism problem characterized by state and local government with constrained finances and subject to serious budget shortfalls, and uneven government regulation of program quality and services. This lack of government administrative and funding capacity in turn undermines the capacity of nonprofits and their ability to provide quality programming and adequate representation. The United Kingdom and Australia have addressed this problem by establishing "compacts" between government and the nonprofit sector that provide a structured avenue for government and representatives of the nonprofit sector to work on funding and regulatory issues of mutual concern.[77] Although the UK-style compact seems unlikely to be introduced in the United States, the lessons of cooperation between government and the nonprofit sector and the commitment of government to specific principles of good practice would seem to be adaptable to the U.S. context, especially at the state level.

Another aspect of these compacts that is relevant to government-nonprofit relations in the United States is the need for active engagement of nonprofit agencies in advocacy on behalf of their agency and their clients and communities. Specific steps for nonprofit agencies to improve their advocacy could include: training and education on advocacy and the broader topic of civic engagement for the board and staff and rethinking their approach to membership and governance. Regarding the former, this training could help overcome the understandable caution of board members on the legal parameters of appropriate civic engagement activity. New approaches to membership such as the inclusion of community members and service users on the board or as voting members of the organizations could help broaden the community support and political constituency of the agency.

The increasingly competitive and performance-oriented funding environment for nonprofit social services will also place serious pressure on nonprofits to balance the push for professionalization and commercialization with the mission orientation, voluntarism, and civic engagement that motivates many staff and volunteers. Smaller community agencies will face especially difficult challenges in negotiating these competing imperatives, and public and private funders will need to invest in nonprofit capacity building and adapt their funding strategies to support effective nonprofits on a sustainable basis. This effort should include more flexible funding strategies and assistance with capital investments. These smaller nonprofits will also need to ensure that greater professionalization does not undermine the community engagement and commitments of the organization.

Overall, the future of nonprofit social services is inextricably intertwined with the future of American social policy. In the United States, we have tried to marry the equity of government with the innovation and community roots of nonprofit organizations by means of extensive public funding through contracts, grants, vouchers, and tax credits, complemented with philanthropic support and, in some organizations, earned income. But the current mixed public-private arrangement lacks the transparency of the government, and the government may not receive appropriate credit for supporting nonprofit programs, since the public may be unaware of the extent of government financial support for nonprofit organizations.[78] Current cutbacks in public and private funding also threaten the sustainability of many important community organizations and programs. Greater transparency and more extensive civic engagement by nonprofit social service agencies and their supporters could help broaden the political support for these organizations and improve their capacity for effective program execution. However, government and, by extension, the citizenry need to recognize that nonprofit social service organizations are critical components of American social policy. Citizens' social rights and life chances hinge upon adequate funding and support.

Notes

1. See Scott W. Allard, *Out of Reach: Place, Poverty, and the New American Welfare State* (Yale University Press, 2009); Steven Rathgeb Smith, "Government Financing of Nonprofit Activity," in *Nonprofits and Government: Collaboration and Conflict,* 2nd ed., edited by Elisabeth T. Boris and C. Eugene Steuerle (Washington: Urban Institute, 2006), pp. 219–56.

2. Gosta Esping-Andersen, *The Three Worlds of Welfare Capitalism* (Princeton University Press, 1991); Lars Skov Henriksen, Steven Rathgeb Smith, and Annette Zimmer, "At the Eve of Convergence? Social Service Provision in Denmark, Germany and the United States," paper delivered at the annual research conference of the Association for Research on Nonprofit Organizations and Voluntary Action, Cleveland, November 19–21, 2009.

3. See Jane Lewis, "Reviewing the Relationship between the Voluntary Sector and the State in Britain in the 1990s," *Voluntas* 10, no. 3 (1999): 255–70; Stein Kuhnle and Per Selle, eds., *Government and Voluntary Organizations: A Relational Perspective* (Aldershot, U.K.: Avebury, 1992); Lester M. Salamon and Helmut K. Anheier, "Social Origins of Civil Society: Explaining the Nonprofit Sector Cross-Nationally," *Voluntas* 9, no. 3 (1998): 213–48; Steven Rathgeb Smith and Michael Lipsky, *Nonprofits for Hire: The Welfare State in the Age of Contracting* (Harvard University Press, 1993); Kirsten A. Grønbjerg and Steven Rathgeb Smith, "Nonprofit Organizations and Public Policies in the Delivery of Human Services," in *Philanthropy and the Nonprofit Sector in a Changing America,* edited by Thomas Ehrlich (Indiana University Press, 1999). pp. 139–72; Ralph M. Kramer, *Voluntary Agencies in the Welfare State* (University of California Press, 1982); Ralph M. Kramer, "Voluntary Agencies and the Personal Social Services," in *The Nonprofit Sector: A Research Handbook,* edited by Walter W. Powell (Yale University Press, 1987). pp. 240–57; Lars Skov Henriksen and Peter Bundesen, "The Moving Frontier in Denmark: Voluntary-State Relationships since 1850," *Journal of Social Policy* 33, no. 4 (2004): 605–25.

4. Alfred J. Kahn, *Social Policy and Social Services,* 2nd ed. (New York: Random House, 1979), p. 20.

5. Kramer, "Voluntary Agencies and the Personal Social Services," p. 240.

6. Alfred H. Katz, *Parents of the Handicapped* (Springfield, Ill.: Thomas, 1961); Robert Wuthnow, *Loose Connections: Joining Together in America's Fragmented Communities* (Harvard University Press, 1998).

7. Allard, *Out of Reach;* Lester M. Salamon, Stephanie L. Geller, and Kasey L. Spence, *Impact of the 2007–09 Economic Recession on Nonprofit Organizations,* Listening Post Project Communiqué No. 14 (Johns Hopkins University, Center for Civil Society Studies, 2009; see www.ccss.jhu.edu/pdfs/LP_Communiques/LP_Communique_14.pdf).

8. Urban Institute, National Center for Charitable Statistics, selected years (www.nccs dataweb.urban.org/tablewiz/tw_bmf.php).

9. U.S. House of Representatives, Ways and Means Committee, *2004 Green Book,* pp. 2–79 (www.gpoaccess.gov/wmprints/green/index.html).

10. U.S. Census Bureau, *State and All Local Employment and Payroll Data, 1997 and 2007* (Washington: 2010) (http://harvester.census.gov/datadissem/Results.aspx).

11. U.S. Census Bureau, *Health Care and Social Assistance: Industry Series: Preliminary Comparative Statistics for the United States (2002 NAICS Basis): 2007 and 2002* (Washington: 2010) (http://factfinder.census.gov/servlet/IBQTable?_bm=y&-geo_id=&-ds_ name=EC0762I2&-_lang=en; accessed July 28, 2010).

12. Henriksen, Smith, and Zimmer, "At the Eve of Convergence?"

13. Neil Gilbert, "The Plight of Universal Social Services," *Journal of Policy Analysis and Management* 1, no. 3 (Spring 1982): 301–16; Kramer, *Voluntary Agencies in the Welfare State;* Henriksen and Bundesen, *Moving Frontier in Denmark;* Henriksen, Smith, and Zimmer, "At the Eve of Convergence?"

14. Ida C. Merriam, "Social Welfare in the United States, 1934–54," *Social Security Bulletin* 18, no. 5 (October 1955): 3–14, 31.

15. Bruce C. Vladeck, *Unloving Care* (New York: Basic, 1980); Gerald N. Grob and Howard H. Goldman, *The Dilemma of Federal Mental Health Policy: Radical Reform or Incremental Change?* (Rutgers University Press, 2006); David J Rothman and Sheila M. Rothman, *The Willowbrook Wars: Bringing the Mentally Disabled into the Community* (New Brunswick, N.J.: AldineTransaction, 2005).

16. Harold L. Wilensky and Charles N. Lebeaux, *Industrial Society and Social Welfare* (New York: Free Press, 1965); Neil Gilbert, "The Transformation of Social Services," *Social Service Review* 51, no. 4 (December 1977): 624–41; Christopher Howard, *The Welfare State Nobody Knows: Debunking Myths about U.S. Social Policy* (Princeton University Press, 2004).

17. Duane Lockard, *The Perverted Priorities of American Politics* (New York: Macmillan, 1971); Michael B. Katz, *In the Shadow of the Poorhouse: A Social History of Welfare in America,* rev. ed. (New York: Basic Books, 1996).

18. Katz, *In the Shadow of the Poorhouse,* p. 266.

19. Anne Kallman Bixby, "Public Social Welfare Expenditures, Fiscal Year 1995," *Social Security Bulletin* 62, no. 2 (1999): 86–94.

20. Michael F. Gutowski and Jeffrey J. Koshel, "Social Services," in *The Reagan Experiment,* edited by J. L. Palmer and I. V. Sawhill (Washington: Urban Institute, 1982), pp. 307–28; Martha Derthick, *Uncontrollable Spending for Social Services* (Brookings, 1975).

21. Bixby, "Public Social Welfare Expenditures, Fiscal Year 1995."

22. Grob and Goldman, *Dilemma of Federal Mental Health Policy.*

23. Gutowski and Koshel, "Social Services."

24. Also Derthick, *Uncontrollable Spending for Social Services.*

25. Gilbert, *Transformation of Social Services.*

26. Scott W. Allard and Steven Rathgeb Smith, "Medicaid and the Funding of Nonprofit Service Organizations," paper presented at the Association for Public Policy Analysis and Management Research conference, Washington, D.C., November 5–7, 2009; Rothman and Rothman, *Willowbrook Wars.*

27. General Accounting Office, *States Use Several Strategies to Cope with Funding Reductions under Social Services Block Grant (SSBG),* publication no. GAO/HEHS-95-122 (Washington: 1984); General Accounting Office, *Report to Congress by the Comptroller General of the United States,* publication no. GAO/HRD-84-68 (http://archive.gao.gov/d6t1/124882.pdf); General Accounting Office, *Medicaid: Spending Pressures Drive States toward Program Reinvention* (Washington: 1995) (www.gao.gov/archive/1995/he95122.pdf).

28. Thomas Gais, Lucy Dadayan, and Suho Bae, *The Decline of States in Financing the U.S. Safety Net: Retrenchment in State and Local Social Welfare Spending, 1977–2007* (Albany: Rockefeller Institute of Government, 2009); Lewin Group and Rockefeller Institute of Government, *Spending on Social Welfare Programs in Rich and Poor States* (Washington: U.S. Department of Health and Human Services, Assistant Secretary for Planning and Evaluation, 2004) (http://aspe.hhs.gov/hsp/social-welfare-spending04/report.pdf).

29. Kaiser Commission on Medicaid and the Uninsured, *Medicaid Home and Community-Based Service Program: Data Update* (Washington: 2009 (www.kff.org/medicaid/upload/7720-03.pdf).

30. David Braddock, Richard Hemp, and Mary C. Rizzolo, *The State of the State in Developmental Disabilities,* 7th ed. (Washington: American Association of Intellectual and Developmental Disabilities, 2008); David Braddock, "Washington Rises: Public Financial Support for Intellectual Disability in the United States, 1955–2004," *Mental Retardation and Developmental Disabilities Research Review* 13 (2007): 169–77; Bruce C. Vladeck, "Where the Action

Really Is: Medicaid and the Disabled," *Health Affairs* 22, no.1 (January–February 2003): 90–100; Smith, "Government Financing of Nonprofit Activity."

31. John Holahan and Arunabh Ghosh, "Understanding the Recent Growth in Medicaid Spending, 2000–2003," *Health Affairs,* Web exclusive, January 26, 2005 (http://content.healthaffairs.org/cgi/reprint/hlthaff.w5.52v1); Tami L. Mark and others, "U.S. Spending for Mental Health and Substance Abuse Treatment, 1991–2001," *Health Affairs,* Web exclusive, March 29, 2005 (http://content.healthaffairs.org/cgi/reprint/hlthaff.w5.133v1); Courtney Burke, *Medicaid Funding for Nonprofit Healthcare Organizations* (Albany: Rockefeller Institute of Government, 2007) (www.rockinst.org/pdf/health_care/2007-06-Medicaid_funding_or_nonprofit_healthcare_organizations.pdf); Rob Geen, Anna Sommers, and Mindy Cohen, *Medicaid Spending on Foster Children* (Washington: Urban Institute, 2005) (www.urban.org/UploadedPDF/311221_medicaid_spending.pdf); Cynthia Andrews Scarcella and others, *The Cost of Protecting Vulnerable Children V: Understanding State Variation in Child Welfare Financing* (Washington: Urban Institute, 2006) (www.urban.org/UploadedPDF/311314_vulnerable_children.pdf); Vladeck, "Where the Action Really Is."

32. U.S. House of Representatives, Ways and Means Committee, *2004 Green Book,* pp. 7-3, 7-4; Pamela Winston and Rosa Maria Castaneda, *Assessing Federalism: ANF and the Recent Evolution of American Social Policy Federalism* (Washington: Urban Institute, 2007) (www.urban.org/UploadedPDF/411473_assessing_federalism.pdf).

33. Gais, Dadayan, and Bae, *Decline of States in Financing the U.S. Safety Net,* p. 6.

34. Allard, *Out of Reach;* Smith, "Government Financing of Nonprofit Activity."

35. C. Eugene Steuerle and Gordon Mermin, *Devolution as Seen from the Budget,* Series A, No. A-2 (Washington: Urban Institute, 1997) (www.urban.org/UploadedPDF/Anf_a2.pdf); Braddock, "Washington Rises"; Scarcella and others, *Cost of Protecting Vulnerable Children V;* Winston and Castaneda, *Assessing Federalism;* Gais, Dadayan, and Bae, *Decline of States in Financing the U.S. Safety Net.*

36. Gais, Dayadan, and Bae, *Decline of States in Financing the U.S. Safety Net,* p. 3.

37. Howard, *Welfare State Nobody Knows;* Allard and Smith, "Medicaid and the Funding of Nonprofit Service Organizations."

38. Center for Medicare and Medicaid Services, *National Health Expenditures by Type of Service and Source of Funds, Calendar Years 1960–2008* (Washington: CMS, 2010) (www.cms.gov/NationalHealthExpendData/02_NationalHealthAccountsHistorical.asp#TopOfPage).

39. John Holahan, Alshadye Yemane, and David Rousseau, *Medicaid Expenditures Increased by 5.3% in 2007, Led by Acute Care Spending Growth* (Washington: Kaiser Commission on Medicaid and the Uninsured, 2009) (http://www.kff.org/medicaid/upload/7978.pdf).

40. Vernon K. Smith and others, *Hoping for Economic Recovery, Preparing for Health Reform: A Look at Medicaid Spending, Coverage and Policy Trend;. Results from a 50-State Medicaid Budget Survey for State Fiscal Years 2010 and 2011* (Washington: Kaiser Commission on Medicaid and the Uninsured, 2010) (www.kff.org/medicaid/upload/8105_ES.pdf); Kaiser Commission on Medicaid and the Uninsured, *State Fiscal Conditions and Medicaid* (Washington: Kaiser Commission on Medicaid and the Uninsured, 2010) (www.kff.org/medicaid/upload/7580-06.pdf); Vernon K. Smith and others, *The Crunch Continues: Medicaid Spending, Coverage and Policy in the Midst of a Recession—Results from a 50-State Medicaid Budget Survey for State Fiscal Years 2009 and 2010* (Washington: Kaiser Commission on Medicaid and the Uninsured, 2009) (www.kff.org/medicaid/upload/7985.pdf). The fiscal burden of Medicaid funding on the states is the topic of Robert Behn and Elizabeth Keating, "Facing

the Fiscal Crises in State Government: National Problem, National Responsibilities," *State Tax Notes* 33, no. 12 (September 20, 2004): 833–47.

41. David Bornstein, *How to Change the World: Social Entrepreneurs and the Power of New Ideas* (Oxford University Press, 2007); Paul C. Light, *The Search for Social Entrepreneurship* (Brookings, 2007); Leslie R. Crutchfield and Heather McLeod Grant, *Forces for Good: The Six Practices of High-Impact Nonprofits* (San Francisco: Jossey-Bass, 2008).

42. National Center for Charitable Statistics, *Government Funding of the Nonprofit Sector 2006/2007 Estimates (Draft)* (Washington: Urban Institute, 2010); personal communication from Tom Pollak, March 11, 2010; Jack Krauskopf and others, "The Helpers Need Help: New York City's Nonprofit Human Service Organizations Persevering in Uncertain Times," survey report prepared by Baruch College School of Public Affairs, Center for Nonprofit Strategy and Management and Baruch College Survey Research (Human Services Council of New York City, 2009) (www.humanservicescouncil.org/documents/9.09_NFP_Report.pdf); Smith, "Government Financing of Nonprofit Activity"; Allard, *Out of Reach.*

43. David Osborne and Ted Gaebler, *Reinventing Government* (New York: Plume 1992); Christopher Hood, "A Public Management for All Seasons," *Public Administration* 69 (1991): 3–19.

44. Robert D. Behn and Peter A. Kant, "Strategies for Avoiding the Pitfalls of Performance Contracting," *Public Productivity and Management Review* 22, no. 4 (June 1999): 470–89; Dall W. Forsythe, ed., *Quicker, Better, Cheaper? Managing Performance in American Government* (Albany: Rockefeller Institute Press, 2001); Carolyn J. Heinrich and Youseok Choi, "Performance-Based Contracting in Social Welfare Programs," *American Review of Public Administration* 37, no. 4 (December 2007): 409–35; Steven Rathgeb Smith, "Nonprofits and Public Administration: Reconciling Performance Management and Citizen Engagement," *American Review of Public Administration* 40 (March 2010): 129–52; Dennis Smith, "Making Management Count: A Case for Theory- and Evidence-Based Public Management," *Journal of Policy Analysis and Management* 28, no. 1 (2009): 497–505.

45. Smith and Lipsky, *Nonprofits for Hire.*

46. Ibid.

47. Andy Goodman, *The Story of David Olds and the Nurse Home Visiting Program* (Princeton, N.J.: Robert Wood Johnson Foundation, 2006) (www.rwjf.org/files/publications/other/DavidOldsSpecialReport0606.pdf); Allen Grossman and Daniel F. Curran, *Harlem Children's Zone: Driving Performance with Measurement and Evaluation* (Boston: Harvard Business Publishing, 2004); Paul Tough, *Whatever It Takes: Geoffrey Canada's Quest to Change Harlem and America* (New York: Houghton Mifflin, 2008).

48. Hokyu Hwang and Walter W. Powell, "The Rationalization of Charity: The Influences of Professionalism in the Nonprofit Sector," *Administrative Science Quarterly* 54 (2009): 268–98, also argue, on the basis of results of a survey of nonprofits in the San Francisco Bay area, that management training was an important contributing factor to the professionalization of nonprofits.

49. Allison J. R. Metz, Karen Blasé, and Lillian Bowie, *Implementing Evidence-Based Practices: Six "Drivers" of Success* (Washington: Child Trends, 2007) (www.childtrends.org/Files/Child_Trends-2007_10_01_RB_6SuccessDrivers.pdf).

50. Oregon Department of Human Services, *Evidence Based Practices in Oregon: An Overview* (Salem, Oregon: Oregon Department of Human Services, 2009) (www.oregon.gov/DHS/mentalhealth/ebp/main.shtml#current).

51. Lester M. Salamon, ed., *The Tools of Government* (Oxford University Press, 2002).

52. Robert K. Prouty, Charlie Lakin, and Kathryn Coucouvanis, "In 2006, Fewer than 30% of Persons Receiving Out-of-Family Residential Supports Lived in Homes of More than Six Residents," *Intellectual and Developmental Disabilities* 45, no. 4 (August 2007): 289–92. p. 1.

53. National Association of State Mental Health Program Directors Research Institute, *FY 2005 State Mental Health Revenue and Expenditure Study Results* (Alexandria, Va.: NRI, 2007).

54. Mark and others, "U.S. Spending for Mental Health and Substance Abuse Treatment, 1991–2001."

55. Center for Medicare and Medicaid Services, *New Freedom Initiative* (Washington: CMS, 2010) (www.cms.gov/NewFreedomInitiative).

56. General Accounting Office, *Medicaid Managed Care: Access and Quality Requirements Specific to Low-Income and Other Special Needs Enrollees* (Washington: 2004) (www.gao.gov/new.items/d0544r.pdf).

57. Richard G. Frank, Howard H. Goldman, and Michael Hogan, "Medicaid and Mental Health: Be Careful What You Ask For," *Health Affairs* 22, no. 1 (January–February 2003): 101–13.

58. Mark E. Courtney, "Managed Care and Child Welfare Services: What Are the Issues?" *Children and Youth Services Review* 22, no. 2 (2000): 87–91.

59. J. Gregory Dees, *The Social Enterprise Spectrum: Philanthropy to Commerce* (Boston: Harvard Business School Publishing, 1996); Kim S. Alter, *Social Enterprise Typology* (Portland, Oregon: Virtue Ventures, 2010) (www.4lenses.org/setypology); Joseph J. Cordes and C. Eugene Steuerle, eds., *Nonprofits and Business* (Washington: Urban Institute, 2009); Angela M. Eikenbery and Jodi Drapal Kluver, "The Marketization of the Nonprofit Sector: Civil Society at Risk?" *Public Administration Review* 64, no. 2 (April 2004): 132–40; Crutchfield and Grant, *Forces for Good.*

60. Howard P. Tuckman, "The Strategic and Economic Value of Hybrid Nonprofit Structures," in Cordes and Steuerle, *Nonprofits and Business,* pp. 129–53; Steven Rathgeb Smith, "Hybridization and Nonprofit Organizations: The Governance Challenge," *Policy and Society,* 29, no. 3 (August 2010): 219–29.

61. Share Our Strength, *Driving Social Change—Community Wealth Ventures, Inc.* (Washington: 2010) (http://strength.org/about; www.strength.org).

62. Crutchfield and Grant, *Forces for Good.*

63. See Christine W. Letts, William P. Ryan, and Allen Grossman, *High Performance Nonprofit Organizations: Managing Upstream for Greater Impact* (New York: Wiley, 1999); Alter, *Social Enterprise Typology;* Dees, *Social Enterprise Spectrum;* Bornstein, *How to Change the World.*

64. For example, Catholic Community Services/Catholic Housing Services of Western Washington (website) provided 1.9 million units of home care in 2009 (see "CCS and CHS Summary of Statistics: 2010," www.ccsww.org/site/PageServer?pagename=about_index).

65. Letts, Ryan, and Grossman, *High Performance Nonprofit Organizations;* Crutchfield and Grant, *Forces for Good.*

66. See also Tough, *Whatever It Takes,* and Grossman and Curran, *Harlem Children's Zone.*

67. Burton A. Weisbrod, "The Nonprofit Mission and Its Financing," *Journal of Policy Analysis and Management* 17, no. 2 (1998): 165–74; Henry B. Hansmann, "The Role of Nonprofit Enterprise," *Yale Law Journal* 89 (1980): 835–901; Eikenbery and Kluver, "Marketization of the Nonprofit Sector."

68. This program is administered by the U.S. Department of Health and Human Services (www.hhs.gov/recovery/programs/scf/index.html).

69. Concerns about service integration and fragmentation have a long history in social services policy. See, for example, Mark Ragan, *Building Better Human Services Systems: Integrating Services for Income Support and Related Programs* (Albany: Rockefeller Institute of Government, 2003); Laurence E. Lynn Jr. "Social Services and the State: The Public Appropriation of Private Charity," *Social Service Review* 76, no. 1: 58–82.

70. For more information on volunteering, see Kennard T. Wing, Thomas H. Pollak, and Amy Blackwood, *The Nonprofit Almanac: 2008* (Washington: Urban Institute, 2008).

71. See Frederica D. Kramer and others, *Implementing the Federal Faith-Based Agenda: Charitable Choice and Compassion Capital Initiatives* (Washington: Urban Institute, 2005); for more specific information on the capacity-building grants of the Compassion Capital Fund, see U.S. Department of Health and Human Services, Administration for Children and Families, "Compassion Capital Fund Fact Sheet" (www.acf.hhs.gov/programs/ocs/ccf/about_ccf/facts.html).

72. Gary Bass and others, *Seen but Not Heard: Strengthening Nonprofit Advocacy* (Washington: Aspen Institute, 2007); Jeffrey M. Berry and David Arons, *A Voice for Nonprofits* (Brookings, 2003); Lester M. Salamon and Stephanie Lessans Geller, *Nonprofit America: A Force for Democracy?* Listening Post Project Communqué No. 9 (Johns Hopkins University, Center for Civil Society Studies, 2008).

73. See Smith and Lipsky, *Nonprofits for Hire.*

74. Chelsea Newhouse, *Report on the Listening Post Project Roundtable on Nonprofit Advocacy and Lobbying,* Listening Post Project Communiqué No. 18 (Johns Hopkins University, Center for Civil Society Studies, 2010).

75. See Berry and Arons, *Voice for Nonprofits.*

76. Kirsten Grønbjerg, *Understanding Nonprofit Funding* (San Francisco: Jossey-Bass, 1993); Laurence E. Lynn Jr., "Social Services and the State: The Public Appropriation of Private Charity," *Social Service Review* 76, no. 1 (March 2002): 58–82; Lester M. Salamon, "Partners in Public Service: The Scope and Theory of Government-Nonprofit Relations," in *Nonprofit Sector,* pp. 99–117.

77. For more information on the compact in the U.K., see www.thecompact.org. See also William Plowden, "The Compact: Attempts to Regulate Relationships between Government and the Voluntary Sector in England," *Nonprofit and Voluntary Sector Quarterly* 32, no. 3 (2003): 415–32; John Casey and others, *Advocacy in the Age of Compacts: Regulating Government-Community Sector Relations—International Experiences,* Working Paper Series No. 76 (University of Technology–Sydney, Centre for Australian Community Organisations and Management, 2008).

78. Steven Rathgeb Smith, "The New Politics of Contracting: Citizenship and the Nonprofit Role," in *Public Policy for Democracy,* edited by Helen Ingram and Steven Rathgeb Smith (Brookings, 1993), pp. 198–221.

5

Arts and Culture

STEFAN TOEPLER AND MARGARET J. WYSZOMIRSKI

The field of arts and culture involves aesthetic, heritage, and entertainment activities, products, and artifacts. It comprises a large, heterogeneous set of individuals and organizations engaged in creating, producing, and presenting arts activities, as well as distributing, preserving, and educating about cultural products. These individuals and organizations may be located in the commercial realm, the nonprofit sector, or the public sector. They may also be embedded in other public or private institutions such as local community centers, public or private universities, or religious institutions. The result is "a large, ubiquitous, economically, and socially significant aspect of American public life."[1]

Although clear delineations are difficult to make in this amorphous field, nonprofit organizations constitute a critically important component of the American arts and culture scene. According to economic impact studies conducted by Americans for the Arts, nonprofit arts organizations may generate as much as $166 billion in combined organizational and audience spending, employ an estimated 2.6 million workers, and support perhaps as much as another 3 million full-time-equivalent jobs outside of the arts.[2] According to Internal Revenue Service data, around 36,000 nonprofit arts, culture, and humanities organizations were operating in the United States as of the mid-2000s, up from just 21,000 in the mid-1990s, representing an average annual growth rate of more than 5 percent.[3] This includes nonprofit visual art galleries; artist organizations; museums; performing arts organizations in dance, theater, opera, and music; humanities organizations and historical societies; folk art and cultural heritage groups; art education organizations; and local arts agencies and art centers.

The nonprofit arts subsector encompasses two basic types of organizations. On the one hand are organizations that engage in amateur and community-based creative activities such as community theater groups, choruses and barbershop quartets, many craft and folk art groups, ethnic cultural societies, and art and music appreciation groups. On the other hand are professional performing, visual, literary, and media arts organizations that are managed by full-time staff and produce or present artworks that meet professional standards for quality and attract paying audiences. The latter professional arts institutions were the traditional focus of arts policymaking, but beginning in the 1990s there was a growing appreciation that the nonprofit arts exist within, and contribute to, a broader creative industry.[4] At the same time, interest in grassroots-based arts and alternative cultural activities began to resurface in the context of both urban redevelopment and a diversifying population. In this chapter we review the state of the nonprofit arts and culture field by charting its scope, structure, and recent trends; explore how the four impulses identified in the introduction to this volume play out in the arts; and discuss prevailing managerial and organizational challenges.

The Nonprofit Role in Arts and Culture

The nonprofit sector plays an important niche role within the larger creative economy. In contrast to many other parts of the sector, nonprofits and commercial providers rarely compete directly with each other. Sometimes, they maintain loose, symbiotic relationships; for example, actors move back and forth between the nonprofit stage and commercial productions, movies, and television; and art museums have stakes in the larger art market dominated by art dealers and auction houses and vice versa. Though vulnerable to economic downturns, the nonprofit arts seem financially relatively stable and the basic revenue structure has remained largely unchanged over the past two decades or so. However, as the arts rely heavily on support from their donors as well as box office and admissions income, there are continuous concerns about arts audiences and future participation trends.

Structure of the Field and the Nonprofit Role

As diverse as the field of arts and culture is, a customary breakdown differentiates the performing arts (such as live theater, dance, musical theater, or musical concerts) from the visual arts (art galleries, museums), and both from the humanities. The latter are the least easy to define, but are frequently understood to encompass activities ranging from cultural heritage and historical inquiry to literary undertakings, such as fiction and poetry. However, all three sometimes overlap. For example, an arts center may sponsor concerts or poetry readings while showing an exhibition of a local visual artists' collective. Some cultural activities, such as a festival showcasing the traditional arts and crafts of a country or world region, escape any attempts of easy classification.

Almost all arts institutions of national and international renown are non-profit in nature (a few exceptions are public—that is, government-affiliated—nonprofit organizations such as the Smithsonian Institution or the National Gallery of Art). This is true for the visual arts (institutions such as the Getty Center in Los Angeles, the Metropolitan Museum of Art in New York) and the performing arts (institutions such as the Chicago Symphony Orchestra, the Metropolitan Opera, and the Martha Graham Dance Company). The very prominence of these examples somewhat masks the fact that nonprofit arts and cultural organizations are niche players in the broader cultural marketplace, which is dominated by commercial popular culture, including publishing, film and television, and music recording (see next section). Nevertheless, the non-profit niche is relatively well defined and not particularly small.

Using data reported in the 2007 Economic Census, figure 5-1 positions the nonprofit arts within the framework of selected industries of the broader cul-tural economy. Nonprofits are predominantly found in the performing arts and the broadly defined museum field (which also includes institutions with living collections, such as zoos, aquariums, and arboreta), where they coexist with a minority commercial presence. A nonprofit presence can also be identified else-where, such as fine arts schools (including dance academies), where nonprof-its capture about one-quarter of the revenues. Revenues from the performing arts and museum fields combined are about $27 billion, equivalent to revenues from the book-publishing industry, with nonprofits accounting for two-thirds. The nonprofit arts generate higher revenues than art dealer sales ($8 billion), the sound recording industry ($15 billion), or independent artists, writers, and performers ($13 billion). On the other hand, the nonprofit arts do not nearly reach the economic scale of the movie industry ($80 billion) or the broadcasting industry ($100 billion).

The nonprofit presence is most pronounced within the performing arts field and the visual arts and museum field (the latter comprising a wide range of organizations from visual arts galleries to parks and historic sites in addition to various kinds of museums exhibiting objects or living collections). The role of nonprofits and the mix of nonprofit and commercial provision differs signifi-cantly between these two fields. Nonprofits clearly dominate the latter. Overall, in the visual arts and museum field, nonprofits account for a little under 90 percent of all establishments and a little over 90 percent of all revenues. These

Figure 5-1. *The Nonprofit Arts in the Context of the Broader Cultural Economy,
Selected Industries*

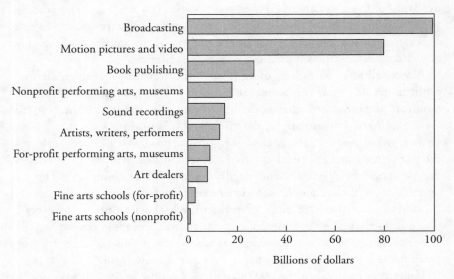

Billions of dollars

Source: U.S. Census Bureau, 2007 Economic Census. Release Date: 10/30/2009. Various Sectors.
"Industry Series: Preliminary Summary Statistics for the United States: 2007."

figures are particularly driven by the economic weight of museums and galleries, of which nine out of ten are nonprofit (figure 5-2 shows the percentage of nonprofits in various cultural subfields). The nonprofit share of historical sites is even higher: 95 percent. Nonprofits are also prevalent among nature parks, with seven out of nine establishments and slightly less than three-quarters of revenues. Within this group of institutions, nonprofits make up the lowest share of zoos and botanical gardens, about two-thirds of all establishments, although nonprofit zoos account for nine-tenths of revenues. Commercial zoo operations—perhaps best typified by the "petting zoo"—tend to be small and do not provide much competition for their much larger nonprofit counterparts, with their focus on education, research, and conservation.

In contrast to the field of museums and similar cultural institutions, the roles of nonprofits and for-profits are much more varied in the performing arts. In most performing arts fields the majority of entities are commercial; nonprofits account for less than half of all establishments and only 40 percent of revenues. The three main performing arts fields—theater, dance, and music—show greatly divergent patterns. The relatively small field of dance is the one where the nonprofit presence is the most pronounced (see figure 5-2). Nonprofits account for three-quarters of establishments and 85 percent of dance revenues. Ballet and

Figure 5-2. *The Nonprofit Share in Major Arts and Culture Subfields, 2007*

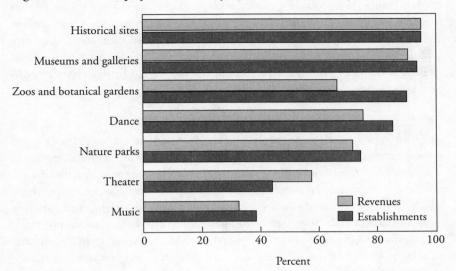

Source: U.S. Census Bureau, 2007 Economic Census, Release Date: 10/30/2009, "Sector 71: EC0771I1: Arts Entertainment and Recreation: Industry Series: Preliminary Summary Statistics for the United States: 2007."

modern dance are an uncontested nonprofit domain, and nonprofits also have a strong presence in folk and other ethnic dance ensembles. Most of the nonprofit activities relate to dance performance rather than to instruction, which accounts for the for-profit dominance among fine art schools (see figure 5-1).

In theater, the majority of establishments, almost 60 percent, are nonprofit, but the situation is reversed with regard to revenues, with nonprofits accounting for only 44 percent of revenues (see figure 5-2). Other than dinner theaters, most commercial theater consists of Broadway shows and traveling productions frequently spun off from them. Off-Broadway and Off-Off-Broadway also have strong for-profit components, but nonprofits become increasingly salient as the distance to Broadway increases. Resident theater companies across the rest of the country are nearly exclusively nonprofit, as are community theater troupes (nine out of ten). Similarly, four out of five children's theaters are noncommercial.[5]

In music, the for-profit presence is even more pronounced. Although nonprofits account for only one-third of establishments and less than 40 percent of revenues (figure 5-2), within the music field, nonprofits occupy distinct "high cultural" niches: opera companies, symphony orchestras, and chamber music organizations are more or less exclusive nonprofit domains, although classical musicians often form smaller ensembles to generate additional earnings by, for example, providing musical entertainment at events. Choral groups are likewise predominantly nonprofit. Outside the classical music field live music performance is essentially a commercial operation. The nonprofit presence is small in jazz and almost nonexistent in dance and stage bands.[6] In sum, arts and culture represents a heterogeneous field that is marked by a pronounced commercial vitality, particularly within the performing arts, as well as firm enclaves of nonprofit dominance.

Financial Trends in the Nonprofit Arts and Culture

As of the mid-2000s, the nonprofit arts and culture field reported annual revenues in excess of $27 billion to the Internal Revenue Service, representing about 2.4 percent of total nonprofit revenues.[7] Although some arts institutions are quite large, they rarely approach the size of hospitals or colleges and universities, which give the health and education fields their economic weight. And although nonprofit arts organizations can be found nearly everywhere, they do not reach the number of agencies that the social services field boasts. Nevertheless, the arts tend to be firmly woven into the fabric of communities. Arts institutions are sources of civic pride and symbols of community identity; they can help center economic development efforts and are invaluable providers of arts education. They can serve as a means of both integration and expression for diverse parts of local communities.

Table 5-1 on page 237 provides an overview of the financial situation of nonprofit arts, culture, and humanities (ACH) organizations. These data capture larger, more formally constituted organizations that report annually to the Internal Revenue Service, but not small-scale avocational groups nor embedded cultural activities. The total $27.4 billion in 2005 ACH revenues breaks down to $7.8 billion (29 percent) for the performing arts, $6.3 billion (23 percent) for museums and related activities, including non–arts museums but excluding non-museum-based visual arts; $2 billion (7 percent) for historical societies; and $11.2 (41 percent) billion for all other cultural organizations. Expenditures are distributed roughly proportionally across the fields with 30 percent for the performing arts, 21 percent for museums, 7 percent for historical societies, and 43 percent for all other fields.

Charting revenue and expenditure growth rates between the mid-1990s and the mid-2000s highlights the contrast between the prosperous late 1990s and the much leaner early 2000s (after the recession of 2001), suggesting some interesting conclusions about the overall financial health of the ACH field. On the one hand, the data suggest that ACH organization finances tend to be cyclical, in contrast to the noncyclical nature of other parts of the nonprofit sector. Thus, cultural nonprofits are prone to boom and bust cycles, depending on the economy at large, and tend to overextend themselves during the good times. On the other hand, the nonprofit ACH field appears to have a substantial financial cushion in the aggregate that dampens the impact of economic crises, at least in the short run.

CYCLICAL NATURE OF FINANCES. Comparing the average annual growth rates for nonprofit ACH revenues and expenditures between the 1995–2000 and the 2000–05 periods suggests that nonprofit arts and cultural organizations experience the impact of economic recessions differently than other parts of the nonprofit sector. As table 5-1 suggests, the annual revenue growth rates remained essentially stable at just above 7 percent for the nonprofit sector at large. Arts and cultural nonprofits by contrast experienced above-average growth rates in the late 1990s (9.9 percent) that then shrank disproportionally in the early 2000s to just 2.4 percent. Although drops in revenue growth occurred everywhere in the ACH field, the intensity of the drops varied significantly by subfield. The museum field had experienced particularly high growth rates in the late 1990s of nearly 14 percent, but growth came to a virtual standstill in the early 2000s at just 0.8 percent. Historical societies showed a similar pattern with growth rates dropping from 12.4 percent to 2.5 percent. In the performing arts, the slowing down of revenue growth was much more moderate, from 8.6 percent to 3.6 percent, and similar to all other ACH activities (8.2 percent to 2.6 percent).

Nonprofit cultural organizations' financial fortunes were closely aligned with the overall economy; thus, they benefited disproportionately from the economic well-being of the 1990s, but began to lose out in equal measure in the economically rougher times of the early 2000s. This cyclical character stands in marked contrast to the anticyclical nature of other parts of the nonprofit sector. Economic recessions tend to increase demand for a wide range of services typically provided by nonprofits because of increased needs, such as emergency shelters and food distribution, job training and placements, or lack of opportunities in the marketplace—for example, increased enrollment in graduate schools resulting from scarcity of viable career opportunities for college graduates.[8] In addition, since significant components of government funding, which support much nonprofit activity outside of arts and culture, are designed to be countercyclical, this helps buttress other nonprofits from the negative impact of economic downturns. All this translates into growing or at least stable overall revenues for nonprofits at large even during economic recessions, as evidenced by the unchanged nonprofit sector revenue growth between 1995 and 2005 (see table 5-1). The revenue picture of cultural organizations is thus much less recession-proof than those of other parts of the nonprofit sector.

POTENTIAL FOR OVEREXTENSION. Moreover, rapid revenue growth such as that experienced by cultural organizations during the 1990s encourages an expansion of services and facilities, which increases future operating costs, requiring additional growth in future revenues. Unless carefully managed, growth can thus undercut the financial viability of a field over the long run by encouraging nonprofits to overextend themselves beyond the limits of available revenues. In fact, concerns about such an overextension in the nonprofit arts have long been voiced, with the museum field a particular area of concern.[9]

Table 5-1 highlights this issue. In the late 1990s, museum expenditures, as well as those of historical societies, grew by an average of nearly 10 percent each year, followed by the performing arts, at 7.4 percent, and all other cultural organizations at 6.7 percent. For the cultural field overall, the growth rate was 7.7 percent, or about one percentage point above the growth rate of the non-profit sector at large. Although expenditures did not grow at quite the speed of revenues in the period, they did not slow down nearly as much as revenues in the economically leaner times of the early 2000s. Annual expenditure growth remained around the 5 percent mark across the board, thus significantly outpacing the greatly reduced growth of revenues in this period. Arguably this left the nonprofit cultural field growing into a financial squeeze well before the onset of the Great Recession of the late 2000s. For the nonprofit arts and culture field, predictions of impending financial crises bookmarked the first decade of the twenty-first century. The decade began with claims of a "perfect storm" resulting from the 2001 crisis and ended with calls for a "bailout" of the arts in the aftermath of the financial crisis of 2007 (inspired by the major economic theme of the day).[10] In between, speculation that structural problems endangered particularly mid-size organizations even in the absence of a specific economic crisis gained considerable attention.[11]

FINANCIAL RESILIENCE. Despite these gloomy predictions, however, the nonprofit arts and culture field at large appears to be managing its finances well enough. Table 5-1 shows the fieldwide surplus (excess of revenues over expenses)—a financial health indicator—for 1995, 2000, and 2005. Generally, cultural organizations generated surpluses double or more than double the size of the reasonable surpluses yielded by nonprofits overall. Whereas nonprofit surpluses were 8 percent in 1995, 11 percent in 2000, and close to 9 percent in 2005, for cultural organizations they were 15 percent, almost 28 percent, and 14 percent, respectively. The scale of nonprofit cultural surpluses was largely driven by museums and historical societies. Museums showed surpluses of one-third of expenditures in 1995, almost 60 percent in 2000, and still close to 28 percent in 2005.

Table 5-1. *Arts, Culture, and Humanities (ACH) Financial Indicators*

Revenues and expenditures	*Perform-ing arts*	*Museums*	*Historical societies*	*All other ACH*	*Total ACH*	*Total nonprofit sector*
Revenues ($ millions, 2005)	$7,807	$6,287	$2,027	$11,234	$27,355	$1,144,022
Average growth, 1995--2000	8.6	13.7	12.4	8.2	9.9	7.2
Average growth, 2000--05	3.6	0.8	2.5	2.6	2.4	7.1
Expenditures ($ millions, 2005)	$7,187	$4,929	$1,562	$10,248	$23,927	$1,053,487
Average growth, 1995--2000	7.4	9.8	9.5	6.7	7.7	6.6
Average growth, 2000--05	5.0	5.3	5.3	4.1	4.7	7.6
Financial health (percent)[a]						
1995	9.7	32.9	30.3	10.1	15.3	8.1
2000	16.1	58.8	48.2	18.2	27.6	11.0
2005	8.6	27.6	29.8	9.6	14.3	8.6

Source: Based on data for public charities reporting to the IRS; see Kenneth Wing, Thomas Pollak, and Amy Blackwood, *The Nonprofit Almanac 2008* (Washington: Urban Institute Press, 2008), tables 5.7 and 5.9.

a. Aggregate excess of revenues over expenses.

Taken together, this suggests that cultural organizations benefited disproportionally from the good economic times of the 1990s, seeing greater than normal revenue growth and much higher surpluses than most other nonprofits. And despite the economic problems of the beginning of the decade and the significant drop in revenue growth, their financial health, as measured by the excess of revenues over expenditures, still looked good by the mid-2000s. However, surplus data need to be interpreted with caution, in the arts perhaps more than in other parts of the nonprofit sector, because tax return–based revenue data do not distinguish between operating and capital revenues. Significant capital campaigns can thus generate something of a distortion, as revenues from, for example, endowment campaigns do not become immediately available for operating purposes, or they accrue long before corresponding expenditures are made, as in the case of campaigns to renovate, expand, or build facilities.[12] Indeed, this would be consistent with the very high surplus rate in the museum field in 2000. Some museums, such as the Metropolitan Museum, had used the 1990s to secure their financial footing by endowment-building efforts, but the prevailing trend was to raise capital support funds for bricks-and-mortar building campaigns.[13] Chronically undercapitalized, museums have arguably come to rely on expansions and related periodic capital campaigns to help cover structural deficits in an escalation of what used to be referred to as "blockbuster economics"—the attempt to generate financial windfalls through the staging of big, highly popular exhibitions every two or three years to plug ongoing budget deficits in the interim.[14] Nominal surpluses—derived from capital campaigns rather than ongoing operating support—could then mask the underlying financial problems while exacerbating them into the future, as expansions induce higher operating costs that require even more future revenues.

Still, the nonprofit arts are likely more stable than often expected. While some, usually smaller, organizations do have to close, the vast majority finds ways to muddle through the crises. True, the Baltimore Opera was forced into liquidation in 2009, but in the same year the Washington National Opera, though forced into significant budget cuts, was not existentially threatened. The relative economic resiliency of arts and culture was shown after the 2001 recession, which had raised grave concerns about a "perfect storm"—a simultaneous drop in individual contributions, corporate and foundation giving, government support, and endowment income. Despite dour predictions and some belt tightening, however, there were few indications that the crisis led to the demise of many cultural organizations.[15]

Revenue Structure and Trends

Table 5-2 shows the overall revenue structure for arts, culture, and humanities organizations. Revenue structures vary considerably among various artistic disciplines; for example, theater companies are much more dependent on box office receipts than art museums are on admissions income. As of 2005, government support amounted to a little over 12 percent, whereas private gifts and grants from individuals, foundations, and corporations amounted to close to 41 percent. Thus, arts and culture nonprofits deviate from the overall nonprofit sector revenue structure, with relatively low levels of government support and a relatively high share of private philanthropy. Similar to the overall picture, though, nearly half of arts and cultural organization revenues (46.7 percent) are derived from various forms of earned income, with private payments (ticket sales, admission fees, tuition charges, and similar fees for service) accounting for 31 percent of total revenues and other earned income (such as endowment and investment income, fundraising events, and business ventures) for another 15 percent.

Although there is some variability over time, data for the near twenty-year period from 1977 to 2005 suggest that the broad revenue categories within the arts and culture are relatively stable (table 5-2), despite both the considerable growth of the nonprofit arts as well as the significant economic ups and downs that occurred during this period. Government support peaked at 15 percent in 1987 and then dropped to less than 10 percent in 1997; private philanthropy reached a high of more than 43 percent in the prosperous late 1990s; and earned income, particularly investment income, briefly dipped in the recession

Table 5-2. *Revenue Structure for Nonprofit Arts, Culture, and Humanities Organizations, 1977–2005*

Percent

Source of income	1977	1987	1997	2005
Government support	11.8	15.0	9.7	12.5
Private philanthropy	41.2	40.0	43.5	40.8
Earned income	47.0	45.0	46.7	46.7
Private payments	29.4	30.0	27.9	31.3
Other earned income	17.6	15.0	18.8	15.4

Sources: For 2005 data see Kenneth Wing, Thomas Pollak, and Amy Blackwood, *The Nonprofit Almanac 2008* (Washington: Urban Institute Press, 2008), table 5.12; for 1977–97 data see Independent Sector and Urban Institute, *The New Nonprofit Almanac & Desk Reference* (San Francisco: Jossey-Bass, 2002), figure 4.13.

of 1987. Nevertheless, the revenue structure of arts and cultural organizations in 2005 was essentially a mirror image of the 1977 revenue structure; the most significant difference was a slight shift toward more box office and admissions income and somewhat less other earned income—with no impact on the overall earned income share. Nevertheless, a number of trends within the main revenue groups merit further discussion.

GOVERNMENT SUPPORT. Toward the end of the first decade of the twenty-first century, government grants to nonprofit arts organizations amounted to some $1.3 billion, of which 63 percent came from local governments, 25 percent from the states, and 12 percent from the federal government through the National Endowment for the Arts (NEA).[16] Although the national funding stream was the smallest of the public funders, the national role was crucial in sparking public support at the state and local levels after the establishment of the NEA and the National Endowment for the Humanities (NEH) in the mid-1960s. Following substantial increases during the 1970s, federal arts funding continued to grow slowly in the 1980s (even though budget erosion occurred in real terms) to a high of $175.9 million in 1992. Following years of controversy that began in 1989 with disputes over funding for sexually explicit art, federal funding lost ground and the NEA's budget was drastically cut in 1996, to $99.5 million. At that time, Congress all but eliminated the agency's ability to fund individual artists directly, except for honorific awards such as the jazz and folk art masters and the highly competitive fellowships for writers of literature. Instead, 40 percent of the NEA budget allocation had to be distributed to state arts agencies. Subsequently, the agency shifted its focus somewhat, from providing through its funding a sort of seal of approval for excellent arts organizations

to outreach through national initiatives such as enabling Shakespeare productions to tour rural America or bringing opera productions to military bases.[17]
Once the NEA was thus on politically safer ground, its budget began to grow
again—to $155 million in 2009—but it never recovered its earlier budget level
in current, let alone real, terms.

Where federal funding was subject to political turbulence, state and local
government support for the arts has proved to be more susceptible to economic turbulence. After recovering from the 1991 recession, state funding
grew quickly through the latter part of the 1990s, reaching a high of $451 mil-
lion in 2001. However, in the aftermath of the 2001 recession state funding
dipped to less than $300 million by the mid-2000s, briefly recovered to $350
million, and then began to drop off again, going into the financial crisis at the
end of the decade. With many states subject to balanced budget constraints, arts
funding is highly sensitive to overall economic conditions and usually does not
rebound until several years into the next economic recovery.[18] Recessions mean
less government support everywhere, but the size of the swings in state-level
appropriations can vary significantly among states, depending on local circumstances. This can be best illustrated by the experience of California and New
York, the two states that approved the largest state arts agency appropriations
in fiscal year 2000: $68 million and $56.7 million, respectively. By FY2010,
New York appropriated $52 million. Although this represented a small nomi-
nal decline over FY2000 (and a much more significant decline in real terms
over the decade), New York's was still the largest state appropriation by far for
2010, followed at some distance by Minnesota ($30 million) and New Jersey
($17 million). In California, by contrast, the onset of the 2001 recession led
almost immediately to calls for the elimination of the state arts council; faced
with budgetary pressures throughout the remainder of the decade, the state did
indeed virtually eliminate arts funding in the end: the appropriation for FY2010
amounted to a mere $4.3 million, a per-capita allocation of $0.12, the lowest
among all fifty states.[19]

At the local level, local arts agencies are the primary channel of public finding. Support from local governments, the largest source of public funds in the
aggregate, was estimated to have grown from $600 million at the beginning of
the 1990s to $800 million at the end. In contrast to both federal and state sup-
port, local support exceeded pre-2001 funding levels by growing to $858 mil-
lion after a brief post-2001 recession dip. Arts funding at the local level is at
least partially rooted in efforts to boost tourism and economic development, but
it is not recession-proof: forecasts for 2010 placed the volume of local arts support at $765 million. There are an estimated five thousand local arts agencies
in the country, most of which are nonprofit organizations that receive public
funds, while some are public agencies. Nine out of ten local agencies administer

their own cultural programming; four out of five provide direct services to artists and arts organizations; six out of ten run arts facilities; and two out of three make grants. Virtually all local arts agencies encourage and fund collaborations with other public and community agencies, especially school districts, parks and recreation departments, libraries, convention and tourism bureaus, neighborhood groups, and chambers of commerce.[20]

PRIVATE PHILANTHROPY. The 1990s proved to be a period of significant growth for private arts philanthropy. Private dollars almost tripled, from less than $4 billion in 1990 (4 percent of all private giving) to $11.4 billion in 2001 (5 percent of all giving).[21] Despite some early concerns about declining average contributions and declining shares of total giving, the 1990s were marked by the availability of ready philanthropic monies that encouraged growth.[22] The 1990s also saw new foundations enter the field of cultural philanthropy, notably the Lila Wallace Reader's Digest Fund, the Doris Duke Charitable Foundations, the Thomas Kenan Institute for the Arts, and artist-funded foundations such as the Andy Warhol Foundation for the Visual Arts and the Robert Mapplethorpe Foundation. In addition, many foundations and corporations began to rethink and adapt their funding strategies and perspectives.[23] In one especially innovative gesture, a group of private foundations supported the creation of a new nonprofit organization called Creative Capital, dedicated to funding experimental, challenging projects in the performing, visual, film-video, and hybrid arts. Another one was the Pew Charitable Trusts' effort at the end of the decade to launch a major cultural policy initiative.

In the 2000s, arts philanthropy quickly rebounded from the 2001 recession, but lacked the more dynamic growth of the 1990s. Philanthropy reached a peak of $13.7 billion, or 4.4 percent of all giving, in 2007 before falling back to $12.3 billion, or 4 percent of all private philanthropy, in still recession-constrained 2009. In terms of qualitative change, corporate and foundation support became more focused on the anticipated impact and outcomes of arts and cultural programming than on altruism or support of art for art's sake.[24] Many such institutional donors aimed to develop a broader systems approach, to take an ecological perspective, and to see the nonprofit arts and humanities as part of a broadly conceived culture sector. Grant makers paid more attention to the promotion of the cultivation of new relationships for arts and cultural organizations with partners outside the cultural realm or in the commercial sector. Others experimented with new program tools and expanded the role of intermediaries such as community foundations and arts service organizations. However, over the course of the decade, institutional funders faced growing pressures to justify the allocation of scarce philanthropic dollars to the arts, which in turn weakened their ability to exert policy leadership in the field. By the end of the

2000s, the Ford and Rockefeller foundations, which had been instrumental in the postwar creation of the nonprofit arts field, had essentially ceased their arts and culture programs.[25]

EARNED INCOME. Mounting pressures to increase earned income resulted in changes in marketing, more emphasis on entrepreneurial activities, and a sharper concern for cultivating new audiences and new donors. Often this new entrepreneurship focused on ancillary activities such as restaurants or gift shops. Other times it involved a technologically driven strategy to digitize and, it was hoped, capitalize on an organization's intellectual property. Although the latter hope fizzled out even before the bust of the dot.com boom, cultural institutions heeded the call to seek greater financial independence through the box office or the admissions booth. For example, the reopening of New York's Museum of Modern Art in 2004 after renovations was accompanied by a rise in the general entrance fee by what the *New York Times* termed "an eye-opening 67 percent, to $20, making MoMA the most expensive major art museum in the United States."[26] In addition, cultural organizations that could also sought to build or bolster endowments, both as a hedge against shifting funding patterns and as a strategy for organizational autonomy in the face of demands from virtually all institutional funders for greater accountability and demonstrable community outcomes.

Audience Development and Participation Trends

Although some forms of high culture have a reputation as elitist and exclusive, arts activities serve a broad swath of the American public. A recent participation survey suggests that more than one third of the adult population attended arts performances or visited arts museums in 2008.[27] However, after generally healthy growth in the 1990s, arts audiences appear to have been shrinking in the 2000s, causing considerable concern about the future viability of parts of the nonprofit cultural infrastructure. These concerns have been augmented by a perceived "graying" of audiences for some art forms and the difficulties in attracting younger and more diverse audiences to them. Arts attendance is also sensitive to economic circumstances; virtually all forms of arts attendance experienced a decline between 2002 and 2008, the onset of the national recession (see figure 5-3). Since the overall economic conditions affect both tourism and the discretionary income of residents, arts participation is sensitive to recessions, and the observed drop in 2008 may thus be as much a short-term reaction to the developing financial crisis at the time as a reflection of a long-term trend.

Art museums, visited by some 51 million adults in 2008, are the most popular type of art institution and the least affected by participation concerns. During the museum boom of the 1990s, the share of the adult population visiting

Figure 5-3. *Arts Attendance Trends, by Subfield, as Percentage of Total Adult Population*

Percent

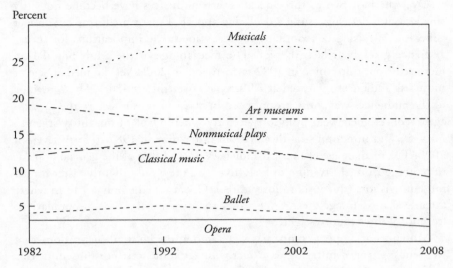

Source: National Endowment for the Arts, *Arts Participation 2008: Highlights from a National Survey* (Washington: NEA, 2009).

these museums grew from 22 percent in 1982 to 27 percent in 1992, where it remained through 2002 until dropping back to 23 percent in 2008.[28]

Plays, musicals, and nonmusical theater constitute the second-largest type of arts participation, with attendance of 46 million. Notwithstanding this fact, the trend in theater visits has been downward since 1980, even before the economic problems of the early 2000s (the only exception is growth of one and a half percentage points in audiences for nonmusical theater during the 1980s). Attendance at nonmusical theater declined from 13.5 percent of the adult population in 1992 to 9.4 percent in 2008, and attendance at musical theater remained more or less stagnant at around 17 percent over the period (see figure 5-3). Ballet and dance attendance (16 million) shows a pattern similar to that of nonmusical theater: some growth during the 1980s and a moderate decline since then. Opera companies, though only reaching a relatively small segment of the population, 5 million, managed to grow and hold on to their audience from the 1980s into the 2000s, before also suffering a decline in 2008. While the relative vitality of opera over the past two decades has been a ray of hope for classical music advocates, classical music in general (symphony and chamber music concerts) is the major arts discipline that has seen the most consistent and the most long-term erosion of its audience. Whereas 13 percent of the adult population attended classical concerts in 1982, the share shrank to 11.6 percent in 2002 and further down to 9.3 percent by 2008 (see figure 5-3).

Over the past two to three decades, arts audiences have become not only smaller but older, suggesting a declining appeal of many art forms to younger generations, raising concomitant concerns about the implications for future audience growth or lack thereof. The median age of the adult population increased from thirty-nine in 1982 to forty-five in 2008, yet the median age of most arts audiences increased at a faster rate over this period.[29] The "graying" of the audiences was most pronounced in classical music, where the median age of concertgoers went from forty to forty-nine; in ballet from thirty-seven to forty-six, and in nonmusical theater from thirty-nine in 1982 to forty-seven in 2008. The median age of musical audiences tracked that of the general population, going from thirty-nine to forty-five, and grew only slightly faster for art museum visitors (thirty-six to forty-three). Opera was the only art form where attendees' median age grew more slowly than that of the general population, from forty-three to forty-eight.

Museums and opera companies were among the cultural institutions that were most engaged in trying to attract younger audiences. For museums, this reflected a greater focus on offering family programs or family-friendly activities in conjunction with regular art exhibitions, thus making museums attractive destinations for younger adults with children. But museums also engaged in targeted efforts to reach and cultivate new generations of patrons by offering opportunities for young professionals to socialize and network.[30] Singles nights and other similar evening events with cash bar and music intended for young adults became an art museum staple in many metropolitan areas. Opera also experienced exceptional growth among audiences in the eighteen-to-twenty-four age group over the past two decades. Many opera companies have aggressively marketed to young audiences by designing subscription programs that combine attendance at opera performances with social interaction. Although opera is still the least commonly attended of the "high" arts, creative marketing efforts did succeed in appealing to young professionals and generation X opera neophytes alike.[31] Nevertheless, opera, like all arts disciplines except for art museums in 2008, also saw a drop in young adult participation below the early 1980s levels.[32]

Factors Shaping the Nonprofit Arts

Lester Salamon (chapter 1, this volume) describes four impulses that shape the nonprofit sector in the early twenty-first century: voluntarism, civic activism, professionalization, and commercialization. To varying degrees, all of these are pertinent in arts and culture.

Voluntarism

Arts and cultural organizations provide a wide range of opportunities for volunteers to participate in governance, and to provide administrative and program support. Volunteers answer the phones during pledge drives for local public broadcasting stations; serve as ushers during theater performances; guide schoolchildren and other groups through museum exhibitions as docents; help out in the costume studio or sometimes participate as supernumeraries in opera productions. Principally, however, the nation's voluntary spirit in the arts is embodied in a pervasive range of avocational activities in which Americans come together to actively make art and enjoy cultural expression. In fact, significant parts of the population are involved in such activities. For example, 15 percent of the adult population enjoy photography as a hobby; 13 percent weave or sew; 9 percent paint or draw; 7 percent write creatively; 6 percent engage in pottery making. Among the performing arts, 5 percent of the adult population sing in choirs or choruses; 3 percent perform classical music; 2 percent dance; and almost 2 percent act in musical and nonmusical plays.[33]

Some of this activity is pursued individually, but much of it takes place in small, informal or semiformal groups that connect people with similar avocational interests. Hobby photographers gather in photography or camera clubs to share, exhibit and judge each other's works. Sewing has traditionally been done in the great communal tradition of the quilting club. Creative writers present and discuss their work in writers' clubs or circles. Amateur actors produce plays in community theaters, schools, or church basements. Musical amateurs perform chamber music in *Hausmusik* settings; and singers not only participate in church and community choirs but may also form barbershop quartets and similar small ensembles.

Unfortunately, the full extent and outlines of this grassroots, avocational activity and how, if at all, it intersects with the more professional cultural infrastructure remains largely unknown. For better or worse, the traditional focus on larger, professional nonprofit cultural institutions has pushed this widespread grassroots activity to the sidelines and left it largely unexplored. Some analysts thus noted that as "long as these activities remain unquantified, they are left out of our understanding of the arts sector and will remain invisible on the radar screens of policymakers. Yet the individual and community impact of the unincorporated arts is substantial. They represent grassroots participation and involve a large number of Americans."[34] This point was echoed elsewhere with regard to the performing arts.[35] Although definitive evidence is still lacking, a number of more limited studies support the point. In a suburban context, for example, one study found that grassroots cultural activities outnumbered larger and more formal organizations by a factor of 2, drew more than one-third of all volunteer efforts in the arts, and attracted 13 percent of all arts and culture attendance.[36]

However hard to quantify, informal cultural activities perform important functions in the community context, and the social impacts of cultural activity are of particular importance in the context of urban neighborhoods.[37] In this regard it is disconcerting that there has been a marked decline across all forms of active participation over the past two decades. For example, the portion of the adult population acting in plays dropped by more than 3.5 percentage points between 1992 and 2008; dance by 6; and weaving and sewing by 12 percentage points. Only photography saw an increase over the period, as the advent of digital technology increased the ease and potential, while reducing the costs, of practicing this art form.[38]

It is possible that this observed decline may be a reflection less of dwindling participation than of the growth of forms of arts participation, particularly among ethnic and racial minorities, that are not well captured by traditional categories.[39] Changing immigration patterns have recently resulted in an increase in the attention drawn to cultural heritage activities such as organizing festivals and providing space to showcase and maintain language, musical, culinary, and other cultural traditions that help preserve community identity within immigrant and other low-income communities.[40] Not only has the pace of immigration increased over the last two decades, but also—unlike the early modern immigration pattern that disproportionately affected America's large urban industrial regions in the Northeast, Midwest, and California—the contemporary wave of immigrants marks a truly national phenomenon. Smaller cities throughout the nation have directly attracted new settlement from abroad and have grown in population because of immigration.

Immigration may also bring changes in cultural sensibilities and diversity over the coming years.[41] In contrast to the earlier waves of mostly European immigration, the new immigration is less likely to cluster around faith-based institutions or other community centers. Rather, much of the civic and social life is organized around more or less informal cultural activity. For example, dance performances or concerts by foreign or immigrant artists are frequently organized by loose networks of individuals and take place in the living rooms or basements of private homes—fully bypassing official grant cycles, established facilities, and mainstream dissemination and distribution channels.[42] These forms of cultural expression remain largely under the radar screen, posing a significant problem for local policymakers and funders. Gaining a better understanding of cultural diversity and need of support in immigrant communities is important for fostering cultural democracy and pluralism and generating spillover effects for mainstream cultural organizations in terms of both developing new audiences and increasing internal diversity.

Civic Activism

Traditionally, the primary client group of civic activism in the arts has been the arts themselves, as opposed to many other fields, in which nonprofits foster civic activism on behalf of disadvantaged client groups such as children, or the homeless. In the post–World War II period activism largely focused on increasing public and private financial resources in an effort to nurture and grow the nascent nonprofit arts and culture infrastructure. Not only did the quest for artistic excellence and particularly broadening access to the arts benefit the population at large, but also the most immediate and direct beneficiaries were arts institutions and to some extent artists themselves. This arrangement first came under fire with the so-called culture wars of the late 1980s and early 1990s, in which the arts featured prominently.

Debates concerning allegedly obscene, pornographic, blasphemous, or otherwise offensive art exhibited in museums and galleries or performed on stage and in theaters raised public awareness and concern about the content of the so-called "high arts" that are generally seen as the purview of the nonprofit arts sector. Advocates for the arts made freedom-of-expression arguments to counter congressional efforts to legislate community decency standards that could have opened the door to public censorship. Although these debates have faded away at the federal level, they still occasionally flare up locally. In one such episode, Mayor Rudolph Giuliani of New York City threatened to cut city subsidies to the Brooklyn Museum over what was reported as blasphemous art in a somewhat sensationalist exhibition.[43] The coincidence of similar debates concerning the commercial arts and entertainment industries—whether television, movies, recordings, or video games—continued to muddy public assumptions about the public's ability to trust the quality of art found in many nonprofit venues as well as in the popular-culture offerings of the entertainment industries.

Nonprofit arts and cultural organizations dealt more successfully with other, less sensational, issues concerning fairness, equity, and public responsibilities. The mobilization of a broad arts education movement since the early 1990s, in tandem with a more general effort to reform education, highlighted the educational mission and potential of cultural organizations even as it revealed the often meager presence of arts in the schools and the frequently underdeveloped capacity of cultural organizations to contribute to a well-rounded public education. The nonprofit arts community not only rose to the general educational challenge but also extended its efforts to targeting at-risk youth, often through after-school programs. Engaging the broader community in efforts to stem and reverse the long decline of arts education nevertheless remains a significant challenge.[44]

Another major concern that has emerged since the 1990s relates to the issue of civic inclusiveness and how well arts institutions reflect and engage all the elements of their communities. The perceived demographic unrepresentativeness of established cultural organizations, such as orchestras and museums, remains a major point of discussion and debate within disciplines and between specific organizations and their local communities. For example, museums began the early 1990s with the American Association of Museums' 1992 report *Excellence and Equity* and enactment of the Native American Graves Protection and Repatriation Act (passed in 1990).[45] Both reflected a growing concern on the part of museum professionals with equity, cultural sensitivity, and the public responsibilities of museums. The AAM report noted: "As public institutions in a democratic society, museums must achieve greater inclusiveness. Trustees, staff, and volunteers must acknowledge and respect our nation's diversity in race, ethnic origin, age, gender, economic status, and education, and they should attempt to reflect that pluralism in every aspect of museums' operations and programs."[46]

The AAM continued this effort with another major undertaking, the Museums and Community initiative at the turn of the millennium.[47] Taking a similar tack, in the early 1990s, the League of American Orchestras (then the American Symphony Orchestra League) brought out its controversial report, *Americanizing the American Orchestra*.[48] Prompted in part by concern for the precarious financial state of orchestras, reports of aging audiences, and accusations of cultural irrelevancy, the report sought to promote change in many aspects of orchestra operations and relations with the public and local communities. These changes were both about ensuring the survival of orchestras as well as about emphasizing their public role. The report noted, "In order to remain a vital and relevant element of American society, the orchestra field as a whole should demonstrate greater inclusiveness and responsiveness to the demographic and cultural evolution of the United States, and individual American orchestras should reflect more closely the cultural mix, needs, and interests of their communities."[49]

However, these pressures fed into a backlash from some who suggest that arts institutions should be primarily about the arts, and that their core artistic and cultural purposes are increasingly and detrimentally being trumped by broader educational, social, and economic agendas.[50] Indeed, the primary focus on civic activism since the 1990s has been to utilize arts and culture to achieve a range of broader purposes. A wave of economic impact studies has sought to establish the arts as a means of furthering economic development and business improvement objectives. In addition, the initial suggestion of a possible "Mozart effect"—the notion that exposure to classical music might improve certain brain functions—and numerous studies suggesting that art making and exposure could improve students' math and reading skills have reignited advocacy efforts on behalf of arts education. The increasing instrumentalization of the arts has therefore led to a new debate about the value of art and the benefits of supporting art for art's sake.

Professionalization

Professionalization and commercialism in the arts—as in perhaps other fields as well—are two interrelated concepts that do not appear alone in the absence of the other—an outgrowth of the fact that the historical roots of much of what is today nonprofit cultural activity are in the commercial realm. In the absence of state-supported cultural institutions like those in Europe, cultural production in the United States was driven by profit-seeking entrepreneurs and impresarios well into the nineteenth century, as exemplified by P. T. Barnum's American Museum in mid-nineteenth-century New York City.[51] Only in the latter half of the nineteenth century did the beginnings of the nonprofit institutional form evolve. High-cultural institutions, such as museums and symphony orchestras, were founded, tightly controlled, and financially dependent on the local urban elites.[52] Wealthy patrons controlled key resources: individual gifts as well as, occasionally, substantial municipal appropriations. These high-cultural nonprofit institutions served as tools of social stratification and expressions of civic prowess, and also as sources of edification for the masses—but they remained largely the exceptions in an otherwise commercial field.

This remained the case until after the Second World War, when a few foundations—including, notably, the Ford Foundation—began to develop arts programs intended to expand artistic offerings and establish the arts as a legitimate area of public policy. These efforts not only spurred foundation giving to the arts but also led to the entrance of the federal government into the field, culminating in the establishment of the National Endowments for the Arts and Humanities in 1965. This in turn fostered the development of new state and local-level public funding agencies. With the entrance of corporations as sponsors in the 1970s, that decade saw the rise of new public and private funding, all geared toward the nonprofit form. The availability of these new funding streams led to the establishment of new nonprofit cultural organizations that could employ professionally trained artists. At the same time, arts professionals who had until then operated proprietary groups and companies began to convert to nonprofit status. For example, commercial dance companies converted to nonprofit status to become eligible for Ford Foundation grants.[53] Colleges and universities that had been coaxed by Carnegie and other foundations to establish new training programs produced the supply of arts professionals needed to make use of these new opportunities.

In addition to a highly professional for-profit arts culture—for example, Broadway musicals, popular music, and film—the postwar era also saw the

substantial growth of a nonprofit arts infrastructure that was just as highly professionalized in its own way. By the turn of the millennium, this growth could
be tracked:

> Dance [troupes] have grown from 28 in 1958 to over 400. Opera compa-
> nies with budgets of over $100,000 have grown from 29 in 1964 to 209
> by 1989. Chamber music groups, most formed in the last twenty years,
> now number around 1,120. Half of America's 8,200 museums have come
> into existence since the 1970s. The nonprofit regional theater movement,
> begun in the 1960s, now consists of more than 900 theater groups. At
> least 37 mixed-arts complexes have sprung up nationally in various urban
> centers in the last twenty years.[54]

One result of the professionalization of the field was a tremendous expansion
of access to arts and culture and of the pursuit of artistic excellence; both results
were the primary policy goals pursued by both public and private funders. But
the professionalization trend arguably also had several unintended consequences
that came increasingly to light in the course of the early 2000s. For one, the
provision of full-time employment opportunities for arts professionals fostered a
"culture of [artistic] performance," in performing arts institutions—specifically,
symphony orchestras. This "performance culture" means that music schools and
conservatories focus narrowly on performance excellence in interpretation and
delivery of the existing music repertoire, and young musicians, upon graduation, bring this focus to their work in the orchestra. Neither the value of artistic
creation—the composition of new music—nor a broader understanding of the
institutional needs of orchestras or the classical music scene at large are being
instilled in new generations of musicians on whom the future viability of classical music depends. The resulting performance culture pushes contemporary
composers to the sideline and causes a lack of musical innovation, and consequently younger and more diverse audiences are not attracted to the art.[55] It has
been suggested that both symphonic and opera musical repertoires have been
contracting rather than expanding.[56]

In addition to the critique that the professionalization of performances came
at the expense of a separation from creation with resulting adverse effects on
audiences, others fault professionalization for leading to a sterilization of the arts
experience. Whereas the performing arts thrived in earlier times in an atmosphere of lively, even raucous, audience responses, the professionalization of the
arts changed audiences from active interpreters to passive recipients of the arts
experience. Arts audiences "have been taught to remain quiet[,] to keep their
feelings hidden inside a calm, still body [and have] been conditioned to wait
to receive meaning from the experts: the artist, the newspaper critic, the professor, and other, more sophisticated patrons."[57] This passive recipient style of

arts participation is increasingly being questioned, for its possibly turning away younger and more diverse audiences. Concerns along these lines have thus led to greater interest in community outreach, on the one hand, and attempts to harness technology to engage audiences in new ways, on the other. For example, the Metropolitan Opera devised a path-breaking way to use new communications technology to broadcast live performances to movie theaters, thereby freeing audiences from the decorum expected within the opera house. But many other cultural institutions are still struggling with finding ways to connect to new audiences by harnessing the power of the new social media.

Commercialism

Concerns about commercialization are not generally widespread within the arts. In fact, the commercial roots of much artistic activity are still evident in the high levels of subscription and individual ticket sales as shares of total revenues in much of the performing arts and in the heavy reliance on earned income by small to mid-size arts organizations in general.[58] Sophisticated "pricing" strategies designed to maximize fee-for-service (box office) income are rarely an area of concern for either patrons or the public at large, even if much of the public is effectively being priced out of attending. The live performing arts do not generate much auxiliary income, as concessions and merchandising stands before and during events have limited revenue potential. Even significant commercial transactions, such as record deals by symphony orchestras, are perceived as enhancing an orchestra's mission to make classical music performances available, and the shrinking of the market for classical CDs and the concomitant loss of recording possibilities for orchestras is perceived as a significant problem.

Whereas other parts of the nonprofit sector have been concerned about a commercialization or marketization threat, the arts discourse has turned this on its head by counseling arts institutions to close a so-called "earnings gap" by finding ways to increase earned income to levels that would ensure financial independence and make them self-sustainable.[59] This sustainability mantra is reinforced by various stakeholders: business-minded corporate executives serving on arts boards of directors; public funders (looking for subsidy reductions); and private funders (concerned about long-term funding obligations). At the same time, arts institutions themselves have been attracted by the prospect of less reliance on public subsidies and private philanthropy, to achieve greater freedom from the restrictions and the volatility of contributed income streams.[60] What is more, past studies of arts demand (and pricing strategies based on them) seemed to broadly suggest that demand for the arts is relatively inelastic and does not react significantly to changes in ticket prices or admission fees. Accordingly, greater levels of commercialization were not necessarily associated with concerns about any negative effects on participation. However, more recent and closer investigation suggests that demand might not be as inelastic as generally thought and that the perceived inelasticity may in large part be due to past nonprofit pricing strategies that kept tickets and admissions at levels below the willingness to pay of audiences and visitors.[61] Thus, whether increases in commercialization since the 1990s may have contributed to declining participation rates remains an issue for further investigation.

Nevertheless, until very recently some of the core concerns about the potential drawbacks to nonprofits of commercialization, such as the threat of mission displacement—the tendency to have decisions driven by economic concerns rather than the mission—have been all but unknown in the field of arts and culture. The cultural institution where the threat of mission displacement is perhaps playing out most publicly is the Public Broadcasting System. Over the past two decades or so, the seemingly increased use of commercials in the form of corporate underwriter messages on PBS stations has sparked substantial criticism of the growing commercialization of "commercial-free" television, which is seen as the final departure from the idealistic educational blueprint that helped establish the public television system in the first place. But criticisms of the occasional close entanglements between culture and corporate patrons remain prevalent elsewhere in the arts as well, as shown by the controversies over the Guggenheim Museum's BMW-sponsored motorcycle and Armani exhibits, and the Brooklyn Museum's mounting of an exhibition of a private collection tied to an advertising firm.[62] In the latter case, a controversy originally sparked by the content of some of the pieces in the show led to the revelation of questionable relations between museums, private collectors, and commercial galleries. Indeed, many questioned the propriety of private art collectors' lending to museums artworks that become the centerpiece of exhibitions in institutions whose luster then lends added cachet and presumably market value to these collections—particularly when the collectors not only seek to sell such works but also to exercise curatorial input in the show. In the aftermath and as part of a periodic ten-year review process, both the American Association of Museums and Association of Art Museum Directors reviewed and revised their codes of ethics to better deal with questions about what constitutes appropriate collector and gallery involvement in exhibition design and funding as well as post-exhibition sales of artworks.

Yet perhaps the most preeminent form of commercialism in the arts has been the extensive merchandising that many prominent museums began during the 1980s. Although museum shops were not unknown before the 1980s, many museums' decisions to pursue retail activities were taken to scale by the 1990s. Although museums did pursue other forms of commercialization—including raising admission fees where feasible, instituting parking fees, and upscaling museum restaurants—merchandising became the strategy of choice for increasing earnings. Museums expanded on-site store space, developed permanent or temporary off-site shops in shopping malls, engaged in mail order, and took merchandising into cyberspace with the development of "e-tailing." At the height of the merchandising boom of the 1990s, retail sales in some cases began to equal or exceed the more traditional revenue streams. However, net profit margins were generally low, investments were risky, and going into the early 2000s, a decommercialization trend became observable.[63] A few prominent museums began to jettison their costly mail-order catalogue operations.

Other Management Concerns

Nonprofit arts and cultural organizations continue to confront new variants of the enduring administrative concerns of marketing and audience development, fundraising, programming, maintaining facilities, and volunteer management. Each of these continuing demands has taken on new aspects in the face of technological innovation, globalization, demographic shifts, changes in governmental relations and public policies, and the blurring of distinctions and interactions with the commercial arts and entertainment sector. Arts and cultural organizations continue to grapple with the challenge of an increasingly heterogeneous American population and the implications of that cultural diversity for everything from marketing and audience development to board recruitment and governance to programming and educational activities.

LEADERSHIP. Many arts organizations were established or grew to prominence during the boom years of the 1960s and 1970s. Now, forty years later, their executive and artistic directors are retiring or succumbing to age, and the issue of leadership has taken on a new urgency as generational turnover has continued to ripple through the sector. Coinciding with the growing complexity and demands of these positions, the turnover has prompted concern about the recruitment of new leaders. As a consequence, a number of arts service organizations have instituted leadership development programs such as the League of American Orchestras' long-running Orchestra Management Fellowship program or the Theatre Communications Group's New Generations grants program for theater leadership. Alternative ways to deal with succession problems, such as using interim directorships effectively, likewise took on greater urgency.[64] Nevertheless, the cultivation of a new generation of cultural policy leaders remains haphazard.

Sometimes the emerging leadership gap is most visible from a field perspective. For example, in 1999 at least twenty art museum directorships at prominent museums were open—a fifteen-year-high. Primary among the reasons cited for the vacancies was a sense that the constant demands of fundraising and marketing have turned the job into a business that is driving art historians and curators from this career path and tarnishing the intellectual and social prestige of being a museum director.[65] Since then, the vacancy rate has not dropped below twenty open directorships; the median age of current directors is rising and the advent of new museums is increasing the demand. As a result, turnover rates are increasing as museums hire directors away from other museums, thereby destabilizing the institutions organizationally and weakening community relations. The competition for the small pool of directors possessing the requisite business and management savvy has also led to a rise in the level of compensation packages offered.[66]

ACCOUNTABILITY. This leadership crisis has in turn led to significant accountability challenges and well-publicized scandals that have pushed the museum world well into the vanguard of nonprofit accountability problems. One of the most significant of these involved the Smithsonian Institution, which broke with tradition by appointing a business executive as its chief executive (called its secretary) in 2000. Lawrence Small came from a banking background and was president of Fannie Mae before coming to the Smithsonian. Small focused on fundraising, corporate sponsorships, and commercial ventures, and his tenure was initially seen as successful, until his compensation and business expensing came under closer scrutiny in 2007. Small came under fire less for his salary, which was in the million-dollar range, than for what the chairman of the Senate Finance Committee, Charles Grassley, colorfully termed a "Dom Perignon lifestyle"—charging a significant housing allowance for a private home rarely used for official functions, private jet and first-class travel, spousal travel expenditures, and other unauthorized business spending.[67] Small resigned in 2007. Shortly afterward the director of the Smithsonian's American Indian Museum was criticized for high travel expenditures.[68] High compensation, lavish spending, first-class travel, and other inappropriate expenditures also brought down Barry Munitz, the chief executive of another major museum complex, the J. Paul Getty Trust, in 2005, just a few years before the Smithsonian scandals.[69] And even more traditional museum directors came under fire. At the Museum of Modern Art, information came to light that trustees had set up a separate trust fund, off the institution's books and outside regular reporting channels, to provide additional compensation to the MoMA's director, Glenn D. Lowry.[70] The practice of many museums of providing tax-free, high-end housing benefits also came under fire.[71]

Beyond these essentially governance-related accountability lapses, the nonprofit arts and culture sector dealt with questions of accountability in the form of calls for greater performance evaluation, the ability to demonstrate effectiveness. This affected nonprofit arts and culture organizations both directly and indirectly. The nonprofit sector as a whole has been grappling with the challenge of developing appropriate measures of its effectiveness (see the introduction and chapter 16 in this volume). This, of course, included arts and cultural organizations—which may face a particularly complicated task since "process is often as important as product, and the impact of creativity and imagination [is] difficult to quantify."[72] Although arts and cultural organizations (and often their funders) are apt to regard evaluation as having a negative connotation, many are beginning to see it as "part of an ongoing learning process."[73]

In truth, cultural organizations have long been operating under a professional review system that involves critical commentary and peer review. But what has become more apparent is that the arts are also operating in a system where political oversight and popular opinion are important. These three evaluation perspectives—professional, political, and popular—have implicit values that are not necessarily congruent.[74] The current interest in evaluation and impact analysis can be seen as a meter of the stage of development of the cultural support system. That is, evaluation is more likely to be useful and prevalent when an old paradigm is waning and a new one is forming—a situation that seems to characterize both the public and private support systems for the arts and culture. From other policy arenas we know that evaluation that involves impact analysis is more likely to be fruitful when programs have a track record and have evolved over years of operational experience. After more than forty years of experience with programs of direct government funding for the arts that were premised on a link between public and private funding, arts policy now has an extensive track record and thus could be regarded as being capable of demonstrating policy impact.[75] But because of unsettled policy priorities and newly emerging policy issues, this demonstration remains past due.

MARKETING AND DEVELOPMENT. Nonprofit arts and cultural organizations also face a challenge, indeed a triple challenge, in the area of marketing and development. As a consequence of changing demographics, organizations must simultaneously (1) keep or increase their share of the aging baby boomers in their audience, even as this cohort revises the image of retiring and invents new stages of life, (2) cultivate generations X and Y and the latest digital generation as new audiences and new donors who have different value preferences than their elders and respond to different information media, and (3) successfully position their institutions in an increasingly competitive leisure and entertainment market.[76] Most performing arts organizations have discovered that traditional subscription packages are outmoded and have instead developed flexible and tailored subscription programs. For example, many arts organizations have created specific categories and events for a new generation of givers, such as the Metropolitan Museum of Art's Apollo Circle for people twenty-one to thirty-nine or the Washington National Opera's Generation O program for students and young professionals between eighteen and thirty-five. In addition, many cultural organizations are exploring generational marketing and brand development. Some organizations are exploring the exploitation of new communications technology and social networking for both fundraising and image enhancement for sponsors. For example, many orchestras now include links at their websites to their large corporate donors, thus connecting orchestra patrons directly to information about the products of corporate donors. In the face of ambitious and virtually perpetual capital and endowment campaigns, fundraisers are confronting growing and incessant demands.

PROGRAMMING. In the programming area, the live performing arts, such as opera and ballet, have commissioned new works as an effort both to support creativity and to attract new audiences. Now the orchestra field is encouraging the commissioning and performance of new works. A growing number of websites dedicated to streaming classical music online are offering concert experiences at their websites—often from international venues and by high-profile artists—that not only may serve classical music lovers but also may draw new audiences into a larger classical music community. The challenge of introducing new works combined with the new opportunities of globalization has meant that arts presenters (individuals or organizations that schedule arts events or organize tours) must engage in more "curatorial" activities to complement performances and presentations. They also face new administrative challenges in managing international tours and dealing with foreign artists and ensembles.[77] In both theater and dance, nonprofit companies strive to create economically successful "hit" programs that can be spun off into a touring company generating profits that can return to the parent company as a form of cross-subsidization. Museums, too, have been drawn to collaboratively mounting touring exhibitions in which costs and collections are shared; sometimes the project is brokered by a state or regional arts agency.

TECHNOLOGY. A special challenge to the nonprofit arts world arises from the technological changes of recent years. The technological environment in which the nonprofit arts must function today and in the immediate future is dramatically different from what it was just a few years ago. The pace of change in the areas of information, networking, and telecommunications is dizzying. It is common to read projections of the likely consequences of such technological innovations for the commercial arts and entertainment industries, or for banking, finance, and insurance services, and the dawning of the information age is also propelling nonprofit arts organizations to rethink many assumptions concerning administrative and financial practices, not to mention posing legal and policy dilemmas. In part such rethinking is simply inescapable. We are all living in a very different and more digital world than we were just twenty years ago. For example, when Bill Clinton became president in 1992, few artists or nonprofit arts organizations had an e-mail address, websites were rare, digital information was largely a subject for scientists, and few homes owned a personal computer. Today the best-seller nonfiction lists are populated with books about digital assets, digital capital, and a digital society.

Artists, nonprofit arts organizations, and commercial cultural corporations are important generators of intellectual property, and in the information age, intellectual property has become a key economic resource. Today, U.S. creative industries constitute the second largest export sector of the nation (outranked only by the defense equipment industry). Nonprofit arts and cultural institutions are implicated in these phenomena in many ways. They are generators of new intellectual property: sometimes these ideas get developed by commercial entertainment industries; other times these ideas and artworks constitute alternative aesthetic choices for the cultural consumer. Nonprofit arts and cultural organizations (including heritage groups and institutions) are also stewards of vast stockpiles of cultural content in the form of museum collections, historical archives, and performing arts repertoires. Such content might be called the "raw material" form of intellectual property—resources that could be converted into digital assets for the information age. But at present, and unlike their "cousins" in the commercial arts and entertainment industries, nonprofit arts entities are content-rich but data-poor.

Thus, for nonprofit arts and cultural organizations, the creative quandary is at least fourfold.[78] First, although they possess substantial intellectual property assets, much of this material requires conversion into digital formats if it is to be fully developed in the information age. Even without digitization, the task of managing intellectual property assets raises new challenges for nonprofit arts organizations. For example, it has become a factor in labor agreements such as the current contract agreement between the American Federation of Musicians and many of the nation's major symphony orchestras, opera, and ballet companies; the contract covers compensation for both the transmission of live performances through "streaming audio" technology and prerecorded audio files that listeners can download.[79]

Second, any large-scale digital conversion is likely to incur significant financial costs, which most nonprofit arts and cultural organizations are not in a position to absorb. Furthermore, commercial arts and entertainment companies with global distribution networks can plan and can take action vis-à-vis intellectual property and technology concerns as though they were investments—and substantial investments, at that. In contrast, nonprofit arts organizations do not have the market scale or global distribution networks of the kind that help the commercial arts to recover their digital production costs, especially when the pace of technological change requires constant updating, which incurs even more costs.

Third, digitization and technological accommodation raise fundamental issues of aesthetics, management, and marketing, particularly for the performing arts. Aesthetically, going digital can rob the experience of some of its key live elements: immediacy, immersion, fresh invention, physicality, ritual, and social interaction.[80] Thus for many in the live performing arts—most of which are situated in the nonprofit sector—a key question is whether their rather ephemeral performances should be transformed into any fixed format and whether the resultant piece becomes something other than the original. Similarly, going digital has profound implications for creative control. As Andrew Taylor points out, "Creative control by the author or artist, the carefully crafted stewardship of great works by arts organizations, and the context of a cultural work torn from its intended means of conveyance, the cultural integrity of ritual or celebratory expression . . . are all issues that lose their foothold in the information age."[81] Meanwhile, there is also a "push" to develop a new marketing role for nonprofit arts organizations, that of cultural experience broker, a role that is more involved and interactive with the audience than the traditional role of presenter.[82] However, arts institutions continue to struggle with handling new social media and engaging and involving digital audiences in meaningful ways.[83] Symphony orchestras have even extended their experiments with text messaging during broadcast performances to live audiences.[84]

Finally, the provision of accurate digitization and media-distributed art by nonprofit arts and cultural organizations requires continuous innovation. Each time a new information format emerges, it raises new challenges for preservation in cultural fields. Take, for example, dance preservation: to record choreography accurately and usefully requires both new technology that can capture movement and sense motion as well as refined computer imaging techniques. Thus nonprofit cultural organizations face the dual challenge of evolving from one technology-based information format to the next in order to keep their creative edge and to compete effectively in the world of e-commerce, while simultaneously preserving, maintaining, and facilitating public access to a legacy of cultural resources that are fixed in older technological media. Technology—especially when combined with intellectual property considerations—presents the nonprofit arts and culture sector with more than an equipment and interconnectivity challenge. Rather, the nonprofit arts and culture sector finds itself in a multifaceted creative quandary over how to adapt to an information-driven, networked, digital era.

Conclusions and Future Trends

Clearly, the past two decades have been a time of considerable challenge and change for nonprofit arts and culture. They have also been decades of significant experimentation and improvisation. Old paradigms—whether financial, administrative, or political—are noticeably in decline, and new operating paradigms are still protean. What steps might now be taken to improve the position and condition of nonprofit arts and culture as well as to strengthen their ability to make positive contributions to American society?

Certainly, nonprofit arts and culture organizations enter the twenty-first century with a heightened awareness of their public role and responsibilities. However, this awareness has not yet crystallized into an advocacy strategy, a set of stable public expectations and attitudes, or a policy agenda. The public discourse is becoming more of a dialogue concerning both the public interest in fostering the arts and culture and the variety of public purposes that the arts and culture can help to advance and address.

These shifts lead in turn to new challenges. Financially, the language and logic of government and philanthropic support have shifted away from subsidy and toward investment and entrepreneurship. Responding to that shift requires conscious attention, targeted programs, and broadened and deepened information sharing. A decade of experimentation has taken place with regard to new funding devices and strategies, including program-related investments, a more active cultural role for community foundations, endowment-building campaigns by organizations, public trust funds for public agencies, the creation of cultural districts and earmarked taxes to support the arts, public service advertisement campaigns, and public awareness marketing campaigns. However, we have little systematic information about the effectiveness or general utility of these devices. Thus the appropriate character of emerging administrative and funding paradigms remains unclear. The same holds true for accountability mechanisms and effectiveness measures. How can a field that is still fragmented by discipline, sector, and geography, by grant makers and grantees, and by service organizations and scholars better share and use information, especially when it is often gathered for different institutional purposes, may be sensitive or proprietary in nature, and is built on different normative assumptions?

A broader perspective both about what the entire arts and culture sector encompasses and about what it can contribute raises different challenges. What are the dimensions and interrelations between the parts of this broadly conceived arts and culture sector? Can the nonprofit arts learn from or partner with the commercial arts when it comes to distribution and delivery systems or investment and venture capital strategies? What role do the avocational, voluntary and community-based arts and cultural institutions play with regard to the development of talent, an audience, and a market for the professional nonprofit arts as well as for the cultural industries? If the arts and culture are both affected by and help to address other societal concerns such as education, quality of life, and community development, how can they be included more consistently in the relevant planning and policy discussions? Nonprofit arts and culture organizations often complain that they are not "invited to the table" when tax policy is being reformed, trade or intellectual property treaties are being negotiated, or technology is being developed. And how can the arts and cultural community share knowledge and experience gained at these various "tables"? Indeed, although financing remains a necessary and persistent concern, the arts and culture sector may find that mechanisms to leverage access to the "right tables," to new players, and to better information are equal requirements of success in the information age.

The nonprofit arts and culture sector along with its public and private supporters may also need to identify new ways of targeting capacity-building efforts. Although it has been traditional to recognize that needs and practices differ from one field to another, it seems increasingly clear that needs vary by the size and age of the organizations. Certainly, the particular problems of mid-size organizations merit special attention. In addition, the organizational and professional development issues that were program targets of an earlier era might now usefully give way to technological development and entrepreneurship as areas of focus.

In this context, it will be interesting to see whether America's nonprofit arts and culture institutions manage to turn the economic crisis that hit the nation in the last years of the 2000s into an opportunity. Although a few institutions had to close their doors as of this writing, a major loss of cultural infrastructure and access to programming will not likely be among the long-term consequences. Similar to the 2001 downturn, the arts field is proving to be financially resilient enough to weather even significant economic crises. Yet, such crises also open windows into the remaining weaknesses and shortcomings and enable organizations to rethink capacity, programming, and technological issues in order to emerge organizationally and managerially stronger in the future. Among other things, over the coming years arts organizations will have gained a new appreciation of the relative value and vulnerabilities of the main components of their revenue mix. Many organizations have come to realize that earned income will not be able to make up for missing subsidies and donative income in times of crisis and that programming needs to expand and diversify rather than contract and rely on old stand-bys, as the Kennedy Center's Michael Kaiser has been counseling throughout the economic crisis.[85]

Finally, the nonprofit arts and cultural sector finds itself triangulated by the forces of decentralization, globalization, and the market at a time when federal support, attention, and leadership have declined. Yet for these very reasons a national-level presence is more necessary than ever: as a partner in intergovernmental affairs, as a negotiator and representative in global matters, and as a mediator and facilitator of the market. Federal cultural agencies tend to have fewer resources and less impact than they used to. Thus they must find new ways to exercise leadership and offer support. Arts service organizations—the trade associations of museums, theaters, orchestras, and so forth—can bring a national and sometimes even international perspective to particular issues or fields, and have the potential to assume a greater leadership and representational role. Coalitions can be assembled across fields, issue areas, sectors, and levels of community to bring together a national perspective and a capacity for effective action. Such network approaches are another consequence of decentralization, diversification, and the successes of development that the nonprofit arts and culture field experienced in the late twentieth century.

Three decades of significant growth followed by two decades of profound change have brought the nonprofit arts and cultural sector to the recognition of a need for even more change and a more positive attitude about accommodating and adapting to the evolving environment. Articulating, integrating, and routinizing the emergent financial, administrative, and political paradigms are now the tasks at hand.

Notes

1. American Assembly, *The Arts and the Public Purpose: Final Report of the 92nd American Assembly, May 29–June 1, 1997* (New York: American Assembly, 1997)

2. Americans for the Arts, *Arts and Economic Prosperity III* (Washington: n.d.). Though economic impact estimates have frequently and usefully been deployed in many industries for policy purposes and to generate support for specific large-scale projects, their validity has sometimes been called into question. With respect to the arts, see Bruce Seaman, "Beyond Economic Impact," in *Arts in a New Millennium: Research and the Arts Sector,* edited by Valerie B. Morris and David B. Pankratz (Westport, Conn.: Praeger, 2003), pp. 77–92.

3. Kenneth Wing, Thomas Pollak, and Amy Blackwood, *The Nonprofit Almanac 2008* (Washington: Urban Institute Press, 2008), table 5.6.

4. Richard Florida, *The Rise of the Creative Class and How It's Transforming Work, Leisure, Community, and Everyday Life* (New York: Basic Books, 2002).

5. See Paul DiMaggio, "Nonprofit Organizations and the Intersectoral Division of Labor in the Arts," in *The Nonprofit Sector: A Research Handbook,* edited by Walter Powell and Richard Steinberg, 2nd ed. (Yale University Press, 2006), pp. 432–61.

6. Ibid.

7. Wing, Pollak, and Blackwood, *Nonprofit Almanac 2008,* table 5.7. Note that census and IRS data seldom correspond very closely, owing in part to differences in coverage and the lack of systematic review of the IRS data.

8. Lester M. Salamon and others, *Public Good/Private Action: Maryland's Nonprofit Sector in a Time of Change* (Baltimore: Johns Hopkins Institute for Policy Studies/Maryland Association of Nonprofit Organizations, 1997); Lester M. Salamon and Wojciech Sokolowski, "Nonprofits and Recessions: New Data from Maryland," January 2010 (ccss.jhu.edu/pdfs/NED_Bulletins/States/MD_33.pdf); Lester M. Salamon and Wojciech Sokolowski, "Texas Nonprofit Employment Update," August 2010 (ccss.jhu.edu/pdfs/NED_Bulletins/States/NED_Bulletin35_Texas_2010.pdf); Lester M. Salamon and Stephanie L. Geller, "Impact of

the 2007–09 Economic Recession on Nonprofit Organizations," June 2009 (ccss.jhu.edu/pdfs/LP_Communiques/LP_Communique_14).

9. See Adrian Ellis, "Museum Boom Will Be Followed by Bust," *The Art Newspaper,* June 18, 2001, cited in Adrian Ellis, "American Museums in Financial Crisis," Forbes.com, 2003 (http://www.forbes.com/2003/05/05/cx_0506hot.html).

10. Michael Kaiser, "No Bailout for the Arts?" *Washington Post,* December 29, 2008, A15.

11. Kevin F. McCarthy and others, *The Performing Arts in a New Era* (Santa Monica: Rand, 2001).

12. Stefan Toepler, "Profiling Cultural Support: Introduction." *Journal of Arts Management, Law and Society* 32, no. 3 (2002): 171–74.

13. Stefan Toepler, "Caveat Venditor? Museum Merchandising, Nonprofit Commercialization and the Case of the Metropolitan Museum in New York," *Voluntas* 17, no. 2 (2006): 95–109.

14. Ellis, "Museum Boom Will Be Followed by Bust."

15. Stefan Toepler and Mark Hager, "Museums and Financial Vulnerability," paper presented at the Twenty-Ninth Conference on Social Theory, Politics and the Arts, Columbus, Ohio, October 9–11, 2003.

16. Angela Han, "Public Funding for the Arts: 2009 Update," *GIA Reader* 20, no. 4 (Summer 2009): 6–7

17. National Endowment for the Arts, *How the United States Funds the Arts,* 2nd ed. (Washington: 2007).

18. Han, "Public Funding for the Arts: 2009 Update."

19. National Assembly of State Art Agencies, *Legislative Appropriations Annual Survey: Fiscal Year 2000* (Washington: 2000); National Assembly of State Art Agencies, *State Arts Agency Funding and Grant Making* (Washington: March 2010).

20. Randy Cohen, "Local Government Support of Arts and Culture," *Journal of Arts Management, Law and Society* 32, no. 3 (2002): 206–21; Americans for the Arts, "Arts Facts . . . Government Arts Funding" (www.artsusa.org/pdf/news/press/2_Govt%20Funding%20 2009.pdf); Americans for the Arts, "Arts Facts . . . Local Arts Agencies" (www.artsusa.org/pdf/get_involved/advocacy/research/2010/laa2010.pdf).

21. Giving USA Foundation, *Giving USA 2009: The Annual Report on Philanthropy for the Year 2008* (Glenview, Ill.: 2010).

22. Nina Kressner Cobb, *Looking Ahead: Private Sector Giving to the Arts and the Humanities* (Washington: President's Committee on the Arts and the Humanities, 1996).

23. Loren Renz, Steve Lawrence, and John Kenziol, *Arts Funding 2000: Funder Perspectives on Current and Future Trends* (New York: Foundation Center, 2000); see also Margaret Jane Wyszomirski, "Philanthropy and Culture: Patterns, Context, and Change," in *Philanthropy and the Nonprofit Sector in a Changing America,* edited by Charles T. Clotfelter and Thomas Ehrlich (Indiana University Press, 1999), pp. 461–80.

24. Renz, Lawrence, and Kenziol, *Arts Funding 2000.*

25. James Allan Smith, "Foundations as Cultural Actors," in *American Foundations: Roles and Contributions,* edited by Helmut Anheier and David Hammack (Brookings, 2010), pp. 262–282; Stefan Toepler, "Roles of Foundations and Their Impacts in the Arts," in Anheier and Hammack, *American Foundations,* pp. 283–304.

26. David Leonhardt, "The Shock of the New Entry Fee," *New York Times,* September 26, 2004 (www.nytimes.com/2004/09/26/arts/design/26leonhardt.html).

27. National Endowment for the Arts, *Arts Participation 2008: Highlights from a National Survey* (Washington: 2009). Although the data do not distinguish between government

(public museums) and commercial (Broadway theater) entities, the overall participation trends are generally applicable to the nonprofit arts and culture field.

28. National Endowment for the Arts, *Arts Participation 2008*.

29. Ibid.

30. See Volker Kirchberg, "Thinking about 'Scenes': A New View of Visitors' Influence on Museums," *Curator: The Museum Journal* 50, no. 2 (April 2007): 239–54.

31. Patrick Giles, "The Gap: Has Generation X Lost Its Way to the Opera?" *Opera News,* February 2000, pp. 29–31.

32. National Endowment for the Arts, *Arts Participation 2008*.

33. Ibid.

34. Monnie Peters and Joni Maya Cherbo, "The Missing Sector: The Unincorporated Arts," *Journal of Arts Management, Law and Society* 28, no. 2 (1998): 117.

35. Kevin McCarthy and others, *The Performing Arts in a New Era* (Santa Monica: Rand, 2001).

36. Stefan Toepler, "Grassroots Associations versus Larger Nonprofits: New Evidence from a Community Case Study in Arts and Culture," *Nonprofit and Voluntary Sector Quarterly* 32, no. 2 (2003): 236–51; Stefan Toepler and Greg Finch, "The Arts and Humanities in Montgomery County: An Empirical Profile," occasional paper 12 (Ohio State University, Arts Policy and Administration Program, Spring 2000).

37. Maria Jackson, "Arts and Culture Indicators in Community Building: Project Update," *Journal of Arts Management, Law, and Society* 28, no. 3 (1998): 201–05; Mark Stern and Susan Seifert, *Cultivating "Natural" Cultural Districts* (University of Pennsylvania, Social Impact of the Arts Project, 2007); Carole Rosenstein, "Cultural Development and City Neighborhoods," policy brief (Washington: Urban Institute, Center on Nonprofits and Philanthropy, 2009).

38. National Endowment for the Arts, *Arts Participation 2008*.

39. Carole Rosenstein, "Diversity and Participation in the Arts: Insights from the Bay Area," research report (Washington: Urban Institute, Center on Nonprofits and Philanthropy, 2005).

40. Carole Rosenstein, "Cultural Heritage Organizations: Nonprofits That Support Traditional, Ethnic, Folk and Noncommercial Popular Culture," research report (Washington: Urban Institute, Center on Nonprofits and Philanthropy, 2006).

41. Pia Moriarty, *Immigrant Participatory Arts: An Insight into Community Building in Silicon Valley* (San Jose: Cultural Initiatives Silicon Valley, 2004); Mark Stern, Susan Seifert, and Domenic Vitiello, *Migrants, Communities, and Culture* (University of Pennsylvania, Social Impacts of the Arts Project, 2008).

42. Divya Kumar, "New Americans, Lasting Art: A Call to Build," *Subcontinental—Journal of South Asian American Public Affairs* 2, no. 2 (2004): 41–54.

43. Lawrence Rothfield, ed., *Unsettling "Sensation": Arts Policy Lessons from the Brooklyn Museum of Art Controversy* (Rutgers University Press, 2001).

44. See Susan J. Bodilly, Catherine H. Augustine, and Laura Zakaras, *Revitalizing Arts Education through Community-Wide Coordination* (Santa Monica: Rand, 2008).

45. American Association of Museums, *Excellence and Equity. Education and the Public Dimension of Museums* (Washington: 1992); Lisa Sharamitaro, "Association Involvement across Policy Process: The American Association of Museums and the Native American Graves Protection and Repatriation Act," *Journal of Arts Management, Law, and Society* 31 (Summer 2001): 123–36.

46. American Association of Museums, *Excellence and Equity*, p. 8.

47. American Association of Museums, *Mastering Civic Engagement: A Challenge to Museums* (Washington: 2002).

48. American Symphony Orchestra League, *Americanizing the American Orchestra: Report of the National Task Force for the American Orchestra. An Initiative for Change* (Washington: American Symphony Orchestra League, 1993).

49. Ibid., p. 37.

50. James Cuno, "Introduction," *Whose Muse? Art Museums and the Public Trust,* edited by James Cuno (Princeton University Press, 2004), pp. 11–26.

51. George Mason University, Center for History and New Media, "The Lost Museum" (http://chnm.gmu.edu/the-lost-museum).

52. Paul DiMaggio, *Nonprofit Enterprise in the Arts: Studies in Mission and Constraint* (Oxford University Press, 1986).

53. Anatole Chujoy, "Philanthropic Foundations and the Dance," in *U.S. Philanthropic Foundations,* edited by Warren Weaver (New York, Harper & Row, 1969), pp. 316–28.

54. Joni Cherbo and Margaret Wyszomirski, "Mapping the Public Life of the Arts in America," in *The Public Life of the Arts in America,* edited by J. Cherbo and M. Wyszomirski (Rutgers University Press, 2000), pp. 3–21.

55. Joseph Horowitz, *Classical Music in America: A History of Its Rise and Fall* (New York: Norton, 2005), p. 534

56. James Heilbrun, "Empirical Evidence of a Decline in Repertory Diversity among American Opera Companies, 1991/92 to 1997/98," *Journal of Cultural Economics* 25, no.1 (2001): 63–72; James Heilbrun, "The Symphony Orchestra Repertory: A Research Note," *Journal of Arts Management, Law and Society* 34, no. 2 (2004): 151–56.

57. Lynne Conner, "In and Out of the Dark: A Theory about Audience Behavior from Sophocles to Spoken Word," in *Engaging Art: The Next Great Transformation of America's Cultural Life,* edited by Steven Tepper and Bill Ivey (New York: Routledge, 2008), p. 115.

58. Stefan Toepler and Greg Finch, *Arts and Humanities in Montgomery County;* Carole Rosenstein, *Cultural Heritage Organizations.*

59. Louise Stevens, "The Earnings Shift: The New Bottom Line Paradigm for the Arts Industry in a Market-Driven Era," *Journal of Arts Management, Law, and Society* 26, no. 2 (July 1996): 101–13.

60. Stefan Toepler, "Culture, Commerce, and Civil Society: Rethinking Support for the Arts," *Administration and Society* 33, no. 5 (2001): 508–22.

61. Bruce A. Seaman, "Empirical Studies of Demand for the Performing Arts," in *Handbook of the Economics of Art and Culture,* edited by Victor A. Ginsburgh and David Throsby (Amsterdam: Elsevier, 2006), pp. 415–72.

62. James Ledbetter, *Made Possible By . . . The Death of Public Broadcasting in the United States* (London, New York: Verso, 1997); Chin-tao Wu, *Privatising Culture: Corporate Art Intervention since the 1980s* (London, New York: Verso, 2002); Mark Rectanus, *Culture Incorporated: Museums, Artists, and Corporate Sponsorships* (University of Minnesota Press, 2002); Rothfield, *Unsettling "Sensation."*

63. Stefan Toepler and Sarah Dewees, "Are There Limits to Financing Culture through the Market? Evidence from the U.S. Museum Field," *International Journal of Public Administration* 28, no. 1–2 (2005): 131–46.

64. Robert Goler, "Interim Directorships in Museums: Their Impact on Individuals and Significance to Institutions," *Museum Management and Curatorship* 19, no. 4 (2001): 385–402; Robert Goler, "Making the Most of the Internal Interim Directorship," *Journal for Nonprofit Management* 7, no.1 (2003): 56–66.

65. Lester M. Salamon, *Holding the Center: America's Nonprofit Sector at the Crossroads* (New York: Nathan Cummings Foundation, 1997).

66. James Abruzzo, "The US Art Museum Management Leadership Gap," *Arts Management Newsletter,* no. 81 (April 2008).

67. Jacqueline Trescott and James V. Grimaldi, "Smithsonian's Small Quits in Wake of Inquiry," *Washington Post,* March 27, 2007.

68. James V. Grimaldi and Jacqueline Trescott, "Indian Museum Director Spent Lavishly on Travel," *Washington Post,* December 28, 2007.

69. Jason Felch, Robin Fields, and Louise Roug, "The Munitz Collection: Getty's Chief Executive Has Been Highly Compensated during a Time of Austerity," *Los Angeles Times,* June 10, 2005.

70. Stephanie Strom, "Donors Sweetened Director's Pay at MoMA," *New York Times,* February 16, 2007.

71. Kevin Flynn and Stephanie Strom, "Plum Benefit to Cultural Post: Tax-Free Housing," *New York Times,* August 9, 2010.

72. Renz, Lawrence, and Kenziol, *Arts Funding 2000,* p. 30.

73. Ibid., p. 31.

74. Cherbo and Wyszomirski, "Mapping the Public Life of the Arts in America," pp. 16–17.

75. Margaret Jane Wyszomirski, "The Arts and Performance Review, Policy Assessment, and Program Evaluation: Focusing on the Ends of the Policy Cycle," *Journal of Arts Management, Law, and Society* 28, no. 3 (1998): 192.

76. Carol Scott, "Branding: Positioning Museums in the 21st Century," *International Journal of Arts Management* 2, no. 3 (2000): 35–39.

77. Aimee Fullman, *The Art of Engagement: Trends in US Cultural Exchange and International Programming* (www.rsclark.org/uploads/SurveyEngagementTrends.pdf).

78. Margaret Jane Wyszomirski, "Public Policy at the Intersection of the Arts, Technology, and Intellectual Property," Occasional Paper 18, background paper prepared for the American Assembly Art, Technology, and Intellectual Property Project (Ohio State University, Arts Policy and Administration Program, 2000).

79. Allan Kozin, "Classical Concerts and Audiences Seek an Audience on the Web," *New York Times,* June 13, 2000, pp. CI, C6.

80. Andrew Taylor, "Pandora's Bottle: Cultural Content in a Digital World," in *The Arts in a New Millennium: Research and the Arts Sector,* edited by Valerie B. Morris and David B. Pankratz (Westport, Conn.: Greenwood Press, 2002)

81. Taylor, "Pandora's Bottle."

82. Andrew Taylor, "The Experience Brokers: The New Role for Arts Administrators in the Information Age," in *Looking Ahead: A Collection of Papers from the International Social Theory, Politics, and the Arts Conference* (Drexel University Press, 1999), pp. 66–71.

83. James Yasko, "Museums and Web 2.0," *Museum News,* July–August 2007; Ximena Loacutepeza and others, "The Presence of Web 2.0 Tools on Museum Websites: A Comparative Study between England, France, Spain, Italy, and the USA," *Museum Management and Curatorship* 25, no. 2 (June 2010): 235–49.

84. Daniel J. Wakin, "Orchestras Seek BFF by Cellphone Texts," *New York Times,* July 21, 2010.

85. Sue Hoye, "Recession Hits Arts Groups Especially Hard," *Chronicle of Philanthropy,* January 2, 2009; Richard Lacayo, "Culture Crunch: The Recession and the Arts," *Time,* June 8, 2009; see also Michael Kaiser, *The Art of the Turnaround: Creating and Maintaining Healthy Arts Organizations* (Brandeis University Press, 2008).

6

Housing and Community Development

AVIS C. VIDAL

Housing and community development is one field in which nonprofit involvement has exhibited some of its most extraordinary growth and creativity. Nonprofits active in this area started from virtually nowhere amid the civic activism of the 1960s and expanded rapidly in number beginning in the 1980s. They have now established themselves as important and increasingly professionalized producers of publicly assisted housing and as important contributors in other ways to improved living environments and economic opportunities in some of the nation's most distressed communities. Moreover, they have done so while avoiding the reckless practices that landed so many for-profit lenders and developers in financial difficulty during the period leading up to the 2008 financial crisis.

Three factors help to account for this success. One is the development and increasing sophistication of a distinctive institutional infrastructure that supports the field. It features nonprofit "intermediary" organizations that have found inventive ways to attract public, private, and philanthropic capital into low-income housing investment, and gradually to expand the field's capacity to engage in a community improvement agenda that extends beyond housing provision. Also at work has been a significant expansion of federal subsidies, which are indispensable to the production of both affordable housing for low-income people and other critical community improvements. Finally, both of these have depended centrally on the increasing ability of national, regional, and local

266

nonprofits to engage in communities in ways that attract and sustain support while protecting investors and low-income residents from unacceptable risks.

Impressive as the growth of nonprofit involvement in the housing and community development field has been, however, it also demonstrates the limits of nonprofit action. Despite substantial expansion over the past thirty years, federal housing subsidies still reach only a fraction of the families eligible for them. Since the supply of unsubsidized low-cost rental units has been contracting for some time, while the incomes of poor renters have been falling, nonprofit housing providers have been fighting a losing battle as the quantity of low-cost housing has increasingly trailed the quantity needed. More broadly, public and nonprofit stimuli to investment in poor communities are commonly inadequate to overcome sustained flight of private capital from such neighborhoods.

To these long-standing challenges the mortgage foreclosure crisis that began in late 2007 and the ensuing financial crisis and recession have added enormous new problems. The nonprofits in this field are consequently beset on two fronts. First, the residents of the types of neighborhoods they serve have been among the most heavily hit by both the ongoing wave of foreclosures and the recession. At the community level, mounting foreclosures and the resulting collapse of home prices mean that even the most capable and highly regarded nonprofit organizations in the field are seeing two decades of community improvement work undermined. Second, because they are engaged in the housing market as full-fledged players, nonprofit housing developers and lenders are inevitably vulnerable to some of the same types of financial difficulties that face their for-profit counterparts, despite careful risk management. Many are experiencing financial stress as a result, and it will be some time before a clear picture emerges of how well they have weathered the storm.

This chapter seeks to tell this story of significant achievement short-circuited by the financial crisis and recession. It provides an overview of the nonprofit role in the housing and community development field, identifies some of the major trends in the field, and assesses the challenges and opportunities that lie ahead.

The Nonprofit Role in Housing and Community Development

Nonprofit participation in housing and community development is distinctive because the nonprofit role blends active engagement in communities, especially local housing markets, with the use of a complex array of public subsidy programs. Understanding their role thus begins with understanding the field and the tools available to practitioners. After laying this foundation in this section, in later sections we examine the nonprofits active in the field and highlight the distinguishing features of their engagement.

The Housing and Community Development Field

"Housing and community development" is not a single field. Rather, "housing" and "community development" each encompasses a broad set of activities that partly overlap.

HOUSING. Housing is a large industry in which nonprofit organizations occupy a small but important niche. The housing industry is commonly stratified along three basic dimensions. The most familiar ones are ownership status (owner-occupied versus rental) and the type of structure (for example, single-family house, duplex, multifamily). The dimension most important for this discussion, however, is subsidy status: whether housing is market-rate, public, or assisted.

Market-rate is housing that households either purchase or rent at prices determined in the marketplace and is the type of housing that predominates in the United States. Most of it is built by for-profit developers and then purchased and managed by owner-occupant households. Large development companies produce most of the units built, but many of the housing producers are small. Private developers build a smaller amount of market-rate rental housing as well, sometimes to hold and manage as an investment, sometimes to sell to for-profit investor or managers.

For-profit developers and owners of rental property also provide housing for low- and moderate-income households. These households fall into three groups:

—Those that can afford market-rate housing because it is offered at a low rent.

—Those that can afford market-rate housing because they receive federal housing subsidies.

—Those that cannot afford it (according to federal guidelines) but have no alternative and therefore must cope with some combination of high rents, over-crowding, and low-quality housing or neighborhoods.[1]

The third group is the largest group of low- and moderate-income renter households because housing subsidies are available for only about one quarter of the households whose income makes them eligible for them.[2] Unfortunately, this group is growing, because renter incomes have been falling while the number of private, low-cost rental units lost from the housing inventory each year generally exceeds the number of new federal subsidies authorized.[3]

Federal housing policymakers have responded to the nation's evolving housing problems in numerous ways over the years, starting in 1937 with the passage of legislation that provided for the creation of public housing.[4] The construction and operation of public housing is subsidized by the federal government, but the housing is owned and operated by local (and occasionally state) public housing authorities (PHAs). Most public housing was built before 1980, and no funds have been available to expand the public housing stock since 1995.[5] Although the earliest public housing developments were built to house working- and middle-class families hard hit by the Great Depression, public housing has increasingly become "housing of last resort." Some developments, referred to as "elderly housing," house low-income senior citizens. Others, called "family developments," are open to all low-income households but are primarily occupied by very low-income, single-parent families.

Much public housing, especially the elderly housing and the family housing located in mid-size and smaller cities and towns, is decent and well maintained. However, the conspicuous physical and social deterioration of some large-scale family developments in large cities (often owned by troubled PHAs) has stigmatized this segment of the assisted housing market. In response, the federal HOPE VI program, begun in 1992 by the Department of Housing and Urban Development (HUD), has supported the demolition and redevelopment of severely deteriorated projects to create better-designed properties for mixed-income tenants. Unfortunately, not all of the housing units demolished in the process have been replaced, so the size of the public housing stock has been reduced.

Since the end of World War II, a changing menu of other programs has provided public subsidies for the production or rental of privately held housing for low- and moderate-income persons and families. The federal government has provided the lion's share of these housing subsidy dollars.[6] Some programs have been available to both for-profit and nonprofit developers; others have been open to (or specifically designed for) one or the other exclusively. Most direct subsidies have focused on assisting renters, although a variety of indirect federal support increases the affordability of home ownership.[7]

Most of the early programs were "supply-side" programs, meaning that they made resources available to housing producers in order to allow them to construct and thus expand the supply of housing that could be occupied by low-income households or persons with special needs. Starting in the 1970s, the federal government gradually began placing more reliance on a "demand-side" approach, providing income-eligible renters with vouchers that can be used to pay private landlords. The chief program of this sort is now called the Housing Choice Voucher (HCV) program, which provides vouchers that tenants can use to help pay for rental housing of their own choice, provided it meets minimum standards.[8]

Currently, the largest federal subsidy in support of the development of low-income rental housing is the low-income housing tax credit (LIHTC), enacted in 1986: it supported the production of about one-sixth of all the multifamily housing (both assisted and market-rate) built between its enactment and 2006.[9] Rather than provide direct financial support, it uses the Internal Revenue Code to stimulate investment in the development of low-cost rental housing. The federal government allocates tax credits to the states, generally to state housing finance agencies, which in turn allocate the credits to eligible housing developments. The credits are sold to private corporations (mainly financial institutions), which use the credits to reduce their federal tax liability. The money paid to purchase the credits becomes equity financing for the rental housing projects, with the stipulation that the housing must remain occupied by low-income tenants for at least fifteen years. The availability of this equity reduces the projects' need for debt financing, enabling them to charge rents that are below market rate, thus making them affordable for low- or moderate-income households. Since LIHTCs do not provide a very deep subsidy, they are commonly combined with other sources of subsidy to further increase afford-ability; the lower the incomes of the tenants targeted by a development, the more likely that development is to need additional sources of subsidy. The most frequently used subsidy supplements are tax-exempt bonds, typically issued by state housing finance agencies, and the Home Investment Partnership Program (HOME), which delivers federal block grants to state and local governments for affordable housing.

Nonprofits have become adept users of LIHTCs, and these subsidies have become a mainstay of the nonprofit housing production system. Nonprofit providers enjoy set-asides in both the LIHTC program (10 percent) and the HOME program (15 percent), which can be used to support both rental hous-ing and affordable home ownership. However, they compete successfully for larger shares of both, especially in places where the nonprofit sector is strong.

Direct federal funding for rental housing production is also available, but it is focused on housing that is affordable to people with special needs and is commonly accompanied by appropriate supportive services. These include the McKinney programs for homeless individuals and families, the Section 811 program for persons with serious mental or physical disabilities, Hous-ing Opportunities for People with AIDS, and the Section 202 program for low-income seniors not assisted by other programs. The Section 202 and 811 programs are specifically targeted to nonprofits. Funding conduits for the McKinney programs are more complex, but most of the housing built and operated under them is ultimately provided by nonprofit organizations, along with the vast majority of the supportive services.

In addition to the existing programs, federal housing policy also reflects the residual effects of a number of programs that have been phased out. Especially notable in this regard are the Section 221(d)(3), Section 236, and Section 8 New Construction and Substantial Rehabilitation programs, all of which sub-sidized development of substantial inventories of affordable rental housing.[10] As the end of the subsidy periods has been reached, the projects' owners have faced the choice of trying to renew their subsidies or converting the develop-ments to market-rate housing. Nonprofit owners, which have developed substantial inventories of this stock, are committed to preserving these units in the affordable-housing inventory.

COMMUNITY DEVELOPMENT. Community development—less clearly defined than housing provision—can cover a lot of ground. It essentially concerns the broader community context within which neighborhood life takes place. A widely used definition of community development is "asset building that improves the quality of life among residents of low- to moderate-income communities, where communities are defined as neighborhoods or multi-neighborhood areas."[11] Assets may take various forms—physical, human, social, financial, and political—and may generate a stream of benefits over time. For example, education and training increase an individual's ability to engage in productive work and to earn income; physical infrastructure improvements (streets, sidewalks, lighting) foster greater neighborhood safety and encourage homeowners to invest in their properties; an active civic association may strengthen ties among neighborhood residents and give them good access to their local city council member. Viewed in this context, housing development is an aspect of community development, since housing is one of the many types of assets whose addition or improvement can strengthen neighborhoods.

For most of the period since the end of World War II, private investors have commonly avoided making new investments and maintaining existing assets in low- and moderate-income neighborhoods, choosing instead to support suburban development. Individual households and entrepreneurs who wanted to invest in lower-income communities, especially in minority neighborhoods, have consistently had greater difficulty gaining access to credit to purchase homes or start businesses than individuals investing in other types of neighborhoods. In many lower-income communities, public-sector investments—in infrastructure, parks, schools, and other public amenities—have not kept pace with the deterioration that comes with age and use. Consequently, the value of these public assets and their ability to produce good services have also declined. This has made community development as important a part of improving living conditions and access to opportunity as the provision of improved housing.

Federal policy in the years following the War on Poverty (the broad term for a bundle of policy initiatives launched by Lyndon Johnson in the 1960s) has paid limited explicit attention to community development, but a number of policies and programs do provide support for this work. The Community Development Block Grant (CDBG) program, begun in 1974, gives states and localities great flexibility in developing programs to support decent housing, community improvements, and improved economic opportunities, as long as these principally benefit low- and moderate-income persons. Nonprofits in this field make extensive use of these programs. In addition, the Community Development Financial Institutions (CDFI) Fund makes competitive awards to certified community development financial institutions (CDFIs) to expand their capacity to support a wide variety of economic development, affordable-housing, and financial services to low-income people and neighborhoods. More than 80 percent of the CDFIs certified as of 2010—mainly loan funds and credit unions—are nonprofit entities. The CDFI Fund also administers the New Markets Tax Credit, which allows certified community development entities to raise equity for a wide range of community development projects in low-income neighborhoods. More broadly, the Community Reinvestment Act (CRA), and subsequent legislation that strengthened it in various ways, requires banks and other depository institutions to lend in the markets from which they receive deposits; over time, this has had the effect of making private capital more readily available in historically red-lined neighborhoods, especially for housing.

Nonprofit Engagement in Housing and Community Development

Nonprofit organizations are actively involved in both housing and community development, though their relative position in the latter field is clearly more dominant.

HOUSING. In the housing field, nonprofit providers initially focused almost exclusively on producing and managing assisted rental housing. Over the past two decades, however, these providers have responded to the combination of resident interest and federal encouragement by broadening programming to include promoting affordable home ownership, especially for first-time buyers.

Several types of nonprofit organizations are involved in housing development and management, and the relationships among them are dynamic and complex.

The first on the scene, and now by far the most numerous, are community development corporations (CDCs), which are community-based organizations (CBOs) with origins in the civic activism of the civil rights movement and the War on Poverty of the 1960s. The number of CDCs has grown dramatically, from a few hundred in the 1970s to an estimated 5,500 in 2005.[12] As their name suggests, CDCs tend to focus on spatially defined target areas, such as one or more urban neighborhoods or a cluster of rural counties. Because of their numbers, the CDCs are the part of the sector positioned to affect directly the greatest number of communities.

Housing is a core activity for the vast majority of these organizations, and the activity for which they are best known, but they typically have broad community improvement missions and are involved in other activities besides housing. Not all are active as developers. The ones that are developers may manage their own rental housing or contract with either private or nonprofit outside management entities; most offer, in addition to housing production, a variety of housing-related services, such as home ownership and financial literacy counseling, home weatherization and repair programs, and resident services.

The continuous entry of fledgling groups has kept the average size of CDCs modest and fairly steady; median staff size has been about seven since the late 1980s. As in the private sector, however, size varies greatly: the larger groups (those with staff sizes in excess of 125) account for the lion's share of total CDC housing production, whereas many smaller groups operate on a smaller scale. In the aggregate, however, the number of housing units produced has grown steadily, reaching about 55,000 units a year by the early 2000s. The number of groups capable of producing a steady stream of units, the number of financial supporters, the number and strength of local partners, and the public visibility and political influence associated with CDCs have all increased correspondingly, with growth coming especially rapidly during the 1990s and continuing into the early 2000s.[13]

A second group of nonprofit housing providers operates at substantially larger scale than the CDCs, although some got their start as CDCs. Since many work throughout an entire city or metropolitan region, they are commonly referred to as regional or area-wide providers. However, some work statewide, others in selected target areas across the country. A few are large faith-based groups, such as Catholic Charities and B'nai B'rith, which, although not specializing in housing, have built substantial numbers of dwellings.

About eighty-five of the largest regional organizations are members of the Housing Partnership Network (HPN) (although many members are not structured as partnerships). These nonprofit providers generally specialize in housing production, management, and related services. Compared to the CDCs, they are larger, better capitalized, and much less likely to be engaged in broad community improvement activities. Some are lenders as well as developers, and a few specialize solely in lending. Although few in number, they are significant producers, the average annual output of HPN members being competitive with the volume produced by for-profit builders of multifamily rental housing. By 2004 the typical HPN developer had built a total of more than 2,650 units.[14] Because of their scale and specialization, they are probably more efficient producers than many of the CDCs, and they are commonly important contributors to regional program development and problem-solving collaborations.

A third group of nonprofit organizations operating in the housing field are the financial intermediaries: a small set of national and local nonprofits, umbrella organizations, and public-private partnerships that support the work of the CDCs and similar groups but that generally do not themselves develop or operate housing. The best-known national intermediaries are the Local Initiatives Support Corporation (LISC), Enterprise, and NeighborWorks, although the field also includes some more specialized ones, such as the Corporation for Supportive Housing. Localities where the nonprofit housing sector is best developed commonly have local intermediaries, often affiliated with one of the national entities. The intermediaries are one of the most distinctive features of the nonprofit housing and community development world. Their creation at the start of the 1980s effectively triggered the dramatic expansion in the number, production, and range of community development activities of the CDCs over the subsequent three decades. Since their founding, LISC and Enterprise have invested more than $20 billion in low-income communities.[15]

The intermediaries' success stems from their ability to meet the particular needs of both the CDCs and their financial supporters. Because of the neighborhoods and residents they serve, CDC projects are often viewed as being financially riskier than conventional developments—and sometimes they are. The intermediaries have established expertise and a track record in assessing risk and in structuring financial packages that both minimize risk and spread unavoidable risk across a sizable group of investors. They package philanthropic support (from both foundations and corporations), below-market rate loans, and tax-induced corporate equity investments (via the LIHTC) and make the proceeds available on a "retail" basis to CDCs and, to a lesser degree, other nonprofit developers. The intermediaries' demonstrated success in facilitating tangible improvements in poor communities while achieving repayment rates that rival those in conventional banking have made them attractive conduits for philanthropic and corporate support, especially from the nation's major banks and insurance companies. In essence, the intermediaries make it possible for funders who know little about assisted housing production or community development to support it effectively. In addition, the national intermediaries have made significant contributions to cultivating local funding partnerships and programs, helping to develop and disseminate promising program models, and educating policymakers about how better to support the sector's work. In partnership with many others, they have also been effective in making the case for expanded federal support for housing and community development—for example, via the LIHTC and the HOME program to support housing, and via the CDFI and New Markets Tax Credit programs to support both housing and other community assets such as community centers, charter schools, and businesses.

Also important to the national supportive infrastructure of the field is Living Cities, a unique collaboration of foundations and financial institutions. Established in 1991 as the National Community Development Initiative, Living Cities initially channeled all its funding through LISC, Enterprise, and their local affiliates with the goal of increasing CDC housing production by strengthening local nonprofit housing production systems, creating and supporting CDC capacity-building programs, providing general operating support, and developing new CDC-sponsored programs. In recent years, Living Cities has begun to work with a wider variety of partners and to engage in program and policy development intended to improve urban neighborhoods via interventions that extend well beyond affordable housing. During its twenty years of operation, the members of Living Cities have invested more than $1 billion to promote community revitalization.[16] Both the intermediaries and this philanthropic collaborative provide numerous lessons that might inform the development of support systems in other fields.

Together, these three groups function as a loosely structured system, or network, of nonprofit housing and community developers. At the national level the major players tend to operate independently but collaboratively. At the local level considerable variation exists. In places where the field is strong and has considerable capacity, production systems are relatively well developed and provide the CDCs with predictable project and organizational support. In other places, relationships may be less well developed and local funding streams less regularized.[17]

Two other groups, not as well integrated into the nonprofit housing system as those just described, are nevertheless important to note. The first are providers of housing for residents with special needs, most of which serve homeless individuals and families. Systematic information about these organizations is lacking, but they are similar to the CDCs, and just as diverse; however, they are far less numerous, and produce a more specialized product.[18] Rather than having a broad community improvement mission, these organizations mainly provide housing and supportive services for disadvantaged populations eligible for distinct federal subsidies (although they also use the LIHTC).

The second group is the CDFIs, a diverse group of about twelve hundred community development loan funds, community development banks, credit unions, and community development venture capital funds that provide financing and financial services to low-income individuals and communities.[19] Roughly paralleling the pattern of growth among CDCs, growth in the number of CDFIs was strong in the 1980s and especially in the 1990s, then dropped sharply in the early 2000s. Almost 1,000 CDFIs were certified by the federal CDFI Fund as of 2012; of these, the loan funds and credit unions (about 85 percent of the total) are overwhelmingly nonprofit. The community development loan funds include many of the already-discussed intermediaries, regional nonprofits, and some of the larger CDCs, which sought federal certification and funds to expand their activities. Almost two-thirds of the financing extended by the loan funds—by far the most common type of CDFI—supports housing development, mainly by nonprofit producers, so they are a core piece of the nonprofit, low-income housing production system. At the same time, the community development banks extend a preponderance of their loans to businesses, the CDFI credit unions focus heavily on housing and consumer lending, the loan funds support both firms and community-service providers, and the venture capital funds invest only in businesses—so they clearly are important to the broader community development agenda. In the aggregate, since the CDFI banks control the most capital, businesses and housing producers receive about equal shares of all CDFI funds. Federally certified CDFIs made loans and investments totaling more than $5 billion in FY2007.[20]

Taken together, this diverse group of nonprofit organizations now plays a considerable role in the production of assisted housing. Walker estimates that nonprofits produced about 34 percent of federally assisted housing (both rental and owner-occupied) built between 1995 and 2002, a total of some 367,900 units, with the balance produced by the private sector. He finds that this share has remained fairly stable since 1999.[21] However, since assisted housing units are such a small portion of the nation's overall housing (most of which is single-family and owner-occupied), the share of the nation's housing stock for which nonprofits are responsible remains less than 1 percent, despite the dramatic nonprofit expansion of the past three decades.

Nonprofit organizations also play a variety of roles in the housing field that go beyond housing development. In these roles, they both facilitate the creation of housing and support the preservation of existing housing assets. Such roles include:

—*Housing repair and improvement.* Many CDCs, especially local Neighborhood Housing Services (NHS) organizations affiliated with NeighborWorks, administer programs to help homeowners improve, repair, or weatherize their homes. Some CDFIs, especially credit unions, support this activity as well.

—*Housing counseling.* CDCs, NHSs, and other types of nonprofits provide credit repair, financial services counseling, and home ownership training to individuals seeking to become first-time home buyers;

—*Housing ownership and management.* In addition to nonprofit developers' management of their own units, some groups, including the large-scale regional producers, have specialized in managing low-cost rental housing developed by others (either nonprofits or for-profits).

—*Community land trusts.* These organizations seek to acquire and hold land in perpetuity for use in providing affordable housing for low- and moderate-income families; their numbers have been growing rapidly in recent years, although most remain small.

—*Housing advocacy.* Housing groups are broadly engaged at all levels of government in policy advocacy for affordable housing; especially when highly visible issues are at stake, they gain support from a wide range of organizations concerned with the well-being of poor and working-class people.

—*Resident councils, mutual housing associations, and condominium associations*. These groups are concerned with project livability once housing is developed; unlike the previously listed organizations they can serve households at all income levels.

COMMUNITY DEVELOPMENT. Most CDCs, some of the regional providers and intermediaries, and many of the CDFIs engaged in the housing sector are also active in other aspects of community development. Among the CDCs, the most common activities that extend beyond housing are community economic development (developing commercial and industrial real estate and community facilities, providing entrepreneurship training, operating micro-enterprise loan funds), community organizing and advocacy, education and training, and programs for youth.[22]

In addition, there is history going back to the settlement houses of the early twentieth century of CBOs engaging in strengthening other types of community assets; such groups include the following:

—*Community organizing groups*. Mobilize residents to build social relationships and cultivate political clout aimed at improving the community.

—*Community and neighborhood associations*. Like the resident councils and others noted earlier, they protect community interests by, for example, fighting for proper zoning or safer streets.

—*Educational and workforce development organizations*. Help residents in low-income communities develop their human capital via activities that range from after-school tutoring for children to job training for adults.

Distinguishing Features of Nonprofit Involvement in Housing and Community Development

Four central features distinguish nonprofit housing producers, particularly the CDCs, from their for-profit counterparts in the housing field.

First and most significant is that they generally engage in a variety of community development activities that extend well beyond housing, whereas for-profit housing developers tend to specialize in housing alone. For-profit developers deal with neighborhood influences by building in the best locations where they can identify development opportunities, and by building at a large enough scale to create the type of neighborhood they seek to market. If they build rental housing, they typically limit their attention to maintaining their own properties. In contrast, CDCs commonly serve communities plagued by disinvestment. Housing development is, for them, part of a broader community development agenda. They tend to take a broad view of "community," and to be concerned about the full spectrum of community issues and needs. This inclination is reinforced by their organizational investment in housing, which creates an incentive for them to be concerned about the behavior of the residents and the conditions in the surrounding neighborhood—an incentive even for large regional providers with a strong housing focus. Indeed, the field as a whole tends to view housing as a means to greater ends: improved communities and stronger families with greater access to opportunity.

Second, the CDCs typically define their mission in terms of a geographic service area; in cities, this is commonly one or more neighborhoods. This means they know their communities very well, but it can have the effect of limiting their development opportunities to those available within their target area. Even though few CDCs have actually "run out" of housing development opportunities, the geographical constraint often makes it more difficult (sometimes impossible) to develop on a large enough scale to maximize their economic efficiency. This is especially an issue in neighborhoods where in-fill housing—small scale developments built on vacant lots amid already existing housing stock—is a priority.

Third, the CDCs are typically smaller and less well capitalized than either the large-scale regional nonprofits or their for-profit counterparts. Most are highly vulnerable to the loss of key senior staff, and have limited financial reserves either to respond to opportunities (such as to acquire key properties when they become available) or to weather adversity. Developing at small scale, as many do, exacerbates this problem. In contrast, the regional producers are generally very sophisticated developers. Compared to the CDCs, they are larger, take on larger developments, and produce at higher levels. This makes them more likely to realize economies of scale and to have portfolios of rental properties that are large enough to manage efficiently. Because they are willing to build anywhere in the region, they are better positioned than the CDCs to facilitate the deconcentration of poor households outside of high-poverty neighborhoods.

Finally, nonprofit developers generally have to engage in more complex financial arrangements than the typical market-rate housing developer. This is the case because producing assisted housing requires using one or more housing subsidies, each of which comes with its own rules and requirements. The LIHTC, in particular, is a complicated program, although it has tended to become less so over time. When the LIHTC was enacted in 1986, prospective purchasers did not understand the program, so demand for the credits was rather modest and the amount of equity their sale raised was also modest. As a result, multiple sources of subsidy (sometimes more than half a dozen) had to be added to the financing package in order to keep rents affordable to income-eligible tenants, and each subsidy program added a new layer of rules and requirements. Over time, as demand for the credits increased and their sale raised more money for projects, financing became simpler. By the mid-2000s, when demand for LIHTCs was strongest, only a small fraction of developments required more than one additional subsidy, and these were commonly targeted to households with near-poverty-level incomes. Nevertheless, financing for LIHTC projects remained much more complicated than the financing for conventional market-rate housing.[23]

In addition to differing from public and for-profit housing providers, non-profit housing groups also differ from nonprofits in other fields in interesting ways. Perhaps the most unusual is the extent to which the nonprofits' role interacts with the operation of the market. In seriously disinvested neighborhoods, one of the CDCs' goals is to get the for-profit and public sectors to do their jobs better. Vis-à-vis the private sector, the challenge is to use sustained, strategic investments in housing and other community assets to re-create viable housing markets that will attract renewed flows of private investment. Accomplishing this requires significant, strategically placed investments in housing sustained over a period of years. In neighborhoods with very high concentrations of poverty, it also sometimes requires production of housing for moderate-income home owners to give the neighborhood more economic diversity and increase its political influence. Corollary activities to strengthen neighborhood shopping districts, encourage investments in public infrastructure such as streetscaping and parks, improve safety, or organize residents are also required. Conversely, in strong housing markets, the nonprofit role shifts to developing and retaining as much affordable housing as possible, especially affordable home ownership opportunities, so that low-income residents are not forced out of the community as new investments make it a more desirable place to live and gain access to employment.

A second distinguishing feature of nonprofit engagement in housing and community development as compared to other spheres of nonprofit activity is the success that this sector has achieved in meeting its financial challenges. Financial viability poses a serious obstacle to nonprofit activity in many other fields, particularly those built around large numbers of small organizations. Success in this field has been strongly driven by the intermediary organizations described earlier. Their efforts have attracted a significant flow of private capital into the work of nonprofit organizations committed to improving low-income neighborhoods and the housing opportunities available to low-income people.

Nonprofits in the housing and community development fields have also made important headway in resolving one of the other perennial challenges facing nonprofit organizations: strengthening their capacity and resilience. This includes well-established approaches such as providing access to first-rate training, timely technical assistance, improved software, and state-of-the-art management systems. But it also extends to longer-term interventions, exemplified by the multiyear capacity-building programs stimulated by Living Cities in more than twenty cities to provide CDCs with operating support in exchange for steady improvement in organizational performance. Most broadly, it entails a systemwide commitment to dealing with problems that have sometimes hindered community development and low-income housing promotion, such as developing standardized systems to simplify financial reporting on complex subsidy programs, investing in training for better property management, and providing best-practice guidance for local governments about how to make their programs and services more user-friendly to CDCs and other small developers.

Major Forces Shaping the Nonprofit Housing and Community Development Field

The past three decades have been a period of enormous growth for the nonprofit housing and community development field. The trajectory of the field was strongly positive up until the advent of the foreclosure crisis. In the wake of the crisis, serious challenges will command considerable attention until housing markets and the national economy recover. Two categories of factors currently are shaping the field: first, factors linked to the foreclosure crisis, which threaten households, neighborhoods, and nonprofit housing and community development organizations in the near-to-medium term (and possibly longer in very weak housing markets); second, longer-term challenges and opportunities that exist independent of the crisis.

Challenges Created by the Foreclosure Crisis

The nonprofit housing and community development system is one of the less visible victims of the mortgage crisis and the subsequent recession. This system is beset on several fronts.

In the wake of the financial crisis, the market for LIHTCs stumbled badly. The financial institutions (including Fannie Mae and Freddie Mac) that had been purchasing most of the credits became more risk-averse and more reluctant to lend and invest, and had fewer profits to shelter. As a result, sales fell sharply, and the credits that sold did so at lower prices and therefore generated less equity. Many projects were stalled. Temporary changes in the LIHTC program did enable states to move forward on projects that were caught in the pipeline. The LIHTC market has rebounded, although not to its peak level; Fannie Mae and Freddie Mac have withdrawn from the market, but many financial institutions have again become profitable and some new investors have entered the market. However, investors are more cautious, and more likely to seek out strong project sponsors and stronger markets. Continued health of the LIHTC program in some form is critical: it is the nation's largest assisted housing production program and is the main instrument used to maintain the affordability of expiring-use properties—properties whose existing subsidy commitments are ending.

Many CDCs experienced financial stress as a result. Developing LIHTC housing is a source of fee income that can be used for operating support. Further, those that responded to federal encouragement and resident demand for more affordable home ownership opportunities were commonly left holding inventory they could not sell, thus adding to their costs. Although few CDCs derive a substantial portion of their income from developer fees, their undercapitalized status means that the loss of any substantial income source can pose a financial threat. Larger CDCs, along with the regional providers and the intermediaries, had to belt-tighten, sometimes substantially, but generally had enough financial depth to be able to weather the storm. Small CDCs were at greater risk. Some had no choice but to fold or leave the development business and find ways to transfer their housing assets to other, stronger, organizations to manage; others (probably fewer) may seek to merge with stronger organizations.

The buyers of CDC-sponsored owner-occupied housing are unlikely to be casualties of the foreclosure crisis if they remain employed, since they commonly received home ownership or financial counseling plus access to affordable fixed-rate mortgages. However, many CDC-served neighborhoods were vulnerable to predatory lenders, and as the foreclosure crisis spread to owners with more mainstream mortgages (including adjustable-rate mortgages), low- and moderate-income owners and their neighborhoods were particularly hard hit. Foreclosures have been widespread, and many more such owners are at risk of losing their homes. They need counseling to enable them to obtain modified mortgage terms and remain in their homes, or to find affordable rental housing if they cannot. The resources and policy tools needed to assist these residents are simply not adequate to serve all who need help, and developing them is a major challenge. Effective workout strategies are complex to craft, and banks, mortgage servicers, and the federal government must take the lead in developing them. But federal efforts have been slow, in part because financial institutions have been reluctant to make major changes, so many at-risk owners have not received adequate help.

The National Foreclosure Mitigation Counseling Program makes major new federal funding available to deal with this issue, although more help will certainly be required. The program funds the NeighborWorks network and many of the regional providers and their partners to both train foreclosure mitigation counselors and provide direct assistance to at-risk home owners. These funds enable CBOs with established expertise in this arena to expand their work.

Some organizations formerly engaged in providing financial literacy and pre-purchase homeownership counseling have struggled to switch gears, however, as this new type of counseling requires significantly different skills and partners.

For nonprofit developers, a core challenge is to deal with the devastating effects widespread foreclosures have on neighborhoods. Foreclosures reduce the value of occupied homes in the neighborhood; this makes it less likely that owners hard-pressed by the recession can refinance their homes or sell them for enough money to pay off the mortgage. This encourages under-maintenance, and even abandonment. Empty homes discourage investment in the community. They also invite vandalism. Stripping empty homes for materials such as appliances, plumbing, wiring, and fixtures that can be sold is commonplace if the new owner (possibly the lender), neighbors, and the police are not vigilant. Costly investments are required to make stripped homes even habitable, much less attractive and affordable. Securing vacant properties, finding responsible owners, making them move-in ready, and returning them to productive use is a formidable challenge, and becomes all the more so if the homes cannot be sold and must be converted to single-family rental housing, which is difficult to manage. Neighborhoods with widespread foreclosures such as those served by CDCs can face the necessity of demolishing many homes that cannot be repaired or rehabilitated; this problem is especially acute in historically weak-market cities. This, too, is unfamiliar work for most nonprofit developers, especially at the scale that is now evident.

Also vulnerable are community development banks and loan funds that have concentrated their lending in these hard-hit neighborhoods. Despite their emphasis on providing affordable mortgages to home buyers and sound underwriting for affordable-housing developments, they cannot help but be affected by falling property values in neighborhoods where foreclosures are widespread. Most of these lenders make mission-appropriate loans across large service areas, but those that have targeted their lending geographically are at risk.[24]

Like the foreclosure crisis itself, these problems are much too large for neighborhood organizations, or even the entire nonprofit housing sector, to respond to alone. Major investments are required, new programs and policies must be developed, and both the public sector—federal, state, and local—and the private sector will have to step up to the plate. The nonprofits can contribute to these efforts, of course. They are actively engaged in helping to develop programs and strategies tailored to local communities, and promising approaches are slowly emerging. Federal stimulus dollars have been critical to this early work, but longer-term, steady sources of financial support for these programs must be found: the CDCs and others seeking to undertake them are already financially stressed for reasons described earlier, and in many neighborhoods the work that needs to be done will take years to accomplish.

Ongoing Long-Term Challenges

Overall, the long-term picture has been strongly positive. As discussed earlier, most standard indicators of the sector's health prior to the foreclosure crisis tell a consistent story. Even though the exponential growth of earlier years is unlikely to be seen again in the foreseeable future, and some organizational consolidation is to be expected, the core of the industry is solid, especially in places where it is well established and enjoys a seasoned support structure of public, private, and philanthropic partners.

At the regional and national levels, the field's institutional infrastructure is firmly established and has proved creative and resilient over time. The non-profit intermediaries and CDFIs have, of course, experienced troubled loans and delayed repayments, which, combined with reduced financial support from foundations and mainstream financial institutions, have made retrenchments necessary. However, careful project selection and underwriting appear to have headed off the widespread defaults observed in other parts of the financial sector. All segments of the system have marshaled their forces to meet the foreclosure-related challenges, but without losing sight of, and working toward, the long-term goal of building healthy low- and moderate-income communities. Housing and financial markets will likely rebound in an uneven fashion, with some places regaining their vigor in pace with the national economy and others stabilizing over a much longer term. As this process unfolds, the field's support structure can be expected to again seek affirmative opportunities to advance that long-term goal.

In the wake of such a massive disruption to the housing market, the specific contours of the field's future remain unclear. However, the strategies that have facilitated the sector's remarkable growth in the past are likely to continue to be important. Affordable-housing production and management will continue to be central, most likely with the emphasis shifting toward rental housing. Continued attention to expanding the funding base will be essential. The field's signature approach to this is developing effective ways to attract and integrate support from public, private, and philanthropic sources. And reflective efforts to build the field continue at all levels, not just by attracting funding but also by strengthening organizational capacity and expanding the range of improvements the field can deliver to communities.

But, in addition to the challenge of overcoming the lingering effects of the recession and the mortgage meltdown, nonprofits in the housing and community development field face a number of other challenges; five of the most critical deserve mention here.

ECONOMIC AND DEMOGRAPHIC CHALLENGES. Nonprofit housing providers are affected by the broader economic and demographic trends shaping the cities and regions in which they operate. Increasing income inequality and the inability of poor unsubsidized households to afford market prices for housing has induced private owners to maintain low-cost units poorly or convert them to more profitable uses. The result has been a sustained loss of low-cost rental units from the national housing stock and a heightened housing affordability crisis for low-income households, despite the sustained expansion of nonprofit housing production over the past three decades. Even under the rosiest of circumstances, federal housing subsidies will continue to reach only a fraction of the affected households who qualify for them. That a significant proportion of the urban poor, particularly poor people of color, live in communities where poor people are highly concentrated only complicates the problem further.

Two major national demographic trends will also have important implications for the nonprofit housing and community development sector. The first is record high levels of immigration. Many cities that have not traditionally been entry portals are seeing increasing flows of immigrant arrivals (see chapter 17, on demographics), and in contrast to previous eras of immigration, suburbs and smaller cities and towns are also becoming destinations. As a consequence, nonprofits engaged in housing and community development face the challenges of providing housing, and sometimes a variety of other programs and services, to groups whose cultures and languages are unfamiliar. Many immigrants arrive with extremely limited resources, yet are often ineligible for the public subsidy and service programs the nonprofits rely on. Communication problems, differences in cultural norms about such matters as the use of residential space, and the newcomers' need for services that the nonprofits may not have provided previously further complicate the task. This is particularly difficult in communities where tension develops between immigrant groups and the nonprofits' traditional constituents.

Second, the aging of the population (also highlighted in chapter 17) will be a growing issue for the field. Most immediately affected are owners of Section 202 housing for the elderly, all of which are nonprofit. About one-third of the residents of Section 202 housing are eighty or older.[25] More than one-fifth of all residents are frail, and an even larger number require assistance with daily tasks. These figures have been rising steadily and will continue to do so. These residents will increasingly need supportive services and dwellings modified to facilitate mobility if they are to remain in their homes; otherwise they will need access to affordable assisted living. Indeed, the need for this type of housing is expected to increase. Substantially larger numbers of seniors receive other forms of housing subsidies, such as Housing Choice Vouchers, Section 236, and public housing; some of them reside in nonprofit-owned housing and will face similar problems.

CHALLENGES OF ENGAGING WITH THE MARKET. Historically, nonprofit and for-profit participants in housing operated quite independently: nonprofits entered the field of housing and community development precisely because the housing and other amenities poor communities needed were not being provided by the market, and they received housing subsidies directly from the public sector. Now the relationships between the two sectors are both more complex and more dynamic.

The LIHTC exemplifies this complexity. When Congress initially authorized LIHTCs in 1986, they were temporary; as a result, for-profit developers were unwilling to invest the time needed to learn how to use them. When Congress made the credits permanent in 1993, private-sector developers became active users of LIHTCs. During the late 1990s and into the 2000s, competition among developers for the annual fixed supply of credits increased. Uncertainty about whether projects would go forward and the costs of delay when proposed projects did not receive funding posed real difficulties for nonprofit developers. At the same time, increased competition among purchasers of the tax credits drove up prices; as discussed earlier, that brought more equity dollars into projects that did receive credit allocations but also attracted increased for-profit interest. However the tax credit program evolves in the future, interdependencies of this type are likely to endure.

Similarly, in attractive cities and neighborhoods, nonprofits seeking to provide affordable housing options compete with for-profits for development opportunities. The higher costs in these areas drive up development costs, making the projects more difficult to do; in very high-cost locations, low-income projects may become financially infeasible. During the boom of the 1990s and early 2000s, as the nonprofits became "priced out" of opportunities in their neighborhoods, they switched gears: helping local families purchase homes so they could capitalize on rising prices and neighborhood improvements, seeking joint ventures with for-profit developers (either to improve local retailing or to build some affordable units into new market-rate housing developments in the community); or moving beyond their initial target areas. The bursting of the housing bubble eased this price pressure, perhaps for quite awhile, but in economically strong cities some form of this dynamic is likely to recur.

FUNDING CHALLENGES. Notwithstanding the substantial growth of federal support for low-income housing, nonprofit housing and community development organizations continue to confront significant funding challenges on two fronts: the funding of actual housing projects, and the funding of the operating costs of the nonprofit agencies that help to develop the housing and engage in other community development activities.

For funding actual projects, sustained federal support, both direct (such as for HOME and CDBG) and indirect (for LIHTC and tax-exempt bonds), are critical over the long term. Absent those dollars, affordable-housing production is not feasible. Federal support for housing programs at a level that sustained the nonprofit role was not a problem in the mid- to late 1990s, an era characterized by sustained economic growth and budget surpluses. But with the resurgence of budget deficits in the aftermath of two wars, the Bush-era tax cuts, a financial bailout, and a deep recession, sustaining funding for low-income housing and communities will be politically challenging, even with a sympathetic administration in the White House. More fundamentally, even if levels of federal support sufficient to sustain the nonprofit development sector can be found, they do not even come close to enabling nonprofits to provide for all households with acute problems in finding affordable housing.

Funding operating support presents a different type of challenge. In some localities, local intermediaries or public-private partnerships provide CDCs with some core operating support, often in exchange for the CDCs' increasing their organizational capacity in some agreed-upon way or meeting other kinds of performance benchmarks. Some local governments use part of their CDBG allocations for this purpose. On the whole, however, raising money for operating costs is an ongoing struggle for many groups, and even if the field sees some consolidation, the typical CDC is likely to remain small and undercapitalized.

ORGANIZATIONAL AND MANAGEMENT CHALLENGES. The nonprofit housing and community development field has been quite proactive about building organizational capacity and performance, especially in localities with numerous CDCs. Before the foreclosure crisis, localities where capacity-building programs were in place saw steady improvements among the groups assisted. In the wake of the crisis, capacity building continues to be critical. In the short term, the capacity to respond to the foreclosure crisis and its effects is clearly inadequate, and the field is actively supporting efforts to help existing organizations undertake new activities such as assisting households during the foreclosure process and dealing with the impact of properties left vacant as a result of foreclosures. At the same time, the crisis has forced belt tightening at all levels of the housing and community development system, from the national to the grassroots, and this has taken a toll. Since most nonprofits' operating costs (as opposed to development costs) primarily cover salaries, staffing cutbacks have been common, eroding organizational capacity that will need to be rebuilt.

More fundamentally, as local housing markets rebound in different ways (or not at all), there will be opportunities to reconsider what kinds of organizational capacities are needed and how they can best be organized. Indeed, conversations about capacity are part and parcel of crafting responses to the foreclosure crisis.

In the new housing landscape, the challenges of sustaining large numbers of small, financially vulnerable producers that cannot achieve economies of scale in production and management call for thoughtful development of new business models that reduce the dependence of smaller organizations on development fee income. Dealing with this issue will be especially important in very weak markets where the legacy of the foreclosure crisis and recession will be long and where preservation of the existing housing stock that remains viable is at least as important as new production.

As ever, nonprofit housing and community development organizations are under pressure to respond to neighborhood and management challenges while maintaining their community roots and developing community leadership. They thus confront some of the tensions facing the nonprofit sector more generally, as highlighted in Lester Salamon's introduction to this volume. The CDC movement was spawned by civic activism, and this is a key source of their legitimacy in speaking for their neighborhoods. As the field has matured it has made systematic efforts to build organizational capacity so that the CDCs can successfully complete financially complex housing developments, manage them well in troubled neighborhoods, and stretch to tackle a wider array of tough community issues. This professionalization has been critical to the successes that have been achieved, but it also creates the potential for tension between sustaining resident involvement and managing work that is technically and financially complex. This challenge is amplified by the fact that tenant and community organizing—the basic method of stimulating and sustaining resident involvement and training new community leadership—are activities that many funders, both public and private, are reluctant to support.

LACK OF PUBLIC RECOGNITION. A final challenge confronting nonprofit housing and community development organizations is lack of public recognition. In most places, CDCs and other nonprofit housing organizations are still not on the general public's radar screen. Even though the foreclosure crisis has made housing a high-profile national issue, affordable housing (like urban policy more generally) has not been a prominent focus of national attention. Although the sector has worked hard at getting the word out and has become better known and more highly regarded as its extent and accomplishments have grown, the achievements of the housing and community development nonprofit sector remain one of the great untold tales of successful nonprofit inventiveness.

Promising Opportunities in the Field

Despite the challenges that are part and parcel of the housing and community development field and that necessarily command attention, the future also holds genuine opportunities for the field.

BROADENING THE PROGRAMMATIC AGENDA. The production of affordable housing and the provision of related housing services has become the core of the nonprofit work in this field because significant funds for this aspect of community development could most readily be tapped. Yet there has long been broad interest in developing systematic capacity to deal with community improvement in a more multifaceted way, and real progress in this direction has been made.

In cities with community development depth—numbers of capable CDCs and well-developed systems of support for them—local intermediaries (often affiliates of the national intermediaries) have crafted systems of support for a CDC agenda "beyond housing." Prime targets of opportunity for this expanded agenda have included the following:

—Greater involvement by the CDCs in economic development, through formal collaborations that enable CDCs to share staff with specialized skills, or the creation of a specialized new organization to serve the commercial development needs of CDCs citywide;

—Community-building activities such as neighborhood planning and advocacy and community and tenant organizing;

—Development of community facilities that can be used by community partners such as clinics or charter schools;

—Incorporation of "green" elements into the construction of CDC-sponsored dwellings to reduce their long-term operating costs, by demonstrating new technologies or integrating new funders and technical assistance providers into the local housing production system.[26]

Foundations, too, have increasingly become interested in this possibility, seeing the CDCs and other CBOs as community agents with demonstrated capacity in neighborhoods where such agents are sometimes in short supply. Their interest has spawned two approaches to enriching the community development agenda. One is to channel funding through a CDC or other "lead agency" that is expected to facilitate an inclusive community "quality-of-life" planning process and draw in neighborhood partners to mount projects and programs to implement the plan. The New Communities Program, launched in 2003 by the MacArthur Foundation and Chicago LISC to stimulate multifaceted community improvement in sixteen Chicago neighborhoods, exemplifies this approach and has served as a prototype for LISC's Building Sustainable Communities initiative. The other enables the national intermediaries to support approaches to community development that have not traditionally been part of the CDC agenda, promoting affordable "green" building. Living Cities is also making substantial investments in developing fresh approaches to broadening the community revitalization agenda. The upshot is the growing possibility of a richer, higher impact role for the field.

How this plays out will doubtless vary from place to place. In some places, CDCs will become more diversified, continuing to add the building of other types of community assets to their housing development and management agendas. In others, the CDC might identify areas of community need and interest and provide the needed facilities, but partner with a specialized service provider to operate the clinic, school, or child-care center. In another model, the CDC could act as a broker (like the "lead agency" role just described), identifying and working with other types of organizations that have experience in providing the community benefits the CDC neighborhood needs. Each of these approaches will require the CDCs to acquire new skills and operating styles, most notably the ability to collaborate with organizations that have expertise in different fields—approaches that are likely to become increasingly important if the Obama administration gains traction with its efforts to break down programmatic "silos" and promote integrated solutions to community problems, as reflected in its Choice Neighborhoods and Promise Neighborhoods initiatives.

ENGAGING REGIONALLY. Public policymakers increasingly recognize that the well-being of neighborhoods and their rural counterparts is inextricably linked to the economic and fiscal health of larger regions. National-level policy research, advocacy, and public education in the nonprofit housing and community development field has taken this insight to heart—and continuing and extending these types of activities is critical.

Engaging effectively in regional policymaking will require nonprofits in the housing and community development field to undertake new kinds of collective action by making common cause with congregations, labor unions, environmental organizations, and others around issues—such as smart growth and living wages—that affect the quality of life in poor neighborhoods but are not actionable at the neighborhood level. There is little doubt that the nonprofits' constituents and communities would benefit from metropolitan, regional, or statewide initiatives that emphasize reinvestment and redevelopment in core urban neighborhoods, or from local government or union-led efforts that "make work pay" a family-supporting wage. CDCs would find moving such agendas difficult to do on their own: financial support for tenant and community organizing is perennially scarce, and many neighborhoods that would benefit from such initiatives are not served by CDCs, so they are poorly positioned to take the lead. But groups of CDCs might be (or could become) well positioned to weigh in effectively on these broader issues, especially if they act through their local, metropolitan, or statewide membership associations.

CAPITALIZING ON TECHNOLOGICAL OPPORTUNITIES. Historically, the housing and community development field has been characterized by small, dispersed organizations that have had limited opportunities to learn from peers and inadequate resources to do more than react to pressing problems. As the field has matured, it has become more highly organized: local and state CDC associations, networks of CDCs affiliated with the national intermediaries, and a variety of trade associations—for example, of CDFIs and the large regional producers—have come together to create opportunities for knowledge sharing. The field has already made a strong start on using new technologies such as social networking and webinars to augment and broaden the range of such connections for policy advocacy, real estate finance training, and other purposes.

Technology also presents a powerful opportunity for the field to become more analytical and strategic about both neighborhood planning and program and policy development. Geographic information systems, fueled by detailed data increasingly pooled from a myriad of sources, facilitate both the analysis of complex urban development patterns and the presentation of analytic results in visually powerful, readily understandable ways. At the city and regional levels, this creates opportunities as diverse as better-informed planning with broader community participation, more effective monitoring of the performance of public programs that affect neighborhoods, and identification of places with common circumstances that might find common cause politically. At the neighborhood level, public access to such data systems (including residents' ability to collect and add their own data) can also be used to engage residents directly in such activities as housing code enforcement and crime prevention. This technology is demonstrating its value in a growing number of places, many of which have joined together in the National Neighborhood Indicators Partnership, and it has tremendous potential to improve both community development practice and public policy support.

Conclusions

Nonprofit housing and community development organizations have enjoyed enormous growth since 1980. Although the sector plays a very small role in the housing industry overall, it is a significant player in the production and management of assisted housing, and it predominates in the field of community development, particularly in disadvantaged neighborhoods. Although continued exponential growth in the number of nonprofit housing producers is unlikely, and some consolidation is a real possibility, there remain ample opportunities for existing organizations and their supporters to become stronger and more effective in communities. And the sector clearly has an important role to play in helping the nation deal with the community impacts of the foreclosure crisis and the collapse of home prices.

Beyond this, the recent experience of nonprofit housing and community development organizations holds important lessons for nonprofit organizations in other fields. Especially important has been the success these organizations have achieved in tapping sizable pools of private capital—and the political support of the diverse stakeholders who provide it—and channeling the resulting resources into nonprofit activities in this field. This success has been due to the availability of federal tax subsidies coupled with the presence of a set of innovative nonprofit intermediary organizations that specialize in packaging these subsidies, marketing them to investors, and then using the proceeds to finance the work of local nonprofit housing producers. The special characteristics of housing do make this function easier to perform in this sphere than in many others. Nonetheless, the progress that the nonprofit housing and community development organizations and their affiliated intermediaries have made in extending their model to fields beyond housing suggests that there are lessons here for nonprofits operating in other spheres where the demands for capital investment have recently escalated. More generally, this experience shows that significant private capital can be generated for the work of nonprofit organizations where the nonprofits are willing to build the requisite links.

Notes

1. Current federal policy deems housing "affordable" if it costs no more than 30 percent of a household's income.

2. Calculated from table A-1a in U.S. Department of Housing and Urban Development, Office of Policy Development and Research, *Affordable Housing Needs 2005* (Washington: 2007).

3. Alex F. Schwartz, *Housing Policy in the United States,* 2nd ed. (New York: Routledge, 2010), pp. 35–39, 45–47.

4. Very modest efforts to move toward public housing date back to World War I, and some states made similar efforts during the 1920s, but serious federal policy was first established with the Wagner-Steagall Housing Act of 1937. See Lawrence M. Friedman, "Public Housing and the Poor," in *Housing Urban America,* edited by Jon Pynoos and others (Chicago: Aldine, 1973).

5. Schwartz, *Housing Policy in the United States,* p. 126.

6. States and localities play important roles in allocating and administering a number of important federal housing programs. Beyond this, many have launched housing programs of their own. These programs vary greatly and the extent of funding for them often varies with the financial health of the supporting jurisdiction. Discussion of these programs lies beyond the scope of this chapter.

7. Some federal subsidies, such as those under the HOME and CDBG programs, can be used to promote home ownership affordable to low-income families, but most federal support for home ownership is indirect. The home mortgage interest deduction is by far the nation's largest housing subsidy, but homes whose owners take the deduction are not generally considered assisted housing.

8. Housing vouchers enable income-eligible households that have them to rent any housing unit they can find that meets basic housing standards and rents for no more than a federally approved "fair market rent"; the voucher pays the difference between the actual rent and 30 percent of the tenants' income—the amount they can officially "afford." Housing

vouchers permit households to pay more than 30 percent of their income as rent, but the households must pay the difference between the market rent and the federally approved fair market rent.

9. Schwartz, *Housing Policy in the United States,* p. 103.

10. The Section 502 and 515 programs, both run by the Farmers Home Administration, also supported development of substantial housing inventories; they are not discussed further because nonprofit participation in these programs was low.

11. Ronald F. Ferguson and William T. Dickens, eds., *Urban Problems and Community Development* (Brookings, 1999), pp. 4–5.

12. Neal R. Peirce and Carol F. Steinbach, *Corrective Capitalism: The Rise of America's Community Development Corporations* (New York: Ford Foundation, 1987); Christopher Walker, "Affordable Housing Production in the Nonprofit and For-Profit Sectors: A Summary of the Statistical Evidence," unpublished working paper, prepared for Local Initiatives Support Corporation, New York, 2009.

13. Walker, "Affordable Housing Production in the Nonprofit and For-Profit Sectors"; Christopher Walker and Mark Weinheimer, *Community Development in the 1990s* (Washington: Urban Institute, 1999).

14. Neil S. Mayer and Kenneth Tempkin, *Housing Partnerships: The Work of Large-Scale Regional Nonprofits in Affordable Housing* (Washington: Urban Institute, 2007).

15. "LISC Online Annual Report 2009" (www.lisc.org/annualreport/2009/message/message.shtml; October 30, 2010); Enterprise Community Partners, *A Good Life Is Affordable: 2009 Annual Report* (Columbia, Md.: 2010).

16. See Living Cities (www.livingcities.org/20years/ [May 1, 2012]).

17. Langley C. Keyes and others, "Networks and Nonprofits: Opportunities and Challenges in an Era of Federal Devolution," *Housing Policy Debate* 7, no. 2 (1996); Walker and Weinheimer, *Community Development in the 1990s;* David J. Erickson, *The Housing Policy Revolution: Networks and Neighborhoods* (Washington: Urban Institute Press, 2009).

18. A sizable fraction of CDCs also produce some special needs housing, even though it is not their major focus, and in some places CDCs are being encouraged to produce some special needs units so that the populations served can be better integrated into the community.

19. CDFI Data Project, *Providing Capital, Building Communities, Creating Impact,* 7th ed., FY 2008 data, 2011 (http://opportunityfinance.net/store/product.asp?pID&@=12535 [May 1, 2012]).

20. Ibid.

21. Walker, "Affordable Housing Production in the Nonprofit and For-Profit Sectors."

22. National Alliance of Community Economic Development Associations, *Rising Above: Community Economic Development in a Changing Landscape* (Washington: 2010).

23. For an excellent explanation of these complex issues, see Schwartz, *Housing Policy in the United States,* pp. 103–10.

24. This type of exposure accounts for the restructuring of Shorebank, the nation's premier community development bank, which was required to close by the FDIC in 2010. Although it is a for-profit institution, its difficulties illustrate the vulnerability of community development lenders committed by their missions to tight geographic targeting. See Rick Cohen, "The Cohen Report: A Community Development Bank Passes," *Nonprofit Quarterly,* August 24, 2010.

25. Barbara A. Haley and others, *Section 202 Supportive Housing for the Elderly: Program Status and Performance Measurement* (Washington: U.S. Department of Housing and Urban Development, 2008), pp. 5, 27.

26. Langley C. Keyes and Avis C. Vidal, *Beyond Housing: Growing Community Development Systems* (Washington: Urban Institute, 2005); Wendy Kellogg and Dennis Keating, "Cleveland's EcoVillage: Green and Affordable Housing through a Collaborative Network," *Housing Policy Debate* 21, no. 1 (2011).

7

Environmental Organizations

CARMEN SIRIANNI AND STEPHANIE SOFER

The environmental movement in the United States traces its organizational roots to the turn of the twentieth century, and some of the membership organizations created during that period—especially the Sierra Club (1892) and the National Audubon Society (1905)—are still major players today. Other organizations, such as the Wilderness Society (1935) and National Wildlife Federation (1936), were established in subsequent decades, but the real explosion of growth that gave birth to the contemporary environmental movement occurred in tandem with other social movements of the 1960s. In the latter half of the 1960s and the first half of 1970s, important new organizations were established, such as the Environmental Defense Fund (1967) and the Natural Resources Defense Council (1970), and some of the existing organizations increased their memberships substantially. As these and other so-called "mainstream" environmental organizations became increasingly professionalized in their staffing, structure, and funding, they became powerful players in the national environmental regulatory regime that emerged at this time. They have been effective in getting many new laws passed and using the courts and regulatory agencies to reduce pollution. This "command-and-control" regulatory paradigm entailed Congress's restricting certain activities, setting definite deadlines for reducing specific pollutants, and mandating the use of specific technologies over others. The U.S. Environmental Protection Agency (EPA) would bear primary responsibility for enforcing these mandates. Should polluters fail to meet requirements and deadlines, the EPA could impose penalties. For their part, citizens could sue polluters and the EPA itself, should the intent or letter of the law not be carried out. Of course, in practice all this proved to be a much more complicated affair than envisioned when the EPA was created, in 1970.[1]

The mainstream environmental organizations, however, have been repeatedly challenged by various groups in the name of greater democratic participation from below and of relative effectiveness in addressing persistent problems, such as ecosystem degradation and environmental injustice, that do not lend themselves as well to the kinds of command-and-control tools and action repertoires preferred by most of the national advocacy organizations. As a result, the field of environmentalism has continued to become more organizationally diverse and dynamic, with new forms of civic engagement and social capital generated in the process. This dynamic diversity stands in contrast to the much more pessimistic reading of environmental organizations one finds in Robert Putnam's *Bowling Alone* and also provides significant alternatives to the decline of the classic multi-tier civic associations analyzed in Theda Skocpol's *Diminished Democracy*. The complex challenges of climate change, which extend across so many institutional actors and social sectors, only reinforce this trend toward continued diversity and dynamism in the field.[2]

In this chapter we explore this organizational diversity in broad strokes. We classify organizations in terms of three major types—advocacy, ecosystem, and education—though it will quickly become evident that in each category there are hybrids and further distinctions. In addition, proliferating across the environmental landscape today are multi-stakeholder partnerships of many sorts that might include one or more environmental organizations from each category, as well as assorted other civic associations, universities, businesses, farming and ranching groups, professional and trade associations, and local, state, and federal agencies. Some of these partnerships are initiated by environmental organizations, which quite frequently have traditional adversaries, while others are convened under the auspices of public agencies or facilitated by third-party neutrals, such as environmental dispute resolution centers. If anything distinguishes the field of environmental organizations today as compared to forty years ago, when the movement surged decisively forward, it is the prevalence of terms such as "partnership" and "network" in environmental protection and natural resource governance. Indeed, a recent report of the National Academy of Public Administration even urged the U.S. Environmental Protection Agency to transform itself into a "partnering agency," and the National Advisory Council for Environmental Policy and Technology recommended that the agency rethink its mission in terms of stewardship, partnership, and collaborative governance.[3]

Our analysis also leads us to project future developments in the field and to pose a series of challenges related to capacity building and policy design in the coming years, specifically how to strengthen partnerships and networks within and across these various organizational types and to do so in ways that enhance the resiliency of the field in the face of climate change.[4]

To pursue these themes, the discussion here will fall into four sections. First, we will examine each of the three major types of nonprofit environmental organizations identified earlier—advocacy, ecosystem, and educational. Second, we will look at the multi-stakeholder partnerships that have emerged in the environmental arena to cope with the growing complexity of environmental problems. Third, we will assess how environmental organizations are being affected by the four broad impulses that the introduction to this book has identified as shaping the evolution of the nonprofit sector in this country. Finally, a concluding section looks to the future and identifies some factors promoting the further development of the nonprofit environmental subsector, but also some of the challenges and limitations this set of organizations confronts.

Major Types of Nonprofit Environmental Organizations

In this section we examine the three core types of environmental organizations, as well as some of the hybrid activities they may pursue. *Advocacy* organizations run the gamut from national (and international) to state and local, and pursue their agendas in a broad array of venues, such as legislatures, administrative agencies, and the courts. *Ecosystem* organizations focus on place-based work, from the scale of a small stream to that of a large landscape or watershed, and may draw on support by state, regional, national, and some international organizations. *Educational* organizations facilitate traditional classroom learning in K–12 schools, as well as hands-on service learning in schools and through community and youth groups, with support from national, state, and local associations of environmental educators.[5]

Advocacy Organizations

Environmental advocacy organizations are the most familiar type, although they are quite diverse, ranging from national organizations with lobbying offices in Washington, D.C., to ad hoc local groups that might advocate against the siting of an incinerator in a particular neighborhood. We place groups in this category if one or more of their core activities is lobbying for specific policy changes before Congress, the White House, governors, state legislatures, city councils, and other local legislative bodies; advocating for rule changes by administrative agencies and serving as a watchdog over implementation; representing environmental interests in the courts; or mobilizing members through grassroots campaigns and protest. Some advocacy groups sponsor activities that fall into the ecosystem and education categories as well or that are of particular significance in the historical formation of the group's identity, such as the Sierra Club's hiking and Audubon's birdwatching.

MEMBERSHIP GROWTH OF NATIONAL ADVOCACY ORGANIZATIONS. Many of the major national environmental advocacy organizations have grown substantially in membership over the course of four decades, though not without periodic slippage (see table 7-1). Overall there are about one hundred environmental advocacy organizations that operate as professionalized public interest organizations at the national level.

NATIONAL ORGANIZATIONAL STRUCTURES. The organizational structures of the major national environmental advocacy groups display certain common features, yet also significant variation. They typically have professionalized their staffs and centralized their leadership over the past decades. They have also come to rely upon direct mail and telemarketing, and increasingly on e-mail and other Internet tools, as predominant methods for recruitment and retention of members, in contrast to face-to-face recruitment through local networks. National organizations that have failed to professionalize in an effective and timely manner, such as Environmental Action, which was founded by the organizers of the first Earth Day in 1970, have suffered demise.[6]

Although national environmental advocacy organizations tend to fill certain issue niches, such as wildlife or toxics, many cover a fairly broad range, and some can be categorized as "full-service" organizations.[7] The Sierra Club is perhaps the best example of this: Sierra Club, Inc., is a nonprofit 501(c)(4) that includes under its broad umbrella the Earth Justice Legal Defense Fund, Sierra Club Foundation, Sierra Club PAC, Sierra Student Coalition, Sierra Club Books, and the Sierra Club Property Management, Inc. (for its headquarters property). The Sierra Club also has twenty-two regional offices, state chapters in every state, a dozen or so regional chapters (including nine in its founding home state of California, where one-third of its members live), and some three hundred local chapters. The National Wildlife Federation is a 501(c)(3) that includes an NWF Endowment, a publications division, nine regional natural resource centers, and independent affiliates in every state (National Wildlife Productions, a film-video division, no longer exists). The National Audubon Society has state chapters in every state, some five hundred local chapters, and a network of local nature centers and sanctuaries.

The Environmental Defense Fund, founded by a small group of lawyers and scientists in the fight against DDT on Long Island, has never had local chapters; its members are simply dues-paying contributors, and decisionmaking resides with the executive director and staff, distributed to some extent through its regional offices. The Natural Resources Defense Council, founded by Yale

Table 7-1. *Reported Membership of Selected Environmental Advocacy Organizations, 1965–2008*

Number of members

Organization	1965–66	1970–71	1975–76	1980–81	1985–86	1991–92	1996–97	2002–03	2008–09
Sierra Club	31,000	124,000	165,000	246,000	378,000	615,000	569,000	736,000	1.3 million
National Audubon Society	40,500	115,000	321,000	400,000	500,000	600,000	550,000	550,000	600,000
National Wildlife Federation	256,000	540,000	612,000	818,000	900,000	997,000	650,000	650,000	4 million program participants
Wilderness Society	28,000	62,000	62,500	52,000	145,000	365,000	237,000	225,000	400,000
Environmental Defense Fund	...	20,000	37,000	46,000	65,000	175,000	300,000	350,000	500,000
Natural Resources Defense Council	...	5,000	n.a.	40,000	65,000	170,000	260,000	450,000	564,000
Clean Water Action	...	...	...	...	400,000	600,000	600,000	600,000	1.2 million
Greenpeace USA	...	...	...	250,000	800,000	2.2 million	400,000	250,000	250,000

Sources: Christopher J. Bosso, *Environment, Inc.: From Grassroots to Beltway* (University Press of Kansas, 2005), pp. 54–55; Kristy A. Harper, *Encyclopedia of Associations*, vol. 1, National Organizations of the U.S., 48th edition (Detroit: Gale Research, 2009); organizations' annual reports 2008–09. Reporting methods are not always consistent across periods or organizations.

n.a. = Not available.

Law School students, was intended from the beginning to function as an environmental law firm on the model of the American Civil Liberties Union or the NAACP Legal Defense Fund.

Professionalization has not come without strain and even periodic grassroots rebellion within some of the major national advocacy groups. The Sierra Club is perhaps most famous for tensions between grassroots activists in chapters and professional staff in the national offices, especially during earlier decades. The national board of directors is elected by the membership in a mail-in ballot, with a participation rate in 2008 of 9.5 percent, about half of the average rate in the 1990s. Leadership, however, resides primarily with the executive director and other key staff. Prior to 1994, the governing structure included the Sierra Club Council, with elected delegates from each of the state and regional chapters, as well as delegates from the 63 committees established by the board of directors. Local, state, and regional chapters, which elect their leadership, also participated in setting issue priorities to be pursued in each new Congress. Budget shortfalls in the early 1990s led to organizational and issue rationalization, though there still remains a vibrant chapter structure and efforts to revitalize leadership development at the grassroots.[8]

FUNDING NATIONAL ADVOCACY. Along with the general growth in membership, most major environmental advocacy organizations have increased revenues substantially, though unevenly, over the past several decades (see table 7-2). Individual membership dues and similar contributions are a significant source of revenue. Several techniques are used to generate such revenues, especially direct mail (and increasingly e-mail), telemarketing, and canvassing. Organizations hire direct-mail firms, especially those with specialties in progressive causes, and these firms often craft the messages themselves, as well as prospect for members through other targeted mailing lists, such as those who buy clothes and gear from L.L. Bean or contribute to the local aquarium or zoo. Telemarketing firms handle phone solicitation campaigns, though these have lost luster due to government restrictions on unwanted telephone marketing calls. Some organizations canvass door-to-door seeking signatures on a petition for a specific issue, along with a contribution or membership. Greenpeace was most famous for this during the heyday of its growth in the 1980s, and the Sierra Club has sustained canvassing over a longer period, though it has often been contracted out to other groups, such as the Fund for Public Interest Research.[9]

In addition to individual contributions, many national environmental organizations raise money by selling various products. These run a wide gamut, including books, videos, educational curricula, T-shirts, tote bags, and various other items. Some of the large organizations also offer "affinity" Visa or Mastercard credit cards as an incentive to join and derive further revenue on charged

Table 7-2. *Revenue Trends of Selected Environmental Advocacy Organizations,*
1991–2009

Million$, except as noted[a]

| | Amount | | | | Percent change, |
Organization	1991	1996	2002	2008–09	1991–2009
Sierra Club and Sierra Club Foundation	$40.6	$56.3	$83.7	$86.7	113
National Audubon Society	38.0	46.9	78.6	82.2	116
National Wildlife Federation	77.3	88.1	102.1	82.4	7
The Wilderness Society	17.0	14.5	18.8	30.4	79
Environmental Defense Fund	15.8	27.0	43.8	134.9	754
Natural Resources Defense Council	16.9	25.4	46.4	71.9	325
Clean Water Fund and Clean Water Action	14.6	1.7	4.4	11.4	–22
Greenpeace USA and Greenpeace Fund	65.0	9.8	25.9	26.2	–60

Sources: Christopher J. Bosso, *Environment, Inc.: From Grassroots to Beltway* (University Press of Kansas, 2005), pp. 97–98; organizations' annual reports, 2008–09.

a. Figures are rounded and unadjusted; they include revenues of both 501(c)(3) and affiliated 501(c)(4) organizations.

purchases. Ecotourism, sometimes tied to service projects, has also become an important source of revenue for some national organizations.

A third major source of revenue takes the form of foundation and corporate grants and government grants and contracts. Despite repeated charges that corporations buy goodwill on the cheap through "greenwashing," most major national environmental advocacy organizations receive significant corporate contributions.[10] Foundations have played a strategic role in shaping the field of environmental organizations since the Ford Foundation's investments in the founding of the Environmental Defense Fund and Natural Resources Defense Council in the late 1960s and early 1970s. Today, there are bigger environmental funders than Ford, such as the Pew Charitable Trusts, as well as the Environmental Grantmakers Association, founded in 1987, to provide networking, research, and strategic thinking across the entire field. In 2007, its 214 member organizations provided grants totaling over one billion dollars, nearly fourteen times the amount awarded by its twelve founding members in 1987 (these figures include grants to all levels and types of environmental organizations and projects). Government grants and contracts have also been important in funding national environmental advocacy organizations, but such funds are typically designated for research, education, ecosystem restoration, and similar projects, rather than for advocacy activities as such.[11]

Foundation priorities in funding certain types of environmental organizations over others have often been questioned by activists and academics alike. The major charge is that foundations are more comfortable with grants that go to mainstream organizations with professional leadership and accountability mechanisms than to more innovative, grassroots, contentious, and radical organizations, leading to a conservative bias in who receives money. This funding bias clearly exists, yet the critique is too often made in a way that is analytically unhelpful and politically misleading. It typically rests on little more than an unquestioned ideological assumption that radical or contentious means better, more effective, and truly transformative, without any credible test of organizational sustainability and political realism or any metric of strategic impact, project performance, movement building outcomes, or reciprocal accountability to institutional partners, donors, or even to grassroots members. These are all questions that foundations must remain alert to as they negotiate priorities with other actors in the broader environmental field. It is no less a democratic challenge than remaining responsive to promising approaches emerging at the grassroots. There is certainly much room to question foundation priorities on various grounds, not the least of which is building the local community and civic leadership capacities to engage in effective and sustained ecosystem, environmental justice, health, and climate partnerships (see next section). Yet assuming that foundations should fund organizations just because they have more radical protest repertoires or discourses (deep ecology, ecofeminism, ecotheology) hardly provides a sound normative or strategic guide to building the field or democratizing environmental politics and policy.[12]

STATE AND LOCAL ENVIRONMENTAL ADVOCACY. State and local advocacy groups have also proliferated in recent years. After steadily losing authority to the federal government in the 1960s and 1970s, states have become increasingly important in the environmental policy system, especially as federal policy became gridlocked during the Reagan years. In addition, policy analysts have recognized that states often possess comparative advantages for policy innovation as the limits of command-and-control became increasingly evident. With rising budgets and administrative capacities, as well as federal support for devolution, state agencies began to tackle a broader range of issues. In recent years, federal gridlock over climate change has also prompted increased action at the state level, thus generating further opportunities and incentives for state environmental groups.[13]

All states have one or more statewide environmental advocacy groups, such as, in Oregon, the Oregon Environmental Council and 1000 Friends of Oregon, in addition to state chapters of the multi-tier national groups such as the Sierra

Club, the National Audubon Society, and the National Wildlife Federation. Some have names that differ from their parent groups; for example, the Vermont Natural Resources Council is the state affiliate of the National Wildlife Federation. Many states also have several other specialized groups working at the state level on issues such as wilderness or forest policy. State PIRGs, affiliates of the U.S. Public Interest Research Group, have also engaged in extensive advocacy on environmental issues, and in 2007 formed Environment America, a federation of twenty-nine state affiliates (Environment Arizona, Environment California, and so forth), plus one from the District of Columbia. State advocacy groups also sponsor voter initiatives and referenda. Like their national counterparts, these groups tend to be professionalized, even in the smaller states.[14]

The number of local advocacy groups has also increased substantially in the past several decades, with the greatest rise among autonomous groups and those affiliated with regional networks, in contrast to local chapters of national organizations. Some of this increase has been among groups advocating for anti-toxics and environmental justice—those protesting hazardous facilities, cleanup plans, unusual disease patterns, and other perceived threats to health and community, especially in poor, working-class, and minority communities. Advocacy of this sort has resulted in a distinct environmental justice movement that makes strong claims to distributional equity, social inclusion, and grassroots participation and challenges environmental and health agencies and national environmental organizations, in addition to corporate polluters.[15]

However, despite the heightened academic and regulatory attention paid to environmental justice, it is not clear how many local groups of this sort actually exist or have been able to sustain themselves beyond their initial oppositional activity. Statewide inventories of local environmental groups tend to show a very substantial undercount of local groups in various organizational directories; the actual level of local engagement may thus be far more robust than some national studies of social capital and civic associations would lead us to believe. Furthermore, such studies do not reveal a substantial percentage of environmental justice groups. They do show that only a very small minority of local advocacy organizations hold radical perspectives or employ disruptive protest tactics. The oft-repeated bifurcation of national mainstream versus local radical environmental organizations is overstated and overly simplistic. The vast majority of local organizations engage in reform advocacy or fall into our two other major organizational categories: those dealing with the ecosystem as a whole, and educational organizations.[16]

Ecosystem-Based Organizations

A second major type of environmental organization is focused on preserving and restoring land and watersheds as integrated ecosystems. The activities of some advocacy organizations fall into this category, but unlike them, ecosystem organizations clearly recognize the limitations on the kind of command-and-control regulation typically preferred by the major national and state advocacy groups, and are generally more amenable to working with traditional adversaries to achieve goals. Watershed associations and land trusts represent two major types of ecosystem organization, though there is considerable diversity within each category, including the degree to which ecosystem goals are salient in their work.[17]

WATERSHED ASSOCIATIONS. Watershed associations, councils, and alliances are groups that form to protect and restore particular streams and rivers and often expand their horizon to include much larger watersheds. Such associations often emerge from various groups that refer to themselves as "friends" or "stewards" of a particular creek or lake, and many begin as single-issue advocacy groups in a fight with a local developer or government agency. What distinguishes these groups as they develop over time is that they adopt a distinctive watershed frame for their work. Formulated over the course of the 1980s and 1990s through mutual learning among networks of watershed movement innovators, academic scientists, policy analysts, legal theorists, and public officials, this frame holds that most if not all the key problems pertaining to water—quality, supply, fisheries, habitat preservation, biodiversity, flood control—need to be understood and dealt with at the level of the watershed: hydrologically defined drainage basins that feed particular water bodies. Watersheds, including smaller watersheds nested in much larger ones, are systems defined by complex interactions among innumerable natural and social dynamics, and only holistic, problem-solving strategies tailored to specific, place-based contexts and engaging civic associations and institutional actors in active stewardship could hope to maintain and restore them. Even though fragmented federal regulations, command-and-control techniques, and massive investments in wastewater treatment have significantly reduced point-source pollution since the Clean Water Act amendments of 1972, watersheds remain at risk owing to nonpoint source pollution, primarily from farms, transportation systems, and urban runoff as well as innumerable everyday activities of ordinary citizens. The familiar regulatory tools are inadequate for nonpoint source pollution and ecosystem restoration. Climate change brings still further complexity and the need for holistic strategies.[18]

The structure of local watershed groups varies considerably. Some are stand-alone groups, while others bring together an array of conservation, education, neighborhood, and other civic groups into a separate 501(c)(3). Still others are multi-stakeholder, including independent watershed and civic groups, plus various farming, ranching, timber and other business and commodity interests, as well as representatives from local, state, and federal agencies. The multi-stakeholder model is more typically (though not consistently) called a "watershed council," and is more prevalent in the West, where the consensus process is often utilized to move beyond policy stalemate and where state agencies might certify and fund the councils, which are usually not incorporated as separate nonprofits.[19]

Dozens, even hundreds, of watershed groups may be concerned with the watersheds that feed water to a larger estuary, a semi-enclosed coastal body of water with one or more rivers or streams flowing into it. A good example is the Chesapeake Bay, whose watershed—64,000 square miles extending over six states and the District of Columbia—has some 678 watershed associations, including the bay-wide Chesapeake Bay Foundation and the Alliance for Chesapeake Bay. The Alliance for Chesapeake Bay neither lobbies nor litigates; it builds the capacity of watershed associations and other citizen groups, local governments, businesses, developers, professional associations, and other institutions to work in partnership to craft sound policy on land use and development and engage in hands-on volunteer monitoring and restoration activities. These include planting trees for riparian buffers on streams or eelgrass in the estuary, removing nonnative species, installing fish ladders or weirs, restoring beach nesting areas, and raising oysters as a project in elementary and middle schools and transplanting them to the bay. The Chesapeake Bay Foundation is a regional advocacy group, but it also engages citizens in volunteer monitoring and restoration, as well as watershed education in classrooms and in the field.

State-level nonprofit intermediaries exist in many states to share information and best practices for volunteer monitoring, watershed and land-use planning, and hands-on restoration, as well as for civic capacity building (leadership, financing, organizing, public communication). These state-level intermediaries emerged as the U.S. EPA's Office of Wetlands, Oceans, and Watersheds, established in 1991, began to actively promote the watershed approach at the state level, and the Kendall Foundation sponsored regional innovators' workshops based on the experience of several leading states (Massachusetts, California, Washington, and Florida). Thus, for example, when the Colorado Water Quality Control Division reorganized around the watershed approach in 1997, the number of independently organized watershed groups, only six in 1996, grew quickly to forty by 1998 and then established the statewide Colorado Watershed Assembly as their coalition, which by 2010 had spurred growth to represent some seventy groups. The assembly sponsors training and an annual conference; in October 2007 it collaborated on the Sustaining Colorado Watersheds Conference with a broad range of other civic groups, including AWARE (Addressing Water and Natural Resource Education) Colorado, the League of Women Voters of Colorado Education Fund, the Colorado Watershed Network, the Colorado Lakes and Reservoir Management Association, and the Colorado Riparian Association. The assembly also publishes an attractive and influential annual report on the state of Colorado's watersheds and the work of its watershed groups. It has lobbied successfully in the statehouse and collaborated with the state water conservation board and water quality control commission to create and manage a grant program for watershed groups funded through a state income tax refund check-off program, which in turn has been used by local groups as a match source for various federal grants. The legislation creating the watershed license plate does likewise and provides each watershed group with an added incentive to reach out to the local community.[20]

Several national intermediaries have also been critical to building the watershed field. The River Network, established in 1988, has become the nation's premier national network of (freshwater) watershed groups, with seven hundred dues-paying local and state "partners" (not branded member chapters, as in the Sierra Club or National Audubon Society) plus several thousand other watershed groups in its far-flung network reach. Its primary role is training and organizational capacity building for local and state watershed associations. It is chief sponsor of the watershed movement's annual River Rally, at once a professional training conference, national strategy meeting, and uplifting movement celebration. The River Network collaborates with a variety of national advocacy organizations, such as American Rivers, but delineates its role within the watershed movement's division of labor thus: "We do not take positions on national or state legislative or regulatory issues, become directly involved in local or state affairs, endorse political candidates at any level, or litigate. These are roles better filled by others—including the local, state and regional groups we serve, other national organizations, and coalitions that form within our network to address specific issues."[21]

Restore America's Estuaries, a national coalition of eleven major estuary-based watershed nonprofits, such as the Chesapeake Bay Foundation and People for Puget Sound, plays a key advocacy role, but also sponsors extensive habitat restoration work by local citizens and, in the case of some of its member organizations, multiple stakeholder groups. The Ocean Conservancy, primarily a national advocacy group focused on such issues as fisheries management and regulation, nonetheless applies an ecosystem perspective in its work and has helped build the capacity for volunteer monitoring among some six hundred local watershed groups in all twenty-eight of the estuaries designated as part of the National Estuary Program.

Because watershed groups place emphasis on collaborative planning and restoration, rather than one-sided advocacy, they qualify for considerable financial support from government agencies. Thus, the River Network has managed several EPA grants designed to build the capacity of local and state watershed associations, as have other intermediaries such as the Center for Watershed Protection, the Southeast Watershed Forum, the International City/County

Management Association, and Trees, Water, and People. Funding might also come to local watershed groups in the form of matching grants through the EPA's National Estuary Program, channeled through the twenty-eight local NEP members, and the Nonpoint Source Program, provided to states. Restore America's Estuaries receives funding for its ecosystem restoration work through the Restoration Center of the National Oceanic and Atmospheric Administration's National Marine Fisheries Service, as do some two dozen other NOAA partners working in all of the 130 U.S. estuaries, including multi-tier associations such as Trout Unlimited. From 2000 to 2005, for instance, Restore America's Estuaries received $8,717,249 from the Restoration Center, which it distributed to local groups; they in turn leveraged $9,136,416 directly and a further $8,404,916 through the partnership. A variety of other federal, state, and local agencies provide funding for capacity building and project-based work among watershed nonprofits, as does the congressionally chartered National Fish and Wildlife Foundation.

Indeed, the watershed movement has benefited from government support in other ways as well. Volunteer watershed monitoring groups have received substantial financial support and technical assistance from the EPA and the Cooperative Extension Service housed in the Department of Agriculture, and its network of land-grant and sea-grant state universities. The EPA has also developed or funded an extensive array of practical watershed tools, typically coproduced with nonprofit watershed partners, including ones for watershed planning, information management, community forums, volunteer monitoring, and community organizing. It has also played a key role in developing the networks that have come to define the watershed movement as a movement, as can be seen in its cosponsorship of important conferences over the past two decades (see table 7-3).

LAND TRUSTS. Land trusts are nonprofit organizations designed to conserve land by undertaking or assisting direct land transactions through purchase, donations, or conservation easements, which are legal agreements that restrict the development and use of land to ensure protection of its conservation values. The land trust thus holds title to the land, brokers sale or resale to public agencies or public-private partnerships, or holds specific management and development rights transferred from the property holder in return for reduced taxes based on the remaining value of the land. Typically the land trust also organizes stewardship of the land through professional staff and volunteers engaged in activities such as weed control, tree and wildflower planting, species inventory, and trail monitoring, as well as watershed restoration. Indeed, easement monitors are increasingly drawn from friends-of-the-stream, adopt-a-park, and kindred groups.[22]

Table 7-3. *Select Watershed Network Building Conferences Cosponsored and Cofunded by the U.S. Environmental Protection Agency*

Conference	Date	Participants
First National Conference of Estuary Groups	1987	Save the Bay (Providence, R.I.) convenes emerging coalitions of estuary groups as National Estuary Program is established.
National Citizen Monitoring Conferences	1988–2000	Biannual conference, 100 to 300 participants, in conjunction with rotating civic partners (Izaak Walton League, Chesapeake Bay Alliance); now part of National Water Quality Monitoring Council network (professional and volunteer monitors).
Watershed '93	1993	1,100 participants from broad range of local, state, and national watershed and conservation groups, tribes, public agencies, university extension services, business and professional associations; hundreds more via satellite broadcast on final day.
Restoring Urban Waters: Friends of Trashed Rivers Conference	1993	Coalition to Restore Urban Waters, with River Network, Izaak Walton League, National Association of Service and Conservation Corps (now Corps Network), and others; 300 participants (followed by three other "trashed rivers" conferences)
Watershed '96	1996	2,000 participants, plus several thousand others at 156 teleconference downlinks, from broad range of local, state, and national watershed and conservation groups, public agencies, university extension, K–12 schools, and business and professional associations.
National River Rally	1995–2008	524 participants in peak year of 2006, convened by River Network, other river advocacy and watershed restoration groups, public agencies. Support from the EPA has fallen off recently, but it still makes tools presentations.
Regional Watershed Forums	1999–2001	Thirteen regional multi-stakeholder lay-professional roundtables, with forty to eighty-five participants each. Some continue as regular roundtables, with state and county offshoots. Forums prepare agenda for National Watershed Forum.
National Watershed Forum	2001	480 participants from broad range of local, state, and national watershed and conservation groups, public agencies, university extension services, and professional associations.
National Conferences on Coastal and Estuarine Habitat Restoration	2003–08	800 to 1,500 participants, broad multi-stakeholder group, convened by Restore America's Estuaries, with Save the Bay, The Nature Conservancy, National Oceanic and Atmospheric Administration, U.S. Fish and Wildlife Service, local and state agencies, business partners.

Source: Carmen Sirianni, *Investing in Democracy: Engaging Citizens in Collaborative Governance* (Brookings, 2009), pp. 170–71.

Although the first land trust was the Trustees of Reservations in Massachusetts, started in 1891, and several dozen land trusts emerged in the first half of the twentieth century, sustained growth emerged only after World War II, as highway construction and suburban sprawl threatened once-remote places, and as rising incomes and shorter workweeks meant that a premium was placed on outdoor recreation. Citizens began to push back and the contemporary environmental movement was born partly from this resistance. Public support for federal land purchases had declined considerably with the end of the Depression, when such purchases were popular tools for economic relief for farmers and job relief for the unemployed, while accomplishing conservation goals through national service programs such as the Civilian Conservation Corps. The land trusts' distinctive response to the political opportunity structure of the 1950s and 1960s, in contrast to the Sierra Club, was expressed early on by Richard Pough, one of the founders of The Nature Conservancy, when he said, "I don't protest anything. If someone comes to me and complains that a majestic forest is about to be cut down, I [tell them], 'Don't cry about the forest. Go out and buy it!'"[23]

Several new statutes in the ensuing decades expanded federal authority to acquire land, but these proved relatively limited, and the Reagan revolution's assertion of private property rights and the limits of federal control, as well as cutbacks in federal staff with conservation skills, generated further opportunities for nonprofits to step into the breach. The scientific ascendance of landscape ecology and conservation biology reinforced the ecosystem frame of managing across large, interconnected landscapes, rather than according to the property boundaries of separate land parcels, in order to preserve species habitat and biodiversity.[24]

The number of land trusts has grown substantially in the past three decades, to a total of more than sixteen hundred in 2005, and their geographical distribution has also become more even on a regional basis (see table 7-4). The number of new acres conserved has also increased considerably. From 2000 to 2005, for instance, newly conserved land rose by 96 percent, from 6,056,624 to 11,890,109 acres, an area twice the size of the state of New Hampshire. Overall, total acreage conserved through private means, including local and state land trusts and the largest land conservation groups, stands at 37 million acres. The number of volunteers increased by 63 percent in this period, to a total of 90,871, and the number of board members to 14,906.[25]

Funding comes from a variety of sources. Private foundations play an important role, with the Ford Foundation again serving as a key strategic investor in the early decades. Land trusts also place much emphasis on cultivating land donors, including those who might wish their land to serve community and conservation values for future generations. Resources have also increased as states

Table 7-4. *Growth and Number of Land Trusts, by Region, 1981–2005*

Region	1981	1990	2000	2005	Percent increase 2000–05
Mid-Atlantic	59	105	174	245	41
Midwest	67	119	186	250	34
Northeast	155	433	497	581	17
Northwest	49 (Northesest and Pacific)	50	69	95	38
Pacific		79	139	217	56
Southeast	62 (Southeast and South Central)	115	117	166	42
South Central		25	11	[Category eliminated]	
Southwest	6	26	80	109	36
Total	368	885	1,263	1,667	32

Sources: Land Trust Alliance, *2005 National Land Trust Census Report* (Washington, 2006); Sally K. Fairfax and others, *Buying Nature: The Limits of Land Acquisition as a Conservation Strategy, 1780–2000* (MIT Press, 2005), p. 179.

stabilized, and in many cases standardized, tax treatment of donated conservation easements and enacted their own easement legislation. Between 1999 and 2003, voters at the local and state level approved $19.2 billion in bond measures for new conservation financing. Corporate investors and partners have also become increasingly important. At the federal level, the biggest source of funding has come from the 1985 Farm Bill and its various revisions, which have provided billions of dollars for reserve programs that pursue ecosystem protection and conservation of wetlands, watersheds, farmlands, forests, and open space.[26]

Lest the "don't protest, buy it" dictum be taken literally, it should be noted that citizen advocacy groups often play an important and sometimes decisive role in securing popular support for bond measures, as well as preventing unwanted development, generating alternatives, and serving as watchdogs. Thus, in the San Francisco Bay Area, the Greenbelt Alliance has served as a strong regional advocate for open space for the past fifty years, often in conjunction with local advocacy groups, even as new land trusts arise to buy or manage land for conservation, recreation, and other purposes. It also serves as the fiscal agent for the Bay Area Open Space Council, a collaborative network of 150 public agencies and nonprofits engaged in preserving and managing open space.[27]

In addition to local trusts, the field comprises regional and national intermediaries and trusts. At the national level, the Land Trust Alliance, founded initially as the Land Trust Exchange in 1982, serves as the major trade association, developing standards and practices, providing training and curriculum, and lobbying for policies that promote land trusts and related conservation goals. The Trust for Public Land has focused specifically on urban land conservation, including community gardens (now part of a burgeoning urban agriculture movement), urban parks, trails, and watersheds. Not itself a membership organization, the Trust for Public Land provides local land trusts and state and local governments with expertise in identifying, planning, and financing land purchases and conservation. When it does purchase land itself, it generally turns management over to a public agency. The American Farmland Trust, founded in 1980, serves as a national advocate, especially around issues in the federal farm bill, but also works on state legislation and provides education and technical assistance for sustainable farming practices, growth management planning, and growing local strategies. The Rails to Trails Conservancy serves similar functions for local projects that convert old rail lines into trails, which receive funding through the U.S. Department of Transportation.[28]

The Nature Conservancy is the premier national land trust organization in the United States and internationally. Founded in 1950 from a spin-off of the Ecological Society of America, it has grown steadily to more than one million members. It has state chapters in every state and a large professional staff, including 720 staff scientists. Over the years, its approach has become increasingly strategic in protecting and restoring ecosystems, rather than just buying land. Its "conservation by design" represents a science-based approach in terms of analyzing relative threats to biodiversity, based on global habitat and ecoregional assessments, building capacities of government and nongovernmental actors for collaborative planning, stewardship, working landscapes, and investing resources in ways that yield optimal and measurable conservation returns.[29]

Environmental Education Associations

Environmental education organizations represent our third major type, and it, too, contains hybrids. The field is constituted by local, state, and national (and some international) organizations and networks that develop or deliver curricula to K–12 schools, where much environmental education occurs, community-based and youth organizations, and institutions such as zoos and aquariums that have broad public education missions. Some organizations are also active in the training of educators, either directly or working in partnership with state associations of science teachers and similar organizations, and likewise address issues of professional standards and best practices. Several major national advocacy organizations—especially the National Audubon Society, the National Wildlife Federation, the World Wildlife Fund, and the Wildlife Conservation Society—have broad educational programs that are not tightly linked to the specific information and communication needs of their advocacy campaigns, and these programs are generally considered an important part of the environmental education field.

One important type of environmental education organization is the national nonprofit with a specialized topical curriculum that it distributes through various other organizations and network partners, as well as through professional training workshops. Project WET (Water Education for Teachers), Project WILD, and Project Learning Tree are the most notable examples. Project WILD (Wildlife in Learning Design) was initiated in 1983 as a project of the Western Regional Environmental Education Council (renamed the Council for Environmental Education in 1996), composed of representatives of state education agencies and natural resource agencies in thirteen western states, and the Western Association of Fish and Wildlife Agencies. Over the next decade, Project WILD developed programs in every state and by 2006 claimed to have reached the one million mark for number of teachers trained. Its network of state coordinators is housed primarily in state agencies with jurisdiction over fish and wildlife, and these coordinators train volunteer facilitators, who provide professional development workshops to teachers. In 2006 in Massachusetts, for instance, the state coordinator oversaw sixty-five volunteer facilitators, mostly teachers and agency professionals working on their own time, who had trained an estimated total of eight thousand teachers in the prior two decades. Project WET was initially established in 1984 by the North Dakota State Water Commission and then moved to Montana State University with funding from the Bureau of Reclamation, part of the U.S. Department of the Interior. These sponsors enabled Project WET to pilot several state projects and then develop a national network of state coordinators, many of them housed in state universities and Extension Services and half housed in state environmental protection and natural resource agencies, even as the project became an independent operating foundation in 2005. Project Learning Tree emerged from the Western Regional Environmental Education Council and the American Forest Institute (now the American Forest Foundation) in the 1970s and subsequently grew into a national organization. In 2006 it had a network of three thousand active volunteers and state coordinators who had trained some five hundred thousand teachers over three decades. These three organizations occupy distinct niches defined by topic (wildlife, water, forests) and also compete to a certain extent in areas of overlap; the Council for Environmental Education now contains several other projects, in addition to WILD. At the state level, however, there is often a good deal of collaboration—for example, a joint newsletter in Colorado, a common summer training institute in New Hampshire—and many teachers have been trained in more than one curriculum.

State associations for environmental education represent another organizational type designed to share pedagogical practice through annual conferences, enhance legitimacy through standards, build institutional capacity, and develop comprehensive strategies, including advocacy for state environmental educational requirements and funding. In addition to their individual member professionals, such associations include a diverse array of other organizations as network affiliates. Typical among them are the state programs of the national projects (WET, WILD, Learning Tree), as well as state and local chapter representatives from national organizations such as the Audubon Society, the National Wildlife Federation, and sometimes the Sierra Club, who often serve as key board members. Other affiliates and board members can include individual public and private schools and universities, representatives of local public school systems and natural resource agencies, and a broad array of nature centers, aquariums, museums, land trusts, camps, zoos, mountain clubs, and the professional and volunteer "interpreters" who work in such organizations, both public and nonprofit. Other environmental education organizations—such as Earth Force, a national organization with nine local and regional offices that emphasize long-term leadership development and community-problem solving models among youth—are also members. In some states, 4-H clubs and local YMCAs might also be affiliates, though these are generally oriented to their own organization's environmental and conservation education curricula and network activities. This is true, too, for the Student Conservation Association and The Corps Network, which engage youths in full-time conservation programs and internships with a broad range of public agencies and nonprofits such as The Nature Conservancy, providing extensive education in the process. Some state environmental education associations and their affiliates also have relatively well developed network links to watershed associations, since much environmental education focuses on water quality, volunteer monitoring, and various service learning and community-based models for watershed problem solving and restoration. The Global Rivers Environmental Education Network, founded in 1984 and now a project within Earth Force, has pioneered in this.[30]

The North American Association for Environmental Education serves as the professional association for these state associations, national projects, and various other affiliates, such as university and Extension Service educators. Founded in 1971 as a group of U.S. community college educators, NAAEE gradually expanded its individual and institutional membership base and then became trinational in 1983. NAAEE has been a core partner in the Environmental Education and Training Partnership, funded through cooperative agreement with the EPA under the 1990 Environmental Education Act. This partnership is a consortium of ten national groups, teacher associations, university centers, and public agencies that provides training and leadership development to educators and assists in building state association and program capacity. The partnership also assists with the development of professional certification, quality assurance, and program evaluation so that environmental education is scientifically accurate, pedagogically sound, and responsive to community needs.[31]

Funding for environmental education is provided through the EPA's Office of Environmental Education, the National Science Foundation, and the U.S. Department of Agriculture, as well as through other federal and state agency grants, foundations, corporations, and fees for service, especially for curricula and teacher training. In-kind state-agency staff support and office space are also important resources for the field. The National Environmental Education Foundation, chartered by Congress in 1990 as a nonprofit, leverages additional private funds to build the field.[32]

Multi-Stakeholder Partnerships and Collaborative Governance

The three major types of environmental organization—advocacy, ecosystem, and education—often function as hybrids with a mix of activities. Multi-stakeholder partnerships are actually designed to include diverse types of environmental organizations, as well as other organized stakeholders, such as public agencies, business and professional groups, schools and universities, and other civic associations and nonprofits. The simplest rationale for multi-stakeholder partnerships is that the increasing complexity of many environmental problems requires a diverse array of community and institutional assets, tools, perspectives, and trust to generate sustainable and measurable problem solving, and that narrow advocacy and adversarialism often result in suboptimal policies and political stalemate. Pathways to partnership vary considerably, as do membership configurations. Some partnerships form only after years of bitter political and legal battles have led to a visible crisis, whereas others emerge through a gradual expansion of networks of piecemeal collaborations on less controversial projects.[33] Indeed, projects are often chosen because they have the potential to draw upon unifying themes in the local culture and community, such as, say, salmon, and so trust can be built before the collaboration is overburdened with more contentious issues.[34] Some partnerships include a broad array of organizations, while others build upon a small core of partners and work through informal relationships rather than formalized public consensus processes. Some enlist extensive participation through association members and ordinary citizens, whereas others rely primarily upon professional staff. Here we consider three types: grassroots ecosystem management or watershed partnerships, environmental justice and community health partnerships, and climate change partnerships.[35]

Grassroots Ecosystem Management Partnerships

One type of partnership might be characterized as the grassroots ecosystem management or watershed partnership. There are no exact estimates of the number of such partnerships, nor of their relative durability, but one leading scholar has estimated some five hundred in existence in the early 2000s across the western region of the United States.[36] If we add similar partnerships in other regions, including various estuary partnerships, the number would be higher still. Such partnerships might include local and state environmental advocacy groups such as the Sierra Club, or leaders emerging from such groups who may have become disillusioned with the results achievable through one-sided advocacy and command and control. Partnerships might also include a range of ecosystem groups, such as a land trust, a watershed association, or a state chapter of The Nature Conservancy, as well as environmental education partners, such as a state university center or an Extension Service office, a state environmental education association, or a local school system. Outdoor recreation groups are often represented, sometimes through chapters of national groups such as Trout Unlimited or Ducks Unlimited. In ecosystem and watershed partnerships, commodity interests—farmers, ranchers, loggers, irrigators, developers—also come to the table, as do representatives of local, state, and federal agencies and local tribes. A robust partnership might have dozens of stakeholders, with a diverse array of organizations within each category.

Ecosystem partnerships employ holistic management approaches based on the premise that integrated ecosystems require place-based, context-specific strategies with much room for proactive and adaptive problem solving. Stakeholders engage in collaborative planning based on nonhierarchical roles and shared information. Consensus-based decisionmaking is designed to build trust and civic respect, as are voluntary projects that engage partners in coproduction, with mutual accountability for carrying out specific tasks. Thus, various sets of partners might monitor the health of a stream, restore riparian buffers, control noxious weeds, design and implement new infrastructure projects, or collaborate in developing sustainable forest products that can be brought to market. Ecosystem partnerships do not seek to subvert national and state laws or undermine the authority of regulatory agencies, but aim to achieve measurable improvement in the health of ecosystems, as demonstrated by community-generated indicators and performance measures, along with other goals, such as creating sustainable local economies, that cannot be achieved very well through fragmented regulations and bureaucratic silos.[37]

Environmental Justice and Community Health Partnerships

Environmental justice and community health partnerships represent a second type of multi-stakeholder partnership. In many cases they emerge as community groups recognize the limits of legal, regulatory, and protest strategies for making measurable improvements in the health of local residents. Indeed, key networks of the environmental justice movement, working through the federally authorized multi-stakeholder policy forum of the National Environmental Justice Advisory Council (NEJAC), have concluded that on issues such as cumulative risk and pollution prevention, a place-based collaborative approach can deliver substantial payoffs for communities most vulnerable to multiple and cumulative risk factors. Two NEJAC reports represent this self-described "paradigm shift." In *Ensuring Risk Reduction in Communities with Multiple Stressors,* the NEJAC workgroup argues that in the presence of multiple physical, chemical, biological, social, and cultural factors—which cumulatively and in the aggregate contribute to distinct vulnerabilities for low-income and minority communities—a multimedia, place-based approach can provide the most effective way to generate a "bias for action" that engages various stakeholders in making quick and tangible improvements. Tackling immediate risks and ones broadly recognized as real problems can enable local actors and institutions, including polluters, to build trust for dealing with more difficult, contentious, or indeterminate issues down the line. Residents can directly contribute to local health diagnoses and practical solutions through participatory action research and community health education campaigns.[38]

In *Advancing Environmental Justice through Pollution Prevention,* NEJAC makes a similar set of arguments. Pollution prevention strategies have advanced significantly in recent years through a broad range of initiatives in cleaner technologies and materials, energy efficiency and green building, transportation and land-use planning, and management and work systems. The Pollution Prevention Act of 1990 and a host of voluntary programs have encouraged this effort. But getting the full benefit of prevention approaches at the community level, especially for those most vulnerable, requires far more intentional collaboration among civic organizations, environmental groups, small and large businesses, health departments, and other local government agencies.[39]

Environmental justice and community health partnerships have been growing in recent years, typically built around several core partners, such as an environmental justice group, community development corporation, community health center, school of public health or nursing, and a chapter of the American Lung Association. The addition of green jobs and climate change to the environmental justice frame promises to expand such partnerships still further. In some cases, city departments of planning and public health collaborate with community groups to leverage partnerships for greater and more systemic impact, as happened in San Francisco when the Eastern Neighborhoods Community Health Impact Assessment, developed through a community visioning and collaborative planning process among two dozen organizations with extensive public participation, was adopted as a citywide tool and disseminated regionally. With funding from EPA's collaborative environmental justice grants and Community Action for a Renewed Environment Program or from various programs within the U.S. Department of Health and Human Services, Centers for Disease Control, and National Institute of Environmental Health Sciences, such partnerships can come to include a much broader range of stakeholders and a wide array of health improvement strategies, combining local knowledge and professional expertise in a rich mix of "street science."[40]

Climate Change Partnerships

Emerging as perhaps what may be the dominant form of partnership in the coming years is the climate change partnership or network, which is a typical component of the rapidly increasing number of city-based climate action plans and of various state strategies. Because climate change represents such a critical challenge having an impact on so many environmental and other policy arenas, partnerships have an especially broad potential reach and operate on multiple levels. They often grow out of ecosystem, environmental justice, community health, smart growth, sustainable city/community partnerships, and other "bottom-up networks," and extend to broad networks of businesses and trade and professional associations such as those for architects and builders.[41]

For instance, the Seattle Climate Action Now Initiative, an effort led by the City of Seattle, involves various kinds of partnerships between city agencies, civic and religious groups, environmental organizations and businesses, the Downtown Seattle Association, and all kinds of museums, theaters, schools, and universities. The initiative also provides tools for individual and family action to reduce their carbon imprint. Sustainable Seattle, the nonprofit that led the way in the early 1990s, has progressively integrated its work with neighborhood associations and neighborhood planning, part of the comprehensive planning process. Seattle neighborhoods and surrounding cities and towns now link their sustainability initiatives, such as Sustainable Ballard, Sustainable South Seattle, and Sustainable Bainbridge, in an area-wide learning network—Sustainable Communities ALL Over Puget Sound (SCALLOPS). The Puget Sound Partnership, a state office that emerged from the region's National Estuary Program, also includes key roles for a broad range of environmental advocacy, ecosystem, and education organizations and networks.[42]

Civic Activism, Professionalism, Voluntarism, and Commercialism

Lester Salamon in chapter 1 of this volume notes that four "impulses"—voluntarism, professionalism, civic activism, and commercialism—tend to define the force field within any given nonprofit arena. The field of environmental organizations is no exception. Civic activism has been a prominent feature from the beginning, since most environmental organizations have been directly linked to the environmental movement generally and sometimes to distinctive movements that have emerged not just to confront corporate and government actors but also to challenge established environmental organizations to be more responsive to grassroots members, engage more effectively with communities of place, and adopt frames and tools outside their normal repertoire. Civic activism is responsible for much of the dynamism in the field, helping to legitimate local knowledge, generate innovative policy frames, and establish new types of organizations. Civic activism has also been critical to the formation of lifelong identities, even among those who might later become professional staff in environmental organizations or public agencies or shift from protest to collaborative problem solving. Some key professional innovators in the watershed arena, for instance, have decades-long biographies of activism that include the nuclear weapons freeze, urban community organizing, and antitoxics protest.[43] Much needed, however, are initiatives to renew civic activism in some of the professionalized national advocacy groups; one such initiative is the Harvard University–Sierra Club Leadership Development Project, which nurtures relational organizing, team-based capacity building, and the mobilization of moral resources through shared narratives.[44]

Professionalism has been a largely positive impulse in the environmental field and its variants are more complex than often recognized. Professionalism has been the sine qua non of effective national and state advocacy, policy development, and organizational maintenance. It has been key to the financing and management of land trusts and the development and legitimation of environmental education in schools. Professionalism has also been a critical ingredient in sustaining many local environmental justice partnerships and bridging forms of local and expert knowledge to enable communities to maintain civic activism. Without professionally facilitated bridges between grassroots activists and health and regulatory professionals in institutional settings, much local civic initiative collapses. Professional leadership and facilitation have also been essential to ecosystem partnerships and networks and often serve as critical ingredients in ensuring "democratic anchorage" of networks in broad-based associations. Civic activism and democratic accountability in partnerships and networks are enhanced considerably when professional staff can facilitate organizing, communication, trust building, and the use of sophisticated information, planning, and performance measurement tools by ordinary citizens in communities of place.[45]

Voluntarism has also been essential in the environmental nonprofit field.[46] Voluntarism can take the relatively simple form of episodic acts, such as a stream cleanup on weekends by kids in a 4-H club or church group. This provides a wide and indispensable portal of entry to environmental engagement and education, often prior to civic activism. On the other end, volunteerism may be an essential part of complex, strategic efforts to preserve land, restore watersheds, and monitor and improve human and ecosystem health. The more strategic the challenge, the more important the organizational and professional capacities to manage volunteers and the more otherwise professionalized organizations need to invest in such capacities, such as a staff person to organize volunteer stewards for land trusts, quality assurance training for volunteer watershed monitoring networks, and online information portals to track carbon reduction by community and institutional volunteers in urban climate action partnerships. Professionals in environmental nonprofits, universities, and government agencies have been increasingly energetic in developing such usable tools, but investment in nonprofit staff capacity is often a critical ingredient in enabling broad and effective use.

The commercial impulse in the environmental field takes a variety of forms. First, to supplement their fundraising strategies, many national advocacy organizations market products such as T-shirts and holiday cards, as well as educational and media products. Some organizations sponsor ecotourism through their own subsidiaries and endorse green products of commercial manufacturers, such as the Sierra Club's endorsement of the Philips Eco TV so that "couch potatoes can do their part for the planet" by reducing their carbon footprints.[47] Second, land trusts engage in commercial purchase and sale of property and negotiate easements that limit the exercise of property rights in the interests of long-term conservation. Third, to the extent that environmental goals can be achieved only by transforming commercial business practices and greening supply chains, some environmental organizations form partnerships with corporations and trade associations. The Environmental Defense Fund has not only pioneered market approaches, such as cap and trade for air pollution emissions and catch shares to promote sustainable fisheries, but also engaged in direct partnerships with corporations and trade associations, beginning with its somewhat controversial partnership with the McDonald's Corporation in 1990 to find ways to reduce, reuse, and recycle on a very large scale. A partnership between the Environmental Defense Fund and the Global Environmental Management Initiative, a nonprofit organization of three dozen leading companies, promotes corporate-NGO partnerships. Such partnership approaches, along with regulatory, information, and other governance tools promoting sustainability and corporate citizenship, have opened ever-greater opportunities for for-profit consulting firms. Indeed, we can no longer claim to effectively analyze the field of environmental organizations as a whole without understanding the role played by corporate actors and the complex learning processes through which many have managed to adjust to regulation and then incorporate green practices more deeply in organizational cultures, often with pressure from and the assistance of nonprofits.[48]

Some tensions exist among these impulses, to be sure. Grassroots civic activists are often suspicious of professionalism in the mainstream movement.

Their challenges often go unheeded or find resonance only after some lag-time. Depending on where one sits in the organizational field and one's overall understanding of the desired shape and trajectory of the environmental movement, this tension either confirms the relative conservatism, even cooptation, of the mainstream organizations or provides evidence of dynamic learning potential within the field as a whole. Similar differences can be found in regard to the commercial impulse. The Environmental Defense Fund was quite roundly criticized by many in the movement for its early collaboration with corporations. But two decades later, many who were once critics can be found among those promoting green business practices and corporate culture change as essential to meeting sustainability and climate challenges.[49]

Looking Ahead

The nonprofit role in the environmental field is likely to grow. Public support for environmental causes has remained strong over the years, and the rising salience of climate change promises to reduce the tendency of other public issues to trump environmental ones, especially as effective climate strategies are progressively linked to economic growth and green job creation—presuming, of course, a favorable political environment. Younger cohorts manifest strong commitment to environmental values and a substantial potential for civic engagement and community problem solving, ranging from increasingly sophisticated geographical information systems (GIS) and planning tools to mobilizing for "days of action" and similar events through other Internet tools. Although the indispensability of regulatory tools will ensure an important role for national and state advocacy groups, the manifest limits of command and control will continue to generate increasing opportunities for ecosystem, education, and partnership strategies.[50]

However, there remain very substantial capacity-building challenges, especially for ecosystem and education organizations and all forms of partnership. For instance, although watershed groups have continued to increase in number, 40 percent of watershed groups surveyed by the River Network in 2005 had no budget, 45 percent were without an annual work plan, and 74 percent lacked a fundraising strategy—a far cry from stable financing.[51] Most watersheds do not yet have robust watershed associations and partnerships capable of complex analysis, planning, and monitoring of results, not to mention sustained collaboration with a broad array of state and local government partners, businesses, and other institutions, even though the National River Restoration Science Synthesis, the most prestigious study of its kind, shows that such associations are the most important factor in ensuring accountability for improved ecosystem outcomes.[52] Most watershed groups are not able to engage substantial numbers of ordinary citizens for ongoing restoration work nor to develop strategies to meet the far more complex set of challenges associated with climate change. National, regional, and state nonprofit watershed intermediaries have had far too few resources to work with the depth and breadth needed. Land trusts, faced with many of the same challenges as watershed associations, likewise lack adequate resources for robust engagement of volunteer stewards, citizen scientists, and easement monitors.

Local groups addressing issues of toxics, health, and environmental justice typically arise in communities with substantial barriers to resource mobilization and have generally been unable to sustain themselves without some government funding. Although environmental justice grants from the EPA, including those from the Office of Environmental Justice, have been important to many local groups, this funding is far from adequate, especially as groups take on more complex challenges requiring sustained multi-stakeholder collaboration and technical capacity. States, especially those with comprehensive environmental justice approaches, are beginning to take up some of the slack in helping to build local civic capacity and promoting collaborative models. But environmental justice is not a statutory program at the EPA that can provide substantial funds to the states to help build such capacity, as is possible with the Clean Water Act's section 319 nonpoint source pollution grants in the Office of Water. There is legitimate scientific uncertainty about the causes and consequences of environmental disparities and risks in poor, working-class, and minority communities, but there can hardly be much doubt that the challenge of environmental justice will take decades to achieve and will require civic capacity building on a fairly substantial scale, which the grassroots movement is highly unlikely to be able to generate from either indigenous resources or private foundations. The latter, however, could invest more strategically in building the capacity of local environmental health and justice partnerships and effective national intermediaries to assist them.[53]

Local and state climate change partnerships are relatively new and no systematic evidence is available yet on how much funding their nonprofit partners have been able to garner from private foundations or local, state, and federal agencies. However, selected evidence in this arena and trends in funding other forms of civic capacity investment suggest that serious shortfalls can be expected, even in cities such as Seattle that have a relatively good record of engaging citizens in neighborhood and sustainability planning.

Federal policy could help with these issues in two general ways. The first is to invest substantial resources in forms of organization that engage in collaborative problem solving and can serve as partners in environmental governance at the local and regional levels. As argued in *Investing in Democracy*, this is not a question of supporting nonprofits that treat citizens as clients or simple objects of technocratic solutions, but of enabling civic leadership development, capacity building, and network governance at a level appropriate to the increasing complexity of problems and diversity of publics. The greatest opportunity to make such investments in the coming years is to include them as an essential component of climate change funding, which will be substantial. While the bulk of federal funding will be in the form of investments in such things as green buildings, alternative energy, and sustainable transportation, federal agencies—and the states and cities that receive federal funding—need to invest in the nonprofit and civic infrastructure to ensure effective partnerships, civic engagement, and collaborative governance. This should be made an explicit part of policy design and grant requirements. The current danger, of course, is that budget cutting to reduce the deficit or to save other programs will lead to a very serious disinvestment in the organizational capacities for democracy and collaborative governance.[54]

Second, the Obama administration should energetically and creatively implement the three core principles of transparent, participatory, and collaborative government that it announced in its first presidential memorandum on January 21, 2009, and has since elaborated in its open government directive, specific cabinet-agency open government plans, and OMB place-based memoranda.[55] This entails much more than making information available and ensuring openness of process. It also requires information systems that citizens and local nonprofits can utilize—indeed, coproduce—for watershed planning, healthy city planning, carbon reduction, and sustainable economic development. It entails better aligning regulatory and market tools with stewardship and partnership strategies, as the National Academy of Public Administration and the National Advisory Council for Environmental Policy and Technology have urged, and as proposed by the multi-stakeholder Partnering with Communities project, cosponsored by the EPA and several other federal agencies, environmental health and justice groups; the Brookings Institution; and the Ash Center for Democratic Governance and Innovation at the Kennedy School of Government. The president needs to exercise vigorous and vigilant leadership to ensure that federal agency heads understand that their mission entails strategic capacity building among civic groups, communities, and nonprofits to facilitate their engaging in effective partnerships. Inspiring calls for bottom-up problem solving during the campaign of 2008 must be matched by federal agencies willing and able to activate the collaborative "we" in "Yes, we can."[56]

Notes

1. For good overviews, see Marc Landy, Marc Roberts, and Stephen Thomas, *The Environmental Protection Agency: Asking the Wrong Questions* (Oxford University Press, 1990), and Daniel J. Fiorino, *The New Environmental Regulation* (MIT Press, 2006).

2. See Robert Putnam, *Bowling Alone: The Collapse and Revival of American Community* (New York: Simon and Schuster, 2000), especially chapters 3 and 9, and Theda Skocpol, *Diminished Democracy: From Membership to Management in American Civic Life* (University of Oklahoma Press, 2002). On some of the conceptual issues in the literature on institutional fields and organizational ecology, which I cannot take up directly here, see Walter M. Powell and Paul J. DiMaggio, eds., *The New Institutionalism in Organizational Analysis* (University of Chicago Press, 1991); Royston Greenwood and others, eds., *The Sage Handbook of Organizational Institutionalism* (Thousand Oaks, Calif.: Sage, 2008); Joel Baum, "Organizational Ecology," in *Handbook of Organization Studies,* edited by Stewart Clegg, Cynthia Hardy, and Walter Nord (London: Sage, 1996), pp. 77–114.

3. National Academy of Public Administration, *Taking Environmental Protection to the Next Level: An Assessment of the U.S. Environmental Services Delivery System—A Report to the U.S. EPA* (Washington: April 2007), 163; National Advisory Council for Environmental Policy and Technology, *Everyone's Business: Working towards Sustainability through Environmental Stewardship and Collaboration* (Washington: Environmental Protection Agency, March 2008). See also Thomas Dietz and Paul C. Stern, eds., *Public Participation in Environmental Assessment and Decision Making* (Washington: National Research Council, 2008).

4. In this essay, we draw on interviews, field research, policy documents, organizational strategy papers, annual reports, and similar documents relating to several research projects over the past fifteen years, in addition to the sources cited.

5. For a different classification based on eleven major discursive frames in the U.S environmental movement, see Robert Brulle and others, "Measuring Social Movement Organization Populations: A Comprehensive Census of U.S. Environmental Movement Organizations," *Mobilization: An International Quarterly Review* 12, no. 3 (2007): 195–211.

6. On organizational structures of national environmental advocacy organizations, see especially Ronald G. Shaiko, *Voices and Echoes for the Environment: Public Interest Representation in the 1990s and Beyond* (Columbia University Press, 1999); Robert Gottlieb, *Forcing the Spring: The Transformation of the American Environmental Movement* (Washington: Island Press, 1993), chapter 4.

7. See Ronald G. Shaiko, "More Bang for the Buck: The New Era of Full-Service Public Interest Organizations," in *Interest Group Politics,* 3rd ed., edited by Allan J. Cigler and Burdett A. Loomis (Washington: Congressional Quarterly Press, 1991), pp. 109–30, and, more generally, Jeffrey M. Berry, *The New Liberalism: The Rising Power of Citizen Groups* (Brookings, 1999). On issue niches among national environmental advocacy organizations, see especially Christopher J. Bosso, *Environment, Inc.: From Grassroots to Beltway* (University Press of Kansas, 2005), chapter 3.

8. See Philip A. Mundo, "The Sierra Club," in *Interest Groups: Cases and Characteristics* (Chicago: Nelson-Hall, 1992), 167–201; William Bret Devall, "The Governing of a Voluntary Association: Oligarchy and Democracy in the Sierra Club," Ph.D. dissertation, University of Oregon–Corvallis, 1970; Marshall Ganz and Ruth Wageman, "Sierra Club Leadership Development Project: Pilot Project Report and Recommendations" (Harvard University, May 2008).

9. See Shaiko, *Voices and Echoes,* chapter 4; Dana Fisher, *Activism, Inc.: How the Outsourcing of Grassroots Campaigns Is Strangling Progressive Politics in America* (Stanford University Press, 2006).

10. For a nuanced analysis of relative degrees of corporate influence on national environmental policy, see Sheldon Kamieniecki, *Corporate America and Environmental Policy: How Often Does Business Get Its Way?* (Stanford University Press, 2006).

11. See Environmental Grantmakers Association, *Environmental Grantmaking Foundations,* 10 volumes (Cary, N.C.: Resources for Global Sustainability, 1992–2005). These figures are adjusted according to the revised (December 22, 2009) "Summary of Tracking the Field, Volume 2: A Closer Look at Environmental Grantmaking" (www.ega.org/news/docs/SummaryFinalDec2k9.pdf). *EGA Journal* and various reports are available on the website of the Environmental Grantmakers Association (www.ega.org).

12. For examples of this radical critique, see Robert J. Brulle and J. Craig Jenkins, "Foundations and the Environmental Movement: Priorities, Strategies, and Impact," in *Foundations for Social Change: Critical Perspectives on Philanthropy and Popular Movements,* edited by Daniel Faber and Debra McCarthy (Lanham, Md.: Rowman and Littlefield, 2005), pp. 151–74; Robert J. Brulle, *Agency, Democracy, and Nature: The U.S. Environmental Movement from a Critical Theory Perspective* (MIT Press, 2000); Mark Dowie, *Losing Ground: American Environmentalism at the Close of the Twentieth Century* (MIT Press, 1995).

13. See Barry G. Rabe, "Power to the States: The Promise and Pitfalls of Decentralization," in *Environmental Policy: New Directions for the Twenty-First Century,* edited by Norman J. Vig and Michael E. Kraft (Washington: Congressional Quarterly Press, 2006), 34–56; Barry G. Rabe, *Statehouse and Greenhouse: The Emergent Politics of American Climate Change Policy* (Brookings, 2004); Christopher McGrory Klyza and David Sousa, *American Environmental Policy, 1990–2006: Beyond Gridlock* (MIT Press, 2008), chapter 7; Denise Scheberle, "Devolution," in *Environmental Governance Reconsidered: Challenges, Choices, and Opportunities,* edited by Robert F. Durant, Daniel J. Fiorino, and Rosemary O'Leary (MIT Press, 2004), 361–92; DeWitt John, *Civic Environmentalism: Alternatives to Regulation in States and Communities* (Washington: Congressional Quarterly Press, 1994).

14. For a far-reaching state study, see William G. Robbins, *Landscapes of Conflict: The Oregon Story, 1940–2000* (University of Washington Press, 2004).

15. Luke W. Cole and Sheila R. Foster, *From the Ground Up: Environmental Racism and the Rise of the Environmental Justice Movement* (New York University Press, 2000); J. Timmons Roberts and Melissa M. Toffolon-Weiss, *Chronicles from the Environmental Justice Frontline* (Cambridge University Press, 2001); Andrew Szasz, *Ecopopulism: Toxic Waste and the Movement for Environmental Justice* (University of Minnesota Press, 1994).

16. See especially Kenneth T. Andrews and Bob Edwards, "The Organizational Structure of Local Environmentalism," *Mobilization: An International Journal* 10, no. 2 (2005): 213–34; Andrew Savage, Jonathan Isham, and Christopher McGrory Klyza, "The Greening of Social Capital: An Examination of Land-Based Groups in Two Vermont Counties," *Rural Sociology* 70, no. 1 (March 2005): 113–31; Willett Kempton and others, "Local Environmental Groups: A Systematic Enumeration of Two Geographic Areas," *Rural Sociology,* 66, no. 4 (2001): 557–78; Erika S. Svendsen and Lindsay K. Campbell, "Urban Ecological Stewardship: Understanding the Structure, Function, and Network of Community-Based Urban Land Management," *Cities and the Environment* 1, no. 1 (2008): 1–31, which finds a marked rise in the formation of stewardship groups in six major northeastern cities since 2000.

17. For the development of the broad framework, see Hanna J. Cortner and Margaret A. Moote, *The Politics of Ecosystem Management* (Washington: Island Press, 1999); Richard O. Brooks, Ross Jones, and Ross A. Virginia, *Law and Ecology: The Rise of the Ecosystem Regime* (Burlington, Vt.: Ashgate, 2002).

18. For the network process of developing the watershed frame, see Carmen Sirianni, *Investing in Democracy: Engaging Citizens in Collaborative Governance* (Brookings, 2009), pp. 31, 159–61. For scientific and management components of the approach, see National Research Council, *New Strategies for America's Watersheds* (Washington: National Academy

Press, 1999); Paul A. DeBarry, *Watersheds: Processes, Assessment, and Management* (Hoboken, N.J.: Wiley, 2004).

19. See Peter M. Lavigne, "Watershed Councils East and West: Advocacy, Consensus, and Environmental Progress," *UCLA Journal of Environmental Law and Policy* 22, no. 2 (2004): 301–10; John T. Woolley, Michael Vincent McGinnis, and Julie Kellner, "The California Watershed Movement: Science and the Politics of Place," *Natural Resources Journal* 42, no. 1 (2002): 133–83; Elizabeth A. Moore and Tomas M. Koontz, "A Typology of Collaborative Watershed Groups: Citizen-Based, Agency-Based, and Mixed Partnerships," *Society and Natural Resources* 16, no. 5 (2003): 451–60; Michael Houck, "Bankside Citizens," in *Rivertown: Rethinking Urban Rivers,* edited by Paul Stanton Kibel (MIT Press, 2007), pp. 179–96.

20. On the dynamics of watershed innovation among local, state, and national associations and state and federal agencies, see Sirianni, *Investing in Democracy,* chapter 5.

21. River Network, *2005–2008 Strategic Plan* (Portland, Ore.: 2005), p. 9.

22. We follow the common terminology here, though some contest the term "land trust" in favor of "conservation trust." See Sally K. Fairfax and Darla Guenzler, *Conservation Trusts* (University Press of Kansas, 2001), whose study includes trusts established in and by government agencies, such as the Dade County Wetlands Trust, as well as mixed public-private trusts, such as the North Dakota Wetlands Trust. On the development of volunteer stewardship and some of the controversies surrounding it, especially in the pioneering Chicago Wilderness projects, see William K. Stevens, *Miracle under the Oaks: The Revival of Nature in America* (New York: Simon and Schuster, 1995); Paul Gobster and R. Bruce Hull, eds., *Restoring Nature: Perspectives from the Social Sciences and Humanities* (Washington: Island Press, 2000). On community farms and forests, see Robert G. Lee and Donald R. Field, eds., *Communities and Forests: Where People Meet the Land* (Oregon State University Press, 2005); Mark Baker and Jonathan Kusel, *Community Forestry in the United States: Learning from the Past, Crafting the Future* (Washington: Island Press, 2003); Jonathan Kusel and Elisa Adler, eds., *Forest Communities, Community Forests* (Lanham, Md.: Rowman and Littlefield, 2003); Brian Donahue, *Reclaiming the Commons: Community Farms and Forests in a New England Town* (Yale University Press, 1999).

23. Richard Brewer, *Conservancy: The Land Trust Movement in America* (Dartmouth College Press, 2003), quotation from p. 189. See also Adam Rome, *The Bulldozer in the Countryside: Suburban Sprawl and the Rise of American Environmentalism* (Cambridge University Press, 2001).

24. See especially Sally K. Fairfax and others, *Buying Nature: The Limits of Land Acquisition as a Conservation Strategy, 1780–2000* (MIT Press, 2005).

25. Land Trust Alliance, *2005 National Land Trust Census Report* (Washington: 2006).

26. See Ernest Cook and Matt Zieper, "State and Local Government Funding for Land Conservation," in *From Walden to Wall Street: Frontiers of Conservation Finance,* edited by James N. Leavitt (Washington: Island Press, 2005), pp. 51–72; Robert Bonnie, "Financing Private Lands: Conservation and Management through Conservation Incentives in the Farm Bill," in Leavitt, *From Walden to Wall Street,* pp. 183–99; William Shutkin, *The Land That Could Be: Environmentalism and Democracy in the Twenty-First Century* (MIT Press, 2000), chapter 6; William J. Ginn, *Investing in Nature: Case Studies of Land Conservation in Collaboration with Business* (Washington: Island Press, 2005); and Story Clark, *A Field Guide to Conservation Finance* (Washington: Island Press, 2007).

27. See Daniel Press, *Saving Open Space: The Politics of Local Preservation in California* (University of California Press, 2002), for a statewide, county-based analysis of open space protection.

28. See Richard Brewer, *Conservancy: The Land Trust Movement in America* (Dartmouth College Press, 2003), chapters 9, 11, 12, and 13.

29. See Brewer, *Conservancy,* chapter 10; Shutkin, *Land That Could Be,* chapter 7; Bill Birchard, *Nature's Keepers* (San Francisco: Jossey-Bass, 2005); Peter F. Cannavò, *The Working Landscape: Founding, Preservation, and the Politics of Place* (MIT Press, 2007); Courtney White, *Revolution on the Range: The Rise of a New Ranch in the American West* (Washington: Island Press, 2008).

30. Susan K. Jacobson, Mallory D. McDuff, and Martha C. Monroe, *Conservation Education and Outreach Techniques* (Oxford University Press, 2006); David Sobel, *Place-Based Education: Connecting Classrooms and Communities* (Great Barrington, Mass.: Orion Society, 2004); Elaine Andrews, Mark Stevens, and Greg Wise, "A Model of Community-Based Environmental Education," in National Research Council, Committee on the Human Dimensions of Global Change, *New Tools for Environmental Protection: Education, Information, and Voluntary Measures,* edited by Thomas Dietz and Paul C. Stern (Washington: National Academies Press, 2002), 161–82.

31. See especially National Environmental Education Advisory Council, *Report Assessing Environmental Education in the United States and Implementation of the National Environmental Education Act of 1990,* prepared for U.S. Congress (Washington: Environmental Protection Agency, December 1996); Marcella Wells and Lynnette Fleming, *EETAP Capacity Building Evaluation: Final Project Report* (Washington: Environmental Protection Agency, August 30, 2002).

32. James L. Elder, *A Field Guide to Environmental Literacy: Making Strategic Investments in Environmental Education* (Rock Spring, Ga.: Environmental Education Coalition, 2003).

33. See Rosemary O'Leary and Lisa B. Bingham, eds, *The Promise and Performance of Environmental Conflict Resolution* (Washington: Resources for the Future, 2003); Julia M. Wondolleck and Steven L. Yaffee, *Making Collaboration Work: Lessons from Innovation in Natural Resource Management* (Washington: Island Press, 2000).

34. See Freeman House, *Totem Salmon: Life Lessons from Another Species* (Boston: Beacon Press, 1999).

35. See Caroline E. Lee, "Is There a Place for Private Conversation in Public Dialogue: Comparing Stakeholder Assessments of Informal Communication in Collaborative Regional Planning," *American Journal of Sociology* 113, no. 1 (July 2007): 41–96; Caroline E. Lee, "Accounting for Diversity in Collaborative Governance: An Institutional Approach to Empowerment Reforms," in *Varieties of Civic Innovation: Deliberative, Collaborative, Network, and Narrative Approaches,* edited by Carmen Sirianni and Jennifer Girouard (Vanderbilt University Press, 2011).

36. Edward P. Weber, *Bringing Society Back In: Grassroots Ecosystem Management, Accountability, and Sustainable Communities* (MIT Press, 2003). See also Daniel Kemmis, *This Sovereign Land: A New Vision for Governing the West* (Washington: Island Press, 2001); Matthew McKinney and William Harmon, *The Western Confluence: A Guide to Governing Natural Resources* (Washington: Island Press, 2004).

37. See Weber, *Bringing Society Back In;* Paul A. Sabatier and others, *Swimming Upstream: Collaborative Approaches to Watershed Management* (MIT Press, 2005); Tomas M. Koontz and others, *Collaborative Environmental Management: What Roles for Government?* (Washington: Resources for the Future, 2004); Mark Lubell, "Resolving Conflict and Building Cooperation in the National Estuary Program," *Environmental Management* 33, no. 5 (2004): 677–91; Mark Lubell and others, "Building Consensual Institutions: Networks and the National Estuary Program," *American Journal of Political Science* 47, no. 1 (2003): 143–58; Mark

Lubell and others, "Watershed Partnerships and the Emergence of Collective Action Institutions," *American Journal of Political Science* 46, no. 1 (2002): 148–63; Anne Taufen Wessels, "Constructing Watershed Parks: Actor-Networks and Collaborative Governance in Four U.S. Metropolitan Areas," Ph.D. dissertation, University of California–Irvine, 2007. For an important comparative analysis of seven cases that argues that conventional politics (salience campaigns, lawsuits, expert planning) and regulatory tools can be more effective than goal setting by partnerships, see Judith A. Layzer, *Natural Experiments: Ecosystem-Based Management and the Environment* (MIT Press, 2008).

38. National Environmental Justice Advisory Council, *Ensuring Risk Reduction in Communities with Multiple Stressors: Environmental Justice and Cumulative Risks/Impacts* (Washington: Environmental Protection Agency, 2004). On the rationale for a fresh approach see Christopher Foreman Jr., *The Promise and Peril of Environmental Justice* (Brookings, 1999). On further complexities and uncertainties see Lisa Schweitzer and Max Stephenson Jr., "Right Answers, Wrong Questions: Environmental Justice as Urban Research," *Urban Studies* 44, no. 2 (February 2007), 319–37. For an overview of community-based methods, see Barbara A. Israel and others, eds., *Methods in Community-Based Participatory Research for Health* (San Francisco: Jossey-Bass, 2005).

39. National Environmental Justice Advisory Council, *Advancing Environmental Justice through Pollution Prevention* (Washington: Environmental Protection Agency, 2003).

40. See Jason Corburn, *Street Science: Community Knowledge and Environmental Health Justice* (MIT Press, 2005); Jason Corburn, *Toward the Healthy City: People, Places, and the Politics of Urban Planning* (MIT Press, 2009); Charles Lee, "Collaborative Models to Achieve Environmental Justice and Healthy Communities," in *Power, Justice, and the Environment: A Critical Appraisal of the Environmental Justice Movement,* edited by David Naguid Pellow and Robert J. Brulle (MIT Press, 2005), pp. 219–49; National Academy of Public Administration, *Putting Community First: A Promising Approach to Federal Collaboration for Environmental Improvement. An Evaluation of the Community Action for a Renewed Environment (CARE) Demonstration Program* (Washington: 2009); Phil Brown, *Toxic Exposures: Contested Illnesses and the Environmental Health Movement* (Columbia University Press, 2007); Van Jones, *The Green Collar Economy* (New York: HarperCollins, 2008).

41. See Kent E. Portney and Zachary Cuttler, "The Local Nonprofit Sector and the Pursuit of Sustainability in American Cities: A Preliminary Exploration," *Local Environment* 15 (2010): 323–39; Hari M. Osofsky and Janet Koven Levit, "The Scale of Networks: Local Climate Change Coalitions," *Chicago Journal of International Law* 8 (Winter 2008): 427; Jason Corburn, "Cities, Climate Change, and Urban Heat Island Mitigation: Localising Global Environmental Science," *Urban Studies* 46, no. 2 (February 2009): 413–27; Kirk Emerson, "Collaborative Public Management and Climate Change: Managing Climate Change in a Multi-Level Governance System," in *Navigating Climate Change Policy: The Opportunities of Federalism,* edited by Edella C. Schlager, Kirsten H. Engel, and Sally Rider (University of Arizona Press, 2011); Kirk Emerson and Peter Murchie, "Collaborative Governance and Climate Change: Opportunities for Public Administration," paper presented at Minnowbrook III Conference, Syracuse University, Maxwell School of Public Administration, Lake Placid, New York, September 2008. See also Kent E. Portney, *Taking Sustainable Cities Seriously: Economic Development, the Environment, and Quality of Life in American Cities* (MIT Press, 2003); Daniel A. Mazmanian and Michael E. Kraft, eds., *Towards Sustainable Communities: Transition and Transformations in Environmental Policy* (MIT Press, 1999); Peter Newman and Isabella Jennings, *Cities as Sustainable Ecosystems: Principles and Practices* (Washington: Island

Press, 2008); Timothy Grewe, Susan Anderson, and Laurel Butman, "Portland, Oregon: A Case Study of Sustainability," *Government Financial Review,* 18 (2002): 8–14.

42. See Sirianni, *Investing in Democracy,* chapters 3 and 5.

43. See Carmen Sirianni and Lewis A. Friedland, *Civic Innovation in America: Community Empowerment, Public Policy, and the Movement for Civic Renewal* (University of California Press, 2001), on biographical pathways of activists in various arenas of civic innovation, including the watershed movement. On activist identities, see also Paul Lichterman, *The Search for Political Community: American Activists Reinventing Commitment* (University of Chicago Press, 1996).

44. See Ganz and Wageman, *Sierra Club Leadership Development Project.*

45. On the concept of democratic anchorage, see Eva Sørensen and Jacob Torfing, "The Democratic Anchorage of Governance Networks," *Scandinavian Political Studies* 28, no. 3 (2005): 195–218; Eva Sørensen and Jacob Torfing, eds., *Theories of Democratic Network Governance* (Basingstoke, U.K.: Palgrave Macmillan, 2007). On the role of professionals in brokering trust in lay and professional networks and enabling sophisticated use of data tools such as GIS systems by empowered communities, see Carmen Sirianni and Jennifer Girouard, "The Civics of Urban Planning," in *The Oxford Handbook of Urban Planning,* edited by Rachel Weber and Randall Crane (Oxford University Press, 2011); Renee E. Sieber, "Public Participation Geographic Information Systems: A Literature Review and Framework," *Annals of the Association of American Geographers* 96 (2006): 491–507.

46. See, for instance, Robert L. Ryan and Robert E. Grese, "Urban Volunteers and the Environment: Forest and Prairie Restoration," in *Urban Place: Reconnecting with the Natural World,* edited by Peggy F. Bartlett (MIT Press, 2005), 173–88.

47. Dan Oko, "Building Better: Cool Products for an Eco Home," *Sierra* (www.sierraclub.org/sierra/200901/cool.aspx).

48. See especially Andrew J. Hoffman, *From Heresy to Dogma: An Institutional History of Corporate Environmentalism,* expanded edition (Stanford, Calif.: Stanford Business Books, 2001); Global Environmental Management Initiative and Environmental Defense, *Guide to Successful Corporate-NGO Partnerships* (Washington: 2008) (http://innovation.edf.org/documents/8818_GEMI-EDF%20Guide%20Final.pdf). See also Daniel C. Esty and Andrew S. Winston, *Green to Gold: How Smart Companies Use Environmental Strategy to Innovate, Create Value, and Build Competitive Advantage* (Hoboken, N.J.: Wiley, 2009); Dietz and Stern, *New Tools for Environmental Protection,* part 3.

49. For an astute analysis of how learning within business firms is contingent on notions of "good citizenship," right-to-know requirements, and social networks linking actors within the firm to the broader community, see Manik Roy, "Pollution Prevention, Organizational Culture, and Social Learning," *Environmental Law* 22 (1991): 189–251. When Roy wrote this article he was serving on the staff of the Environmental Defense Fund, whose strategy as a mainstream nonprofit was evolving decisively.

50. See Deborah Lynn Guber, *The Grassroots of a Green Revolution: Polling America on the Environment* (MIT Press, 2003); Cliff Zukin and others, *A New Civic Engagement: Political Participation, Civic Life, and the Changing American Citizen* (Oxford University Press, 2007); Dana R. Fisher and Marije Boekkooi, "Mobilizing Friends and Strangers: Understanding the Role of the Internet in the Step It Up Day of Action," *Information, Communication, and Society* 13, no. 2 (March 2010): 193–208; "Transition to Green: Leading the Way to a Healthy Environment, a Green Economy, and a Sustainable Future," November 2008, environmental transition recommendations for the Obama administration endorsed by

twenty-nine environmental and conservation groups (http://docs.nrdc.org/legislation/files/leg_08112401a.pdf [March 4, 2010]).

51. Wendy Wilson and Pat Muñoz, *Sustainable Financing for Watershed Groups,* U.S. EPA Watershed Academy, live webcast, March 22, 2006 (www.cluin.org/conf/tio/owsusfund_032206 [March 4, 2010]).

52. Emily S. Bernhardt and others, "Restoring Rivers One Reach at a Time: Results from a Survey of U.S. River Restoration Practitioners," *Restoration Ecology* 15, no. 3 (2007): 482–93; Margaret Palmer and others, "River Restoration in the Twenty-First Century: Data and Experiential Knowledge to Inform Future Efforts," *Restoration Ecology* 15, no. 3 (2007): 472–81

53. On funding sources within the environmental justice movement based on survey data from local groups, see Robert J. Brulle and Jonathan Essoka, "Whose Environmental Justice? An Analysis of the Governance Structure of Environmental Justice Organizations in the United States," in Pellow and Brulle, *Power, Justice, and the Environment,* pp. 205–18; Jo Marie Rios, "Environmental Justice Groups: Grassroots Movement or NGO Networks? Some Policy Implications," *Policy Studies Review* 17, nos. 2–3 (2000): 179–211.

54. Sirianni, *Investing in Democracy,* chapter 6.

55. President Barack Obama, "Transparency and Open Government: Memorandum for the Heads of Executive Departments and Agencies," January 21, 2009 (www.whitehouse.gov/the_press_office/TransparencyandOpenGovernment/ [January 21, 2009]). See also U.S Office of Management and Budget, "Open Government Directive," memorandum, December 8, 2009 (www.whitehouse.gov/omb/assets/memoranda_2010/m10-06.pdf); The White House, "Developing Effective Place-Based Policies for the FY 2011 Budget," memorandum, August 11, 2009 (www.whitehouse.gov/omb/assets/memoranda_fy2009/m09-28.pdf). Specific cabinet agency plans were released in April 2010.

56. See Sirianni, *Investing in Democracy,* chapter 6; Carmen Sirianni and others, *Partnering with Communities: Perspectives from Scholarship* (Harvard University, Kennedy School of Government, Ash Center for Democratic Governance and Innovation, April 2010).

8

International Assistance

ABBY STODDARD

I n the provision of aid to foreign populations suffering the effects of war, natural disasters, or chronic poverty, private nonprofit organizations play a crucial operational and advocacy role. Commonly referred to in the international aid field as nongovernmental organizations (NGOs), these entities not only undertake independent charitable activities but also serve as the main implementers of governments' foreign assistance programs. Over the past four decades, NGOs have matured and professionalized, earning a reputation for speed, flexibility, deployment capacity, and programming innovation beyond the reach of most governmental actors. In addition, their grassroots orientation and their staffs' firsthand knowledge of local conditions have earned them the stamp of credibility and a measure of influence in national and international policymaking circles.

The proliferation of complex humanitarian emergencies and the widespread shrinking of the public sector role that characterized the post–Cold War period increased the need for and the growth of international assistance organizations. These organizations have increasingly ventured into environments of active conflict or catastrophic state failure, and as a result have found themselves literally and figuratively under fire. New forms of intrastate conflict, characterized by

This chapter is a revised and updated version of the chapter by Shepard Forman and Abby Stoddard that appeared in the 2003 edition of this book.

self-perpetuating illicit economies and heavy civilian tolls, have created hazardous working conditions and wrenching moral dilemmas for humanitarian organizations. They have also inflicted enormous damage on family livelihoods and national development efforts, most notably in Africa. In addition to these politically rooted crises, the AIDS pandemic, the global food crisis, and the proliferation of small-to-medium-scale natural disasters associated with climate change have also increased the need for, and the challenges to, international assistance providers. Heightened visibility of NGOs, combined with inflated expectations as to what they can and should attempt to accomplish, has at times provoked criticism from both practitioners and outside observers about the performance, transparency, and accountability of these organizations. This in turn has spurred far-reaching reforms in the field. The tension between voluntarism and professionalism seen in other parts of the nonprofit sector is continually evident in the international aid subsector as well, as organizations strive to improve performance with data-driven and results-oriented programming while at the same time attempting to remain true to the altruistic ethos and independent spirit of international aid that bridles against regimentation and bureaucratization. Civic activism, or advocacy, as it is termed in the international assistance parlance, has grown in importance to NGOs as evidenced by the proliferating policy and advocacy departments among organizations and their campaigns for public outreach and political change. This is countered and complicated by certain commercialist trends in the NGO community. In particular, the rise in large-scale government contracts taken on by some NGOs (particularly in the reconstruction settings of Afghanistan and Iraq) has led some organizations to assume roles and relationships to the donor government (a government that funds foreign aid implemented through NGOs) very much resembling those of sector government contractors. For NGOs operating in foreign aid contexts, the general blurring of the lines between assistance and commercial or military activities remains a source of concern and internal debate.

In this chapter we will describe the basic characteristics of the nonprofit international relief and development subsector and explore the features of the international context that have shaped its important role in developing world crises. In the process, we will identify the external events and internal pressures that over the past four decades have transformed much of the subsector from an arena of well-meaning amateurs into a professionalized network of technical experts, dominated by a small number of very large and influential agencies.

The Key Role of Nonprofits in the International Assistance Field

The first internationally oriented assistance organizations in the United States appeared during the interwar period, and the field continued to grow slowly after World War II. The aim of these early organizations was to provide emergency relief supplies to war victims in Europe. This changed with decolonization after World War II, as the emergence of many newly independent, and underdeveloped, nations triggered a movement for economic development assistance, so that throughout the 1960s and '70s the focus of NGOs shifted to poverty reduction efforts in the third world. Widespread disappointment with the initial government-to-government approach to development, which had resulted in high-profile, wasteful projects or outright diversion of aid monies by corrupt governments, shone a light on NGOs as an alternative vehicle for progress.[1] Using a bottom-up approach, international NGOs working at the village level represented a strategy for development upward from the local communities, which many donors embraced.

During this period NGOs continued to respond to natural and conflict-related emergencies, but their access to victims was constrained by politics and limited technological and logistical capacity. The role of primary aid provider in conflict situations was still the undisputed province of the International Committee of the Red Cross. The founding of Médecins Sans Frontières (Doctors Without Borders) in 1971 marked a turning point in relief assistance, forging a path for greater independent action by NGOs. Committing itself to the "humanitarian imperative," this new breed of organization sought to provide relief to victims wherever they happened to be, with or without waiting for consent of the warring parties and thus challenging the principles of sovereignty and noninterference. By the late 1970s a boom had begun in the relief and development field, likely fueled in part by amendments to the U.S. Foreign Assistance Act in 1973, which created the mechanisms and policy impetus for increased government funding of private voluntary organizations through small-scale assistance grants rather than large-scale government-to-government transfers. The growth in the number of NGOs gained increased momentum over the next twenty years as a consequence.[2]

The last decade of the twentieth century witnessed unprecedented levels of humanitarian crisis. Not only were there three times as many natural disasters in the 1990s as there were in the 1960s, but the 1990s also marked a high point for state fragmentation and violent civil conflicts (see table 8-1).[3] Only two of the world's twenty-seven major armed conflicts in 1999 were wars between nations.[4] Although the number of intrastate conflicts has decreased in more recent years, chronic and regionally based conflicts continue to thwart development and keep populations on the brink of humanitarian catastrophe. Africa in particular has been beset by the twin phenomena of "failed states" and "complex emergencies," where long-standing environmental and food security problems are exacerbated by fighting or by the outright collapse of central authority. The modus operandi of combatants in such conflicts has been to inflict damage and

Table 8-1. *Trends in Humanitarian Emergencies*

Decade	Number of emergencies (natural disasters and complex emergencies)	Number of people affected (millions)
1970s	1,182	553
1980s	2,796	1,258
1990s	5,031	1,973
2000s (to date)	6,840	2,074

Source: EM-DAT: The OFDA/CRED International Disaster Database (www.emdat.be), Université Catholique de Louvain, Brussels, Belgium.

exert control on civilian areas and populations rather than on opposing military forces, resulting in unprecedented numbers of civilian casualties, refugees, and internally displaced persons. Finally, global climate change has contributed to an upsurge of floods, droughts, storms and other moderate-scale natural disasters, which do not receive the attention that massive calamities such as 2005's Indian Ocean tsunami do but which, combined, cause billions of dollars' worth of damage and disrupt vast numbers of lives.[5] After both natural and man-made disasters, the burden of post-crisis recovery sets back years of development progress in the countries where the disasters occurred.

Along with burgeoning humanitarian need, the 1990s saw greatly increased access by independent relief agencies to victims. The end of the cold war ushered in a new era of cooperation on the Security Council and a willingness to take action on humanitarian grounds. By essentially loosening the principle of national sovereignty and promoting international "humanitarian intervention" to safeguard stability and individual human rights, the council's actions helped to further legitimize the work of private relief agencies.[6] In addition, these NGOs were now accorded the freedom to operate in formerly "closed" societies transitioning from communism.

The increased need and opportunity for humanitarian aid stimulated a doubling of relief funding from industrialized countries, and an explosion of new NGOs in the late 1980s and '90s. Organizations already doing development work in the field found that their existing infrastructures and local knowledge made them well placed to respond to emergent needs as they arose, while scores of new organizations were created in the wake of each new humanitarian disaster for the express purpose of launching a rapid response delivery of relief aid. The number of international relief and development organizations based in the United States grew from fifty-two organizations in 1970 to over four hundred by 1994.[7] By the end of 2008, the United States Agency for International Development (USAID) registered 584 U.S.-based NGOs as funding partners, up from 439 in 2000,[8] the largest number of such organizations in any OECD nation. The combined revenue and in-kind support from public and private sources for these 584 organizations totaled over $27 billion in 2007—more than the total amount of U.S. official development assistance.[9]

The U.S.-based NGOs represented on the USAID registry range widely in organizational size and scope of work, with the smallest operating on budgets of under $10,000, and the largest having budgets in the hundreds of millions. Some of these organizations focus on issues peripheral to development assistance, such as environmental conservation or political democratization, and others have chosen a single issue or activity, such as adoption, or a specific country or region. An untold number of other small NGOs exist outside the USAID partnership, and it is common for many to spring up around a particular emergency and then dissolve or reappear in a different institutional form. The largest U.S. consortium of relief and development organizations, the Washington D.C.-based NGO consortium InterAction, narrows the field somewhat by requiring membership dues and entry criteria, and counts 190 members, still a sizable number. Yet even with proliferating aid organizations in the 1990s, the bulk of global aid dollars and materials continue to be channeled through a small group of large and long-standing NGOs. Of a roughly estimated four thousand NGOs based in the global North at the turn of the current century, the ten largest accounted for an estimated 20 percent of combined NGO revenue.[10] Among these giants are four of the largest American relief and development NGOs: CARE USA, Catholic Relief Services, Save the Children USA, and World Vision. These four organizations—two of them religious in orientation and two secular—are examples of broad-based, "multisectoral" relief and development agencies that undertake a wide range of program activities in which they are joined by the larger community of NGOs, some of which also do work across a variety of program areas and others of which specialize in one or two.

Principal Program Areas within International Assistance

There are three principal—and somewhat interrelated—program areas in the international assistance field: development assistance, humanitarian assistance, and recovery and rehabilitation.

Development Assistance

The aim of development assistance, geared toward long-term poverty reduction, is to build local capacities, support livelihoods, and create sustainable improvements in quality of life. Such projects include technical assistance in agriculture, education, small business development and micro-credit initiatives, primary health care with an emphasis on maternal and child health, nutrition, and food security. In attempting to understand and eliminate the root causes of poverty and underdevelopment, the development assistance portion of the development field has also come to focus on civil society strengthening, democratization, and press freedom, reproductive health and family planning, and human rights. Issues of gender inequality, environmental degradation, and HIV/AIDS, critical "cross-cutting" issues whose impacts must be considered and integrated into all aspects of programming, are given varying levels of attention and resources by NGOs.

Increasingly, the major international NGOs working in development assistance are nationalizing their country offices and devolving their programming to local partner organizations. The growing self-sufficiency of global South development organizations in mounting their own development efforts has their international counterparts doing less direct implementation of assistance and more technical assistance and resource provision.[11]

Humanitarian Assistance

Humanitarian assistance refers to relief efforts to save lives and mitigate damage caused by natural disasters and complex political emergencies, including armed conflict. Often this takes place within the context of refugee movements or large-scale internal displacement of populations, where rapid provision of basic goods and services is required. The major subsectors of this field are emergency food aid, health care interventions, shelter, and water and sanitation services.

Most of the larger United States–based NGOs that undertake emergency humanitarian response are also involved in long-term poverty reduction activities in their areas of operation, including a wide range of assistance activities focusing on the development of food resources, shelter, health, sanitation, agriculture, micro-enterprise, and infrastructure. These multi-mandate organizations have discovered the strategic and cost advantages to launching emergency response in areas where they already maintain an operational presence, logistical infrastructure, networks of contacts, and partnerships in the community. Furthermore there is now widespread recognition that the two sets of activities are functionally and conceptually interdependent. Poverty, overpopulation, and environmental degradation can increase a country's vulnerabilities to disaster, and, conversely, disasters have an antithetical effect on development. Thus development seeks to reduce a country's vulnerability to disasters, and relief aid, appropriately targeted, can help provide a solid foundation for rehabilitation and ongoing development.

Recovery and Rehabilitation

During the 1990s the relief and development communities recognized a third set of needs to be met besides the urgent, life-saving activities of acute humanitarian crises and the long-term poverty fighting: post-crisis recovery and rehabilitation programs, undertaken in "stable development contexts." This large, somewhat gray, area of international assistance encompasses elements of both types of programming as well as activities specific to early recovery and reconstruction assistance such as infrastructure repair, peaceful reintegration of displaced populations, property rights mediation, and support for the recurrent costs of maintaining the public sector, such as civil servants' salaries. Research has shown the critical importance of the post-crisis period, particularly after armed conflict, when populations need to see tangible evidence of improvements in their lives to avoid the very real risk of backsliding into instability and violence.[12] Governments and international organizations have for years grappled with a de facto gap during the recovery period between acute crisis relief and development aid in terms of funding and institutional mandates, with the result that the critical activities of early recovery have been under-resourced. Although most large donors continue to categorize activities into "relief," "recovery," and "development," this distinction has been challenged by most practitioners as outmoded and counterproductive. Since relief, recovery, and development activities are in reality all interrelated and overlapping, treating them as separate stages along a continuum results in funding and service gaps, and the threat of backsliding into renewed crisis.[13]

Characteristics of the Relief and Development Nonprofit Subsector

The international relief and development organizations represent a unique subsector of U.S. nonprofits. Although a few also engage in some domestic programming, the bulk of their work is carried out overseas, in poor or war-torn countries. The majority of their employees (between 85 and 95 percent in most cases) are developing-country nationals. To operate effectively these organizations and their employees must navigate relationships with host country governments and local authorities, occasionally with warring parties, and with a range of international bodies and political actors. Also unlike other nonprofits, these organizations, especially those engaged in humanitarian relief efforts in conflict situations, face serious security risks and have suffered increasing casualties to their personnel. In recent years NGOs have had to grapple with such matters as hostage taking, and the effects of psychological stress and burnout of field staff.

There are unique dynamics within the relief and development community as well. U.S. international relief and development organizations exist as part of a complex transnational community of NGOs and other international actors. The NGOs are essentially private organizations, each following its own distinctive normative mandate in a highly politicized environment. Some observers make the argument that the diversity and independence of the members of this community is a thing to be valued, as the key to NGOs' operational advantage in the field. As a senior staffer of InterAction put it, "Civil society is by nature diverse, and the last thing we want is to make it monolithic. Varied opinions help make us innovative, and challenge us to perform better."[14] At the same time, however, aid organizations have recognized that their objectives are too large to accomplish independently, and that if they truly want to have a positive effect on the lives of their beneficiaries, their work will have to be strategically and operationally coordinated with that of their counterparts. For this reason aid practitioners have made efforts to identify the common core principles of humanitarian assistance and to promote constructive cooperation in the field and at the headquarters level.[15] This is no easy task, as cultural differences abound among the NGOs, along both organizational and regional lines.

Despite occupying a unique position in the U.S. nonprofit sector, international aid organizations nonetheless share common features and challenges with their domestic counterparts. These include a changing funding landscape, an ongoing—though ambivalent—pursuit of professionalism, and the difficulties in defining their relationships with government, be it as partners, petitioners, or lobbyists. These commonalities as well as the distinctive aspects of internationally operating NGOs will be explored below.

Factors Shaping the NGO Position in the Field

At the dawn of the twenty-first century, the international environment was characterized by both economic globalization and conflict and state failure. This combination of factors thrust aid NGOs into unaccustomed prominent roles, some for which they were never intended or adequately prepared. The 9/11 attacks and the transformations in the U.S. global military security agenda that followed created a further set of conditions in the form of a subset of aid environments (specifically Afghanistan and parts of the Middle East) where NGOs are marginalized and buffeted by competing political forces. Aid funding on the whole has continued to increase, but with new contribution modalities, and with sources and recipients that do not always favor the mission and interests of the NGO community. The lingering effects of the 2008 banking crisis and resulting economic recession are further disrupting NGO budgets and program planning. Security of personnel has deteriorated in many areas, and violent attacks on aid workers have proliferated over the past several years. All of these factors have shaped the recent evolution of the international NGO sector, whose members continue to seek solutions and develop new modes of working with local communities and partners—and with each other—in an increasingly polarized global arena. These factors and the NGOs' responses and adaptations are discussed in this section.

Globalization and the Shrinking Public Sector

On the development side, globalization has had both direct and indirect effects on the work of NGOs. It has opened new doors for fundraising and private sector partnerships. New technology that has suddenly become available and affordable to NGOs, such as portable satellite communications systems, has helped increase NGO access to victims and improved their logistical capacity to provide assistance. And of course the Internet has revolutionized fundraising. To give just one example, CARE USA generated upwards of $5 million in small online donations from private citizens in the first ten days after the Indian Ocean tsunami.[16] At the same time, while globalization has been hailed as a boon to developing countries, creating new jobs and educational opportunities, raising the standard of living and building bridges to the modern industrialized world, it also seems to have increased rather than decreased inequities within states, creating new forms of poverty and social tensions just as it creates new forms of wealth. In the post–cold war period fundamentalist free market economic theories ruled the day, proponents of the "Washington consensus" argued for rapid privatization of national economies, and states undergoing fiscal crisis found an enabling philosophy for cutting back on social services. The shrinking of the public sector and fraying of the social safety net occurred all over the world, including in many nominally socialist countries. National governments and the United Nations have increasingly called on international aid agencies and local NGOs to meet the resulting social needs, and are faced with ever-widening gaps to fill in places where they have been working for decades.[17]

The global economic recession that began in 2008 is exacerbating these problems. The recession is anticipated to have particularly devastating effects on developing countries, particularly coming as it has on the heels of a global crisis of rising food prices. As of autumn 2010 the direct and indirect implications of the recession for the international relief and development NGOs were not yet clear, but signs pointed to a likely contraction of the sector's major players against a backdrop of increased need on the ground.

Post–Cold War Conflict Patterns and the Post-9/11 Security Environment

New challenges have also confronted the international assistance organizations as a result of the end of the cold war and the attacks of September 11, 2001. During the 1990s, relief agencies found themselves in the unenviable position of representing the *primary* response of the international community to many of the emergencies resulting from the violent civil conflicts that emerged in the aftermath of the cold war. The breakup of the USSR ended the Security Council's long-standing deadlock between the veto powers of the United States and the Soviet Union, resulting in a spate of new peacekeeping activity.

More than triple the amount of UN peacekeeping operations were approved after 1988 than had been mandated in the prior forty years of the UN's existence. However, these missions suffered from persistent underfunding and disputes over command and control. Absent the geostrategic contest between the superpowers, governments had little by way of a compelling national interest in the outcome of most of these conflicts, and the United States in particular was loath to run the risk of troop losses after the early experience with humanitarian intervention in Somalia. Despite the passage in 2006 of the UN resolution enshrining the "Responsibility to Protect," Russia, the People's Republic of China, and a number of developing countries on the Security Council continue in various ways to oppose the idea of forceful "humanitarian intervention" on the grounds that it violates the principle of sovereignty.[18] The tendency of the Western democracies to support humanitarian aid operations while eschewing deeper political or military commitments prompted accusations that they were using aid as a "humanitarian fig leaf" to conceal their inaction. In Bosnia, Rwanda, and Somalia it became clear that without resolute political action, including security measures as necessary, relief work could become both dangerous and futile.

Since 9/11, however, NGOs in some settings have faced the opposite problem. Political and military interests are paramount for the United States in the protracted conflict settings of Afghanistan and Iraq (and in certain short-term emergencies such as Lebanon in 2006) and aid actors must take pains to dissociate themselves from the political agendas that would compromise their core principles of independence and neutrality. It has been especially difficult for U.S.-based NGOs to project independence and neutrality when the majority of their funding comes from the U.S. government. The U.S. government not only has been a party to the conflict in Afghanistan and Iraq but also has made it a point of policy in recent years to use aid as an integral component of its hearts-and-minds strategy, and to consider the NGO providers as "force multipliers."[19]

Funding and Partnerships

Equally significant developments confront U.S.-based NGOs in the area of finance. NGOs require substantial funding for large-scale assistance projects. For example, even a short-term three-to-six-month project grant from the Office of U.S. Foreign Disaster Assistance (USAID's relief wing) can easily top $1 million. The United States government, by far the largest aid donor among governments in absolute terms, contributed $21.8 billion worth of international relief and development assistance in 2007.[20] Roughly a quarter of this official development assistance (ODA) was channeled through NGOs.[21] This reflects in part the credibility and legitimacy that has accrued over the past few decades to these nonprofit, nonstate actors operating in the international sphere.

Figure 8-1. *U.S. NGO Funding Levels for Fiscal Years 2000 to 2006*

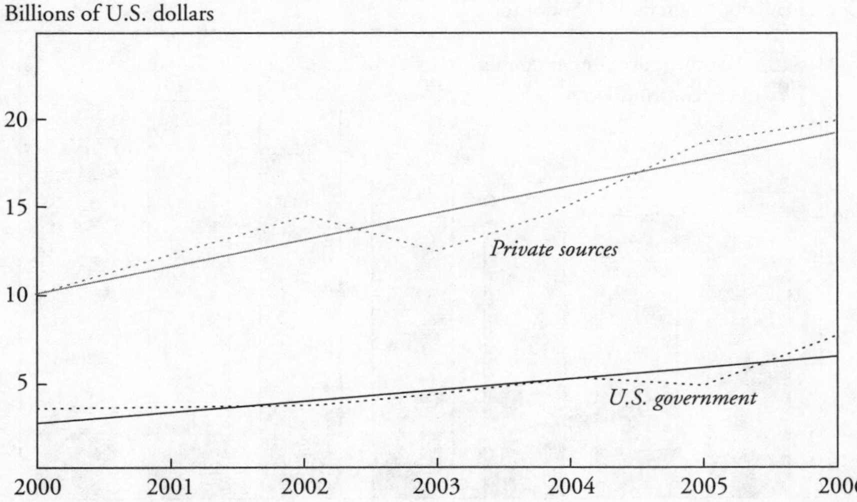

Billions of U.S. dollars

Source: USAID, *Report of Voluntary Agencies,* 2000 to 2006.

Unlike the major European NGOs, until recently most of the U.S. relief and development organizations have traditionally relied heavily on the U.S. government for the bulk of their resources. (See figure 8-1.) At the beginning of the decade, the four largest and most prominent U.S. relief and development NGOs listed earlier (CARE, Catholic Relief Services, Save the Children, and World Vision) accounted for nearly 47 percent of total U.S. government annual support to NGOs, and all but one of the four, World Vision, relied on U.S. government sources for more than 50 percent of their funding.[22]

The proportion of official government assistance that is channeled through NGOs is in fact understated, since a large percentage of what is given as a direct grant to an international agency such as the UN High Commissioner for Refugees is typically then distributed to NGOs in the form of subgrants and implementing partnerships. These international agencies represent another important source of funding for NGOs and provide a locus of coordination for aid efforts. And UN agencies, like national governments, depend on NGOs to carry out much of the end-stage service delivery and to move quickly to identify and access populations in need.

Overall aid funding from governments has trended upward over the past several years, with a spike in 2005 owing to the tsunami response (see figure 8-2). Combined official development assistance (ODA) from the government donors reached $109 billion in 2007, with the U.S. contribution accounting for

Figure 8-2. *U.S. Share of Total International Aid Funded by Governments*

Constant (2006) billions of U.S. dollars

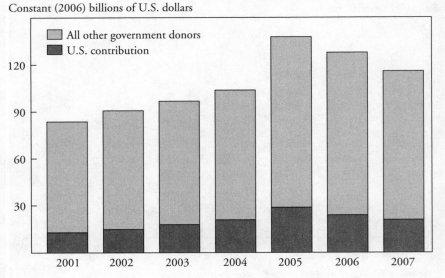

Source: OECD/DAC International Development Assistance Statistics (www.oecd.org/dac/stats, March 2008).

roughly 20 percent of the total.[23] Only a handful of governments have met or exceeded the ODA target of 0.7 percent of national budgets (the United States, which never committed to the target, has never gotten higher than 0.23 percent and is now at .16 percent) but this movement has already served to help raise the tide of international assistance funding. For NGOs, the increases in government funding have been more evident in humanitarian relief, as opposed to the development side.

Although the Bush administration greatly increased U.S. government spending for development, much of this expenditure went in the form of contracts to for-profit firms, such as Development Alternatives International and Chemonics.

On the humanitarian relief side (typically about 10 percent of overall aid), new international financing mechanisms such as the UN's expanded Central Emergency Relief Fund (CERF) and the country-level Common Humanitarian Funds (CHFs) have allowed donor governments to pool their contributions in a single fund that is allocated by UN officials to their aid agencies and NGO partners. What these humanitarian funding mechanisms provide for donors, apart from facilitating coordination of planning and allocation on the part of the operational agencies, is a convenient vehicle to funnel larger volumes of aid with fewer transaction costs on the part of the donor agency. In other words, they are able to make fewer large contributions instead of multiple individual grants, each of which requires processing and administrative oversight. Although the new mechanisms have been credited with raising humanitarian funding levels for NGOs, they have been an even greater boon to the UN agencies, which act as the pass-through or umbrella grantors to the NGOs—thus gaining both administrative overhead funds from the grant and an important coordinating role in the aid programming—who then do the actual implementation of aid projects. For NGOs this has meant adjusting to receiving a larger share of their humanitarian funding through UN subgrants, and in some cases coping with delays and inefficiencies that result, including the phenomenon of multiplying overheads, as the money passes through the intermediary levels, as opposed to going to the end user directly.[24] With such large sums coming from government donors, the autonomy of the recipient organization may also understandably be called into question. Similarly, political advocacy by an NGO arguably becomes problematic when the government that is being lobbied is also the organization's single largest donor, though as we will see later, many NGOs seem to have circumvented this dilemma.

In addition to friction with donor governments, there is a constant friction in the relationship between NGOs and international organizations, even as the two sides recognize their mutual dependence. There has been a decisive shift in the pattern of donor funding, from principally bilateralized aid (governments making grants to specific organizations for specific countries and purposes) and more multilateral, unrestricted funding to UN agencies' core budgets or international pooled funds such as the UN's Central Emergency Response Fund (CERF). This dynamic has kept NGOs and UN agencies in a low-level competition with each other over donor resources. Another source of tension is that UN agencies are mandated to set up operations in any and all areas of need, whereas NGOs are free to pick and choose their countries of operation. UN personnel argue that this results in too many agencies responding in situations that attract media interest, and a dearth of agencies responding to the "forgotten emergencies," leaving gaps in basic service provision.

To cope with these problems, NGOs have pushed to make their voices heard in international forums and to a considerable extent have succeeded. The aid architecture in the UN has expanded in recent years to include formal and semiformal structures for NGO participation and consultation.[25] In addition, the Security Council has on occasion invited NGO representatives to advise on matters related to ongoing humanitarian crises. Although some organizations have complained that NGO participation tends to be more symbolic than real, nevertheless the influence NGOs have had in these intergovernmental forums has grown.

In the face of these challenges associated with government funding, recent years have seen NGO efforts to diversify their resource base by taking advantage

Table 8-2. *Funding Sources of American NGOs*[a]

	FY2003		FY2006	
Organization	Income (US$ millions)	Percent from private sources	Income (US$ millions)	Percent from private sources
World Vision	686	71	944	74
CARE USA	523	25	656	23
Catholic Relief Services	484	22	562	38
Save the Children (U.S.)	241	44	355	55

Source: USAID, *Report of Voluntary Agencies,* 2003 and 2006.
a. Includes U.S. government–donated food and freight costs.

of new fund-raising technologies as well as of the emergence of significant new private donors for development, such as Bill Gates and Warren Buffett. These efforts have clearly begun to pay off, as can be seen in table 8-2, which shows the growth of the private share of support for some of the largest U.S. NGOs. These changes have also helped boost the development side of the funding equation for NGOs. The majority of development funds for the U.S.-based NGOs now derive from these private sources.

The global financial crisis that unfolded in 2008 has clearly threatened some of these gains, however, since the major private contributors to NGOs had most of their resources invested in the stock market. The crisis has also diminished the endowments and other investment assets of nonprofits. So far the NGO community has yet to experience major cutbacks in personnel or programming, but at least some downsizing appears imminent, as 2009 budgets and plans had to be revised downward to accommodate the new financial reality.[26] At least one major organization has spoken of a hiring freeze and potential layoffs to be implemented in the near future.[27]

Finally, a long-standing financing concern for all but the very largest organizations is the general lack of endowments and reserve funds. This problem is particularly acute in the area of emergency humanitarian relief, where the nature of donor-agency financing results in costly and less effective outcomes.[28] The basic dilemma is that most emergency grants are negotiated and awarded only after the onset of a disaster. NGOs wishing to respond in the critical early days and weeks of the emergency are forced to use their own funds, but most have inadequate reserves. The dearth of unrestricted advance funding has also prevented NGOS from establishing organizational preparedness capacities such as standby personnel and relief supply stockpiles. Certain partnership framework funding mechanisms do exist between NGOs and donors to provide the necessary upfront funding to overcome this dilemma, but they are few, ad hoc, and underutilized.[29] The newly rolled out CERF and CHF mechanisms have gone some way toward addressing this preparedness gap on a systemic level, but they are not a complete solution for the individual NGOs. Since the new financing mechanisms were introduced, NGOs and observers have called for donors to renew efforts to establish advance funds or framework partnerships for NGOs to draw down resources and take quick action in emergencies.[30]

For U.S.-based NGOs, government partnerships encompass not only the donor relationship with the United States government but also with the national governments in the countries of operation, and with the "international public sector," meaning the United Nations and other multilateral, regional, and subregional organizations that exist to provide what can be thought of as transnational public goods. NGOs have historically had a complex relationship with local authorities. Designed to serve the people directly at the local community level, they have long been seen by some national governments as a threat to sovereignty. At times NGOs have been accused of being covers for spies, or simply pawns for furthering the cold war agendas of their own national donors. Conversely, some governments nowadays may lean too heavily on NGOs to provide the services that governments no longer provide. Whether in socialist countries transitioning to a market economy or failing states with weak or corrupt governments, there is a global trend of weakened state capacity and political will to provide public goods.[31] NGOs have had to ask themselves whether they are providing a necessary stopgap or merely letting governments in recipient countries get a free ride with their services, creating greater dependencies on external assistance.[32] In extreme cases involving the complete collapse of central authority, such as in Somalia and Haiti, NGOs and international agencies have had to step in to form a virtually new public sector, providing everything from infrastructure maintenance to education and health care services.

Security

Staff security has become another issue of vital importance to NGOs over the past two decades. A decisive juncture came during the Somalia crisis in the early 1990s, when NGOs were forced to "militarize" themselves by traveling in armored vehicles or under the escort of heavily armed local mercenaries. (A sobering discovery made around this time was that the insurance policies that NGOs had heretofore used for their overseas staff covered only accidents and medical conditions, not "acts of war" such as sniper fire or mine explosions.) The murder of the Red Cross workers in Chechnya in 1996 was also seen as a turning point in the operational reality of relief agencies. A 2006 study on aid worker violence undertaken by the Humanitarian Policy Group revealed that the rate of violent attacks against aid workers had increased 20 percent since 1997.[33] In the ten years since 2000 over 1,700 aid workers have been the victims of armed attacks, and there have been over 700 fatalities.[34] International aid work is among the most hazardous of civilian occupations, coming in at fifth place, after such professions as loggers and fishermen. Unlike these other professions, however, much of the risk to aid workers comes in the form of intentional violence.[35]

Far from being protected by their neutral humanitarian status, aid workers have increasingly become targets for violence in conflict settings, and a growing body of literature on the "war economies" in modern-day conflicts suggests that such risks will not abate as long as there are parties to the conflict who benefit politically and economically from continued mayhem.[36] Newly globalized threats, such as that embodied by Al Qaeda, have targeted the international aid system, which is disproportionately populated by Western organizations and donor governments, and is accused of pursuing Western political agendas and cultural values. The threat is enhanced by the fact that in many remote locations aid workers represent the sole international presence and are a soft target. In addition, aid operations involve cash and resources for the taking, so that in Afghanistan, Darfur, and Somalia, the criminal element has colluded with political actors in kidnappings and armed robberies of aid workers.

These escalating risks of assassination, kidnapping, armed raids, bombing, harassment or arrest by local authorities, and road banditry have come on top of the familiar threats of robbery, rape, traffic accidents, and health dangers such as malaria and HIV. There is also risk inherent in the nature of field work in underdeveloped areas, such as dealing with large sums of cash, transporting food or other material supplies, and hiring and firing local staff.

Beginning in the mid-1990s NGOs began looking seriously at their security status, and designed field security protocols and awareness-raising events for staff. Many have hired in-house security professionals to oversee organizational training or as adjuncts to country offices. Additionally, over the past few years a growing, and highly controversial, trend has emerged in the form of NGOs' contracting with private sector security companies for protective and security consulting services.[37] Without question the level of professionalism and expertise in security matters has risen within the community, as has the sophistication of available tools. However, the NGOs walk a difficult line in their security planning and management, particularly in terms of their security coordination with other organizations. Many remain reluctant to communicate security information and concerns for fear of damaging their public image or scaring off scarce recruits.[38]

Security risk management—and the considerable costs thereof—will continue to be a critical area for NGOs. Security issues also compound the tension between voluntarism and professionalism in the humanitarian arena— the subject of the subsequent section. The informal, independent, even adventurous, image of the aid worker roughing it in dangerous conditions has not always yielded easily to the changes seen in organizations' security stances. While a few organizations have opted for a protective response to "harden the target," including in some cases the use of armed guards, armored vehicles, and the like, many others have tried very different styles of adaptation, opting instead to take an ultra-low-profile approach, where all branding is removed from offices and vehicles and programming takes place in an almost covert fashion. Still others have relied on the principle of fostering acceptance with the local community and reaching out to all actors as the best way to ensure security for their staffs. Each of the approaches and adaptations entails potential drawbacks and dangers, so in highly insecure environments NGOs are forced to weigh short- and long-term risks to their personnel against the needs of beneficiary populations.

Performance, Professionalism, and Accountability

In security management, and in most other areas of activity, international aid organizations have increasingly professionalized and formalized their operational practice, following the trend toward professionalization that characterizes the nonprofit sector as a whole. As organizations age and grow they move from a voluntaristic, do-gooder spirit to one embodying expertise and experience. Like their domestic counterparts, therefore, NGOs have in the past several years put renewed emphasis on improving the quality, integrity, and measurable outputs of their programming. These changes unfolded in response to both self-assessment and external criticism. Indeed the nonprofit international assistance community found itself exposed to a variety of often scathing accusations, which peaked in volume in the 1990s: of overdependence on large government grants; of being donor-driven as opposed to need-based in programming; of using poor accounting and evaluation practices; of lacking objective measures and quantifiable data on progress; and of under-investing in organizational learning and operations research.[39]

These critiques led to the current growing emphasis on impact measurement and evidence-based planning and analysis in international aid work. The Paris Declaration on Aid Effectiveness, of March 2, 2005, adopted by senior officials of thirty donor countries and sixty recipient countries as well as international aid agencies and the World Bank, lays out commitments by governments and their partner organizations to monitor the effectiveness of aid programs and measure progress and results against specific indicators.[40] Most large donors now insist that results-oriented program design, illustrated by logical framework matrices, be clearly demonstrated in grant proposals. Interagency working groups on evaluation share empirical methodologies and develop software and other tools for field use. Increased attention to gender dynamics, cultural and religious factors, and community participation has also characterized the evolution of relief and development programming in the past two decades. Organizations such as CARE, Oxfam, and others have adopted a "rights-based approach" to relief and development, and have developed programming frameworks that focus on food and income security at the level of the individual household, and these have had significant impact on the entire field.

On the humanitarian side, the movement to improve performance standards was kick-started after the Rwandan refugee crisis of 1994. The humanitarian efforts in the camps in Zaire (now Democratic Republic of the Congo) saw some significant achievements by aid organizations in containing a cholera outbreak and providing food and shelter to approximately 2 million refugees. At the same time, it witnessed a veritable "relief circus," with literally hundreds of NGOs scrambling for a piece of the action and competing for funds and air time, legions of inexperienced and untrained international volunteers, and several examples of unsound health practices. Leaving aside the later controversy involving the takeover of the camps by individuals responsible for the Rwandan genocide, many practitioners felt the initial response amounted to an operational and ethical failure on the part of the aid community. *The Joint Evaluation of Emergency Assistance to Rwanda,* a collaborative effort by donors, NGOs, and UN bodies to document the crisis and relief efforts, found numerous shortcomings in preparedness, coordination, and quality of services.[41] The *Joint Evaluation* spawned an interagency standardization movement to improve the quality of aid by identifying best practices. The centerpiece of this movement, the interagency Sphere Project, put forth the *Humanitarian Charter and Minimum Standards in Disaster Response.*[42] The charter concerns agency behavior and adherence to the basic principles of humanitarian assistance, and the minimum standards apply to water and sanitation, nutrition, food aid, shelter and site planning, and health services.

On a basic level, the U.S. NGO consortium InterAction established early on a set of written standards for its members—a "financial, operational and ethical code of conduct" under which its NGO members are required to self-certify each year.[43] This process is meant to encourage compliance and self-evaluation to identify areas for improvement.[44] Such standard setting has a great deal to do with "enhancing the public trust" of relief and development agencies, which has been unquestionably damaged by recent scandals exposed in the press.[45] These include the lucrative but controversial practice of child sponsorship; in 1998 a series in the *Chicago Tribune* uncovered widespread accounting discrepancies and misrepresentation to donors. Ethical objections to child sponsorship, raised both within and outside the aid community, are that it exploits children through graphic depictions of suffering and hopelessness, and panders to a paternalistic desire for gratitude on the part of the donor. Another blow to NGOs came when some agencies were charged with abetting the corporate "dumping" of expired pharmaceuticals and otherwise inappropriate aid commodities onto disaster victims. In general, gifts in kind are still a matter of intense debate among the NGO community, as many argue they are at best cost-inefficient to transport, and can displace local producers.

For NGOs accountability once meant simply telling their donors how their aid dollars were spent. This practice resulted in donor-driven projects more concerned with fulfilling donor requirements than with the actual needs and long-term benefit of the target population. Increasingly, relief and development NGOs are attempting to be equally accountable to their "customers" or "clients" in developing countries, in other words, the people they are there to assist. An independent office or ombudsman for humanitarian accountability was at one time proposed as a way to encourage NGO compliance with best practices in programming and adherence to humanitarian assistance principles.[46] The body that was ultimately established in 2003 is called the Humanitarian Accountability Partnership, whose members voluntarily commit to "meeting the highest standards of accountability and quality management."[47]

In some of their personnel concerns, the international NGOs probably do not differ much from other U.S. nonprofits. For instance, there is the eternal question of how to attract and retain qualified individuals at salary scales considerably lower than those in the private sector. Yet there are also many issues unique to internationally oriented organizations; one of them is the inherent difficulty of managing field staff from great distances. Different NGOs have struck their own balance between "supervision" and "support" in the headquarters-field relationship, depending on how centralized they require their decision-making process to be. Another problem posed by maintaining expatriate staff in overseas missions is in trying to govern aspects of a staff member's private life, which in the domestic setting would be considered strictly off limits. In the field, staff members are never truly off-duty, and must be cognizant that their public behavior and romantic relationships, and even privately expressed opinions, may have an impact on the safety or success of their mission.

A host of issues revolves around the employment of locally hired professionals and support staff. Indigenous national staffers are the backbone of NGO operations in almost every country, and in the majority of missions they now fill all the positions, or all but the most senior. The disparity between national and international staff pay scales and benefits has long been a subject of debate. On the whole, NGOs pay their national staff at levels consistent with local salary levels—those at the upper end of the scale, in order to attract skilled workers, which may be in short supply, and to remain competitive with other NGOs and UN agencies. The rationale is that paying salaries equivalent with those of international staff would skew the local economy and contribute to "brain drain" from the local public and private sectors. Yet the ethically questionable result is that a local and an international staff member may be paid vastly different salaries for doing very similar jobs. The NGO community has yet to confront this issue head on. The *NGO Field Coordination Protocol* deals with salary issues, but more with the purpose of preventing competitive outbidding of local staff among NGOs than addressing questions of equity between expatriates and locals. Health and life insurance benefits for local staff are also problematic, since many carriers that cover international staff will not offer policies for local hires, or only at prohibitive rates. NGOs have dealt with the insurance problem through a variety of jury-rigged solutions, depending on the local circumstances, including purchasing local policies if available, ad hoc arrangements with local health providers, self-insurance schemes, or, in many cases, simply not insuring their local staff at all. One proposed solution to both the salary and benefits problems is for NGOs to accept two common principles: provide all staff members performing comparable work with equal benefits and working conditions, and pay salaries set "with reference to previous earnings and the prevailing rates in the country of origin."[48] NGOs have not yet seriously explored this or other options as a matter of joint policy.

More generally, as NGOs have grown and taken on more corporate-like structures and bureaucratic procedures, a culture clash of sorts has developed between the values of voluntarism and professionalism in the relief and development community (as Lester Salamon suggests has occurred in other nonprofits, in chapter 1 of this volume). To lose the voluntarism element, some say, would be robbing the NGOs of their unique role and motivation. NGOs worry about losing their organizational soul and succumbing to the global "commercial zeitgeist," the creeping "corporatization" of culture.[49] But it could also be argued, conversely, that professionalization is not simply a by-product of the inevitable bureaucracy and standardization that accompany organizational growth, but rather a moral imperative. If NGOs are truly to be accountable to their beneficiaries, then they are ethically obligated to provide the highest-quality, most cost-effective services possible. In circumstances where promoting the voluntaristic spirit is at odds with that obligation (for instance, sending volunteers on missions where their presence will be more of a logistical burden than a value), ethics dictates that voluntarism be sacrificed in favor of a professionalized operation. In international health programming this conflict can take the form of a clash between the divergent values of *public health* (raising the overall health status of the population) on the one hand, and *medicine* (treating individual patients with the highest level of care available) on the other.[50] Certain organizations that have built their reputation and public profile on sending volunteer physicians overseas feel compelled to continue this practice, under the rationale of "promoting voluntarism." Although long-standing reputable organizations such as Médecins Sans Frontières have accomplished notable success with their partially volunteer missions, other organizations appear to exist more for the benefit of the volunteer physicians than the beneficiaries, with significant money spent on the volunteers' costly travel for short-term field missions (sometimes called "humanitarian tourism"), even in cases where the more cost-effective and ultimately more beneficial alternative would be to retain the services of local health professionals and simply provide them with the materials and pay they need.

The increased security risk to NGO personnel has also contributed to the professionalization movement. In addition to the moral responsibility that NGOs feel for the safety of their staff, and therefore insist that they be well-trained professionals, now liability issues resulting from injuries and deaths have created a legal responsibility around the issue of duty of care (the legal obligation of employers to protect employees from harm), particularly for NGOs based in the highly litigious United States.

Political Influence and Advocacy

The professionalization phenomenon, which saw the evolution of NGOs from intrepid charity workers to expert practitioners, has also affected how NGOs relate to governments, and vice versa. NGOs engage in a variety of advocacy efforts on behalf of their beneficiaries and of their own ability to gain access to and serve people in need. Vis-à-vis the U.S. government NGO advocacy ranges from public statements and lobbying of Congress to behind-the-scenes briefings and informal communications with government officials. The most important asset NGOs have to leverage in their advocacy efforts is their firsthand field-level information and contextual knowledge of the aid settings. This is particularly important in crisis contexts where security conditions often make it impossible for diplomatic personnel and other international political actors to move freely outside the capital city, and the humanitarian aid workers frequently become the eyes and ears on the ground for governments and the United Nations.[51] The power of this information, and the reputations many organizations have gained as technical experts, have given the operational assistance NGOs a measure of influence among policymakers that is well beyond that of most other international nonprofits.

Although the direct policy impact is less clear, NGOs also consider public outreach and education to be a crucial element of their advocacy efforts. This generally requires a more complex and nuanced discussion of poverty and development issues than is possible in sound bites or "tear-jerker" appeals for contributions. Avoiding the easy but exploitative ploys has become for some organizations a measure of their integrity. (One NGO has even promised on its direct mail envelopes that the reader will not be subjected to pictures of starving children within.)

Despite international criticism over the large portion of their funding that comes from U.S. government sources, and the expectation that this would inevitably hinder independence in programming and policy stance, U.S.-based NGOs have acted in concerted opposition to the U.S. government on a number of issues: the deliberate targeting of humanitarian aid to favor one side of a conflict (Sudan and Bosnia); the U.S. Export-Import Bank's lending program to African nations to support the sale of U.S.-manufactured AIDS drugs, which even at the reduced rate are much more expensive than locally produced generic products; and the use of military personnel, armed but not in uniform, to deliver humanitarian assistance in Afghanistan Provincial Reconstruction Teams.

However, there remains some confusion among U.S. NGOs as to what the law allows when it comes to advocacy and lobbying. Perhaps as a result they have been more reluctant than their domestic counterparts to expand into a greater range of advocacy activities, in particular to engage the public in policy advocacy and build constituencies for relief and development issues.

Advocacy directed at a developing country government on behalf of its own citizens is a trickier matter, for NGOs essentially operate at the pleasure of the host government or local authorities. When faced with evidence of grievous government neglect or outright human rights abuses, NGOs must decide whether to remain silent and continue to work, or to speak out and potentially jeopardize their programs and personnel. As a partial solution, many relief and development NGOs have established formal and informal partnerships with local and international human rights organizations whereby any information impugning the local government can be passed along discreetly to a local human rights organization for public action.

Challenges in Relating to Political and Military Actors

Political relationships become especially problematic for NGOs operating in conflict situations. In the camps for Rwandan refugees in Zaire from 1992 to 1994, it became increasingly evident that interspersed with innocent civilians were a large number of ex-army and militiamen responsible for perpetrating the genocidal massacres in Rwanda that preceded the overthrow of the state and the refugee exodus. The NGOs working in the camps became aware that these men were still armed and were using the camps as a safe haven to regroup and to launch periodic cross-border attacks into Rwanda. The *génocidaires* were exercising control over the other refugees who served as their human shield, terrorizing them against returning to Rwanda, redistributing the food rations, and generally dictating daily life in the camp. As acts of violence inside the camp became commonplace, the NGOs appealed to the international community to provide military protection to disarm and separate the *génocidaires* from the general population. When this was not forthcoming, the aid organizations had to decide whether their presence in the camps and their continued provision of material aid was doing more harm than good. Finally, the NGO Médecins Sans Frontières, after much internal debate, took the difficult decision to halt operations and withdraw from the camps. They were later followed by a few other large NGOs, such as the International Rescue Committee, Oxfam, and CARE. Other organizations remained, concerned that the innocents in the camps would be left helpless if they withdrew.

Such are the agonizing dilemmas that can confront NGOs providing humanitarian assistance in complex emergencies. Over the past several years much organizational soul searching has gone on in an attempt to clarify mission principles and political stances, and find ways to incorporate themes of justice and human rights in relief work.

To be sure, humanitarian organizations have always operated within a highly political environment while espousing a normative value system intended to transcend politics. The classic archetype of a relief organization, the Red Cross, projects itself as a purely neutral and apolitical agency providing impartial assistance and protection to civilian victims, with the express consent of the parties to the conflict. The International Committee for the Red Cross was officially recognized in the Geneva Conventions as a neutral organization providing impartial aid in conflicts under a protected emblem. It thus derives its mission and operating principles and status from a basis in international law.

Owing to its unique history, structure and legal status, the Red Cross is a different sort of organizational entity than an NGO. Yet at least four of the Red Cross's seven "fundamental principles" of humanitarian assistance are all seen, with varying degrees of emphasis, in the mission statements and practices of NGOs working in humanitarian assistance. Those four concepts, sometimes referred to as "core" principles of humanitarian aid, are *humanity* (prevention and relief of suffering), *neutrality* (not taking sides), *impartiality* (providing aid indiscriminately, based on need alone), and *independence* (freedom from influence of a foreign government and not pursuing a political or religious agenda). With these criteria satisfied, the reasoning once went, an agency could expect to deliver aid without interference by combatants. Naturally, any humanitarian action will in some way affect the course of conflict so cannot be said to be truly neutral, yet the banner of completely neutral apolitical humanitarianism was a convenient "fiction" that allowed NGOs to operate.[52]

The reality of modern conflict confounds these principles. Now the combatants are less likely to be opposing national armies and more often are loosely organized armed bands or paramilitaries. The belligerents flout the rules of war by deliberately targeting civilians (and occasionally aid workers), and manipulate assistance for strategic advantage or even as an end in itself. The fiction of neutrality has largely unraveled, and NGOs have been forced to rethink their position. Many organizations have adopted the "do no harm" approach, which acknowledges aid's potential for negative impacts in conflicts and seeks to minimize it, while maintaining as neutral a stance as possible. Others have abandoned the concept of neutrality altogether, adopting a stance of solidarity with the victims. This is the approach most commonly associated with organizations belonging to the "French Doctors' Movement" such as Médecins Sans Frontières and Médecins du Monde. A third or middle-way course attempts to straddle the two, in that it strives to target the root causes of conflict and to use humanitarian aid move toward peaceful outcomes, yet "resists taking sides." Indeed, at the end of the 1990s relief and development practitioners were captivated for a brief period by the idea of active "political humanitarianism," the idea that aid could be instrumental not only in recovery and peace-building efforts, but in peacemaking and conflict resolution as well. The watchword became "coherence" with the political actors, specifically the United Nations. Since then, the pendulum has swung back somewhat, and many practitioners, disillusioned with experiences in Afghanistan and Central Africa, have decided that integration with political actors requires too great a compromise of humanitarian ethics.[53] The talk is now more about "complementarity"—finding ways to coordinate effectively with political and military actors while maintaining independence and staying true to principles.

In conflict settings where there is no great power interest at stake, the NGOs, along with the humanitarian agencies of the UN, have been effectively thrown into the breach left open by the international political community, expected to function without adequate protection for their workers or the populations they serve, and are then often blamed for undesirable outcomes. NGOs have come to the reluctant realization that their options are in fact severely limited, and their role in protection and peace building is essentially passive in the absence of the political will and concerted international action needed to achieve sustainable peace. Conversely, in areas considered strategically important to the United States and its allies in the fight against "global terror" in the post-9/11 era, international assistance has been overridden by political and military objectives, and NGOs must take pains to avoid being used or appearing to be used as political tools. Aid workers have also expressed concern about the U.S. military's taking on aid roles of its own, further reducing the neutral "humanitarian space" in which NGOs try to operate. The latest U.S. National Security Strategy names development assistance as one of the "three pillars" of U.S. foreign policy, along with diplomacy and defense.[54] An unwelcome (to the aid community) manifestation of this policy framework has been the increase in Department of Defense funding resources allocated for "humanitarian assistance." Although the volume of U.S. assistance funding managed by USAID has not decreased, the Defense Department's percentage of U.S. official development assistance rose from 5.6 percent in 2002 to over 20 percent in 2005.[55] In addition, NGOs are very leery about the U.S. military's new regional command being established in Africa (AFRICOM). Organizations fear that the AFRICOM's stated goals of using aid as a key tool in providing a bulwark against terrorist elements in this region will at best blur the lines between aid and military interests, and at worst will result in poorly designed and executed assistance projects.

Faith Based versus Secular Aid Traditions

One of the impacts of the Bush administration on the character of U.S. foreign aid was the emphasis it placed on religious charitable organizations, particularly evangelical Christian NGOs. By establishing the Office of Faith-Based Initiatives, which worked to strengthen religious charities, while at the same time closing down USAID's Office of Private and Voluntary Cooperation, which served to bolster small and medium-size NGOs in general, the administration provoked accusations that it was discriminating in favor of these religious NGOs. Accord, a consortium of Christian NGOs (formerly the Association of Evangelical Relief and Development Organizations, or AERDO) in 2010 had a membership of over seventy organizations (up from forty in 2006), many but not all of which are also members of the U.S. NGO consortium InterAction, and USAID reports show an increase in the number and size of grants made to these faith-based NGOs during the same period.[56]

Although religious and secular aid organizations have a long history of working well together in the field, the proselytizing mission of the evangelical movement has created tensions with the secular NGO community, which maintains as a primary principle that aid must be given to those in need regardless of religious, political, or other considerations. Although it is a far less frequent occurrence nowadays, occasionally complaints still surface about an organization that combined proselytizing with aid work in a way that placed conditions on receipt of aid by needy people. In general, the feeling among NGOs is that their objectives are better served by promoting harmony across the whole community and increasing diversity among the organizations working toward common goals. Outside of the Western secular and Judeo-Christian tradition, however, this has been difficult to achieve. For instance, InterAction recently enthusiastically welcomed the international Muslim NGO Islamic Relief as a new member, but it has found attracting significant additional representation of Islamic faith-based groups difficult.

The Likely Future Role of International Nonprofits in the Field

Against this backdrop, the uncertainty of the global economic environment at the time of this writing makes the immediate future of international nonprofit relief and development organizations hard to predict. Many fear that foreign aid funding may be among the first government budget cutbacks, and private charitable giving may suffer as well in the short term because of the economic crisis. Looking to the longer term, however, it is reasonable to expect a continuation of a few key trends.

Slowing of Growth of the NGO Sector

The growth in numbers of new NGOs, after slowing down in the 1980s and '90s, will likely slow further in the next few years.[57] Rising start-up costs and dwindling share of funding for new organizations effectively deterred any significant further expansion during the recent combination of major complex emergencies like Darfur and a massive natural disaster like the Indian Ocean tsunami. The virtual oligopoly of the dozen or so largest NGOs has solidified and accounts for an ever greater proportion of the international resources for assistance. Many major donors, such as USAID, exhibit a preference for NGOs with which they have prior working relationships and in which they have confidence. An additional barrier to entry for new NGOs may be the perception of heightened security risks to personnel in the field. Continued security challenges will necessitate a greater emphasis on professional training, and in some circumstances a more coordinated security stance.

Continued Standardization, Professionalization, and Homogenization

The tide of professionalization, performance enhancement, and coordination of operations and standards across the aid community seems likely to continue and gain strength, as NGOs increasingly feel pressured to conform to international performance standards. For smaller, younger NGOs especially, the desire for legitimacy and credibility with donors and counterparts will push them toward adherence to such norms. Although many hail this evolution as necessary and desirable, others have raised alarms that increasing homogenization threatens the vitality, innovative capacity, and flexibility for which NGOs first made their mark.

Increasing Role of the Private Sector in International Assistance

The importance of private sector actors, particularly corporations, to international assistance has surged and seems poised to grow further. Many corporations are starting their own foundations, or contributing technical or in-kind assistance to relief and development efforts. But already for years large multinationals have explored opportunities for assisting populations in the developing world, where new markets for their products are emerging or anticipated. This movement, dubbed "global corporate citizenship," brings societal needs and concern for the public good within a firm's overall business strategy.

Participating in development projects helps large firms stay attuned to local cultures and conditions as a matter of good business sense, since in many cases "the company may be multinational but its approach is multilocal."[58]

Acknowledging their lack of expertise in the area of development assistance, the corporations are partnering with UN agencies and NGOs. BP Amoco in Angola, Chevron in Kazakhstan, and many others have used such development partnerships to increase their standing with local governments, burnish their public image, and nurture growing markets. The head of AT&T's foundation, Reynold Levy, formerly the president of the International Rescue Committee, predicts, "More companies will join the early pioneers of overseas giving. To do otherwise isn't just uncharitable; it would deprive these companies of an important business asset."[59]

NGOs are approaching these new relationships thoughtfully and cautiously, with an eye toward the potential pitfalls as well as the benefits. A number of complex and strategic "cross sector alliances" have sprung up in recent years, such as those between CARE and Starbucks, and ACCION International and Citibank, where both parties identify and exploit complementarities of mission and values, with an eye to maximizing the interests of both the aid partners and aid recipients. James Austin of Harvard Business School has written about a "collaboration continuum," in which these alliances may pass through three distinct stages: the philanthropic stage (a corporation is solicited by an NGO for donations), the transactional stage (where resources are exchanged through specific activities, such as event sponsorship or cause-related marketing), and the integrative stage (there is a higher level of engagement, communication, and integration between staffs, missions, and activities.)[60] Within these multilayered relationships NGOs can use their leverage with the multinational to push for business policies and practices they deem more developmentally sound than what the corporation would otherwise pursue.

A bigger challenge for NGOs than such private-public alliances is corporate contractors' stepping into post-crisis or reconstruction settings and taking on aid functions themselves. The U.S. government's reconstruction efforts in Afghanistan and Iraq ushered in a wave of for-profit contractors operating alongside, and at times in competition with, NGOs. Corporate vendors have long been a fixture of emergency response, providing the relief commodities, equipment, and overseas transport for large and small aid agencies and doing billions of dollars' worth of business annually with UN peacekeeping operations alone.[61] However, the vast amounts of money flowing through contracts for the post-9/11 post-conflict reconstruction campaigns have taken private sector participation to a new level. For instance, in the first year of the Iraq war, the U.S. government contracted with for-profit firms to undertake reconstruction activities to the tune of more than $1 billion—in contrast to $0.3 billion slated for nonprofit grants.

Improving the Nonprofit Sector's Capacity

The Obama administration's goals and expectations for international assistance are far-reaching, even if reduced since 2008 by the recession. Among other things, NGOs and observers of international aid have decided that the time is ripe to push for major reform or replacement of the Foreign Assistance Act of 1961, the basis of the current highly fragmented U.S. aid architecture. Before Obama took office NGOs were also set to push for a doubling of foreign aid from the United States, which remains around 0.2 percent of gross national income, even though they had given up, for the time being, on the 0.7 percent of GNI target as unrealistically ambitious in terms of what the U.S. government would be willing to do. Now, given the scale of the U.S. budget deficit in the wake of the bank bailouts and the economic stimulus package, it is unclear whether this goal of doubling the percentage to around 0.4 percent is still considered realistic, or whether it will be placed on the back burner.

NGO representatives hope that political and military actors will draw the lines more clearly between the domains of assistance, politics, and soldiering, and the military will end its forays into aid delivery. NGOs would also like to see USAID's staffing increased to its level prior to Clinton era personnel cutbacks, and its director given cabinet-level status.

In terms of changes to their own organizations and community, the international assistance NGOs would do well to keep attention focused on a few key areas:

—*Evidence-based and results-driven planning, programming, and evaluation.* NGOs in all aid sectors have acknowledged they must improve their performance in the areas of needs assessment, program monitoring, and evaluation. These are performed reasonably well at the individual project level, but they are done poorly or not at all at the organization, national, and sector levels. To strengthen NGOs' capacities in this area—a goal recognized by both governments and their grantees in the Paris Declaration—the NGOs will need to work together to establish and flesh out common criteria for performance and specific indicators to measure their progress.

—*Staff care and local staff security.* Typically the most complex and dangerous NGO missions, such as Darfur, are staffed primarily by younger, less-experienced personnel. The senior international NGO staffers have earned the right to choose non-hardship posts, and the more junior hires have an interest in paying their dues to move up the ladder. Unfortunately this situation is inherently prone to mishaps, high turnover, and a good deal of staff stress and burnout. Career-pathing and staff-care initiatives are needed to ensure that personnel with the right skills and experience are matched to the challenges of the particular mission, and that staff are given the appropriate support (including generous rest and recreation). Preventing staff turnover by making appropriate staff assignments, and offering incentives for seasoned staff to accept the hardship assignments (increased pay, frequent home leave allowance, and so on)—although it may add to costs in the short term—is more cost-effective to the organizations in the long run if staff can operate safely and effectively in difficult environments. The threats to and risk factors facing local, national staff must be more carefully assessed and care taken to give these personnel security resources comparable to those of international staff. The 2006 operational security study cited earlier found that national staff were suffering higher rates of casualties as organizations withdrew or evacuated their internationals and left local staff and partners to run aid programs in highly insecure environments, often on the mistaken assumption that nationals were inherently less vulnerable than internationals.[62]

—*Long-term, strategic devolution of responsibility to local actors.* As a long-term goal, the future of the international system for relief and development lies not with the NGO sector of the advanced, industrialized countries of the global North, which for the moment has maximized its capacity for growth (though not for effectiveness and quality), but rather with the global South. Nationalization or localization of relief and development assistance has been happening piecemeal throughout the NGO sector. Whether this is done through training individual professionals, mentoring existing local organizations, or spinning off former country offices into independent NGOs, the goal is to transfer responsibility and "ownership" of the assistance from international agencies to local authorities and organizations. The larger organizations, such as CARE and World Vision, have made the greatest progress in this area, which has occurred mostly in the context of development activities as opposed to emergency assistance; in the latter area building local capacity receives a great deal more lip service than actual action and resources. Investment is key to such devolution. Successful devolution will not happen by itself, but requires the leap from reactive action to long-term strategic planning and capacity building.

Indeed, scarce resources and inefficient funding arrangements make serious long-term planning practically impossible for all but the most well-endowed NGOs. However, if these organizations genuinely support the idea of a lower-cost, locally based response capacity, they need to adopt a forward-looking, proactive approach. A fundamental first step is the realignment of the governance structures so that the organization may draw on diverse national, as well as regional and global, perspectives.

Conclusions

The past decade has been by turns elevating, solidifying, and humbling for the international assistance NGOs. David Rieff and other observers of the field have alluded to the "hubris" of humanitarian practitioners, who refuse to recognize the limitations of their organizations in the face of the tremendously complicated situations in which they now operate. More realistic expectations of the proper roles and potential impact of NGOs are required of both policymakers and the NGOs themselves. This is especially true in complex emergencies, where humanitarian action without political action has proved ineffectual at best, disastrous at worst.

Fortunately, international relief and development has always been a highly introspective and self-critical field, with its NGO members capable of innovative and adaptable response to new challenges. And unfortunately, the persistence of poverty and violent conflict in the developing world means there is no shortage of opportunities for experiential learning and operations research at the field level. Indeed, the most far-reaching analyses of the issues of relief and development assistance tend to emanate from individuals directly involved in its implementation. The world of well-meaning amateurs has given way to an epistemic community of well-trained professionals. Gone, too, is the old model of relief and development as charity from the global North to recipients in the South. Development and, to a lesser degree, relief assistance is being increasingly devolved—though arguably not fast enough—into global networks of international affiliates and locally based capacities.

Notes

1. Vernon Ruttan, *United States Development Assistance Policy: The Domestic Politics of Foreign Economic Aid* (Johns Hopkins University Press, 1996), pp. 476–77.

2. Marc Lindenberg and J. Patrick Dobel, "The Challenges of Globalization for Northern International Relief and Development NGOs," *Nonprofit and Voluntary Sector Quarterly* 28, no. 4 (1999): 4–24.

3. Kofi Annan, *Facing the Humanitarian Challenge: Towards a Culture of Prevention* (New York: UN Department of Public Information, 1999), p. 2.

4. Taylor Seybolt "Major Armed Conflicts," in *SIPRI Yearbook 2000: Armaments, Disarmament and International Security* (Oxford University Press and Stockholm International Peace Research Institute, 2000).

5. For specific figures, see data available at Centre for Research on Epidemiology of Disasters, International Disaster Database (www.emdat.be/database).

6. Security Council resolutions 688 and 794, pertaining to humanitarian intervention in northern Iraq and Somalia, have been seen as precedent-setting decisions, essentially eroding the principle of nonintervention in sovereign states in the interest of humanitarianism and human rights.

7. Marc Lindenberg, "Declining State Capacity, Voluntarism, and the Globalization of the Not-for-Profit Sector," *Nonprofit and Voluntary Sector Quarterly* 28, no. 4 (1999): 147–67.

8. USAID, "Private Voluntary Organizations" (www.pvo.net/usaid); USAID, *Report of Voluntary Agencies* (VOLAG reports), 2000–08; Thomas Dichter, "Globalization and Its Effects on NGOs: Efflorescence or a Blurring of Roles and Relevance?" *Nonprofit and Voluntary Sector Quarterly* 28, no. 4 (1999): 40.

9. Organization for Economic Cooperation and Development, International Development Assistance Committee (OECD-DAC), development statistics (www.oecd.org/dac/stats); USAID, *2008 VOLAG: Report of Voluntary Agencies* (http://pdf.usaid.gov/pdf_docs/PNADN444.pdf).

10. Janet Salm, "Coping with Globalization: A Profile of the Northern NGO Sector," *Nonprofit and Voluntary Sector Quarterly* 28, no. 4 (1999): 83–103.

11. For instance the Grameen Bank, established in the late 1970s as a microcredit program for the poorest of the poor, is now the largest rural lending institution in Bangladesh, with more than 7.6 million loan recipients, primarily women.

12. Shepard Forman and Stewart Patrick, eds., *Good Intentions: Pledges of Aid in Post-Conflict Recovery* (Boulder: Lynne Rienner, 2000).

13. Shepard Forman, Stewart Patrick, and Dirk Salomons, *Recovering from Conflict: Strategy for an International Response* (New York University, Center on International Cooperation, 2000).

14. Linda Poteat, senior program manager for disaster response at InterAction, author interview, December 18, 2008.

15. See Nicholas Leader, "The Politics of Principle: The Principles of Humanitarian Action in Practice," report prepared for the Overseas Development Institute's Humanitarian Policy Group (London: ODI, March 2000). The report cites examples of NGO cooperation around principles of engagement, including the Code of Conduct for the International Red Cross and Red Crescent Movement and NGOs in Disaster Relief (1992), the Principles and Protocols of Humanitarian Operation (Liberia, 1995), and the Agreement on Ground Rules in South Sudan (1994).

16. Abby Stoddard, *Humanitarian Alert: NGO Information and Its Impact on US Foreign Policy* (Bloomfield, Conn.: Kumarian Press, 2006), p. ix.

17. Lindenberg, "Declining State Capacity, Voluntarism, and the Globalization of the Not-for-Profit Sector."

18. Security Council Resolution 1674, April 28, 2006.

19. U.S. Department of State and U.S. Agency for International Development, *Security, Democracy, Prosperity: Strategic Plan Fiscal Years 2004–2009, Aligning Diplomacy and Development Assistance* (Washington:, 2003); Secretary of State Colin Powell, "Remarks to the National Foreign Policy Conference for Leaders of Nongovernmental Organizations," Loy Henderson Conference Room, U.S. Department of State, Washington, October 26, 2001.

20. OECD, Development Co-operation Directorate (DCD-DAC), "Aid Statistics" (www.oecd.org/dac/stats)..

21. U.S.-based NGOs registered with USAID received $2.6 billion in USAID grants, contracts, and material assistance, and $5.2 billion in grants from other U.S. government agencies as well as other governments and international organizations. See USAID, "2008 Report of Voluntary Agencies" http://pdf.usaid.gov/pdf_docs/PNADN444.pdf).

22. Ibid.

23. OECD, Development Co-operation Directorate (DCD-DAC), "Aid Statistics."

24. Abby Stoddard, "International Humanitarian Financing: Review and Comparative Assessment of Instruments," final report of a study for the Good Humanitarian Donorship initiative, commissioned by the Office of U.S. Foreign Disaster Assistance (Washington: Humanitarian Outcomes, July 2008).

25. NGOs are represented by their major U.S. and European consortia as well as individually in UN-based networks such as the Inter-Agency Standing Committee (IASC) on humanitarian affairs.

26. Sylvain Browa, director of global partnerships at InterAction, and Michael Rewald, vice president for global support and partnership at CARE, interviewed by author, December 2008.

27. Ibid.

28. Lester Salamon and Associates, "The Preparedness Challenge in Humanitarian Assistance," unpublished background paper prepared for the Center on International Cooperation, New York University, 1999 (www.nyu.edu/pages/cic/projects/humanassist/publication.html).

29. Examples include prearranged rapid-response consortia such as the Indefinite Quantities Contract signed between the Office of U.S. Foreign Disaster Assistance and the NGOs CARE, International Medical Corps, and International Rescue Committee and earmarked advance funds for emergencies such as the State Department Bureau for Population, Refugees and Migration's memorandum of Understanding with IRC. Salamon and Associates, "Preparedness Challenge."

30. The NGO position was put forward in a variety of forums and organizational statements, and is encapsulated in the Inter-Agency Standing Committee, "Discussion Paper on Ways Forward on Humanitarian Financing," IASC 72nd Working Group Meeting, Rome, November 21–28, 2008.

31. Lindenberg and Dobel, "Challenges of Globalization for Northern International Relief and Development NGOs."

32. Alex de Waal, *Famine Crimes: Politics and the Disaster Relief Industry in Africa* (Indiana University Press, 1997).

33. Abby Stoddard, Adele Harmer, and Katherine Haver, *Providing Aid in Insecure Environments: Trends in Policy and Operations* (London: Overseas Development Institute, Humanitarian Policy Group, September 2006).

34. Humanitarian Outcomes, *Aid Worker Security Database,* "AWSD Summary Table of Incidents as of 17 Sep 2010" (www.aidworkersecurity.org/resources/AWSDsummarytable ofincidents17Sep2010.pdf).

35. Stoddard, Harmer, and Haver, *Providing Aid in Insecure Environments,* p. 4.

36. See Mats Berdal and David Keen, "Violence and Economic Agendas in Civil Wars," *Millennium* 26, 3, 1997: 715–818; William Reno, *Warlord Politics and African States* (Boulder, Colo.: Lynne Rienner, 1998).

37. Abby Stoddard, Adele Harmer and Victoria DiDomenico, "The Use of Private Security Providers and Services in Humanitarian Operations," HPG Policy Brief 33 (London: Overseas Development Institute, Humanitarian Policy Group, September 2008).

38. Koenraad Van Brabant, "Security Training: Where Are We Now?" report (London: Overseas Development Institute, 1999).

39. Michael Edwards and David Hulme, *Making a Difference—NGOs and Development in a Changing World* (London: Earthscan, 1992).

40. OECD, "Paris Declaration on Aid Effectiveness: Ownership, Harmonisation, Alignment, Results and Mutual Accountability," endorsed at the High Level Forum, Paris, February 28–March 2, 2005 (www.oecd.org/dataoecd/11/41/34428351.pdf).

41. Steering Committee of the Joint Evaluation of Emergency Assistance to Rwanda, *The International Response to Conflict and Genocide Lessons from the Rwanda Experience* (London: Overseas Development Institute, 1996) (www.reliefweb.int/library/nordic/index.html).

42. For more on the Sphere Project, see Sphere Project, *Humanitarian Charter and Minimum Standards in Disaster Response* (London: Oxfam Publishing, 2000).The Sphere Project was a collaboration of the major umbrella groups of aid organizations in Europe and the

United States, including the Steering Committee for Humanitarian Response, InterAction, VOICE, the International Committee of the Red Cross, the Red Crescent Movement, and the International Council of Voluntary Agencies. Phase I of the project culminated in the publication of "Humanitarian Charter and Minimum Standards in Disaster Response." The minimum standards cover the areas of water and sanitation, nutrition, food aid, shelter and site planning, and health services. The charter calls for agencies to adhere to humanitarian principles such as those embodied in International Humanitarian Law, and reaffirms their commitment to International Federation of the Red Cross and Red Crescent Movements and the ICRC, "Code of Conduct for the International Red Cross and Red Crescent Movement in NGOs in Disaster Relief" (Geneva: 1994) (www.ifrc.org/Docs/idrl/I259EN.pdf).

43. See InterAction, "PVO [private voluntary organizations] Standards" (www.gdrc.org/ngo/pvo-stand.html).

44. Barkley Calkins, "Improving InterAction's PVO Standards through the Pursuit of Excellence," *Monday Developments* 18, no. 19 (2000): 4.

45. Ibid.

46. Humanitarian Ombudsman Project, "An Ombudsman for Humanitarian Assistance?" *Disasters* 23, no. 2 (June 1999): 115–24.

47. For more information on the Humanitarian Accountability Partnership (HAP International) see their website (www.hapinternational.org/default.aspx).

48. Dirk Salomons, "Building Regional and National Capacities for Leadership in Humanitarian Assistance" (New York University, Center on International Cooperation, 1999) (www.nyu.edu/pages/cic/projects/humanassist/publication.html).

49. Dichter, "Globalization and Its Effects on NGOs," p. 52.

50. Bradford Gray, "World Blindness and the Medical Profession: Conflicting Medical Cultures and the Ethical Dilemmas of Helping," *Milbank Quarterly* 70, no. 3 (1992): 535–56.

51. Abby Stoddard, *Humanitarian Alert: NGO Information and US Foreign Policy* (Bloomfield, Conn.: Kumarian Press, 2006).

52. Leader, *Politics of Principle.*

53. Paula R. Newberg, "Politics at the Heart: The Architecture of Humanitarian Assistance to Afghanistan," Carnegie Paper No. 2 (Washington: Carnegie Endowment for International Peace, July 1999) (www.carnegieendowment.org/publications/index.cfm?fa=view&id=686).

54. U.S. Department of State and U.S. Agency for International Development, *Security, Democracy, Prosperity: Strategic Plan Fiscal Years 2004–2009, Aligning Diplomacy and Development Assistance* (Washington: 2003).

55. Organization for Economic Cooperation and Development, "The United States: Development Assistance Committee (DAC) Peer Review," 2006, pp. 12–13.

56. USAID, *Reports of Voluntary Agencies,* from 2000 to 2008.

57. Lindenberg, "Declining State Capacity, Voluntarism, and the Globalization of the Not-for-Profit Sector," p. 155.

58. D. Logan, and M. Tuffrey, "Striking a Balance between McStandardization and Local Autonomy," *@lliance* 5, no. 2 (2000): 6.

59. Reynold Levy, *Give and Take: A Candid Account of Corporate Philanthropy* (Allston: Harvard Business School Press, 1999), p. 187.

60. James Austin, *The Collaboration Challenge: How Nonprofits and Businesses Succeed through Strategic Alliances* (San Francisco: Jossey-Bass, 2000), pp. 20–26.

61. Ann Cooper, "To Vendors, the UN Is Just Another Customer," *Wall Street Journal,* September 26, 1997.

62. Stoddard, Harmer, and Haver, *Providing Aid in Insecure Environments.*

9

Religious Congregations

MARK CHAVES

There are more than 300,000 religious congregations—churches, synagogues, mosques, and temples—in the United States. More than 60 percent of American adults have attended a service at a religious congregation
within the past year, and about one-quarter attend services in any given week.
Although their exact manner of legal incorporation varies among states and
religious groups, congregations, like most other kinds of membership organizations, reside almost wholly within the nonprofit sector, if by nonprofit
sector we mean organizations that do not distribute surplus income to their
boards, employees, or members. And while at times they engage in commercial activities, contemporary American congregations do not span the nonprofit, for-profit, and government sectors to the same extent as other types
of organizations, such as hospitals, child-care centers, social service providers,
and schools.

Contemporary American congregations also do not span the boundary
between nonprofit and government to the same extent as congregations in other
times and places. In some other societies, religious congregations are at least
partly under the auspices of government in officially established state churches,
and this was the case here, too, at earlier points in our history. Today, however,
contemporary American congregations are voluntary membership organizations, and this fact fundamentally shapes their current situation and the nature
of the challenges facing their leaders.

362

The Diversity of Religious Congregations

Assessing the overall health of religious congregations in the United States is greatly complicated by variation among congregations.[1] One important dimension of that variation is size. Congregations and denominations define congregational "members" differently, making it difficult to meaningfully examine congregations' size in terms of official membership. The number of regular participants, whether or not those participants are official members of the congregation, provides a better picture of congregations' size. Most congregations are small: 56 percent of U.S. congregations have fewer than one hundred regular participants, counting both adults and children, and 71 percent have fewer than one hundred regularly participating adults.

The smallness of most congregations represents only half the story, however, since the size distribution of American congregations is highly skewed. There are relatively small numbers of very large congregations with sizable budgets and multiple staff, but there are many more small congregations with much more modest budgets and only one—or no—full-time staff person. This skew is such that, although most congregations are small, most people are associated with medium-to-large congregations. The median congregation has only seventy-five regular participants, but the median person is in a congregation with four hundred regular participants. Approximately half of all those who attend religious services are in only the largest 10 percent of congregations. David Horton Smith has pointed out that, like the natural universe, the nonprofit universe has much "dark matter" that is not visible through the usual lenses, which focus on the largest organizations.[2] This certainly is true of congregations.

Resource distributions are similarly skewed. The median congregation has an annual budget of only $86,000, but the median person is in a congregation with an annual budget of $280,000. Thirty-five percent of congregations, containing 12 percent of religious service attenders, have no full-time staff; 13 percent, with 5 percent of the people, have no paid staff at all. Only 29 percent of congregations have more than one full-time staff person, but two-thirds of the people are in those congregations. Clearly, congregations with no full-time staff face challenges qualitatively different from those facing congregations with several full-time staff.

Observers of American religion occasionally speculate about the amount of wealth controlled by religious organizations. Although some congregations hold very substantial endowments, the well-endowed congregation is a rarity. Only about 60 percent have any savings or reserve fund, and the median person's congregation has savings of only $20,000. Only 5 percent of congregations have endowments or savings that total at least twice their annual operating budget; only 10 percent have at least a one-year cushion. Although this might make congregations slightly more secure than most other nonprofit organizations—one analyst estimates that only 2 percent of nonprofit organizations have endowments sufficient to cover at least two years of budget—it is clear that the well-endowed religious congregation is atypical.[3] Like the income distribution, the wealth distribution among congregations is highly skewed. Some congregations hold significant wealth, but the vast majority operate on the money raised each year.

Another major source of variation among congregations is their denominational affiliation, or lack thereof. Individuals do not belong directly to denominations. They belong to congregations, most of which are attached to umbrella religious organizations, the denominations. The character of these attachments varies substantially. In some denominations, congregations are wholly independent local organizations, owning their own property, fully in charge of decisions about hiring clergy and other staff, and in no way subject to the authority of a denomination's regional or national bodies. In other denominations, congregational property is legally owned by the denomination, clergy are assigned to congregations by denominational officials, and congregational policies and practices are subject to denominational oversight. Many varieties and mixed forms exist between these two extremes, and these organizational variations can dramatically shape developments within a denomination. In the hierarchical Catholic Church, for example, revelations of the sexual abuse of children and adolescents by Catholic priests were accompanied by charges of cover-up by higher-level church authorities and lawsuits aimed at people and institutions beyond the local parish, developments that would not occur in the same way if a clergyperson in an independent congregation were accused of similar abuse. And recent debates about the acceptability of homosexual clergy are particularly acute in some denominations in part because congregations are disputing their denominations' ownership claims on congregational property. In the Episcopal Church, the conflict over homosexuality has been exacerbated further by that denomination's membership in the Worldwide Anglican Communion.

However hierarchical or nonhierarchical the relations between congregations and denominations might be, denominations are themselves complex organizations. More accurately, denominations are sets of concrete organizations tied to each other in complex and variable ways. In addition to congregations, denominations might contain regional associations of congregations, regional or national representative assemblies, colleges, seminaries, foreign missions agencies, publishing companies, clergy pension companies, social service organizations, Washington lobbying operations, church development offices, and so on. The extent to which these concrete organizations are tightly or loosely connected to one another, and to congregations, varies substantially across denominations.

Congregations relate in very different ways to different parts of their denominations. For some denominational activities, such as periodic national assemblies or conventions, congregations are both sources of delegates and (in denominations in which such assemblies exercise religious authority over congregations) recipients of directives. For other activities, such as denominational publishing houses, congregations are the primary market for the denominational agency's products or services. Although this chapter does not fully catalogue the ways in which denominations might shape the challenges facing congregations, readers should keep in mind that denominations differ in ways that are relevant to congregational life, and broad developments might have variable consequences for congregations after they filter through different denominational structures.

Table 9-1 gives, in broad categories, the distribution of American congregations' denominational affiliations. The table shows this distribution from two perspectives. The first column gives the percentage of people in congregations associated with a particular denomination. The second column gives the percentages of congregations associated with each denomination without respect to how many people are in those congregations. These two percentages differ most in the case of Roman Catholics. Twenty-eight percent of religious service attenders in the United States attend Catholic congregations, yet only 6 percent of U.S. congregations are Catholic. The difference between these two numbers reflects the fact that Catholic congregations are much larger, on average, than other congregations.

Another circumstance that can be inferred from table 9-1 is worth emphasizing: 19 percent of congregations, containing 13 percent of those who attend religious services, are formally affiliated with no denomination. If the unaffiliated congregations were all in one denomination, they would constitute the second largest in number of participants (behind only the Roman Catholic Church) and the largest in number of congregations (except for the Roman Catholic Church, table 9-1 collapses specific denominations into religious families, so this point is not immediately obvious). Although most congregations are attached to denominations, a noticeable minority of American congregations are not formally affiliated with any denomination. Some of these independent congregations even operate as sole proprietorships.

The number of independent congregations appears to be increasing. In 2006–07, 13 percent of attenders were in congregations without a denominational connection, up from 10 percent in 1998. Research on congregations in one New England city found that more recently established congregations were much more likely to be nondenominational than congregations established longer ago. Moreover, denominational affiliations are not always salient to congregations and their members even when they exist. For example, nearly two-thirds of Protestant megachurches belong to a formal national denomination,

Table 9-1. *Denominational Distribution of U.S. Congregations, 2006–07*

Denominational affiliation[a]	Percentage of attenders in congregations with listed affiliation	Percentage of congregations with listed affiliation
Roman Catholic Church	28	6
Baptist conventions and denominations	17	23
No denominational affiliation	13	19
Methodist denominations	9	9
Lutheran and Episcopal denominations	8	7
Denominations in the reformed tradition[b]	5	6
Pentecostal denominations	4	12
Other Christian denominations[c]	12	15
Jewish	2	1
Non-Christian and non-Jewish	2	2
Total	100	100

Source: National Congregations Study, 2006--07 (see note 1 in this chapter).

a. Except for the Roman Catholic Church, these categories represent multiple distinct denominations. The largest Protestant denominations are the Southern Baptist Convention, with which 11 percent of congregations and 8 percent of churchgoers are affiliated, and the United Methodist Church, with which 7 percent of congregations and 8 percent of churchgoers are affiliated. Jewish synagogues, and congregations that are neither Christian nor Jewish, are categorized as Non-Christian and Non-Jewish, respectively.

b. Includes Presbyterian, Reformed, United Church of Christ, Disciples of Christ, and Unitarian congregations.

c. This category includes congregations affiliated with denominations but not elsewhere classified in this table.

but many hide or downplay those connections. How independence from any denomination alters the challenges facing congregations, and how the increasing presence of independent congregations creates challenges for the sector as a whole, are open questions that this chapter does not attempt to answer.[4]

Although size and denomination may be the most basic ways in which congregations vary, they are not the only important sources of variation. Some congregations draw their membership mainly from the immediately surrounding neighborhoods, while others—those Nancy Ammerman calls "niche" congregations—draw certain kinds of people from all over a city.[5] Some are rural, others are urban. Congregations also vary in their ethnic, social-class, and age composition, and in many other ways.

Key Challenges for American Religious Congregations

This diversity of American religious congregations makes it difficult to generalize about them. Nevertheless, it is possible to discern some aspects of congregation life that are widely shared if by no means universal. This section attempts to assess the state of America's religious congregations, paying special attention to four key challenges: maintaining a membership base, securing adequate financial resources, recruiting talented leaders, and finding the right balance between member- and public-serving roles. These challenges demonstrate that congregations are indeed grappling with the four impulses that this volume suggests are shaping America's nonprofit sector: voluntarism, commercialism, professionalism, and civic activism. Religious congregations' reliance on members' voluntary participation and donations makes them one of the few truly voluntaristic parts of the nonprofit sector, but the challenges of maintaining a membership base and securing adequate financial resources illustrate both the limits of voluntarism and the attractions of commercial activity as a way to meet some of those challenges. The challenge of recruiting talented religious leaders and debates about the relative value of professional training versus religious zeal show that the voluntarism-professionalism tension so prevalent in other parts of the sector also extends to congregations. And the challenge of finding the right balance between member- and public-serving roles illustrates how the impulse toward civic activism plays out in congregations. None of these challenges is new for congregations—indeed, each is a perennial challenge for American religion—but they take different forms at different times. The goal of this chapter is to describe what these challenges look like today and, where possible, to say something about where they are likely to push congregations in the coming years. Let us look at each in turn.

Maintaining a Membership Base

Religious congregations are voluntary membership organizations, and their fortunes are directly affected by demographic changes that influence participation in voluntary associations in general, as well as by forces that influence religion in particular. Conventional religious belief remains very high in the United States: more than 90 percent of Americans believe in some sort of higher power, more than 60 percent have no doubts about God's existence, almost 70 percent definitely believe in heaven, and almost 60 percent definitely believe in hell.[6] Attendance at religious services also is high by world standards, though many fewer people regularly attend religious services than profess religious belief, and attendance has changed more over time than belief. There is more to religious involvement than participation in organized religion, and media reports sometimes make it appear that new and unconventional forms of religiosity are swamping more traditional practice. However, religious involvement in the United States still mainly means attending weekend worship services.

Weekly attendance at religious services has been stable since 1990, with about 27 percent of people attending services on a given weekend. At the same time, the percentage of people who *never* attend religious services, while still relatively small, has increased from 13 percent in 1990 to 22 percent in 2008.[7] Attendance declined between 1960 and 1990. According to time-use studies, weekly attendance declined from approximately 40 percent in 1965 to approximately 27 percent in 1993. Other surveys also show declining attendance over this period, especially for Catholics. Overall, then, weekly religious service attendance declined in the several decades leading up to 1990 but has remained essentially stable since then, although there are signs of an ongoing softening in attendance, including a still-increasing percentage of people who never attend, a declining percentage of children being raised by religiously active parents, and the fact that today's young people attend services at lower rates than did individuals of comparable age in earlier decades.[8]

Robert Putnam's work on civic engagement, *Bowling Alone: The Collapse and Revival of American Community,* places the post–World War II decline in religious participation in a broader context. His findings suggest that the decline in religious participation is but one part of a broader decline affecting a whole range of civic and voluntary associations that are close cousins to religious congregations. In this light, it probably is a mistake to proceed as if the membership problems facing some congregations are peculiar to religion.

Evidence also converges on an important demographic aspect of this trend: recent generations attend religious services at lower rates than did previous generations when they were the same age. Putnam found this pattern across a strikingly wide range of activities, including church attendance. More recently, Robert Wuthnow found that fewer people who were twenty-one to forty-five years old in 2000 attended services than did those in the same age demographic in the 1970s, a decline that is largely attributable to lower marriage and fertility rates among the more recently born cohort.[9] We see lower levels of participation in voluntary associations, including congregations, but not because individual people became much less involved over the past three or four decades. Rather, younger cohorts of individuals do less of this activity than older cohorts, and those born earlier are inexorably leaving the scene, being replaced by less civically engaged recent generations. Even if not a single individual changes his or her behavior over time, it still is possible for widespread social change to occur via generational turnover, and this seems to have happened with civic engagement in general, and with religious participation in particular.

There is, of course, variation in these patterns across religious groups, perhaps the most important of which is between evangelical and mainline Protestants. It is well-known that evangelical or conservative Protestant denominations have grown in recent decades while more liberal denominations have declined, and in 2006 there were twice as many individuals affiliated with conservative denominations as with theologically more liberal denominations (28 percent and 14 percent, respectively). Observers often attribute this shift to people fleeing mainline denominations for the supposedly warmer confines of evangelical churches, but recent research shows that perhaps as much as 80 percent of this shift is produced by differential fertility rather than by religious switching. In every birth cohort for which we have the relevant data, women affiliated with conservative Protestant denominations have more children than women affiliated with mainline Protestant denominations.[10]

Religious switching is relevant to the different fortunes of evangelical and mainline Protestants, but not in the way many people think. The most important trend in religious switching is that conservative denominations lose fewer people to mainline denominations than they did in previous decades, perhaps because upward social mobility no longer prompts switching from being, say, Baptist, to being Presbyterian or Episcopalian. Evangelical denominations and congregations have, with their participants, become firmly middle class. Conservative denominations also lose fewer people to secularity. Conservative Protestant denominations have been doing better than mainline and liberal denominations in recent decades, but not because many people have switched from one to the other. The main dynamic is demographic, and this fact has implications for both mainline and evangelical congregations. For mainline congregations, evangelical competitors should not be a primary concern; the main membership challenge arises from low fertility rates and increasing losses to secularity. For evangelicals, birth rates also are declining (along with the gap between their fertility and mainline fertility), and the rate at which evangelicals lose people to secularity and to religions other that Protestantism, although still lower than for the mainline congregations, is increasing. The variations described here notwithstanding, both mainline and evangelical congregations face demographic challenges to their membership base in the coming years.[11]

Although variations within American religion are interesting and important, the key point in the current context is that the growth of evangelical denominations, with their higher levels of religious participation, is not sufficient to offset mainline losses and thereby change the general picture. Compared to, say, 1955, the general picture is one in which fewer people engage weekly in religious activity, but without believing less in the supernatural, and without becoming less concerned about spirituality. This pattern is not limited to the United States. On the contrary, it characterizes many countries around the world. Although the United States has more participation in organized religion than almost all other advanced industrial societies, and although advanced industrial societies vary quite widely in their aggregate levels of religious participation and religious belief, many of these countries have experienced the same basic trends in recent decades: down on religious participation, stable on religious belief, and up on thinking about the meaning and purpose of life. (Some ex-Communist societies show increases in both participation and belief—a subject for another time.)[12]

Although cohort differences in religious participation suggest that many congregations will have smaller pools of active members in coming years, another demographic trend will push in the opposite direction. Religious participation increases with age, and so the projected aging of the American population over the coming decades is good news for congregations. It remains to be seen whether the bump in overall participation produced by an aging population will offset the downward pressure exerted by the inexorable replacement of older people by their children and grandchildren who are less likely to be married, less likely to have children, and less civically engaged.[13]

Increased immigration is another demographic development affecting the membership base of congregations. About half of religious service attenders now attend a congregation with at least some recent immigrants (up from 40 percent in 1998); 64 percent now attend a congregation with at least some Hispanics (up from 57 percent in 1998); and 50 percent now attend a congregation with at least some Asians (up from 39 percent in 1998). Recent immigrants may not be dramatically influencing the majority of congregations, but they are noticeably shaping a minority of congregations. Six percent of congregations—containing 16 percent of religious service attenders—have a worship service at which Spanish is the primary language, or the service is bilingual in Spanish and English. The growing Hispanic population in the United States is especially consequential for Catholic churches. Within the last year, one-quarter of Catholic congregations held a worship service in which Spanish was the primary language, or that was bilingual in Spanish and English. And when congregations lobby elected officials or participate in demonstrations or marches, immigration is among the most common issues they pursue, almost always on the pro-immigrant side.

Although the current immigration wave is different from the wave in the early twentieth century in that recent newcomers are more likely to be from Latin America and Asia, there is continuity in that immigrant religion remains an important vehicle both for preserving ethnic identity and for facilitating assimilation. Recent immigration also is partly responsible for increasing numbers of non-Judeo-Christians in the United States. There probably are twice as many Muslims, Buddhists, and Hindus in the United States today as there were in the 1970s. The percentage of people claiming a religion other than Christian or Jewish remains small—about 2.5 percent—but their numbers are growing.

As important as it is for American congregations, recent immigration is only one aspect of a broader globalization of American religion. American religion, of course, always has had an international aspect, from colonists who left other countries for religious reasons, to connections between American religious groups and global religious institutions, traditions, and movements, to international connections forged by missionaries. It is difficult to know whether increasing flows of people, resources, and ideas across international borders have increased religious congregations' transnational connections. Whether or not these connections are increasing, a sizable minority of American congregations make international connections beyond their affiliations with global churches and beyond the increased presence of immigrants. In 2006–07, for example, 25 percent of congregations, containing 42 percent of religious service attenders, sent a group of members to another country on a short-term trip to help people in need. One analyst estimates that American congregations donated $7 billion to relief and development work in other countries in 2006. Overall, it is safe to say that ethnic and religious pluralism, along with globalization, will continue to pose both opportunities and challenges for American religious congregations.[14]

Responding to ethnic and religious diversity is a perennial challenge for congregations. Incorporating and managing computer technologies that provide new ways to communicate with current and potential members is a new challenge. Of everything that was measured in both the 1998 and the 2006–07 waves of the National Congregations Study, a survey of a nationally representative sample of religious congregations, congregations' computer technology use was the aspect of their operations that changed the most.[15] The number of congregations with websites increased from 18 percent in 1998 to 44 percent in 2006–07. The number using e-mail to communicate with members increased from 22 percent to 60 percent. And the number using visual projection equipment in their worship services increased from 12 percent to 27 percent. These are very large increases. They imply that each year since 1998 on average another 10,000 congregations created a website. Seventy-four percent of attenders are now in congregations with websites, 79 percent are in congregations that communicate with members via e-mail, and 32 percent are in congregations using visual projection equipment in the main worship service.

Will the growth of the Internet lead people to substitute virtual religion for face-to-face involvement in congregations? It is too soon to know for sure, but perhaps televised religion offers an instructive analogy. Research from the 1980s, at the height of televangelism's popularity, showed that, except for some elderly and infirm people who would not be able to attend conventional churches anyway, religious television is watched disproportionately by people who are regular churchgoers.[16] Religious television does not tend to compete with congregations; it is better understood as a kind of entertainment that supplements congregation-based religious practice rather than replacing it. It seems likely that Internet religion will supplement rather than replace face-to-face religious involvement.

Congregations' enthusiastic embrace of new information technologies raises other questions as well. Is congregations' increasing cyber visibility changing the way people look for, assess, and choose a congregation? How do congregations decide what to emphasize about themselves on their websites? Since the profusion of congregational websites makes congregations more visible to each other as well as to current and prospective members, will congregations monitor and influence each other more? Will this increased visibility reduce diversity in congregational practice and theology? Creating and maintaining a website requires resources, whether in volunteer time, staff time, or money. How does increasing technology use affect time and money allocations within congregations? Is computer technology increasing the cost of running a congregation? Does the use of e-mail to communicate with members create a new inequality within congregations between computer-savvy younger people and less well connected elderly? In short, these technologies are diffusing rapidly across congregations, and they present congregations with new challenges as well as new opportunities to communicate with current and prospective members.

A final observation relevant to the challenge of maintaining a membership base is that American churchgoers are increasingly concentrated in the very largest churches. I noted earlier that people and resources are concentrated in the largest congregations, but that concentration began to intensify in the 1970s, and this trend continues. This intensification is evident in the increasing number of very large churches across the country, but it goes beyond the stereotypical megachurch. This concentration is occurring in every Protestant denomination on which we have data. It is occurring in large and small denominations, in conservative and liberal denominations, and in growing and declining denominations. And it is occurring because churchgoers are shifting from small and medium-sized churches into larger churches, not because the very largest churches are attracting the otherwise unchurched. The main competitive dynamic within contemporary American Protestantism, then, probably is the competition for members between very large and small to medium congregations, a competition that the very large congregations appear to be winning. This increasing concentration also has enhanced religion's visibility in American public life, a subject to which I will return.[17]

Securing Adequate Financial Resources

Religious congregations, perhaps more than other components of the nonprofit sector, have to grapple with the limits of voluntarism, especially when it comes to their dependence on members' voluntary contributions. This dependence requires congregations to provide services that their people want, and there is a sense in which part of members' donations to congregations may be understood as a payment for services rather than as an outright donation. Moreover, member contributions sometimes fall short, in which case congregations may turn to commercial activity, especially renting space to non-affiliated groups, to make ends meet.

The vast majority of congregational income comes from individual donations. Three-quarters of congregations receive at least 90 percent of their income from individual donations, and about 85 percent of all the money going to religious congregations comes from individual donations. This extreme reliance on individual donations sets congregations apart from the other types of nonprofit organizations examined in this volume, all of which rely more heavily on government grants and fee-for-service income and for which individual donations constitute only a minor source of income. This contrast arises mainly because congregations are the only membership organizations examined in this volume. Like other membership organizations, congregations are much less affected by shifts in government funding or by competition from for-profit providers than are other parts of the nonprofit sector, and they are much more affected by trends in individual giving.

A conceptual question arises here: Should individuals' monetary contributions to congregations be considered donations or dues? Jewish synagogues have explicit dues systems; Christian churches do not. But the conceptual issue is not resolved simply by saying that Jews pay dues while Christians make donations. If my "donation" to a church mainly supports activities directly beneficial to me—rituals and other events that I attend, religious education for my children, people to visit me when I am sick, an attractive setting for family weddings, and so on—how is this donation conceptually different from the dues I pay to my health club? Most congregations, of course, do more than provide services only to members, even if it is only a little more, so a monetary gift to a congregation probably should be conceptualized as part dues and part true charitable donation. The question then becomes: How much of the money given to congregations should be considered dues and how much should be considered true charitable gifts?

One approach to this question is to treat donations to congregations as true charitable gifts to the extent that a congregation spends its money in ways that benefit people other than members. Jeff Biddle, drawing on data from a variety of sources, estimated that "America's congregations spend 71 percent of their income on mutual benefit activities and 29 percent on philanthropic activities." This estimate probably overstates congregations' spending beyond their own walls. Other calculations suggest that congregations spend only between 10 and 15 percent of their income on things other than running the local congregation. But these low estimates assume that all of the money that congregations give to their denominations and other mission organizations is for charitable purposes, and they assume that none of the money that congregations spend on their own operations benefits people beyond the membership. Neither of these assumptions is accurate. Some of the money that congregations send to their denominations supports organizational infrastructure and activities aimed mainly at members, such as seminary education for future leaders, regional and national offices of a denomination, or annual meetings of the denomination. Some money spent on a congregation's local operations benefits people other than members, as when a clergyperson or other paid staff member spends time on a community project or when a community group uses a congregation's building for little or no charge. And this accounting misses other kinds of publicly beneficial action commonly taken by congregations, such as when they gather a special collection for an unbudgeted charitable purpose such as disaster relief, or when they organize members for volunteer work of various sorts. One recent attempt to take more of this activity into account concluded that congregations spent 23 percent of their annual budgets on social and community service. The most prudent conclusion given the current state of knowledge is that between 10 and 30 percent of congregational income is spent in ways that benefit nonmembers. Hence, we can conceptualize individual donations to congregations as between 70 and 90 percent dues and between 10 and 30 percent true charitable gift.[18]

Burton Weisbrod's "collectiveness index" helps us compare congregations to other organizations in this regard. This index measures the percentage of an organization's revenue that comes from contributions, gifts, and grants rather than from either sales or membership dues. The logic is that an organization is more publicly beneficial the more it benefits individuals beyond its own customers, members, or constituents, and income from contributions, gifts, and grants measures that propensity. Calculations of congregations' "collectiveness" that come out on the high side place congregations in the same vicinity as organizations primarily engaged in welfare (which score 43), advocacy (40), instruction and planning (37), and housing (31). Calculations that come out more on the low side still place congregations in the respectable company of Meals on Wheels (16), as well as organizations primarily engaged in legislative and political education (18), or education (18).[19]

Because religious congregations depend almost entirely on donations from individuals, declining participation ought to produce declining revenue. But this does not seem to be happening. Per capita religious giving among those individuals attached to congregations has increased in recent decades, outpacing inflation and producing an overall *increase* in the total amount of income received by congregations. An analysis of overall giving in twenty-five denominations finds that total giving, adjusted for inflation, increased 79 percent between 1968 and 2005. Evangelical giving is higher than mainline giving, but the trend is the same across the board. Those who remain in congregations are as generous as ever, perhaps more so, producing overall increases in the total number of dollars received by American congregations.[20]

At the same time, there is a long-term decline in the proportion of their incomes that people give to their congregations. That proportion hovered around 3 percent through the 1960s, and has declined to about 2.5 percent today. Consistent with that trend, gifts to religion also are a declining proportion of all charitable giving. Religious organizations received 49 percent of all charitable donations in the period from 1970 to 1974 but only 36 percent in 2005–09.[21] It seems that supporting religious organizations is a lower priority for Americans than it was before, even as giving to religion continues to outpace inflation.

Although total giving to congregations has outpaced inflation in recent decades, congregations have been using more and more of their income to maintain their local operations. An analysis of spending in twenty-five denominations found that the percentage of congregations' income spent on local operations rose from 79 percent in 1968 to 85 percent in 2005. In-depth studies of several denominations find similar, or more dramatic, shifts toward spending on congregations' internal operations.[22] Higher clergy salaries are part of this trend. Clergy salaries vary substantially across religious traditions, with Catholic priests the lowest paid and Jewish rabbis the highest paid. Overall, the median annual salary, in constant 1999 dollars, for full-time clergy with graduate degrees rose from $25,000 in 1976 to $40,000 in 1999, outpacing inflation.[23] It also seems likely that increases in other expenses, such as health insurance and energy, have led congregations to spend more and more simply to maintain their basic operations. In recent decades, it seems that people remaining in congregations are giving more mainly in order to meet these internal budgetary needs.

If increased giving to congregations mainly responds to the increased costs of organizational maintenance, then such increased giving should not be interpreted as an easing of financial pressure on American congregations. As mentioned, only about 60 percent of congregations have any savings, and only 10 percent have as much as a one-year cushion of monetary savings. Moreover, finances are one of the top two issues around which congregations seek help from their denominations or other outside consultants (the other is personnel). In 2006–07, 13 percent of all religious service attenders were in congregations that sought outside consulting on financial matters. Of those congregations seeking outside consulting of any sort, 22 percent sought it about financial matters. Many congregations feel financially pressured, notwithstanding the aggregate increase in overall contributions.

Financial pressure is not new for American congregations. Indeed, it would be difficult to find a moment in American religious history when there was no hand-wringing about the financial health of many congregations. Although there certainly is variation over time in the size of congregations' income streams—the 1930s, unsurprisingly, was a particularly difficult decade for congregations—the fact of financial pressure for many congregations seems to change less than the typical strategies for relieving that pressure. Pew rents, dues systems, sales of goods, investment income—not to mention, in an earlier day, public support through taxation—all, in greater or lesser degree, have been part of congregations' funding streams.

The most important source of secondary income for many congregations, after individual donations, is the sale or rent of property or space in their buildings. Although only a minority of congregations—21 percent, containing 31 percent of religious service attenders—received income from the sale or rent of buildings or property in 2006–07, this is substantially more than the number receiving income from their denominations (12 percent in 1998), from foundations (4 percent in 1998), or from government (4 percent in 2006–07). Congregations that received income from all such nondonation sources received it in amounts that are not trivial for small organizations. In 2006–07, 30 percent of congregations with income from the sale or rent of buildings or property received at least $12,000 from this source, 20 percent received at least $30,000, and 10 percent received at least $50,000 from this source. Moreover, about 40 percent of congregations receiving sale or rental income received at least 5 percent of their annual income from this source, and one-third received at least 10 percent. Although income from this source remains small for the majority of congregations, for a notable minority it is an important way to make ends meet.

Very few congregations receive income from commercial activity other than renting or selling their property or facilities, but some large congregations have launched more extensive commercial ventures. A 2007 analysis conducted by the *New York Times* of online public records of more than 1,300 megachurches found churches engaged in commercial enterprises such as shopping centers, basketball schools, property management, investment partnerships, limousine service, and food service.[24] This sort of commercial activity is much less common than congregations selling or renting property or building space, but it is a development to be watched. Because large rather than small congregations tend to engage in commercial activity, this activity sometimes occurs on a scale that can have real economic consequences for communities as well as for the sponsoring churches. This activity also raises accounting and tax issues that need to be confronted.

Recruiting Talented Leaders

Perhaps the most important challenge raised for congregations by demographic trends, financial pressures, and other long-term social change is that of attracting quality leadership. Defining "quality leadership" is, of course, difficult, and it is especially difficult for clergy because there are qualitative differences among the employers of clergy, congregations, and religious denominations, concerning the kinds of training, skills, and personal characteristics that make for high-quality congregational leaders. Some congregations and religious traditions value religious zeal in clergy more highly than their level of formal education, and there is a long-standing tension in American religion between supporters and resisters of clergy professionalization (as is the case in other parts of the nonprofit sector, made clear in this volume's introductory chapter).[25]

In some ways the clergy are more professionalized than ever. Sixty percent of clergy who lead congregations graduated from a seminary or theological school, a percentage that, according to the historian Brooks Holifield, is higher than for any previous generation of clergy since the American Revolution. At the same time, some indicators suggest a long-term continuing decline in the average talent of individuals choosing clerical careers. For example, of all individuals who take the Graduate Record Examinations (GREs), the number saying they were headed to seminary declined 20 percent between 1981 and 1987. In addition, the average verbal and analytical GRE scores of prospective seminary students declined during the 1980s, a decade in which average scores rose for all test takers. Prospective seminary students scored significantly lower than national averages on the quantitative and analytical sections of the GRE, although only male prospective master of divinity students scored lower than the national average on the verbal section of the test. More generally, the gender differences in GRE scores among prospective seminary students are substantial, with females consistently outperforming males, a fact that may be a basis for optimism, since clergy are increasingly female. In 2006, women were 31 percent of the enrollment in master of divinity programs. In some denominations one in five congregations are now led by clergywomen, although overall only 10 percent of American congregations are led by females.[26]

A similar trend is evident among both Phi Beta Kappa members and Rhodes Scholars—granted, much more select groups than all those who take GRE exams. Four percent of Phi Beta Kappa members who graduated from college in the late 1940s became clergy, a figure that dropped to 2 percent for early 1970s college graduates and to 1 percent for early 1980s college graduates. Eight percent of American Rhodes Scholars between 1904 and 1909 became clergy, dropping to 4 percent in 1955–59 and to 1 percent in 1975–77.[27]

Neither GRE scores nor career choices of Phi Beta Kappa members or Rhodes Scholars are definitive measures of trends in the average talent level of America's clergy, and many gifted individuals continue to enter the priesthood, ministry, and rabbinate. Still, it is noteworthy that all three of these measures, however imperfect, point in the same direction. More broadly, various social changes influencing the status and authority of clergy seem to have reduced the attractiveness of spending one's life leading a religious congregation, especially for recent college graduates. From 1962 to 1999, the average age of seminarians increased from 25 to 35.[28] Were it not for the entrance into seminaries of women and individuals pursuing ordained congregational leadership as a second career, finding a leader would be even more challenging for congregations than it currently is.

One consequence of the increase in second-career clergy and the decline in recent college graduates pursuing this career is the aging of those who lead congregations. The median age of sole or senior pastors increased from forty-nine in 1998 to fifty-three in 2006–07. Today, only 10 percent of American congregations are led by someone who is less than forty years old, down from 15 percent in 1998. We do not yet fully grasp the consequences for congregations of this aging of their leadership pool or, a related factor, the presence in it of increasing numbers of second-career people.

The challenge of attracting quality leadership is not shared equally by all congregations. As is the case with participation, there are major differences across religious traditions in attracting leadership. Jewish congregations—which generally pay their clergy much better than Christian congregations—appear to be least affected by this challenge.[29] The Roman Catholic Church appears most affected. In every tradition, however, the challenge of attracting quality leadership is most acute for rural congregations and for the smallest and least well-off congregations, whether rural or urban. Although only the Catholic Church is widely perceived to have a severe shortage of clergy, Protestant congregations are in fact more likely than Catholic congregations to be without full-time leadership. Thirty-eight percent of Protestant congregations (comprising 17 percent of Protestants) are without full-time religious leadership, compared with 26 percent of Catholic congregations (containing just 5 percent of Catholics).

Perhaps Protestant denominations do not perceive themselves as experiencing an acute clergy shortage because in most denominations the total number of clergy continues to exceed the total number of congregations. But many ordained clergy do not work in congregations. The United Methodist Church reported 34,397 congregations in 2005 and 45,158 total clergy, but only 24,613 clergy were serving in congregations.[30] The same pattern is evident in many Protestant denominations. In other words, although there are sufficient qualified clergy to meet the labor needs of congregations, substantial numbers of congregations are unable to attract those clergy, mainly, it is safe to say, because they are unable to provide adequate compensation or because they are located in places where many clergy prefer not to live.

The demographic changes already described probably mean that a growing number of congregations are too small to be able to employ a full-time clergyperson. This clearly is occurring in at least one major denomination, the

Evangelical Lutheran Church in America, which in 1998 had 270 more congregations with fewer than fifty attenders than it had in 1988. Consequently, the number of Lutheran congregations without pastors increased over this period from 10 percent in 1988 to 19 percent in 1998. Of the congregations in this denomination with fewer than 175 members, 38 percent had no pastor.[31] Part of the problem is a decline in absolute numbers of ordained clergy and new clergy recruits, but that decline is not sufficiently large to account wholly for the increase in congregations without a preacher. It seems likely that this kind of situation—in which the allocation of clergy is as problematic as the overall supply, and perhaps more so—characterizes other denominations as well.

Small and rural congregations long have been disadvantaged in the labor market for clergy, but this disadvantage is exacerbated by two recent developments. First, the growth of two-career families further constrains the geographic mobility of clergy, making rural congregations less attractive than they might be if meaningful employment for a spouse were not an issue. Second, the increasing number of individuals entering the ministry in midlife, as a second career, enhances labor supply problems for small and rural congregations because such individuals often require higher salaries and are less geographically mobile than younger people.

The main point here is that the challenges of attracting high-quality leadership are unequally distributed among congregations. The congregations hit hardest by demographic changes will be those crossing a threshold below which they can no longer attract the kind of leadership they would like to have. Denominations have responded to this challenge in a variety of ways, including appointing clergy to lead several small churches, developing or emphasizing ways for congregations to be led by other than fully ordained, seminary-trained clergy, and entering ecumenical agreements that make it easier for congregations in different denominations to share a clergyperson. None of these responses is likely to alter the underlying dynamics that have made full-time congregational leadership a less common career choice for recent college graduates, and some of these developments are pushing congregational leadership, if not the ordained clergy role itself, in a less professional direction. All in all, it is safe to say that the challenge of recruiting talented, professionally trained leaders will not get any easier in the coming years.

Finding the Balance between Member-Serving and Public-Serving Roles

A fourth challenge confronting congregations is to find a balance between member-serving and public-serving roles. This perennial challenge was highlighted in recent years by a movement to encourage new partnerships, including financial partnerships, between government and religious organizations doing antipoverty work. This movement's first major national success occurred in

1996 when the Personal Responsibility and Work Opportunity Reconciliation Act (PRWORA)—welfare reform, for short—required states that contract with outside organizations for the delivery of social services using funding streams established by this legislation to include religious organizations as eligible contractees. It forbade states to require that a religious organization "alter its form of internal governance" or "remove religious art, icons, scripture, or other symbols" as a condition for contracting to deliver services, and it stipulated that contracting religious organizations shall retain "control over the definition, development, practice, and expression of its religious beliefs."[32] Similar language has been included in legislation affecting other funding streams.

George W. Bush's faith-based initiative further advanced this movement. In the opening days of his administration, President Bush signed executive orders establishing offices of faith-based and community initiatives in the White House and five federal agencies, and he proposed legislation applying the PRWORA provisions to additional programs. Similar initiatives occurred at state and local levels throughout the country.[33]

Despite considerable fanfare and controversy, these initiatives broke little new ground. Religiously based nonprofit organizations, now sometimes called faith-based organizations, always have been significant players in our social welfare system, and government agencies have long funded organizations like Catholic Charities, Salvation Army, Lutheran Social Services, and many other religiously based organizations to deliver social services. The legality of government funding for this sort of religious organization was well established and not affected by PRWORA or by any subsequent policy change associated with the faith-based initiative. Well before PRWORA became law, moreover, religious social service providers wishing to maintain a religious atmosphere or religious content in their programming—and not all, perhaps not even most, religious social service providers wish to do this—commonly did so openly and with little if any interference from their government funder.[34]

Among other goals, the faith-based initiative attempted to increase the amount of government funding going to organizations such as congregations whose primary purpose is to provide religion to their members, not social services to their clients. Like government funding to religiously based social service agencies, there is nothing new about congregations receiving government support for their social service work, but only a small minority of congregations ever have sought or received such support. Had the faith-based initiative succeeded in directing meaningful amounts of public money to religious congregations, and in the process expanded their involvement in social services in general and in publicly funded human services in particular, this would have constituted a notable change in the role of religious congregations in our social welfare system.

There were reasons to be skeptical that the faith-based initiative could increase congregations' involvement in social services or collaborations with government in such work, and we now know that the skepticism was justified. The second wave of the National Congregations Study found that congregations were no more likely in 2006–07 to engage in social services, receive public funding for social service projects, or collaborate with government on social service projects than they were in 1998. Congregations are somewhat more interested in social services and in government funding than they used to be—the faith-based initiative did capture people's attention and, to some extent, their imaginations—but this initiative did not change congregational involvement in social services in any discernible way.

From one perspective, congregational involvement in social services is substantial. Virtually all do something that can be considered social service, social ministry, or human service work, and congregations report a wide variety of specific kinds of help they offer to people in need. In the 2006–07 NCS, which probed for congregations' social service activities more deeply than did the 1998 NCS, 82 percent reported some sort of activity. Congregations most commonly engage in feeding people (42 percent), home building, repair, or maintenance projects (20 percent), and clothing distribution (16 percent). Serving the homeless also is among the more common human-service activities pursued by congregations (12 percent). These broad categories encompass a wide range of specific activities and involvement levels. Congregational involvement in feeding people includes, for example, donating money to a community food bank, supplying volunteers for a meals on wheels project, organizing a food drive every Thanksgiving, operating food pantries or soup kitchens, and setting aside space for community gardens. Similar variety is evident among housing programs and programs to serve the homeless. Regarding housing, specific activities include providing volunteers to repair the homes of the needy, assisting first-time homebuyers with congregational funds, participating in neighborhood redevelopment efforts, and building affordable housing for senior citizens. By far the most common housing-related activity engaged in by congregations is participation in Habitat for Humanity projects, in which groups of volunteers build or rehabilitate an apartment or house for a low-income family. Thirty percent of the housing-related activities reported by congregations refer to Habitat for Humanity projects. Regarding serving the homeless, congregational involvement includes donating money to a neighborhood shelter, providing volunteers who prepare dinner at a shelter on a rotating basis with other congregations, and even providing shelter for homeless women and children in the congregation's building. The most common activity is providing money or volunteers to shelters administered by other organizations.

Although congregations engage in an impressive range of human-service activities, the limits of that activity also are clear. Very few congregations have programs aimed at victims of domestic violence (4 percent), immigrants or refugees (1 percent), substance abusers (3 percent), or those looking for jobs (1 percent). Only 11 percent of all congregations have a staff person devoting at least a quarter time to social service projects. The median dollar amount spent by congregations directly in support of social service programs in 2006–07 was about $1,300. This level of spending, which does not take into account the value of staff time, volunteer time, or donations to denominations, represents about 2 percent of the average congregation's total annual budget. Even volunteer involvement in social services is small-scale for most congregations, with the median active congregation involving only thirteen volunteers in these efforts. Social service activity is disproportionately engaged in by the largest congregations: the largest 10 percent of congregations account for half of all the money spent by congregations directly on social services. Most congregational involvement in social service activity occurs in collaboration with other community organizations.[35]

National and local studies of how clergy spend their time also consistently find that the most time-consuming activities for clergy are sermon preparation and worship leadership, church administration (including attending church meetings), visits with members, and education and teaching, in that order. Community and civic involvement takes up only one to two hours per week. In short, the vast majority of congregational resources are spent producing religion and maintaining the congregation itself, not providing social services to a broader community. Only a small proportion of congregations have the desire and the capacity to operate social service programs in any serious way.[36]

Most congregations focus primarily on their religious activities; the faith-based initiative hasn't changed this. The vast majority of congregations' resources support worship services, religious education, and pastoral care for their own members. Virtually all also do something that can be considered social service, social ministry, or human service work, and a small percentage do quite a lot of this, but for the vast majority of congregations such activity remains a minor and peripheral part of what they do.

In calling attention to the limits of this role, I do not mean to trivialize congregations' contributions in the human services arena. These limits notwithstanding, congregations clearly occupy an important place in our social welfare system. Two points of context should be borne in mind. First, since a small percentage of a large number equals a large number, the small percentage of congregations deeply engaged in social services translates into a rather large absolute number. There are more than 300,000 congregations in the United States. Even if only 1 percent of them are deeply engaged in social services, that represents at least 3,000 congregations. So a small percentage of actively involved congregations still adds up to a substantial amount of activity.

Second, congregations' level of social service involvement compares favorably to levels of effort observed in other organizations whose main purpose, like congregations, is something other than charity or social service. In what other set of organizations whose primary purpose is something other than charity or social service do the majority engage in at least some social service, however peripherally? In what other organizational population do as many as 42 percent somehow help to feed the hungry, 16 percent distribute clothing, 12 percent serve the homeless, or 11 percent have staff devoting at least quarter time to social service activities? What other organizations whose primary purpose is something other than social service devote, on average, more than 2 percent of their income to social services? To offer one comparison, corporations devote only 1 percent of their pretax profits to charity. In absolute terms the $14.1 billion in charitable donations given by corporations in 2009 probably amounts to more than the total amount given by congregations, but not much more. If we use the conservative estimate mentioned earlier—that beyond the 2 percent in direct cash outlays on social services, 10 percent of congregational income is spent in ways that benefit nonmembers—it would mean that $10 billion of the $101 billion given to religious organizations in 2009 benefited nonmembers. This estimate is too high since $101 billion was given to all religious organizations, not just congregations. Still, in qualitative terms, congregations' public-serving activity compares well to the charitable activity of other organizations whose main purpose is neither charity nor social service.[37]

Moreover, there is a kind of community service for which congregations are particularly, perhaps uniquely, well suited: organizing small groups of volunteers to conduct relatively well-defined tasks on a periodic basis. Examples abound: fifteen people spend several weekends renovating a house, five people cook dinner at a homeless shelter one night a week, ten young people spend two summer weeks painting a school in a poor community, ten adults spend a week doing relief and repair work in a post-hurricane city, and so on. Of congregations engaged in social service activity, 90 percent support this activity in the form of volunteer labor from the congregation. In this light, it is not an accident that the highest levels of congregational involvement occur in arenas such as food and housing that also have organizations (such as homeless shelters and Habitat for Humanity) able to take advantage of congregations' capacity to mobilize small numbers of volunteers to carry out well-defined tasks. Volunteer-based action has limits, of course, and attempts to push congregation-based volunteers beyond these limits (such as attempting to engage them in open-ended mentoring relationships with women transitioning from welfare to work) are fraught with difficulties.[38] But congregations are and will continue to be valuable partners, especially to social service organizations able to use what congregations are best able to supply: small groups of volunteers charged with tasks that are well defined and bounded in scope and time.

Politics is another arena in which congregations engage in public-serving activity. As with social services, many congregations engage in some kind of political activity, but few make it central to their identity and work. In line with congregations' distinctive way of participating in social services, mobilizing volunteers, the most common kind of political activity for congregations is offering opportunities for individual political participation (such as petition campaigns, lobbying, or demonstrating). In 2006–07, 30 percent of attenders were offered such opportunities during a worship service. The next most common political activities to which religious service attenders were exposed were registering voters (27 percent of attenders are in congregations that did this), distributing voter guides (26 percent of attenders), and organizing or participating in a demonstration or march in support of or opposition to some public policy (20 percent of attenders). Congregations participate in other political activities at lower rates: 16 percent of attenders are in congregations with a political discussion group, 15 percent are in congregations that lobbied elected officials; 12 percent and 7 percent were in congregations that had an elected government official or a political candidate, respectively, as a visiting speaker. Fifty-nine percent of attenders are in a congregation that participated in at least one of these political activities in the last year. Congregations have increased their participation level in only one of these activities since 1998: the percentage of people in congregations involved with voter registration increased from 12 percent in 1998 to 27 percent in 2006–07.

The 2006–07 survey showed that when congregations participated in demonstrations or marches or when they lobbied elected officials, the issues they most commonly addressed were abortion (29 percent of lobbying or marching congregations); war, peace, or international aid (16 percent); domestic poverty or human welfare (12 percent); gay and lesbian issues (12 percent); and immigration (9 percent). Congregations in different religious traditions tend to focus on different issues. Catholic and white evangelical Protestant churches are most active concerning abortion; black Protestants are most active on poverty and education issues; white liberal Protestant churches are most active on poverty issues and supporting gay and lesbian rights, and also on international issues; Jews and other non-Christian congregations are most active on international issues.

Although congregations are quite visibly present in political debates and conflicts on some of these issues, this visibility is produced by the actions of only a small minority of congregations. Only 14 percent of people attended a congregation that lobbied or marched to protest abortion in 2006–07. Only about 5 percent attended a congregation that lobbied or marched about international issues, domestic poverty or social welfare policies, or gay and lesbian rights. Also, congregational political action is more one-sided on some of these issues than on others. Almost all congregational demonstrating or lobbying about abortion is against abortion rights, and almost all congregational political action on immigration is pro-immigrants. Most congregational political activity on gay and lesbian issues is anti–gay rights, but the political pressure congregations try to exert on gay and lesbian issues is not as one-sided as it is on abortion and immigration: 57 percent of congregations that name this issue worked against gay rights; 36 percent worked in support of gay rights; the remaining 7 percent worked on this issue, but we could not determine which side of the issue they were on.

Many observers see American religion increasing its public presence and political influence in recent years. Religiously active people long have been more conservative generally than more secular people, and religiosity is indeed more tightly connected to political and certain kinds of social conservatism than it used to be. Looking first at political ideology, in the 1970s, 19 percent of respondents who attended religious services at least weekly said that their political views were conservative or extremely conservative, compared to 13 percent of less frequent attenders. In the first decade of the twenty-first century, 32 percent of weekly attenders said they are conservative or extremely conservative, compared to only 16 percent of less frequent attenders. Over recent decades, infrequent religious service attenders have become only slightly more politically conservative while weekly attenders have become much more conservative. The gap between these groups has widened considerably.

The picture is similar for political party identification. In the 1970s, 9 percent of weekly attenders said that they were strong Republicans, compared to 7 percent of less frequent attenders. The comparable numbers after 2000 are 19 percent and 10 percent, respectively. Weekly attenders have moved from being nearly indistinguishable from others in their political party affiliations to being nearly twice as likely as others to call themselves strong Republicans. This is a significant change over a thirty-year period.

Religiosity also has become more tightly connected to several kinds of social conservatism. The trend in thinking on abortion is particularly interesting. The General Social Survey, an ongoing national survey of American adults, asks respondents whether or not they think it should be possible for a pregnant woman to obtain a legal abortion in seven situations: if there is a strong chance of serious defect in the baby, if she is married and does not want any more children, if the woman's own health is seriously endangered by the pregnancy, if the family has very low income and cannot afford any more children, if she became pregnant as a result of rape, if she is not married and does not want to marry the man, and if the woman wants it for any reason. Opposing legal abortion in any of these situations is strongly correlated with religious service attendance, but these correlations have become stronger in recent decades for only two of these items: abortion in the case of rape and in the case of serious defect in the baby. In the 1970s, 29 percent of weekly attenders opposed legal abortion in cases of rape, compared with 12 percent of less frequent attenders. In the 2000–06 surveys, 42 percent of weekly attenders opposed legal abortion in this situation, compared with 16 percent of less frequent attenders. The trend is similar for abortion in cases of serious fetal defect. Similar to political conservatism, the attitude gap between weekly and infrequent attenders has widened substantially on these two items because more frequent church attenders have become more conservative. None of the other abortion items changes in this way, however. There is no general widening of the gap between attenders and nonattenders in those abortion attitudes. Rather, it seems that the most religiously active people have increased their attitudinal distance from the rest of the population only with respect to the two situations in which support for legal abortion in the rest of the population is greatest.

Like opposing abortion in cases of rape or serious defect, disapproval of premarital sex and homosexuality also became more tightly connected to religious service attendance in recent decades. There is, however, an important difference between these trends in views about sexuality and those about abortion. Concerning abortion-related issues, the population at large has grown somewhat more conservative since the 1970s, and the correlation with church attendance has increased because the most religious people have become especially conservative over time. Concerning sexuality issues the population is trending in a liberal direction, but the most religious people are either resisting liberalization (in the case of premarital sex), or liberalizing more slowly than others (in the case of homosexuality). In the 1970s, 53 percent of weekly religious service attenders but 23 percent of infrequent attenders said that premarital sex is always wrong; the 2000–2006 numbers are 55 percent and 17 percent, respectively. Weekly attenders are about as conservative on premarital sex today as they were in the 1970s, but less frequent attenders have become somewhat less conservative on this issue. Both frequent and infrequent attenders have become more liberal about homosexuality: 85 percent of 1970s weekly attenders said that homosexuality is always wrong compared to 67 percent of infrequent attenders, whereas since 2000 the comparable numbers are 79 percent and 50 percent, respectively. On this issue, less religiously active people have liberalized faster.[39]

In sum, the connection between frequent religious service attendance and political and social conservatism is increasingly tight. For some attitudes the connection has grown tighter because the most religiously active people have become more conservative over time. For other attitudes the connection has grown tighter because the most religiously active people are liberalizing more slowly than others. I do not believe that these trends amount to an increasingly divisive culture war. In a group of one hundred regular churchgoers, thirty-two are politically conservative and seventy-nine believe that homosexuality is always wrong, whereas in a group of one hundred nonattenders, sixteen are politically conservative and fifty believe that homosexuality is always wrong. These are real differences, but most people in both groups consider themselves politically moderate, liberal, or only slightly conservative, and most (or nearly most) people in both groups still believe that homosexuality is always wrong. Recall also that when it comes to attitudes about homosexuality, both groups are trending in the liberal direction. The increasingly tight connection between religiosity and conservative attitudes comes about only because one group is liberalizing faster than the other, not because the groups are heading in opposite directions. These nuances lead me to refrain from interpreting these trends as indicating dangerously increasing polarization in American society. Still, the attitudinal distance between the most and least religiously active people in U.S. society has increased in recent decades. The public may not be more polarized on these issues than it was previously, but differences of opinion now line up with religious differences more than they did before.

The tighter connection between religiosity and political and social conservatism probably is a consequence of political conservatives' successful mobilization of religious organizations in recent decades. This mobilization has increased religion's visibility in politics at every level. Religion's social and political visibility also has been increased by another trend that I described earlier: the increasing concentration of churchgoers within very large churches. This concentration has increased religion's visibility, and possibly its social and political influence, even in the face of stable or declining religiosity among individuals. One two-thousand-person church is more visible than ten two-hundred-person churches; one two-thousand-person church presents a more attractive audience for a politician than ten two-hundred-person churches; the pastor of a two-thousand-person church gets an appointment with the mayor more easily than the pastors of two-hundred-person churches; and so on. Thus, increasing religious concentration creates the impression that more people are turning to religion when the real change is in religion's social organization. Organizational concentration can lead to real increase in the social and political influence of religious congregations and their leaders, if only because it creates more very large congregations and more leaders of very large congregations with which to contend. But we should recognize that if congregations' social and political influence has been increasing, it is because of the political mobilization of churches and because of this change in religion's social organization, not because of increases in the underlying levels of religious belief and practice in American society.

Conclusions

Congregations mainly produce religion, serve their own members, and use the vast majority of their collective resources to maintain themselves as religious organizations. Consequently, the most significant challenges facing congregations are the ones most directly relevant to their core condition as religious voluntary membership associations. Of the four impulses shaping America's nonprofit sector (as outlined in chapter 1 of this volume), the challenges related to voluntarism and professionalism are most important to congregations. Reasonable people might disagree about whether religious involvement is stable or declining, but it unambiguously is not increasing. Financial stress is common among congregations, and there are troubling signs about the current state of religious leadership. All in all, it is difficult to see how these developments could be construed as good news for this component of the nonprofit sector, and it is safe to say that congregations will continue to grapple with the limits of voluntarism, and more and more congregations will struggle to adhere to the model of having a full-time leader with graduate-level professional training.

Congregations' main struggle is to maintain themselves, but almost all also engage in some kind of activity aimed at serving a wider public. Only a minority pursues such activities in a way that can be considered central to their mission, but congregations still probably promote more civic engagement and activism than any other type of membership organization. Will congregations' levels of civic engagement or activism change in the coming years? The Bush administration's faith-based initiative did not make congregations more involved in social services or more likely to collaborate with government on human service projects. If there was something distinctively different about congregations' response to human need in recent years, it was the outpouring of aid from congregations in response to the devastation caused overseas by the December 2004 earthquake and tsunami and, closer to home, Hurricane Katrina in August 2005. Congregational response to these disasters probably is behind the small uptick in 2005 in church members' giving that went toward "benevolences" rather than towards congregational maintenance (measured as a proportion of church income).[40]

Regarding civic activism, the last several decades have seen an increasingly tight connection between religious participation and political and social conservatism, but with the exception of increased congregational involvement in voter registration efforts, there is no overall increase in congregations' political activism between 1998 and 2006–07. Religious congregations remain civically and politically active on both the right and the left. We may see some shift in the specific issues on which congregations focus their political energy. I would not be surprised, for example, to see immigration and the needs of immigrants become even more prominent for congregations. But I do not expect a significant increase in congregations' overall level of political involvement. Indeed, there are some signs of a backlash in American society to the highly visible religiously based political activism of recent decades. Interestingly, the number of people who strongly agree that "religious leaders should not try to influence how people vote in elections" increased from 30 percent in 1991 to 37 percent in 1998, and the number who strongly agree that "religious leaders should not try to influence government decisions" increased from 22 percent in 1991 to 31 percent in 1998. Michael Hout and Claude Fischer connect the faster pace since 1990 of the long-term increase in the percentage of people saying that they have no religion—at 16 percent in 2006—to disenchantment with religion's increased political visibility. It appears that the American public has become somewhat less enamored of at least some kinds of explicit religious involvement in the public sphere.[41]

All things considered, impulses toward both meeting human need and civic activism will continue to challenge many congregations to reflect on the appropriate balance between their member-serving and public-serving roles, and current events will pull them into action on one or another specific activity or issue. But the balance between congregations' member- and public-serving roles that we currently see will remain fairly steady into the future.

Notes

1. Unless otherwise noted, statistics reported in this chapter are from the National Congregations Study (NCS), a survey of a nationally representative sample of religious congregations. The NCS (www.soc.duke.edu/natcong) was first conducted in 1998; a second wave was conducted in 2006–07. In each wave, a nationally representative cross-section of congregations was generated by asking respondents to a national survey of individuals to report the name and location of the religious congregation they attend, if they attend religious services. A forty-five-minute telephone survey was then done with a key informant, usually clergy or other staff, within each named congregation. The response rate was 80 percent in 1998 and 78 percent in 2006–07. For more detail about NCS methodology, see Mark Chaves and Shawna Anderson, "Continuity and Change among American Congregations: Introducing the Second Wave of the National Congregations Study," *Sociology of Religion* 69 (Winter 2008):415–40, and Mark Chaves and others, "The National Congregations Study: Background, Methods, and Selected Results," *Journal for the Scientific Study of Religion* 38 (December 1999):458–76.

2. David Horton Smith, "The Rest of the Nonprofit Sector: Grassroots Associations as the Dark Matter Ignored in Prevailing 'Flat Earth' Maps of the Sector," *Nonprofit and Voluntary Sector Quarterly* 26 (1997): 114–31.

3. On the 2 percent estimate see Evelyn Brody, "Charitable Endowments and the Democratization of Dynasty," *Arizona Law Review* 39 (Fall 1997): 873–948, n. 62.

4. Peter Dobkin Hall, "Vital Signs: Organizational Population Trends and Civic Engagement in New Haven, Connecticut, 1850–1998," in *Civic Engagement in American Democracy*,

edited by Theda Skocpol and Morris P. Fiorina (Brookings Institution and Russell Sage Foundation, 1999), pp. 211–48, especially p. 233; Scott Thumma and Dave Travis, *Beyond Megachurch Myths: What We Can Learn from America's Largest Churches* (San Francisco: Jossey-Bass, 2007), pp. 26–27.

5. Nancy Ammerman, *Congregation and Community* (Rutgers University Press, 1997).

6. These numbers are from the General Social Survey (GSS; www.norc.org/GSS+ Website), a sociological survey used to collect data on demographic characteristics and attitudes of residents of the United States. The survey is conducted face-to-face with an in-person interview by the National Opinion Research Center at the University of Chicago. See James A. Davis, Tom W. Smith, and Peter V. Marsden, *General Social Surveys, 1972–2006: Cumulative Codebook* (Chicago: National Opinion Research Center, 2007).

7. The weekly attendance number is based on time-use studies reported in Stanley Presser and Mark Chaves, "Is Religious Service Attendance Declining?" *Journal for the Scientific Study of Religion* 46 (September 2007): 417–23 (which see for more details on attendance trends since 1990). The "never attend" figures are the author's calculations, based on the General Social Survey data (see note 6).

8. On longer-term trends in time-use data, see Stanley Presser and Linda Stinson, "Data Collection Mode and Social Desirability Bias in Self-Reported Religious Attendance," *American Sociological Review* 63 (February 1998): 137–45. On trends in other survey data, see Robert D. Putnam, *Bowling Alone: The Collapse and Revival of American Community* (New York: Simon and Schuster, 2000), especially p. 71; Claude S. Fischer and Michael Hout, *Century of Difference: How America Changed in the Last One Hundred Years* (New York: Russell Sage Foundation, 2007), pp. 203–25; and Mark Chaves, *American Religion: Contemporary Trends* (Princeton University Press, 2011). For comparisons across age cohorts, see Sandra L. Hofferth and John F. Sandberg, "Changes in American Children's Time, 1981–1997," in *Children at the Millennium: Where Have We Come From, Where Are We Going? Advances in Life Course Research*, edited by Timothy Owens and Sandra Hofferth (New York: Elsevier Science, 2001), pp. 193–229; and Robert Wuthnow, *After the Baby Boomers: How Twenty- and Thirty-Somethings Are Shaping the Future of American Religion* (Princeton University Press, 2007), p. 53.

9. Wuthnow, *After the Baby Boomers*.

10. The trend numbers are the author's calculations, based on General Social Survey data (see note 6). The observation that fertility differences largely account for this trend is from Michael Hout, Andrew Greeley, and Melissa J. Wilde, "The Demographic Imperative in Religious Change in the United States," *American Journal of Sociology* 107, no. 2 (September 2001): 468–500.

11. All the empirical facts in this paragraph are from Hout, Greeley, and Wilde, "Demographic Imperative in Religious Change."

12. Ronald Inglehart and Wayne E. Baker, "Modernization, Cultural Change, and the Persistence of Traditional Values," *American Sociological Review* 65 (February 2000): 19–51; Pippa Norris and Ronald Inglehart, *Sacred and Secular: Religion and Politics Worldwide* (Cambridge University Press, 2004).

13. For additional discussion of the consequences for congregations of an aging population, see Anthony E. Healy, "Picturing the 21st Century," *Visions* 3, no. 1 (January–February 2000): 4–8.

14. The observation that immigrant religion continues to be important for both ethnic preservation and assimilation is from Fenggang Yang and Helen Rose Ebaugh, "Transformations in New Immigrant Religions and Their Implications for Global Religious Systems,"

American Sociological Review 66 (April 2001): 269–88. For more on new immigrant religion see R. Stephen Warner and Judith G. Wittner, eds., *Gatherings in Diaspora: Religious Communities and the New Immigration* (Temple University Press, 1998); Helen Rose Ebaugh and Janet Saltzman Chafetz, *Religion and the New Immigrants: Continuities and Adaptations in Immigrant Congregations* (Walnut Creek, Calif.: AltaMira Press, 2000); and Robert Wuthnow, *America and the Challenges of Religious Diversity* (Princeton University Press, 2005). For estimates of the Muslim, Buddhist, and Hindu populations in the United States, see Darren E. Sherkat, "Tracking the 'Other': Dynamics and Composition of 'Other' Religions in the General Social Survey, 1973–1996," *Journal for the Scientific Study of Religion* 38 (1999): 551–60; Tom W. Smith, "Religious Diversity in America: The Emergence of Muslims, Buddhists, Hindus, and Others," *Journal for the Scientific Study of Religion* 41 (2002): 577–85; Tom W. Smith, "The Muslim Population in the United States: The Methodology of Estimates," *Public Opinion Quarterly* 66 (2002): 404–17. For more on transnational religious connections, see Robert Wuthnow and Stephen Offutt, "Transnational Religious Connections," *Sociology of Religion* 69 (2008): 209–32. The $7 billion estimate is from David Sikkink and Stephen Armet, "Overseas Giving by U.S. Congregations," unpublished manuscript, University of Notre Dame, Department of Sociology.

15. See note 1 for more information on the National Congregations Study.

16. Steve Bruce, *Pray TV: Televangelism in America* (New York: Routledge, 1990), chapters 5 and 6.

17. For more on this increasing concentration see Mark Chaves, "All Creatures Great and Small: Megachurches in Context," *Review of Religious Research* 47 (2006): 329–46.

18. Jeff E. Biddle, "Religious Organizations," in *Who Benefits from the Nonprofit Sector?* edited by Charles T. Clotfelter (University of Chicago Press, 1992), pp. 92–133. Compare the estimates in Dean R. Hoge and others, *Money Matters: Personal Giving in American Churches* (Louisville: Westminster John Knox, 1996), p. 34, and John L. Ronsvalle and Sylvia Ronsvalle, *The State of Church Giving through 2005* (Champaign, Ill.: empty tomb, inc., 2007), p. 13. The 23 percent estimate is from Ram A. Cnaan, *The Invisible Caring Hand: American Congregations and the Provision of Welfare* (New York University Press, 2002), p. 88.

19. Burton A. Weisbrod, *The Nonprofit Economy* (Harvard University Press, 1988), pp. 76–78.

20. Ronsvalle and Ronsvalle, *State of Church Giving through 2005*, p. 17.

21. Religious giving as a percentage of income is from ibid., figure 1 (www.emptytomb.org/fig1_07.html [August 3, 2010]). Religious giving as a percentage of all giving is from the Center on Philanthropy at Indiana University, *Giving USA, 2010: The Annual Report on Philanthropy for the Year 2009* (Glenview, Ill.: Giving USA Foundation, 2010), p. 42.

22. Ronsvalle and Ronsvalle, *State of Church Giving through 2005*, p. 13. For studies of congregational spending in specific denominations see Roger J. Nemeth and Donald A. Luidens, "Congregational vs. Denominational Giving: An Analysis of Giving Patterns in the Presbyterian Church in the United States and the Reformed Church in America," *Review of Religious Research* 36 (1994): 111–22; D. Scott Cormode, "A Financial History of Presbyterian Congregations since World War II," in *The Organizational Revolution: Presbyterians and American Denominationalism*, edited by Milton J. Coalter, John M. Mulder, and Louis B. Weeks (Louisville: Westminster John Knox, 1992), pp. 171–98; United Church Board for Homeland Ministries, *The State of the UCC, 1997* (Cleveland: 1997).

23. The facts about clergy salaries are from Jackson W. Carroll, *God's Potters: Pastoral Leadership and the Shaping of Congregations* (Grand Rapids, Mich.: Eerdmans, 2006), pp. 88–94. Carroll draws mainly on Becky R. McMillan and Matthew J. Price, "How Much Should We

Pay Our Pastor? A Fresh Look at Clergy Salaries in the 21st Century," research report (Durham, N.C.: Duke Divinity School, Pulpit & Pew, 2003).

24. Diana B. Henriques and Andrew W. Lehren, "Megachurches Add Local Economy to Mission," *New York Times*, November 23, 2007, p. A1.

25. For more on tension over the professionalization of clergy, see Carroll, *God's Potters*, pp. 19–21, and E. Brooks Holifield, *God's Ambassadors: A History of the Christian Clergy in America* (Grand Rapids, Mich.: Eerdmans, 2007).

26. Holifield, *God's Ambassadors*, p. 332. The GRE results are from Jerilee Grandy and Mark Greiner, "Academic Preparation of Master of Divinity Candidates," ETS Occasional Report (Princeton, N.J.: Educational Testing Service, Fall 1990). The percentage of female seminarians is from the Association of Theological Schools, *Fact Book on Theological Education* (Pittsburgh: Association of Theological Schools, 2007). The percentage of churches led by clergywomen in 2006 is 22.5 in the Evangelical Lutheran Church in America, 22.8 in the United Methodist Church, and 20.6 in the Presbyterian Church–USA. These numbers are from personal correspondence with Kenneth Inskeep, of the Evangelical Lutheran Church in America, Scott Brewer, of the United Methodist Church, and Jack Marcum, of the Presbyterian Church (U.S.A.).

27. The Phi Beta Kappa data are from Howard R. Bowen and Jack H. Schuster, *American Professors: A National Resource Imperiled* (Oxford University Press, 1986). The Rhodes Scholar data are the author's calculations using *A Register of Rhodes Scholars, 1903–1981* (Oxford: Alden Press, 1981).

28. Carroll, *God's Potters*, pp. 72–73.

29. Anthony Ruger and Barbara G. Wheeler, *Manna from Heaven? Theological and Rabbinical Student Debt*, Auburn Studies 3 (New York: Auburn Theological Seminary, 1995), p. 5.

30. Eileen W. Lindner, ed., *Yearbook of American and Canadian Churches, 2008* (Nashville: Abingdon, 2008).

31. Evangelical Lutheran Church in America, Division for Ministry, *Ministry Needs and Resources in the 21st Century* (Chicago: 2000).

32. *A Guide to Charitable Choice: The Rules of Section 104 of the 1996 Federal Welfare Law Governing State Cooperation with Faith-Based Social-Service Providers* (Washington and Annandale, Va.: Center for Public Justice and Christian Legal Society's Center for Law and Religious Freedom, 1997), pp. 28–29.

33. For more on the faith-based initiative's history, implementation, and consequences see Derek Davis and Barry Hankins, eds., *Welfare Reform and Faith-Based Organizations* (Baylor University, J. M. Dawson Institute on Church-State Studies, 1999); Ram A. Cnaan, *The Newer Deal: Social Work and Religion in Partnership* (Columbia University Press, 1999); Bob Wineburg, *Faith-Based Inefficiency: The Follies of Bush's Initiatives* (Westport, Conn.: Praeger, 2007); David Kuo, *Tempting Faith: An Inside Story of Political Seduction* (New York: Free Press, 2007); Rebecca Sager, *Faith, Politics, and Power: The Politics of Faith-Based Initiatives* (Oxford University Press, 2010).

34. Stephen Monsma surveyed international aid agencies and child-service agencies in 1993–94. For organizations that both received government funding and reported that they engaged in religious practices, the majority of religious practices that they engage in—62 percent for the international aid agencies and 77 percent for the child-service agencies—were done openly. Only 11 percent of religiously affiliated, government-funded child-service agencies reported having to curtail religious activities, and only 22 percent of publicly funded international religious aid agencies reported experiencing any sort of pressure or problem about their religious activities. Most, perhaps all, of the activities about which problems were

reported, such as requiring attendance at religious services, are the kind of sectarian worship, instruction, or proselytizing activities that are prohibited even by the legislative and executive actions associated with the faith-based initiative. See Stephen Monsma, *When Sacred and Secular Mix: Religious Nonprofit Organizations and Public Money* (Lanham, Md.: Rowman and Littlefield, 1996).

35. The 2006–07 wave of the National Congregations Study probed more deeply about congregations' social service activities than did the 1998 NCS. Consequently, more congregations reported some sort of activity in 2006–07 than in 1998, and I report those larger numbers here. However, when responses to the 2006–07 questions are analyzed in a way that makes them comparable to responses to the less probing 1998 questions, we see that this activity has not increased since 1998.

36. On clergy's use of time, see Carroll, *God's Potters*, p. 102; Barbara Brown Zikmund, Adair T. Lummis, and Patricia Mei Yin Chang, *Clergy Women: An Uphill Calling* (Louisville: Westminster John Knox, 1998); and Sandi Brunette-Hill and Roger Finke, "A Time for Every Purpose: Updating and Extending Blizzard's Survey on Clergy Time Allocation," *Review of Religious Research* 41 (1999): 47–63.

37. The facts about corporate giving and the total amount of giving to religion in 2009 are from Center on Philanthropy at Indiana University, *Giving USA 2010*, pp. 4, 6, 32.

38. For a case study illustrating the limits of open-ended volunteering, see Paul Lichterman, *Elusive Togetherness: Religious Groups and Civic Engagement in America* (Princeton University Press, 2004), ch. 5.

39. All of the numbers reported in the previous four paragraphs are my calculations, based on the General Social Survey, combining the 1970s surveys and the 2000 to 2006 surveys (see note 6).

40. Ronsvalle and Ronsvalle, *State of Church Giving through 2005*, p. 16. This is only the second annual increase in this number since 1968.

41. The numbers in this paragraph are my calculations based on the General Social Survey (see note 6); Fischer and Hout, *Century of Difference*, pp. 193–94; Michael Hout and Claude S. Fischer, "Why More Americans Have No Religious Preference: Politics and Generations," *American Sociological Review* 67 (2002): 165–90.

10

Civic Participation and Advocacy

ELIZABETH T. BORIS AND MATTHEW MARONICK

A merican democracy draws its strength and legitimacy from the participation of its citizens in the governance of the nation. Constitutionally guaranteed freedoms of speech and association ensure that citizens can participate in democratic governance. Participation can be direct, by voting and petitioning public officials, and indirect, through associations that advocate for individual, group, business, and public concerns. Nonprofit advocacy for and against public policies directed toward elected officials, government agencies, and the courts is a long-standing American tradition. It is a vital instrument of pluralism and a cornerstone of this country's representative democracy.

Nonprofits mediate civic participation by providing structures and networks, both face-to-face and online, which enable individuals to participate in civic life as volunteers, members, activists, board members, and donors. Through associations, people interact and build organizational skills and self-confidence. They create networks of trust and affiliation—social capital—that allow individuals to work together to solve community problems, promote causes, and seek redress or change through the policy process.

Associations mobilize information to educate and inform the public on a host of issues, both to influence attitudes and to change behavior. Nonprofits

We are grateful for Petya Kehayova and Katie Roeger's programming and number crunching, and for Dan Oran's editing.

may represent interests and values in the political system by lobbying Congress or litigating in the courts, for example, for or against gun control or stem-cell research. Some organizations promote civic engagement in nonpartisan get-out-the-vote activities; others conduct partisan efforts to influence elections. Nonprofits also lobby for and against laws that affect their status and for government resources to serve their constituents. All of these activities are aspects of nonprofit advocacy.

The current status of civic participation and nonprofit advocacy is the topic of this chapter. Since the last edition of this book, Internet activism has fundamentally altered both civic participation and advocacy. The Internet has emerged as a potent force for engaging millions of people in causes and in civic affairs. Social media, blogs, and chat rooms have added interactivity to electronic advocacy communications. People share ideas, mobilize around a cause, and create communities of interest. There has been a corresponding change in the ways that many nonprofit organizations conduct their outreach and educational activities and promote individual and collective activism. Channeling the energy and idealism reflected in decentralized online efforts into effective action is a major challenge for nonprofit advocates. The explosion of Internet activism for diverse causes, coupled with the civic engagement evident in the 2004 and 2008 presidential elections, compels reexamination of the concerns raised by Robert Putnam and others about the implications for democracy of declining civic participation and voting rates.[1] During the 2004 presidential campaign it became apparent that the Internet was potentially a powerful new tool used by nonprofit advocates and political campaigns to engage people in civic and political activities. What remained to be seen was whether Internet outreach could successfully motivate a broad cross-section of Americans to participate in partisan and nonpartisan electoral and campaign activities and, ultimately, to vote. The presidential campaign of 2008 and the Tea Party movement initiated in 2009—have settled that debate. Individuals have been mobilized online to take concrete action offline. The question now is whether those activists will maintain some level of civic participation. Will the new media continue to induce people to participate in pluralistic democracy? To what extent will nonprofits use these new media to engage people in public-benefit activities? This chapter provides an overview of civic participation facilitated by nonprofit organizations and their public-interest advocacy activities with special sections on civil rights and antipoverty. The major focus of the chapter is on public charities, the largest group of nonprofits. Both public charities and private foundations are classified by the Internal Revenue Service (IRS) as 501(c)(3) organizations eligible to receive tax-deductible contributions. We will also examine advocacy activities of 501(c)(4) social welfare organizations, which are not eligible for tax-deductible contributions.

Civic Participation

"Civic participation" refers to activities by individuals who attempt to affect governance at a variety of levels. Voting is the critical act of civic participation, but individuals and organizations participate in many other ways, from non-partisan petitioning for better government services and passage of legislation to political activities such as campaigning for candidates and running for public office (although partisan activities are limited to certain types of nonprofits). Voluntary organizations often activate and mediate civic participation both directly and indirectly. Through participation in such groups, people "learn grassroots skills and build relationships in community, religious, and workplace associations in ways that are transferable to politics."[2]

Many types of nonprofits facilitate civic participation with the goal of strengthening democracy, and they do so in a variety of ways. Traditional civic membership groups such as the League of Women Voters, Parent Teacher Associations, Jaycees, and Kiwanis, have active members who work on "good government" and policy initiatives to strengthen, for example, local school funding. Civil rights groups such as the National Association for the Advancement of Colored People (NAACP), the National Puerto Rican Coalition (NPRC), the National Council of La Raza, and the Urban League often mobilize their members to vote, attend community meetings, and monitor political activities. Organizations that serve immigrants provide training for citizenship tests and encourage new Americans to vote and become involved in community affairs. The paradigm is shifting from civic participation mediated mostly by the large structured membership organizations to participation mediated by a wider variety of organizations, many set up for that purpose, and by information networks, coalitions of organizations, and individuals who blog their ideas to the world. A plethora of new organizations describe their activities as strengthening democracy by promoting voting, civic participation, and community problem solving. Some groups, such as America Speaks, Everyday Democracy and Kids Voting USA, involve youth and underserved populations in democratic governance by encouraging them to vote. They organize citizen campaigns and support research projects connected with civic engagement.

Promoting national service is another facet of the civic engagement movement. This movement focuses on volunteer service, but also has a change component and a strong civic responsibility component. Groups may support a national movement to get all youths involved in service activities, advocate to strengthen service programs and funding of the Corporation for National and Community Service, and conduct and disseminate research.

The 2008 national election marked the coming of age of electronic civic participation and political organizing. Nonprofits of every description engaged in voter education and joined coalitions to get out the vote. They worked with political parties and many other organizations and coalitions to provide information, assist with voter registration, drive people to the polls, monitor vote counts and recounts, check out complaints, and much more. Thousands of individuals gave money online and volunteered. Turnout increased and higher numbers of youths, African Americans, and Latinos participated in the ultimate civic act, voting, than in recent presidential elections.[3] Members of another strand of online activism sought to ensure a fair and unbiased election by closely monitoring voting machines and attempts to disenfranchise particular groups. Those in a third strand analyzed and communicated policy pronouncements. The nonpartisan Urban Institute–Brookings Institution Tax Policy Center, for example, posted almost daily estimates of the costs of various candidates' tax proposals at its website (www.taxpolicycenter.org).

Information was decentralized and civic action was democratized. Individuals and organizations from across the ideological spectrum communicated at will, empowered by the low cost and high satisfaction of participating in the political dialogue. Small organizations and individuals had a large presence because transaction costs for electronic communications were minimal. The important outcome was that many people took concrete action—volunteering, debating, contributing, and voting—facilitated by a wide variety of nonprofits in addition to the electoral campaigns.

Despite this outpouring of public participation via electronic communications media, there is a serious question about who is left out. Is there a significant digital divide that is growing with increased income inequality and poverty? Differential access to the Internet could be the Achilles' heel of the new e-participation paradigm. New technology such as smart cell phones, however, may be the answer to low cost and widespread access to electronic communications. The one sure thing is that technology is evolving very quickly.

Advocacy

Advocacy is generally understood to encompass activities and communications designed to influence public policy. It can be for individuals, for specific populations or causes, for the self-interest of an organization or sector, or for broad public benefits. Citizen advocacy groups such as Common Cause, Mothers against Drunk Driving, Focus on the Family, and League of Conservation Voters attempt to change public attitudes and public policies. Some focus on specific issues, such as preventing drunk driving; others on broader issue areas, such as promoting civil rights, family values, or environmental protection. Larger groups may have professional staff and sophisticated organizational structures and communications to mobilize members. Some public interest organizations—such as the Conservation Fund, the Center on Budget and Policy Priorities, and most policy institutes—do not have members. They may use staff, volunteers, donors, and professional lobbyists to advocate. Smaller advocacy organizations are often led entirely by volunteers who mobilize individuals to act. The interests of business corporations are promoted through usually well-funded trade associations such as the Chamber of Commerce that advocate on their behalf. Nonprofit service providers often do not have expertise or resources to advocate but they may belong to associations or coalitions that carry their messages.

Nonprofit policy advocacy is affected by a variety of laws and regulations that define permissible forms and levels of advocacy activity for particular types of nonprofit organizations.

Issue Identification and Agenda-Setting Advocacy

Nonprofit organizations can engage in unlimited research, education, and dissemination of information about social and economic issues and problems. They can also recommend solutions and send their information and analyses to the general public and to public policymakers. The use of websites and electronic communications has lowered the cost and broadened the scope of nonprofit public education activities. Electronic newsletters with e-links to publications can be blasted to thousands of people with the click of a mouse. These activities form the core of advocacy for many nonprofit organizations, although some do not think of such information sharing as "advocacy."

Administrative Advocacy

Nonprofits may provide insights and information on public programs to government agencies and advocate for changes. They often monitor the implementation of government programs to provide feedback to program directors, policymakers and the public.

Lobbying

Lobbying is advocacy targeted to influence specific legislation. In its broadest sense, lobbying involves attempts to influence the public policy decisions of regulatory, administrative, or legislative bodies. Virtually all nonprofit organizations are permitted to lobby, but 501(c)(3) public charities may not lobby to influence specific legislation as their primary activity and they must report their lobbying expenditures on their annual IRS Form 990. Private foundations may only lobby to protect their own interests. The 501(c)(4) social welfare organizations are not limited in their lobbying and they do not have to report their expenditures, but they are not eligible to receive tax-deductible donations.

Although lobbying is permitted for 501(c)(3) nonprofits, they may not spend a substantial amount of time or money on those activities. Unfortunately, the IRS does not define "substantial." This is a source of concern because the penalty for violating this regulation is loss of public charity 501(c)(3) tax-exempt status, which carries with it the right to receive tax-deductible donations. To mitigate this problem, the IRS provides a simple one-page form for public charities to make the 501(h) election, which provides a formula to calculate an exact lobbying expenditure limit. For public charities that choose to come under the 501(h) rules, total lobbying limits are set at 20 percent of the first $500,000 of "exempt-purpose expenditures" (defined as all expenses except fundraising, capital expenditures, unrelated business and investment expenses) to a cap of $1 million on total lobbying expenditures.[4] Unfortunately the value of the election has eroded as this cap has not been raised since the law was enacted in 1976. Only a small proportion of charities elect to come under the 501(h) provision.

Under the 501(h) rules, public charities must report two types of lobbying expenditures: *direct* and *grassroots*. Direct lobbying refers to communication of a point of view on a specific piece of legislation to a legislator, an employee of a legislative body, or another government employee who may participate in the formulation of legislation. Grassroots lobbying includes attempts to encourage the general public, beyond the group's membership, to contact legislators about specific legislation.[5] The cap on grassroots lobbying is set at 25 percent of an organization's total lobbying limit, and because total lobbying is capped at $1 million, grassroots lobbying is effectively capped at $250,000.[6]

Nonpartisan Electoral Activities

Public charities and social welfare organizations are permitted to undertake voter education and voter registration drives and may sponsor nonpartisan candidate forums. They may also engage in nonpartisan issue advocacy and participate in referenda and initiative campaigns. Organizations may poll voters, develop legislative report cards, and publicize issues that appear on the ballot.

Partisan Electoral Advocacy

Public charities are prohibited from doing "express advocacy," defined as advocacy for the election or defeat of candidates for public office. Social welfare organizations may expressly advocate for or against candidates only to their members, but this must not be their primary organizational activity.[7] Social welfare 501(c)(4) organizations, unions 501(c)(5), and professional and trade 501(c)(6) organizations, may not contribute directly to campaigns, but may do so through "connected" political action committees (PACs). Section 527 political organizations are permitted to conduct partisan electioneering activities; they must disclose donors, expenses, and contributions to the IRS. They can contribute (within certain limits) to PACs, campaigns, and parties.[8]

The regulatory framework for nonprofit advocacy is complex and evolving. The complexity deters many, but larger nonprofit organizations have learned to structure their advocacy activities to fit the contours of the laws, particularly in the electoral arena. Sophisticated nonprofit advocacy organizations often align with different types of organizations so that their cause has the benefit of all the permitted structures—501(c)(3) charitable organizations and foundations, 501(c)(4) social welfare organizations, PACs, and 527 organizations. The resulting multi-organizational alignments of advocates are cumbersome and not well documented.

The Supreme Court decision in *Citizens United* v. *Federal Election Commission* in January 2010 declared unconstitutional laws that barred corporations from expressly advocating for or against a candidate for office. The impact of this ruling is yet to be studied, and the ruling is likely to be challenged, but it appears that social welfare 501(c)(4) nonprofit corporations may now conduct express advocacy without setting up political action committees, which may result in the restructuring of some advocacy organizations.

Scope of Nonprofit Advocacy and Lobbying

Recent survey research updates our understanding of nonprofit advocacy and substantiates the findings presented in the previous edition of this book (2002). Charities allocate very little of their resources to advocacy and report very low levels of lobbying expenditures on their 990 forms. Although many may engage in public education or reach out to inform public officials, they shy away from describing those activities as advocacy and only rarely admit to lobbying for specific legislation. Three-quarters of nonprofits surveyed in 2000 engaged in public policy activities, but their reported involvement was inconsistent and at low levels.[9] Nonprofits reported that advocacy was important to their mission, but avoided characterizing policy activities as efforts to influence government. Further, they did not have a good grasp of the lobbying rules. The top barriers to policy participation were reported as lack of resources, complexity of the regulations, and skills needed to conduct advocacy. Among groups that received government grants, three-quarters perceived that government funding was a barrier to policy participation. Respondents also viewed foundation grants as restricting advocacy activities. Paradoxically, nonprofits with higher proportions of government and foundation revenues tended to be more involved in policy activities. Contrary to common wisdom, this study and others documented that organizations funded by government were not deterred from advocacy. Those organizations tend to be larger and more professionalized and to have a more direct stake in government decisions.

A more recent (2008) Johns Hopkins Listening Post Project survey found that nearly three-quarters of respondents reported some type of policy advocacy or lobbying, with three-fifths doing some activity monthly or more. Consistent with other research, resources deployed were minimal: 85 percent of the non-profits surveyed devoted less than 2 percent of their resources to lobbying or advocacy. Barriers cited were: lack of time (70 percent), lack of appropriate staff skills (45 percent), and the fact that coalitions handle this function (36 percent). Government funding was positively associated with advocacy, and foundation funding was negatively related.[10]

The important role of coalitions in nonprofit advocacy is often overlooked. Membership in a coalition or association permits nonprofits to project their voices on issues that matter to them without devoting a great deal of staff time or resources. Organizations can participate by writing letters, signing petitions, serving on committees, and joining in coalition-orchestrated lobby days with a minimum of expense and expertise, because coalition staff with considerable knowledge of the law and legislative processes guides their activities. The Johns Hopkins Listening Post Project survey cited earlier found that 89 percent of organizations surveyed reported belonging to a coalition or intermediary and 87 percent of these indicated that the coalition was involved in advocacy or lobbying.[11]

Reported Lobbying Expenditures among 501(c)(3) Organizations

The only government data on 501(c)(3) public charity advocacy activities are the lobbying expenses reported on their IRS Forms 990. These data have the advantage of being annual and mandated by law, but they have the disadvantage of capturing only one aspect of advocacy that nonprofits may undertake. They also have the same limits as surveys because many organizations are reluctant to categorize their activities as lobbying or they do not understand how to differentiate those activities. Despite these limits, these data provide a consistent barometer of lobbying trends among nonprofit organizations.

Although the number of nonprofits that report lobbying expenses and the amounts they spend remain quite low, since the mid-nineties these expenditures have increased and more nonprofits report lobbying expenses (table 10-1 shows trends in nonprofits' lobbying expenditures from 1996 to 2006). Data from the National Center for Charitable Statistics (NCCS) reveal that from 1996 to 2006 the number of 501(c)(3) organizations reporting lobbying expenses grew from 2,625 (1.3 percent of all) to 6,502 (2 percent), outpacing the growth in the number of new nonprofits. While this is still a very small percentage of organizations, almost all types of nonprofits registered an increase in lobbying expenses. Amounts spent for lobbying more than doubled (in constant 1996 dollars), from $139.7 million in 1996 to $382.4 million one decade later. Lobbying expenditures in 2006 were about .08 percent of total expenses for the

Table 10-1. *Expense Trends for Reporting 501(c)(3) Organizations That Lobby,*
1996–2006

2006 U.S. dollars, except as noted

Indicator	1996	2001	2006
Number of all reporting charities	199,368	264,411	326,804
Number of reporting charities with lobbying expenses	2,625	4,282	6,502
Percent of all reporting charities reporting lobbying expenses	1.32	1.62	1.99
Mean lobbying expenses	53,245	57,622	58,807
Median lobbying expenses	9,421	10,869	9,340
Total lobbying expenses	139,769,157	246,737,587	382,362,797
Total expenses of lobbying organizations	179,797,239,677	257,785,824,868	488,342,927,990
Total lobbying expenses as a percentage of total expenses	0.08	0.10	0.08

Source: National Center for Charitable Statistics Core Files, 1996–2006.

6,502 organizations that actually engaged in lobbying, the same proportion as in 1996. The mean lobbying expenditure in 2006 was $58,807, up from $53,245 (adjusted for inflation) in 1996.

Most organizations, however, spent more modest amounts on lobbying activities. The median in 2006 was $9,340 (see table 10-2). About 41 percent of organizations spent $5,000 or less. The number of groups spending $100,000 or more on lobbying was nearly 14 percent in 2006, a 47 percent increase over the roughly 9.5 percent of organizations that spent that much in 1998. Fewer than 2 percent of nonprofits that lobby spent more than $500,000 on those activities. Lobbying is clearly not an activity that is widespread among public charities and few spend significant amounts on lobbying.

Health, education, and human services organizations represent the bulk (73 percent) of reported lobbying expenses. However, traditional advocacy organizations spent higher proportions of their budgets on lobbying measured as a percentage of their expenses: civil rights (1.51 percent), environment and animals (0.69 percent), and community improvement and capacity-building organizations (0.71 percent). Religious organizations reached 0.53 percent whereas human services organizations reported that only 0.21 percent of their budgets was spent in lobbying. The larger organizations are the dominant lobbyists among public charities.

The big change over the decade is that in 2006 health organizations, including hospitals and other health care services, made up a greater proportion of

Table 10-2. *Ranges of Total Lobbying Expenses for Reporting 501(c)(3) Organizations That Lobby, 2006*

Amount spent on lobbying (2006 U.S. dollars)	Number of organizations	Percent of organizations
1–5,000	2,679	41.20
5,001–25,000	1,630	25.07
25,001–100,000	1,303	20.04
100,001–500,000	781	12.01
More than 500,000	109	1.68
Total	6,502	100.00

Source: National Center for Charitable Statistics Core Files, 2006.

the lobbying expenditures of the nonprofit sector, about 48 percent, up from about 40 percent in 1998 (see table 10-3). Lobbying expenses did not increase as a percentage of health expenses, but the proportion of all health organizations reporting lobbying expenses, 5.2 percent, was higher than reported by environmental organizations (3.6 percent). Only among civil rights organizations and anti-poverty groups were there higher proportions of organizations engaged in lobbying.

Lobbying expenditures are a very small fraction of total hospital expenditures, 0.03 percent for the one in four that lobby. Nonprofit hospitals are on the defensive, making the case for maintaining their charitable status and against charges that they are too commercial. Medicare and Medicaid reimbursement rates and proposed changes in those programs and in access to nonprofit bonds are also likely drivers of hospital lobbying and advocacy activities.

As table 10-4 shows, health-related nonprofits dominate the top ten public charity lobbyists in terms of expenses. This is not surprising because hospitals and other health care organizations also dominate the whole nonprofit sector's expenditures, accounting for 57 percent.

501(c)(4) Social Welfare Organizations as Advocacy Organizations

Social welfare organizations that come under the IRS 501(c)(4) category are often referred to as advocacy organizations because of their freedom to lobby and advocate without budgetary limits. Among the largest and best-known social welfare advocates are the American Civil Liberties Union, the National Rifle Association, AARP, NOW, and the NAACP. Civil rights is the primary focus of the largest group of 501(c)(4) organizations that engage in advocacy, 27 percent of the total. Human-service groups are a distant second, 19 percent of the organizations, followed by community improvement, at 12 percent. Table 10-5 shows the top ten social welfare advocacy organizations.

Table 10-3. *Total Lobbying and Organizational Spending by Reporting 501(c)(3) Organizations, by Type of Organization, 2006*

Type of organization	Percent of total organizations reporting (n = 326,804)	Percent of organizations in category that lobby	Total expenses for all reporting organizations	Organizations that lobby			
				Total expenses	Lobbying expenses	As a percentage of total expenses	Percent of total lobbying expenses
Arts, culture, and humanities	11.05	1.18	24,448,309,743	5,519,118,084	15,476,338	0.28	4.05
Education	17.98	1.57	188,906,083,541	85,036,567,309	55,917,870	0.07	14.62
Environmental and animal related	4.16	3.61	9,985,751,558	3,851,444,666	26,460,060	0.69	6.92
Health							
Hospitals	1.26	26.36	510,216,920,655	281,439,590,768	97,258,516	0.03	25.44
Other health	11.54	2.89	184,104,930,543	69,738,544,664	85,858,961	0.12	22.45
Human services	33.76	1.35	157,295,308,747	19,443,735,125	41,748,295	0.21	10.92
International, foreign affairs, and national security	1.83	1.97	23,572,787,436	5,515,294,930	13,691,300	0.25	3.58
Public, social benefit							
Civil rights, social action, advocacy	0.65	7.01	1,775,244,613	592,351,368	8,945,252	1.51	2.34
Community improvement, capacity building	4.72	1.59	12,151,798,393	1,059,190,547	7,485,722	0.71	1.96
Philanthropy and voluntarism	4.73	0.97	20,865,855,543	3,820,006,922	10,438,709	0.27	2.73
Research institutes/services	0.87	4.08	16,460,514,719	9,037,232,700	10,387,802	0.11	2.72
Public, society benefit, multipurpose, and other	1.02	3.80	9,339,348,087	2,526,562,389	5,182,459	0.21	1.36
Religion related, spiritual development	6.10	0.41	9,689,187,421	590,178,525	3,137,031	0.53	0.82
Mutual or membership benefit organizations	0.24	1.01	2,261,860,291	171,762,805	311,249	0.18	0.08
Unknown	0.09	1.01	41,668,308	1,347,188	63,233	4.69	0.02

Source: National Center for Charitable Statistics Core Files, 2006.

Table 10-4. *Top Ten Reporting 501(c)(3) Organizations,*
Based on Total Lobbying Expenses, 2006

Organization	Expenditures (2006 U.S. dollars)		Lobbying as a percentage of total expenses
	Lobbying	Total	
American Cancer Society (National Home Office)	13,897,200	372,198,513	3.60
American Cancer Society (Affiliates)	7,902,970	908,244,429	0.86
American Heart Association	4,385,965	601,384,364	0.72
Kaiser Foundation Health Plan	4,384,279	26,497,277,100	0.02
Humane Society of the United States	4,165,695	81,661,328	4.85
Nature Conservancy	4,091,752	667,488,665	0.61
Catholic Healthcare West	3,880,686	4,985,277,455	0.08
Cancer Therapy and Research Center	1,822,162	67,225,819	2.64
Sutter Health	1,600,790	349,663,055	0.46
Medstar Health	1,486,477	57,679,706	2.51
Total	47,617,976	34,588,100,434	0.14

Source: National Center for Charitable Statistics Core Files, 2006.

A review of 501(c)(4) organizations reveals that most are not active advocacy organizations. Of the 24,937 social welfare organizations filing IRS Form 990 in 2006, only 1,042 described their activities in terms related to advocacy, a proportion similar to that in earlier studies.[12] The largest social welfare organizations tend to be in the health care field. Social welfare 501(c)(4) advocacy organizations are smaller and younger than the 501(c)(3) civil rights and antipoverty organizations examined in this chapter. Almost half were created between 1993 and 2006 and about 64 percent had annual expenses less than $250,000. Since there are effectively no limits on the ability of a 501(c)(4) to lobby, these organizations do not have to report their lobbying expenditures to the IRS. Only 47 (4.5 percent) of the 501(c)(4) advocacy organizations identified as engaging in advocacy had expenses of $5 million or more.[13] Many of these large 501(c)(4) advocacy organizations are related to a separate incorporated 501(c)(3) organization. The separation allows the costs of lobbying and advocacy activities to be segregated and thus not subjected to the expenditure limitations that 501(c)(3) organizations face. This may account for the small size and recent creation of many 501(c)(4) advocacy organizations.

Major Forces Shaping Civic Participation and Nonprofit Advocacy

Public-interest advocacy is pervasive and powerful despite the limited dollars organizations report spending on advocacy and lobbying. Unlike businesses

Table 10-5. *Top Ten Reporting 501(c)(4) Social Welfare Advocacy Organizations, Based on Total Expenses, 2006*
2006 U.S. dollars

Organization	Total expenses
AARP	903,288,338
National Rifle Association of America	177,628,869
Harvard Pilgrim Health Care of New England	172,287,430
Californians against Higher Taxes	92,875,151
Sierra Club	79,261,306
Rotary International	67,307,290
International Association of Lions	52,091,484
American Israel Public Affairs Committee	47,329,333
National Association for the Advancement of Colored People (Group Return)	42,823,139
American Civil Liberties Union	28,975,560
Total	1,663,867,900

Source: National Center for Charitable Statistics Core Files, 2006.

with multi-billion-dollar budgets that allow them to hire lobbying firms with direct access to policymakers, most nonprofits use public education and softer forms of advocacy, relying on their public-benefit purposes to carry the day. Yet, nonprofits have shaped public consciousness of major issues throughout our history on topics as diverse as the abolition of slavery, benefits for military veterans, and suffrage for women.[14] But organizations that advocate face a host of challenges, both perceived and real. Lack of resources and organizational capacity tops the list of barriers. Charting a way through a complex regulatory landscape is also a daunting obstacle for many nonprofits.[15] The four impulses shaping contemporary nonprofits as charted in this volume—voluntarism (including philanthropy), professionalism, commercialism, and civic activism—all shape nonprofit advocacy. Civic activism, however, is the key impulse that motivates individuals to get involved and advocate.

Civic Activism

"Civic activism" refers to activities that engage individuals and groups with government and with one another to affect democratic governance and the quality of life in their communities, the nation, and the world. This impulse is on the upswing, as discussed earlier, and is the one that most animates civic participation and public interest advocacy. Civic activism and volunteerism are not separate—they overlap. Some voluntarism is for civic purposes and is facilitated by nonprofit advocates mobilizing volunteers for all sorts of activities.

Voluntarism

Volunteers have traditionally played key roles in nonprofit advocacy. They are important resources for many types of advocacy organizations, especially for those involved in community organizing, antipoverty, environmental, and civil rights issues, where members help to mobilize the general public to act for their causes. Many coalitions and campaigns rely on community volunteers to work on their issues. High school and college community service opportunities have reinforced volunteering and have involved recruits in a range of service and advocacy organizations. Recent U.S. presidents have all encouraged volunteering, civic engagement, and national service.[16] There is some evidence that those who engage in national service programs are more active in their communities and more likely to engage in public service work than comparison groups.[17] Research also documents that most nonprofits have a limited capacity to manage effectively a large influx of volunteers, such as retiring baby boomers.[18] Serving on nonprofit governing boards is another common form of voluntarism. Research suggests that board members sometimes play a role in advocating for the needs of their nonprofits.[19] According to the first national survey of nonprofit governance, however, only about one third of nonprofit boards are somewhat or very active in influencing public policy.[20]

Professionalism

Although much of the nonprofit sector consists of small, mostly volunteer-led organizations (44.9 percent of reporting public charities have expenditures of less than $100,000), professionalism is a reality for mid-sized and large nonprofits. Some observers suggest that professionalism has driven out civic engagement and stifled advocacy, but the reality is not that simple, because the nonprofit sector is so diverse and because communication and managerial skills can promote effective advocacy. The largest and most professionalized organizations are likely to lobby and advocate when policy issues affect them. Health organizations, as noted earlier, are a good example. The high level of congressional interest in their finances and public benefits means that they are more likely to lobby than many other types of nonprofits (see table 10-3). The larger question is whether they, and others that lobby, do so for programs that benefit the public, broadly defined, or only for their institutional interests. In many cases, organizations probably equate the two. Resources for job training, preschools, universities, and hospitals can all be described as enhancing the public good.

An important part of professionalism for nonprofit advocates involves segmenting their activities into complex multi-organizational structures to comply with regulations that limit the types of advocacy that different types of organizations may undertake. Coordinating and managing such a structure requires legal and management skills as well as resources.

Commercialism

Analysts have suggested that the growth of nonprofit revenues from contracting with government and fee-for-service activities has resulted in a chilling of nonprofit advocacy by those involved. Although the evidence is mixed, the research discussed earlier does not support widespread chilling, nor does more recent research on human service organizations that contract with government.[21] Proposed changes in government programs and budgets that affect resources available to serve their clients are important policy issues for nonprofits that are dependent on government contracts and fee income, which often originates from government sources through vouchers, Medicaid, or Medicare. Nonprofits may try to influence those issues, much as the business sector advocates for resources directly and through 501(c)(6) trade associations. For example, the health care and higher education sectors are highly dependent on fee-for-service revenues, and they spend more on lobbying than many other types of nonprofits (although it's still a small part of their budgets).

Reliance on commercial, fee-based income has undoubtedly induced some types of nonprofits to adopt some methods typically used by businesses, including marketing and communications approaches. The dilemma is that when nonprofits lobby for resources, they are sometimes perceived as just another "special interest" and weaken their special status as public-interest advocates. Yet nonprofits are also urged to lobby because those they serve often do not have other champions in the political process. This is perhaps why coalitions that involve cross-sector partnerships and faith organizations are increasingly important. These types of coalitions provide moral legitimacy that helps deflect criticisms that nonprofits are advocating for their interests rather than voicing the needs of those they serve.

Nonprofit Advocacy in Operation: Civil Rights and Antipoverty Organizations

Using data compiled from the IRS Forms 990 housed at NCCS, the authors identified samples of civil rights and antipoverty organizations and explored their finances and program information for descriptions of advocacy activities for the period 1998 to 2006.[22] Civil rights organizations document, organize, lobby, and litigate against discriminatory policies and practices and for laws that protect and guarantee the civil rights of their constituencies—racial and ethnic populations, women, children, aged, disabled, gay, lesbian, and many other groups. Among the newer groups are conservative civil rights organizations that advocate against affirmative action programs.

Antipoverty advocacy groups lobby and engage in related activism to catalyze public policies against growing inequality and rising poverty rates. Antipoverty organizations include those that deal with such issues as homelessness, hunger, and job security. Among antipoverty advocates are many faith-based groups as well as formal and informal cross-sector coalitions.[23]

There is a strong overlap and collaboration between civil rights and antipoverty groups. Civil rights organizations often promote public policies to address the economic security of marginalized groups, and antipoverty organizations often promote the civil rights of poor people who do not have access to needed resources as a result of various types of discrimination. Many organizations combine both civil rights and poverty in their missions, and over thirty organizations are members of both the Coalition on Human Needs and the Leadership Conference on Civil Rights.

Civil Rights Organizations

Civil rights organizations have diverse causes, structures, and strategies, making it difficult to generalize about them. The National Association for the Advancement of Colored People (NAACP), one of the oldest and best-known civil rights advocates, has used a variety of strategies and collaborated with many other organizations to break down legal barriers and end de facto discrimination faced by African Americans since it was founded in 1909. The Mexican American Legal Defense and Educational Fund, founded in 1968, has conducted similar work. Newer civil rights groups that are fighting battles for their constituents include the National Gay and Lesbian Task Force Foundation, the Human Rights Campaign Foundation, and Voices for America's Children. The conservative values movement of the 1980s and 1990s fueled the creation of groups such as the Christian Coalition, Promise Keepers, and others that promote traditional Christian values at the individual, social, and political levels.

The activities of civil rights groups may be directed toward changing or enforcing laws, modifying corporate or government behavior, or educating individuals and changing individual behavior; examples of the latter are campaigns to promote sexual abstinence among teens. Some organizations are known for litigating, others for lobbying and public education, still others for voter registration and get-out-the-vote campaigns. They often work in coalitions on issues of common concern.

The number of 501(c)(3) public charity civil rights organizations in the National Center for Charitable Statistics database grew from 1,394 in 1996 to 2,139 in 2006. Even in this set of activist organizations, the number that reported lobbying expenditures was quite small, although it doubled from 74 (5.5 percent) in 1996, to 150 (7 percent) in 2006. Total lobbying expenditures rose over the decade, from about $2.3 million to $8.9 million in 2006 dollars, and increased as a share of total expenses from 1.06 percent to 1.51 percent.

Table 10-6. *Expense Trends for Reporting 501(c)(3) Civil Rights Organizations That Lobby, 1996–2006*
2006 U.S. dollars

| | | | All civil rights organizations that lobby | | |
Circa year	Total number	Number reporting lobbying expenses	Total lobbying expenses	Lobbying expenses as a percent of total expenses	Mean lobbying expenses
2006	2,139	150	8,945,252	1.51	59,635
2001	1,792	126	6,223,085	1.25	49,390
1996	1,345	74	2,327,189	1.06	31,448

Source: National Center for Charitable Statistics Other Core Files, 1996–2006.

Among 501(c)(3) civil rights groups that reported lobbying expenses, the mean lobbying expenditures (in 2006 dollars) came close to doubling, rising from $31,448 in 1996 to $59,635 in 2006. Lobbying as a proportion of expenses rose from 1 percent to 1.5 percent during the decade from 1996 to 2006 (see table 10-6).

Civil rights groups range in size from very small volunteer entities working on local problems to very large membership groups with multi-million-dollar budgets, but the majority are small and young. Six in ten had revenues of less than $250,000 in 2006 and over half (56 percent) were created since 1993, a slightly higher proportion than the sector as a whole (51 percent). The largest organizations tend to be older; 65 percent of those with more than $5 million in expenses were formed before 1985. The larger and older organizations are also more likely to lobby than younger ones with fewer resources. These data suggest that the age and size of organizations may be important indicators of the propensity to lobby.

REPRESENTATION. Civil rights groups that directly represent the rights and interests of their members can speak authoritatively about their needs. Many of these groups started as small kitchen-table protest groups. The well-known ones have usually evolved into professionally staffed entities, often with members who may or may not meet on a regular basis, although they may have local and state chapters and offices in several locations. The extent to which they can mobilize their members for policy work is one measure of their legitimacy and power.

STRATEGIES. Civil rights organizations often use direct action strategies to gain attention and take advantage of the passion of their members. Public demonstrations, marches, and marathons have traditionally been employed because

Table10 -7. *Top Ten Reporting 501(c)(3) Civil Rights Organizations,*
Based on Total Lobbying Expenses, 2006

Organization	Expenses (2006 U.S. dollars)		Lobbying expenses as a percentage of total expenses
	Lobbying	Total	
American Civil Liberties Union Foundation	838,223	55,283,210	1.49
National Association for the Advancement of Colored People	671,996	24,933,630	2.62
People for the American Way Foundation	600,000	16,329,211	3.54
National Council of La Raza	560,540	28,388,455	1.94
Anti-Defamation League of B'nai B'rith	453,985	59,681,822	0.75
NARAL Pro-Choice America Foundation	414,228	5,172,033	7.42
Human Rights Campaign Foundation	400,000	9,147,096	4.19
National Gay and Lesbian Task Force Foundation	388,453	7,441,773	4.96
Legal Momentum	290,769	5,038,570	5.46
Mexican American Legal Defense and Educational Fund	277,429	5,704,343	4.64
Total	4,895,623	217,120,143	2.21

Source: National Center for Charitable Statistics Core Files, 2006.

they involve members, get the message out, and bring money in. Examples include the Million Mom March (gun control), Million Man March (family values), and May Day March for Immigrant Rights. Newer strategies include a strong presence on the Internet offering their members and the public opportunities to learn about issues and respond to action alerts on pending public policies through e-mail letters and other actions. For example, the National Council of La Raza developed a powerful online presence to promote citizenship and mobilize its constituents for educational and workforce campaigns. Litigation is another powerful tool for rights-based work. The American Civil Liberties Union has used litigation throughout its history to protect constitutional rights. Litigation can help to build a body of law around a particular issue as well as to keep an issue alive in the public's mind. The top ten 501(c)(3) civil rights organizations that lobby are among the best known in the country (see table 10-7). Even among these groups, however, the amounts reported for lobbying are only small percentages of their budgets. Two of the groups are aligned with organizations among the top 501(c)(4) social welfare advocates, the NAACP, and the American Civil Liberties Union. This division of labor keeps the public charities safely within the lobbying limitations imposed by law.

Rights groups often work in coalitions to achieve their goals. The Leadership Conference on Civil Rights, for example, is a membership organization of nearly two hundred national organizations of all types, representing people of color, women, children, older Americans, human rights groups, civil rights groups, gays, lesbians, individuals with disabilities, labor unions, and religious groups. This coalition is engaged in a campaign to reclaim civil rights. Another example is the conservative American Civil Rights Coalition, a 501(c)(4) organization with the goal of ending racial and gender preferences. Among its members are the Heritage Foundation, the Center for Equal Opportunity, the Independent Women's Forum, and others.

STRUCTURE. Civil rights groups tend to have complex organizational structures designed to carry out their strategies. These structures are necessary for groups that decide to be politically active, as explained earlier. Almost all of the larger civil rights and social action groups have affiliated organizations, mainly either 501(c)(3)s or 501(c)(4)s, although larger ones also have 527s and PACs. Eight of the top ten civil rights organizations have affiliated political action committees. Many have offices and chapters throughout the United States.

NOW (National Organization for Women) is an example of a 501(c)(4) organization with a multi-organizational structure that includes a separate 501(c)(3) foundation and more than one PAC. It also has chapters all over the country and acts on a variety of issue areas: against racism, sexism, and violence against women, and for economic justice. It engages members on the social networking site Facebook and through Twitter and is part of the Community Reinvestment Coalition, which involves over thirty organizations in town hall discussions about the recession.

RESOURCES. Revenues of civil rights organizations increased over the decade of our study. The makeup of their revenues is strikingly different from that of the nonprofit sector as a whole, and within the civil rights subsector, the patterns are different for those that lobby and those that do not. Direct and indirect support, including contributions from the general public, foundations, corporations, and federated campaigns, constituted the majority of revenues for civil rights and social action groups, about 56 percent of revenues in both 1998 and 2006. Among those that lobby, however, reliance on direct and indirect public support has grown, going from about 60 percent in 1998 to almost 75 percent by 2006. In contrast, for the nonprofit sector as a whole, direct and indirect contributions were less than 13 percent of revenues in 2006, up about one percentage point over 1998.

Compared to the nonprofit sector as a whole, civil rights organizations also relied less on fee-for-service income and more on government grants. In 2006, government grants provided about 17 percent of civil rights organizations' revenues, and program fees provided 12 percent (see table 10-8). Among the groups that lobby, however, reliance on government grants declined significantly between 1998 and 2006, from 21 percent to 9 percent, while staying about the same, 21 percent, for those that did not lobby. The reasons for the decline require further investigation but may indicate a strategy of nonprofits' distancing themselves from government support or government's limiting its support for nonprofits that lobby. The reluctance of some nonprofits to lobby for fear of alienating government sponsors may have some basis.

Because many civil rights organizations represent specific groups of people (ethnic and racial groups, the disabled, gays and lesbians, gun owners, and so forth), many make direct fundraising appeals to these target constituencies. Receiving funds from these populations, even in small amounts, serves two purposes. First, it provides the groups with unrestricted funds that may be used for general support or lobbying and political activities, unlike government, corporate, or foundation grants, which are often project-specific and prohibit such use. Second, financial support from the people who stand to benefit from an organization's efforts translates into legitimacy in the political process.

SUMMARY. Civil rights organizations represent a diverse mix of people and causes. Collectively these groups cover the entire breadth of the political spectrum and engage millions of people in their causes. The resources at their disposal are relatively meager, especially in comparison to corporate lobbying budgets, but they have the power of passion that allows them to leverage volunteers and donations into civic activism. Their growing sophistication in terms of organizational structures and use of electronic media have enhanced their visibility and allowed them to work more strategically alone and collectively in campaigns for their causes. Online fundraising, while still in its infancy, is a potential financial lifeline for these organizations. Their impact is obvious, but documenting it with hard data is still in its infancy, although there are attempts to build the necessary tools.[24]

Antipoverty Organizations

Antipoverty efforts involve secular and religious organizations, unions, and coalitions that also include business entities and government. Faith groups from liberal and conservative traditions are deeply involved in poverty alleviation and to a certain extent in advocacy, and bring moral weight to the antipoverty fight. Antipoverty organizations have a long and venerable history, but fewer than 10 percent of them were founded before 1969, and 38 percent of all antipoverty advocacy groups in our sample were created after 1993.

Table 10-8. *Sources of Revenue for Reporting 501(c)(3) Civil Rights Organizations by Lobbying Activities, 1998–2006*

Circa year	Type	Number	Total revenue (2006 U.S. dollars)	Direct public support	Indirect public support	Government grants	Program service revenue (incl. govt. fees and contracts)	Membership fees	Other revenue
							Percentage of total revenue		
2006	Lobbying organizations	150	675,044,236	70.68	4.11	9.13	8.14	1.84	6.05
	Non-lobbying organizations	1,989	1,416,083,541	44.26	3.03	21.51	13.61	1.23	16.36
	Total	2,139	2,091,127,777	52.79	3.38	17.53	11.84	1.43	13.03
2001	Lobbying organizations	126	551,007,639	66.50	1.83	16.66	8.47	2.84	3.71
	Non-lobbying organizations	1,666	1,140,356,028	51.00	4.80	20.15	13.46	1.62	8.96
	Total	1,792	1,691,363,667	56.05	3.83	19.01	11.84	2.02	7.25
1998	Lobbying organizations	108	439,907,023	59.09	1.18	21.16	7.85	2.16	8.55
	Non-lobbying organizations	1,386	789,355,207	47.17	6.38	21.19	13.05	1.39	10.81
	Total	1,494	1,229,262,230	51.44	4.52	21.18	11.19	1.67	10.00

Source: National Center for Charitable Statistics Core Files, 1998–2006.

Poverty became more visible in the past decade as celebrities such as former President Bill Clinton, Bill Gates, and others turned their attention and their resources toward the needs of poor people in less-developed countries. Concerts and online appeals to help victims of floods, the tsunamis, earthquakes, and wars sensitized many Americans to the devastating impacts of poverty worldwide. This chapter will not cover international poverty organizations, but the worldwide movement to address poverty undoubtedly helped to heighten consciousness of the issue in this country.

Poverty in the United States reemerged as a political issue during the 2004 political campaigns and was forcefully brought into public consciousness following the devastation caused by Hurricane Katrina in fall 2005, when vivid images of poor people who had lost everything played on television day after day. Poverty alleviation gained even more traction with the economic downturn that began in 2007 and the devastation of Haiti in the earthquake of 2010. Nonprofits reported the growing demand for basic necessities as people lost their homes and jobs. Think tanks documented the growing poverty rates and advocates tried to bring attention to the dimensions of the problem and to potential remedies. Civic Enterprises reported that there was a significant increase in media coverage of poverty in 2007 and 2008.[25] The dominant focus, however, was on the financial crisis that enveloped the whole U.S. economy.

By late 2008 there were 37 million Americans, including 13 million children, living in poverty, and that number was growing absolutely and as a percentage of the population, even before the economic collapse of 2008. Considering the income required for basic needs, some advocates argued that a family of three should be considered "poor" if it had an income twice as high as the current poverty line, $16,000.

Antipoverty organizations approach the issues from a variety of perspectives. Some advocate for relief—money for food, shelter, and health care—or for specific legislation and monitor and track such programs as Food Stamps, housing vouchers, and job training. Others embrace a holistic view of poverty and advocate for economic justice, working for a menu of structural changes, including access to health care, freedom to organize in unions, and actions to stem income inequality. Community organizing groups work with community members to promote living-wage campaigns, school reform, and housing.

In our sample of 444 antipoverty advocacy groups, 72 percent are human services organizations; in distant second place (11.5 percent) are community improvement organizations. Antipoverty groups tend to be somewhat older than the typical nonprofit and older and larger than civil rights organizations. Sixty-two percent of antipoverty groups were created before 1993, compared with almost 44 percent of civil rights organizations and 49 percent of all nonprofits. Fifteen percent reported expenses of more than $5 million, compared to 3 percent of civil rights groups. As is true in the nonprofit sector generally, revenues are highly concentrated in the largest organizations. Over 84 percent of all expenditures for antipoverty groups are made by the largest sixty-eight organizations.

REPRESENTATION. Community organizers, congregations, and faith-based providers can speak with some authority and legitimacy about the status of their constituencies. Some mainline religious organizations have professional government relations offices that lobby on a regular basis. Secular nonprofit human services providers are generally more reticent advocates, especially in the legislative and political arenas. Progressive think tanks and civic engagement organizations generally focus on data and policy solutions, drawing the public in through their websites, publications, and meetings, often testifying at congressional hearings and briefing government agencies on poverty issues.

Community organizing groups often have local and national networks that may include individuals, organizations, churches, public agencies, and private businesses that advocate for the needs of communities. People Improving Communities through Organizing (PICO) and the Industrial Areas Foundation (IAF) are faith-based networks. A study of faith-based community organizing reveals a robust field of organizations with thousands of volunteers dealing with issues relating to schools, housing, economics, social services, health care, race relations, public finances, and others. Over half were involved in electoral politics, hosting candidate forums, voter education, and registration.[26]

STRATEGIES. The ideological baggage of the last three decades, symbolized by the discourse around the "deserving" and "undeserving" poor, and "faith-based" interventions to change lives, as well as the battles over welfare reform and immigration reform resulted in framing terminology that largely played down structural issues causing poverty as well as the racial, ethnic, gender, and class connotations that the image of "the poor" carries. Much of the public policy discussion was cast in specific policy terms—job training, affordable housing, food security, health insurance, and educational reform. In an era of conservative ascendancy, few advocated for "the poor" and for addressing the overlapping structural issues affecting poverty, which implies a larger government role in making social policy to alleviate poverty. Even among some religious advocates, concern with economic justice took a backseat to advocacy targeted on specific issues, for example, hunger. The 2008 electoral campaigns talked about the needs of "Main Street" and the "middle class"; poverty and the needs of the poor were barely mentioned.

There is now some evidence of an increased willingness to speak openly about poverty in the United States. In 2007 the initiative Spotlight on Poverty and Opportunity was funded by a group of foundations to raise the visibility of poverty in the national electoral campaigns. It highlighted poverty data from the Census Bureau and sponsored policy forums on the issues. Recent efforts at the national, state, and local levels have set goals to reduce poverty rates. The national campaign Half in Ten, convened in 2008 by the Center for American Progress Action Fund, the Leadership Conference on Civil Rights, and the Coalition on Human Needs, seeks to cut poverty in half in a decade. The Half in Ten campaign used its website to mobilize members to communicate with presidential candidates about poverty in 2008.

State and regional commissions to engage leadership groups to confront poverty have also emerged around the country in the last few years. Ten governors received grants from the National Governors Association to hold poverty summits by summer 2009 and many state and local governments are adopting antipoverty goals.

At the national level, there has been similar consciousness raising. In January 2008 a Sense of the Congress resolution passed that calls for reducing poverty by half in the coming decade. It states that "policy initiatives addressing poverty have not kept pace with the needs of millions of Americans" and cites the "moral responsibility" of the country to meet the needs of those in poverty.[27] This resolution is a reference point for antipoverty advocates.

These initiatives indicate growing awareness that poverty is a serious national problem and that it will take community and government action to alleviate it. Implementing public education campaigns and building leadership coalitions seem to be dominant strategies, but community organizing is an ongoing strategy throughout the country. Whether there will be concerted action to address the structural issues through public policies is not clear.

The data from our study suggest significant growth in antipoverty organizations and in their lobbying activity. Among antipoverty advocates more than 14 percent reported lobbying expenses, a much higher rate than among other types of organizations, but this is still a small proportion engaging directly in trying to shape legislation.[28] The amount spent on lobbying by the sixty-four groups that reported such expenses was $2.7 million in 2006, much higher than was reported by the thirty-six who spent $584,145 on lobbying in 1996. Lobbying actually fell from 0.77 percent of the whole sample's collective expenditures in 1996 to 0.28 percent by 2006, as more and larger groups joined the cohort. The mean lobbying expenditure was $42,350 in 2006, compared to $16,226 in 1996 (in 2006 dollars).

Homelessness and housing is a focus of at least five of the top ten antipoverty advocates that report lobbying expenses (see table 10-9). America's Second Harvest (now called Feeding America) is the largest in this group.

ORGANIZATIONAL STRUCTURE. Coalitions seem to be the most typical structure used by antipoverty activist groups. Since the secular antipoverty advocate organizations are mostly small 501(c)(3) human services organizations, their

Table 10-9. *Top Ten Reporting 501(c)(3) Anti-Poverty Organizations, Based on Total Lobbying Expenses, 2006*

	Expenses (2006 U.S. dollars)		Lobbying expenses as a percentage of total expenses
Organization	Lobbying	Total	
America's Second Harvest, the Nation's Food Bank Network	538,430	639,029,321	0.08
Center on Budget and Policy Priorities	513,664	15,475,960	3.21
Community Preservation Corporation	300,000	59,163,969	0.50
Horizons for Homeless Children	169,683	6,602,858	2.51
Coalition on Homeless and Housing in Ohio	119,126	1,211,490	8.95
Housing Partnership Network	90,000	6,557,221	1.35
Children's Defense Fund	75,725	22,473,495	0.34
Western Center on Law and Poverty	70,196	2,684,778	2.55
National Coalition for Homeless Veterans	66,537	777,158	7.89
Public Policy and Education Fund	55,138	1,413,643	3.75
Total	1,998,499	755,389,893	0.26

Source: National Center for Charitable Statistics Core Files, 2006.

strength comes from numbers and the visibility they gain from cross-sector collaborations with religious congregations, unions, businesses, and governments. Some organizations have members, but judging by the revenues, these are not major sources of support.

Poverty alleviation is not a primary mission for any of the top ten 501(c)(4) advocacy organizations, although some may join coalitions and support antipoverty campaigns. Multi-organizational structures are not as evident among antipoverty groups and they do not appear to have a very strong online presence. There is, however, an effort to encourage more lobbying by promoting the creation of social welfare groups. The Center for Community Change created the Campaign for Community Change, a 501(c)(4) organization, to do its lobbying. The center has also developed a 501(c)(4) incubator program to help other organizations create such 501(c)(4) lobbying entities.

RESOURCES. Resources available for groups dedicated to antipoverty advocacy are a small fraction of the nonprofit sector, but this cohort grew over the period from 1998 to 2006 and its revenues have been increasing at a faster rate than that of the whole nonprofit group. The revenues of these antipoverty advocates rose from about $986 million in 1998 to about $2.2 billion in 2006. The sources of revenue provide a striking contrast to the nonprofit sector as a whole: about 44 percent of its revenues come from direct public support, up from 22 percent in 1998. Among those that report lobbying expenditures, revenues grew from $198 million in 1998 to $991 million in 2006 with almost 78 percent of revenues coming from direct public support and insignificant amounts in indirect public support (0.33 percent) in 2006. This compares to almost 13 percent of direct and indirect public support for all public charities and 8 percent for all that lobby.

Antipoverty advocates received a higher proportion of government grants than the sector as a whole, about 33 percent in 2006, down from 42 percent in 1998. The difference between those that lobby and those that do not is striking. In 1998 lobbying groups received almost 34 percent of revenues from government grants and nonlobbying groups, 42.5 percent. In 2001 lobbying groups' proportion of revenues from government grants had declined to 10.8 percent, whereas nonlobbying groups' percentage had increased to 55 percent. In 2006 lobbying groups experienced a further decline, to 9.5 percent, while nonlobbying groups declined to 50.8 percent. There was clearly shifting of organizations and of government grants, but further research will be required to determine the reasons for these trends.

Fee-for-service income (including that from government) is a much lower proportion of revenues for these organizations, 18 percent, compared to that for the whole sector, 68 percent. Fee-for-service revenues are even lower for antipoverty advocates that lobby, about 11 percent, but the proportion of income from fees rose over the eight years (see table 10-10).

Conclusions

It is apparent that many new organizations and structures dedicated to promoting civic participation and civic activism have sprung up. Many of them seek to promote a more responsive and inclusive democracy. Whether this newfound energy will survive the current economic crisis and the lull between elections is an open question. The online tools that are fueling engagement are relatively inexpensive and can be used to raise revenues. Social networking sites are new and only in the past few years have started promoting civic engagement, activism, and donating to causes. How their activism will evolve is unclear, but they do inspire creativity and experimentation. Such efforts have the potential to keep issues in front of millions of young persons, making causes a part of their everyday life in ways that older Americans never experienced.

Although nonprofit policy advocacy continues to be a low-level effort across the sector, increased levels of lobbying expenditures may indicate some impact of the efforts to promote advocacy through education, training, and distribution of guides and tools. Encouraging organizations and their boards of directors to understand the regulations and engage in advocacy must continue, but there

Table 10-10. *Sources of Revenue for Reporting 501(c)(3) Anti-Poverty Advocacy Organizations by Lobbying Activities, 1998– 2006*

				Percentage of total revenue					
Circa year	Type	Number	Total revenue (2006 U.S. dollars)	Direct public support	Indirect public support	Government grants	Program service revenue (incl. govt. fees and contracts)	Membership fees	Other revenue
2006	Lobbying organizations	64	991,015,262	77.62	0.33	9.46	10.71	0.14	1.73
	Non-lobbying organizations	380	1,269,097,656	18.31	2.13	50.80	23.77	0.21	4.78
	Total	444	2,260,112,918	44.32	1.34	32.67	18.05	0.18	3.44
2001	Lobbying organizations	60	713,985,869	79.22	0.53	10.82	7.04	0.15	2.23
	Non-lobbying organizations	353	1,053,521,607	17.16	3.14	55.01	20.32	0.19	4.17
	Total	413	1,767,507,476	42.23	2.09	37.16	14.96	0.17	3.39
1998	Lobbying organizations	44	198,337,153	48.14	1.47	33.70	9.76	0.46	6.46
	Non-lobbying organizations	299	788,292,361	15.60	3.29	44.69	22.22	0.20	14.00
	Total	343	986,629,514	22.14	2.93	42.48	19.71	0.25	12.48

Source: National Center for Charitable Statistics Core Files, 1998-2006.

should also be a focus on strengthening and building the capacity of the coalitions, professional associations, and membership associations that many nonprofits rely upon to focus their efforts and represent them.

Civic participation and advocacy have entered a new era. Nonprofits must grasp the implications of the powerful electronic tools now available and develop their capacity to use them effectively. Maximizing their capacity to achieve their missions and contribute to the democratic process requires no less.

Notes

1. Robert Putnam, *Bowling Alone: The Collapse and Revival of American Community* (New York: Simon and Schuster, 2000).

2. Elizabeth J. Reid, "Nonprofit Advocacy and Political Participation," in *Nonprofits and Government: Collaboration and Conflict,* edited by Elizabeth T. Boris and C. Eugene Steuerle (Washington: Urban Institute, 1999), p. 292.

3. "Trends by Race, Ethnicity, and Gender: Youth Turnout," Center for Information and Research on Civic Learning and Engagement (CIRCLE), Tufts University (www.civicyouth.org/?page_id=235).

4. Bob Smucker, "Nonprofit Lobbying," in *The Jossey-Bass Handbook of Nonprofit Leadership and Management,* edited by Robert D. Herman (San Francisco: Jossey-Bass, 2005).

5. For more information on government regulation of charitable lobbying, see Gail M. Harmon and others, *Being a Player: A Guide to the IRS Lobbying Regulations for Advocacy Charities* (Washington: Alliance for Justice, 2000).

6. The value of these limits has declined over the years, leading to efforts to raise them and to erase the somewhat artificial distinction between grassroots and direct lobbying.

7. Reid, "Advocacy and the Challenges It Presents for Nonprofits," in *Nonprofits and Government: Collaboration and Conflict,* 2nd ed., edited by Elizabeth T. Boris and C. Eugene Steuerle (Washington: Urban Institute, 2006), p. 359.

8. Ibid.

9. Gary D. Bass and others, *Seen but Not Heard: Strengthening Nonprofit Advocacy* (Washington: Aspen Institute, 2007).

10. Lester M. Salamon and Stephanie Lessans Geller, "Nonprofit Advocacy: A Force for Democracy?" Listening Post Project Communiqué No. 9 (Johns Hopkins University, Center for Civil Society Studies, September 2008).

11. Ibid., p. 15.

12. See Elizabeth Boris and Rachel Mosher-Williams, "Nonprofit Advocacy Organizations: Assessing the Definitions, Classifications and Data," *Nonprofit and Voluntary Sector Quarterly* 27, no. 4 (1998): 488–507, and Jeff Krehely and Kendall Golladay, "The Scope and Activities of 501(c)(4) Social Welfare Organizations: Fact versus Fantasy," paper presented at the thirtieth annual ARNOVA (Association for Research on Nonprofit Organization and Voluntary Action) conference, Miami, Florida, 2001.

13. Program descriptions on IRS Forms 990 and Internet searches were used to identify organizations engaged in advocacy.

14. Jeffrey M. Berry, *The New Liberalism* (Brookings, 1999), and Andrew Rich, *Think Tanks, Public Policy, and the Politics of Expertise* (Cambridge University Press, 2006).

15. Elizabeth J. Reid, "Advocacy and the Challenges It Presents for Nonprofits," in Boris and Steuerle, *Nonprofits and Government,* pp. 343–71.

16. "Activating the Next Generation," *USA Today,* December 9, 2004, p. 10D.

17. Corporation for National and Community Service and Abt Associates, "Still Serving: Measuring the Eight-Year Impact of AmeriCorps on Alumni" (Washington and Cambridge, Mass.: May 2008).

18. Mark A. Hager and Jeffrey L. Brudney, *Volunteer Management Practices and Retention of Volunteers* (Washington: Urban Institute, 2004).

19. Judith R Saidel and Sharon L Harlan, "Contracting and Patterns of Nonprofit Governance," *Nonprofit Management & Leadership* 8, no. 3 (Spring 1998): 243–59.

20. Francie Ostrower and Melissa Stone, "Boards of Nonprofit Organizations: Research Trends, Findings, and Prospects for the Future," in *The Nonprofit Sector: A Research Handbook,* 2nd ed., edited by Walter W. Powell and Richard Steinberg (Yale University Press, 2006).

21. Bass and others, *Seen but Not Heard;* Elizabeth T. Boris and others, *Human Service Nonprofits and Government Collaboration: Findings from the 2010 National Survey of Nonprofit Government Contracting and Grants* (Washington: Urban Institute, 2010).

22. To create the sample that was used in our study of civil rights and antipoverty nonprofits our methodology was as follows:

501(c)(4) advocacy groups: Following the strategy used by Krehely and Golladay, "Scope and Activities of 501(c)(4) Social Welfare Organizations," to identify 501(c)(4) organizations that advocate, we used the National Center for Charitable Statistics 2006 Core Data File created from the IRS Return Transaction File for 501(c)(4) organizations and sorted by activity codes and keywords that indicated advocacy, lobbying, and litigation (available at the website of the National Center for Charitable Statistics www.nccs.urban.org). We also incorporated all 501(c)(4) organizations in the National Taxonomy of Tax Exempt Entities located within the "R (civil rights, social action, and advocacy) designation" as well as all 01 codes designating advocacy-related activities within other exempt listings. This methodology resulted in 1,042 social welfare 501(c)(4) organizations that reported advocacy activities.

Civil rights organizations: We used the National Taxonomy of Tax Exempt Entities codes for civil rights and social action organizations defined as all organizations located within the R (Civil Rights, Social Action, and Advocacy) designation.

Antipoverty organizations: To create our sample of 444 organizations, we used National Center for Charitable Statistics 2006 Core Data File created from the IRS Return Transaction File of Form 990 data. We extracted organizations by purpose and by program descriptions employing keyword searches of terms relevant to poverty and advocacy. We excluded organizations associated with international nonprofit work, hospitals, higher-education programs, and grant-making institutions.

23. If those entities do not file a Form 990 their data are not presented here (see n. 22).

24. See Urban Institute, "Outcome Indicators Project" (www.urban.org/center/cnp/projects/outcomeindicators.cfm).

25. Tom Freedman and others, "Reaching New Heights: The Issue of Poverty in the 2008 Campaign—A Study of Print Media," report prepared by Freedman Consulting LLC, *Spotlight on Poverty and Opportunity,* 2008 (www.naktv.net/Spotlight/SpotlightMediaStudy.pdf).

26. Mark R. Warren and Richard L. Wood, *Faith-Based Community Organizing: The State of the Field* (New York: Interfaith Funders, 2001).

27. Center for American Progress, "House Embraces Poverty Goal," press release, January 25, 2008 (www.americanprogress.org/issues/2008/01/poverty_goal.html [March 4, 2009]).

28. Data compiled by the National Center for Charitable Statistics from its IRS Form 990 data files (www.nccs.urban.org).

11

Infrastructure Organizations

ALAN J. ABRAMSON AND RACHEL McCARTHY

I n addition to the nonprofit daycare centers, soup kitchens, hospitals, and universities with which most people are familiar, America's nonprofit sector also includes a variety of infrastructure organizations (IOs) that support these other organizations by improving their effectiveness and representing them in the policymaking process. Like similar organizations that support the business and government sectors, IOs serving the nonprofit sector are numerous and diverse. They include organizations that support nonprofits in particular fields (for example, the American Hospital Association and League of American Orchestras) and organizations that serve the entire nonprofit sector or at least large portions of it (for example, Independent Sector, Council on Foundations, and National Council of Nonprofits).

As the nonprofit sector has grown in scale and importance in recent decades, the evolution and strengthening of the sector's infrastructure organizations have become matters of increasing concern. Nevertheless, there has been little systematic analysis of these membership, advocacy, educational, research, management assistance, and other IOs that promote the health of the nonprofit sector.

Cici Fong helped with background research for this chapter. Audrey Alvarado, Robert Bothwell, Sara Engelhardt, Mark Rosenman, and Naomi Wish were very generous with their time in commenting on drafts of the 2002 edition of this chapter; Lester Salamon provided invaluable, detailed comments on chapter drafts for both the 2002 and 2012 editions.

This chapter seeks to help fill this gap by examining the growth of nonprofit infrastructure over the past several decades, identifying the major challenges now facing infrastructure organizations, and suggesting priority directions for their future development.

To do so, we focus on the "nonprofit" portion of nonprofit infrastructure, with less coverage of the numerous government and for-profit entities that also support nonprofits and philanthropy. In particular, the focus is on IOs that reach across the entire charitable—501(c)(3) and 501(c)(4)—spectrum of the nonprofit sector, or at least very large portions of it, rather than those that support a single subsector. Thus, not covered in this chapter are IOs seeking to strengthen organizations in a particular industry (for example, the American Association of Museums) or those serving specific population groups or causes (for example, the National Council of La Raza, which works with organizations serving Hispanic Americans).

Unfortunately, the writing of this chapter was handicapped by significant gaps in the available information.[1] To help ground the discussion, therefore, the analysis supplements the available data and written material with two dozen interviews of infrastructure leaders and others that were conducted by one of the authors in 2000, 2008, and 2009.[2] Even so, what follows should be considered an early effort to assess the world of nonprofit infrastructure that others will want to improve on.

What we found in our research and describe in the pages that follow is that nonprofit infrastructure organizations experienced a golden era of growth starting in the 1970s, but that this era of growth has given way in the 2000s to new challenges of consolidation. The period of growth was driven largely by the sector's interest in having stronger representation in the policymaking process and by the professionalization of the nonprofit field, which is one of the overarching impulses that is highlighted in this volume. As will be discussed, IOs were established and called on particularly to defend sector interests in Washington and in state capitols and to advance the professionalization of the nonprofit field.

Although some IOs continue to form and grow, many other IOs now face difficult tests. There is some worry that IOs are not serving the sector as effectively as they should. Of special concern are the quality of services that IOs are providing and their lack of vision and boldness in addressing the important challenges facing the nonprofit sector. Inadequate financial support is an issue for many IOs and may underlie the other weaknesses. Now that a functional nonprofit infrastructure has been established, the biggest challenge for IOs, their leaders, members, funders, and other stakeholders is to consolidate the gains achieved and to strengthen and extend in new ways what has already been created.

Overview of Nonprofit Infrastructure Organizations

Nonprofit infrastructure organizations mushroomed in number and size in the last quarter of the twentieth century, but such organizations have existed, in a limited form, for quite some time. By the late 1800s, local organizations called charity organization societies, modeled after similar societies in Britain, were established in many U.S. cities to coordinate the efforts of independent charitable groups. Charity organization societies sought to maximize philanthropic results, avoid overlapping service provision, ensure accurate knowledge of all charity recipients, coordinate services to those in need, and expose impostor recipients as well as fraudulent institutions—all functions that echo those of nonprofit support organizations today.[3] The hope was that such information sharing and coordination would protect deserving recipients and legitimate institutions from the suspicion and scrutiny that occur in the absence of built-in safeguards and accountability measures.[4] In other words, the charity organization societies were to serve a kind of "policing" function for the charitable sector.

Many subsector infrastructure organizations besides the charity organization societies also have long histories. The American Hospital Association, Association of American Colleges (now the National Association of Independent Colleges and Universities), and the American Association of Museums date from the turn of the nineteenth century. More relevant for this chapter, some sector-wide organizations have also been in existence for many decades: the National Charities Information Bureau (founded in 1918), which has now merged into the BBB Wise Giving Alliance; American Association of Fund-Raising Counsel (1935); Council on Foundations (1949); Foundation Center (1956); and the National Society of Fund Raising Executives (1960), which has been renamed the Association of Fundraising Professionals.

Despite their long history, IOs did not emerge as a discrete set of organizations with major roles in the sector and recognized public importance until the 1970s. Perhaps most significant was the establishment of Independent Sector in 1980. Independent Sector has come to be seen as perhaps the most important overarching infrastructure organization—the Chamber of Commerce for the nonprofit sector—with an ambitious mission to represent, serve, and advocate for the whole nonprofit sector, or at least the 501(c)(3) and 501(c)(4) portions of it.

Since the 1970s, the scope and dimensions of the IO population have grown, almost commensurate with the expansion of the overall nonprofit sector. In the last two decades of the twentieth century, IOs multiplied in number and significantly increased their capacity to provide support and services to nonprofit organizations. To do so, however, they had to overcome some special obstacles.

First, IOs that seek to serve the nonprofit sector as a whole have to over-come the subsector orientation of many nonprofits. In fact, it is subsector IOs that serve many of the infrastructure needs of nonprofits, especially around pub-lic policy and professional development. Nonprofits and their staffs naturally turn to their subsector associations for advocacy on field-specific policy issues (for instance, health care, postsecondary education, youth development, child care, housing, community development, arts, and so forth) and for professional networking opportunities. Subsector associations have experienced significant growth in recent decades with the result that many of these organizations are now large, well-established institutions with considerable capacity for meeting member needs. In this context, sector-wide IOs have the significant challenge of demonstrating their added value, or they will not develop the needed member-ship or client base.

Another problem for sector-wide IOs is that many also face a significant free-rider problem, a problem they share, of course, with the subsector organiza-tions, though to a greater extent. IOs that seek to provide collective benefits that improve the nonprofit sector as a whole (for example, favorable tax treatment of charitable contributions or positive public attitudes toward charities) have dif-ficulty getting individual nonprofits to pay dues to defray the costs of obtaining collective benefits that the latter can enjoy whether or not they pay for them.

Overcoming the subsector orientation of nonprofits and the free-rider prob-lem remain difficult tasks for many IOs, but IOs have found ways to meet these two important challenges. In fact, the final decades of the previous century were a golden era for many nonprofit infrastructure organizations. To better understand the scope of the IO field and the ways in which sector-wide IOs have responded to the pull of subsectors and the free-rider problem, the following pages describe IOs in more detail, grouping organizations according to their key features:

—The clients they serve (the sector as a whole or individual nonprofits and their staffs)

—The services they provide (advocacy, research, technical assistance, educa-tion and training, and other services)

—Their program areas of focus (accountability, governance, fundraising, and other areas).[5]

IOs Serving the Nonprofit Sector as a Whole

IOs that serve the nonprofit sector as a whole provide advocacy, public educa-tion, research, and other services.

ADVOCACY AND PUBLIC EDUCATION. Sector advocates represent the inter-ests of the nonprofit sector as a whole in the policymaking process. At the national level the most prominent sector advocate is Independent Sector, which was founded in 1980 as a national membership organization for both grant makers and grant seekers. Within the nonprofit community, Independent Sector, which now has approximately 550 members, is perceived as the voice of big nonprofits and foundations. Many Independent Sector members are themselves large, national associations of nonprofits (for example, the American Hospital Association, Alliance for Children and Families, YMCA of the United States, Catholic Charities USA, and United Way of America). Among the large, nationally oriented foundation members are the Ford Foundation, the Charles Stewart Mott Foundation, and the Carnegie Corporation of New York.

Independent Sector currently focuses on advocating on behalf of the nonprofit sector in the policy process, promoting ethical practice and effectiveness in the nonprofit sector, and providing a meeting ground for nonprofit leaders. Earlier in its history, Independent Sector also played an important role in helping to grow the nonprofit research field and improving the quality of leadership in the nonprofit sector.

As a membership organization, Independent Sector faces many of the same organizational challenges that confront other membership associations. An often-difficult challenge is the inability of membership associations to exclude nonmembers from enjoying the collective goods the associations provide.[6] In the case of Independent Sector, its successes in public policy are collective goods that are available to all nonprofits, whether or not they pay Independent Sector's sometimes hefty membership dues.

Independent Sector and other membership organizations employ a variety of approaches to deal with this collective action problem. One strategy is to have a small group of concerned foundation members shoulder a disproportionate share of Independent Sector's budget. This allows other members to pay less than they otherwise would have to in order to sustain Independent Sector's activities. Thus, grants and contributions have made up the largest portion of Independent Sector's annual revenues in many recent years.

In addition to counting heavily on its foundation supporters, Independent Sector also relies on "solidary incentives" to get and keep dues-paying members.[7] Although some nonprofits may be tempted to forgo membership in Independent Sector because they can get a free ride, the interest of many nonprofit organizations in being good nonprofit citizens and showing solidarity with other nonprofits can override their narrow cost-benefit calculations and lead them to join.

Where Independent Sector provides services to and advocates on behalf of both grant makers and grant seekers, the Council on Foundations focuses especially on grant makers. The Council on Foundations seeks to promote organized philanthropy, improve its effectiveness, and enhance understanding of it. It also is a membership organization, with nearly 1,800 foundation and corporate grant-making members. Even though Council on Foundations members represent a relatively small fraction of the country's more than 75,000 grant-making foundations, these foundations account for about one-half of the total assets of all U.S. foundations.[8]

To deal with its free-rider problems, the Council on Foundations employs some of the same strategies as Independent Sector but also makes heavier use of selective benefits that only members can obtain. For example, the Council on Foundations offers legal consultation, training sessions, an annual conference, and specialized information resources primarily to its members. Nonmembers can take advantage of some of these services, but generally only at much higher prices than members.

The Council on Foundations, which speaks for a broad range of medium-size and large foundations, also enhances its attractiveness to potential members by supporting affinity groups, which are groups of funders with a common interest in a particular program area, population, or cause, such as health, children, Hispanics, HIV/AIDS, or economic and social conditions in low-income communities. Affinity groups began to form in the early 1980s, and the Council on Foundations now recognizes thirty-nine of them.

Unlike the Council on Foundations, the Association of Small Foundations represents foundations with few or no paid staff. Another important foundation IO is the Philanthropy Roundtable, which brings together conservative funders.[9]

The National Council of Nonprofits (formerly the National Council of Nonprofit Associations) and the Forum of Regional Associations of Grantmakers are national organizations that seek to expand the capacity of state-based and regional associations of nonprofits and grant makers via public policy initiatives and the promotion of a cohesive vision that emphasizes the importance of nonprofits and philanthropy.

The National Committee for Responsive Philanthropy (NCRP) was founded in 1976 in response to concerns about the limited ability of low-income and disenfranchised populations to secure philanthropic support. Its mission is to make philanthropy more responsive to struggling populations, more relevant to public needs, and more accountable and transparent in order to create a more democratic society. OMB Watch is a nonprofit research, educational, and advocacy organization that focuses on budgetary issues, regulatory policy, nonprofit advocacy, access to government information, and activities at the U.S. Office of Management and Budget. OMB Watch, together with the NCRP, the Alliance for Justice, and Independent Sector, led the effort in 1995 to defeat the proposed Istook Amendment, which would have limited the lobbying activity of nonprofits that receive federal funding.

At the state and local level, state and regional nonprofit associations, such as the Minnesota Council of Nonprofits and the North Carolina Center for Nonprofits, as well as regional associations of grant makers, such as the Council of Michigan Foundations and Donors Forum of Chicago, perform many of the same advocacy and member assistance functions on sector-wide issues as national advocates.

RESEARCH. Research conducted at universities and other institutions enhances the nonprofit sector by improving understanding of nonprofit activities. In the past three decades, the number of academic and other research centers dedicated to the study of the nonprofit sector has increased significantly.[10] Among the leading nonprofit research centers are the Center on Philanthropy at Indiana University, the Center for Civil Society Studies at Johns Hopkins University, the Hauser Center for Nonprofit Organizations at Harvard University, and the Center on Nonprofits and Philanthropy at the Urban Institute.

With the expansion in the number of nonprofit research centers and researchers has come corresponding growth in the organizations that serve the field of nonprofit research. Through the 1990s and into the 2000s, the Nonprofit Sector Research Fund at the Aspen Institute awarded grants to support research on nonprofit issues. The Association for Research on Nonprofit Organizations and Voluntary Action (ARNOVA) and the International Society for Third-Sector Research (ISTR) are membership associations for nonprofit researchers that serve the sector by acting as clearinghouses for information on the nonprofit sector and promoting the expansion of knowledge about the sector. *Nonprofit and Voluntary Sector Quarterly, Voluntas,* and *Nonprofit Management and Leadership* are the leading academic journals focused on nonprofit research.

Infrastructure Organizations Serving Individual Nonprofits and Their Staffs

Organizations that seek to strengthen individual nonprofits and their staff make up the other major category of IOs. Reflecting their missions and clientele, these organizations rely more heavily on fees for service than the sector-wide IOs, which depend more on foundation grants and membership dues.

EDUCATION. Universities and other educational institutions seek to provide nonprofit managers with appropriate skills and knowledge. The recent increase in education courses dealing with nonprofit management has been striking. Whereas in 1990 only 17 universities offered a graduate-level concentration in the management of nonprofit organizations, by March 2009 168 colleges and universities offered graduate degree programs with a concentration in nonprofit management.[11] The rapid increase in nonprofit management education programs reflects support for the development of specialized educational programs responsive to the particular needs of the nonprofit sector. The increase also indicates an emerging need for highly trained professional nonprofit managers with various forms of technical expertise.

MANAGEMENT TRAINING AND SUPPORT. Management support organizations provide management assistance to nonprofit organizations with the goal of improving organizational effectiveness. Management support organizations were providing training for more than 250,000 nonprofit managers in 1997, and this was a conservative estimate.[12] Training, management consulting, and information programs are the primary functions and services of management support organizations.[13]

The evolution of nonprofit management as a distinct field and the provision of nonprofit management assistance by specialized providers began in the late 1960s.[14] A 1979 study described the field of nonprofit management as small and fragmented.[15] But nearly twenty years later, in 1998, a directory identified almost seven hundred nonprofit management support organizations in the United States that receive philanthropic support.[16] Many additional management support providers are independent consultants, for-profit consulting firms, or government agencies.

Nonprofit management support organizations are a diverse group whose members serve nonprofits with varied missions. Although these organizations are becoming more highly specialized and professionalized in accordance with overarching trends in the sector, they often act as multifunctional service providers for nonprofit organizations in a particular geographic region.[17] Comprehensive management support for all nonprofit organizations and communities is still not available, but the multiplication of management support organizations has helped to reduce the barriers to access, and their reported successes have led to higher demand for their services.[18] Indeed, management support organizations and professionals from around the country have established their own IO, the Alliance for Nonprofit Management, which was formed in the late 1990s from the merger of the Nonprofit Management Association and Support Centers of America. The Alliance is now being hosted by CompassPoint Nonprofit Services in San Francisco.

Many national support organizations specialize in a particular management function. BoardSource, formerly the National Center for Nonprofit Boards, aims to increase the effectiveness of nonprofit organizations by strengthening their boards of directors. Its programs promote knowledge of effective board practices and advocate for the value of board service and the importance of effective governance. The nonprofit technology field has its own group of specialized support organizations, including the Nonprofit Technology Network (NTEN), CompuMentor (TechSoup), and NPower. The Alliance for Justice provides legal information on the rules pertaining to advocacy, civic participation, and voter registration to nonprofits and foundations. In the same general area, the Center for Lobbying in the Public Interest (CLPI) trains nonprofit staff to advocate and lobby more effectively, educates nonprofit staff and their stakeholders about the importance of advocacy, and works to protect nonprofit lobbying rights. The national Points of Light Institute and its HandsOn Network promote and facilitate volunteerism and civic engagement. Several new organizations—including the Social Enterprise Alliance and the Community Wealth Ventures, a for-profit subsidiary of the nonprofit Share Our Strength—have emerged over the last decade or more to help nonprofits become more effective at earning revenue through social enterprise activities.

An important new wave of general nonprofit support organizations has been established in recent years, heavily influenced by or even spun off from for-profit management consulting practices. This new group of consulting firms includes the Bridgespan Group, FSG Social Impact Advisors, Rockefeller Philanthropy Advisors, the Center for Effective Philanthropy, and others. In addition to providing one-on-one services to their nonprofit, foundation, and donor clients, many of these organizations also produce research reports for the broader nonprofit field.

PROFESSIONAL DEVELOPMENT. The Association of Fundraising Professionals (formerly the National Society of Fund Raising Executives), American Association of Fund-Raising Counsel, and American Society of Association Executives are all professional societies that seek to strengthen nonprofits and philanthropy by promoting the use of best professional practices and adherence to a code of ethics and accountability. The Young Nonprofit Professionals Network (YNPN) brings young nonprofit staff together for professional development and networking through its twenty-five local chapters.

PROVISION OF INFORMATION RESOURCES. A broad range of IOs provide information about nonprofit and foundation operations. This information enhances the accountability of nonprofits and foundations, informs the decisionmaking of grant makers and grant seekers, supports the work of researchers, facilitates communication within the nonprofit sector, and promotes public understanding of nonprofits. GuideStar and the National Center for Charitable Statistics at the Urban Institute make available detailed data about nonprofits on the basis largely of information reported on Form 990, which nonprofits file with the U.S. Internal Revenue Service. The Foundation Center fosters public understanding of foundations by collecting, organizing, analyzing, and disseminating information about foundations and other grant-making entities. The multitude of resources provided by the Foundation Center allows grant-seeking organizations to obtain information on myriad potential funders in one place. The BBB Wise Giving Alliance, formed from the 2001 merger of the National Charities Information Bureau and the Philanthropic Advisory Service of the Council of Better Business Bureaus' Foundation, promotes informed giving by providing information on organizations' activities, governance, staffing, and finances to grant makers so they can make informed decisions about the organizations receiving their awards. Charity Navigator evaluates the financial health of more than five thousand of the United States' largest nonprofits. The Standards for Excellence Institute, an operating division of the Maryland Association of Nonprofit Organizations, also seeks to promote nonprofit accountability by encouraging nonprofit adherence to its fifty-five performance standards. Nonprofits that meet the standards are awarded a Seal of Excellence.

A variety of nonprofit and for-profit periodicals report on the nonprofit sector and philanthropy. Major general-audience journals are the *Chronicle of Philanthropy, NonProfit Times, Nonprofit Quarterly,* and *Stanford Social Innovation Review.* The nonprofit Fieldstone Alliance publishes a broad range of books on nonprofit management, as does Jossey-Bass, which is an imprint of the for-profit publishing house John Wiley & Sons. A growing number of electronic newsletters, Internet sites, and blogs are also serving the public, nonprofit practitioners, and researchers. E-newsletters such as *Philanthropy News Digest, Philanthropy Journal,* and *Blue Avocado* cover the nonprofit and philanthropic communities. Examples of research-oriented websites are the Catalog of Nonprofit Literature and the Philanthropic Studies Index, which are managed by the Foundation Center and the Indiana University Center on Philanthropy, respectively.[19]Among the many blogs that discuss nonprofit issues are *Philanthropy 2173,* by Lucy Bernholz; *White Courtesy Telephone,* by Albert Ruesga and others; and *The Cohen Report,* by Rick Cohen.[20]

FINANCIAL INTERMEDIARIES. A final category of IOs serves nonprofits by providing them with financial resources. Financial intermediaries raise funds from individuals, foundations, and other donors and then redistribute the funds to nonprofit organizations through grants or loans. United Way of America and its nearly 1,300 local affiliates are important long-standing sources of funding for many nonprofits around the country. Network for Good is an online website that makes it easy for donors to give to any charity. The Nonprofit Finance Fund was established in 1980 to strengthen nonprofits' financial health and help them build facilities and expand and sustain their operations. New Profit, Venture Philanthropy Partners, and Social Venture Partners are a few of the new venture philanthropy funds that bring together individual investors to support the efforts of social entrepreneurs to scale their innovative social ventures. These funds employ a model of philanthropy that emphasizes highly engaged donors who bring not only their checkbooks but also their management expertise to their nonprofit grantees; support for nonprofit capacity building and general operations rather than just funding for specific projects; long-term commitments to grantees; and an insistence on measurable results.[21]

Historical Overview of the Recent Growth of Nonprofit IOs

Why has the nonprofit infrastructure expanded in recent decades? As the nonprofit sector has grown, it has invited more attention, and challenge, from hostile policymakers and others; IOs are a vehicle for responding to these challenges. With the overall growth of the sector, more nonprofit staff members have been concerned about their work and careers. IOs also are a vehicle for responding to this heightened professionalism.

Public Policy Challenges

Public policy challenges have been instrumental in fostering the growth of nonprofit IOs. As the overall nonprofit sector has expanded, it has attracted increased attention from policymakers and others. However, this attention often has been hostile to nonprofits, especially foundations. The nonprofit community established and supported IOs to lead the response to this negative attention.

1945 TO 1969: EARLY POLICY CHALLENGES AND NONPROFIT RESPONSES. In response to concern about the growing influence of private foundations and their lack of accountability, Congress undertook several investigations of foundation activity in the post–World War II period. In the late 1940s, there was evidence, as one noted historian concluded, that "some foundations served the donors' business interests better than they served philanthropy." A 1948 inquiry by Senator Charles Tobey of New Hampshire found some foundations providing venture capital for industry, protecting family control of businesses, and advancing unethical business practices. As one observer put it, after all the unscrupulous business activity, "there might even be something left over for occasional gifts to charity." Tax code reforms enacted in 1950 corrected some of the worst abuses.[22]

In 1952, the U.S. House of Representatives established the Cox Committee to examine the possibly "un-American and subversive activities" of foundations.[23] When the Cox Committee's findings proved unsatisfying to foundation foes, the House created the Reece Committee in April 1954 to mount a comprehensive inquiry into the motives for establishing foundations and the influence of foundations on public life. Although the investigation did not attract much attention and was discredited after the fall of the rabid anti-Communist senator Joseph McCarthy, it underscored the vulnerability of the tax-exempt world.[24]

As a consequence of these investigations, several large foundations recognized the need for greater preparedness to defend themselves in the event of future inquiries. The Ford Foundation distributed grants to encourage scholarly investigation of the role of philanthropy in American life, and the Carnegie

Corporation and Russell Sage Foundation took the lead in establishing the Foundation Library Center to serve as a strategic repository of knowledge about foundations and to ensure that foundations had "glass pockets," as one Carnegie trustee, Russell Leffingwell, put it.[25] Other foundations, however, especially some of the small ones, viewed with suspicion initiatives to gather information on their assets and activities.[26]

In the 1960s, Congressman Wright Patman launched a populist attack that challenged the very nature of philanthropy and nonprofit organizations in the United States. Patman's persistence, combined with rising taxes and government's search for additional revenue, resulted in intense inquiries into the tax-exempt status of nonprofit organizations.[27] A 1965 U.S. Treasury Department study found major problems in six areas of foundation practice: donors enriching themselves through financial transactions with their foundations (self-dealing); long delays before foundation resources were used to benefit charities; heavy foundation involvement in business activities; donor use of foundations to control property; foundation involvement in financial transactions unrelated to charitable functions; and a too narrow base of foundation management.[28]

Despite this heightened scrutiny, "the defenders of charitable tax-exempt organizations were remarkably *un*unified in their efforts to defend themselves," wrote the historian Peter Dobkin Hall in 1992.[29] The Foundation Library Center was limited by its primary function as an information-gathering organization. The Council on Foundations, which was established in 1964 through a restructuring of the National Council on Community Foundations (formerly the National Committee on Foundations and Trusts for Community Welfare), continued to serve mainly smaller foundations, which had been the clientele of its predecessor organization. The council was not a unifying force for the foundation community as a whole and lacked the stature and resources to be influential in the congressional arena.[30] Beyond the Foundation Library Center and Council on Foundations, other organizations did not have the scope or capabilities to address the relevant issues.[31]

In the face of the continuing political vulnerability of foundations, Alan Pifer of the Carnegie Corporation wanted to move beyond just strengthening the foundation community, arguing that to survive, foundations and other components of the nonprofit community had to join together to fight for their common needs. He was concerned that nonprofits failed to understand that underlying the congressional attacks on foundations was the potential for an assault aimed at all private charitable institutions.[32] Nonprofit organizations, with their diversity of goals and activities, did not see themselves as part of a unified sector with common needs. In a 1969 speech, Pifer urged that a "broad, national effort be made by private, charitable organizations generally, acting in concert, to reassert their basic unity and to reaffirm to the American people, to the Congress, and the Executive Branch their essential role in our national life."[33]

1970 TO 1980: THE FILER COMMISSION AND THE EMERGING INFRASTRUCTURE. The congressional hearings and government reports of the 1960s culminated in the Tax Reform Act of 1969, which imposed a variety of new restrictions on foundations. The foundation community now was motivated to respond.[34] Among the philanthropic community's multiprong responses were the establishment of additional regional associations of grant makers and the launching of the Commission on Private Philanthropy and Public Needs (the Filer Commission), chaired by John Filer, chief executive officer of the Aetna Life and Casualty Company.

The Filer Commission was organized in the mid-1970s by prominent philanthropists and foundation leaders. John D. Rockefeller III, who had become a leader of the Rockefeller family's philanthropic activities and who was especially concerned about the lack of unity in the foundation community, played a key role in organizing the effort.[35] The Filer Commission undertook a comprehensive, multidisciplinary assessment of the nonprofit sector and developed new information about nonprofit organizations and their role in American life.[36] This represented the first broad-scale effort to explain the societal role of nonprofits to the public as well as to the sector itself.

The positive reaction to the Filer Commission helped to improve the general standing of foundations and to create a perception of nonprofit organizations as part of a unitary sector and not just members of distinctive subsectors, such as health and education.[37] Through its work the Filer Commission forged a "security link" between foundations and the rest of the nonprofit world.[38] In addition, it helped to stimulate substantial amounts of research on the nonprofit sector, led to the creation of the first nonprofit academic center at Yale University, and set the stage for the founding of the National Center for Charitable Statistics.[39]

The Filer Commission also triggered the creation of the Donee Group, which consisted of representatives of advocacy and other nonprofits concerned about the lack of foundation responsiveness to disenfranchised populations. The Donee Group influenced the outcomes of the commission's work by demanding a more inclusive research agenda that was not focused only on grant-maker concerns. The work of the Donee Group was later picked up by the National Committee for Responsive Philanthropy, which continued to support advocacy groups and underrepresented populations.

Perhaps most important for our purposes here, the Filer Commission also outlined the need for an infrastructure that went beyond the subsector associations already in place. Among the Filer Commission's final recommendations was an initiative to establish a permanent, quasi-governmental body "necessary for the growth, perhaps even the survival, of the sector as an effective instrument of individual initiative and social progress."[40]

When it became clear that there was insufficient support for this recommendation, two existing organizations, the National Council on Philanthropy and the Coalition of National Voluntary Organizations—the former founded in the mid-1950s and the latter created in the 1970s to focus on tax reform and cooperation across the sector—commissioned Brian O'Connell, former executive director of the Mental Health Association, to identify "ways in which they might collaborate to better address their mutual interests in philanthropy and voluntary action."[41] The upshot was that the two organizations merged in 1980 to form Independent Sector, whose membership included both grant makers and grant seekers and whose first head was Brian O'Connell. The Filer Commission thus stimulated not only the development of sector identity and research on nonprofit activities but also the establishment of infrastructure to support the growing sector.

1981 TO 2011: RECENT POLICY CHALLENGES AND THE FILLING OUT OF THE INFRASTRUCTURE. Independent Sector's mission to promote the whole nonprofit sector was given added urgency by the inauguration of Ronald Reagan in January 1981. Nonprofits faced a "double whammy" in the Reagan era: federal funding of nonprofits was reduced at the same time that nonprofits faced greater demand for services from clients negatively affected by government cutbacks. Although the new administration supported adding a charitable deduction for taxpayers who were not itemizing their other deductions, it also proposed dramatic tax rate cuts that would reduce incentives to give.

The funding and regulatory crisis of the early 1980s finally sparked a larger-scale mobilization of the sector. According to Peter Dobkin Hall, the federal cutbacks in a time of recession, combined with other threats to the nonprofit sector, drew nonprofits into a common defense.[42] Unlike the temporary coalitions mobilized against specific government initiatives in the late 1960s and 1970s, the mobilizations of the 1980s represented a shift toward less ephemeral, more established institutional responses to general threats against the sector.

In the early 1980s, Independent Sector stimulated research about the impact on nonprofits of budget cuts proposed by the Reagan administration, although it did not take a stand on the Reagan budget plans.[43] New IOs emerged in the 1980s and into the 1990s with the purpose of promoting the health of the nonprofit sector by uniting nonprofit organizations and creating forums for research, communication, public education, and legislative defense. Moreover, previously established organizations extended their reach and activities during this period to address the new public policy issues more effectively.[44]

In addition to the Reagan budget reductions of the early 1980s and the Newt Gingrich–inspired Contract with America cuts of the mid-1990s, legislative challenges for the nonprofit sector during this period included tax reform that eliminated the deductibility of charitable contributions for non-itemizers, tax rate reductions that reduced incentives to give, and restrictions on lobbying by nonprofit organizations.[45]

Nonprofits were perhaps most united and vocal in opposing the attempts to limit their advocacy and lobbying activity, which were led by Representative Ernest Istook Jr., a Republican from Oklahoma.[46] The so-called Istook amendment and its numerous legislative cousins sought specifically to constrain the advocacy activities of nonprofits receiving government support. Some important infrastructure organizations and alliances emerged or were strengthened in response to this challenge, including the Alliance for Justice, OMB Watch, the Let America Speak coalition, and the Advocacy Institute. These entities helped to lead the nonprofit fight against the Istook amendment and have assisted nonprofits to become better advocates.[47]

Trends toward devolution—the shift of federal government authority to the state and local levels—also spurred the expansion of nonprofit infrastructure in the 1980s and 1990s. In response to devolution, nonprofits supported the establishment of state nonprofit associations to protect their interests at the increasingly important state level. State nonprofit associations have proved to be important monitors of state-level regulatory changes affecting nonprofits.[48] As the nonprofit expert Dennis Young put it, federal devolution initiatives seemed "to be the same kind of catalyst for organizing nonprofits at the state level in the 1990s that congressional attacks on foundations in the 1960s were for galvanizing collective action by the sector at the national level."[49]

In the 2000s a new round of exposés of unethical and even illegal nonprofit activity led to new challenges. And, once again, nonprofit IOs were an important part of the sector's defense. The decade began with the American Red Cross's coming under fire for suggesting that it would hold some money donated for 9/11 relief in reserve to meet future needs.[50] In 2003, with this controversy still fresh, the *San Jose Mercury News* and *Boston Globe* ran articles on questionable foundation practices, and the *Washington Post* ran a scathing series on The Nature Conservancy.[51] Foundations were seen as spending excessive amounts on executive and trustee compensation.

Congress considered legislation during 2003 to exclude foundation salaries, travel, and administrative expenses from counting toward the mandatory 5 percent of assets that foundations are required to pay out in grants or other "qualifying distributions."[52] Foundations hired a high-powered lobbyist to fight the proposed legislation, and the bill stalled in Congress. In 2004, however, congressional examination of the nonprofit sector picked up steam again. Under

Senator Charles Grassley's leadership, the Senate Finance Committee held hearings on nonprofit activities, and the committee staff issued a "staff discussion draft" white paper with a broad range of recommendations to reform nonprofit and foundation practices. For example, nonprofit boards should have between three and fifteen members; foundation trustees could not be compensated; a nonprofit's Form 990 should include a detailed description of the organization's annual performance goals and measures of its success in meeting prior goals.[53]

In response to the Senate activity, Independent Sector established the Panel on the Nonprofit Sector to recommend actions to strengthen the governance, ethical conduct, and transparency of charitable organizations. The panel and its many work groups, advisory committees, and task forces issued a series of reports with recommendations about how Congress, the IRS, and the nonprofit sector itself could enhance the sector's accountability.[54]

Ultimately, only relatively modest changes in nonprofit law were enacted in the 2000s. The Pension Protection Act of 2006 included some provisions to encourage greater charitable giving—individuals seventy and a half years of age and older were allowed to donate up to $100,000 from their IRAs without having to count the donation as taxable income—and other measures to enhance accountability, such as expanded mandatory e-filing of Form 990 and reform of the process for appraising and valuing donated property. More notably, a group of younger sector leaders came together under the banner of the "America Forward" coalition to push through the Edward M. Kennedy Serve America Act of 2009, which significantly expanded AmeriCorps and other national service programs, established a new Social Innovation Fund to help seed and scale up nonprofit programs, and authorized funding to improve nonprofits' organizational capacity.

Still, many of the more dramatic proposals to reform the nonprofit sector that had been discussed in the 2004 Senate Finance Committee white paper and elsewhere were not passed into law. Perhaps a more significant consequence of the recent policy challenges to the sector than the legislation passed has been the reenergizing of Independent Sector as the lead organization for defending the sector's interests in the federal policy process.

Professionalization

IOs have grown in response not only to policy challenges but also to the professionalization of the nonprofit field. "Professionalization" refers to a shift away from amateur or personalized responses to needs or problems and toward technical and often standardized approaches to providing services that reflect expert knowledge gained through specialized training.

As the introductory chapter in this volume indicates, moves toward professionalization within the nonprofit sector began as early as the late 1800s but have accelerated sharply in recent decades. This recent trend contributed to the rapid expansion of the professional development infrastructure and further movement away from what Hall has called "methodless enthusiasm."[55]

The Tax Reform Act of 1969 played a major role in this trend. Much of the debate preceding enactment of the law focused on the perceived inefficiency and lack of accountability of nonprofits and foundations as well as a series of financial abuses by foundations in the 1960s. The Tax Reform Act expanded Internal Revenue Service oversight of nonprofit organizations in a variety of areas, including fiscal practices. When the law was finally implemented, nonprofit organizations had to reconfigure their financial operations and management styles in order to conform. Even leading foundations had to hire specialized staff to address the emerging procedural requirements.[56]

The expansion of government contracting with nonprofits was an additional spur toward professionalization. Nonprofits had to improve their internal management processes to meet government contracting requirements and were sometimes obligated to hire specially trained professionals to deliver government-funded services.[57]

However, government regulations were not solely responsible for the professionalization of the sector, nor was professionalization entirely forced on nonprofits. The push toward professionalization also came from within the sector.[58] Many nonprofit leaders embraced the movement toward professionalization in the interest of developing expert staff capable of handling the complicated challenges that nonprofits were being called on to address. Professionalization also served the interests of nonprofit staff members who had received specialized training.

Increased professionalization also was a response to several scandals that roiled the sector in the nineties; one scandal involved the head of United Way of America, William Aramony, who in 1995 was convicted of fraud, tax evasion, and conspiracy. The higher visibility and potency of nonprofit organizations, in conjunction with the publicized scandals involving inadequate reporting and misuse of funds, made nonprofits targets for public scrutiny and necessitated further responsiveness from the sector, which sought to standardize accounting practices, promote accounting transparency, and implement other professional processes.[59]

IOs established to provide a central voice for the sector also became vehicles for disseminating information on best practices, effective training methods, standards of accountability, and organizational effectiveness. Increases in professionalization required institutional mechanisms to dispense information and convene discussions on issues relating to the efficacy and accountability of the sector. IOs emerged in part to meet this need.

The expansion of the sector, the challenges of both increased government regulation and decreased government funding, and the public scrutiny of the sector and its processes created a propitious environment for the growth of IOs. Infrastructure organizations such as Independent Sector promised to provide common meeting ground, resources to enhance professional development and organizational capacity, and permanent capacity to respond to public policy challenges. Nonprofit organizations therefore united under the auspices of infrastructure organizations to both defend and promote themselves and, by extension, to protect and enhance the health of the sector.

Current Challenges and Future Directions

Today, after an extended period of infrastructure growth, membership organizations represent nonprofits and foundations at the national, state, and local levels; management support organizations cover much of the country; nonprofit educational and research centers have multiplied; and there is more media coverage of nonprofit issues. With the essential elements of infrastructure in place, the major task for IOs and their stakeholders now and into the future is to strengthen existing IOs, build on the gains of recent decades, and provide a more compelling and convincing argument for the country's stake in the health of the sector these organizations represent. More specifically, IOs currently face two kinds of challenges: improving their own organizational performance, and helping the nonprofit community as a whole better address the critical issues it now confronts.

Challenges to IOs as Organizations

The first set of challenges now facing IOs relates to their own organizational needs to secure their financial base, demonstrate their value, improve their performance, and work more effectively with one another.

FINANCIAL SUSTAINABILITY: A MORE SECURE FUNDING BASE. Although existing data do not permit a simple comparison of nonprofit, business, and government infrastructure, it seems likely that there is an underinvestment in the infrastructure of nonprofits relative to that of the other sectors. With a few notable exceptions—including Independent Sector, the Council on Foundations, the Foundation Center, and some other infrastructure organizations—many IOs are relatively fragile organizations, dependent for their revenue either on relatively poor nonprofits who are hard-pressed to pay IOs for the services the IOs provide or on foundations that have been on the whole relatively modest and inconsistent supporters of IOs and who have become even more reluctant funders in the down economy. By most accounts, the nonprofit infrastructure does not have the resources it needs to support the nonprofit sector properly.[60]

The need for IOs to diversify their resource base has become much more urgent in recent years because several of the few foundations that had supported them have significantly reduced their IO funding. Two of the largest, the Atlantic Philanthropies and the David and Lucile Packard Foundation, dropped the infrastructure field as a major area of funding in the last decade. While the Bill and Melinda Gates Foundation is an important, new IO funder, other foundations reduced their support because of shifting priorities and endowments that shrank in value because of the recession.

One hopeful sign is the possibility of increased government support for at least some IOs. The huge 2009 economic recovery act included $50 million in funding for a Strengthening Communities Fund in the U.S. Department of Health and Human Services. The fund supports nonprofit groups that provide training and management assistance to charities serving low-income and disadvantaged populations.[61] The Serve America Act, which was also enacted in 2009, authorized a Nonprofit Capacity Building Program in the U.S. Corporation for National and Community Service to help small and medium-size charities get needed training and management assistance.[62] Unfortunately for capacity-building advocates, the Strengthening Communities Fund received no funding for fiscal year 2011, which runs from October 1, 2010, through September 30, 2011, and the Nonprofit Capacity Building Program was allocated just under $1 million. For FY 2012, which begins October 1, 2011, President Obama proposed a modest $20 million for the Strengthening Communities Fund and no funding for the Nonprofit Capacity Building Program.

New ideas are needed about how to fund IOs. One proposal floated informally in the last decade was to have government "tax" all registered nonprofits and then use the money to support nonprofit IOs. In addition, many more foundations and individual donors must educate themselves about the value of infrastructure activity and fund IOs. A 2009 report by the *Nonprofit Quarterly* discusses the possibility of having foundations tax themselves or "tithe" a percentage of their grant money to IOs. To promote efficiency, many foundations and other donors might contribute to a common funding pool to support IOs rather than funding IOs directly on their own. IOs should also explore increasing their earned income, although IOs that hold conferences and provide data, financial, and professional services may have more options in this area than IOs which focus on research, policy development, and advocacy.[63]

In any case, significant funding challenges are now the norm for many IOs. Unless IOs develop new funding sources to replace the lost foundation dollars, they will have to reduce their activities or go out of business, with potentially significant negative consequences for the health of the nonprofit sector.

TELLING THEIR STORY, MAKING THEIR CASE. The financial woes of IOs have been compounded by the fact that many IOs—and their stakeholders—have a hard time identifying the value they add and telling their story. It is often difficult for IOs to gauge their impact on the individual nonprofits and the broader nonprofit community that they serve. And, not surprisingly, it is even harder for IOs to pinpoint their influence on the societal problems that their nonprofit clients are trying to address.

An important underlying challenge is that many IOs are delivering hard-to-measure services—advocacy, research, education, management support, and others—and establishing their value-added with any precision is difficult. However, advances have been made in recent years in assessing these services.[64] Improvements in evaluation practices—and more attention paid to actually evaluating IO activities—will help IOs better gauge their impact and tell more convincing, positive stories about themselves.

A somewhat different problem is that IOs and the services they deliver are often seen as "boring" compared to the more interesting work in particular policy fields like education, health, or the arts which compete for funder attention. Nonprofit infrastructure is like the plumbing that is mostly out of sight but which is critical to the smooth functioning of any structure. The problem, as one funder put it, is that, "No one wants to fund the plumbing." IOs must develop more interesting, persuasive case statements about their value-added to keep existing donors and attract new ones.[65]

QUALITY: IMPROVING IO PERFORMANCE. While developing better methods for assessing IO performance should be a priority for IOs and their stakeholders, until better information is available nonprofit leaders will judge IOs on the basis of impressions. Unfortunately, these impressionistic judgments now reflect concerns about IO performance. In particular, too many IOs are seen as passive or otherwise slow to respond to changing sector needs; afraid of controversy; behind the times with their use of new information and management technologies; not operating at sufficient scale; and/or providers of low-quality services. Overall, the consensus is that many IOs should be performing at higher levels.

Management assistance is one area of concern with regard to performance. Today, almost anyone can hang out a shingle and claim to be a nonprofit management assistance provider. Beyond the market test, there is little or no assurance that assistance providers are delivering quality services. Many providers do not have relevant training and experience, the field lacks meaningful standards of practice, and the base of knowledge on which providers can draw is inadequate.[66] Moreover, management support providers too often give generic assistance that is inadequately customized to the needs of individual organizations.

To cope with concerns about the quality of management assistance being offered, IOs operate programs that seek to improve practice in this area. The Alliance for Nonprofit Management promotes quality in nonprofit capacity building and convenes management assistance providers to break down their isolation.[67] BoardSource sets standards for quality in management that can guide assistance providers. Grantmakers for Effective Organizations was founded in 1997 to help foundations improve the effectiveness of the nonprofits they work with.[68] These organizations and others that are addressing issues of standards and accountability in the field of management assistance have produced significant reports and research. However, their analyses must be aggregated, analyzed, and properly disseminated and implemented to yield benefits for the sector.

In the nonprofit research field, which is another area of concern, recent decades have been a period of tremendous growth, with dramatic increases in the number of nonprofit scholars and academic centers. Unfortunately, only a modest number of university-based scholars have won promotion or tenure because of their nonprofit research, and nonprofit academic centers generally receive only minimal financial support from their universities, relying heavily instead on "soft" grant money from foundations.

The failure of universities to fully embrace nonprofit scholars and academic centers results in part from the relative newness of the field of nonprofit research, and there is likely to be greater acceptance over time. However, nonprofit scholars are also being penalized for their too-frequent failure to meet accepted standards for research in the social sciences and other fields. One major concern, for example, has been the overuse of case studies that limit the generalizability of research findings.

To advance the field of nonprofit research, large databases are needed that will enable researchers to go beyond single case studies.[69] Nonprofit researchers must be trained to use—and then actually use—the sophisticated methodologies that are now being employed in the social sciences to analyze large data sets. In addition, to expand the pool of high-quality nonprofit researchers, funders and others must increase their outreach to promising scholars engaged in disciplinary networks (for example, American Political Science Association, American Sociological Association, American Economics Association) as well as interdisciplinary activities (for example, ARNOVA).[70]

Another important concern about nonprofit research is its lack of relevance for and inaccessibility to policymakers and nonprofit practitioners. The lack of policy- and practice-relevant research is an important handicap for policymakers and nonprofit managers and leaders and hinders their job performance.[71] While building "basic" knowledge about nonprofit activities is important, scholars, practitioners, policymakers, and funders must also collaborate to build bridges between academic research and communities of practice and policy.[72]

OVERLAPS: INCREASING COLLABORATION. At a time of reduced foundation resources and in response to the overlapping responsibilities and persistent fragility of many IOs, funders and others have encouraged IOs to explore collaboration and even merger. Many continue to wonder, for example, about whether Independent Sector and state nonprofit associations (and the Council on Foundations and regional associations of grant makers) should be folded together or at least work more closely with one another. In the area of nonprofit data and research, the Foundation Center, National Center for Charitable Statistics, and GuideStar have some overlap, and many nonprofit education and research institutes work on similar issues.

In reality, reducing redundancy by merging turf-conscious IOs can be difficult. Moreover, eliminating all redundancy through mergers is probably not even desirable, since duplicative capacity and competition can be beneficial. In fact, actual mergers have been rare, although some organizations (for example, the National Council of Nonprofits) have spent considerable time exploring possibilities.

Compared with mergers, collaborations, both formal and informal, may be a more promising way to minimize the negative consequences of the current overlaps. In recent years, the Urban Institute, Foundation Center, and GuideStar collaborated on a multi-year study of foundation expenses and compensation.[73] The Council on Foundations, Foundation Center, and ARNOVA have worked together on a diversity initiative. The Electronic Data Initiative for Nonprofits brought together a broad range of partners to advocate for an expeditious, smooth transition to electronic filing of nonprofits' tax forms. Nonprofit research centers at Arizona State University, Indiana University, and Grand Valley State University have joined forces as the AIM Alliance to develop standardized research protocols, jointly publish and disseminate research findings, cross-deliver flagship programs, and cross-participate in other significant events. In 2010, the National Council of Nonprofits and the Urban Institute collaborated on a national study of nonprofit-government contracting and grants. The Aspen Institute's Program on Philanthropy and Social Innovation is hosting a group of data and research-oriented IOs to explore issues of mutual concern, including an interest in having government do more to support nonprofit data and research.

Many of these and other collaborations have been helped along by encouragement from funders. Leadership changes at some IOs have also opened the door to discussion of new collaborations. A series of meetings earlier in the decade of 30-35 IO executives and IO funders helped these leaders get to know each other better, which generally is a prerequisite for collaboration. However, these larger meetings as well as informal lunch-time meetings of the half-dozen member Infrastructure Exchange Group quickly ran their course, partly because of frustration with the lack of clear outcomes. With the end of these meetings, many IOs leaders still do not know each other very well, and lack of familiarity and trust remain obstacles to collaboration.

Another obstacle to collaboration is the significant earned revenue that some IOs are able to raise. IOs that receive substantial funding from foundations are generally open to at least considering recommendations from their donors about exploring possible collaborations. However, IOs that rely more on earned revenue than foundation grants are less susceptible to foundation encouragement. More fresh thinking is needed about how to overcome these and other obstacles to sensible IO collaboration.

Challenges for IOs in Supporting the Overall Nonprofit Sector

IOs face major tests not only in raising their own organizational performance but also in fulfilling their mission to help the broader nonprofit sector meet the numerous important challenges it faces.

IMPROVING ACCOUNTABILITY AND EFFECTIVENESS. An important challenge for the broad nonprofit sector is the ever-increasing pressure on nonprofits to increase their accountability and impact. Spurred by recent declines in public trust of nonprofits, IOs are now seeking new ways of enhancing nonprofits' accountability and performance.

"Accountability" is an especially elusive term, and there is no clear consensus on exactly what "accountability" is or how it can be achieved (see chapter 16 of this volume). Under the rubric of accountability, IOs and others are seeking to increase the amount of financial and other information that nonprofits and foundations make available to the public, ensure ethical behavior, enhance board oversight, and secure compliance with relevant government laws and regulations. In pursuit of accountability, IOs are contemplating or actually undertaking a variety of initiatives, including the development of codes of ethics, governance-related education and training, and the certification of responsible behavior. For example, the Maryland Association of Nonprofit Organizations has developed a Standards for Excellence program that sets high standards and promotes excellence and accountability for nonprofits through self-regulation. In 2007, Independent Sector's Panel on the Nonprofit Sector released its report on ethical practices, with a discussion of thirty-three principles to ensure responsible behavior by nonprofits.[74] To be sure, while IOs are increasing their efforts in the area of accountability, some argue that it is essentially impossible for the sector to regulate itself and that only government can truly hold nonprofits accountable.[75]

There are also many IO initiatives aimed at helping nonprofits improve their effectiveness. Reflecting the current interest in this area, two IOs focused specifically on helping nonprofits and foundations become more effective, the Center for Effective Philanthropy and Grantmakers for Effective Organizations, have grown rapidly over the past decade even while many other IOs are shrinking or barely holding their own. Interest in improving nonprofit effectiveness has been spurred by the multiplication of efforts to rate and report on nonprofit performance and accountability. There are now a variety of "rating" agencies— including the BBB Wise Giving Alliance, Charity Navigator, GuideStar, Kiva, the Center for High Impact Philanthropy at the University of Pennsylvania, Great Nonprofits, and others—that evaluate nonprofits on different aspects of their accountability and effectiveness.

The challenge to IOs to assure nonprofit accountability and effectiveness is enormous. They have been called on to set standards and benchmarks; consult with, educate, and train nonprofit leaders and boards; monitor compliance; and punish transgressions. Although this responsibility is immense, the ever-expanding nonprofit sector cannot increase its value to society simply by growing. If IOs and the sector fail to pay more attention to accountability and performance issues, they will risk losing the public support that is critical to the health of the sector.

COMMUNICATING A COMPELLING VISION FOR THE OVERALL NON-PROFIT SECTOR. If IOs and the overall nonprofit sector do not meet the current accountability and performance challenges they face, they risk further damage to public confidence in and support of the nonprofit sector. Already, public understanding of nonprofits seems only modest, and public confidence in nonprofits appears to be falling, at least according to surveys conducted by the nonprofit scholar Paul Light.[76]

Some uncertainty about the rationale for the nonprofit sector compounds the public education and confidence problems. Are nonprofits really operating any differently than for-profits in some areas? For example, journalists have written some cutting articles about the uncharitable activity of nonprofit hospitals, and congressional investigations and hearings have probed whether nonprofit hospitals are, in fact, any different than their for-profit competitors and whether they continue to deserve tax-exempt status.[77] In its recent extended debate on health care reform legislation, Congress considered including a provision that would have required nonprofit hospitals to provide a minimum annual level of charitable care.[78] Congress pulled back from this requirement in the legislation it finally passed in March 2010, but it did mandate that nonprofit hospitals conduct a "community health-needs assessment" at least once every three years and that the IRS review each nonprofit hospital's community benefit work every three years.[79]

Sector blurring, the fading of distinctions between nonprofit and for-profit organizations, clearly complicates the communication challenge for nonprofit leaders. If for-profits are increasingly providing services that nonprofits have traditionally provided, the question for some becomes: Why do we need a non-profit sector?[80]

One way for nonprofits to respond to sector blurring is to downplay their service-providing activities and emphasize their other, perhaps more distinctive, roles as builders of civil society and as advocacy groups. This approach seems to have gained some currency over the last decade, but it may be problematic. IOs are apt to have a difficult time communicating the distinction between nonprofits and for-profits as long as program service fees, which are the natural source of revenue for for-profits, also constitute the largest portion of nonprofit revenues.[81]

To articulate the importance of the nonprofit sector effectively to the public, infrastructure organizations need to enunciate clearly the correlation between the healthy functioning of the nonprofit sector and the healthy functioning of American society. In other words, a vital nonprofit sector must be understood as an essential building block of an engaged citizenry, a just society, and a healthy democracy. Nonprofit leaders have been drawn to the work of Robert Putnam, the author of *Bowling Alone: The Collapse and Revival of American Community*, for ideas about the role that nonprofits might play in building, or rebuilding, American civil society.[82] The challenge of developing and communicating a compelling vision for the sector is an important task for nonprofit and IO leaders in the years ahead.

FRAMING A BOLDER APPROACH TO PUBLIC POLICY. In light of the public's limited understanding of the nonprofit sector and its declining confidence in the sector's performance, it is perhaps not surprising that IOs have advanced relatively modest, narrowly focused, defensive public policy agendas on the nonprofit sector's behalf in recent decades. Rather than promoting their own proposals, IOs often have been in a reactive, defensive mode, fending off attacks such as the proposed Istook amendment in the mid-1990s and the Grassley-led initiatives in the mid-2000s. This reactive, tactical, crisis-oriented mode has had some payoff for IOs, and the nonprofit sector has fared relatively well in recent times. Independent Sector gets high marks from many sector leaders for neutralizing the probes by Senator Grassley.

Yet there is still widespread sentiment that IOs should be bolder, more proactive, and more strategic in advancing sector interests regarding nonprofit-government relations and other issues. For example, IOs could have been much more active in developing and advocating for a nonprofit policy agenda in the 2008 presidential election. In fact, IOs were virtually invisible during the campaign season. Indeed, two impressive, recent nonprofit policy-related initiatives, the "Serve America" legislation and the proposals outlined in the "Forward Together" Declaration, were developed largely outside mainstream IOs.[83]

For IOs to be more proactive, it will be necessary for them to overcome inertia and the lack of consensus among their constituent members, especially the large foundations that do much to set the sector's policy agenda. When members themselves are content with the way things are or when they disagree, as they often do, it is difficult for IOs to break the inertia of the status quo and take bold policy initiatives.

Another obstacle to more aggressive policy work by sector-wide IOs is the subsector orientation of many nonprofits. Nonprofits are concerned primarily with policy developments in their own fields—health, education, human services, or the arts. These subsector-specific interests are generally advanced by subsector associations, which may represent for-profits in the subfield as well as nonprofits. Only secondarily do individual nonprofits focus on issues that cut across nonprofit subsectors and turn to sector-wide IOs for assistance.

IOs may also shy away from active public policy activity because many sector leaders seem wedded to an old "philanthropic" model of the nonprofit sector that emphasizes the sector's reliance on philanthropic support. This view fails to take sufficient account of the current importance of government funding in the balance sheet of nonprofits and the stake that nonprofits now have in government action. Nonprofit leaders and IOs must recognize just how much they are affected by government action, how much they have to offer government, and therefore how much they need a more proactive public policy.[84]

In this context, it is interesting to note the only relatively modest support that nonprofits and foundations gave to the Nonprofit Sector and Community Solutions Act of 2010 (H.R. 5533), which was proposed by Representative Betty McCollum, a Democrat from Minnesota, in June 2010. The proposed legislation recognized the ongoing partnership between the federal government and the nonprofit sector and sought to strengthen it by establishing two new federal entities, the U.S. Council on the Nonprofit Sector and the Interagency Working Group on the Nonprofit Sector, and expanding federal support for nonprofit data and research. The legislation made little headway in part because Rep. McCollum's Democratic party lost its majority status in the November 2010 election but also because of opposition from some nonprofit and foundation leaders concerned that the McCollum proposal might have other, less friendly amendments added to it as it moved through Congress or that, once established, a new federal office on the nonprofit sector would become an unwieldy bureaucracy that would increase regulation of nonprofits.

To secure passage of this or other pro-sector legislation, IOs and other nonprofit advocates will have to resolve differences among sector leaders and will also need to find new ways to enhance the nonprofit sector's standing with elected officials and other policymakers. Because nonprofits cannot endorse political candidates or make campaign contributions, sector advocates currently operate in the policy process with one or even two hands tied behind their backs. Some interesting recent efforts to increase nonprofits' political standing are the Nonprofit Congress, a project of the National Council of Nonprofits; the work of the Nonprofit Voter Engagement Network; and the V3 Campaign and CForward PAC, which are both initiatives launched by Robert Egger, a Washington, D.C.-based nonprofit leader. Unfortunately, many of these initiatives have received only modest donor support. More foundation backing has been forthcoming for strengthening policy work at the larger IOs, Independent Sector and the Council on Foundations. These are all promising developments, but more active steps are needed.

MEETING THE NONPROFIT SECTOR'S LEADERSHIP AND FUNDING CHALLENGES. A newer challenge that has come into sharper focus in recent years is a leadership crisis in the sector that is projected to get worse. A broad range of studies point to a variety of current or future workforce-related problems for nonprofits: burnout among current executive directors, ambivalence in the next generation about filling leadership positions, challenges in recruiting diverse staff, cross-generational tensions, and a projected shortfall in the availability of individuals qualified to be senior nonprofit leaders in the years to come (see also chapter 18 of this volume).[85] Some IOs—including Idealist, Bridgestar, and the Nonprofit Leadership Alliance (formerly American Humanics)—are moving to address these leadership challenges, but clearly there is room for other IOs to help with this emerging problem.[86]

In addition to this human resource challenge, the sector has long-standing, persistent financial resource problems. At least some IOs seem to be taking new interest in helping nonprofits with their need for adequate, stable funding. With the lid on government funding (except for the recent bump derived from stimulus-related funding) and with philanthropic support not yet increasing as projected, more nonprofits are turning to earned revenue for needed financial resources. Several IOs, including the Social Enterprise Alliance, Community Wealth Ventures, and others, have emerged to help nonprofits navigate the tricky world of earned revenue. Other IOs, such as the Nonprofit Finance Fund, are seeking to develop and channel new resources to nonprofits, while still others are conducting research about how to significantly expand funding for nonprofits.[87]

MAKING IO SERVICES MORE AVAILABLE TO UNDERSERVED NONPROFITS. Despite the growth of IOs in recent decades, there are still some important holes, or weak spots, in the nonprofit infrastructure. Existing IOs do not entirely meet current needs, and action is needed to fill these gaps.[88]

Management support is not obtainable in numerous locales, including many rural and poor areas, and even when it is available it is unaffordable for many nonprofits, especially small and medium-sized organizations.[89] Another important gap at the state and local levels in many areas is the absence of strong IOs focused on advocating for the nonprofit sector as a whole. This weakness is especially troubling in this devolutionary era when public policy decisions of importance to the nonprofit sector are increasingly being made at the state and local levels. It is appropriate that state nonprofit associations and regional associations of grant makers have been established and are taking on more responsibility in many areas. However, such associations are still lacking in quite a few jurisdictions and remain weak in many of the places where they do exist.

Many state and regional nonprofit associations are relatively young organizations that are struggling to build membership bases and obtain financial support.[90] Like other membership associations, their advocacy activities are handicapped by the free-rider problem. Potential members of state nonprofit associations can benefit from the policy work of the associations without joining them. To compensate for the lack of support from free riders, strong state nonprofit associations have developed support from foundation grants and other sources of revenue to supplement membership dues, but such strong associations are few in number. Overall, despite the best efforts of the National Council of Nonprofits and others, nonprofit infrastructure is uneven at the state level, and the nonprofit sector has not adjusted adequately to devolutionary trends. Since bills affecting the nonprofit sector are introduced in state legislative bodies at significantly higher rates than they are in the federal Congress, enhancing the capacity of state-level policy infrastructure is imperative.[91]

A final gap, though one that may be closing, is the lack of sufficient infrastructure to grow philanthropy and increase its impact. Few organizations are working, especially at the national policy level, to increase the overall level of charitable giving in the United States. Of course individual nonprofits seek to increase donations to their own organizations, and this activity does much to raise the total volume of philanthropic giving. Community foundations and other intermediary funders are also working to expand donations. However, currently there are few organizations whose primary mission is to increase the aggregate level of philanthropy in this country, especially by means of national-scale, policy-based approaches. As a result we probably have less philanthropy than we could have. Researchers at Boston College predict a $40 trillion transfer of wealth by those who pass away in the first half of this century, some portion of which will be used for philanthropic giving. Yet, there exists no national organization whose primary job is to maximize the share of that transfer that goes to philanthropy rather than to heirs, government, or other purposes.[92]

A related gap is that there are also still relatively few IOs working with donors to make their giving more effective.[93] Although the number of organizations working to educate donors—including Rockefeller Philanthropy Advisors, the Philanthropic Initiative, Philanthropy Workshop West, the Aspen Institute's Program on Philanthropy and Social Innovation and others—is increasing, their market penetration with donors is still relatively modest, and there is definitely room for more growth. There is also need for more agencies, such as BBB Wise Giving Alliance, GuideStar, Charity Navigator, and GreatNonprofits, that provide information about and may even rate nonprofits and thereby signal donors about where their philanthropy can have the most impact. If philanthropy is to continue playing an important role in the nonprofit sector, new IOs must emerge or existing IOs must expand to help philanthropy maintain and increase its overall size and effectiveness.[94]

Concluding Thoughts

At the beginning of a new decade, nonprofit infrastructure organizations stand at something of a crossroads. In recent decades IOs have come a long way, successfully overcoming the significant hurdles of the free-rider problem and the subsector orientation of many nonprofits to develop into important, supportive institutions giving voice to sector-wide interests and helping improve the effectiveness of many nonprofit organizations.

However, despite this progress, infrastructure organizations are facing an array of tough challenges. IOs confront some difficult tests for themselves as organizations, including the need for a more secure funding base, the need for improved performance, and the need for increased collaboration. At the same time IOs are being called on to help the nonprofit sector as a whole address some thorny challenges, including the sector's need to adhere to high ethical and performance standards; the sector's need to communicate a more compelling vision regarding its role in society; the sector's need for a stronger, more proactive voice in the policy process; the sector's need to address gaps in human and financial resources; and the sector's need to better meet the problems of underserved populations.

IOs have enjoyed some notable successes in recent years, but they have also sometimes seemed unimaginative and timid in responding to the significant challenges they face. In terms of the overall themes of this volume, as IOs continue to professionalize their own operations and advance the professionalization of the nonprofit field, they must work to avoid the rigidity, narrowness, and indifference that are the dark side of professionalism. IOs must take care to retain in their own organizations and promote in the broader nonprofit sector the dynamism, passion, and openness to change that have long been hallmarks of the nonprofit sector. And for this they will need the continued, and even expanded, support of their members, funders, and other stakeholders.

Notes

1. The limited literature on nonprofit infrastructure includes Union Institute, *Mission Possible: 200 Ways to Strengthen the Nonprofit Sector's Infrastructure* (Washington: 1996); "Funding Infrastructure: An Investment in the Nonprofit Sector's Future" (special issue on infrastructure) *Nonprofit Quarterly* 12 (2004); "Building the Power Grid" (special issue on infrastructure), *Nonprofit Quarterly* 15, no. 4 (Winter 2008); David Brown and others, "The Nonprofit Quarterly Study on Nonprofit and Philanthropic Infrastructure," report for *Nonprofit Quarterly,* 2009 (www.nonprofitquarterly.org/images/infrastudy.pdf [June 1, 2009]).

2. Alan Abramson conducted these interviews. The analysis offered in this chapter is also informed by his long involvement with many of the organizations discussed in these pages. In particular, he has worked on nonprofit issues at the Urban Institute, the Aspen Institute, and George Mason University, and has served on the boards of directors of the Association for Research on Nonprofit Organizations and Voluntary Action and the National Council of Nonprofits and on advisory committees for Independent Sector and the Council on Foundations. He also has served as a consultant to Independent Sector on federal budget issues.

3. Amos G. Warner, *American Charities: A Study in Philanthropy and Economics* (1894; reprint, New York: Arno Press and New York Times, 1971).

4. Ibid., p. 363.

5. For an actual map of the U.S. nonprofit infrastructure, see David O. Renz, "The U.S. Nonprofit Infrastructure Mapped," *Nonprofit Quarterly* 15, no. 4 (Winter 2008): 17–20.

6. See Mancur Olson, *The Logic of Collective Action: Public Goods and the Theory of Groups* (Harvard University Press, 1971), pp. 36—52; and James Q. Wilson, *Political Organizations* (New York: Basic Books, 1973), pp. 30–55, for detailed discussions of the organizational challenges of providing collective goods.

7. See Wilson, *Political Organizations,* pp. 39–45, for discussion of "solidary" incentives.

8. Council on Foundations membership figures are available on the council's website (www.cof.org/files/Bamboo/about/whoweare/documents/Who-We-Are.pdf [May 23. 2011]). According to the latest estimates from the Foundation Center, assets of all U.S. foundations totaled $622 billion in 2010; see Steven Lawrence and Reina Mukai, "Foundation Growth and Giving Estimates: Current Outlook, 2011 Edition" (New York: Foundation Center, 2011), p. 5 (http://foundationcenter.org/gainknowledge/research/pdf/fgge11.pdf [May 20, 2011]).

9. Until recently, another affinity group, the National Network of Grantmakers, advocated for progressive grant makers, but it has now closed.

10. Dennis R. Young, "Games Universities Play: An Analysis of the Institutional Contexts of Centers of Nonprofit Study," in *Nonprofit Management Education: U.S. and World Perspectives,* edited by Michael O'Neill and Kathleen Fletcher (Westport, Conn.: Praeger, 1998), p. 119. The Nonprofit Academic Centers Council has fifty member academic centers (www.naccouncil.org/members.asp [May 22, 2011]).

11. Naomi B. Wish and Roseanne M. Mirabella, "Curricular Variations in Nonprofit Management Graduate Programs," *Nonprofit Management and Leadership* 9, no. 1 (1998): 99; Roseanne M. Mirabella, "Nonprofit Management Education: Current Offerings in University-Based Programs," Seton Hall University website (http://academic.shu.edu/npo/ [May 23, 2011]).

12. Rick Smith, "Building the Nonprofit Sector Knowledge Base: Can Academic Centers and Management Support Organizations Come Together?" *Nonprofit Management and Leadership* 8, no. 1 (1997): 90.

13. Ibid., p. 90.

14. John McKiernan, ed., *Directory of Management Support Providers for Nonprofit Organizations* (Denver: Applied Research and Development Institute International, 1998), p. 23.

15. Cited in ibid., p. 23.

16. Ibid., p. 15.

17. Ibid., p. 18.

18. Ibid., pp. 23–24; see also Thomas E. Backer, Jane Ellen Bleeg, and Kathryn Groves, "The Expanding Universe: New Directions in Nonprofit Capacity Building" (Encino, Calif.: Human Interaction Research Institute, 2004).

19. Foundation Center, "Catalog of Nonprofit Literature" (http://cnl.foundationcenter. org), and "Philanthropic Studies Index" (http://cheever.ulib.iupui.edu/psipublicsearch).

20. The *Chronicle of Philanthropy* has compiled a useful list of nonprofit blogs (http:// philanthropy.com/giveandtake [May 27, 2009]).

21. For an influential early discussion of venture philanthropy see Christine W. Letts, William Ryan, and Allen Grossman, "Virtuous Capital: What Foundations Can Learn from Venture Capitalists," in *Harvard Business Review on Nonprofits* (Harvard Business School Press, 1999). For a broader discussion of the new tools and actors that have surfaced in the philanthropic arena in recent years, see Lester M. Salamon, ed., *New Frontiers of Philanthropy: The New Tools and New Actors Reshaping Philanthropy* (San Francisco: Jossey-Bass, forthcoming in 2012).

22. Robert H. Bremner, *American Philanthropy*, 2nd ed. (University of Chicago Press, 1988), p. 165.

23. See Eleanor L. Brilliant, *Private Charity and Public Inquiry: A History of the Filer and Peterson Commissions* (Indiana University Press, 2000), pp. 13–23; Peter Dobkin Hall, *Inventing the Nonprofit Sector and Other Essays on Philanthropy, Voluntarism, and Nonprofit Organizations* (Johns Hopkins University Press, 1992), pp. 67–68.

24. Hall, *Inventing the Nonprofit Sector*, pp. 68–69.

25. Ibid., p. 69, citing F. Emerson Andrews, *Foundation Watcher* (Lancaster, Pa.: Franklin and Marshall College, 1973); James Allen Smith, "The Foundation Center Fifty Years On," in *Philanthropy in the 21st Century: The Foundation Center's 50th Anniversary Interviews*, edited by Mitch Nauffts (New York: Foundation Center, 2006).

26. Hall, *Inventing the Nonprofit Sector*, pp. 69–70.

27. Ibid., pp. 70–71.

28. Bremner, *American Philanthropy*, pp. 181–82.

29. Hall, *Inventing the Nonprofit Sector*, p. 72.

30. Ray La Montagne (Rockefeller family associate), memo to John D. Rockefeller III, September 21, 1964, cited in Hall, *Inventing the Nonprofit Sector*, p. 72.

31. Darlene Siska, "Building a Sector," *Foundation News and Commentary* 40, no. 2 (1999): 50; Brilliant, *Private Charity and Public Inquiry*, p. 55; La Montagne memo, p. 72.

32. Alan Pifer, *Philanthropy in an Age of Transition: The Essays of Alan Pifer* (New York: Foundation Center, 1984), p. 44.

33. Ibid., p. 53.

34. Among the new regulations aimed at foundations were a prohibition of self-dealing transactions, new payout rules, limits on excess business holdings, a tax on foundation investment income, reduction of the charitable deduction for contributions of capital gain property to most private foundations, and new restrictions to prevent foundation influence on campaigns or legislation. See Thomas A. Troyer, *The 1969 Private Foundation Law: Historical Perspective on Its Origins and Underpinnings* (Washington: Council on Foundations, 2000), pp. 18–22.

35. See Brilliant, *Private Charity and Public Inquiry,* pp. 39–52, 99–110, and elsewhere, and Hall, *Inventing the Nonprofit Sector,* pp. 73–80, for discussions of the evolution of John D. Rockefeller III's views on the philanthropic community and its need for reform and unity.

36. Peter Dobkin Hall, "A Historical Overview of the Private Nonprofit Sector," in *The Nonprofit Sector: A Research Handbook,* edited by Walter W. Powell (Yale University Press, 1987), p. 20.

37. William G. Bowen and others, *The Charitable Nonprofits* (San Francisco: Jossey-Bass, 1994), p. 41.

38. Paul N. Ylvisaker, "Foundations and Nonprofit Organizations," in Powell, *Nonprofit Sector,* p. 375.

39. Virginia A. Hodgkinson, "Creating a Third Sector of American Life," in *Toward a Stronger Voluntary Sector: The "Filer Commission" and the State of Philanthropy* (Indiana University, Center on Philanthropy, 1996), p. 4.

40. Commission on Private Philanthropy and Public Need, *Giving in America: Toward a Stronger Voluntary Sector* (New York: 1975), p. 26.

41. Brian O'Connell, *Powered by Coalition: The Story of the Independent Sector* (San Francisco: Jossey-Bass, 1997), p. 21.

42. Hall, "Historical Overview," p. 21.

43. On the federal budget's impact on the nonprofit sector in the early 1980s, see Lester M. Salamon with Alan J. Abramson, *The Federal Government and the Nonprofit Sector: Implications of the Reagan Budget Proposals* (Washington: Urban Institute, 1981), and Lester M. Salamon and Alan J. Abramson, *The Federal Budget and the Nonprofit Sector* (Washington: Urban Institute Press, 1982).

44. Hall, "Historical Overview," p. 21.

45. Dennis R. Young, "Complementary, Supplementary, or Adversarial? A Theoretical and Historical Examination of Nonprofit-Government Relations in the United States," in *Nonprofits and Government: Collaboration and Conflict,* edited by Elizabeth T. Boris and C. Eugene Steuerle (Washington: Urban Institute, 1999), p. 60.

46. See Carol De Vita, "Nonprofits and Devolution: What Do We Know?" in Boris and Steuerle, *Nonprofits and Government,* pp. 229–30.

47. Elizabeth J. Reid, "Nonprofit Advocacy and Political Participation," in Boris and Steuerle, *Nonprofits and Government,* p. 316.

48. Ibid., p. 316.

49. Young, "Complementary, Supplementary, or Adversarial?" p. 61.

50. See, for example, David Barstow, "A Nation Challenged: The Charities; In Congress, Harsh Words for Red Cross," *New York Times,* November 7, 2001.

51. See, for example, Eric Nalder, "CEO's Rewards at Non-Profit," *San Jose Mercury News,* April 27, 2003; "Some Officers of Charities Steer Assets to Selves," *Boston Globe,* October 9, 2003, and subsequent articles in the six-part "Charity Begins at Home" series; and David B. Ottaway and Joe Stephens, "Nonprofit Land Bank Amasses Billions," *Washington Post,* May 4, 2003, and subsequent articles in the three-part "Big Green: Inside the Nature Conservancy" series.

52. See 108th Congress, H.R. 7: The Charitable Giving Act of 2003 (http://thomas.loc.gov/cgi-bin/query/z?c108:H.R.7).

53. Senate Committee on Finance, "Staff Discussion Draft: Proposals for Reform and Best Practices in the Area of Tax-Exempt Organizations" (Washington: June 22, 2004), pp. 1–19.

54. For the panel's reports, see Independent Sector, Panel on the Nonprofit Sector, "Strengthening Transparency, Governance, and Accountability of Charitable Organizations:

A Final Report to Congress and the Nonprofit Sector" (June 2005), "Supplemental Report" (April 2006), and "Principles for Good Governance and Ethical Practice: A Guide for Charities and Foundations" (October 2007) (www.nonprofitpanel.org/Report/index.html; free to users logged in).

55. Hall, *Inventing the Nonprofit Sector,* p. 91. On the origins of professionalization among nonprofits, see Eleanor L. Brilliant, *The United Way* (Columbia University Press, 1990), pp. 20–21; Warner, *American Charities,* pp. 402–03; Roy Lubove, *The Professional Altruist: The Emergence of Social Work as a Career, 1880–1930* (New York: Atheneum, 1980).

56. Hall, *Inventing the Nonprofit Sector,* p. 91; Brilliant, *Private Charity and Public Inquiry,* p. 101.

57. Lester M. Salamon, "Partners in Public Service: The Scope and Theory of Government-Nonprofit Relations," in Powell, *Nonprofit Sector,* pp. 114–15.

58. Ibid.

59. Robert O. Bothwell, "Trends in Self-Regulation and Transparency of Nonprofits in the U.S.," *International Journal of Not-for-Profit Law* 2, no. 3 (March 2000) (/www.icnl.org/ www.icnl.org/knowledge/ijnl/vol2iss3/sg_2.htm [October 27, 2010]).

60. See, for example, Union Institute, *Mission Possible,* pp. 37–46. In recent years, even some of the larger IOs have had to cut spending because of recession-induced reductions in their own funding.

61. Suzanne Perry, "Details Posted about Stimulus Money for Nonprofit Management Help," *Chronicle of Philanthropy,* May 14, 2009.

62. Suzanne Perry, "Fight Continues for Federal Program to Help Small Charities," *Chronicle of Philanthropy,* May 20, 2009.

63. Tom Clough, David Brown, and David Renz, "Financial Models for Infrastructure," in Brown and others, "*Nonprofit Quarterly* Study on Nonprofit and Philanthropic Infrastructure," pp. 57–64.

64. On new approaches to evaluating policy advocacy, see Harvard Family Research Project, "Advocacy and Policy Change," *The Evaluation Exchange* 13, no. 1 (Spring 2007). On evaluating management assistance see Deborah Linnell, "Evaluation of Capacity Building: Lessons from the Field," report (Washington: Alliance for Nonprofit Management, 2003).

65. For a thoughtful case statement for nonprofit infrastructure see Cynthia Gibson and Ruth McCambridge, "Why Every Foundation Should Fund Infrastructure," *Nonprofit Quarterly* 12 (2004, special issue on infrastructure): 8–15.

66. Thomas E. Backer, "Strengthening Nonprofits: Foundation Initiatives for Nonprofit Organizations," in *Building Capacity in Nonprofit Organizations,* edited by Carol J. De Vita and Cory Fleming (Washington: Urban Institute, 2001), pp. 44, 64, 66–67, 89.

67. Alliance for Nonprofit Management, "About the Alliance" (www.allianceonline.org/ about/index.php [June 1, 2009]).

68. See Grantmakers for Effective Organizations, "About GEO" (www.geofunders.org/ aboutgeo.aspx [May 20, 2011]).

69. See, for example, Colin B. Burke, "Nonprofit History's New Numbers (and the Need for More)," *Nonprofit and Voluntary Sector Quarterly* 30, no. 2 (June 2001): 174–203; Charles T. Clotfelter, Paul J. DiMaggio, and Janet A. Weiss, "Resources for Scholarship in the Nonprofit Sector: Studies in the Political Economy of Information, parts 1 and 2," *American Behavioral Scientist* 45, nos. 10 and 11 (June and July, 2002). An important existing resource for scholars is the Form 990 database that has been created by the National Center for Charitable Statistics at the Urban Institute. Important data-related breakthroughs have also been made by Lester Salamon and his team of researchers at Johns Hopkins University in their

Comparative Nonprofit Sector Project and in their work with the United Nations Statistics Division and the International Labour Organization to create a systematic body of data about the nonprofit sector and volunteering internationally. The Johns Hopkins research team has also successfully tapped the enormous body of data on U.S. nonprofit employment gathered by the federal Bureau of Labor Statistics and state labor agencies through the Quarterly Census of Employment and Wages. What has been lacking in at least some of these initiatives is systematic funding to sustain the efforts, active support from infrastructure organizations for them, and easier access from government agencies to data they have collected..

70. See also "Advancing Nonprofit and Philanthropy Research: Perspectives from a July 2001 Meeting Convened by the Nonprofit Sector Research Fund," Nonprofit Sector Research Fund Working Paper Series, The Aspen Institute, 2001.

71. Smith, "Building the Nonprofit Sector Knowledge Base," p. 91; Thomas J. Billitteri, "Research on Charities Falls Short," *Chronicle of Philanthropy,* November 27, 1997, p. 33.

72. The W. K. Kellogg Foundation's $13.5 million Building Bridges Initiative, which ran from 1997 to 2002, was an example of such an effort. See Katheryn W. Heidrich and Robert F. Long, "The Story of the Building Bridges Initiative" (Battle Creek, Mich.: W. K. Kellogg Foundation, 2004) (www.centerpointinstitute.com/Resources/Documents/Story%20of%20 the%20BBI.pdf [June 1, 2009]). Among the few research initiatives that speak to the needs of nonprofit leaders and policymakers is the Listening Post Project at Johns Hopkins University, which monitors in a systematic and timely way how nonprofits in the United States are responding to a broad range of challenges. Another example of useful applied research is the Urban Institute–National Council of Nonprofits 2010 collaboration on a national study of nonprofit-government contracting and grants in the human services. See Elizabeth T. Boris and others, "Contracts and Grants between Human Service Nonprofits and Governments" (www.urban.org/publications/412229.html [May 20, 2011]) and National Council of Nonprofits, "Government Contracting Crisis" (www.govtcontracting.org [May 20, 2011]). In October 2010 and June 2011, ARNOVA (Association for Research on Nonprofit Organizations and Voluntary Action) convened nonprofit scholars and leaders to identify areas of inquiry where new research is most needed to address concerns about public policies' impact on nonprofits. See Association for Research on Nonprofit Organizations and Voluntary Action, "Public Policy for Nonprofits: Executive Summary of the Report on ARNOVA's Symposium of October 2010" (Indianapolis: ARNOVA, 2011) (www.arnova.org/pdf/ ARNOVA%20Symposium%20Executive%20Summary%20–%20Final.pdf [May 20, 2011]) and "Finances of Nonprofits & Public Policy: A Report from a Symposium" (http://arnova-conference.org/doc/Finances%20of%20NP%27s%20and%20Public%20Policy%20–%20 Executive%20Summary.pdf [January 27, 2012]).

73. Elizabeth T. Boris and others, "What Drives Foundation Expenses and Compensation? Results of a Three-Year Study," report sponsored by the Urban Institute, the Foundation Center, and GuideStar, 2008 (www.urban.org/UploadedPDF/411612_foundation_expenses. pdf).

74. Independent Sector, Panel on the Nonprofit Sector, "Principles for Good Governance and Ethical Practice."

75. Joel Fleishman, "Public Trust in Not-for-Profit Organizations and the Need for Regulatory Reform," in *Philanthropy and the Nonprofit Sector in a Changing America,* edited by Charles T. Clotfelter and Thomas Ehrlich (Indiana University Press, 1999), pp. 188–91.

76. See Paul Light, "How Americans View Charities: A Report on Charitable Confidence, 2008," *Issues in Governance Studies* 13 (Brookings Institution). For another analysis of public confidence in charities that finds little evidence of a "crisis in confidence," see Michael

O'Neill, "Public Confidence in Charitable Nonprofits," *Nonprofit and Voluntary Sector Quarterly* 38, no. 2 (April 2009): 237–69.

77. See, for example, Jonathan Cohn, "Uncharitable?" *New York Times,* December 19, 2004.

78. Robert Pear, "Hospitals Mobilizing to Fight Proposed Charity Care Rules," *New York Times,* June 1, 2009.

79. Suzanne Perry and Grant Williams, "Health Centers, Hospitals to See Changes under Law," *Chronicle of Philanthropy,* April 4, 2010 (http://philanthropy.com/article/Health-Centers-Hospitals-to/64922/ [May 20, 2011]).

80. For a summary of research on the role of nonprofits in the health care field, see Aspen Institute, Nonprofit Sector Research Fund, "The Vital Role of Nonprofits in American Healthcare: Benefits and Challenges," *Snapshots,* no. 39 (August 2005): 1–4.

81. Elizabeth T. Boris, "The Nonprofit Sector in the 1990s," in Clotfelter and Ehrlich, *Philanthropy and the Nonprofit Sector,* p. 14. It should be noted, however, that nonprofit revenues from program service fees include both fees paid directly by nonprofit clients and the significant fees paid by government on behalf of nonprofits' needy and elderly clients.

82. Robert D. Putnam, *Bowling Alone: The Collapse and Revival of American Community* (New York: Simon and Schuster, 2000); Robert D. Putnam, "Bowling Alone: America's Declining Social Capital," *Journal of Democracy* 6, no. 1 (1995): 65–78; Robert D. Putnam, *Making Democracy Work: Civic Traditions in Modern Italy* (Princeton University Press, 1993).

83. The Serve America legislation had significant input from the America Forward Coalition (www.americaforward.org). For information about the Serve America Act see Corporation for National Community Service, "Edward M. Kennedy Serve America Act of 2009" (www.nationalservice.gov/about/serveamerica/index.asp [May 20, 2011]). "Forward Together: Empowering America's Citizen Sector for the Change We Need," was a declaration developed in 2009 by participants in a seminar organized by the Listening Post Project at Johns Hopkins University's Institute for Policy Studies, Center for Civil Society Studies (www.ccss.jhu.edu/index.php?section=content&view=9&sub=5&tri=102).

84. The "Forward Together" declaration (see previous note) explicitly recognizes the value of the nonprofit sector to society, the sector's interdependence with the other sectors, and the need to strengthen nonprofit-government and other partnerships.

85. Jeanne Bell, Richard Moyers, and Timothy Wolfred, "Daring to Lead 2006: A National Study of Nonprofit Executive Leadership," research report prepared for CompassPoint Nonprofit Services and Eugene and Agnes E. Meyer Foundation, 2006 (www.meyerfdn.org/downloads/4DaringtoLead2006d.pdf); Marla Cornelius, Patrick Corvington, and Albert Ruesga, "Ready to Lead? Next Generation Leaders Speak Out," report prepared for the Annie E. Casey Foundation, Eugene and Agnes E. Meyer Foundation, Idealist.org, and CompassPoint Nonprofit Services, 2008 (www.meyerfoundation.org/downloads/ready_to_lead/ReadytoLead2008.pdf); Frances Kunreuther, Helen Kim, and Robby Rodriguez, *Working across Generations: Defining the Future of Nonprofit Leadership* (San Francisco: Jossey-Bass, 2008); Lester M. Salamon and Stephanie Lessans Geller, "The Nonprofit Workforce Crisis: Real or Imagined?" Listening Post Project Communiqué No. 8 (Johns Hopkins University, Institute for Policy Studies, Center for Civil Society Studies, 2007); Thomas J. Tierney, "The Leadership Deficit," *Stanford Social Innovation Review* (Summer 2006), pp. 26–35 (www.ssireview.org/articles/entry/the_leadership_deficit).

86. For a national workforce agenda for nonprofits see Stephanie Lessans Geller and Lester M. Salamon, "A Nonprofit Workforce Action Agenda: Report on the Listening Post Project Roundtable on Nonprofit Recruitment and Retention," Listening Post Project Communiqué

No. 10 (Johns Hopkins University, Institute for Policy Studies, Center for Civil Society Studies, 2008).

87. See also Salamon, *New Frontiers of Philanthropy.*

88. Hodgkinson, "Creating a Third Sector of American Life," p. 44; Union Institute, *Mission Possible,* pp. 37–46.

89. Brown and others, "*Nonprofit Quarterly* Study on Nonprofit and Philanthropic Infrastructure," p. 12.

90. National Council of Nonprofit Associations, *Strategic and Operational Plan: 2000–2002* (Washington: December 1999), p. 2.

91. Ibid.

92. John J. Havens and Paul G. Schervish, "Why the $41 Trillion Wealth Transfer Is Still Valid: A Review of Challenges and Questions," report (Boston: Boston College, Social Welfare Research Institute, January 2003) (www.bc.edu/content/dam/files/research_sites/cwp/pdf/41trillionreview.pdf [March 8, 2010]); Richard C. Morais, "Huge Wave in Charitable Giving Still Coming," *Forbes.com,* October 2, 2009 (www.forbes.com/2009/10/02/estate-tax-bill-gates-boston-college-personal-finance-bc.html [July 21, 2010]).

93. William and Flora Hewlett Foundation and McKinsey & Company, "The Nonprofit Marketplace: Bridging the Information Gap in Philanthropy," white paper, 2008 (www.hewlett.org/uploads/files/whitepaper.pdf).

94. For an exploration of the revolution now under way in new philanthropic approaches that offers some promise for the future, see Salamon, *New Frontiers of Philanthropy.* Three new books offering advice to donors and nonprofits about how to improve their effectiveness are Leslie R. Crutchfield, John V. Kania, and Mark R. Kramer, *Do More Than Give: The Six Practices of Donors Who Change the World* (San Francisco: Jossey-Bass, 2011); Mario Morino, *Leap of Reason: Managing to Outcomes in an Era of Scarcity* (Washington: Venture Philanthropy Partners, 2011); and Thomas J. Tierney and Joel L. Fleishman, *Give Smart: Philanthropy That Gets Results* (New York: PublicAffairs, 2011).

12

Foundations and Corporate Philanthropy

LESLIE LENKOWSKY

In January 2008, in a widely publicized speech at the World Economic Forum in Davos, Switzerland, the founder of Microsoft Corporation, Bill Gates, called for a new way of helping the world's poor: "creative capitalism." It would rely more extensively on economic incentives to address the problems of developing countries than on government or philanthropic aid. "Such a system would have a twin mission," he argued, "making profits and also improving lives for those who don't fully benefit from market forces. To make the system sustainable, we need to use profit incentives whenever we can."[1] Government and philanthropy would still have significant roles to play, but the most important task for the future would be "finding approaches that meet the needs of the poor in ways that generate profits and recognition for business."[2]

What was most surprising about this speech was not what was said, which echoed ideas that have been advanced previously by the Grameen Bank founder, Muhammad Yunus, and many others, but who said it.[3] Perhaps more than anyone since Andrew Carnegie and John D. Rockefeller, Gates symbolizes American philanthropy. He had endowed the world's largest grant making organization, the Bill and Melinda Gates Foundation. With the addition of Warren Buffett's contributions, it was scheduled to spend an unprecedented amount annually—some $3 billion. Within a few months, Gates himself planned to leave Microsoft to run the foundation full-time. Yet, he used what was likely to be his last appearance at Davos as a corporate chief executive to extol the

459

virtues of business for solving problems that were usually regarded as within the domain of philanthropic and government activity.

Bill Gates's speech was surprising also because the first decade of the twenty-first century had mostly been a good one for institutional grant makers in the United States and elsewhere.[4] Institutional philanthropy is grant making conducted by organizations, rather than directly by individuals. Although they could also be included as forms of individual giving, federated givers such as United Way of America and funds run by for-profit investment firms such as the Fidelity Charitable Gift Fund can also be included in this category.[5] Between 1999 and 2009, the giving of this group—composed principally of independent, corporate, and community foundations—rose by 43 percent, from $23.3 billion to $33.3 billion, after adjusting for inflation.[6] Community foundations, which are endowed by gifts from residents of a particular geographical area, led the way, with a 75 percent increase. At 41 percent growth, independent foundations, which typically are funded by an individual or family, lagged behind but accounted for half of the rise in giving. Corporate foundations, established by businesses, were donating 26 percent more by the end of this period than they were at the beginning.[7]

With such substantially greater resources at their disposal than in the past, institutional grant makers looked better positioned than ever to respond to the kinds of proposals made by Bill Gates.[8] By the close of 2008, the number of institutional grant makers in the United States stood at an all-time high of 75,595, and nearly 30 percent of the largest ones had been created during the first decade of the twenty-first century.[9] Institutional philanthropy accounted for 15.2 percent of American charitable giving, compared to 12 percent in 2000.[10]

Even as Gates was speaking in Davos, however, the United States economy was weakening and grant-making organizations would feel the consequences. In 2009, giving by independent, community, and corporate foundations fell by 8.4 percent, or nearly $4 billion.[11] Even though this reduction was more moderate than many had expected, it brought an end to a long period of expansion. Indeed, the Foundation Center reported that giving by institutional grant makers had previously gone down in only three other years since 1975.[12] Many organizations reduced their spending, especially on administrative costs, and a large number of other grant makers—nearly 40 percent, according to the Foundation Center's estimate—dipped into their endowments to maintain their budgets. Americans donated 15.6 percent less to foundations in 2008 than they had the year before and the number of new foundations rose by just 0.5 percent, the smallest annual growth rate in a generation.[13] Institutional grant makers were also encountering a variety of political storms. In 2004, in a move led by Iowa's Senator Charles Grassley, the United States Congress launched its most extensive investigation of foundations and other parts of the nonprofit sector since the 1960s, when Congressman Wright Patman of Texas presided over nearly a decade of hearings that resulted in the Tax Reform Act of 1969, which imposed a variety of legal restrictions on grant makers that were often characterized as "punitive." This time, legislators focused on whether foundations were using enough of their resources for charitable activities, or whether they were instead providing too many personal benefits to donors, trustees, and staff, such as excessive salaries.

Institutional grant makers also faced accusations of devoting too little money to helping the needy. In 2004, a California research group released a study concluding that less than 10 percent of foundation grants went to "communities of color."[14] Additional research focused on racial, gender, and other forms of diversity among trustees and staffs, as well as grant recipients. Legislation inspired by these investigations that would have required grant makers to reveal more fully how they were using their resources was proposed. It nearly passed the California legislature and versions were considered in Florida and other states, as well as in the United States Congress.[15] Longtime watchdog organizations such as the National Committee for Responsive Philanthropy called upon grant makers to adopt new "criteria" for their grant making that would send more of their money to organizations that helped the "underserved."[16]

Perhaps most interesting, questions as to the proper role of philanthropies also arose from within institutional philanthropy. In the 1990s, a growing number of wealthy individuals and families who had earned their fortunes in the high-tech economic boom became more involved in grant making. As was true of earlier generations of donors, they brought not only new resources but also new ideas, which in this case owed much to their business backgrounds, especially with venture capital firms. They charged that foundations were devoting too much of their resources to funding specific programs, rather than supporting capacity building in the organizations they wanted to assist. They also criticized donors for not paying enough attention to evaluation, neglecting to invest their time and expertise (along with their money) in helping grantees, and focusing more on short-term successes than on sustainable results. The approach this new generation of philanthropists favored—usually called "venture philanthropy" or "high-engagement philanthropy"—also implied that prior experience in institutional philanthropy might be less useful in grant making than knowledge of business ideas and techniques, especially the approaches used by venture capitalists.[17]

Bill Gates's remarks at Davos took this critique a step further. If institutional philanthropy could be improved by adopting business practices, businesses, he seemed to be saying, could attain philanthropic goals, such as helping the needy, while still being profitable.[18] Other high-tech magnates, such as eBay's founders, Pierre Omidyar and Jeffrey Skoll, expressed similar views.[19] So did two influential strategists, Michael E. Porter and Mark R. Kramer, who stated: "When a well-run business applies its vast resources, expertise, and management talent to problems that it understands and in which it has a stake, it can have a greater impact on social good than any other institution or philanthropic organization." Moreover, they predicted, "corporate social responsibility" was likely to become "increasingly important to companies' competitive success" in the future.[20]

Thus, by the end of the first decade of the twenty-first century, institutional philanthropy found itself in a contradictory situation. Its resources were greater than ever before and, if past experience was any guide, were likely to resume growing after the recession was over, though possibly at a slower rate.[21] But it was also facing a series of questions about what it was supporting, how it was governed, and how effective it was in solving social problems. Despite a serious economic downturn, institutional philanthropy had never been so healthy. Yet it had not been so challenged since at least the 1960s.

The roots of this state of affairs can be found in the conflicting impulses that have long shaped the nonprofit sector in the United States, as outlined in the introduction to this volume.

On the one hand, the growth of "civil associations" (as Alexis de Tocqueville called them in *Democracy in America*) reflected the willingness of Americans, in a country that embraced the ideas of equality and limited government, to join together to express views and take action on matters of public concern.[22] By contrast, in "aristocratic countries," Tocqueville wrote, "great undertakings" are done by "a few very powerful and wealthy citizens."[23] Although wealthy citizens in the United States had assumed an "aristocratic" philanthropic role in the early nineteenth century, the activist and voluntarist impulses of the general public produced a larger, livelier, and more diverse variety of voluntary organizations in the United States than in other countries and played an important role in sustaining democratic political life.

In addition, two other forces have also affected the development of the nonprofit sector: commercialism and professionalization. Even at the time of Tocqueville's visit in the 1830s, a growing merchant class was already using its wealth to create institutions such as schools, libraries, and hospitals that, though privately run, were intended to provide a variety of public services to the citizenry. In addition, starting in the middle of the nineteenth century, there was an increase in efforts to improve charitable work by incorporating new knowledge, especially from the sciences. Implicit, and sometimes explicit, in this effort, known as "scientific philanthropy," was the idea that trained professionals could do a better job in running nonprofit groups than civic-minded and well-meaning amateurs.

The development of institutional philanthropy reflected the commercial and professional impulses shaping the nonprofit sector more than the civic and voluntarist ones. Starting with the establishment of the Russell Sage Foundation in 1906 and the Rockefeller Foundation and Carnegie Corporation a few years later, wealthy donors and their advisers embraced the idea that research and analysis could be useful in guiding decisions about what to support. The establishment of the Cleveland Foundation in 1914 brought community foundations into existence, organizations whose leaders believed in the value of social surveys and other methods of investigation for informing their grant making. Influenced by early-twentieth-century principles of "scientific management," major industrial corporations, such as American Telephone & Telegraph and the Ford Motor Company, began to provide a variety of health, social, and educational services for their employees and the communities in which they operated.

Commercial and not just social motives also influenced those who established early philanthropic entities. John D. Rockefeller's philanthropy was partly driven by concerns about his public image, badly tarnished by exposés of his business practices. Community foundations were usually set up by banks, which sought to increase the assets under their management by attracting money for community social projects. Corporate donations were designed not just to provide help that was unavailable from government or other sources at the time, such as retirement pensions or medical care, but also to improve the productivity of a company's workforce and resist unionization.

The result was that the advent of institutional philanthropy marked a new approach to giving. Previous giving had often been a matter of a person's deciding voluntarily how to contribute time or money to a charitable goal. These gifts could be far-sighted and far-reaching, but for better or worse they reflected the often particular—and sometimes paternalistic—interests and intentions of their donors.[24] With notable exceptions, most of such giving was focused on the communities where the givers lived or worked. Partly because religious organizations made up such a substantial portion of the nonprofit sector, a large share of donations was also directed toward them rather than toward nonsectarian social purposes.[25]

The new grant-making organizations changed that pattern. Drawing on their own business experience, donors hired growing numbers of trained experts or practitioners to assist them in making grants.[26] Rather than give money mostly for immediate local needs, they transferred their funds to organizations that built up endowments so that the organization could continue to operate beyond the donors' lifetimes and deal with problems on a long-term basis, such as education for Negroes (the word then used for African Americans) in the South, the quality of American medicine, labor relations, population growth, and many others, which exceeded the scope of smaller or periodic gifts. Support for religious charities became of lower priority for these foundations.

By the 1960s, the largest and most influential grant makers had embraced this model of giving. James Douglas and Aaron Wildavsky later called them the "knowledgeable foundations" because they understood their missions to be supporting the development and application of expertise to problems of broad public concern.[27] The champions of institutional philanthropy's point out that the professionalization of grant making, while not without its problems, seems to have compiled an enviable record of achievement.[28]

But from the beginning, it was also subject to criticism. Attacks often came from populists on the political left and right, who claimed that institutional philanthropy was actually a means of advancing the interests of the wealthy patrons who provided the funding and typically approved the grants, rather than impartially serving the public's interests. These critics achieved their greatest success with the Tax Reform Act of 1969; during nearly a decade of investigations and hearings, proposals that threatened to require foundations to spend all their money and cease operating after they had existed for a number of years received serious consideration. Congress ultimately rejected those proposals but it did enact a series of rules designed to regulate grant making by foundations, including a requirement that they spend—"pay out"—a certain minimum amount of money each year.

Not just the practice of but also the assumption behind institutional philanthropy—that professionalization could improve grant making—has faced several different kinds of criticisms. On the left, or "progressive," end of the political spectrum, organizations such as the National Committee for Responsive Philanthropy have charged that the experts who work for or advise grant-making organizations are really philanthropic mandarins, out of touch with the people they should be trying to help and more adept at creating bureaucratic hurdles than achieving social change. From the political right has come the complaint that the staffs of institutional grant makers do not actually know as much as they claim; cling to outmoded, often technocratic ideas; or pursue agendas that fail to address social problems effectively and may also be at odds with what the donors who underwrote their organizations would have wanted to do. Legislators and regulators have looked suspiciously at the amount of money spent on professional grant-making staffs and consultants or placed into the large endowments that sustain the organizations beyond their donors' lifetimes, and have asked whether more shouldn't be going directly, and more quickly, to organizations directly providing public services.

Underlying these criticisms is an arguably less-than-impressive record of accomplishment by grant-making organizations in recent years.[29] Determining success in philanthropy is never a simple task, yet a number of recent, high-profile foundation efforts in a variety of fields have generally been judged disappointing. Perhaps the most notable was a $500 million "challenge" by the Annenberg Foundation, announced in 1993, whose aim was improving urban school systems. The results are widely acknowledged to have been negligible.[30] And the Robert Wood Johnson Foundation, after investing nearly $90 million over a fifteen-year period in its "Fighting Back" program to deal with community drug and alcohol abuse problems, conceded that its efforts had been unsuccessful.[31] Several other foundations have reached similar conclusions about other major initiatives, and some have made their conclusions public.[32]

To be sure, grant-making organizations could still point to a variety of achievements, although they are often relatively modest.[33] They also continued to undertake ambitious initiatives, such as the Bill and Melinda Gates Foundation's effort to eradicate malaria and other deadly diseases, a campaign that looked much like those undertaken by institutional philanthropy in its early years during the first third of the twentieth century. A number of foundation leaders and observers felt that the cure for what ailed institutional philanthropy was to become more strategic in its efforts, not less—which usually meant more professional.[34]

But others felt that the problems of institutional philanthropy were more fundamental and required changing the model on which it had been built. These critics argued that grant makers, instead of relying on applying scientific or professional expertise, should enlist more involvement from, and have boards and staffs more representative of, those they were seeking to help, should play a more activist role than just making grants to help solve the problems that concern them, and should become more entrepreneurial in their efforts.[35] In other words, institutional philanthropy needed to do more to incorporate the kinds of civic and voluntarist impulses that had long characterized other parts of the American nonprofit sector but not the most notable grant-making organizations.

In short, following a period of unprecedented growth, the resources of grant-making organizations may have been more plentiful than ever, but how they should be deployed was increasingly debated. By 2007, foundations and other institutional donors accounted for little more than 3 percent of the total revenues of publicly supported 501(c)(3) organizations, which are the only kind of nonprofits that can receive foundation grants.[36] But for over a century, they had been playing an important role in the American nonprofit sector, serving not only as financial intermediaries between donors and organizations but also, in theory and often in practice, adding expertise, perspective, continuity, and risk-taking capacity. Critics from outside and within the institutional philanthropic world, however, charged not only that institutional philanthropy was failing to deliver on its promise but also that the value of the approach to grant making it had historically embodied no longer seemed as clear-cut as it once had.

Let's look more closely at the current state of these organizations, the validity of the criticisms leveled against them, and the kinds of changes that may be coming.

The World of Institutional Philanthropy

To discuss institutional philanthropy in the United States as though it had a single identity or expressed a particular approach to grant making vastly over-simplifies the large and complicated array of organizations that the field comprises. Whereas the best-known organizations subscribe to a highly professionalized operational style, the vast majority of foundations are effectively family checkbooks in an institutional form. Most have been endowed by an individual, family, or corporation, but many raise money from the general public and their existence thus depends on maintaining the public's goodwill. A significant number do not make grants at all, but operate their own programs. And many organizations that call themselves foundations do not properly belong in the world of grant makers, since they are effectively fundraising arms for one or more closely affiliated nonprofits.[37]

Still, it is useful to think of institutional philanthropy as consisting of intermediary bodies that collect money from donors and then grant it to charities, or use it for charitable purposes, following procedures that to some degree are independent of the original donors' and recipients' aims.[38] Foundations, corporate giving programs, charity federations, and other kinds of organizations meet these criteria. They serve, in effect, as bankers to the charitable world, collecting money from depositors (donors) and paying it to recipients (charities) on the basis of criteria that they have established and apply.

Rationale

Why should contributors give money to these "banks" when they could just as easily make contributions directly to the charities of their choice? For some donors, the reasons are personal: creating a lasting memorial, deferring giving to the future, or reducing the tax consequences of large increases in income or capital. These goals can also be attained without using an intermediary organization, but just as banks help to make their depositors' funds more productive by investing them, institutional philanthropy allows donors potentially to add value to their gifts to the nonprofit sector.

Some grant-making organizations provide expertise and other kinds of help to people who think they would be unable to contribute responsibly on their own (perhaps because they lack information or have too many resources to dispense without assistance). Others may enable donors to be more confident that their gifts are going to high-priority uses (whether in a community or in, say, the treatment of a disease), because a trustworthy organization can weigh programs against alternatives, often using research methods.

Grant-making organizations can also produce economies of scale, for example, when they aggregate relatively small sums of money that might otherwise go to shareholders and deposit them into a corporate foundation, or collect donations from local businessmen, professionals, or employees for a community foundation or federated fund. And some institutions can create "economies of time" by allowing funds contributed in one period to be available in another period, when they might do more good, and without the time limits that are usually placed on trusts. By establishing and administering substantial funds that are controlled by neither their donors nor the government, grant-making organizations can also provide the equivalent of a venture capital fund for the nonprofit world that can be accessed for innovative, risky, or unpopular causes.

Regardless of the personal motives of contributors, what has made institutional philanthropy attractive and important for donors is the possibility that it will improve their ability to support charities, including by professionalizing their grant making decisions. For that reason, public policy encourages it, such as by exempting from taxation the returns on assets donated to an intermediary. (If the assets had been left in the donor's bank account to appreciate to be used later for direct giving, the returns would have been taxed until they were contributed to a charity.) And because of their potential to have greater impact than individual philanthropy, public policy has carefully watched grant making organizations, sometimes even limiting what they can do, such as by restricting their ability to support political activities more tightly than that of publicly supported charities.

Major Components

What are the contours of institutional philanthropy? And how is it evolving? This section describes the major components of institutional philanthropy.

FOUNDATIONS. Foundations are the most prominent grant-making organizations—the ones most people think of as exemplifying institutional philanthropy. Over 75,000 foundations awarded nearly $45 billion in grants in 2007.[39] Although all foundations share some features, they are conventionally understood as falling into four separate types: independent, operating, community, and corporate.

Most foundations are independent and are established by individuals or families. They range widely in size. Sixty percent (or 46,000) had endowments below $1 million in 2007. Just sixty-nine independent foundations, or 0.1 percent of the total, exceeded $1 billion in assets, but these accounted for one-quarter of the total giving by foundations, held nearly 90 percent of all assets dedicated to institutional philanthropy, and employed 90 percent of all foundation staff.[40] (Foundations with endowments exceeding $10 million made up 10 percent of all independent foundations, and were responsible for three-quarters of total gifts.) Gates, Ford, Rockefeller, and Carnegie are some of the best-known upper-tier names. For the most part these are the foundations that seek the advantages of professionalization for their philanthropic work. The rest were created largely to facilitate charitable giving by a one- or two-generational family.

Most foundations are grant-making bodies that use their resources to provide support for other charitable organizations, such as universities, museums, hospitals, and social service agencies, but nearly 3 percent—or roughly 5,000—are operating foundations, which means that they principally conduct their own programs rather than provide support for other nonprofit groups.[41] Among the best known of these operating foundations are the Open Society Institute and the J. Paul Getty Trust. The largest operating foundations, those with endowments of at least $10 million, account for 6 percent of all operating foundations but make 80 percent of total expenditures. Typically they have sizable, highly professional staff, well-developed organizations, and long-standing missions.[42] Though rooted in their donor's concerns, they normally develop institutional features, such as specialized departments and programs, that make them look more like publicly supported charities than grant-making intermediaries.

The two other types of foundations receive their resources not from a wealthy individual or family but from a broader group of people. One is the community foundation, which obtains its assets from contributors in a particular community. Community foundation organizations are legally classified as "public charities" and receive more favorable tax treatment than other kinds of foundations.[43] They pool the funds of smaller givers into larger endowments, which can exist indefinitely and employ staff or consultants to advise on giving. In effect, community foundations seek to extend the benefits of institutional philanthropy to those who lack the means or desire to establish their own grant-making foundation.

Of the over 700 community foundations that exist today, more than 450 were established after 1980. Although they make up less than 1 percent of grant-making organizations, in 2007 they held about 8 percent of total foundation assets and made nearly 10 percent of all grants. As with the independent foundations, the larger community foundations (such as the New York Community Trust and the San Francisco Foundation) account for well over 90 percent of assets and grants in the subgroup.[44] Community foundations are also far more likely to employ professional staff than are other grant-making foundations.[45]

A new and important type of foundation that is a kind of hybrid of the operating and community types of foundations is the conversion foundation. Typically created after a publicly supported nonprofit institution, such as a hospital, insurance plan, or higher education financing agency is acquired by a for-profit company, these organizations use the proceeds of the sale for their endowments (ostensibly on the grounds that the money was partly the fruit of donations and tax exemptions, and thus should be kept in community-serving purposes). Their programs usually combine grant making with the provision of services, often under the leadership of professionals from the predecessor institution.

Although they did not really begin to appear until the early 1980s, the number of health care conversion foundations now exceeds 190, with endowments ranging from $2.4 million to $3.5 billion, and assets that totaled over $14 billion in 2007.[46] About half are organized as private foundations principally engaged in grant making. The rest are public charities that operate various kinds of health-related programs.[47]

Conversion foundations exist outside of health care, too. Although estimates are difficult to come by since they are of more recent vintage, one of them—the Lumina Foundation for Education, created from the sale of a student loan guarantor, USA Group, to SLM Corporation in mid-2000—was ranked among the top fifty foundations in assets in 2007.

CORPORATIONS. For-profit companies occupy their own niche in the world of institutional philanthropy. Among the nation's 75,000 foundations, nearly 2,500 are sponsored by businesses. In 2007, although these corporate foundations held just 3 percent of the assets of foundations, they made almost 10 percent of the grants, totaling approximately $4.4 billion.[48]

Not all companies create endowed foundations, but those that do so aim to ensure that their grant making will not suffer too much from business downturns by committing assets to underwrite their giving programs. The rest completely or partially support their foundations through annual grants from corporate earnings. The corporate share of institutional philanthropy has declined since the 1980s, largely because giving by other kinds of foundations has risen more rapidly than corporate grant making. Spending by corporate foundations (in constant dollars) has fluctuated since 1987, but in 2007 it was more than twice what it was twenty years earlier. (Giving by corporate foundations actually rose between 2007 and 2008, a period of economic downturn.)[49] Corporate foundations' assets have grown threefold, partly because investment returns have been robust and also because businesses have been committing more money to their foundations than the foundations have been paying out.[50] Except for community foundations, business foundations are more likely than other grant-making institutions to have professional and support staff, although corporate downsizing has made the difference smaller than it used to be.[51]

Foundation giving accounts for only a portion of corporate philanthropic activity. The rest of the nearly $16 billion that businesses gave in 2007 went directly to charities, often through company units specializing in public affairs or human resources and sometimes in goods or services rather than in cash. The most generous givers are typically those, such as pharmaceutical and computer companies, whose products make up a large share of their donations. Many corporations also devote a sizable portion of their charitable giving to matching employee gifts to colleges, universities, charity federations, and other kinds of nonprofit organizations, rather than develop their own philanthropic programs. Matches may be made both from their foundations and directly. In a sense these donations reflect individual rather than institutional priorities, but businesses often see them as a way of enhancing employee morale, productivity, or other corporate goals.

In addition to the contributions of cash and in-kind products, corporations make donations in the form of free publicity, meeting space, marketing assistance, lending executives and other help for charities, corporate sponsorships of special events and other nonprofit activities, royalty and licensing fees paid to charities in connection with product marketing, and political contributions to issue-oriented advocacy groups. Although sponsorships are rarely included in most tallies of corporate giving, IEG, a company that advises companies on sponsorships, estimates that businesses spent $15 billion on sponsorships in 2007. Two-thirds of this amount went to underwriting sporting events, such as football bowl games, and the balance went for the arts, festivals, membership organizations, and other purposes.[52] Thus, businesses spent almost as much on this form of support for activities that benefit the nonprofit sector as they did on direct giving.

FEDERATIONS. Businesses often play a central role in another form of institutional philanthropy: charity federations, which are joint appeals undertaken as a local campaign. In 1913, in order to make fundraising more efficient and expand the number of contributors to the city's charities, the Cleveland Chamber of Commerce persuaded fifty-three organizations to coordinate their appeals for support through an annual campaign. Unless the giver designated a particular group, the money raised was allocated by a governing board composed of representatives of the participating charities, business leaders, and other philanthropists, according to their assessment of Cleveland's priorities.

This was the first modern United Way.[53] Within a few years the idea had spread to a dozen more cities, and by the end of the 1920s, joint appeals in more than 129 communities raised close to $60 million.[54] By the end of World War II, more than 1,000 local United Ways were in existence, and the number has continued to grow, totaling roughly 1,300 locally based organizations by the end of the century. Despite a series of problems in recent years, their fundraising drives still brought in $4.2 billion in contributions in 2007.[55]

United Ways are only one kind of charity federation. A number of religious denominations have long maintained organizations to raise money from their members and distribute it among denominational charities according to priorities determined by the group's board and staff. Among the most successful have been Jewish federations, operating in over 500 localities and raising collectively more than $3 billion in gifts and endowment funds annually for Jewish charities.[56] Similar to the United Ways, a national organization sets policies, provides support, and loosely coordinates their efforts. Most local federations also engage in planning around religious needs and direct their contributions accordingly.

The so-called "alternative funds" are another type of charity federation. Created mostly since the 1980s, they conduct fundraising campaigns, often in the workplace, on behalf of small groups of charities usually linked by a common interest, such as the arts, the environment, education, health care, or disaster relief, or by a common group of beneficiaries, such as women or minorities. According to Emily Barman, these "communities of purpose" (in contrast to the "communities of geography" represented by United Way organizations) numbered 150 and together raised about $140 million in 2001.[57] Although practices vary widely, they normally distribute the funds they raise in response to requests from member agencies or other eligible groups.

Finally, a number of health organizations, such as the American Cancer Society, American Lung Association, and the March of Dimes, operate as federations. Using a variety of methods, local chapters raise money, a portion of which supports the work of the affiliates and the rest of which is allocated according to national priorities, such as for research or public information efforts. These organizations typically rank among the nation's most successful charities in fundraising. In 2007, for example, the American Cancer Society and its chapters raised over $1 billion; two-thirds of this amount was used for "program services." Altogether, Americans donated over $4 billion to the 23 health federations on the Philanthropy 400 list compiled by *The Chronicle of Philanthropy*.[58] That places the health charity federations on a par not only with United Way, but also with corporate and community foundations.

GIFT FUNDS. The most recent innovation in institutional philanthropy is also the most controversial. In 1992 a Massachusetts mutual fund company, Fidelity Investments, began offering its clients the opportunity to create a charitable gift fund. The Internal Revenue Service classified these funds as publicly supported charities—or 501(c)(3) organization—so in exchange for agreeing to use the fund only for philanthropic contributions, the donor could immediately receive a tax deduction for the money deposited in the fund, which would be exempt from tax as it grew. The fund's donor (or his designated successor) could later determine where and when the contributions would be made; Fidelity's trustees and staff reviewed and set certain limits on the grants (such as restricting them to organizations located in the United States), and also retained the right to disapprove them.

Community foundations have used such donor-advised funds for years, but the adoption of this technique by for-profit investment firms was an innovation—one that turned out to be an immediate success. Within four years, more than 6,000 donor-advised accounts, worth more than $500 million, had been established in Fidelity's Charitable Gift Fund; by 2007, the number of accounts topped 42,000 and assets topped $4.6 billion. In its 2007 fiscal year, the fund made nearly $1 billion in grants, four times as much as the largest community foundation did.[59] Other financial companies, including the Vanguard Group, Morgan Stanley Smith Barney, Schwab, and T. Rowe Price, set up similar funds.[60]

To many in the world of institutional philanthropy, Fidelity's Charitable Gift Fund looks more like a collection of bank accounts for individual donors than a grant-making organization. Although it provides the same tax advantages as giving to a community foundation or charity federation, it makes no pretense of trying to pool and allocate contributions according to priorities determined by the fund's trustees or staff. Apart from making at least one donation every seven years, donors are not required to give some of the money they put in their accounts to charity annually, as would be the case if they had created their own foundations.

As Fidelity's Charitable Gift Fund grew and spawned imitators, demands for regulations requiring it to act more like a grant-making organization began to be heard. In response to these concerns, Fidelity and the other funds have moved modestly toward the institutional philanthropy model. The Charitable Gift Fund now aims to distribute to charity an amount equal to at least 5 percent of its net assets each year. To reach this goal, it can if necessary draw on individual accounts that give less to create a special fund, controlled by its trustees. (In fact, since the Charitable Gift Fund was established it has spent an average of more than 20 percent of its assets annually.) If a donor dies without naming a successor, the money in his account goes to the trustees' fund.[61]

At the same time, community foundations have increased the number and size of donor-advised funds in their endowments. In 2007, *The Chronicle of Philanthropy's* survey reported nearly 21,000 donor-advised funds at community foundations; five years earlier, slightly more than 15,000 existed. The value of the assets in them had increased substantially as well. Indeed, half of the $2 billion endowment of the Silicon Valley Community Foundation, the nation's largest, was in donor-advised funds.[62] Depending on the conditions attached to them, which are set in accord with the policies of each organization after negotiation with donors, the growth of these funds could restrict the ability of community foundations to use them for what its trustees and staff considered high-priority community needs. Instead, they would be constrained by what their donors felt was important, a model of philanthropy that looks more like the traditional type of individual philanthropy than the institutional version.

Patterns of Giving

The patterns of giving by grant-making organizations look very different from those of charitable giving overall, which is dominated by individual contributions and bequests.

For example, in 2009 account holders with the Fidelity Charitable Gift Fund gave one-quarter of their donations to community- and human-services organizations and nearly another quarter to education; just 11 percent went to religious groups.[63] By contrast, according to *Giving USA,* of the $304 billion Americans contributed to charity in 2009, one-third went to religious organizations and only 13 percent to education. Another 9 percent went to human services agencies and 8 percent to public-society benefit groups (see table 12-1).[64] These differences may be due chiefly to differences between people who set up accounts with the Fidelity Charitable Gift Fund and those who contribute to charities directly in what they prefer to support. But people who use an organization for their grant making, even one as loosely directed as Fidelity's, may also regard their Fidelity accounts as serving different aims or using different criteria than they use for the rest of their personal giving.

The giving patterns of other forms of institutional philanthropy deviate even more from the overall giving pattern than charitable funds do. For example, the larger foundations gave little more than 2 percent of their grant funds to religious groups in 2008, but nearly 22 percent to education. Community foundations donated a slightly larger share to religion (4.5 percent) and education (23.4 percent), while corporate foundations gave less to religion (0.6 percent) and slightly more (22.5 percent) to education.[65] Most United Way grants go to well-established health and social service agencies, while religious federations typically specialize in supporting secular charities with a denominational background, such as those providing educational and welfare services to coreligionists and international relief. Alternative funds are more likely to support groups whose activities involve political advocacy, although they underwrite many traditional charities too.

These funding priorities have changed little in the past decade. Several of the major categories of support tallied in the Foundation Center's annual review of larger foundations saw increases or reductions of about five percentage points or more in the share of grant dollars received in 2008 compared to 1998. However, except for independent foundations, which are now giving more to health than they are to education or community-service agencies, the order of institutional philanthropy's priorities remains the same as it was a decade ago.[66]

Table 12-1. *Total and Institutional Giving as a Percentage of Grant Dollars,*
by Source and Destination, 2008

Source	Religion	Education	Health	Community service[a]	Other
All sources[b]	33	13	7	17	30
Independent foundations	2.1	21.8	25.5[c]	19.8[c]	31
Community foundations	4.5	23.4	13.3[c]	31	27.8
Corporate foundations	0.6	22.5[c]	14.2[c]	38.2	24.6
Fidelity Charitable gift fund	10.9[c]	23.6	7.2	24.9[c]	33.4

Source: Steven Lawrence and Reina Mukal, *Foundation Giving Trends: Updates on Funding Priorities* (New York: Foundation Center, 2010), p. 37; Giving USA Foundation, *Giving USA 2010: The Annual Report on Philanthropy for the Year 2009* (Glenview, Ill.: 2010), p. 4; Fidelity Investments, 2009 Annual Report: Upholding the Spirit of Giving, p. 6.

a. Includes human services and public or society benefit.

b. 75 percent individual; 8 percent bequests.

c. Change of plus or minus five percentage points (rounded) since 1998.

Grant-making organizations also made a shift in the types of support they provided. During the 1990s only a small fraction of grant dollars from the foundations sampled by the Foundation Center—usually around 12 percent—went for general support of charities, while nearly half was earmarked for program support. In 2008, funding for general support had risen to 19.2 percent, though half continued to underwrite particular programs. This shift came at the expense of funding for capital items, such as buildings and equipment, which declined to 15.8 percent of total grant making in 2008 from nearly one-quarter a decade earlier.[67] Although no comparable tallies exist for individual donors, most personal gifts are used for general support (although a not insignificant share, especially from upper-income donors, also funds endowments and capital investments).

The independent foundations in the Foundation Center's sample were more likely to finance particular programs than to provide general support. On the other hand, the community and especially corporate foundations surveyed were inclined to underwrite continuing operations, although a larger share of funding by these two types of grant makers could not be categorized.[68] Colleges and universities received nearly 20 percent of foundation funding, a decline from nearly 25 percent a decade ago. Although human-services agencies obtained just 12 percent of funding from the top 1,400 grant making organizations, they received one-quarter of all grants.[69]

These independent foundations also gave a greater portion of their funds— nearly 30 percent—to recipients categorized as economically disadvantaged. Community and corporate foundations favored children and youth, who received about 20 percent of their gifts.[70] In the past ten years, the share of

Table 12-2. *Geographic Distribution of Grants Awarded and Grants Received by Region, 1998 and 2008*
Number of grants

Region	Grants awarded 1998	Grants received 1998	Grants awarded 2008	Grants received 2008
Northeast	35.7	27.3	25.5	26
Midwest	27.2	22.3	18.7	16.1
South	19.8	29.8	19.9	33.1
West	17.3	20.5	35.9	24.7

Source: Foundation Center, "Geographic Distribution of Grant Dollars Awarded and Grant Dollars Received by State, circa 1998" (http://foundationcenter.org/findfunders/statistics/pdf/03_fund_geo/1998/08_98.pdf [September 27, 2010]); Foundation Center, "Geographic Distribution of Grants Awarded and Grants Received by State, circa 2008" (http://foundationcenter.org/findfunders/statistics/pdf/03_fund_geo/2008/08_08.pdf [September 27, 2010]).

funding for children and youth has grown slowly, but funding for the economically disadvantaged has risen rapidly, especially since 2005.[71] Over half of all gifts in the Foundation Center's most recent tabulation are not directed at identifiable groups or are reported as intended for the public as a whole.

Perhaps the most dramatic change in the pattern of institutional philanthropy during the past decade has been location (see table 12-2). In 1998, grantmaking organizations in the northeastern United States surveyed by the Foundation Center accounted for 35 percent of gifts from institutional philanthropy, and organizations in the West accounted for 17 percent. A decade later, nearly the reverse was true: institutional grant makers in the West gave 36 percent of the gifts made by institutional philanthropists, while the share in the Northeast had declined to 25.5 percent. The rapid growth of the West's economy, accompanied by decisions of prominent residents, such as Bill and Melinda Gates, to create or expand foundations is undoubtedly the chief explanation of this shift.

It is unclear what difference in the impact of philanthropy on the ground this shift in the geographical source of money will make. Unlike individual donors, who typically support organizations in their communities or with which they are familiar, institutional philanthropy enables donors to range farther afield, giving them the capacity to become involved with problems in states and countries other than their own. Thus, despite the sizable growth in grants awarded by grant makers located in the West, the share of foundation gifts received by organizations in that region only increased from 20.5 percent to 24.7 percent during the decade. By comparison, in the South, where poverty and other social problems have been more severe, the share of philanthropic giving has not changed since 1998, yet the proportion of foundation grants that went to the South grew from 20 percent in 1998 to 33 percent in 2008.

If institutional philanthropy was meant to be more than the lengthened shadow of the people or businesses whose contributions support it, it seems to have succeeded. At the very least, it has diversified the pattern of support for charitable endeavors, thus reinforcing a central rationale for charitable intermediaries. But in the eyes of its critics, that may no longer be enough.

Institutional Philanthropy's Four Greatest Challenges

Despite, or perhaps because of, its growing prominence among the sources of donations for the nonprofit sector, institutional philanthropy has faced ever more questions since the turn of the twenty-first century. Four major challenges stand out; each is important not only in its own terms but also because each raises questions about the value of professionalization in giving. Yet a close look at each issue suggests that the case for institutional philanthropy is stronger than the case against it.

How Much Payout?

From its earliest days, institutional philanthropy has been faulted because it diverted contributions away from organizations that actually provided services and toward intermediaries and their staffs that would release the money a little at a time. Most recently this criticism has centered on the annual "payout" rate imposed by the Tax Reform Act of 1969, which currently requires foundations to spend annually an amount equal to 5 percent of the value of their assets (including administrative costs and other items—except investment expenses—as well as grants). As economic growth during the 1990s produced higher returns on foundation investments, a variety of organizations urged Congress to increase that percentage so that more money would be going to grantees. The foundation community opposed this change, claiming that when inflation and cyclical fluctuations in asset values were taken into account, spending more than 5 percent would erode grant makers' endowments and leave them with less ability to meet unknown challenges in the future.[72]

After several years of debate, Congress took no action. The response of institutional grant makers to the prolonged economic downturn in the United States suggests that it was right to leave the "payout" rate alone. From the start of the recession in December 2007 to its end in June 2009, broad-based stock market indices such as the S&P 500 fell by more than one-third. Even after a modest rebound, they remained substantially below the level they had reached three years earlier. Foundation endowments declined accordingly, winding up 14 percent lower at the end than at the start of the recession, and if it had not been for an estimated $31 billion in new gifts to foundations in 2009, the drop would have been even sharper.[73]

Despite the recession, however, giving by institutional philanthropy actually rose by 5.4 percent in 2008, the first full year of the economic slump, and the 8.4 percent decline in 2009 was smaller than the decline in foundation assets.[74] The main reason institutional philanthropy did not fall more rapidly was the rule requiring foundations to spend an amount equal to 5 percent of the value of their assets on grants and administrative expenses. By the Foundation Center's estimate, one-quarter of grant-making organizations meet this requirement by using a two- to five-year rolling average of their investments. As a result, spending in 2008 was affected by the much higher asset-values of the previous years, especially for the larger foundations, which are more likely to adopt this approach. In fact, the relatively shallow recession at the beginning of the decade led more grant makers to use the averaging method as well as a variety of other more conservative strategies for managing their portfolios, which helped cushion their spending after economic conditions worsened later in the decade.[75]

Grant-making organizations also adjusted their activities in response to the nation's financial turmoil. Along with reducing administrative costs, many shifted funding priorities to meet emergency needs. In July 2009, the Foundation Center reported that the amount of "crisis-related" grants and investments made by a sample of foundations it was tracking had more than tripled since January.[76] A September 2010 survey found that 41 percent of foundations "have made grants, program-related investments (PRIs) and/or provided other types of support specifically to address problems related to the economic crisis."[77] Smaller family foundations increased their giving beyond required levels.[78] After falling in 2008, corporate giving rose in 2009 (although grants from corporate foundations declined).[79]

With unemployment remaining high and poverty rising, the need for continued support from institutional philanthropy in 2010 and beyond remained substantial. Yet as the years in which asset values were reduced start to affect payout calculations, many foundations have lower absolute spending requirements (if they are spending no more than the 5 percent payout formula requires). If they want to continue responding to the nation's economic travails, they will face more difficult decisions in the future, including possibly having to spend more than the law obliges them to.

In spite of these financial challenges, institutional grant makers appear remarkably sanguine about the future. According to a January 2010 Foundation Center survey, more than half (61.1 percent) of large foundations expected to keep their giving steady, or increase it, in 2010 ("a prospect that would have seemed incredibly optimistic at the nadir of the market" in the middle of 2009).[80] In September 2010, another survey found similar plans for 2011, with 80 percent of large foundations anticipating making no change or raising their grant-making level. Although many had taken steps to cut costs, few saw the economic downturn as having a "lasting impact" on their funding priorities. Less than 1 percent of the respondents had decided to "spend down" their endowments because of the recession's toll, while 4 percent indicated it had caused them to decide to maintain their assets in perpetuity to ensure that their funds would be available for future emergencies.[81]

Because of these endowments, foundations, including corporate ones, were able to readjust their priorities and increase their spending when faced with growing financial strains in the nonprofit sector. To be sure, the decline in institutional philanthropy from 2007 through 2009 was greater than that of individual giving. Nevertheless, *Giving USA* reports, "the ratio of giving to assets in 2009 was the highest it has been since 1985," with the "payout" rate for independent foundations actually reaching 6.8 percent.[82] Absent a healthier economy, institutional philanthropy might not be able to continue operating at this level. But if foundations had been required to spend more when their endowments were growing robustly, they might have had more difficulty sustaining support when it was necessary to do so, and the impact of the 2007–09 recession on the nonprofit sector might have been even greater than it was.

Who Receives Grants?

The recession caused institutional philanthropy not only to spend more but also to allocate funds differently. Forty percent of the foundations surveyed by the Foundation Center in September 2010 reported they had made changes in their funding priorities, providing more assistance to "safety net activities and vulnerable populations." Some also had shifted toward giving more operating support and away from concentrating on funding specific programs.[83]

However, less than 10 percent of the respondents expected these changes to be permanent. That would not come as a surprise to another set of critics. For them, the problem of institutional philanthropy is not how much it gives away, but how little funding normally goes to the needy and minority groups—despite the professed ambitions of many grant makers to promote social change—and how much goes to promoting programs benefiting the better-off. Institutional philanthropy's critics charge that it is rife with particularism, and usually helps organizations that are already successful or are unlikely to advocate radical measures, notwithstanding its spokespersons' claims to the contrary.

Is this true? According to data compiled by the National Committee for Responsive Philanthropy (NCRP), between 2004 and 2006 only one-third of the grant dollars expended by a sample of 809 large foundations went to groups serving the poor and other "marginalized communities."[84] Half of the grant makers analyzed gave less than 20 percent of their funds to these groups. Only 13 percent donated more than 50 percent to disadvantaged groups, the figure NCRP judged a "benchmark for Philanthropy at its Best."[85]

The Greenlining Institute leveled similar charges against foundations concerning their meager support for minority-led nonprofits. Just 12 percent of the nearly12,000 grants national foundations awarded in 2005 that the organization studied, and only 8 percent of the dollars, went to groups headed by members of minority groups. In California, where the Greenlining Institute is based, the record was somewhat better, with almost 18 percent of the grants and 12 percent of the dollars being given to minority-led groups. Even so, the institute reported "a great disparity in minority giving among the sampled foundations" in comparison to funds aimed at other portions of the population, which it blamed in subsequent reports on the underrepresentation of minority-group members on the boards and staffs of grant-making organizations.[86]

The Foundation Center, taking a broader perspective, reported that grants for "social justice" from a sample of 1,000 larger foundations reached the highest level in 2008 since it began keeping track, $3.7 billion, or nearly 15 percent of the total awarded by these grant makers that year.[87] It defined "social justice" philanthropy as "the granting of philanthropic contributions to nonprofit organizations based in the United States and other countries that work for structural change in order to increase the opportunity of those who are the least well off politically, economically, and socially."[88] Much of the activity recorded by the Foundation Center was accounted for by just one foundation, the Bill and Melinda Gates Foundation, which made twenty-two of the twenty-five largest "social justice" grants recorded.[89] Without it, "social justice" spending would have been closer to 10 percent of total grant making, as it had been for a decade.

Reports such as these were behind so far unsuccessful efforts in state legislatures as well as the United States Congress to prompt institutional philanthropists to provide more support for supposedly underserved groups.[90] Yet the record of grant-making foundations in assisting these groups does not support the view that such prodding is necessary. Most of the information about institutional philanthropy's beneficiaries comes from data collected by the Foundation Center, an organization created in 1956 to give information to the public about the work of grant makers. However, the reports it receives are not always easy to interpret. In some cases, intended beneficiaries are unidentified, or are categorized in general terms, such as for "women" or "children." In addition, often it is not possible to know whether particular groups, such as minorities or the poor, will benefit from grants that are made to achieve a broad purpose, such as medical research, without knowing the incidence of the medical or other problems in those populations.

In a study for the Philanthropic Collaborative, the economist Philip D. Swagel sought to correct for these difficulties, using a sample of 200 health-related grants. Surprisingly, he discovered that in addition to the 31.4 percent of grants that were clearly described as helping one or another underserved group, between 46.9 percent and 64.1 percent of the remaining donations could properly be categorized as helping such groups also. Using a mid-range estimate of likely beneficiaries, he judged that two-thirds of the awards he examined helped the needy.[91] Swagel admits that the definitional problems can be formidable, but suggests that foundations may have a better record of assisting the underserved than their critics contend.

The Foundation Center undertook a similar effort to examine funding for minority groups in California. After recategorizing grants from fifty large foundations in the state that were not explicitly designated for "populations of color," the study concluded that in 2005, 39 percent of the "domestically focused" awards and 33 percent of the money aimed to benefit minorities, about twice the proportion estimated using grant makers' own reports. Moreover, during the previous ten years, the share of grants targeted toward minority groups and the economically disadvantaged, many of whom are minorities, had been rising steadily. Although only one out of seven grants went to specifically "minority-serving nonprofit organizations," these constituted just part of the funding given by the fifty large California foundations to assist "populations of color."[92]

Much the same point can be made about the Foundation Center's own analysis of "social justice" grant making. Far more organizations—including think-tanks, universities, and religious groups—are interested in "structural change" in American society and the rest of the world than those explicitly or chiefly dedicated to that goal. (And some, most notably the small but influential group of so-called "conservative" groups, would also contest the definition the Foundation Center uses of "social justice.")[93] Many of these also receive funding from institutional philanthropy.

Nor does institutional philanthropy seem to be slighting underserved groups in staffing. A survey of ninety-five of the members of Philanthropy New York, the association of New York City–area grant makers, showed that 43 percent of staff were "people of color." Being relatively new to the profession, these individuals were more likely to be found in administrative and support or program officer positions than higher up in the administrative hierarchy; their representation among CEOs and board members was considerably smaller. On the other hand, women made up a majority of all staff categories and 45 percent of directors.[94] A survey of the staffs of Council on Foundations members in 2008 reported by the Association of Black Foundation Executives found similar results, as did an Urban Institute survey of nonprofit organizations (not just grant makers) in California.[95]

Whether minority representation in institutional philanthropy is adequate or still needs improvement, and whether funding for "social justice" is satisfactory or should be expanded, are ultimately matters of judgment. Like other kinds of philanthropy, institutional grant making inevitably reflects the interests and concerns of its donors, directors, and staffs, but its rationale is rooted in the possibility of going beyond those horizons by using the expertise of professionals to expand the vision of those who establish, govern, or work for foundations and other kinds of grant makers. Despite the charges from the Greenlining Institute and others, the institutional philanthropic approach seems to be consistent with addressing problems facing the needy and minorities today, as it was in the past. Moreover, as members of these groups become professionals themselves, they are also entering and even creating grant-making organizations.[96] Efforts to make the leadership of institutional philanthropy look more like and rely more for guidance on its intended beneficiaries is by no means guaranteed to lead to more, or more effective, activism on behalf of those who most require its help.

Who Governs Institutional Philanthropies?

Even after the passage of the Tax Reform Act of 1969, institutional philanthropy still possessed an extraordinary degree of independence in how it operated. As long as foundations and other grant makers met the "payout" requirement, avoided giving significant financial benefits to their donors, top executives, and others who managed them, and stayed away from partisan election campaigns and funding efforts to enact legislation, they were essentially self-governing. The only means for public oversight was the possibility of an IRS audit or an investigation by a state attorney general.[97] Institutional philanthropy's defenders have frequently cited its freedom as a critical feature that enables organizations to act on the expertise of their directors and staff as to what needs to be done, rather than to depend on and thus be accountable to and swayed by customers, voters, or large numbers of contributors.

This autonomy was subjected to closer scrutiny starting in the 1990s, after a number of well-publicized scandals enveloped the nonprofit sector. Nationally prominent organizations such as the American Red Cross, the Smithsonian Institution, and the Nature Conservancy became the subject of newspaper exposés and congressional hearings. Grant-making organizations, most notably the J. Paul Getty Trust (whose president was accused of a range of offenses) also came under fire, leading the president of the Council on Foundations, Dorothy S. Ridings, to wonder whether we might soon be seeing foundation officials taken into a courtroom in handcuffs.[98]

The scandals typically involved one or another kind of misuse of funds by officials of charitable organizations, often to provide personal benefits for themselves or members of their families. Charges of excessive compensation of directors and staff members and accusations of imprudent or self-serving investment policies also figured prominently.[99] To make matters worse, these allegations came against the backdrop of exposures of fraudulent activity at several large companies, including Enron and Tyco, which led to the passage of the

Sarbanes-Oxley Act of 2002 (P. L. 107-204), which created new governance requirements for publicly traded corporations. In the name of enhancing confidence in the nonprofit sector, proposals for establishing an analogous set of rules for it, including grant-making organizations, were put forward.[100]

In June 2004, the Senate Finance Committee launched a series of hearings on the need for greater oversight of charities.[101] Among the items under consideration were measures regarding the use of assets, compensation of staff and trustees, and public disclosure of investment and grant-making actions. The potential usefulness of a national accreditation system for nonprofits, including grant makers, was also discussed.[102] Testifying before the Committee, Internal Revenue Service Commissioner Mark W. Everson noted that his agency had not conducted an in-depth examination of foundations since the 1980s. Because of the "steady growth in what had been a fairly stable sector," it was planning to launch a new "initiative" to assess how well grant-making organizations were complying with existing laws.[103]

The hearing, followed by several subsequent meetings, rang alarm bells throughout the nonprofit sector. A variety of organizations sought to respond to what they feared would be increased and potentially damaging restrictions on their activities. The most prominent effort to neutralize the apparent offensive against nonprofits was a panel of grant makers, charity executives, and scholars that was convened by the organization Independent Sector. The group issued a detailed report to Congress in June 2005.[104] It stopped short of calling for a new federal agency to police the philanthropic world, as some had sought; instead it recommended a number of smaller legal changes, better enforcement of existing laws, and more effective self-regulation by nonprofit organizations of all types. Meantime, a survey of nonprofit social service, arts, and civic organizations that was carried out by the nonprofit Listening Post Project at Johns Hopkins revealed that most surveyed organizations already had in place most of the governance and accountability protections being suggested by the Finance Committee chairman and were often governed by several layers of ethical standards.[105]

When Congress eventually acted, it endorsed a cautious approach. Although the Pension Protection Act of 2006 (P. L. 109-280) did affect institutional philanthropy by enacting new standards for donor-advised funds that aimed at preventing those who set them up from using them for personal benefit (especially important to community foundations), it mostly addressed abuses by individual contributors, such as overvaluing in-kind gifts. The IRS's plans for looking more closely at private foundations were overtaken by a broader examination of executive compensation in the nonprofit sector. After surveying more than 1,200 organizations, including 200 foundations, the agency concluded that although there were inaccuracies in reporting information in about 30 percent of the cases, compliance with existing rules seemed to be satisfactory. Just 5 percent of the foundations reviewed were found to be paying "excessive" compensation and 60 percent already possessed conflict-of-interest policies.[106]

The IRS study was not based on a random sample of organizations and so its results are not generalizable, but an Urban Institute study of a more representative group of 5,100 nonprofits (not all grant makers) reached essentially the same conclusion. The authors of the latter study concluded that adopting governance reforms like those in the Sarbanes-Oxley Act would require considerable changes in some cases, but little in others, "because most nonprofits are already in voluntary compliance or because they must comply with other regulations that resemble Sarbanes-Oxley provisions."[107] In particular, larger organizations were more likely to have established independent audit committees, "whistleblower" protections, and other good-governance measures than smaller ones.[108]

These findings reinforced what the New York attorney general's office had told Congress in an unsuccessful effort to persuade it to ban foundations with less than $20 million in assets. Despite the headlines that the scandals of the 1990s generated, larger, more established foundations were more likely to follow recommended practices in corporate governance than the smaller, "noninstitutional" members of the grant-making world.[109] Although some of the accusations leveled against grant-making organizations had merit (under pressure from the Council on Foundations and California's attorney general, the Getty Trust replaced its president and adopted new operating guidelines), professionalization generally served more as an asset for philanthropic governance than a source of problems.[110]

How Effective Are Institutional Nonprofits?

Foremost among the claims on behalf of professionalization in philanthropy is that it can lead to more effective giving. Advocates of professionalization argue that grant makers are more likely to achieve a greater impact as a result of developing and applying expertise than they would be if they relied on more subjective and, by implication, less informed judgments. Although a donor need not create a foundation or other kind of institution to take advantage of professionalization, doing so allows for continuity and accrual of knowledge necessary to deal with complex issues. For that reason, the benefits of professionalization have often been viewed as linked to creating organizations with an existence that could extend beyond the lifetimes of their funders.

Yet this view has always been controversial. In two influential articles written at the end of the 1920s, Julius Rosenwald, a businessman who built the Sears, Roebuck Company and was a leader in the early years of institutional philanthropy in the United States, argued that grant-making organizations set up to exist "in perpetuity" may actually be less effective than those with limited lifetimes. In the latter, both directors and staff, knowing that they had only a finite period in which to accomplish their goals, might be more inclined to innovate and take risks. Rosenwald's view was that institutional philanthropy, far from enhancing the value of professionalization, could diminish it, if preserving a grant-making organization indefinitely took precedence over achieving the purposes for which it had been set up.[111]

In the 1960s, largely because of populist fears about concentrations of wealth, Congress considered a proposal to require limited lifetimes for foundations, but failed to enact it. Most donors have also rejected Rosenwald's perspective and set up their foundations or other grant-making organizations to continue after their deaths.

During the first decade of the twenty-first century, however, concerns about the effectiveness of institutional philanthropy have given the idea new life. Also, several prominent philanthropists have embraced it, including Bill Gates, whose foundation is due to shut down fifty years after he and his wife die; Charles Feeney, whose Atlantic Philanthropies is due to end in 2017; and Warren Buffett, who gave the bulk of his fortune to the Bill and Melinda Gates Foundation on the condition that each increment be spent in the year it was received, not placed in the foundation's endowment. In addition, to improve the impact of grant-making organizations, more rigorous evaluations and a series of steps have been called for that usually are referred to collectively as venture philanthropy, because they seek to apply the techniques of venture capitalists to philanthropic purposes.

Despite the prominence of the advocates of these new directions in grant making, their appeal should not be exaggerated. Despite the interest they have aroused, much of institutional philanthropy has not endorsed them. Although Julius Rosenwald's ideas about perpetuity have enjoyed a revival, surveys suggest that leaders of only a small percentage of organizations—the Urban Institute and the Foundation Center both estimate around 10 percent—actually intend to curtail the organizations' lifetimes, although twice as many indicated they were undecided or considering doing so.[112] These figures are comparable to the results of a 1980s study done by the Council on Foundations and Yale University's Program on Non-Profit Organizations.[113] Moreover, the Urban Institute's researcher observed, in most cases the plans had little to do with "overall philanthropic mission, strategy and impact."[114]

Likewise, only a relatively small portion of the philanthropic world appears to have embraced the major practices associated with "venture philanthropy," such as using assets rather than just grants to accomplish goals, supporting operating costs, and becoming involved directly in the activities of grantees. Although "program-related investments"—support in the form of investments, loans, and other potentially risky transactions using endowment funds—have been increasing, less than two hundred private and community foundations made one or more such investments in 2006–07. Their total value was $742 million, less than 5 percent of the amount grant-making organizations gave away.[115] Funding from foundations for the capital expenses of nonprofits has also been declining for most of the decade, and although support for operating costs, as opposed to specific programs, has been rising, it remained below 20 percent of the awards by large grant makers in 2008.[116]

One-quarter of large foundations conducted "direct charitable activities" in 2007, with around 60 percent of them reporting an increase in such efforts over the previous five years. The most common type of "direct charitable activity" was running conferences or cultural events for groups other than board members or staffs, and providing technical assistance and training to grantees was the second most frequent.[117] According to one survey, the number of "giving circles"—which enable members to pool their contributions, and require that they also contribute time to working with charities—more than doubled between 2004 and 2006. But the amount they granted, $65 million, was a minuscule share of giving by institutional philanthropy.[118]

A similar pattern emerges in looking at foundation involvement in supporting "public policy–related" initiatives. One-quarter of a group of over 1,300 grant makers surveyed by the Foundation Center reported funding such activities, with half having increased them since 2005. Still, the amount of money spent was small. Forty percent of the foundations devoted less than 5 percent of their spending to improving public information, monitoring government performance, research, and other methods of promoting policy changes.[119]

Surprisingly, even calls for institutional philanthropy to do more to assess its work are far from being fully heeded. Grantmakers for Effective Organizations (GEO) is an association of 350 organizations whose goal is to promote "grant-making practices that improve nonprofit results." Yet GEO's 2008 survey of over 3,500 staffed foundations revealed that only half of them "formally evaluated" what they funded, the same proportion as that found by a 2003 Urban Institute study. Just one-third reported using the information they obtained from the study to adjust their grant making.[120]

GEO is one of several organizations that have been created or expanded since 2000 to promote more strategic practices in giving.[121] More grant-making organizations may adopt them in the future, or they may develop other ways of trying to increase the impact of their efforts. But change in institutions always occurs slowly, even in philanthropic ones that are committed to taking a professional approach to their work. Moreover, effectiveness is not just a matter of adopting the right techniques; it also depends upon having realistic aims and knowing how to attain them. Initiatives undertaken by institutional philanthropy have not always possessed these qualities, often because their goals have been overly ambitious and the steps necessary to achieve them, too complex.[122]

It is ironic that for organizations whose rationale is rooted in a belief in the value of applying expertise to grant making, improving effectiveness may be their biggest challenge.

The Future of Institutional Philanthropy

The challenges of ensuring effectiveness may be why successful entrepreneurs such as Bill Gates, Pierre Omidyar, and Jeffrey Skoll are expressing skepticism about the usefulness of grant-making organizations. Others apparently share this view. Research done by the Center on Philanthropy at Indiana University for the Bank of America shows that only about 15 percent of "high net-worth households" either have established private foundations or intend to do so within a few years.[123] Donations for particular activities or charities now make up a larger portion of contributions to philanthropic federations, and donor-advised funds make up a greater share of gifts to community foundations than donations to foundations. Both types of donations are intended to give direction to trustees and staffs of these grant-making organizations and to restrict, at least temporarily, their ability to support projects that they consider worthwhile but that are not in line with the donors' intentions.

Corporations are increasingly providing assistance to nonprofit groups through one or another means that allows them to advance their business interests, not just serve philanthropic purposes. This "social entrepreneurship," as it is sometimes called, has grown explosively in popularity, not only in the United States, but especially internationally. Its advocates are critical of traditional giving and seek ways to employ commercial methods to foster social change.

These trends do not indicate that the century-old era of institutional philanthropy is coming to an end. Existing and new foundations and other grant-making organizations will continue to operate and provide considerable amounts of support to the nonprofit sector. The tensions that have always existed between the knowledge-driven traditions of large grant-making organizations and the activist and voluntarist spirit of community-oriented American philanthropy will not be resolved soon, or at all, even if the balance may have shifted toward the latter in recent years.

Yet for all the shortcomings of professionalization, donors that rely on enlisting expert associates to make money are unlikely to cast experts aside when it comes to giving money away. The confidence in the ability to improve giving that led Andrew Carnegie to create a foundation to "promote the advancement and diffusion of knowledge and understanding" and John D. Rockefeller to aspire through his foundation "to promote the well-being of mankind throughout the world" will continue to inspire others to seek better ways of using their fortunes to benefit the public.

Notes

1. Bill Gates, "A New Approach to Capitalism," in *Creative Capitalism: A Conversation with Bill Gates, Warren Buffett, and Other Economic Leaders,* edited by Michael Kinsley and Conor Clarke (New York: Simon & Schuster, 2008), p. 10.

2. Ibid., p. 12.

3. Muhammad Yunus, Nobel lecture, Oslo, December 10, 2006 (http://nobelprize.org/nobel_prizes/peace/laureates/2006/yunus-lecture-en.html [May 25, 2010]).

4. Although this chapter deals exclusively with developments in the United States, the past decade has also seen the growth of institutional philanthropy in other parts of the world, including China, Europe, and Latin America. See, for example, Qiusha Ma, *Non-Governmental Organizations in Contemporary China: Paving the Way to Civil Society?* (London and New York: Routledge, 2006); Kenneth Prewitt and others, eds., *The Legitimacy of Philanthropy Foundations: United States and European Perspectives* (New York: Russell Sage Foundation, 2006); Lester M. Salamon, *Rethinking Corporate Social Engagement: Lessons from Latin America* (Sterling, Va.: Kumarian Press, 2010).

5. See Leslie Lenkowsky, "Foundations and Corporate Philanthropy," in *The State of Nonprofit America,* edited by Lester M. Salamon (Brookings, 2002), pp. 363–65.

6. Steven Lawrence and Reina Mukai, *Foundation Growth and Giving Estimates: Current Outlook,* 2010 edition (New York: Foundation Center, 2010), p. 1. Conversion to 2008 dollars was achieved by using the deflator for the services component of personal consumption expenditures as provided in the 2011 National Income and Product Accounts, table 1.1.9 (www.bea.gov/national/nipaweb/TableView.asp?SelectedTable=13&Freq=Qtr&FirstYear=2006&LastYear=2008 [April 11, 2011]).

7. Lawrence and Mukai, *Foundation Growth and Giving Estimates,* 2010 edition, p. 1. For 2000, see Foundation Center, "FC Stats—Grantmaker National Growth Trends" (http://foundationcenter.org/findfunders/statistics/gm_growth.html [June 27, 2010]).

8. Lenkowsky, "Foundations and Corporate Philanthropy," p. 357. See also Joel L. Fleishman, *The Foundation: A Great American Secret—How Private Wealth Is Changing the World* (New York: PublicAffairs, 2007).

9. Ibid., p. 4. The Foundation Center defines "larger foundations" as those with assets of at least $1 million or those making grants of $100,000 or more.

10. For foundation data see Foundation Center, "FC Stats—Grantmaker National Growth Trends" (http://foundationcenter.org/findfunders/statistics/gm_growth.html [June 27, 2010]). For charitable giving, see Giving USA Foundation, *Giving USA2009: The Annual Report on Philanthropy for the Year 2008* (Glenview, Ill.: 2009), p. 210.

11. Lawrence and Mukai, *Foundation Growth and Giving Estimates,* 2010 edition, p. 1.

12. Ibid., p. 1. Two of those years were 2002 and 2003, but in each, the decline was estimated to have been less than half of one percent.

13. Lawrence and Mukai, *Foundation Growth and Giving Estimates,* 2010 edition, pp. 4, 9.

14. Will Pitz and Rinku Sen, *Short Changed: Foundation Giving and Communities of Color* (Oakland, Calif.: Applied Research Center, 2004), p. 4.

15. Ian Wilhelm, "Group Pushes Foundations to Give More to Minorities and the Poor," *Chronicle of Philanthropy,* March 3, 2009 (http://philanthropy.com/article/Group-Pushes-Foundations-to/63032 [May 29, 2010]). In response to this effort, the Florida legislature in May 2010 enacted a law prohibiting the state government from requiring foundations to appoint board members or make grants on the basis of race, religion, income level, sexual orientation, and other specified characteristics (http://acreform.com/article/ACR_bill_protect_foundation_giving).

16. Niki Jagpal, "Criteria for Philanthropy at Its Best: Benchmarks to Assess and Enhance Grantmaker Impact," report (Washington: National Committee for Responsive Philanthropy, 2009).

17. In 2007 the Ford Foundation chose as its new president Luis A. Ubinas, a consultant with McKinsey & Company, who had no previous grant-making experience. See Stephanie Strom, "Ford Foundation Selects Its New Leader from Outside the Philanthropic World," *New York Times,* August 14, 2007; see also *High-Engagement Philanthropy: A Bridge to a More Effective Social Sector: Perspectives from Nonprofit Leaders and High-Engagement Philanthropists* (Washington: Venture Philanthropy Partners and Community Wealth Ventures, 2004).

18. Gates praised the late C. K. Prahalad's book, *The Fortune at the Bottom of the Pyramid: Eradicating Poverty through Profits* (Philadelphia: Wharton School, 2007).

19. Lewis D. Solomon, *Tech Billionaires: Reshaping Philanthropy in a Quest for a Better World* (Piscataway, N.J.: Transaction, 2009).

20. Michael E. Porter and Mark R. Kramer, "Strategy and Society—The Link between Competitive Advantage and Corporate Social Responsibility," *Harvard Business Review,* December 2006, p. 92.

21. Holly Hall, "Charitable Giving Might Not Melt Down, Philanthropy Scholar Predicts," *Chronicle of Philanthropy,* October 8, 2008.

22. Alexis de Tocqueville, *Democracy in America,* trans. Harvey C. Mansfield and Delba Winthrop (University of Chicago Press, 2000), pp. 489–92.

23. Ibid., p. 490.

24. Andrew Carnegie is probably best remembered for his important series of grants to create public libraries in the United States and elsewhere, but his belief in the value of music for the working class also led him to donate 7,689 church organs during his lifetime, even though he was not particularly religious himself. See David Nasaw, *Andrew Carnegie* (New York: Penguin, 2006), pp. 607–8.

25. In 1889, John D. Rockefeller began supporting the growth of what became the University of Chicago. His goal was to help establish a Baptist university in the Midwest. See Ron Chernow, *Titan: The Life of John D. Rockefeller, Sr.* (New York: Random House, 1998), pp. 307–28.

26. In 1886, Rockefeller created what is generally considered one of the first industrial research laboratories in the United States at the Standard Oil Company. It allowed him to refine crude oil from Ohio and Indiana, which had been considered below commercial grade. See Chernow, *Titan,* pp. 285–87.

27. Aaron Wildavsky and James Douglas, "The Knowledgeable Foundations," in *The Future of Foundations: Some Reconsiderations* (New Rochelle, N.Y.: Change Magazine Press, 1978), pp. 10–43.

28. See, for example, Warren Weaver, *U.S. Philanthropic Foundations: Their History, Structure, Management, and Record* (New York: Harper & Row, 1967), part 2.

29. Helmut K. Anheier and David Hammack, eds., *American Foundations: Roles and Contributions* (Brookings, 2010).

30. Barbara Cerrone, "When Reach Exceeds Grasp: Taking the Annenberg Challenge to Scale," in *Reconnecting Education & Foundations: Turning Good Intentions into Educational Capital,* edited by Ray Bacchetti and Thomas Ehrlich (San Francisco: Wiley, 2007), pp. 139–61.

31. Paul Brest and William Harvey, *Money Well Spent: A Strategic Plan for Smart Philanthropy* (New York: Bloomberg Press, 2008), pp. 3–4.

32. Stephanie Strom, "Foundations Find Benefits in Facing Up to Failures," *New York Times,* July 26, 2007.

33. Joel L. Fleishman, J. Scott Kohler, and Steven Schindler, *Casebook for the Foundation: A Great American Secret* (New York: PublicAffairs, 2007).

34. Fleishman, *The Foundation;* Brest and Harvey, *Money Well Spent;* Peter Frumkin, *Strategic Giving: The Art and Science of Philanthropy* (University of Chicago Press, 2006).

35. See, for example, Mary Ellen S. Capek and Molly Mead, *Effective Philanthropy: Organizational Success through Deep Diversity and Gender Equity* (MIT Press, 2006); Angela M. Eikenberry, *Giving Circles: Philanthropy, Voluntary Association, and Democracy* (Indiana University Press, 2009); Leslie R. Crutchfield, John V. Kania, and Mark R. Kramer, "Do More than Give: The Six Practices of Donors Who Change the World," unpublished ms.; Helmut K. Anheier and Diana Leat, *Creative Philanthropy* (London and New York: Routledge, 2006).

36. Lester M. Salamon, *America's Nonprofit Sector: A Primer* (New York: Foundation Center, 2011).

37. United States laws generally define a foundation by what it does not do: it is an organization established for charitable purposes that does not raise money from the general public.

38. This definition would exclude organizations such as the Heritage Foundation or the Sierra Club Foundation, which raise money from donors but use it for their own programs. Private operating foundations, which are considered part of institutional philanthropy, also spend their funds on their own programs and typically do not raise money from the general public.

39. Steven Lawrence and Reina Mukai, *Foundation Yearbook: Facts and Figures on Private and Community Foundations,* 2009 edition (New York: Foundation Center, 2009), p. vii. This chapter generally uses 2007 or 2008 data, which are the most complete currently available.

40. Ibid., p. 13; Foundation Center, "Foundation Staff Positions by Asset Range 2009 (New Criteria)" (http://foundationcenter.org/findfunders/statistics/pdf/12_fs_fr/2009/staffing/saa_09.pdf [July 27, 2010]).

41. Steven Lawrence and Reina Mukai, *Foundation Growth and Giving Estimates: Current Outlook,* 2009 edition (New York: Foundation Center, 2009), p. 9.

42. Lawrence and Mukai, *Foundation Yearbook,* 2009 edition, p. 42.

43. Community foundations are tax-exempt under section 501(c)(3) of the Internal Revenue Code, which means that donors may deduct up to 50 percent of their adjusted gross income for annual contributions to them. Other foundations are exempt under this section and also section 509(a), which limits contributions to them to 30 percent of adjusted gross income and imposes other rules as well, such as a payout requirement.

44. Lawrence and Mukai, *Foundation Yearbook,* 2009 edition, p. 40.

45. Foundation Center, "Foundation Staff Positions by Type of Foundation: 2007" (http://foundationcenter.org/findfunders/statistics/pdf/12_fs_fr/2007/staffing/stype_07.pdf [August 22, 2010).

46. Foundation Center, "Aggregate Financial Data for New Health Foundations, 2007" (http://foundationcenter.org/findfunders/statistics/pdf/01_found_fin_data/2007/fdn_type/agg_health.pdf [August 22, 2010]).

47. Grantmakers in Health, "A Profile of Foundations Created from Health Care Conversions," June 2009 (www.gih.org/usr_doc/2009_Conversion_Report.pdf [August 22, 2010]).

48. Lawrence and Mukai, *Foundation Growth and Giving Estimates,* 2009 edition, p. 9.

49. Ibid.

50. Foundation Center, "Change in Corporate Foundation Giving and Assets, 1987–2007" (http://foundationcenter.org/findfunders/statistics/pdf/02_found_growth/2007/01_07.pdf [August 22, 2010]).

51. Foundation Center, "Foundation Staff Positions by Type of Foundation: 2007" (http://foundationcenter.org/findfunders/statistics/pdf/12_fs_fr/2007/staffing/stype_07.pdf [August 22, 2010]).

52. "Sponsorship Spending Recedes for First Time; Better Days Seen Ahead," *IEG Sponsorship Report* 28 (December 21, 2009): 24. Corporations are limited by law in the amount of economic benefit they can receive from sponsorships, a limitation that does not apply to their advertising.

53. For a history of United Way, see Emily Barman, *Contesting Communities: The Transformation of Workplace Charity* (Stanford University Press, 2006).

54. Peter Dobkin Hall, "Community Foundations in America, 1914–1987," in *Philanthropic Giving: Studies in Varieties and Goals,* edited by Richard Magat (Oxford University Press, 1989), p. 186.

55. "The Philanthropy 400," *Chronicle of Philanthropy,* October 30, 2008, p. 10.

56. Jewish Federations of North America, "About Us" (www.jewishfederations.org/section.aspx?id=31 [February 23, 2011]).

57. Barman, *Contesting Communities,* pp. 71–72; for amounts raised, see ibid., chapter 3.

58. "Philanthropy 400," p. 10.

59. Fidelity Investments, *2009 Annual Report: Upholding the Spirit of Giving,* p. 6.

60. Noelle Barton and Elizabeth Schwinn, "Growing Concerns and Assets," *Chronicle of Philanthropy,* May 29, 2008.

61. Fidelity Charitable Gift Fund, "Gift Fund Policy Guidelines," program circular (www.charitablegift.org/docs/Gift-Fund-Policy-Guidelines.pdf [August 23, 2010]).

62. Barton and Schwinn, "Growing Concerns and Assets."

63. Fidelity Investments, *2009 Annual Report: Upholding the Spirit of Giving,* p. 6.

64. Giving USA Foundation, *Giving USA2010: The Annual Report on Philanthropy for the Year 2009* (Glenview, Ill.: 2010), p. 4.

65. Steven Lawrence and Reina Mukai, *Foundation Giving Trends: Updates on Funding Priorities,* 2010 edition (New York: Foundation Center, 2010), p. 37.

66. This largely reflects the impact of the Bill and Melinda Gates Foundation, which donated nearly $2 billion to health care organizations in 2008, four times as much as the next-largest institutional donor. See Lawrence and Mukai, *Foundation Giving Trends,* 2010 edition, p. 13.

67. Ibid., p. 31.

68. Ibid., p. 36.

69. Ibid., p. 29.

70. Foundation Center, "Distribution of Grants by Population Group and Foundation Type circa 2008" (http://foundationcenter.org/findfunders/statistics/pdf/08_fund_pop/2008/17_08.pdf [September 27, 2010]).

71. Foundation Center, "Foundation Grants Designation for Certain Populations Groups, circa 1998" (http://foundationcenter.org/findfunders/statistics/pdf/08_fund_pop/1998/16_98.pdf [September 27, 2010]).

72. Thomas J. Billitteri, "Money, Mission and the Payout Rule: In Search of a Strategic Approach to Foundation Spending," Nonprofit Sector Research Fund Working Paper Series (Washington: Aspen Institute, July 2005).

73. Lawrence and Mukai, *Foundation Growth and Giving Estimates,* 2010 edition, p. 2; Giving USA Foundation, *Giving USA 2010,* p. 6.

74. Ibid., p. 1.

75. Steven Lawrence, "Foundations Address the Impact of the Economic Crisis," *Foundation Center,* April 2009, pp. 4–5.

76. "The Foundation and Corporate Response to the Economic Crisis: An Update," *Foundation Center,* July 2009, p. 1.

77. Steven Lawrence, "Moving beyond the Economic Crisis: Foundations Assess the Impact and Their Response," research advisory (New York: Foundation Center, November 2010), p. 3 (http://foundationcenter.org/gainknowledge/research/pdf/researchadvisory_economy_201011.pdf [August 26, 2011]).

78. Foundation Source, "Small to Mid-Size Foundations Exceed Minimum Distribution Requirement by Large Margin," June 29, 2010 (www.foundationsource.com/content/small-mid-size-foundations-exceed-minimum-distribution-requirements-large-margin [July 16, 2010]).

79. Giving USA Foundation, *Giving USA 2010,* p. 5; Lawrence and Mukai, *Foundation Growth and Giving Estimate,* 2010 edition, p. 6.

80. Lawrence and Mukai, *Foundation Growth and Giving Estimates,* 2010 edition, p. 3.

81. Lawrence, "Moving beyond the Economic Crisis," p. 3.

82. Giving USA Foundation, "Giving by Foundations," *GivingUSA 2010,* pp. 8–9.

83. "Moving beyond the Economic Crisis," p. 2.

84. Jagpal, "Criteria for Philanthropy at Its Best," p. 23. The report defines "marginalized communities" as "the economically disadvantaged; racial or ethnic minorities; women and girls; people with AIDS; people with disabilities; aging, elderly and senior citizens; immigrants and refugees; crime/abuse victims, offenders and ex-offenders; single parents; and LGBTQ citizens" (p. 26, note 1).

85. Ibid., p. 24.

86. Christian Gonzalez-Rivera and others, *Funding the New Majority: Philanthropic Investment in Minority-Led Nonprofits* (Berkeley: Greenlining Institute, 2008), p. 4 (www.greenlining.org/publications/pdf/372 [December 6, 2010]); Christian Gonzalez-Rivera, "Diversity on Foundation Boards of Directors," issue brief (Berkeley: Greenlining Institute, 2009), p. 2 (www.greenlining.org/publications/pdf/458 [December 6, 2010]).

87. "Key Facts on Social Justice Grantmaking" (New York: Foundation Center, April 2010) (http://foundationcenter.org/gainknowledge/research/pdf/keyfacts_social_2011.pdf [August 26, 2011]), p. 1.

88. Ibid., p. 4.

89. Ibid., p. 1.

90. Wilhelm, "Group Pushes Foundations." After becoming chairman of the Senate Finance Committee in 2007, Senator Max Baucus of Montana launched an effort to encourage foundations to provide more funding in rural areas. See Rachael Swierzewi, *Rural Philanthropy: Building Dialogue from Within* (Washington: National Committee for Responsive Philanthropy, 2007).

91. Phillip Swagel, *Broad Benefits: Health-Related Giving by Private and Community Foundations* (Washington: Philanthropic Collaborative, 2009) (www.philanthropycollaborative.org/BroadBenefits061109.pdf [December 6, 2010]).

92. Lawrence T. McGill, Algernon Austin, and Brielle Bryan, *Embracing Diversity: Foundation Giving Benefiting California's Communities of Color* (New York: Foundation Center, 2008), pp. v–vi.

93. See Alice O'Connor, "Foundations, Social Movements, and the Contradictions of Liberal Philanthropy," in Anheier and Hammack, *American Foundations,* pp. 328–46.

94. Lawrence T. McGill, Brielle Bryan, and Eugene D. Miller, *Benchmarking Diversity: A First Look at New York City Foundations and Nonprofits* (New York City: Philanthropy New York and the Foundation Center, 2009), pp. 8–9.

95. Association of Black Foundation Executives, "2008 Staff Demographic Data for Professional (26) and Administrative Positions (9) in Philanthropy" (New York: 2010); Carol J. DeVita and Katie L. Roeger, *Measuring Racial-Ethnic Diversity in California's Nonprofit Sector* (Washington: Urban Institute, 2009) (www.urban.org/UploadedPDF/411977_CA_Diversity.pdf [December 6, 2010]).

96. According to a Council on Foundations study, *Career Pathways to Leadership: 2009 Baseline Report* (Arlington, Va.: Council on Foundations, 2009), 20 percent of a sample of foundation CEOs selected between 2004 and 2008 came from "diverse racial and ethnic groups" (p. 9).

97. John Simon, Harvey Dale, and Laura Chisolm, "The Federal Tax Treatment of Charitable Organizations," in *The Nonprofit Sector: A Research Handbook,* 2nd edition, edited by Walter W. Powell and Richard Steinberg (New Haven & London: Yale, 2006), note, however, that because their funds typically come from a private party, such as an individual, a family, or a corporation, institutional nonprofits have been more tightly regulated than other nonprofit organizations (pp. 283–84).

98. Francie LaTour and Beth Healy, "AG in Conn Begins Probe: 2 Foundations for Charities Are Eyed," *Boston Globe,* November 11, 2003.

99. Leslie Lenkowsky, "The Politics of Doing Good: Philanthropic Leadership for the Twenty First Century," in *Taking Philanthropy Seriously: Beyond Noble Intentions to Responsible Giving,* edited by William Damon and Susan Verducci (Indiana University Press, 2006), pp. 50–61. The financial swindle perpetrated by Bernard Madoff had a significant impact on a number of foundations, especially those established by Jewish donors. See Niki Jagpal and Julia Craig, *Learning from Madoff,* rev. ed. (Washington: National Committee for Responsive Philanthropy, 2009).

100. See, for example, Joel L. Fleischman, "Public Trust in Not-for-Profit Organizations and the Need for Regulatory Reform," in *Philanthropy and the Nonprofit Sector in a Changing America,* edited by Charles T. Clotfelter and Thomas Ehrlich (Indiana University Press, 2001), pp. 172–97; Marcus S. Owens, "Charity Oversight: An Alternative Approach," Working Paper No. 33.4 (Harvard University, Hauser Center for Nonprofit Organizations, October 2006).

101. United States Senate Committee on Finance, "Charity Oversight and Reform: Keeping Bad Things from Happening to Good Charities," June 22, 2004.

102. United States Senate Committee on Finance, "Staff Discussion Draft," June 2004.

103. "Written Statement of Mark W. Everson, Commissioner of Internal Revenue, before the Committee on Finance, United States Senate, Hearing on Charitable Giving Problems and Best Practices, June 22 (http://finance.senate.gov/imo/media/doc/062204metest.pdf [December 18, 2010]), p. 6.

104. Panel on the Nonprofit Sector, *Strengthening Transparency, Governance, Accountability of Charitable Organizations: A Final Report to Congress and the Nonprofit Sector* (Washington: Independent Sector, 2005).

105. Lester M. Salamon and Stephanie Geller, *Nonprofit Governance and Accountability,* Listening Post Project Communiqué No. 4 (Johns Hopkins University, Center for Civil Society Studies, May 2005).

106. Internal Revenue Service, "Report on Exempt Organizations Executive Compensation Compliance Project—Parts I and II," March 2007 (www.irs.gov/pub/irs-tege/exec._comp._final.pdf [December 18, 2010]).

107. Francie Ostrower and Marla J. Bobowick, *Nonprofit Governance and the Sarbanes-Oxley Act* (Washington: Urban Institute, 2006), p. 1.

108. Another Urban Institute study of the 10,000 largest foundations concluded that the size of the foundation, the number of people it employed, and the degree to which it was engaged in staff-intensive activities were the principal factors affecting its administrative expenses. See Elizabeth T. Boris and others, *What Drives Foundation Expenses and Compensation? Results of a Three-Year Study* (Washington: Urban Institute, Foundation Center, and Philanthropic Research, Inc., 2008).

109. Frank Brieaddy, "Small Private Charities Targeted," *Syracuse Post Standard,* July 28, 2003; Grant Williams, "Making Philanthropy Accountable," *Chronicle of Philanthropy,* June 26, 2003.

110. J. Paul Getty Trust, "J. Paul Getty Membership Status in Council on Foundations Restored," press release, April 17, 2006.

111. Julius Rosenwald, "Principles of Public Giving," *Atlantic Monthly,* May, 1929, pp. 599–606; Julius Rosenwald, "The Trend away from Perpetuities," *Atlantic Monthly,* December 1930, pp. 741–49.

112. Francie Ostrower, *Limited Life Foundations: Motivations, Experiences and Strategies* (Washington: Urban Institute, 2009), p. 2; Loren Renz and David Wolcheck, *Perpetuity or Limited Lifespan: How Do Family Foundations Decide?* (New York: Foundation Center, 2009), p. vii.

113. Teresa Odendahl, ed., *America's Wealthy and the Future of Foundations,* p. 74.

114. Ostrower, *Limited Life Foundations,* p. 1. However, the Urban Institute study did note that donors more concerned about preserving their philanthropic intentions were more likely to favor limiting the lifetimes of their foundations than those who were less concerned.

115. Steven Lawrence, "Doing Good with Foundation Assets," *The PRI Directory,* 3rd edition (New York: Foundation Center, 2010).

116. Lawrence and Mukai, *Foundation Giving Trends,* 2010 edition, pp. 30–31. However, a Center on Philanthropy survey of foundations found that nearly 70 percent made grants for overhead costs when requested by grantees. See Patrick Rooney and Heidi Frederick, "Paying for Overhead Study" (Center on Philanthropy at Indiana University, 2007).

117. Loren Renz and Rachel Elias, *More than Grantmaking: A First Look at Foundations' Direct Charitable Activities* (New York: Foundation Center, 2007).

118. Jessica E. Bearman, *More Giving Together: The Growth and Impact of Giving Circles and Shared Giving* (Washington: Forum of Regional Associations of Grantmakers, 2007), p. 2.

119. Foundation Center, "Key Facts on Foundations' Public Policy-Related Activities" (New York: December 2010).

120. Grantmakers for Effective Organizations, *Is Grantmaking Getting Smarter?* (Washington: 2008), pp. 6–7.

121. Others include the Center for Effective Philanthropy, FSG Social Impact Consultants, the Bridgespan Group, Venture Philanthropy Partners, and the Grantmaking School of the Johnson Center for Philanthropy at Grand Valley State University. Existing organizations such as the Council on Foundations, the Philanthropy Roundtable, the Forum of the Regional Associations of Grantmakers, and the Association of Small Foundations have increased their programming on ways of improving grant-making effectiveness.

122. Education reform is a good example. See Cerrone, "When Reach Exceeds Grasp: Taking the Annenberg Challenge to Scale."

123. Center on Philanthropy at Indiana University, *The 2010 Study of High Net Worth Philanthropy: Issues Driving Charitable Activities among Affluent Households* (Indianapolis: 2010), p. 69. This figure has changed little from earlier waves of the survey in 2005 and 2007. A "high-net-worth" household is defined as one with a household income above $200,000 or net worth exceeding $1 million, excluding the value of the residence.

13

Individual Giving and Volunteering

ELEANOR BROWN AND DAVID MARTIN

Americans give hundreds of billions of dollars each year to support a wide range of causes, and most of this money flows through nonprofits. In addition, individuals support nonprofit organizations by donating billions of hours of volunteer labor. Although these levels of giving are remarkable, for much of the nonprofit sector private philanthropy—giving and volunteering by individuals—is not a major source of income. In this chapter, we describe personal giving and volunteering, the forces that shape them, and their significance in the funding streams of nonprofit organizations in various parts of the nonprofit sector.

Because it focuses on two forms of voluntarism, this chapter illuminates some interactions between voluntarism and the other impulses shaping the nonprofit sector—commercialism, professionalism, and civic activism—whose influences are traced throughout this book. We see that levels of personal giving are affected by factors other than the revenue needs of the nonprofit sector, so that growth in giving may not keep pace with the growth of the sector, increasing the attractiveness to nonprofit organizations of commercial sources of revenue. Changes in the composition and habits of the volunteer work force influence the extent to which nonprofits rely on professionals rather than volunteers, and emerging patterns of volunteering are blurring the lines between volunteering and other forms of civic activism.

Giving and Volunteering: An Overview

In 2007, individuals in the United States gave about $229 billion to organizations, most of it to nonprofits, and in 2006 volunteered an estimated 12.9 billion hours.[1] Converting these hours into a monetary equivalent using average nonfarm hourly wages, roughly $216 billion in time was volunteered.[2] This outpouring of giving and volunteering constitutes a remarkable flow of resources. For perspective, a country that had an annual gross domestic product equal to the combined value of annual American giving and volunteering would rank about twentieth in the world, just behind Sweden and Belgium.

Relative to the United States' economy, U.S. individual giving in the first decade of the twenty-first century has hovered around 2 percent of personal income. In 2007, individual giving constituted 2.1 percent of personal income; in 2008, a year of economic crisis and uncertainty, the ratio fell to 1.9 percent.[3] (As steep as that decline was, the ratio of individual giving to personal income in 2008 was still higher than in any year during the quarter century between 1973 and 1997. The rise in giving as a fraction of personal income that began in 1998 came disproportionately in the form of noncash contributions.)[4] Subtracting taxes from personal income yields disposable income; the fraction of disposable personal income represented by individual giving has fluctuated narrowly around 2.3 percent over the past decade.

To investigate the importance of this level of individual giving to the nonprofit sector, we look first at the importance of individual giving relative to private giving from all sources. Inter vivos giving—gifts given by individuals during their lifetimes—accounts for about three-quarters (74.8 percent in 2007) of all private giving. The rest comes from foundations (12.6 percent of total giving), bequests (7.6 percent), and corporations (5.1 percent). Total private monetary giving in 2007 was $306.4 billion.[5] (If one adds this total private giving number to the cash equivalent of volunteering to generate a hypothetical country's GDP, that country now passes Belgium and Sweden in the rankings.) Bequests are, of course, a form of individual giving, but because the determinants of bequests are somewhat different from the determinants of inter vivos giving, and in any event data about bequests tend to arise in different contexts from data on annual giving, social scientists tend not to lump the two forms of giving together.

Stacking these estimates of giving against estimates from the national income accounts of the level of nonprofit outlays shows that total private giving represents about 30 percent of the total outlays of the nonprofit sector.[6] This number is useful in comparing the sizes of the organized nonprofit sector and the volume of individual philanthropic initiative, but it overstates, by a factor of 2, the importance of private giving relative to what we see in data reported by

Table 13-1. *Nonprofit Activity with Private Contributions as a Percentage of Nonprofit Revenue, 2005*

International and foreign affairs	67.3
Environment and animals	48.0
Arts, culture, and humanities	40.8
Other	40.0
Human services	16.4
Education	14.9
Health	4.0
All	12.3

Source: Kennard T. Wing, Thomas H. Pollak, and Amy Blackwood, *The Nonprofit Almanac*, 2008 (Washington: Urban Institute Press, 2008), chapter 5.

individual nonprofit organizations. What accounts for this difference? Not all private contributions go to nonprofits; public universities, hospitals and museums are examples of organizations outside the nonprofit sector that attract private donations. Even more important in understanding the data is the fact that not all nonprofits are required to file financial reports with the IRS, and among the exempted organizations are religious congregations. Religious congregations rely heavily on gifts from individuals, and one third of private giving goes to support religion. Only a tiny fraction of this giving and of these congregations are represented in the detailed IRS data that let us examine the importance of charitable contributions in the revenue streams of individual nonprofits.[7]

Looking at the available data and keeping in mind that they exclude most religious congregations and most nonprofits too small to be required to report to the IRS, we find that private contributions account for 12.3 percent of nonprofit revenue, and that reliance on private giving varies widely across the sector.[8] Table 13-1 shows the importance of private giving to the revenue of nonprofit organizations by type of activity. Private giving is relatively unimportant in health services, where fees for services, including payments from government programs such as Medicare and Medicaid, are a major source of revenue. Educational nonprofits charge tuition, and many of them have substantial investment income from endowments. The most donation-reliant areas of nonprofit activity, environmental and international causes, are ones that take up charitable causes for which governmental support may be perceived to be modest relative to global levels of need. The arts also rely heavily on private donations.

The importance of private giving to the operation of the nonprofit sector depends not just on the level of giving but also on the details of the gifts. First, gifts may come with strings attached, and these restrictions on the use of the gifts may—or may not—affect their value to the organization. For example, financial aid is a popular target for gifts to colleges and universities; as long as the college can remove unrestricted funds from its preferred financial aid budget and replace them with the restricted gifts, the restriction on the use of gifts enhances the donors' satisfaction at no cost to the institution. Gifts in the form of matching grants may leverage further fundraising successes, bringing more than their face value to the organization. More generally, though, conditions for the receipt of gifts and restrictions on their disposition tend to reduce their value to the recipient organization by directing resources away from the organization's self-defined areas of greatest need.

Similarly, gifts in kind, such as donations of works of art to a museum, generally but not always differ in important ways from unrestricted gifts of cash. On occasion, gifts in kind represent coveted resources not generally available for purchase, such as a historical site or a particular work of art that is integral to a collection. To the extent that donors insist on their gifts' being directed to activities that are low on nonprofits' priority lists, however, the face value of the gift can overstate its actual value to the organization. For example, an art museum that is strapped for funds to cover its operating expenses may receive a gift of art with the stipulation that it not be immediately resold or that it be displayed in an expensive manner; the effect of such a gift is substantially different from a gift of cash of the same face value. Still other in-kind gifts are much like gifts of cash, such as shares of stock and nearly obsolete used cars donated with an eye to tax savings and a ready understanding that they will be converted to cash.

Sometimes restrictions on the use of gifts are imposed by the organizations themselves. Gifts to some institutions, such as universities, may routinely be added to the organization's endowment, with only a small fraction of their value contributing to operating expenses in any given year. If the institution has immediate revenue needs but is loathe to draw down its endowment and unwilling or unable to borrow against it, the amount of current giving can overstate the charitable revenues available to meet current funding imperatives.

Although volunteer labor is itself a form of in-kind gift, we treat gifts of money and gifts of time as distinct forms of philanthropy. Volunteer labor is an important resource for the nonprofit sector: in 2008, an estimated 61.8 million people volunteered a median amount of time equal to one hour a week.[9]

Like gifts of money, volunteering is more important to some areas of economic activity than to others. The area most likely to attract volunteers is religion; in 2008 just over one third (35.1 percent) of the people doing volunteer work name religion as their principal locus of volunteering. Youth and education is the principal area of volunteering for 26 percent of volunteers, followed by community service, and by health (see table 13-2).

The most common tasks undertaken by volunteers are fundraising, tutoring or teaching, and general labor. There are differences in tasks by gender and by

Table 13-2. *Principal Field of Volunteering Reported by Volunteers, as Percentage of All Volunteering, 2008*

Religious	35.1
Youth education	26.0
Social or community service	13.5
Health	8.2
Civic, professional, or international	5.5
Sport, hobby, culture, or arts	3.3
Environment, animals	2.0
Public safety	1.3
Other or unknown	5.2

Source: U.S. Bureau of Labor Statistics, Volunteering in the United States, 2008, table 4 (http://data.bls.gov/cgi-bin/print.pl/news.release/volun.t04.htm).

race and ethnicity. Men are more likely to coach or referee youth sports and to offer managerial and technical assistance, and women are more likely to tutor or teach and to prepare food. African Americans are more likely to undertake church-related volunteering such as ushering or ministerial work and less likely than others to engage in fundraising, and Asian Americans are more likely to be involved in tutoring and teaching.[10]

Like other gifts in kind, volunteer labor is not a perfect substitute for cash in the pockets of nonprofits. In many circumstances, volunteers have an advantage over the paid staff who might have been hired with donated money. For example, a fundraising call from a volunteer who believes in an organization may be more convincing than a call from someone who is being paid to tout it. Parents who volunteer in their children's classrooms may be more motivated to achieve results than paid aides would be. On the other hand, volunteers may not bring the skill mix most needed by a nonprofit, and there may be limitations on the extent to which nonprofits can exploit the skills they do bring, owing, for example, to union rules or state regulations.

A further complication that comes with volunteers is the need to manage and to motivate them. More than a third of the people who volunteered in 2006 did not volunteer in the following year; David Eisner and his colleagues estimate that these lapsed volunteers had given about 1.9 billion hours in 2006, or roughly $38 billion in labor services.[11] Mark A. Hager and Jeffrey L. Brudney identify dimensions of volunteer management that have positive effects on volunteer retention and find that many volunteer-utilizing nonprofits have not adopted these management practices. Significant in reducing volunteer turnover are screening procedures that match volunteers with suitable volunteer assignments, a practice adopted "to a large degree" by 45 percent of the surveyed nonprofits;

regularly recognizing the contributions of volunteers, for example with award ceremonies, a common practice among 35 percent of nonprofits; and providing volunteers with training and professional development, an enticement offered to volunteers by just 25 percent of nonprofits who utilize volunteers.[12]

Besides annual giving and volunteering, individuals can direct resources to the nonprofit sector at the end of their lives through charitable bequests. Because the largest bequests can be very large, the amount of giving transmitted through bequests varies by a substantial percentage from year to year. In rough numbers, the amount of giving to nonprofit causes via bequest is about one tenth the amount given by living persons.[13] About half of the charitable money given via bequest goes to philanthropic organizations such as private and community foundations and federated giving organizations such as the United Way.

What Influences Individual Giving?

Philanthropy is a widespread practice in the United States, but levels of participation vary widely. Over the course of a year, roughly two-thirds of households make at least $25 in charitable donations, making giving the rule rather than the exception.[14] The amounts people give vary with household income, but there is also a striking degree of variability in levels of giving within income classes. For example, in 1995 the median percentage of income given away by tax itemizers with incomes between $50,000 and $100,000 was just 1.4 percent, while at the 95th percentile of generosity within this group the portion of income given away was 10.0 percent. The differences are even more striking at higher levels of income: among itemizers with annual incomes between $1 million and $2.5 million, the median percent of income given to charity was 0.8 percent, in contrast to 14.0 percent at the 95th percentile of generosity.[15] Clearly, income is not the only factor affecting how much people give.

Religious organizations are the most frequently chosen recipients of individual giving and volunteering, and attendance at religious services is a strong predictor of charitable giving. Charitable giving also tends to increase with education, and with measures of embeddedness in one's community, such as years of residence, homeownership, and civic engagement. Within households, the relative influence of husbands and wives over charitable giving seems to vary with their relative economic clout more generally, with consequences for how charitable dollars are doled out. Husbands tend to concentrate charitable giving and behave strategically with respect to taxes, whereas wives distribute charity across more types of charitable activity and respond less to tax incentives.[16]

Recent research suggests that habits of charity are passed on within families from one generation to the next, just like other economic characteristics such as levels of income and wealth. The degree of family resemblance in giving habits across generations is about as strong, in the case of religious giving, as the family resemblance in levels of income and wealth. In the case of giving to secular causes, the correlation in levels of giving within families from one generation to the next is smaller but still significant, similar to the family resemblance across generations in levels of consumption.[17] This implies that policies that increase giving in one generation can have a positive effect on future generations' levels of giving as well.

Even though most households give something, high-income and high-wealth households account for a very large fraction of total giving, as they do of total income. In 2000, for example, the 7 percent of households with the highest incomes were responsible for 50 percent of charitable giving; similarly, the 7 percent of households with the highest levels of wealth gave 50 percent of all charitable giving.[18] To understand what shapes the charitable flow of resources to the nonprofit sector, then, we pay special attention to the philanthropic behavior of high-income households.

The distinction between high-income households and average households is a meaningful one: well-to-do households' giving behavior differs from that of other households in ways that are relevant to public policy and to the fundraising strategies of nonprofit organizations. In particular, the evidence suggests that high-income households are particularly sensitive to the tax consequences of their gifts, paying attention both to the level of taxes and to prospective changes in tax law.

Economists expect taxes to affect levels of giving in multiple ways. First, taxes reduce giving by reducing how much money people have in their pockets to spend. Second, for households that itemize deductions in the calculation of their income tax liability, taxes affect the trade-off between personal consumption and charitable giving. When a household decides whether or not to spend another tax-deductible dollar on charity, the choice is to give the dollar to charity or to split it between paying income tax and spending the rest on something else. If people don't enjoy paying their taxes and the tax rate on that extra dollar (which we refer to as the marginal tax rate) is, say, 35 percent, then the choice is seen as a choice between giving a dollar to charity or spending 65 cents on themselves. Economists call this cost of giving in terms of forgone consumption the "tax price" of giving, and calculate it as one minus the tax rate that applies to an individual's last dollar of income. The higher this marginal tax rate, the lower the tax price of giving and the more we expect people to give.

To see the usefulness of this notion of a tax price of giving, revisit the trend we noted earlier in this chapter in the share of personal income going to individual giving. Giving's share rose in the late 1990s; this corresponds to a time at which people experienced large gains in the stock market. The tax code allows itemizers donating appreciated stock to deduct the current value of the stock, with no tax liability for capital gains. The fraction of individual giving made up of noncash donations rose dramatically in the late 1990s, rising from 18 percent in 1995 to a peak of 33.6 percent in 2000.[19] When the composition of people's incomes shifts to include a greater proportion of income in forms with low tax prices of giving, it is not surprising that the level of giving goes up.

To recap: when charitable gifts are deductible from taxable income, economists expect increased *average* tax rates to *depress* giving by lowering income and increased *marginal* tax rates to *increase* giving by reducing its price.

It is not just this year's taxes that affect this year's giving. It matters whether taxes have been higher or lower in the near past, and whether they are expected to go up or down in the near future. One way in which tax changes affect giving is through habituation. People's charitable giving this year depends not only on their current circumstances but also on the charitable commitments they have made in the recent past. This means that recent past tax rates have an influence on current giving. For example, if marginal tax rates were higher in the recent past than they are now, giving may be higher now as well, because the low tax price of giving in the past encouraged people's charitable commitments, and those commitments help to buoy current giving even when the now-lower tax rates mean that giving now comes at a higher cost in terms of personal consumption.

A second way in which tax changes affect giving is through the strategic timing of gifts. If tax rates are anticipated to fall next year, for example, there is an incentive to move gifts one might have made next year into the current year, because the value of the tax deduction is greater. This is the commonly accepted explanation of the huge spike in charitable giving seen in 1986, just before the tax rate reductions of the Tax Reform Act of 1986 went into effect, dropping top tax rates over the next two years from 50 percent to 28 percent. Giving by millionaires spiked in 1993 and 1994, consistent with delaying gifts when in 1992 Bill Clinton had campaigned for president saying that he would raise taxes on the rich, which he did; starting in 1993, the top marginal rate rose from 31 percent to 39.6 percent.[20]

A third important consideration is whether people think a change in tax rates, or in their incomes, is temporary or permanent. An increase in income that is thought to be a temporary blip may not cause people to adjust their spending habits as much as a permanent change would do. Similarly, a temporary change in tax rates might invite donors to shift their giving from one year to another in search of tax advantages but might not lead them to make permanent changes to their levels of charitable giving. The distinction between permanent and transitory movements is theoretically important, but disentangling permanent and transitory movements, and people's expectations of what is temporary and what is permanent, represents an analytical challenge.

Given the many ways in which taxes can affect giving—not to mention the complication that giving can affect tax rates if charitable deductions are great enough to move a taxpayer from one bracket to another—it is tricky, even with good data, to sort out statistically the effects of income and tax price on charitable giving. Nevertheless, by examining over half a million federal personal income tax returns from 1979 to 2005 and using a variety of statistical techniques, Jon Bakija and Bradley Heim find several patterns in the response of charitable giving behavior to changes in state and federal income taxation. To capture the impact of taxes on the behavior of well-to-do taxpayers, high-income households were oversampled. The average income for households in the data set is more than $1 million, and the average level of annual charitable giving is $140,000. Their study therefore is well suited to examining the behavior of the households of most importance to the nonprofit sector as a whole. Bakija and Heim find that high-income households are more responsive to changes in the tax incentives to give than are less affluent households. Households with incomes of $1 million or more show evidence of strategic timing of their gifts. If tax rates are scheduled to increase, for example, wealthy households will postpone some of their giving in order to take advantage of the larger future tax deduction. In contrast, giving by households with annual incomes below $500,000 does not appear to be strategically timed to take advantage of changing tax rates.[21]

Lower-income households may not be timing their gifts to take advantage of changes in tax laws, but their levels of charitable giving do respond to their income, their wealth, and, for those who itemize deductions, their tax rates. Giving increases with household income; giving as a proportion of income increases over most of the income distribution, but middle-income households give a somewhat smaller fraction of their income, on average, than do both poorer and more affluent households. While it is not surprising that high-income families, having proportionately more discretionary income, would give away a higher fraction of income on average than do middle-income families, the relative generosity of poorer families deserves comment. Two groups of lower-income families that are especially generous, and to whom the generosity of their income bracket can largely be attributed, are those who give to religious organizations and those who have low incomes but high levels of wealth, primarily retirees.

Controlling for a household's average level of income, variability in income from year to year is associated with less giving than we see from households with more stable income flows.[22]

In considering the giving behavior of retirees and other donors whose levels of giving depend on their wealth, huge drops in the value of the stock market appear to augur bad times for nonprofits that depend on donations, especially from wealthy households, whose gifts are frequently in the form of non-cash assets whose tax advantage rises with capital gains.[23] John Havens and Paul Schervish point out, however, that personal wealth is not as volatile as the stock market. About two-thirds of household assets are in forms other than stocks, such as real estate, bank accounts, and motor vehicles. In the downturn from 1999 to 2002, when the Dow Jones Industrial average fell by 27 percent, household wealth fell by just 7 percent. In the first half of 2008, when the Dow fell by 13.5 percent; household wealth fell by 4.5 percent. Havens and Schervish suggest a rule of thumb that "a 30 percent drop in the Dow is statistically associated with a 6 percent decline in the value of household net worth and a 4 percent decline in charitable giving."[24]

Around these trends there is, of course, substantial divergence in the experiences of individual nonprofit organizations. Tracking a sample of seventy-seven large nonprofits that rely on direct marketing through the twelve months ending in mid-2009, a recent survey found dramatic median declines in dollars of charitable giving received, acquisition of new donors, and charitable revenues per donor. Even in this crisis-ridden period, however, 18 percent of the nonprofits in the survey experienced positive growth in charitable dollars, a third increased their numbers of donors, and a third experienced increases in dollars given per donor.[25]

Scholars have also investigated the extent to which potential donors respond to the behavior and circumstances of nonprofits themselves. One question they have investigated is whether donors react negatively to nonprofits' financial reports showing that a large proportion of their revenues is spent on administration and fundraising rather than on service delivery. If they were more fully informed, potential donors might more reasonably care how an organization is likely to spend the additional donations they are contemplating; it is quite possible that administrative and fundraising overhead are high on average but low at the margin where decisions are being made. In the absence of this preferred information, it is an empirical question whether donors seem to take cues from reported average levels of administrative and fundraising costs. Some studies find a negative statistical relationship between the proportion of revenue going to overhead costs and the level of donations received by American nonprofits. Other studies find little relationship.[26] Daniel Tinkelman and Kamini Mankaney propose that a negative relationship between administrative costs and donations is more likely to be found for nonprofit firms whose data on administrative costs are "decision useful." With a large data set and careful attention to econometric detail, they drop from the data nonprofit organizations that are so young that the financial anomalies associated with start-up make recent data unrepresentative of their likely future circumstances, as well as firms that report implausibly low administrative costs and firms that do not to a significant degree rely on donations. Using their data set comprising firms whose data convey reliable information to donors, they find robust negative relationships between nonprofit organizations' administrative costs and charitable contributions received.[27] Woods Bowman argues, further, that donors have even more reason to be concerned with changes in an organization's overhead than with its level, and finds evidence that donors respond negatively to increases in the proportion of budget going to overhead.[28]

A second circumstance to which donors might respond is the nonprofit organization's access to government grants. When a nonprofit receives a grant, to what extent (if at all) do donors respond by giving less; conversely, when public support is cut do private donations increase? The literature on this topic has produced a wide range of answers; one careful study that followed 430 local service nonprofits for ten years found crowd-out of about half, that is, that when taking into account the consequent fall in private donations, a dollar of government grant increased nonprofit revenue by about half a dollar.[29]

While this may sound at first like terrible news for nonprofits, subsequent research suggests that nonprofits may actually be contributors to this negative relationship between government grants and private giving. When government support dries up, nonprofits can respond by stepping up their fundraising efforts, and when government support expands, fundraising can slack off. James Andreoni and Abigail Payne looked for such a response in fourteen years of data on 233 nonprofits in the arts and 534 nonprofits in social services, and found large changes, as predicted, in fundraising expenditures in response to changing levels of government support. There were proportionately greater responses in the arts, which are more heavily dependent on donations, than in social services.[30]

What Influences Levels of Volunteering?

In 2008, almost 62 million Americans volunteered. In spite of the breadth of this participation, however, volunteering, unlike charitable donations of money, is the exception rather than the rule: between one-quarter and one-third of households have at least one adult who over the course of a year does volunteer work on at least one occasion.[31] Among the population of volunteers, there was significant variation in the amount of time volunteered, with half the volunteer population giving one hour a week or less on average, and about a third of the volunteer population giving two hours per week or more.[32]

Like charitable giving, volunteering increases with education and with markers of community involvement, such as the presence of children in the household and attendance at religious services. The correlation between an individual's volunteering and his or her overall civic and group involvement is high—higher, for example, than the correlation between giving to religious and to secular causes, or between giving and volunteering—suggesting that people who tend to get involved in activities around them tend to be volunteers.[33]

Women volunteered at greater rates than men, with 29.4 percent of women volunteering at some point in the previous year, compared with just 23.2 percent of men. For both men and women, rates of volunteering are low during early adulthood. In the age range twenty-five to thirty-four, only 22.8 percent of the population volunteers; this jumps by more than a third, to 31.3 percent, in the age group thirty-five to forty-four. Consistent with this movement through the life cycle, we see that parents of school-age children are more likely to have volunteered in the past year than are adults with no children or whose youngest child is younger than six years old.[34]

This picture of the relationship between volunteering and age changes somewhat if we shift from looking at who volunteered at least once during a year's time to looking at the likelihood of volunteering on an average day. This shift distinguishes sporadic volunteering, responding to occasional circumstances, and episodic volunteering, such as picking up trash in the forest every year on Earth Day, from steady, frequently recurring volunteering, such as delivering meals to shut-ins every week. This distinction is important to nonprofits interested in attracting a stable and committed volunteer workforce. Data from 2003 through 2007 suggest that men and women age sixty-five and over are most likely to volunteer their time for no pay to an organization on an average day.[35]

Older Americans are volunteering more than they used to. A rise in volunteering among older Americans relative to their middle-age counterparts was noted in the 1990s. Kristin A. Goss concluded in 1999 that although increased health and educational attainment among the elderly are contributing factors, the members of what has been called the "long civic generation"—those born in the first third of the twentieth century, whose members had a high level of community engagement when compared to later generations constituted an extraordinary generation in later-life volunteering as in so many other ways.[36] It comes as good news, then, that relatively high rates of volunteering among citizens age sixty-five and over have persisted as we move through the first decade of the twenty-first century. In 2005, when the youngest of the "long civic generation" turned seventy-five, volunteering within the age group sixty-five years and older was higher among the younger members of the age group.[37] The high level of volunteering in the over-sixty-five age group was no longer attributable only to the exemplary citizenship of the generation born before 1930, and it appears that rates of volunteering among the retirement-age population will remain higher than they were before the rates started to rise in the 1990s.

Volunteering varies dramatically by educational attainment; persons with at least a bachelor's degree volunteer at a rate (42.2 percent) more than twice that (19.1 percent) of persons for whom a high school diploma is their highest qualification. Thirty-four percent of part-time workers volunteer, a significantly higher rate of volunteering than that among full-time workers (28 percent), the unemployed (22 percent), and persons not in the labor force (22 percent).[38]

Economists have occasionally expressed puzzlement over the relationship between rates of volunteering, education, and employment. Wages increase with education; why, then, aren't highly educated citizens inclined to give money in place of their valuable time? And why aren't people who are not working more inclined to volunteer, given that a big time demand, work, doesn't impinge upon them? The economist's instinct that the value of time matters is not wholly misplaced: although the more highly educated are more likely to volunteer, they volunteer in briefer stints of time than their less educated fellow volunteers.[39] What is missing in this view centered on the opportunity cost of time is the powerful role in influencing both volunteering and giving played by what social scientists have come to call social capital, as we discuss in a later section.

Trends in Giving and Volunteering

In looking for trends in giving and volunteering, we quickly come up against the unglamorous and policy-wonkish question of where our data come from and whether they are comparable over time. Many of the data sources that in the twenty-first century give us our best estimates of giving and volunteering are different from the sources we relied upon a decade earlier. In the 1990s, scholars looking for nationally representative surveys of giving and volunteering gratefully relied on the biennial surveys of giving and volunteering sponsored by Independent Sector. These data are no longer collected, and several alternative sources have sprung up in their place. The Bureau of Labor Statistics has begun regular data collection on volunteering as part of its large-scale Current Population Survey (CPS). The BLS has also collected time diary data in the American Time Use Survey (ATUS), begun in 2003; the ATUS data can be linked to the CPS data. The venerable Panel Study of Income Dynamics, a high-quality data set that has followed families and their descendants since the late 1960s, has included questions on giving and volunteering since 2001. Some high-quality data sources, such as IRS data on charitable donations reported on personal income tax returns and estate tax filings and the Federal Reserve Board's Survey of Consumer Finances, have been available continuously, but they provide more information on the charitable giving of higher-income households (who are more likely to itemize their donations, have taxable estates, and give at least $500 annually to charity) than on that of the population overall.

Whether or not we can document them as "trends," some developments in giving and volunteering—or in our understanding of giving and volunteering—stand out as the new millennium gets under way. Changes in technology bring more Americans to the Internet, tantalizing nonprofits with the generosity of online and phoned-in responses to natural disaster but exposing them to the easy disappearance of these donors with whom no rapport has been created and sustained. Changes in the income distribution of the United States have placed more money in the hands of the super-rich, whose capacity for philanthropic works is vast. Volunteering has been shaped by institutional changes that spur volunteering even as they blur the line between volunteering and other forms of civic activism. Finally, scholars have learned more about the links between social capital—the networks of association and the norms of trust and reciprocity that embed individuals in their communities—and individuals' levels of giving and volunteering. We consider these developments in turn.

Online donations are growing in number and importance. The year 2001 was a watershed for Internet giving. In that year Americans responded to the disasters of September 11 with an outpouring of donations to relief agencies, giving more than $100 million online by the end of the year. In 2001, the proportion of the large nonprofit firms included in the Chronicle of Philanthropy's Philanthropy 400 that had online donation capabilities mushroomed from roughly half at the beginning of the year to 80 percent by the year's end.[40]

Nevertheless, a survey of 2,333 American adults taken three and a half years later, in July 2005, found that only 14 percent had made an online donation within the previous twelve months, even though over 90 percent of respondents in each age bracket described themselves as daily users of the Internet.[41] That sparse use of the Internet for charitable giving would soon change, with another outpouring of financial support for disaster relief efforts in the wake of Hurricane Katrina in August 2005 and the Pakistan earthquake in October 2005. Disaster relief highlighted the strengths of Internet giving: nonprofit organizations are able to update information rapidly on their websites and donors are able to respond immediately to need. Online donations to relief organizations and animal welfare groups grew rapidly in 2005 and 2006; more recently, other areas of nonprofit activity have seen online giving grow in importance. At a January 2009 forum of large nonprofits interested in online giving, the median proportion of an organization's donors giving online was nine percent, and the median proportion of charitable donations received online was 11 percent.[42]

Internet donors tend to be younger, have higher incomes, and be more highly educated than donors who exclusively make their donations offline.[43] They are more likely to focus on national and international causes and less on local matters. A growing proportion of first-time donors are online donors. Nonprofits find Internet donors a mixed blessing, when compared to direct-mail donors: gifts received online are on average bigger than gifts received through direct mail but, at any level of giving, online givers are less likely to renew their giving. Because both online and direct-mail donors of larger gifts tend to be more loyal, overall one-year retention rates for online and direct-mail donors have been found to be similar.[44]

The option of making a donation online gives donors a way to respond immediately with timely aid in urgent, rapidly unfolding situations. In contrast to the general finding that being asked to give is a key motivator for donors, over half of online donors in the 2005 survey said they had never been contacted online to give; rather, eighty-nine percent cited news reports as triggers that frequently or sometimes spurred their Internet giving. Consistent with this picture of Internet givers' decisions to give being triggered through an awareness of events conveyed outside of nonprofits' solicitations for funding, Adrian Sargeant and others find no relationship between the strength of the case for support made on a nonprofit's website and any aspect of its fundraising performance.[45]

Even swifter and more immediate than the option of online giving is the ability to make charitable donations by sending a text message from a cell phone. A one-word text message can commit a small amount of money, typically $10, to a specified charity or group of charities; the cost of the gift is added to the phone bill. The flat amount of money is small, the decision of how much to give to whom is streamlined, and the technology is swift and at hand. In this environment, the prospective donors have little incentive to pause and devote time and effort to investigating the organizations to which their money goes. When phone companies seek confirmation of a gift and ask whether the donor wants to receive follow-ups from the nonprofit, the texting donor can decline, assuring anonymity vis-à-vis the nonprofit and protection from follow-up contacts that might be regarded as spam. The donor-donee relationship that seems tenuous in the case of Internet donations becomes, in the case of anonymous text-message donations, downright ephemeral.

Just as the terrorist attacks of 2001 spurred the use of Internet-based giving, the devastating earthquake in Haiti in January 2010 underscored the power of texting. In the first week after the earthquake, the Red Cross received $22 million in $10 pledges made via cell phone text messaging. These text message donations accounted for 20 percent of the first week's donations to the Red Cross.[46] The cell phone has further democratized philanthropy, mobilizing a large corps of independent donors who in the course of leading electronically connected lives—watching a football playoff game or a benefit concert, chatting online with other players in a Facebook game—pause for a moment to express solidarity and compassion through giving.

One consequence of the growing use of electronic media in charitable giving is that large nonprofits in areas such as disaster relief are increasingly likely to find their relationships with donors mediated by third parties. The response to the January 2010 earthquake in Haiti highlighted this intermediation as celebrities, television networks, and phone companies rallied the public and directed their donations. Mediation between nonprofits and donors is nothing new, of course: local charities have long relied on federated giving organizations such as the United Way and United Jewish Appeal. The new mediators to whom nonprofits must appeal, however, are those able to connect to people and businesses pausing in their normal pursuits to respond quickly to extraordinary circumstances. In such an environment, public reputations and personal connections will matter more, and donor solicitations and careful compliance with transparent standards less, to the fundraising successes of nonprofits.

If the Internet and cell phone connectivity have allowed substantial numbers of Americans to respond rapidly and on their own initiative to events as they unfold, vast accumulations of wealth have allowed the richest Americans to make very large donations deliberately, either on their own initiative or in collaboration with nonprofit organizations that spend years cultivating relationships with them. The Slate 60 is an annual list of the year's sixty largest American charitable contributions (including bequests); to make the list in 2008, a person needed to give away at least $25 million. The contributions by the Slate 60 in 2008, which included several large bequests, totaled $15.78 billion, more than double the $7.79 billion value of the top sixty contributions made in 2007. Impressive as these totals are, Warren Buffet dwarfed them single-handedly with his 2006 gifts, valued in the Slate list at $43.5 billion.[47]

These enormous gifts derive from the increasingly enormous fortunes being amassed by the very richest Americans. By "very richest" we refer to a group far more exclusive than, say, the richest 1 percent of the population: the top 1 percent is so unexclusive that in 1998 it included households with annual incomes below a quarter of a million dollars. The top 1 percent of the top 1 percent (0.01 percent), however, contains about 13,100 households with annual incomes above $3.6 million. The last quarter of the twentieth century saw a dramatic reemergence of concentrations of income at the tip of the income distribution pyramid. In 1973, the top 0.01 percent had 0.5 percent of all household income, or 500 times the average income. In the quarter century from 1973 to 1998, the share of income going to the top 0.01 percent of the income distribution increased fivefold, to 2.57 percent. Such concentrations of income approach the levels seen before World War I, but there has been a shift in the sources of this income, away from capital income (such as dividends and rents) toward entrepreneurial and labor income (including stock options paid as part of a compensation package), to the point where by 1998 the top 0.01 percent of the income distribution was getting twice as much of its income from labor as it was from capital.[48]

The initiative and innovation that give rise to new entrepreneurial fortunes is evident in the evolving culture of philanthropy among America's superrich. Catch phrases such as "venture philanthropy" and "philanthrocapitalism" have emerged to capture the hands-on, risk-taking, ground-breaking directions of the philanthropy of many of the superrich. One illustration of this "new philanthropy" can be found in the guiding principles of the Bill and Melinda Gates Foundation. Among their fifteen guiding principles are these markers of initiative and entrepreneurial spirit: "#1: This is a family foundation driven by the interests and passions of the Gates family"; "#7: We take risks, make big bets, and move with urgency. We are in it for the long haul"; and "#11: Delivering results with the resources we have been given is of the utmost importance—and we seek and share information about those results."[49]

As a bigger share of income goes to households at the top of the income distribution, a bigger share of the nation's charitable dollars goes to causes favored by higher-income households. Religious giving constitutes a bigger proportion of household giving among households of modest incomes, and as their share of personal income has declined, so too has the share of charitable giving going to religious causes. Although the absolute level of charitable giving to religion has continued to climb, as a proportion of private contributions to nonprofits it has fallen from over half in the mid-1980s to less than a third in 2005–2006. Over the same period there was substantial growth in the fraction of giving going to foundations, to international affairs, and to support the environment, causes favored by more highly educated, higher-income households.[50]

If developments in charitable giving are linked to new technologies and the changing distribution of income, developments in volunteering seem to be shaped by shifts in the civic arena. Volunteering increased among young people as schools emphasized community service; volunteering has increased among older Americans as improved health, greater educational attainment, and the good example of America's most civically engaged generation have made their way into the upper age brackets. Full-time volunteering has become more common; ever more months-long opportunities for full-time public service are sponsored by the Corporation for National and Community Service, and ever more volunteers take up these opportunities . Decades of focus on community service programs in secondary schools have paid off, and volunteering is now common among high school students. A study conducted by the Corporation for National and Community Service in 2005 concluded that 58 percent of American high school students volunteered at some point during the year, roughly the same rate found by Independent Sector in its surveys of teen volunteering conducted in 1992 and 1996.[51] An important determinant of teenage volunteering is exposure to community service at school: 38 percent of high school students had undertaken some form of community service as part of a school activity. Besides the significant influence of exposure to community service at school, teenagers are more likely to volunteer if they attend religious services, and if their parents volunteer.[52]

As we have seen, most adult volunteers give an average of one hour a week or less to volunteer activities, and much of their volunteering is sporadic or episodic. Alongside this preponderance of loosely attached, occasional, and brief volunteering, however, has emerged the phenomenon of full-time, "stipended" public service. AmeriCorps assigns its members to projects for ten to twelve months and provides a stipend of "a modest living allowance" to enable participants to forgo paid employment during their term of service. The number of Americans participating each year in AmeriCorps is scheduled to expand from 88,000 in 2010 to 250,000 in 2017.[53]

The public service elicited by public programs such as school-based community service requirements and the AmeriCorps program raise the issue of what constitutes volunteering. A typical definition of volunteering refers to unpaid work, undertaken voluntarily under the aegis of a formal organization, for the benefit of people beyond the volunteer's circle of family and friends.[54] Under this definition, compulsory community service is not volunteering. What about AmeriCorps and other paid service? Can stipended service be construed as volunteer work?

The question of remuneration for volunteers arises most starkly in cases in which people leave their homes to offer free labor services at a remote site, as in the outpouring of volunteer assistance for the relief and clean-up efforts in the wake of Hurricane Katrina. When volunteers give their time away from home, there are financial costs involved—volunteers need food and shelter—and our definition of volunteering might usefully distinguish between stipends that address these costs and payments that reward the labor itself. The rise of full-time volunteering suggests that we expand our definition of a volunteer to include people who donate their time through an organization for no remuneration except that which directly facilitates their volunteering, be it a lunch provided on the job, reimbursement for the cost of gasoline, or shelter when volunteering away from home. People who receive housing when they travel to New Orleans for the clean-up effort and, like AmeriCorps workers, receive modest living stipends would then fit within the definition of volunteers (although AmeriCorps workers' eligibility for education vouchers constitutes a form of remuneration that fails the test of directly facilitating volunteering).

Wherever we decide to draw the boundaries around what we call volunteering, the point remains that cultures of volunteerism and many kinds of civic activism are closely linked, and the forces that encourage one will almost certainly encourage the other. One way to explore these links is through the notion of social capital, the networks of association and the attitudes of trust and trustworthiness that bind individuals into the social fabric of their communities. Individuals' stocks of social capital have been found to be related to various forms of pro-social behavior, and recently attention has turned to the relationships among social capital and giving and volunteering. Amornrat Apinunmahakul and Rose Anne Devlin find that time spent with family and friends has a positive association with the charitable giving of men, and that the number of organizations they belong to has a positive association with the charitable giving of women. Membership in clubs and other organizations has a bigger impact on people's levels of volunteering than it does on their charitable gifts of money.[55] Brown and Ferris find that different dimensions of social capital are important for different kinds of personal philanthropy: religiosity increases giving to religious causes, civic and social networks increase giving to secular causes, and habits of informed and responsive citizenship combined with attitudes of trust are important determinants of people's levels of volunteering.[56]

The Future of Giving and Volunteering

In 2008 and subsequent years, recession wreaked havoc on the U.S. economy. Charitable giving, adjusted for inflation, fell by 6.3 percent in 2008 from its level the year before. Except for the decline in giving between 1986 and 1987 (caused by the acceleration of giving into 1986 in order to receive tax deductions before the Tax Reform Act of 1986's lower tax rates went into effect in 1987), this is the largest single-year decline in giving on record.[57] The near-term future of individual giving as the economy emerges from crisis will be shaped by many factors, including the performance of the economy, changes in federal income taxation, and underlying social trends.

On the economic front, charitable giving will rebound as household incomes stabilize and as housing and stock market wealth regain some of their lost value. People pushed by the recession out of full-time work into part-time employment may fill some of their spare time with volunteering, but people pushed into unemployment will tend to volunteer less as their social ties and social standing are diminished. Employment tends to rebound more slowly than GDP, so nonprofits that rely on small donations from benefactors of modest means may see their donations rebound more slowly than nonprofits whose donor base is more affluent.

With the federal budget deficit standing at $1.4 trillion, higher taxes for high-income households seem a conspicuous potential source of government revenue. Two proposals endorsed at various times by President Obama, an income tax increase on high-income households and a cap on the rate at which charitable gifts can be deducted, have implications for charitable giving. Higher tax rates for high-income individuals will lower the tax price of giving for households that are responsible for a large fraction of the donations that reach American nonprofits; this is predicted to increase giving once the higher tax rates go into effect, but to depress giving beforehand, as people time their gifts to coincide with years that offer more valuable tax deductions. In contrast, proposals to cap the rate at which charitable gifts can be deducted from taxable income cancel, or even reverse, this dynamic. A cap at the current top tax rate would eliminate the tax price and timing effects on charitable giving of an additional top tax bracket, leaving only the depressive effect of higher average income tax rates on the disposable incomes of the rich.

At the time of this writing, the political future of the estate tax is uncertain. The drive for federal revenue will almost certainly lend pressure to reinstate the estate tax. This is good news for nonprofits; the higher the estate tax rate, the greater are the incentives to bequeath wealth to tax-deductible nonprofit activities.

Although the deficit may lead to tax increases that make tax-deductible donations more attractive, the federal budget deficit itself must be reckoned with. To the extent that we incur deficits now, we saddle our children and our children's children with the prospect of higher taxes in the future. To the extent that we care about our children and our children's children, these concerns will direct our dollars away from charitable purposes and into the pockets of our progeny.

In this gloomy environment, nonprofit organizations interested in private donations as a funding source can enhance their prospects in several ways. While levels of generosity vary dramatically across households, giving and volunteering remain widespread habits, and we can expect these established habits of giving to buoy generosity during economic downturns. This suggests that nonprofits should be especially attentive to their established donors, and that they seek ways to develop ties with new donors who come to them through the relationship-sparse medium of the Internet.

The economic and political challenges of the coming decade are daunting, yet there are underlying social trends that increase our philanthropic potential. Rising levels of educational attainment are associated with increased personal giving. The increasing connectivity of younger citizens through electronic media may draw young people into habits of philanthropy; the longer-term effects on philanthropy of expressive gifts of small amounts at grocery counters and through text messages remain to be seen. Alongside these casual forms of giving, the formation of family foundations among the wealthy and networks such as giving circles among the general population continue to create vehicles for informed, strategic philanthropy. Finally, the improved health and vitality of the large cohort of senior citizens reaching retirement age should be very good news for nonprofit organizations with the capacity to engage talented, dedicated volunteers.

Notes

1. Giving USA Foundation, *Giving USA 2008* (Glenview, Ill.: 2009), p. 9.

2. Kennard T. Wing, Thomas H. Pollak, and Amy Blackwood, *The Nonprofit Almanac, 2008* (Washington: Urban Institute Press, 2008), p. 97.

3. Individual giving data from Giving USA Foundation, *Giving USA 2009* (Glenview, Ill.: 2010), p. 217; personal income data from U.S. Department of Commerce, Bureau of

Economic Analysis, National Income and Product Accounts, table 2.1, as revised October 29, 2009 (www.bea.gov/national/nipaweb/TableView.asp?SelectedTable=43&FirstYear=2009& LastYear=2010&Freq=Qtr).

4. Wing, Pollak, and Blackwood, *Nonprofit Almanac,* table 3.10, p. 93.

5. Giving USA Foundation, *Giving USA 2008,* p. 9.

6. Wing, Pollak, and Blackwood, *Nonprofit Almanac,* p. 17.

7. Giving USA Foundation, *Giving USA 2008,* page 89; and Wing, Pollak, and Blackwood, *Nonprofit Almanac,* table 5.8, p. 157.

8. Wing, Pollak, and Blackwood, *Nonprofit Almanac,* table 5.5, p. 146.

9. U.S. Department of Labor, Bureau of Labor Statistics, "Volunteering in the United States, 2008," publication USDL 09-0078, January 23, 2009 (www.bls.gov/news.release/ volun.nr0.htm).

10. U.S. Department of Labor, "Volunteering in the United States, 2008," table 5.

11. David Eisner and others, "The New Volunteer Workforce," *Stanford Social Innovation Review* 7, no. 1 (Winter 2009): 32–37.

12. Mark A. Hager and Jeffrey L. Brudney, *Volunteer Management Practices and Retention of Volunteers* (Washington: Urban Institute, 2004).

13. John J. Havens, Mary A. O'Herlihy, and Paul G. Schervish, "Charitable Giving: How Much, by Whom, to What, and How?" in *The Nonprofit Sector: A Research Handbook,* 2nd ed., edited by Walter W. Powell and Richard Steinberg (Yale University Press, 2006), pp. 542–67 (chapter 23).

14. Center on Philanthropy (Indiana University), "Center on Philanthropy Panel Study— Household Giving and Volunteering Reports" (www.philanthropy.iupui.edu/Research/ COPPS/COPPS_2006.aspx; February 24, 2009);

15. Gerald E. Auten, Charles T. Clotfelter, and Richard L. Schmalbeck, "Taxes and Philanthropy among the Wealthy," in *Does Atlas Shrug?* edited by Joel B. Slemrod (New York: Russell Sage Foundation, 2000), pp. 392–424 (chapter 12).

16. James Andreoni, Eleanor Brown, and Isaac Rischall, "Charitable Giving by Married Couples: Who Decides, and Why Does It Matter?" *Journal of Human Resources* 18, no. 1 (Winter 2003): 111–33.

17. Mark Wilhelm and others, "The Intergenerational Transmission of Generosity," *Journal of Public Economics* 92 (October 2008): 2146–56.

18. Havens, O'Herlihy, and Schervish, "Charitable Giving."

19. Wing, Pollak, and Blackwood, *Nonprofit Almanac,* table 3.10, p. 93.

20. Jon Bakija and Bradley Heim, "How Does Charitable Giving Respond to Incentives and Income? Dynamic Panel Estimates Accounting for Predictable Changes in Taxation," National Bureau of Economic Research Working Paper 14237 (Cambridge, Mass.: NBER, August 2008).

21. Ibid.

22. Patricia Hughes and William Luksetich, "Income Volatility and Wealth: The Effect on Charitable Giving," *Nonprofit and Voluntary Sector Quarterly* 37, no. 2 (June 2008): 264–80.

23. Gerald Auten, Charles T. Clotfelter, and Richard L. Schmalbeck, "Taxes and Philanthropy among the Wealthy," in *Does Atlas Shrug? The Economic Consequences of Taxing the Rich,* edited by Joel B. Slemrod (New York: Russell Sage Foundation, 2000), pp. 392–424 (chapter 12) .

24. John Havens and Paul Schervish, "Giving in Today's Economy," *Trusts and Estates,* January 1, 2009, pp. 42–45 (see link at www.trustsandestates.com/toc/toc_010109).

25. Helen Flannery, Rob Harris, and Carol Rhine, "Index of National Fundraising Performance: 2009 Second Calendar Quarter Results," report (Minneapolis: Target Analysis

Group, September 2009) (www.blackbaud.com/files/resources/downloads/cam/TargetIndex ResultsSummaryQ22009.pdf).

26. Burton Weisbrod and N. Dominguez, "Demand for Collective Goods in Private Non-profit Markets: Can Fundraising Expenditures Help Overcome Free-Rider Behavior?" *Journal of Public Economics* 30 (1986): 83–96; C. Okten and Burton Weisbrod, "Determinants of Donations in Private Nonprofit Markets," *Journal of Public Economics* 75 (2000): 255–72.

27. Daniel Tinkelman and Kamini Mankaney, "When Is Administrative Efficiency Associated with Charitable Donations?" *Nonprofit and Voluntary Sector Quarterly* 36, no. 1 (March 2007): 41–64.

28. Woods Bowman, "Should Donors Care about Overhead Costs? Do They Care?" *Nonprofit and Voluntary Sector Quarterly* 35, no. 2 (June 2006): 288–310.

29. Abigail Payne, "Does the Government Crowd Out Charitable Donations? New Evidence from a Sample of Non-Profit Firms," *Journal of Public Economics* 69, no. 3 (1998): 323–45.

30. James Andreoni and A. Abigail Payne, "Do Government Grants to Private Charities Crowd Out Giving or Fundraising?" *American Economic Review* 93, no. 3 (June 2003): 792–812.

31. Center on Philanthropy (Indiana University), "Center on Philanthropy Panel Study—Household Giving and Volunteering Reports"; U.S. Department of Labor, Bureau of Labor Statistics, "Volunteering in the United States, 2008."

32. Ibid., table 2.

33. Eleanor Brown and James M. Ferris, "Social Capital and Philanthropy: An Analysis of the Impact of Social Capital on Individual Giving and Volunteering," *Nonprofit and Voluntary Sector Quarterly* 36, no. 1 (March 2007): 85–99.

34. U.S. Department of Labor, Bureau of Labor Statistics, "Volunteering in the United States"; U.S. Department of Labor, Bureau of Labor Statistics, American Time Use Survey, "Charts by Topic: Volunteer Activities" (www.bls.gov/tus/charts/volunteer.htm).

35. Ibid.; U.S. Department of Labor, Bureau of Labor Statistics, "Volunteering in the United States."

36. Kristin A. Goss, "Volunteering and the Long Civic Generation," *Nonprofit and Voluntary Sector Quarterly* 28, no. 4 (December 1999): 378–415.

37. Stephanie Boraas White, "Volunteering in the United States, 2005," *Monthly Labor Review,* February 2006, pp. 65–70.

38. U.S. Department of Labor, Bureau of Labor Statistics, "Volunteering in the United States, 2008."

39. U.S. Department of Labor, Bureau of Labor Statistics, American Time Use Survey, "Charts by Topic: Volunteer Activities."

40. Juan L. Gandia, "Nonprofit Organizations' Use of the Internet: A Content Analysis of Communication Trends on the Internet Sites of the Philanthropy 440," *Nonprofit Management & Leadership* 18, no. 1 (Fall 2007): 59–76.

41. Craver, Mathews, Smith & Company, "Keep Your Postage Meter: The Status of Online Giving in America," DonorTrends White Paper, October 2005 (http://craver mathewssmith.com/wp-content/uploads/2008/07/onlinegivingwhitepaper_final.pdf).

42. Helen Flannery, Rob Harris, and Carol Rhine, "2008 DonorCentrics Internet Giving Benchmark Analysis" (Minneapolis: Target Analysis Group, January 2009).

43. Craver, Mathews, Smith &Company, "Keep Your Postage Meter"; Helen Flannery and Rob Harris, "2006 donorCentrics Internet Giving Benchmarking Analysis" (Minneapolis: Target Analysis Group, January 16, 2007) (www.docin.com/p-94176332.html [August 27, 2011]).

44. Flannery, Harris, and Rhine, "2006 donorCentrics Internet Giving Benchmarking Analysis."

45. Adrian Sargeant, Douglas C. West, and Elaine Jay, "The Relational Determinants of Nonprofit Web Site Fundraising Effectiveness: An Exploratory Study," *Nonprofit Management & Leadership* 18, no. 2 (Winter 2007): 141–56.

46. Thomas Heath, "Cellphone Donations Surpass $22 Million; Red Cross's Previous Text Message Record was $400,000," *Washington Post,* January 19, 2010, p. A10.

47. Rachael Larimore, "The 2008 Slate 60: The Largest American Charitable Contributions of the Year," Slate.com, January 26, 2009 (www.slate.com/id/2209476).

48. Thomas Piketty and Emmanuel Saez, "Income Inequality in the United States, 1913–1998," *Quarterly Journal of Economics* 118, no. 1 (February 2003): 1–39.

49. Bill and Melinda Gates Foundation, "Guiding Principles" (www.gatesfoundation.org/about/Pages/guiding-principles.aspx).

50. Wing, Pollak, and Blackwood, *Nonprofit Almanac,* table 3.2, pp. 74–75.

51. Virginia A. Hodgkinson and Murray S. Weitzman, "Volunteering and Giving among Teenagers 12 to 17 Years of Age" (Washington: Independent Sector, 1997).

52. Robert Grimm Jr., and others, *Building Active Citizens: The Role of Social Institutions in Teen Volunteering* (Washington: Corporation for National and Community Service, November 2005).

53. Corporation for National and Community Service, "The Edward M. Kennedy Serve America Act Summary; Public Law 111-13, enacted April 21, 2009" (www.nationalservice.gov/pdf/09_0421_serveact_summary.pdf).

54. For an investigation of the four issues considered by one definition of volunteering— free choice, remuneration, mediation by an organization, and the identity of beneficiaries— see Ram Cnann, Femida Handy, and Margaret Wadsworth, "Defining Who Is a Volunteer: Conceptual and Empirical Considerations," *Nonprofit and Voluntary Sector Quarterly* 25, no. 3 (September 1996): 364–83.

55. Amornrat Apinunmahakul and Rose Anne Devlin, "Social Networks and Private Philanthropy," *Journal of Public Economics* 92, nos.1 and 2 (February 2008): 309–28.

56. Eleanor Brown and James M. Ferris, "Social Capital and Philanthropy: An Analysis of the Impact of Social Capital on Individual Giving and Volunteering," *Nonprofit and Voluntary Sector Quarterly.*

57. Giving USA Foundation, *Giving USA 2009,* p. 211.

PART III

Major Challenges

14

Commercialization, Social Ventures, and For-Profit Competition

DENNIS R. YOUNG, LESTER M. SALAMON,
AND MARY CLARK GRINSFELDER

T he end of the twentieth century witnessed a fundamental questioning of the traditional welfare state in Western industrial countries, the fall of communism in Central Europe and the states of the former Soviet Union, and the disappearance of authoritarian regimes in many developing countries. Underlying all of these events has been a profound disaffection with government, which has helped to create new opportunities and responsibilities for the private sector—both for-profit and nonprofit—to address societal problems and improve the welfare of citizens.

No sooner did free market capitalism claim center stage in this unfolding drama, however, than it began to reveal its excesses. With government in retreat or under the control of free market enthusiasts and with regulatory protections muted or neutered, some corporations, especially in sectors such as finance, housing, and energy, threw caution to the wind and ultimately plunged the U.S. and global economies into a free fall, from which they have yet to fully recover as of this writing.

While these developments have stunned the commercial impulses coursing through the global economy, however, they have hardly stopped it in its tracks. Nor have they obliterated the powerful hold these impulses have come to have on the nation's nonprofit sector. At the same time, these recent developments have injected a note of caution into the nonprofit sector's embrace of the market mantra and reawakened it to the importance of the values that set it apart from commercial enterprise.

The nonprofit sector's complex relationship with market forces is not, of course, a new story. Nonprofit organizations have been involved in commercial transactions from the sector's earliest days. Religious orders, for example, have long marketed wine, and orphanages have taken in laundry to help cover their costs. But the scope, scale, and variety of the penetration of commercial impulses into the nonprofit sector took on a whole new dimension in the two decades leading up to the 2008 economic crisis and remain quite powerful in its wake. This is apparent in the substantial growth of fee income as a source of nonprofit revenue, in the expanded involvement of nonprofits in the sale of ancillary goods and services, in the considerable proliferation of business-nonprofit partnerships, and in the widespread growth of an enterprise culture within nonprofit organizations. Indeed, the whole concept of a separate non-profit sphere has come under serious question as interest has grown in a new kind of entity—the social enterprise—that marries business means to nonprofit ends through the creation of social purpose business enterprises.

This chapter explores this important trend toward commercialization within the nonprofit sector in more detail, identifying the forces that are giving rise to it and assessing its implications for the sector's operation and role. To do so, the discussion falls into three parts. The first part examines the forces that have propelled nonprofits into greater engagement with the private market economy. The second part explores how nonprofits have responded to these forces, documenting the extent of nonprofit adoption of the dominant market culture. The third part assesses the implications of these developments for the role and character of nonprofit organizations and asks whether limits to these trends loom on the horizon.

The central conclusion emerging from this analysis is that nonprofits have accommodated themselves quite well to the commercial pressures they are confronting, reinventing themselves in often creative ways. At the same time, this development is posing a variety of new challenges and dangers for the sector. Nonprofit organizations seem to be finding ways to deal with these dangers, although egregious counterexamples do exist. At the same time, it is far from clear whether public understanding, or approval, has kept pace with the scope of the changes under way, with the result that the sector's most precious asset of all—the public's trust—may increasingly be at risk.

The Pressures for Commercialization

The fact that nonprofit organizations have turned increasingly to the market over the past two decades should come as no surprise given the pressures under which these organizations have been operating and the opportunities to which they have been exposed. Broadly speaking, six factors seem to be propelling nonprofit organizations toward greater integration with the prevailing market system.

Fiscal Squeeze

In the first place, nonprofits have long confronted a significant fiscal squeeze as a result of the relatively limited level, and generally tepid growth, of their traditional form of financial support—charitable giving—and the significant cutbacks that occurred in the early 1980s in government support, which had fueled the sector's substantial growth in the previous two decades. While charitable giving is probably higher in the United States than in most other nations, it has rarely exceeded 2 percent of the nation's gross domestic product, and less than half of these contributions are available for social welfare purposes (health, education, and welfare).[1] The level of private giving declined as a share of national income from the 1970s to the 1990s—from an average of 1.86 percent in the 1970s to 1.78 percent during the 1980s and to 1.72 percent in the early 1990s before turning up during the years of the dot.com bubble and the stock market gains that resumed during the housing boom of the middle of the twenty-first century's first decade. But these numbers include giving to foundations, giving to endowments, giving of works of art, and giving to various federated campaigns that turn around and give it to operating charities, thus counting the same dollars twice. The share of giving actually available to nonprofits to cover their annual operating costs is thus a pale reflection of these totals. Indeed, it stood at roughly 10 percent of total nonprofit service and expressive organizations' operating income as of 2007.[2] And following the severe economic recession that began in 2008, overall giving turned sharply down, declining by 5.6 percent in real dollar terms between 2007 and 2008.[3]

Although their charitable support remained limited, nonprofits benefited enormously in the 1960s and early 1970s from a significant expansion of government involvement in the field of social welfare, much of which was channeled through nonprofit organizations. The result was a massive surge in nonprofit activity and substantial growth in the scale and reach of the sector. By 1980 government accounted for well over 30 percent of a considerably larger base of nonprofit income.[4] But with the election of Ronald Reagan in the early 1980s, this expansion of government support slowed considerably and, in some fields, was completely reversed. Nonprofits therefore found themselves in a fiscal squeeze. Although, as Lester Salamon shows in chapter 1 of this book, public sector support for nonprofit organizations subsequently resumed its growth, accounting for 31.3 percent of total nonprofit revenue in 1997 and 38 percent as of 2007, that support changed significantly in form.[5] Instead of grants and contracts to nonprofit providers, which were cut, government support increasingly came through programs such as Medicaid and Medicare, which provide reimbursement "vouchers" to the "customers" that nonprofits serve. As a consequence, nonprofit organizations more and more found themselves in a commercial-type relationship even to secure government support. Moreover, in much of the social sector, costs have been rising faster than inflation. For example, price indexes for education and medical care, substantially reflecting underlying cost inflation, rose 35.7 percent and 24.0 percent, respectively, between 2000 and 2005, compared to 13.4 percent for the consumer price index.[6]

Expanded Demand

While experiencing a significant squeeze in their charitable and government support, nonprofit organizations have faced higher demand for their services. In part this demand has originated with the poor and disadvantaged, long an important constituency of the nonprofit sector. But social and demographic changes have also generated demands from other segments of the population, many of whom can afford to pay for the services they receive, either on their own or with the aid of public subsidies.

The continued rapid aging of the population, for example, has significantly increased the demand for a variety of elderly care services, from nursing home care to home health services. The over-sixty-five population is projected to double in size and to increase from 12 to 20 percent of the population between 2003 and 2030.[7] Similarly, the changing role of women in American society has substantially increased the demand for child care and related services. From 1975 to 2000 the labor force participation rate of mothers with children under eighteen rose from 47 to 73 percent, receding only slightly to 71 percent between 2004 and 2006.[8] Changes in the structure of American families have ratcheted up the need for various types of counseling and supportive services. With one out of three marriages ending in divorce by the mid-1990s, up from 5 percent in the early 1960s, child care, psychiatric counseling, crisis intervention, and associated activities are in much higher demand.[9]

Taken together, these and related social and demographic developments have put a premium on the kinds of services that nonprofit organizations have traditionally provided. In the process, they have helped to create a much broader market for nonprofit organizations' services.

Increased For-Profit Competition

One important effect of this growing market for nonprofit services has been the attraction of for-profit competition into fields once dominated by nonprofit providers. This has turned on its head the long-standing small business concern about unfair competition from nonprofits in traditional for-profit fields. An overriding concern now is the increased competition from for-profits in traditional nonprofit fields. In many of these fields, moreover, for-profits have certain structural advantages. For example, for-profits can focus more easily than nonprofits on the most profitable segments of particular service markets, neglecting the populations unable to pay or at most severe risk, whereas non-profits often retain a mission-oriented focus, which obliges them to serve those in greatest need. In some fields, such as health care, this can drive up the costs of care for the remaining clients because it increases the level of risk involved. In addition, for-profits have access to sources of capital that are unavailable to nonprofits—most particularly equity capital generated through the sale of stock. Equity capital tends to be cheaper since it involves an ownership stake in a company. Because nonprofits do not have owners who can share in any prof-its earned, this source of capital is not accessible to them. The more important access to capital is in a given field (for example, to build new facilities or acquire technology), the greater is the comparative advantage of for-profit businesses. Fortunately, some recent developments to provide greater access to capital mar-kets for nonprofits show some promise of addressing this issue, as we see more fully below, though these developments remain rather embryonic.[10]

Reflecting this situation, for-profit firms have been expanding more rapidly than nonprofits in a variety of traditional fields of nonprofit endeavor. As Sal-amon shows in chapter 1, between 1977 and 1997 the nonprofit share of child care jobs declined from 54 to 38 percent, and that of home health care jobs declined from 70 to 28 percent.[11] Nonprofits in these two fields managed to hold their own a bit better in the subsequent decade from 1997 to 2007, but only partly. Thus between 1997 and 2007 the for-profit share of home health care jobs went from 72 percent to 77 percent, of clinic jobs from 35 percent to 40 percent, of continuing-care retirement community jobs from 29 percent to 43, and of jobs in the formerly nonprofit-dominated field of children and fam-ily services from 9 percent to 31 percent. Moreover, similar developments were evident in other fields.[12]

The federal welfare reform legislation of 1996 facilitated some of these changes by opening a new arena for for-profit involvement in the areas of employment counseling, job training, and placement services, all of them tra-ditionally nonprofit markets. Large corporations such as Lockheed Martin IMS entered the social services market as master contractors, exploiting their access to high-speed computing technology to manage large caseloads and to process clients through complex networks of nonprofit and for-profit service providers. Indeed, welfare reform helped to transform public welfare into a major growth industry for for-profits. Maximus, Lockheed Martin IMS, and other for-profit corporations have capitalized on the new arrangements to expand their business operations. The Lockheed Martin IMS story is particularly interesting because it also reflects the changing priorities in public policy in the aftermath of the cold war. As the number of defense contracts dwindled during the 1980s and 1990s, Lockheed Martin IMS picked up the slack in its parent company's defense-related operations by contracting for delivery and administration of welfare services. This strategy proved to be quite a success, at least initially. Lockheed Martin IMS experienced a significant jump in the number of government welfare department clients, from none to twenty-five, following the passage of welfare reform in 1996.[13]

For-profit firms have even penetrated the field of charitable giving, as financial service firms such as Fidelity and Merrill Lynch have begun offering donor services similar to those developed by community foundations.[14] In less than five years the Fidelity Charitable Gift Fund alone attracted more capital into donor-advised funds than is held by the nation's largest community foundation, and by 2007 the thirty-eight commercially originated donor-advised funds were approaching the entire universe of over 600 community foundations in the donor-advised fund assets they had under management.[15]

To be sure, the competition between nonprofits and for-profits is not always a one-way street. Rather, it can ebb and flow. In the 1960s and 1970s nonprofit nursing homes lost ground to for-profit homes as Medicaid increased its coverage and for-profits were better positioned to tap into the capital markets to construct the facilities required to respond. Similarly, in the early 1990s nonprofit hospitals and health maintenance organizations lost ground to their for-profit counterparts that were able to invest in the information-processing equipment needed to make managed care work. In each of these fields, however, nonprofits have regained ground in more recent years, as reductions in the reimbursement rates under Medicare and Medicaid and pressures from private insurance companies have squeezed profit margins to the point where for-profit providers no longer find it so attractive to operate.

Similar problems have affected for-profit involvement in the welfare reform arena. Lockheed Martin IMS struggled in Miami-Dade County, where it failed to make a significant impact on caseloads. The county government has since handed the contract for welfare-to-work services over to a local community college.[16] In Kansas the state's transformation of child and family services has come under attack not only from liberal critics, who argue that public welfare should not be left up to firms whose primary motive is profit, but also from the businesses themselves. *Governing* magazine reported that "Kansas's story isn't really about privatization; it's about a rushed, no-holds-barred effort to build a public-private social services system using managed care principles, as well as struggles to recover from the fallout."[17] Unlike other states, Kansas bypassed small-scale, experimental initiatives and chose instead to undertake sweeping reform. The change resulted in confusion, as state officials struggled to learn new roles as contract managers rather than caregivers and as the newly empowered private firms found themselves swamped by the demands of public welfare programs with which they had little previous experience.

As their traditional businesses returned, therefore, some of the new for-profit entrants into the welfare business bailed out. Thus for example in July 2001 Lockheed Martin sold its IMS affiliate to Affiliated Computer Services Inc. as part of a corporate realignment designed to divest the company of noncore businesses, demonstrating in the process one of the disadvantages of for-profit entry into human service fields, where durability of provision is a prime need.[18] Nevertheless, the growing prominence of for-profits in a number of traditionally nonprofit fields has called into question the competitive advantages and disadvantages of the nonprofit form.[19]

Growing Competition among Nonprofits

Not only are nonprofits encountering increasing competition from for-profit firms, they are also facing increasing competition from other nonprofits. Such competition has long been at least implicit in service fields such as higher education and the arts, where nonprofits compete for clients and patrons among themselves as well as with for-profits. But the pressures of rivalry and competition have long been balanced by expectations of collaboration and pursuit of broader community interests, expectations that have been reinforced by the funding community—especially community foundations and federated fundraising organizations—which encourages both improved individual organizational performance as well as collaboration and consolidation in the interests of achieving greater overall efficiency and effectiveness.

Currently, however, the balance between collaboration and competition may be tipping toward competition. In health care and higher education, in particular, nonprofit institutions now invest heavily in advertising and marketing so as to outpace their competition, whether the competition be from for-profits or other nonprofits. The competition is not only for clients, moreover. It extends as well to competition for charitable contributions. With the development of the Internet and services such as GuideStar, donors are being empowered to become active shoppers in the arena of charitable giving, requiring nonprofits to make their cases more forcefully to distinguish themselves from their peers. Nonprofits also must compete for affiliations with for-profit corporations that offer their websites for Internet giving. Cisco Systems and America Online are two corporations that have made significant investments in online giving services, an area that is likely to continue to grow.[20] Among the top 400 nonprofits the establishment of online giving entities rose from 50 percent in 2001 to 90 percent in 2005.[21]

Traditional institutions for coordination of charitable giving, especially at the community level, are themselves experiencing the forces of disaggregation and competition. United Ways, which once enjoyed monopoly access to corporate payroll deduction systems, are now forced to share that access with alternative funds and even individual charities. Moreover, donors have insisted on having more say over the allocation of their charitable dollars to federated fundraising organizations, resulting in donor-choice systems that allow donors to designate their gifts to particular charitable causes.[22] This in turn increases the pressure on individual nonprofits to promote themselves vis-à-vis their nonprofit competitors. Finally, the entire corporate economy has become more decentralized after the downsizing of large corporations in the 1980s and the growth of entrepreneurial small businesses. Individual nonprofits must therefore target a broader field of business ventures for their fundraising appeals. The implications for nonprofits are mixed. According to a recent study of corporate giving, while large corporations give more on average than small businesses, small businesses are more likely to give.[23]

Broader Availability of Corporate Partners

In addition to being pushed into commercial activities by the increased competition from for-profit enterprises, nonprofits are also being pulled into the commercial orbit by increased corporate willingness to cooperate with nonprofits in joint undertakings. This development is part of the broader transformation of the corporate economy during the past several decades, as corporations have come to emphasize quality and identity—traditional nonprofit concerns—and not simply cost and efficiency as central values in a competitive global economy. To retain skilled staff and attract loyal customers, corporations have found it desirable to bolster their corporate image by identifying their organizations with socially useful undertakings. Forging partnerships with nonprofit organizations is one way to do this. Cause-related marketing, collaborative projects, and related undertakings are all manifestations of this phenomenon, as corporations make themselves available to nonprofit organizations not simply as donors, but as full-fledged partners willing to integrate their partnerships with nonprofits into their overall corporate strategies.[24]

Increased Demands for Accountability

Finally, the pressures nudging nonprofit organizations in the direction of the market arise as well from the expanded expectations of measurable performance on the part of the various stakeholders of the nonprofit sector. One consequence of competition from for-profit providers is that nonprofit organizations have been forced to pay more attention to efficiency and effectiveness in order to compete successfully for customers. Potential corporate partners and other institutional donors, including government agencies, are also seeking concrete measures of nonprofit performance as a condition of continued support. Thanks to new technologies, individual donors too are able to shop around and are demanding information on how nonprofits spend their money and do their work before parting with their charitable dollars.

These demands for accountability are arising, moreover, against the backdrop of an important shift in public philosophies about the causes of social problems. Where formerly such problems were perceived as the product of lack of opportunity and skills, increasingly they are viewed as the product of lack of initiative and will. This shift has put nonprofits, with their traditional "helping" orientation, on the defensive and moved employment-oriented organizations into an advantaged position.[25] To remain relevant in this climate, nonprofits have had to put more emphasis on demonstrating results in order to justify and protect the benefits they enjoy under public policy.[26]

The Response: The Move toward the Market

In response to this combination of pressures and opportunities, nonprofit organizations are drawing far closer to the market economy than perhaps at any time in their history. To be sure, not all components of the nonprofit sector are responding to these developments in the same way, and even within particular fields there are immense differences among organizations. The growing market involvement of nonprofit organizations is a complex and multifaceted phenomenon, with various strands interwoven into a rich tapestry. Nevertheless, a new reality is slowly coming into focus—a self-propelled, social problem-solving sector that has loosened its moorings to both traditional charity and government support and become much more tightly connected to the market system, while still trying to remain committed, however tenuously, to the pursuit of public benefit. The picture remains blurred and filled with crosscurrents, but the emerging pattern seems clear enough to describe in general terms.

The Growing Reliance on Earned Income

Perhaps the most salient aspect of the growing involvement of nonprofit organizations with the market is their steadily expanding reliance on fee income. Thus Salamon finds that, in 2007, 52 percent of the income of nonprofit service and expressive organizations (that is, all but religious congregations, foundations, and other funding intermediaries) came from private fees (compared to 38 percent from government and 10 percent from philanthropy).[27] What is more, between 1997 and 2007 private fees accounted for 58 percent of what was fairly substantial nonprofit growth. While some components of the nonprofit sector are more reliant than others on commercial fees (such as education, at 72 percent), even fields in which such fees were much less in evidence one or two decades ago, such as social services, now report levels of fee support that, at 45 percent, are near the sectorwide average.

Even this understates the commercial involvement of the nonprofit sector, however, since the character of government support has changed markedly over recent years (as noted in previous chapters). In particular, a much larger share of government support is reaching nonprofits through voucher programs that deliver their assistance directly to consumers rather than to the nonprofit producers of services. As a consequence, nonprofits are increasingly having to compete for clients in the market even for government support.

Nonprofit reliance on fees and charges is not an exclusively U.S. phenomenon, either. Lester Salamon and Wojciech Sokolowski find that, on average, 53 percent of the revenue of nonprofits in thirty-four countries scattered widely around the world derive from fees and charges, compared to 34 percent from government and 12 percent from philanthropy.[28] Some twenty-four of the thirty-four countries' nonprofit sectors are fee dominant—that is, more dependent on fees and charges than on any other source of income. Revealingly, though, most of these are in Asia or the developing world. By contrast, in most of Western Europe the nonprofit sector gets most of its support from public sector sources, reflecting the pervasiveness of government-nonprofit partnerships in that part of the world.

Most of the earned income that U.S. nonprofits receive takes the form of fees and charges for the mission-related services that nonprofits provide: tuition in education, box office receipts in the arts, charges for hospital stays and services, fees for counseling in social services, and so on. Some of this income, however, also derives from ancillary commercial activities not necessarily associated with core mission–related activities. For example, museums run gifts shops in shopping centers and airports, colleges offer travel services for their alumni, and YMCAs rent out their facilities for private parties. Determining the extent of such unrelated business income is difficult, however. By law, nonprofit organizations are obligated to pay taxes on such unrelated business income and to file a special tax form, the 990-T unrelated business income tax (UBIT) return, if they receive at least $1,000 in gross unrelated business income in a given year.

Unfortunately, the data resulting from such returns are a poor indicator of the extent of unrelated business income, for several reasons. First, certain categories of earned income are excluded from UBIT, including passive investment income, royalties, and activities performed by volunteers or for the convenience of the nonprofit's clientele (such as on-campus conveniences for students). Second, the rules on unrelated business income are liberal and allow nonprofits to declare income as related rather than unrelated within very broad boundaries. Revenue generated by Girl Scout cookie sales and on-premises museum gift shop sales are considered related income, for example, although one might argue that they are peripherally related to the organizations' missions. Reflecting this, Lewis Segal and Burton Weisbrod find that only between 1 and 10 percent of nonprofits, depending on the field, file the required form 990-T.[29] Third, nonprofits have broad discretion in allocating costs between related and unrelated activities so as to minimize their tax liabilities on unrelated income activity. Thus in 1997 only half of the 39,302 organizations filing an unrelated business income form reported any net income from their unrelated business activities, and the total net income for UBIT filers as a whole was actually negative, as total expenses allocated to unrelated activities exceeded total revenues![30]

However, this picture is gradually changing. For example, the number of organizations filing form 990-T increased 19 percent between 2003 and 2006. In 2006 nonprofits produced $11.3 billion gross unrelated business income, a 19 percent increase over 2003. Net reported unrelated business income increased 152 percent from 2003 to 2006, yielding $556.3 million in taxes in 2006.[31] Such data suggest that the scale and nature of enterprise activities and the number of institutions engaged in such activities have grown substantially beyond the feeble beginnings charted by James Crimmins and Mary Keil in the early 1980s.[32] But it remains notable that, of the 43,250 organizations required to file 990-Ts for 2006, only roughly half reported any net income from their unrelated business activities.

Social Purpose Enterprise

Not only have nonprofit organizations turned to the market to supplement their incomes, but they also are integrating the market into the pursuit of their social missions in a more fundamental way.[33] For example, rather than training disadvantaged individuals and sending them out cold into the private labor market, some nonprofit training agencies have begun creating their own small business ventures to help reintegrate their disadvantaged or structurally unemployed clientele into the mainstream economy. The venture is thus not a sideline or a mere source of revenue but an integral component of the agency's program, directly related to the pursuit of its mission.

This development has given rise to a new type of social institution known variously as social purpose enterprises, social ventures, and community wealth enterprises.[34] Such enterprises can take at least four forms.[35] These include traditional *sheltered workshops* of the sort historically operated by Goodwill Industries and that often enjoy government preferences, *open-market enterprises* that compete in the marketplace without governmental preference, *franchises* that operate within the context of a national corporation, and *program-based enterprises* that grow out of a nonprofit organization's social service programs.

Many of these enterprises function largely to provide protected employment opportunities to disadvantaged populations. For example, Asian Neighborhood Design employs low-income individuals in a furniture-manufacturing business, Barrios Unidos employs Latino youth in a screen-printing business, and Community Vocational Enterprises employs people with psychiatric disabilities in janitorial, food service, clerical, and messenger service businesses. Other examples include the Greyston Bakery in Yonkers, New York, a for-profit subsidiary of the Greyston Foundation, which trains and hires unemployable workers in its gourmet bakery business; the New Community Corporation in Newark, New Jersey, which provides job training and employment to inner-city residents as well as needed retail services to underserved neighborhoods through its various for-profit business enterprises such as franchised grocery and convenience stores, restaurants, and print and copy shops; and Pioneer Human Services, a nonprofit in Seattle, which operates a variety of business enterprises, including an aircraft parts manufacturer, food buying and warehousing services, and restaurants, in which it trains, employs, and rehabilitates ex-offenders, chemically dependent individuals, and persons on probation or under court supervision. These cases, and many others such as Juma Ventures, San Francisco Clean City Coalition, Triangle Residential Options of Substance Abusers, and DC Central Kitchen, are still in business as of this writing and have relatively long histories of successful operation.[36] These business ventures are logically connected to the mission of the nonprofit only as a means to provide training and employment opportunities for their clientele, not because their particular products are especially relevant to that mission. The point of the ventures is to create a commercial environment in which to nurture client success and (at least incidentally) to generate resources to sustain the organization.

The concept of social purpose enterprise has also been extended beyond the employment sphere to include business ventures that contribute directly to nonprofit, mission-related, outputs as well as to revenues and mission-related employment. In Mexico, for example, social purpose enterprises emphasize the relief of poverty rather than the provision of employment per se.[37] Other social purpose enterprises address social issues such as the environment and community transportation. For example, the Orange County Community Distribution Center in Florida serves an environmental conservation mission by warehousing discarded materials and providing them to local nonprofits at reduced cost, employing and training inmates on work release in the process. Similarly, the Bikestation Coalition in California promotes bicycle use to address community transportation and environmental objectives by offering various services to cyclists, including valet bicycle parking, changing rooms, and repair services.[38] Finally, microenterprise has become an important market-based strategy for addressing issues of poverty and economic development. Basically, under this strategy, foundations and other nonprofits (and increasingly, commercial firms) offer small business loans to emerging entrepreneurs in impoverished communities in the belief that their businesses will grow and help lift communities out of poverty. One interesting example is Habitat for Humanity in Atlanta, which is launching a microloan program in partnership with the Calvert Foundation that will allow individuals to invest in, rather than simply donate to, Habitat.[39]

These various experiences with commercial enterprise on the part of nonprofit organizations are beginning to put nonprofit commercial activity into a new light. No longer conceived simply as a revenue-generation strategy, these ventures treat market engagement as the most effective way to pursue a nonprofit organization's mission, to provide marketable skills to the structurally unemployed, or to change behavior in an environmentally sensitive way.

The concept of a social venture has taken an even broader form in Europe, where it includes cooperatives and worker-owned or worker-controlled enterprises. Clearly such ventures do not adhere to the central criterion of a nonprofit entity in the American setting—that is, one that does not distribute its profits to its members or owners. Far more important in Europe is the way an organization is governed and what its purpose is rather than whether it strictly adheres to the nondistribution constraint of a formal nonprofit organization. A social enterprise in these terms is thus any organization that is private, that enjoys managerial autonomy, that produces and sells collective goods, that earns income partly from sales and not solely from donations, and that grants some meaningful degree of control to key stakeholders, such as workers, users, volunteers, and consumers, regardless of whether the organization distributes profits to them.[40]

Reflecting this, some analysts are finding the nonprofit form too restrictive to capture the scope of new social enterprise activity. In Mexico, for example, social enterprise is not restricted to a particular sector but rather refers to "efforts of government, nonprofit organizations, and businesses directed toward the creation of novel schemes that take into consideration the global frame of a free market economy to induce programs to help alleviate regional development lags and poverty."[41] Reflecting this line of thinking as well, the Organization for Economic Cooperation and Development has formulated a definition of social enterprise that emphasizes intent rather than a particular organizational form. Thus a social enterprise is defined as "any private activity conducted in the public interest, organized with entrepreneurial strategy, but whose main purpose is not the maximization of profit but the attainment of certain economic and social goals, and which has the capacity for bringing innovative solutions to the problems of social exclusion and unemployment."[42]

While in the United States the social enterprise movement has not overturned conventional notions of the nonprofit sector, a stream of opinion is emerging that characterizes the nonprofit sector and its related business ventures as a continuum of activity between market and philanthropy, arguing for a more general understanding of social enterprise than a strict divide between nonprofits and for-profits would comfortably allow.[43] This argument is centered on the observation that some socially focused enterprise activity takes place outside the formal nonprofit realm as well as through interactions and combinations of nonprofit and for-profit activity. One example is the "giving malls" that have sprung up on the Internet. Thus iGive.com offers customers the opportunity to shop from over 400 affiliated merchants and to direct up to 39 percent of every purchase (although the typical donation is 3 percent) to more than 18,000 nonprofits, often local chapters of large national nonprofit organizations. The chance to be associated with a good cause is not lost on retail giants like Amazon, L.L. Bean, Barnes & Noble, Office Max, eBay, and Dell. During its nine years in existence, iGive.com has helped distribute nearly $2 million to 30,000 charitable causes. According to Thomas Reis and Stephanie Clohesy, "There are hundreds—and perhaps thousands—of examples throughout the U.S. of organizations that are experimenting with enterprise or market-based approaches for solving problems that are weaving together profitmaking activities with social change purposes."[44]

In response, some proponents of the new social entrepreneurship chafe against the strictures of the nonprofit form and are beginning to push for the creation of a new type of organizational structure that can better accommodate their socially driven business ventures. In particular, the L3C, a new, low-profit, limited-liability company that combines features of nonprofit and for-profit corporations, has been created.[45] L3C legislation has been enacted in eight states and two Indian territories and was under consideration in eleven other states as of 2010. More than 500 L3Cs had been created as of 2012, and investment in these organizations is under way by some foundations as a potentially efficient way to engage in program-related investments.[46]

Along with this development of social enterprises has come a host of new financing entities and instruments to channel not just philanthropic grants but also private investment capital into these new entities. This development has been greatly encouraged by two recent policy innovations: the Community Reinvestment Act, which requires depository institutions to demonstrate to federal regulatory authorities that they are channeling a meaningful portion of their loan resources to disadvantaged communities in their service areas; and the creation of tax incentives for investments in so-called community development finance institutions, which then use these resources to invest in social enterprises and other developmental activities in these disadvantaged communities. Over 1,300 of these institutions are in existence, handling billions of dollars of capital. And they have been joined by dozens of other capital aggregators— social purpose secondary markets, bond funds such as the Calvert Foundation, social enterprise brokers, social stock exchanges, and social impact bonds. These developments suggest that the relationship between the nonprofit sector and the market may be entering a new phase. Indeed, we may be seeing the emergence of what Salamon terms a "new frontier of philanthropy and social investing."[47]

Nonprofit-Business Collaboration

A third important manifestation of the penetration of the market into the operations of nonprofit organizations takes the form of nonprofit-business partnerships. Even nonprofit organizations that are not engaged in enterprise activity or fee-for-service operations may still engage the market indirectly through cooperative relationships with for-profit corporations. As noted, the pressures of global competition have put a premium on reputational capital in order for corporations to attract customers, retain high-level staff, and ensure the kind of public support they need to operate. For a variety of reasons, these pressures have led corporations to see nonprofit organizations as important strategic partners. As one practitioner notes, "A company's relationship to the Third Sector is only partly charitable in impulse. In varying measure, nonprofits represent markets, sources of employees, pools of research and expertise, and sources of community goodwill for companies."[48]

Just as corporations have discovered the strategic value of working with nonprofits, nonprofits have come to understand how relationships with corporations can be helpful programmatically as well as financially. As a consequence, over the past decade the stereotypes of corporate altruism, on the one hand, and nonprofit suspicion of business, on the other, have all but evaporated.[49] In their place have come new concepts of strategic fit and new forms of interaction that go well beyond simple philanthropic giving.[50] Corporate involvement with nonprofit organizations now also involves the provision of equipment, space, and contacts; employee volunteer programs; loaned executives; event sponsorship; cause-related marketing; complex royalty and licensing arrangements; and even joint ventures.[51] Underlying these relationships is the belief that corporate-nonprofit ties, properly conceived, can serve the strategic missions of both the corporation and the nonprofit so that both sides gain something of value. Examples of such strategic partnerships include the following:[52]

—The Merck Corporation has had a fifteen-year partnership with the United Negro College Fund, under which the corporation provides scholarship funds, mentors, and internships to promising minority students. In return, Merck gains access to bright minority students with an interest in science.

—Ralston Purina provides support to the American Humane Association for the Pets for People program, which helps provide care and adoption for more than 1.5 million pets annually. This effort, in addition to gaining the corporation a reputation for philanthropy, increases the market for its pet foods.

—Under growing criticism that its packaging was creating environmental problems, McDonald's teamed up with the Environmental Defense Fund to design packaging and processes that are environmentally friendly. McDonald's thus fended off environmental criticism, and the Environmental Defense Fund made a significant breakthrough in its mission.

—American Express entered into a partnership with Share Our Strength under which American Express contributes 2 cents for every swipe of an American Express card to Share Our Strength for it to use in relieving international hunger, thus boosting use of the American Express credit card and providing Share Our Strength with additional funds to spend on its program.

—The Nature Conservancy works closely with Georgia Pacific to manage wetlands owned by the corporation. Through this arrangement, Nature Conservancy advances its mission of protecting large and important environmental resources, while Georgia Pacific gains access to the Nature Conservancy's expertise and improves its relationship with the general public.

Other such business-nonprofit partnerships include those between Starbucks and CARE, to improve the economic and educational prospects for people in coffee-growing regions in Ethiopia, Costa Rica, Guatemala, and Indonesia; between Nike and Portland's Children's Museum, to produce imaginative architecture for children; between Coca-Cola and Reading Is Fundamental, to promote literacy; and between Tyson Foods and Share Our Strength to alleviate hunger.[53]

The potential benefits to business corporations of collaborating with appropriate nonprofit partners take several possible forms. Corporations polish their public images, gain access to special expertise or future talent, create demand for their products, and motivate their employees by providing opportunities for volunteering and community service. In turn, their nonprofit partners gain access to substantial financial, personnel, and other corporate resources, obtain wider forums in which to broadcast their messages and appeals, and in some cases influence consumers in ways that directly support the nonprofit's mission. For example, when the American Cancer Society associates itself with the Florida citrus industry and offers the use of its name and logo on citrus products and commercials, it helps to increase the consumption of citrus fruit, a contributor to cancer prevention. Similarly, the affiliations between the American Lung Association and the American Cancer Society with manufacturers of smoking patches, and the affiliation between Prevent Blindness and makers of protective eyewear, directly contribute to the health-related missions of those organizations.[54]

Gauging the extent of such corporate-nonprofit partnerships is difficult. Clearly not all nonprofits have equal access to them, nor are all corporations fully engaged. Indeed, the globalization of the economy, while increasing the pressures on corporations to attend to their corporate images, has paradoxically also distanced many corporations from the communities they serve as a consequence of the extensive mergers and acquisitions that globalization has also encouraged. Moreover, corporate partnerships are not without risk for both nonprofits and corporations. For example, American Express's partnership with Share Our Strength, intended to relieve international hunger, has been criticized for spending more money on advertising the campaign than on contributing to the cause. Such arrangements, if not carefully researched, can tarnish the image of a nonprofit as well as undermine the corporate brand. Nevertheless, something fundamental has happened to the relationship between corporations and nonprofit organizations over the past two decades—a change in the direction of closer working relationships, and the scope of the change is quite extensive.[55]

A Changing Nonprofit Culture

The engagement of nonprofits with the dominant market culture is not limited to increased reliance on fee revenues, experimentation with commercial ventures, and partnerships with for-profit firms. It pervades the very manner in which nonprofits conduct their day-to-day affairs. Nonprofits are no longer bashful about aggressively advertising their services or competing for charitable contributions. They are more forthright in paying the going wage rate in labor markets to secure the talent they need to operate or to hire fundraising consultants or development staff in order to secure greater shares of gifts and grants. They administer a variety of planned giving options, sometimes competing with for-profit financial institutions to secure the investments of older donors. And they are increasingly preoccupied with performance, with demonstrating their ability to serve their missions efficiently and effectively.

In short, in response to the challenges they are facing from the market, nonprofits are internalizing the culture and techniques of market organizations and are making them their own. This is resulting in changes in internal processes, in organizational structures, and ultimately in the culture and ethos of the organizations. Management practices, organizational values, and the very language that nonprofits use have been changing dramatically, signaling that nonprofits are becoming very different kinds of organization than they were in the past and that their market involvement is likely to continue.

One manifestation of this change is the transformation in nonprofit attitudes toward entrepreneurship and management. Twenty years ago, the term *entrepreneurship* was virtually unknown in the nonprofit sector, and where it was applied, it was thought to be irrelevant or even pejorative. Entrepreneurship was something that pertained to the for-profit sector, not to nonprofits. People in the nonprofit world never fully separated the generic idea of entrepreneurship from its association with for-profit activity, even when research stressed the generic character of entrepreneurship and linked it to nonprofit organizational success.[56] Similarly, nonprofits traditionally put little emphasis on management or on hiring people with special management expertise. Nonprofit managers were normally professionals in their various service fields—the arts, social work, health care, education, and so on—who incidentally took on administrative responsibility as their careers evolved.

Growing competition from the for-profit sector, declining public revenue, and increased calls for accountability beginning in the early 1980s have changed this markedly, however.[57] In response, nonprofits have firmly embraced managerialism.[58] As a consequence, the number of courses in nonprofit management has soared. More than a hundred universities now offer degree or certificate programs in nonprofit management, and numerous others offer nonprofit management courses within traditional public administration, business administration, or other degree programs.[59] In the process, nonprofit management has become a respected career path, and nonprofit manager, a legitimate profession.[60]

One by-product of this development has been a further infiltration of the language and the practice of the market into nonprofit operations. Nonprofit organizations are increasingly encouraged to identify their market niches, to maximize their comparative advantages, to think of their clients as customers, to devise marketing plans, and to engage in strategic planning.[61] Pressured by both public and private funders, nonprofit organizations have had to focus on measurable outcomes and impact, on assessing their performance, and on demonstrating their cost-effectiveness.[62]

The particular difficulties of United Way are of special interest in this connection. The Aramony scandal of the early 1990s gave impetus to reforms that moved the nonprofit sector further in the direction of the market culture. Measuring performance and social impact has become a theme for United Way since then and is stressed by the national organization for adoption by local United Way affiliates.[63] Moreover, the United Way monopoly has been broken in the payroll deduction systems of private and public sector employers, and more heed is now taken in the United Way system to demands by donors to have more say over the allocation of the funds they contribute through payroll deduction systems.[64] A similar observation can be made about community foundations and other federated fundraising organizations. Donor choice has thus surfaced in the charitable realm as a manifestation of the concept of consumer sovereignty in the market paradigm.

In response to these pressures, nonprofits, through federated fundraising systems or as individual organizations, have taken to promoting particular aspects of their programming to suit donor preferences. Admittedly, this may simply represent a contemporary example of a long-standing nonprofit practice of identifying particular aspects of an organization to "sell" to particular donors for a given "price." But nonprofits seem to be moving more and more to taking a product differentiation approach to solicitation, allowing donors to designate their gifts, and often affix their names, to particular initiatives or assets. This is yet another aspect of the market culture that has become firmly rooted in contemporary nonprofit organizations.

Elements of this market culture have also spread to the world of foundations, perhaps the chief institutional embodiment of organized philanthropy. A new generation of philanthropists, many associated with the burgeoning technology-based economy of the 1990s, has pushed for a more activist and cost-effective approach to charitable giving modeled on the operations of venture capitalists.[65] Central to this venture philanthropy approach is an emphasis on measurable results, on achievement of a positive rate of return on charitable investments, and on engagement of the donor in helping to ensure the effective management of the funded organization. Indeed, some advocates of this approach now talk of a full-blown nonprofit capital market in which funders manage portfolios of social investments that exhibit varying degrees of diversification for risk and return, use a combination of grant and loan instruments to implement their investments, try to maximize the social returns on their investments, and use rating services to assess these social returns.[66] Clearly, this is a new language, and a new conception, of what philanthropy is all about.

Not only is the cultural transformation under way in the nonprofit sector evident in the changing language and practice of agency management; it also is evident in a significant transformation of agency structures. A major restructuring of nonprofit organizations appears to be under way. In part, this has manifested itself in complex interconnections among agencies. Under pressure to collaborate, coordinate, and consolidate their operations as competition increases, as greater size becomes advantageous in order to stand out in the more competitive landscape, and as major funders seek ways to allocate their funds strategically for greatest impact, nonprofits have responded with a variety of restructuring initiatives, sharing, transferring, or combining services, resources, or programs among agencies in a variety of ways.[67] Such restructuring includes simple one-time programmatic collaborations, longer-term administrative consolidations and joint ventures, complex "holding company" arrangements, and out-and-out mergers.[68] The upshot is a much more dense and complex network of relationships among nonprofit agencies.

At the same time, the internal structure of individual nonprofit organizations has also become increasingly complex. Here the pressures are partly legal and partly managerial. Advocacy organizations that combine education with lobbying are establishing separate 501(c)(3) and (c)(4) organizations to ensure that they can attract tax-deductible gifts for their advocacy work while still being free to engage in lobbying when this becomes necessary. Similar pressures are convincing service agencies to segment their various services into separately incorporated entities in order to shield them from liability in case of challenge or to separate funding streams in order to simplify cost accounting. A family and children's service organization that operates a residential treatment home financed in part by Medicaid as well as a day care center and a counseling center supported largely by private fees might therefore choose to restructure its service activities into separately incorporated 501(c)(3)s and to manage the resulting conglomerate as a holding company with separate boards for the individual subsidiaries. The expanding involvement of nonprofit organizations in for-profit ventures has naturally accelerated this development, as nonprofits find it desirable to organize separately incorporated for-profit subsidiaries to handle their venture activities. Evidence exists suggesting a considerable elaboration of the internal structure of nonprofit agencies, with numerous programs and funding streams, multiple organizational components, and complex combinations of nonprofit and for-profit activity.[69] Increasingly, this is clearly not the traditional nonprofit sector.

Summary: The New Governance

In short, the market system and the market culture have penetrated nonprofit organizations in many ways. Growing reliance on fee income, expanded experimentation with enterprise activities, broader partnerships with for-profit companies, growing adoption of management practices characteristic of business enterprises, and increasing organizational complexity all signal a fundamental shift in orientation that will be difficult to reverse. At the same time, the recent economic crisis has significantly shaken the market's claims to being the preferred institutional framework for organizing social and economic activity. As a result of the great recession of 2008–09, nonprofits have faced especially great challenges, many of them related directly or indirectly to failures of the market, including losses in the value of endowments and investment income, reductions in the capacity of both citizen and institutional donors for charitable giving, pullbacks in government funding deriving in part from reductions in taxable revenues, and increases in the need for services by stressed constituencies. In the process, the recession and financial crisis have helped create a greater awareness of the distinctive strengths and values of the nonprofit form, albeit a nonprofit form that has absorbed important characteristics of business practice.

It seems unlikely, however, that the recent challenges to faith in the market will cause a significant rollback in the penetration of market forces into the nonprofit sector. The new market orientation of nonprofit organizations is driven not so much by changes in ideology as by pragmatism. Given the pressures on public budgets, nonprofits have sought, with some success, other means of financial support. Given the revolution in technology, nonprofits are adapting to the demands for information and donor empowerment. At the same time, given increasingly sophisticated and intense competition in the business world, for-profits are turning to nonprofits to seek a value edge in attracting customers and retaining staff.

The result is not so much a disappearance of sectoral lines (they were never as distinct as our mythologies would lead us to believe) as a greater recognition of sectoral interdependencies and of the common ground all three sectors—nonprofit, government, and business—share. Hence classic sectoral distinctions have become less important and less inhibiting, as nonprofit sector leaders and social entrepreneurs consider new approaches to social problem solving. It is now more natural to think outside the box in business, in government, and in the nonprofit sector, especially when it comes to problems such as poverty, education of minority groups, community development, and social justice that have not responded to old programs and old solutions. The criterion for organizing solutions to social problems is moving away from sectoral mandates—the "government should do it" theme of the War on Poverty, "the voluntary sector should do it" notion of the Reagan administration, or the "business will take care of it" posture of some free market enthusiasts. Rather, the more recent call is "whatever works"—a nonformulaic, nonlegalistic, nonpolitical, noncategorical approach to getting the job done.

This suggests the emergence of a new governance, a new approach to solving public problems. The heart of this approach is an emphasis not on the differences among the sectors but on both the opportunities and the need for collaboration among them. It is in this context that business, markets, and nonprofits are becoming intertwined and that new organizational forms are emerging.[70]

Implications and Conclusions

The commercialization and marketization of the nonprofit sector detailed here offer important opportunities but also carry enormous risks for the nonprofit sector, for those it serves, and for American society. How the balance between the opportunities and the risks plays out may well determine the future of this set of institutions and its ability to continue making its distinctive contributions to our national life. Indeed, this may well determine whether the existing legal definition of a nonprofit organization, with its stress on the nondistribution of profits, still makes sense.

The opportunities are enticing if not yet clearly defined. By engaging market forces and strategies in a more substantial way, marketization offers the nonprofit sector access not only to more resources but also to the energy and creativity that the market system has long represented. Empowered with earned income, nonprofits may become more fully independent than either government support or reliance on the whims of wealthy donors has ever made possible. Beyond this, engagement with the market opens possibilities for lever-aging enormous private resources and talents for social sector purposes. The record of nonprofit low-income housing organizations detailed in chapter 6 provides a powerful lesson in this regard. Finally, and not inconsequentially, given the ascendance of the norms of efficiency and effectiveness in our society, adoption of the trappings of business management may help to erase popular images of nonprofit ineffectiveness and establish instead the image of organiza-tions that have learned how to bring the most efficient means to the service of the most valued ends.

Set against these opportunities, however, are substantial risks and uncertain-ties. First, and most obvious, is the distinct possibility that the pressures of the market will entice the nonprofit sector to lose its way and surrender precisely those values that make it so vital—its commitment to quality, to free expression, to serving those in greatest need, and to doing what is right as opposed to what is popular or commercially viable. This concern has already arisen forcefully in several areas of nonprofit activity, including health care and higher education. For example, an article in the *Atlantic Monthly* bewails the "kept university," a reference to the fact that the research and teaching agendas of private, nonprofit universities are now being influenced by the commercial needs of private corpo-rations, which not only skew those agendas toward work of commercial value (to the neglect of basic research and less applied activities) but also influence long-standing mission-related practices and institutional values such as public access to research-generated knowledge.[71] Inevitably, the more the nonprofit sector is forced to rely on fees and charges, the more it will be tempted to orient its services to those able to pay.

Many of the cause-related marketing and joint venture arrangements between nonprofits and for-profit firms discussed in this chapter raise these issues in stark form. The more closely a reputable nonprofit is willing to identify itself with a particular product or company, the more the arrangement will be worth to that company and the more that company will be willing to remunerate the non-profit. But such exclusive arrangements can compromise a nonprofit's objectiv-ity. The American Cancer Society receives substantial grants from the Florida citrus growers and from Smith-Kline Beecham in exchange for understandings that it will not associate itself with other producers of citrus or smoking patches. By comparison, the American Heart Association receives much more modest fees for attaching its heart-healthy seal to various food products that meet its nutritional standards.

The growing closeness of nonprofits and corporations, while creating many benefits, is not without risk to participating nonprofits. In particular, a non-profit may be perceived as neglecting or harming its mission if it identifies itself with questionable products, with disreputable organizations, or exclusively with products that may not be the very best for its intended beneficiaries. In the case of the American Medical Association and the Honeywell Corporation, leaders of the American Medical Association lost their jobs for entering into an exclusive relationship that appeared to offer advance endorsements of yet-to-be-tested medical devices. Similarly, the American Association of Retired Persons has been questioned for entering into special relationships with health insurers that may not always offer the best coverage for older people. In response to similar concerns, the American Association of Museums issued a code of ethical standards for museums entering into arrangements with owners and dealers of art collections to protect against situations in which private parties would stand to benefit financially from the display of their art in the museum and in which they might use financial incentives to influence the museum's decisions regarding the art to be exhibited. Many nonprofits, particularly smaller ones, remain leery of such involvements because they lack the expertise or sophistication to avoid such pitfalls. Other nonprofits have yet to identify corporations that provide the appropriate strategic fit with their own particular cause. Further, issues of organizational size influence the propensity to partner on both sides of the market. Smaller nonprofits may not be well enough known or may not represent large enough constituencies to be attractive to corporate sponsors. Nonprofits with unpopular constituencies, such as ex-offenders or the mentally ill, might similarly be unattractive to corporations. To the extent that the nonprofit sector becomes dependent on the market for its sustenance and legitimacy, crucial functions and values could be lost. Indeed, there is a danger that nonprofits will find themselves smothered in the corporate embrace.

Equally significant is the impact that the marketization of the nonprofit sector can have on the sector's public support. To be sure, the public seems to be demanding higher standards of performance from nonprofit organizations, and the adoption of market-oriented management techniques may help to achieve this. But to the extent that adoption of business methods—including competitive salaries, charges for services, and marketing to paying customers—obscures the distinction between nonprofit and for-profit firms, it opens the nonprofit sector to serious charges of neglecting its social mission. This is particularly true given the limited effort that so far has been put into educating the public and key opinion leaders about the changes under way. In this kind of setting, the nonprofit sector could easily find itself exposed to damaging and untrue claims in the press and the public policy arena, jeopardizing its special tax and other advantages in the process.

These issues naturally arise most sharply in relation to the new social ventures that have gained popularity in recent years in both the United States and Western Europe. Such ventures consciously blur the distinction between nonprofit and for-profit forms. Indeed, in their European incarnation, these ventures relax or eliminate what has long been the principal defining feature of nonprofit organizations in the American setting—their inability to distribute profits to their owners or members. Instead, such organizations are granted special tax and other privileges as long as they serve socially useful ends and provide meaningful opportunities for input to employees and other stakeholders.

Controversial though this approach may be, it holds useful lessons for the American nonprofit scene. It has long been recognized in the United States that the nonprofit form per se does not guarantee responsible behavior or effective performance. The nondistribution constraint must always be carefully policed to avoid inurement, and even then it is difficult to guarantee that nonprofits are truly driven by mission rather than self-serving goals.

This does not mean that we can ignore organizational form and simply embrace the market as a suitable vehicle for serving social objectives. The evidence is strong that nonprofits serve different groups of clientele and provide different varieties of service than for-profits.[72] They also promote other important values related to diversity, expression, and innovation.[73] Preserving a set of institutions that adheres to incentives that are not wholly market driven thus seems essential even as these institutions incorporate managerial practices that market institutions pioneered. At least nonprofits can take comfort in the fact that the transmission of best practices across sector lines remains a two-way street.

Notes

1. U.S. Social Security Administration, *2000 Annual Statistical Supplement to the Social Security Bulletin,* p. 120.

2. Lester M. Salamon, *America's Nonprofit Sector: A Primer,* 3rd ed. (New York: Foundation Center, 2012).

3. *Giving USA 2009* (Indianapolis: Giving USA Foundation, 2009), p. 214.

4. Lester M. Salamon and Alan J. Abramson, *The Federal Budget and the Nonprofit Sector* (Washington: Urban Institute, 1982), p. 44.

5. For 1997 figures, see Murray S. Weitzman and others, *The New Nonprofit Almanac and Desk Reference* (San Francisco: Jossey-Bass, 2002), p. 91.

6. Jane C. Wei-Skillern and others, *Entrepreneurship in the Social Sector* (Thousand Oaks, Calif.: Sage Publications, 2007), p. 2.

7. Wan He and others, "65+ in the United States: 2005," Current Population Report (U.S. Census Bureau, 2005), p. 6.

8. U.S Bureau of Labor Statistics, *Women in the Labor Force: A Databook* (U.S. Department of Labor, 2007), p. 1. Unmarried mothers have higher labor force participation rates than married mothers.

9. Lester M. Salamon, *America's Nonprofit Sector: A Primer,* 2nd ed. (New York: Foundation Center, 1999), pp. 161–62.

10. For a detailed analysis of these developments, see Lester M. Salamon, ed., *New Frontiers of Philanthropy: A Guide to the New Actors and New Tools That Are Transforming Philanthropy and Social Investing* (San Francisco: Jossey-Bass, 2012).

11. Based on data from U.S. Census Bureau, *Census of Service Industries, 1997.*

12. U.S. Census Bureau, *Economic Census 1997;* U.S. Census Bureau, *Economic Census 2007.* See also Salamon, *America's Nonprofit Sector,* 2nd ed.

13. Robert B. Denhardt and Janet V. Denhardt, *Public Administration: An Action Orientation,* 6th ed. (Belmont, Calif.: Thomson Wadsworth, 2009), p. 113.

14. Thomas K. Reis and Stephanie Clohesy, "Unleashing New Resources and Entrepreneurship for the Common Good," paper prepared for the International Society for Third Sector Research conference, Dublin, Ireland, July 2000, p. 9.

15. Andrew W. Hastings. "Donor Advised Fund Market: An Analysis of the Overall Market and Trends" (Jenkintown, Pa.: National Philanthropic Trust, 2008) (www.nptrust.org). See also Rick Cohen, "Corporate-Originated Charitable Funds," in *New Frontiers of Philanthropy,* edited by Lester M. Salamon (San Francisco: Jossey-Bass, 2012).

16. Jonathan Walters. "The Welfare Bonanza," *Governing Magazine,* January 2000 (www.governing.com/topics/health-human-services/Welfare-Bonanza.html).

17. Rob Gurwitt, "The Lonely Leap," *Governing Magazine,* July 2000 (www.governing.com/topics/health-human-services/Lonely-Leap.html).

18. See www.lockheedmartin.com/news/press_releases/2001/LockheedMartinAgrees SellIMSCorporat.html.

19. John H. Goddeeris and Burton A. Weisbrod, "Conversion from Nonprofit to For-Profit Legal Status," in *To Profit or Not to Profit,* edited by Burton Weisbrod (Cambridge University Press, 1998), pp. 129–48.

20. Reis and Clohesy, "Unleashing New Resources," p. 16.

21. Wei-Skillern and others, *Entrepreneurship in the Social Sector,* pp. 73, 75.

22. Sharon M. Oster, *Strategic Management for Nonprofit Organizations* (Oxford University Press, 1995), pp. 272–86.

23. Business and Civic Leadership Center, *Report on the State of Corporate Community Investment* (Washington: U.S. Chamber of Commerce, 2008) (http://bclc.uschamber.com/sites/default/files/resources/files/edareportpdf.pdf). See also Caroline Preston, "Most Small Companies Make Charitable Donations, Survey Finds," *Chronicle of Philanthropy,* November 2008.

24. Reynold Levy, *Give and Take: A Candid Account of Corporate Philanthropy* (Harvard Business School Press, 1999), pp. 3–15; Jane Nelson, *Business as Partners in Development* (London: Prince of Wales Business Leaders Forum, 1996), pp. 52–54; David Logan, Delwin Roy, and Laurie Ruggelbrugge, *Global Corporate Citizenship: Rationale and Strategies* (Washington: Hitachi Foundation, 1997), pp. 6–18; Lester M. Salamon, *Rethinking Corporate Social Engagement: Lessons from Latin America* (Sterling, Va.: Kumarian Press, 2010).

25. Lester M. Salamon, *Partners in Public Service: Government-Nonprofit Relations in the Modern Welfare State* (Johns Hopkins University Press, 1996), pp. 211–13.

26. Elaine Morley, Elisa Vinson, and Harry P. Hatry, "Outcome Measurement in Nonprofit Organizations: Current Practices and Recommendations" (Washington: Independent Sector, 2001); Paul C. Light, *Making Nonprofits Work* (Brookings, 2000).

27. Salamon, *America's Nonprofit Sector,* 3rd ed. Other data sources convey a grossly misleading picture of nonprofit finances by failing to adjust data provided on nonprofit form 990 filings to take account of the fact that these forms report government voucher payments such as Medicare and Medicaid as well as much of government contract payments to nonprofits as "program service revenue." In addition, they include contributions to foundations and federated funders as well as the contributions these entities make to operating nonprofits as part of nonprofit revenue, thereby counting the same dollars twice. See for example Kennard T.

Wing, Thomas H. Pollak, and Amy Blackwood, "Trends in Private Giving and Volunteering," in *The Nonprofit Almanac 2008* (Washington: Urban Institute, 2008), pp. 115–17.

28. Lester M. Salamon and S. Wojciech Sokolowski, *Global Civil Society: Dimensions of the Nonprofit Sector,* vol. 2 (Bloomington, Conn.: Kumarian Press, 2004), p. 30.

29. Lewis M. Segal and Burton A. Weisbrod, "Interdependence of Commercial and Donative Revenues," in Weisbrod, *To Profit or Not to Profit,* pp. 105–28.

30. Margaret Riley, "Unrelated Business Income Tax Returns, 2004," *Statistics of Income Bulletin* 27, no. 3 (Winter 2008): 76.

31. Jael Jackson, "Unrelated Business Income Tax Returns, 2006," *Statistics of Income Bulletin* 29, no. 3 (Winter 2010): 150.

32. James C. Crimmins and Mary Keil, *Enterprise in the Nonprofit Sector* (New York: Rockefeller Brothers Fund, 1983), p. 11.

33. Edward Skloot, "Enterprise and Commerce in Nonprofit Organizations," in *The Nonprofit Sector: A Research Handbook,* edited by Walter W. Powell (Yale University Press, 1987), pp. 380–93; Edward Skloot, ed., *The Nonprofit Entrepreneur* (New York: Foundation Center, 1988); Jed Emerson and Faye Twersky, eds., *New Social Entrepreneurs* (San Francisco: Roberts Enterprise Development Fund, 1996); Dennis R. Young, "Commercialism in Nonprofit Social Service Associations," in Weisbrod, *To Profit or Not to Profit,* pp. 195–216.

34. *Social Purpose Enterprises and Venture Philanthropy in the New Millennium,* 2 vols. (San Francisco: Roberts Enterprise Development Fund, 1999); see vol. 1, p. 2.

35. Emerson and Twersky, *New Social Entrepreneurs,* pp. 6–7.

36. For additional discussion of these and other examples of social ventures, see *Social Purpose Enterprises.* See also www.dccentralkitchen.org, www.community-wealth.org/strategies/panel/social/models.html.

37. Gabriela Perez-Yarahuan, "Social Enterprises: Who Benefits?" paper prepared for the International Society for Third Sector Research conference, Dublin, Ireland, July 2000.

38. See the Bikestation Coalition website, www.bikestation.org.

39. Chris Megerian, "Plan Turns Habitat for Humanity into an Investment: Individuals Will Be Able to Buy Stake in Nonprofit's Microloan Program," *Atlanta Journal Constitution,* July 24, 2008 (www.ajc.com/business/content/business/stories/2008/07/23/habitat_for_humanity_investing.html).

40. Carlos Borzaga and Alceste Santuari, eds., *Social Enterprises and the New Employment in Europe* (University of Trento, 1998), p. 75. See also Martha Nyssens, ed., *Social Enterprise: At the Crossroads of Market, Public Policies, and Civil Society* (London: Routledge, 2006).

41. Perez-Yarahuan, "Social Enterprises," p. 12.

42. Organization for Economic Cooperation and Development, *Social Enterprises in OECD Countries* (Paris: OECD, 1998), p. 10.

43. J. Gregory Dees, "Enterprising Nonprofits," *Harvard Business Review* 76, no. 1 (1998): 55–67.

44. Reis and Clohesy, "Unleashing New Resources," p. 7.

45. The principal advantage of the L3C form is that it creates a type of organization that can earn and distribute profits without having the obligation to maximize profits, which is a responsibility of board members under standard corporate legal provisions. The availability of this legal form is also thought to facilitate the making of so-called program-related investments by foundations, which are investments that can earn a return and still count toward foundation payout requirements—but only if the return is not the major objective of the investment. On the law of social ventures, see Marc Lane, *Social Enterprise: Empowering Mission-Driven Entrepreneurs* (Chicago: American Bar Association, 2011).

46. "The L3C: Low-Profit Limited Liability Company Research Brief" (Washington: Community Wealth Ventures, 2008), pp. 1–3; L3C—An Update by Keren Raz (http://charity lawyerblog.com).

47. Salamon, *New Frontiers of Philanthropy.* For a discussion of the social stock exchange idea, see the Social Enterprise Alliance website (www.se- alliance.org/news_evolution_se.pdf).

48. Levy, *Give and Take,* p. 17.

49. Dwight F. Burlingame and Dennis R. Young, eds., *Corporate Philanthropy at the Crossroads* (Indiana University Press, 1996).

50. James R. Austin, *The Collaboration Challenge* (San Francisco: Jossey-Bass, 2000).

51. For discussions of this mode of corporate engagement with nonprofits, see Craig Smith, "The New Corporate Philanthropy," *Harvard Business Review* 72, no. 3 (1994): 105–16; Levy, *Give and Take,* pp. 39–57; Austin, *Collaboration Challenge.*

52. See the following websites: www.merck.com/newsroom/news-release-archive/corporate-responsibility/2010_0621.html; www.purina.com/animal-welfare/animalwelfare.aspx; www.edf.org/pressrelease.cfm?contentID=11452; www.strength.org/our_partners/american_express/; www.kochind.com/files/020910GPWaunaMilldonation.pdf; http://news.starbucks.com/article_display.cfm?article_id=119.

53. See the following websites: http://news.starbucks.com/article_display.cfm?article_id=119; www.joinred.com/aboutred; www.rif.org/us/donate/supporters/coca-cola-company.htm; www.tysonhungerrelief.com/our-commitment/.

54. Dennis R. Young, *Commercial Activity and Voluntary Health Agencies: When Are Ventures Advisable?* (Washington: National Health Council, 1998), p. 13.

55. For a discussion of the unusual form such partnerships have taken in Latin America, see Salamon, *Rethinking Corporate Social Engagement.*

56. Dennis R. Young, *If Not for Profit, for What?* (Lexington, Mass.: D. C. Heath, 1983), pp. 21–41.

57. Crimmins and Keil, *Enterprise in the Nonprofit Sector;* Skloot, "Enterprise and Commerce in Nonprofit Organizations," pp. 380–93.

58. On the concept of managerialism and the managerial revolution in American business, see Alfred D. Chandler Jr., *The Visible Hand: The Managerial Revolution in American Business* (Harvard University Press, 1977), pp. 1–12, 484–98. Managerialism here refers to the emergence of complex, multiple-unit organizations and an emphasis on management and managers, as opposed to owners or boards, to ensure organizational performance. For a fuller explication of managerialism, see chapter 1 of this volume.

59. Roseanne M. Mirabella, "University-Based Educational Programs in Nonprofit Management and Philanthropic Studies: A 10-Year Review and Projections of Future Trends," *Nonprofit and Voluntary Sector Quarterly* 36, no. 4 (2007): 11S–27S.

60. Michael O'Neill and Kathleen Fletcher, eds., *Nonprofit Management Education* (New York: Praeger, 1998), pp. 1–10.

61. For a useful summary of these concepts as they apply to the nonprofit sector, see Kevin P. Kearns, *Private Sector Strategies for Social Sector Success: The Guide to Strategy and Planning for Public and Nonprofit Organizations* (San Francisco: Jossey-Bass, 2000).

62. Paul Brest, *Money Well Spent: A Strategic Plan for Smart Philanthropy* (New York: Bloomberg Press, 2008); Light, *Making Nonprofits Work,* pp. 68–77; Patricia Patrizi and Bernard McMullan, "Realizing the Potential of Program Evaluation," *Foundation News* 40, no. 3 (1999): 30–35; Gary Walker and Jean Grossman, "Philanthropy and Outcomes," in *Philanthropy and the Nonprofit Sector in a Changing America,* edited by Charles Clotfelter and Thomas Ehrlich (Indiana University Press, 1999), pp. 449–60.

63. Light, *Making Nonprofits Work,* pp. 19–22.

64. Oster, *Strategic Management for Nonprofit Organizations,* pp. 277–86.

65. Christine Letts, William P. Ryan, and Allen Grossman, "Virtuous Capital: What Foundations Can Learn from Venture Capitalists," *Harvard Business Review* 75, no. 2 (1997): 2–7.

66. Jed Emerson, "The U.S. Nonprofit Capital Market: An Introductory Overview of Developmental Stages, Investors, and Funding Instruments," in *Social Purpose Enterprises,* vol. 2, pp. 187–216; Michael E. Porter and Mark R. Kramer, "Philanthropy's New Agenda: Creating Value," *Harvard Business Review* 77 (November/December 1999): 121–30. See also Salamon, *New Frontiers of Philanthropy,* which develops the concept of the foundation as a "philanthropic bank."

67. Amelia Kohm, David LaPiana, and Heather Gowdy, *Strategic Restructuring: Findings from a Study of Integrations and Alliances among Nonprofit Social Service and Cultural Organizations in the United States,* discussion paper (Chicago: Chapin Hall Center for Children), p. 1; Jane Arsenault, *Forging Nonprofit Alliances* (San Francisco: Jossey-Bass, 1998).

68. For examples, see Joseph J. Cordes, Zina Poletz, and C. Eugene Steuerle, "Examples of Nonprofit-For-Profit Hybrid Business Models," in *Nonprofits and Business,* edited by Joseph J. Cordes and C. Eugene Steuerle (Washington: Urban Institute, 2009), pp. 69–82.

69. Ibid.

70. For further elaboration, see Lester M. Salamon, "The New Governance and the Tools of Government Action: An Introduction," in *The Tools of Government: A Guide to the New Governance,* edited by Lester M. Salamon (Oxford University Press, 2002), pp. 1–18.

71. Eyal Press and Jennifer Washburn, "The Kept University," *Atlantic Monthly,* March 2000, pp. 39–54.

72. Burton A. Weisbrod, *The Nonprofit Economy* (Harvard University Press, 1988).

73. Bradford H. Gray, *The Profit Motive in Patient Care* (Harvard University Press, 1991), pp. 332–33.

15

Devolution, Marketization, and the Changing Shape of Government-Nonprofit Relations

KIRSTEN A. GRØNBJERG AND LESTER M. SALAMON

R elations between the nonprofit sector and government—always complex, multifaceted, and in flux—have undergone significant changes in the United States over the last several decades. In the process, the implicit partnership that characterized these relations during much of American history, and that was fundamentally expanded during the 1960s and 1970s, has been substantially redefined. In the more than three decades since 1980, America's nonprofit sector has grown massively, but it has also had to contend with a withering series of challenges in its dealings with government: retrenchment and marketization of government funding, expansion of the types of organizations eligible to compete for this funding, further devolution of government decision-making to the fifty states, narrowing of the tax advantages nonprofits have available, expanded local efforts to capture revenues from nonprofits, tightening of government regulation, and risks to core mission objectives as a result of pressures to lower the unit cost of services.

Although the election of Barack Obama, a former community organizer, gave rise to hopes among many that the nation might return to the pattern of government-nonprofit partnership that characterized earlier periods, the nation's economic crisis, the growing deficits resulting from the Bush-era wars and tax cuts, and the return of a virulent antigovernment political climate quickly dashed those hopes and left nonprofits in the same no-man's-land, or worse, so far as its relationship with government is concerned. As the second

549

decade of the twenty-first century dawns, therefore, nonprofits find themselves under increasing fiscal strains, with little hope that cash-starved governments at federal, state, or local levels will come to their rescue, as in the past, and with the realization that these economic strains are coupled with new assaults on tax incentives for giving, which could limit private charitable support as well.

This chapter examines the recent evolution of government-nonprofit relations in the United States and the prospects for the future. To put the discussion into context, however, it begins by outlining the multiple arenas of government-nonprofit interaction and the historical pattern of government-nonprofit ties. It then investigates the recent changes that have occurred in each of the various arenas. A concluding section then examines the implications of the recent changes and offers some recommendations for improving the relations between government and the nonprofit sector in the years ahead.

Arenas and Patterns of Government-Nonprofit Relations

Government-nonprofit relations in the United States are complex and dynamic, and have been from the very beginning. These relations are embedded in the economic and political structures of American society and in the political ideologies that have come to guide our national consciousness, shaping our concepts about the proper role of government, the virtues of markets, and how central a role private initiative should play. Disentangling the realities from the myths in this field is difficult, but it is essential. After all, simplistic explanations that fail to capture essential dimensions are poor guides for interpreting new developments or for making choices about the future.

A useful starting point for clarifying these relationships is to recognize that government-nonprofit relations operate on more than one level and in multiple arenas. What is more, variations also exist across localities and across fields or components of the sector. It is quite possible, therefore, that different perceptions of these relations can result from focusing on different levels, arenas, localities, or fields.

Perhaps most important for our purposes here is the mismatch that has long existed between the ideological or normative perception of the government-nonprofit relationship, on the one hand, and the empirical or factual realities of this relationship, on the other. For better or worse, the nonprofit sector has been the ideological battleground for a long-running debate in American thinking about the appropriate role of government in responding to social and economic needs. Much of the discussion of government-nonprofit relations has thus occurred at the ideological level. Advocates of a limited state have championed the nonprofit sector as an alternative mechanism for responding to social ills and emphasized strict separation between government and voluntary groups.

Advocates of greater governmental involvement, on the other hand, have downplayed the importance of nonprofit organizations and emphasized instead the need for government action to cope with social and economic problems. Neither side, therefore, has had an ideological interest in emphasizing the possibilities for cooperation between the sectors. Rather, the rhetoric of separation and conflict has dominated at the ideological level, obscuring what has been a pattern of extensive and substantial partnership in practice.

In addition to the confusion that results from viewing government-nonprofit realities through a heavy ideological prism, other difficulties arise from observing the different arenas in which government and nonprofit organizations interact. Four such arenas are in evidence: government funding of nonprofits, government tax policy toward nonprofits, government regulation of nonprofits, and substantive government policy more generally. In the arena of government spending, government decisions impact nonprofit organizations in two different ways: indirectly, by affecting the need for nonprofit services; and directly, by determining the resources nonprofits have available to help meet the resulting needs.

Nonprofit organizations are also affected both directly and indirectly in the arena of government taxation policies. Nonprofits are typically exempted from taxation in the United States, but the range of activities so exempted and the range of taxes—income, sales, property—from which exemptions are provided can vary over time and among jurisdictions.[1] Tax policies also affect the donations that nonprofits receive from individuals and corporations. Donations to charities eligible for exemption under section 501(c)(3) of the tax code are deductible from the taxable income of individual taxpayers and corporations within certain limits, which means that the value of these deductions to donors varies with the tax rate. Similarly, contributions to such organizations have also been deductible from estates in computing estate taxes, which have historically been fairly high in the United States so as to avoid the creation of an aristocracy of wealth.

In the regulatory arena, government actions determine the types of organizations eligible for tax-exempt status, the procedures under which they secure this status, the types of activities these organizations can undertake, and the kinds of public disclosure they must make. Thus, religious congregations have historically not been required to seek official designation as tax-exempt entities, whereas nonreligious organizations typically are required to file for such status with the Internal Revenue Service. Similarly, constraints of various sorts have been placed on the political and legislative activity of charitable nonprofit organizations, that is, those eligible to receive tax-deductible gifts, but not on other types of tax-exempt entities.

Finally, nonprofit organizations have a deep stake in the broader *policies* that governments pursue. As noted in the overview chapter to this book and in chapter 10, policy advocacy is one of the principal functions of the nonprofit sector and one of the major contributions these organizations make to American society. Indeed, one of the great strengths of the American democratic system is the freedom it affords individuals to come together in organizations to promote their definition of the common good, including pressuring government to respond to disadvantaged groups or attend to what they see as urgent problems. But many nonprofits, most notably those that are registered as charities, run up against limitations when this activity crosses from advocacy into lobbying, though the distinction between these two is often blurred, with varying definitions in different pieces of legislation.

Given these multiple arenas, it is quite possible for government and nonprofit organizations to be at odds in one arena while cooperating in others. Thus, for example, Planned Parenthood has been a recipient of sizable federal government grants while being vehemently opposed to recent federal policies prohibiting family planning organizations from distributing condoms in their overseas work.

Background: A Heritage of Cooperation

While it is difficult to generalize about government-nonprofit relations across all arenas and all fields of service, it seems fair to conclude that the general tenor of these relations at the operating level has been cooperative throughout most of U.S. history, even though a rhetoric of conflict and separation has dominated at the ideological level. The historian Waldemar Nielsen puts it as well as anyone: "Throughout most of American history government has been an active partner and financier of the Third Sector to a much greater extent than is commonly recognized. . . . Collaboration, not separation or antagonism, between government and the Third Sector . . . has been the predominant characteristic."[2]

Although some early colonies resisted the formation of nonprofit institutions, and such institutions were outlawed for a time in early Massachusetts history, government has generally protected the right of citizens to associate. The first nonprofit organization on American soil, Harvard College, was thus not only chartered by the Massachusetts Bay Colony but also made the recipient of a dedicated commonwealth tax, the *colledge corne*. This pattern was replicated, moreover, in the design of other venerable nonprofit educational institutions, such as Columbia, Dartmouth, and Yale.[3] As state governments expanded their functions in the latter nineteenth century in response to the twin challenges of urbanization and industrialization, this pattern of government support of private institutions was extended as well, at first into the health field and later into social services more broadly. A 1901 survey found, in fact, that "except possibly two territories and four Western states, there is probably not a state in the union where some aid [to private charities] is not given either by the state or by the counties and cities."[4] The federal government followed the same approach in its dealings with the District of Columbia. By 1892 half of the funds that Congress allocated for aid to the poor in the District went to private charities, and these private institutions also absorbed two-thirds of the funds the District allocated for the construction of charitable facilities.[5] Rather than crowding out nonprofit service providers, as is sometimes charged, government supported the sector by providing it with funds to operate.

None of this is to say that the relationships between government and the nonprofit sector were without their tensions as well. While governments at various points challenged the wealth that nonprofit institutions sometimes amassed, nonprofits vigorously challenged public neglect of poverty and distress.[6] Yet even when protests were most in evidence, the objective was typically not to replace government but to energize and enlist it for such purposes as abolishing slavery, granting women the right to vote, restricting consumption of alcohol, or regulating the employment of children.

In other cases, nonprofit advocacy efforts served to mobilize government to finance initiatives that nonprofits were then empowered to carry out—such as care of the poor or provision of foster care. The upshot was the development of a distinctive, but by no means unique, American approach to addressing public problems, an approach that one of the present authors terms third-party government.[7] The central feature of this approach is the reliance by government on a variety of third parties to carry out functions that the public wants to be performed but is reluctant to have government directly carry out, whether it is extension of loans to homebuyers, provisioning of the military, construction of roads and bridges, pursuit of scientific research, or poverty alleviation. These third parties include commercial banks, industrial corporations, highway construction companies, and in the human service, education, and health fields, nonprofit organizations.

When the federal government was finally persuaded to address the health, employment and training, community development, and social service problems of the nation during the Great Society era of the 1960s and 1970s, therefore, it was only natural that it would use this same approach. The upshot was a substantial enlargement of the already existing pattern of government-nonprofit cooperation but bringing the national government into the arrangement for the first time in a major way. In the process, government helped stimulate a massive expansion of the nonprofit sector. Indeed, much of the nonprofit sector as we know it today, at least in the human service arena, took shape as a result of this growth in government support. In some cases, government stimulated the creation of such organizations where none existed (such as the Community Action Agencies fostered by the War on Poverty, Area

Table 15-1. *Sources of U.S. Nonprofit Organizations' Revenue,*
Exclusive of Religious Congregations, 1977
Percent

	Amount of revenue			
Type of nonprofit	Government	Fees, investments	Private giving	Total
Health	32	53	14	100
Education and research	18	67	15	100
Social and legal services	54	13	33	100
Civic and social	50	19	31	100
Arts and cultural activities	12	47	41	100
Total	31	51	18	100

Source: Authors' estimates based on data in Murray S. Weitzman, Nadine Tai Jaladoni, Linda M. Lampkin, and Thomas H. Pollack, *The New Nonprofit Almanac and Desk Reference* (San Francisco: Jossey-Bass, 2002).

Agencies on Aging, community mental health centers, and regional planning agencies in health and metropolitan development). Elsewhere, government relied on already existing nonprofit hospitals, higher education institutions, family service agencies, and day care centers.

Between 1960 and 1980, as a consequence, the operating expenditures of American nonprofit organizations increased nearly tenfold in current dollar terms and more than doubled in constant dollar terms, jumping from less than 4 percent of the nation's gross domestic product to nearly 6 percent.[8] Outside of religious congregations, by 1977 government had easily surpassed private giving from individuals, corporations, and foundations combined as a source of nonprofit income (see table 15-1). Among social service organizations, moreover, government moved into first place.

For the most part, this newly expanded government support flowed directly to the nonprofit agencies themselves. While much of it took the form of grants or contracts for particular services rather than the general purpose funding of earlier eras, the grants or contracts were often on terms that were highly favorable to the nonprofit organizations. Thus, for example, expanded federal funding of university-based scientific research during and after World War II operated through project grants to researchers that were largely controlled by the academic research community and carried with them substantial overhead support to the host institutions.[9] Other support was provided for the capital construction needs of universities and hospitals. Even the consumer-side vouchers created during this period, such as Medicare and Medicaid, used cost-based reimbursement systems that were highly advantageous to the recipient institutions, essentially committing the federal government to reimburse them for their costs.[10]

Not only did federal funding of nonprofit organizations blossom during this period, but so did other facets of government-nonprofit relations. Most notable here was the federal government's encouragement and subsequent responsiveness to nonprofit advocacy and promotion of social and political rights. This was evident in the passage of the civil rights and voting rights acts and in the opening of greatly expanded opportunities for class action suits in such fields as consumer rights and environmental protection. Thanks to these openings, nonprofit organizations representing black Americans, Native Americans, Hispanics, older Americans, welfare recipients, migrant farmworkers, women, gays and lesbians, people with disabilities, consumers, and environmentalists were able to push for much fuller participation in the nation's social, political, and economic life.

These more intense interactions also produced their share of tensions and challenges, of course. The numerous and substantial funding relationships inevitably created the need for greater formality and structure. The result was a loss of flexibility for both parties.[11] What is more, the sheer number and variety of government programs created major coordination problems for both recipient organizations and government agencies, increasing the transaction costs for both sides.[12] Nevertheless, this period represented in many respects a golden era of government-nonprofit cooperation.[13]

Recent Developments: Retrenchment, Marketization, Devolution, and Regulation

Set against this backdrop, the last several decades, stretching from the early 1980s through the first decade of the twenty-first century, have witnessed a significant deterioration in government-nonprofit relations. To be sure, not all the developments have been negative; indeed, the number of registered charities more than doubled during this period, as did the real value of their total estimated revenues, and some of the negative impacts have been the product of misunderstanding the real relationships that exist.[14] Yet even with these caveats it is hard not to view this recent period as one of growing tension and uncertainty. What is more, this tension and uncertainty was evident in more than one of the arenas of government-nonprofit interaction.

The Arena of Government Spending

Especially troublesome developments have occurred in the arena of government funding, where a combination of retrenchment and shifts in the structure of government funding have imposed significant strains on nonprofit organizations. Indeed, five major developments are evident in this arena.

RETRENCHMENT. Perhaps the signal development of this thirty-year period since the early 1980s has been a sharp reversal in the policy of increasing direct government support of nonprofit organizations. This reversal was initiated in the early 1980s by the Reagan administration, which took the rhetoric of conflict and competition between government and the nonprofit sector, which has long dominated the ideological picture of this relationship, as an accurate portrayal of reality. The administration claimed to strengthen the nonprofit sector by getting government out of its way, overlooking the extent to which these two sectors had forged mutually supportive bonds during the previous 150 years. Although only a portion of the budget cuts the Reagan administration proposed were enacted, the result was still a significant decline (by 25 percent) in the real value of government support to nonprofit organizations in the early 1980s, and spending was still below the 1980 level in real dollar terms as of 1994. Indeed, by the mid-1990s, when the Contract with America Congress ushered in a new round of cuts, the real value of direct federal support to nonprofit organizations was 19 percent below its 1980 level in the fields of education and social services, 17 percent below in the field of international assistance, and 42 percent below in the field of community development.[15]

Moreover, beginning in 2002, the Bush administration proposed additional significant cuts in discretionary programs of interest to nonprofits.[16] For example, the president's 2008 budget proposals included the elimination of the Community Services Block Grant and the Commodity Supplementary Food Program, as well as cuts of 10 percent or more in funding for the Corporation for Public Broadcasting, Community Development Block Grants, Low-Income Home Energy Assistance Grants, the Corporation for Community and National Service, AmeriCorps, Learn and Serve America, the National Civilian Service Corps, the National Service Trust Fund, the Points of Light Foundation, Juvenile Justice, the Social Service Block Grant, and various job training and employment programs.[17] The proposed cuts were only to a minor extent offset by proposed major increases (12 percent or more) in a handful of programs, including the Institute of Museum and Library Services, Homelessness Assistance Grants, grants to local health care centers, the National Science Foundation, and the president's much-touted Office of Faith-Based and Community Initiatives and related Compassion Capital Fund (targeted to faith-based organizations). This latter initiative brought new focus and visibility to the role of faith-based organizations in providing services; however, the level of funding allocated to the initiative was relatively small and was more than offset by cuts in other programs areas.[18] While not all of the president's proposed cuts were enacted, and the catalogue of federal domestic assistance still includes more than 600 federal programs for which nonprofit organizations are potentially eligible, the repeated threats have created continuing uncertainty about the future of federal funding of nonprofit organizations, at least through the numerous so-called discretionary programs.[19]

SHIFT TO CONSUMER-SIDE SUBSIDIES. The one bright spot in this otherwise bleak picture of actual or threatened cuts in federal support to nonprofit organizations has been the so-called entitlement programs, such as Medicare and Medicaid. Generally speaking, the entitlement programs continued to grow during the period of supposed retrenchment. In fact their growth escalated. As Salamon notes in chapter 1 of this volume, part of this was due to the natural expansion of costs and the natural growth of the eligible populations. But a far larger part was due to the considerable expansions that occurred in the late 1980s and throughout the 1990s in the services and populations covered by these programs. For example, Medicaid coverage was extended to fifty distinct subgroups during this period, ultimately boosting the program's coverage from 21.6 million people in 1980 to 40.6 million by 1998 and to 58.3 million in 2008.[20]

Also at work were successful state attempts to shift more of their human service spending from declining federal discretionary grant and contract programs to the growing Medicaid voucher program, which provided a more generous federal matching rate and a more open-ended funding stream.[21] In the process, Medicaid was transformed into a virtual social service block grant, financing a broad range of social service programs for persons with disabilities, single mothers and their children, and other populations. Despite the budgetary stringency, therefore, overall federal spending in fields in which nonprofits are active continued to grow, and nonprofit revenue from government grew with it. This growth was quite robust in the period between the late 1980s and the late 1990s but then slowed somewhat in the more recent period between 1997 and 2007, as federal and state authorities sought to restrain the rapid expansion of the major entitlement programs as well, largely by reducing reimbursement rates. Still, between 1997 and 2007, government support of nonprofit organizations expanded by 38 percent after adjusting for inflation, slightly more than the 34 percent growth in the country's GDP but well below the overall 53 percent growth of total nonprofit revenues. As a consequence, from a high of 42 percent of total nonprofit revenue as of 1997, government support shrank to 38 percent as of 2007, with the remainder coming from private fees (52 percent) and private charity (10 percent).

Quite apart from the scale of government support to nonprofit providers, these changes triggered a fundamental shift in its basic form. Most of the discretionary programs that absorbed the bulk of the cuts were so-called producer-side subsidies; that is, they delivered their benefits in the form of grants and contracts to the providers of services, many of them nonprofit organizations. By contrast, the major entitlement programs are consumer-side subsidies; that is, they deliver their benefits, in the form of vouchers, directly to the consumers of services, who then—in something approaching an open market—have the option of choosing their providers. The budget policies of the thirty-year period following 1980 thus decisively changed the balance between producer-side subsidies and consumer-side subsidies toward the latter, with over 77 percent of federal support to nonprofit organizations taking this form by 2007. These developments forced nonprofit organizations into unaccustomed competition for "customers" with for-profit organizations, which have far greater experience with marketing their services.

Also working in the same direction was the increased reliance on a variety of other indirect tools of government action, such as loan guarantees and tax subsidies. These tools gained popularity in the prevailing antigovernment, antitax climate of the 1980s and 1990s.[22] Indeed, the price of securing support for government efforts to deal with child poverty, day care services, low-income housing needs, and a host of other problems in the latter 1980s and into the 1990s was to utilize such indirect tools. This is hardly entirely new, of course. The tax deduction for medical expenses and the exclusion of scholarship aid from taxable income, for example, have long been established features of the tax code. But the use of such tools in fields in which nonprofits are active expanded considerably over the past several decades with the addition or extension of programs such as the child care tax credit, the credit for student loan interest payments, the low-income housing tax credit, health savings accounts, and education savings accounts.

By 2010 tax expenditures, loan guarantees, and direct loans amounted to $484.1 billion in federal assistance in fields in which nonprofits are active. This amount is roughly equivalent to the more than $500 billion in direct government support flowing to nonprofits and double their scale two decades earlier, as shown in table 15-2. This includes a 45 percent increase in the value of tax expenditures and a striking eightyfold rise in the value of direct loans, largely reflecting the replacement of the long-standing federal college student loan guarantee program with a direct loan program. As table 15-3 indicates, moreover, the range of activities covered by these tax and lending programs is exceedingly broad, from housing to medical assistance, and from foster care to workforce training. In many fields, in fact, the value of activities supported through these indirect tools exceeds that of activities supported by the outright spending programs. In day care, for example, the $3.5 billion in subsidies made available to middle-income and lower-middle-income families through the child and dependent care tax credit in 2010 exceeds the roughly $2.1 billion in

Table 15-2. *Growth in Federal Tax Expenditure and Loan Programs Relevant to Nonprofit Organizations, 1990–2010*
Constant 2010 dollars (billions)

Tool	1990	2010	Percentage change, 1990–2010
Tax expenditures	201.2	292.5	45.4
Direct loans	0.2	149.4	84,846.2
Loan guarantees	47.3	42.3	−10.6
Total	248.7	484.1	94.7

Source: U.S. Office of Management and Budget, *Budget of the U.S. Government, FY 2012*, Supplemental Tables; U.S. Office of Management Budget, *Budget of the U.S. Government, FY1992*, Special Analyses.

subsidies provided to poor families through the Child Care and Development Block Grant.[23]

This shift in government support from relatively predictable producer-side grants and contracts to consumer-side vouchers, tax credits, and loan guarantees has been justified on the grounds that it gives consumers more choice and fosters efficiency by forcing providers to compete for clients in an open market. Also at work, however—especially in more recent years—has been the realization that government assistance delivered to faith-based charities has an easier time passing legal muster when delivered indirectly through consumer-side subsidies than when delivered through direct grants or contracts, because with the indirect forms the government cannot as easily be accused of supporting religion.[24]

MARKETIZATION. This shift toward consumer-side subsidies has complicated the work of nonprofit organizations, injecting a much higher degree of uncertainty into their operations, intensifying pressures on organizations to market their services, requiring a broad array of additional nonprofits beyond those in the health field to master the substantial intricacies of Medicaid and Medicare reimbursement processes, and threatening mission-critical functions by forcing nonprofits to compete on the basis of the lowest unit cost of services. In addition, however, it has attracted for-profit firms into arenas in which nonprofits have historically operated. As noted in chapter 14, moreover, these firms have had an advantage in generating capital and thereby in responding to the increased demand that the expanding government voucher programs have generated.

Also working in the same direction have been a number of other governmental measures to promote for-profit involvement in government contract work, including that for human services. Thus a 1983 Office of Management and Budget circular established an elaborate process requiring federal agencies

Table 15-3. *Major Federal Tax Expenditure and Loan Programs of Relevance to Nonprofit Organizations*
Constant 2010 dollars (millions)

Tax expenditures (outlay equivalent)	Amount
Insurance companies owned by nonprofits	200
Low-income housing credit	5,650
Empowerment zone	730
New markets tax credit	720
Scholarship income exclusion	2,760
HOPE tax credit	
Lifetime learning tax credit	3,490
American Opportunity Tax Credit	15,110
Education Individual Retirement Accounts	60
Student loan interest deduction	1,480
Higher-education expense deduction	760
State prepaid tuition plans	1,390
Student loan bond interest deduction	550
Nonprofit education facilities bond interest	2,340
Credit for holders of zone academy bonds	190
Interest on savings bonds used for education	20
Parental exemption for expenses of students over nineteen	2,960
Charitable contribution deduction (education)	3,930
Employer educational assistance	680
Special deduction for teacher expenses	160
Discharge of student loan indebtedness	20
Qualified school construction bonds	80
Work Opportunity Tax Credit	1,110
Welfare-to-work tax credit	20
Employer-provided child-care exclusion/credit	1,230
Adopted foster-care assistance	460
Adoption credit	660
Exclusion of foster-care payments	420
Child credit	23,030
Child and dependent-care credit	3,470
Employer medical insurance contributions	160,110
Self-employed medical insurance	5,680
Medical savings accounts	1,790
Charitable contribution deduction (health)	3,850
Medical expense deduction	9,090
Hospital construction bond interest	3,530
Parsonage allowance deduction	660

Tax expenditures (outlay equivalent)	Amount
Other charitable contributions	34,080
Subtotal, tax expenditures	292,470
Loan guarantee commitments (2010)	
Family education loan program	42,141
Community development loan guarantees	150
Subtotal, loan guarantees	42,291
Direct Loan Disbursements (2010)	
Rural housing insurance fund	2,178
Rural community facilities direct loans	399
Historically black college capital financing	263
Direct student loan program	74,709
TEACH Financing account	104
Student loan acquisition account	24,432
Temporary Student Loan Purchase Authority	31,963
State Housing Finance Agency Direct Loan	15,309
Community development credit union revolving fund	4
Subtotal, direct loan disbursements	149,361
Total	484,122

Source: U.S. Office of Management and Budget, *Budget of the U.S. Government, FY 2012,* Supplemental Tables.

to open even more of their activities to "the competitive market-place," meaning particularly private businesses.[25] Although these moves were characterized as "privatization" and were justified by "public choice" economic theories, their real impact, given the prevailing widespread practice of government reliance on private nonprofit organizations, was to increase for-profit competition for many of the grants and contracts that nonprofit organizations were already receiving. At the same time, earlier preferences for nonprofit organizations in key fields were weakened or phased out. Thus for example in the health field the Medicare licensure requirement for for-profit (but not nonprofit) home health facilities and the start-up assistance to nonprofit health maintenance organizations were eliminated. As noted below, the welfare reform legislation of 1996 further added to these developments by setting in motion a movement of for-profit firms into the welfare reform arena as "master contractors" for complex welfare-to-work programs. The Bush administration's efforts to implement its Faith-Based Initiatives may have moderated these pressures somewhat in view of the difficulties it revealed on the part of small community-based and sectarian organizations in competing for federal and state contracts and in gaining access to Medicaid funding, but it is not clear how much progress was made in this direction.[26]

PERFORMANCE MEASUREMENT AND MANAGED CARE. Not only have the instruments being used to channel public support to nonprofit organizations changed, but so too have the internal operations of some of the existing instruments, often in ways that make them more challenging for nonprofits. Thus, for example, the retrospective cost-based reimbursement system long used to finance the Medicare and Medicaid programs was replaced in the early 1980s by a prospective payment system, which established fixed rates for particular medical procedures and required institutions to meet these costs or suffer losses on their publicly subsidized services. In many cases, nonprofits charged that the new rates took too blanket an approach and failed to cover the special costs that nonprofits incurred as a result of their mission-critical activities, such as teaching and research for university-based hospitals.

A related challenge is represented by the growth of managed care systems in several service fields, most notably health and now also human services, as detailed by Steven Smith and by Bradford Gray and Mark Schlesinger in chapters 2 and 4 (this volume). Under these systems, both public and private third-party payers, such as insurance companies, establish set fees for coverage of particular classes of client for particular ranges of service and then hold nonprofit and for-profit providers accountable to provide the services at these preset fees. The growth of managed care presents profound challenges for nonprofits. The successful operation of managed care systems requires large pools of clients in order to balance risks. But this requires sophisticated information-processing equipment, which nonprofits often lack the investment capital to acquire. Inevitably, therefore, these developments have attracted for-profit competitors into key service fields. What is more, nonprofits have had to find ways to reconcile their missions of providing quality care with reimbursement structures that frequently drive them toward lowest-cost service.

There is also evidence that federal (and state) reimbursement rates for other key government programs in which nonprofits are involved have failed to keep up with costs. A recent survey of nonprofit human service agencies by the Urban Institute, for example, finds that two-thirds of respondents report that government payments for services failed to cover the full costs, and of these, 44 percent considered this to be a "big problem."[27] Significant proportions of these organizations also report facing matching requirements on government grants and contracts, and a majority report unrealistic limits on coverage of administrative or overhead costs. As a result of these practices, nonprofits end up losing money on the government-supported services they offer, since their costs exceed the government support they receive.

Passage of the Government Performance and Results Act of 1993 has had a similar effect. The point of this legislation was to measure the tangible performance of government operations at all levels. However, since cost and efficiency considerations are easier to measure than quality or equity ones, the overall result has been to give an implicit advantage to for-profit providers, which tend to focus on these market-oriented criteria. All of this has changed the ground rules for nonprofit service providers. The momentum has shifted from efforts to deliver effective services toward cost control, efficiency, and minimum standards of care. In the process, for-profit providers, who are accustomed to competing on precisely these terms, have gained the competitive advantage.

WELFARE REFORM AND CHARITABLE CHOICE. The fifth major factor affecting the public sector funding environment for nonprofit organizations has been welfare reform (now into its second decade) and the accompanying expansion of so-called charitable choice. The impact here, however, has been complex and by no means unidirectional.

In its basic design and thrust, the welfare reform legislation that passed in 1996 appeared to be largely hostile to nonprofit organizations. This legislation put a lid on federal payments to states for welfare assistance and stipulated that states had to move welfare recipients off the welfare rolls and into jobs within five years. It thus shifted the focus of this major federal income support program from services and income support to work readiness and employment, not fields in which traditional nonprofit social service agencies have a particular comparative advantage.

Reflecting this, many states moved early in the welfare reform implementation process to enlist for-profit companies, including a number of defense contractors such as Lockheed Martin, to assist them in managing the complex process of moving welfare recipients into jobs, thus intensifying the competition between nonprofit agencies and for-profit companies in the human service arena. Thus, early analysis by Richard Nathan and Thomas Gais shows that almost one-third (31 percent) of the states contracted out their administrative design of employment and training programs and one-fifth contracted out the policymaking responsibilities for this field.[28] The corresponding percentages for pregnancy prevention services were 21 and 15 percent. As Peter Frumkin and Alice Andre-Clark report, during this early period, at least, a growing number of these administrative contracts were with for-profit entities, so that many nonprofits no longer interacted directly with government when they delivered publicly financed services, but instead interacted with a for-profit contractor.[29] Indeed, case studies of these new types of contracting regimes show the complexities involved, especially if perverse incentives for shifting risks from one contracting party to another are to be avoided.[30] It also seems clear that smaller agencies have found these new regimes more difficult to operate within than have the larger, more established ones.[31] What is more, while these lines of business were attractive to the large defense contractors when their regular business was slow, once their core business picked up steam they lost little time exiting the difficult world of welfare case management. Thus, for example, Lockheed Martin sold its welfare case management business to Affiliated Computer Services Inc. in July 2001 after encountering difficulties in its Florida and Kansas operations.[32]

Additional competition for nonprofits resulted from the so-called charitable choice provisions in the welfare reform bill. These provisions specifically authorized the funding of so-called faith-based organizations—religious congregations and other avowedly sectarian organizations—in an effort to help welfare recipients overcome dependence and secure paying jobs. The arguments advanced for these provisions are similar to those that underlay the marketization initiatives of this period—that sacramental organizations are more cost effective than traditional nonprofit agencies in achieving welfare reform's objectives. This was so, advocates argued, both because they mobilize the power of faith to change human behavior and because they have access to religiously inspired volunteers, making it possible for them to avoid payments to nonprofit professionals.[33] In this sense, the charitable choice provisions were a not-so-subtle rebuke of the professionally staffed nonprofit organizations presumably "feeding at the federal trough" and an effort to push the nonprofit sector back toward its presumed voluntary roots by privileging organizations that exemplify the ideal of a truly voluntary sector supported largely by private charity and committed volunteers. These arguments were then extended beyond the welfare reform arena through the second Bush administration's Faith-Based Initiatives, which sought to open more of the federal funding stream to faith-based organizations through executive orders and administrative reforms, including the establishment of faith-based initiatives in each of the major federal agencies.

Ironically, however, because of constitutional restrictions on direct funding for sacramental programs and a general preference for free-market models, the administration pursued its Faith-Based Initiatives through consumer-side funding mechanisms. Consequently, the initiatives not only politicized religion and disadvantaged mainline nonprofit service providers but also served to draw the most "mission-based" segment of the nonprofit sector—that is, faith-based organizations—into the growing tide of market-based and marketlike entities already competing for public benefits.

While the basic structure of welfare reform thus posed significant challenges to the nonprofit sector, however, the actual evolution of the program turned out to produce some important windfalls. This was so because the economic boom of the late 1990s created extraordinary employment opportunities for welfare recipients, leading to an unexpected drop in welfare rolls—from 5 million families in 1995 to 2 million in 2000.[34] Since the welfare reform legislation guaranteed that federal payments to states would remain at their pre-1996 levels for at least five years, the drop in the rolls translated into a fiscal windfall for the states. Thus by 1999 the median state spent only 54 percent of its combined federal TANF money and state "maintenance of effort" funds on cash assistance, a quarter of the states spent less than 45 percent, and Wisconsin, which had implemented its welfare reform program very early, spent only 28 percent.[35] The remaining funds could therefore be channeled into a variety of supportive services. Similarly, Rob Geen reports that state TANF spending for child welfare services increased by $1.5 billion, or 170 percent, over the 1996–2000 period and that by 2000 states were spending $9.9 billion in federal funds (including federal TANF dollars) on child welfare services, up by 36 percent from 1996.[36] More in-depth analysis of four states (California, Georgia, Missouri, and Wisconsin) shows that cash assistance had declined by 29–51 percent over the 1995–99 period, while expenditures for most types of services increased during the same period, in most cases significantly.[37] Other, more recent, data point to significant differences among the states. Thus Olivia Golden finds that, while total spending for child welfare increased nationally between 1996 and 2002, fourteen states saw total spending on child welfare decline, sixteen states saw drops in federal spending, fourteen states saw drops in state spending, and five states saw drops in local spending.[38]

As a result, for a relatively brief period during the late 1990s into 2001, some nonprofits in some states were able to find new funding at the state level as the combination of a growing economy and the 1996 welfare reform legislation allowed states to shift funds to work readiness and employment programs. However, these are not fields in which traditional nonprofit social service agencies have a particular comparative advantage. In addition, as other researchers note, many of those types of agencies encountered significant increases in demand for services.[39] Moreover, the recession of 2001, combined with continuing growth of Medicaid and jumps in welfare rolls, brought sharp cuts in an array of more traditional social service programs at the state level.[40]

IMPLICATIONS FOR NONPROFIT FUNDING. If the funding environment for nonprofit agencies grew more challenging and complex during the past thirty years, however, the agencies seem to have found ways to cope with the resulting challenges. Thus, the number of charities registered with the IRS has shown continuing and substantial growth since 1977, with annual growth increasing from 14,600 per year for the 1977–87 period to 27,100 per year for the

Figure 15-1. *Number and Growth of Charities Registered with the IRS,
1977–2007*

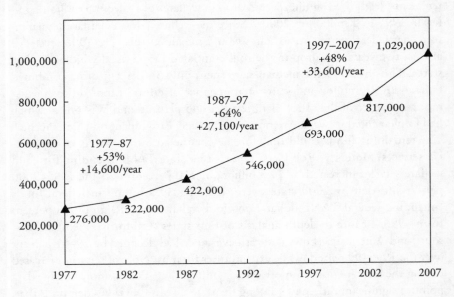

Source: *Nonprofit Almanac,* Independent Sector and Urban Institute, various editions.

1987–97 period and 33,600 per year over the 1997–2007 period, and then
jumping to an average of 45,000 per year between 2007 and 2010 (see figure
15-1). Aggregate revenues of reporting charities (those that file financial information with the IRS) have also increased markedly, from $699 billion in 1992
to $1.3 trillion in 2007 (all in constant 2007 dollars), an average annual increase
of 4.3 percent. Government support kept pace with this increase overall, but this
obscures a significant difference between the early part of the period (between
1992 and 1997), when the annual average increase of government support was
6.1 percent a year as the expansions of the Medicaid program kicked in) and the
more recent period (1997–2007), when the average annual increase of government support was a more modest 3.3 percent, as constraints on Medicaid and
Medicare reimbursements plus other cutbacks in discretionary programs limited
growth. Reflecting this, as shown in figure 15-2, government support declined
slightly as a share of nonprofit revenue, from 42 percent of total nonprofit revenue in 1997 to 38 percent in 2007, though it still exhibited a robust absolute
growth of nearly 40 percent after adjusting for inflation.

Harder to determine is what the cost of this success has been in terms of
the traditional functions of the nonprofit sector since so much of the overall
gain was fueled by commercial fees. What is more, there is a serious question

Figure 15-2. *Shares of Nonprofit Revenue, 2007 versus 1997*

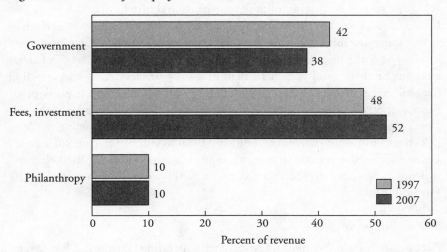

Percent of revenue

Source: Author's estimates based on Form 990 microdata files accessed through the Internal Revenue Service at www.irs.gov and related sources. For further detail, see chapter 1, note 112.

about whether these gains can be sustained into the foreseeable future. The mid-to-late 1990s was a boom period for the economy and hence for government revenues. The early years of the new century, by contrast, were a period of lagging economic growth, which intensified with the banking and housing crises of 2007–08 and the subsequent deep recession from which the economy has still not recovered as of this writing. Coupled with significant tax cuts (discussed more fully below) and massive federal spending for the wars in Iraq and Afghanistan, the result was to turn federal budget surpluses into record federal deficits.

Fortunately for nonprofit organizations, the economic stimulus program that the Obama administration managed to steer through Congress during its first year in office significantly buffered significant portions of the nonprofit sector, as well as the state and local governments on which they heavily rely, from some of the impact of the recession. In addition, the administration managed to get congressional approval for a substantial expansion of the national service program and for the creation of a modest $50 million Social Innovation Fund. However, the congressional elections of 2010 ushered in a new wave of conservative stalwarts, whose mission is to slash government spending and cut back on publicly funded services. While states were able to draw on their "rainy day" funds to keep overall spending relatively flat during the 2001 recession, it seems unlikely that they will be able to keep the storm clouds at bay as the nation enters the second decade of the new century.[41] Indeed, it was only the availability of federal funding through the American Recovery and Reinvestment Act that allowed states to overcome revenue shortfalls of $60 billion, $80 billion, and $84 billion for fiscal years 2009, 2010, and 2011, respectively.[42] While state government revenues are likely to stabilize and perhaps even grow modestly for the next several years, states will have $38 billion less in federal stimulus funds in fiscal year 2012 than in fiscal year 2011, and new spending cuts will be necessary. Forecasts for local government finances are equally pessimistic, especially given anticipated declines in property taxes because of the collapse of the housing market. Indeed, city fiscal officers express the highest level of concern in twenty-five years about the fiscal health of their jurisdictions.[43] Given expanded conservative strength in the Congress after the 2010 election, it is highly unlikely that further federal rescue efforts will be launched in the foreseeable future.

The Taxation Arena

Accompanying the changes in government spending during the last several decades have been dramatic changes in taxation policies that have also had significant, and generally mixed, implications for nonprofit organizations. These changes have taken many different forms and have shifted somewhat over time. What is more, they have affected both the taxation of nonprofit organizations themselves and the donations they receive from the public.

TAX RATE AND DEDUCTION CHANGES. Most dramatic, perhaps, have been the changes in individual income tax rates. Income tax rates not only determine how much money taxpayers have to contribute to charity (the income effect) but also the out-of-pocket cost of such gifts (the price effect). Although this is only one of many factors influencing donor giving decisions, generally speaking the price effects are thought to be stronger than the income effects. This means that lowering tax rates is likely to reduce charitable giving since it increases the out-of-pocket cost of the gift—that is, the net cost of the gift after taking account of what the taxpayer would have paid in taxes had she not made the gift.[44]

Generally speaking, tax rates have been in decline over the past thirty years, especially for upper-income taxpayers, who make the bulk of the charitable donations, at least outside of giving to religious congregations.[45] Thus the Reagan administration pushed through significant income tax rate reductions in 1981, and these were extended in 1986. While these reductions were partly reversed during the first Bush administration, the second Bush administration successfully pushed through further deep cuts in tax rates for upper-income taxpayers under the Economic Growth and Tax Relief Reconciliation Act of 2001. These were further extended and expanded under the Jobs and Growth Tax Relief Reconciliation Act of 2003. In addition, a 1993 act tightened administration of the charitable contribution provisions by requiring written substantiation for gifts of $250 or more. The so-called Pension Protection Act of 2006 now requires taxpayers to have written documentation of all contributions; it also tightened requirements for certain types of contributions, such as stuffed animals, used clothing, and household items.

Other changes in tax legislation increased the incentives to give; these changes include the institution for a short period in the early 1980s of a special charitable deduction for those who do not otherwise itemize their deductions and the elimination in 1993 of gains on appreciated property from the alternative minimum tax base. The 2006 Pension Protection Act also included more generous rules for conservation easements and corporate donations of food and information technology, partly in an effort to deal with the impact of Hurricanes Katrina and Wilma. The act also provided the opportunity for people over the age of seventy and a half to transfer part or all of their minimum required IRA withdrawals to charities tax free. Finally, some states, most notably Arizona, Michigan, and North Carolina, have experimented with providing incentives in the form of tax credits for contributions to charities serving low-income populations.

However, the impact of these incentives is not clear, and the overall effect of the tax rate changes has been to reduce tax rates, especially for better-off taxpayers, and thereby to increase the out-of-pocket cost of charitable giving.[46] So, too, a proposal introduced in the Obama administration's fiscal year 2010 budget, and reintroduced in the fiscal year 2012 proposal issued in February 2011, would move the country further in this direction by reducing the tax rate on charitable gifts made by families earning over $250,000 to 28 percent instead of the current 35 percent rate such taxpayers currently pay. This means that the out-of-pocket "cost" of a $1,000 gift would increase from $650 to $720.

ESTATE TAXES. Also significant have been changes in estate taxes. Such taxes have historically been fairly high in the United States in order to avoid the creation of an aristocracy of wealth in the country. As a consequence, wealthy individuals have had strong incentives to make charitable bequests and create charitable foundations rather than see their estates go to the government at their death.

Beginning in the early 1980s, however, steps were taken to reduce these taxes. Thus the 1981 Economic Recovery Tax Act reduced the maximum tax on estates from 70 percent to 50 percent over a period of years, increased the exemptions from this tax, and permitted a complete exemption for spouses. The Tax Act of 1997 further increased the estate tax exemption, and the tax act enacted in 2001 as part of the Bush administration's tax program began a full phaseout of this tax to be completed by the end of 2009.[47] The phaseout ended in 2010, and the tax was scheduled to be reinstated in 2011 to its 2001 level.

However, an eleventh-hour compromise between President Obama and congressional Republicans reinstated the tax, but at a considerably more favorable rate to wealthy taxpayers. In addition, more favorable gift tax provisions were enacted that will allow even the small proportion of wealthy individuals potentially affected by the estate tax to evade it by distributing their wealth to their heirs as gifts before the estate tax comes into play.[48] How this will affect the formation of foundations in the future is hard to predict, but it certainly reduces the financial incentives to do so.

PROPERTY AND SALES TAX EXEMPTIONS. Other forces are at work challenging the direct tax exemptions that nonprofit organizations enjoy, at least at the state and local level. These exemptions cover all three major forms of state and local taxes: income, sales, and property. The nature and extent of these exemptions vary widely, however, among states and localities.[49] Perhaps because of this, little is known about the extent to which they subsidize nonprofit activity or what their true impact is on local government finances.[50] However, as work by Evelyn Brody and H. Woods Bowman makes clear, nonprofit assets include extensive real estate property, as much as $900 billion in 1997 (not counting extensive church holdings), which is not nearly as much as is owned by governments but is still quite a substantial amount.[51] If all this real estate property were exempt from property taxes (which is not the case, since some holdings are used for commercial purposes and states and localities vary in how they treat nonprofit real estate), the value of this tax exemption would be $8–13 billion, or about 1.3–2.1 percent of total nonprofit revenues and equivalent to about 7 percent of all property taxes. However, the impact varies greatly across municipalities and states.[52]

As the title of Brody's edited volume, *Property-Tax Exemption for Charities: Mapping the Battlefield,* suggests, the exemption has been highly contentious for a number of years.[53] The battle erupted most prominently in Pennsylvania, where a 1985 Supreme Court decision narrowed considerably the criteria under which nonprofit organizations could claim exemption from local property taxes as "purely public" charities. This emboldened local property tax assessors to threaten nonprofit organizations with loss of property tax exemptions unless they made "payments in lieu of taxes" (PILOTs). In the late 1980s and early 1990s, therefore, the scope and scale of these PILOT programs expanded considerably in Pennsylvania, attracting increased attention from other jurisdictions and from the nonprofit sector. The initial challenge receded as nonprofit groups turned up the political heat and local politicians came to understand the limited revenue likely to come from this source so that only a small fraction (seven of fifty-one) of the largest cities in the nation were soliciting payments in lieu of taxes from nonprofit organizations as of the late 1990s, and most of these focused only on certain subsets of the sector.[54] Moreover, recent research suggests that nonprofit property holdings have a significant positive impact on the surrounding community.[55]

However, as state and local fiscal circumstances continue to deteriorate, pressures have mounted to reconsider the exemptions that nonprofit organizations receive from these various taxes, especially given the growing scale of nonprofit operations and the increasing nonprofit reliance on commercial fees and charges.[56] While hospitals have come under particularly close scrutiny, the impact is being felt also by other charities relying extensively on fee income.[57] Thus in *Under the Rainbow Child Care Center, Inc.* v. *County of Goodhue* the Minnesota Supreme Court held in December 2007 that nonprofits must provide goods or services free or at considerably reduced rates as a substantial part of their operations in order to meet the criteria for property tax exemption as a "purely public charity" under Minnesota law.[58]

What is more, jurisdictions have found inventive ways to skirt the nonprofit resistance to property taxes and payments in lieu of these taxes by shifting the funding of more community services from general purposes taxes to user fees. Reflecting this, a recent survey by the Johns Hopkins Listening Post Project finds that 63 percent of a sample of mostly midsized and large nonprofits in the human service, community development, and arts fields were paying some kind of user fee, field-specific tax, or PILOT as of the latter part of 2010, with additional pressures from budget-challenged state and local governments in the offing.[59]

The Regulatory Arena

The third arena of nonprofit-government interaction has also witnessed a considerable squeezing of nonprofit freedom of action in recent years. This is somewhat ironic given the overall deregulation climate in national policy. While substantial parts of the business sector have been deregulated, nonprofits have confronted an increase in regulation in certain crucial spheres. Three of these spheres deserve particular mention: charitable fundraising, advocacy, and nonprofit management practices.

REGULATION OF FUNDRAISING. Nonprofit access to charitable donations, one of the distinctive features of the nonprofit sector, has been under "a barrage" for some time.[60] In response to concerns about charitable fundraising practices that surfaced in the wake of 9/11, all but four states now have some form of regulation of charitable solicitations, with some local jurisdictions having their own ordinances. These regulations usually cover the use of professional fundraisers; commercial co-ventures; securing permits, licenses, or registrations for fundraising activities; and financial reporting.[61] These regulations vary considerably from state to state, making it necessary for any charity operating in more than one state to alter its mode of operation in each state. Thus for example any organization seeking charitable donations or managing charitable trusts in the state must be registered with the attorney general's office in Illinois. Next door, in Indiana, only professional fundraisers or others raising funds on behalf of another organization need to register. Moreover, the growing use of the Internet and web portals to solicit and receive charitable donations requires charities to track the state location of donors to determine whether the charity needs to register in particular states.[62]

There are also more aggressive efforts to regulate the ways in which nonprofits raise funds. Indiana nonprofits, for example, may only use their own volunteers or staff, not contractors, to seek donations via telemarketing techniques from the roughly one-third of the state's households that have signed up for a no-calls service through the attorney general's office. Other states have also imposed restrictions on the use of telemarketing, sometimes including and sometimes excluding charitable solicitations.

Federal regulation of fundraising has also been tightened, especially under the Pension Protection Act of 2006, and now includes requirements that charitable gifts be substantiated in writing, that noncash contributions (such as used cars, clothing, and household goods) be in "good condition" to be deductible, and that the organization's application for exempt status and its annual financial information returns be available to the general public upon request.[63] In addition, a number of court cases have clarified or complicated applicable rules at both the federal and state levels. While these regulatory provisions potentially serve the salutary purpose of buttressing public confidence in nonprofit institutions, they have nevertheless increased substantially the legal and regulatory burdens for these organizations.

REGULATION OF ADVOCACY. Nonprofit organizations have also been under increased regulatory pressures with regard to their policy advocacy activities, another crucial function of the nonprofit sector. Restriction of nonprofit "lobbying" has long been a part of the basic federal tax exemption law, which bars charitable nonprofit organizations (501(c)(3) organizations) from lobbying as a "substantial part" of their activities. However, lobbying in the tax law is defined rather narrowly to mean directly or indirectly attempting to influence the passage of particular pieces of legislation or administrative actions. Beginning in the early 1980s, however, efforts have been made to broaden this restriction. The first of these was an Office of Management and Budget circular (A-122) on nonprofit cost-accounting developed by the Reagan administration in 1982–83 and ultimately promulgated in 1984. This circular essentially prohibits nonprofits from using federal grant dollars to support "political advocacy," a concept that embraced more than the narrower concept of lobbying.[64] A subsequent

OMB circular (A-133), issued in 1990, tightened the audit process nonprofits must use in order to ensure that this prohibition is enforced.

The Lobbying Disclosure Act of 1995 imposed additional restrictions on nonprofit organizations in the political advocacy arena. Most seriously, the act prohibits nonprofit 501(c)(4) organizations—the ones specifically permitted to engage in lobbying—from engaging in such activity if they receive any federal grants, loans, or awards. In addition, the act requires nonprofit organizations that employ at least one person who spends at least 20 percent of his or her time on lobbying activities to register with the secretary of the Senate and the clerk of the House of Representatives. There have also been repeated, but so far unsuccessful, efforts to put further restrictions on nonprofit policy advocacy activity by restricting nonprofits that receive federal funds from a wide range of policy advocacy activities. Some of these proposals would define political advocacy so broadly as to prevent nonprofits from engaging in litigation and from participating in administrative agency proceedings, activities that have long been considered fundamental forms of expression in a free society.

Nonprofits have also been impacted by repeated efforts to regulate campaign financing. Thus the Bipartisan Campaign Reform Act of 2002, which aims to limit the role of soft-money contributions to political parties and candidates, also banned the use of money to pay for electioneering communications by corporations, labor unions, and eventually also incorporated nonprofit issue organizations. On the other hand, the Federal Election Commission's regulatory restrictions on 527 political groups in 2004 helped spur expanded use of 501(c)(4) social welfare organizations for election purposes. Some of these, the so-called "qualified nonprofit corporations" that fit criteria established by the FEC in connection with the 1986 *Massachusetts Citizens for Life* Supreme Court case, are exempt from the ban on corporate spending for express advocacy and also are not required to report any contributions used for express advocacy unless the donors have specifically earmarked funds for this purpose.[65]

The Honest Leadership and Open Government Act of 2007, passed in the wake of the Jack Abramoff lobbying scandal, now requires the clerk of the House of Representatives to make lobbying filings available on the Internet (and increased penalties for failure to comply). As a result, it is now much easier for friend and foe alike to track the political activities of nonprofit institutions and associations that meet the filing requirements. During the 2008 presidential election, the Internal Revenue Service also gave special attention to the political advocacy of congregations.

Regulations at the state level have weakened politically active membership organizations, for example, by limiting the collective bargaining rights of public employees through a raft of so-called paycheck protection measures. The latter, now enacted in several states, require nonprofit organizations to obtain permission from their members before using membership dues, or payroll deductions, for "political activities," a term that is defined quite broadly. Though aimed specifically at labor unions, such provisions impact many other types of nonprofit organizations as well, including workplace solicitation organizations such as the United Way.[66] These developments have put a chill on at least some nonprofit engagement in policy deliberations and have left nonprofits that choose to engage in policy advocacy with considerably expanded paperwork burdens.[67] One consequence has been to shift nonprofit advocacy activities from individual agencies to specialized nonprofit coalitions or advocacy consortia, which can distance the advocacy work from the hands-on activity and client contact of operating organizations. The restrictions are all the more troubling for nonprofits, moreover, in view of the recent Supreme Court ruling in *Citizens United* v. *Federal Election Commission,* which removed all restrictions on corporate financing of election campaigns.[68]

REGULATION OF MANAGEMENT. The Enron and WorldCom financial scandals that began to unravel in 2001 have also had significant implications for the nonprofit sector. Not only did some key management requirements in the Sarbanes-Oxley Act of 2002, passed in response to the scandals, apply to large nonprofits, but the events brought renewed attention to transparency and accountability by all types of institutions.[69] The most prominent of these developments were the U.S. Senate Finance Committee hearings on charities and charitable giving ("Charity Oversight and Reform: Keeping Bad Things from Happening to Good Charities") that began in June 2004. Chaired by Senator Chuck Grassley of Iowa, the committee heard testimony and received written comments from a long list of prominent philanthropic institutions and others, along with numerous accounts of self-dealings and management practices, which if not actually illegal were at least of questionable ethics.

Generally speaking, testimony from leading nonprofit organizations paints a picture of general probity in the operation of the nation's major nonprofit institutions, and this perspective finds support in a survey of nonprofit management and accountability practices conducted by the Johns Hopkins Listening Post Project. According to this survey, the vast majority of nonprofit human service, arts, and community development organizations already had in place the governance practices and ethical standards being recommended by the Senate Committee. Nevertheless, in response to the hearings and to prevent new draconian regulations (at one point the Senate Finance Hearing contemplated imposing "best practices" on nonprofits, such as limiting the size of boards to no more than fifteen members), Independent Sector, the national umbrella group representing the nation's nonprofit organizations, convened a nonprofit panel in October 2004 and, with the encouragement of the Senate Finance Committee, set out to develop a series of recommendations for Congress to improve the oversight and governance of charitable organizations. The panel issued its preliminary report in June 2005 (*Strengthening Transparency, Governance, and Accountability of Charitable Organizations*), a supplementary report in April 2006, and a final report in October 2007 (*Principles for Good Governance and Ethical Practice: A Guide for Charities and Foundations*).[70]

Many of the issues identified in the Senate Finance Committee hearings and in the reports by the nonprofit panel were incorporated into the Pension Protection Act of 2006, which also authorized the IRS to revise form 990, the financial information report that exempt organizations with annual revenues in excess of $25,000 (limit increased to $50,000 in fiscal year 2010) are required to file, and also required all other exempt entities to annually report to the IRS or risk losing their tax-exempt status.[71] The new form 990, the first major revision to the form in years, was introduced in draft form in June 2007. The IRS allowed only six months for public comment but nevertheless received more than 700 letters and 3,000 pages of comments. The final revisions were formally introduced in April 2008, with final instructions published in December 2008. The form now requires reporting nonprofits to indicate whether they have specific management practices in place. These practices are not required, and the IRS's own advisory group has urged caution in how they are presented, but these are now clearly expected practices.[72]

The revisions to form 990 also reflect other requirements included in the USA Patriot Act of 2001 and Executive Order 13224 (signed on September 23, 2001) in response to the terrorist attacks on September 11, 2001. The act's many provisions expand federal authority for surveillance, enforcement of old and new immigration laws, and monitoring of financial activities. In particular, the act criminalizes financial contributions to suspected foreign terrorist organizations and effectively requires foundations and international aid and relief organizations to closely monitor the published lists of suspected terrorist organizations to make sure they are not inadvertently supporting organizations and individuals suspected of terrorist connections. In December 2005 the U.S. Treasury released a draft of "voluntary best practices" (finalized in October 2006), which outlines specific management practices that charities were advised to follow in order to adhere to the act. The revised form 990 now also includes a supplementary form (schedule F) that all nonprofits must complete if they maintain an office, employees, or agents outside of the United States, with details (name, type of entity, purpose, amount, manner of disbursement, method of evaluation of noncash assistance) on all grants and other assistance to organizations/entities and individuals outside of the United States. They must also report if they have an interest in, or signature or other authority over, any foreign financial accounts.[73]

Although nonprofit reactions have been remarkably muted in responding to the Patriot Act and its fairly significant implications for civil rights, the sector has otherwise responded vigorously to most of these new regulatory challenges to fundraising, advocacy, and management. Indeed, there is now a well-developed industry that tracks the proposals and mobilizes the sector to respond. However, only the largest and most well-connected nonprofits are likely to be able to keep abreast of developments at the federal, state, and local levels, leaving the more volunteer-driven nonprofits to fend for themselves.

The Policy Arena

These regulatory developments have naturally complicated nonprofit involvement in the policy arena, but they are hardly the only source of such complication. The shift in forms of government action detailed earlier has also played a part. As government has come to use a broader range of tools to carry out its mandates, especially tools that involve less direct action and more complex network structures, it becomes more difficult to track who is involved or how to assess the overall outcomes of policy initiatives.

For nonprofits this has necessitated mastering a much wider array of forms of interaction with the public sector and often learning how to interact with a much wider array of government agencies. Thus nonprofit child welfare organizations accustomed to dealing with social service grant programs must now find their way through the complex intricacies of the health field to tap funding that is now available only through Medicaid. Indeed, these new forms of public action have produced what Salamon in a recent volume terms the "new governance," which is characterized by complex collaborations among a variety of public and private actors and requires new activation, orchestration, and modulation skills on the part of both government and its for-profit and nonprofit partners.[74] Public administration theory and practice and nonprofit management training are only now beginning to catch up with these developments, and there are still relatively few guidelines for how to carry out public policy initiatives under these new structures and no well-established principles for analyzing their operations.

Nonprofits have become increasingly immersed in policy issues well beyond those that affect the organizations directly, moreover.[75] These debates now occur across a much broader array of policy arenas than previously; indeed, nonprofits appear to be playing a central role in many of the hot political issues of our day. They serve to mobilize citizens and shape political action on a full range of social issues, such as civil rights, abortion, gun control, death penalty, gay/lesbian marriage, affirmative action, immigration reform, privacy/safety, and English as a second language. But they are now also active in arenas more closely related to science and health that have also gained prominence in recent years: antismoking policies, genetically modified food, stem cell research, climate change, and alternative energy sources. As detailed in chapter 10 of this volume, these debates have also drawn in more diverse participants than ever before, including not only traditional corporate and public-interest issue groups but also grassroots organizations and their industry-financed counterparts (the so-called Astroturf organizations). It is an open question whether the result is a more "civil" society or a more vocal and strident one.

These observations highlight two somewhat contradictory developments about the role of nonprofits in civic activism. On the one hand, nonprofits have played a highly visible role in responding to major disasters that overwhelmed government (such as the 9/11 terror attacks and Hurricanes Katrina and Wilma) by mobilizing volunteers and charitable contributions. They have also played an active role, for better or worse, in shaping increasingly confrontational policy debates. However, in other respects, the decade of the 2000s revealed a remarkable lack of civic activism. For example, the United States has waged a highly unpopular war, yet there has been precious little popular protest. Similarly, while popular protests have arisen in much of Western Europe over government austerity measures, in the United State voices on the left were surprisingly silent until the Occupy Wall Street movement belatedly arose while the Tea Party movement emerged on the right with the aid of substantial corporate contributions pushing for cuts in government spending, more generous tax breaks for the wealthy, and curtailment of collective bargaining rights for public employees.

The nonprofit sector's ability to play an effective policy advocacy role has been hindered in recent years by the significant devolution of policymaking authority to state and local government triggered by the 1996 welfare reform legislation and earlier block grant legislation. The resulting decentralized decisionmaking has made the task of responding to policy changes more difficult for nonprofits involved in service provision—and more demanding.[76] While the rise of state-level nonprofit associations detailed in Alan Abramson's analysis of the evolving nonprofit infrastructure (chapter 11, this volume) doubtless helps nonprofits deal with this fragmented policy playing field, the need for coalitions, policy analysis capability, and lobbying to influence the growing array of decision points has grown far beyond what these infrastructure organizations can offer. The recent passage of a major health reform law further complicates the situation by vesting so many of the key decisions at the state level. Nonprofits are therefore having to run harder to stay in the same place, and this at a time of growing restrictions, or at least scrutiny, not only of their advocacy activities but also of their fundraising and management practices and the significant loosening of restrictions on the campaign contribution activities of business corporations.

Conclusion: Toward a New Government-Nonprofit Compact

The past thirty years have thus been a time of enormous tension for the nonprofit sector in its pivotal relations with government. After a period of rapidly expanding cooperation, nonprofits have had to deal with a significant retrenchment in public funding, a widespread diversification of the forms of public assistance, a shift from producer-side to consumer-side subsidies, the loss of their "preferred-provider" status in many government programs, increased demands for efficiency, less favorable tax regimes, increased regulatory pressures, and a far more fragmented policy arena.

From the evidence at hand, it appears that nonprofits have responded effectively to these challenges but at some cost to their basic character and operations, as suggested in the overview chapter in this volume. Among other things, this set of changes has contributed to the increased competition nonprofits are experiencing from for-profit providers, a growing marketization and commercialization of the sector, the fragmentation of decision points at which nonprofits must aim to influence the policy environment, increased scrutiny and regulation of some crucial nonprofit functions, and a squeezing of important mission-critical functions.

The picture of government-nonprofit relations that has emerged over the past thirty years is thus a mixed one. Certain components of the nonprofit sector—primarily those providing public-benefit services—have increased in size and become more deeply engaged with government. However, the mechanisms by which these relationships are carried out have diversified beyond the grants and contracts of the 1960s and are now increasingly marketlike in structure. Nonprofits that wish to tap the significant revenues that government is pouring into priority service fields must therefore also become more marketlike themselves in order to compete for the clients and patrons into whose hands the allocation of funding among providers has now been placed in many government programs. Meanwhile, under severe fiscal pressures, states and localities have narrowed the scale of administrative costs they are willing to allow, have ratcheted down reimbursement rates, and in many cases have delayed payment.

Nonprofits therefore find themselves in a no-win situation. On the one hand, they are being pressured by both public and private funders to become more marketlike in their operations in order to compete more effectively with for-profit firms enticed into traditional nonprofit markets by new forms of government payment. On the other hand, to the extent that they succumb to these pressures, nonprofits are finding themselves accused by public officials and the press of departing from their charitable missions and becoming just another claimant on government resources, thereby surrendering their claim to tax-exempt status and access to tax-deductible contributions.

To escape this dilemma, a new paradigm is needed to guide government-nonprofit relations in the years ahead, one that treats the collaboration between government and the nonprofit sector not as a regrettable necessity but as a highly positive feature of a modern, pluralistic society that encourages active engagement by all sectors in the resolution of societal problems. Central to such a new paradigm is a clearer recognition by government at all levels of its stake in the effective operation of the nonprofit sector in view of the crucial role nonprofits still play in the delivery of publicly financed services and the important contribution they make in keeping American democracy vital and responsive. In a sense, government needs to take the same nurturing approach to the nonprofit sector that it takes to the defense industry.[77] This would require, among other things, a deliberate governmental investment in improving the capacity of nonprofit sector organizations, efforts to ensure a level playing field for nonprofits in accessing the capital needed to remain competitive with for-profit firms, and greater recognition in government reimbursement rates of the costs of maintaining the mission-critical advocacy and charity care functions that make nonprofits distinctive. In turn, nonprofits need to accommodate the public sector's growing need to demonstrate effective performance in its programs.

Other countries recognize the need for such a new approach to government-nonprofit relations and have forged compacts to systematize the new collaborative philosophy.[78] Although no such official effort has been undertaken in the United States, one group of nonprofit leaders issued a declaration in early 2009 calling for just such a new partnership to address the challenges facing this country. Ultimately endorsed by close to 500 nonprofit leaders representing at least 100,000 nonprofit organizations across the country, this "Forward Together" declaration proposes a significant government investment in citizen-sector capacity to innovate and perform, encouragement of new models of nonprofit finance, including a social innovation fund, to offset the disadvantage nonprofits face in generating investment capital, and the creation of a Commission on Cross-Sector Partnerships to improve government-nonprofit relations at all levels.[79]

Several of these ideas were incorporated into the Serve America Act passed by Congress early in 2010, though at relatively meager levels of support. Although a proposal for a government-nonprofit commission was originally incorporated in this act, it was ultimately pulled prior to passage, though the idea has resurfaced in a proposed bill introduced by Congresswoman Betty McCollum.[80] Meanwhile, however, many of the difficulties that have convinced nonprofit leaders that such a serious resetting of government-nonprofit relationships is needed persist and, in many respects, deepen.[81]

If the latter part of the twentieth century marked the resurgence of the market as the mechanism for addressing public problems following an era of much heavier reliance on the state, it also demonstrated that the market is no more a panacea for societal ills than is sole reliance on government. Indeed, deregulation of the housing, banking, and other financial markets played a significant role in plunging the U.S. and world economies into the deep 2007–09 recession and demonstrates the need for much closer government oversight. The twenty-first century thus could well mark a new era of realism, one that recognizes the virtues of collaboration not only between government and the nonprofit sector, but also between both of these and at least some segments of the business sector as well. The challenge before us is to confront this reality and build systems that can take advantage of what each sector has to offer without subverting what makes them distinctive. This is a significant challenge, to be sure, but one that simply must be met.

Notes

1. Thus for example nonprofit organizations pay federal income taxes on their "unrelated business income," and foundations pay an excise tax on their assets. See Bruce Hopkins, *The Law of Tax-Exempt Organizations,* 9th ed. (Hoboken, N.J.: John Wiley and Sons, 2007), pp. 15–20.

2. Waldemar Nielsen, *The Endangered Sector* (Columbia University Press, 1979), pp. 14, 47.

3. John S. Whitehead, *The Separation of College and State: Columbia, Dartmouth, Harvard, and Yale, 1776–1876* (Yale University Press, 1973), pp. 3–16.

4. Frank Fetter, "The Subsidizing of Private Charities," *American Journal of Sociology* (1901/02), p. 360.

5. Amos Warner, *American Charities: A Study in Philanthropy and Economics* (New York: Thomas Y. Crowell, 1894), p. 337.

6. For a discussion of these conflicts, see Peter Dobkin Hall, *Inventing the Nonprofit Sector* (Johns Hopkins University Press, 1992), pp. 20–36.

7. See Lester M. Salamon, "Rethinking Public Management: Third-Party Government and the Changing Forms of Public Action," *Public Policy* 29: 255–75; Lester M. Salamon, *Beyond Privatization: The Tools of Public Action* (Washington: Urban Institute, 1989); Lester M. Salamon, "The New Governance and the Tools of Public Action," in *The Tools of Government: A Guide to the New Governance,* edited by Lester M. Salamon (Oxford University Press, 2002).

8. Murray S. Weitzman and others, *The New Nonprofit Almanac and Desk Reference* (San Francisco: Jossey-Bass, 2002), p. 26.

9. Donald K. Price, *The Scientific Estate* (Harvard University Press, 1965); David H. Guston and Kenneth Keniston, *The Fragile Contract: University Science and the Federal Government* (MIT Press, 1994).

10. For an excellent analysis of the design of the Medicare program and its accommodation of the concerns of hospitals, see Herman Miles Somers and Anne Ramsay Somers, *Medicare and the Hospitals: Issues and Prospects* (Brookings, 1967).

11. See for example Harold W. Demone Jr. and Margaret Gibelman, eds., *Services for Sale: Purchasing Health and Human Services* (Rutgers University Press, 1989); Steven Rathgeb Smith and Michael Lipsky, *Nonprofits for Hire: The Welfare State in the Age of Contracting* (Harvard University Press, 1993).

12. Kirsten A. Grønbjerg, *Understanding Nonprofit Funding: Managing Revenues in Social Services and Community Development Organizations* (San Francisco: Jossey-Bass, 1993).

13. For further detail, see Lester M. Salamon, "Partners in Public Service: The Scope and Theory of Government-Nonprofit Relations," in *The Nonprofit Sector: A Research Handbook,* edited by Walter W. Powell (Yale University Press, 1987), pp. 99–117; Lester M. Salamon,

Partners in Public Service: Government-Nonprofit Relations in the Modern Welfare State (Johns Hopkins University Press, 1995).

14. Registered charities grew by 88 percent, from 546,000 in 1992 to more than 1 million in 2007; total revenues rose from $561 billion in 1992 to $1.1 trillion in 2005 in constant 2000 dollars, or by 96 percent, with government grants and payments increasing almost as fast (90 percent), from $170 billion to $323 billion in constant 2000 dollars. Data on the number of registered charities are from the first edition of this volume, supplemented by analysis of the Business Master File of IRS-registered tax-exempt entities available at the National Center for Charitable Statistics at the Center on Nonprofits and Philanthropy, Urban Institute. Financial data are from Kennard T. Wing, Thomas H. Pollak, and Amy Blackwood, *The Nonprofit Almanac 2008* (Washington: Urban Institute, 2008), pp. 134–37. These data likely understate the extent of government support due to the fact that the major data source used, the 990 form filed by nonprofits with the Internal Revenue Service, includes government Medicare and Medicaid payments as "program service revenue," that is, fees; this source only partially corrects for that.

15. Lester M. Salamon and Alan J. Abramson, "The Federal Budget and the Nonprofit Sector: Implications of the Contract with America," in *Capacity for Change? The Nonprofit World in the Age of Devolution,* edited by Dwight F. Burlingame and others (Center on Philanthropy, Indiana University, 1996), p. 8.

16. Discretionary programs are programs whose spending levels are set through annual appropriations from Congress. They differ from so-called entitlement programs, the spending levels of which are determined automatically by the number of eligible persons who show up seeking benefits. The Social Service Block Grant is an example of a discretionary program, whereas Medicare and Medicaid are examples of entitlement programs.

17. Elizabeth Schwinn, "Bush's Budget Plan," *Chronicle of Philanthropy,* February 27, 2007; Brennen Jensen and Suzanne Perry, "A Budget Squeeze Hits Charities: Bush's 2009 Plan Calls for Cuts in Social Services and the Arts," *Chronicle of Philanthropy,* February 21, 2008.

18. See *The Quiet Revolution: The President's Faith-Based and Community Initiative: A Seven-Year Progress Report* (White House, February 2008) as well as an overview of reactions to the report by Anne Farris and Claire Hughes, "At Finish, Bush Faith-Based Initiative Gets Mixed Reviews," paper prepared for Roundtable on Religion and Social Welfare Policy, Rockefeller Institute, November 18, 2008. More detailed analysis is available in Lisa M. Montiel and David J. Wright, *Getting a Piece of the Pie: Federal Grants to Faith-Based Social Service Organizations* (Albany: Rockefeller Institute, 2006).

19. The online catalog is available at www.gsa.gov/fdac/.

20. U.S. House of Representatives, *2000 Green Book* (Committee on Ways and Means, 2000), pp. 892–93; Teresa A. Coughlin, Leighton Ku, and John Holahan, *Medicaid since 1980: Costs, Coverage, and the Shifting Alliance between the Federal Government and the States* (Washington: Urban Institute, 1994), p. 2; U.S. Bureau of the Census, *Statistical Abstract of the United States: 2010,* table 147 (www.census.gov/compendia/statab/2011/tables/11s0147.pdf).

21. Total Medicaid spending (excluding SCHIP expansion and SCHIP) stood at $308.9 billion in 2006, up from $200.5 billion in 2000 and $73.7 billion in 1990 (www.cms.hhs.gov/NationalHealthExpendData/02_NationalHealthAccountsHistorical.asp#TopOfPage).

22. For a general discussion of these alternative tools of public action, see Lester M. Salamon, "The New Governance and the Tools of Public Action: An Introduction," in *The Tools of Government: A Guide to the New Governance,* edited by Lester M. Salamon (Oxford University Press, 2002), pp. 1–47. For a discussion of tax expenditures and loan guarantees, see Christopher Howard, "Tax Expenditures," in Salamon, *The Tools of Government,* pp. 410–44;

and Thomas H. Stanton, "Loans and Loan Guarantees," in Salamon, *The Tools of Government*, pp. 381–409.

23. Data on tax expenditures for child care are from U.S. Bureau of the Census, *Statistical Abstract of the United States 2011*, p. 322; information on the Child Care and Development Block Grant is from www.gpoaccess.gov/usbudget/fy10/pdf/appendix/hhs.pdf, p. 488.

24. For more detailed analyses of these issues, see Ira C. Lupu and Robert W. Tuttle, *The State of the Law 2008: A Cumulative Report on Legal Developments Affecting Government Partnerships with Faith-Based Organizations* (Albany: Rockefeller Institute, 2008).

25. Office of Management and Budget, "Enhancing Governmental Productivity through Competition: A New Way of Doing Business within the Government to Provide Quality Government at Least Cost," p. 15, quoted in Donald Kettl, *Shared Power: Public Governance and Private Markets* (Brookings, 1993), p. 46.

26. For a review of these issues, see Courtney Burke, James Fossett, and Thomas Gais, *Funding Faith-Based Social Services in a Time of Fiscal Pressure* (Albany: Rockefeller Institute, 2004); Lisa Montiel, *The Use of Public Funds for Delivery of Faith-Based Human Services: A Review of the Research Literature Focusing on the Public Funding of Faith-Based Organizations in the Delivery of Social Services*, 2nd ed. (Albany: Rockefeller Institute, 2003); Carol De Vita and Pho Palmer, "Church-State Partnerships: Some Reflections from Washington, D.C." (Washington: Urban Institute, September 2003); Montiel and Wright, *Getting a Piece of the Pie*.

27. Elizabeth T. Boris and others, *Human Service Nonprofits and Government Collaboration: Findings from the 2010 National Survey of Nonprofit Government Contracting and Grants* (Washington: Urban Institute, 2010), p. 13.

28. Thomas L. Gais and others, *Implementation of the Personal Responsibility Act of 1996: Commonalities, Variations, and the Challenge of Complexity* (Albany: Rockefeller Institute, 2000).

29. Peter Frumkin and Alice Andre-Clark, "When Missions, Markets, and Politics Collide: Values and Strategy in the Nonprofit Human Services," *Nonprofit and Voluntary Sector Quarterly* 29, no. 1 (2000): 141–63.

30. Sheena McConnell and others, *Privatization in Practice: Case Studies of Contracting for TANF Case Management* (New York: Mathematica, 2003); Barbara S. Romzek and Jocelyn M. Johnston, "State Social Services Contracting: Exploring the Determinants of Effective Contract Accountability," *Public Administration Review* 65, no. 4 (2005): 436–49; Kristin S. Seefeldt and others, "Nonprofits That Serve Welfare Recipients: Contractual Relations and Agency Effects" (Washington: Aspen Institute, 2001).

31. Michael Reisch and David Sommerfeld, *Assessing the Impact of Welfare Reform on Nonprofit Organizations in Southeast Michigan* (Washington: Aspen Institute, 2001); Seefeldt and others, "Nonprofits That Serve Welfare Recipients."

32. See summary in Robert B. Denhardt and Janet V. Denhardt, *Public Administration: An Action Orientation*, 6th ed. (Belmont, Calif.: Thomson Wadsworth), p. 113.

33. Sheila Suess Kennedy, "Constitutional Competence of Nonprofit Managers," paper prepared for the annual meetings of the Association for Research of Nonprofit Organizations and Voluntary Action, Miami, November 29–December 1, 2001.

34. Sheila Zedlewski, "Are Shrinking Caseloads Always a Good Thing?" Policy Brief 6, Short Takes on Welfare Policy (Washington: Urban Institute, 2002).

35. Gais and others, "Implementation of the Personal Responsibility Act of 1996," p. 16.

36. Rob Geen, "Shoring up the Child Welfare–TANF Link," Policy Brief 7, Short Takes on Welfare Policy (Washington: Urban Institute, 2002).

37. Gais and others, "Implementation of the Personal Responsibility Act of 1996."

38. Olivia Golden, "Assessing the New Federalism—Eight Years Later" (Washington: Urban Institute, 2005).

39. David Sommerfeld and Michael Reisch, "The 'Other America' after Welfare Reform: A View from the Nonprofit Sector," *Journal of Poverty* 7, nos. 1/2 (2003): 69–95; Rebecca Joyce Kissane and Richard Krebs, "Assessing Welfare Reform, over a Decade Later," *Sociology Compass,* nos. 1/2 (2007): 789–813.

40. For more detailed analyses, see Woods Bowman, *Fiscal Crisis in the States: Its Impact on Nonprofit Organizations and the People They Serve* (Washington: Aspen Institute, 2003); Thomas Gais, Courtney Burke, and Rebecca Corso, *A Divided Community: The Effects of State Fiscal Crisis on Nonprofits Providing Health and Social Assistance* (Albany: Rockefeller Institute, 2003); Courtney Burke, James Fossett, and Thomas Gais, *Funding Faith-Based Social Services in a Time of Fiscal Pressure* (Albany: Rockefeller Institute, 2004).

41. Elaine Maag and David F. Merriman, "Understanding States' Fiscal Health during and after the 2001 Recession," *State Tax Notes,* August 6, 2007.

42. National Governors Association, "State Budget Update, November 2008"; National Conference of State Legislatures, "State Budget Update: November 2010" (www.ncsl.org/documents/fiscal/november2010sbu_free.pdf); Elizabeth McNichol, Phil Oliff, and Nicholas Johnson, "Recession Continues to Batter State Budgets: State Responses Could Slow Recovery" (Washington: Center on Budget and Policy Priorities, 2010).

43. Christopher W. Hoene and Michael A. Pagano, *City Fiscal Conditions in 2010* (Washington: National League of Cities, 2010).

44. To illustrate, for a taxpayer in a 50 percent tax bracket, the out-of-pocket cost of making a gift to charity would be $0.50, since the taxpayer would have had to pay $0.50 in taxes anyway had she not made the gift. If the tax rate falls to 33 percent, the out-of-pocket cost of the gift goes up to $0.67, since the taxpayer would have had to pay only $0.33 in taxes had she not made the gift.

45. For a detailed discussion of these changes, see Alan J. Abramson, Lester M. Salamon, and C. Eugene Steuerle, "Federal Spending and Tax Policies: Their Implications for the Nonprofit Sector," in *Nonprofits and Government: Collaboration and Conflict,* 2nd ed., edited by Elizabeth T. Boris and C. Eugene Steuerle (Washington: Urban Institute, 1999), pp. 121–33.

46. Waller Margy, "Charity Tax Credits: Federal Policy and Three Leading States" (Washington: Pew Forum on Religion and Public Life, 2001); Carol J. De Vita and Eric C. Twombly, "Charitable Tax Credits: Boon or Bust for Nonprofits?" Policy Brief 16, Charting Civil Society (Washington: Urban Institute, 2004); Brennen Jensen, "Alaska Passes Law Aimed at Increasing Charitable Giving," *Chronicle of Philanthropy,* June 26, 2008.

47. The tax rate fell from 55 percent in 2001 to 45 percent in 2009 and then to zero in 2010. The amount excluded from federal estate taxes increased from $675,000 in 2001 to $3.5 million in 2009. There was no tax at all in 2010.

48. The new law provides a $5 million exemption from estate taxes beginning in 2011 and a tax rate of 35 percent on estates above that level. See Paul Sullivan, "Estate Tax Will Return Next Year, but Few Will Pay It," *New York Times,* December 17, 2010.

49. John L. Mikesell, "Sales Taxation of Nonprofit Organizations: Purchases and Sales," in *Sales Taxation: Critical Issues in Policy and Administration,* edited by William F. Fox (Westport, Conn.: Praeger, 1992), pp. 121–30.

50. John L. Mikesell, "Tax Expenditure Budgets, Budget Policy, and Tax Policy: Confusion in the States" (School of Public and Environmental Affairs, Indiana University, 2002).

51. Evelyn Brody, ed., *Property-Tax Exemption for Charities: Mapping the Battlefield* (Washington: Urban Institute, 2002); H. Woods Bowman, "Reexamining the Property Tax

Exemption," *Land Lines* 15 (2003): 3. Also see Donald A. Krueckeberg, "Free New Jersey: The Burden of Property Tax Exemptions," *New Jersey Policy Perspective,* December 2004.

52. Michael A. Pagano, "Financing Infrastructure in the 21st Century City: 'How Did I Get Stuck Holding the Bag?'" (Great Cities Institute, University of Illinois at Chicago, 2006); David Sjoquist and Rayna Stoycheva, "The Property Tax Exemption for Nonprofits," Working Paper 08-15, Andrew Young School of Policy Studies (Georgia State University, 2008); Krueckeberg, "Free New Jersey"; Harvy Lipman, "The Value of a Tax Break: Charities in the Nation's Big Cities Receive at Least $1.5 Billion a Year in Property-Tax Subsidies," *Chronicle of Philanthropy,* November 23, 2006; Harvy Lipman, "Cities Take Many Approaches to Valuing Tax-Exempt Property," *Chronicle of Philanthropy,* November 23, 2006.

53. Brody, *Property-Tax Exemption for Charities.*

54. Pamela Leland, "PILOTs: The Large-City Experience," in Brody, *Property Tax-Exemption for Charities,* pp. 202–06.

55. Wolfgang Bielefeld and others, "The Location of Nonprofit Organizations Influences Residential Housing Prices: A Study in Marion County, Indiana" (Indianapolis: Center for Urban Policy and the Environment, SPEA, IUPUI, 2006); Ingrid Gould Ellen and Ioan Voicu, "Nonprofit Housing and Neighborhood Spillovers," *Journal of Policy Analysis and Management* 25, no. 1 (2006): 31–52.

56. Robert Egger, "Next on the Board's Agenda: Fighting State Cuts," *Chronicle of Philanthropy,* June 26 2008.

57. Heather O'Donnell and Ralph Martire, "An Analysis of the Tax Exemptions Granted to Cook County Non-Profit Hospitals and the Charity Care Provided in Return" (Chicago: Center for Tax and Budget Accountability, 2006); Stephanie Strom, "Exemptions for Charities Face New Challenges," *New York Times,* May 26, 2008.

58. For a summary of the case, see Rick Cohen, "The Case of Under the Rainbow Child Care Center vs. Goodhue County," *Nonprofit Quarterly,* January 9, 2008 (www.nonprofit quarterly.org/index.php?option=com_content&view=article&id=257:the-case-of-under-the-rainbow-child-care-center-vs-goodhue-county&catid=149:rick-cohen&Itemid=99).

59. Lester M. Salamon and Stephanie Geller, "Taxing the Tax-Exempt Sector—A Growing Danger for Nonprofit Organizations," Listening Post Communiqué 21 (Center for Civil Society Studies, Johns Hopkins University, 2011).

60. Bruce Hopkins, *Starting and Managing a Nonprofit Organization: A Legal Guide,* 5th ed. (New York: John Wiley and Sons, 2008), p. 131.

61. For a summary of these regulations, see Giving USA Foundation, *Annual Survey of State Laws Regulating Charitable Solicitations, as of January 1* (Center on Philanthropy, Indiana University, 2008); Multi-State Filer Project, *Unified Registration Statement* (www.multi statefiling.org/e_tpforms.htm).

62. For more information, see the National Association of State Charity Officials, The Charleston Principles: Guidelines on Charitable Solicitations Using the Internet, March 2001 (www.nasconet.org/wp-content/uploads/2001/05/Charleston-Principles-Final.pdf).

63. Hopkins, *Starting and Managing a Nonprofit Organization,* p. 139.

64. Harmon, Curran, and Spielberg, "Regulation of Advocacy Activities for Nonprofits That Receive Federal Grants" (Washington: Alliance for Justice).

65. Peggy Gavin and Deanna Gelak, "Lobbying Disclosure Databases: A User's Guide," *Online* 32, no. 5 (2008): 34–38; "Fast Start for Soft Money Groups in 2008 Election: 527s Adapt to New Rules, 501(c)(4)s on the Upswing" (Washington: Campaign Finance Institute, 2008).

66. OMB Watch, "Paycheck Protection Proposals in Congress and the States: Varying Impacts on Charities" (Washington)(www.ombwatch.org/las/1998/paypro.html); OMB

Watch, "State Charity Regulation Proposals Listed" (Washington) (www.ombwatch.org. article/artuckeorubt/2861/1.

67. Michael B. Trister, and Holly B. Schadler, "Bipartisan Campaign Reform Act of 2002: Provisions Affecting Nonprofit Advocacy Organizations" (Washington: Alliance for Justice, 2002) (www.afj.org/bcrabriefingfinal.html); National Council of Nonprofits, "State Nonprofit Policy Updates," *Nonprofit Policy News,* November 2008 (www.councilofnonprofits. org/news/nonprofit-policy-news-archive/nonprofit-policy-news-november-2008.

68. Adam Liptak, "Justices, 5-4, Reject Corporate Spending Limit," *New York Times,* January 21, 2010.

69. Provisions in the Sarbanes-Oxley law that applied to some nonprofits included sections related to insider transactions and conflicts of interests, independent and competent audit committees, the responsibility of auditors, certified financial statements, disclosure, whistle-blower protection, and document destruction. Nonprofits were also affected by a series of new restrictions on charitable deductions written into the Pension Protection Act of 2006. These included an increase in excise taxes and penalties for foundations, limits on deductions for façade easements, recapture of tax benefits for contributions not used for exempt use, limits on deductibility of clothing and household items donated, and substantiation of donations regardless of amount. For further detail, see Independent Sector, "Analysis of Charitable Reforms and Incentives in the Pension Protection Act of 2006" (Public Law 109-280) (2007).

70. For information about the panel and its efforts, see www.nonprofitpanel.org.

71. As of June 30, 2010, some 293,000 registered exempt organizations had failed for three consecutive years to file form 990-N, which is required of organizations with revenue of less than $25,000; another 28,000 had failed to submit financial information on form 990 for a similar period. See Amy Blackwood and Katie L. Roeger, "Here Today, Gone Tomorrow: A Look at Organizations That May Have Their Tax-Exempt Status Revoked" (Washington: Urban Institute, 2010). In June 2011 the IRS announced that 275,000 nonprofits had actually lost their exempt status (the count now stands at 380,000). For more information, see Kirsten A. Grønbjerg, Kellie McGiverin-Bohan, Kristen Dmytryk, and Jason Simons, *IRS Exempt Status Initiative: Indiana Nonprofits and Compliance with the Pension Protection Act of 2006* (Bloomington: School of Public and Environmental Affairs, University of Indiana, 2011) (www.indiana.edu/~nonprof/results/database/IRSRevocation.html).

72. IRS form 990 now requires tax-exempt entities to indicate whether the organization made any significant changes to its organizational documents since the prior form 990 or became aware during the year of a material diversion of the organization's assets; contemporaneously document meetings held or written actions undertaken during the year by the governing body and each committee with authority to act on behalf of the governing body; provide a copy of form 990 to the organization's governing body before it is filed and describe the procedures, if any, used to review the form; have a written conflict-of-interest policy; have their officers, directors or trustees, and key employees disclose on an annual basis interests that could give rise to conflicts; have a written whistle-blower policy and a written document retention and destruction policy; have a process for determining compensation of key executive staff that includes review and approval by independent persons, comparability data, and contemporaneous substantiation of the deliberation and decision and describes the process; and explain whether and how the organization makes its governing documents, conflict-of-interest policy, and financial statements available to the public. For more information, see Boggle, *The Pension Protection Act of 2006;* Grant Williams, "IRS Urged to Use Caution in Stomping out Wrongdoing by Charity Boards," *Chronicle of Philanthropy,* June 13, 2008;

Advisory Committee on Tax-Exempt and Government Entities, *Report of Recommendations* (Washington: 2008).

73. See Christine Aube, "The Patriot Act and the Nonprofit Sector: Charitable Organizations after 9/11" (Washington: Philanthropic Research, 2006) (www. guidestar.org/news/features/patriot_act.jsp#2). For the list of suspected terrorist entities, see www.ustreas.gov/offices/enforcement/ofac/programs/terror/terror.pdf. For the U.S. Department of the Treasury's "Updated Anti-Terrorism Guidelines: Voluntary Best Practices for U.S.-Based Charities," see www.treas.gov/offices/enforcement/key-issues/protecting/charities-intro.shtml.

74. Salamon, "The New Governance and the Tools of Public Action: An Introduction," pp. 1–47.

75. See for example Jeffrey Berry, *The New Liberalism: The Rising Power of Citizens Groups* (Brookings, 1999); Elizabeth J. Reid, *Structuring the Inquiry into Advocacy*, vol. 1, *Nonprofit Advocacy and the Policy Process: A Seminar Series* (Washington: Urban Institute, 2000).

76. See, for example, Gais and others, "Implementation of the Personal Responsibility Act of 1996"; Thomas L. Gais and B. Kent Weaver, "State Policy Choices under Welfare Reform," Policy Brief 21, Welfare Reform and Beyond (Brookings, 2002); Sheila R. Zedlewski, Pamela Holcomb, and Amy-Ellen Duke, "The Story of 13 States: Assessing the New Federalism" (Washington: Urban Institute, 1998).

77. See for example Joe Nocera, "From Pentagon, a Buy Rating on Contractors," *New York Times,* February 12, 2011, p. B1 (www.nytimes.com/2011/02/12/business/12nocera.html).

78. See for example J. Casey and others, "Regulating Government–Community Sector Relations—International Experience with Compacts," *Voluntary Sector Review* 1, no. 1 (2010): 59–79; Commission on the Compact, *Compact Relations between the Government and the Voluntary and Community Sector in England* (www.Thecompact.org.uk/shared_asp_files/GFSR.asp?NodeID=100318).

79. See www.ccss.jhu.edu/forward/ForwardTogetherDeclaration.pdf.

80. A Bill to Strengthen the Partnership between Nonprofit Organizations and the Federal Government, and for Other Purposes, H.R. 5533, 111 Cong. 2 sess. (2011).

81. See, for example, Boris and others, *Human Service Nonprofits and Government Collaboration.*

16

Accountability in the Nonprofit Sector

KEVIN P. KEARNS

A t the time of this writing, the spotlight of media scrutiny was not flattering to several nonprofit organizations in this author's home city. Headlines in local newspapers blared out various misdeeds and lackluster performance by nonprofit organizations including embezzlement by the executive director of the funds of a small organization that provides household goods and toys to needy families, spending on lavish entertainment and executive perks by a large nonprofit college loan organization, the inappropriate awarding of a college degree by a prestigious private university, and debates about what constitutes adequate performance by a nonprofit health care giant.[1] In addition, both the mayor and the county executive waged a war of words in the local newspapers, asserting that large, land-owning nonprofit organizations have a moral obligation to do more than is currently the case to help pay for government services, even though they are not technically liable for property taxes.

As these stories indicate, nonprofit accountability is very much in the news. But it turns out that accountability is a far more complex topic than is often assumed, embracing compliance with laws and regulations, ethical behavior of professional staff, vigilant and transparent governance, the exercise of prudence and good judgment in spending, and appraisals of organizational performance by a variety of stakeholders, some of whom cannot even agree on what "good" performance entails.

In this chapter, taking a broad view of the elusive subject of nonprofit accountability, I examine three major questions:

1. What does it mean for nonprofits to be accountable and what are the most important types of accountability facing nonprofits? There will always be vigorous debate on this issue, but this chapter focuses on three types of accountability: legal accountability, financial accountability, and performance accountability.

2. How do multiple and conflicting expectations of the nonprofit sector create tensions with respect to the way accountability is defined and measured? The four impulses introduced by Lester Salamon in chapter 1 are quite useful in dissecting these tensions.

3. Can the quality of the public discourse on nonprofit accountability be improved? This chapter concludes with some thoughts on how to frame the public discourse on nonprofit accountability in a more constructive way.

Dimensions of Accountability

The academic literature on accountability in the nonprofit sector is relatively recent.[2] Yet it benefits from a much older and extensive literature from other fields such as business, social work, political philosophy, and especially public administration.[3] This literature provides a useful starting point, emphasizing three aspects of accountability. First, nonprofits must account to various oversight bodies for their compliance with legal requirements. Second, nonprofits must account to donors and various funding organizations for their use of financial resources. Third, nonprofits must account to many stakeholders for their performance in meeting social needs and wants, and this often places them in the difficult position of responding to implicit as well as explicit standards of performance.

Legal Accountability

A legal approach to accountability focuses on the imperative for a nonprofit organization to answer for—literally, give an *account* of—its compliance with rules, laws, regulations, procedures, or other codified standards of performance. Jay Shafritz, for example, defines accountability as "the extent to which one must answer to a higher authority—legal or organizational—for one's actions in society at large or within one's organization."[4]

If we embrace this definition, the following ingredients must be in place if people and organizations are to give an account of their performance in a literal sense:

—There must be a rule, law, regulation, internally sanctioned procedure, or organizational policy that is accepted by all stakeholders as a valid and legitimate standard of performance.

—There must be some type of overseeing authority that is recognized by all stakeholders as legitimate and qualified to judge compliance or performance relative to the standard.

—The oversight body must itself have sufficient internal capacity, including resources and management expertise, to effectively and fairly monitor compliance.

—All stakeholders must embrace the oversight system that accurately tracks compliance or performance relative to the standard as well as reporting procedures that capture the relevant information and convey it in a timely manner to the overseeing authority.

—There should be appropriate sanctions for noncompliance and rewards for compliance.

—Ideally, there should be a feedback loop that gives organizations the opportunity to learn from their mistakes and to improve their future performance.

These ingredients of a fully functioning system of legal accountability appear fairly straightforward, but upon close inspection it is clear that having all of them in place at any given time is a rather tall order. Even under the best of circumstances, some of the elements may be present while others are incomplete or absent altogether. For instance, no one disputes that the Internal Revenue Service has the legitimate authority to oversee nonprofit organizations and to enforce various federal regulations related to their exemption from federal corporate income tax. It has been well documented, however, that the IRS lacks the resources and management capacity to effectively perform its oversight role.[5] Therefore, the media and some self-appointed watchdog organizations have sprung up to fill the gap created by the meager enforcement resources of the IRS. But these self-appointed watchdogs are not necessarily recognized as legitimate by important stakeholders.

It is beyond the scope of this chapter to provide a technically detailed discussion of the growing array of legal and financial standards to which nonprofits are held accountable by various federal, state, and local oversight agencies.[6] Instead, I will focus on just a few legal issues that have strategic importance to nonprofit organizations.

CORPORATE STATUS AND STRUCTURE. The leaders of a nonprofit organization must decide at the outset whether or not they wish to incorporate their enterprise as a charitable nonprofit organization in the state in which they are domiciled. Most, but not all, nonprofit organizations choose to formally incorporate rather than operate as an unincorporated entity. This is because formal recognition as a corporation by the appropriate government oversight body brings with it benefits beyond the tax exemption itself, which more than compensate for the many obligations and responsibilities that come with governmental oversight. For example, a corporation is a distinct legal entity that can provide important legal and financial protections for the staff and board. Moreover, formal recognition as a corporation sends a powerful message to potential supporters who want assurances that the mission of the organization will survive after the personal involvement of its founders has ended.

If the founders of the organization choose the route of formal incorporation, they will likely seek recognition as a tax-exempt corporation from the appropriate tax regulator at the state level and the Internal Revenue Service at the federal level. Section 501(c)(3) of the Internal Revenue Code, and corresponding provisions in state laws, delineate broad charitable purposes deserving of preferential tax treatment, typically involving religious, charitable, scientific, or educational purposes. Although 501(c)(3) organizations are the primary focus of this and most books on the nonprofit sector, there are many other sections of the federal tax code that allow for some type of special tax treatment by the federal government, including certain types of social and recreational clubs, trade and business associations, labor unions, and advocacy organizations.[7]

GOVERNANCE. An important distinction between nonprofit and for-profit corporations relates to the legal obligations of the governing board. The governing board of a for-profit corporation is ultimately accountable to the owners or shareholders of the firm. On the other hand, the board of a nonprofit is accountable to the general public, presumed to be the surrogate "owners." Nonprofit board members are legally bound to fulfill three types of obligations:

1. *Duty of obedience.* Board members must make decisions that are consistent with and help to promote the mission of the organization. Members of a nonprofit governing board serve as stewards or protectors of the organization's mission. The board is ultimately responsible for ensuring that the mission is pursued in accordance with applicable federal, state, and local laws.

2. *Duty of care.* Board members must exercise reasonable care by educating themselves regarding how best the organization can meet its mission, actively participating in decisions, and showing good faith when making decisions on behalf of the organization. Board members need not be experts on all topics related to the organization, but in the event of a controversy, they must be able to prove that they have exercised reasonable prudence in fulfilling their duties.

3. *Duty of loyalty.* Nonprofit board members must put the interests of the organization above their own interests when making decisions that affect the organization. If placed in a position where there is a potential conflict between their personal interests and those of the organization, they must remove themselves from the decision or, when the conflict is irreconcilable, resign their position on the governing board.

These legal standards of nonprofit governance seem unambiguous, yet one can envision circumstances where board members might feel torn between their accountability to the general public, or to other constituencies, and their duty to the organization itself. This tension is especially problematic for board members who are elected or politically appointed to the position and therefore may feel obligated to represent the interests of a certain "constituency" as well as the interests of the organization as a whole. Board members of an advocacy organization might be torn between their passions for civic activism ("the cause") versus the cold realities of keeping the organization on solid financial ground ("the money").[8]

There is strong evidence suggesting that most nonprofit governing boards are aware of and are performing their legal duties related to stewardship of the mission and of the key resources of the organization.[9] But powerful external stakeholders, including the Senate Finance Committee, have suggested that nonprofit governing boards should do more—they should be more involved in establishing basic organizational and management policies, setting program objectives, and approving compensation for all management positions, and they should exercise closer oversight of organizational finances.[10] The available research suggests that governing boards are far less involved in these types of strategic governance activities than in the basic legal oversight activities.[11]

The tension with respect to governance and accountability involves three groups of stakeholders with different expectations. Oversight organizations want governing boards to be relatively more involved in management functions in order to avert some of the high-profile scandals that have plagued both the nonprofit and for-profit sectors. Nonprofit managers, on the other hand, are wary of more board involvement in their functions. They have concerns about the ability of governing boards to be competently engaged in activities such as setting program objectives.[12] Board members themselves may feel caught in the middle between these two sets of expectations. On the one hand, they are increasingly aware of their obligations and even the legal risks that accompany their volunteer activity. On the other hand, they are reluctant to take on added responsibilities deemed to be the purview of management.

Some authors have tried to resolve this tension by proposing governance frameworks that draw sharp lines between "management" and "policy" functions.[13] However, most experts on governance suggest that the roles and responsibilities of managers and governing boards overlap and that the management team and the governing board must work side by side on operational issues, strategic issues, and continuous revitalization of the organization.[14] There is a growing body of empirical evidence suggesting that certain board development practices—such as careful recruitment programs, orientation sessions for new board members, and periodic evaluation of the board—lead to higher levels of board competence and better-functioning boards.[15]

COMMERCIALIZATION AND THE NONDISTRIBUTION CONSTRAINT. Most nonprofit organizations do not rely solely, nor even primarily, on charitable contributions. Instead, they derive their revenues from a variety of sources, including private donations, government grants and contracts, and fees for service.[16] Indeed, for many years, earned income has been among the fastest-growing sources of revenue, not just in commercialized nonprofits such as hospitals and private schools but also in traditionally "charitable" nonprofits such as social service agencies.[17]

Advocates of social entrepreneurship propose that nonprofits should leverage their core competencies to generate earned income while simultaneously pursuing their mission. The so-called double (or even triple) bottom line espoused by those who advocate social entrepreneurship has significantly enlarged the accountability challenge for entrepreneurial nonprofit organizations as they pursue not only social outcomes but financial (the second bottom line) and environmental (the third bottom line) outcomes as well.[18]

Some observers caution that profit making by nonprofit organizations can lead to mission drift or can stretch an organization beyond its core competencies.[19] Here, too, there is tension created by misunderstanding and divergent expectations. When it comes to light that a nonprofit organization has generated a substantial profit, either from its charitable purpose or some type of related or unrelated business enterprise, the media and the public may express surprise or even outrage. Many of us have heard friends or colleagues exclaim, "I thought nonprofit meant *no* profit!" Yet profit generation by nonprofit organizations is, in most instances, perfectly legal, provided excess revenues are reinvested in the core charitable mission of the organization and not distributed to employees or board members. It is this *nondistribution constraint* that prevents staff from benefiting unreasonably from the nonprofit's financial performance. When revenues are generated from an enterprise that is not related to the charitable purpose, then the organization is liable for Unrelated Business Income Tax (UBIT) at a rate that is comparable to what any for-profit corporation would pay on its earnings.

Again, as with the governance standards described earlier, one can easily envision nonprofit leaders being torn between competing conceptions of accountability with respect to commercialization. Balancing the charitable purpose with the commercial realities of the nonprofit sector requires constant vigilance. This is especially true in highly competitive nonprofit industries such as health care, child care, and education, where nonprofits compete for their survival not only with each other but often with for-profit firms.[20]

The economic recession that began in 2008 added fuel to debates about the accountability of commercial nonprofits, especially those that own substantial parcels of tax-exempt property in fiscally distressed communities. As states and localities felt the blow of the recession, we witnessed more intense local pressure on nonprofit organizations, particularly large nonprofits such as hospitals and universities, to provide some sort of voluntary contribution to strained governmental coffers or perhaps even to surrender their tax-exempt status.[21]

Accountability for Financial Probity

The second aspect of accountability, accounting for the acquisition and use of financial resources, would appear at first glance to be the simplest type of accountability. After all, one simply needs to account for the acquisition and use of financial resources. But in fact financial accountability is a multifaceted concept.

FINANCIAL ACCOUNTING AND EXTERNAL OVERSIGHT. Like any prudently managed enterprise, nonprofit organizations maintain various records and produce financial documents that provide tangible evidence of their financial accountability according to well-established accounting methods and processes. Financial accounting documents are used by outside stakeholders to evaluate the financial condition of the organization and its compliance with commonly accepted accounting rules and standards, such as those established by the Financial Accounting Standards Board (FASB).[22] The two essential questions are: Where did the money come from and how was it spent?

Examples of financial accounting documents that answer those questions include balance sheets, income statements, and cash-flow statements. These documents provide testimonials regarding the categorization and use of unrestricted, temporarily restricted, or permanently restricted funds and net assets. These and other methods of financial accounting are used by a variety of external stakeholders, including: donors and prospective board members who rightly want to exercise due diligence prior to making financial or personal commitments to the organization; donors and government contractors who wish to ensure that funds invested in a nonprofit organization have been properly designated, isolated, and accounted for; and nonprofit organizations themselves to prepare IRS Form 990, the financial reporting form that most nonprofits must file annually with the Internal Revenue Service. In an attempt to enhance accountability reporting, the IRS revised Form 990, requiring nonprofits to supply more information on their finances, governance, program performance, and management operations.

In cases where one nonprofit organization is acquired by another or when a nonprofit organization is converted to or purchased by a for-profit firm, financial accounting documents also are critically important in determining the net worth of the organization and thus the extent to which the general public (the surrogate owners of a nonprofit corporation) should be "compensated" for the transaction via creation of a conversion foundation or some other mechanism. This issue was especially significant in the late 1980s through the mid-1990s, when a large number of nonprofit hospitals were purchased and converted to for-profit health care firms. Many observers claimed that the nonprofit hospitals were sold under severe financial pressure and that their assets consequently were systematically undervalued, resulting in "fire sale" bargains and windfall profits for the acquiring firms.[23] State attorneys general often became mired in discussions with auditing and financial experts regarding arcane algorithms for determining the fair market value of a nonprofit hospital.

MANAGERIAL ACCOUNTING. Nonprofit organizations engage in managerial accounting when they produce financial records that are used primarily by internal managers for purposes of planning, cost analysis, pricing of services, financial control of operations, and various measures of efficiency. For example, budget documents translate the organization's long-range strategic plans and annual operating plans into financial terms. A business plan is another type of managerial accounting tool, which contains both financial and nonfinancial information about new programs or business ventures being considered by a nonprofit organization.

FINANCIAL POLICY STATEMENTS. Many nonprofit organizations maintain a variety of policy documents detailing the governing board's philosophy with respect to the management and stewardship of financial assets. For example, a formal statement of investment policies and procedures should give the board's investment objectives and priorities, the level of investment risk that the board is willing to tolerate, the performance benchmarks for the portfolio, and the designation of the person(s) responsible for monitoring investments and reporting their performance to the governing board.

Investment policies of nonprofit governing boards have come under public scrutiny after some prominent nonprofit organizations fell victim to volatile economic markets or were duped by the fraudulent promises of unscrupulous investment brokers. In late 2008 we learned that many prominent Jewish charities and other nonprofit organizations were hurt by an audacious Ponzi fraud perpetrated by investment wizard Bernie Madoff.[24] Observers may wonder, "Where was the board? How could they have made such a blunder with their investments?" Madoff is not the first investment manager to take advantage of unsuspecting nonprofits. Thirteen years earlier some very prominent nonprofit institutions were duped by another outlandish Ponzi scheme known as the

Foundation for New Era Philanthropy, which was engineered by William Bennett. Bennett promised his investors astonishingly high returns on their investments, using new accounts to pay obligations on old accounts, thereby building the credibility of the scheme.

Other financial policy statements include a risk management policy, which itemizes various types of institutional risk exposure, and an executive compensation policy, which specifies how compensation for top executives of the organization is to be determined.[25]

The tensions with respect to financial accountability are the result of varying opinions regarding what type of financial information should be maintained and to whom this information should be reported. Recent debates have focused on IRS Form 990, which nonprofit organizations must submit annually as an accountability document to the federal government. In December of 2007 the IRS published its new version of Form 990, which collects significantly more information than the earlier version of the form about executive compensation, program expenses and revenues, fundraising activities and impacts, governance, political activity, and other aspects of nonprofit operations.

Also, there is extensive debate at all levels of government, including the states, regarding the extent to which nonprofits should be required to comply with the provisions of the so-called Sarbanes-Oxley Act, which was enacted in 2002 in response to corporate accounting scandals. Currently nonprofit organizations must comply with only two provisions of the act, those pertaining to whistle-blower protection and document retention. But some policymakers are calling for more extensive application of the many provisions of this complicated oversight mechanism to nonprofits.[26]

Some self-appointed watchdog organizations, such as the Better Business Bureau's Wise Giving Alliance, have issued guidelines to help citizens and potential donors evaluate the credibility and accountability of nonprofit organizations.[27] Some of the standards of good financial management applied by organizations such as the Better Business Bureau may not be applicable to all types of nonprofit organizations. Nonetheless, media sources and other opinion leaders often cite these best standards, thereby placing great pressure on nonprofit organizations to adopt them.

There are many other standards of financial probity and ethics, far too numerous to discuss here, that apply to, or can be adapted to, nonprofit organizations. Fortunately, nonprofits have at their disposal a growing number of resources for information and best practice guides on various types of legal and financial accountability and sample policy guidelines. For example, BoardSource publishes *Nonprofit Policy Sampler,* which contains a very useful set of sample policy statements regarding compliance with legal requirements, good governance practices, financial accountability, and ethical standards of good conduct.[28]

Accountability for Performance

Accountability for legal requirements and financial probity are, as we have seen, far from simple. There are ambiguities, multiple expectations and standards, and enforcement challenges even in these relatively straightforward types of accountability. An even more challenging standard of accountability relates to nonprofit performance in mission accomplishment, program effectiveness, and meeting stakeholder expectations.

Barbara Romzek and Melvin Dubnik state that "accountability involves the means by which . . . agencies and their workers manage the diverse expectations generated within and outside the organization."[29] This definition of accountability is much broader than the legalistic or financial probity definitions introduced earlier in the chapter. It recognizes that accountability includes compliance with legal mandates or accounting for the use of financial resources. But it implies that there are other standards of accountability as well, such as responsiveness to community needs, fidelity to certain values, efficiency in the use of charitable resources, and effectiveness in mission accomplishment that may or may not be legally binding. These accountability standards come from diverse stakeholders— donors, contractors, vendors, board members, other volunteers, citizens, and employees—all of whom have implicit or explicit expectations of the nonprofits that touch their lives. The expectations originate not just from outside constituencies or formally charged overseers but also from within the organization.

The Romzek and Dubnik definition acknowledges that these expectations can and should be actively managed by nonprofit organizations and the people who work in them. This aspect of the definition is particularly insightful because it implies that nonprofit organizations should be proactive, or strategic, by attempting to influence and shape the expectations for which they are ultimately held accountable. In this sense, a major responsibility of the organization's leaders is to continuously monitor societal expectations, trace their origins and likely trajectory, and try to position their organizations strategically to respond effectively not only today but in the future.

This broader conceptualization challenges the principal-agent conception of accountability common in much current thinking, which views nonprofits as answerable to various overseers via externally imposed accountability mechanisms. Rather, it suggests a stewardship theory, according to which nonprofits take it upon themselves to define accountability expectations and adopt mechanisms to fulfill their stewardship role in society.[30] As should be evident by now, in this chapter I argue that both types of accountability are equally important.

Demonstrating accountability for performance is particularly challenging because many of the basic building blocks of a good accountability system discussed earlier in this chapter are missing or in dispute, with the following possible results:

—The performance standard applied to the nonprofit organization may be ambiguous or even unattainable.

—The oversight and enforcement body may be absent or not widely accepted as legitimate.

—The measurement and reporting systems for many aspects of nonprofit performance are likely to be imperfect.

—The level of control that the organization actually has over its performance may be limited.

—The sanctions and rewards may be only tangentially related to the organization's performance.

—In many cases regarding performance there is not a useful feedback loop that the organization can use for continuous improvement.

Complicating things further is the fact that "performance" itself has multiple meanings. Procedural performance means carrying out organizational functions in a way that is consistent with sector precepts of openness and participation. Output-oriented performance refers to the delivery or provision of a specified amount of activity or services (number of clients served, symphonies performed, trainings held, or trainees graduated). Performance in terms of outcomes achieved refers to the actual impact that the organization is having on those it serves or on society as a whole. Increasingly, the trend in performance measurement is toward outcomes, but it is far from clear that organizations have the capabilities to provide such evidence.[31]

Performance accountability has been conceptualized and monitored in the nonprofit sector in various ways. I discuss them here, progressing from most to least complex.

ACCOUNTABILITY FOR MISSION FIDELITY AND ACCOMPLISHMENT. In theory, holding nonprofit organizations accountable for accomplishment of their mission seems to be a natural activity, but in practice it is very difficult to do. Mission fidelity can be achieved by preventing mission drift (drifting off the stated mission) or mission creep (expanding the mission in an unplanned fashion). In an effort to prevent mission drift, many nonprofits have drafted and published a set of values and operating philosophies to complement their mission statement. These accompanying documents can provide a beacon of sorts to guide the organization along the path toward its mission.[32] Even with these tools, however, there is sometimes a fine line between mission growth (a consciously planned expansion of an organization's mission) and mission creep (incrementally expanding the mission without careful planning).

Mission accomplishment is even trickier to assess than mission fidelity. Many nonprofit organizations have ambitious, even unattainable, missions. For example, the mission of the Greater Pittsburgh Community Food Bank is "eliminating hunger and developing collaborative strategies to encourage self-reliance in Southwestern Pennsylvania." Unfortunately, eliminating hunger is a mission that may never be fully accomplished. There are even enormous obstacles to measuring simple progress toward that ambitious mission. Data on hunger would need to be gathered from myriad agencies, then collated and tracked over time. Issues of validity and reliability of the data, though they present some obstacles, are not as great as issues of causality, which could be intractable. If we were to observe reductions in hunger in the Pittsburgh region, how would we know that this positive outcome has been caused by actions of the Food Bank rather than the actions of many other hunger-related organizations in the region or, more likely, the cumulative effects of economic factors that combine to create better opportunities for people in need? Often mission accomplishment is expressed in terms of surrogates such as consumer satisfaction or vignettes of individual clients whose lives were impacted by the organization, not in terms of genuine metrics.

Performance monitoring techniques such as the Balanced Scorecard have been advocated as a way to track progress toward mission accomplishment.[33] Developed for use as a strategy control device in the private sector, the Balanced Scorecard combines traditional quantitative performance indicators with qualitative indicators (for instance, organizational learning and improvement) to provide organizations with a kind instrument panel, like that on a car's dashboard, that can be used for continuously monitoring progress toward mission accomplishment. It does this by breaking down the mission into a series of incremental steps embedded in a strategy "map"; each small step has a presumed causal relationship to subsequent steps toward the mission, leading to accomplishment of the mission. The strategy map represents a series of cause-effect hypotheses that the organization continuously tests and refines. As intriguing and useful as this technique may be, it is important to remember that the Balanced Scorecard is little more than a representational model of the mission, broken down into its constituent elements.[34]

The difficulty of demonstrating successful fulfillment of mission has opened nonprofits to a significant dilution of public trust in the eyes of a number of observers. For example, a number of media professionals and a few scholars have made widely publicized claims that the public is losing confidence in "the nonprofit sector" at an alarming rate.[35] Some have focused on how public confidence in the nonprofit sector was shaken following the terrorist attacks of September 11, 2001, when organizations like the American Red Cross were exposed to public criticism for their fundraising practices and their response to the crisis.[36] Others have noted, however, that such discussions must take better account of the enormous diversity of the nonprofit sector. For example, Michael O'Neill notes that citizen loss of confidence in the health care system does not mean they also have lost confidence in symphony orchestras, universities, or the Girl Scouts. Indeed, although O'Neill's evidence suggests that public confidence in the health care system as a whole has dropped, he finds no significant decline in public confidence in many other types of nonprofits, including private elementary and secondary schools, private colleges and universities, nonprofit social service agencies, and organizations engaged in the arts and humanities, advocacy, and international relations.[37]

ACCOUNTABILITY FOR PROGRAM PERFORMANCE. Many nonprofit organizations pursue their ambitious missions through a portfolio of programs and services. Demonstrating accountability for the performance of these programs is technically difficult, but it is vastly more manageable than demonstrating accomplishment of the total organization-wide mission.[38]

Foundations, local United Way affiliates, government agencies, and other funders have for many years demanded that nonprofits provide meaningful information on client outcomes, program effectiveness, and program efficiency. In some cases these funders are quite explicit about the type of outcome and impact information they demand as a condition of future support. Also, funders like the United Way generally provide technical advice and assistance to agencies as they try to comply with the program evaluation requirements. Tools such as logic models are sometimes supplied by the funder.

Foundations, on the other hand, seem to be less helpful to grantees when it comes to program evaluation. They usually offer short-term grants of one or two years and rarely provide sufficient overhead to fund rigorous evaluation of programs or even reasonably sophisticated compliance mechanisms to assure that the grant was administered effectively and efficiently. In many communities local foundations do not adequately coordinate their grant-making strategies with each other, resulting in competitive and duplicative grant making. Also, foundations have been reluctant to provide general operating support, which might be used by charities to develop greater management and administrative capacity to monitor their own performance. To be fair, many foundations are thinly staffed by generalists who must themselves manage a bewildering portfolio of grantees, requiring grant officers to speak multiple languages as they interact with nonprofit professionals. This knowledge deficit further complicates efforts to engage nonprofit leaders in meaningful dialogue on how to account for performance in program outcomes.[39] A publication from Grantmakers for Effective Organizations (GEO) laments: "Program officers don't have enough time to develop and sustain honest, open and productive relationships with their grantees. . . . The burdens grant making organizations place on their staffs have profound influence on their ability to help nonprofits succeed."[40] But nonprofits also bear responsibility for some of the failure of performance-oriented accountability systems. Lehn Benjamin found that the accountability process is complicated by a number of factors:

—Efforts by nonprofits to construct and control the performance information they give to overseers in a way that prevents probing inquiry and inspection.

—The tendency of nonprofit organizations to blame non-performance on forces beyond their control.

—Power imbalances between players that can distort the information and the manner in which it is conveyed and interpreted.

—The failure of the accountability system to generate and promote learning, correct errors, and improve performance.[41]

Further, the interaction of multiple professional perspectives—grant officers, agency leaders, clinical specialists—can produce tension with respect to program objectives and the methods used to account for program performance.

ACCOUNTABILITY FOR INDUSTRY STANDARDS. A slightly more manageable form of performance accountability occurs when an organization compares itself to its peers in the "industry" in which it operates. Typically, this is accomplished through some type of benchmarking technique, in which an organization identifies comparable organizations that share common key characteristics such as size, clientele, budget, and so on.

Virtually any type of performance might be compared with these benchmark organizations: process performance (inputs generated), output performance (efficiency), or outcome performance (community impact). Quite often, a nonprofit organization will use the organizational life-cycle in selecting benchmark organizations that are at approximately the same stage in their development. For example, start-up organizations are quite different from organizations that are in the growth stage; conversely, growing organizations face different strategic issues than mature organizations.[42]

Alternatively, an organization might choose to compare itself with industry leaders, with full knowledge that it might not compare favorably. In this approach, the organization tries to identify organizations that are recognized for their innovative practices, their superior organizational processes, or their exemplary performance. Such comparisons might be used to identify gaps in current performance as part of a strategic planning or goal-setting process. Alternatively, such a comparison might be used to make a claim for more resources that ostensibly are necessary to achieve the superior performance of the industry leaders.

Sometimes industry standards are codified in the form of accreditation requirements; this is the case for hospitals, universities, some types of child-care organizations, and many other nonprofits. These organizations are subject to periodic peer review by representatives of the accrediting organization.

UNINTENDED CONSEQUENCES OF PERFORMANCE ACCOUNTABILITY. Performance-based accountability systems carry with them some unintended consequences that are worth mentioning, if only briefly.

A major concern is whether performance-based accountability systems have resulted in a homogenized nonprofit sector in which organizations not only begin to look more and more like each other, but also like for-profits operating in the same fields, robbing nonprofits of their distinctive structures, styles, and cultures. This *institutional isomorphism* can result from organizations' benchmarking their performance against one another's and complying with relatively uniform practices of program evaluation and outcome measurement, perhaps imposed by government contractors and other funders.[43]

Another potential by-product of performance-based accountability systems is manipulation of the system, whether intentional or not, by nonprofit organizations and the people who work in them. Performance-based accountability systems may tempt nonprofit organizations to select only clients who are most likely to succeed (a practice known as "creaming"), set performance targets that are artificially low and easily obtained, or select indicators and measures that are easy to interpret as success.[44]

Finally, there is the concern that performance-based accountability systems do not allow room for organizations to learn from their failures. Alnoor Ebrahim has been highly critical of performance-focused accountability systems that are applied in the field of international aid and development. His claim is that too much attention is focused on measures of output and efficiency, with far too little attention paid to helping international aid organizations learn from their experience (including their mistakes) and improve their performance.[45]

Accountability and the Four Impulses

The previous section noted that there are significant ambiguities and tensions with respect to all three ways of measuring accountability. In theory they may seem unambiguous, but in practice they are interpreted through the lens of myriad forces—economic, political, social—and a bewildering array of stakeholders who bring to the task different interests, perceptions, and assumptions.

In chapter 1 of this volume, Lester Salamon describes these various forces and stakeholders influencing the nonprofit sector in terms of four impulses or ideologies—voluntarism, professionalism, civic activism, and commercialism—that have influenced the roles played by nonprofit organizations, the ways they are organized and governed, and the strategies they use to achieve their objectives. Salamon notes that there are tensions among these four ideologies—that they tend to pull nonprofit organizations in various directions that are not always completely compatible. These ideologies also have an impact on how I define and measure accountability, sometimes imposing competing and even conflicting definitions of accountability, thereby making it even more difficult to carry on productive discourse about how to enhance accountability in the nonprofit sector. Table 16-1 provides a summary of essential questions about accountability as viewed through the lens of each of Salamon's four impulses: to whom are nonprofit organizations accountable, and for what are they accountable?

Even a cursory review of table 16-1 reveals that the four ideologies push and pull the nonprofit sector toward particular conceptions of accountability, not all of which are perfectly compatible. In the following section I explore how Salamon's four impulses can help us clarify some of the tensions in public discourse on accountability in the nonprofit sector and thus provide a foundation for improving that discourse. Rather than repeat the descriptions of the four impulses, the reader should refer back to the excellent discussion provided by Lester Salamon in chapter 1.

Accountability and Voluntarism

In the ideology of voluntarism as defined by Salamon, accountability is measured in terms of individual positive outcomes and anecdotes of personal transformations. Within the voluntarism frame of reference, anecdotal evidence is perfectly legitimate as a tool for establishing accountability, perhaps even desirable, as "proof" that the value-based methods are effective.

This view of accountability brings voluntarism into conflict with other impulses, especially professionalism and commercialism, two ideologies that view accountability in terms of objective empirically based evidence of outcomes.

From a purely objective and scientific perspective, I might argue that voluntarism that has a focus on values and anecdotal evidence provides a distorted lens for studying accountability. On the other hand, not many of us would argue with the success of Alcoholics Anonymous, an entirely volunteer-based and values-driven program with no organized infrastructure and surely no objective evidence of its effectiveness in transforming the lives of its members. The AA movement (one cannot call it an "organization" because its principles shun formal organization and authority) relies on anecdotes and personal testimonials of transformation. These personal and idiosyncratic stories are told and retold in multiple languages in tens of thousands of AA meetings around the world every day. Accountability is taken at face value and now widely recognized and respected even by the professional medical community, whose clinical treatments of alcoholism have for decades been largely futile. By all accounts, this grassroots program, with its strong spiritual components, has transformed the lives of chronic alcoholics, even those whom the medical community had long ago forsaken as hopelessly addicted.

Nonprofit leaders should not allow the growing emphasis on professionalism and commercialism to completely eclipse the historic values of voluntarism. Certainly many of the underlying values of the voluntarism ideology have meaning, including the notion that some types of accountability cannot be quantified in aggregate terms but must be observed in the transformed lives of individuals and communities. Indeed, as Albert Einstein noted: "Everything that can be counted does not necessarily count; everything that counts cannot necessarily be counted."[46]

Accountability and Professionalism

According to Salamon, the ideology of professionalism is concerned with demonstrating programmatic outcomes and organizational success in mission accomplishment. Professionalism also implies personal standards of accountability. As individuals, professionals are loyal to the methods of their craft, their trade, their guild, and they view themselves as accountable to the extent that they leverage the methods of their profession to help accomplish the mission of the organization and meet the standards set by their profession.

There is no escaping the reality that the nonprofit sector is now managed principally by a growing cadre of highly trained professionals from the fields of management, marketing, fundraising, program design and evaluation, clinical specialists of all types, accountants and finance experts, policy analysts, logistics specialists, lobbyists and professional advocates, and many other specialties.

From the standpoint of accountability, I and others must ask how (or if) the training received by this emerging professional class of future nonprofit employees is preparing them for the accountability challenges and opportunities they will face on the job.

Naomi Wish and Rosanne Mirabella have been vigilant in tracking the impact of professional training programs on the nonprofit sector.[47] In their early study in 1999, they found that the coursework of nonprofit curricula were heavily focused on the internal environment of the organization, not its relationship to the external community or its broader role in society.[48] Thus, the skills of budgeting, accounting, human resource management, finance, statistical analysis, and decision analysis took precedence over "boundary-spanning" skills such as advocacy, strategic planning, and external relations. A more recent analysis suggests that schools are making some progress in developing courses that address boundary-spanning activities and managing external relations, but there seems to be ample room for additional progress.[49]

Table 16-1. *Accountability and the Four Impulses*

	Voluntarism	Professionalism	Commercialism	Civic activism
To whom are nonprofits accountable (stakeholders)?	Value-based communities such as advocacy groups or religious groups, who bring passion and conviction to bear on the mission of the organization (for example, YMCA, Catholic Charities).Volunteers, who have historically provided a significant portion of the human capital for nonprofit organizations Individual donors and members, who voluntarily provide support for the mission	Professional staff, who bring specialized skills to bear on the mission Professional associations that exert a guild philosophy (for example, "best practices") on professionals who work in the sector Clients, who are increasingly knowledgeable about the services they receive and demand professionalism Industry groups that promulgate and enforce performance standards Government funders and institutional donors, who demand professional approaches to the mission	The marketplace, by pursuing missions that not only meet a need (gap in services) but also respond to a market demand (someone is willing to pay to fill the gap) Strategic partners and investors, venture philanthropists, social entrepreneurs, and others who expect a social return on their investment Clients and beneficiaries, who expect to be treated like customers	Citizens, volunteers, and supporters who view nonprofits as a vehicle for social change Coalitions and partner organizations that seek complementary outcomes Beneficiaries of nonprofit's mission, including future generations
What are nonprofits accountable for (performance expectations of stakeholders)?	Providing a vehicle for the expression of values (including religious values) in the social sphere Embracing or at least accommodating value-based explanations of social problems and issues	Accomplishing the mission via theory-based services and logic models derived from professional standards (secular versus value-based) Results and outcomes that are empirically validated and address causes as well as symptoms of problems	Growing the organization's market share, sales, vouchers, and financial sustainability; leveraging external investments; generation of community wealth Social return on investment	Changing the allocation of valued goods in society and the rules by which those goods are allocated

	Transforming the lives of individuals, in the short term through material assistance or values counseling, and in the long term through personal transformation and self-help Providing a way to reduce the role of government in the lives of people	Continuous organizational learning and improvement Meeting professional guild standards of individual performance such as certification, licensing Meeting industry standards of organizational performance such as accreditation Meeting standards of good governance, efficiency, ethical management such as codes, and financial probity	Exploitation of niche markets and leveraging the comparative advantage of the organization Accountable for spawning the entrepreneurial culture through replication, franchising, or other growth strategy	Holding people and organizations accountable in informal, consensual, and networked-based structures
Challenges to effective accountability	"Soft" data on outcomes that are based on anecdotes of individuals who have been transformed by their encounter with the nonprofit Concerns about government support (for example, separation of church and state)	Replication of professional and industry standards across many organizations, which may stymie innovation, lead to organizational isomorphism, and push organizations toward measurable short-term results and away from long-term advocacy and social change	Market incentives and partners, possibly leading to mission drift and loss of nonprofit's distinctiveness	

Source: Author's compilation.

The concern is that nonprofit professionals who have been trained in the type of educational environment just described, though quite adept at the type of process control skills needed for compliance-focused accountability, may be less equipped to deal with the total spectrum of accountability challenges they will face, especially those arising from competing values and expectations of diverse external stakeholders. Indeed, Paul Light's research suggests that public and nonprofit sector workers believe their formal education shortchanged them in these boundary-spanning skills that are so central to the broader notions of accountability described above.[50]

The premises of professionalism sometimes are at odds not only with voluntarism but also the impulse of commercialism. The health care industry, for example, has taken commercialism to an extreme level. In order to survive, hospitals must combine into massive vertically integrated health care systems, aggressively market their services, secure control of inputs and supply chains, and establish partnerships with networks of doctors and other health care professionals. Cost control and efficiency are rewarded as well as successful marketing, new product development, and technological innovation.

Yet data suggest that a growing number of health care professionals who work in these increasingly commercial enterprises are dissatisfied with the high-pressure, cost-conscious culture created by the commercial environment of the modern health care industry. For example, research suggests that primary-care physicians feel pressured to see more patients, spend less time per patient, and adhere to other productivity benchmarks imposed by insurers and managed-care overseers. Many of these physicians consciously choose to ignore these benchmarks, with adverse financial consequences.[51] They are forced to choose between their own professional standards of accountability and accountability standards imposed by the commercial marketplace.

Accountability and Civic Activism

Citizens have historically viewed nonprofits as "mediating structures," meaning that they are smaller, more tolerant, more innovative, and more accessible vehicles for effecting social change than do government bureaucracies.[52]

With respect to legal accountability, there are constraints on civic activism with which nonprofit organizations must comply, most of which deal with lobbying defined as an attempt to influence a particular legislative initiative at the federal, state, or local level. However, compliance with legal restrictions is only one part, perhaps the easy part, of the accountability environment with respect to civic activism. Giving sanction to any type of civic activism is indeed a solemn responsibility, never to be taken lightly. Rarely is civic activism by a nonprofit organization noncontroversial.

In 2002 the Grable Foundation, the Heinz Endowments, and the Pittsburgh Foundation withdrew a grant of $11 million from the Pittsburgh Public School District, sending shock waves through the philanthropic and educational communities in Pittsburgh and around the nation.[53] Technically, the action was taken because the school district had failed to comply with the terms of a particular grant, which was intended to introduce a new literacy program to the schools. On the surface, the three foundations used the legal contract to hold the district accountable for its nonperformance.

But beneath the surface there is a remarkable story of civic activism by the three foundations and their leaders. At that time, the Pittsburgh School Board was a governing body torn by ideological and racial disputes. That the board was dysfunctional is an understatement. Repeated efforts by mediators, consultants, and the news media failed to have an effect on the boorish and counterproductive behavior of the school board. The staff and the trustees of the three foundations took it upon themselves to take a dramatic step to highlight the issues and to mobilize a wide variety of public resources to deal with the problem.

The withdrawal of $11 million was only moderately consequential in the school district's huge annual budget, but symbolically, the action was dramatic and pivotal. A blue ribbon study commission was formed, parents became organized and mobilized, the media focused its energies and exerted substantial public pressure for change, and political leaders exerted personal and institutional influence. Eventually, the leadership and composition of the school board and the central administration changed hands and now the Pittsburgh Public Schools seem to be back on track toward high performance.

Despite the generally positive outcome of the action, there were critics of the three foundations who believed that this type of philanthropic muscle flexing smacked of arrogance. Others believed that three private nonprofit organizations had no business being engaged in civic advocacy of this type, essentially meddling in local politics.

Thus, civic activism creates special accountability challenges arising from competing conceptions of the public interest, historical boundaries between public and private action, and the ambiguity of outcomes, some of which may not be apparent for many years into the future.

Accountability and Commercialism

The commercialism ideology in nonprofits has given rise to accountability measures such as the Unrelated Business Income Tax, prohibition of excessive compensation, and stricter reporting of nonprofit revenues and expenditures. Yet the most challenging accountability questions arising from the commercialism impulse in the nonprofit sector revolve around mission drift and the extent to which commercialization has eroded the charitable values upon which the nonprofit sector was built.[54] Have nonprofits become too like businesses? Are they abandoning consumers who cannot pay for their services? Have they lost sight of the charitable "culture" that attracts volunteers and donors to their ranks in the first place?

The empirical research on these questions is mixed and somewhat difficult to interpret, because of the variability of nonprofits' missions. Commercial nonprofits, such as hospitals, that rely extensively on earned income for their existence can be expected to respond differently to commercial pressures than purely charitable nonprofits such as homeless shelters.[55] There are studies that show that nonprofit and for-profit hospitals are not significantly different in their commitment to providing uncompensated care.[56] Also, there is research suggesting that the boards of nonprofit hospitals provide no special incentives for CEOs to engage the hospital in charitable activities.[57] In other words, the boards of nonprofit hospitals care deeply about profits just as the boards of for-profit hospitals do.

In more traditional charities that rely extensively on donations, the issue of commercialism is intermingled with the question of organizational survival, suggesting that human service organizations turn to earned income out of necessity or to enhance their financial self-sufficiency. In the child-care industry nonprofit providers are struggling mightily to defend themselves against for-profit competitors. Government reimbursements and vouchers to needy families rarely cover all of the fixed and variable costs of providing child care. Thus, nonprofit child-care centers are tempted to seek out more and more families who have the ability to pay the full market price so that their fees can subsidize the below-market fees paid by needy families. It is a delicate balancing act. If they drift too far toward middle- or high-income families that have the ability to pay market rates, they jeopardize their charitable mission and risk losing the investment of donors and volunteers. On the other hand, if they commit themselves too heavily to needy clients, they run the risk of insolvency.[58]

Beyond this, as Baorong Guo's study of sixty-seven human service agencies suggests, commercial revenues do not necessarily contribute to the organization's ability to attract donors or volunteers or to fulfill its mission.[59] Similarly, Angela Eikenberry and Jodie Drapal Kluver conclude that commercialization of traditional nonprofits may have negative consequences for their ability to leverage social capital to achieve their missions.[60]

Commercialism complicates the accountability discussion because it opens the door to a whole new set of stakeholders whose interests may or may not be compatible with the charitable purposes and goals of nonprofits. Venture philanthropists, entrepreneurs, product design and marketing specialists, and paying customers combine to create a melting pot of commercial interests on both the supply and demand sides of the equation. Nonprofits must take care to ensure that commercial activities are consistent with the organization's mission and core competencies. They should use portfolio management methods to demonstrate exactly how earned income streams from some programs and services contribute to the support of programs that do not cover their costs.[61] Nonprofits should engage only in competitive strategies that can be fully defended on ethical grounds.[62]

Conclusions

In this chapter I have made the claim that accountability is a multifaceted concept that includes, first and foremost, the imperative for nonprofits to be in compliance with the laws and regulations imposed by outside authorities and the requirements of financial probity. But increasingly, accountability has also come to mean meeting the expectations of performance generated by stakeholders and by historical impulses that have shaped the sector almost since its inception.

Looking ahead, several issues present promising areas for research and also potential concerns for nonprofit leaders:

Accountability in Networked Delivery Systems

Many nonprofits are now part of a complex supply chain of organizations—governments, businesses, and nonprofits—involved in the delivery of goods and services. As these networked systems become more intricate, even globalized, the challenge of holding individual parts of the system accountable for their respective functions grows more and more complicated.[63] Networks involve webs of unilateral, bilateral, and multilateral responsibilities and interdependence. The technical aspects of government contracting and subcontracting for the delivery of networked services simply cannot keep pace with the growing complexity of interorganizational relationships and performance expectations. The possible scenarios of oversight, compliance, success, and failure are almost endless and therefore too complex for even the most carefully constructed performance contract to account for. Consequently, early research is suggesting that successful networks somehow develop a shared culture of accountability based on trust, goal congruence, shared values, and reciprocity.[64]

The question is whether these networks can be trusted to develop their own self-regulating culture and mechanisms when compliance-oriented tools such as contracts cannot be structured to reflect the complexity of the task. If the financial crisis of 2008 is any predictor, we have cause for grave concern.

Accountability and Grant Makers

Grant-making organizations are now under the glare of public scrutiny and have been challenged to develop stronger mechanisms for holding themselves and their grantees accountable for performance.

In *The Foundation: A Great American Secret,* Joel Fleishman argues that many foundations have not responded well to calls for greater accountability. In Fleishman's opinion, many foundations have done a poor job of selecting investments, specifying meaningful performance targets, sharing information with each other and with the public about successes and failures, and contributing to the general knowledge about what types of charitable programs succeed and what types fail.[65] There are also case studies illustrating how foundations sometimes catalyze large-scale efforts and investments in social initiatives, only to change their priorities when they lose patience with outcomes that may have longer horizons. This approach can leave grantees in the lurch, having themselves invested significant resources to "match" the foundation grants, only to be abandoned.[66]

Clearly, Fleishman has hit upon a subject in need of more empirical research, complemented by a more open public dialogue.

Accountability and Organizational Capacity

Nonprofit accountability cannot be meaningfully discussed without attention to the issue of organizational capacity. Most nonprofits are very small and their ability to design and implement accountability systems like those discussed in this chapter is limited.

For many nonprofits, the demand for services far exceeds the resources available to meet those demands. This has become painfully clear during the economic crisis. Thus, nonprofit boards and staff members are reluctant to commit scarce resources to building administrative infrastructure when the mission itself seems to be underfunded. They fear negative public reaction if they devote scarce resources to administrative investments such as better information systems to track needs and program performance, better human resource strategies to build skills in program evaluation and project management, or better process control systems like Balanced Scorecards and logic models to measure causal links between actions and results.

We are reminded of the scathing and relentless public criticism of the American Red Cross following the September 11 attacks when it announced that a portion of its wildly successful Liberty Fund would be devoted to building administrative infrastructure.

The paradox of accountability is that some of those who are screaming the loudest for enhanced accountability in nonprofit organizations are also those who have been most intolerant of making the necessary investments in the administrative infrastructure to achieve the goal. People who are interested in enhancing the accountability of nonprofit organizations must also be willing to help them build the internal capacity to meet higher standards of performance.

Performance: A Longer-Term Perspective

Foundations and other grant makers have, with the best of intentions, created a kind of accountability "monster" by focusing almost exclusively on short-term program funding as opposed to general operating support and by insisting that nonprofit organizations demonstrate short-term outcomes.[67]

A small but vocal group of foundations are challenging this prevailing strategy among grant makers.[68] Paul Shoemaker, of Social Venture Partners in Seattle, is among those who are calling for a return to long-term perspectives, arguing that nonprofits should be given support to pursue impacts and goals that defy measurement, at least with the metrics that the language of business schools and strategic philanthropy have pressed upon us. Shoemaker has argued that grant makers should relax or abandon their funding restrictions and provide substantially more unrestricted operating grants.

General operating support could be tailored to the life cycle of the organization. Nonprofits at the start-up stage need venture capital, funding for program development, marketing, and program testing and refinement. At the growth stage organizations need help building their internal operating systems, their boards, and going to scale with their programs. At the mature stage, nonprofits need help reinvesting in innovation and learning, or perhaps in preparing for executive transitions.

Tailoring operating support to the organization's need at different stages in its life cycle offers grant makers and grant seekers alike a clear set of performance targets, and may offer grant makers an intriguing opportunity to strategically specialize in certain types of grants on the basis of their interests and comparative advantages. Indeed, several of the foundations that have moved to general operating support work closely with their grantees to develop very specific benchmarks of success.

Regardless of specific strategies and tactics for enhancing accountability, it is imperative that the public dialogue on this issue continue in a way that is nuanced and informed, not driven by shrill generalities and ideological bias. The four impulses presented by Salamon in this volume and applied to the topic of accountability provide one way to frame the discourse, to surface assumptions and values, and to reasonably scrutinize proposals for change.

Notes

1. Tracie Mauriello, "Senator's Wife Charged with Theft," *Pittsburgh Post-Gazette,* August 15, 2008, p. B1; Brad Bumsted, "Audit Shows Excessive Spending by PHEAA," *Pittsburgh Tribune Review,* August 19, 2008, p. 1; Anya Sostek, "Committee to Probe CMU Master's Degree," *Pittsburgh Post-Gazette,* September 5, 2008, p. 1; Patricia Sabatini, "UPMC's Profits Take a Nose Dive," *Pittsburgh Post-Gazette,* August 22, 2008, p. A1.

2. Kevin Kearns, *Managing for Accountability: Preserving the Public Trust in Public and Nonprofit Organizations* (San Francisco: Jossey-Bass, 1996), pp. 3–44. See also David R. Buckholdt, and Jaber F. Gubrium. "Practicing Accountability in Human Service Institutions," *Journal of Contemporary Ethnography* 12, no. 3 (October 1983): 249–68; Carol Estes and others, "How the Legitimacy of the Sector Has Eroded," in *The Future of the Nonprofit Sector: Challenges, Changes, and Policy Considerations,* edited by Virginia Hodgkinson, R. W. Lymann, and Associates (San Francisco: Jossey-Bass, 1989); Dennis R. Young, "The Influence of Business on Nonprofit Organizations and the Complexity of Nonprofit Accountability," *American Review of Public Administration* 32, no. 1 (March 2002): 3–19; David C. Hammack, "Accountability in Nonprofit Organizations: A Historical Perspective," *Nonprofit Management & Leadership* 6, no. 2 (Winter 1995): 127–39.

3. The famous debate in 1940 and 1941 between Herman Finer and Carl Friedrich regarding the merits of external controls versus self-policing has set the tone for discourse on accountability in government for seventy years. See Herman Finer, "Administrative Responsibility in Democratic Government," *Public Administration Review* 1, no. 4 (Summer 1941): 335–50, and Carl Friedrich, "Public Policy and the Nature of Administrative Responsibility," in *Public Policy,* edited by Carl Friedrich (Harvard University Press, 1940).

4. Jay Shafritz, *The HarperCollins Dictionary of American Government and Politics* (New York: HarperCollins, 1992), p. 4.

5. Patricia Read, "Testimony of Independent Sector to the U.S. Senate Appropriations Committee, Financial Services and General Government Subcommittee," May 23, 2007, pp. 2–3.

6. There are many authoritative sources of technical information regarding various standards of fiscal accountability and transparent governance. See, for example: Marion Fremont-Smith, *Governing Nonprofit Organizations: Federal and State Law and Regulation* (Harvard University Press, 2004)

7. For a useful illustration of the legal steps to be followed in the founding of a nonprofit organization, see Thomas Silk, "The Legal Framework of the Nonprofit Sector in the United States," in *The Jossey-Bass Handbook of Nonprofit Leadership and Management,* 2nd ed., edited by Robert D. Herman and Associates (San Francisco: Jossey-Bass, 2005), pp. 63–80.

8. Michael Worth, *Nonprofit Management: Principles and Practice* (Thousand Oaks: Calif.: Sage, 2009), pp. 62–66.

9. Lester M. Salamon and Stephanie Geller, "Nonprofit Governance and Accountability," Listening Post Communiqué No. 4 (Johns Hopkins University, Institute for Policy Studies, Center for Civil Society Studies, Listening Post Project, 2005).

10. Ibid., citing U.S. Senate Finance Committee, "Staff Discussion Draft" (June 22, 2004).

11. Ibid.

12. Ibid., pp. 3–4.

13. John Carver, *Boards That Make a Difference,* 3rd ed. (San Francisco: Jossey-Bass, 2006).

14. Richard Chait, William P. Ryan, and Barbara E. Taylor, *Governance as Leadership: Reframing the Work of Nonprofit Boards* (New York: Wiley, 2005).

15. William Brown, "Board Development Practices and Competent Board Members: Implications for Performance," *Nonprofit Management and Leadership* 17, no. 3 (Spring 2007): 301–17.

16. Lester M. Salamon, *America's Nonprofit Sector: A Primer* (New York: Foundation Center, 1999).

17. Lester M. Salamon, "The Marketization of Welfare: Changing Nonprofit and For Profit Roles in the American Welfare State," *Social Service Review* 67, no. 1 (March 1993): 16–39.

18. Peter C. Brinckerhoff, *Social Entrepreneurship: The Art of Mission-Based Venture Development* (New York: Wiley, 2000); Alex Nicholls, "Measuring Impact of Social Entrepreneurship: New Accountabilities to Stakeholders and Investors?" Working Paper (Oxford University, Said Business School, Skoll Center for Social Entrepreneurship, 2005) (www.built-environment.uwe.ac.uk/research/ESRCseminars/pdfs/alex_nicholls_seminar4.pdf [September 28, 2009]).

19. Burton Weisbrod, "The Pitfalls of Profits," *Stanford Social Innovation Review* 2, no. 3 (2004): 40–47; compare with Marshall Jones, "Multiple Sources of Mission Drift," *Nonprofit and Voluntary Sector Quarterly* 36 no. 2 (June, 2007): 299–307.

20. Kevin P. Kearns, "Market Engagement and Competition: Opportunities, Challenges and the Quest for Comparative Advantage," in *Wise Decision Making in Uncertain Times: Using Nonprofit Resources Effectively,* edited by Dennis Young (San Francisco: Jossey-Bass, 2006).

21. For a comprehensive historical discussion of the property tax exemption, see Evelyn Brody, ed., *Property Tax Exemptions for Charities: Mapping the Battlefield* (Washington: Urban Institute, 2002).

22. A useful technical discussion of financial accounting is provided by Robert N. Anthony and David W. Young, "Financial Accounting and Financial Management," in Herman and Associates, *Jossey-Bass Handbook of Nonprofit Leadership and Management,* pp. 466–512.

23. Jack Needleman, Deborah Chollet, and Jo Anne Lamphere, "Hospital Conversion Trends," *Health Affairs* 16, no. 2 (March–April 1987):187–95

24. Eleanor Laise and Dennis Berman, "Impact on Jewish Charities Is Catastrophic," *Wall Street Journal,* December 16, 2008.

25. Melanie Herman, "Risk Management," in Herman and Associates, *Jossey-Bass Handbook of Nonprofit Leadership and Management,* pp. 560–82.

26. BoardSource and Independent Sector, *The Sarbanes-Oxley Act and Implications for Nonprofit Organizations* (Washington: BoardSource, 2006) (www.boardsource.org/dl.asp?document_id=558).

27. Better Business Bureau, *Standards for Charity Accountability* (Arlington, Va.: Council of Better Business Bureaus, 2008).

28. Barbara Lawrence and Outi Flynn, *The Nonprofit Policy Sampler* (Washington: Board-Source, 2006).

29. Barbara Romzek and Melvin Dubnik, "Accountability in the Public Sector: Lessons from the Challenger Tragedy," *Public Administration Review* 47, no. 3 (1987): 228.

30. Ralf Caers and others, "Principal-Agent Relationships on the Stewardship-Agency Axis," *Nonprofit Management and Leadership* 17, no. 1 (Fall 2006): 25–47.

31. Joanne Carmen and Kimberly Fredericks, "Evaluation Capacity and Nonprofit Organizations: Is the Glass Half-Empty or Half-Full?" *American Journal of Evaluation* 31, no. 1 (2010): 84–104; Joanne Carman, "The Accountability Movement: What's Wrong with This Theory of Change?" *Nonprofit and Voluntary Sector Quarterly* 39, no. 2 (2010): 256–74.

32. Kevin Kearns, "Mission Statement," entry in *The International Encyclopedia of Public Policy and Administration,* edited by Jay Shafritz (Boulder: Westview Press, 1998), pp. 1412–14.

33. Robert S. Kaplan, and David P. Norton, "The Balanced Scorecard—Measures That Drive Performance," *Harvard Business Review* 70, no. 1 (1992): 71–79; Robert S. Kaplan

and David P. Norton, *The Strategy Focused Organization: How Balanced Scorecard Companies Thrive in the New Business Environment* (Boston: Harvard Business School Press, 2000); Robert S. Kaplan, "Strategic Performance Measurement and Management in Nonprofit Organizations," *Nonprofit Management and Leadership* 11, no. 3 (2001): 353–70.

34. Hanne Norreklit, "The Balance on the Balanced Scorecard—A Critical Analysis of Some of Its Assumptions," *Management Accounting Research* 11, no. 1 (2000): 65–88.

35. Paul C. Light, "Rebuilding Trust in Charity," *Christian Science Monitor*, May 16, 2002, p. 9; Suzanne Perry, "Public Confidence in Nonprofit Groups Slides Back, New Survey Finds," *Chronicle of Philanthropy*, April 3, 2008, p. 12.

36. Jacqueline L. Salmon, "Nonprofits Show Losses in the Public's Trust," *Washington Post*, September 9, 2002, p. A2.

37. Michael O'Neill, "Public Confidence in Charitable Nonprofits," *Nonprofit and Voluntary Sector Quarterly* 38, no. 2 (2009): 237–69.

38. Allison H. Fine, Colette Thayer, and Anne T. Coghlan, "Program Evaluation Practice in the Nonprofit Sector," *Nonprofit Management & Leadership* 10, no. 3 (Spring 2000): 331–39.

39. Joanne Carmen, "Nonprofits, Funders, and Evaluation: Accountability in Action," *American Review of Public Administration* 39, no. 4 (July 2009): 374–90.

40. Grantmakers for Effective Organizations, *Listen, Learn, Lead: Grantmaker Practices That Support Nonprofit Results* (Washington: 2006), p. 9.

41. Lehn Benjamin, "Account Space: How Accountability Requirements Shape Nonprofit Practice," *Nonprofit and Voluntary Sector Quarterly* 37, no. 2 (June 2008): 201–23.

42. Susan Stevens, *Nonprofit Lifecycles: Stage-Based Wisdom for Nonprofit Capacity* (N.p.: Stagewise Enterprises, 2002).

43. Paul DiMaggio and Walter W. Powell, "The Iron Cage Revisited: Institutional Isomorphism and Collective Rationality in Organizational Fields," *American Sociological Review* 48, no. 2, (1983): 147–60; compare with Ramanath Ramya, "Limits to Institutional Isomorphism: Examining Internal Processes in NGO-Government Interactions," *Nonprofit and Voluntary Sector Quarterly* 38, no. 1 (February 2009): 51–76.

44. Debra Mesch and James McClelland, "Managing for Performance and Integrity," in *Wise Decision-Making in Uncertain Times: Using Nonprofit Resources Effectively*, edited by Dennis R. Young (New York: Foundation Center, 2006), pp. 33–54.

45. Alnoor Ebrahim, "Making Sense of Accountability: Conceptual Perspectives for Northern and Southern Nonprofits," *Nonprofit Management & Leadership* 14, no. 2 (Winter 2003): 191–212.

46. Albert Einstein, quoted in Charles G. Koch, *The Science of Success: How Market-Based Management Built the World's Largest Private Company* (Hoboken, N.J.: Wiley, 2007).

47. Naomi Wish and Rosanne Mirabella, "Educational Impact of Graduate Nonprofit Degree Programs," *Nonprofit Management and Leadership* 9, no. 3 (1999): 329–40.

48. Ibid., p. 338.

49. Roseanne Mirabella, "University-Based Educational Programs in Nonprofit Management and Philanthropic Studies: A 10-Year Review and Projections of Future Trends," *Nonprofit and Voluntary Sector Quarterly* 36, no. 4 (December 2007): S11–S27.

50. Paul Light, *The New Public Service* (Brookings, 1999).

51. Jeffrey Solomon, "How Strategies for Managing Patient Visit Time Affect Physician Job Satisfaction," *Journal of General Internal Medicine* 23, no. 6: 775–80.

52. Peter L. Berger and Richard John Neuhaus, *To Empower People: The Role of Mediating Structures in Public Policy* (Washington: American Enterprise Institute, 1977).

53. Barry Varela, "Three Foundations and the Pittsburgh Public Schools," Foundation Impact Case Series (Duke University, Terry Sanford Institute of Public Policy, 2007).

54. Dennis R. Young, "The Influence of Business on Nonprofit Organizations and the Complexity of Nonprofit Accountability," *American Review of Public Administration* 32, no. 1 (2002): 3–19.

55. Henry Hansmann, "Economic Theories of Nonprofit Organizations," in *The Nonprofit Sector: A Research Handbook,* edited by Walter W. Powell (Yale University Press, 1987), pp. 27–42.

56. Frank Sloan "Commercialism in Nonprofit Hospitals," in *To Profit or Not to Profit: The Commercial Transformation of the Nonprofit Sector,* edited by Burton Weisbrod (Cambridge University Press, 1998), pp. 151–68.

57. James Brickley and R. Lawrence Van Horn, "Managerial Incentives in Nonprofit Organizations: Evidence from Hospitals," *Journal of Law and Economics* 45 (April 2002): 227–49.

58. Kevin Kearns, "Market Engagement and Competition," in Young, *Wise Decision Making in Uncertain Times.*

59. Baorong Guo, "Charity for Profit? Exploring the Factors Associated with Commercialization of Human Service Nonprofits," *Nonprofit and Voluntary Sector Quarterly* 35, no. 1 (2006): 123–38.

60. Angela Eikenberry and Jodie Drapal Kluver, "The Marketization of the Nonprofit Sector: Civil Society at Risk?" *Public Administration Review* 64, no. 2 (2004): 132–40.

61. Kevin Kearns, "Income Portfolios," in *Financing Nonprofits: Putting Theory Into Practice,* edited by Dennis R. Young (Lanham, Md.: AltaMira Press, 2007): 291–314.

62. I. C. McMillan, "Competitive Strategies for Not-for-Profit Organizations," *Advances in Strategic Management,* volume 1 (Greenwich, Conn.: JAI Press, 1983).

63. Stephen Goldsmith and William Eggers, *Governing by Network: The New Shape of the Public Sector* (Brookings, 2004); Lester M. Salamon, "Introduction: The New Governance and the Tools of Public Action," in *The Tools of Government: A Guide to the New Governance,* edited by Lester M. Salamon (Oxford University Press, 2002), pp. 1–51.

64. Barbara Romzek "Accountability and Contracting in a Networked Policy Arena: The Case of Welfare Reform," in *Accountable Governance: Promises and Problems,* edited by George Fredrickson and Melvin Dunnick (Armonk, N.Y.: M. E. Sharpe, 2010).

65. Joel Fleishman, *The Foundation: A Great American Secret* (New York: PublicAffairs, 2007).

66. Susan A. Ostrander, "Innovation, Accountability, and Independence at Three Private Foundations Funding Higher Education Civic Engagement, 1995–2005," *Nonprofit Management and Leadership* 18, no. 2 (Winter 2007): 237–53.

67. For a discussion of the limitations of short-term evaluations of complex social interventions, see Lester M. Salamon, "The Time Dimension in Policy Evaluation: The Case of the New Deal Land Reform Experiments," *Public Policy* (Spring 1979): 129–83.

68. Denise Carluso, "Can Foundations Take the Long View Again?" *New York Times,* January 6, 2008.

17

Demographic and Technological Imperatives

ATUL DIGHE

Sociologists have observed that societal development consists of a cycle of technological development followed by an era of adjustments and re-creation of a new normal as a result of the technology boom. The previous century is a good example. A person magically transported forward in time from 1900 to 1950 would have gone from the world of the horse-drawn buggy to rocket ships blasting into space; from the telegraph to the television; from old-fashioned artillery and horses to nuclear warheads. The amazing technological advances in a fifty-year period of time boggle the mind. Similarly, many baby boomers born before or around 1950 had been witness to amazing changes to society by 2000: races and ethnic groups interacting and working together; women with access to leadership positions in government and business; the sexual revolution.

If the future is anything like the past, we are in the midst of another era of amazing technological change—one that will reshape how we work, learn, and interact with each other, and surely one that once again will have an impact on our social institutions, including the nonprofit sector.

We are in the midst of a historically unique demographic, technological, and cultural transformation. This transformation has implication for all of our institutions, and they may be especially pronounced for the country's nonprofit institutions, as a result of these institutions' commitment to innovation, their responsiveness to shifts in other sectors, and their involvement in many of the fields, such as health care and education, where the pace of change is especially fast.

616

It used to be possible to know a great deal about the future, because in times when change came more slowly the future was bound to be fairly similar to the present and the recent past. Now, however, prediction beyond a few years ahead is less and less possible for most important things because technological change is creating so much discontinuity and novelty. But the need for foresight, problem prevention, and anticipatory problem solving is greater than ever before. There are unprecedented dangers ahead that we need to head off and unprecedented opportunities that we can only grasp if we see them clearly.

We can be better prepared for whatever the future may bring by scanning for trends and emerging developments and exploring alternative futures. With the accelerating pace of change, nonprofit organizations, like their counterparts in business and government, need to reshape their structures, cultures, stakeholder interactions, and information systems to foster continuous learning and capacity for rapid self-organization.

It is critical that nonprofit organizations have a sense of the most important questions to raise about the future as well as a sense of the likely answers to them. The future is fundamentally uncertain, yet there are potential directions, even if they may be conflicting and multiple in nature. Without a concerted effort to remain focused on the future, nonprofit organizations run the risk of losing importance in the fluctuating world of the early twenty-first century.

One area for study is technological trends. Perhaps more so than ever before, technology is shaping the future. Like demographic trends, technological trends can be forecast, and, what is more important, their potential impacts can be explored.

Another appropriate approach is to discern trends in the racial, gender, and ethnic makeup of the population or workforce of a particular region or country. Such trends can be forecast fairly confidently. Exploring the possible implications of demographic trends often leads to new and occasionally surprising insights into the future.

A final area for study is cultural trends. Often spurred by demographics and technological changes, cultural trends shape who we are and how we interact.

Identifying existing trends and emerging developments sets the stage for thinking about the future. This chapter explores key technological, demographic, and cultural trends affecting the nonprofit sector. The information is meant to serve as a starting point for a constructive conversation about the future. The trends discussed here are by no means comprehensive; rather they are examples of the types of dynamic change the future holds.

Technology's Tomorrow Is Here Today

Smaller, faster, cheaper has become the motto for a technologically driven era in the early twenty-first century. Amazingly, the ways in which we communicate, learn, and live our daily lives is in many instances fundamentally different from the way things were a mere few years ago. In the past decade, information needed to get from point A to point B has evolved from paper maps to mapping websites to real-time GPS systems on our smart phones. We have seen the arrival and passing of web 1.0 and web 2.0 and the dawning of web 3.0 in which user-generated content in the form of text, photo, and videos is stored, searched, and shared in a "cloud" available for the entire world to access. The implications of technological change are occurring so rapidly that in many cases we as a society are not even fazed or impressed by the ways in which our lives are impacted. Here we focus on several of these implications of particular relevance to nonprofit organizations.

Distributed Learning

One of these implications is having significant effects in the field of education. There is growing recognition that the days of the "sage on the stage" model of face-to-face education are numbered. Schools and training institutions are scrambling to develop new capabilities in distance education or are setting up new virtual universities. Lifelong learning and the need to retrain for new career opportunities are creating a large new student demographic: adults from nineteen to ninety-nine. These initial steps will eventually bring about the next paradigm for education and training—distributed learning.[1] In the future, learning will be distributed across time, location, age, subject matter, teaching or learning style, and the nonprofit, for-profit, and government sectors.

Many in the education community have already discovered that face-to-face interaction places strict limitations on the scope of learning. Such interaction is restricted to predetermined times, predetermined places, and predetermined materials. The new paradigm of distributed learning relies on new communication technologies to overcome these limitations. Asynchronous communication allows education to be distributed across time through the use of e-mail, online discussion forums, and blogs. The ubiquity of Internet access transcends any geographic limitations on participation and allows education to occur among a geographically dispersed body of students. Arriving shortly on the scene will be technological breakthroughs such as artificial intelligence tutors, high-quality voice synthesis, and biofeedback input devices all delivered on hand-held smart phones or ultra-portable tablet computers.

Although we are still years away from a fully immersive learning simulation environment along the lines of the holodeck in *Star Trek,* advances in technology are revolutionizing education. New discoveries in the field of neuroscience are helping us to understand how we learn on an individual basis. Wireless technologies such as tablet computers, smart phones, and electronic books and paper have redefined communication and hence redefined education. The expectations of a generation of schoolchildren who have grown up with a ubiquitous World Wide Web, computers in every classroom, and Power Point slides for every lecture are very different from those of previous generations. In short, the information age has placed its permanent stamp on education—from this point forward education must make full use of available technology not just to supplement the learning experience but to be an integral component of it. Terms used in the Internet world, such as twenty-four/seven, anytime/anyplace, customizable, and user-friendly interface, have become key descriptors of learning in the twenty-first century.

As education models evolve toward distributed learning, nonprofit organizations will need to engage their stakeholders in a dialogue about their educational and training needs and the best ways those needs can be fulfilled. Keeping in mind issues such as equity and access to technology, nonprofit organizations can help their stakeholders to navigate the increasingly diverse set of educational options available in the marketplace.

As innovation drives the reinvention of the education process itself, nonprofits that lack access to technological resources may find themselves at a severe disadvantage in the marketplace. Distributed learning will attract a whole host of new competitors from both the nonprofit and for-profit sectors. Rapid innovation will lead to experimentation, and to both successes and failures. The successful educational and training organization (nonprofit or otherwise) will be able to integrate the best new technologies and innovations with timeless educational principles such as reliance on proven relevant content and time-tested teaching methods such as the Socratic method.

Clean Tech

Technology is not simply an external force to which we must respond. It can also be molded and shaped. Inventors, visionaries, entrepreneurs, employees, investors, consumers, politicians, regulators, and environmentalists are all involved in this molding and shaping, and nonprofit organizations can also be part of this process. One potential example of this is the shift to so-called clean technologies such as green buildings—energy-efficient buildings with healthful indoor environments and high levels of visual, thermal, and acoustic comfort.

In the United States, buildings use one-third of our total energy and two-thirds of our electricity. Greening our buildings is one of the highest-impact strategies available for reducing the environmental effects of economic growth and heading off global warming.

Patricia Griffin, president of the Green Hotels Association, points out that nonprofit organizations can easily and simply influence the evolution of the whole lodging industry by consciously spending their dollars for meetings and conferences with hotels that are working to green their properties.[2] Going green can be as simple as the sheet chaining cards now found in thousands of hotel guest bathrooms, which ask guests to consider using their linens more than once. Or it can involve more ambitious renovations like the one undertaken by the Boston Plaza hotel. Occupancy rates increased and brought an additional $2 million in business after the hotel installed energy-efficient lighting, water-efficient showerheads, Thermopane windows, and a comprehensive recycling program.[3]

New construction provides an opportunity to show what can be done. For example, the Olympic Village at the 2000 Summer Olympics in Sydney, Australia, had such good passive cooling design that its rooms were comfortable without conventional air conditioning. The money saved on cooling was used to install a kilowatt of solar cells on the roof of each unit.[4] Over the last several years retail concerns such as Safeway Grocery Stores and Macy's have announced plans to install solar panels atop their newly renovated stores in California, generating over 20 percent of the locations' energy needs. Safeway and other like-minded retail organizations believe that participating in the green tech movement will not only save on operating costs but also will help them to connect with consumer desires to support organizations with a "sustainability ethos."[5]

A growing body of case studies shows that green designs usually cost no more to build than conventional designs and have much lower operating costs. For example, in a review of thirty newly built green schools, the construction cost was found to be only 2 percent higher than that of conventional buildings, but operating an energy-efficient building saves about $70 per square foot, or about $100,000 per year, in energy costs alone.[6] The most surprising finding is the savings that result from the satisfaction and performance of the people who use the building. Better indoor air quality, daylight that reaches into the interior of the buildings, and other aspects of green design reduce absenteeism, improve worker productivity, and boost occupancy. A 1 or 2 percent increase in an office's labor productivity produces the same bottom-line benefit as eliminating the entire energy bill.[7]

Green buildings are a good example of an area in which nonprofit organizations can save money while acting in an environmentally conscious manner. Another area in which organizations can both save money and positively affect energy consumption is transportation and logistics. Hybrid vehicles have become mainstream over the last decade. Technological advances in battery storage and the further development of a hybrid-electric vehicle infrastructure will only help to accelerate this trend and potentially impact nonprofits as both users and promoters of hybrid technologies.

Google's nonprofit wing, google.org, is in the midst of conducting an interesting experiment with hybrid vehicles. Google.org has configured a fleet of hybrid cars to serve as portable power plants while the engines idle. Google employees drive the special cars to work and plug them into the "local Google campus grid." While their owners are at work the vehicles work as well. Google.org hopes the experiment can serve as a model of how organizations can align green business principles with profitable business practices as the vehicles pay for themselves with the clean energy they produce during the day while serving as strong recruitment and retention drivers for their employees during off-work hours.[8]

In fact hybrid fleet vehicles are forecasted to reach nearly 750,000 by 2015.[9] As organizations of all types, including nonprofits, funnel their transportation and logistics expenditures toward more "green" solutions, the needed infrastructure changes are sure to follow.

Nonprofit organizations can use their collective clout to raise awareness of important environmental issues, while at the same time advocating and using energy-efficient, cost-saving approaches. Green building and hybrid vehicles are two areas of rapid growth and acceptance in today's marketplace. Nonprofit organizations can help accelerate the trends toward greater use of clean technologies such as these not only through their advocacy but also through their actions.

Biomolecular Convergence

The most far-reaching scientific and technological advances sometimes can be found at the intersection of disparate industries or disciplines. Walter Truett Anderson observes in his book *Evolution Isn't What It Used to Be* that we are now witnessing a convergence between the biosciences and electronics—a bionic convergence.[10]

The biosciences, also known as life sciences, are any of the several branches of science, such as biology, medicine, ecology, or anthropology (a social/life science) that deal with living organisms and their organization, life processes, and relationships to each other and their environment. Electronics is the field of engineering and applied physics dealing with systems and devices that depend on the flow of electronics for the generation, transmission, reception, and storage of information. As biosciences and electronics converge, the advancement of each is accelerated as developments in one domain are applied to the other. Today, electronics has the strongest influence on the biosciences. For example, the planet is now enveloped by an electronic skin of sensors that collect, store, and interpret information about our planet and its living creatures. The human genome project—which Paula Gregory of the National Center for Human Genome Research estimated was 40 percent an information technology project—would not have been possible without powerful computers.

In the future, the tide of influence will likely shift, and the biosciences will become the stronger force. For example, the future of electronics may include computers that metaphorically and literally are biological: artificial limbs or organs that have direct connections to the brain and biosensing "smart skin" that can monitor blood-sugar levels of people with diabetes and administer insulin if needed.[11]

Many sciences are operating at smaller and smaller scales and are converging on the molecule and the atom as a focal point. The end result may be the development of nanotechnology, which is manufacturing at the scale of a nanometer, or one billionth of a meter. Today according to the National Nanotechnology Initiative, over 20,000 scientists are working on technologies and applications of molecule-size machines called assemblers that are able to build objects atom by atom. Nanotechnology is radically altering our world. Leading researchers believe that we can literally change the molecular nature of waste products and pollution and transform them into useful fuels and structures. Materials engineers are creating new materials that are molecularly flawless and fifty times stronger than steel. The manufacturing paradigm is actually shifting from a fixed location process to a "desktop" process with nanomachines constructing and deconstructing items one atom at a time. We could develop airborne artificial immune systems that could be programmed to recognize and eliminate all known threats, more effective methods for water purification, and approaches to cleaning up bio-hazard and chemical spills.[12]

Much less fanfare has been generated by MEMS—microelectromechanical systems. MEMS are microchips that not only think, like those in personal computers, but also sense and act. Incorporating tiny sensors, probes, lasers, and actuators, these micromachines may underpin the generation of medical, electronic, and communication devices and spawn entirely new technologies.

MEMS are being developed in more than 600 laboratories worldwide, and the technology is already in widespread use (for example, in automobile airbags). MEMS technology is also being used to create biosensors that offer "hospital labs on a chip" and gene chips that rapidly and efficiently acquire, analyze, and manage genetic information. Currently, MEMS technology is widely used as pressure sensors in the medical sector to monitor blood pressure in IV lines, respiratory monitoring in ventilators, and in kidney dialysis machines.[13] These advances, which could have dramatic positive impacts on the treatment of disease and the prevention of illness, will also significantly affect the current health care system. Testing and diagnostic processes that currently require a lot of time, money, and equipment could be completed instantly by biosensors the size of a postage stamp. Nanotechnology would allow us to attack disease on the molecular level as opposed to the microscopic level. Self-regulating artificial limbs and organs can be created that will open entirely new possibilities for the handicapped as well as those seeking performance enhancements. Parallel breakthroughs in nanotechnology and MEMS coupled with a better understanding of genomics could render our current paradigm of health care, and the institutions that support it, completely obsolete.

Scientific exploration and discovery in the biosciences are far ahead of any societal dialogue about the ethics and appropriate uses of those types of technologies. "Can we do it?" is the driving question in our scientific community, not "Should it be done?" Perhaps the best example of the ethical difficulties that lie ahead is the ongoing debate on stem-cell research. Some scientists point to preliminary findings that research using stem cells could yield significant medical and commercial value; meanwhile, other scientists and many politicians caution against their use, citing ethical considerations. Further complicating the discussion is the question of the use of federal dollars to fund research in such a complicated and controversial field.[14]

The nonprofit sector could become a resource by providing a safe space in which to discuss the implications of these types of scientific advances. Nonprofit organizations can promote a much-needed and still far too limited dialogue about our future. In helping society to think through (and policymakers to plan for) the emerging technological breakthroughs, nonprofit organizations can fill a vital need.

Social-Networking Activism

Networked computing and global telecommunications are making possible truly global markets and global companies. The digital revolution and the new social media–Internet-based communications tools used to facilitate relationship building—is also giving rise to new kinds of civic accountability that impose novel checks and balances on the power of global corporations. For example, when the labor practices in Nike's Vietnamese factories were exposed to the world, first in cyberspace and then on CNN, a global firestorm of public opinion was unleashed demanding change. Home Depot was forced to commit itself publicly to stop sourcing timber from endangered forests as the result of a social-networking coordinated campaign led by the Rain Forest Action Network and Greenpeace, but involving hundreds of environmental organizations and grassroots groups around the world. In a world of radically expanding connectivity, there appears to be no way for companies in any industry to try to shield themselves from initiatives of this kind.[15]

Social-networking activism is also providing effective in influencing international policies and structures, which in turn affect the operations of corporations. For example, an informal network of more than 700 human rights groups around the world coordinated their activities online to formulate and push forward a global treaty to ban land mines, over the opposition of many governments. Their effort was recognized with the Nobel Peace Prize in 1997. Less well known are the efforts of a similar network of nongovernmental organizations that played a major role in the establishment on the International Court of Justice in 1999. Initiatives of this nature are proving so powerful that they deserve to be viewed as an important aspect of the emerging process of global governance and social change.

We appear to be evolving toward a situation where virtually all private-sector companies of any significant size will be under constant scrutiny by hundreds of nongovernmental organizations around the world. The cost to companies that become targeted by global social activism networks can be extremely high, including the loss of brand value, the disappointment of major stakeholders, and the loss of market share.

Furthermore, the potential impact of social media on government cannot be understated. In the 2008 and 2010 American elections, social media outlets such as Twitter, Facebook, and various blogs played a heavy role in fundraising, campaigning, and issue awareness among voters. In the 2010 election, the burgeoning Tea Party movement tapped into social media outlets to "organize" their message, including a series of face-to-face rallies.[16] Internationally, the 2009 election in Iran serves as a good case study of the impact of open social media networks in otherwise tightly state-controlled societies. In that election, despite the efforts of the Iranian government to suppress and control information regarding the prevalence and passion of those protesting, Twitter messages were giving fellow Iranians as well as the rest of the world a true glimpse into government action.[17]

As is the case with any technological advance, there are upsides and downsides. Not all social-networking activism is for the good. These new technologies allow terrorist groups to recruit, train, and in some instances execute their agendas. In the brutal terrorist attacks in Mumbai in November 2008, social media were used by the terrorists to organize and coordinate their attack. The terrorists even monitored Twitter and other social media feeds from those trapped inside the Taj Mahal Hotel to more effectively carry out their mission.[18]

Of particular interest to the nonprofit community will be the growing use of social media to connect supporters with cause-driven organizations. Beginning in 2009 Chase Bank established its community giving fund, which uses Facebook to identify organizations to receive a share of upwards of $5 million every year. In 2010 over 2.5 million people participated in the process, driving the selection of about 200 nonprofits to be the recipients of between $20,000 to $250,000.[19] Understanding the dynamics of social-networking social activism will be crucial to the success of any nonprofit organization wishing to effect societal change. Harnessing the ability to influence global citizens, corporations, and governments can give the nonprofit community the ability to overcome many—but likely not all—resource disadvantages. The nonprofit organizations that best understand this trend and technologies will be able to exert a tremendous amount of leverage on behalf of their particular viewpoints and agendas.

Demographic Destinies

In addition to these technological developments, nonprofits also face a series of dramatic demographic shifts. Many of these demographic shifts are easily identifiable, giving us quantifiable glimpses into the future. However, along with the comfort of "knowing" the numerical shape of the future comes a high level of discomfort in not being able to know how these demographic destinies will play out. For example, we know that the minority populations in the United States will continue to grow in the future; however, we do not know how this emerging "minority majority" will affect our collective society. We know that we soon will have five major generational cohorts interacting in the marketplace; we do not know whether generational synergies will develop or whether generational outlooks will divide us. We know that life expectancy in the developed world is increasing; we do not know how our social institutions will adapt to this challenge. So, although we can seek to understand our demographic destinies, we also must use this new understanding to inform our human choices.

A Minority Majority

The census 2000 snapshot of America showed that, taken together, Latino American, Asian American, African American, Native American, and other ethnic groups had increased from 23 to 30 percent of the total U.S. population between 1990 and 2000.[20] And that was just a foretaste of things to come. By 2006 the U.S. Census Bureau was able to report that one-third of the residents in the United States were members of a minority group.[21] More than one-half of the people added to the U.S. population between July 2008 and July 2009 were Hispanic.[22] Our society has a "diversity generation gap": more than 40 percent of our nation's young people are minorities.[23] As those young people grow up, we will experience the most dramatic demographic transition in our history. More than five-sixths of all new employees in the next generation will be women and non–Euro Americans. Demographers forecast that by mid-century, America will have a "minority majority."[24]

Dramatic evidence of the change our society is experiencing is the fact that immigrants, and even first-generation Latino Americans, no longer need to learn English to function and thrive in our economy. In the past, immigrants who left home were "gone for good." Today, with global telecommunications and travel, the reinforcement of home values is just a phone call, text message, or Facebook posting away. In fact, many people are rediscovering their cultural roots, others are trying hard to preserve the best of their cultures, and still others delight in the "new" cultural diversity. In fact, there is a large increase in the number of people who identify themselves as multiracial or multiethnic and reject conventional demographic categories.[25]

A process of mutual adaptation is under way in which the mainstream culture, too, is in flux, trying to accommodate the entire mixture of diversity and the growing desire to maintain much of that diversity. The most fascinating developments to watch will be the cultural fusions, where new forms of everything from food and entertainment to business practices and worldviews emerge as the United States innovates at the intersection of multiple cultures. The 2000 census for the first time gave people an opportunity to choose more than one race to describe themselves, and nearly 7 million people did so. Intermarriage rates are soaring, and the number of multiracial children is growing accordingly. By 2050, 21 percent of Americans will be claiming mixed ancestry, according to projections made by the demographers Jeffrey Passel and Barry Edmonston.[26]

In fact, many of the old racial categories we place people into are now becoming irrelevant. Paola Menozzi and Alberta Piazza , in *The History and Geography of the Human Genes,* set out a genetic atlas of the world that demonstrates the genetic absurdity of traditional concepts of race. Their findings virtually eliminate the category of Caucasians. Most European Caucasians are a genetic combination of roughly 35 percent African and 65 percent Asian, even in populations whose gene pools were in place in 1500, before the Americas were colonized.[27] Another recent study determined that there is more genetic diversity on the African continent than on any other.[28] Race is obsolete as a meaningful biological distinction, but racial and ethnic differences still matter at a cultural and personal level. But our old categories often blur important differences and keep us from seeing the diversity within groups in a single accepted category. For example, Americans with Cuban, Puerto Rican, or Mexican heritage may all be called Hispanics or Latinos, but each group's culture is appreciably different from that of the others.

Seeing that the meaningful differences between people are not biological but cultural and personal reaffirms the importance of defining diversity to encompass cultural background, age, values, outlooks, and many other dimensions. Nonprofit organizations can facilitate this type of dialogue in society at large and serve as the nexus for this new blended society. In helping minority groups to preserve the best that their unique cultures offer while learning from the best of others, nonprofit organizations can help build a productive multiracial society. Nonprofit organizations focused on serving the needs of a specific segment of the minority population need to pay special attention to these trends. As multi-ethnic identities grow in number and acceptance, organizations focused on a single ethnic group will need to change and adapt in order to stay relevant. In bridging the gap of cultural misunderstandings by promoting the common good for society, nonprofit organizations can help to create a better society for us all.

Understanding the Generational Constellation

Generational labels can rankle us on a fundamental level because they are inevitably oversimplifications.[29] Each generation can be broken into many subgroups. Even the labels and the years used to define them vary from analysis to analysis. People born on the cusp of two generations often blend the experiences of both. The rich of each generation have very different life experiences than the poor. As more people live longer lives, and patterns of education, work, and leisure become more flexible, the life experiences of different generations may blur together. Ultimately, everyone is a unique individual. Nevertheless, generational labels can serve as a starting point from which to explore the specific characteristics and attitudes of an individual or group of people.

THE GIS (BORN 1900–24). This group is so named because of the dominant role its members played in World War II.

THE SILENT GENERATION (BORN 1925–45). Sandwiched between two dominant generations—the GIs and the baby boomers—members of the silent generation often developed strong negotiating skills.[30] The silent generation produced many of the twentieth century's greatest legislators. Their distinctive leadership role has often involved fine-tuning the institutional order and negotiating between the larger generations around them. They have excelled at bringing people together and modifying the extremes on either side of divisive controversies. The flexible, consensus-building leadership of the silent generation opened many of the paths that baby boomers later traveled, providing leaders ranging from Martin Luther King Jr. and Gloria Steinem to Colin Powell.

THE BABY BOOM GENERATION (BORN 1946–64). The statistical spike in the number of babies born immediately following World War II, when the troops came home, gave rise to the largest generation in American history and the first to be accorded its own name, the baby boom; it was destined to be influential if for no other reason than its size.[31] The social movements for civil rights, women's rights, ecology, and other causes that took place in the formative years of many baby boomers' lives created a sense of idealism. The coming-of-age passions of the baby boom generation calmed as its members took on jobs, started families, and pursued the material comforts of an affluent society. Now many members of this generation are dealing with both their aging parents and their children of all ages, from older members of generation X to budding millennials. Older baby boomers are moving toward career peaks. People who in their youth flaunted their individualism and challenged the moral vacuity of America's institutions now find themselves spending much of their time attending consensus-oriented meetings and managing the types of institutions against which they once rebelled.

The baby boom generation redefined the succeeding life stages as they passed through them, and it is now poised to redefine retirement. Many retirement-age baby boomers—enjoying longer, healthier lifespans in conjunction with varying financial needs—are now choosing to extend their careers in a variety of ways. Some simply stay on their current career path, while others are looking to apply their experience to new, complex social challenges such as education reform and cause-based philanthropic activities. As this generation ages it will have interesting impacts on the nonprofit community in the roles of leaders, primary contributors, volunteers, and recipients of nonprofit-organization services.

GENERATION X (BORN 1961–81). Generation Xers constitute the first wave of the baby boom generation's offspring.[32] They are a highly diversified generation; one in three belongs to an ethnic minority, compared to one in four individuals in the general population. Generation Xers are a smaller generation than their parents, as reflected in another term used to describe them: the baby bust generation. The sheer numbers and cultural dominance of the baby boom generation can be disheartening to a small generation trying to stake out its own identity. Some of their ranks are emerging as the hard-driving entrepreneurs behind the development of new high-tech companies. But having experienced the consequences of their parents' hectic work lives, many generation Xers intentionally seek balance, looking for flexible jobs with tangible outcomes that leave them time to "have a life."

THE MILLENNIAL GENERATION (BORN 1982–2001). The millennial generation's parents were older baby boomers and generation Xers. These were the "babies on board" of the early Reagan years, the "Have you hugged your child today?" sixth-graders of the early Clinton years, the teens of Columbine and, most recently, the high school class of 2000. By 2004 they started entering the workforce and making their presence felt on college campuses. William Strauss, the coauthor or *Millennials Rising,* lists seven important traits of this generation: sheltered, confident, group-oriented, special, achieving, pressured, and conventional.[33]

Millennials offer a sharp contrast to the perception of their predecessors, generation X. Where generation Xers are ironic and cynical, millennials are enthusiastic and idealistic. The drive and passion of the millennial generation will become increasingly important for nonprofit organizations, since millennials are inclined to build and support institutions. Baby boomers tried to tear down dominant cultural institutions, and generation Xers ignored them, but the millennial generation is going to want to rebuild and reform them.

THE DIGITAL GENERATION (BORN 2002–TO BE DETERMINED). The digitals know only a world of ubiquitous computing and WiFi connectivity. As this generation matures and enters society as consumers and producers of digital content, its impact on society will be interesting to watch.

GENERATIONAL SYNERGY. To make their best contribution, these age groups or generations need to work together effectively. To do that, people in each generation need to know something of the life experiences, outlooks, and motivations of each of the other generations around them in the workplace. Each of these generations brings a distinctive culture to the workplace, and their unique needs will evolve over time. The challenge for nonprofit organizations is twofold: to identify and meet the needs of each generation and to develop generational synergies among members of the five cohorts.

Each generational cohort will rely on the nonprofit sector in different ways. The silent generation may need assistance to deal with all of the issues related to aging (for example, health care, retirement finances, advocacy for government benefits), while baby boomers will continue to advocate for social justice issues but will also need assistance with retirement issues. Both the silent generation and the baby boomers could serve as a prime source of funding as well as a large pool of volunteers for nonprofit organizations. Meanwhile, generation Xers and the millennial generation could view nonprofit organizations as vehicles to bridge the gap between haves and have-nots and to advocate for environmental issues.

In addition to meeting the unique needs of each generational cohort, nonprofit organizations, because of their relatively small scale and value orientation, could serve a larger, and perhaps more important, purpose—modeling as well as fostering intergenerational synergy. Facilitating mentoring relationships between the silent generation, generation Xers, baby boomers, and the millennial generation could help each generation to build on its strengths and experiences for the greater good. Fostering intergenerational synergy may, in fact, prove to be one of the nonprofit sector's major contributions to society.

The Changing Definition of Aging

Understanding changing features of the aging process will be key to understanding demographic trends for the foreseeable future. Average life expectancy in the developed world is rising dramatically. A child born today can expect to live nearly thirty years longer than a child born in 1900. Reflecting this, between 2010 and 2030 in the United States the size of the sixty-five-plus population will grow by more than 75 percent.[34] Indeed, with breakthroughs in anti-aging medicine and greater knowledge of disease prevention, living to a healthy 100 years old may not be as rare as it once was. As a result, the number of centenarians is expected to grow from around 100,000 today to 5 million over the next fifty years.[35]

The challenges to society are vast. Never before has such a high proportion of people been living such long, healthy lives. Before the baby boomers there has never been a generation moving toward older age that is so large in proportion to the total population. Finally, there has never before been an older generation whose members have been expected to live longer, healthier and more active lives during their golden years.[36]

Organizations attuned to the unique needs of aging baby boomers will enjoy success in the future. Nonprofit organizations that focus on elder care, such as nursing home care, home health care, and retirement or residential care, will experience a growth in demand. However, with this growth in demand will come more for-profit competitors. Residential patterns will also be affected by retiring baby boomers' choices. For example, over the past few years, small to mid-size college towns have become one of the most popular locations for retirement communities because they combine access to high-quality health care with cultural and educational opportunities.

In fact, the very definition of "old" will change, as baby boomers inscribe the new definition with their life-style choices over the next twenty to thirty years. A new paradigm of life will develop, replacing the old linear paradigm of education-work-retirement with a new cyclical one of learn-contribute-reflect. People will cycle in and out of different learning experiences, different careers, and different forms of reflection.

Nonprofit organizations can play a key role in helping people to reinvent themselves repeatedly. Today's commonly held assumptions about what "old," "retirement," and "a student" means will no longer hold true. Adult education—providing people with meaningful educational and volunteering opportunities and facilitating the development of society's potential—will be key areas for nonprofit involvement.

Fusion Family

The pace of life is accelerating, and free time is becoming one of the most precious commodities for working adults. This acceleration, which some pundits have dubbed "the great blur," is a key force driving lifestyle changes in the American family. Family lifestyles are increasingly being defined by the way in which families approach this critical issue of creating and enjoying some free, unstructured time. What is emerging is a range of family lifestyles bounded by two new approaches, outsourcing and downshifting, that appear to pull in opposite directions.[37]

In the context of family life, outsourcing refers to using money to purchase essential but time-consuming family services. This is often made possible by the incomes from two-career couples or driven by necessity due to increased geographic separation of extended family members and the growth of single-parent households. Daycare and home childcare are the primary family functions that are commonly outsourced, with cleaning and laundry services to a somewhat lesser extent. However, in recent years the scope of family activities that are being subcontracted has expanded considerably. Private tutoring for children is available at neighborhood learning centers or online. Personal assistants will come to your house and precook meals for your family. Services will plan your child's birthday party or assemble family albums from a box of random pictures. As these services become more common and inexpensive, the line between family and family services will grow less distinct.

Downshifting involves limiting the material consumption of the family (which involves accepting a lower income), in order to gain more time to pursue wider personal interests or a more extensive family life. Whether it is a desire to quit the rat race, live a more holistic and sustainable life-style, or allow a parent to stay at home with a child full-time, downshifters are willing to trade material wealth for a better quality of life. Families are beginning to move beyond the suburbs to rural small towns to enjoy the peaceful and unhurried lifestyle of the country. A movement toward voluntary simplicity provides advice and justifications for stepping off the treadmill of the corporate career path. Growing numbers of children are being home-schooled by full-time parents, who are willing to forgo a free public education for their children. The rising popularity of telecommuting, temping, and independent consulting will enable growing numbers of dissatisfied workers to choose a new balance between work, play, and home.

Not only is a range of family lifestyles emerging, but the very structure of the modern family is changing as well. The traditional two-parent nuclear family with a married father and mother living under the same roof with the children is becoming increasingly rare in American society, owing to a combination of premarital sex leading to single parenthood, and no-fault divorce. Four new family structures are in the process of joining the two-parent nuclear family as recognized family forms:

THE GAY AND LESBIAN FAMILY. Same-sex marriage is now legal in five states and Washington, D.C., and another dozen states are considering making it legal. Numerous lawsuits and legal movements on both sides of the issue will shape the nature of this family form in the coming years. Ironically, gay and lesbian couples are fighting for legal rights enjoyed by partners in a traditional marriage, while heterosexual couples seem to be moving away from this ideal.[38]

THE EXTENDED AND BLENDED FAMILY. Once more, as it was a century ago, it is increasingly common for multiple generations to be housed under one roof.

Reasons can include using grandparents for childcare, providing home care for an aging parent, and housing a child unable to afford an apartment after college. Furthermore, blended families, resulting from divorce and remarriage, and adult children's returning home to live with their parents for economic reasons make this category one that seems to be on the rise. In fact, according to recent census data, about 8 percent of all children live in a household that includes at least one grandparent.[39] In a postindustrial era, these extended families are re-creating family structures that generally are associated with the pre-industrial era.[40]

THE SINGLE-PARENT FAMILY. The single-parent family is already a common family form, and it spans the entire range of income levels, from the single mother on welfare to the successful single career woman who decides to start a family.

THE SINGLE-PERSON HOUSEHOLD. The proportion of households consisting of one person living alone increased from 17 percent in 1970 to over 25 percent in 2005. Economic pressures such as the 2008–09 recession may slow this trend, yet shrinking household size remains a long-term demographic direction for the U.S. population.[41]

These new types of family structures and living patterns will challenge nonprofit organizations to reevaluate the mix of stakeholders they serve. Although some family needs, such as child advocacy, will exist regardless of the form of family, nonprofit organizations might discover that new types of families also have new, unmet needs. Furthermore, an expansion in the demand for family services means that nonprofit organizations, more than ever before, will confront stiff competition from the for-profit sector.

Culture of Tomorrow

Whereas demographics and technological trends shape how and what our future might look like, cultural trends reflect society's ability to adapt to its changing environment and our ability as individuals to create something greater than ourselves. Cultural trends inform us of what values we might hold highest in the future and how we might choose to interact and influence each other. They speak of how we will define ourselves and about our highest aspirations for the future.

Values-Driven Cultural Segments

The term "cultural segments" refers to a subsegment of the population that has a common set of beliefs and priorities. Enabled by technology and a clearer sense of what matters to each individual, values-driven cultural segments are emerging in our society. Driven by values, and facilitated by technologies that permit the creation of cultural communities that defy geography, these segments are making their impact on the marketplace of products, politics, and ideas.

The burgeoning Tea Party movement is having an impact on the policies and politics of both major political parties. Driven by an ethos of a smaller government, this values-driven cultural segment is using technology to help organize regional and local rallies in support of its cause and its candidates.

So-called cultural creatives are emerging as a new demographic subculture in America and other developed nations. In extensive surveys and focus groups conducted over the past decade, the sociologist Paul Ray has identified a large cluster of Americans who embrace core values that set them apart from their peers. These values include a preference for holistic thinking, cosmopolitan attitudes, integrated lifestyles, and social activism.[42]

The green movement of the 1990s has fully manifested itself in a sustainability-driven consumer segment whose values are reshaping the marketplace. During the economic downturn of 2008–09 consumer spending dropped dramatically across the board, yet consumer packaged-goods companies such as P&G and Clorox actually saw an increase in sales of their sustainable and green product lines, despite a higher per product cost compared to traditional products. A move toward renewable energy may actually become a reality over the next twenty years in large part due to a values shift toward a pro-environmental stance among a growing number of consumers and businesses.[43]

Learning Culture

In the decade since the turn of the millennium, learning has emerged as one of the key skills that individuals and institutions will need in order to cope with the opportunities and challenges of the twenty-first century.[44] The old models of education are becoming increasingly irrelevant in an economy that places a higher value on skills and abilities than on formal credentials. New communication technologies are putting vast quantities of educational resources online, enabling learning activities to escape the confines of schools and classrooms. We are beginning to evolve toward a learning society that extends learning far beyond classrooms, transforming learning into an activity pursued throughout all of our institutions and throughout the course of our lives.

The need for continuous learning has never been greater. We live in an era where skills are constantly evolving in order to adapt to the rapid changes in technology and the economy. The great challenges we face as a society, from stopping global warming to fostering equitable and sustainable global development, can only be met by collectively "learning our way into the future." As we move toward a model of lifelong learning, nonprofit organizations are in an opportune position to provide educational resources to support continuous learning. Schools are at a competitive disadvantage because of their orientation around a formal curriculum, not around offering extended learning support services. Nonprofit organizations can play a central role in the learning society, shaping environments that are supportive of learning communities.

Virtual Global Communities of Interests

Despite the assertions of scholars such as Robert Putnam, the author of *Bowling Alone*, we are not experiencing a rapid erosion of social cohesion. In fact, some would argue that virtual global communities of interest such as the social-networking website Facebook are redefining community and uniting society. With over 500 million members and counting, Facebook has emerged as a potent example of the power of social media to create community.

Nonprofit organizations will be wise to understand and, when appropriate, harness the power of virtual global communities of interest. Millions of dollars were raised within days of the 2010 Haitian earthquake via text messages and virtual pledges on Facebook and the like. Real-time Twitter feeds and YouTube video postings have allowed global human rights watchdog groups to monitor elections, document injustices, and create support for their causes. During the 2008 presidential campaign, Barack Obama used a multimodal social media strategy to tap into the fundraising and volunteer power of virtual communities of interest to fuel his successful presidential bid.

Ubiquitous access to the Internet via wireless smart phones and tablet computers allows us to find, interact with, and develop meaningful relationships with like-minded individuals who share a common passion, unaffected by geographical separation. Status updates and Twitter feeds let us share our lives (from the mundane to the profound) in a way never previously possible. Fostering a community of supporters, fundraisers, and volunteers may have never been easier for a nonprofit organization. Yet the global reach of these virtual communities means that on some level the competition for attention and financial support from caring individuals may also never have been greater. Successful nonprofit organizations will have to learn how to create their own or become affiliated with complementary virtual communities of interest in order to fully harness the power of this trend.

Conclusion: The Impact of Future Trends on Four Key Impulses Shaping the Future of Nonprofits

All of our experience is with the past, but all of our decisions are about the future. Leaders at every level have usually assumed that their past experience is a fairly reliable guide to the future. This can no longer be taken for granted. Today, in area after area, we are confronted by true uncertainty; we do not know what will happen, but we know that it will happen quickly.

Technological changes, demographic destinies, and the culture of tomorrow will have profound impacts on our society and hence on any and all of our social institutions, including nonprofit organizations. The implications of these trends for the nonprofit sector can be conveniently seen in the impact they are likely to have on the four impulses shaping the nonprofit sector identified in chapter 1 of this volume:

1. *Volunteerism.* Aging baby boomers and caring millennials will be drawn to support causes and organizations they believe in by devoting to them their most precious resource, their time. The challenge for nonprofit organizations will be to communicate how their missions align with the specific values a given volunteer holds and to demonstrate a proven track record of impacting society. By using emerging forms of organizational and community-building tools such as social media websites, nonprofit organizations will be able to attract volunteers from a much larger population than ever before. However, nonprofits must also realize that the competition for volunteer hours will be steep and geographically dispersed. The sheer number of potential volunteers will increase in the coming years, yet nonprofits' need for very specific skill sets will also increase, leading to a furthering of the professionalism of the nonprofit community.

2. *Professionalism.* Online educational opportunities and a growing learning culture will allow nonprofit employees to further sharpen their professional skills. Giving the employees of nonprofit organizations access to the latest portable educational platforms, such as smart phones and tablet computers, will facilitate real-time learning. Professional education will increasingly be available through nontraditional learning organizations using Web 2.0 user-generated content, which should drive down the cost of professional development. Leading-edge nonprofit organizations will develop methods for using the existing professional skills of their volunteer base to further enhance organizational capabilities.

3. *Civic activism.* The near-term future may well become known as the era of social media–driven civic activism, in which Tweets, texts, status updates, photos, and videos have become central facets of the activist's toolkit. Empowered and emboldened by the media, younger people, especially the millennial and digital generations, will become the most civic activism–focused generation in human history. Overall this is a positive development for the nonprofit community, but nonprofit organizations will need to use these technologies to foster long-term relationships with the donor and volunteer communities. The ease of outreach and connection will increase the overall awareness levels of society to a broad host of needs, issues, and causes. Social media–enhanced civic activism will create the conditions for numerous professionally run nonprofit and for-profit "issue of the week" organizations to rise and not only grab headlines but also resources and volunteers, to the potential detriment of long-standing nonprofits.

4. Commercialism. The nonprofit organization will face increased levels of competition in the coming years from civic-minded entrepreneurs. With low to no start-up and operating costs and the potential to capture revenue from a more civic- and values-driven society, "doing well by doing good" could create the environment in which for-profit organizations with missions comparable to those of traditional nonprofits can thrive. These new competitive elements coupled with those creating businesses to take advantage of marketplace trends will also drive the successful nonprofit to behave more like a business in order to recruit and retain talent, attract volunteers, and remain relevant in the face of changing market pressures

Nonprofit organizations must lead the way if we are to create a future that narrows the gaps between the haves and the have-nots, addresses environmental issues, eliminates poverty and disease, and allows for each individual an unencumbered opportunity to maximize his or her unique contribution to society. To do so, they must first understand the underlying forces they will have to contend with. This chapter has provided some markers to help them with this task.

Notes

1. Chris Dede, "Distance Learning to Distributed Learning: Making the Transition" (www.educase.edu/nlii/articles/dede.html [September 2001]).

2. "Green" Hotels Association, "Why Should Hotels Be Green/What Are Green Hotels?" (http://greenhotels.com/index.php [August 29, 2011]).

3. Ibid.

4. "Eco-Friendly Olympics" (www.dfat.gov.au/australia2000/olympics [April 2001]).

5. "Safeway to Install Solar Panels on 23 Stores" (www.environmentalleader.com/2007/09/14/safeway-to-install-solar-power-panels-on-23-stores [November 2010]).

6. "Going Green: Environmentally Friendly Schools Pay Off" (www.csba.org/NewsAndMedia/Publications/CASchoolsMagazine/2008/Spring/InThisIssue/GreenSchools.aspx [December 2010]).

7. Chris Salmans, "Does Green Pay Off?" (www.century21.ca/chris.salmans/chris.salmans/Blog/Does_Green_Pay_Off [December 2010]).

8. RechargeIt.org, "Our Fleet" (www.google.org/recharge/dashboard [November 2010]).

9. "Hybrid Fleet Vehicle Sales Expected to Soar" (www.smartmeters.com/the-news/1195-hybrid-fleet-vehicle-sales-expected-to-soar.html [November 2010).

10. Walter Truett Anderson, *Evolution Isn't What It Used to Be* (San Francisco: Freeman, 1997).

11. "Smart Insulin Molecule" (www.sciencedaily.com/releases/2010/04/100412151834.htm [November 2010).

12. "National Nanotechnology Initiative" (www.nano.gov/html/about/home_about.html [November 2010).

13. "MEMS Clearinghouse" (www.memesnet.org [November 2010).

14. "The Stem Cell Debate" (www.pbs.org/wgbh/nova/miracle/stemcells.html [November 2010).

15. Rainforest Action Network: Action Center (www.ran.org/action [June 2001]).

16. Joseph Gilbert, "Tea Party Express Rolls into Worcester for Last-Minute Rally" (www.examiner.com/tea-party-in-boston/tea-party-express-rolls-into-worcester-for-last-minute-rally [November 2010).

17. Evgeny Morosov, "Iran Elections: A Twitter Revolution" (www.washingtonpost.com/wp-dyn/content/discussion/2009/06/17/DI2009061702232.html [November 2010]).

18. Timon Singh, "How Social Media Was Used during the Mumbai Attacks," Next Generation Online (website) (www.ngonlinenews.com/news/mumbai-attacks-and-social-media [November 2010]).

19. JP Morgan Chase & Co., "Chase Community Giving Announces Winning Charities" (investor.shareholder.com/jpmorganchase/releasedetail.cfm?releaseid=487739 [November 2010]).

20. U.S. Census Bureau, Newsroom, "Census 2000 Shows America's Diversity," press release, March 12, 2001 (www.census.gov/newsroom/releases/archives/census_2000/cb01cn61.html [February 25, 2011]).

21. U.S. Census Bureau, Newsroom, "Nation's Population One-Third Minority," press release, May 10, 2006 (www.census.gov/newsroom/releases/archives/population/cb06-72.html [February 25, 2011]).

22. U.S. Census Bureau, Newsroom, "Hispanic Heritage Month 2010," Facts for Features, July 15, 2010 (www.census.gov/newsroom/releases/archives/facts_for_features_special_editions/cb10-ff17.html [November 2010]).

23. U.S. Census Bureau, "Hispanic Heritage Month 2010: September 15–October 15" (http://www.census.gov/newsroom/releases/archives/facts_for_features_special_editions/cb10-ff17.html [April 17, 2011]).

24. U.S. Census Bureau, "Back to School 2010" (www.census.gov/newsroom/releases/archives/facts_for_features_special_editions/cb10-ff14.html [April 17, 2011]).

25. U.S. Census Bureau, Censusscope, "Multiracial Population," map (www.censusscope.org/us/map_multiracial.html [February 25, 2011]).

26. Barry Passel and Jeffrey Edmonston, *Immigration and Ethnicity: The Integration of America's Newest Arrivals* (University Press, 1994).

27. Paola Menozzi and Alberta Piazza, *The History and Geography of Human Genes* (Princeton University Press, 1994).

28. Science Daily (website), "African Genetics Study Revealing Origins, Migration and 'Startling Diversity' of African Peoples" (www.sciencedaily.com/releases/2009/04/090430144524.htm [April 17, 2011]).

29. For more information on the generational constellations, see Robert Olsen and Atul Dighe, *Exploring the Future* (Washington: ASAE Press, 2001).

30. William Strauss and Neil Howe, *Generations: The History of America's Future, 1584 to 2069* (New York: William Morrow, 1992).

31. Ibid.

32. Ibid.

33. William Strauss and Neil Howe, *Millennials Rising: The Next Great Generation* (New York: Vantage, 2000).

34. U.S. Census Bureau, "Back to School."

35. "Americans Hold Great Expectations for Their Personal Aging, New Survey Reveals," Senior Journal (website), June 13, 2001 (http://seniorjournal.com/NEWS/Aging/2001/06-14-1AttitudeAging.htm [February 25, 2011]).

36. Ken Dychtwald, *Age Power: How the 21st Century Will Be Ruled by the New Old* (San Francisco: Jeremy Tarcher, 2000).

37. Patti Hathaway, "Focus to the Future," *Change Agent* (online journal) 6, no. 1 (www.thechangeagent.com/pdfs/chng6_1.pdf [February 25, 2011]).

38. "Same Sex Marriage," Wikipedia entry (en.wikipedia.org/wiki/Same-sex_marriage [November 2010]).

39. U.S. Census, Newsroom, "Americans Marrying Older, Living Alone More," press release, May 25, 2006 (www.census.gov/newsroom/releases/archives/families_households/cb06-83.html [November 2010]).

40. U.S. Census Bureau, Newsroom, "Grandparents Day 2006: September 10" (www.census.gov/newsroom/releases/archives/facts_for_features_special_editions/cb06-ff13.html [April 17, 2011])

41. U.S. Census Bureau, Newsroom, "Americans Marrying Older, Living Alone More."

42. Paul Ray and Sherry Ruth Anderson, *Cultural Creatives: How 50 Million People Are Changing the World* (San Francisco: Harmony, 2000).

43. "P&G Ups 2012 Green Products' Sales Targets," Environmental Leader (website), March 26, 2009 (www.environmentalleader.com/2009/03/26/pg-expands-sustainability-targets-by-2012/ [November 2010]).

44. For more information on the learning culture, see Olsen and Dighe, *Exploring the Future.*

18

Nonprofit Workforce Dynamics

MARLA CORNELIUS AND PATRICK CORVINGTON

O rganizations are only as good as their members. The ability of the non-profit sector to accomplish the critical work in which it is involved—serving children, resolving social inequities, working to heal the environment, promoting the arts, and the other myriad issues that are the province of the sector—may be most dependent on the ability of nonprofit organizations to continue to attract the right talent. As Jim Collins makes clear, getting the right people on the bus may be the most important first step in achieving organizational greatness.[1]

The frequently mentioned demographic shift that our nation's labor market has begun to experience—the retirement of the baby boomer generation—is a prevalent concern, one that is driven by pure arithmetic. As the boomers exit the workforce, generation Xers are expected to ascend the ranks and fill the vacancies left behind. But the baby boomer generation comprises 76 million people, whereas generation X is significantly smaller: just 48 million people. (The baby boom generation is commonly defined as the cohort of people born between 1946 and 1964. Generation X is usually defined as those born between 1965 to 1980.) Over the past several years, researchers have focused on this demographic shift, looking specifically at how it will impact the nonprofit sector. A series of studies has provided ample evidence that a dramatic exit of boomers will result in a leadership vacuum. The difference in cohort size has resulted in increased efforts to acquire and retain top talent, now a driving concern across all sectors.

In the private sector, this so-called "war for talent" has propelled companies to create career pipelines, offer incentives, and establish various organizational structures to meet the needs of a changing and demanding workforce.[2] The public sector faces similar challenges. From front-line to managerial talent, recruitment and retention issues have driven federal, state, and local agencies to think of creative ways to remain competitive in the talent market.[3]

Some studies state that as many as 75 percent of executive directors may leave their jobs within the next five years.[4] Other research predicts the nonprofit sector will need to find an additional 640,000 new executives—2.4 times the number currently employed—over the next decade or it will experience a leadership shortfall and a dangerous destabilization of nonprofits as vacating executive directors leave positions unfilled.[5]

The fear of an impending mass exodus of leaders from the sector has naturally led to rising concerns about how to identify new leaders, and workforce issues have become high priorities for those thinking about the sector's future. As the nonprofit sector attempts to prepare for this generational shift, individuals are initiating sectorwide discussions about the issues, analyzing trends, and proposing recommendations. These efforts have produced a growing body of research and publications on the processes by which organizations prepare for, manage, and successfully weather executive transitions. Leveraging this opportunity, management consultants, thought leaders, and philanthropic organizations have produced prodigious volumes on the issue; executive transitions and succession planning manuals consequently abound, full of recommendations on such leadership development efforts as mentoring, training, improving recruitment, and finding ways to tap into the passion and motivation of young leaders. Among the questions regularly posed are these: Where will our future nonprofit leaders come from? How is the sector going to prepare them? What role does succession planning play in their development and training? "Building bench-strength" has become a term of art for the purposeful grooming of successors to positions of organizational leadership.

The approach taken thus far, however, is problematic in two significant ways. First, the collective response has been driven by a crisis framework. Although this frame has prompted some helpful responses by creating a sense of urgency around the issue of strong nonprofit leadership and workforce, it has focused attention on the *quantity* of nonprofit workers rather than the *quality,* and on filling existing positions rather than on rethinking the structure of nonprofit work.[6] The crisis frame dominates to such a degree that many organizations have embraced the notion of a crisis while *not* in fact experiencing the crisis of which they speak. They are concerned about being able to attract a workforce, but have not had significant challenges in filling positions.[7] Although some organizations have reported little difficulty in attracting staff, it is difficult to ascertain whether or not organizations are attracting the *right kind of talent*. Is the talent pool from which they are drawing limited by widely held negative opinions of employment in the sector, such as long hours for little pay, poor management, and lack of professional development? In short, is our nation's top talent self-selecting out of the nonprofit sector?

The second problem is that most responses have been targeted at individuals (leadership development programs and skills building) rather than at organizations or the sector as a whole. For example, recent data show that young people remain committed to the work of the sector but organizational and structural barriers prevent them from making this commitment enduring.[8] This suggests that talent and workforce issues may be rooted more in organizations than in individuals. This argument is supported in many of the publications and guides cited in this chapter that point to the need for interventions at the sectoral and governmental levels to effect a lasting impact on broader workforce issues. This is promising in that it may broaden our understanding of mitigating influences and focus our attention not just on individual approaches but also on strategies geared to the infrastructure of organizations and the sector surrounding them.

The notion of a workforce crisis in the sector might be overstated. In fact it might be better stated as a workforce *concern*—one that can be mitigated with the right set of interventions. What cannot be avoided is the recognition that nonprofit organizations' current operating mode is potentially at odds with the kind of work environment and culture that members of the future talent pool want.

Overview of the Nonprofit Workforce

Our aim in this chapter is to explore the current state of nonprofit leadership and talent within the nonprofit workforce and suggest a course of action to ensure that the sector continues to attract a healthy and vibrant pool of talented leaders. To do this, first we'll examine different features of the sector.

Sector Size and Scale

The nonprofit sector has experienced a steady period of employment growth over the past decade, most notably in educational services, nursing and residential care, and social assistance. Surprisingly, this employment growth occurred even during periods when the *overall* employment growth in the United States declined. For example, between 2002 and 2004, the nonprofit sector experienced fairly robust growth in employment of 5.0 percent while employment overall declined by 0.2 percent.[9] In real numbers, the sector employed 9.4 million paid workers and another 4.7 million volunteer full-time equivalents, for a total workforce of 14.1 million.[10] Thus, a significant percentage of the United States' total workforce—10.5 percent—is employed by a nonprofit. These

Figure 18-1. *Nonprofit Paid Employment, by Field*

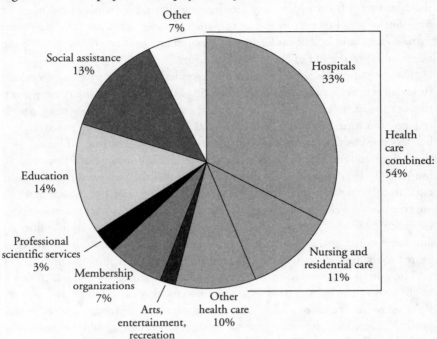

Source: Lester M. Salamon and S. Wojciech Sokolowski, "Employment in America's Charities: A Profile," *Nonprofit Employment Bulletin* 26 (Johns Hopkins University, Insitute for Policy Studies, Center for Civil Society Studies, 2006), p. 10.

workers are distributed across our nation's 1.4 million nonprofits, which span an enormous range of organizations, activities, budget sizes, and social causes (see figure 18-1 for a breakdown of nonprofit employment by field).[11]

The nonprofit giants, hospitals and institutions of higher learning, are the largest employers: about one-third of nonprofit workers are employed in hospitals and another 13.9 percent are in education.[12] These large employers often skew our understanding of the workforce landscape. Although they employ the largest numbers of people, they do not make up a majority of the organizations. Nonprofits with more than $500 million in revenue account for less than 0.1 percent of organizations but more than 27 percent of the sector's assets and revenue.[13] In fact, most nonprofit organizations are quite small; 74 percent are operating with expenses under $500,000.[14] Without question, large institutions provide essential services and play an important role in maintaining the health of this sector. However, the majority of our nonprofits, smaller entities that in the aggregate make up the nation's civil-society sector, deliver many of the human safety-net services on which underprivileged and disadvantaged populations rely.

There is great variety in the types of nonprofits and also in the types of positions found within organizations; thus the skills, education, experience, and career trajectories of nonprofit personnel vary greatly. The nonprofit sector employs scientists, social workers, financial analysts, artists, program assistants, educators, and lobbyists, to name just a few professionals employed in nonprofits. The workforce issues that have come to the forefront of the nonprofit sector's attention—recruitment, retention, employee satisfaction, and career development—are profoundly different depending on the nature of the specific organization. For example, the career path of a director in a small theater group is quite different from that of a finance manager in a large economic development corporation. Similarly, a community health clinic is not competing for staff on equal footing with a large health care company. Yet the full spectrum of dissimilar positions is grouped together under the all-inclusive term "nonprofit workforce."

Employee Satisfaction

The significant differences in the kinds of organizations that make up the nonprofit sector make it impossible to generalize about the nonprofit workforce and prescribe a single course of action for improved workforce development. Despite this challenge, a body of recent research provides some useful data about employee satisfaction as well as the emerging issues that employees face.

Myriad studies have found that the nonprofit sector offers desirable employment for individuals looking for meaningful and fulfilling work. This is partly evidenced by the trend of nonprofit employment growth described earlier. It is noteworthy that the sector continues to attract people despite continuous media reports depicting nonprofits as work settings characterized by low pay, long hours, and staff burnout. Sector leaders who have never been an executive director and want to continue their career doing mission based social sector work are called "next-generation nonprofit leaders." In the first national study of these next-generation nonprofit leaders, *Ready to Lead? Next Generation Leaders Speak Out,* a report released in 2008, 53 percent of respondents stated their commitment to remaining in the nonprofit sector. Remarkably, only 5 percent reported a commitment to leave the nonprofit sector for their next job.[15] Moreover, when asked in which sector respondents' ideal next job would be, 62 percent indicated that it would be a job in the social sectors—those combining nonprofit, philanthropy, and government-related work (see table 18-1). Approximately one in three next-generation leaders report that they aspired to leadership positions, stating that they would like to become executive directors at some point in the

Table 18-1. *Sector for Job Seekers' Ideal Next Job*
Percent

Nonprofit	47
Philanthropy or foundation	9
Government	6
Social sectors subtotal	62
For-profit	5
Self-employed	10
No preference	20
Do not plan to seek future employment	3
Total	100

Source: Marla Cornelius, Patrick Corvington, and Albert Ruesga, "Ready to Lead? Next Generation Leaders Speak Out," national study (San Francisco: CompassPoint Nonprofit Services, 2008).

future.[16] This is particularly interesting considering the prevailing concern that the sector is likely to experience a shortfall of leaders in the coming years.

The research also contains reports of high levels of job satisfaction and commitment to doing mission-driven work. Eighty-seven percent of respondents in the *Ready to Lead* survey reported that they are learning and growing in their nonprofit jobs and 75 percent said that their work was personally fulfilling.[17] A study of human-services nonprofit staff found that "98 percent of respondents said helping people was an important consideration for taking their job, 93 percent said the same about serving their community, and 92 percent about the opportunity to do challenging work." In this same study, 97 percent reported having pride in telling others what they do for a living.[18]

Workforce Challenges

Although the appeal of nonprofit work evidenced by these data is an effective draw deftly employed by nonprofit recruiters, there is reason to believe that the success of that recruitment tack may be temporary. After organizations initially attract talent, *retaining* talent proves more challenging. Staff turnover and position vacancy rates are the result of many complex factors, but one significant factor is how well nonprofits take care of their employees—by providing them with adequate compensation and benefits, opportunities for advancement, and the ability to maintain a healthy work-life balance. It is in these more qualitative areas of employee satisfaction that the data reveal a number of organizational hiring challenges and employee disincentives indicating that the future of the nonprofit workforce could be more challenged than other data might suggest. As indicated in the table below, data suggest that there are a number of

Table 18-2. *Concerns of Nonprofit Employees: Possible Barriers to Retention and Recruitment*

Percent

Concerned about quality-of-life issues	66
Feel underpaid	69
Financial concerns about committing to a career in the nonprofit sector	64
Feel underutilized at work	58
Believe organization is not good at promoting from within	40

Source: Marla Cornelius, Patrick Corvington, and Albert Ruesga, "Ready to Lead? Next Generation Leaders Speak Out," national study (San Francisco: CompassPoint Nonprofit Services, 2008).

employee concerns related to financial stability, promotional opportunities, and quality of life that require further exploration (see table 18-2).

Career Advancement

The smaller nonprofit organizations that many consider the backbone of the sector may face the most challenges in attracting the talent they need. Multi-million-dollar institutions have layered hierarchies and are typically well financed. They have human resource departments, training budgets, and professional staff development plans. Even though in many cases the budgets for the human resources function are stressed and underfunded, these functions are staffed. In most cases these departments are at least able to support the basic human resource functions: administering benefits, conducting talent searches, and coordinating professional development activities. Member and affiliated organizations typically have access to the resources of their national parent agencies. Associations often have annual conferences as well as smaller convenings, which serve as staff development opportunities for member organizations.

Smaller organizations face a significantly different reality. They usually have flat hierarchies that provide little in the way of career advancement. Resources are notoriously scant, forcing them to operate so close to the margins that they are unable to invest sufficiently in their professional infrastructure. Furthermore, smaller organizations rarely have dedicated human resources staff to provide employees with the same benefits as larger organizations. Often the traditional human resources functions become an additional burden of the executive director or one more task for an "office manager" type of employee. The combination of poor human resource administration, anemic benefits, few opportunities for career advancement, reports of burnout, and perceptions of inadequate pay can hamper an organization's ability to attract and retain talent.

The professionalization of the nonprofit sector is still a relatively new phenomenon. There are some nonprofit professional specializations, such as fundraising, that have established certifications and professional associations, but these are the minority.[19] Whereas larger institutions usually provide systems and infrastructure to support professional development and advancement, the far more numerous small organizations with flat organizational structures offer little in the way of articulated career paths and opportunities for promotion. This has reportedly created a "glass ceiling" effect that frustrates workers and obscures the opportunities that do exist. To exacerbate the issue, nonprofit organizations routinely hire outside candidates for executive-level positions, reinforcing the perception that career paths do not exist within organizations. To top it off, next-generation leaders report a lack of support and mentoring from their current supervisors and executive directors.[20] This perceived lack of support, and at times lack of clarity about how to advance (not just in an organization but also in the field), can leave some feeling lost, frustrated, and unable to find a path forward.

Compensation

One of the most significant disincentives to nonprofit employment as reported by both recruiting organizations and employees is the *perception* of low pay and the assumption that inadequate compensation packages are to be expected in many nonprofit jobs. The inability to offer competitive salaries was reported to be the top reason that recruitment was challenging for 87 percent of nonprofit employers in one study. This was followed closely by the inability to offer competitive benefits, reported by 65 percent of hiring organizations.[21] Moreover, individuals wishing to make their careers in the nonprofit sector are concerned about their long-term earning potential or financial security, particularly when reports of low executive director salaries indicate that salaries do not necessarily increase with tenure.[22]

When next-generation leaders were asked if they had financial concerns in committing to a career in the nonprofit sector, 64 percent said yes. When asked what factors contributed to this concern, 48 percent said that they feared they would not make enough money to retire comfortably and 37 percent reported that they believed they would not be able to support themselves or a family if the rest of their career is spent in the sector. Student loan debt is also a significant contributor to financial concerns. Another report found that the current generation of college graduates is entering the nonprofit workforce with greater financial obligations than any previous generation—74.5 percent are graduating with debt incurred for their education, a higher proportion than for graduates entering the private sector or government.[23]

But are these very real concerns based in reality? Data indicate that they are fueled mostly by myth and hearsay. In fact, data suggest that nonprofit employees "actually have higher average wages than for-profit workers in industries in which both are extensively engaged."[24] It appears that public perception, therefore, is rooted in the fact that many nonprofits are in fields that pay less than other fields, such as health and child care, regardless of the sector. Even though not clearly substantiated, the poor-pay perception is prevalent and it informs existing as well as potential employees' employment concerns and affects their actual career decisions in very concrete ways.

Quality of Life

Executive directors have long been reporting high stress and burnout as leading contributors to job dissatisfaction, and recent studies of other nonprofit staff have consistent findings of dissatisfaction among these respondents.[25] Sixty-six percent of next-generation leaders reported quality-of-life issues as predominant reasons that they would not pursue an executive-level position.[26] Long hours, high stress, and crisis-filled environments are characteristics of nonprofit culture that have come to be expected. Nonprofit organizations are often described as having a "culture of sacrifice" or a "culture of martyrdom." Past generations might have accepted this aspect of the job, but younger generations do not appear to be as willing to do so.

Executive directors have not always served as the best role models for potential younger employees. The overworked, harried, and stressed-out executive director has almost become a caricature of leadership in the nonprofit sector. Executive directors regularly complain about the difficulties of fundraising, managing their boards of directors, and the constant struggle of managing under-resourced organizations.[27] This lifestyle holds little appeal for young people following—or not following—in their footsteps. Economic demands have increased as family structures have changed, and current organizational structures and behaviors may not work as well for today's nonprofit employees. Young people report wanting to live differently than their parents did. Specifically, they want to spend more time with their families, be involved in a variety of civic activities outside of work, and proactively avoid burnout—in short, they want to lead more balanced lives. In contrast to the nonprofit sector, the private for-profit sector has responded by providing different opportunities for their employees to have the flexibility they require.[28]

Quality-of-life concerns are also exacerbated by current economic pressures. A recent report on the impact of the current recession on nonprofits found that organizations employed a number of staff-related "belt-tightening strategies" to remain financially viable. Among the numerous cost-cutting activities, 41 percent of organizations have postponed filling new positions, 34 percent have eliminated staff positions, and 33 percent have implemented salary freezes.[29] Many of these strategies will undoubtedly add further stresses to the burdens carried by existing staff.

I Want to Make a Difference

The nonprofit sector was once known as a locus of innovation. Now, under-capitalization may have led to the sector's becoming a lackluster performer in some areas. "Sector agnosticism"—meaning, that many individuals do not have a preferred sector in which to work—is seen as a growing trend.[30] As reported in "Ready to Lead," a substantial 42 percent of respondents stated that they have no sector preference for employment, suggesting that the type of work or specific opportunity matters more than the type of organization where the work happens to be located. Many experts in workforce issues attribute sector agnosticism to the fact that the nonprofit sector is no longer the only place where one can do mission-based work. It is certainly the case that there are many attractive opportunities for mission-related work in public systems and in the private sector, where there are often more resources for innovation. Green technology is one example.

What is important to underscore is an important shift in the attitudes of some younger workers: they want to do work that furthers social justice. This type of work was once the province of the nonprofit sector, but now such opportunities can increasingly be found in any sector.

Clearly people have varied experiences working in nonprofits. For some people, nonprofit jobs are just jobs that provide a paycheck, but for most people working in the nonprofit sector, it provides an opportunity to use their jobs as a vehicle to do something meaningful in their lives. It is perhaps this element of idealism and driving desire to have meaning that creates conflict for some people in the nonprofit sector. In focus groups conducted in the context of the studies *Up Next* and *Ready to Lead* as well as other focus groups, many spoke of the dissonance in the values expressed by organizations and the culture and climate within those organizations. For example, there are organizations working to alleviate poverty while simultaneously paying "poverty wages." Similarly, there are organizations working on issues of race, civil rights, and cultural competence whose staff are themselves experiencing inequities within their organizations. What might be experienced in the private sector as the mundane and normal challenges of any job could become points of contention and job dissatisfaction for those employed in a nonprofit that is felt to be not living up to its values.

Contextual Factors: Additional Workforce Dimensions

Nonprofit organizations face a number of other workforce challenges in addition to the challenges of attracting and retaining next-generation leaders. Some of these are executive leadership transition, generational conflict, the workforce pipeline, and the current economy.

Executive Leadership Transitions

Many transition studies have focused on executive directors, meaning that specifically leadership transition has been the main subject of the research. From these studies we have data evidencing a significant exodus of leadership, with 75 percent of nonprofit executive directors claiming that they will leave their posts within five years. Many executives might not actually leave in the near term, but they will certainly leave eventually, one way or another. However, the fact that these leaders will be leaving their positions may be less central than their *reasons for leaving.* What is striking, and most speaks to the culture and environment in which nonprofits operate, is that the reasons executives cite for wanting to leave are related to burnout. Executive directors report two primary reasons for burnout. Boards of directors contribute to executive stress and job dissatisfaction because of their lack of engagement with the organization, unmet expectations in terms of their governance responsibilities, and a general lack in board leadership and support of the executive director. Second, executive directors report high levels of frustration caused by imbalanced power relationships between funders and the nonprofit. These dynamics cause executives to spend inordinate amounts of time on fundraising activities and meeting unreasonable funder demands.[31]

Generational Conflict

Research on generational conflict in the workforce has highlighted the cultural tensions between baby boomers and younger generations. Much of this tension results from a combination of factors: personality conflicts related to leadership style, differing definitions of employee commitment and ambition, and differing opinions about problem-solving strategies and techniques. The research is often from the perspective of next-generation leaders and their perception that their leadership capabilities are frequently overlooked or dismissed by baby boomer bosses. Many find themselves in what they experience as intolerable work environments where martyrdom is the work ethos fueled by executive directors who have a strong attachment to their organizations and little desire to relinquish the reins.[32]

Workforce Pipeline: Getting a Nonprofit Job

Pipeline research is about why people are attracted to working in the sector and how they access work in it. Pipeline research has highlighted the challenges to those inclined to work in the sector to easily find their way into paid positions at nonprofit organizations—the lack of an "on ramp" to the sector. These studies often focus on young people who are graduating from college and are early entrants into the workforce, and often discuss the lack of ease young people have in finding jobs in the nonprofit sector.[33] But pipeline research is not just about younger people. As the baby boomers reach retirement age, the pipeline research has also turned its attention to people who are looking for second careers in the nonprofit sector. So-called "encore careers" (the term was coined by Marc Freedman of Civic Ventures) are becoming more and more desirable to individuals who either are not ready to stop working or, increasingly, cannot afford to retire, given the decimation of the value of their retirement accounts in light of the recent and ongoing economic crisis.[34]

The Economic Climate at the End of 2011

Indeed, it is difficult to think of a nonprofit sector and its workforce that has not been profoundly influenced by the current economic crisis. In the midst of this ongoing crisis, the United States nonprofit sector finds itself in a particularly challenging paradox: there has been an extraordinary spike in demand for services while there has also been an equally significant decline in philanthropic and some public resources.

Federal, state, and local governments are experiencing dramatic budget shortfalls. It is thought that organizations can expect either significant cuts to existing contracts or drastically delayed payments. These delayed payments, at times many months behind schedule, are placing additional stress on undercapitalized nonprofits. The Center on Budget and Policy Priorities projects that as of fiscal year 2010 state budget deficits will stand at a combined $100 billion, forcing states to drastically reduce services to some of their most vulnerable residents, specifically in the areas of health care and education.[35] Although federal assistance can lessen the negative impact of state budget cuts on vulnerable populations and the nonprofits that serve them, current economic projections indicate that an immediate and permanent 20 percent reduction in expenditures for all federal programs may be necessary in order to close the federal fiscal gap in the next four years.[36] Additionally, in the face of the declining value of retirement accounts and foundation endowments, institutional and individual donors are also cutting back on donations and grants. As the economic crisis continues, individuals working in nonprofits still have job security concerns, despite some indications that improvements are on the horizon. Couple such concerns with still-shaky financial markets and we are likely to see financial constraints on nonprofits for some time to come.

It is unknown exactly how the economic climate might be changing the life of nonprofit organizations, but it appears to be exacerbating the existing pressure on undercapitalized organizations. For many organizations already under stress, the current economic pressures may result in organizations significantly scaling back their work or closing altogether. This climate and the resulting decline in retirement savings may cause many who were contemplating retirement or at least shifting out of their current positions as executive directors to stay in their current positions longer than originally planned.

We know that many organizations facing declining or uncertain funding prospects are waiting to fill vacant positions and others are instituting staff layoffs. This will inevitably result in further understaffing within already lean organizations. This continued shrinking of staffs while service demands increase might fuel the notion that the nonprofit sector is an unattractive place to work, particularly for those seeking leadership positions. In the end, the deepening economic challenges and resulting further undercapitalization of the sector may propel those inclined to work in the sector to make different choices.

As dire as the current economic situation is for nonprofit organizations, the cyclical nature of the economy suggests that the economy will improve, and with it organizations will bounce back. The question remains: Will organizations continue to operate in a scarcity mind-set or will they grow, rise to the challenge, and innovate? The choices they make may be particularly critical as the sector struggles to maintain its footing through an economic recovery.

Strategies for the Long Haul

Because multiple factors influence workforce issues, no single strategy can mitigate all the concerns and solve all the problems of the nonprofit workforce. To ensure a better future for both nonprofits and their current and future staffs, it will be necessary to intervene on multiple levels to improve the workforce in the nonprofit sector: individual, organizational, sectoral, and governmental.

What Can Individuals Do?

Many nonprofit organizations do not have resources to help guide individual employees, and so individuals who take control of their own careers may be at an advantage. There is a lot that individuals can do to advance their own careers and prospects. Most workforce interventions and special training opportunities are accessible to individuals as individuals. They provide many opportunities for young people to develop skills outside their own organizations. Specific activities that have proved to be attractive and effective tools for skills development and career advancement include leadership development programs, technical management training, mentoring, and coaching. In addition to these fairly traditional strategies, career development opportunities also exist in volunteer and board service positions. Joining a board of directors is an ideal way to prepare for leadership positions, yet only 2 percent of nonprofit organizations have board members younger than thirty years of age, and just 36 percent of organizations have board members between thirty and forty-nine years of age. Board service provides direct access to new networks of community leaders and executives. Many of these individuals are likely sources for references and mentors. Younger staff must abandon the rescue myth that a mentor will serve as an illuminating influence guiding them through the opaqueness of nonprofit career pathing. In fact, those who demonstrate the ability to lead themselves will be able to lead others most effectively.

What Can Organizations Do?

Organizations and current executives can draw on a host of strategies to create work settings that attract good people who will want to join and to which they'll commit their careers. Organizations can no longer rely on the nonmonetary benefits of mission-related work as a supplement to noncompetitive wages and benefits. Adhering to an organizational budget that does not provide for competitive salaries, cost-of- living increases, and attractive benefits drastically erodes an organization's competitive advantage in the labor market.

As younger workers enter the labor market, organizations will also need to tackle organizational cultures that prevent healthy work-life balance. Current executives will need to model more balanced work schedules and take care not to imply that long hours and weekends are the means to advancement. Executives should also reevaluate internal systems and structures that alienate and frustrate people. Next-generation research has shown that overly hierarchical and paternalistic organizational structures, leadership that resists change and transparency, and top-down decisionmaking—the hallmarks of many organizations staffed by baby boomers—foster environments that emerging leaders find unappealing.

A combination of two important variables, treatment of employees and compensation, may prove fatal for many organizations if both are negative. Just one variable with a negative profile without the other may prove tolerable for nonprofit staff. An organization's inability to provide competitive salaries may be balanced out by a work environment in which people feel valued, feel that they are making a difference and that their work is important. They may be willing to make the trade-off of lower compensation for the ability to do meaningful work. But if poor compensation is combined with a poor work environment, people will make alternative choices when possible.

Although many organizations may have difficulty dealing with their financial challenges, particularly given the current economy, they can take clear and affirmative steps toward tackling the culture of their organizations. In fact, dealing with these issues could go a long way toward alleviating many of the challenges faced by executive directors. By building stronger teams and practicing shared leadership that extends responsibility down and laterally, executive directors might find that they have talented staff waiting for the opportunity to step up and make a difference. In fact, there is anecdotal evidence that when this has happened, it can be transformative for organizations.[37]

It is prudent for executives and boards to engage in succession-planning activities to prepare for planned and unexpected departures. Less often recognized is that succession planning also entails intentional, planned, and strategic leadership development of current employees throughout the organization. This process helps not only to create stronger organizations but also to articulate growth and development paths for emerging leaders needing assistance and support in their careers.

What Can Be Done at the Sectoral Level?

The nonprofit sector is made up of an intricate web of infrastructure and intermediary organizations that provide services, support, funding, and advocacy on behalf of nonprofits. By conservative estimate, there are seven hundred management support organizations in the United States and forty-one state nonprofit associations with approximately 200,000 members.[38] Despite this support infrastructure, the thousands of organizations that make up the nonprofit sector's infrastructure are fragmented and undertake little coordinated or collective action. Collaboration and robust partnerships aimed at improving workforce issues are nearly nonexistent—those that do exist are fledgling at best. Efforts are thwarted by competing agendas, competition for scant resources, and a lack of sectorwide leadership to unite interests and provide direction. Clearly, an organized infrastructure can have an important impact on the sector as a whole, whatever issue it takes on. This infrastructure, mobilized around workforce issues, could be catalytic in providing a sectorwide response through coordinated strategies. For example, coordinated efforts at conferences including programming for younger staff, scholarships for attendance, and similar actions could serve as simple yet powerful tools for providing leadership and professional development opportunities. Beyond basic programmatic interventions, an organized infrastructure can speak with one voice about a set of potential remedies to address many of the workforce challenges rooted in the structural issues faced by the sector. Specifically, a coordinated approach around developing a more rational capital market for the sector may begin to address issues of fundraising and sustainability. Additionally, as stated earlier, the challenges of creating adequate benefit structures abound. A coordinated strategy to deal with these issues has a natural home with nonprofit infrastructure organizations.

What Governmental Entities Can Do

There are few challenges for the nonprofit sector that are unaffected by public policy, yet the sector generally shies away from proactively seeking to use this potential for effecting positive change. Two categories of the workforce issues described here are tied directly to federal and state policy and fall into two categories: capitalization and structural barriers. First, we know that public dollars pay for much of the nonprofit sector's activities; Medicare and Medicaid alone provide more funds to nonprofits than philanthropy does. Yet as the public sector faces revenue shortfalls and there are increasing budget constraints, it is likely that reimbursement rates will continue to decline, which will force nonprofits to continue to do more with less and exacerbates workforce challenges. Second, the data clearly show the challenges of student debt and its impact on the ability of some to commit to a career in the nonprofit sector. Existing vehicles such as the College Cost Reduction Act of 2007, the Public Service Loan Forgiveness Program, and 20/220 Pathway for Economic Hardship Deferment would mitigate student debt pressures for those willing to make the commitment to working in the nonprofit sector. For seniors, the Pension Protection Act of 2006 includes public policy interventions to address retirement insecurity.[39] Fully exploring public policy options that would relieve operating pressures for nonprofits could very well be the single most important intervention on behalf of the nonprofit sector. Absent public policy intervention, nonprofits are playing at the margins.

Conclusion

It is difficult to imagine just how the nonprofit sector will be transformed by a combination of historic events, the worst economic crisis since the Great Depression, and the election of the first African American president, who has deep roots in the nonprofit sector. What is clear, however, is that there will be change. The current economic crisis looms large, and even some well-regarded and established nonprofits are beginning to lay off staff and close their doors. At the same time there is an equally powerful movement afoot of young people drawn to service. For years, national service has been an important and powerful way to attract young people to the work of the nonprofit sector. Now more than ever, there is a growing wave of enthusiasm for being part of the solution to society's problems, and in many cases, the solution is in the nonprofit sector.

If nonprofit sector leaders can effectively advocate for government support through proposed and nascent economic stimulus activities, the marrying of government investment in the nonprofit sector with a wave of committed and enthusiastic young people could be transformative for the sector. If this potential is realized, organizations might not need to worry about how to transform themselves to meet the needs of the incoming workforce because young people coming into the sector will themselves create and transform organizations. Indeed, they always have.

Notes

1. Jim Collins, *Good to Great and the Social Sectors* (Colorado: Author, 2005), p. 13.

2. For a discussion of the war for talent see "The War for Talent," *The McKinsey Quarterly* 3 (1998): 44–57, and "The Battle for Brainpower," *The Economist,* October 6, 2006.

3. Dr. Mary B. Young, "Building the Leadership Pipeline in Local, State and Federal Government," report, International City/County Management Association (Washington: ICMA, 2005; free download at www.icma.org).

4. See Adams & Associates, "Community-Based Organizations and Executive Leadership Transitions: A Survey of Annie E. Casey Community-Based Grantees" (Baltimore: Annie E. Casey Foundation, 2003); Jeanne Bell, Rick Moyers, and Tim Wolfred, "Daring to Lead 2006: A National Study of Nonprofit Executive Leadership" (San Francisco: CompassPoint Nonprofit Services, 2006); P. Teegarden, "Nonprofit Executive Leadership and Transitions Survey 2004" (Silver Spring, Md.: Managance Consulting, 2004).

5. Thomas J. Tierney, "The Nonprofit Sector's Leadership Deficit" (San Francisco: Bridgespan Group, 2006).

6. Frances Kunreuther and Patrick A. Corvington, "Next Shift: beyond the Nonprofit Leadership Crisis" (Baltimore: Annie E. Casey Foundation, 2007).

7. Lester M. Salamon and Stephanie L. Geller, "The Nonprofit Workforce Crisis: Real or Imagined?" Listening Post Communiqué No. 8 (Johns Hopkins University, Center for Civil Society Studies, Listening Post Project, 2007).

8. Marla Cornelius, Patrick Corvington, and Albert Ruesga, "Ready to Lead? Next Generation Leaders Speak Out" (San Francisco: CompassPoint Nonprofit Services, 2008), pp. 16–20.

9. Salamon and Geller, "Nonprofit Workforce Crisis."

10. Lester M. Salamon and S. Wojciech Sokolowski, "Employment in America's Charities: A Profile," Nonprofit Employment Bulletin No. 26 (Baltimore: Johns Hopkins University, Center for Civil Society Studies, 2006).

11. Kennard T. Wing, Thomas H. Pollak, and Amy Blackwood, *The Nonprofit Almanac 2008* (Washington: Urban Institute, 2008).

12. Salamon and Sokolowski, "Employment in America's Charities."

13. Shelly Cryer, *The Nonprofit Career Guide* (St. Paul: Fieldstone Alliance, 2008), p. 21.

14. Ibid., p. 21.

15. Marla Cornelius, Patrick Corvington, and Albert Ruesga, "Ready to Lead? Next Generation Leaders Speak Out," research study (San Francisco: CompassPoint Nonprofit Services, 2008), p. 12.

16. Ibid., p. 7.

17. Ibid., p. 12.

18. Paul C. Light, "The Health of the Human Service Workforce," Center for Public Service report (New York: Center for Public Service, Robert F. Wagner Graduate School of Public Service, March 2003), p. 7.

19. For information on professional fundraising, see the website of the Association of Fundraising Professionals (www.afpnet.org).

20. Cornelius, Corvington, and Ruesga, "Ready to Lead?" pp. 20–22.

21. Salamon and Geller, "Nonprofit Workforce Crisis."

22. Bell, Moyers, and Wolfred, "Daring to Lead 2006," pp. 17–20.

23. Amanda Ballard, "Understanding the Next Generation of Nonprofit Employees: The Impact of Educational Debt," study conducted for the Building Movement Project (New York, 2005), p. 2.

24. Lester M. Salamon, "What Nonprofit Wage Deficit?" *Nonprofit Quarterly*, Winter 2002, p. 61.

25. Bell, Moyers, and Wolfred, "Daring to Lead 2006."

26. Cornelius, Corvington, and Ruesga, "Ready to Lead?" p. 18.

27. Bell, Moyers, and Wolfred, "Daring to Lead 2006."

28. Institute for Corporate Productivity, "I4CP Study: Flexible Work Arrangements Gaining More Attention in the Workplace" (www.i4cp.com/print/news/2009/08/17/i4cp-study-flexible-work-arrangements-gaining-more-attention-in-the-workplace [August 29, 2011]).

29. Lester M. Salamon, Stephanie L. Geller and Kasey L. Spence, "Impact of the 2007–09 Economic Recession on Nonprofit Organizations," Listening Post Communiqué No. 14 (Johns Hopkins University, Center for Civil Society Studies, Listening Post Project, 2009).

30. Cornelius, Corvington, and Ruesga, "Ready to Lead?" p. 3.

31. Ibid.

32. See Frances Kunreuther and Patrick A. Corvington, "Next Shift: Beyond the Nonprofit Leadership Crisis," study conducted for the Building Movement Project (Baltimore: Annie E. Casey Foundation, 2007; free download at www.buildingmovement.org/news/entry/3).

33. Cryer, *Nonprofit Career Guide*, p. 1.

34. See Marc Freedman, *Encore: Finding Work That Matters in the Second Half of Life* (New York: PublicAffairs, 2007).

35. Nicholas Johnson, Elizabeth Hudgins, and Jeremy Koulish, "Facing Deficits, Many States Are Imposing Cuts That Hurt Vulnerable Residents," report (Washington: Center on Budget and Policy Priorities, November 2008).

36. Richard Kogan, Kris Cox, and James Horney, "The Long Term Fiscal Outlook Is Bleak," report (Washington: Center on Budget and Policy Priorities, December 2008).

37. A point made by Patrick Corvington of the Annie E. Casey Foundation at a conference, "Organizational Transformation," held at the Annie. E. Casey Foundation, Baltimore, 2007.

38. Paul Connolly and Peter York, "Building the Capacity of Capacity Builders: A Study of Management Support and Field-Building Organizations in the Nonprofit Sector" (New York: Conservation Company, 2003), p. 13.

39. See "Summary of the College Cost Reduction and Access Act (H.R. 2669)" (www.nasfaa.org/publications/2007/g2669summary091007.html). The Pathway for Economic Hardship Deferment is a debt-relief plan for medical students that provides for three years of deferment of payments on loans that equal more than 20 percent of an individual's income. For an explanation see "Department of Education Defers Medical Student Loan Deferment" (www.calphys.org/html/cc557.asp). For an explanation of the Pension Protection Act of 2006, see Joint Committee on Taxation, "Technical Explanation of H.R. 4, the 'Pension Protection Act of 2006,' as Passed by the House on July 28, 2006, and as Considered by the Senate on August 3, 2006 (JCX-38-06)" (www.dol.gov/ebsa/pdf/x-38-06.pdf).

19

For Whom and for What? Investigating the Role of Nonprofits as Providers to the Neediest

PASCALE JOASSART-MARCELLI

In the 1830s, the practice of forming voluntary associations to serve the multiple and diverse needs of the population struck Alexis de Tocqueville as distinctively American.[1] Subsequently, many observers would note the presumably unique role of charitable organizations in American society, ranging from pioneer communities, abolitionist associations, and settlement houses to today's large-scale and vertically integrated hospitals, universities, and social-service agencies. Although the nature of charities has changed dramatically over time, it has generally been assumed that such organizations primarily serve the needs of the poor. Today's nonprofit sector is no different than early mutual aid societies in the sense that it is often perceived as the provider of last resort, when family, friend, and government supports fail. Nonprofits may be the only source of assistance to families that have lost their shelter, aliens who fear deportation, victims of domestic violence, or mentally disabled patients abandoned by the health care system. This representation of the nonprofit sector as benevolent is so ingrained in our culture that the motives and purposes of philanthropy and charity are rarely questioned. The purpose of this chapter is to assess this belief

This chapter builds on the chapter written by William Díaz for the first edition of *The State of Nonprofit America*. Although he died in 2002, Díaz's work continues to influence research on Latino populations and equity issues in the nonprofit sector. The author would like to thank Jennifer Wolch for comments and suggestions on an earlier draft.

in the benevolence of the nonprofit sector in light of available evidence. The central conclusion that emerges is that this belief is largely a myth and that a social policy that is based on it entails serious dangers.

The idea of a charitable nonprofit sector that would meet the needs of the poor better than other institutional arrangements reflects several ideological and cultural traits of United States politics. The emphasis on aid to the poor is strongly embedded in the country's Judeo-Christian religious tradition, which calls upon people to give to those in need.[2] Few passages in the Bible illustrate the importance of taking care of the needy better than Matthew 25:35–37: "For I was hungry and you gave me food, I was thirsty and you gave me something to drink, I was a stranger and you welcomed me, I was naked and you gave me clothing, I was sick and you took care of me, I was in prison and you visited me." It is often assumed that the moral values of charity and caring for those in need will lead people to organize and provide for one another and thus make the need for government redistribution moot. This is best illustrated by the media coverage of natural disasters such as Hurricane Katrina or the recent California fires. In both cases, the food and clothing donations of individuals throughout the United States and the efforts of nonprofit organizations received disproportionate attention and were often portrayed as more efficient initiatives than those of governments.

Indeed, a widespread distrust of large government underlies this idea that small-scale voluntary organizations promulgating American values of efficiency, localism, and self-sufficiency will suffice to respond to the country's problems of poverty and deprivation. The conservative agenda for social policy, which reflects the doctrine conservatives call compassionate conservatism, relies on the assumption that the needs of the poor will be better served by the "thousand points of light . . . all the community organizations that are spread like stars throughout the Nation, doing good," than by the federal government.[3]

Despite this culturally and ideologically embedded perception that nonprofits primarily serve the poor and disadvantaged, and do so with great efficiency, the available evidence fails to support these claims. There appears to be a disjunction between the myth of the nonprofit sector's benevolence and the reality of what it is willing and able to do to support people in need. Important questions remain regarding whose needs the nonprofit sector really serves and how these needs are being served. This chapter focuses on these equity concerns.

In the past three decades, the role of nonprofit organizations in serving the disadvantaged has been increased as a result of important policy changes affecting both the so-called welfare state and the nature of the voluntary sector itself. As a result of these policy changes, the United States is characterized by a complex government welfare system that subsidizes private and nonprofit social services providers (see chapter 15, this volume). Yet federal devolution and cutbacks of important social programs have put increasing pressure on the nonprofit sector as provider of last resort.[4] In addition, a number of policies—including the Workforce Investment Act (WIA), Temporary Assistance for Needy Families (TANF), and the Low-Income Housing Tax Credit (LIHTC), have specifically carved out a role for nonprofit organizations, as either substitutes for or partners with government agencies. Chapter 15 in this volume, by Kirsten Grønbjerg and Lester M. Salamon, discusses the complexity of the relationships between the public and nonprofit sectors, and highlights both the tensions and the opportunities for partnership. Debates on the nature of these relationships notwithstanding, there is no doubt that nonprofits are expected to play an increasingly important role in the provision of services to the poor.[5] However, the assumption that they will be able to do so without government assistance is likely to lead to further social inequalities.

If poverty is an appropriate indicator of need, there are valid reasons to be concerned about the ability of the nonprofit sector to play a critical role in social policy. Most recent census figures from the Current Population Survey indicate that in 2007 more than 37 million people lived in households with income below the official poverty threshold ($21,027 for a family of four), and the number of children and immigrants living in poverty experienced a sharp increase over 2006. Women and minorities are disproportionately affected by poverty.[6] For example, in 2007, 25 percent of blacks and 22 percent of Latinos were living in poverty, compared to 10 percent of whites. These figures are even more troubling if we consider the inadequacy of the official poverty threshold to reflect current economic hardship.[7] Raising poverty thresholds to 150 percent of the official limits in order to reflect rising costs of living and working produces poverty rates of 22 percent for the entire population, 38 percent for Latinos, and 37 percent for blacks.

Since the early 1970s, the gap between the top 20 percent and the bottom 20 percent of the household income distribution has increased dramatically. Despite small improvements in the income of the bottom fifth in recent years following changes in minimum-wage regulations, inequality has continued to grow as a result of disproportionately high rates of income growth for the top 20 percent.[8]

On top of this, the 2008–09 recession has pushed additional families into economic distress. The mortgage crisis has created severe financial hardship for many families that have lost their homes and joined those in precarious housing conditions. Rising unemployment figures and returning troops from the wars in Iraq and Afghanistan heighten the need for workforce development, health care services, and housing. This chapter focuses on whether, and how, the nonprofit sector is meeting these needs and those of disadvantaged populations in general.

Three Spheres of Interaction between Nonprofits and the Poor

There are three primary ways in which the nonprofit sector can contribute to the well-being of disadvantaged populations. First, it can provide services that would not be otherwise available, because of a lack of supply by other sectors of the economy, limited accessibility, or prohibitive cost. Second, nonprofits can advocate for the needs of low-income and minority populations. Doing so is critical to the development of antipoverty policies. Third, the nonprofit sector can play an important role in creating social capital in disenfranchised communities by promoting trust, community involvement, and voluntarism. "Social capital" here refers to the resources associated with social networks and institutionalized relationships.[9] Yet in each of these spheres there are significant questions about the benevolence of nonprofit organizations. First, there are concerns about the type of services provided by nonprofits and the targeted beneficiaries. Are nonprofits as charitable as is commonly believed? What type of services do they provide? Whose interests do they serve? Do the types and purposes of nonprofit organizations vary geographically?

Second, there are concerns that the nonprofit sector may not effectively address the root causes of poverty and inequality. Although nonprofits provide temporary assistance to populations in need through the distribution of goods and services, their role in promoting civic activism and policy change is less well understood. How important is the role of antipoverty nonprofits in lobbying and advocating for policies addressing the needs of low-income populations?

Third, although nonprofit activity is often associated with social capital and social networks, it is unclear whether and how nonprofits actually build social capital in poor communities. To what extent do disadvantaged groups participate in community-based nonprofits through voluntarism and philanthropy? How does involvement in such organizations empower specific groups and create positive spillovers for their community?

The ability of the nonprofit sector to provide antipoverty services, advocate for equitable policy, and build social capital in poor neighborhoods needs to be seen in the context of the evolving relationship between governments and nonprofits and the changing nature of the nonprofit sector. For instance, is the ability of the nonprofit sector to address the needs of the poorest affected by federal devolution and recent trends towards greater commercialization and professionalism among nonprofits? This issue also has important geographic implications to the extent that financial resources are inversely related to financial needs, and consequently, availability and accessibility to services may be limited in poorer locales. An analysis of the nonprofit sector's ability to serve those with greatest needs thus requires an investigation of equity issues at multiple levels, ranging from the nation to regions, communities, and organizations.

The remainder of this chapter is organized around a critical examination of the three potential contributions of the nonprofit sector to a poverty reduction agenda, including antipoverty service delivery, policy advocacy, and social-capital creation. I argue that nonprofits lack the financial resources to effectively meet the needs of the poor and are falling short on their potential to serve and empower marginalized populations, particularly in geographically isolated areas of concentrated poverty. Consequently, the recent social policy changes that mistake for reality the myth of a nonprofit sector primarily focused on charity to the poor are likely to result in the reproduction of poverty through increasingly unmet needs.

In the following sections we examine in greater depth the three ways the nonprofit sector interacts with the poor and poor communities.

Nonprofits as Providers of Services to the Poor

The lack of available information means that determining who benefits from the nonprofit sector is not an easy task. The main sources of data on nonprofit services, the Economic Census, undertaken every five years by the Census Bureau, and annual Internal Revenue Service data on tax-exempt organizations, focus on organizations rather than on their clients. Thus, with the exception of in-depth surveys of specific segments of the industry or regions, information regarding the demographic characteristics of the populations served by public charities is not readily available. In addition, neither of these data sources include information on religious organizations, whose missions may lead them to serve people in need; they are not required to file for IRS tax-exempt status, and are considered "out-of-scope" by the Economic Census.

Self-reported primary organizational purposes reflect the nature of services provided, and thus may hint at the type of populations served.[10] Such information must be used with caution, however. For example, the assumption that social service organizations primarily serve the poor may not reflect reality. Nonprofit child-care centers may provide services to needy populations such as low-income single mothers required to work by restrictions on welfare benefits. Many, however, offer exclusive early-childhood development services for high-income families. In contrast, arts organizations are typically expected to benefit the middle and upper classes. Yet, there are examples of nonprofits promoting arts among marginalized populations, including inner-city youths and cultural minorities.

The most recent Internal Revenue Service data available indicate that in 2006, there were 328,075 reporting public charities in the United States, with approximately a third of organizations involved in the provision of human services (see table 19-1).[11] However, this subset of organizations accounts for only 13 percent of all nonprofit spending. In a survey of nonprofit social service providers,

Table 19-1. *Public Charities and Expenditures, 2006*[a]

Type	Number of organizations	Percent of organizations	Percent of expenditures
Arts	36,649	11.15	2.12
Education	57,273	17.42	16.69
Higher education	2,040	0.62	11.19
Other	55,233	16.8	5.50
Environment	13,801	4.2	0.85
Health	42,200	12.84	58.73
Hospital	4,613	1.4	43.14
Other	37,587	11.44	15.59
Human services	111,105	33.8	13.22
International	6,151	1.87	2.20
Mutual benefit	858	0.26	0.19
Public and Societal benefit	40,497	12.32	5.20
Religion	19,447	5.92	0.77
Unknown	709	0.22	0.03
All public charities	328,690	100	100

Source: National Center for Charitable Statistics, "Public Charities," *IRS Core File 2006* (Washington: Urban Institute, 2008).

a. Organizations are grouped by major National Taxonomy of Exempt Entities (NTEE) category.

Salamon found that only 27 percent of such organizations reported serving mostly poor clients and an additional 20 percent indicated that some of their clients were poor.[12] For the majority, less than 20 percent of their clients were in poverty. Recent trends toward professionalization and commercialization of nonprofits, which are increasing the pressure on nonprofit social service providers to be self-sufficient and to demonstrate effectiveness, seem likely to reduce their willingness to serve very poor people with multiple and complex needs.

Health nonprofits account for over half of expenditures by reporting public charities, although only a small fraction is allocated to serving the needs of the poor and uninsured. For instance, earlier studies found that, on average, nonprofit hospitals served lower proportions of low-income patients than state hospitals did.[13] Bradford H. Gray and Mark Schlesinger, in chapter 2 of this volume, highlight a number of recent conflicting developments that on the one hand require additional evidence that nonprofit health providers meet their community benefit obligations but on the other intensify competition for funding with for-profit hospitals and thus limit resources available to help the poor. Education nonprofits represent another significant share of organizations and expenditures, but they tend to serve children from more affluent families, and

Table 19-2. *Antipoverty Nonprofit Organizations and Expenditures, 2006*

| | Organizations | | Expenditures | |
Type	Number	Percent	Billions	Percent
Antipoverty	39,505	12.04	76.00	6.31
Other	288,570	87.96	1,126.00	93.69
Total	328,075	100	1126.23	100

Source: National Center for Charitable Statistics, "Public Charities," *IRS Core File 2006* (Washington: Urban Institute, 2008).

from fewer minority families, despite recent efforts to increase racial and economic diversity among students and faculty (see chapter 3, this volume).[14]

Although no clear conclusion may be drawn from these broad categories, the core codes of the National Taxonomy of Exempt Entities (that is, NTEE-CC) can be used to identify organizations most likely to provide antipoverty services.[15] These include homeless shelters, low-income and subsidized rental housing, food banks and pantries, soup kitchens, job-training programs, sheltered employment, community clinics and mental health centers, hot lines and crisis intervention services, family and human services, ethnic and immigrant centers, urban and community economic development programs, and others. In 2006, almost forty thousand organizations, or 12 percent of all reporting public charities in the NCCS (National Center for Charitable Statistics) data, were estimated to provide services to the needy (see table 19-2). However, many of these organizations have smaller budgets and together only represent 6 percent of all nonprofit expenditures. These findings suggest that antipoverty activities are not the principal focus of nonprofit organizations in the United States.

In contrast, the majority of nonprofits are involved in activities—described by Julian Wolpert as amenity services such as education, culture, and health care—that disproportionately benefit higher-income populations.[16] Private universities, museums, and operas are often described as elitist.[17] Even popular organizations such as the YMCA have been criticized by for-profit health clubs for catering to the affluent and abusing their tax-exempt privilege. According to Wolpert, this imbalance between antipoverty or equity-based services and amenity services is particularly high in suburban communities, where higher levels of generosity translate into greater support for local amenities.[18] In contrast, in central cities, a greater proportion of nonprofits support charitable purposes, but here, resources are significantly lower, especially in light of the high needs for services in concentrated poverty areas. These trends, combined with the financial pressures described in the following section, lead to a very uneven distribution of antipoverty nonprofit activity among regions and neighborhoods, whereby needs in the poorest communities are rarely met.[19]

Determining the race and ethnicity of nonprofit clients or service recipients is even more challenging than estimating their poverty status. Most studies investigating equity questions related to race and ethnicity focus on organizations that clearly identify themselves as serving specific populations.[20] The Mexican Legal Defense and Education Fund and the National Association for the Advancement of Colored People are prominent examples of such organizations. Yet there also exist many smaller so-called indigenous, or community-based, institutions that have historically served the needs of ethnic and racial minorities and immigrants from diverse countries.[21]

Indigenous organizations, or agencies created by disadvantaged groups to serve their particular needs, have had a critical yet ambiguous role in promoting equal access to opportunities in the United States. In a society where economic and political participation has been limited by unequal rights and discriminatory practices, nonprofits have emerged to provide for the needs of disadvantaged minorities and advocate on their behalf. Beginning in the early eighteenth century, mutual aid societies and other associations developed to serve the needs of freed slaves, Native Americans, new immigrants, and women.[22]

In 2006, included in the Internal Revenue Service's NCCS core data were about fourteen hundred ethnic and immigrant centers that were working alongside churches and less formal organizations to help immigrants with a broad range of issues. There were also more than a thousand civil rights organizations, although those focusing on minority rights are increasingly overshadowed by those advocating for the rights of children, women, lesbians and gays, and disabled individuals. As disadvantaged groups become less marginalized, they are likely to receive more support from institutional philanthropy and become more successful in advocating for the needs of their members.[23] Thus, the challenge remains to support the smaller and struggling organizations that are advocating for the most disenfranchised groups.

The early mutual aid and benevolent societies, in addition to providing services to their communities, often had a larger purpose of promoting integration and assimilation of their members in mainstream society. To this end they often adopted a moralizing stand, promoting traditional values in an effort to show that minorities—the recipients of their assistance—were "deserving" of equal opportunities. Many organizations, particularly those linked to churches, engaged in paternalistic antipoverty efforts aimed at controlling individuals deemed inferior, different, or deviant.[24]

The historically moralizing attitude of indigenous and other charitable organizations continues to be reflected in the types of services provided by antipoverty nonprofits today. In a context where cultural explanations of poverty dominate, initiatives designed to alter the behavior of the poor are favored over those providing financial aid or direct material support.[25] Thus, a number of voluntary organizations are involved in providing public education, motivation, and inspiration, which has led to a "spiritualization" of social services. According to David Wagner, these types of social services are based less on the needs of the poor than on the convictions of donors and volunteers.[26]

This focus on personal transformation rather than material assistance is particularly characteristic of religious charities, which, as noted earlier, are typically excluded from official statistics. According to Luis E. Lugo, faith-based organizations provide a qualitatively different type of service that "addresses matters of the heart and draws on spiritual and moral resources largely beyond the reach of government."[27] Cash is practically never given by religious organizations, which instead favor labor-intensive services provided by their volunteers. Estimates of the proportion of religious organizations' spending directed to social services, including food, shelter, and counseling, range from 10 to 20 percent.[28] Despite these trends, important distinctions exist among religious traditions of charity. Although evangelical and conservative Protestant churches tend to primarily serve the needs of their members, liberal Protestant, Jewish, and Catholic churches are more likely to serve anyone in need.[29] Attitudes toward unwed mothers, alcoholics, addicts, and people with AIDs also differ dramatically among religious organizations.[30]

This moralization and spiritualization of nonprofit services can be linked to the continued pull of the voluntarism impulse in the nonprofit sector cited by Lester Salamon in the introduction to this volume. At the same time, the increased professionalization of the sector has brought a greater emphasis on therapeutic services. As volunteers have been progressively replaced by social workers, providers have come to be seen as professionals or experts in understanding what the poor need, lending them some authority in counseling individuals on their behavior and emphasizing the need for personal responsibility.[31]

This focus on individual treatment driven by the professional impulse undercuts efforts to alter structures of political and economic power.[32] Similarly, Ruby Takanishi argues, this "mantra of empowerment" through education and social-capital-building efforts actually diverts attention and resources from the structural causes of poverty such as labor and housing markets, and rarely leads to actual empowerment.[33]

In short, the assumption that nonprofits primarily serve the needs of the poor and marginalized does not appear to be supported by the existing evidence. A minority of secular and religious charitable organizations is involved in antipoverty activity, and the types of services provided may not in fact adequately serve the most pressing needs of low-income people and society as a whole. Although thousands of volunteers and nonprofit workers throughout America help millions of hungry and sick persons, unemployed workers, homeless families, and neglected children, their efforts are unfortunately insufficient to adequately address the needs of the poor in a highly polarized society. This is not a new finding. Indeed, in the United States, the creation of the welfare state can be linked to the progressive realization that private charities were unable, certainly on their own, to fully deal with the needs of the poor in a rapidly industrializing and urbanizing society.[34]

Nonprofit Advocacy for Antipoverty Policies

Given that the nonprofit sector alone cannot solve the problems of poverty, one of its most important contributions may be to shape public policy by generating knowledge about poverty and advocating on behalf of the poor—that is, pursue social change through discussion, information, demonstration, or protest. Nonprofits can also lobby for social change—attempt to influence particular government legislation. Lobbying, however, is heavily regulated, and many organizations are reluctant to participate in such activities. Although advocacy is less heavily regulated than lobbying, it requires a significant mobilization of resources, severely limiting the nonprofit sector's ability to advocate for the needs of minority and low-income populations.

Quantifying the participation of nonprofits in lobbying activity is challenging. In general, nonprofits that are engaged extensively in activities designed to influence policy for the promotion of "social welfare" are registered with the IRS as 501(c)(4)s. These organizations differ from public charities, 501(c)(3)s, in their ability to lobby and in the fact that donations made to them are not tax-deductible. In many cases, however, the distinction between 501(c)(3) and 501(c)(4) entities is blurry, for the IRS itself is unclear about what defines lobbying.[35] Studies show that only a small proportion of 501(c)(4)s actually participate in lobbying efforts.[36] In 2003, less than 6 percent of the 121,000 social welfare organizations registered in the United States self-identified as advocacy organizations.[37] Among the remaining entities several claimed to be involved in the following activities: inner- city or community activities (10.9 percent), civil rights activities (1.9 percent), job training (0.3 percent), and antipoverty work (0.1 percent). Others included primarily health organizations such as HMOs and local associations of employees, which rarely address the needs of the poor or the uninsured.

According to the data gathered by Jeff Krehely and Kendall Golladay, the majority of the ten largest advocating entities are not actively promoting any policies targeting the poor or other disadvantaged groups.[38] In 1999, these included a number of health care organizations, the Aircraft Owners and Pilots Association, Greenpeace, the American Israel Public Affairs Committee, and the National Right to Life Committee. However, the top-ten list also included the National Association for the Advancement of Colored People and the American Civil Liberties Union, which have been active in the defense of civil rights. Not far down the list, one could find the National Rifle Association and other institutions that play an active role in shaping public opinion and mobilizing voters in ways that rarely benefit the poor. Given the diversity of 501(c)(4) organizations, there is an urgent need for research on their role in promoting public policy and participation.[39]

Public charities represent a much larger component of the nonprofit sector: more than 800,000 organizations representing over 60 percent of all registered nonreligious tax-exempt organizations. Their ability to lobby is limited by the tax code, and according to 2006 NCCS Core IRS data, less than 1 percent of public charities report any expenditures associated with lobbying activity. This proportion is even lower among organizations involved in antipoverty efforts (see chapter 10 in this volume, by Elizabeth T. Boris and Matthew Maronick). However, many of these organizations are involved in advocacy efforts designed to sensitize the public to issues of poverty and social justice in order to increase support for their causes.

Among institutions with 501(c)(3) status, foundations are usually more involved in research and policy development than are public charities, which primarily focus on service delivery. Yet they are often hesitant to support social change. According to Emmett Carson, foundations have often provided innovative leadership in health and education, but rarely in the area of social justice advocacy.[40] Reliance on the benevolence of the wealthy is unlikely to lead to major social change in favor of the poor. At the end of the nineteenth century, Andrew Carnegie's Gospel of Wealth called for wealthy entrepreneurs to use their fortunes to alleviate poverty. As Robert H. Bremmer argues, however, this "philanthropy was less the handmaid of social reform than a substitute for it."[41] Indeed, increased philanthropy was meant to reduce the role of governments and prevent drastic changes to the existing social order. During the 1980s and 1990s, a similar agenda was promoted by a number of conservative foundations that saw an expansion in the role of nonprofits, including faith-based organizations, in the delivery of social services as an efficient alternative to large government. In other words, philanthropy has been critical in "subsidizing" the practice of limited government and maintaining a social status quo. This perspective ignores the fact that many nonprofits need government resources to operate and reach their goals. Instead, it views governments as an obstacle in the development of individual and community responsibility.[42] Thus, by supporting the myth of a benevolent and charitable nonprofit sector focused on alleviating poverty, conservative philanthropic organizations indirectly contribute to cutbacks in government funding and the reproduction of poverty.

Results from the Johns Hopkins Listening Post Project, which surveyed over 872 nonprofit organizations, indicate that three out of four public charities are involved in some form of advocacy, yet very small proportions of their budgets are allocated to these activities, which primarily involve minor forms of engagement such as signing petitions or writing to state and local government officials.[43] In addition, advocacy activities rely primarily on the work of executive directors and rarely include volunteers, staff members, and clients, a situation that limits opportunities for community building. These findings are consistent with those of Gary Bass and his colleagues, who argue that the potentially critical role of nonprofit advocacy in shifting public policy in favor of the poor and disenfranchised is primarily limited by a lack of financial resources and staff or volunteer skills.[44]

Some commentators have suggested that the connections between governments and nonprofits, particularly in the area of antipoverty services, may discourage organizations involved in the day-to-day delivery of services from actively challenging existing policies because nonprofit reliance on public funding for their livelihood may make them reluctant to engage in activities that would jeopardize their relationship with governments.[45] Findings from several studies suggest, however, that the fear of losing public funding is not a major factor limiting advocacy activity.[46] Indeed, organizations that receive public funds tend to be more active in advocacy than those without such support, perhaps because of the additional resources that such funding provides.[47] Nevertheless, in this context advocacy and lobbying efforts are more likely to focus on the renewal or expansion of grants and contracts rather than the empowerment of the local communities that the organizations serve. Here again, the professionalism of nonprofits is working against the interests of the poor by trumping civic activism. As Takanishi puts it, nonprofits tend to follow public policy rather than alter it.[48]

Nonprofits and the Creation of Social Capital in Poor Communities

The limited participation of community members in both advocacy and service delivery just noted leads to the question of what causes communities to be actively involved in antipoverty efforts and successfully to meet the needs of local residents. Recent neo-Tocquevillian arguments portray nonprofits as important agents in the creation of civil society and social capital.[49] For instance, Robert Putnam argues that voluntary organizations generate social capital by building social networks of reciprocity and trust, which in turn can lead to social action,[50] but it is debatable whether social capital is simply the product of association. Perhaps social capital—that is, the resources associated with social networks—is also a prerequisite for the development of effective community-based organizations. In that case, it is not clear how voluntary organizations are promoting the creation of social capital that will lead to empowerment of disenfranchised communities. There seems to be an implicit and somewhat naïve assumption that participation in voluntary associations will yield benefits regardless of the political and economic structures.[51] Yet both participation and its intended consequences are shaped by these structures.

First, community participation depends on the existence of social networks and the capacity of local nonprofits to engage residents. Citizen engagement hinges upon the ability of citizens to participate in the needs assessment and decisionmaking processes. It also relies on the expected returns that such participation would bring. To the extent that people do not feel that their voices are being heard or that their efforts could lead to any significant changes, they will have limited incentives to join, organize, and participate in community-based organizations.

Evidence suggests that few advocacy nonprofits are located in inner-city areas, where a high proportion of low-income and minority households reside. According to Grønbjerg and Paarlberg, advocacy nonprofits are more likely to be located in smaller communities with lower poverty rates, less religious diversity, and a greater proportion of people locally employed.[52] Combined with the limited resources of nonprofit social services providers, the underrepresentation of advocacy groups in low-income communities undermines the idea of voluntary organizations as the foundation of civil society and the source of social capital needed to empower various groups to participate in democracy.

Second, despite the potentially positive effects of minority participation in nonprofit activity, there is evidence that antipoverty nonprofit organizations may not promote diverse citizen engagement for a number of reasons.[53] Unlike the bowling associations and friends of the library groups emphasized by Putnam, social service organizations have fewer volunteers and members to build social capital.[54] Thus, instead of a bottom-up approach, whereby a few local residents organize and start grassroots organizations, many nonprofit social service providers use a top-down approach, with foundations or supporting organizations shaping the agenda and activities.

This is undoubtedly related to the increased professionalization of the nonprofit sector emphasized in the introduction to this volume. According to Yeheskel Hasenfeld and Richard A. English, "A significant unanticipated consequence of the increased professionalization of human service organizations has been the alienation of clients, particularly the impoverished and lower classes, from the services provided by these organizations."[55] Instead of engaging in spontaneous community-building efforts, nonprofit organizations involved in antipoverty efforts mostly administer programs, while getting little input from the communities they aim to serve. Over the past forty years, civic activism has been replaced with a therapeutic approach to social services that privileges the individual relationship between the client and the social worker.[56] Within that framework, there is little room for social-capital building and empowerment of low-income communities.

Existing research on the board and staff composition of many nonprofits suggests that minorities continue to be underrepresented in the decisionmaking process.[57] For instance, in a national survey of 2,000 organizations, Jeanne Bell, Richard Moyers, and Timothy Wolfred found that 82 percent of nonprofit executives were white. Foundations are characterized by a similar lack of diversity, with approximately 80 percent of staff and 90 percent of board members identified as white in 1998.[58] There are also important distinctions in the position, pay, and tenure of racial and ethnic minorities and women on the staffs and boards of directors of nonprofits, which may reduce their ability to effectively meet the needs of the communities they presumably represent. This might explain why grant making by large foundations to minority-led and minority-serving organizations is disproportionately low. In 2006, 10 percent of grants (and 7 percent of funding) made by a sample of 1,263 large foundations went to organizations serving ethnic or racial minorities. Immigrants and refugees received 1 percent of grants made by these institutions.[59]

In short, although nonprofit organizations have the potential to create social networks of trust, evidence that they effectively do so is lacking. This is primarily due to the limited amount of resources and capacity to encourage participation, the professionalization of the sector, and the underrepresentation of minorities in the decisionmaking process.

Obstacles Faced by Nonprofits in Serving the Poor

How can we explain the relatively limited nonprofit support for the poor in any of the three spheres in which such support is supposed to occur? Part of the answer lies in the political-economic context in which nonprofits operate, including recent federal devolution and increased professionalization and commercialization of the nonprofit sector, all of which have a profound impact on the resources available to serve people in need.

Public charities receive funding from a variety of sources, including private contributions from individuals or foundations; government grants, contracts, and vouchers; service fees from diverse agencies; membership dues; and asset revenues such as rents. The role of governments is particularly important for antipoverty nonprofits, supporting a significant share of the limited focus nonprofits have given to the poor over the past forty years. Using the NTEE-CC classifications discussed earlier and the 2006 National Center for Charitable Statistics Digital Data, we can isolate the revenue sources of antipoverty and other nonprofit organizations.

These data sources indicate that government grants constitute almost 30 percent of revenue for antipoverty nonprofits, compared to eight percent for other organizations (see figure 19-1). These grants include awards from the

Figure 19-1. *Funding Sources of Antipoverty and Other Nonprofits, 2003*

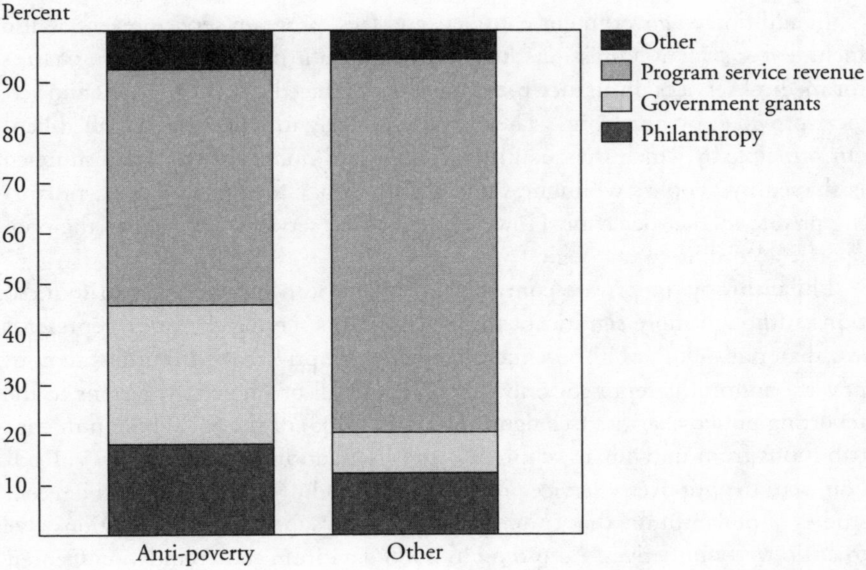

Source: National Center for Charitable Statistics, "Public Charities," *Digitized Data* 2006 (Washington: Urban Institute, 2008).

U.S. Department of Housing and Urban Development, Temporary Assistance to Needy Families, Medicaid and Medicare, and many smaller programs that actively operate through nonprofits.[60]

But these data grossly understate the role of government contributions, which increasingly take the form of voucher payments and contracts listed under program service revenues—the largest source of income for nonprofits. These types of arrangements are particularly important for organizations serving low-income populations.[61] For example, workforce development nonprofits often receive funds from government agencies according to the amount of counseling and job-training activities they provide. Similarly, community clinics get reimbursed by Medicaid for the services they deliver. Homeless shelters may receive a fee from state or local governments on the basis of the number of overnight stays by their clients. Without these contracts, it is unlikely that such services would be delivered by the nonprofits at all. Thus, for many anti-poverty nonprofits, government contributions, including direct grants as well as fees from service contracts, represent the major source of revenue, underscoring the critical relationship between the public and nonprofit sectors.[62] Additional government support also comes in the form of tax credits and tax-exempt bond financing, and may not be obvious from the financial statements of nonprofits.

In addition to government contracts and fees, program service revenues also include fees such as admission charged by nonprofit museums, tuition, charges for medical services, insurance premiums, and reduced prices for goods and services provided by nonprofits. These are more likely to reflect the so-called benefit principle by which the quantity of public and nonprofit amenities supplied is shaped by people's willingness and ability to pay for these services, mirroring private market behavior. However, few of the services provided to the poor operate according to that logic.

Philanthropy, or private contributions from both individuals and foundations, although more significant for organizations serving the poor, represents less than one-eighth of all revenues. Furthermore, private contributions to antipoverty nonprofits represent only 10 percent of all private contributions to the reporting public charities (see figure 19-1). In 2003, of the $120 billion in contributions from individuals, churches, and foundations to nonprofits, $11 billion went to antipoverty service providers. This finding is corroborated by recent studies of philanthropy that emphasize the limited support that foundations give to antipoverty initiatives. According to 2006 data from the Foundation Center, 20 percent of grants made by foundations were directed to antipoverty purposes or to organizations focusing on the poor.[63] Between 10 and 20 percent of religious giving, the largest category of private giving, was allocated to such uses.[64]

A number of recent developments have affected the resources available to nonprofits to address poverty-related needs. First, during the past three decades, federal devolution has reduced the amount of federal moneys allocated to antipoverty programs. This has had the effect of expanding demands placed on nonprofits while reducing the resources they have available to support them.[65] Although in some instances public resources were reallocated to the nonprofit sector through contracts and block grants, in most cases more had to be done with less.[66] Indeed, several observers have noted the pernicious role of nonprofit organizations in getting governments "off the hook" by providing an ultimate safety net, yet the nonprofit sector, lacking adequate resources, is incapable of providing equal services to all in need. The expectation that philanthropy will compensate for the cuts in public monies is not anchored in reality. Evidence suggests that for every lost public dollar, only a few cents are raised through philanthropy.[67] Private giving may compensate for cuts in federal support of nonprofits, but it is clearly insufficient to make up the overall federal cuts in social services and antipoverty programs.[68] The idea that the nonprofit sector could serve as a substitute for governments has imposed tremendous costs on the poor, who have experienced severe cuts in public services without any comparable increase in nonprofit outreach or material aid.

The professionalization of the nonprofit sector identified in the introduction is also affecting the sector's ability to raise revenues to meet poverty-related needs. Over the past decade, governments at all levels have increased their accountability and performance requirements (see chapter 16 in this volume, by Kevin P. Kearns). This has led to a further formalization and bureaucratization of organizations dependent on government fees. Despite the benefits of transparency, there are unintended consequences associated with this transformation. First, smaller organizations with limited resources are often unable to attract the staff qualified to compete for public funding and meet the administrative requirements. These are likely to be the small-scale, community-based grassroots organizations that provide services in some of the nation's poorest neighborhoods. In addition, performance requirements provide an incentive to serve individuals who are more likely to succeed in getting a job or becoming self-sufficient. Hard-to-employ populations, including single parents, drug addicts, the mentally disabled, and chronically homeless are less likely to receive services that require a long-term commitment. Thus, people with the greatest need are in danger of being abandoned by a system where organizations are under great pressure to minimize costs and report positive outcomes for large numbers of clients. In addition, professionalization has led to a shift away from community organizing and advocacy effort toward administration of service delivery.

In recent years, nonprofit activities have also become increasingly commercialized, leading to a rise in market-based approaches to both service delivery and fundraising (see chapter 14, this volume).[69] It is not surprising that service revenues represent the major source of income, since nonprofits increasingly rely on fees to cover the costs of the services they provide. Fees act similarly to prices in determining the equilibrium between supply and demand in a market system. This practice has important equity implications, since it excludes people unable to afford the fees. Although wealthier residents may be willing to pay for education, health care, and the arts in their communities, low-income people are less able to do so, even for basic services such as food and shelter. In addition, this pricing mechanism ensures that those who benefit from nonprofit services are also those who pay for them, and thus limits redistribution from wealthy to low-income users. To partly offset these inequities, some organizations use sliding fee scales, so that fees vary in proportion to income, but this practice of higher-income users subsidizing lower-income users remains rare.

Similar detrimental consequences are associated with the increasing use of commercial for-profit activities, such as museum and university stores and restaurants, to subsidize nonprofit operations. Certainly these innovative practices generate additional funds for cultural and educational nonprofits, but they rarely benefit those serving the poor. In fact, the need to generate revenue through sales is likely to reshape activities and redirect resources, including volunteers, away from direct service provision for low-income individuals. Given the extent to which public funds have declined, however, nonprofits are often left with few other revenue options.

Commercialization in fundraising has evolved even more rapidly, with the emergence of new capital assets financing nonprofit activity in the fields of housing and community development, and the continued growth of technology-based philanthropy. These developments may increase the amount of resources available to nonprofits, but whether they will promote an expansion of antipoverty activity in the voluntary sector is unclear. For instance, the use of technology in promoting charitable giving accentuates the role of marketing and promotion, and thus favors larger institutions. Causes such as disaster relief and medical research, and organizations involved in those activities such as the Red Cross and the American Cancer Society, continue to receive a large share of private donations. Similarly, corporate philanthropy often seeks out prestigious and well-known organizations such as art museums and universities as a strategy to increase the corporations' visibility. According to Grønbjerg and Smith, the doubling of corporate donations in the last two decades of the twentieth century did not lead to any increase in funding for health and human services.[70]

The commercialization of the nonprofit sector also refers to the growing competition between nonprofits and for-profit organizations in a number of industries, including education, health care, and social services. Heightened competition for both clients and public resources can lead to improvements in the quality of services, but it can also create incentives to cut costs. Under these circumstances, nonprofit organizations providing services to "hard-to-serve" populations with long-term and complex needs are less likely to successfully win the battle for government funds.

These transformations in the nature of the voluntary sector and its relationship with government affect not only the quantity and type of services provided but also their geographic distribution.[71] To the extent that nonprofits are largely locally supported, the residential segregation patterns that divide metropolitan areas by income and race are likely to lead to uneven access to nonprofit services.[72] Federal devolution has heightened these disparities by withdrawing funds and shifting responsibilities to lower levels of governments, which are characterized by different levels of fiscal capacity.[73] Thus, poorer municipalities are less likely to have the resources necessary to support an active antipoverty nonprofit sector than under a national redistributive system. The commercialization and professionalization of the nonprofit sector has also put increasing pressure on smaller inner-city social service organizations that do not have the resources to compete with larger nonprofit (or in some cases for-profit) organizations that have greater administrative and marketing capacity. Ultimately, donors and volunteers are interested in supporting their communities rather than the welfare of others. Devolution has been instrumental in accentuating the spatial segregation between needs and resources.

Analysis of the distribution of nonprofit resources in the Los Angeles region suggests the creation of a three-tier urban landscape in which high-income suburban communities have an active nonprofit sector involved almost exclusively in the production of local amenities, middle-class communities support antipoverty efforts alongside other activities, and poor areas focus primarily on social services.[74] However, owing to their substantially larger poverty populations, the latter end up with lower levels of antipoverty nonprofit services per capita. Recent research by Lester Salamon and Wojciech Sokolowski analyzes trends in the geographic distribution of nonprofit employment within five mid-Atlantic states and provides evidence of an increasing suburbanization of nonprofit jobs.[75] This is explained in part by the fact that nonprofits follow the money by marketing their services to paying customers who disproportionately reside in the suburbs, thereby increasing the demand for staffers and nonprofit workers in these areas. For example, in recent years, a number of nonprofit organizations have emerged to provide recreation and after-school opportunities on public parks in southern California. The majority of those are located in suburban communities.[76]

There is mounting evidence that poverty concentration leads to significant social costs, creating structural barriers to economic opportunities for local residents, and imposing disproportionate fiscal stress on local governments.[77] Under these circumstances, the uneven distribution of nonprofit resources and their limited presence in extremely poor neighborhoods is likely to contribute to the reproduction and possible increase of existing intra-metropolitan socioeconomic disparities. This problem affects a variety of communities and populations, as the landscape of concentrated poverty itself shifts from inner-city, largely African American zones to a more variegated set of inner suburban and even exurban areas with more diverse populations.[78] Unless regional efforts are made to reduce socioeconomic polarization and reliance on higher levels of government to provide antipoverty services can be increased, it is unlikely that the nonprofit sector will have more than a marginal effect in meeting the needs of the poorest.

Conclusion

Almost a decade ago, William Díaz concluded, "Contrary to conventional wisdom, by and large, the nonprofit sector does not address the needs of the poor and disadvantaged very well."[79] Since then, unfortunately, little has changed to contest this conclusion.

Poverty and inequality remain stubbornly high in the wake of the recent economic crisis, yet, as the data presented here suggest, only a small proportion of nonprofits directly serve the needs of the poor. Similarly, few nonprofit organizations identify minority groups as their primary clients. Indeed, the majority of nonprofits are involved in the production of amenities such as education, recreation, arts, culture, and health that disproportionately benefit middle- and high-income individuals and communities. In addition, organizations that are involved in antipoverty activities rarely address the structural forces underlying poverty, especially for racial and ethnic minorities. This is partly driven by the scarcity of resources that prevents organizations from engaging in costly long-term social change. It also reflects a desire, at least by some, to alter the behavior of the poor through counseling and education rather than material assistance. This so-called "spiritualization" of social service has been heightened by the expanding role of faith-based organizations and the reduction of government support. In contrast to public agencies, nonprofits have more flexibility in defining the populations they serve and often discriminate against those they see as "undeserving" poor.[80]

Nonprofits do not operate in a vacuum, and to understand their role in serving the poor we must consider the larger social, economic, and political structures in place. The invaluable role of nonprofits in providing last-resort assistance to the millions of people who experience economic and social hardship has been weakened by continuing trends in the devolution of federal responsibility for antipoverty policy, and new developments in the professionalization and commercialization of the nonprofit sector. These changes have had deep impacts on organizations that, in addition to facing greater demands linked to cuts in public services, must increasingly compete for public and private funds with other service providers. Geographic disparities in voluntary and philanthropic resources, combined with a shift from federal to state and local poverty management policies, have resulted in a very uneven distribution of nonprofits and a consequent spatial gap between needs and resources. Absent greater participation from higher tiers of government, these disparities will continue to have profound implications for the economic well-being of the poor, especially people living in areas of concentrated poverty.

The significance of the role of governments in sustaining nonprofit antipoverty activity points to the importance of advocacy on behalf of the poor and other disadvantaged groups. However, small organizations working for low-income communities often lack the resources and capacity to effectively influence policy. This in turn weakens the legitimacy of these organizations and reduces citizen participation.

The history of the United States is rich with examples of nonprofit leaders and volunteers fighting to defend the rights of people discriminated against, challenging existing policies, demanding social change, and serving the poor and disenfranchised in multiple other ways. Although these efforts are admirable, they represent a small share of nonprofit activity and do not justify the withdrawal of public resources from antipoverty programs that has occurred in the past three decades. Nonprofits cannot alleviate poverty alone, and the role of government remains essential. Assuming that nonprofits are both willing and able to meet the needs of the poor is a dangerous policy. Instead, policymakers must focus on how nonprofits and governments can work more effectively together and with the clients they serve to assess the real needs of poor people and communities, and to develop, implement, and evaluate programs to better serve these needs.

Notes

1. Alexis de Tocqueville, *Democracy in America* (Cambridge: Sever & Francis, 1831).

2. Peter D. Hall, "Religion, Philanthropy, Service, and Civic Engagement in Twentieth-Century America," in *Gifts of Time and Money: The Role of Charity in America's Communities*, edited by Arthur Brooks (New York: Rowman & Littlefield, 2005).

3. George H. W. Bush, Inaugural Address, 1988; Marvin Olaski, *Renewing American Compassion: How Compassion for the Needy Can Turn Ordinary Citizens into Heroes* (Washington: Regnery, 1996).

4. See Julian Wolpert, "Decentralization and Equity in Public and Nonprofit Sectors," *Nonprofit and Voluntary Sector Quarterly* 22 (1993): 281–96.

5. See Elizabeth T. Boris and C. Eugene Steuerle, eds., *Nonprofits and Government: Collaboration and Conflict* (Washington: Urban Institute Press, 2006); Jennifer R. Wolch, *The Shadow State: Government and Voluntary Sector in Transition* (New York: Foundation Center, 1990); Lester M. Salamon, *Partners in Public Service: Government-Nonprofit Relations in the Modern Welfare State* (Johns Hopkins University Press, 1995).

6. U.S. Census Bureau, *Current Population Survey: Annual Social and Economic Supplement* (Washington: 2007).

7. Pascale Joassart-Marcelli, "Working Poverty in Southern California: Towards an Operational Measure," *Social Science Research* 34, no. 1 (2005): 20–43.

8. Lawrence Mishel, *State of Working America 2006/2007* (Washington: Economic Policy Institute, 2007).

9. Pierre Bourdieu, "The Forms of Capital," in *Handbook of Theory and Research for the Sociology of Education*, edited by J. Richardson (Westport, Conn.: Greenwood Press, 1986).

10. Kirsten A. Grønbjerg, "Using NTEE to Classify Non-Profit Organizations: An Assessment of Human Service and Regional Applications," *Voluntas* 5, no. 3 (1994): 301–28.

11. National Center for Charitable Statistics, *IRS Core File 2006* (Washington: Urban Institute, 2008); reporting public charities are organizations other than foundations that are registered with the IRS under the 501(c)(3) tax-exemption code, with gross receipts above $25,000, excluding foundations and mutual benefit organizations, that file the required Form 990.

12. Lester Salamon, "Social Services," in *Who Benefits from the Nonprofit Sector?* edited by Charles Clotfelter (University of Chicago Press, 1992).

13. David S. Salkever and Richard G. Frank, "Health Services," in Clotfelter, *Who Benefits from the Nonprofit Sector?*

14. Saul Schwartz and Sandy Baum, "Education," in Clotfelter, *Who Benefits from the Nonprofit Sector?*

15. Pascale Joassart-Marcelli and Jennifer Wolch, "The Intrametropolitan Geography of Poverty and the Nonprofit Sector in Southern California," *Nonprofit and Voluntary Sector Quarterly* 32, no. 1 (2003): 70–96.

16. See Julian Wolpert, *Patterns of Generosity in America: Who Is Holding the Safety Net?* A Twentieth Century Fund Paper (New York: Twentieth Century Fund Press, 1993); Julian Wolpert, "Communities, Networks, and the Future of Philanthropy," in *Philanthropy and the Nonprofit Sector in a Changing America*, edited by Charles Clotfelter and Thomas Ehrlich (Indiana University Press, 1999).

17. Dick Netzer, "Arts and Culture," in Clotfelter, *Who Benefits from the Nonprofit Sector?*

18. See Wolpert, *Patterns of Generosity in America*; Wolpert, "Communities, Networks, and the Future of Philanthropy."

19. Joassart-Marcelli and Wolch, "The Intrametropolitan Geography of Poverty and the Nonprofit Sector in Southern California"; Kirsten Grønbjerg and Laura Paarlberg, "Community Variations in the Size and Scope of the Nonprofit Sector: Theory and Preliminary Findings," *Nonprofit and Voluntary Sector Quarterly* 30 (2001): 684–706. Laura Peck, "Do Antipoverty Nonprofits Locate Where People Need Them? Evidence from a Spatial Analysis of Phoenix," *Nonprofit and Voluntary Sector Quarterly* 37 (2008): 138–52.

20. William Díaz, "For Whom and for What? The Contributions of the Nonprofit Sector," in *The State of Nonprofit America*, edited by Lester Salamon (Brookings, 2002); William Díaz, "Philanthropy and the Case of the Latino Communities in America," in Clotfelter and Ehrlich, *Philanthropy and the Nonprofit Sector in a Changing America*.

21. Hector R. Cordero-Guzman, "Community-Based Organizations and Migration in New York City," *Journal of Ethnic and Migration Studies* 31 (2005): 889–909; Chi-Kan Richard Hung, "Immigrant Nonprofit Organizations in U.S. Metropolitan Areas," *Nonprofit and Voluntary Sector Quarterly* 36 (2007): 707–29.

22. See Díaz, "For Whom and for What?"; Díaz, "Philanthropy and the Case of the Latino Communities in America"; and Emmett Carson, "The Roles of Indigenous and Institutional Philanthropy in Advancing Social Justice," in Clotfelter and Ehrlich, *Philanthropy and the Nonprofit Sector in a Changing America*.

23. See Díaz, "For Whom and for What?"; Díaz, "Philanthropy and the Case of the Latino Communities in America"; and Carson, "Roles of Indigenous and Institutional Philanthropy in Advancing Social Justice."

24. See Carson, "Roles of Indigenous and Institutional Philanthropy in Advancing Social Justice."

25. Herbert Gans, *The War against the Poor: The Underclass and Antipoverty Policy* (New York: Basic Books, 1995); Frances Fox Piven and Richard Cloward, *Regulating the Poor: The Function of Public Welfare*, 2nd updated ed. (New York: Vintage, 1993).

26. See David Wagner, *What's Love Got to Do with It? A Critical Look at American Charity* (New York: New Press, 2000).

27. Luis E. Lugo, *Equal Partners: The Welfare Responsibility of Governments and Churches* (Washington: Center for Public Justice, 1998), p. 18.

28. Eleanor Brown, "Patterns and Purposes of Philanthropic Giving," in Clotfelter and Ehrlich, *Philanthropy and the Nonprofit Sector in a Changing America*, is the source of the 10 percent estimate; John McCarthy and Jim Castelli, "Religion-Sponsored Social Service Providers: The Not-So-Independent Sector," Nonprofit Sector Research Fund Working Paper (Washington: Aspen Institute, 1998), is the source of the 20 percent estimate.

29. McCarthy and Castelli, "Religion-Sponsored Social Service Providers"; Hall, "Religion, Philanthropy, Service, and Civic Engagement in Twentieth-Century America"; and Thomas

Harvey, "Government Promotion of Faith-Based Solutions to Social Problems: Partisan or Prophetic?" Nonprofit Sector Research Fund Working Paper (Washington: Aspen Institute, 1997).

30. Hall, "Religion, Philanthropy, Service, and Civic Engagement in Twentieth-Century America"; Wagner, *What's Love Got to Do with It?*

31. Roy Lubove, *The Professional Altruist: The Emergence of Social Work as a Career* (Harvard University Press, 1965).

32. See ibid.; John H. Ehrenreich, *The Altruistic Imagination: A History of Social Work and Social Policy in the United States* (Cornell University Press, 1985).

33. Ruby Takanishi, "Children in Poverty: Reflections on the Roles of Philanthropy and Public Policy," in Clotfelter and Ehrlich, *Philanthropy and the Nonprofit Sector in a Changing America.*

34. Theda Skocpol, *Social Policy in the United States: Future Possibilities in Historical Perspective* (Princeton University Press, 1995); Ehrenreich, *Altruistic Imagination*; Michael B. Katz, *In the Shadow of the Poorhouse: A Social History of Welfare in America* (New York: Basic Books, 1996).

35. Elizabeth Reid, "Nonprofit Advocacy and Political Participation," in Boris and Steuerle, *Nonprofits and Government.*

36. Ibid.; Jeff Krehely and Kendall Golladay, "The Scope and Activities of 501(c)(4) Social Welfare Organizations: Fact versus Fantasy," paper presented at the 2001 research conference of the Association for Research on Nonprofit Organizations and Voluntary Action (ARNOVA), Miami (November 30, 2001).

37. National Center for Charitable Statistics, *IRS Core File 2004* (Washington: Urban Institute, 2006).

38. Krehely and Golladay, "Scope and Activities of 501(c)(4) Social Welfare Organizations."

39. Ibid.; Elizabeth Reid, "Social Welfare Organizations, Politics, and Regulation," in *In Search of the Nonprofit Sector*, edited by Peter Frumkin and Jonathan Imber (New Brunswick, N.J.: Transaction, 2004); Elizabeth Boris and Jeff Krehely, "Civic Participation and Advocacy," in Salamon, *State of Nonprofit America.*

40. See Carson, "Roles of Indigenous and Institutional Philanthropy in Advancing Social Justice."

41. Robert H. Bremmer, *American Philanthropy*, 2nd ed. (University of Chicago Press, 1998), p. 102.

42. Dennis R. Young, "Complementary, Supplementary, or Adversarial? A Theoretical and Historical Examination of Nonprofit-Government Relations in the United States," in Boris and Steuerle, *Nonprofits and Government.*

43. Lester Salamon and Stephanie Lessans Geller, "Nonprofit America: A Force for Democracy," Listening Post Communiqué No. 9 (Johns Hopkins University, Center for Civil Society Studies, Listening Post Project, 2007).

44. Gary Bass and others, *Seen but Not Heard: Strengthening Nonprofit Advocacy* (Aspen: Aspen Institute, 2007).

45. Smith, "Government and Nonprofits in the Modern Age."

46. Salamon and Geller, "Nonprofit America: A Force for Democracy"; and Bass and others, *Seen but Not Heard.*

47. Mark Chaves, Laura Stephens, and Joseph Galaskiewicz, "Does Government Funding Suppress Nonprofits' Political Activity?" *American Sociological Review* 69, no. 2 (2004): 292–316.

48. Takanishi, "Children in Poverty," p. 352.

49. Michael Foley and Bob Edwards. "Escape from Politics? Social Theory and the Social Capital Debate," *American Behavioral Scientist* 40, no. 5 (2004): 550–61.

50. Robert Putnam, "Bowling Alone: America's Declining Social Capital," *Journal of Democracy* 6, no. 1 (1995): 65–78; Robert Putnam, *Bowling Alone: The Collapse and Revival of American Community* (New York: Simon & Schuster, 2000).

51. Foley and Edwards, "Escape from Politics?"; James DeFillipis, "The Myth of Social Capital in Community Development," *Housing Policy Debate* 12, no. 4 (2001): 781–806.

52. Grønbjerg and Paarlberg, "Community Variations in the Size and Scope of the Nonprofit Sector."

53. Díaz, "For Whom and for What?"

54. Putnam, *Bowling Alone*; Smith "Government and Nonprofits in the Modern Age"; Theda Skocpol, "Advocates without Members: The Recent Transformation of American Civic Life," in *Civic Engagement in American Democracy*, edited by Theda Skocpol and Morris Fiorina (Brookings, 1999).

55. Yeheskel Hasenfeld and Richard A. English, *Human Service Organizations: A Book of Readings* (University of Michigan Press, 1974) p. 20.

56. See Lubove, *Professional Altruist.*

57. Díaz, "For Whom and for What?"; Díaz, "Philanthropy and the Case of the Latino Communities in America"; Julia Parshall and others, *Philanthropy in a Changing Society: Achieving Effectiveness through Diversity* (New York: Rockefeller Philanthropy Advisors, 2008); Judith Y. Weisinger, "Understanding the Meaning of Diversity in a Nonprofit Organization," paper delivered at the annual conference of the Association for Research on Nonprofit Organizations and Voluntary Action (ARNOVA), Washington, D.C. (November 2005).

58. Jeanne Bell, Richard Moyers and, Timothy Wolfred, "Daring to Lead: A National Study of Nonprofit Executive Leadership" (San Francisco: CompassPoint and Meyer Foundation, 2006); Lynn Burbridge, "Diversity in Philanthropy: The Numbers and Their Meaning," in *Meaning and Impact of Board and Staff Diversity in the Philanthropic Field: Findings from a National Study*, edited by Chris Cardona (New York: Joint Affinity Group, 2002).

59. Foundation Center, "Foundation Grants Designated to Special Population Groups, circa 2006," Foundation Center's Statistical Information Service (www.foundationcenter.org/findfunders/statistics/pdf/08_fund_pop/2006/16_06.pdf).

60. Steven R. Smith, "Government Financing of Nonprofit Activity," in Boris and Steuerle, *Nonprofits and Government.*

61. Smith, "Government Financing of Nonprofit Activity"; Steven R. Smith and Michael Lipsky, *Nonprofits for Hire: The Welfare State in the Age of Contracting* (Harvard University Press, 1993); Wolch, *Shadow State.*

62. Lester M. Salamon and Alan Abramson, "The Federal Budget and the Nonprofit Sector: Implications of the Contract with America," in *Capacity for Change? The Nonprofit World in the Age of Devolution*, edited by Dwight Burlingame and others (Indiana University, Center on Philanthropy, 1996); Wolch, *Shadow State*; Salamon, *Partners in Public Service*; Smith, "Government and Nonprofits in the Modern Age."

63. Foundation Center, "Foundation Grants Designated to Special Population Groups, circa 2006."

64. Eleanor Brown, "Patterns and Purposes of Philanthropic Giving," in Clotfelter and Ehrlich, *Philanthropy and the Nonprofit Sector in a Changing America,* p. 226.

65. Carol De Vita, "Nonprofits and Devolution: What Do We Know?" in Boris and Steuerle, *Nonprofits and Government*; Wolpert, "Decentralization and Equity in Public and Nonprofit Sectors."

66. Alan J. Abramson, Lester M. Salamon, and C. Eugene Steuerle, "The Nonprofit Sector and the Federal Budget: Recent History and Future Directions," in Boris and Steuerle, *Nonprofits and Government.*

67. Richard Steinberg, "Can Individual Donations Replace Cutbacks in Federal Social-Welfare Spending?" in Burlingame and others, *Capacity for Change.*

68. Abramson, Salamon, and Steuerle, "Nonprofit Sector and the Federal Budget."

69. See Estelle James, "Commercialization and the Mission of Nonprofits," in Frumkin and Imber, *In Search of the Nonprofit Sector.*

70. Grønbjerg and Smith, "Nonprofit Organizations and Public Policies in the Delivery of Human Services."

71. See Joassart-Marcelli and Wolch, "Intrametropolitan Geography of Poverty"; Grønbjerg and Paarlberg, "Community Variations in the Size and Scope of the Nonprofit Sector"; Peck, "Do Antipoverty Nonprofits Locate Where People Need Them?"

72. Wolfgang Bielefeldt, James C. Murdoch, and Paul Waddell, "The Influence of Demographics and Distance on Nonprofit Location," *Nonprofit and Voluntary Sector Quarterly* 26 (1997): 207–25; Wolfgang Bielefeldt, Patrick Rooney, and Kathy Steinberg, "How Do Need, Capacity, Geography, and Politics Influence Giving?" in *Gifts of Time and Money: The Role of Charity in America's Communities*, edited by Arthur Brooks (New York: Rowman & Littlefield, 2005). See Wolpert, "Decentralization and Equity in Public and Nonprofit Sectors," and Wolpert, "Communities, Networks, and the Future of Philanthropy."

73. De Vita, "Nonprofits and Devolution: What Do We Know?"; Pascale Joassart-Marcelli, Juliet Musso, and Jennifer Wolch, "The Fiscal Consequences of Poverty Concentration in a Metropolitan Region," *Annals of the Association of American Geographers* 95, no. 2 (2005): 336–56.

74. See Joassart-Marcelli and Wolch, "Intrametropolitan Geography of Poverty"; Jennifer Wolch and R. K. Geiger, "The Distribution of Urban Voluntary Resources: An Exploratory Analysis," *Environment and Planning A* 15 (1983): 1067–82.

75. Lester Salamon and Wojciech Sokolowski, "Nonprofit Organizations: New Insights from QCEW Data," *Monthly Labor Review*, September 2005, pp. 19–26.

76. Pascale Joassart-Marcelli, Jennifer Wolch, and Zia Salim, "Building the Healthy City: The Role of Nonprofits in Creating Active Urban Parks," *Urban Geography*, forthcoming.

77. William J. Wilson, *When Work Disappears: The World of the New Urban Poor* (New York: Knopf, 1996); Joassart-Marcelli, Musso, and Wolch, "Fiscal Consequences of Poverty Concentration."

78. Nathan J. Sessoms and Jennifer R. Wolch, "Measuring Concentrated Poverty in a Global Metropolis: Lessons from Los Angeles," *Professional Geographer* 60, no. 1 (2008): 70–86.

79. Díaz, "For Whom and for What?" p. 532.

80. Wolch, *The Shadow State.*

Contributors

Alan J. Abramson is professor of public and international affairs at George Mason University and director of the university's Center for Nonprofit Management, Philanthropy, and Policy.

Elizabeth Boris is director of the Center on Nonprofits and Philanthropy at the Urban Institute.

Eleanor Brown is professor of economics at Pomona College.

Mark Chaves is professor of sociology at Duke University.

Marla Cornelius is senior project director with CompassPoint Nonprofit Services.

Patrick Corvington is formerly with the Annie E. Casey Foundation.

Atul Dighe is a senior director of Finance & Strategy Practice at the Corporate Executive Board.

Bradford H. Gray is principal research associate at the Urban Institute.

Kirsten A. Grønbjerg holds the Efroymson Chair in Philanthropy at the Center on Philanthropy and is professor of public and environmental affairs at Indiana University.

Pascale Joassart-Marcelli is assistant professor in the Department of Geography, San Diego State University.

Pearl Rock Kane is the Klingenstein Family Professor in the Department of Organization and Leadership at Teachers College, Columbia University, and director of the Esther A. and Joseph Klingenstein Center.

Kevin Kearns is professor of public and international affairs at the University of Pittsburgh.

Leslie Lenkowsky is professor of philanthropic studies and public policy at the School of Public and Environmental Affairs, Indiana University.

Matthew Maronick is a PhD candidate at the University of Chicago.

David Martin is a senior analyst with Cornerstone Research.

Rachel McCarthy is a former research coordinator with the Aspen Institute and is now a producer for *The Story with Dick Gordon,* a public radio program distributed nationally by American Public Media.

Lester M. Salamon is a professor at Johns Hopkins University and director of the Johns Hopkins Center for Civil Society Studies.

Mark Schlesinger is associate professor at Yale University's School of Medicine and a fellow at Yale's Institution for Social and Policy Studies.

Lisa Scruggs is an associate at the law firm Jenner and Block.

Carmen Sirianni is professor of sociology and the Department of Sociology chair at Brandeis University.

Stephanie Sofer is a former research assistant with Brandeis University.

Steven Rathgeb Smith is Nancy Bell Evans Professor of Public Affairs, Evans School of Public Affairs, University of Washington.

Donald M. Stewart is a visiting scholar at the Erikson Institute.

Abby Stoddard is a founding partner at Humanitarian Outcomes and senior program adviser on Humanitarian Action at the Center on International Cooperation, New York University.

Stefan Toepler is associate professor of nonprofit studies at George Mason University.

Avis Vidal is professor of urban planning and chair of the Department of Geography and Urban Planning at Wayne State University.

Margaret J. Wyszomirski is professor of both art education and public policy and director of the Arts Policy and Administration Program at Ohio State University.

Dennis R. Young is professor of public administration and urban studies, Andrew Young School of Policy Studies, Georgia State University.

Index

AA. *See* Alcoholics Anonymous

AAM. *See* American Association of Museums

AARP, 403, 543

Abramoff, Jack, 573

Abramson, Alan J., 423–58, 577

Academic community, 42, 66, 106. See also Education issues; *individual academic institutions*

ACCION International, 355

Accord, 353

Accountability: accountability environment, 32–33; accountability mechanisms, 37; civic activism and, 601–02, 604–05, 606–07; commercialism and, 601–02, 603, 604–05, 606, 607–09; commercialization and the nondistribution constraint, 592–93; definition of, 588, 596, 609; demands for nonprofit accountability, 528–29; financial accountability, 593–95, 596; financial policy statements, 594–95; grantmakers and, 609–10; improving accountability and effectiveness, 445–46; industry standards accountability, 600–01; legal accountability, 588–93, 596, 606; long-term perspective of, 611; managerial accountability, 594; mission fidelity and accomplishment, 597–99, 607–09; in networked delivery systems, 609; organizational capacity and, 610; performance accountability, 596–601; professionalism, 601–02, 603–06; standards and expectations of, 596–97, 600–01, 606; voluntarism and, 601–03, 604–05, 606. *See also* Nonprofit sector; *individual organization types*

ACH. See Arts, culture, and humanities

ACLU. *See* American Civil Liberties Union

Addressing Water and Natural Resource Education (AWARE; Colorado), 304

Advancing Environmental Justice through Pollution Prevention (report; NEJAC), 315

Advocacy and lobbying: administrative advocacy, 398; advocacy for antipoverty policies, 413, 415–19, 660, 664, 666–68; challenges of, 406; civic activism and, 406, 419; civil rights organizations and, 408–13, 414; coalitions and, 400, 407, 408, 409, 412, 417–18; commercialism and, 408; definition of, 74n9, 397; *501*(c)(*4*) social welfare organizations and, 403, 405, 406t; forces shaping civic participation and nonprofit advocacy, 405–08; governing boards and, 591; group organization, 412; issue identification and agenda setting, 398; Istook amendment and, 35, 428, 437; lobbying, 38, 74n9, 398–99, 408–13, 417, 419, 428, 666; nonprofit advocacy, 394–95, 397–98, 551–52, 555, 573–74, 577, 666–68; organizational structure, 412, 417–18; partisan electoral advocacy, 399–400; regulation of, 572–74; reported lobbying expenditures among *501*(c)(*3*) organizations, 401–03, 404, 405t, 418t, 420; representation, 410, 416; resources and financial pressures, 299–301, 406, 409, 412–13, 414, 415–16, 418–19; scope of nonprofit advocacy and lobbying, 400–01; strategies for, 410–12, 416–17; voluntarism and, 406–07, 410. *See also* Corporate and business issues; Environmental issues; Nonprofit sector; Professionalism

Advocacy Institute, 437

AERDO (Association of Evangelical Relief and Development Organizations). *See* Accord

AFDC. *See* Aid to Families with Dependent Children

Affiliated Computer Services Inc., 527

Afghanistan, 330, 336, 338, 344, 350, 352, 355, 567

Africa, 330, 331, 350, 352, 353

AFRICOM. *See* U.S. Africa Command

Agriculture, Department of (DOA), 306, 313

AHA. *See* American Hospital Association

Aid to Families with Dependent Children (AFDC), 204
AIM Alliance, 444
Aircraft Owners and Pilots Association, 666
Alabama, 205
Alcoholics Anonymous (AA), 195, 602–03
Alegent Health School of Radiologic Technology, 143
Alliance for Chesapeake Bay, 304
Alliance for Children and Families, 195, 427
Alliance for Justice, 428, 430, 437
Alliance for Nonprofit Management, 430, 442–43
Alliance of Community Health Plans, 121
Allied Computer Services Inc., 564
AMA. *See* American Medical Association
Amazon, 534
America Forward coalition, 438
American Association for the Advancement of Science, 148
American Association of Fund-Raising Counsel, 425, 431
American Association of Museums (AAM), 248, 252, 424, 425, 543
American Association of Retired Persons. *See* AARP
American Cancer Society, 471, 536, 542, 674
American Civil Liberties Union (ACLU), 299, 403, 411, 666
American Civil Rights Coalition, 412
American Express, 57–58, 536, 537
American Farmland Trust, 310
American Federation of Musicians, 257
American Forest Foundation. *See* American Forest Institute
American Forest Institute, 311
American Forests, 58
American Heart Association, 542
American Hospital Association (AHA), 121, 122, 423, 425, 427
American Humane Association, 535
American Humanics. *See* Nonprofit Leadership Alliance
Americanizing the American Orchestra 1990s (report; League of American Orchestras), 248
American Indian Museum, 254
American Israel Public Affairs Committee, 666
American Lung Association, 315, 471, 536
American Medical Association (AMA), 543
American Recovery and Reinvestment Act of *2009* (ARRA), 169, 173–74, 176, 178, 209, 441, 567–68
American Red Cross: disaster relief by, 674; as a formal public charity, 195, 197, 200; Haitian earthquake and, 509; murder of workers in Chechnya, 343; as a neutral, apolitical organization, 351; post-September *11, 2001,* 37, 437, 481, 598–99, 610. *See also* International Committee of the Red Cross
American Rivers, 305
Americans for the Arts, 229
American Society of Association Executives, 431

American Symphony Orchestra League. *See* League of American Orchestras
American Telephone & Telegraph. *See* AT&T
American Time Use Survey (ATUS), 507
America Online, 527
America Speaks, 396
AmeriCorps, 192–93, 205, 217–18, 438, 512, 556
Ammerman, Nancy, 366
Ancilla College, 143
Anderson, Walter Truett, 621
Andre-Clark, Alice, 563
Andreoni, James, 505
Andover. *See* Philips Academy Andover
Andy Warhol Foundation for the Visual Arts, 241
Angola, 355
Annenberg Foundation, 465
Antioch College, 151
Apinunmahakul, Amornrat, 512–13
Apollo (education company), 150
Aramony, William, 439, 538
Area Agencies on Aging, 553–54
Arizona, 569
Arizona State University, 444
ARNOVA. *See* Association for Research on Nonprofit Organizations and Voluntary Action
ARRA . *See* American Recovery and Reinvestment Act of *2009*
Arts, culture, and humanities (ACH): accountability in, 254–55; advocacy in, 62, 248–49; arts nonprofits, 44, 47, 52, 53, 66, 229, 249–50; audience development and participation, 242–44, 250–51; challenges of, 247–48; characteristics of, 229, 234; civic activism and, 247–49; commercialism and marketing, 251–53, 255–56, 258; contracts, 257; culture and recreation nonprofits, 46, 48, 52, 53; earned income, 238–39, 242, 252–53; employment in, 229; factors shaping the nonprofit arts, 244–53; for-profit organizations in, 232, 233, 249; fundraising and, 56, 256; future issues of, 258–61; government involvement in, 231, 238, 239–41, 249, 260–61, 505; growth of, 229–30; immigration and, 246; leadership in, 39, 253–54; management concerns, 253–58; performance culture of, 250; private philanthropy and, 238, 241–42; professionalization, 249–51; revenues and fiscal pressures of, 11, 231, 233–42, 249, 251, 497, 530; role and structure of nonprofits in, 230–33; technology in, 255–58; voluntarism in, 245–46. *See also* National Endowment for the Arts; National Endowment for the Humanities; Nonprofit sector; *individual arts and cultural venues*
Ash Center for Democratic Governance and Innovation, 321
Asia, 530
Asian Neighborhood Design, 532
Aspen Institute, 58, 429, 444
Association for Healthcare Philanthropy, 55

Association for Research on Nonprofit Organizations and Voluntary Action (ARNOVA), 443, 444
Association of American Colleges, 425. *See also* National Association of Independent Colleges and Universities
Association of American Colleges and Universities, 147
Association of Art Museum Directors, 252
Association of Black Foundation Executives, 480
Association of Evangelical Relief and Development Organizations (AERDO), 353
Association of Fund-Raising Professionals (AFP), 55, 431. *See also* National Society of Fund-Raising Executives
Association of Small Foundations, 57, 428
Associations, 13, 121, 394, 398. *See also individual associations by name*
AT&T, 355, 463
Atlantic Monthly, 542
Atlantic Philanthropies, 151, 441, 484
ATUS. *See* American Time Use Survey
Austin, James, 355
AWARE. *See* Addressing Water and Natural Resource Education

Bakija, Jon, 503
Balanced Scorecard, 598, 610
Baltimore, 48–49
Baltimore Opera, 238
Banking crisis of *2008*. *See* Great Recession
Barman, Emily, 471
Barnes & Noble, 534
Barnum, P. T., and the American Museum, 249
Barrrios Unidos, 532
Bass, Gary, 668
Bay Area Open Space Council, 309
Bayh-Dole Act (*1980*). *See* Patent and Trademark Amendments of *1980*
BBB (Better Business Bureau) Wise Giving Alliance, 425, 431, 446, 451, 595
Bell, Jeanne, 670
Beloit College, 151
Benevolent societies, 664
Benjamin, Lehn, 600
Bennett, William, 594–95
Bernholz, Lucy, 432
Berry, Jeffrey, 61, 63
Better Business Bureau (BBB). *See* BBB Wise Giving Alliance
Biddle, Jeff, 373
Bikable Communities, 52
Bikestation Coalition, 532
Bill and Melinda Gates Foundation, 151, 441, 459, 465, 468, 479, 511
Biosciences, 621–23
Bipartisan Campaign Reform Act of *2002*, 573
Block grants. *See* Grants
BLS. *See* Bureau of Labor Statistics
Blue Avocado, 432

B'nai B'rith, 273
BoardSource, 430, 443, 595
Boris, Elizabeth T., 394–422, 667
Boston Associated Charities, 17
Boston College, 450
Boston Globe, 437
Bowling Alone: The Collapse and Revival of American Community (Putnam), 295, 368, 447, 634
Bowman, H. Woods, 505, 570
Boys and Girls Club, 195, 200
BP Amoco, 355
Bremmer, Robert H., 667
Breneman, David, 147
Bridgespan Group, 431
Bridgestar, 449
Broadway and Off-Broadway theater, 233, 249
Brody, Evelyn, 570
Brookings Institution, 321
Brooklyn Museum, 247, 252
Brown, Eleanor, 495–517
Brown University, 139, 144
Brown v. Board of Education (1954), 141
Brudney, Jeffrey L., 499
Buffett, Warren, 342, 459, 484, 510
"Build Market Share for God" (PowerPoint), 55
Bureau of Labor Statistics (BLS), 507
Bureau of Reclamation (DOI), 311
Bush (George H. W.; Bush I) administration, 568
Bush, George W., 380
Bush (George W.; Bush II) administration: faith- and community-based charities and, 36, 192, 216, 218, 353, 556; foreign aid and, 353; government spending for development and, 340; New Freedom Initiative of, 212; tax cuts, budget cuts, and wars of, 24, 148, 556–57, 568–69. *See also* Faith-Based and Community Initiative
Bush, Vannevar, 149
Business issues. *See* Corporate and business issues
Business Roundtable, 64

California, 106, 199, 240, 304, 461, 479, 480. *See also* University of California
Calvert Foundation, 533, 534
Campaign for Community Change, 418
Campus Compact, 218
Cara Program, 178–79
CARE USA: cross-sector alliance of, 355, 536; funding sources for, 339, 342t; Indian Ocean tsunami and, 337; localization of relief, 357; as a multisectoral relief agency, 333; programming framework of, 346; in Rwanda, 351
Carnegie, Andrew, 151, 459, 486, 488n24, 667
Carnegie Classification of Institutions of Higher Education, 144, 147, 148, 181n36
Carnegie Corporation of New York, 427, 433–34, 463, 468
Carnegie Foundation for the Advancement of Teaching, 144, 249
Carson, Emmett, 667

Catalog of Nonprofit Literature, 432

Catawba University, 146

Catholic Charities, 195, 199, 200, 214, 273, 380, 427

Catholic Church, 364, 365, 368, 370, 375, 378, 384, 665. *See also* Religious congregations and organizations

Catholic Community Services of Western Washington, 214–15

Catholic Health Association (CHA), 103, 106, 121

Catholic Hospital Association (CHA), 122

Catholic Housing Services, 214–15

Catholic Relief Services, 333, 339, 342t

Cause Marketing Forum, 58

CBOs. *See* Community-based organizations, 272

CCC. *See* Civilian Conservation Corps

CCF. *See* Compassion Capital Fund

CDBGs (Community Development Block Grants). *See* Grants

CDC. *See* Centers for Disease Control

CDCs. *See* Community Development Corporations

CDFIs. *See* Community Development Financial Institutions

Census Bureau (U.S.), 197, 416–17, 625, 661

Center for American Progress Action Fund, 417

Center for Civil Society Studies (Johns Hopkins), 429

Center for Community Change, 418

Center for Effective Philanthropy, 431, 445

Center for Equal Opportunity, 412

Center for High Impact Philanthropy (U. of Pennsylvania), 446

Center for Lobbying in the Public Interest (CLPI), 430–31

Center for Watershed Protection, 305

Center on Budget and Political Priorities, 397–98, 650

Center on Nonprofits and Philanthropy (Urban Institute), 429

Center on Philanthropy (Indiana U.), 429, 486

Centers for Disease Control (CDC), 316

Central Emergency Relief Fund (CERF; UN), 340, 341, 343

CForward PAC, 449

CHA. *See* Catholic Health Association; Catholic Hospital Association

Chamber of Commerce (U.S.), 64, 398

Charitable organizations and giving: advocacy by, 667–68; charitable bequests, 500; charitable choice, 563–65; civil rights organizations, 409; competition and, 527; contributions to suspected terrorists, 575; definitions of charity, 105–07; donor-choice systems, 528; economic factors in giving, 501–04; faith-based charities, 36; for-profit firms and, 526; fundraising and funding of, 30, 55, 670; incentives for giving, 72, 569; Internet and cell phone giving, 72, 337, 508–09, 510; patterns and levels of giving, 473–76, 500; registered charities and revenues, 581n14,

661–62, 667; regulation of, 571–76; role of charitable organizations in American society, 657; scandals of, 37; tax-exemption status of, 7; U.S. economic climate and, 650–51. *See also* Faith-based organizations; Grants; Foundations; Nonprofit sector; Philanthropy; Religious congregations and organizations

Charity care, 126–27

Charity federations, 470–71

Charity Navigator, 432, 446, 451

Charity organization societies, 425

"Charity Oversight and Reform: Keeping Bad Things from Happening to Good Charities" (Senate hearings), 574

Charles Stewart Mott Foundation, 427

Charter Medical, 118

Chase Bank, 624

Chaves, Mark, 362–93

Chechnya, 343

Chemonics, 340

Chesapeake Bay Foundation, 304, 305

Chesapeake Bay watershed, 61, 304

CHFs. *See* Common Humanitarian Funds

Chevron, 355

Chicago, 288

Chicago Tribune, 346

Chicago Local Initiatives Support Corporation (LISC), 288

Chicago Symphony Orchestra, 231

Child Care and Development Block Grant, 26

Children's issues: child and family services, 526; child care, 40, 525, 608, 631, 661; child welfare services, 565; child welfare workers, 38–39; family structure, 40; foster care, 41; out-of-wedlock births, 40

Children's Museum (Portland), 536

Child Welfare League of America, 195

China. *See* People's Republic of China

Christian Coalition, 409

Christian Right. *See* Conservatives and conservatism

Christian values, 409

Chronicle of Higher Education Almanac, 147–48

Chronicle of Philanthropy, 57, 432, 472, 508

Cisco Systems, 527

Citibank, 355

Citizen engagement, 61

Citizens United v. *Federal Election Commission* (*2010*), 38, 64, 400, 574

City Year, 58, 192–93, 205, 215, 217, 221

Civic activism, engagement, and participation: anti-poverty activism, 669; characteristics of, 15t, 17–18; civic participation, 394, 396–97; commercialization and, 20; decline in, 368; role of nonprofits in, 577; social-networking activism, 623–24, 635. *See also* Accountability

Civic affairs, 11

Civic Enterprises, 415

Civil associations, 462, 669

Civilian Conservation Corps (CCC), 308

Civil rights, 272, 403, 408–13, 414, 555. *See also* Advocacy

Civil society, 42, 669

Clark University, 146

Clean Water Act and Amendments of *1972*, 303, 320

Clean Water Action, 298, 300t

Clean Water Fund, 300t

Cleveland, 163

Cleveland Chamber of Commerce, 470

Cleveland Foundation, 463

Cleveland Orchestra, 12

Clinton, Bill, 257, 415, 502

Clinton (Bill) administration, 217

Clohesy, Stephanie, 534

CLPI. *See* Center for Lobbying in the Public Interest

CNCS. *See* Corporation for National and Community Service

Coalition on Human Needs, 409, 417

Coalition on National Voluntary Organizations, 436

Coca-Cola, 58, 536

Cohen Report, The (blog), 432

Cohen, Rick, 432

Cold war, 332, 337

College Board, 142, 159

College Cost Reduction Act of *2007*, 654

College Navigator website, 152

Collins, Jim, 639

Colorado, 37, 304–05, 311

Colorado Lakes and Reservoir Management Association, 304

Colorado Riparian Association, 304

Colorado Water Quality Control Division, 304

Colorado Watershed Assembly, 304–05

Colorado Watershed Network, 304

Columbia/HCA, 115. *See also* Health Corporation of America

Columbia University, 139, 144, 552

Commercialism: accountability and, 601–02, 603, 604–05, 606, 607–09; characteristics of, 15t, 18–19; future of, 636; nonprofit sector, 462, 521–44, 592–93, 662, 670, 673–74, 676

Commission on Higher Education (Truman), 142

Commission on Private Philanthropy and Public Needs (Filer Commission), 435–36

Commodity Supplementary Food Program, 556

Common Cause, 397

Common Humanitarian Funds (CHFs), 340, 343

Commonwealth Institute of Funeral Service, 143

Communities, 109–10, 668–69, 673. *See also* Housing and community development

Community Action Agencies, 553–54

Community Action for a Renewed Environment Program, 315

Community-based organizations (CBOs), 272, 281–82

Community-based service, 167, 218, 221

Community benefits and health. *See* Health and health care issues

Community Chests, 16, 200. *See also* Philanthropy; United Way

Community development banks and finance institutions, 275–76, 282, 534

Community Development Block Grants (CDBGs). *See* Grants

Community Development Corporations (CDCs), 272–75, 277–80, 282, 286, 287, 288–89

Community Development Financial Institutions (CDFIs), 272, 274, 275–76, 277, 283

Community economic development, 277

Community land trusts, 276

Community Mental Health Centers Act of *1963*, 202

Community Psychiatric Centers, 118

Community Reinvestment Act (CRA; *1977*), 272, 534

Community Reinvestment Coalition, 412

Community service, 205, 498. *See also* Volunteering and voluntarism

Community Vocational Enterprises, 532

Community Voice Mail, 215

Community Wealth Ventures, 69, 213

Compassion Capital Fund (CCF), 216, 218, 556

CompassPoint Nonprofit Services, 430

CompuMentor (TechSoup), 430

Cone/Roper surveys, 58

Congress (U.S.), 61, 64, 433. *See also* Senate Finance Committee

Connecticut, 140, 199. *See also* Yale University

Conservation Fund, 397–98

Conservatives and conservatism: abortion and church attendance, 385–86; Christian Right, 63–64, 409; compassionate conservatism, 658; government subsidies and, 26, 567, 568; social welfare services and, 35, 36, 667; view of nonprofit sector of, 4, 5, 14, 34, 36. *See also* Bush (George W.) administration; Faith-Based and Community Initiative; Faith-based organizations; Reagan (Ronald) administration

Contract with America, 23, 24, 437, 556

Cooperative Extension Service (DOA), 306

Corinthian (education company), 150

Cornelius, Marla, 639–56

Cornell University, 144

Corporate and business issues: access to corporate payroll deduction systems, 528; bottom-of-the-pyramid businesses, 69; charitable giving of, 383, 528; collaboration and partnerships with nonprofits, 43, 57–59; corporate philanthropy, 674; corporate status and structure, 589–90; financing of election campaigns, 38, 400, 574; flexible purpose corporate forms, 53; foundations and charitable giving of, 469–70; global corporate citizenship, 354–55; governance and the governing board of, 590–92; green practices, 318; growth in business organizations, 46; limited liability company (L3C), 534; lobbying and advocacy by, 61, 64; microenterprise and microlending, 532–33; multinational corporations, 62; nonprofit-business collaboration, 535–37;

partnerships with nonprofits, 528; political action committees (PACs), 64; social purpose enterprises, 531–35; support for the arts, culture, and the humanities, 249; support of environmental organizations, 300

Corporation for National and Community Service (CNCS), 217, 218, 396, 441, 511, 556

Corporation for Public Broadcasting, 556

Corporation for Supportive Housing, 273–74

Corps Network, The, 312

Corvington, Patrick, 639–56

Council for Aid to Education, 151

Council for Environmental Education, 311. *See also* Western Regional Environmental Education Council

Council of Better Business Bureaus, 431–32

Council of Michigan Foundations, 428–29

Council on Foundations, 57, 423, 425, 427–28, 434, 440, 444, 449, 480, 483, 484

Council on the Nonprofit Sector (U.S.), 448

Cox Committee (*1952*; U.S. House of Representatives), 433

CNCS. *See* Corporation for National and Community Service

CPS. *See* Current Population Survey

CRA. *See* Community Reinvestment Act

Creative Capital, 241

Crimmins, James, 531

Crises and conflicts, 331–32

Crow, Brandon, 179

Crutchfield, Leslie R., 214

Cultural segments and trends, 632–34. *See also* Occupy Wall Street movement; Tea Party movement

Current Population Survey (CPS), 507, 659

Darfur, 344, 354, 356

Dartmouth College, 139, 140, 552

David and Lucile Packard Foundation, 441

Day care and day care providers, 26, 28, 558–59

D.C. *See* District of Columbia

DC Central Kitchen, 532

Defense, Department of (DOD), 352–53

Delancey Street, 213

Dell, 534

Demand. *See* Economic issues

Democratic Republic of the Congo. *See* Zaire

Democracy, 61, 246, 394–96, 447

Democracy in America (Tocqueville), 13, 462

Demographic issues: age and aging, 370, 378, 524, 629–30; birth rates, 369; cultural subgroups, 41; demand for nonprofit services, 39–40; demographic challenges, 283–85, 639; fusion families, 630–32; generational conflict, 649; generational constellations and labels, 627–29, 639; generational synergy, 629; generation gap, 625; information concerning, 661; life expectancy, 89, 625, 629; minority majority, 625–26. *See also* Immigration

Denison University, 146

Developing countries, 337, 338, 343, 344, 354, 358, 530

Development Alternatives International, 340

Devlin, Rose Anne, 512–13

Díaz, William, 675

Dighe, Atul, 616–38

Diminished Democracy: From Membership to Management in American Civic Life (Skocpol), 295

District of Columbia (D.C.), 48, 553

DHHS. *See* Health and Human Services, Department of

DOA. *See* Agriculture, Department of

DOD. *See* Defense, Department of

DOI. *See* Interior, Department of

Donee Group, 435

Donors Forum of Chicago, 428–29

Doris Duke Charitable Foundations, 241

DOT. *See* Transportation, Department of

Douglas, James, 464

Downtown Seattle Association, 316

Drucker Foundation's Self-Assessment Tool, 55

Dubnik, Melvin, 596

Ducks Unlimited, 314

Earth Day, 297

Earth Force, 312

Earth Justice Legal Defense Fund, 297

Eastern Neighborhoods Community Health Impact Assessment, 315

eBay, 534

EBP. *See* Evidence-based practice

Ebrahim, Alnoor, 601

Ecological Society of America, 310

Economic Census, 231, 661

Economic Growth and Tax Relief Reconciliation Act of *2001*, 568

Economic issues: access to investment capital, 31; banking crisis, 24; blockbuster economics, 237–38; capacity building, 216–17; creative capitalism, 459; cyclical nature of ACH finances, 234–38; demand, 31, 111, 112, 114, 118, 124, 251–52, 524; dues versus donations, 373; earned and personal income, 213–15, 238–39, 242, 503–04, 508, 513; economic challenges, 283–86; economic rebound, 283; equity capital, 113–14, 119, 525; family downshifting, 631; family outsourcing, 630–31; federal budget deficit, 513, 514; fiscal centralization, 205; for-profit sector bankruptcies, 59; free-market capitalism, 521; giving as percent of personal income, 496, 501; growth of commercial income, 47–49; household assets, 504; income distribution, 659; inflation, 375; markets and marketing, 57–59, 66, 67, 126; microfinance, 69; private investment capital, 50; privatization, 561; profits and profit making, 119; public choice economic theory, 561; recessions, 235, 567; reputational capital, 535; richest Americans, 510–11; social investing, 534–35,

539; stock market, 101, 503–04, 523, 525; transfer of wealth, 43; U.S. gross domestic product (GDP), 44, 45; value of time, 507; venture activity, 5153; "Washington consensus," 337. *See also* Commercialism; Endowments; Globalization; Great Recession of *2008–09*; Poverty

Economic Opportunity Act of *1964*, 35

Economic Recovery Program, 205

Economic Recovery Tax Act (*1981*), 569

Ecotourism, 300, 318

Eddie Bauer, 58

Edmonston, Barry, 626

Edmund Rice High School, 158, 161, 164, 166

Edna McConnell Clark Foundation, 207

Education, Department of, 152

Education Gospel, 146–47

Education issues: accountability, 143; demand for skilled labor, 174; distributed learning, 618–19; enrollment in for-profit and nonprofit institutions, 30, 137; financial aid, 558, 646; learning culture, 633–34; legislation, 142; nonprofit organizations, 46, 47, 50, 54, 137–38, 662–63; nonprofit paid employment in, 642; price index for, 524; private and public organizations, 140; revenues and fiscal pressures, 2, 56, 497, 530; segregation and integration, 141; technological advances, 618; voluntarism, 498, 506–07

Education issues—higher education: academic health centers, 148; accountability, reporting, and standards, 152–53, 155, 606; arts training programs, 249; black, Hispanic, Asian, and other schools, 141, 144; challenges of, 145–55; for clergy, 377–78; community colleges, 142, 167; competition, 527; costs and expenditures, 145–46, 150, 153–54; curricula, 147; early origins, 139–40; endowments, 498; enrollment, 138, 141, 142, 143, 150; faith-related schools, 144; financial aid, 138, 139, 142–43, 145, 150, 152, 155, 497–98; for-profit schools, 149–50, 152, 153–55; future of, 155–56; GI Bill, 141; government involvement, 140–43, 147–49, 152–53, 155, 554; institutional isomorphism, 153–55; "kept" universities, 542; land-grant universities, 144–45; liberal arts schools, 144, 146–47, 151, 155; marketing of patented discoveries, 56, 149; net cost/price calculator, 152, 153; nonprofit management courses, 538; nonprofit schools, 138–39, 143–55; normal schools, 141; peer review process, 149; private-philanthropy priorities, 150–51, 155; private schools, 138–39, 141–42, 143–56; public schools, 141–42, 143, 144, 153–55; research universities, 144–45, 147–49, 155, 554; revenues and fiscal pressures, 151, 474, 497–98, 554; student loan programs, 558, 646, 654; tuition, 145–46, 150, 153; vocational schools, 143, 155; women's schools, 144

Education issues—K-*12*: Catholic schools, 157–58, 160–64, 165; challenges to, 160–64, 165; charter schools, 160, 162, 163, 165, 183n90; common schools, 158; conservative Christian schools, 159–60, 183n87; costs and expenditures, 163–64; country day schools, 159; curricula, 158–59, 162, 310, 312; diversity of private schools, 157; early origins, 156–57, 158; enrollment, 157, 158, 159, 160–61; environmental education, 310–13; faculty, 161–62; financial aid, 161; fundraising, 164; government involvement, 159; independent boarding and day schools, 158–59, 160–64, 165; nonprofit schools, 160; "prep" schools, 159; private-philanthropy priorities, 151; private schools, 156–57, 160–66; proprietary schools, 159; Protestant ethos of mass education, 156; public schools, 156, 162, 164–66; school choice and competition, 162–63; standardized testing, 162; tuition, 156, 161, 163, 164; volunteering, 511; vouchers, 162–63

Education issues—workforce development and training: accountability, 168, 169–71, 179; adaptation and change, 173–75; choice and individual training accounts (ITAs), 171–72, 175; challenges, 175–79; collaboration and subcontracting, 172–73; community-based organizations, 167–68, 170, 171, 175, 178; community colleges, 167–68, 175; competition, 167–68, 171, 175, 179; costs and expenditures, 170; demand-driven workforce development systems, 176–77; early origins, 166; for-profit organizations, 167–68, 175, 178; funding, 178–79, 186n136; government involvement, 166, 167, 168–73, 177–79; incentives for, 171; nonprofit organizations, 166–68, 170, 171–72, 175, 177, 178, 179, 186n136; private organizations, 167; training for the hardest to serve, 177–79. *See also* American Recovery and Reinvestment Act of *2009*; Job training; One-Stop career centers; Workforce Investment Act

Edward M. Kennedy Serve America Act of *2009*, 205, 217–18, 438, 447, 579

Egger, Robert, 449

Eikenberry, Angela, 608

Einstein, Albert, 603

Eisner, David, 499

Elections and campaigns, 573

Elections and campaigns—specific: *2004*, 395, 415; *2008*, 395, 396–97, 417, 447, 624, 634; *2010*, 448, 567, 568, 624

Electronic Data Initiative for Nonprofits, 444

Electronics, 621–23

Employment issues: career advancement, 645–46; compensation, 646–47; demographic shifts in the American workforce, 174–75; employee satisfaction, 643–44, 648; employer demand-driven development systems, 176–77; employment in for-profit sector, 29, 30t; employment in nonprofit sector, 8, 29, 30t, 48, 53–54, 197, 198; encore careers, 650; "gainful employment" education programs, 152; generational conflict, 649; getting a nonprofit job, 649–50; health insurance, 27; new economy and, 35; nonprofit workforce dynamics, 639–54; pipeline research, 649–50; public employment in public welfare, 199; quality of life, 647; sector project strategies, 177; social purpose enterprises, 531–32; strategies for the long term, 651–54; U.S. employment growth, 641; welfare reforms, 564–65; workforce challenges and turnover, 644–45; workforce development and training, 167–69; workforce intermediaries, 168; working women, 40, 524. *See also* Education issues—workforce development and training; Job training; Labor and union issues; Nonprofit sector

Endowments: of the Bill and Melinda Gates Foundation, 484; of community foundations, 472; of educational nonprofits, 497, 498; of foundations in general, 476, 478; grant makers endowments, 476, 478; of health care conversion foundations, 469; Jewish federations and, 471; losses in value of, 540, 650; private giving and, 523, 650; program-related investments and, 484

English, Richard A., 669

Enron, 574

Ensuring Risk Reduction in Communities with Multiple Stressors (report; NEJAC), 315

Enterprise, 273–74

Entitlement programs, 22, 557–59. *See also* Medicaid; Medicare

Environmental Action, 297

Environmental Defense Fund, 294, 297, 298, 300, 318, 319, 536

Environmental Grantmakers Association, 300

Environmental issues: activism, professionalism, voluntarism, and commercialism, 316–19, 320–21; advocacy organizations, 296–302; anti-toxics and environmental justice, 302, 320; challenges of, 295, 316, 319–21; civic activism, 316–17; classification of organizations, 295, 296; climate change, 295, 301, 303, 315, 316, 319–20, 321, 330, 332; command-and-control regulatory paradigm of, 294; early origins, 294–95; ecosystem-based organizations, 296, 302–10, 313–14; educational organizations, 296, 310–13; environmental justice and community health partnerships, 314–16, 320; for-profit consulting firms, 318; future of, 319–21; governmental involvement, 300–01, 308, 311–12, 320, 321, 497; greening of buildings, 619–20; growth of, 297; land trusts, 306, 308–10, 318, 320; membership of, 298; multi-stakeholder partnerships, 295, 313–16; nonprofit organizations, 46, 50, 621; organizational structure of, 297, 299; pollution, 303, 315; revenues and fiscal pressures of, 299–302, 305–06, 308–09, 312–13, 315–16, 317, 319, 320–21, 497; transportation, 620–21; watershed associations and conferences, 303–06, 307, 319–20. *See also* Environmental Protection Agency

Environmental Education Act (*1990*), 312

Environmental Education and Training Partnership, 312–13

Environmental Protection Agency (EPA), 294–95, 305, 306

Environment America, 302

EPA. *See* Environmental Protection Agency

Episcopal Church, 364. *See also* Religious congregations and organizations

Equity and fairness, 207–08

Ethics and ethical issues, 107, 252, 348, 352, 431, 445, 595

Europe: eligibility for social services, 202; European Caucasians, 626; government-nonprofit partnerships in, 530; higher learning in, 139; NGOs in, 339; nonprofit social service organizations in, 221; protests in, 577; public safety net in, 200; social ventures in, 533, 543–44; state-supported cultural institutions in, 249; U.S. assistance to, 331

Evangelical Lutheran Church, 378–79. *See also* Religious congregations and organizations

Everson, Mark W., 482

Everyday Democracy, 396

Evian, 58

Evidence-based practice (EBP), 209

Evolution Isn't What It Used to Be (Anderson), 621

Excellence and Equity (report; American Association of Museums; *1992*), 248

Executive Order *13224* (Bush II), 575

Facebook, 412, 624, 634

Faith-Based and Community Initiative, 218, 380–81, 388, 561–62, 564

Faith-Based organizations, 36, 68, 353, 416, 559, 564. *See also* Education issues—higher education; Religious congregations and organizations

Family Violence Prevention Fund, 58

Fannie Mae. *See* Federal National Mortgage Association

Farestart, 213

Farm Bill (*1985*), 309

FASB. *See* Financial Accounting Standards Board

FEC. *See* Federal Election Commission

Federal Election Commission (FEC), 573

Federal Election Commission v. Massachusetts Citizens for Life, Inc. (*1986*), 573

Federal Home Loan Mortgage Corporation (FHLMC; Freddie Mac), 280

Federal National Mortgage Association (FNMA; Fannie Mae), 280

Feeney, Charles, 484

Ferrall, Victor E., Jr., 147

Ferris, James M., 513

FHLMC. *See* Federal Home Loan Mortgage Corporation

Fidelity Charitable Gift Fund, 30, 460, 471–72, 473, 526

Fidelity Investments, 55–56, 471–72, 526

Fieldstone Alliance, 432

"Fighting Back" program, 465

Filer Commission. *See* Commission on Private Philanthropy and Public Needs

Filer, John, 435

Financial Accounting Standards Board (FASB), 593

Fischer, Claude, 389

Fleishman, Joel, 610

Florida, 163, 304, 461

FNMA. *See* Federal National Mortgage Association

Focus on the Family, 397

Forces for Good (Crutchfield and Grant), 214

Ford Foundation, 241–42, 249, 300, 308, 427, 433, 468

Ford Motor Company, 463

Foreclosures, 282. *See also* Housing and community development

Foreign aid. *See* International assistance; Nongovernmental organizations; *individual organizations*

Foreign Assistance Act and Amendments (*1961, 1973*), 331, 356

Form *990* for Tax-Exempt Organizations (IRS): as an accountability document, 103, 104–05, 124–25, 595; fee income on, 214; hospitals and, 102, 107, 122, 124, 129; limitations of, 103; lobbying expenditures on, 398; mandatory filing of, 438, 593; revisions of, 102, 575, 593, 595; unrelated business income, 530

For-profit sector: access to investment capital by, 31; expansion of, 111–13; fraudulent practices of, 59; health care domains in, 92, 94; political influence of, 102; requirements of, 585n71; trustworthiness of, 94–95. *See also* Health and health care issues

For-profit sector—as a competitive challenge to the nonprofit sector: commercialization, 674; growth of for-profit involvement, 28–31, 100–01, 524–27; marketization, 558, 559, 561–62; meeting the for-profit competition, 59–60, 446–47

Forum of Regional Associations of Grantmakers, 57, 428

"Forward Together" Declaration, 447

Foundation, The: A Great American Secret (Fleishman), 610

Foundation Center, 425, 431, 432, 440, 444, 460, 473, 474, 475, 477, 478, 479, 480, 484, 485, 672

Foundation for New Era Philanthropy, 594–95

Foundation Library Center, 434

Foundations: accountability of, 610; advocacy by, 63, 667; assets of, 452n8; characteristics of, 467; charity federations, 470–71; criticisms of, 464–65; cultural philanthropy, 241; definition of, 489n37; diversity in, 670; endowments of, 467–68, 469, 476, 478; Filer Commission and, 435; financing of nonprofit lobbying by, 38; geographic distribution of, 475; institutional philanthropy and, 467–69; market culture and, 539; patterns of giving, 473–76; payout and payout rate of, 476, 477–78, 496; program evaluation

by, 599–600; public policy challenges to, 433–38; regulation and governance of, 453n34, 464, 476, 481–83; religious organizations and, 471, 473; scandals, 437–38; Spotlight on Poverty and Opportunity, 416–17; types of, 467; U.S. economy and, 460, 476–78. See also Association of Small Foundations; Council on Foundations; Grants; Living Cities; Philanthropy; *individual foundations by name*

Foundations—specific types: charity federations, 470–71; community foundations, 460, 463, 468, 472–73, 474, 483n43; conversion foundations, 468–69; family foundations, 466, 477; independent foundations, 460, 468, 474–75, 478; knowledgeable foundations, 464; operating foundations, 468; private foundations, 241, 308, 320, 395, 398, 433, 469, 482, 486

Foundations—support: support for IOs, 441; support of arts, culture and the humanities, 249; support of environmental organizations, 300, 301; support of higher education by, 151; support of housing and community development by, 288; support of social services by, 193, 208, 215, 216, 669

4-H Clubs, 312, 317

Fourth sector, 69

Freddie Mac. *See* Federal Home Loan Mortgage Corporation

Freedman, Marc, 650

French Doctors' Movement, 352

Friedman, Milton, 165

Frumkin, Peter, 563

FSG Social Impact Advisors, 431

Fuelner, Edward, 34

Functions: advocacy function, 12; community-building function, 13; expressive function, 12–13; service function, 11–12; value guardian function, 13

Fund for Public Interest Research, 299

Gais, Thomas, 563

GAO. *See* Government Accountability Office

Gates, Bill, 342, 415, 459–61, 475, 484, 486

Gates Foundation. *See* Bill and Melinda Gates Foundation

Gates, Melinda, 475, 484

GEO. *See* Grantmakers for Effective Organizations

General Social Survey (GSS), 385, 390n6

Generations. *See* Demographic issues

Genetic issues, 626

Geneva Conventions, 351

Georgetown College, 146

Georgia, 565

Georgia Pacific, 536

Getty Center, 231

Getty Trust. *See* J. Paul Getty Trust

GI Bill. *See* Servicemen's Readjustment Act of *1944*

Gifts. *See* Philanthropy; *individual recipients*

Giloth, Robert, 178

Girl Scouts, 530–31

Girls Incorporated, 58

Giving USA, 473, 478

Global Environmental Management Initiative, 318

Globalization, 43, 253, 256, 260, 336–37, 370–71, 536–37

Global Rivers Environmental Education Network, 312

Global terror, 352

Golden, Olivia, 565

Golladay, Kendall, 666

Goodwill Industries, 177, 195, 197, 200, 213, 531

Google, 620–21

"Gospel of Wealth" (article; Carnegie), 667

Goss, Kristin A., 506

Governing magazine, 526

Government—federal: acquisition of land by, 308; climate change and, 301; distrust of, 658; effects on for-profit sector, 59, 60; federal budget deficit, 513, 514, 567, 650; federal devolution, 437, 450, 549, 577, 659, 670, 672, 674–75, 676; federal government, 97, 166, 200, 201, 204, 301, 553; federally funded scientific research, 148–49; impact of social media on, 624; local governments, 37, 200, 201, 202–03, 204, 240–41, 568; professionalism and, 16–17; role of, 550–51; social programs of, 35, 657–58; social welfare expenditures of, 21–27, 523; subsidies of, 24–27, 30–31, 49–51, 557–58; third-party government, 553. *See also* Education issues; Health and health care issues; Taxes and taxation issues; Vouchers; *individual administrations*

Government—government-nonprofit relations: adaptation to public funding, 49–51; advocacy and, 63; background of, 4–5, 552–55; changes in, 549, 555, 556–59, 674; contracting regimes and, 563–64, 671; government-fueled fiscal growth, 21–27; government spending and nonprofit funding, 10, 34–35, 72, 448, 505, 523–24, 529, 530, 555–68; marketization, 559, 561–62; patterns of government-nonprofit relations, 550–52; professionalism and, 16; public policies and, 576–77; regulation of advocacy, 572–74; regulation of fundraising, 571–72; regulation of management, 574–76; regulation of politically active nonprofits, 573–74; reimbursement and, 562–63; taxes and taxation issues, 6–7, 37–38, 51, 102, 439, 551, 558–59, 560–61, 568–71; toward a new government-nonprofit compact, 70–71, 577–80; welfare reform and charitable choice, 563–65; workforce issues, 653–54

Government—state governments: American Recovery and Reinvestment Act and, 567–68; arts, culture, and the humanities and, 249; associations for environmental education of, 311–12; budget deficits, 650; challenges to nonprofit tax exemptions, 37; Community Development Block Grants, 271–72; environmental policy issues, 301, 320; Extension Services, 311, 314; health-care organizations and, 97, 104, 113; low-income

housing tax credits and, 269–70; managed care and, 212; Medicaid and, 557; rainy day funds, 567; social services and, 49, 200, 201, 202–03, 204, 209–10, 211; support for the arts and culture, 240; support for nonprofits, 22; support of private institutions, 552–53; welfare reform and, 23–24, 563, 565; workforce development, 166. *See also* Medicaid

Government Accountability Office (GAO), 103

Government Performance and Results Act (GPRA; *1993*), 32, 563

Grable Foundation, 607

Grand Valley State University, 444

Grant, Heather McLeod, 214

Grantmakers for Effective Organizations (GEO), 32, 443, 445, 485, 599–600

Grants: accountability and grant makers, 609–10; changes in, 473; criticism of grant making, 464–66; endowed organizations, 463–64; geographic distribution of, 475, 674–75; grant recipients, 478–81; institutional grantmakers, 460–61; patterns of giving, 473–76; politics, policies, and regulation, 460–61, 464, 467; types of support provided, 474; U.S. economy and, 460, 477–78. *See also* Forum of Regional Associations of Grantmakers; Foundations; Government—government-nonprofit relations; Philanthropy

Grants—specific: assistance grants, 331; block grants, 26, 78n48, 202, 270, 557, 577, 672; categorical grants, 202; Child Care and Development Block Grant program, 26, 78n48, 558–59; Community Development Block Grant (CDBG) program, 271, 556; Community Service Block Grant program, 202, 556, 581n16; corporate grants, 413; emergency grants, 342; foundation grants, 400, 413, 433, 443, 445, 450, 461, 599, 670; government grants, 239, 400, 412–13, 417, 419, 552, 554, 670–71; Homelessness Assistance Grants, 556; local health care centers grants, 556; Low-Income Home Energy Assistance Grants, 556; matching grants, 498; New Generations theater grants, 253; Nonprofit Sector Research Fund, 429; private philanthropic grants, 208; social justice grants, 479–80; Social Service Block Grant, 556, 557

Grassley, Charles ("Chuck"; R-Iowa), 103, 122, 254, 437–38, 447, 460–61, 574

Gray, Bradford H., 59, 66, 89–136, 562, 662

Great Depression of *1929*, 268–29, 308, 336

Greater Pittsburgh Community Food Bank, 598

GreatNonprofits, 451

Great Recession of *2007–09*: accountability of commercial nonprofits and, 593; arts and, 48, 242, 260; charitable giving and, 513, 523; corporate role in, 521; deregulation and, 579–80; funding for low-income housing, 286; green movement and, 633; household size and, 632; international assistance and, 336, 337; job training and placement, 166, 167, 173–74, 176, 178;

nongovernmental organizations and, 342; non-profit sector and, 215, 521–22, 540, 567, 650–51; philanthropy and, 476–77; poverty and, 415, 659, 675–76; social services and, 209; spending cuts, 193; stock market indices and, 476
Great Nonprofits, 446
Great Society, 21–22, 23, 553
Greenbelt Alliance, 309
Greenlining Institute, 479, 481
Greenpeace USA, 298, 299, 300t, 623, 666
Green, Rob, 565
Gregory, Paula, 621
Greyston Foundation bakery, 52, 213, 532
Griffin, Patricia, 619
Grinsfelder, Mary Clark, 521–48
Grønbjerg, Kirsten A., 549–86, 659, 669, 674
Grubb, W. Norton, 146–47, 167
GSS. *See* General Social Survey
Guggenheim Museum, 52, 252
GuideStar, 431, 444, 446, 451, 527
Guiliani, Rudolph, 247
Guo, Baorong, 608

Habitat for Humanity, 205, 381, 533
Hacker, Jacob, 63–64
Hager, Mark A., 499
Haiti earthquake (*2010*), 343, 415, 509–10, 634
Half in Ten, 417
Hall, Peter Dobkin, 434, 436
Hands On America, 217
HandsOn Network, 431
Harlem Children's Zone, 205, 208, 215, 217, 218
Harvard Business Review, 44
Harvard College and University, 12, 42, 138, 139, 140, 144, 429, 552
Harvard University-Sierra Club Leadership Development Project, 317
Hasenfeld, Yeheskel, 669
Hauser Center for Nonprofit Organizations (Harvard U.), 429
Havens, John, 504
HCA. *See* Hospital Corporation of America
HCV. *See* Housing Choice Voucher program
Health and Human Services, Department of (DHHS), 315–16, 441
Health and health care issues: abortion, 384, 385–86; academic health centers, 148; accountability, 102–05, 124–25, 606; advocacy and, 402–03, 404, 405t, 407; challenges of, 89–90, 91, 95–96, 98–118, 124, 128–30; charity and charitable roots of, 96–97, 104, 105, 471; chronic medical conditions and, 109–10; commercialism, 606; community benefits and health, 106, 110, 120, 124–27, 289; competition in, 527; costs, 98–99, 102–03, 525; deinstitutionalization, 203; depro-fessionalization of medical services, 108–09; of developmentally disabled persons, 24, 193–96, 203, 211–12, 215; domains of, 90, 91–94, 110–18; drug and alcohol treatment, 197; dumping of

unprofitable patients, 99; elder care, 630; facility closures, 102; fee-for-service plans, 26–27; fiscal and revenue pressures, 96, 98–100, 102–03, 497; for-profit organizations, 100–02, 111–13, 114–15, 116, 118–22, 129–30; fraudulent behavior in, 120, 124, 129; government involvement, 97–98, 100, 111, 112, 118, 127, 197; health maintenance organizations (HMOs), 31, 66, 101–02, 111, 112–13, 118, 526; home health care, 31, 111, 112, 118, 197, 212, 525; hospice care and centers, 112, 115–16; innovation in, 95–96; investor-owned corporations, 100–02, 117, 119, 124; joint ventures of, 52, 120–21; life cycle in, 118–20, 127–27; limited public under-standing, 107–08; managed care, 26–27, 33, 99–100, 108, 117, 212, 526, 562; medical costs, 98; mental health care, 197, 199, 212; mergers, 99; nonprofit organizations, 44, 45, 47, 50, 53, 66, 89–91, 110–30, 562, 662; nonprofit paid employment in, 642f; organizational practices and structure, 120–22; paradox of, 89; physical medicine, 112; price index for, 524; private-sector share of, 28–29; psychiatric services, 117; public confidence in, 599; quality-of-care protec-tion, 112; report cards, 108; role of nonprofits in healthcare, 91–97; social services and, 197, 199; substance abuse, 40; technology and, 112, 622–23; trustworthiness and professional values in, 94–95, 108–09, 123–24, 127, 129; utilization review, 99; voluntarism, 498. *See also* Hospitals; Nonprofit sector; Patient Protection and Afford-able Care Act; Population health
Health and health care issues—nursing homes: accountability of, 104; charity care in, 126; demographic and social changes and, 40, 41, 524, 630; fraud and, 59, 95; federal support, 22; investor-owned companies and, 101; Medicaid and, 77n40; Medicare and, 113–14; multifacility systems, 121; nonprofit and for-profit organiza-tions, 12, 110, 113, 116–17, 123, 526; report cards for, 108
Health and health care issues—specific diseases and disorders: acquired immunodeficiency syndrome (AIDS), 330, 350; cholera, 346; end-stage renal disease, 111; malaria, 465
Health insurance: consumer choice and, 108; con-sumer cooperatives, 100; costs and, 98; domain life cycles and, 126; gaps in, 129; government role in and, 33, 97, 100; hospital insurance pro-grams, 97; insurance exchanges, 97, 100; insured and uninsured patients, 89, 97, 98, 102–03, 105; levers of control of, 98; national health plans, 99; nonprofit insurance plans, 100; for psychiatric care, 117; vulnerability to fraud and abuse, 94, 95. *See also* Medicaid; Medicare; Patient Protec-tion and Affordable Care Act
Heim, Bradley, 503
Heinz Endowments, 607
Heritage Foundation, 412

Herzlinger, Regina, 37, 44

Higher Education Act of *1965*, 142, 143

Higher Education Act Amendments (*1972*), 142

Higher Education Opportunity Act (*2008*), 152

Hill-Burton Act. *See* Hospital Survey and Construction Act

Historical societies. *See* Arts, culture, and humanities

History and Geography of the Human Genes, The (Menozzi and Piazza), 626

HMO Act of *1973*, 108, 113

HMOs (health maintenance organizations). *See* Health and health care issues

Holifield, Brooks, 377

HOME. *See* Home Investment Partnership Program

Home and Community Based Waiver program, 203

Home Depot, 623

Home Investment Partnership Program (HOME), 270, 274, 286

Homosexual issues, 384–85, 386–87, 631

Honest Leadership and Open Government Act of *2007*, 573

Honeywell Corporation, 543

HOPE VI program, 269

Hospital Corporation of America (HCA), 118. *See also* Columbia/HCA

Hospitals: academic medical centers, 106; accountability of, 102–04; acute care in, 205; advocacy and lobbying by, 403; business activities of, 52, 56; certificates of need and, 114; charges for, 530; charitable and community benefit activities of, 102, 106–07; commercialism and, 606; competitive practices of, 96; expectations for accountability for, 102; for-profit sector and, 526; fraudulent practices of, 59, 117, 118; investor-owned hospital companies, 98, 113–14, 115, 117, 118; Medicare and, 98; nonprofit sector and, 90, 110–11, 114–18, 446, 526; numbers of hospital beds, 114, 119; paid nonprofit employment in, 642; private- and for-profit sector share of, 28–29, 111–12, 114–15, 116–18; professionalism and transformation of, 16; reporting practices of, 103; sale and conversion to for-profit firms, 594; tax exemptions for, 104, 106; uncompensated care by, 608. *See also* Health and health care issues; Medicaid; Medicare

Hospitals—specific: community hospitals, 119; dialysis centers, 111–12; general hospitals, 113–15; nursing homes, 59, 116–17, 123; private hospitals, 16; psychiatric hospitals, 110–11, 117–18; rehabilitation hospitals, 28, 111, 112. *See also* Health and health care issues—nursing homes

Hospital Survey and Construction Act (Hill-Burton Act; *1946*), 105, 113, 114

Housing and community development: advocacy for, 276; challenges of, 279–87; community development, 271–80; competition and, 285; demographic trends and, 284; financial intermediaries, 273–75, 279, 283; financial viability, 279; foreclosure crisis and, 267, 280–82, 283,

286–87; for-profit organizations, 277–80, 285; future promising opportunities in the field, 287–90; government involvement in, 266–67, 268–71, 278, 281, 282, 284, 285–86, 291; growth of, 290; housing industry, 268–80; housing markets, 279; institutional infrastructure of, 266–67; major forces shaping the field, 280–90; organization and management, 286–87; providers of housing to the disadvantaged, 275; private sector issues, 273; public housing, 268–69, 284; public policies, 289; revenues and fiscal pressures of, 280–81, 285–87, 288, 290–91; role of nonprofit organizations in, 49–50, 72, 266, 267–80, 285, 288; technology, 289–90. *See also* Home Investment Partnership program; Housing Choice Voucher program; Low-Income Housing Tax Credit program; *headings under Community and Communities*

Housing and Urban Development, Department of (HUD), 269, 670–71

Housing Choice Voucher program (HCV), 269, 284

Housing Opportunities for People with AIDS, 2370

Housing Partnership Network (HPN), 273

Hout, Michael, 389

HPN. *See* Housing Partnership Network

HUD. *See* Housing and Urban Development, Department of

Human genome project, 621

Humanitarian Charter and Minimum Standards in Disaster Response, 346

Humanitarian Accountability Partnership, 347

Humanitarian Policy Group, 343

Humanitarian tourism, 349

Human Rights Campaign Foundation, 409

Human services. *See* Social services

Hurricane Katrina (*2005*), 388, 415, 508, 512, 569, 577, 658

Hurricane Wilma, 569, 577

IAF. *See* Industrial Areas Foundation

Idealist, 449

IEG, LLC, 58, 470

iGive.com, 534

Illinois, 37, 572

Immigration, 41, 246, 284, 370–71, 385, 388–89, 396, 625

Independent Sector: advocacy by, 427; foundations and, 449; Grassley-led initiatives and, 447; as a national umbrella group, 17, 423, 425, 426–27, 436, 440, 444; Panel on the Nonprofit Sector, 438, 445; professionalization and, 57; recommendations for governance of nonprofits, 482, 574–75; surveys of, 507, 511

Independent Women's Forum, 412

Indiana, 572

Indiana University, 42, 429, 444

Indiana University Center on Philanthropy, 432

Individual training accounts (ITAs). *See* Education issues—workforce development and training

Industrial Areas Foundation (IAF), 416
Infrastructure Exchange Group, 444
Infrastructure organizations (IOs): accountability of, 443, 445; advocacy and public education by, 426–29, 446–47; challenges and future directions of, 424, 425–26, 427, 433, 440–51; clients served by, 426–32; collaboration, 443–45; education and management support for nonprofits by, 429–32, 439, 442, 449–50; government involvement, 436–37, 439–40, 441, 445; growth and consolidation of, 424, 425, 426; historical overviews of, 425–26, 433–40; journals, 429, 432; leadership of, 444; overview of nonprofit IOs, 425–32; provision of information resources, 431–32; public policies and, 433–38, 447–49; research, 429, 443; revenues and fiscal pressures of, 424, 432, 440–41, 443, 445, 450–51; services of, 442; state nonprofit associations, 437, 449–50
"Inside Higher Education" (essay; Ferrall), 147
Institute of Medicine (IOM), 114–15
Institute of Museum and Library Services, 556
Integrated Postsecondary Education Data System (IPEDS), 152
Intellectual property, 34, 242, 257–58, 260
InterAction, 333, 336, 346, 353
Interagency Working Group on the Nonprofit Sector, 448
Interior, Department of (DOI), 311
Internal Revenue Code, 7. *See also* Taxes and taxation
Internal Revenue Service (IRS), 103, 112, 439, 446, 565, 573, 589, 661
International assistance: characteristics of the nonprofit subsector and, 335–36; civic activism and advocacy in, 330; crises and challenges to, 330, 331–32, 334–35, 336, 337–38, 349, 352; government involvement, 331, 338–40; humanitarian aid, 340–41; international crises and, 329–30; official development assistance (ODA), 338, 339–40; peacekeeping and, 337–38, 352, 355; principal program areas within, 333–35; revenues and fiscal pressures of, 336, 338–43; role of nonprofits in, 329–33; role of private sector in, 354–55; sovereignty and intervention, 332, 338, 358n6; voluntarism and, 330. *See also* Nongovernmental organizations; Professionalism
International City/County Management Association, 305–06
International Committee of the Red Cross, 331, 351. *See also* American Red Cross
International Court of Justice, 623–24
International nonprofit organizations, 46, 50
International Rescue Committee, 351
International Society for Third-Sector Research (ISTR), 429
Internet: activism of, 60, 395; advocacy on, 398, 415, 417, 419, 421; education and, 618; elections of *2008* and, 396–97; fundraising and charitable giving and, 72, 337, 508–09, 510, 527; giving malls on, 534; lobbying filings on, 573;
nonprofits and, 432; religious congregations and organizations and, 371–72; social media and networking, 412, 623–24; virtual global communities of interests, 634. *See also* Google; Technology
Investing in Democracy (Sirianni), 320
IOM. *See* Institute of Medicine
IOs. See Infrastructure organizations
IPEDS. *See* Integrated Postsecondary Education Data System
Iran, 624
Iraq, 330, 338, 355, 567
IRS. *See* Internal Revenue Service
Islamic Relief, 353
Istook amendment, 35, 428, 437, 447
Istook, Ernest, Jr. (R-Okla.), 437
ISTR. *See* International Society for Third-Sector Research
ITAs (Individual training accounts). *See* Education issues—workforce development and training

Jaycees, 61, 396
Jewish Family Services, 195, 199
Jewish federations and charities, 471
Jewish synagogues and congregations, 373, 375, 378, 384, 665. *See also* Religious congregations and organizations
Joassart-Marcelli, Pascale, 67, 657–81
Jobs and Growth Tax Relief Reconciliation Act of *2003*, 568
Jobs for Veterans Act (*2002*), 178
Job training: advocacy organizations and, 666; antipoverty organizations and, 415, 416, 663; economic recessions and, 235; enhancement of the public good and, 407; government support for, 671; job training legislation, 168–78, 525, 659; purpose of, 169; as a social service, 194, 204, 532. *See also* Education issues—workforce development and training; Employment issues; Personal Responsibility and Work Opportunity Reconciliation Act of *1996*
Job Training Partnership Act of *1982*, 168
Johns Hopkins University, 12, 42, 138, 144, 148, 429
Johns Hopkins Listening Post Project, 31, 54–55, 62, 63, 220, 401, 482, 571, 574, 667–68
Johnson, Lyndon B., 22, 271
Johnson (Lyndon B.) administration, 200–201
Joint Evaluation of Emergency Assistance to Rwanda, The, 346
J. Paul Getty Trust, 468, 481, 483
Juma Ventures, 532
Jumpstart, 218
Juvenile Justice, 556

Kaiser, Michael, 260
Kaiser Permanente, 100
Kane, Pearl Rock, 137–91
Kansas, 526–27
Kanter, Rosabeth, 44, 58

Kaplan (education company), 150
Kazakstan, 355
Kearns, Kevin P., 587–615, 673
Keil, Mary, 531
Kendall Foundation, 304
Kennedy (John F.) administration, 200–01
Kennedy School of Government, 321
Kids Voting USA, 396
King, Martin Luther, Jr., 627
Kiva, 446
Kiwanis, 61, 396
Kluver, Jodie Drapal, 608
Kramer, Mark R., 461–62
Krehely, Jeff, 666

Labaree, David, 147
Labor and union issues, 64, 168, 174–75, 257,
    573–74. *See also* Employment issues
Land mines, 623
Land Trust Alliance (Land Trust Exchange), 309–10
Land trusts. *See* Environmental issues
Langton, Stuart, 20
Lazerson, Marvin, 146–47
Leadership Conference on Civil Rights, 409, 412,
    417
League of American Orchestras, 248, 253, 423
League of Conservation Voters, 397
League of Women Voters, 61, 396
League of Women Voters of Colorado Education
    Fund, 304
Learn and Serve America, 556
Lebanon, 338
Leffingwell, Russell, 434
Legal issues. *See* Accountability
Legitimacy. *See* Nonprofit sector
Lenkowsky, Leslie, 459–94
Let America Speak (coalition), 437
Levy, Reynold, 355
Liberal Education and America's Promise initiative,
    147
Light, Paul, 446, 606
LIHTC. *See* Low-Income Housing Tax Credit
Lila Wallace Reader's Digest Fund, 241
LISC. *See* Local Initiatives Support Corporation
Living Cities, 274–75, 279–80, 288
Liz Claiborne, 58
L.L. Bean, 299, 534
Lobbying. *See* Advocacy and lobbying
Lobbying Disclosure Act of *1995*, 38, 573
Local Initiatives Support Corporation (LISC),
    273–74, 288
Lockheed Martin, 563, 564
Lockheed Martin IMS, 525–26, 527
Los Angeles, 675
Low Income Housing Tax Credit (LIHTC). *See* Taxes
    and taxation issues—Low Income Housing Tax
    Credit
Lowry, Glenn D., 254
Lubove, Roy, 36

Lugo, Luis E., 665
Lumina Foundation for Education, 469
Lutheranl Church, 378–79. *See also* Religious congre-
    gations and organizations
Lutheran Social Services, 195, 199, 200, 380

MacArthur Foundation, 288
Macy's, 620
MADD. *See* Mothers Against Drunk Driving
Madoff, Bernie, 594
Maine, 37
Manchester's Craftsmen Guild, 213
Mankaney, Kamini, 504–05
Mann, Horace, 156
March of Dimes, 471
Maronick, Matthew, 394–422
Martha Graham Dance Company, 231
Martin, David, 495–517
Maryland, 106
Maryland Association of Nonprofit Organizations,
    209, 432, 445
Marycrest International University, 151
Marymount College, 143
Massachusetts, 37, 106, 156, 304, 311
*Massachusetts Citizens for Life. See Federal Election
    Commission v. Massachusetts Citizens for Life, Inc.*
Massachusetts Institute of Technology, 144
Mattel, 58
Maximus, 525
May Day March for Immigration Rights, 411
McCarthy, Joseph, 433
McCarthy, Rachel, 423–58
McCollum, Betty (D-Minn.), 448, 579
McDonald's Corporation, 318, 536
McDonnell, Lorraine M., 167
McKinney programs (housing), 270
McReynolds, James (Supreme Court justice), 156
Médecins du Monde, 352
Médecins Sans Frontières (Doctors Without Borders),
    331, 348, 351
Medicaid: academic health centers and, 148; choice
    and, 108; community agencies and, 205; com-
    munity benefits and, 124; consumer-side sub-
    sidies and, 25–26; coverage by, 97; economic
    retrenchment and, 24; effects of, 106; for-profit
    organizations and, 59; government support
    and, 49, 50, 554–55, 557, 670–71; growth and
    expansion of, 23, 77n40, 77n42, 526, 557, 565;
    incentives of, 101; investment opportunities
    and, 113; managed care and, 212; mental health
    expenditures of, 212; nonprofit organizations
    and, 205, 654; nursing homes and, 117, 526;
    provision of care and, 98; reductions in, 148;
    social services and, 193, 203–05, 214, 221. *See
    also* Entitlements
Medicaid—rates, reimbursement, and payments:
    cost-based reimbursement system, 113–14,
    554–55; funding for nonprofits, 654, 671;
    government payment and reimbursement rates

for, 215, 526, 557; increases in expenditures, 204–05; prospective reimbursement system, 562; as a quasi-voucher system, 210; total spending, 581n21

Medical issues. *See* Health and health care issues; Hospitals

Medicare: academic health centers and, 148; budget cuts and, 24; choice and, 108; costs and, 98; coverage by, 77n40, 97; effects of, 106; end-stage renal disease program coverage by, 111; fraud in, 95; government support and, 50, 554–55, 557, 561, 670–71; growth of, 22, 25–26; health maintenance organizations and, 101–02; home health care benefit of, 31, 112, 561; hospice benefit of, 112, 115, 116; incentives of, 101, 112; investment opportunities and, 113–14; nonprofit organizations and, 654; nursing homes and, 117; psychiatric hospitals and, 117; reductions in, 148; rehabilitation hospitals, 112. *See also* Entitlements

Medicare—rates, reimbursement, and payments: capital payment rules, 118, 119; cost-based reimbursement system, 66, 98, 112, 113–15, 554–55; funding for nonprofits, 654; government reimbursement rates for, 526; prospective reimbursement system, 117, 562

Meléndez, Edwin, 176

Membership organizations: citizen participation, 61; civic participation, 396; environmental movement and, 294; Independent Sector and, 426–27; Leadership Conference on Civil Rights and, 412; politically active organizations, 573; religious congregations and, 362, 367, 373, 388; social service organizations and, 219–20

MEMS. *See* Microelectromechanical systems

Menozzi, Paola, 626

Merck Corporation, 535

Merrill Lynch, 526

Metropolitan Museum of Art, 12, 231, 237, 255

Metropolitan Opera, 231, 251

Mexican American Legal Defense and Educational Fund, 409, 664

Mexico, 532, 533

Meyerson, Martin, 155–56

Miami-Dade County (Fla.), 526

Michigan, 569

Microelectromechanical systems (MEMS), 622

Middle East, 336

Millennials Rising (Strauss), 628

Million Man March, 411

Million Mom March, 411

Milwaukee (Wisc.), 163

Minnesota, 106, 240

Minnesota Council of Nonprofits, 428–29

Minnesota Supreme Court, 571

Mirabella, Rosanne, 603

Missouri, 565

Montana State University, 311

Moral and ethical issues. *See* Ethics and ethical issues

Morgan Stanley Smith Barney, 472

Morrill Acts (*1862, 1890*), 140–41, 144–45

Mothers Against Drunk Driving (MADD), 397

Moyers, Richard, 670

Mumbai (India), 624

Munitz, Barry, 254

Museum of Modern Art (MoMA), 242, 254

Museums, 530–31, 543. *See also* Arts, culture, and humanities

Museums and Community initiative, 248

Music and musicians. *See* Arts, culture, and humanities

Mutual aid societies, 657, 664

NAACP (National Association for the Advancement of Colored People), 61, 396, 403, 409, 411, 664, 666

NAACP Legal Defense Fund, 299

NAAEE. *See* North American Association for Environmental Education

Nathan, Richard, 563

National Academy of Public Administration, 295, 321

National Academy of Sciences, 114

National Advisory Council for Environmental Policy and Technology, 295, 321

National Association of Independent Colleges and Universities (NAICU), 146, 150, 425

National Association of Independent Schools, 159

National Audubon Society, 294, 297, 298, 300t, 301–02, 310, 312

National Center for Charitable Statistics (NCCS; Urban Institute), 9–10, 196, 401, 409, 431, 435, 444, 663, 664, 667, 670

National Center for Education Statistics (NCES), 138, 143, 145, 152, 162

National Center for Nonprofit Boards. *See* BoardSource

National Charities Information Bureau, 425, 431

National Civilian Service Corps, 556

National Committee for Planned Giving, 55

National Committee for Responsive Philanthropy (NCRP), 428, 435, 461, 464, 478

National Committee on Foundations and Trusts for Community Welfare. *See* National Council on Community Foundations

National Community Development Initiative. *See* Living Cities

National Congregations Study (NCS), 371, 381, 389n1

National Council of La Raza, 61, 396, 411, 424

National Council of Nonprofits (former National Council of Nonprofit Organizations), 423, 428, 444, 449, 450

National Council on Community Foundations, 434

National Council on Philanthropy, 436

National Defense Education Act (*1957*), 142

National Endowment for the Arts (NEA), 239–40, 249

National Endowment for the Humanities (NEH), 239, 249
National Environmental Education Foundation, 313
National Environmental Justice Advisory Council (NEJAC), 315
National Estuary Program (NEP), 305, 306, 316
National Fish and Wildlife Foundation, 306
National Foreclosure Mitigation Counseling Program, 281
National Gallery of Art, 231
National Gay and Lesbian Task Force Foundation, 409
National Governors Association (NGA), 417
National Institute of Environmental Health Sciences (NIEHS), 316
National Institutes of Health (NIH), 148, 149
National Marine Fisheries Service, 306
National Medical Enterprises, 118
National Nanotechnology Initiative, 622
National Neighborhood Indicators Partnership, 290
National Oceanic and Atmospheric Administration (NOAA), 306
National Organization for Women (NOW), 61, 403, 412
National Puerto Rican Coalition (NPRC), 396
National Rifle Association (NRA), 403, 666–67
National Right to Life Committee, 666
National River Restoration Science Synthesis, 319
National Science Foundation (NSF), 149, 313, 556
National Service, 396
National Service Trust Fund, 556
National Society of Fund-Raising Executives, 55, 425, 431
National Taxonomy of Exempt Entities (NTEE-CC), 663, 670
National Wildlife Federation (NWF), 294, 297, 298, 300t, 301–02, 310, 312
National Wildlife Federation Endowment, 297
National Wildlife Productions, 297
Native American Graves Protection and Repatriation Act (*1990*), 248
Nature Conservancy, The, 308, 310, 312, 314, 437, 481, 536
Natural Resources Defense Council, 294, 297, 298, 299, 300
NCCS. *See* National Center for Charitable Statistics
NCES. *See* National Center for Education Statistics
NCRP. *See* National Committee for Responsive Philanthropy
NCS. *See* National Congregations Study
NEA. *See* National Endowment for the Arts
NEH. *See* National Endowment for the Humanities
Neighborhood Housing Services (NHS), 276
NeighborWorks, 273–74, 276, 281
Network for Good, 432
NGA. *See* National Governors Association
NGOs. *See* Nongovernmental organizations
NEJAC. *See* National Environmental Justice Advisory Council

NEP. *See* National Estuary Program
New Communities Program, 288
New Community Corporation, 532
New Era Philanthropy, 37
New Freedom Initiative, 212
New Generations grants program, 253
New Hampshire, 37, 140, 311
New Jersey, 240
New Profit, 69, 432
New York City, 247, 249
New York Community Trust, 468
New York State, 37, 106, 163, 240
New York Times, 242, 376
NGOs. *See* Nongovernmental organizations
NGO Field Coordination Protocol, 348
NHS. *See* Neighborhood Housing Services
NIEHS. *See* National Institute of Environmental Health Sciences
Nielsen, Waldemar, 14, 552
NIH. *See* National Institutes of Health
Nike, 536, 623
NOAA. *See* National Oceanic and Atmospheric Administration
Nobel Peace Prize, 53, 623
Nongovernmental organizations (NGOs): advocacy and lobbying by, 330, 349–50; challenges of, 341–42, 346–53, 356–58; characteristics of the nonprofit subsector, 335–36, 358; commercialism of, 330; development assistance and, 334, 340; factors shaping the NGO position in international assistance, 336–53; financial and revenue resources of, 331, 333, 337, 338–43, 350, 353–54, 356, 357; fundamental principles of, 351–52; future role of, 353–57; government involvement with, 330, 331, 341, 343, 349–50, 356; growth in numbers of, 332–33; humanitarian assistance and, 334, 340–41, 342, 344–45, 351–52; improving the capacity of, 356–57; performance, professionalism, and accountability, 345–49, 354; political and military actors and, 350–53, 356; private sector and, 354–55; recovery and rehabilitation and, 334–35; role and focus of, 329, 331, 332, 336; scandals of, 346–47; scrutiny by, 623–24; staff security and, 343–45, 349, 352, 354, 357; technology and, 337; United Nations and, 341; visibility of, 330; voluntarism and professionalism, 344–45, 348. See also International assistance; *individual organizations*
Nonpoint Source Program, 306
Nonprofit and Voluntary Sector Quarterly, 429
Nonprofit Capacity Building Program, 441
Nonprofit Congress, 449
Nonprofit Finance Fund, 432, 449
Nonprofit Leadership Alliance, 449
Nonprofit Management and Leadership, 429
Nonprofit Management Association, 430
Nonprofit Policy Sampler (BoardSource), 595
Nonprofit Quarterly, 57, 441

Nonprofit sector: access to investment capital by, 31; advocacy and lobbying role of, 60–64, 65, 71, 219–20; boards of directors, 145, 220, 299, 419, 430, 649, 651–52; changing culture of, 537–40; changing interpretations of health and health care, 108–10; charitability and community service of, 105–08; competition issues of, 6, 71, 527–29, 540–41, 564–65, 578; components of, 6; consumer choice, 108; contracts of, 439; definition, identities, style, and impulses of, 3–4, 6–20, 32, 44, 65, 66, 67, 68–69, 70, 462, 543–44; demand for services of, 39–41, 524; demographic shifts and, 625–32; disadvantages to small agencies, 67–68; effectiveness of, 31–33, 483–86; executive compensation in, 482–83; executive directors of, 39, 63, 640, 643–45, 647, 649, 650–51, 652–53, 668; functions of, 11–13, 39–41, 67, 68; future scenarios, 68–73, 635–36; governance of, 540–41; growth of, 44–59, 64–65, 354, 462, 549, 565–67; human resources and employment in, 38–39, 48–49, 53; leaders and leadership in, 20, 39, 54, 56, 66–68, 73, 100, 449–50, 640, 643–44, 647, 649, 652–53; legitimacy and trust of, 34–38, 68, 73, 94–95, 446–47, 522, 598–99; minority and racial diversity and, 626, 670; mission of, 597–99; networked delivery systems and, 609; nonprofit-business collaboration, 535–37; opportunities of, 39–43; organization and organizational structures of, 15t, 16, 17, 18–19, 56–59, 449–50; political activities of, 38, 61, 394–95, 396–97, 448, 551, 574; property holdings of, 570–71; public expectations of, 34, 37, 68, 72, 107–08; responses of, 5–6; role of, 14, 17–18, 110–18, 447, 525, 551–52; scandals of, 439, 481–82; size of, 7–10; social purpose enterprises of, 531–35; special interest argument, 34–35; strategies of, 14, 15t, 17, 18; tax-exempt status of, 434, 439, 446–47; technology and, 33–34, 42–43, 619–24; types and categories of nonprofits, 7, 8–10; volunteer labor and, 498–500; workforce dynamics of, 639–54. *See also* Accountability; Advocacy and lobbying; Civic activism; Commercialism; Education issues; Employment issues; For-profit sector—as a competitive challenge to the nonprofit sector; Health and health care issues; Infrastructure organizations; Philanthropy; Professionalism; Taxes and taxation issues—*501*(c)(*3*) and *501*(c)(*4*) organizations; Volunteering and voluntarism

Nonprofit sector—challenges: competition challenge, 28–31, 524–28, 561–62; disadvantaging small agencies, 67–68; effectiveness challenge, 31–33; fiscal challenge, 21–28, 523–24, 565–68; growing identity crisis, 66; human resource challenge, 38–40, 449, 644–45, 648–50; increased demands for accountability, 528–29; increased demands on managers, 66–67; legitimacy challenge, 34–38; loss of public trust, 68; making

services more available, 449–51; mission creep, 67; performance management, 173, 207, 208, 209; responses to, 5–6, 65–66, 70, 73, 529–40, 578; technology challenge, 33–34; trend toward commercialization, 522–44; U.S. economy and, 650–51; welfare reform, 563–65

Nonprofit sector—as providers to the neediest: advocacy for antipoverty policies, 660, 664, 666–68, 669, 676; antipoverty nonprofit organizations, 669; belief in benevolence of the sector, 657–59, 675–76; creation of social capital in poor communities, 660, 668–70; ethnic, minority, and immigrant centers, 664; moralization and spiritualization of services, 664–65; need for government assistance, 659, 667, 668, 670–72, 676–77; obstacles faced in serving the poor, 670–75; provision of services to the poor, 660, 661–66, 675–77; revenue sources and, 670–74; three spheres of interaction between nonprofits and the poor, 660–61

Nonprofit sector—revenue and fiscal pressures: aggregate revenues of, 566; commercialization, 47–59, 65, 522–44; costs, 33, 531, 562; donations, 608; fee and earned income, 529–30, 541–42, 566, 571, 592, 608, 672, 673; fiscal squeeze, 523–24; government support, 670–72; Great Recession and, 521–22, 540, 549–50; individual giving, 496–97; mission creep and, 67; move toward the market, 529–44, 578; overall sector growth, 44–45; philanthropy, 529, 530, 667, 672; regulation of fundraising, 571–72, 578; resources of civil rights organizations, 412–13; sources of revenue, 10–11, 554, 592, 670–71, 673; spending by, 504–05, 554; strengthening nonprofit finance, 71–72; total resources, 8–9; unrelated business income, 530–31. *See also* Nonprofit sector—challenges; Government—government-nonprofit relations

Nonprofit Sector and Community Solutions Act of *2010*, 448

Nonprofit Sector Research Fund (Aspen Institute), 429

Nonprofit Sector Strategy Group (Aspen Institute), 58

Nonprofit Technology Network (NTEN), 430

Nonprofit Times, 57, 432

Nonprofit Voter Engagement Network, 449

North American Association for Environmental Education (NAAEE), 312

North Carolina, 569

North Carolina Center for Nonprofits, 428

North Dakota State Water Commission, 311

Notre Dame College, 151

Novartis, 58

NOW. *See* National Organization for Women

NPower, 430

NPRC. *See* National Puerto Rican Coalition

NRA. *See* National Rifle Association

NSF. *See* National Science Foundation

NTEE-CC. *See* National Taxonomy of Exempt Entities
NTEN. *See* Nonprofit Technology Network
Nurse Home Visiting program, 208
Nursing homes. *See* Health and health care issues—nursing homes; Hospitals—specific
NWF. *See* National Wildlife Federation

Obama, Barack, 321, 513, 549, 634
Obama (Barack) administration: cap on tax deductions, 38, 569; economic stimulus program, 567; faith-based organizations and, 218; international assistance and, 356; open government directive of, 321; performance management and, 208; solutions to community problems, 289; Strengthening Communities Fund, 216; support for community colleges, 186n126; support for social innovation, 42, 53, 192, 205. *See also* American Recovery and Reinvestment Act of *2009*; Patient Protection and Affordable Care Act
Obamacare. *See* Patient Protection and Affordable Care Act
OBRA. *See* Omnibus Budget Reconciliation Act
Occupy Wall Street movement, 64, 577
Ocean Conservancy, 305
O'Connell, Brian, 436
OECD. *See* Organization for Economic Cooperation and Development
Office Max, 534
Office of Environmental Education (EPA), 313
Office of Environmental Justice (EPA), 320
Office of Faith-Based and Community Initiatives, 353, 556
Office of Management and Budget (OMB), 38, 428, 559, 561, 572
Office of Private and Voluntary Cooperation, 353
Office of U.S. Foreign Disaster Assistance (USAID), 338
Office of Water, 320
Office of Wetlands, Oceans, and Watersheds (EPA), 304
Office of Social Innovation, 192, 205
Olympic Games and Village (*2002*), 620
OMB. *See* Office of Management and Budget
OMB Watch, 428, 437
Omidyar, Pierre, 461–62, 486
Omnibus Budget Reconciliation Act (OBRA; *1981*), 202
O'Neill, Michael, 599
One-Stop career centers, 172–73
1000 Friends of Oregon, 301
onPhilanthropy (website), 58
Open Society Institute, 468
Orange County Community Distribution Center, 532
Orchestra Management Fellowship program, 253
Orchestras. *See* Arts, culture, and humanities
Oregon, 37, 209
Oregon Environmental Council, 301

Organization for Economic Cooperation and Development (OECD), 333, 533
Owen-Smith, Jason, 149
Oxfam, 346, 351

Paarlberg, Laura, 669
PACs. *See* Political action committees
Pakistan earthquake (*2005*), 508
Panel on the Nonprofit Sector (Independent Sector), 438
Parent Loan for Undergraduate Student (PLUS) program, 143
Panel Study of Income Dynamics, 507
Parent Teacher Associations (PTAs), 396
Parents As Teachers, 218
Paris Declaration on Aid Effectiveness (*2005*), 345, 356
Partnering with Communities project, 321
Passel, Jeffrey, 626
Patent and Trademark Amendments of *1980* (Bayh-Dole Act), 56, 149
Patient Protection and Affordable Care Act (PPACA; Obamacare; *2010*), 95, 97, 100, 104–05, 126, 129, 446, 577
Patient Self-Determination Act (*1991*), 116
Patman, Wright (D-Texas), 434, 460–61
Payne, Abigail, 505
PBS. *See* Public Broadcasting System
Pell, Claiborne (D-R.I.) and Pell grants, 142
Pennsylvania, 37, 570
Pennsylvania State University (Penn State), 139, 144, 153–54
Pension Protection Act of *2006*, 438, 482, 569, 572, 575, 585n68, 654
People for Puget Sound, 305
People Improving Communities through Organizing (PICO), 416
People's Republic of China, 338
Performance measurement, 32
Performing arts. *See* Arts, culture, and humanities
Personal Responsibility and Work Opportunity Reconciliation Act of *1996* (PWRORA; welfare reform), 23, 26, 30, 36, 41, 204, 380, 525, 526, 561, 563
Pets for People program, 535
Pew Charitable Trust, 241, 300
Pew Foundation, 151
PHAs (Public housing authorities). *See* Housing and community development
Philanthropic Advisory Service, 431
Philanthropic Collaborative, 479
Philanthropy 400, 508
Philanthropic Initiative, 450–51
Philanthropic Studies Index, 432
Philanthropy: challenges of, 476–86; criticism of, 465–66, 476, 478; definition of, 466; developments in, 43, 55–56; donor-choice systems, 528; effectiveness of institutional nonprofits, 483–86; future of giving and volunteering, 486, 513–14; geographic distribution of, 475; gifts and gift

funds, 471–73, 496; growth of charitable giving, 450; history of, 462; infrastructure organizations and, 450–51; institutional philanthropy, 460–86; major components of, 467–73; overview of giving and volunteering, 496–500; patterns of giving, 473–76; payout rate, 476–78, 481; private and personal philanthropy, 495–14, 672; rationale for, 466–67, 480–81; regulation and governance of, 481–83; religious organizations and, 463; restrictions on, 497–98; shifting priorities of, 150–51; social justice philanthropy, 479; social services and, 199, 672; staffing for, 480; support for the nonprofit sector and, 10–11, 27–28, 48; suburbanization of, 48; technology-based philanthropy, 674; trends in giving and volunteering, 507–11; venture/high-engagement philanthropy model, 32, 432, 461, 484–85, 510–11, 539; of the wealthy, 667; what influences individual giving, 500–05. *See also* Charitable organizations and giving; Community chests; Foundations; Grants; National Committee for Responsive Philanthropy; Volunteering and voluntarism

Philanthropy *400*, 508

Philanthropy Journal, 432

Philanthropy News Digest, 432

Philanthropy New York, 480

Philanthropy 2173 (blog), 432

Philanthropy Roundtable, 428

Philanthropy Workshop West, 450–51

Philips Eco TV, 318

Phillips Academy Andover (Andover), 159

Physicians: end-of-life treatment and, 116; expectations of, 129; joint ventures and, 121; kick-backs to, 118; modern health-care industry and, 112, 606; non-profit physician groups, 60; protection of patients and, 94, 108; volunteer physicians, 348–49. *See also* Health and health care issues; Hospitals

Piazza, Alberta, 626

PICO. *See* People Improving Communities through Organizing

Pierce v. Society of Sisters (1925), 156, 165

Pierson, Paul, 63–64

Pifer, Alan, 434–35

Pioneer Human Services, 52, 214, 215, 532

PIRGs. *See* Public Interest Research Groups

Pittsburgh, 598

Pittsburgh Foundation, 607

Pittsburgh Public School District, 607

Planned Parenthood, 552

Plessy v. Ferguson (1896), 141

PLUS. *See* Parent Loan for Undergraduate Student program

Points of Light Foundation, 217, 556

Points of Light Institute, 431

Political action committees (PACs), 399, 400, 412

Political issues: corporate financing of election campaigns, 38; cost of medical care, 109; funding for social services, 203; government-nonprofit

relations, 550; government spending and, 24; growth of nonprofit infrastructure organizations, 433–38; influence of for-profit sector, 102; international politics, 62; nonprofit sector activity and visibility, 42, 219; political advocacy of nonprofits and NGOs, 38, 341; poverty in the U.S., 415; regulation of nonprofit organizations, 37; relief work, 338; religious organizations, 384–87; support for art, culture, and the humanities, 239–40; tax exemptions, 104

Pollution Prevention Act of *1990*, 315

Population health, 109–10. *See also* Health and health care issues

Porter, Michael E., 461–62

Pough, Richard, 308

Poverty: advocacy by anti-poverty groups, 403, 408–09, 413, 415–19; concentration of, 675; in the developing world, 358; development assistance and, 333–34; globalization and, 337; microenterprise and, 532–33; nonprofit sector and, 35–36, 67, 672; social services and, 35; in the United States, 160, 413, 415–19, 658, 659. *See also* Nonprofit sector—as providers to the neediest

Powell, Colin, 627

Powell, Walter, 149

PPACA. See *Patient* Protection and Affordable Care Act

Prevent Blindness, 536

Princeton University, 12, 138, 139, 144

Principles for Good Governance and Ethical Practice: A Guide for Charities and Foundations (report; Independent Sector), 574–75

Professionalism: advocacy and, 60–61, 407, 410; in the arts and culture, 249–51; deprofessionalization of medicine, 108–09; in environmental organizations, 294, 297, 299, 302, 317; future of, 635; government and, 16–17; of grant making, 464; in housing and community development, 286–87; implications of, 15t; in infrastructure organizations, 424, 438–40, 451; of institutional philanthropy, 465, 467; in international assistance, 330, 345–49; managerial professionalization, 54–57; in nonprofits, 53–57, 65, 438–39, 462, 603, 662, 665, 668, 670, 676; overprofessionalization argument, 36; in philanthropy, 483, 484; professionalism impulse, 35; in religious congregations and organizations, 367, 377; in security efforts, 344–45; in social services, 202, 207, 208–09, 222, 669, 673. *See also* Accountability; Nonprofit sector

Program on Non-Profit Organizations (Yale), 484

Program on Philanthropy and Social Innovation (Aspen Institute), 444, 450–51

Project Learning Tree, 311, 312

Project Match, 171

Project WET (Water Education for Teachers), 311, 312

Project WILD (Wildlife in Learning Design), 311, 312

Promise Keepers, 409
Property-Tax Exemption for Charities: Mapping the Battlefield (Brody), 570
Protestant denominations, 365–66, 368–69, 369, 372, 378, 384, 665. *See also* Religious congregations and organizations
PTAs. *See* Parent Teacher Associations
Public Broadcasting System (PBS), 252
Public funding. See Government; Nonprofit sector; *"government involvement" under individual subject headings*
Public housing authorities (PHAs). *See* Housing and community development
Public Interest Research Groups (PIRGs), 302
Public sector. *See* Government
Public Service Loan Forgiveness Program, 654
Public Welfare Amendments of *1962*, 201
Puget Sound Partnership, 316
Putnam, Robert, 60, 295, 368, 395, 447, 634, 668
PRWORA. *See* Personal Responsibility and Work Opportunity Reconciliation Act of *1996*

Racial and minority issues: children of color in Catholic schools, 161; children of color in the United States, 160; church attendance, 370; foundation support for minority-led nonprofits, 479; integration and assimilation, 664; a minority majority, 625–26; participation in nonprofit activities, 669, 670; poverty, 659, 676; race as a biological distinction, 626; social services, 200. *See also* Demographic issues
Rails to Trails Conservancy, 310
Rain Forest Action Network, 623
Ralston Purina, 535
Ray, Paul, 633
Reading Is Fundamental, 536
Ready to Lead? Next Generation Leaders Speak Out (report; CompassPoint), 643–44, 648
Reagan, Ronald, 22, 42, 202, 523
Reagan (Ronald) administration, 22, 23, 38, 112, 202, 308, 436–37, 556, 568
Red Cross. *See* American Red Cross; International Committee of the Red Cross
Reese Committee (*1954*; U.S. House of Representatives), 433
Regulations. *See* Advocacy and lobbying; Charitable organizations and giving; Foundations; Government—government-nonprofit relations; Grants; Nonprofit sector—revenue and fiscal pressures
Reis, Thomas, 534
Religious congregations and organizations: anti-poverty services of, 664–65; challenges of, 362, 366–72, 388; civic activism and, 367, 382, 388–89; commercialization of, 367, 373, 376, 522; competition in, 372, 373; concentration of, 387; congregations and denominations, 364–66; conservative Christian schools, 159–60; contributions to, 497; diversity of, 363–66; evangelical and conservative denominations, 368–69, 374,

385; globalization and international connections of, 370–71; government involvement in, 373, 379, 380, 392n34; leadership in, 376–79, 382, 388; megachurches, 365-66, 372, 376; membership base of, 367–72; nonprofits, 47; political issues and activities of, 384–87, 388–89, 573; private Catholic schools, 157–58; religious switching, 369; religious Internet and television, 371–72; revenues, spending, and fiscal pressures of, 363–64, 372–76, 382, 388, 500–01, 503, 511, 513; Second Vatican Council, 157, 158; service roles, 379–87, 389, 392n34; as tax-exempt entities, 551, 661; voluntarism and, 367, 372, 381, 383–84, 388, 498, 500; weekly attendance in, 362, 367–68, 369; welfare reform and, 379–80. See also Professionalism; *individual churches and congregations*
Research, 148–49. *See also* Education issues—higher education
Residential care facilities, 56
Restoration Center (NOAA), 305, 306
Restore America's Estuaries, 305, 306
Rice High School. *See* Edmund Rice High School
Ridings, Dorothy S., 481
Rieff, David, 357–58
River Network, 61, 63, 305, 319
River Rally, 305
Robert Maplethorpe Foundation, 241
Robert Wood Johnson Foundation, 465
Rockefeller Foundation, 150–51, 241–42, 463, 468
Rockefeller Philanthropy Advisors, 431, 450–51
Rockefeller, John D., Sr., 144, 459, 463, 486, 488nn25-26
Rockefeller, John D., III, 435
Roman Catholics. *See* Catholic Church
Romzek, Barbara, 596
Rosenwald, Julius, 483–84
Rudolph, Frederick, 140
Ruesga, Albert, 432
Russell Sage Foundation, 433–34, 463
Russia, 338. *See also* Union of Soviet Socialist Republics
Rutgers, the State University of New Jersey, 139
Rwanda, 338, 346, 350–51
Ryan, William, 31–32

Safeway Grocery Stores, 620
Sage Colleges, 146
Salamon, Lester M., 3–86 , 128, 244, 287, 316, 348, 521–86, 601–02, 603, 659, 661–62, 665, 675
Salvation Army, 195, 197, 200, 213, 380
San Francisco, 309, 315
San Francisco Clean City Coalition, 532
San Francisco Foundation, 468
San Jose Mercury News, 437
Sarbanes-Oxley Act of *2002*, 481–82, 483, 574, 585n68, 595
Sargeant, Adrian, 509Save the Children USA, 333, 339, 342t

SCALLOPS. *See* Sustainable Communities ALL Over Puget Sound

Scandals, 37, 439, 574, 587, 591, 594–95. *See also* Foundations; Nongovernmental organizations

Schedule H. *See* Form *990* for Tax-Exempt Organizations

Schervish, Paul, 504

Schlesinger, Mark, 59, 66, 89–136, 562, 662

Schwab, 472

Science: The Endless Frontier (report; 1944; Bush), 149

Scott, Richard, 115

Scruggs, Lisa, 137–91

Seattle Climate Action Now Initiative, 316

Second Chance Act (*2007*), 178

Section *8* New Construction and Substantial Rehabilitation program (housing), 270–71

Section *202* program (housing), 270–71, 284

Section *221*(d)(*3*) program (housing), 270–71

Section *236* program (housing), 270–71, 284

Section *811* program (housing), 270–71

Security Council (UN), 332, 337, 338

Segal, Lewis, 531

Senate Finance Committee (U.S.): nonprofit accountability, 254; nonprofit expenditures, 102, 103, 104; nonprofit governing boards, 591; nonprofit oversight, 482, 574–75; reform of nonprofits and foundations, 437–38. *See also* Congress (U.S.)

September *11, 2001*, 336, 337, 508, 509, 571, 575, 577, 598–99, 610. *See also* Terrorism

Serve America Act. *See* Edward M. Kennedy Serve America Act

Servicemen's Readjustment Act of *1944* (GI Bill), 141

Settlement house movement, 17

Sewanee, the University of the South, 146

Sexuality issues, 386, 409. *See also* Homosexual issues

Shafritz, Jay, 588

Share Our Strength, 58, 213, 218, 431, 536, 537

Shoemaker, Paul, 611

Shore, Billy, 57, 58

Sierra Club, 61, 294, 297, 298, 299, 300t, 301–02, 308, 312, 314, 318

Silicon Valley Community Foundation, 472

Sirianni, Carmen, 63, 294–328

Skocpol, Theda, 60, 295

Skoll, Jeffrey, 461–62, 486

Slate *60*, 510

SLM Corporation, 469

Small, Lawrence, 254

Smith, David Horton, 363, 674

Smith-Kline Beecham, 542

Smithsonian Institution, 231, 254, 481

Smith, Steven Rathgeb, 192–228, 562

Social capital, 42, 394, 508, 512, 660, 668. *See also* Nonprofit sector—as providers to the neediest

Social Enterprise Alliance and Community Wealth Ventures, 431, 449

Social enterprises and entrepreneurs: changing nonprofit culture and, 537–40; commercial methods to foster social change and, 486; community support and, 219; institutional innovation and, 53; interest in community service and, 218; social service agencies and, 205; use of the market by, 36, 43, 522, 592

Social innovation, 205

Social Innovation Fund, 53, 438, 567

Social media and networking, 623–24

Social policies: advocacy and, 220; benevolence of the nonprofit sector and, 658, 661; conservative agenda for, 658; employment and welfare, 35; nonprofit social services agencies and, 192–93, 206; poverty and, 416, 659, 661; in Europe and Australia, 221; in the U.S., 222

Social purpose enterprise, 531–35

Social Security Act of *1935*, 116–17, 202

Social Security Act Amendments (*1962*), 35, 202

Social services: accountability and regulation, 206–09; advocacy for, 221–22; addressed in Europe and Australia, 200, 221; boom-and-bust cycles of, 59; challenges and opportunities of, 196, 206–20; community-based agencies, 192, 194, 205, 207, 211, 216, 219, 221; competition in, 202, 209–13, 215, 222; contracts of, 206–07, 208, 209, 210–11, 212, 216, 219; cooperation and coordination among, 217; costs and expenditures of, 207; early origins of, 200–03; eligibility for, 202; employment in, 197, 198, 199; failure of, 35; faith-based agencies, 192, 216, 218; formal agencies, 195–96; for-profit organizations and, 197, 198, 199, 205, 211, 213, 215; future of, 193, 220–22; government involvement, 192–93, 195, 196, 197, 199, 201–08, 209, 212, 215, 221; health care and, 197, 199; human safety-net services, 643; informal organizations, 194–95, 196; managed care and, 27, 33, 212–13; mapping nonprofit social services, 194; mergers, 217; nonprofit advocacy and, 62; religious organizations and, 379–84; reporting and nonreporting agencies, 196; role of, 193; scope of the nonprofit social services sector, 196–99; social services policy and nonprofit organizations, 200–06, 669; spiritualization of, 664–65, 676; subcontracting for, 203; therapeutic approach to, 669; transformation of, 41; voluntarism and civic engagement in, 202–03, 205, 207, 217–20. *See also* Medicaid; Medicare

Social services—nonprofit organizations: commercial income of, 47, 608; competition and the market for social services, 209–13; future of, 220–22; growth of, 46, 192; Medicaid and, 49; nonprofit organizations and social services policy, 200–06; professionalization of, 54; regulation and accountability, 206–09; scope of the nonprofit social services sector, 196–99; spiritualization of, 664–65; types of organizations, 194–96; voluntarism, community service, and civic engagement, 217–20

Social services—revenues and fiscal pressures: foundation support, 474–75; government support, 192–93, 197, 199, 200–05, 206, 208, 209–11, 212–13, 218, 219, 220, 221, 222; private fees, 200; private philanthropy, 197, 199, 205–06, 208, 218, 219, 222; revenue diversification and organizational restructuring, 213–17; types of services and, 194, 195, 196
Social Services Block Grant (SSBG), 202
Social Venture Partners, 432
Social ventures, 19, 31, 43, 51, 52, 432, 531–35, 543–44
Social welfare, 21–27, 403, 405, 411, 523
Social work, 16, 35, 36
Sofer, Stephanie, 63, 294–328
Sokolowski, S. Wojciech, 530, 675
Somalia, 338, 343, 344
Southeast Watershed Forum, 305
Soviet Union. *See* Union of Soviet Socialist Republics
Spelman College, 141
Sphere Project, 346, 360n42
Spotlight on Poverty and Opportunity, 416–17
SSBG. *See* Social Services Block Grant
SSI. *See* Supplemental Security Income
Stafford loans, 143
Standards for Excellence Institute and program, 432, 445
Stanford, Leland, 144
Stanford Social Innovation Review, 57, 432
Stanford University, 144
Starbucks, 355, 536
Steinem, Gloria, 627
Stewart, Donald, 137–91
Stoddard, Abby, 329–61
Stokes, Donald E., 149
Strauss, William, 628
Strayer (education company), 150
Strengthening Communities Fund, 216, 441
Strengthening Transparency, Governance, and Accountability of Charitable Organizations (report; Independent Sector), 574–75
STRIVE, 217
Student Conservation Association, 312
Summers, David, 44
Supplemental Security Income (SSI), 23, 49, 214
Support groups, 195
Support Centers of America, 430
Survey of Consumer Finances (Federal Reserve Board), 507
Susan G. Komen for the Cure, 58
Sustainable Bainbridge, 316
Sustainable Communities ALL Over Puget Sound (SCALLOPS), 316
Sustainable Seattle, 316
Sustaining Colorado Watersheds Conference (*2007*), 304
Swagel, Philip D., 479–80
Swarthmore, 138

Takanishi, Ruby, 665, 668
TANF. *See* Temporary Assistance for Needy Families
Tax Acts of *1997, 2001,* 569–70
Taxes and taxation issues: alternative minimum tax base, 569; charitable donations, 20, 436, 437, 467, 501–03, 513–14, 550, 551, 568–69; *colledge corne,* 552; community foundations, 468; donated conservation easements, 309; estate taxes, 514, 569–70, 583nn47-48; *501*(h) provisions, 399; health and education savings accounts, 558; legislation, 568–69; lobbying, 38, 437; major federal tax programs, 560–61; minimum IRA withdrawals, 569; New Markets Tax Credit, 272, 274; payments in lieu of taxes (PILOTs), 570–71; property and sales tax exemptions, 570–71, 593; property taxes, 102, 568; reforms and nonprofits, 433; scholarship aid, 558; section *527* organizations, 399–400, 412; tax credits, 25, 26, 50, 72, 142, 558–59; tax cuts, 24, 25; tax deductible donations, 156–57, 196, 501–02; tax deductions, 38, 72, 142, 558, 568–69; tax-exempt bond money, 210; tax expenditures, 78n47; tax incentives, 71; tax price of giving, 501, 513, 568, 583n44; tax rates, 502–03, 568; tax subsidies, 558; unrelated business income tax (UBIT), 530–31, 592, 607. *See also* Form *990* for Tax-Exempt Organizations; Government; Internal Revenue Code; Internal Revenue Service; Pension Protection Act of *2006*
Taxes and taxation issues—exemptions: challenges and justification for, 37–38, 97, 102, 103; criteria for, 106; documentation for, 90; for nonprofit health care providers, 129; for nonprofit HMOs, 112–13; for nonprofit hospitals, 115; for nonprofit, private schools, 156–57; trustworthiness and, 95
Taxes and taxation issues—Low Income Housing Tax Credit: community development corporations (CDCs) and, 274; development of, 278–79; effects of, 659; financial crisis and, 280–81; low-income housing and, 72, 286; nonprofit development organizations and, 49–50; for-profit and nonprofit developers and, 285; stimulation of investment in low-cost rental housing, 269–70
Taxes and taxation issues—section *501*(c)(*3*), section *501*(c)(*4*), and section *501*(c)(*6*) organizations: advocacy organizations, 61–62, 539, 573, 666–67; antipoverty organizations, 417–18; civil rights organizations, 412; election purposes and, 573; environmental organizations, 303; formal agencies, 195–96; holding companies, 540; increased numbers of, 46; lobbying by, 38, 56, 63, 74n9, 398–99, 401–03, 408, 409–10, 411t, 572–73; National Wildlife Federation, 297; partisan electoral advocacy and, 399–400; private schools, 156–57; public charities and private foundations, 395; registration, 196; revenues and income of, 50, 51, 465; Sierra Club, 297; social

service and welfare organizations, 215, 216, 395; tax-deductible donations to, 7, 156–57
Tax Reform Acts: *1969*, 38, 63, 435, 439, 461, 464, 476, 481; *1986*, 502, 513. *See also* Tax Acts
Taylor, Andrew, 258
Teach for America, 162, 192–93, 205
Tea Party movement (U.S.), 42, 395, 577, 624, 633
Technology: in the arts and culture, 256–58; bimolecular convergence, 621–23; challenges of, 33–34, 43, 174, 623; clean and green technology, 619–21; communications technologies, 62, 633; cultural segments and, 632–33; digitization, 52, 257–58; dot.com phenomenon, 43; in housing and community development, 289; improvements in physical medicine and, 112; information technology, 33, 562; in international assistance, 337; opportunities of, 43; in political activism, 396–97; in religious organizations, 371–72; societal development and, 616–18; tracking and, 208. *See also* Internet; Nonprofit sector
TechSoup. *See* CompuMentor
Temporary Assistance for Needy Families (TANF), 204, 565, 659, 670–71
Tenet, 115
Terrorism, 624. *See also* September *11, 2001*
Thatcher, Margaret, 42
Theater. *See* Arts, culture, and humanities
Theatre Communications Group, 253
Third Sector. *See* Nonprofit sector; Volunteering and voluntarism
Third World, 331
Thomas Kenan Institute for the Arts, 241
Timberland, 58
Tinkelman, Daniel, 504–05
Title IV (Higher Education Act), 152
Title XX (Social Security Act), 202
Tobey, Charles (R-N.H.), 433
Tocqueville, Alexis de, 5, 13, 462, 657
Toepler, Stefan, 39, 229–65
Transportation, Department of (DOT), 310
Treasury, Department of, 434
Trees, Water, and People, 305–06
Triangle Residential Options of Substance Abusers, 532
Trout Unlimited, 306, 314
T. Rowe Price, 472
Truman, Harry S., 142
Trustees of Dartmouth College v. *Woodward* (1819), 140
Trustees of Reservations (Mass.), 308
Trust for Public Land, 310
Tsunami (Indian Ocean, *2004*), 332, 337, 339, 354, 388, 415
20/220 Pathway for Economic Hardship Deferment, 654, 656n39
Twitter, 61, 412, 624, 634
Tyson Foods, 536

Under the Rainbow Child Care Center, Inc. v. *County of Goodhue* (*2007*), 571
UN High Commissioner for Refugees, 339
Union of Soviet Socialist Republics (USSR), 337. *See also* Russia
Unions. *See* Labor and union issues
United Jewish Appeal, 510
United Methodist Church, 378. *See also* Religious congregations and organizations
United Nations (UN), 332, 337–38, 340, 341, 343, 352, 355
United Negro Fund, 535
United States (U.S.): budget deficits of, 193, 238, 286, 356, 513, 514, 650; charitable giving in, 523; conflict patterns and security environments, 337–38; democratic strength and legitimacy of, 394; international relief organizations in, 332–33; military security agenda of, 336, 352; nongovernmental organizations and, 343, 349–50, 352; official development assistance of, 339–40; poverty in, 160, 413, 415–19; religious congregations in, 370, 382–83; safety net in, 200; social enterprise movement in, 532–34; social services in, 221; structural change in, 480; welfare state in, 666. *See also* Government; Religious congregations and organizations
United Way: accountability of, 538; access to corporate payroll deduction systems, 528; as a federated giving organization, 427, 460, 470, 510; funding by, 201–02, 205–06, 207, 432; patterns of giving, 473; performance measurement and, 32, 207; scandal of, 37; social problems and, 193. *See also* Community Chests
University of California, 58, 144–45
University of Chicago, 138, 144
University of Illinois, 144–45
University of Maryland, 144–45
University of Michigan, 148
University of Minnesota, 144–45
University of Wisconsin, 144–45
Up Next (study), 648
Urban Institute, 42, 196, 429, 444, 480, 483, 484, 485, 562
Urban Institute Brookings Institution Tax Policy Center, 397
Urban League, 61, 396
U.S. *See* United States
U.S. Africa Command (AFRICOM), 353
U.S. Agency for International Development (USAID), 332–33, 352, 354, 356
USA Group, 469
USAID. See U.S. Agency for International Development
USA Patriot Act of *2001*, 575–76
U.S. Export-Import Bank, 350
U.S. National Security Strategy, 352
U.S. News & World Report, 145
USSR. *See* Union of Soviet Socialist Republics

Vanguard Group, 472
Venture Philanthropy Partners, 432
Vermont, 534
Vermont Natural Resources Council, 302
VHA, Inc., 121. *See also* Voluntary Hospitals of America
Vidal, Avis C., 266–93
Voices for America's Children, 409
Voluntas, 429
Volunteering and voluntarism: civic participation and, 396; common tasks of, 498–99; definition of, 512; elderly population and, 41; in faith-based organizations, 564; future of giving and volunteering, 513–14, 635; limitations and complications of, 499–500; national service, 396; in nonprofit advocacy, 407; overprofessionalization and, 36; overview of giving and volunteering, 496–500; principle fields of, 498, 499t; public support for, 42; Reagan administration and, 22; role in the nonprofit sector, 14–17, 53, 564, 665; role in the social services, 202–03, 205, 207; trends in volunteering, 511–13; voluntary associations and organizations, 668–69; volunteer labor, 498; what influences levels of volunteering, 505–07. *See also* Accountability; Community service; Nonprofit sector; Philanthropy; Social services
Voluntary Hospitals of America (VHA), 103, 106, 122. *See also* VHA, Inc.
Voluntary Support of Education (survey), 151
Volunteers of America, 195, 200
Voters and voting, 396–97, 399
Voting rights, 555
Vouchers: AmeriCorps education vouchers, 512; anti-poverty organizations, 415; child care, 199, 210, 608; GI Bill and, 141; housing, 210, 269, 284, 291n8; as a market-based, consumer-side subsidy, 19, 25–26, 530, 554–55, 558, 559, 671; Medicaid and Medicare, 78n49, 210, 214, 523–24, 554–55, 557; nonprofit *501(c)(3)* organizations and, 50; political issues, 26; as "program service revenue," 214; school choice, 162–63; as targeted assistance, 78n47
V3 Campaign, 449

Wagner, David, 665
Walker, Christopher, 276
Wall Street Journal, 102
War on Poverty (*1960s*), 271, 272, 553
Washington (D.C.). *See* District of Columbia
Washington National Opera, 238, 255
Washington Post, 437
Washington State, 304
Watershed councils, 303–04
Watersheds. *See* Environmental issues
Weisbrod, Burton, 374, 531

Welfare and welfare reform: child welfare field, 38–39; government social welfare spending, 23–24, 26–27; welfare-to-work programs, 208, 211, 526, 561; workforce development and training, 168–69, 186n135. *See also* Personal Responsibility and Work Opportunity Reconciliation Act of *1996*; Workforce Investment Act
Western Association of Fish and Wildlife Agencies, 311
Western Regional Environmental Education Council, 311. *See also* Council for Environmental Education
White Courtesy Telephone (blog), 432
WIA. *See* Workforce Investment Act
WIBs. *See* Workforce Investment Boards
Wildavsky, Aaron, 464
Wilderness Society, 294, 298
Wildlife Conservation Society, 310
William and Mary, College of, 139
Winner-Take-All Politics (Hacker and Pierson), 63–64
Wisconsin, 37, 565
Wish, Naomi, 603
Wolfred, Timothy, 670
Wolpert, Julian, 663
Wordlaw, Robert, 171
Workforce Investment Act (WIA; *1998*), 168–78, 659
Workforce Investment Boards (WIBs), 176
World Bank, 345
WorldCom, 574
World Economic Forum (*2008*), 459
World Vision, 333, 339, 342t, 357
Worldwide Anglican Communion, 364. *See also* Religious congregations and organizations
World Wildlife Fund (WWF), 310
World War II, 21, 249, 269, 271, 308, 330–31, 368, 470
Wuthnow, Robert, 368
WWF. *See* World Wildlife Fund
Wyszomirski, Margaret J., 39, 229–65

Yale-New Haven Hospital (Conn.), 102
Yale University, 42, 138, 139, 140, 144, 435, 484, 552
YNPN. *See* Young Nonprofit Professionals Network
Yoplait, 58
Young, Dennis R., 437, 521–48
Young Nonprofit Professionals Network (YNPN), 431
YMCA, 312, 427, 530, 663
YWCA, 195
YouthBuild, 192–93, 205, 215, 221
YouthBuild Transfer Act (*2006*), 178
YouTube, 634
Yunus, Muhammad, 53, 459

Zaire, 346, 350–51